Application Development for IBM WebSphere Process Server 7 and Enterprise Service Bus 7

Build SOA-based flexible, economical, and efficient applications

Swami Chandrasekaran

Salil Ahuja

[PACKT] enterprise
professional expertise distilled
PUBLISHING

BIRMINGHAM - MUMBAI

Application Development for IBM WebSphere Process Server 7 and Enterprise Service Bus 7

First published: July 2010

Production Reference: 1010710

Published by Packt Publishing Ltd.
32 Lincoln Road
Olton
Birmingham, B27 6PA, UK.

ISBN 978-1-847198-28-0

www.packtpub.com

Cover Image by Tina Negus (tina_manthorpe@sky.com)

Credits

Authors
Swami Chandrasekaran
Salil Ahuja

Reviewers
Xinyu Liu
Steve Robinson
Prabu Swamidurai

Acquisition Editor
Sarah Cullington

Development Editors
Dhwani Devater
Reshma Sundaresan

Technical Editors
Alfred John
Neha Mallik

Copy Editor
Leonard D'Silva

Editorial Team Leader
Aanchal Kumar

Project Team Leader
Lata Basantani

Project Coordinator
Poorvi Nair

Proofreader
Lynda Sliwoski

Indexer
Monica Ajmera Mehta

Production Coordinator
Alwin Roy

Cover Work
Alwin Roy

About the Authors

Swami Chandrasekaran works for IBM as an Industry Executive Architect for its Software Group—Industry Solutions. He provides architectural leadership for IBM tooling / product suite and works with its global customers in delivery of best in class solutions. His expertise includes next-generation networks, OSS/BSS, SOA, Dynamic BPM and modern web-based architectures, and TM Forum Frameworx (NGOSS). He has travelled to almost 24 countries and is constantly sought after within the company for his technical leadership and client skills. His credits include technical and strategic interface with various senior executive and institutions, including Fortune 100/500 companies and international clients. He is the SME and Co-Lead Architect for the WebSphere Telecom Content Pack.

He has presented at several conferences, authored articles within IBM, articles featured in *BearingPoint Institute for Thought Leadership*, and also holds several patent disclosures. He previously worked for BearingPoint and also for Ericsson Wireless Research. He lives with his wife Ramya and daughter Harshitha in Dallas, Texas. He is an avid video gamer and during his free time he likes to write at `http://www.nirvacana.com`. He holds a Master's in Electrical Engineering from the University of Texas, Arlington.

There are many people whom I would like to thank. I thank my IBM management team for encouraging and allowing me the time needed to write this book. I'd like to thank all my mentors and my family members including my in-laws who have helped and guided me over the last several years. I'd like to thank the staff at Packt Publishing, including Poorvi Nair, Sarah Cullington, Reshma Sundaresan, and Dhwani Devater for their assistance in this effort. Finally and most importantly, I thank my wife, Ramya and daughter, Harshitha for encouraging me to take this immensely challenging journey and for all the weekends and time they have sacrificed so that this book could become a reality.

I dedicate this book to my parents, my Gurus, and Ramya.

Salil Ahuja currently works for IBM as a Technical Lead in their AIM Customer Programs group. He has been working in the IT industry for over eight years in a variety of positions ranging from development to client services. As a certified IBM SOA Designer, he has spent the majority of his career consulting with large healthcare players on the design, implementation, and delivery of standards-based enterprise SOA solutions. In his current role, he works with premium IBM clients to educate and enable them on the leading edge technologies within the IBM Business Process Management portfolio. Salil is a sought after expert on HIPAA and Health Level 7 Clinical Data Architecture, and has presented to various IBM labs on healthcare information exchange in the provider payer space.

He lives in Austin, Texas with his wife Priyanka. In his spare time he enjoys the outdoors, theater, and playing or watching basketball whenever possible. He can be contacted on LinkedIn at `http://www.linkedin.com/pub/salil-ahuja/0/b92/186`.

This book is a result of a collaborative effort and I would like to acknowledge those who helped make it possible. First, I thank IBM management for approving the undertaking of this book project and Packt publishing for helping materialize the book. Also, I would like to extend thanks to my co-author, Swami Chandrasekaran, for bringing this opportunity to me. We worked countless hours to make this book a reality. I could not have completed this book without the continuous support from my mentors, friends, and family - thank you to all of you. Specifically, I would like to thank my parents, Sudha and Suvir, and my brother, Nitin, for their constant support and encouragement that allows me to continuously take on new challenges like this. And lastly, a very special thanks to my wife Priyanka - thank you for your encouragement, understanding, and patience that gave me the space and enviroment that allowed me to write this book.

I dedicate this book to my parents - Sudha and Suvir, who have always put my needs before theirs and laid the foundation for the life that I have built.

About the Reviewers

Xinyu Liu had his graduate educations at the George Washington University. As a Sun Microsystems certified enterprise architect, he has intensive application design and development experience on JavaEE, JavaSE, and JavaME platforms.

He works in a healthcare company as a key technical contributor in its IT department. During his years of service, new application design and implementation methodologies and strategies were established under his effort. He also leads the effort to transition to a Portal, BPM, SOA-oriented architecture, in addition to the setting up of an enterprise-wide knowledge repository based on Drools rule engine and a content management system on top of Alfresco.

He is a writer for Java.net and Javaworld.com on different topics, including JSF, Spring Security, Hibernate Search, Spring Web Flow, and the new Servlet 3.0 specification.

He also worked on the review of the books *Spring Web Flow 2 Web Development* and *Grails 1.1 Web Application Development*, both by Packt Publishing.

Special thanks to my son, Gavin Liu and my wife, Xiaowen Zhou.

Steve Robinson is currently employed as Chief Technology Officer for a Boutique management consultancy in London. Previously, he was an international WebSphere consultant and he has been a consultant for both IBM Lotus Notes and Microsoft. NET technologies. Steve has been working in IT for over 15 years and has provided solutions for many large-enterprise corporations worldwide including IBM, Lloyds Banking Group, BSkyB, and PricewaterhouseCoopers in both the middleware and Internet technology space. He recently published a book entitled *WebSphere Application Server 7.0 Administration Guide*. Steve also runs and supports `http://www.webspheretools.com`, a very popular knowledge site dedicated to WebSphere and related tools.

Prabu Swamidurai is a WebSphere consultant specializing in large scale WebSphere implementations in the "Big 4 Banks" and financial and retail industries in the UK. He has worked in Fortune 500 companies in the Europe and the Middle East region for the past 12 years, focusing on IBM WebSphere technologies.

Prabu is certified in several IBM products including WebSphere Application Server, Process Server, ESB, DataPower, MQ, and Message Broker. He has a unique reputation for creating and implementing highly-sophisticated automated build and deployment tools for these products and technologies with his clients. He has a Master's degree in Physics and Computer Science.

He can be contacted via his web portal `www.websphereSpcialist.com`.

I would like to thank my loving wife Latha; without you I would not be the person I am today. I also dedicate this book to my children Alwin and Ajeet who in their own unique ways gave me encouragement, enjoyment, and delight throughout the review of this book. I also would like to thank my mother (Jeya) for her dedication, love, and support.

Table of Contents

Preface

By adopting an SOA approach in Business Process Management (BPM), you can make your application flexible, reusable, and adaptable to new developments. This book introduces basic concepts of Business Integration, SOA Fundamentals, and SOA Programming Model, and implements them in numerous examples.

You will learn to analyze business requirements and rationalize your thoughts to see if an SOA approach is appropriate for your project. Using the principles of Business Process Management, Service Oriented Architecture, using IBM WebSphere Process Server 7(WPS), and WebSphere Enterprise Service Bus 7 (WESB), the authors guide you through building an Order Management application from scratch.

What this book covers

Chapter 1, Introducing IBM BPM and ESB, discusses the core capabilities needed for a process integration approach, IBM's SOA Reference Architecture, and IBM's Business Process Management platform including WebSphere Process Server (WPS) and WebSphere Enterprise Service Bus. It also discusses IBM's BPM enabled by SOA lifecycle methodology.

Chapter 2, Installing the Development Environment, takes you through the process of installing and setting up the WID development environment. During the course of setting up the environment, it takes a quick peek into some of the fundamentals of WID, key concepts, and terms. It takes us through a crash course in using WID and also shows us how to navigate using WID as well as some of the key activities that one would perform and how to perform them.

Chapter 3, Building your Hello Process Project, discusses the fundamental SOA programming model concepts and helps us understand how these concepts apply in the context of WID/WPS/WESB. It also discusses, in detail, the Service Component Architecture (SCA). It also rounds up the SOA programming model discussions with BPEL. It also provides instructions on building our first business process-based application—Greeting Solution. Though the application does a simple job, the purpose of building this application is to understand how to go about using WID, the various capabilities of WID, and how to apply these capabilities. It also briefly touches upon logging, debugging, and troubleshooting basics and exporting projects from WID.

Chapter 4, Building your Hello Mediation Project, provides an overview of WESB-based programming fundamentals including Service Message Objects (SMO) and Mediation Flows. It helps us to build our first HelloMediationModule. Instructions are provided to create, implement, and assemble the HelloMediationModule and HelloProcess. These modules are then deployed on the WebSphere Process Server, which is a part of the WID Unit Test Environment.

Chapter 5, Business Process Choreography Fundamentals, discusses the various aspects and functions of WPS and WESB that are absolutely and fundamentally essential. The topics covered are Business Process (WS-BPEL), Business Objects, Business Rules, State Machines, Visual Snippets, Compensation, Fault Handling, and Control Structures .

Chapter 6, Mediations Fundamentals, performs an in-depth study of mediation flows, mediation primitives, and adapters. It walks us through the various aspects and concepts about Mediation primitives and Service Message Objects that are absolutely fundamental and essential. The other topics that this chapter touches upon are Adapters and Dynamic routing.

Chapter 7, Sales Fulfillment Application for JungleSea Inc., guides you through the steps involved in architecting the new Sales Fulfillment Application. It also identifies the appropriate WPS and WESB components that will have to be built.

Chapter 8, Walk the Talk, provides details around the assembly phase of the IBM SOA Reference Architecture. It discusses how to assemble components to catalog their interface and data types in shared libraries that can then be leveraged by the different modules of the Sales Fulfillment Application.

Chapter 9, Building the Order Handling Processes, guides us through how to build the Process Services modules, namely, ProcessServices-OrderHandling and ProcessServices-CustomerInterfaceManagement, and the associated businesses processes (BPELs). It starts with the creation of shared libraries and then provides a top-down breakup of the process, business, and access services that will be developed and assembled for the Sales Fulfillment Application. It covers several

topics including BPEL development steps, using business rules in the process, implementing human tasks, usage of control structures, fault handling including compensation, correlation sets, and discusses how to test the business processes end-to-end, once the Business Service and Access Service modules have been built.

Chapter 10, Integration with Various Applications, walks you through the implementation of the first working version of the Sales Fulfillment Application along with all the business service modules (with the associated components) and the corresponding Access Services (with the associated components). Then it discusses how to perform unit testing and component testing. It also helps in the implementation of the Business and Access Service modules. It also provides a step-by-step method to implement them and unit test them.

Chapter 11, Business Space, provides an overview of the Business Space and touches upon some of the basic concepts and functionalities to help you get started.

Chapter 12, Deployment Topologies, provides information regarding the fundamental aspects to take into consideration when choosing a deployment topology. It discusses the fundamentals behind WebSphere Application Server Network Deployment (WAS ND), which is the base foundation platform for the IBM BPM portfolio of products including WPS and WESB. Then it discusses clustering, how to do vertical and horizontal clustering, and briefly looks at the databases used by WPS. It also discusses the several deployment patterns available from IBM and how, from them, we can choose the Remote Messaging and Remote Support topology pattern (gold topology) as the production topology.

Chapter 13, Management, Monitoring and Security, shows us how to perform some of the most common solution administration tasks, including how to use the admin console and various activities we can perform using it. Then it discusses installing versioned SCA modules and how to monitor the applications deployed on WPS/WESB. It also discusses various tools and capabilities provided in WID/WPS/WESB to monitor the applications and components.

Appendix, WID, WPS, and WESB Tips, Tricks, and Pointers will be a random yet useful collection of typical questions, how-tos, and tips on different topics when developing with WID, WPS, and WESB. It will cover some of the most common questions related to WID tooling, managing, and administering the runtime. This chapter is meant to be a quick reference where we scratch the surface of some advanced topics that warrant a book by itself. It aims to provide you with the right pointers so that you can get to the appropriate information and not have to search for it.

What you need for this book

This book covers building an application using the principles of BPM and SOA and using WPS and WESB. The various detailed aspects, features, and capabilities of the product will be conveyed though examples. It will also provide pragmatic guidance on various aspects in relation to building the SOA application.

The software needed for this book is

Operating system: Windows or Linux

WebSphere Integration Developer v7

- This includes an Integrated WebSphere Process Server and WebSphere Enterprise Service Bus test environments

- For software requirements on Windows refer: `http://www-01.ibm.com/support/docview.wss?rs=2308&context=SSQQFK&uid=swg27016958`

- For software requirements on Linux refer: `http://www-01.ibm.com/support/docview.wss?rs=2308&context=SSQQFK&uid=swg27016957`

Who this book is for

This book is for SOA architects, designers and developers who have a basic understanding of SOA concepts and would like to learn more about building solutions and applications using IBM WebSphere Process Server and WebSphere Enterprise Service Bus.

Conventions

In this book, you will find a number of styles of text that distinguish between different kinds of information. Here are some examples of these styles, and an explanation of their meaning.

Code words in text are shown as follows: "In WID the service component definition is included in the `<SERVICE_NAME>.component` file."

A block of code is set as follows:

```
DataObject customerInfo) {} function with the following code:
public DataObject requestCreditApproval(DataObject customerInfo) {
    ServiceManager serviceManager = ServiceManager.INSTANCE;
    BOFactory boFactory = (BOFactory)serviceManager.
locateService("com/ibm/websphere/bo/BOFactory");
    DataObject customerCreditApproval = boFactory.create("http://
Ch6Library","CustomerCreditApproval");  customerCreditApproval.
setString("id",customerInfo.getString("id"));
```

Any command-line input or output is written as follows:

```
manageprofiles(.bat)(.sh) -backupProfile -profileName profile_name
-backupFile backupFile_name -username user_name -password password
```

New terms and **important words** are shown in bold. Words that you see on the screen, in menus or dialog boxes for example, appear in the text like this: "Click on the **Add** button and then click on the **Finish** button."

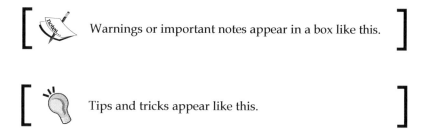

[Warnings or important notes appear in a box like this.]

[Tips and tricks appear like this.]

Reader feedback

Feedback from our readers is always welcome. Let us know what you think about this book—what you liked or may have disliked. Reader feedback is important for us to develop titles that you really get the most out of.

To send us general feedback, simply send an e-mail to `feedback@packtpub.com`, and mention the book title via the subject of your message.

If there is a book that you need and would like to see us publish, please send us a note in the **SUGGEST A TITLE** form on `www.packtpub.com` or e-mail `suggest@packtpub.com`.

If there is a topic that you have expertise in and you are interested in either writing or contributing to a book on, see our author guide on `www.packtpub.com/authors`.

Customer support

Now that you are the proud owner of a Packt book, we have a number of things to help you to get the most from your purchase.

> **Downloading the example code for this book**
>
> You can download the example code files for all Packt books you have purchased from your account at `http://www.PacktPub.com`. If you purchased this book elsewhere, you can visit `http://www.PacktPub.com/support` and register to have the files e-mailed directly to you.

Errata

Although we have taken every care to ensure the accuracy of our content, mistakes do happen. If you find a mistake in one of our books—maybe a mistake in the text or the code—we would be grateful if you would report this to us. By doing so, you can save other readers from frustration and help us improve subsequent versions of this book. If you find any errata, please report them by visiting `http://www.packtpub.com/support`, selecting your book, clicking on the **let us know** link, and entering the details of your errata. Once your errata are verified, your submission will be accepted and the errata will be uploaded on our website, or added to any list of existing errata, under the Errata section of that title. Any existing errata can be viewed by selecting your title from `http://www.packtpub.com/support`.

Piracy

Piracy of copyright material on the Internet is an ongoing problem across all media. At Packt, we take the protection of our copyright and licenses very seriously. If you come across any illegal copies of our works, in any form, on the Internet, please provide us with the location address or website name immediately so that we can pursue a remedy.

Please contact us at `copyright@packtpub.com` with a link to the suspected pirated material.

We appreciate your help in protecting our authors, and our ability to bring you valuable content.

Questions

You can contact us at `questions@packtpub.com` if you are having a problem with any aspect of the book, and we will do our best to address it.

1 Introducing IBM BPM and ESB

JungleSea Inc. is a fictitious online retailer who sells a wide range of products including books, digital media, and electronics. They have a wide network of suppliers and partners, who participate in their ecosystem. JungleSea is under constant pressure to respond quickly to tactical changes happening in the market place, while adopting new business and operating models for rapid strategic change. Architects within JungleSea have been a big proponents of a **Business Process Management** (**BPM**) enabled by a **Service Oriented Architecture** (**SOA**) approach to help business and IT decisions to be aligned better. By adopting a BPM-SOA approach, they have, over time, demonstrated how they were able to reach the flexibility, reuse, and adaptability that made them better prepared to compete and win against their competitors. The SOA approach also gave them the potential to lower costs (from reuse), and increase revenue (from adaptability and flexibility). JungleSea Inc. had already selected and decided that it would use IBM **WebSphere Process Server** (**WPS**) and IBM **WebSphere Enterprise Services Bus** (**WESB**) as its core platform for its BPM enabled by SOA.

JungleSea's IT, like any other organization, has multi-faceted, multi-skilled, and multi-leveled employees. From time to time, they hire new people to infuse new blood and thinking into the system. Quite naturally, a BPM-enabled SOA approach can get overwhelming for new hires. This book is about taking the reader through a mentorship journey. The style of the book will be such that the reader will be introduced to the fundamental concepts, then walk them through numerous examples, and finally the journey of building an application using the principles of BPM and SOA and using WPS and WESB.

Alongside the journey, we will be using WPS and WESB as the vehicle to build the SOA application; the various detailed aspects, features, and capabilities of the product will be conveyed though examples. It will also provide practical and pragmatic guidance on various aspects in relation to building the SOA application. Every section will have solutions to common problems and pitfalls. The purpose of this book is to enable the reader to assume the role of the mentee (one who is being mentored; source: Merriam-Webster) and how he/she is introduced to various concepts in SOA, BPM Integration, and so on, and how we apply all these concepts while building a solution. The style of the book is:

- A reference book that's organized into chapters, so you can flip right to what you need
- A text that addresses the core concepts and practical ideas in BPM, enabled by SOA approach
- A primer for getting started with BPM using WPS and WESB
- A step-by-step guide for implementing BPM using WPS and WESB successfully
- A compilation of WPS and WESB related resources that you can go to for additional help or continued education

In the first part, we will focus on the basics and overview of the key and essential concepts that a reader will require to go forward with the book. We will give a crash course on Business Integration, SOA Fundamentals, and SOA Programming Model. Then we will have the environment set up. Then, to give the reader a feel for the product, build the first Hello Process (with WPS) and Hello Mediation (with WESB) applications.

In the second part, we will build an SOA-based Order Management Application (named Sales Fulfillment Application) for JungleSea Inc. We will guide the reader through the various aspects and functions of WPS and WESB, which are absolutely necessary, through numerous practical examples. Then we will analyze the business requirements and rationalize our thoughts to see if an SOA approach is the right way. Then we will build SOA-based architecture, do a top-down decomposition, and identify use cases (and scenarios), business processes, and services/components.

In the third and final part, having built the SOA Application for JungleSea Inc., we will take the reader through various non-functional topics including Administration, Governance, Management, Monitoring, and Security. We will also discuss deployment topologies for WPS and WESB, performance tuning, and recommended practices. Finally, we will address a series of 'How Do I' questions that a reader typically ask.

In this chapter, we will:

- Discuss how a BPM enabled by the SOA approach is the key to achieving success.
- Discuss the key building blocks for a business process-driven integration enabled by SOA.
- Briefly discuss the value of reference architectures and IBM SOA reference architecture.
- Map the key building blocks of BPM enabled by SOA approach with the IBM SOA reference architecture.
- Demonstrate what an instantiated solution architecture that has adopted IBM SOA reference architecture would look like.
- Start introducing WebSphere Process Server and where it fits in the larger context of SOA. Also discuss its platform architecture and some of the common usage scenarios it will be used in.
- Discuss Enterprise Service Bus (ESB) and some of the key capabilities to look for in an ESB. We then introduce WebSphere Enterprise Service Bus Server and where it fits in the larger context of SOA. We also discuss its platform architecture and some of the common usage scenarios it will be used in.

What is Service Oriented Architecture (SOA)?

There is no single unique and easy way to define or explain SOA. Given a room full of C-level executives, IT Managers, IT-Architects, and developers with each asked to give a one sentence explanation of what SOA is, for sure, each answer will be different. What is the fundamental message behind SOA? What is it trying to achieve and what does it provides the adopter with? This will help the reader to be able to define or explain it correctly. Let's list some of most common facts he/she may have heard about SOA:

- It's a style for building loosely coupled and distributed applications
- It's all about service providers providing services to service consumers that conform to contracts
- It provides a programming model based on standards defined by various standard bodies including OASIS, WS-*, and so on

> **Service Oriented Architecture** (**SOA**) is a set of architectural styles, patterns, principles, procedures, and criteria for building solutions and applications.
>
> Such applications exhibit the following characteristics:
>
> - Loosely coupled from operating systems, programming languages, and protocols
> - Expose coarse grained Business Services that can be mapped to business capabilities
> - Business Services are Modular, Encapsulated, and Reusable
> - Can be Composed, Orchestrated, or Choreographed
> - Services expose standardized interfaces
> - Services are described though contracts and hence discoverable
> - Leverages a standards-compliant middleware

The process of adopting an SOA is a journey and possibly an *ever-evolving, ever-learning, never ending one*. With SOA, you progress and mature over time to reach a state where you can truly achieve the benefits, as promised.

Process, Business Services, and Components—the core constructs

Business Processes represent the flow of activities required to complete a business process, which, in turn, help achieve a business objective. They are orchestrations, choreography, or compositions of Business Services targeted to achieve business goals.

Business Service, to be more precise, represents a discrete business function that makes meaningful sense to an organization. A Business Service can be composed of one of the many fine-grained functions or atomic services, and by the true definition of SOA, encapsulation, it can dynamically behave depending on how it is invoked. Services form the building blocks of SOA and should be reusable, decoupled, exposed in a standardized fashion, and derived from disparate IT resources.

Components realize and provide services from one or more applications and these components are wrapped into the Business Services. Components help realize not only the functionality of the services they expose, but also ensure that their Quality of Service (QoS) is good, as guaranteed by the service provider. The following figure depicts how all of the above are interrelated and interconnected at a very high level.

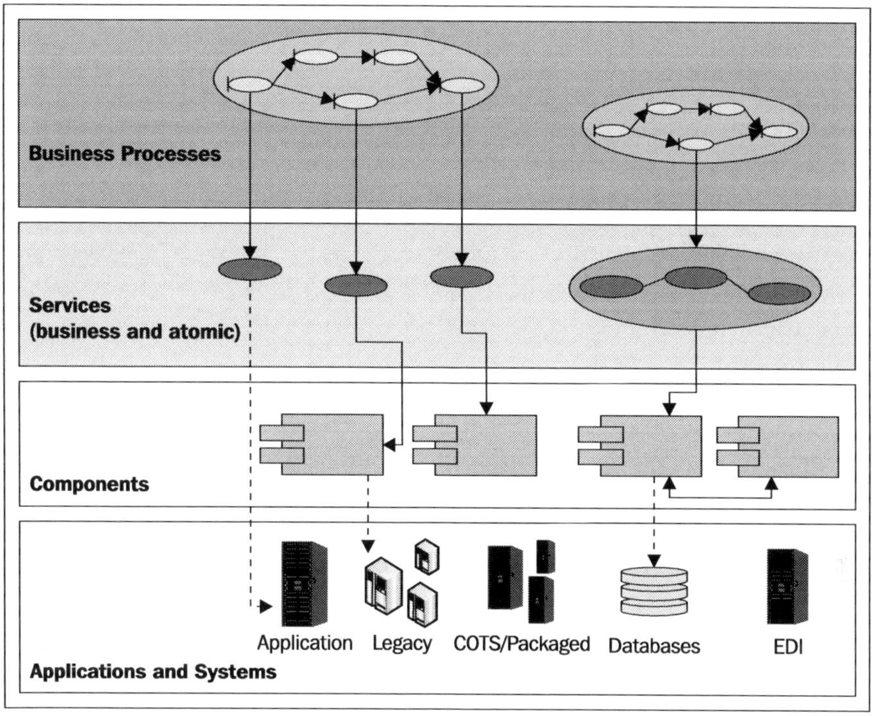

Achieving success through BPM enabled by SOA

A fact of reality in many organizations today is that they have many applications which are disparate in terms of technology, programming languages based on which they were written, capabilities exposed through interfaces, services, or APIs, and so on. To create a purchase order in an order entry system, we will need information about the customer from customer information management systems, product information from product catalog, and so on and so forth. Hence there is a constant struggle to make all the applications integrated.

IT is under constant pressure to address these requirements for managing layer upon layer of legacy systems that may or may not interoperate with any degree of simplicity. This is where integration comes in and helps connect applications together with the right communications , data semantics and server infrastructure as well as the right business process capabilities to give IT and enterprise leaders the ability to create composite applications that meet new flexible and dynamic business needs.

Getting the integration right is one of the key aspects of getting SOA right, and it enables the integration of the disparate applications. Integration is only one half of the struggle; there are several techniques and modes in which you can integrate applications. They include but are not limited to:

- Presentation-based integration that provides interaction and collaboration capabilities
- Process-driven integration that helps streamline business processes
- Information-centric integration for unified access to information from heterogeneous data sources
- Bare bones connectivity-based integration

A **Business Process Management** (BPM) approach enabled by SOA is key to achieving operating efficiencies and gaining a competitive advantage for any organization. Organizations need a BPM enabled by SOA framework, which will allow them to constantly evolve their collaborative process automation and process improvement approaches. So what is this BPM enabled by SOA framework and what will it comprise?

Business Process Management (BPM)

You may have been reading a lot about Business Process Management. What is it? BPM is a discipline that focuses on process modeling, design, automation, management, and continuous improvement. It is not a technology or a product. It covers the full range of application-to-application, inter-application, workflow, and person-to-person process management, including process modeling, design, automation, monitoring, management, and continuous improvement. The core and basic components of BPM include (but are not limited to):

- Modeling and simulation
- Policies and Rules
- Collaboration through human task processing
- Content-centric processing
- Process execution including choreography and orchestration
- **Business Activity Monitoring** (BAM)
- **Support for common Business Objects** (BOs)

- Intuitive process definition tool
- Customizable work portal
- Historical process analysis
- Wide range of integration capabilities and adapters
- Process Tracking and Notification
- Process Performance Analysis
- System Scalability and Process Performance
- Provision for parallel human task approvals
- Capability to work with and modify in-flight processes

Building blocks of BPM enabled by SOA framework

Businesses very well understand that their core (and differentiating) business processes will have to be automated (post integration) and be able to externalize these from end applications. Process-driven integration is about bringing people, processes, information, and systems together using the Business Process management (BPM) approach enabled by an SOA approach. This approach requires a solid technology platform and of course an over-arching methodology that will offer you prescriptive guidance on how to deliver solutions. So what are these core building blocks? They include:

- Business Process Modeling
- Business Process Execution
- Business Policies and Rules
- Enterprise Service Bus
- Business Process Monitoring
- Information Model (the semantic model)

Now let's look briefly at each of these core building blocks/capabilities that are needed for achieving success in a business process-driven integration provided, as shown in the following figure:

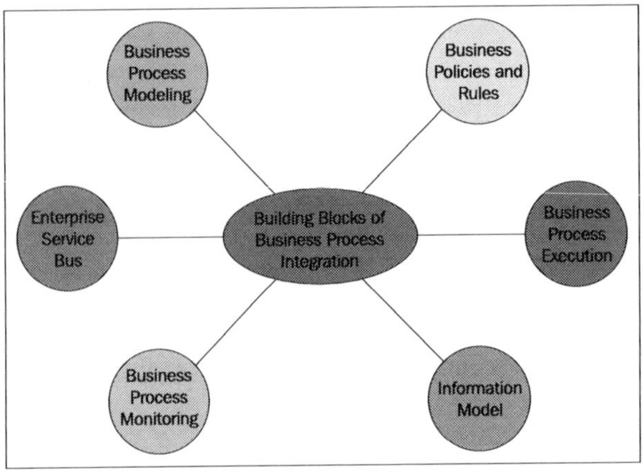

Business Process Modeling

This is the starting point where you discover and document the various other business process(s) (using a modeling notation such as **Business Process Modeling Notation BPMN**) that might exist on paper or even in the minds of some subject matter experts and document it with business modeling. Also, once the processes are modeled, you will have the ability to run model simulations and try out various 'what-if' scenarios to forecast what would happen if you altered the process. Based on these simulations, you arrive at an optimal process design. The process modeling exercise also helps to identify the SOA services that will have to be specified, realized, and also in many cases, reused.

Business Process Execution (including Choreography)

Once the business processes have been modeled, they will have defined in an executable format (such as **Business Process Execution Language** (**BPEL**)) and deployed on a standard-based process execution platform that supports both the business process execution environment and the packaging of business tasks as services. The assembly, sequencing, orchestration, and choreography of existing services and new services results in the realization of a deployable process model. This assembly should be based on industry standards such as **Service Component Architecture** (**SCA**). The execution platform must also support human interaction for both participants in the business process and administrators of the business process.

The runtime should also provide a variety of administrative capabilities required to configure the environment for the applications that are installed.

Enterprise Service Bus

Enterprise Service Bus (ESB) provides the underlying connectivity and backbone infrastructure for SOA to connect applications. An ESB is essentially an architecture pattern that provides capabilities including connectivity, communications, message queuing, message routing, message transformation, reliable messaging, protocol transformation and binding, event handling, fault handling, message level security, and so on. It enables loose coupling between service consumers and service providers, and thus enhances the ability to rapidly change and introduce new Business Services into the environment. An ESB typically would leverage a service registry and repository to provide information about service endpoints.

Business Policies and Rules

Policies and rules can make the business processes highly flexible and responsive. A business policy represents a key piece of domain knowledge, externalized from a business process and is applied when a particular request context is met. An example could be, all purchase orders that include order items such as *Oxygen Canisters* are deemed critical orders, order amount worth over *$1000* has to be shipped overnight, and so on. Metadata elements such as "order item" and "order amount" are deemed as the business domain vocabulary and values of which can change (you can add "Defibrillator" along to the critical items list), which will have to be externalized from the business process.

A business rule is a statement that defines or constrains some aspect of the business. They are typically atomic and cannot be broken down further. An example would be, say, in a loan origination business process, at each step of the process, business analysts identify rules that must be met by the loan staff and underlying systems. In traditional banking systems, these rules reside within the loan origination system itself, so changing the rules means modifying the application. When the rules are abstracted from the loan origination systems, they reside in a business rules engine. As a result, bank management can identify those activities that change rapidly, such as decisions relating to FICO® scores, and then, instead of changing the process and its underlying application, they change only the decision point within the business process, which in turn resides in a business rules engine (external to the process itself). This capability adds agility to the process by reducing the time, costs, and resources necessary to respond to changing conditions.

Business Process Monitoring

While the business processes are deployed and are executing, data must be captured that provides information about the processes. This data can be analyzed to determine if the business processes are performing as expected. Both business-related information and IT-related information can be captured for monitoring. You should also be able to visually define dashboards based on **Key Performance Indicators (KPI)**, which are based on the monitor model deployed for the business process, providing a visual display of the business process status.

Information Model

For a process-driven integration approach coupled with SOA to succeed, a common and enterprise level information model is required, which becomes the basis for the messages exchanged between processes and services, and also serves as the glossary for the business policies and rules. When dealing with applications that have disparate data and information models, use of this common information model shields the business processes away from the gory details of each and every individual system. The ESB provides capabilities to transform from this Canonical Data Model to the target system's format. The Canonical data model minimizes dependencies between integrated applications that use different data formats. Typically, one could leverage industry standards such as Tele Management Forum's Shared Information/Data Model (**SID**) and so on to define the information models.

> A mind map is a diagram used to represent words, ideas, tasks, or other items linked to and arranged around a central keyword or idea. Mind maps are used to generate, visualize, structure, and classify ideas, and as an aid in study, organization, problem solving, decision making, and writing.

A mind map, as shown in the following figure, sums up all the previous concepts.

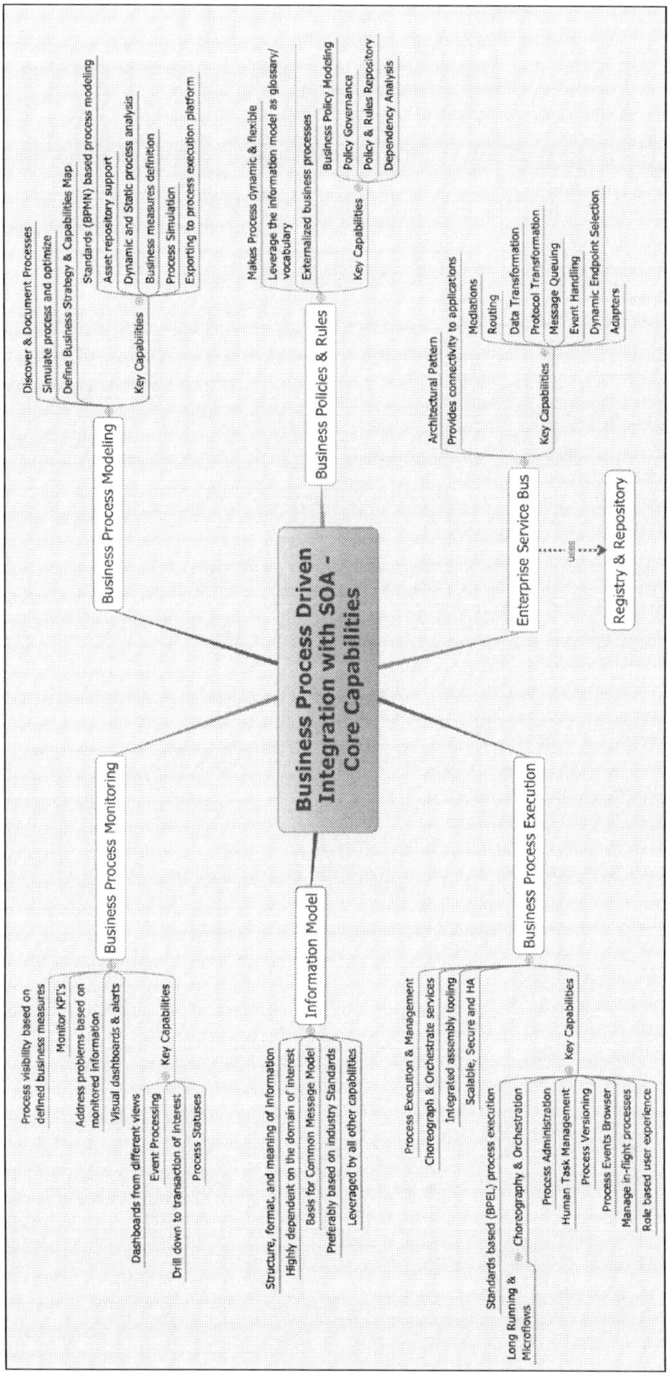

IBM SOA Reference Architecture

IBM's SOA Reference Architecture defines a vendor and technology agnostic set of comprehensive IT capabilities that are required to support your SOA at each stage in a typical SOA life cycle. When an organization defines a solution architecture based on this reference architecture, they would not need all of the capabilities needed initially. But over time, to be successful in SOA, all the capabilities need to be evolved and added.

What is Reference Architecture?

A Reference Architecture captures the essence of the architecture of a collection of systems. It models the abstract architectural elements in the domain or a solution area, independent of the technologies, products, and protocols that are used to implement the domain. It differs from a reference model in that a reference model describes the important concepts and relationships in the domain focusing on what distinguishes the elements of the domain. Thus reference architecture is useful for:

- Providing a common ground domain model
- Basis for realizing an architecture vision
- Providing key architectural guidance and a blueprint as a baseline

Reference architecture is typically abstract and is abstract for a purpose. You typically instantiate or create solution/system architectures based on the reference architecture. Example reference architecture includes Unisys 3D Blueprints, IBM Insurance Application Architecture, and NGOSS reference architecture from the TM Forum, and so on.

Key elements of IBM SOA Reference Architecture

The IBM Software Reference Architecture is a reference model that lets you leverage information, applications, and tools as services in an interoperable, system-independent way. The subsequent diagram shows the IBM SOA Reference Architecture organized around the key capabilities required for building any SOA-based solution.

- *Development Services* provide the capabilities in terms of development tools for the end users to efficiently complete specific tasks and create specific output based on their skills.
- *Interaction Services* provide the user interaction capabilities required to deliver the Business Services and data to end users.
- *Process Services* provide the control, management, choreography, and orchestration of the business processes that interact with multiple services.
- *Information Services* provide the capabilities required to federate, unionize, and transform data from one or multiple applications or data sources and expose them as services.
- *Enterprise Service Bus* delivers all the connectivity capabilities required to leverage and use services implemented across the entire organization.
- *Business Innovation and Optimization Services* provide the monitoring capabilities and manage the runtime implementations at both the IT and business process levels.
- *Business Application Services* are services provided by existing applications or ones that will have to be exposed by the applications itself including third-party systems.
- *Access Services* allow access to the end applications, legacy applications, pre-packaged applications, enterprise data stores (including relational, hierarchical, and nontraditional, unstructured sources such as XML and Text), and so on using a consistent approach. These typically leverage the business application services.
- *Infrastructure Services* provide security, directory, IT system management, and virtualization capabilities to the SOA solution.
- *Partner Services* provide the capabilities for the efficient implementation of business-to-business processes and interactions.

So what is the relationship between the process integration, key capabilities needed for successful process integration, SOA, IBM SOA reference architecture, IBM WebSphere Process Server, and IBM WebSphere Enterprise Service Bus? The answer is pretty obvious. The book is about how you build SOA solutions with these two products and these two products indeed provide a majority of the capabilities, if not all, which are essential to a successful SOA. Now let's delve into what these two products are all about.

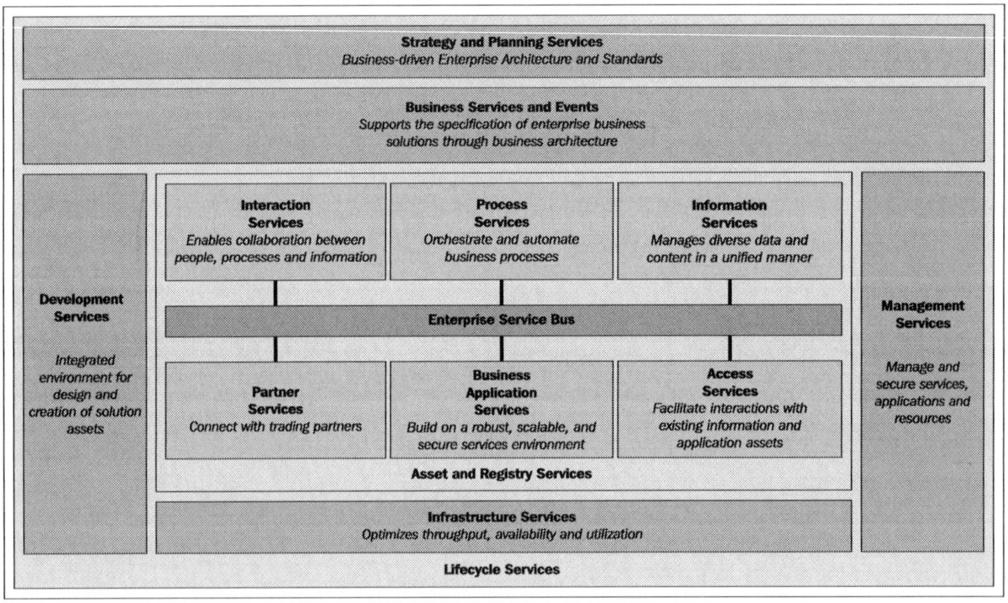

Having defined the essential elements for a BPM enabled by SOA approach, having explained the need for a reference architecture, and in particular, what IBM's SOA reference architecture is all about how does it all come together? How would a (reference) solution architecture, based on the IBM SOA Reference Architecture, look? The following figure shows one such instantiation of the "BPM enabled by SOA" solution architecture. It incorporates all of the building explained above, as categorized and organized into the appropriate IBM SOA reference architecture buckets/layers. Also, what each layer and each building block should have as capabilities within itself is explained.

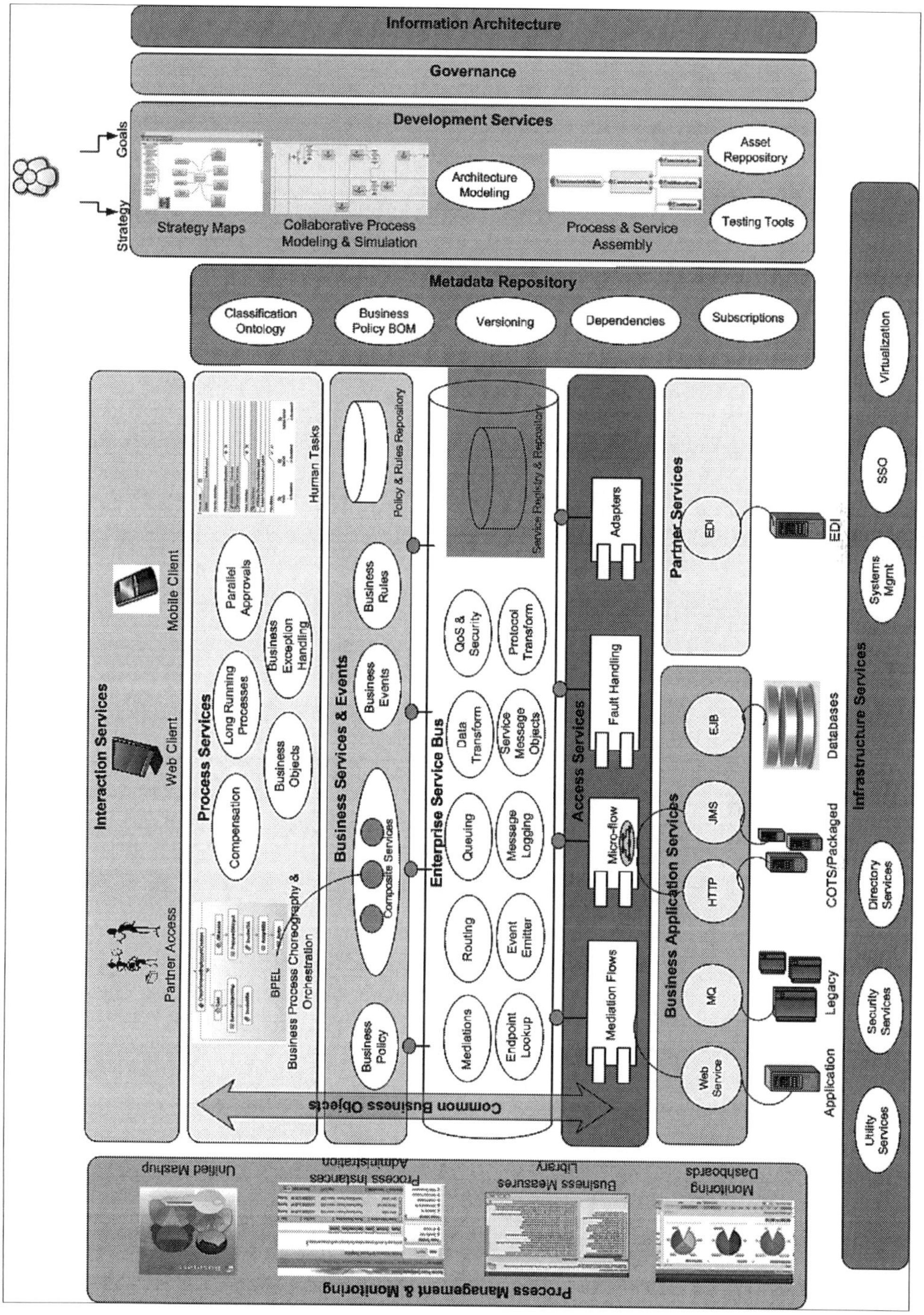
Information Architecture
Governance
Development Services
Strategy
Goals
Strategy Maps
Collaborative Process Modeling & Simulation
Architecture Modeling
Process & Service Assembly
Asset Reppository
Testing Tools
Metadata Repository
Classification Ontology
Business Policy BOM
Versioning
Dependencies
Subscriptions
Interaction Services
Partner Access
Web Client
Mobile Client
Process Services
BPEL
Business Process Choreography & Orchestration
Compensation
Long Running Processes
Business Objects
Parallel Approvals
Business Exception Handling
Human Tasks
Business Services & Events
Business Policy
Composite Services
Business Events
Business Rules
Policy & Rules Repository
Enterprise Service Bus
Mediations
Endpoint Lookup
Routing
Event Emitter
Queuing
Message Logging
Data Transform
Service Message Objects
QoS & Security
Protocol Transform
Service Registry & Repository
Common Business Objects
Access Services
Mediation Flows
Micro-flow
Fault Handling
Adapters
Business Application Services
Web Service
MQ
HTTP
JMS
EJB
Partner Services
EDI
Application
Legacy
COTS/Packaged
Databases
EDI
Infrastructure Services
Utility Services
Security Services
Directory Services
Systems Mgmt
SSO
Virtualization
Process Management & Monitoring
Unified Mashup
Process Instances Administration
Business Measures Library
Monitoring Dashboards

Introducing IBM WebSphere Process Server (WPS)

> In this book we will cover WebSphere Integration Developer v7.0, WebSphere Process Server v7.0, and WebSphere Enterprise Service Bus v7.0 built on top of IBM WebSphere Application Server-ND v7.0.0.7.

WebSphere Process Server (**WPS**) is one of the key and core products in the IBM WebSphere BPM suite. Referring back to the key capabilities needed for a successfully process-driven integration approach enabled by SOA, WPS addresses capabilities including Business Process Execution, Business Rules, Enterprise Service Bus, and a key enabler for Business Process Monitoring. WPS platform provides a standards-based uniform programming model for representation of data, invocation of services, and structure of composite applications. It provides a unified tooling, namely, **WebSphere Integration Developer** (WID) for the visual development of composite applications.

Role of WPS in SOA

As explained in the previous sections, process integration is fundamentally built on the concept of an SOA. In recent times, most of the applications expose web services. These services, which may be very fine-grained or atomic in nature, will have to be assembled into coarse-grained services that make meaningful sense to the business. A process-driven integration leverages these Business Services as business tasks in the larger choreography or orchestration of a business process. Because of the fact that fine-grained atomic services are assembled into coarse-grained business services, the use of the service is independent of the IT infrastructure needed to accomplish the task. Each Business Service then becomes a building block that, when combined with other Business Services, can become the fundamental building block to realize an end to end business process. The structuring of business processes, in this way, provides a flexible solution to real business problems, allowing the creation of new and modified processes easily. You can use WPS to develop and execute standard-based, component-based Business Integration applications using an SOA approach. The use of standards-based technology, including Web Services, helps to make the SOA vision a reality.

WPS leverages a programming model, which is very fundamental to understanding how applications are developed in WPS and WID (as explained earlier, WID is the integrated development environment for WPS). The programming model has three parts:

1. **Invocation Model**—*defines how invocations of processes and services are made.*

   Invocation is the way in which a request is made from one piece of code to another. Programmatically, there are several methods of invocation including REST, HTTP, EJB stateless session beans, JAX-WS, JAX-RPC, JDBC for communicating with databases, JMS for messaging, and so on. WPS has adopted the Service Component Architecture (SCA) specifications as the basis for its invocation model. SCA is a set of specifications that describe a model for building applications and systems using an SOA approach. SCA divides the steps in building a service-oriented application into two major parts:

   - The implementation of components which expose (export) services and consume (import) other services
   - The assembly of sets of components to build business applications, through the wiring of references to services

   SCA uses **Service Data Objects** (SDO) to represent the business data that forms the request and response values of service and/or components. SCA supports bindings to a wide range of access mechanisms used to invoke services and also through both synchronous and asynchronous programming styles.

2. **Data Model**—*defines how data can be represented*

   Programmatically, there are several ways to represent data—EDI message, JDBC row set, JMS message, **Java Persistence API** (JPA), and so on. WPS has standardized the way in which data is represented and will be using **Business Object (BO).** BOs are extensions of Service Data Objects (SDO) to provide an abstraction layer for data access. Business Objects include some extensions that are very important for integration solutions and further describe the data that is being exchanged between Service Component Architecture-based services. This includes metadata-like change history or information on the context of the data such as update, create, delete, and so on.

3. **Composition Model**—*how you put together a series of invocations*

   WPS has adopted Business Process Execution Language (BPEL) as the way to define the overall business process. When the business process accesses data, it does so by making calls to SCA services passing Business Objects.

We will venture into more details about SCA, SDO and BO, and BPEL in the coming chapters.

Platform architecture

WPS at its core is built on WebSphere Application Server, providing a robust application server runtime with capabilities that the process server implementation can exploit such as Java Message Service (JMS) messaging and enterprise beans. It can also make use of the application server qualities of services such as transactions, security, and clustering. The following image shows the platform architecture of WPS and the different components it is made up of.

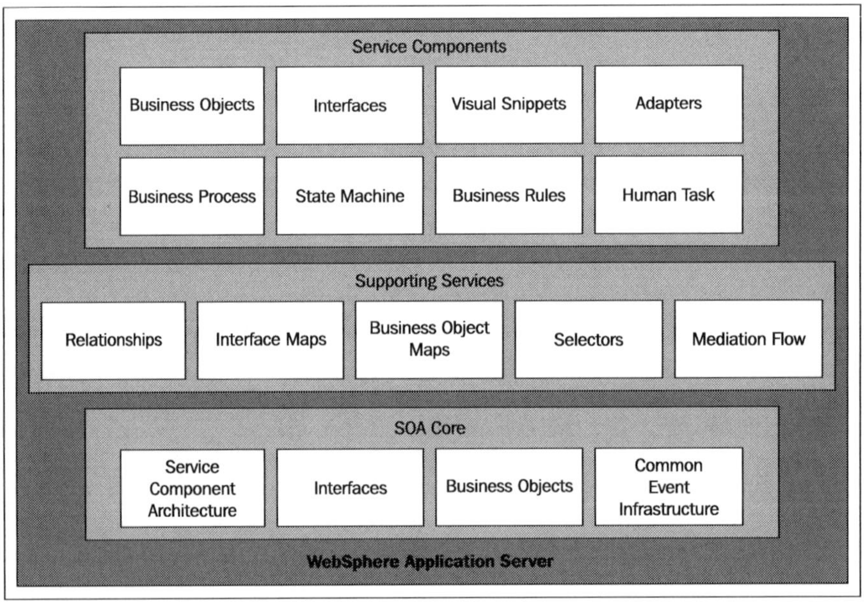

The components in the WPS platform architecture can be categorized as follows:

- SOA Core

  The foundation of SOA includes the main components, namely, the Service Component Architecture (SCA), Business Objects (BOs), and the **Common Event Infrastructure** (**CEI**). The CEI provides the foundation architecture for the management and handling of events produced by business processes. This is essential for enabling the monitoring of business processes with products such as the WebSphere Business Monitor.

- Supporting Services

  On top of the SOA Core are a set of Supporting Services, which provide the transformation primitives required when building SOA solutions using SCA and BO. These include:

  - Interface maps which enable mapping to semantically similar but syntactically different interfaces.
  - Business object maps, which enable the transformation of business data between fields of Business Objects.
  - Relationships enable the correlation and synchronization of data representing the same business entity stored in multiple backend systems.
  - Selectors provide for a dynamic invocation of a target.
  - Java to invoke Java code.

- Service Components

  Service Components provide different component types that can all be assembled together when building an SOA solution.

  - Business Processes, which are defined using BPEL, realize an executable version of a business process in which the different activities of the process are carried out by making calls to the individual SCA services that implement the specific activities.
  - Human Tasks provide the human task capabilities for people to participate and collaborate with the business processes. Human tasks can be integrated directly into the BPEL.
  - Business State Machines are another way of modeling a business process that are highly event-driven and are well suited to being thought of in terms of a state transition diagram. The Business State Machine component allows you to model the business process using similar constructs as UML 2.0 state machine support and then generates BPEL for the implementation.
  - Business rules enable the implementation and enforcement of business policy business rules and also for them to be managed independently from other aspects of an application. There are two styles of business rules, if-then rule sets and decision tables. A Web client is provided where the parameters of business rules can be changed by a business user using a natural language.
  - Adapters are used for integration with various applications and backend systems that are external to the WPS. Adapters are categorized into technology and application adapters. These adapters are compliant with the Java Connector Architecture (JCA) 1.5 specification.

Common BPM adoption scenarios

In the collection of patterns for e-business, IBM has leveraged its vast experience from its architects and solutions and developed various classes and categories of patterns that can be applied to create solutions rapidly, whether for a small local business or a large multinational enterprise. The site `http://www.ibm.com/developerworks/patterns/` breaks down these pattern assets into the following elements:

- Business patterns
- Integration patterns
- Custom designs
- Application and Runtime
- Product mappings
- Guidelines

All of the above integration patterns give interesting insight into how to integrate applications and data within an individual business pattern. At its highest level, application integration by itself is divided into Process Integration and Data Integration patterns.

Now let's look at some of the most common BPM adoption patterns, and more specifically, how WPS can be adopted in real-life client scenarios. IBM's BPM adoption patterns are classified into the following broad categories:

- *Process Automation*—Streamline and automation of manual business processes to gain and hence optimize costs and efficiency. Examples include:
    - Automation of insurance rate-quote-issue process across multiple product lines
    - Customer billing and invoice inquiry or dispute process automation in the telecommunications industry
    - Order handling business process automation applicable to several vertical industries
    - Member/Patient claims handling processes automation in healthcare
    - Automation of student registration/on-boarding in education

- *Capture Insights for Effective Actions*—Achieve visibility through monitoring and capturing new insights to seize opportunities and mitigate risks. Business Activity Monitoring (BAM), in combination with role-based dashboards, augments and helps deliver this capability. Examples include:
    - Define time-bound KPIs on loan origination and approval business processes in the banking industry and act on them.
    - Detecting the root cause of service activation failures in the Telecommunication industry and acting on them.
    - Based on strategically defined business goals to improve customer satisfaction (defined as KPI) and improve customer problem handling business processes.
    - Define fraud detection rules (too many withdrawals on an account from ATM, high rate of claims requests, and so on) and act on them appropriate by automating the detection and acting upon processes.
- *Discover and Design*—Unlock valuable process opportunities and uncover critical improvement areas by focusing on high return on investment (ROI) areas. Examples include:
    - Leveraging existing SOA service models and industry content to rapidly enable process modeling and automation efforts. IBM's Industry Content Packs is a good example here.
    - Define library of KPI models based on the particular industry's information model, business terms and concepts and use it as a means to measure and monitor strategic business goals.
    - Leverage third-party content, collaborate on process models and bring them into your ecosystem.
- *Adapt and Respond Dynamically to Change*
    - Based on changing customer and market opportunities, make changes on-the-fly to business processes. Example would be adding new channels from which an order handling process can invoke dynamic behavior for certain types of customers.

> In the white paper titled "BPM Process Patterns: Repeatable Design for BPM Process Models"—BPTrends May 2006, Dan Atwood has discussed, in detail, six categories of process design patterns.

Introducing IBM WebSphere Enterprise Service Bus (WESB)

> Note: WebSphere Process Server includes WebSphere Enterprise Service Bus.

An Enterprise Service Bus (ESB) is *fundamentally an architectural pattern*. As explained through the IBM SOA reference architecture, from an SOA point of view, an ESB provides the connectivity layer between services and serves as the core backbone for the SOA—it's the nervous system. The service consumers in a service interaction are connected to the ESB, rather than directly to one another including the service provider. When the service request connects to the ESB, the ESB takes responsibility for delivering its requests, using messages, to a service provider offering the required function and quality of service. The ESB facilitates requester provider addresses despite mismatched protocols, interaction patterns, or service capabilities. An ESB can also enable or enhance monitoring and management. The ESB provides virtualization and management features that implement and extend the core capabilities of SOA. So what are the core capabilities that an ESB should support? The fundamental capabilities of an ESB include:

- Message processing
- Mediations and Communications
- Service interactions
- Integration
- Quality of services
- Security
- Service level
- Management and autonomic services
- Infrastructure intelligence

Role of WESB in SOA

SOA mandates that the service providers and the service consumers be loosely coupled and support the use of explicit interfaces. This flexibility enables IT change with very limited impact such as the update or replacement of a given Business Service or the development of a new composite solution which leverages existing services. That is, the power of the ESB enables you to realize the full value of SOA.

As shown in the following figure, interposing the ESB between the participants in an SOA ecosystem enables you to modulate their interactions through a logical construct called mediation. Mediations operate on messages in transit between service consumers and service providers. For complex interactions, mediations can be chained sequentially. The following figure lists the core capabilities that are provided by WESB and how they interact with the various backend applications and how they expose them to the service consuming layers north of it (Process Services and Business Services). In some cases, Interaction Services can also become consumers of these WESB mediations. But it is always preferable to have the mediation wrapped into Business Services because more than likely, you would want to expose core business functions to the service consumers. In doing so, you can account for service variability within the Business Service through the use of business policies and rules. An example would be that WESB can expose mediations that manipulate customer data from one or many customer information management systems. Which customer information system is chosen will depend on the business context of the request (examples include customer location - North America or Europe, type of customer—residential or commercial, service level agreements with the customer, or request priority and so on). All these account for service variability behavior and how the service should behave based on a combination of such cases. Having such a kind of processing logic within the WESB mediation flows is not preferable for the simple reason being it can change as business conditions change. Hence WESB, in an SOA architecture, should be positioned to deal with the hardcore integration and connectivity needs and should not be overloaded with capabilities it is not meant to do architecturally.

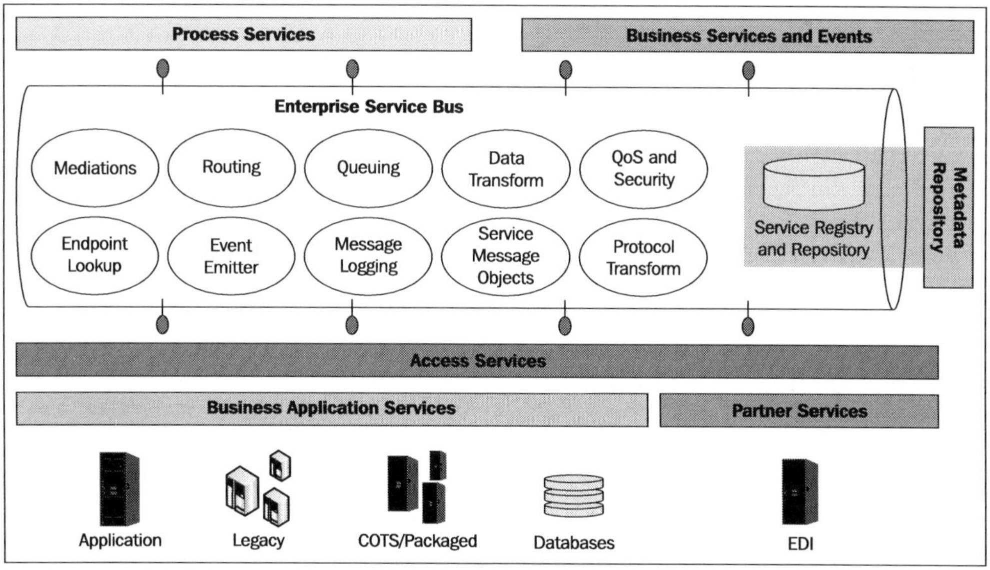

Platform architecture

As depicted in the core platform architecture for WPS (as mentioned earlier WPS includes WESB), WESB is also built on top of WebSphere Application Server. WESB mediation flows provide routing, transformation, and logging operations on the messages. The information that governs their behavior is often held in headers flowing with the business messages. WESB also adopts the same programming model as WPS (explained in the previous sections), but also introduces the Service Message Object (SMO) pattern for SDOs to support this pattern of operating on the messages, including its headers. We will discuss in detail about SMO in the coming chapters.

As shown in the WPS platform architecture, mediation flows belong to the support services. The mediation flows provide capabilities that include:

- Centralizing the routing logic so that service providers can be exchanged transparently
- Performing tasks such as protocol translation and transport mapping
- Acting as a facade to provide different interfaces between service consumers and providers
- Adding logic to provide tasks such as logging

The following figure is an example of a **mediation flow** that provides routing, transformation, and logging operations on the messages through the use of **Mediation primitives**. Mediation primitives are the smallest building blocks in WESB and are contained within a mediation flow. With Mediation primitives, you can change the format, content, or target of service requests, as well as log messages, perform database lookups, and so on and so forth. WESB can interconnect a variety of different service consumers and providers using standard protocols including JMS, SOAP/HTTP, SOAP/JMS, HTTP, and so on. It supports web services standards including WS-Security and WS-Atomic Transactions. It also includes **Universal Description Discovery and Integration** (UDDI), Version 3.0 that can be used to publish and manage service end point metadata, which enables service definitions to be made available to client applications. WESB also supports IBM WebSphere Service Registry and Repository and is used for cases where you may have to do dynamic endpoint lookup.

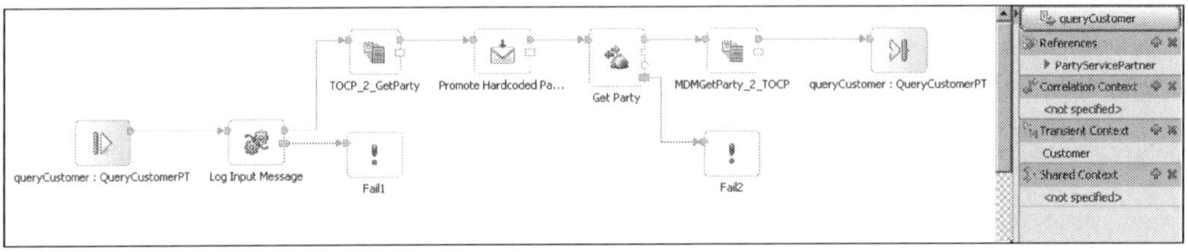

Common WESB usage scenarios

There are three categories of usage patterns when building WESB-based solutions:

1. Interaction patterns
2. Mediation patterns
3. Deployment patterns

Now let's look in more detail at some of the most common usage scenarios that belong to the preceding categories that WESB can be used in.

Interaction patterns

These are the very basic set of patterns that allow service interactions to occur via the WESB. Types of interactions include:

- Synchronous
    - request/response
    - one-way or notifications
    - request/multi-response
- Asynchronous
    - request/response
    - publish/subscribe
    - anonymous or one-way to publish messages, and so on

Mediation patterns

These are the next level of message exchange and manipulation patterns. This category of patterns typically deals with message mediations and having to "work on" the messages before allowing service interactions to occur. Some example message exchanges include:

- **Protocol Switch/Transformation**—typically dealing with protocol transformation, for example, receiving a JMS request from a service consumer and going to a service provider who supports MQ.
- **Data Transformation**—transforms and translates the incoming message from one schema format to the target schema format. You may have to perform and apply data validation, integrity, and transformation rules.

- **Data Enrichment**—augments or enriches the incoming message payload by fanning-out and fetching data from one to many sources and fanning-in.
- **Content Based Routing**—routes the message from a service consumer to one among the many service providers based on some message content.
- **Message Observer**—monitors and observes messages (non-invasively) as they pass through the mediation by applying filters. Examples could be watching out for too many ATM transactions on the same account, observing response time from a particular backend application, and monitoring for SLA breaches, logging, and auditing messages.

Deployment patterns

This category of patterns deals with how WESB can be deployed in a variety of ways including, federated, brokered, and so on.

- **Global ESB**: All services share one namespace, and each service provider is visible to every service requester across a heterogeneous, centrally administered, geographically distributed environment. Used by departments or small enterprises where all the services are likely to be applicable throughout the organization.
- **Directly connected ESB**: A common service registry makes all of the services in several independent ESB installations visible. It is used where services are provided and managed by a line of businesses but made available enterprise-wide.
- **Brokered ESB**: Bridge services that selectively expose requesters or providers to partners in other domains regulate sharing among multiple ESB installations that each manages its own namespace. Service interactions between ESBs are facilitated through a common broker that implements the bridge services. Used by departments that develop and manage their own services, but share a few of them or selectively Access Services provided across the enterprise.
- **Federated ESB:** One master ESB to which several dependent ESBs are federated. Service consumers and providers connect to the master or to a dependent ESB to Access Services throughout the network. Used by organizations that want to federate a set of moderately autonomous departments under the umbrella of a supervising department.

WESB selection checklist

It's quite possible for an organization to have multiple ESB configurations/topologies. It's all driven by business needs and the ESB topologies may change as business requirements change. The flexibility and "service virtualization" provided by the ESB is achieved through what architects call "separation of concerns", the clear separation between the applications which run the business (including Business Services and business processes) and the ESB (the infrastructure for connecting applications and services together).

> IBM has three ESB products in its offering portfolio:
>
> - WebSphere Enterprise Service Bus
> - WebSphere Message Broker is used in scenarios where the infrastructure has heterogeneous applications with standard and non standard interfaces, protocols, and data formats
> - WebSphere DataPower Integration Appliance XI50 is Appliance-based ESB for simplified deployment and hardened security

When selecting WESB, here are some of the most typical considerations or topics to consider include:

- Focus on standards-based interactions using XML, SOAP, and WS*
- Mediate and integrate to existing systems using JMS, MQ, Web Services, and so on
- Support for protocols including HTTP, MQ, JMS, RMI, and so on
- Need for message transformation using XSLT
- Use WPS for process choreography and orchestration (common tooling, runtime infrastructure)
- Your team has skills with WebSphere Application Server Administration and Java coding
- Reliability and extensive transactional support are key requirements

IBM's SOA Foundation lifecycle

The IBM SOA Foundation is an integrated open standards-based set of IBM software, best practices, and patterns. The key elements of the IBM SOA Foundation are the SOA life cycle (model, assemble, deploy, manage), reference architecture, and SOA scenarios. IBM's SOA Foundation lifecycle consists of the following iterative phases and some of the key activities performed:

- Model
    - Gather key business requirements, objectives, and success criteria
    - Model business processes based on requirements and objectives
    - Identify KPIs and instance metrics
    - Perform business process model simulations
    - Service discovery and identification
- Assemble
    - Service Components Assembly based on business design
    - Service specification, realization, and implementation
    - Business process assembly and implementation leveraging new and existing services and components
    - End application connectivity including routing, message transformation, protocol transformation, and so on
    - Creating the monitoring model based on KPIs
- Deploy
    - Preparation of the hosting/operational environment
    - Integration testing of solution
    - Software configuration management activities
- Manage
    - Administer deployed applications, processes, services, and components
    - Monitor KPIs and instance metrics
    - Feed real-time monitor metrics to fine-tune the business process model

    - Plan for growth based on operational performance and metrics
    - User security

- Govern (that spans all phases)
    - Process and service lifecycle governance
    - Ensure process controls and compliance

When developing SOA-based solutions, you can adopt the SOA lifecycle by mapping what activities are performed in which phase and also identify which tools and products can be used to fulfill activities in that phase. The lifecycle, as shown in the following figure, outlines the key IBM products that could be used to fulfill some of the key activities in each phase to deliver the solution. *Products marked in bold are the ones we will be covering in this book.*

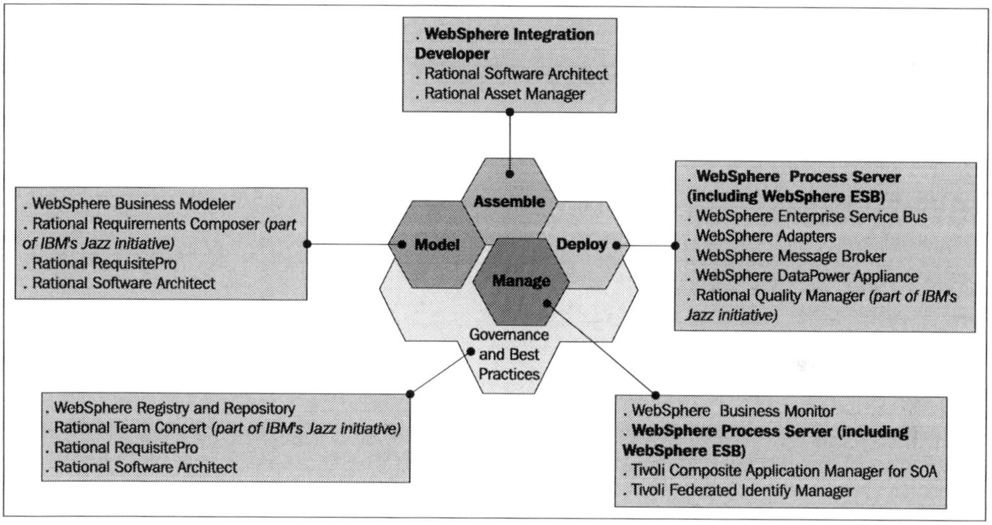

IBM's BPM enabled by SOA method

As mentioned earlier, SOA is not a technology but glue that cements the holistic relationship between IT and business. BPM again is a practice of focusing on the improvement of operations efficiencies within an organization by modeling, automating, and monitoring their core business processes. Both BPM and SOA are an art into themselves. Some of the key concerns, questions, and topics that arise when venturing into the adoption of BPM and SOA may include:

- How to identify process metrics and KPIs which are not only aligned with my core business performance objectives, but also help me constantly improve?
- How can I set up and implement a process governance and management framework?
- How to identify an implementation of a continuous and iterative BPM process optimization cycle that improves business and process agility?
- How to realize the value of applying BPM to deliver business processes?
- What are the set of phases, associated activities, and deliverables that I should adopt for the BPM solution development and management?

So when I'm building solutions with a BPM enabled by SOA approach, what are the lifecycle phases and what do I typically do in each of the lifecycle phases? Also, how and where do WPS, WESB, and potentially other products from IBM apply to each of the lifecycle phases? Let's look at IBM's BPM enabled by SOA methodology.

IBM's BPM enabled by SOA methodology provides a structured set of activities that you can manipulate and use in the build out of SOA and BPM based solutions. By using the method correctly, you can be assured that the solution including the business processes and Business Services will be aligned with business goals and that it creates a framework for continuous improvement. As shown in the following figure, the BPM enabled by the SOA method has five primary phases, which are as follows:

- Envision
    - Define strategy maps
    - Identify process capabilities and processes
- Assess
    - Collect understanding of current processes, process performance, and process enablers

- Define
    - Model future business processes, future process performance, and supporting process enablers
    - Validation of models and design
- Execute
    - Build, test, and deploy business processes, process performance monitoring and reporting, and supporting process enablers (technology, organization, and knowledge)
- Optimize
    - Operating, monitoring, and managing operational processes and their supporting process enablers (technology, organization, and knowledge)
- Governance spans all phases

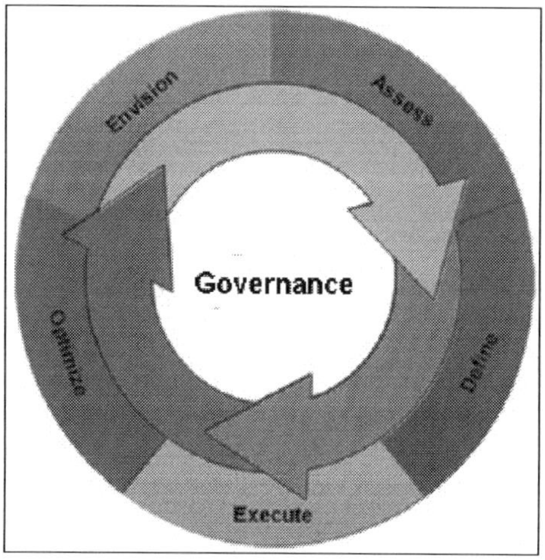

For detailed information on IBM's BPM enabled by SOA methodology, refer to the IBM Redpaper, *Business Process Management Enabled by SOA* by Anthony Catts and Joseph St. Clair:

`http://www.redbooks.ibm.com/abstracts/REDP4495.html?Open`

Summary

In this chapter, we discussed why when building IT solutions a process-driven integration combined with an SOA approach is critical for achieving dynamism. We also discussed the core capabilities needed for a process integration approach, IBM's SOA reference architecture, and IBM's Business Process Management platform including WebSphere Process Server (WPS) and WebSphere Enterprise Service Bus. We saw how WPS fits in an SOA approach, how it helps deliver an SOA infrastructure to orchestrate, mediate, connect, map, and execute the underlying IT functions and systems. We also discussed the ESB as a pattern and essential considerations to make when choosing an ESB. Then we discussed how WESB complements an SOA approach, how it enables connectivity and messaging capabilities, and hence provides a smart approach to SOA. We then discussed the IBM SOA lifecycle, various activities performed in the appropriate phases, and products from IBM that help accomplish activities within phases. Finally, we discussed IBM's BPM enabled by SOA lifecycle methodology, which can be used as a practical method when building SOA-based solutions.

2

Installing the Development Environment

Having given an overview of what Business Integration is and the fundamentals of SOA and BPM, we will now show how to install and set up your integrated development environment WebSphere Integration Developer (WID) and how to get started developing SOA applications using the WebSphere Process Server (WPS) and WebSphere Enterprise Service Bus (WESB). We will briefly discuss about WID and explain how it is the authoring environment for WPS and WESB. We will then guide you through how to start working with the tool, explain some of the fundamental concepts associated with WID, perform the various basic tasks like creating workspaces and projects, working with modules, exporting and importing projects—all that is necessary for building, testing, and deploying SOA-based BPM and integration solutions across the WebSphere Process Server, WebSphere ESB, and WebSphere Adapters.

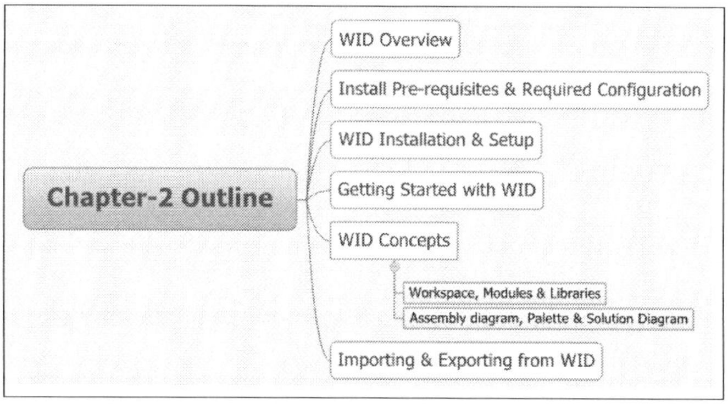

This chapter aims to help you with the following topics:

- Overview of WID and how and where it fits in the larger BPM and SOA Application development lifecycle
- Go over the installation requisites and configuration
- Install and set up WID including a unit test environment
- Starting WID and getting started with the tool
- Explain some of the fundamental concepts around workspace, modules, libraries, assembly diagram, palette, and solution diagram
- Importing and Exporting projects into and from WID

WebSphere Integration Developer overview

When you start working with WID, one of the first questions that you would ask at the outset is, "*What is WebSphere Integration Developer (WID)?*".

Let's first address that question. WID is part of the WebSphere BPM suite and is the Eclipse-based authoring environment to build SOA and BPM-based solutions. WID is primarily used in the assembly, implementation, and testing of Service Component Architecture (SCA)-based applications. It supports both top-down and bottom-up assembly-driven approaches in building the SOA and BPM-based applications.

The fundamental construct in a WID-centric world are **components**. Components are services, which are assembled to form end-to-end applications. In WID, the focus is on the assembly of components. The implementation of components can be done later or can be reused from capabilities exposed by existing IT systems. Users of WID typically produce artifacts or components such as business processes, state machines, data transformations, mediation flows, adapters, and so on, which are assembled together visually, to form a solution. WID provides the visual environment to build these artifacts and make the users focus on business logic implementation, by providing this layer of abstraction, and not worry about the component implementation. It also provides integrated testing, debugging, and deployment capabilities. WID provides an embedded unit test environment onto which the applications can be deployed for testing and validation. And last but not the least, solutions that are created using WID are based on the most common and prevalent industry standards such as Java Message Service (JMS), Business Process Execution Language (BPEL), Web Services, Simple Object Access Protocol (SOAP), Java EE Connector Architecture (JCA), and so on. The relationship of the various components as they apply to the WID tooling is shown in the following figure:

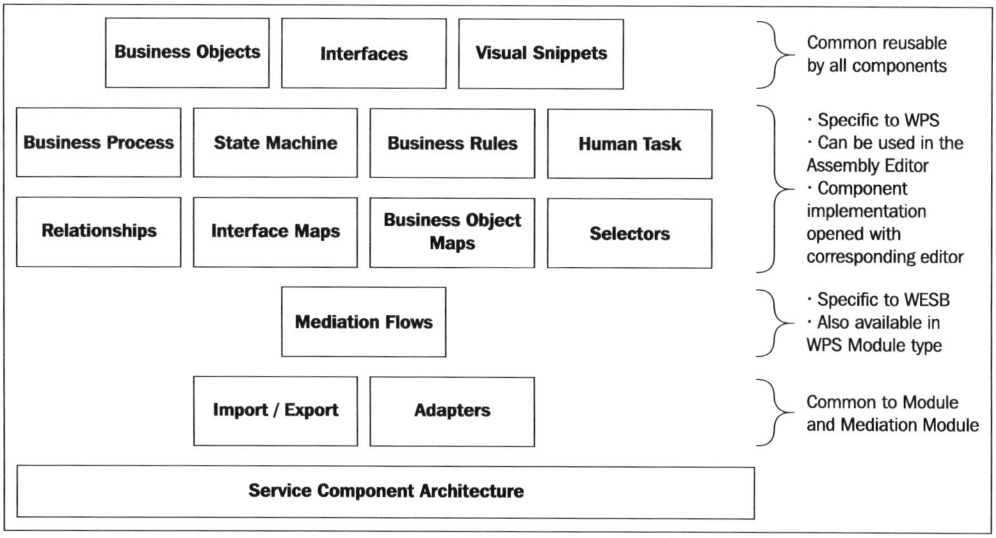

The preceding figure gives you an appreciation for the wide variety of components available in WID and how they relate to WPS and WESB. It also layers the components from a top-down perspective and provides an insight into their reuse.

Using the WID assembly editor, one can assemble, implement, and deploy service components to build SOA-based applications and hence solutions these applications belong to. These components can be grouped into **modules** or **mediation modules**, and specify which service interfaces are exposed by the components and hence the module to outside consumers. Services that are available include imported components such as Java beans or Web services and service components that WPS and WESB provide. Modules are then connected to form complete integration solutions.

So how does WID fit into the typical lifecycle-phases-roles involved in the Business Integration approach? Business Integration fundamentally has very strong ties to BPM and SOA, and enables the adopter of a Business Integration approach to identify, consolidate, and optimize business processes. Business Integration projects can have different flavors or different entry points.

1. **People/Portal Centric** features allow for human interaction.
2. **Application Integration Centric** features enable integration and collaboration between different systems, services, and applications independent of their underlying platform and language.
3. **Process Automation Centric** features help optimize and automate processes.

4. **Pure Play Connectivity** features allow to service providers to expose their existing application capabilities or functions on a standardized enterprise bus.
5. **Legacy Modernization** features help modernize and increase efficiency and accessibility of older legacy systems.

A typical Business Integration project lifecycle will consist of the following the phases:

1. Model
2. Assemble
3. Deploy
4. Manage
5. Govern

Typical roles involved during a Business Integration project will include:

1. Business/Process Analyst
2. Integration Architect
3. Integration Specialist
4. Component Developer
5. Infrastructure Administrator

When dealing with a Business Integration approach, the three pillars to its programming model include:

1. Business Process Choreography or Orchestration—how various components can be "stitched" together.
2. Business Data Objects—what is transferred between components.
3. Service Component Architecture—set of specifications which describe a model for building applications and systems using an SOA approach.

So in short, WID is an integrated development environment that provides the necessary capabilities and tools to:

1. Support all the phases (except for modeling of business processes, where a true process modeling tool like IBM WebSphere Business Modeler would help).
2. Support different roles and correspondingly support their activities.
3. Help develop Business Integration solutions based on the various standardized technologies mentioned as the three pillars.

4. It also helps to deploy the solutions to the WebSphere Process Server or the WebSphere Enterprise Service Bus.
5. The four phases are shown in the following image:

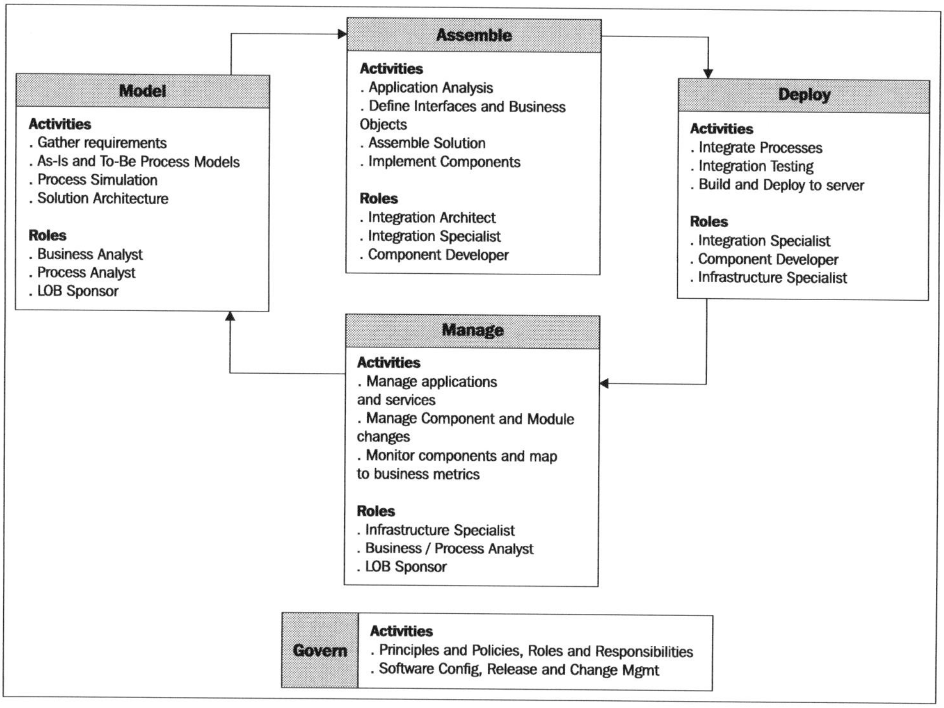

The preceding diagram illustrates the Business Integration life cycle, typical activities (which is highly condensed), and roles involved in building an integrated business application.

Of particular focus are the activities and roles involved in building, testing, and deploying applications using WebSphere Integration Developer as shown in the following figure:

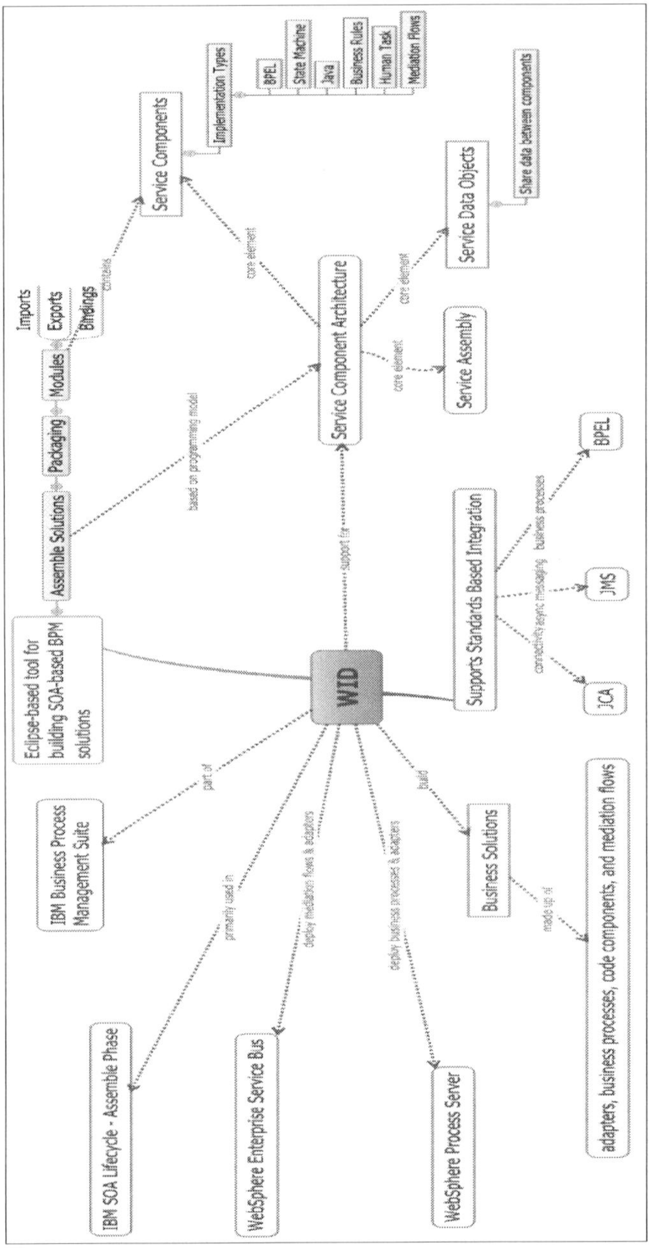

Prerequisite configuration

The following machine specifications are required for a Windows-based machine to host WebSphere Integration Developer v7.0:

- Most current processor (at least 1GHz or more, which is the norm these days)
- Recommended memory of 3 GB
- Windows XP or Windows Vista Operating System
- Atleast 7.5 GB free hard drive space for the installation
- Apart from the Internet Explorer browser, Firefox could also be an option
- Adobe Flash Player 9
- User must have administrator privileges

> For more detailed information on the system software and hardware requirements, please visit the product **System requirements** page:
>
> `http://www-01.ibm.com/software/integration/wid/sysreqs/?S_CMP=rnav`
>
> For more information about how to a get copy of the WebSphere Integration Developer inquire at:
>
> `http://www-142.ibm.com/software/dre/h2b/buildh2bpage.wss?synkey=F131134I92520H03`

Installing WID on Windows

Even if you have an existing compatible Eclipse platform environment, installing WebSphere Integration Developer into it is not supported! However, WID can co-exist with other/previous versions of WID.

Though there are several installation topologies and scenarios that are possible, for this book, we use a standalone version of WID with the necessary **unit test environment** (**UTE**) with embedded test environment servers. The next section will cover more details on installation.

> If you are migrating from a previous version of WID, referred to as version-to-version migration, please refer to the detailed guidance provided in the WID product Info Center, under **Migrating to WebSphere Integration Developer** section.
>
> `http://publib.boulder.ibm.com/infocenter/dmndhelp/v6r2mx/index.jsp`

IBM Installation Manager

IBM Installation Manager is a unified tool that we will use to install the WebSphere Integration Developer packages on our workstation. It will also be used to update and modify other packages and fixes over time. It keeps track of what we install, software components that have already been installed, and components that are available for installation. It searches for updates and installs the latest version of the WebSphere Integration Developer product packages. You should use the Installation Manager to modify, uninstall, and roll back product packages. The following mind map shows the capabilities of the IBM Installation Manager:

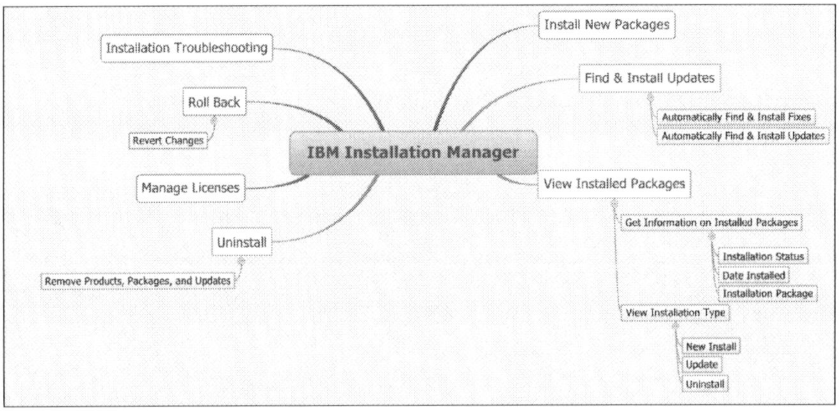

Starting the Installation

Based upon your license with IBM, you may have DVDs for the WID installation or download it from Passport Advantage. If you download from Passport Advantage, you need to get all five image parts of WebSphere Integration Developer V 7.0 Multiplatform Multilingual. Please ensure that these binaries are available on the installation machine. The following mind map gives an overview of the sequence of installation steps that we will walk through:

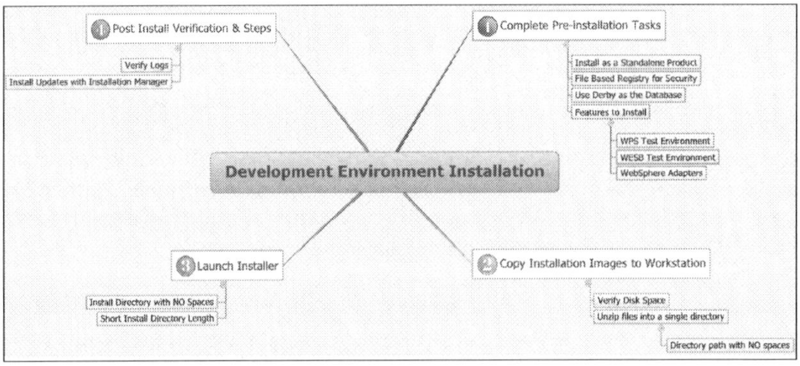

After verifying the prerequisites and copying the install images to your server, we begin the third step, as described in the preceding mind map. In this step, we use the Installation Manager to install WID V 7.0. The Installation Manager in turn has a three-step process:

- The first step opens a wizard to install IBM WebSphere Integration Developer tooling.
- The second step does a silent installation of the WebSphere Application Server in the test environment.
- The last step installs WPS over the WebSphere Application Server.

Having unzipped all of the installed images `ZIP` files (that would add up to five), into the same directory location (for example, `D:\WID_Install`), launch the installation launchpad program found under `disk1/launchpad.exe`.

Here are the steps to install IBM WebSphere Integration Developer V 7.0:

1. Select **Install IBM WebSphere Integration Developer V 7.0**, as shown in the following screenshot:

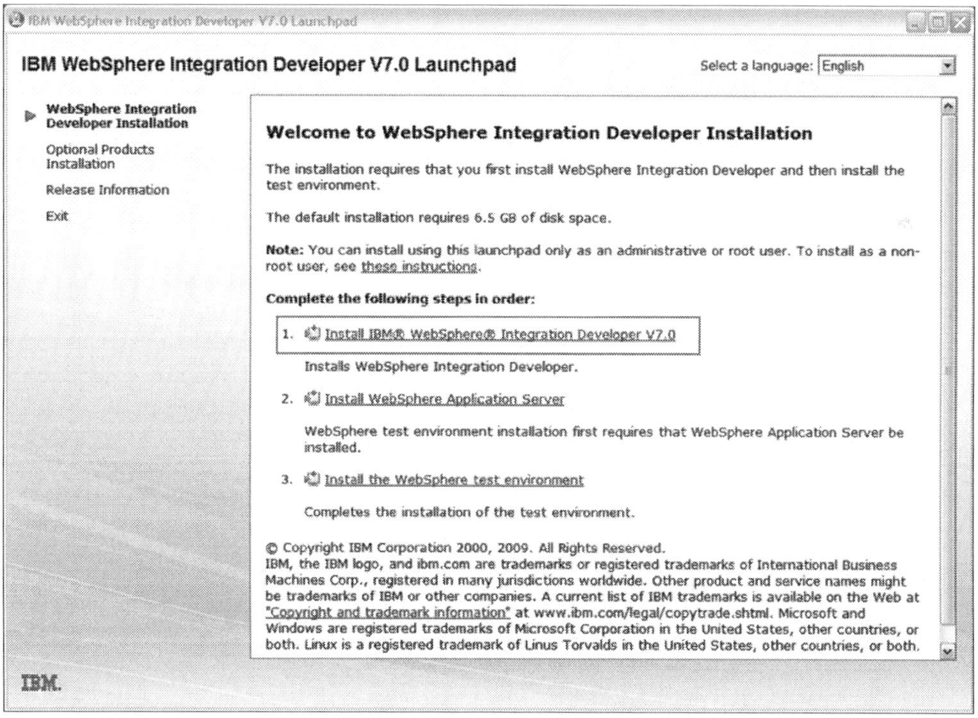

2. The **IBM Installation Manager** wizard will be launched. Select the components you want to install. In this case, it will install **IBM WebSphere Integration Developer Version 7.0.0.0** so click on the **Next** button as shown in the following screenshot:

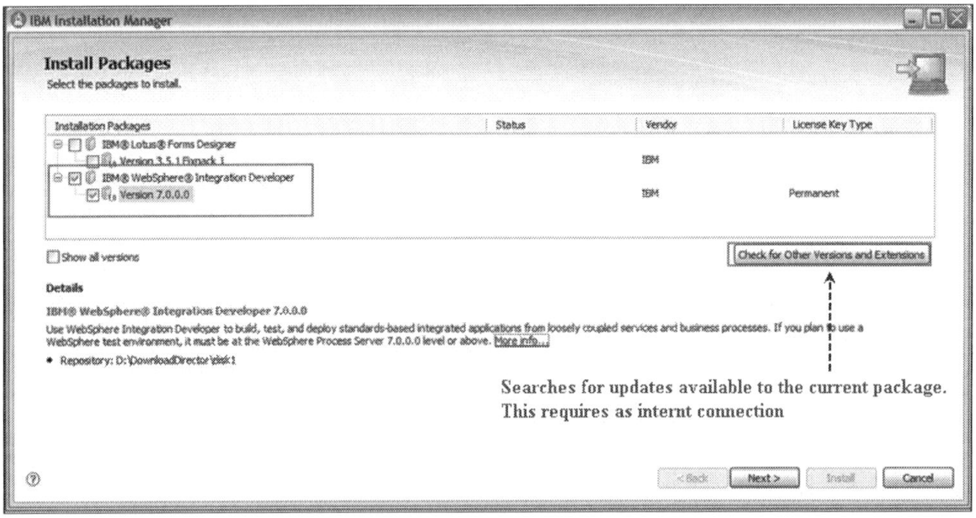

3. On the license agreement page you need to accept the terms of use in order for the **Next** button to appear. Once you accept, click on the **Next** button.
4. If this is a clean machine and this the first time you are installing, the **IBM Installation Manager** screen will appear. It is recommended to change locations as shown in the following screenshot:

> One of the most critical and common advice is to have no spaces in the directory locations where various components would be installed under. Also you get a warning about the 259 character limit for Windows path lengths. If the directory path is too long you may see the error message *The URL length is greater than the Windows limit of 259 characters.*
>
> Another piece of advice is that you can specify the shared resources directory only the first time you install a package. All subsequent Installation Manager installations will use this directory. Hence it is critical to allot sufficient space and to select this location carefully.

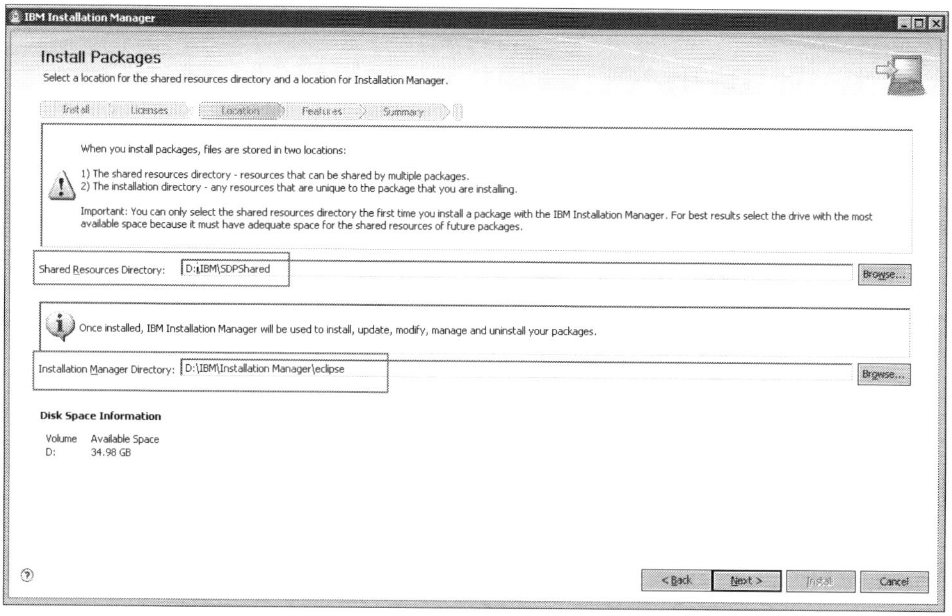

5. Similarly, on the next page select the location of the WID install directory (for example, `D:\IBM\WID7`) and click on the **Next** button.
6. On language selection, by default, **English** is selected. You may choose another language as needed and then click on the **Next** button.
7. On select features, you may add features as needed. For the purpose of this book we have kept the default selections as shown in the following screenshot and then click on the **Next** button.

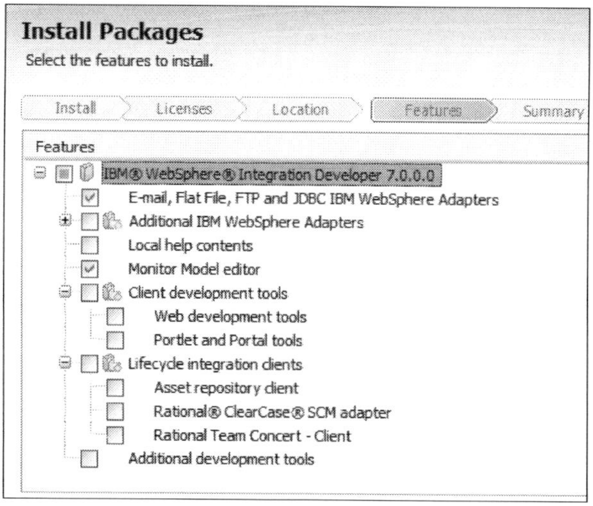

8. Review the summary of your selections and click on the **Install** button.
9. Once the installation completes successfully close the Installation Manager and return to the launch pad.

This completes the first step of the Installation Manager as you have installed only the tooling successfully. You still need to install the UTE, even though the UTE is not required we do recommend it.

Setting up UTE

After installing WID, you will have the option to install an integrated test environment for both the WebSphere Process Server (WPS), and/or the WebSphere Enterprise Service Bus (WESB) profiles, as explained in the next section.

> A **profile** is used to define a separate runtime environment, with separate command files, configuration files, and log files. We will dicuss in more detail about profiles and other related concepts in *Chapter 12, Deployment Topologies*

Typically, you can define three different types of environments:

1. stand-alone server
2. deployment manager
3. managed node

With profiles you can have more than one runtime environment on your system, without having to install multiple copies of the WID. You can create, augment, or modify profiles using the **Profile Management Tool** that will be available once you install WID.

> For more information refer: `http://publib.boulder.ibm.com/infocenter/dmndhelp/v7r0mx/topic/com.ibm.wbit.help.inst.doc/topics/t_instute.html`

WPS and WESB Integrated test environment

If you choose a WPS profile, you will be able to deploy, debug, and test Service Component Architecture (SCA)-based SOA applications that contain BPEL-based business processes, human tasks, state machines, business rules, selectors, Java components, and so on. You can also add WESB mediation flows to a module and test them. More specifics about these SCA component types will be covered in the later chapters.

You can consider the WPS profile as a superset that can run all types of components and should be used in instances when you have solutions that contain a mix of WPS-based and WESB-based modules. The WESB profile is a subset of the WPS profile. Hence you cannot run BPEL business processes, human tasks, business rules, state machines selectors, and so on using a WESB profile. There is no harm in choosing to create both these profiles during the installation setup and have them available in the WID environment.

The steps to install a WPS-integrated test environment for version 7.0 are as follows:

1. On the launch pad click on step 2—**Install WebSphere Application Server**. This will give you a warning to close the Installation Manager before proceeding. It is critical to ensure that the Installation Manager is closed, or else your WebSphere Application Server will fail. Click on the **OK** button on the warning box to begin the installation.

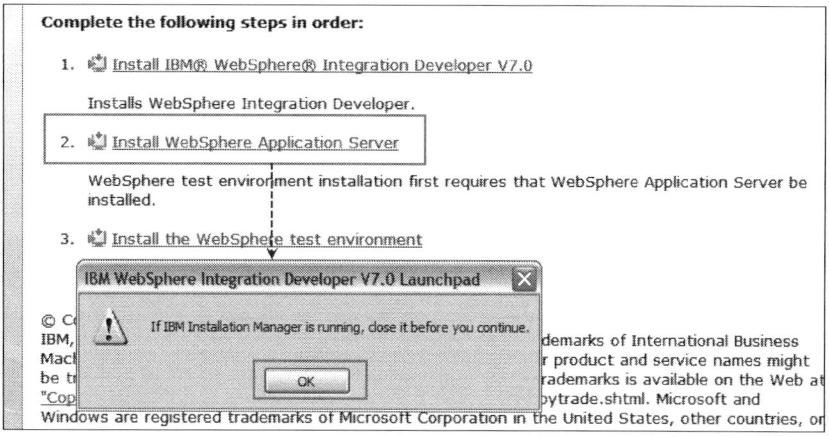

2. You will see an installation progress begin at the bottom of the launch pad. Please be patient as this may take a few minutes.

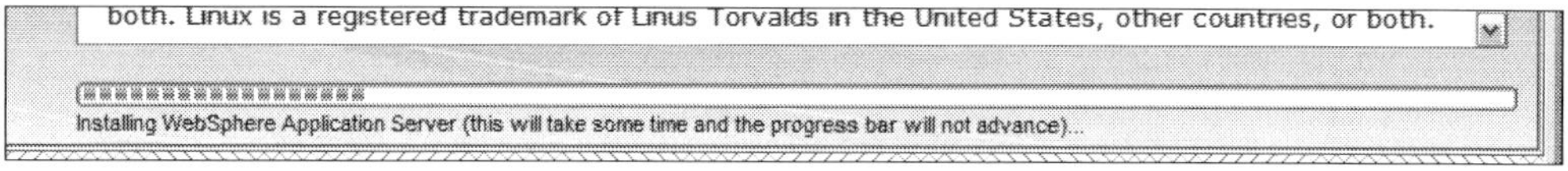

3. Once the installation is complete you will be given an Installation successful dialog box. Click on the **OK** button on the dialog box.
4. On the launch pad now click on step 3—**Install the WebSphere test environment**. This will launch the Installation Manager.

5. On **Install packages** screen select the packages you want to install. By default, the WPS and its underlying dependencies SCA and WAS feature packs are selected, as shown in the following image. Click on the **Next** button.

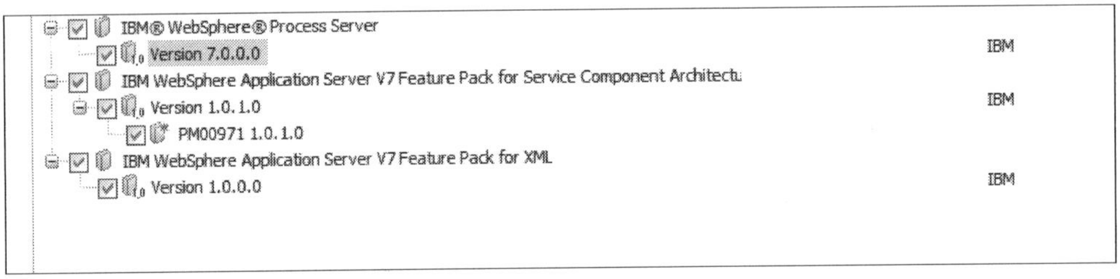

6. The installation wizard's steps are the same as the WID installation we covered above. On the feature installation page you are given the option to install a WPS or WESB or both standalone development profiles. For the purpose of this book, we go with the default WPS standalone development profile selection, as shown in the following screenshot. On the next page, you will need to define the admin user credentials for the WPS profile and provide a username and password (admin / admin is the default username and password. You are free to change this what you prefer).

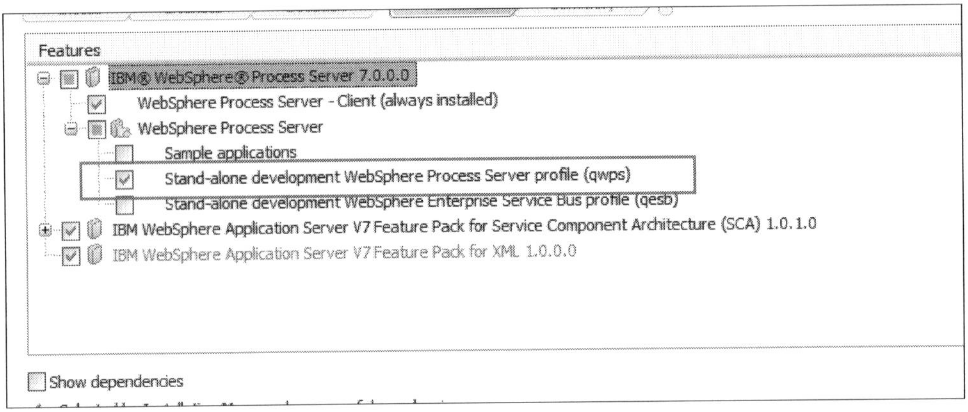

7. Once you complete installing the test environment, you may close the launch pad screen. This completes your WID installation.

Verifying the installation

Since we chose to install IBM Installation Manager during the WID setup, it will be available post installation to update and modify other packages and fixes over time. You can view the Installation status at any time by going to **IBM Installation Manager | File | Installation History** and looking at the summary of the installation details. Also all the installation log files for the installation are available under the following location, `C:\Documents and Settings\All Users\Application Data\IBM\Installation Manager\logs`.

Using IBM Installation Manager you can import these log files and go though the installation logs that were done over a period of time. You can do this by starting **IBM Installation Manager | View Log | Import log file** (icon on top-right) and selecting the log file of interest to view/examine the detailed results of an installation session.

Post installation activities

We strongly recommend that you use the IBM Installation Manager post installation to find any updates and to apply them.

> Internet access is required to install the updates with IBM Installation Manager. As these packages may be large in size (often several hundred MB) it would be helpful to have more bandwidth available for the process.

Using the **Update** icon in the IBM Installation Manager main screen, if updates are found (iFix or FixPak, Feature Packs, or Updates), the appropriate updates are selected and installed. Installation status and logs can be found, as described in the previous section.

Uninstalling WID

Installation Manager can also be used to uninstall products and packages. Make sure the package being uninstalled is not dependent on another package.

> For more information, go to `http://publib.boulder.ibm.com/infocenter/dmndhelp/v7r0mx/topic/com.ibm.wbit.help.inst.doc/topics/t_uninstall_offering.html`

Getting Started with WID

The following mind map provides a detailed layout of the different features in WID that you will use to develop integrated SOA and BPM solutions.

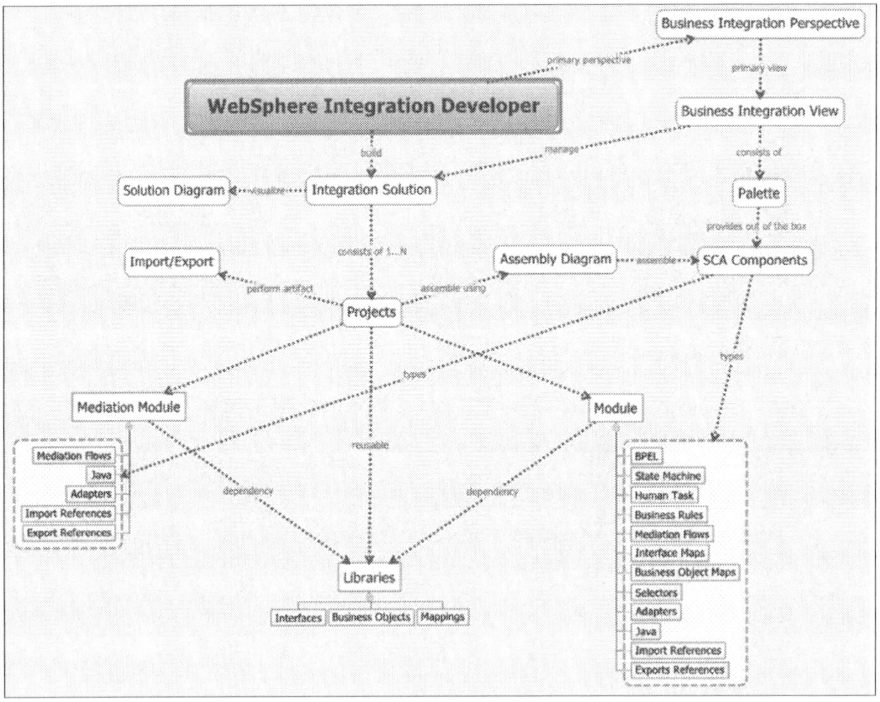

Business Integration perspective is the default perspective that provides rich features to visually define business processes and solutions through simple drag-and-drop technology. It lets you efficiently manage your integrated solutions that consist of projects and libraries, as shown in the preceding map. More details about the layout of this perspective are covered later in the chapter. Let's now start WID and take a closer look at the product.

Starting WID

You can start WID from the **Start | Programs** by selecting the WebSphere Integration Developer shortcut or from the command line by executing `% WID_HOME% \wid.exe`. After starting WID a splash screen will appear as shown in the following screenshot:

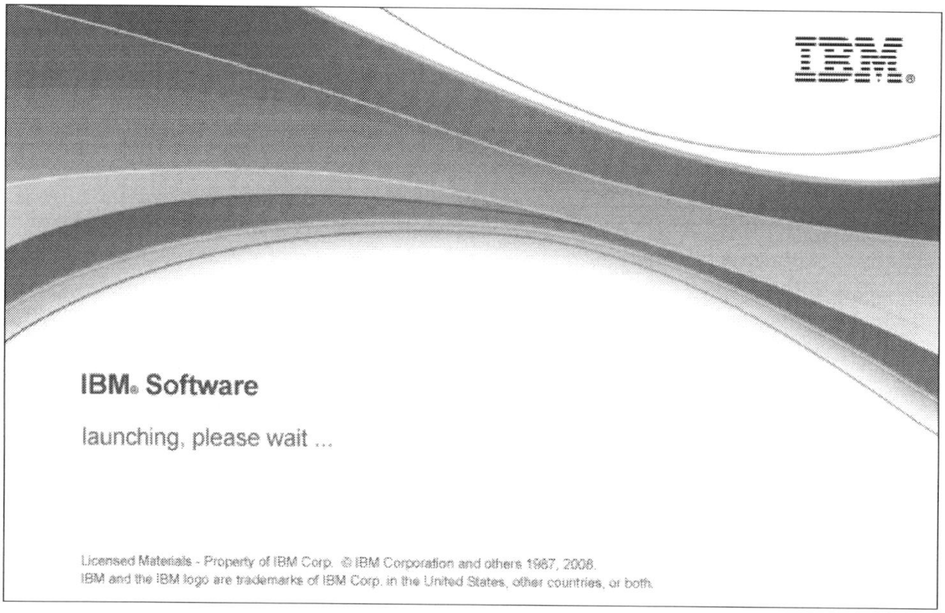

After the splash screen, you will be asked to provide a workspace path. Here are few suggestions to help you choose the right workspace location:

- We recommend not to go with the default location and to change the location to something short and manageable. For example, we recommend `C:\AllWork\ws1`. On Windows-based machines this becomes more important due to the 259 character limit on the fully qualified path.
- You can create multiple workspaces based on your development needs. From a usability and manageability perspective it is always better to keep all workspaces in the same location, which would be `C:\AllWork`.
- Finally, do not place the workspace folder within the production install folder. This is to prevent deletion or corruption of your work if the product is uninstalled or updated.

One of the first things you will notice if you have not used a product based on Eclipse 3 (for example, Eclipse Web Tools Project, Eclipse SDK, and so on), is the welcome screen that is shown when you start a new workspace. From this screen you can access information about the product overview, cheat sheets, tutorials, samples, new features, migration information, and web resources. If you close the Welcome screen, you can always open it again by selecting **Help | Welcome** from the menu bar.

There is another new feature added in Eclipse 3 that is important to know. This feature is referred to as progressive disclosure, though you may also hear it associated with the term "Capabilities". Progressive disclosure is a way to hide certain product features based upon your role. For example, if a user is not working on web services development, it is possible to hide the associated wizards and tools by disabling the web services development capabilities. Capabilities that are not enabled can be enabled either when the feature is first accessed, or by enabling the appropriate capability through the **Preferences** menu.

Business Integration perspective

The primary perspective in WebSphere Integration Developer is the Business Integration perspective as shown in the following screenshot:

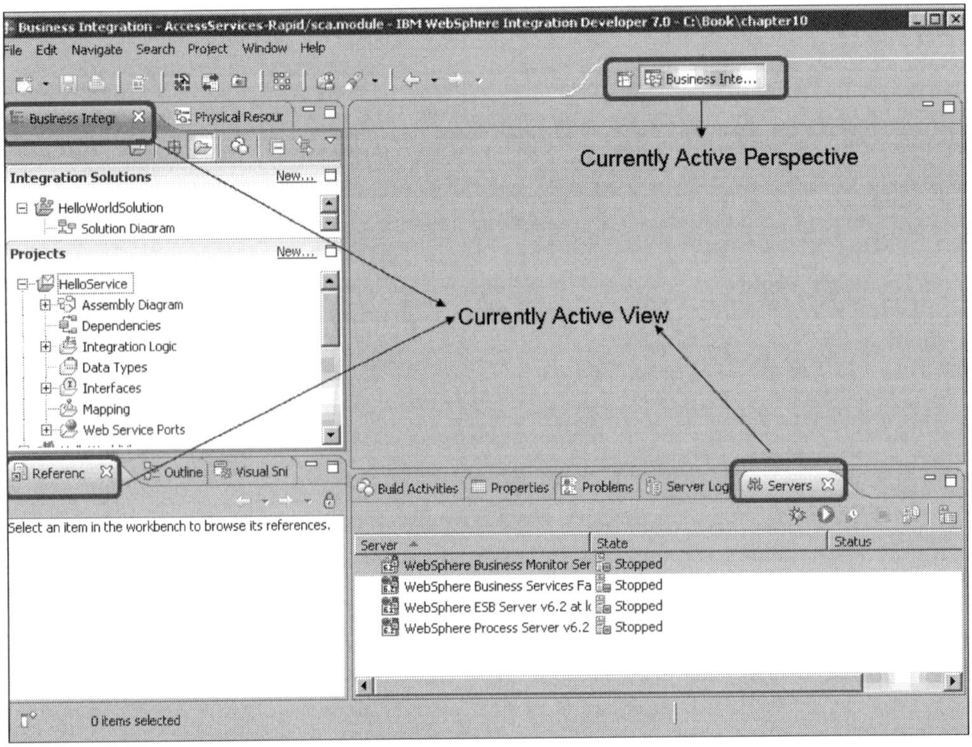

The majority of your Business Integration work is done from this perspective and it is the default perspective when the product is launched.

Available views

The primary view in the Business Integration perspective is the Business Integration view. This view is used to manage and view all Business Integration resources. The resources shown in this view provide a logical grouping of resources and hide artifacts that are not essential for business integration development. It is important to note that this view only shows a logical representation of the resources in the workspace that are related to Business Integration work, and there is not a one-to-one relationship to physical resources on the file system. Both module and library projects are visible from the Business Integration view.

Working with Modules and Libraries

There are two important project types when doing Business Integration development in the WebSphere Integration Developer, as shown in the following screenshot:

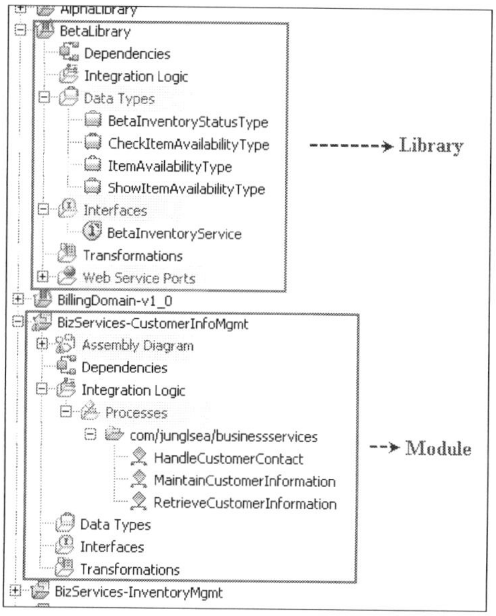

A module project represents a basic unit of deployment and is a composite of service components, imports, and exports. Modules can contain various components (BPEL, Mediation Flow, Java, and so on) within a module and can pass their data by reference. There are two types of modules—modules and mediation modules. A module (considered a superset is also referred to as a Business Integration module) contains many component types that support a business process. A mediation module contains one or more mediation flow components, plus zero or more Java components that augment the mediation flow component. A module can contain mediation flow components also.

A module is a Business Integration project type for developing SCA-based applications. A module is a basic unit of deployment to the WebSphere Process Server runtime environment, and as such, is packaged in an **Enterprise Archive (EAR)** file. The `EAR` file contains all the SCA-based artifacts packaged in a `JAR` file, J2EE projects, such as Web and EJB modules, dependent Java projects, and any dependent Libraries packaged as `JAR` files. Also included in this project are other Business Integration artifacts that make up the overall application. This would include BPEL definitions, interface definitions, and XML schema definitions.

> For more information on `EAR` files please refer to
> `http://en.wikipedia.org/wiki/EAR_(file_format)`

A library project is also another type of Business Integration project. Unlike the module project, a library project is not a deployable unit. The library project holds artifacts that can be shared between multiple modules. Implementations, interfaces, business objects, business object maps, roles, relationships, and other are held within a library. It is important to note, however, at runtime that the library is not shared. In this case, the library is deployed individually with the module that is dependent upon it.

Another important difference between a module and library project is the type of artifacts that can be contained in each project type.

Specifically, library projects only contain interfaces, business objects and graphs, business object maps, and relationships. Library projects do not include other types of Business Integration resources such as SCA artifacts. A library project is created to store artifacts that are shared between module projects. If a module is dependent upon a particular library project, that project must be added to the dependency list for the appropriate module using the dependency editor.

Solution diagram

The integration solution diagram organizes and displays how modules, mediation modules, libraries, and other dependent projects connect. The Business Integration view is split between projects and integration solutions, as shown in the following screenshot:

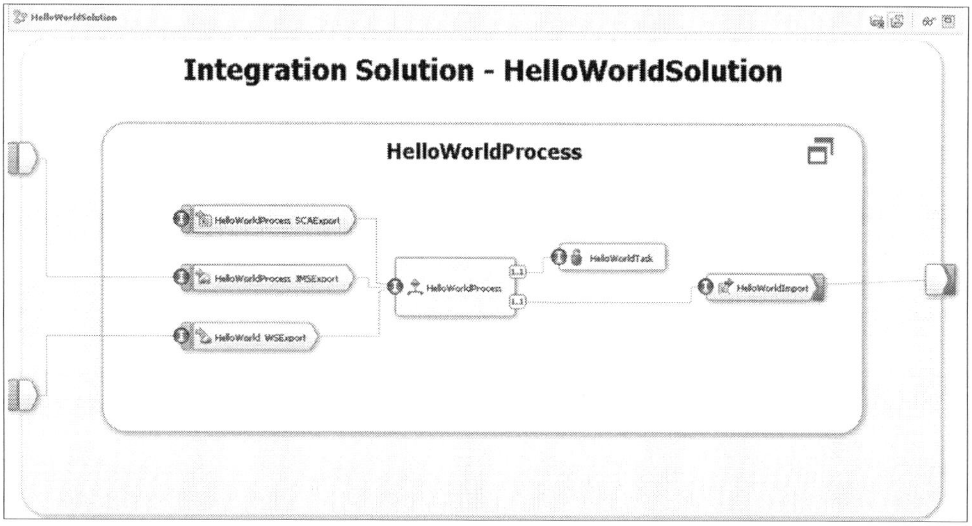

The integration solutions section helps users organize multiple modules, mediation modules, libraries, and other dependent projects into one scope. This is a development/design time concept only and the servers/runtime still will not have any visibility into this concept. The second and most important part of the integration solution is the diagram. It allows you to visualize how modules, mediation modules, libraries, and other dependent projects connect.

Assembly Diagram

The primary tool for defining and assembling SCA artifacts is the assembly editor. This editor will allow you to visually assemble SCA applications such as components, exports, imports, and standalone references, and to wire them together to build composite applications/solutions. A sample assembly diagram would look like a figure as shown in the following screenshot:

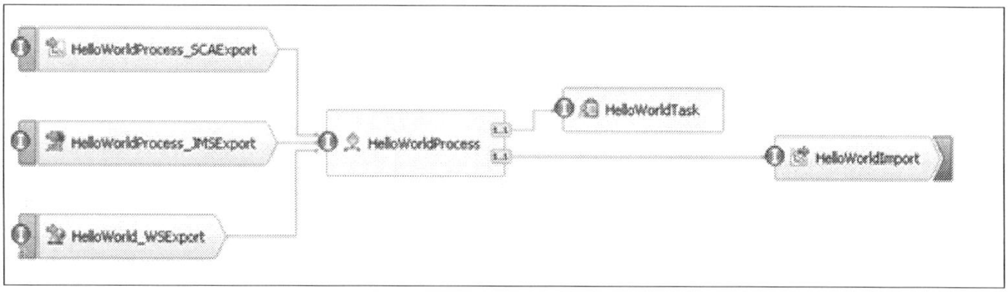

When using the assembly editor, there are several development approaches. First, you can build your SCA application using a top-down development model. In this case, you use the assembly editor to diagram and model your application visually before you implement the components and create any associated component business logic. You drag and drop the preferred SCA componets to the assembly diagram. Once the SCA components are added to the assembly diagram, you can assign interfaces and even create new interface definitions for each component from within the assembly editor.

In the bottom-up development model, you start by implementing the components individually, by defining your business logic. The components can be implemented as a business processes, business state machines, business rules, or human tasks. Or you can import existing components or services exposed by end applications by dragging them and dropping them onto the assembly diagram. As part of this process, the appropriate interfaces and references are automatically added to the components. You complete the assembly by wiring the SCA elements together.

Finally, in the middle development model, you define the elements in the assembly diagram and their implementations in parallel. As with the top-down approach, you create the assembly diagram in the assembly editor. But unlike the top-down approach, you do not generate implementations from the elements in the diagram. Instead, you select the appropriate implementation that you created in parallel. Be aware that the parallel activities, creating the diagram and creating their implementations, are not done in isolation.You must know the interfaces and references for each element in order to create its implementation, and vice versa. The point is that you do not have to wait for one activity to finish before you begin with the other.

Palette

On the left of the assembly editor is a palette that allows you to add various SCA components to the assembly diagram. The palette groups elements into drawers that can then be expanded and collapsed. The primary drawer is labelled components and is expanded in this screen capture. Within the expanded view there are three groupings.

- The first grouping is for those SCA components that provide business logic, which are human tasks, Java, business processes, business rule groups, and business state machines.
- The second group is for those SCA artifacts that provide access to services, specifically imports, exports, and standalone references.
- The third grouping is for components that provide supporting logic, which are interface maps and selectors. The two collapsed drawers at the bottom of the palette are for outbound and inbound adapters which provide access to imports and exports associated with specific adapter types.

Favorites allows you to create your own grouping of the components and adapters you regularly use, allowing you to work from that drawer without having to open the others. The canvas area of the assembly diagram shows the various components that make up the SCA application in the module project.

Imports and Exports

The following screenshot shows an example of Import and Export SCA components.

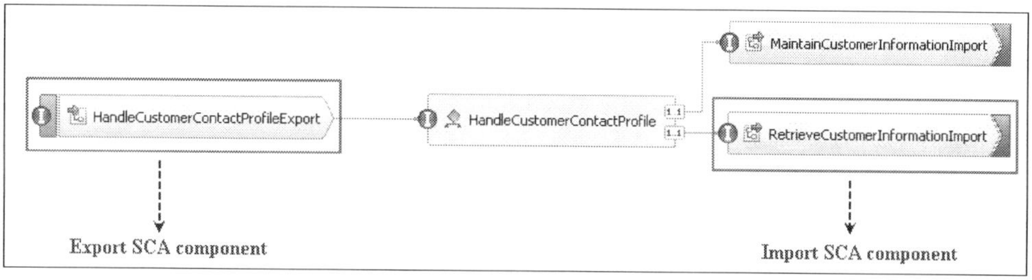

An **import** allows you to use functions that are not a part of the module that you are assembling. Imports are used in an application in exactly the same way as local components. Imports have interfaces that are the same as, or a subset of, the interfaces of the remote service that they are associated with so that those remote services can be called. To share the interfaces between modules, put the interfaces into a library. Then, for both modules, add a dependency on the library to use its resources.

Imports and exports require binding information, which specifies the means of transporting the data from the modules. An import binding describes the specific way an external service is bound to an import component. For an import that is generated from an export, the binding type of the import will be specified for you. Imports can use the following bindings, which can be remote or local:

- SCA
- Web service
- HTTP
- Messaging (JMS, MQ JMS, generic JMS, MQ)
- Stateless session bean
- EIS

If you are creating the import using the palette in the assembly editor, you will have to specify a binding type for the external service in order to test it. Bindings specify the means or the technology protocol used for transporting data into or out of a module.

> For more information on binding types and selecting appropriate binding types refer to `http://publib.boulder.ibm.com/infocenter/dmndhelp/v7r0mx/index.jsp?topic=/com.ibm.websphere.wps.doc/doc/tadm_installversionedsca.html`

An export is a published interface from a component or import that offers its service to the outside world, for example, as a Web service. Exports have interfaces that are the same as or a subset of the interfaces of the component or import that they are associated with so that the published service can be called. An export dragged from another module into an assembly diagram will automatically create an import. Exports that are shown under the module assembly in the Business Integration view can also be used to create imports in other modules. Each export has an address (which is a URL, for example: `http://localhost:9080/BenefitEligibilityModuleWeb/sca/BasicValidationExport`) at which it will be deployed on the server. The export can be exposed at that address.

Imports and exports require binding information, which specifies the means of transporting the data from the modules. When you use the **Generate Export** action from the menu of a component, you need to select the binding so that the binding is generated when the export is created.

References and wires

There are two types of wires. The first type of wire comes from a Partner Reference (the source) that is defined for a component or standalone reference node and goes to a component or import (the target). In this case, the wire identifies the component or import (target) that is accessed when the source component uses that partner reference. By default, a partner reference only allows one wire leading from it unless the partner reference's multiplicity property is changed to 0...n.

The second type of wire comes from an Export Wire (the source) and goes to a component or import (the target). In this case, the wire identifies the (target) component that provides the service. An export can only have one wire leading out of it.

The following screenshot shows the two types of wires:

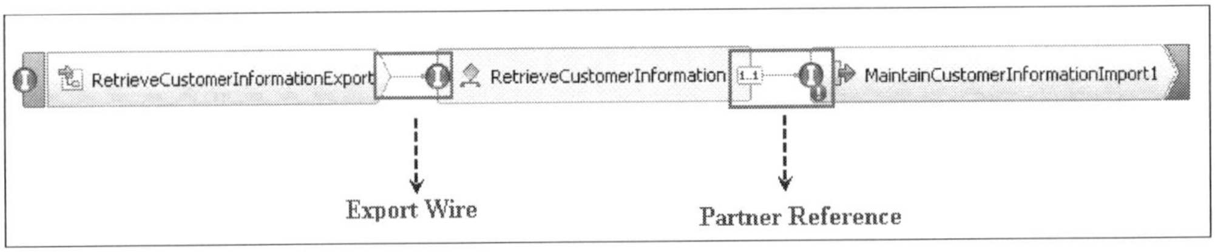

Dependency editor

If a module or mediation module needs to use resources from a library or if a library needs to use resources from another library, you have to open the module or library with the dependency editor and add a dependency on the required library, as shown in the following screenshot:

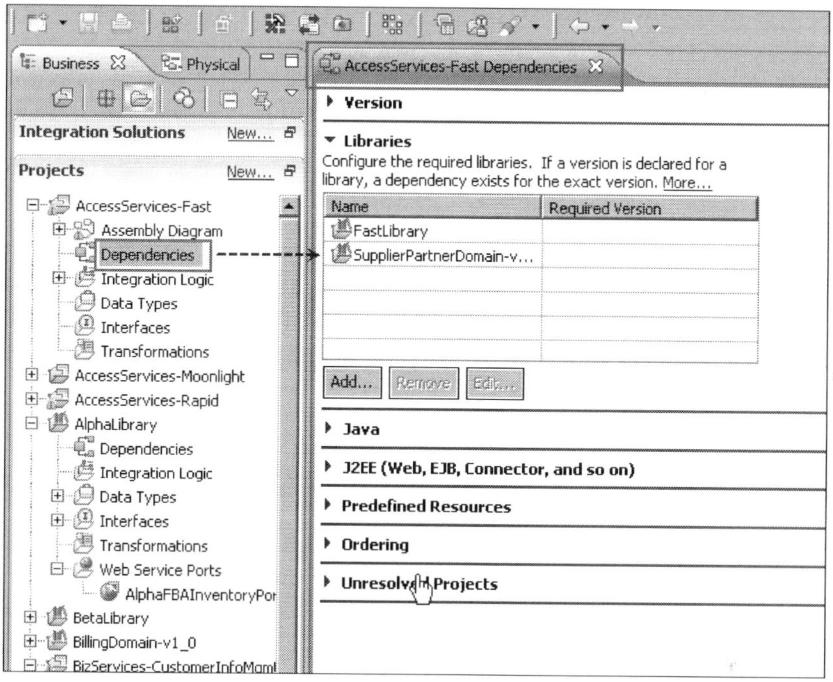

Business objects and interfaces are examples of the resources that you would want to share. Libraries must be deployed with modules that have dependencies on them so that the resources are available during runtime. With the dependency editor, you can add dependencies on libraries and Java projects and also add dependencies on J2EE projects.

Words of wisdom — tips, tricks, suggestions, and pitfalls

- Use shorter directory paths. Beware of the Windows 259 character limit. Also, there are no spaces in directory paths.
- If you experience a failed WID installation, identify where and why the installation failed by referring to the installation logs, as mentioned in the preceding sections. Before attempting another install, uninstall any existing versions using IBM Installation Manager, restart the machine, and run the install setup process again. You can also roll back a particular upgrade, FixPak, or iFix using the IBM Installation Manager.
- If you come across a situation where the IBM Installation Manager is not able to find any `repository.config` files: in this case manually add the `repository.config` file from the installation images extraction location `disk1\IM_win32`. You can do this by going to **File | Preferences | Repositories | Add Repositories** and adding the `repository.config` files.
- Use IBM Installation Manager to find and install any iFix, FixPak, Feature Packs, or updates. Do perform this activity periodically to find any updates to the product and apply all the key updates.
- After updating WID or after applying any iFix or a FixPak, it's recommended that you start with a `-clean` option. You can do this from the command line by issuing `% WID_HOME% \wid.exe -clean`. This option will rebuild the Eclipse repository, and it also does things like removing and regenerating manifest files, cached binaries, JXE information, and runtime plugin registry.
- You can use the **Profile Management Tool** (**PMT**) found under `%WTE_HOME%\`\runtimes\bi_v7\bin\ProfileManagement, run `pmt.bat` to create a standalone server profile, a deployment manager profile, or a custom profile. `WTE_HOME` refers to the path where the WebSphere Test Environment was installed.
- It's highly recommended that you back the test environment profiles on a periodic basis. You can back up the profile using the `manageProfiles.bat` tool found under `%WTE_HOME%\ runtimes\bi_v7\bin directory`. A typical backup command may look like:

  ```
  manageProfiles.bat -backupProfile -profileName wps -profilePath
  %WID_HOME%\pf\wps -backupFile "%fileName%"
  ```

- You can restore corrupted test environment profiles in from these backups at any time.

- Avoid modifying module dependencies outside the dependency editor.
- It is highly recommended that you use a software configuration management system like ClearCase, CVS, or Subversion to manage you modules.

Summary

In this chapter, we went through the process of installing and setting up the WID development environment. During the course of setting up the environment we quickly took a peek into some of the fundamentals of WID, key concepts, and terms. We also did a crash course in using WID and showed how to navigate using WID, some of the key activities one would perform and how to perform them. Now the reader is all set to start building the first set of applications using WID, as well as the WPS and WESB test environments.

3

Building your Hello Process Project

It's time to build our first business process application. Adhering to the long-lasting tradition of writing "Hello World" as the first program when we start learning a new language, framework, or application, we will build a Hello World business process. We will start with an overview of the Service Component Architecture (SCA) standard and Service Data Object (SDO) standard and how they relate to building applications using an SOA approach using WID. Getting the fundamentals about SCA and SDO will provide the reader with an understanding of how to begin to build, test, and deploy business process applications.

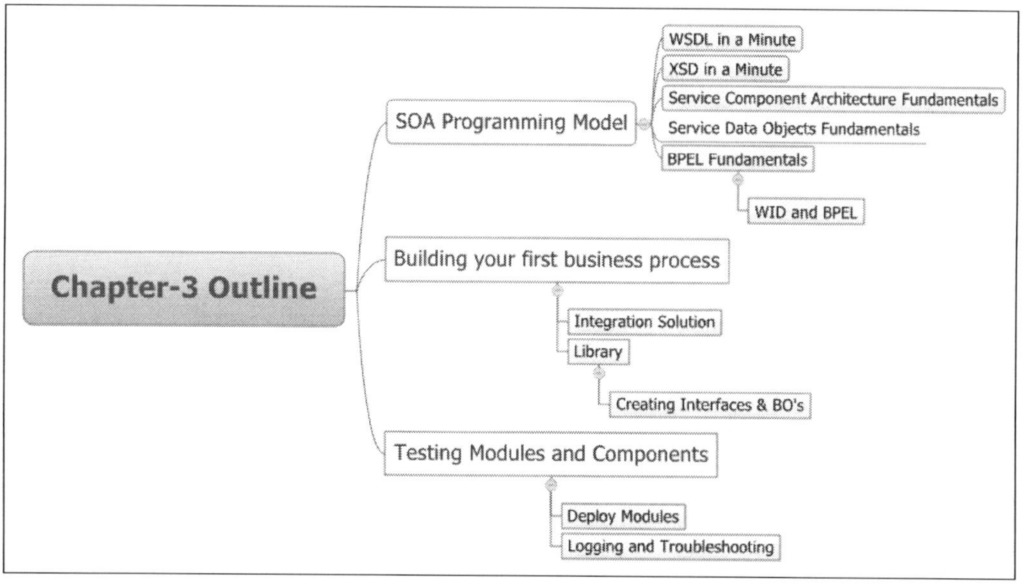

By the end of this chapter the aim is to have the reader enabled on the following items and topics:

- Overview of SOA programming model fundamentals including Service Component Architecture (SCA), Service Data Objects (SDOs)
- Also recap/reinforce the fundamental topics including WSDL, XSD, WS-BPEL
- Building the first module project in WID
- Deploying the module on a server and testing the project
- Logging, debugging, and troubleshooting basics
- Exporting projects from WID

SOA programming model

There is no single unique and easy way to define or explain SOA. Given a room full of executives, IT Managers, ITArchitects, and developers with each asked to give a one-sentence explanation of what SOA is, for sure each answer will be different. Its very important to understand the fundamental message behind SOA, what it is trying to achieve and what it provides the adopter. Here are some of most common facts you may have heard about SOA:

- It's a style for building loosely coupled and distributed applications
- It's all about service providers, providing services to service consumers that conforms to a common interface much like an agreement
- It provides a programming model based on standards defined by various standards bodies including the Organization for the Advancement of Structured Information Standards (OASIS), WS-* and so on

> OASIS is a not-for-profit consortium that drives the development, convergence, and adoption of open standards including WS-BPEL, WS-*, and UDDI. For more information on OASIS refer to:
> `http://www.oasis-open.org/who/`

So what are the needs and the fundamentals behind the SOA programming model? An SOA programming model derives from the basic concept of a service. Fundamentally, a service represents a discrete and yet a meaningful function, that makes larger sense to the business. Developers build services, use services, and develop solutions that aggregate services. They typically compose or assemble services into Integration Solutions.

> A **Service** or a **Business Service,** to be more precise, represents a discrete business function that makes meaningful sense to organizations. A Business Service can be composed of one of many fine-grained functions or atomic services, and by the true definition of SOA, it can behave dynamically depending on how it is invoked (context) and what it is invoked with (content). Services form the building blocks of SOA and are/should be reusable, decoupled, exposed in a standardized fashion, and derived from disparate IT resources.

The process of building a service-oriented architecture (SOA) is a journey and possibly an ever-evolving, ever-learning, never ending one. With SOA, you progress and mature over time to reach a state where you can truly achieve the benefits as promised. When you start building SOA-based solutions, you seldom create a solution that comprises of architectural elements from scratch. You inherit existing applications and its infrastructure, packages, and legacy applications, vendor/third party applications. You build and integrate solutions around these.

So why is that we are talking about SOA concepts, fundamentals and philosophy in the context of explaining what WID, WPS, and WESB is all about? In order to effectively build solutions, and applications with WID/WPS/WESB, you will have to understand a few key fundamental concepts and how these concepts apply in the context of WID/WPS/WESB, in order for you to use the appropriate features from the product. Since Web Services is "one" of the key enablers of SOA from a technology perspective (and also a core feature supported by WID/WPS/WESB), we will delve a little deeper into the fundamentals of concepts behind Web Services. We will brush up on the fundamental constructs and elements of a web service including:

- Web Services Description Language (WSDL)
- XML Schema Definition (XSD)
- Binding

Since WSDL and XSD are very much fundamental to building solutions with WID/WPS/WESB, we are going to be dealing with them in and out in the forthcoming sections.

Web Services Description Language (WSDL) in a minute

The following figure shows the mind map of a WSDL and describes the various concepts and its parts. A **WSDL** is an **Extensible Markup Language** (**XML**) based document that describes a web service and is also used to locate it. In a nutshell, WSDL is an XML grammar for specifying a public interface for a web service. This includes the following:

- Information on all publicly available **operations**/functions which can be invoked
- Data type information for all XML messages that are used to invoke the operations/functions
- **Binding** information about the specific transport protocol used. The binding can be either a Remote Procedure Call (RPC) style binding or a document style binding. The SOAP binding can have an encoded use or a literal use. This gives you four style/use models:
    - RPC/encoded
    - RPC/literal
    - Document/encoded
    - Document/literal

  Document/literal (Web Services Interoperability standard) for the most part is the preferred choice of WSDL style when using WID/WPS/WESB, because a document/literal style of web service (or WS-I compliant) allows web services to be interoperable across platforms, applications, and programming languages.
- Address information for locating the specified service.

> There is an excellent article *Which style of WSDL should I use?* by Russell Butek, which discusses the various WSDL binding styles and when to use what at:
> `http://www.ibm.com/developerworks/webservices/library/ws-whichwsdl/`

WSDL is not necessarily tied to a specific XML messaging system, but it does include built-in extensions for describing SOAP services. Any special datatypes used are embedded in the WSDL file in the form of XML Schema Definition (XSD). The service consumer or client application can then use SOAP to actually call one of the functions listed in the WSDL. WSDL document defines services as a collection of network endpoints or ports. In WSDL, the **abstract** definition of endpoints and messages are declared separately from their **concrete** network deployment or data format bindings. As shown in the following mind map, the abstract definition elements include:

- Types—describes all data types that are used.
- Message—defines the information exchanged, whether request or response. It can contain one or more parts or elemental pieces.
- PortType—defines the abstract set of operations of the service. It can define one or more operations. It supports four basic patterns of operations—request/response, one-way, solicit-response, notification.

The concrete definition elements include:

- Binding—describes the concrete specifics of how service will be implemented on the wire. It maps the specific information encapsulated in the portType to the specific implementation.
- Service—specifies the address for invoking the specific service, such as the URI.

A WSDL is generally published to a service registry and repository to be discovered and consumed by a client application. A service registry and repository (like WebSphere Registry and Repository) allows the services defined by a WSDL to be governed by promoting visibility and reducing redundancy in an SOA.

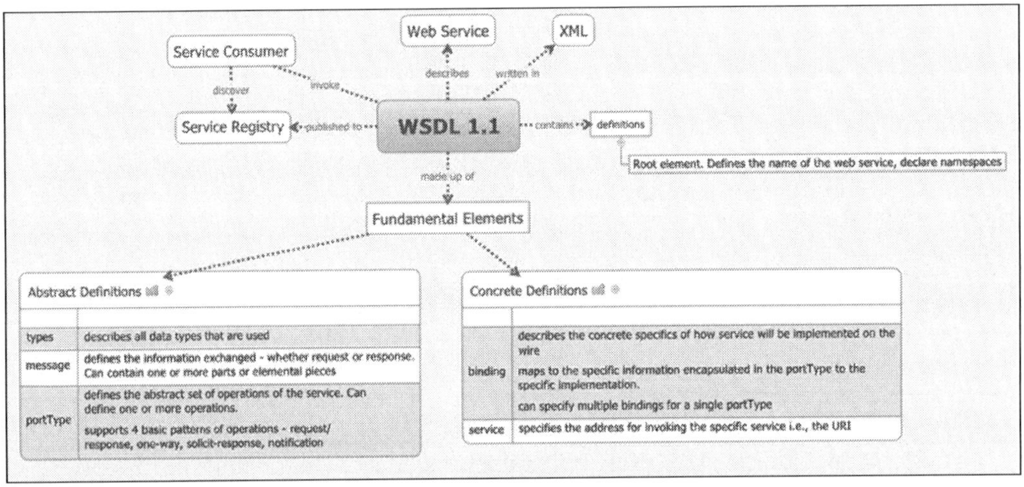

Having breezed through the fundamental concepts behind a WSDL, what will a WSDL look like when you open it in WID v7.0? The following diagram depicts a sample WSDL opened using the WID WSDL editor. In the following sections and also later in the book we will go into the details on how to create a WSDL or interface using WID. But for now we want to give you a glimpse into how a WSDL appears graphically in WID and the different relevant parts that we discussed above.

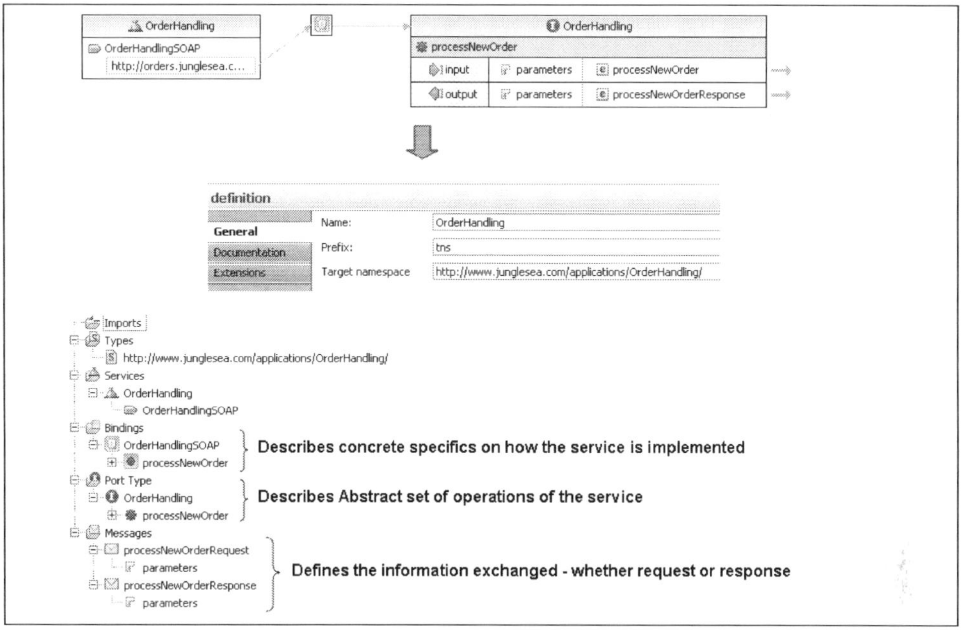

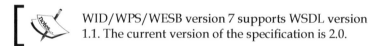

> WID/WPS/WESB version 7 supports WSDL version 1.1. The current version of the specification is 2.0.

XML Schema Definition (XSD) in a minute

XML Schema Definition (XSD) is the de-facto XML-based language used to express the structure and content of XML documents. XSD defines the elements, attributes, and data types that conform to the **World Wide Web Consortium** (**W3C**) XML Schema Part 1: Structures Recommendation for the XML Schema Definition Language. XSD defines the structure of an XML document by defining what each element must or may contain. Here are some quick notes for your reference about XSDs:

- Elements are the fundamental building block of XML. XSD's define the structure of these elements
- Element can be of simple type or complex type
- Simple types can be atomic (for example, strings and integers) or non-atomic (for example, lists)
- An element of complex type can contain child elements and attributes
- An XSD is composed of the top-level schema element, whose definition must include the namespace, `http://www.w3.org/2001/XMLSchema`

- The schema element contains type definitions and attribute and element declarations
- Complex types may have mixed content—a combination of text and child elements

Let's take a look at a simple XML schema as depicted and seen using the WID v7.0 XML Schema editor. In the following sections and also in the later chapters we will go into detail on how to create a XSD or business objects using WID. But for now we want to give you a glimpse into how a XSD appears graphically in WID and the different relevant parts that we discussed above.

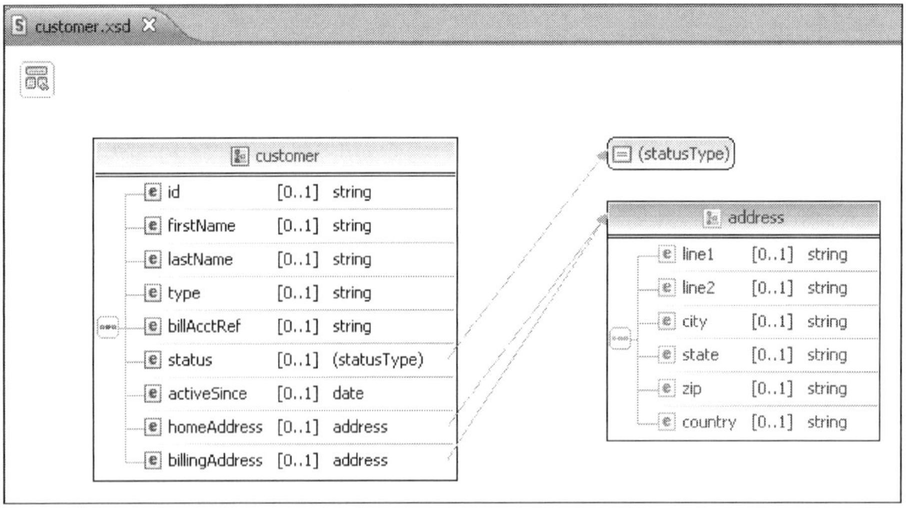

Service Component Architecture (SCA)

So what's the story behind Service Component Architecture (**SCA**)? Why would you want to use it? What are the fundamentals behind SCA? How does it fit in the context of WID/WPS/WESB? Let's begin to answer these questions.

We design and build applications for JungleSea Inc.(for example order management, customer care, customer billing, and so on) so they can run their business effectively and efficiently. Applications can be looked at as a collection of software components that are assembled or integrated together for a particular purpose. Ideally you should have the freedom to implement the different components in the technology of your choice. However, at times you may have to inherit or work with existing systems and technologies or work with third parties who have a different set of technologies. When you adopt an SOA approach to building applications, these components can be viewed as services. When we look at the constructs that make up a service, two things immediately come to mind:

1. The *What* part—data that should be passed to the service and data received back from the service.
2. The *How* part—what is the mechanism to realize the service and how it can be invoked or can be made available to a service consumer.

For each of the above two questions, there are many standards and programming models and, at times, it may get too overwhelming. This is where a **Service Component Architecture (SCA)** model comes in and mitigates these complexities. SCA is not another programming language nor replacement, but rather gives a *model* to assemble and build SOA applications by choosing any technology-specific implementation approach. The fundamental goal and premise of SCA is to separate business logic from infrastructure logic. WID provides the *design time environment* to build SCA-based applications using a bottom-up (expose services out of existing applications and make them available through the enterprise service bus) or top-down approach (a more business driven approach to identifying the right set of services needed to achieve a larger goal, capability, or solution). WID therefore enables architects and developers to spend more time working on solving a particular business problem rather than focusing on the details of which implementation technology to use.

Defining SCA

Service Component Architecture (SCA) is a set of specifications which describe a model for building applications and systems using an SOA approach. SCA extends and complements prior approaches to implementing services, and SCA builds on open standards such as Web services.

SCA divides up the steps in building a service-oriented application into two major parts:

1. The **implementation** of components which expose (**export**) services and consume (**import**) other services.
2. The **assembly** of sets of components to build business applications, through the **wiring** of references to services.

SCA uses Service Data Objects (SDOs) to represent the business data that forms the request and response values of services, providing uniform access to business data to complement the uniform access to Business Services offered by SCA itself. SCA supports bindings to a wide range of access mechanisms used to invoke services. The complete set of SCA specifications can be found at:

`http://www.osoa.org/display/Main/Service+Component+Architecture+Specifications`

SCA emphasizes the decoupling of service implementation and of service assembly from the infrastructure capabilities, from technology or programming language specifics and from the details of the access methods used to invoke services. SCA components operate at a business level and use a minimum of middleware-specific APIs. The basic elements of SCA include:

- Service Components
- Service Assembly
- Service Data Objects

The basic building block in SCA is the service component and represents a Business Service that publishes or operates on business data. The following image depicts the essential pieces of a service component definition. A service component can have one or more interfaces with which it is associated. The interfaces associated with a service component advertise the business operations associated with this service. These interfaces can be specified as either Java interfaces or WSDL port type interfaces. The arguments and return types for these interfaces are specified as simple Java types, Java classes, Service Data Objects, or XML Schemas (for WSDL port type interfaces). Also associated with a service component definition is an implementation. As the following figure indicates, there are multiple language and component types available for implementing a service component.

> When specifying a component interface you cannot mix Java and WSDL port type interfaces on the same service component definition.

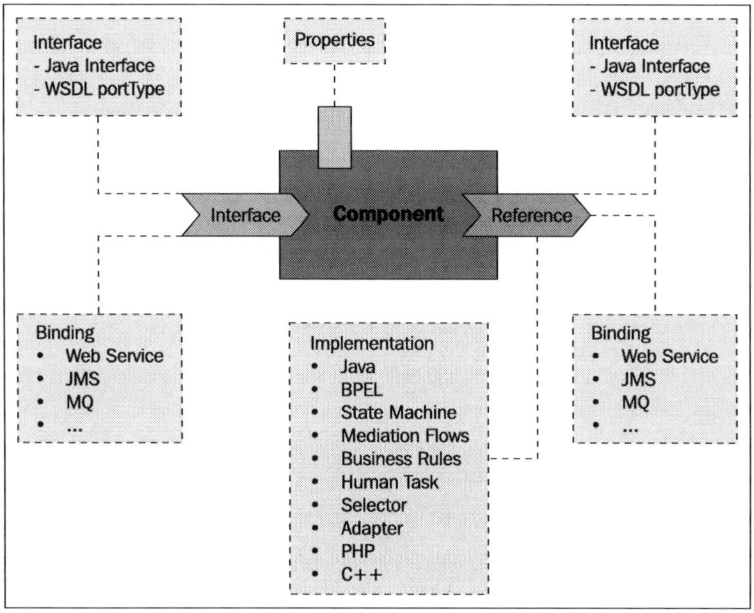

A Service Assembly deals with the aggregation of components and the linking of components through *wiring* or **wires**. Think of the assembly model as how, when building a kitchen, someone would assemble various components including kitchen cabinets, sink, appliances, counter top, and so on. The Assembly Model is independent of implementation language. An analogy would be: You don't care how and where the dishwasher is engineered, manufactured, and built but rather focus on the features, functions, and durability.

SCA uses **Service Data Objects (SDO)** to represent the business data that forms the request and response values of services, providing uniform and consistent access to business data to complement the uniform access to Business Services offered by SCA itself.

An SCA application can be made up of one or many components. Components can be combined into **composites**, a *logical* construct. The following figure depicts how an SCA-based order handling application is made up from two composites, Order Processing Composite and third party shipping composite.

In WID, a composite can be compared to a **Service Module**, which in essence becomes the basic unit of deployment and administration in WPS or WESB (SCA runtime). In the figure shown below is the blown up, detailed view of the SCA-based order handling application. A Service module typically contains the following artifacts:

- Module Definition
  - SCA specification defined deployment model for packaging components into a service module. In WID the **sca.module** file contains the definition of the module.
  - In the figure below the "Order Processing Composite" and "Third Party Shipping Composite" are the modules.
- Service Components
  - Each service component can be implemented in various ways (BPEL, Mediation Flow Component, State Machine, Java, and so on), specified by the implementation definition.
  - Service components can invoke other service components or imports defined in the current service module as defined by an appropriate reference.
  - A component can have 1..N interfaces.
  - Each service component definition can have zero or more references to other services.
  - In the following figure "Order Validation Component" and "Order Handling Component" are the service components whose implementations are BPEL and state machine respectively.
  - In WID the service component definition is included in the `<SERVICE_NAME>.component` file.
- Imports
  - Allows SCA components in one module to invoke SCA components in other modules.
  - A service module can have zero or more imports included with Imports have a name and a set of 1..N interfaces.
  - Binding attribute describes how the external service is bound to the current module.
  - Once an import has been defined, other services from within the module can reference the imported service as if it was a regular service component defined in the module.

    - In the following figure the "Order Handling Component" imports a component from the "Third Party Shipping Composite" through a reference.
    - In WID, import definition is included in the <IMPORT_NAME>.import file.
    - As explained in *Chapter 2, Installing the Development Environment,* imports can use the following bindings, which can be remote or local:
        - SCA
        - Web service
        - HTTP
        - Messaging (JMS, MQ JMS, generic JMS, MQ)
        - Stateless session bean
        - EIS
- Exports
    - Allows SCA components in a module to expose their capabilities to components in other modules.
    - In order to invoke any of the services in the order handling application, by any client (SCA or non-SCA) the service must be exposed with an export.
    - A service module can have zero or more **exports** included with it.
    - Export components include a name and a target attribute.
    - Binding attribute describes how the service is bound externally.
    - In the figure below, the "Order Validation Component" has an export named "Order Validate Export".
    - In WID import definition is included in <EXPORT_NAME>.export file.
    - As explained in *Chapter 2* exports binding can be

- References
    - Inline
    - Standalone
        - A service may also include a standalone references file that includes references to services in the same module that can be used by SCA and non-SCA services.
        - As shown in the following diagram, we have a standalone reference wired to the order validation component.
- Interfaces, Business Objects, Java classes, and other components

In WPS or WESB, an SCA service module is packaged and deployed as a Java Enterprise Edition (JEE) Enterprise Archive (EAR) file. It can also contain other JEE modules, WAR files, and so on. Non-SCA artifacts including Java Server Pages (JSP), HTML, and so on can also be packaged in the module, enabling one to invoke SCA services through the SCA client programming model using a standalone reference.

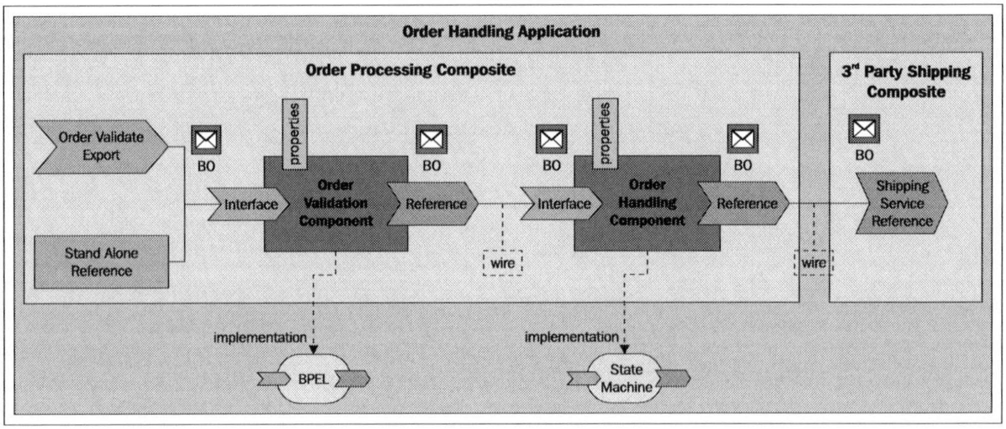

Service Component Definition Language

Service Component Definition Language (**SCDL**) is an XML-based definition language used to define all SCA artifacts in a project. The WebSphere Integration Developer *generates* the appropriate SCDL definitions when building an SCA-based application. SCDL typically describes the components a particular composite contains and specifies how they relate to one another. As explained in the previous section, SCDL definitions are organized across several files depending on the type of artifact (for example, `sca.module` or `<SERVICE_NAME>.component` file and so on).

SCA and SDO Cheat Sheet

1. SCA is a set of specifications which describe a model for building applications and systems using SOA.
2. Emphasizes the decoupling of service implementation and of service assembly from the details of infrastructure capabilities and from the details of the access methods used to invoke services.
3. SCA components operate at a business level and use a minimum of middleware APIs.
4. SCA supports service implementations written using any one of many programming languages, including both conventional object-oriented and procedural languages such as Java™, PHP, C++, COBOL; XML-centric languages such as BPEL and XSLT; and declarative languages such as SQL and XQuery.
5. SCA and SDO were developed by the Open Service Oriented Architecture group (osoa.org).

Service Data Objects (SDO)

SCA gives us a universal model to define Business Services. The Service Data Object (SDO) provides the technology to represent a universal model for data that flows between components in an SCA. Each SCA component passes and exchanges data with each other in a neutral fashion by passing SDOs. Data objects are the preferred form for data and metadata in SCA. The fundamental concept in the SDO architecture is the data object, a data structure that holds primitive typed data and/or other data objects. The data object also holds references to metadata that provides information about the data included in the data object.

SDOs allow the integration developer to focus on working with business artifacts. In fact, service data objects are transparent to the integration developer. They are defined by a service data objects Java Specification Request (JSR) and for more information refer to the link:

`http://www.jcp.org/en/jsr/detail?id=235`

In the SDO programming model, data objects are represented by the `commonj.sdo.DataObject` Java interface definition. This interface includes method definitions that enable clients to get and set the properties associated with the DataObject. Another important concept in the SDO architecture is the data graph, a structure that encapsulates a set of data objects. From the top-level data object contained in the graph, all children data objects are reachable by traversing the references from the root data object. Another important feature included in the data graph is a change summary that is used to log information about what data objects and properties in the graph have changed during processing. **The WebSphere Process Server implements the SDO specification by way of business objects.**

The following mind map summarizes the various concepts behind an SCA application. Please take time to go through it and recollect some of the concepts explained in the previous sections.

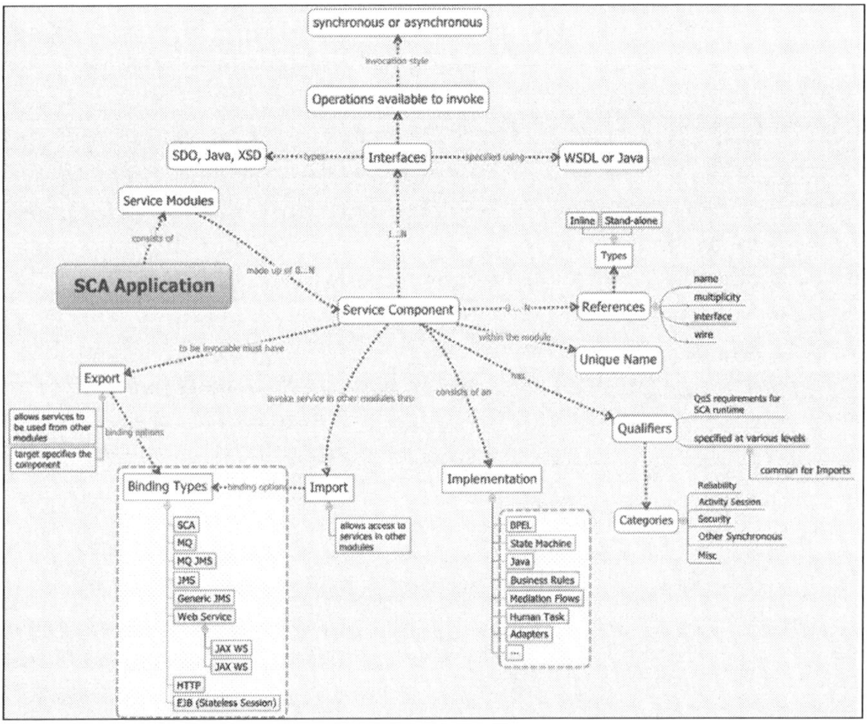

Business Process Execution Language (WS-BPEL)

A business process is the set of business-related activities, tasks, rules, and conditions invoked and executed in a defined sequence to achieve a business goal. We mentioned in *Chapter 1, Introducing IBM BPM and ESB* that a business process-driven approach to building applications driven by SOA is key to agility, loose coupling and flexibility. WID and WPS is a core enabler of this BPM enabled by SOA. Modeling business processes in a *standardized* format and transforming the models to a *standardized* executable/deployable format deploying them on an execution engine like WPS is pivotal to the success of a BPM enabled by SOA approach. Though there are several process modeling notations available (UML activity diagrams, XPDL, and so on), Business Process Modeling Notation (BPMN) is the most comprehensive process modeling notation that has been developed yet, and is under the umbrella of Object Management Group (OMG). BPMN is automatically mapped to Web Services Business Process Execution Language (WS-BPEL, or more shortly BPEL) which is the de-facto standard for executing business processes. WS-BPEL (is also referred to as BPEL and the two will be interchangeably used going forward in this book) provides a grammar for describing the behavior of a Business Process including interactions within the process, with external partners and also with other processes. BPEL is an XML-based programming language to describe high-level business processes. BPEL allows you to define **choreography** (inter-company or inter-organization) or **orchestration** (intra-organization) interactions to be described easily and thoroughly such that a company "Shipper Express" can provide a shipping and logistics related Web Services and company JungleSea Inc. can use it with a minimum of compatibility issues. With BPEL you can define an "order to ship" choreography that uses a web service to validate the order, check inventory, fetch the shipping rates to a particular zip code, track shipments, perform order status inquiry, and so on. WS-BPEL uses service interfaces as a means to connect the different steps within the process. It uses XSDs and XPATH as a means to define the data objects that are used by the processes. The main elements of a WS-BPEL (explained in the later sections), which define and detail how a business process is organized, include:

- Partner links
  - The services with which a business process interacts are modeled as partner links in WS-BPEL.
- Variables
  - Provide the means for holding messages that constitute a part of the state of a business process.
  - The messages held are often those that have been received from partners or are to be sent to partners.

  - Variables can also hold data that are needed for holding state related to the process and never exchanged with partners.
  - WS-BPEL uses three kinds of variable declarations: WSDL message type, XML Schema type (simple or complex), and XML Schema element.
- Correlation sets
  - Correlation is used to track the multiple, long-running exchanges of messages that typically take place between a BPEL process and its partner services.
  - Correlation sets help to route messages to the appropriate process instance based on the contents of the message body, thus enabling the process instance to hold a conversation with the partner service.
- Fault handlers
  - Fault handling in WS-BPEL is designed to be treated as "reverse work," in that its aim is to undo the partial and unsuccessful work of a scope in which a fault has occurred.
- Compensation handlers
  - WS-BPEL allows scopes to delineate that part of the behavior that is meant to be reversible in an application-defined way by specifying a compensation handler.
- Event handlers
- Activities
  - These allow you to define processing logic.

In a WS-BPEL process, , by default each and every service component invocation is done in a stateless manner, without any context of other previous invocations of the same service component. In a WS-BPEL based business process, *state* can be built up as the different service components are invoked and the results of one service can be used in the invocation of another service. When all service components have been invoked, the overall business transaction is complete.

WID and WS-BPEL

So where does WID/WPS fit in with WS-BPEL (hence forth referred to as BPEL)? BPEL is one of the options that are provided in WID to implement an SCA component. Once you model a business process using BPEL you will need to deploy the BPEL process on a BPEL runtime engine that can interpret the business process modeled, invoke the appropriate services, maintain state, handle faults and associated compensations, and also support long-running processes than can span days or weeks or even months. We will be getting into these topics as we progress into the later chapters.

WID/WPS v7.0 supports WS-BPEL version 1.1 specification completely and version 2.0 partly. Majority of WS-BPEL 2.0 language elements are available in WID/WPS version 7.0. Additional value-add functions in WPS/WID even go beyond the standard.

- Here is the link to BPEL specification v1.1,

  `http://www.ibm.com/developerworks/library/specification/ws-bpel/`

- Here is the link to BPEL specification v 2.0,

  `http://docs.oasis-open.org/wsbpel/2.0/OS/wsbpel-v2.0-OS.html`

As you very well know WS-BPEL (or BPEL used interchangeably) provides the ability to express stateful, long-running interactions between Web services. IBM was the author of the original proposal for the BPEL specification, one of the first vendors to support BPEL and supports WS-BPEL throughout its products including,

  - WebSphere Business Modeler
  - WebSphere Integration Developer
  - WebSphere Process Server
  - WebSphere Business Monitor

The WS-BPEL 2.0 specification can found at `http://docs.oasis-open.org/wsbpel/2.0/wsbpel-v2.0.html` and was approved in April 2007. IBM is a major contributor to the WS-BPEL 2.0 standard. Diane Jordan from IBM has been the chair of the OASIS technical committee and several others from IBM in the technical committee.

When you are building a business process in WID, the fundamental WS-BPEL activities you work with as provided in WID business process editor palette are shown in the table below. You would use a combination of these activities to visually build your business process that accomplishes a particular function or goal.

Activity	Icon in WID	Description
Receive	Receive	Wait for input from an external interface partner
Reply	Reply	Send a response back to the one-way or request-response operation initiator
Invoke	Invoke	Call a a one-way or request-response operation
Assign	Assign	Update value of variable or assign new values
Throw	Throw	Signal a Fault
Rethrow	Rethrow	Rethrow a fault caught in one scope to an another enclosing scope
Wait	Wait	Wait for a given time period
Compensate	Compensate	Used in Fault handler to call a compensation handler
Terminate	Terminate	Stop the process while running
Empty	Empty Action	Empty action object used as a place holder
Snippet	Snippet	Write Visual expressions or Java code
Human Task	Human Task	Send a task to a person to work on
Structures	Scope Parallel Activities Sequence Choice While Loop Repeat Until Loop For Each Generalized Flow	Various control structures used in BPEL programming

For more information on WS-BPEL, refer to the following:

1. *Business Process Driven SOA using BPMN and BPEL* by *Kapil Pant, Matjaz Juric.*
2. *SOA and WS-BPEL* by *Yuli Vasiliev*, Packt Publishers.

Once the processes have been assembled and in WID, you deploy them to the WPS runtime. WPS provides a robust runtime environment including the Business Process Choreographer (BPC) which is responsible for all aspects of BPEL business process execution. BPC can support both short-running and long-running business processes. Services can be invoked either synchronously or asynchronously. Using WPS through WID, you can also make use of the additional extensions like micro-flow, event and compensation handlers, compensate activity, and rethrow. You can also make use of enhancements provided for executing long-running business processes where transaction capabilities are an important consideration.

Building your first business process

Let's get into action and build our first simple Hello World solution that would return an interactive greeting. As simple as it sounds, you would need to understand how to use the WID tooling and in the due course relate it back to the various concepts we have been talking about. Since we don't want to build anything one off, we will begin with a solution-oriented approach to building applications in WID. Though the application we are building is simple, let's start looking at it from a solution point of view. So the requirements for our first application are:

- It should be capable of getting user input and more specifically their first name, last name, and age
- It should return a customized greeting based on their age
    - Ages 25 and younger it should return—"What's up <name>!"
    - Ages 26 to 65 it should return—"What's happening, <name>!"
    - Ages 65 and above it should return—"Good Day to you <name>!"
- The solution should be exposed via Web Services

I know this is a very simple application that could be written in a few lines of Java code or any other programming language of choice. But the point here is to build this as your first WID application using business process (BPEL) components that will allow you to understand the various features of WID and how to use them. Now having given the requirements, there is a capability in WID that you can make use of to organize multiple modules, mediation modules, libraries, and other dependent projects into one scope. This capability is called **Integration Solution**. It provides a diagrammatic representation of how modules, mediation modules, libraries, and other dependent projects are connected/inter-connected.

> Integration Solution is a development time concept only and the servers have no idea about them. The servers still will view an integration solution as a set of `.ear` files.

Let me first give you a ten-step, high-level to plan to build our first Hello World module. As we proceed we will work on each step in more detail. It is important for you to gain an understanding for the high level before executing it. Don't panic and try to do all these steps now; we will be covering each of these steps in detail as we proceed with this section.

1. Start WID and switch to Business Integration perspective.
2. Create an Integration Solution named *Greeting_Solution*.
3. Create a Library project named *GreetingLibrary*. Create Business Objects and Interfaces in the *GreetingLibrary* for the initial BPEL component we will specify in step 5 and implement in step 6.
4. Create a Module project named *Greeting* and add as project reference the Library created in step 1.
5. Add Module and Library to the Integration Solution as project references.
6. Create and wire the BPEL component.
7. Implement the BPEL component.
8. Add Web Service and SCA exports to the BPEL component.
9. Test the Module.
10. Deploy the Module to the WebSphere Process Server.

To start, let's open WID (as explained in *Chapter 1*, we installed it under `C:\IBM\WID7`). From the **Start** menu select **Start | Programs | IBM WebSphere Integration Developer | IBM WebSphere Integration Developer v7.0 | WebSphere Integration Developer v7.0**.

When WID starts it will ask you for a **workspace** location. Let's specify it as `C:\workspaces\ch3`.

> It's advisable to have short directory paths. Beware of the Windows 259 character limit. There can be no spaces in directory paths.

On the **Welcome** page click on the arrow next to **Go to the Business Integration perspective** in the top right-hand corner to start using WID.

Creating the Integration Solution

In a **Business Integration** perspective, within the **Integration Solution** section, click on the **New Integration Solution.** Give the name. Enable the **Focus the new integration solution in the Business Integration view** checkbox. Click on the **Finish** button.

The following screenshot shows the **New Integration Solution** wizard page:

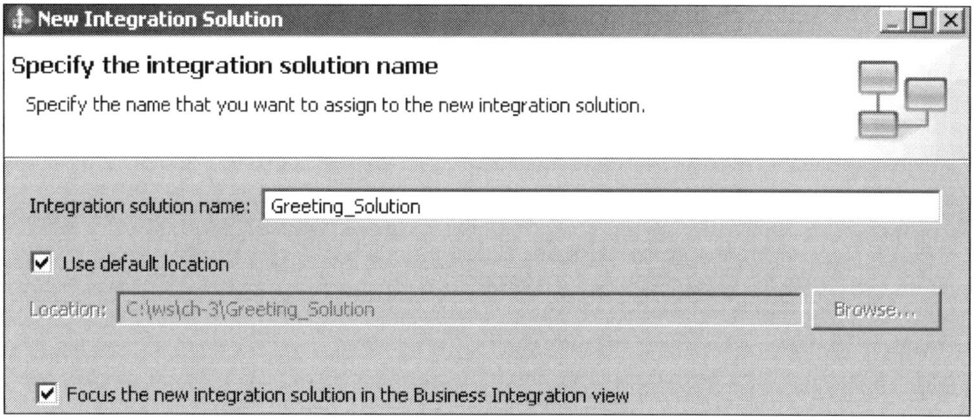

Creating library project

Now that a solution has been created, you can proceed to create the libraries required for this solution. A library project is used to store these resources that are required by other projects and hence has reuse potential. Libraries contain:

- Business Objects
- Interfaces
- Transformations
- Mediation Subflows

Once you create a library project, it can be *added as a dependency* in the module or a mediation module project. A library *cannot* be deployed by itself to WPS or WESB. But you can add a library to the module and select to *deploy it with the module* option. There can be nested library dependencies also meaning library-A can be dependent on library-B.

In the Business Integration perspective, within the Projects section:

1. Click on **New** Business Integration project and select **Library** from the wizard menu.
2. Give the **Library name** as **GreetingLibrary**.

3. Proceed to next and by default you should see the library being included in the **Greeting_Solution Integration Solution**.
4. Click on the **Finish** button.

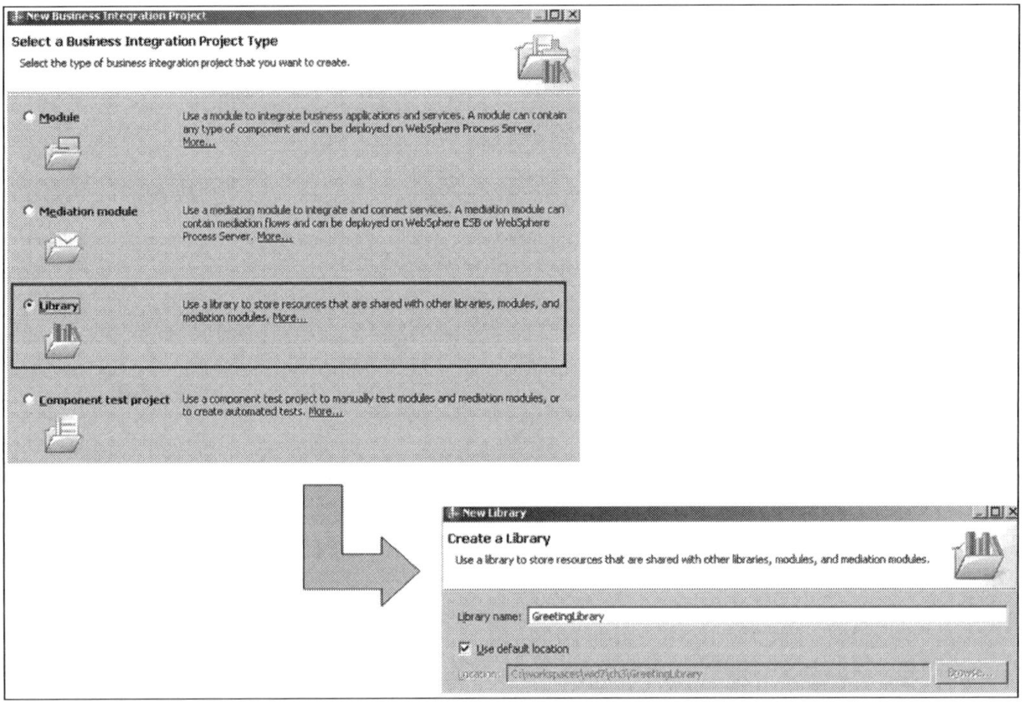

The new library is created, and you can view the structure of the library project in the Business Integration view.

Creating and visualizing Business Objects

Business Objects (BO) represent one of the fundamental building blocks of a Business Integration solution. They represent the data payload that is being passed back and forth between the various services and hence components. Using WID you can create and visualize these BO using the business object editor. Since we have the intention of sharing the business object among modules, we will create it in the *GreetingLibrary* library. To create a *Party* business object in the *GreetingLibrary*, follow these steps:

1. Right-click on the **Data Types** folder and select **New | Business Object** from the context menu.
2. Give the Business Object the name **Party**. Give the folder name **com/junglesea/solution/greeting/bo** and then click on **Finish**.

> For every component or artefact you create in the Business Integration perspective, you will be asked for standard information including:
>
> 1. Module or library
> 2. Namespace
> 3. Folder
> 4. Name
> 5. Inherit from

> Module or library should be autopopulated based on the module/library in which you are creating it. Folder can be left blank, but that is strongly not recommended. Give a suitable namespace such as structure.

Once you do this, the Party BO will be created in the `Data Type root` folder (further under the folder structure `com/junglesea/solution/greeting/bo`) and then opened and presented in the BO Editor.

Now let's add fields/elements to the Party BO. With the business object editor, you can add, delete, and reorder fields and change the type of a field. To add a simple field to the business object, do the following:

3. In the business object editor, click the **Add a field to a business object** icon.
4. Replace the default name, **field1**, with the name of the field (that is, FirstName), as shown in the following figure.
5. Add two more fields; **LastName** and **Location**. If you notice this, by default all of the above fields will have a type `xsd:string`.
6. Add one more field **Age** and change the type to `xsd:int`, by clicking on **String** and selecting the `xsd:int` type. This will then enable a field which will represent the age of the person and store it as integer type.

> When creating a business object field you are given the option of selecting the type to be a simple data type, an existing business object, or a new business object.

7. Save and close the BO Editor.

> You can save in WID using *Ctrl+S* or you can save all unsaved content using *Ctrl+Shift+S*.

The following diagram recaps the steps we have taken in order to implement Party Business Object:

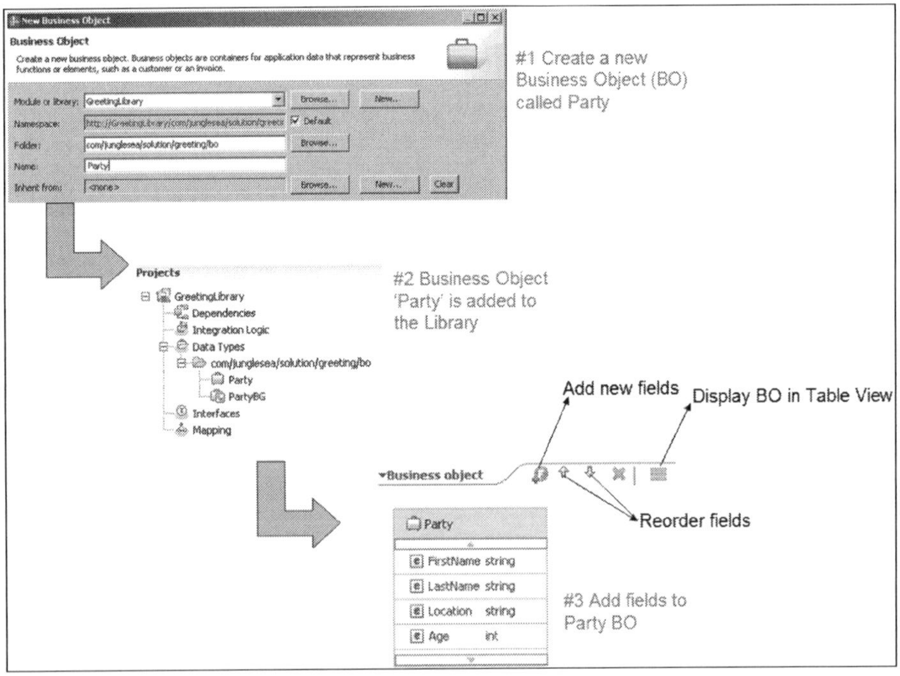

> You can also create a business graph of your business object when you right-click the business object and select "Create a Business Graph" from the context menu. More about Business Graphs will be covered in *Chapter 5, Business Process Choreography Fundamentals*.

Creating and visualizing interfaces

Every component in a module will have to be specified with interfaces. The interfaces specify the inputs and outputs of each component and hence determine which data can be passed from one component to another. An interface is created independently from the implementation of the component and can also be created for a component which has no implementation (implementation is done later). To create a HandleGreetingMessage Interface in the **GreetingLibrary** do the following:

1. Right-click on the **Interfaces** folder and select **New | Interface** from the context menu.
2. Provide a name for the folder as **com/junglesea/solution/greeting/interfaces** and name the interface as **HandleGreetingMessage** and click on the **Finish** button. Once you do this, the interface will be created in the Interfaces and then automatically opened and presented in the Interface Editor.
3. You will notice that there are no operations in the interface. The next task is to add operations and specify the appropriate inputs and outputs. To add a new operation and parameters to the interface, in the interface editor, click the **Add Request Response Operation** icon.
4. Change the operation name to *returnGreeting*. Note that you can also add additional inputs, output fields, and also a Fault section.
5. Change the Input(s) name with a meaningful name like *inputPartyInfo*. You can also change the name of this field in the **Properties** view. Click on the **string** value in the **Type** field. Then, scroll down and select the **Party** business object.
6. Change the Output(s) name to *outputGreetingMessage* and leave the type to be **string**. Save and close the interface editor. The following diagram recaps the preceding steps taken to implement a new interface called *HandleGreetingMessage*.

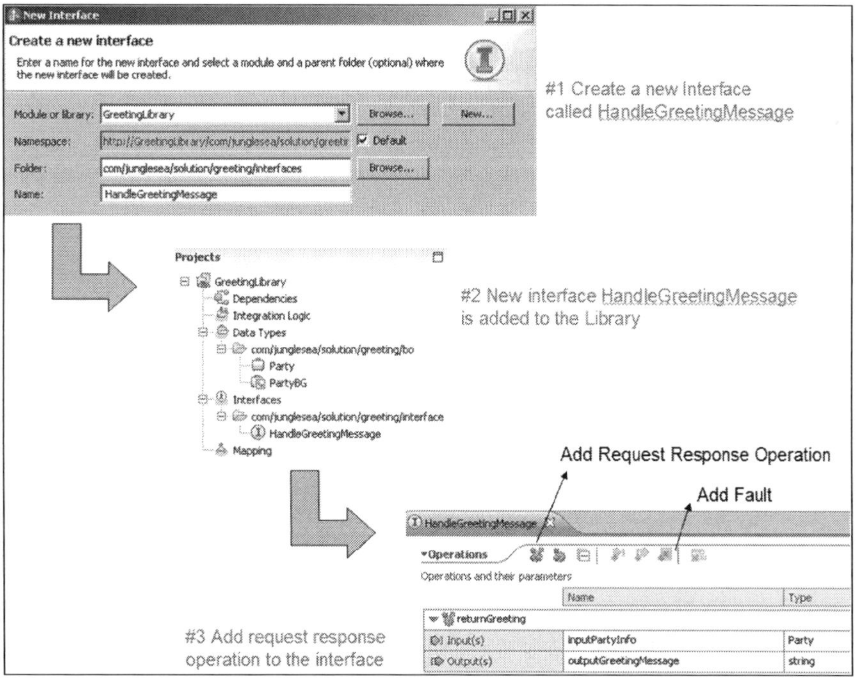

Creating the Hello Process BPEL

All the common assets like the interface and business object have been created in the library. Next you will create the solution called Hello Process BPEL. In order to create a Hello process BPEL you will need to:

1. Create a new module called *Greetings*.
2. Create a new business process component named *HelloProcess*.
3. Implement the *HelloProcess* process.

Now let's take a closer look at each step.

Creating a new module called HelloProcess

The first step is to create a module to define our solution. In Business Integration perspective, within the Projects section:

1. Right-click on **New** and select **Module** from the context menu. Give the **Module** name as **Greetings**.
2. Proceed to next and select **GreetingLibrary** under **Libraries** list.
3. Proceed to next and check **Select an Integrated solution** focused on *Greeting_Solution* and then click on the **Finish** button.

Creating a business process component HelloProcess

After the module has been defined, create a business process component named HelloProcess for the solution. In Business Integration perspective, within the Projects section:

1. Right-click on **Greetings** | **New** and select **Business Process** from the context menu.
2. Give the folder name as `com/junglesea/solution/greeting/process` and the name *HelloProcess*.
3. Proceed to next and select the process type as **microflow**.
4. Proceed to next and enable the **Select an interface** radio button, browse and select the **HandleGreetingMessage** interface.
5. Click on the **Finish** button. The **Process Editor** window will open to enable you to edit and implement *HelloProcess*. The steps are detailed in the following diagram:

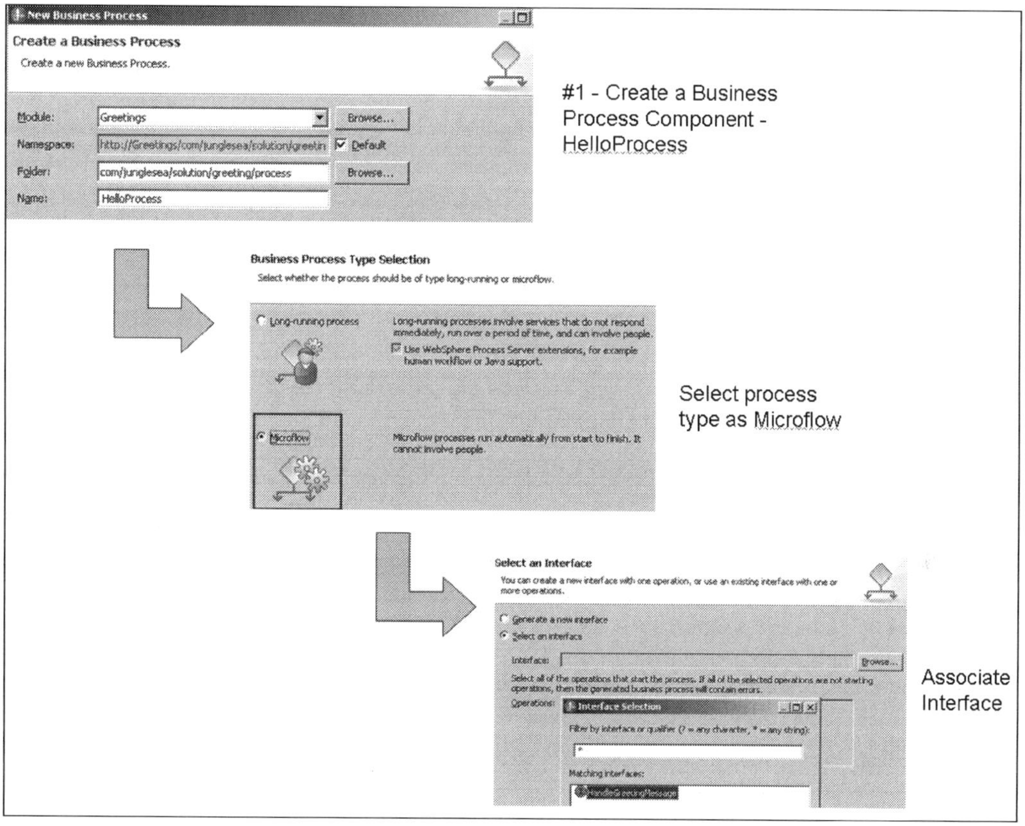

Implementing the HelloProcess process

Now we will start implementing the BPEL process component. Here are the steps to implement the business process:

1. In the business process editor, from the palette select the "Choice" activity and drag and drop it to the business process editor between the Receive and Reply activities.
2. Replace the default **Display Name** with the name "CheckPartyAge". The **Display Name** field can also be changed in the **Description** section of the **Properties** view; a change of the display name will as well update the **Name** field. Now let's add case statements, each checking and handling a particular age range.

3. Click on the **Case** activity within the **Choice** activity scope, and in the **Properties** view, give the name for this case as "LessThan25". Click on the **Details** tab and choose the expression language to be of type **XPath 1.0**. Here we will write an XPath expression to check the age of the party. Using an XPath expression you will be able to reference parts of the variables or business objects of a BPEL. An XPath expression may reference simple data types (for example. strings and integers) as well as complex data types. In our case we will check the Age in the Party business object that comes as an input to the business process (remember we set this as the input when we defined the interface and operation). The XPath expression can will be `$inputPartyInfo/Age <= '25'`.
4. Under this **Case** element, drag-and-drop a snippet from the palette and name it "SayGreeting-WhatsUp". The visual snippet editor displays a diagrammatic representation of the Java and let's you graphically create and manipulate snippets of Java code. In the visual snippet canvas you can assemble various out-of-the-box activities that WID provides to compose your visual snippet. WID provides many commonly-used snippets as part of the product and as shown next. You can also refer to methods from custom Java classes/libraries in the visual snippet.

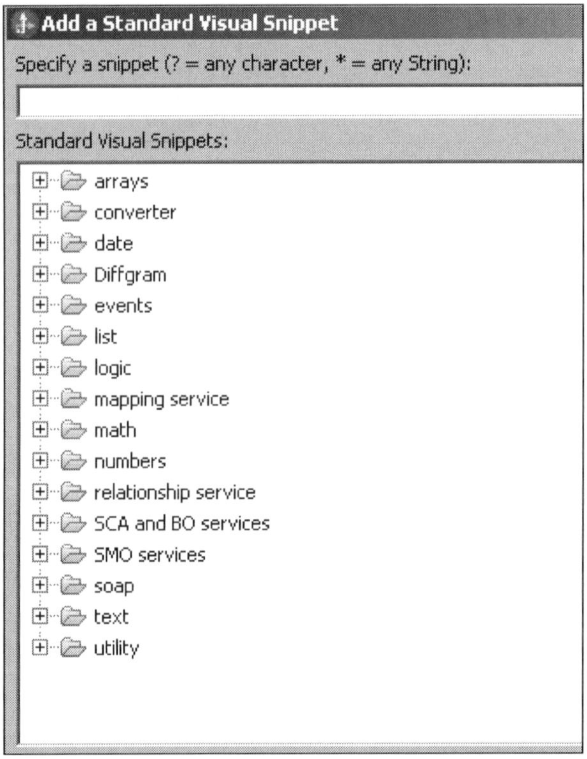

5. Under the **Properties** view for this snippet, we will compose a visual snippet expression as shown in the following screenshot:

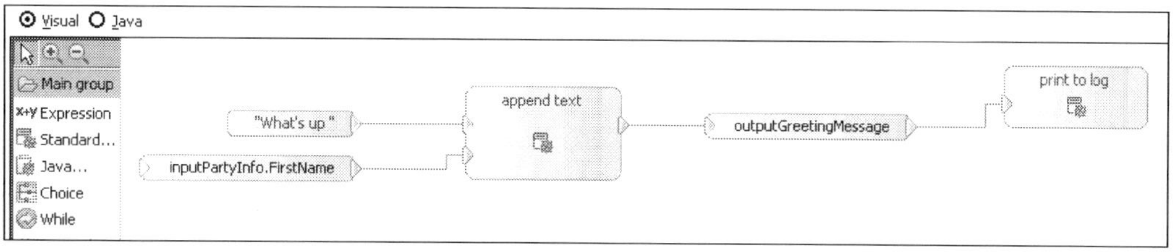

6. Now we will add one more case by clicking on the **CheckPartyAge** choice activity and in the action bar that appears, clicking on **Add Case** element. We will name this **MoreThan25LessThan65**. The XPath expression will be `($inputPartyInfo/Age >= '26')` and `($inputPartyInfo/Age <= '65')`. We will repeat what we did in step 5 by adding a visual snippet named "SayGreetingWhatsHappening" and an associated expression which will look as shown in the following screenshot:

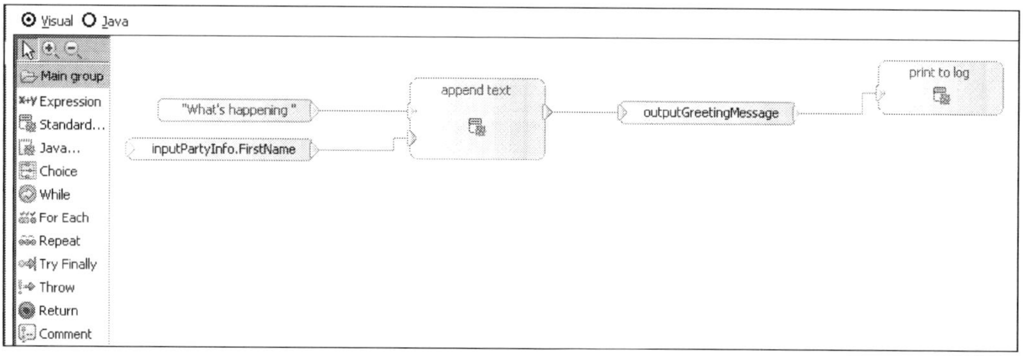

7. Then add an otherwise element (for over 65) and add an expression as shown in the following screenshot:

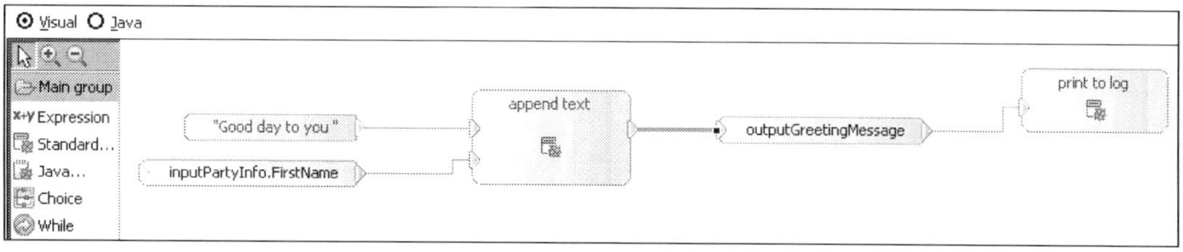

8. Save all your settings. This completes the implementation of the process.

9. Finally, your BPEL process will look as shown in the following screenshot:

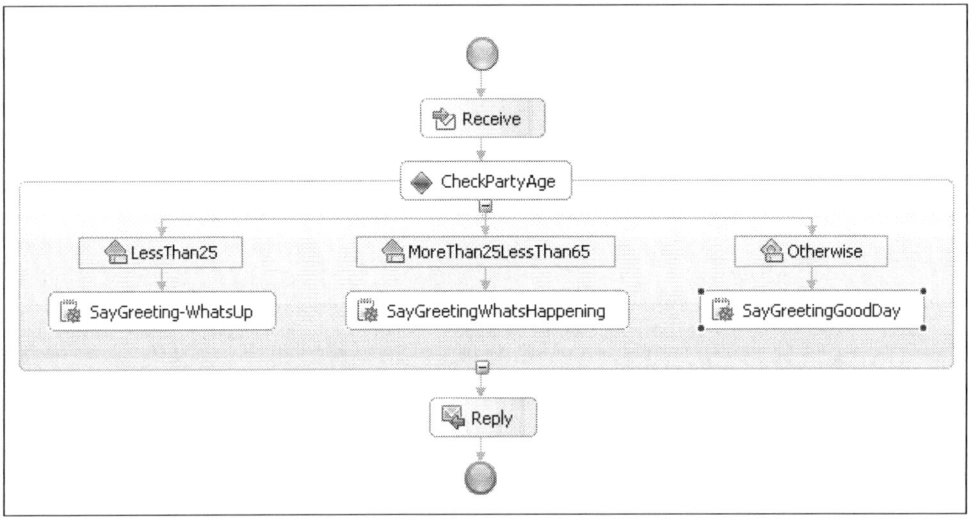

For more information on XPath 1.0, see `http://www.w3.org/TR/xpath`

This brings us to the next step where you will learn how to assemble the SCA solution and expose (via export) the BPEL process as a Web Service. Remember that Web Service is one of the many options WID makes available to you.

You could potentially use a rules component to compute the age and provide the appropriate greeting to display. This could be easily achieved by having the HelloProcess component call this rules component. We will get to doing this later in the book. You are now getting a sense of the flexibility that this architecture provides you.

To expose the process as a web service, here are the steps to follow:

1. Double-click on **Assembly Diagrams** under **Greetings** project.
2. Drag **HelloProcess** business process component to the assembly diagram and it will appear in the assembly diagram canvas as shown in the following screenshot:

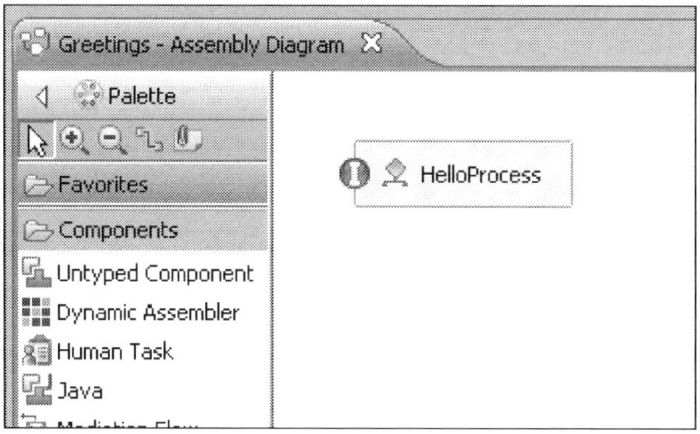

3. Right-click on **HelloProcess**, select **Generate Export** | **Web Service Binding**, select the default transport protocol as **SOAP 1.1/HTTP using JAX-RPC**, and then click on the **OK** button.
4. Save the assembly diagram and after doing the above, your assembly diagram would appear as shown in the following screenshot:

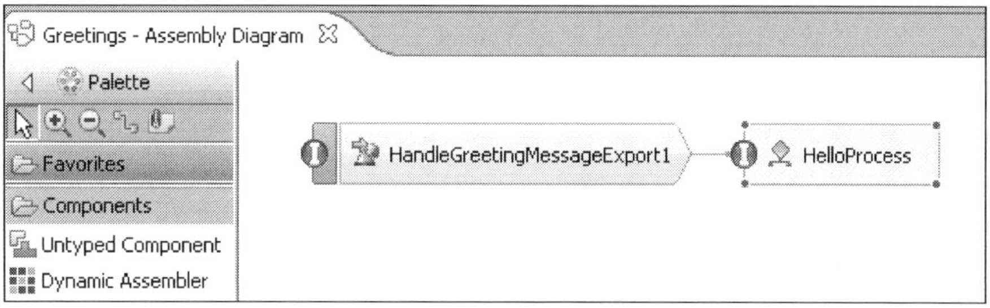

Congratulations! You have assembled and implemented your very first integration solution. Next you need to test this solution.

Testing modules and components

In the previous chapter when we installed WID, we also installed the WebSphere test environment that provided an embedded version of WebSphere Process Server to enable the developers quickly test their applications. With WID, you can test your modules by performing either unit testing or component testing. In unit testing, you choose the components and interfaces that contain the operations that you want to test, then you test the operations one at a time in the integration test client.

For deployment, WID allows you to specify a particular WPS, and with a single action, applications can be published to the server and started in preparation for testing. If updates are made to an application, the changes can also be scheduled to be published to a server for testing. Applications can also be exported from IBM WebSphere Integration Developer and be installed using the administrative console or the wsadmin command line interface, which we will cover in detail in *Chapter 13, Management, Monitoring, and Security*. First we will have to start the WPS unit test server by going to the **Servers** view, clicking on **WebSphere Process Server v7.0 at localhost**, and clicking on the start button on the top right as shown in the following screenshot:

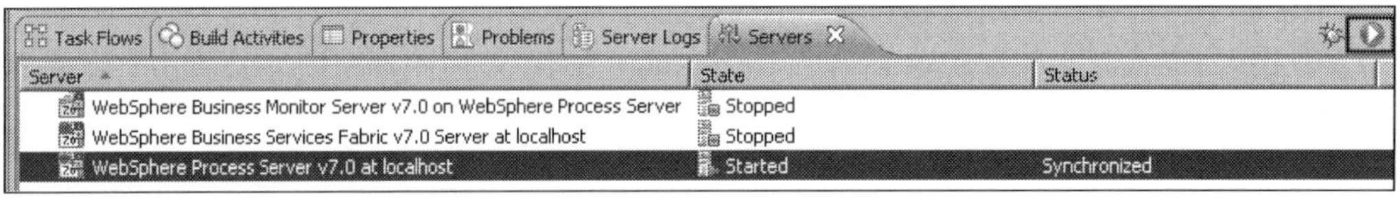

Deploying the modules

We will now deploy the *Greetings* module on your WPS test environment.
In **Servers** view

1. After the server has been started, which may take a few minutes, right-click on **WebSphere Process Server v7.0 at localhost**, and select **Add and Remove Projects**.
2. As shown in following figure, select **GreetingsApp**. Click on the **Add** button and then click on the **Finish** button.

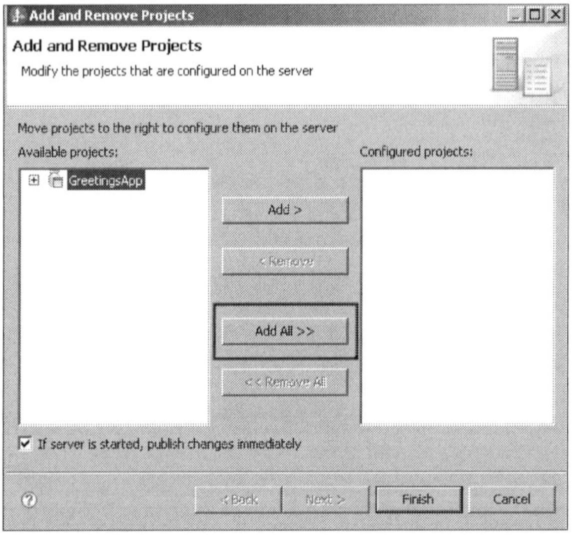

3. The **GreetingsApp** will now get deployed and published on the WebSphere Process Server. You will able to verify this by seeing it listed under **WebSphere Process Server v7.0 at localhost**, as shown in the following screenshot:

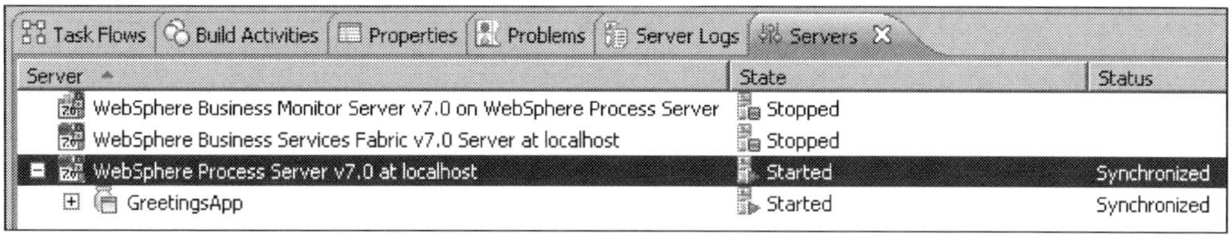

Executing the modules

After deploying the modules, the next step is to execute the modules. We will use the integration test client to unit test the Greetings modules and more specifically test the interface operations of the HelloProcess component.

1. To test the component, go to the assembly diagram and right-click on the web service export and click **Test Component**.
2. As shown in the following screenshot, this will launch the **Integration Test Client** where you can specify the component, interface to test, and the values to be used for different unit test cases.

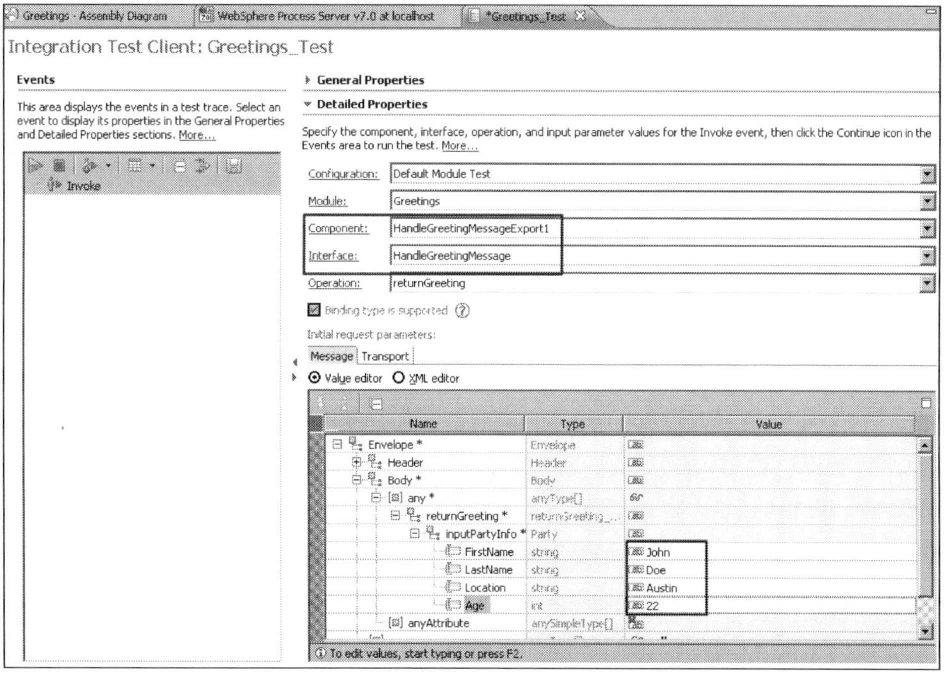

3. Enter the following details as test values:

FirstName	John
LastName	Doe
Location	Austin
Age	22

4. The process executes and returns with a custom greeting: **What's up John** Congrats on your first hello world BPEL.
5. If you want to rerun the operation and specify new input parameter values, right-click the top-level **Invoke** event in the **Events** area and select **Rerun with Auto Emulate**. Specify different values and test the process component.
6. The following diagram summarizes the testing results for different test cases and for each case what the greeting message was:

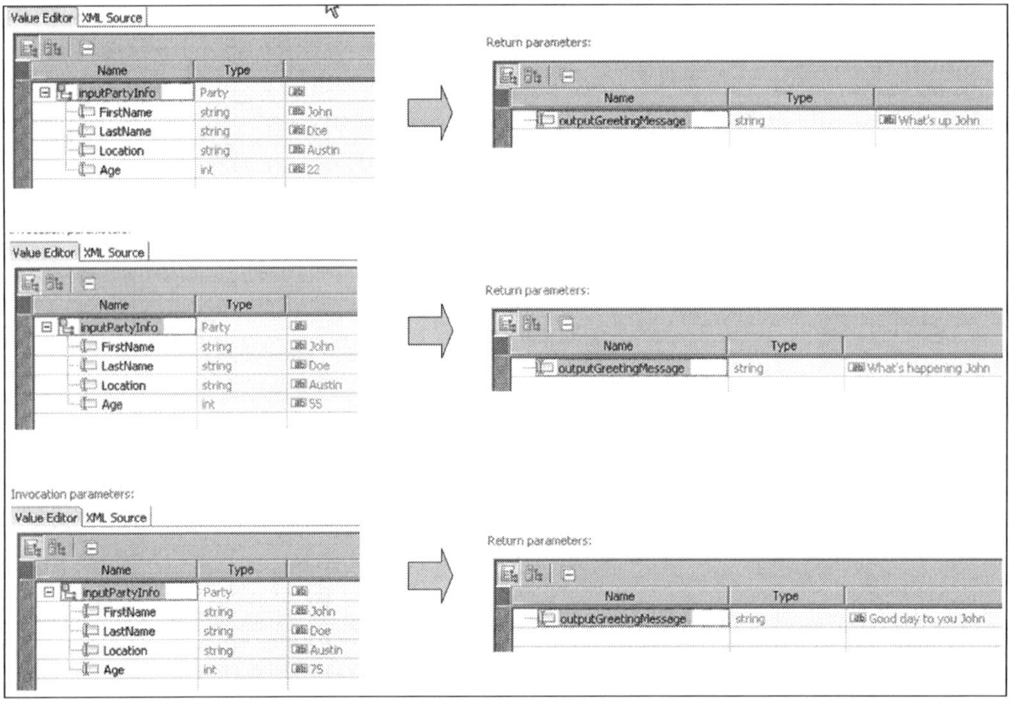

Congratulations! You have now completed developing and testing your SCA solution. Now you must keep in mind that there will be times that things do not flow as smoothly as above and you will need to diagnose runtime issues. For this I would like to show you the trouble-shooting tools available in WID.

Logging and troubleshooting

For development issues, WID provides the **Problems** view. All development errors are listed here. Further it also provides quick fix to common issues. A quick fix can be applied by right-clicking on an error and selecting **Quick Fix.** You may also select **Show Help** that brings up a more detailed explanation of the issue. WID also takes advantage of the Eclipse **Dynamic Help** feature that searches the help content to provide information about the item in focus or highlighted.

For runtime issues, WID provides **Sever Logs** (`%WTE_HOME%\\runtimes\bi_v7\profiles\qmwps\logs\server1`) and **Console** views to give you insight into the execution of WPS. These are listed under the Windows menu in the toolbar. These views essentially expose the `SystemOut.log` of the underlying Process Server. Server logs view provides a more user-friendly view while Console view displays the raw logfile text. Any errors in the execution of the process can be seen here.

Words of wisdom — tips, tricks, suggestions, and pitfalls

- Installation paths: Long installation paths can cause the installer to fail. If this happens, check the `log.txt` file in the `temp` directory. You can also have path length problems later on when applications are installed or updated. Long path lengths do not always show up directly as errors; what you will see is an error message about path or file not found, or a class not found when the class is in a long-named package.
- `Eclipse.ini` settings: In `WID_HOME/eclipse.ini`, Xmx will set the max JVM heapsize while Xms is the minimum heapsize. We recommend that you to set the following (say on a machine with 3GB Memory):
    - -Xms512m
    - -Xmx1024m
- Open `%WID_INSTALL_PATH%\eclipse.ini` in notepad and make the changes highlighted as shown next:

```
-vm
C:\IBM\WID62\jdk\jre\bin\javaw.exe
-vmargs
-Xquickstart
-Xms512m
-Xss2048k
-Xmaxf0.1
-Xminf0.05
```

```
-Xmx1024m
-Xgcpolicy:gencon
-Xscmx96m
-Xshareclasses:singleJVM,keep,nonfatal
-Xnolinenumbers
-XX:MaxPermSize=512M
-Dsun.java2d.noddraw=true
```

- Cleaning up logs: Periodically clean the logfiles under `%WID_HOME%/ pf\wps\logs\server1` and also `%WID_HOME%/ pf\wps\logs\ffdc`.

Summary

In this chapter we started with an explanation about the fundamental SOA programming model concepts and understood how these concepts apply in the context of WID/WPS/WESB. We quickly refreshed our fundamentals in WSDL and XSD. Then we discussed in detail about Service Component Architecture (SCA). To quickly recollect, SCA is neither another programming language nor replacement, but rather gives a model to assemble and build SOA applications by choosing any technology-specific implementation approach. The fundamental goal and premise of SCA is to separate business logic from infrastructure logic. WID provides the design time environment to build SCA-based applications. The Service Data Object (SDO) provides the technology to represent a universal model for data that flows between components in an SCA. Finally we rounded up the SOA programming model discussions with BPEL. BPEL is an XML based programming language used to describe high-level business processes. BPEL allows you to define choreography (inter-company or inter-organization) or orchestration (intra-organization) interactions to be described easily and thoroughly. BPEL is one of the options that are provided in WID to implement an SCA component.

After getting the fundamental concepts right, we started building out first business process based application—Greeting Solution. Though the application was doing a simple job, the purpose of building this application was to understand how to go about using WID, the various capabilities of WID, and how to apply these capabilities. We discussed how to create Integrated Solutions, creating modules and libraries, assembling and wiring components, implementing the BPEL component, navigating through and using the business process editor -- and finally, after developing the business process, how to deploy and test it. Then we briefly touched upon logging, debugging, and troubleshooting basics and exporting projects from WID. We hope by the end of this chapter you have began to get your feet wet and will be ready for more detailed concepts in the forthcoming chapters.

4

Building Your Hello Mediation Project

This chapter will be along similar lines as the previous chapter, where you will build your first HelloWorld **WebSphere Enterprise Service Bus (WESB)** mediation application and WESB mediation flow-based application. This chapter will then give an overview of **Service Message Object (SMO)** standards and how they relate to building applications using an SOA approach. At the completion of this chapter, you will have an understanding of how to begin building, testing, and deploying WESB mediations including:

- Overview of WESB-based programming fundamentals including WS-*? standards and Service Message Objects (SMOs)
- Building the first mediation module project in WID
- Using mediation flows
- Deploying the module on a server and testing the project
- Logging, debugging, and troubleshooting basics
- Exporting projects from WID

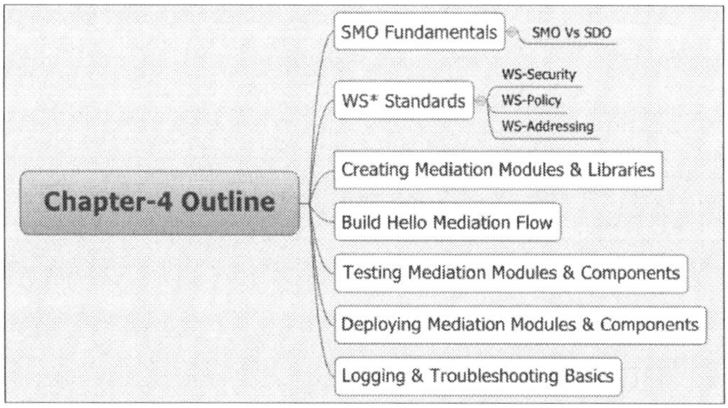

WS standards

Before we get down to discussing mediation flows, it is essential to take a moment and acquaint ourselves with some of the Web Service (WS) standards that WebSphere Integration Developers (WIDs) comply with. By using WIDs, user-friendly visual interfaces and drag-and-drop paradigms, developers are automatically building process flows that are globally standardized and compliant. This becomes critical in an ever-changing business environment that demands flexible integration with business partners.

Here are some of the key specifications that you should be aware of as defined by the Worldwide Web Consortium (W3C):

- WS-Security: This is one of the secure standards used to secure Web Service at the message level, independent of the transport protocol. To learn more about WID and WS-Security refer to `http://publib.boulder.ibm.com/infocenter/dmndhelp/v7r0mx/topic/com.ibm.wbit.help.runtime.doc/deploy/topics/cwssecurity.html`.
- WS-Policy: A framework that helps define characteristics about Web Services through policies. To learn more about WS-Policy refer to: `http://www.w3.org/TR/ws-policy/`.
- WS-Addressing: This specification aids interoperability between Web Services, by standardizing ways to address Web Services and by providing addressing information in messages. In version 7.0, enhancements were made to WID to provide Web Services support for WS-Addressing and Attachments. For more details about WS-Addressing refer to `http://www.w3.org/Submission/ws-addressing/`.

What are mediation flows?

As we discussed in *Chapter 1, Introducing IBM BPM and ESB* in an SOA, service consumers and service providers use an ESB as a communication vehicle. When services are loosely coupled through an ESB, the overall system has more flexibility and can be easily modified and enhanced to meet changing business requirements. We also saw that an ESB by itself is an enabler of many patterns and enables protocol transformations and provides mediation services, which can inspect, modify, augment and transform a message as it flows from requestor to provider. In WebSphere Enterprise Service, mediation modules provide the ESB functionality.

The heart of a mediation module is the mediation flow component, which provides the mediation logic applied to a message as it flows from a service consumer to a provider. The mediation flow component is a type of SCA component that is typically used, but not limited to a mediation module. A mediation flow component contains a source interface and target references similar to other SCA components. The source interface is described using WSDL interface and must match the WSDL definition of the export to which it is wired. The target references are described using WSDL and must match the WSDL definitions of the imports or Java components to which they are wired. The mediation flow component handles most of the ESB functions including:

- Message filtering which is the capability to filter messages based on the content of the incoming message.
- Dynamic routing and selection of service provider, which is the capability to route incoming messages to the appropriate target at runtime based on predefined policies and rules.
- Message transformation, which is the capability to transform messages between source and target interfaces. This transformation can be defined using XSL stylesheets or business object maps.
- Message manipulation/enrichment, which is the capability to manipulate or enrich incoming message fields before they are sent to the target. This capability also allows you to do database lookups as needed.
- If the previous functionalities do not fit your requirements, you have the capability of defining a custom mediation behavior in JAVA.

The following diagram describes the architectural layout of a mediation flow:

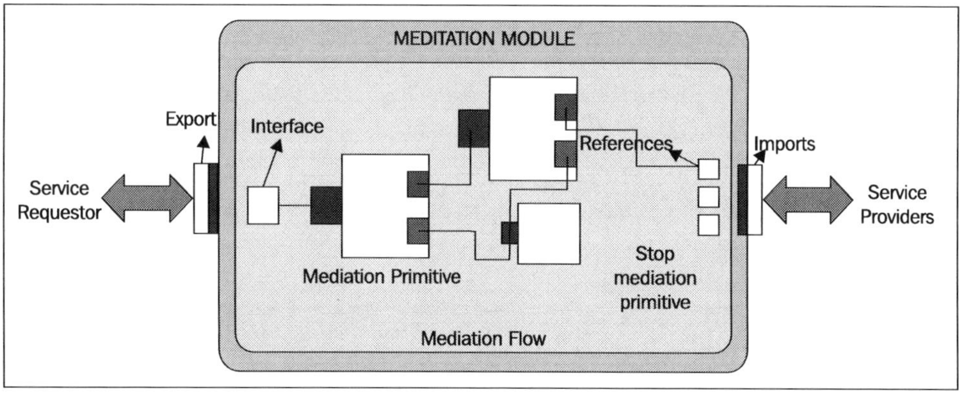

In the diagram, on the left-hand side you see the single service requester or source interface and on the right-hand side are the multiple service providers or target references. The mediation flow is the set of logical processing steps that efficiently route messages from the service requestor to the most appropriate service provider and back to the service requestor for that particular transaction and business environment. A mediation flow can be a request flow or a request and response flow. In a request flow message the sequence of processing steps is defined only from the source to the target. No message is returned to the source. However, in a request and response flow message the sequence of processing steps are defined from the single source to the multiple targets and back from the multiple targets to the single source. In the next section we take a deeper look into message objects and how they are handled in the mediation flows.

Mediation primitives

What are the various mediation primitives available in WESB?

Mediation primitives are the core building blocks used to process the request and response messages in a mediation flow.

- Built-in primitives, which perform some predefined function that is configurable through the use of properties.
- Custom mediation primitives, which allow you to implement the function in Java.
- Mediation primitives have input and output terminals, through which the message flows. Almost all primitives have only one input terminal, but multiple input terminals are possible for custom mediation primitives.
- Primitives can have zero, one, or more output terminals.
- There is also a special terminal called the fail terminal through which the message is propagated when the processing of a primitive results in an exception.

The different types of mediation primitives that are available in a mediation flow, along with their purpose, are summarized in the following table:

Service invocation	
Service Invoke	Invoke external service, message modified with result

Routing primitives	
Message Filter	Selectively forward messages based on element values
Type Filter	Selectively forward messages based on element types

Routing primitives	
Endpoint Lookup	Find potential endpoint from a registry query
Fan Out	Starts iterative or split flow for aggregation
Fan In	Check completion of a split or aggregated flow
Policy Resolution	Set policy constrains from a registry query
Flow Order	Executes or fires the output terminal in a defined order
Gateway Endpoint Lookup	Finds potential endpoint in special cases from a registry
SLA Check	Verifies if the message complies with the SLA
UDDI Endpoint Lookup	Finds potential endpoints from a UDDI registry query

Transformation primitives	
XSL Transformation	Update and modify messages using XSLT
Business Object Map	Update and modify messages using business object maps
Message element setter	Set, update, copy, and delete message elements
Set message type	Set elements to a more specific type
Database Lookup	Set elements from contents within a database
Data Handler	Update and modify messages using a data handler
Custom Mediation	Read, update, and modify messages using Java code
SOAP header setter	Read, update, copy, and delete SOAP header elements
HTTP header setter	Read, update, copy, and delete HTTP header elements
JMS header setter	Read, update, copy, and delete JMS header elements
MQ header setter	Read, update, copy, and delete MQ header elements

Tracing primitives	
Message logger	Write a log message to a database or a custom destination
Event emitter	Raise a common base event to CEI
Trace	Send a trace message to a file or system out for debugging

Error handling primitives	
Stop	Stop a single path in flow without an exception
Fail	Stop the entire flow and raise an exception
Message Validator	Validate a message against a schema and assertions

Mediation subflow primitive	
Subflow	Represents a user-defined subflow

Service Message Objects (SMO)

The primary function of a mediation flow is to operate on a message between endpoints, where a service requestor and a service provider are those endpoints. However, this presents a problem. The first point is that a message can take on many different forms because the protocol used to send a message, whether JMS or Web services, can vary. Also, each message is different depending upon the interface and operation associated with the message and whether this is the request side or response side of the interaction between the requestor and provider.

The next point to understand is that within the mediation flow, mediation primitives are used to operate on the message. Mediation primitives examine and update the message contents and therefore must understand what is contained in the message. The solution is to provide mediation primitives with some kind of a common representation of a message, and that is what a Service Message Object does. SMOs provide a common representation of a message that accounts for differing protocols and differing interfaces, operations, and parameters that the message represents. SMOs are built using Service Data Object (SDO) technology. SDO uses a schema that describes the basic structure of an SMO which is composed of three major sections.

The body of the message represents the specific interface, operation, and parameters relevant to this message. The headers section of the message represents information about the protocol over which the message was sent. The context section represents data that is important to the internal logic of the flow itself. Each of these major sections of the SMO is examined in more detail in subsequent slides. The data within an SMO is accessed using SDO, specifically the SDO DataObject, which enables access using XPath, the generic DataObject APIs, and some SMO-specific APIs that are aware of the SMO schema.

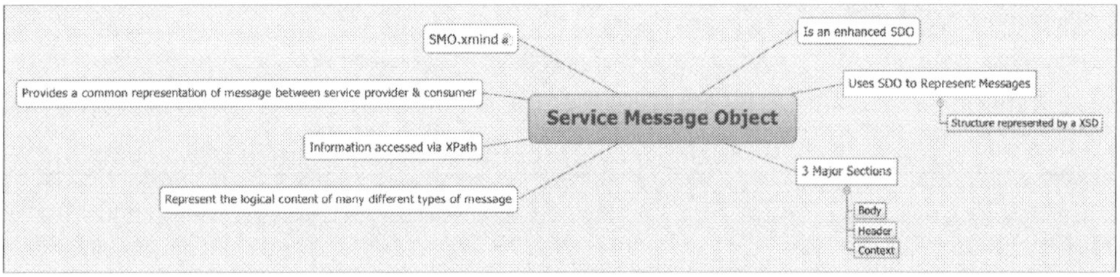

The service requestor and service provider interact with the bus through the bindings for the exports and imports of the mediation service module. The data representing the message depends on the binding used for exports and imports. If the primitives in the mediation flow component had to support the data representation for all the various bindings, it would be difficult to implement primitives. For this reason, the first thing the runtime does is that it converts the binding-specific data into common data structure, called Service Message Objects (SMO).

The SMO interface extends the DataObject interface, which is defined by the Service Data Object (SDO), similar to other business objects used in WebSphere Process Server. SMO includes the message headers, message data (payload) and context information and provides an interface to access and modify the SMO data, including headers, payload, and context information. In addition, the SDO data can be accessed using the XPath reference mechanism. The mediation module input contains binding-specific data representation. The mediation module output import binding dictates the data representation that must be sent to the output message. As a result, there is a lack of consistency in data representation and if the mediation flow primitives had to handle all the different data representation, it would become a huge challenge. To solve this problem, the data from binding-specific interaction is converted to a common data structure called the Service Message Object (SMO).

If the mediation primitives in a message flow require a temporary area to save data for other primitives down the message flow or need data set in the request flow to be available during the response flow, context information is used as a scratch pad. There are two types of context information: Transient context, as the name suggests, is temporary and available only on the specific request flow or the response flow but is not carried from the request to the response flow, and is therefore stored in memory. Correlation context is the second type of context data that is available for the duration of the complete request/response flow. Data set in the request flow is available for all the primitives in the response flow. Any primitive can modify the context information and downstream primitives in the message flow will have access to that information. The context data are represented as data objects and the structure is inserted in the SMO structure at the start of the mediation flow.

Creating mediation modules

You now have an understanding of the basic concepts of mediation and mediation flows. Let's try implementing these concepts in a simple HelloMediationModule.

For this we shall build upon our example from the previous chapter. In the previous chapter we had built a simple HelloProcess integration solution. We will use the HelloProcess requirements as the basis and will build a mediation flow based solution that will satisfy the following requirements:

- It should be capable of getting user input and more specifically their first name, last name, and age

- It should return a customized greeting based on their age
    - Ages 25 and younger it should return—"What's up <FirstName LastName>! Congrats on your first hello world mediation flow"
    - Ages 26 to 65 it should return—"Hey <FirstName LastName>! Congrats on your first hello world mediation flow"
    - Ages 65 and above it should return—"Greetings <FirstName LastName>! Congrats on your first hello world mediation flow"
- The solution should be exposed through Web Services

If you remember, we used a XPath object within the BPEL to develop the logic to return the custom greeting message. In this example, we shall build this logic in a mediation flow using the message filter primitive along with the use of a correlation context and message element setter primitive we just learnt.

Creating the Hello Mediation Flow

In order to create Hello Mediation Flow,

1. In a new WID workspace, create a new Integration Solution in WID, **File | New | Integration Solution** and name it **Greeting_Solution**.
2. Import the GreetingLibrary that we created in the previous chapter
3. Click on **File | New** and select **Mediation Module** from the context menu. Give the module the name **HelloMediationModule** and the name of the mediation component as GreetingsFlow as shown in the following figure:

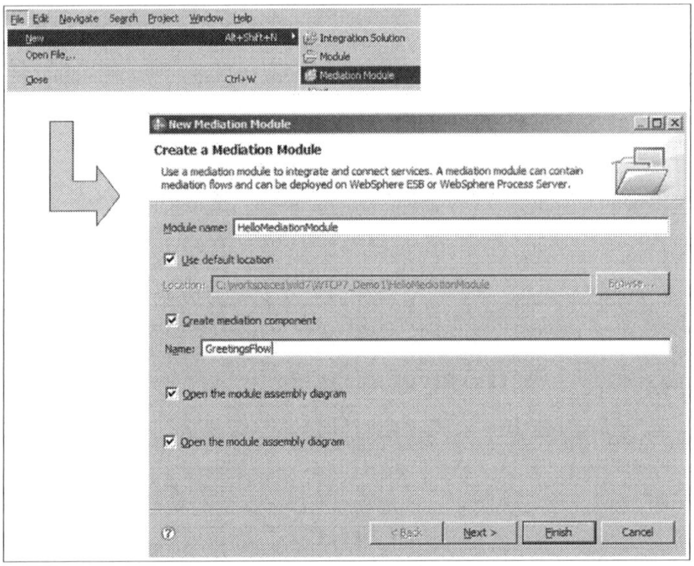

4. Specify the **GreetingLibrary** in the required libraries wizard screen and proceed to next.
5. Make this mediation module part of the **Greeting_Solution** Integration Solution. Click on the **Finish** button.

Upon clicking **Finish** the mediation module gets created and the Assembly diagram opens for the new mediation module. On the canvas of this assembly diagram you will notice that the GreetingsFlow mediation flow component has been created. We will specify the HandleGreetingMessage as the interface on this mediation flow component.

This can be done by as shown in the following steps:

1. Right-click on **GreetingsFlow** | **Add...** | **Interface** | **HandleGreetingMessage**. Click on the **OK** button, as shown in the following diagram:

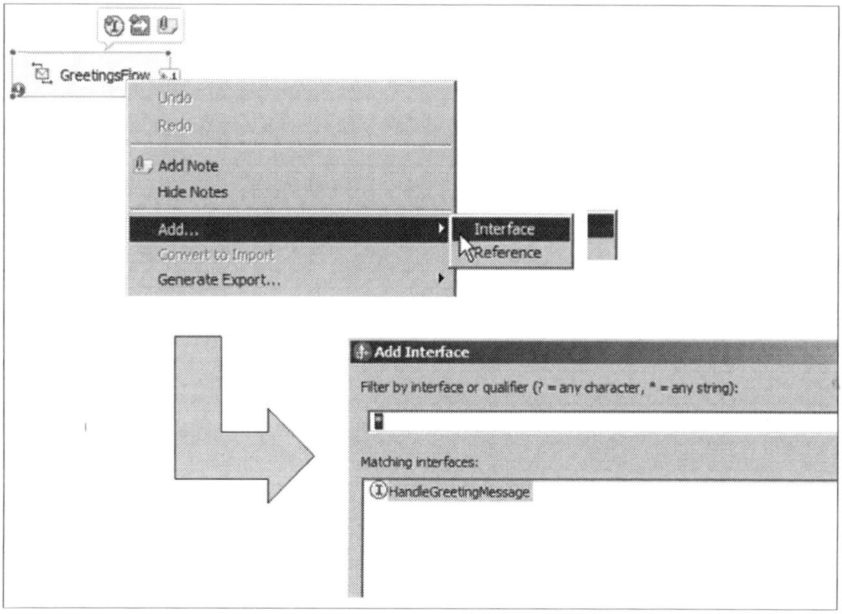

2. Right-click on **HelloMediationModule | Generate Export... | Web Service Binding | SOAP1.1/HTTP.** Click on the **OK** button, as shown in the following screenshot:

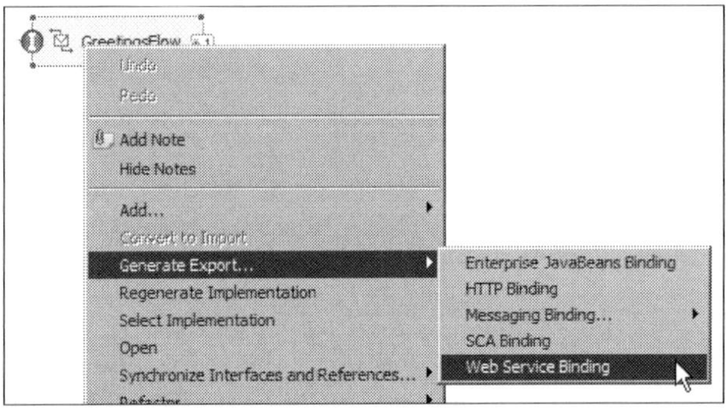

The **Assembly Diagram** should now look like the following screenshot:

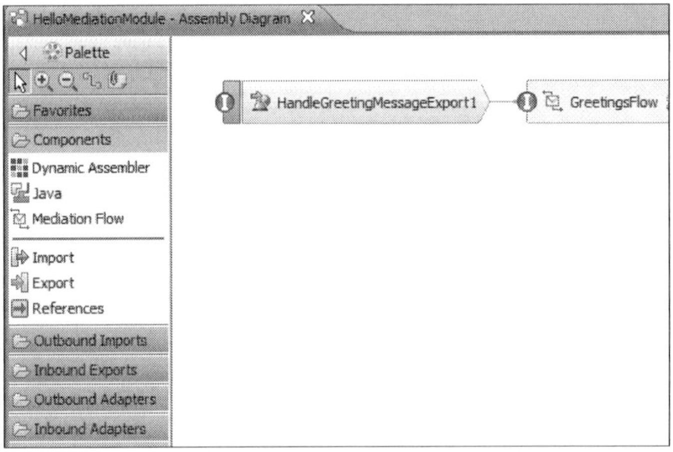

Implementing the HelloMediationModule

1. Right-click on **HelloMediationModule**. Select **Generate Implementation** and then select **New Folder** (or you can double-click on the component). Enter the name of the new folder as **com.junglesea.solution.greeting.mediation** and click on the **OK** button.
2. This will open the mediation flow overview. Click on the **returnGreeting** operation and select **Blank Mediation Flow**, as shown in the following screenshot:

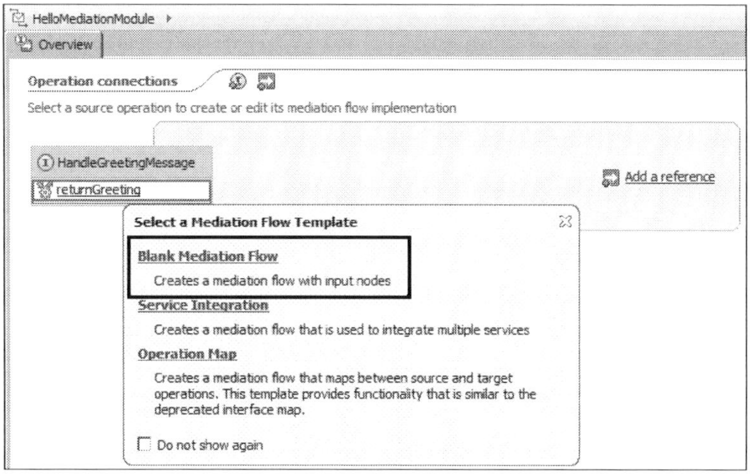

3. The mediation flow editor should now be open. We shall cover details about this editor in *Chapter 6, Mediations Fundamentals*. For now we shall focus on building the GreetingsFlow and getting a basic understanding of mediation flow components.

4. We will first use a "Message Filter" primitive to route the incoming message based on age value. continue with this bullet. In the palette of the mediation editor under **Routing** category, select and drag the **Message Filter** primitive onto the canvas. Rename the message filter primitive to **AgeBasedFilter** by clicking on the **MessageFilter1** text below the component, as shown in the following screenshot:

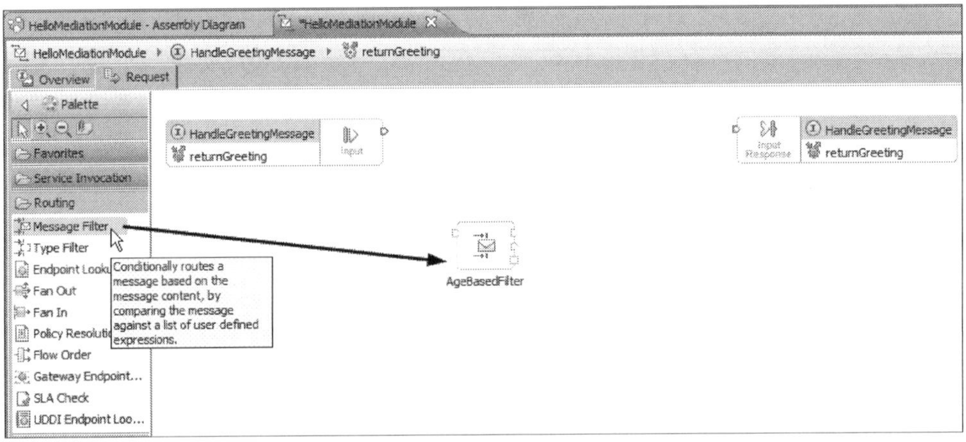

> Message Filter primitive is used to route messages to target based on a pre-defined condition or filter. In our example we will use this primitive to check the age in the incoming message and accordingly route the message to one of the three custom mediation primitives that will print the response greeting in *Chapter 6, Mediations Fundamentals* covers more in-depth details.

5. Select **AgeBasedFilter** and open **Properties**, and select the **Terminal** tab on the left-hand side. Rename the Output terminal **match1** to **LessThan25**. Right-click on **Output terminal** (shown in the following figure) and select **Add Output Terminal**, and add one more output terminals named **MoreThan25LessThan65** as shown in the following screenshot:

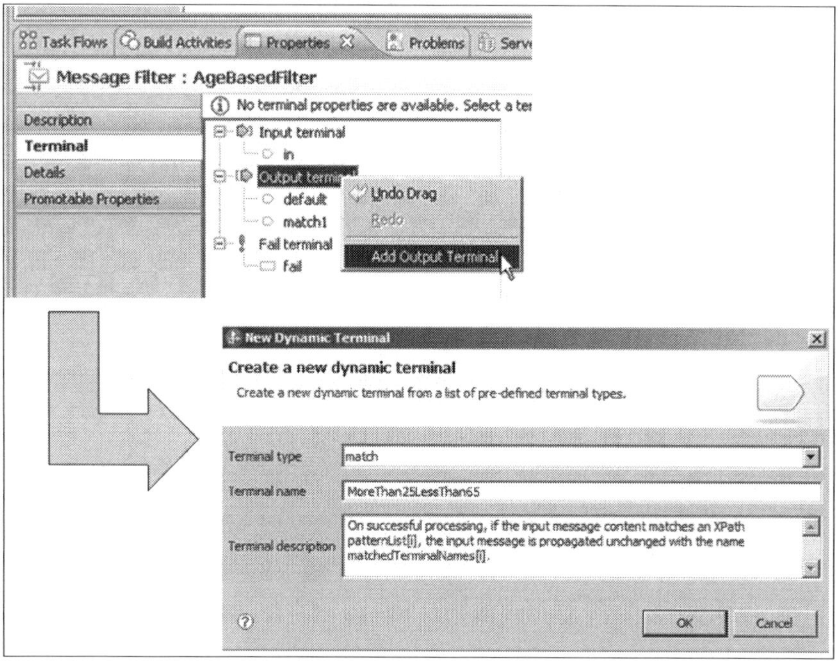

6. Wire the **Input** node to the **AgeBasedFilter** primitive.
7. From the palette of the mediation editor under the **Transformation** category, select and drag the **Custom Mediation** primitive on to the canvas. Name this primitive **SayGreetingWhatsUp**. Repeat the same and create two more custom mediation primitives named **SayGreetingWhatsHappening** and **SayGreetingGoodDay**.
8. Wire the **AgeBasedFilter** primitive default terminal to the **SayGreetingGoodDay** custom mediation primitive . Similarly wire **LessThan25** and **MoreThan25LessThan65** terminals to the **SayGreetingWhatsUp** and **SayGreetingWhatsHappening** custom mediation primitives respectively.

9. Now let's specify the age based message filtering patterns. Select the **AgeBasedFilter** primitive and open **Properties** and select the **Details** tab on the left-hand side. Click on the **Add** button as shown in the following screenshot:

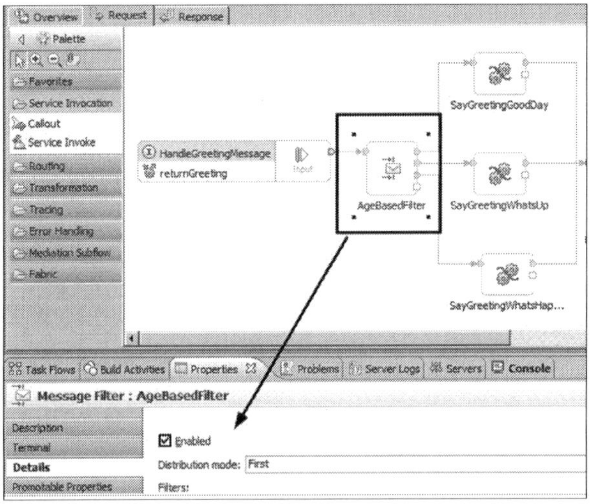

10. In the **Add/Edit** properties dialog box enter the pattern **/body/returnGreeting/inputPartyInfo/Age[self::node()<=25]**.
11. As shown in the following screenshot select **Terminal name** as **LessThan25** and click on the **Finish** button.

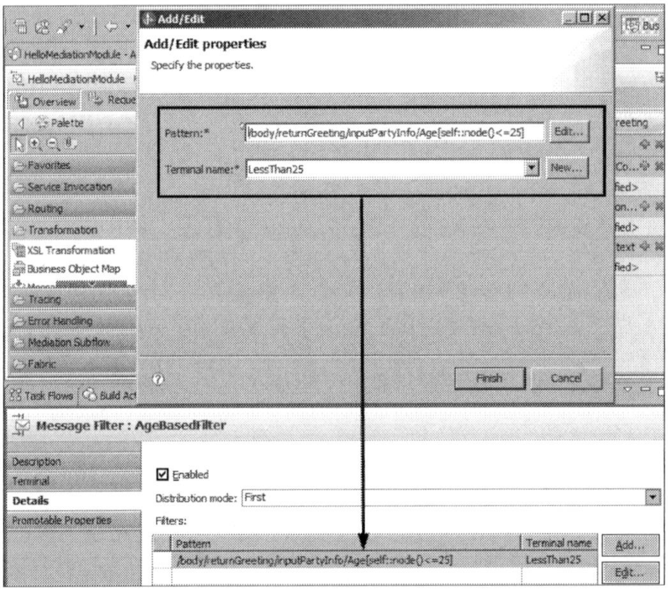

12. Repeat the preceding steps to add the **/body/returnGreeting/inputPartyInfo/Age[self::node()>25 and self::node()<=65]** matching pattern to the **MoreThan25LessThan65** terminal.
13. We will define a correlation context named **greetingMessageCtx** to store the greeting message so that it can be used to hold the greeting message and can be mapped to the response message – **outputGreetingMessage**. Correlation context's are for passing values from the request flow to the response flow inside a mediation flow. Think of them as temporary variables that are accessible in both the request and response flows with a mediation flow.

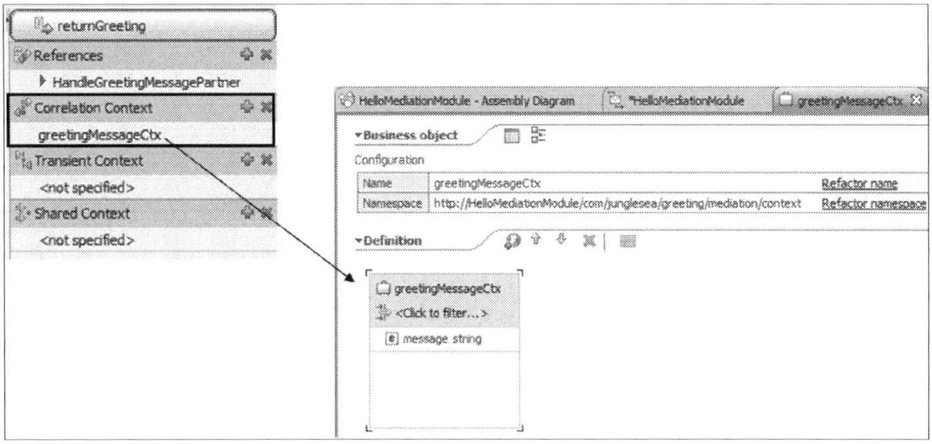

14. Then specify within the custom mediation primitives the greeting messages to return. Go to **SayGreetingGoodDay** primitive and switch to the **Visual** implementation model and add the logic as shown in the following figure. As you can see we use the **append text** standard utility function to create the response message and then store it in the **greetingMessageCtx** correlation context we defined in the previous step.

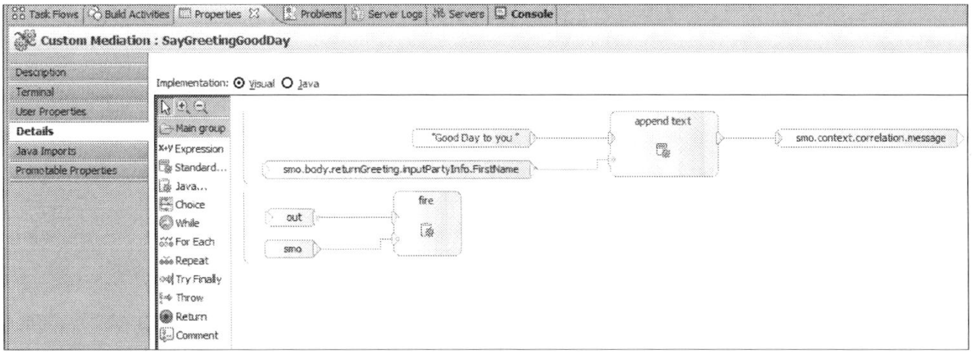

15. Repeat the same steps for the **SayGreetingWhatsHappening** and **SayGreetingGoodDay** custom mediation primitives as shown in the following screenshot:

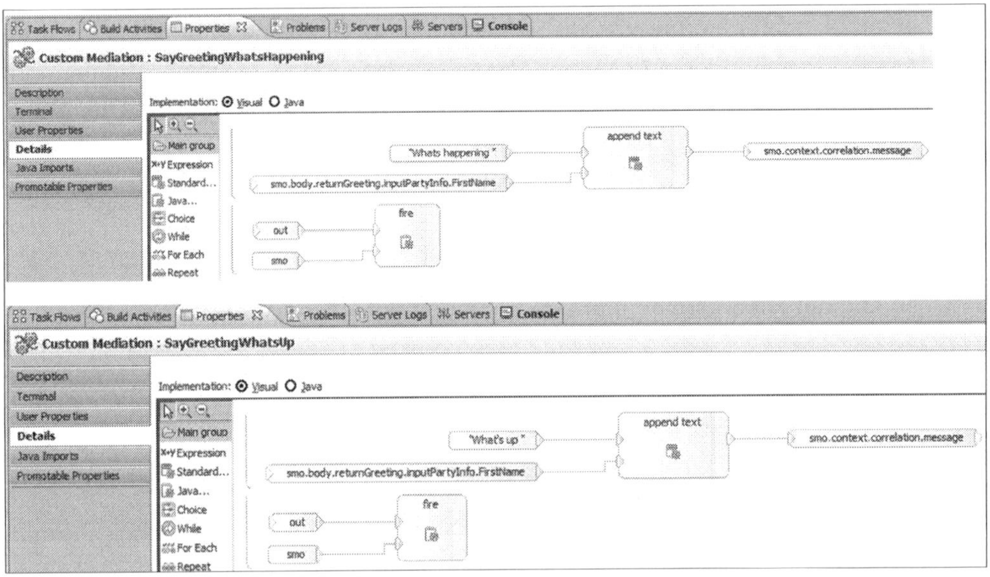

16. From the palette of the mediation editor under **Service Invocation** category, select and drag the **Callout** primitive on to the canvas. A callout node is an end point in the request flow. It sends the processed message to the target operation and in our case this will be sent back as the response. Wire the output of the **SayGoodDayGreeting** custom primitive and go to the **Callout** node. If you look you will see a response flow that will get added when you add the Callout. Repeat the same for the **SayGreetingWhatsUp** and **SayGreetingWhatsHappening** custom primitives.
17. Go to the response flow and add a **Message Element Setter** primitive (that will copy the value of the greeting from the correlation context to the response element) in between the callout response and input response. Your mediation response flow will look as shown in the following screenshot.

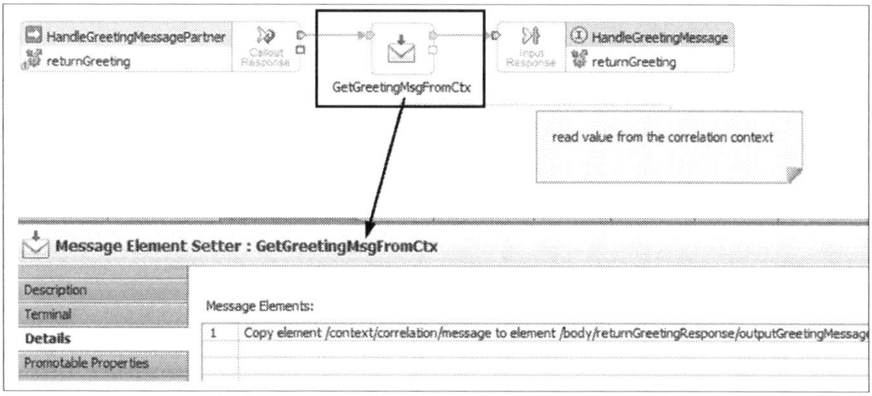

Congratulations! You have now created your first mediation module. We will now unit test the mediation flow.

Testing modules and components

In the last chapter, we tested the HelloBPEL process using the WID unit test environment (UTE) that is installed as a part of WebSphere Integration Developer and consists of a separate installation of the WPS and WESB. We have also talked about the fact that the WebSphere Process Server is built on WebSphere Application Server and contains an Enterprise Service Bus. This helps this server to provide the ideal environment to test **HelloMediationModule**.

Deploying the modules

You will now deploy your **HelloMediationModule** on your WebSphere Process Server UTE environment (or the WESB server if you have it set up). In the **Server** view,

1. Click on the **Servers** tab, and start the WPS server by clicking on the green play button and wait for the server to start. This may take a few minutes.

2. Right-click on **WebSphere Process Server v7.0**, select **Add and Remove Projects**. Select **HelloMediationModuleApp**, and then click on **Add | Finish**. The **HelloMediationModule** will now get deployed and published on the WebSphere Process Server. You will be able to verify this by seeing it listed under **WebSphere Process Server v7.0**, as shown in the following screenshot:

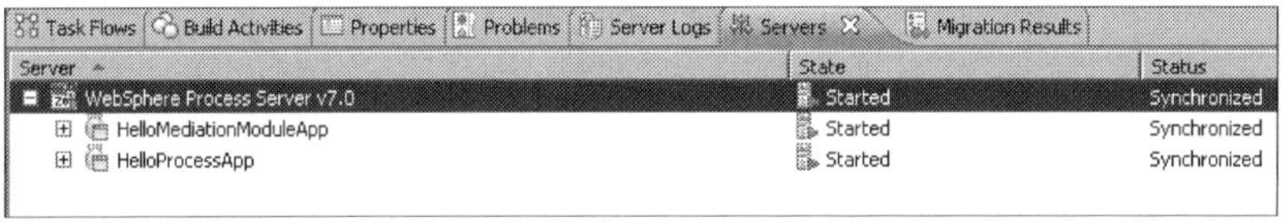

Executing the modules

After deploying the modules, the next step is to execute the modules. Similar to how we did in the previous chapter, we will use the integration test client to unit test the HelloMediationModule module and more specifically test the interface operations of the GreetingsFlow mediation flow component.

1. Right-click anywhere in the assembly diagram and select **Test Module**. This will bring up the **Integration Test Client** editor. Enter appropriate values and press the play button that will execute the module and you will be able to see the greeting message depending on the age you entered.
2. In the following figure the request values and the appropriate response messages are shown when the mediation module is executed.

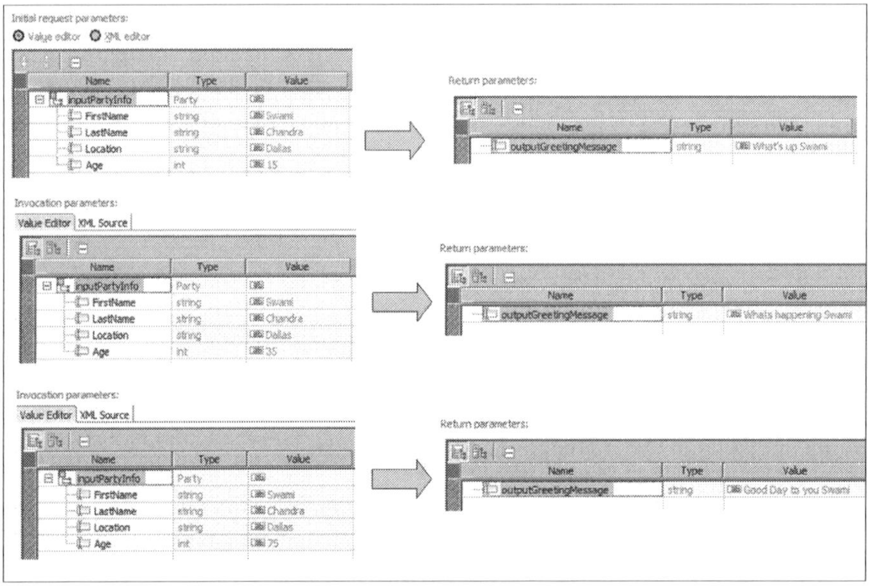

Summary

This chapter gave an overview of WESB-based programming fundamentals including Service Message Objects (SMO) and Mediation Flows. This discussion gave the fundamentals to build our first mediation flow component. Instructions were provided to create, implement and assemble the HelloMediationFlow. This mediation module was deployed on the server and unit tested using the WID Unit Test Environment.

5
Business Process Choreography Fundamentals

We have concluded Part 1 of our journey and have thus enabled you by imparting the fundamental concepts in Business Integration, SOA, BPM, and ESB. We went through the process of installing and setting up the WID development environment and installing and configuring it properly. We also guided you through building the first BPEL-based module and also a mediation flow component-based mediation module. It's action time now! In the second part of the journey we will build an SOA-based Order Management Application for the fictitious company—JungleSea Inc. To prepare for this, we will first guide you through the various aspects and functions of WPS and WESB that are absolutely and fundamentally essential.

We intend to impart this knowledge and information to you with a *What, When, and How* approach. Topics covered include Business Process (WS-BPEL), Business Objects, Business Rules, State Machines, Visual Snippets, Compensation, Fault Handling, and Control Structures. We will walk-through each of these aspects, functions, and features with examples so that you can relate to them and their usage applicability. By the end of this chapter, the goal is to prepare you for selecting and using the right tool from the toolbox when building applications for WPS and WESB, which can be built, unit tested, and debugged using WID.

The mind map that outlines this chapter's topics is shown in the following screenshot:

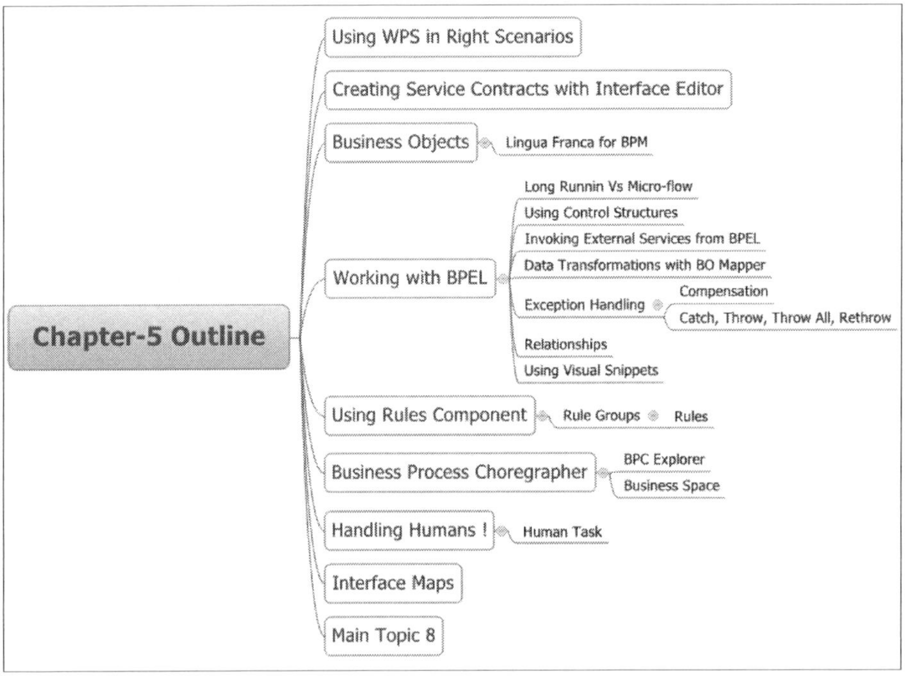

Using WPS in the right scenarios

According to the article, *The Forrester Wave*: *Business Process Management For Document Processes, Q3 2007* by *Craig Le Clair* and *Colin Teubner*, there are four categories of business processes:

1. Integration Intensive: Typically used in cases to perform process automation with minimal interaction/intervention. Common adoption patterns include straight through processing and application integration.
2. People Intensive: Typically used in cases to perform process automation with mostly interactive or task-based interaction. Adoption requires the use of a rich user interface.
3. Decision Intensive: Typically used in cases to perform process automation, along with heavy use of a decision-based interaction. The complex decision logic is externalized from the business process and typically created and maintained in a business rules management system (such as IBM ILOG).
4. Document Intensive: Processes automation is very document-centric and task-oriented. Process lifecycle and tasks are oriented managing the lifecycle of a piece or a collection of content.

You have, so far, seen how WPS and WESB provide capabilities to build business process solutions and mediation solutions respectively. WPS provides a wide range of capabilities and can be used in different scenarios and for different purposes. You may ask when to choose WPS over WESB and also some of the most common usage types for WPS. To understand when to choose WPS appropriately requires you to understand the various business process types and patterns. Let me provide some guidance on when to use WPS and for which scenarios:

- Synchronous Transactional Process
    - Orchestration of rapidly responding services.
- GUI Intensive Process
    - An external GUI-driven navigational flow and data aggregation rather than in WPS.
- Human Task Oriented Process
    - Predominantly based around task-based human interaction. BPEL processes guide the flow of control from one task to the next. Most processes are expected to go though a significant number of user tasks before completion.
- Asynchronously Initiated Transactional Process
    - This is a process invoked by a consumer in a fire and forget fashion such that the consumer need not wait for a response. If the transaction fails, it is the responsibility of the operations team to resolve the issue—the user does not need to retry.
- Briefly Persisted Process
    - This is a special use for a long-running process where the process completes relatively swiftly. Process lifespan is deliberately short (seconds, maybe minutes), such that process versioning issues can be avoided. The process must be designed to complete in a timely fashion, so no human tasks are allowed and error handling can or preferably handled outside of the process in a seperate component.
- Versioned Long-lived Process
    - A multi-transactional process and associated instances that often span days or weeks. It can therefore be assumed that the process cannot be re-installed to make changes.

- Content Management Process
    - A special use of a long-running process where the process lifecycle and tasks are centred around a piece or a collection of content or documents.

> For more information on selecting WPS for process-based solutions refer to *Solution design in WebSphere Process Server: Part I and II*—by *Kim. J. Clark* and *Brian. M. Petrini.*
>
> `http://www.ibm.com/developerworks/websphere/library/techarticles/0904_clark/0904_clark.html`
>
> `http://www.ibm.com/developerworks/websphere/library/techarticles/0908_clark/0908_clark.html`
>
> For information on how to combine BPM and SOA and using them together to build a more flexible dynamic enterprise, refer to *Dynamic SOA and BPM: Best Practices for Business Process Management and SOA Agility* by *Marc Fiammante* (author Swami Chandrasekaran's mentor) *ISBN-10: 0137018916.*

Creating service contracts with interface editor

We explained pretty well what a WSDL is in *Chapter 3, Building your Hello Process Project*,and if you remember, it's the document that describes a Web Service which is also used to locate it. In a nutshell, WSDL is an XML grammar for specifying a public interface for a Web Service. So what capabilities does WID provide for me to create interfaces?

Also as explained in Chapter 3, the fundamental building block(s) in an SOA-based business solution are the Service Components Architecture (SCA) components. We also explained that these SCA components can be assembled and wired together using the WID assembly diagram and deployed to WPS or WESB.

The SCA components can be implemented using different implementation types, which can include business processes (BPEL), business rules, Java, and so on. The components, by themselves, apart from its implementation, have one or more interfaces. You also know that in the WID assembly diagram, the components appear as rectangular icons. The interface provides the input and output of a component. To users of a service component, all that matters is its interface, which dictates how to use it. Technically, an interface can be created independent of the implementation of the component. WID is flexible in the sense that it lets you build interfaces either before or after component implementation with the same results.

For an interface, you can specify a preferred interaction style as synchronous or asynchronous. The interfaces that are defined on the component are defined in the synchronous form and asynchronous support is also generated for them.

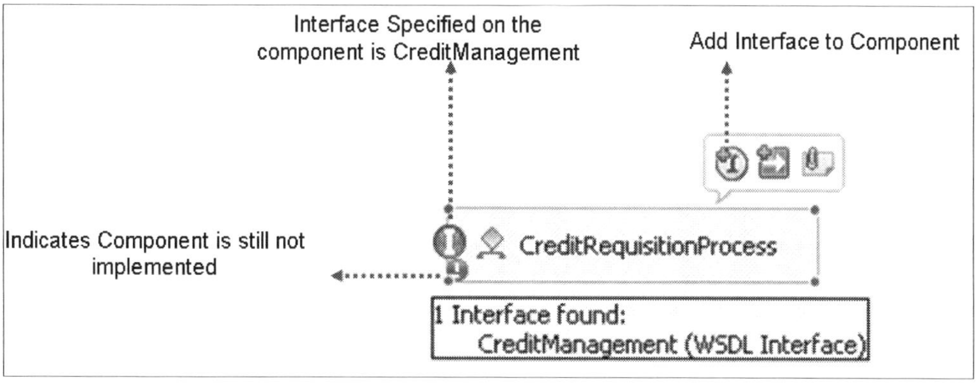

Interfaces link the different components in a module. The inputs and outputs of each component, specified by the interface, determine which data can be passed from one component to another. We also saw in *Chapter 2, Installing the Development Environment* and *Chapter 3, Building your Hello Process Project* that in order to share the interfaces between modules, we have to put the interfaces into a library. So how do you go about creating these interfaces? Well, let me first explain our three approaches to creating interfaces:

- Top-down
- Bottom-up
- Meet-in-the-middle

Before I start explaining, you may ask, "Why do we need three approaches? Why can't I just use the tool to create interfaces?" The three key elements of an SOA include business processes, services, and components that realize services. The promise of SOA is in creating loosely-coupled, business-aligned services that, because of the separation of concerns between description, implementation, and binding, provide unprecedented flexibility in responsiveness to new business threats and opportunities. So how do you identify these SOA services and secondly how can you make sure that two people sitting next to each other do not write the same service? Thirdly, and finally, how can you make sure that the service you developed makes meaningful sense to the business and can indeed be reused? Basically you don't want to blindly build components and services.

IBM's **Service Oriented Modeling and Architecture** (**SOMA**) for example is a modeling and design method for identification, specification, realization, implementation, and deployment of services for an SOA. SOMA recommends a process that is a combination of top-down, bottom-up, and middle-out techniques of domain decomposition, existing asset analysis, and goal-service modeling. SOMA provides an approach to building an SOA that aligns to the business goals and directly ties the business processes to underlying applications through services, which will help the business realize benefits more rapidly.

In a *top-down* view, a blueprint of use cases provides the specification for services. This top-down process is often referred to as domain decomposition. In the *bottom-up* portion of the process or existing system analysis, existing systems are analyzed and appropriate service candidates are identified, which will support the use cases. The *middle-out* view consists of steps to validate goals and unearth other services not captured by either top-down or bottom-up service identification approaches. It's therefore very important in an SOA approach that you adopt such a technique to properly identify and specify interfaces.

So we took a segue, but it was worth the effort. We will now continue with how to create interfaces using WID. An interface consists of one or more operations. An operation is a description of an action implemented by the component. An operation may be a request-response type, or a one-way type, meaning only an input is sent and there is no response needed. Each operation defines the data in the form of input, output, and fault. Each operation may have one or more faults to handle error conditions. A one-way operation only has an input. The binding style specifies the protocol and data format of the operation. The following screenshot shows an interface created in WID named **CreditManagement**:

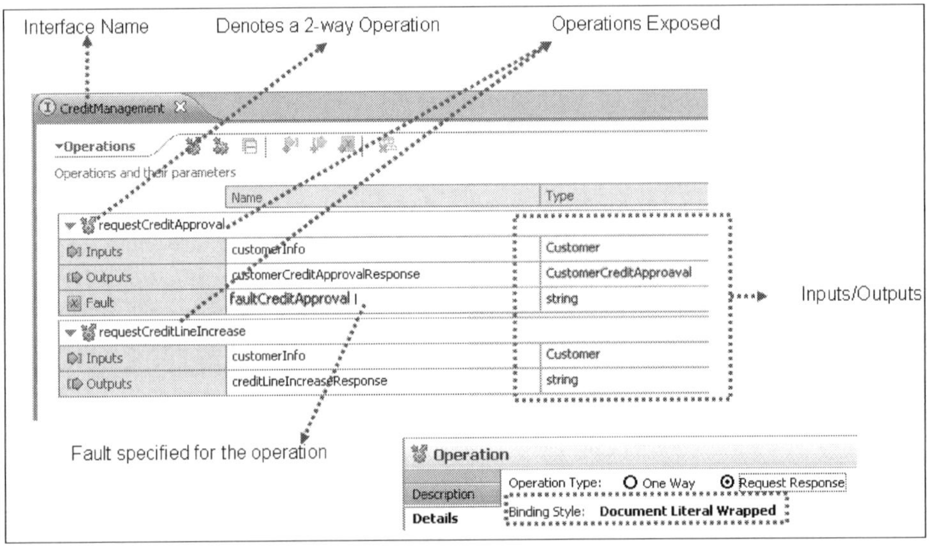

The different parts of **CreditManagement** (interface) are shown in the following interface editor:

Operation Name	requestCreditApproval	Allows a request for a credit application to be made and responds appropriately with the results.
Operation Type	request-response	One-way is the other type.
Inputs	Customer	This is a business object that contains information about the customer.
Outputs	CustomerCreditApproval	Detailed response business object that contains information about the credit check response.
Fault	faultCreditApproval	A string describing the error returned.
Binding Style	Document Literal	Document literal wrapped is the default binding style when creating interfaces with WID. Document literal RPC are tolerated.

So here are the steps to create the previous interface in WID:

1. In a new workspace, create a new library in WID (as explained in Chapters 2 and 3) named **Ch5Library**.

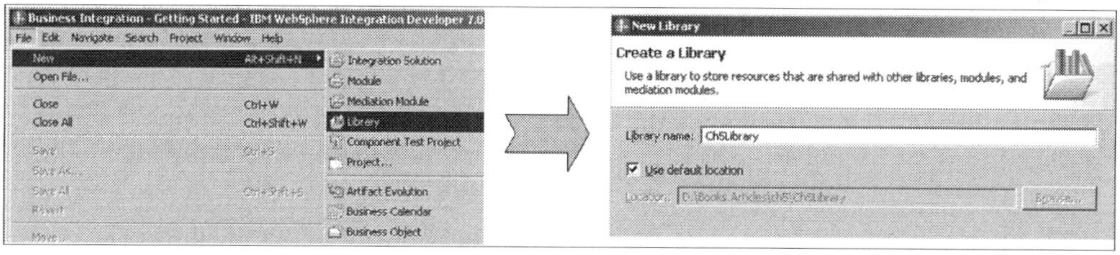

2. Right-click the **Interfaces** option in the **Ch5Library**, and from the pop-up menu, select **New | Interface**. Provide a name for the interface, **CreditManagement** in this case, in the name field. You can also provide the folder name (which is analogous to packages and becomes the basis for the namespace) **com/junglsea/interfaces** and click on the **Finish** button. You will now see an empty interface in the interface editor.

> As you can see from the following diagram, the namespace for this component is based on the module name. You are free to follow any other naming scheme.

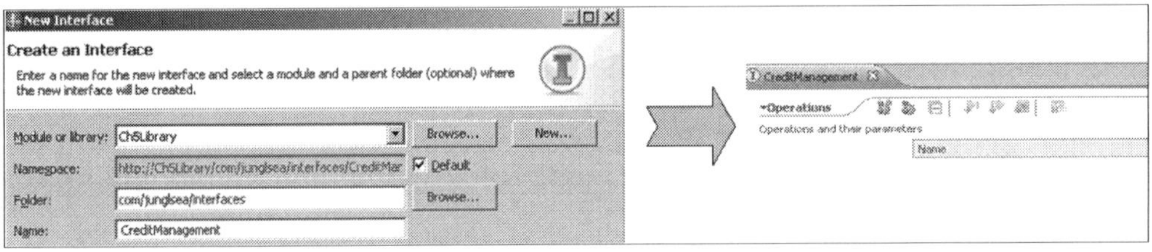

3. Add operations to the empty interface. Click on the **Add Request Response Operation** icon. A request-response operation with an input and an output is created. Rename **operation1** to **requestCreditApproval**.

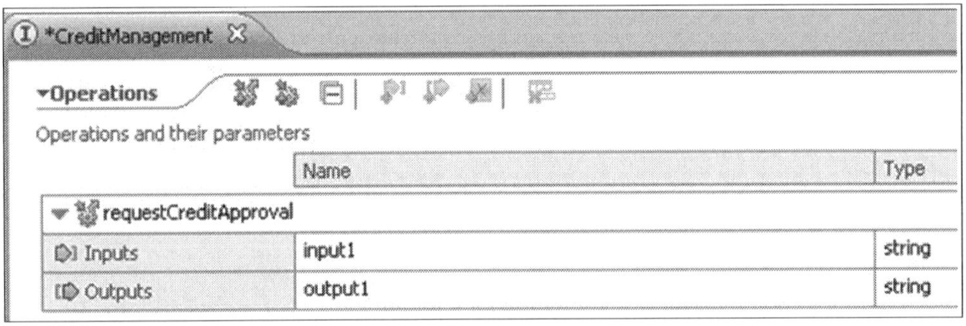

4. Change the **Inputs** and **Outputs**. By default, the **Type** is set to a **string** primitive type. You can change this to any primitive or any other complex data type. Change **input1** to **customerInfo** and let us change the type of the input, to a new one in the next step.
5. When you click on the string type, you will see a context menu pop-up and select the default string. From the context menu, select **New**, and you would see a wizard for a new business object come up. Provide a meaningful name, in this case, **Customer**. You would see an empty business object, customer window open. You can add elements of primitive or complex types. We will see how to create and work with business objects in the next section. The type of inputs is now changed.

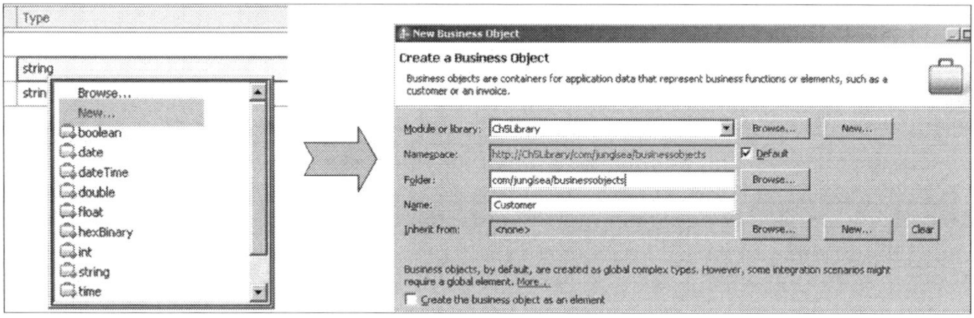

6. Repeat step 5 for **Outputs**, and in this case, name it **customerCreditApprovalRespose** of complex type CustomerCreditApproval, which will have to be created.
7. Now let's define the Customer BO by adding the following fields to it:
    - id (string)
    - firstName (string)
    - lastName (string)
    - title (string)
    - dateOfBirth (date)
    - suffix (string)
8. You can do this by opening the BO using the business object editor and adding fields by clicking on the **Add a field to a business object** button. You can specify the name and the type of the field, which can be a primitive or a complex type.
9. Similarly, we will define the CustomerCreditApproval BO by adding the following fields. As you can see, we have specified creditInput and creditResponseSummary to be of a complex type.
    - creditInput (CreditInput)
        - person (Person)
            - ssn_identifier (string)
            - fName (string)
            - lName (string)
            - dob (date)
        - requestIntiateDate (date)
        - vendor (string)
        - additionalInfo (string)

- creditResponseSummary (CreditResponseSummary)
    - creditScore (double)
    - creditSummary (string)
    - vendor (string)
    - processedDate (date)
    - additionalInfo (string)

10. Once we create the previous two BOs, they will appear in the business object editor, as shown in the following screenshot:

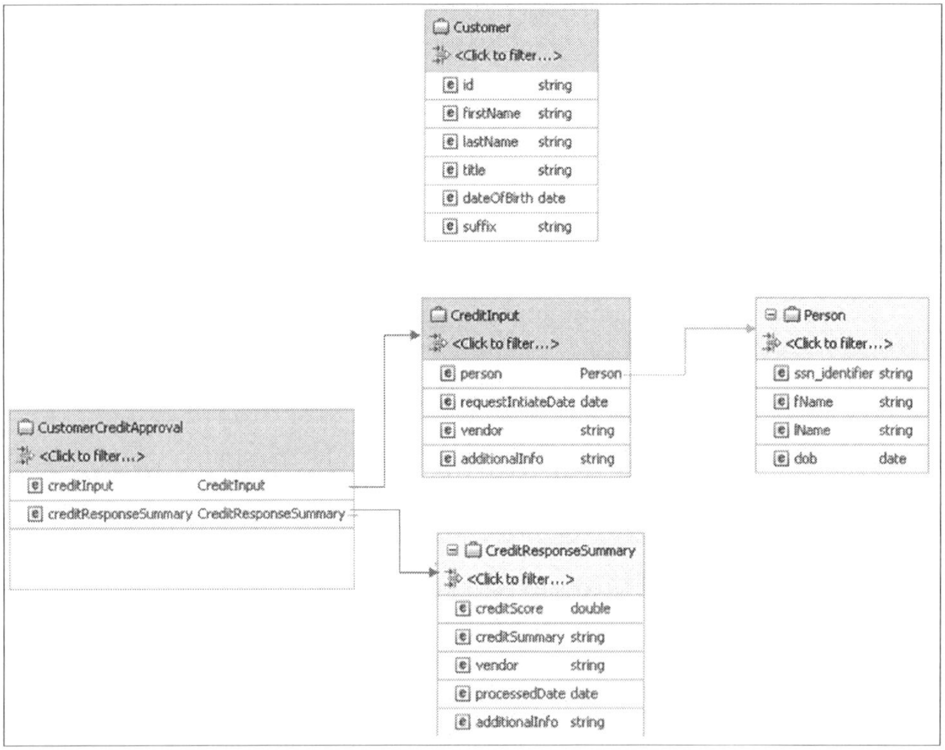

Now to the interface, let's add an explicit fault to the operation using the **Add Fault** icon. Name the fault as **creditApprovalFault** and leave the type as **string**. From the menu bar, select **File | Save**. Congratulations, you have now created your interface in WID. Now all components that implement this interface will be able to throw these named exceptions to a service consumer.

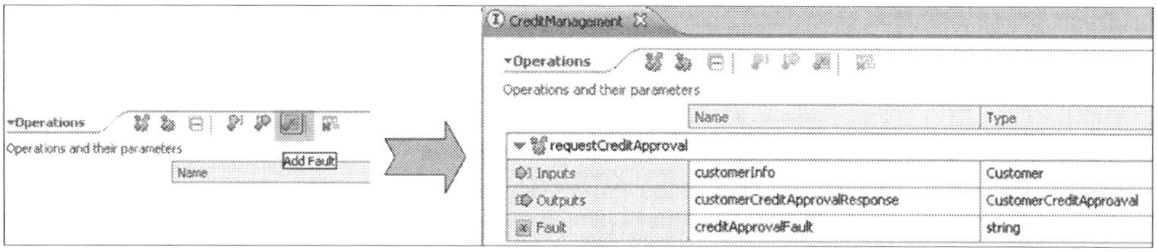

We have now completed the steps needed to create an interface visually using WID. You can view the WSDL source of the interface created by right-clicking on the interface and selecting **Open With | WSDL Editor**. In the window that opens, you can switch between a graphical and source view. Here are a few items for your observation:

- To see the properties of the interface, click anywhere outside the table. The properties of the interface are open in the properties view. The PortType name, namespace, folder, and documentation fields are shown and can be modified.
- By default, the **Binding Style** for an interface created in WID is a document-literal wrapped (we discussed the different types of WSDL in Chapter 3 and also gave reference to an article, *Which style of WSDL should I use?*). You can see this for yourself by clicking on the operation name and then looking at the properties view. Document-literal RPC are tolerated. A document/literal style of web service (or WS-I complaint) allows web services to be interoperable across platforms, applications, and programming languages.
- You can add a description about the interface or the operation or the inputs and outputs in the "description" text area, visible under the properties view.
- You can also specify valid and meaningful namespaces (by default, the module or library name becomes the namespace prefix).
- Operation types can be changed. Right-click the operation you want to change, and from the context menu, select **Operation Type**. Choose the type of operation you would prefer.

Development approach with WID

So with respect to WID and interfaces creation, when do you choose a top-down versus bottom-up versus meet-in-the-middle development? Here are some guidelines:

Top-down:

- You are starting from scratch.
- No existing interfaces to work with.

- You (using the assembly diagram) model your application before you create any backing business logic. Once the SCA components are added to the assembly diagram, you can assign interfaces and even create new interface definitions for each component from within the editor.
- Once the SCA components are defined with their interfaces and references, you generate components with no implementations and edit them to add your business logic.
- The above example is a top-down development approach.

Bottom-up

- Already have an interface created as a WSDL file, most likely from an application vendor or an existing web service provider.
- In this case, you import it into a module or drag-and-drop the WSDL into the module or library.
- You then define business logic for implementing SCA components including BPEL processes, business state machines, business rules, and human tasks by leveraging existing WSDL and web services.

Meet-in-the-middle

- You have an interface that either exactly matches the interface's needs for a component or is close to what you need.
- Once you do this, you can open the WSDL using the interface editor and do all the necessary modifications.
- Meet-in-the-middle development is all about reverse engineering.

Lingua Franca for BPM — Business Objects

We explained Service Data Objects (SDO) in Chapter 3. So where can we place the overall need for business objects in the context of building business processes and also SOA? As you very well know, the core of the BPM approach is the business processes; be it system-to-system, inter or intra systems, or workflow and person-to-person process management. Business processes need a standardized and systematic language to communicate within and with other external processes or services. This lingua franca or the systematic language is **Business Objects**. These Business Objects represent the data that is produced, manipulated, and exchanged between activities within the business processes and transferred to external services or other business processes that the parent business process invokes.

Typically and more fundamentally, these business objects should be in a form that is understood by the business (it should not to be defined by technical folks!). Another purpose of these business objects is to provide data abstraction to the SCA-based business applications.

From an IBM WebSphere Process Server point of view, as explained and discussed in Chapter 3, **Service Data Objects (SDO)** represent the business data that forms the request and response values of processes and services, providing uniform access to business data.

Now how do these business objects become a key enabler of an SOA? The whole point of adopting an SOA approach is to build business applications. If you look at the three pillars of an SOA (as explained in *Chapter 1, Introducing IBM BPM and ESB*)—processes, services, and data—there needs to be a way to represent the data that is exchanged between processes and services. Data is often an ignored stepchild in the world of SOA. As processes and services are assembled into larger business applications, data is very critical to the agility and loose coupling of the business application architecture itself. Imagine if you had five different versions of a customer entity and worse if it changes by region, line of business (LOB), and so on, within the same organization. Hence in WPS (and in WESB too) the data that is exchanged between business components is the business objects, and it is based upon the SDOs.

These business objects provide data abstraction by allowing an organization to create an enterprise-level business object that represents a Customer entity for example and specify what information this Customer BO can hold and how that information should be accessible. Each field has a name, type, cardinality, and other optional properties. Also, you can create business graphs from BOs, which provide a wrapper around a BO or a hierarchy of BOs to have information such as change summary and event summary information related to the BOs. Thus a business graph allows you to address the issue of five versions of a Customer entity. All of these add up to providing the loose coupling and agility to SOA. In WPS, business objects provide additional capabilities that SDO does not provide.

The following image (which we had discussed in detail in Chapter 3) shows the detailed view of the SCA-based order handling application. It depicts how BOs (as depicted by the blue mail envelope icon) are used in the various points of the SOA-based order handling application, especially between business processes, services, and components. These BOs are used as the primary business data structure used not only by the business processes, but also by the interfaces used by the processes and also the services and other components. This provides an organization to uniformly define the various business entities in a consistent way and be reused by various interfaces and hence components.

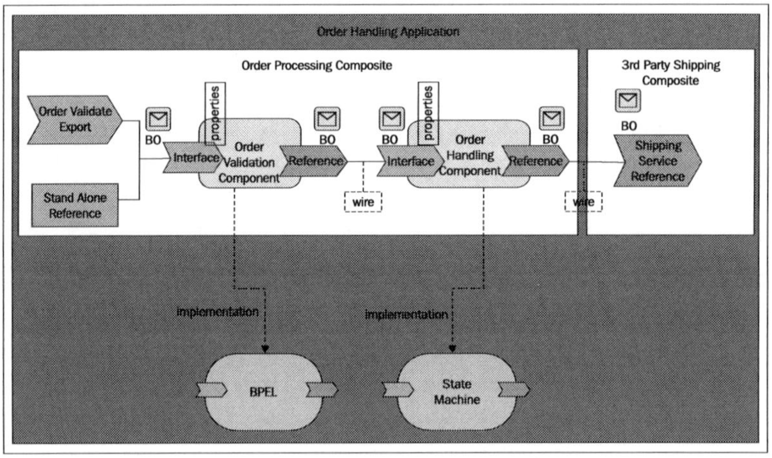

The following mind map provides a summary of some of the key concepts related to business objects that you need to remember:

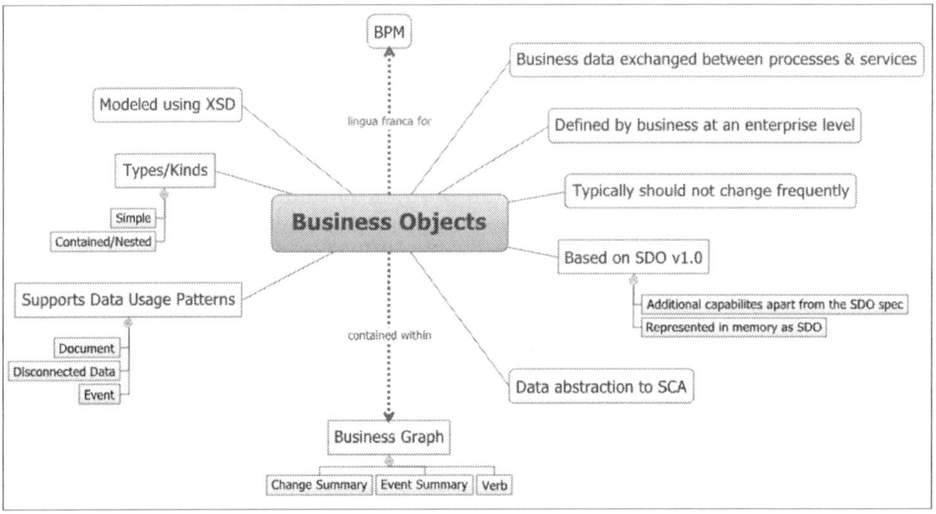

Now to complement the preceding mind map, let's list down the key points for each of the concepts.

- **Business Object (BO)**
    - Fundamental data structure that forms the request and response values of processes and services, providing uniform access to business data.
    - Within WPS represented in memory with the SDO type `commonj.sdo.DataObject`.
    - One business object can inherit another business object, that is, one can be a superset of another.
    - Shown next is a raw XML representation of a business object defined in WID. We have provided a consistent definition of a Customer entity and when we add this to a library project, this BO can be used across projects. Hence this BO approach allows you to overcome (of course with some discipline) the issues related to having multiple versions of an entity and uniformly define entities (as BOs) across the enterprise.

```
<?xml version="1.0" encoding="UTF-8"?>
<xsd:schema targetNamespace="http://Ch5Library"
        xmlns:xsd="http://www.w3.org/2001/XMLSchema">
        <xsd:complexType name="Customer">
                <xsd:sequence>
                        <xsd:element minOccurs="0" name="id"
type="xsd:string"/>
                        <xsd:element minOccurs="0"
name="firstName" type="xsd:string"/>
                        <xsd:element minOccurs="0"
name="lastName" type="xsd:string"/>
                        <xsd:element minOccurs="0" name="title"
type="xsd:string"/>
                        <xsd:element minOccurs="0"
name="dateOfBirth" type="xsd:date"/>
                </xsd:sequence>
        </xsd:complexType>
</xsd:schema>
```

- **Business Graph (BG)**
    - Similar to the concept of the data graph in the SDO architecture, a structure that encapsulates a set of data objects.
    - Is a wrapper for business objects and contains additional or enhanced information such as:
        - Change Summary
            - Used for denoting/recording changes to a BO contained within a BG.
        - Event Summary (enhanced for WPS)
        - Verb (enhanced for WPS)
            - Standard verbs include Create, Update, Delete, UpdateWithDelete, Retrieve.
    - Business Graph complex type, provided by WPS, is the part of the business graph that provides the change summary and event summary to a business graph.
    - To create a BG in WID, right-click on the BO and select "Create a Business Graph".
    - So why do we need BGs? A couple of data patterns distinctively bring out the need for BGs, which are:
        - Disconnected Data Pattern
            - Consider this scenario: A business process (say BP) contains invocations to many services (say SVC-1 and SVC-2). The same business object (Customer) is used to exchange data between SVC-1 and SVC-2. To maintain data concurrency between SVC-1 and SVC-2, a data graph can be used, especially in cases where the invocation of SVC-2 may change Customer and will have to be subsequently communicated to SVC-1.
        - Event Pattern
            - Used especially in data synchronisation cases, where a combination of event summary and verb can keep different south-bound applications in synch.
- Business Object Type Metadata
    - Metadata to annotate BO.
- Business Object Services
    - Set of APIs provided to enhance some of the existing SDO v1.0 capabilities.

- APIs to create, copy, show equality, serialize, and de-serialize business objects, also access a business graph event or change summary.

> Here are some useful references to understand business objects:
>
> *Examining business objects in the WebSphere Process Server*
>
> `http://www.ibm.com/developerworks/websphere/library/techarticles/0603_tung/0603_tung.html`
>
> *SOA programming model for implementing Web services, Part 2: Simplified data access using Service Data Objects*
>
> `http://www.ibm.com/developerworks/webservices/library/ws-soa-progmodel2.html`

Working with Business Process (WS-BPEL)

A business process is the set of business-related activities, tasks, rules, and conditions invoked and executed in a defined sequence to achieve a business goal. As explained in Chapter 3, WS-BPEL or BPEL provides a grammar for describing the behavior of a business process including interactions within the process with external partners and also with other processes. BPEL is one of the options provided in WID to implement an SCA component. The Business processes can be either long-running or microflows. Once you model a business process using BPEL, you will need to deploy the BPEL process on a BPEL runtime engine that can interpret the business process modeled, invoke the appropriate services, maintain state, handle faults and associated compensations, and also support long-running processes that can span days, weeks, or even months. *What is the difference between long-running processes and microflows?* Let's look at the specifics behind the business process types and their differences.

Long-running processes and microflows

There are different ways in which you can design and implement a business process or BPEL. The implementation types can be broadly classified under the following categories:

- Short-running process
- Long-running process

A long-running business process, like its name suggest, is essentially interruptible. The process steps can have their own transaction scope and typically wait for external invocations or events to trigger them. These triggers can be external invocations, or response to an asynchronous invocation or the completion of a human task. A long-running process has the following characteristics:

- Persisted briefly
- Made up of several transactions, each task can have its own transaction scope
- Made up of synchronous and asynchronous services including human tasks
- Can support compensations and state restore

On the other hand, a short-running or microflow, which is IBM's extension to the BPEL specification, runs in one physical transaction or thread. It runs within a global transaction or as part of an activity session. A microflow has the following characteristics:

- Non-interruptible
- Runs in a single unit of transaction
- Short-running
- No state persistence
- Can be asynchronously initiated but cannot invoke outbound services using asynchronous protocols

Recollect that in Chapter 3, we created our first HelloWorld BPEL process, which was of type microflow. The reason we selected a microflow process was because we wanted to create a single synchronous transaction process without the capabilities of handling multiple transactions executed over an extended period of time. If we did in fact need a process to handle multiple transactions executed over a longer period of time or a process capable of human interaction, we would have used the long-running process option. You may ask me, "What is a transaction?" A transaction can be thought of as the set of activities that complete the execution of a single business process that may accomplish or add to a larger business goal. For example, when you go to buy something at a store, you execute a checkout transaction. You provide your goods for purchase to the checkout clerk, who then scans them and presents you with the bill. You pay the bill and take your goods. This completes the transaction. Now it is important to realize that the checkout transaction is just a part of a larger scale of a good business goal. Hence a transaction may satisfy the business goal by itself or multiple transactions may be needed to satisfy the goal. Now let's create a cheat sheet that you can refer to as needed.

Long-running Process	
Purpose	"A long running process executes over an extended period of time and is much more flexible and resilient than a microflow. Interruptible business processes and asynchronous business processes are examples of long running processes" `http://publib.boulder.ibm.com/infocenter/dmndhelp/v7r0mx/index.jsp`
When	You will use a long-running processes for any of the following types of business processes: Processes that do not respond immediately Processes that require to run over a period of time Processes that involve human interaction Strongly recommended that you reduce the number of long-running processes invoked.

Microflow	
Purpose	"A microflow is a process that is contained within a single transaction. This is ideal for situations where the user is expecting an immediate response." `http://publib.boulder.ibm.com/infocenter/dmndhelp/v7r0mx/index.jsp`
When	If you have a short series of steps to model and want them executed very quickly in the runtime environment, then use a microflow. If you want your processes to handle high-volumes and be made up of non-blocking activities. Used in cases where you want to incorporate integration logic that entails the invocation of more than one operation on an end application API or atomic service in a particular sequence. Series or collection of microflows can be orchestrated or choreographed into a long-running process, which naturally allows you to decompose a business process. Performance differential is a factor of 10 or even more. Maintenance is a lot easier (no worry about in-flight or running instances) and no requirements for versioning.

Let's proceed with how to implement a simple long-running process using WebSphere Integration Developer | Business Integration perspective. This will help give a practical example of the WS-BPEL concepts and help appreciate the difference in the various options available. Let's consider a business use case that will help explain these various features. JungleSea Insurance (a subsidiary of JungleSea Inc.) wants to implement a new eligibility business process. One of their requirements is to have the ability to auto-approve claims for members up to the age of 65 years and then have an administrator review claims of members above the age of 65. The mind map shown in the following figure summarizes the business logic and steps to implement this use case.

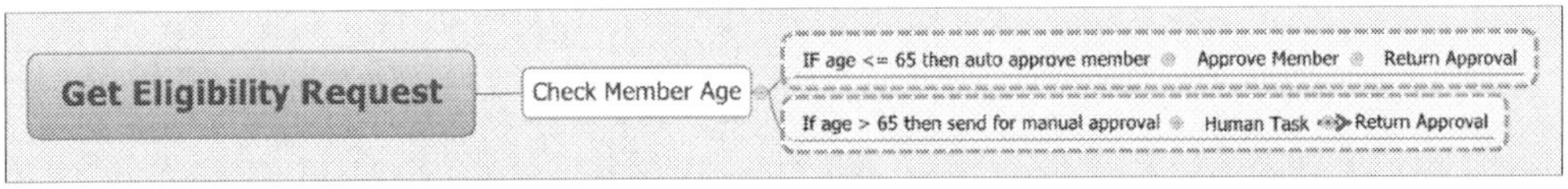

Having read through a lot of theory from the first part of this book, we would like you to work and implement this use case using a business process component in WID. So here is a quiz: "What should your first step be, based on what you have learned?". I would expect an answer like "Create a library!" You need to create a library that will contain the business objects and interfaces used in this business process. Now let's go through the steps to implement this:

1. Create a new library called **EligibilityCheckLibrary.** Add a new business object called **MemberInfo** with three fields: **FirstName string, LastName string**, and **Age int**, as shown in the following screenshot:

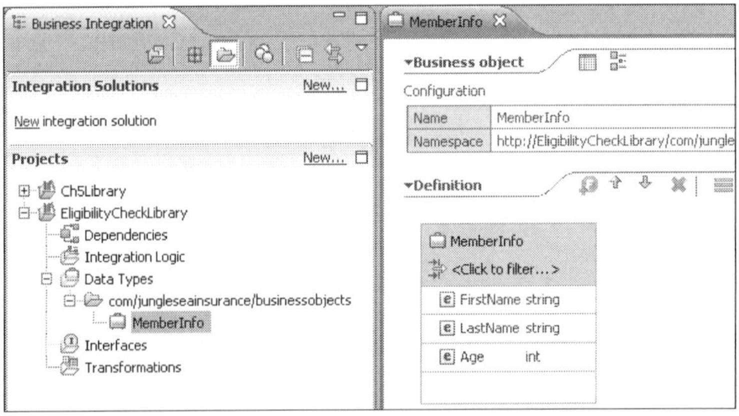

2. Create an interface in the library called **EligibiltyCheck** and **add an** operation named **checkEligibility** with the input parameter member of type **MemberInfo** and output parameter **validateEligibilty** of type **boolean.**

Once you have created the business objects and interface you are ready to begin creating the business process for this use case. For this use case we will use a long-running process because it involves interaction with humans. A microflow process would not give this capability. In order to build a long running process:

3. Create a new module called **EligibilityCheck** with a dependency to the **EligibilityCheckLibrary**.
4. Right-click on **Integration Logic** in the **Business Projects** window. Select **New | Business Process**. Give the process the name **PerformEligibilityCheck** and folder `com/jungleseainsurance/solution/eligibilityCheck/process`. Select **Long-running process**, as shown in the following screenshot. As you can see, we are going to select using IBM's extensions to the human tasks and Java support.

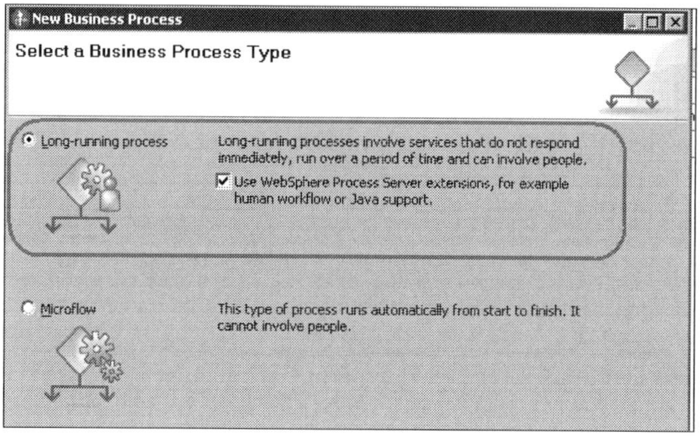

5. Associate interface **EligibiltyCheckInterface** and the operation with this process. Click on the **Finish button.**
6. Drag-and-drop the **PerformEligibilityCheck** component to the assembly diagram.

On clicking **Finish**, the business process wizard closes and the business process editor opens. You will notice that a template process with a **Receive** and **Reply** activity has already been created. Hence the process is currently capable of receiving an eligibility request and replying back. However, the business logic of the approval process is still missing. The first step of the business process based on the mind map is a decision point where a choice needs to be made based upon the incoming service request. Before you implement the Business Process, let's first understand control structures that are provided by WID in the business process editor.

Using control structures in your processes

Control structures in the BPEL process provide the ability to make decisions, repeat steps, or split the process flow. In WebSphere Integration Developer, these activities are listed under **Structures** in the left column **Palette.** Here is a mind map and a cheat sheet to help you understand the various activities available to you while creating a process flow and their use:

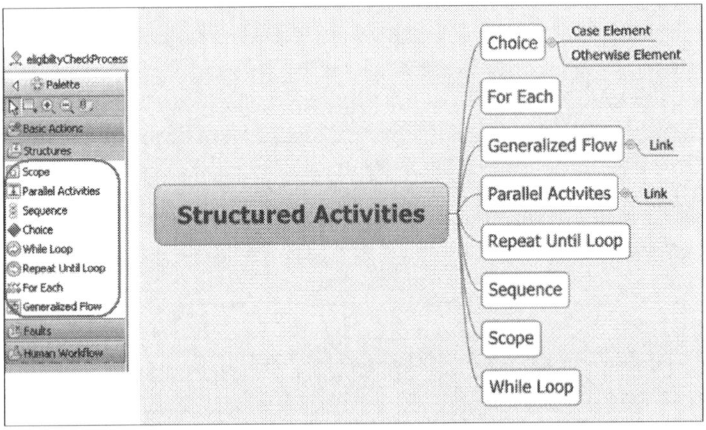

The business process editor, as shown in the following image, consists of the following distinct areas/parts in its screen real estate:

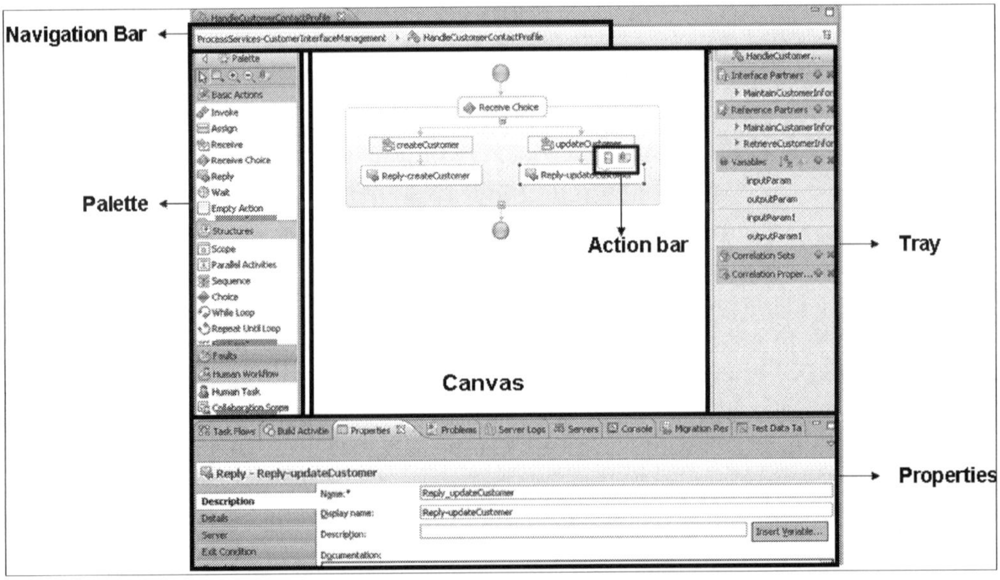

- **Palette**—provides various objects and primitives that can be (dragged-and-dropped) and used in the construction of a business process (or a business state machine)
- **Canvas**—the white area where you visually assemble objects from the palette to build a business process
- **Action bar**—small dialog pop up that appears when you hover you mouse over certain activities in your business process (for example, when you hover over an invoke activity, you will see an action bar that pops up giving options to add a fault handler or a compensation handler)
- **Tray**—displays the interface and reference partners, variables, correlation sets, and correlation properties associated with the business process that you are building
- **Properties view**—displays properties of any selected object from the canvas or tray
- **Navigation bar**—helps you to navigate between different levels in a business process or jump back to the assembly diagram

Now let's look at each of the control structures in detail, listed through the following table:

Activity	Description
Choice	This activity is used to make a choice between two or more control paths and then follow the appropriate one. The path that first satisfies the defined conditions is selected. The conditions used to select a particular path are defined in a case element. If no conditions qualify, then use an otherwise element to define the default path.
For Each	This activity is a loop construct that repeatedly runs the activities that it contains either sequentially or in parallel for a specified number of iterations. It further gives you the flexibility to define **Early Exit Criterion** to exit the loop early, if some special conditions apply. This activity is usually used when dealing with an array of objects. More details can be found at : `http://www-01.ibm.com/support/docview.wss?rs=2307andcontext=SSQH9Manduid=swg27011753`

Activity	Description

Generalized Flow	This activity is used to nest other process activities within it and controls the execution order of those activities. It has the ability to use **conditional links** to loop back to previous activities in the sequence and to use **fault links** to handle faults that occur in the business process. It is important that a generalized flow has exactly one start activity, but it can have more than one end activities.
	If your process requires more flexibility, simplified fault handling, or cyclic flows, consider using a generalized flow.
	For details see:
	`http://publib.boulder.ibm.com/infocenter/dmndhelp/v6r2mx/index.js`
	`p?topic=/com.ibm.wbit.620.help.bpel.ui.doc/topics/tcyclic.html`

Parallel Activity	This activity is used to nest other process activities that need to run concurrently. A **link** is used to connect the activities that it contains. All the paths within the activity are run simultaneously, and the end activity will not fire until all the control paths have completed. In long-running processes, avoid accessing the same BPEL variable in parallel branches because this can result in undesired behavior of the BPEL variable. It is preferable to use separate variables for each parallel control path. For details see: `http://publib.boulder.ibm.com/infocenter/dmndhelp/v6r2mx/topic/com.ibm.wbit.620.help.bpel.ui.doc/tasks/tparal.html`
Repeat Until Loop	This activity is used to repeat one or more activities for as long as specific conditions are valid. The conditions are evaluated at the end of the cycle of activities. The activities in the repeat cycle are performed at least once.
Scope	This activity is used to group behavior of one or more activities in your process. This can be used for granting user administrative privileges over the running order of the activities that are nested within the scope.
Sequence	This activity is used to define a series of activities into your process that will run sequentially.
While Loop	This activity is used to repeat one or more activities as long as specific conditions are valid. The conditions are evaluated at the beginning of the activity. Hence the activity is skipped if the condition is not met on entry. The activities in the repeat cycle may not be run even once if the associated conditions are not satisfied.

You will next add a **Choice** activity to check the age of the member and define the process steps accordingly, that is, whether the member be auto-approved or will need to be approved manually.

1. Continuing with the steps to implement the **PerformEligibilityCheck** process, drag the **Choice** activity onto the canvas, rename it to **Check Age**, and lay it in-between the **Receive** and **Reply** activity, as shown in the following screenshot:

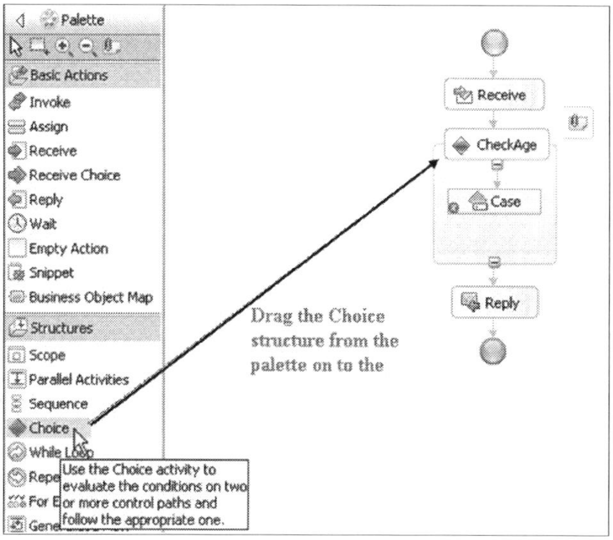

2. Rename the default **Case** to **AutoApproval**. Add another case by clicking on the action bar that appears when you click on the **Case** element and rename it to **ManualApproval**, as shown in the following image. Save your work.

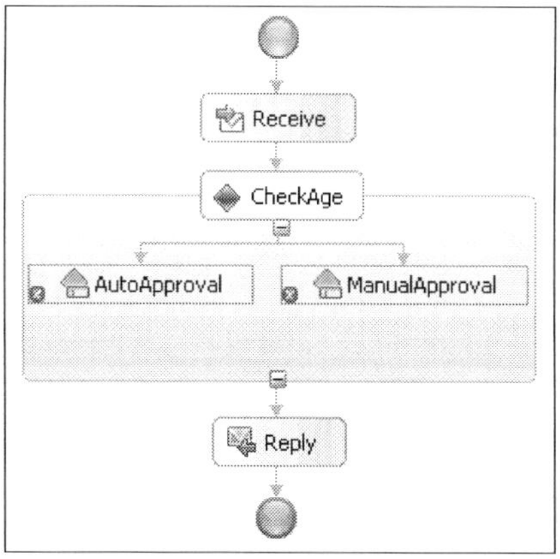

3. Now we will have to specify the selection expressions on each of the Case statements. Click on **AutoApproval**. Select **Properties | Details** view. Click on **Create New Condition**. Enter condition **member.Age > 0** and **member.Age<= 65**, as shown below. Note, as explained in Chapter 3, we can also use XPath expressions to evaluate conditions. It's your choice in the end which option to use.

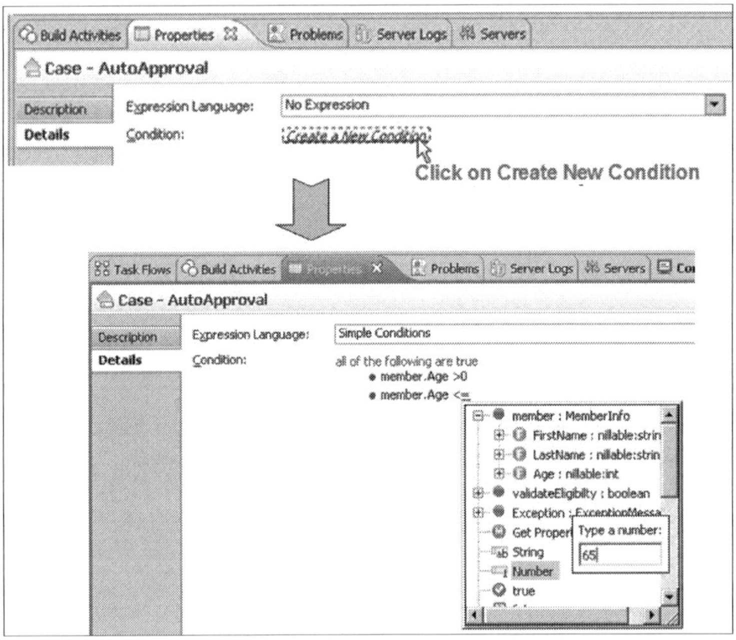

4. We will now specify what activity to perform when this condition is met using a Java snippet. From the palette, drag-and-drop a **Snippet** activity (naming it **SetApprovalofEligibility**) under the **AutoApproval** case. In the visual snippet editor (you can get to this by clicking on the **Snippet | Properties | Details** view), drag-and-drop the **validateEligibility** from the **Variables** section and assign a value of **true**. This is shown in the following figure:

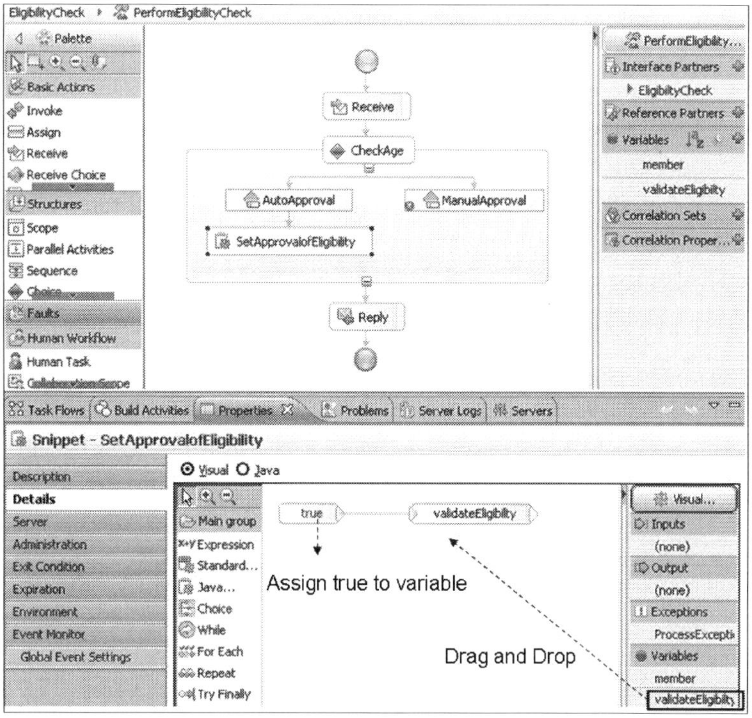

5. Similarly, add a condition to the **ManualApproval** case **Input.Age >= 65**.

With the steps done so far we have completed the aspects of checking for age from the incoming request. The process will now the check the age in the incoming message request and select the path accordingly.

So what happens once the manual process path is selected? As per our requirements, this request needs to be sent for approval by a human. We still have to implement this requirement. To do so, we will use an Invoke activity and decouple the implementation of the human task from the process flow. This will help make the process flow independent of the activity handling manual process. This makes our solution extremely flexible. Later it also allows us to replace the human task with another component such as Java Snippet, for example, automate the process or perform additional steps. We shall pause here to understand the invoke activity.

Invoke external services using Invoke activity

While creating a business process in the business process editor of WID | Business Integration perspective, some basic actions are listed under the palette in the left column. One of these actions is the **Invoke** activity, as shown in the following screenshot. This activity allows the business process to call an operation on specific partner service. This call may be a request/response (synchronous) call or a one-way (asynchronous) call.

The developer now has the flexibility to define both external and internal services. This allows for loosely-coupled business processes that separate the implementation and definition of the service. The invoke activity is only aware of the interface and operation of the service. The actual location of the service is wired later in the assembly diagram and can be changed, as needed, without impacting the business process.

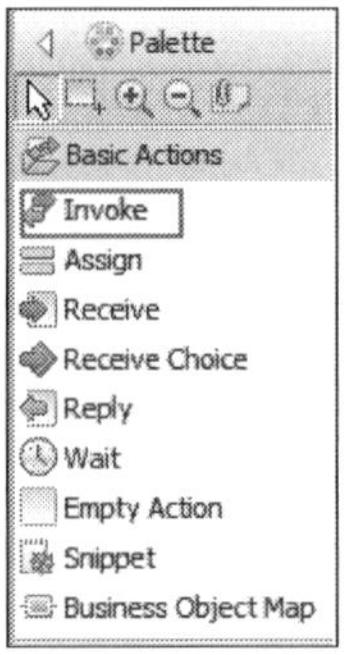

Now continuing with the implementation of our **PerformEligibilityCheck** process, we can add an invoke activity to our business process. Later in this chapter, we will implement the human task.

1. Wire an **Invoke** activity (named **ApproveSeniorEligibility**) under the **ManualApproval** case. Create a new **Reference Partner** named **ApproveEligibility** associated with **EligibilityCheck** interface. This can be done by clicking on the **ApproveEligibility** | **Properties** | **Details** | **Partner** | **Browse** | **New**.

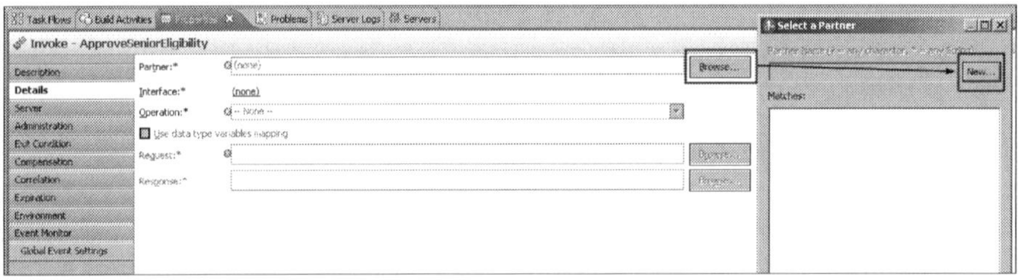

> Invoke can be either synchronous or asynchronous.
>
> - In a synchronous style of invocation, a request to the target is made by the consumer/requestor and the response is received immediately in the same thread.
> - In an asynchronous style of invocation, the consumer/requestor sends the request in one thread and will receive the response in a totally different thread. A response is optional (one-way operation) or can be received explicitly by the client (deferred response) or implicitly sent by the server (callback).

2. Now the **ApproveSeniorEligibility** activity is associated to the **ApproveEligibility** reference partner. Select operation **EligibilityCheck**. Specify the input and output variables to be used for this reference. You will specify the process variables member and **validateEligibility** as the input and output respectively, by clicking on **none** in the **Read from Variable** column, and from the pop-up, specifying the variable. After performing these steps, your process will look as shown in the following screenshot:

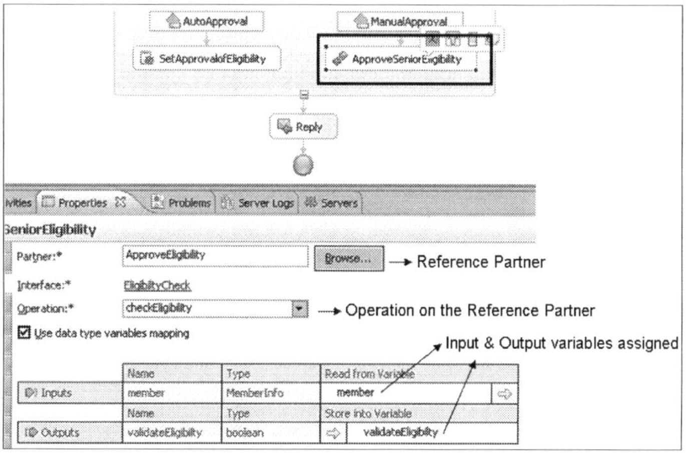

3. Save the process and verify that there are no problems listed in the **Problems** window.

Data mapping using Business Object Maps

Now let's take a pause from implementing the **PerformEligibilityCheck** process and take a look at some of the other key concepts that you will encounter. These concepts will be particularly useful in the later chapters when we build a Sales Fulfillment Application. We will now see how to use Business Object Maps (BO Maps) in a business process to map data between objects. Not all applications are built with the same semantics. So most when building SOA applications, and more specifically when integrating into these different applications, it is more than likely that there wil be a need to transform the data into a format that the receiving application can consume through the interface it exposes.

A BO Map helps you map from one business object to another business object format "visually". BO Maps are in business processes, mediation flows, and can also be inserted between components in a module. A Business Object map assigns values to target business objects based on values in source business objects. You can create and edit business objects maps using the business object mapping editor. To create a new BO Map, here are the high-level steps:

1. Right-click on the **Ch5Library** that we created earlier in this chapter and, select **New | Data Map**.

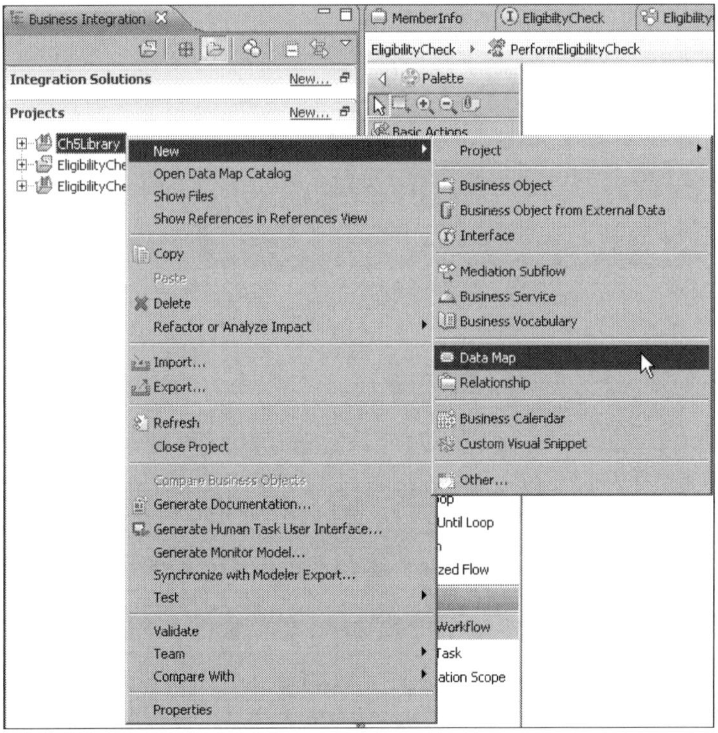

2. From the **Data Map** wizard, select the data map to be of the type Business Object Map. As shown in the following diagram, provide a folder name (**/com/junglsea/datamaps/bomaps**) and a name for the BO Map (**Customer_To_CustomerCreditApproval**). Continue with the wizard and specify the input and output business objects that you want to transform data between. As shown in the following image, we will specify the Customer as the input BO and CustomerCreditApproval as the output BO. Note that we created these business objects earlier in the chapter.

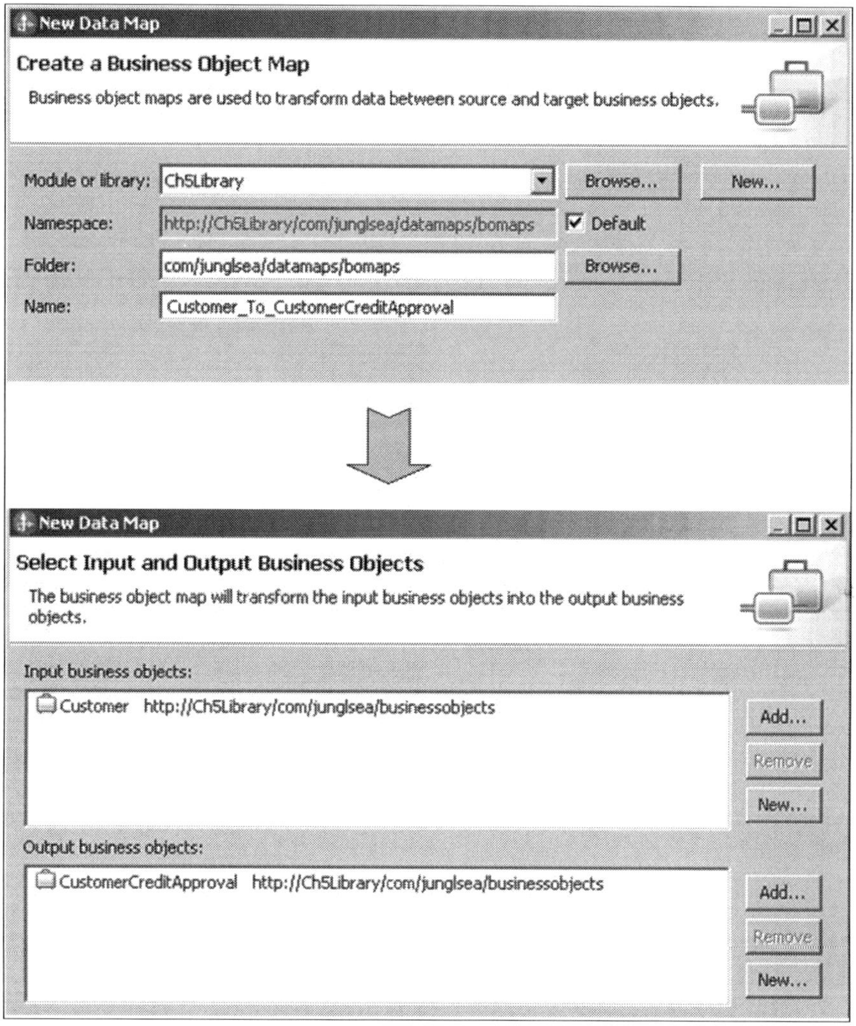

3. Having followed the previous two steps, you can now visually drag-and-drop from the source BO to a target BO. Now, as shown in the following diagram, you can map by individual element(s) from the source BO to the target CustomerCreditApproval BO and have the option of performing a simple move or more complex transforms. You can add variables to a BO Map that can be used in the transformation. The variables can be a simple data type, BO, or even a Java class object map using the business object mapping editor.

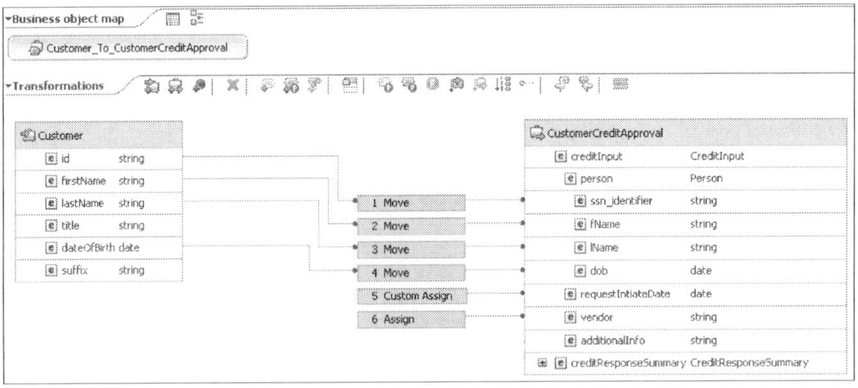

We have thus far seen how to create and edit BOs using the BO editor in WID. You can also edit the BOs from the BO Map editor. In the BO Map editor, you can select the BO (input or output), right-click, and select Edit Business Object. Note that the graph view is the default view.

As shown in the following image, from the toolbar of the BO Map editor you can also do the following:

- Create a reverse data transform map (**CustomerCreditApproval_To_Customer** in our case)
- Show the change summary or event summary on BOs and go back to the five versions of a Customer BO we discussed earlier
- Filter and show only transformed fields or untransformed fields
- Sort by transformation run order
- Add multiple BOs in the input or output from which you can transform from and to

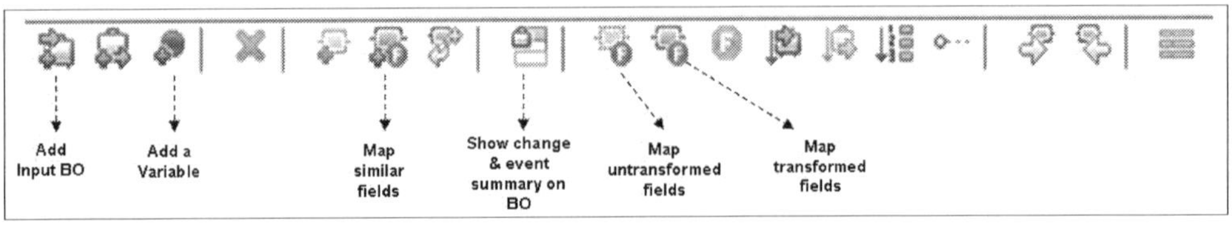

The various transformation or mapping types available to you in a BO Map are:

- Move: Assigns the value in the source to the target.
- Extract: Source value must be a string. This extracts a portion of the string and assigns it to the target based on a delimiter.
- Join: Combines the values of two or more sources into one, and assigns it to the target. The target of a Join transform must be a string.
- Submap: Source and target must be business objects (that is, they must be complex types). You can reuse other BO Maps here.
- Custom: You can define custom logic for mapping the input(s) and output(s) by using Java code.
- Assign: Sets a constant value to the output.
- Relationship: This type of transform performs relationship management. The source and target of a Relationship transform must also be of complex types.
- Relationship Lookup: This is used for relationship management between static cross-referencing data. The source and target of a Relationship Lookup transform must be simple types.
- Custom Assign: This type of transformation is similar to Custom, except that it does not take any input. It is also similar to Assign, except that you can use more logic in assigning the values using Java (using the text or visual editors).
- Custom Callout: This type of transformation is similar to Custom, except that it does not take any output. It may be useful for initialization before executing any transforms.

> In the BO Map editor, you can perform automatic mapping of similar fields by clicking on the Map similar fields toolbar icon, which finds matches between similar inputs and outputs, as opposed to exact inputs and outputs. Transforms that have similar names and exact XSD complex types are created. You can change the sensitivity of the business object string name comparisons by adjusting the Field name similarity threshold that you can change in the WID preferences.

Exception handling in Business Processes

Poor exception handling implementations can thwart even the best designs. An exception condition occurs when an object or component, for some reason, can't fulfill a responsibility. The longer you avoid exceptions, the harder it is to wedge cleanly-designed exception handling code into working software. There is a nice paper that discusses in detail about the importance of exception handling, *Toward Exception-Handling Best Practices and Patterns*, by *Rebecca J. Wirfs-Brock, IEEE Software, vol. 23, no. 5, pp. 11-13, Sep./Oct. 2006, doi:10.1109/MS.2006.144*. Agreeing on a reasonable exception handling style for your application and following a consistent set of exception handling practices is crucial to implementing software that's easy to comprehend, evolve, and refactor. An exception condition occurs when an object or component, for some reason, can't fulfill a responsibility. Exceptions can occur due to:

- Pre-conditions not met
- Required parameters missing
- Malformed arguments
- Inconsistent state
- Unavailable resources, or coding or logic errors
- Security exceptions
- Runtime exceptions due to the runtime platform

If a fault is not caught:

- Navigation of the process discontinues
- Process could end in a failed state, which does not allow administrative repair actions

The solution: Use fault handlers and fault links to catch and programmatically deal with fault conditions

SCA exception types

The SCA programming model and hence WPS supports two types of exceptions:

1. Service Runtime Exception:
    - Undeclared exceptions that are used to signal an unexpected condition in the runtime
    - Typical exceptions that can happen including NullPointer, a server failure, or a network loss on a call to an external web service

- To handle these types of exceptions, you have three choices:
  a. Catch them and perform some alternative logic
  b. Catch the exception and let it be rethrown to your client
  c. You may remap the exception to a business exception or user defined exceptions; this is a strongly recommended practice

  The following are the four current subclasses of ServiceRuntimeException:

  i. ServiceExpirationRuntimeException
  ii. ServiceTimeoutRuntimeException
  iii. ServiceUnavailableException
  iv. ServiceUnwiredReferenceRuntimeException

2. Service Business Exceptions
   - Exceptions that are defined on the interfaces (WSDL) and represent known and declared exceptions
   - When designing a component, it's your responsibility to specify the different exceptions/faults a component can throw and hence a service consumer can appropriately:
     a. Catch the exceptions thrown back to them
     b. Handle the exceptions through alternate logic

We strongly recommend that you define the appropriate faults in the interface that would be thrown from the component.

Compensation

As mentioned several times, microflows execute within a single unit of transaction, and normal rollback logic will handle most cases. However, there are cases where a fault handler might need to compensate work that has already been accomplished. All or part of this work would need to be reversed. A compensation handler specifies compensation logic and is typically defined for a scope or an invoke activity and hence callable from a fault handler. Compensation activity triggers compensation and allows you to trigger compensation handlers. You cannot define a compensation handler and a compensation action at the same time. We will discuss compensation in detail in the later chapters.

Catch, Catch All, Throw, Rethrow, and Terminate

Within a business process component, you can perform fault propagation using throw, rethrow, and reply within a fault handler.

- Catch: Used to intercept and deal with a specific kind of fault. You can use as many of these elements as you need.
- Catch All: Use this element to intercept and deal with any fault that is not already defined in an existing catch element. You can only use one of these per fault handler.
- Throw: Indicates a problem that a business process flow cannot handle and is typically used to throw an exception corresponding to an internal error condition. You can use a throw activity within the normal flow of a business process or within a fault handler to allow an outer fault handler to handle the fault. A throw activity can throw one of the standard BPEL faults or a custom fault. The throw activity is required to provide a name for the fault and can optionally include a variable with data providing further information about the fault.
- Rethrow: Used when the current fault handler cannot handle the fault and wants to propagate it to an outer-scoped fault handler. In the absence of a rethrow activity, a fault propagated to a higher level using a throw activity would be a new fault. When a rethrow activity is invoked, the fault is the same instance. The rethrow activity is available only within a fault handler because only an existing fault can be rethrown.
- Terminate: This node within a business process marks the end of a process. Every process, subprocess, and loop must have at least one terminate node.

When a fault occurs, WPS runtime (BPC container, to be more specific) needs to match and associate the fault with a fault hander. As specified in the BPEL spec, the BPC uses the following rules to select the catch activity that processes a fault.

- If the fault has no associated fault data, the BPC uses a Catch activity with the matching fault name. Otherwise it uses the default CatchAll element.
- If the fault does have associated fault data, the BPC uses a Catch activity with a matching fault name and variable values. If there is no fault name specified, then it uses a Catch with a matching fault type. Otherwise, it uses the default Catch All element.
- If you do not define a Catch All handler anywhere in the fault handler chain, the fault reaches the global business process level and the process ends in a failed state, which is obviously undesirable.

One objective of good process design and implementation is to handle all exceptional conditions. It is an admittedly lofty goal to anticipate all exceptional scenarios at the inception of process development. Remember to include time in the development cycle for additional fault-handler development as the process moves through testing and even after production deployment. When designing fault handlers, consider the following options:

- Catch a fault and try to correct the problem, allowing the business process to continue to normal completion.
- Catch a fault and find that it is not resolvable at this scope. Now, you have additional options:
    - Throw a new fault
    - Rethrow the original fault to allow another scope to handle it
    - Reply with a fault to the process initiator
    - Invoke a human task to correct the issue
    - If the fault handler cannot resolve the issue, you might need to rollback and compensate

Exception handling suggested practices

In WPS, you will encounter with an application fault (Service Business Exceptions) or a System Fault (Service Runtime Exceptions). Handling exceptions in business processes and also in a mediation flow component will have to be a combination of application and system fault handling techniques.

1. Let's continue with the implementation of **PerformEligibilityCheck** business process. We will add a user-defined fault to the **CreditManagement** interface and will name the fault as **invalidMemberDataException**. To add a fault to an interface:
    a. Open the interface using the interface editor
    b. Click on the operation (**checkEligibility** in this case)
    c. Click on **Add Fault** from the action bar
    d. For the exception type, define a new business object named "ExceptionMessage" with the following elements
        i. **exceptionId**
        ii. **exceptionName**
        iii. **exceptionCategory**

iv. **exceptionDateTime**

v. **description**

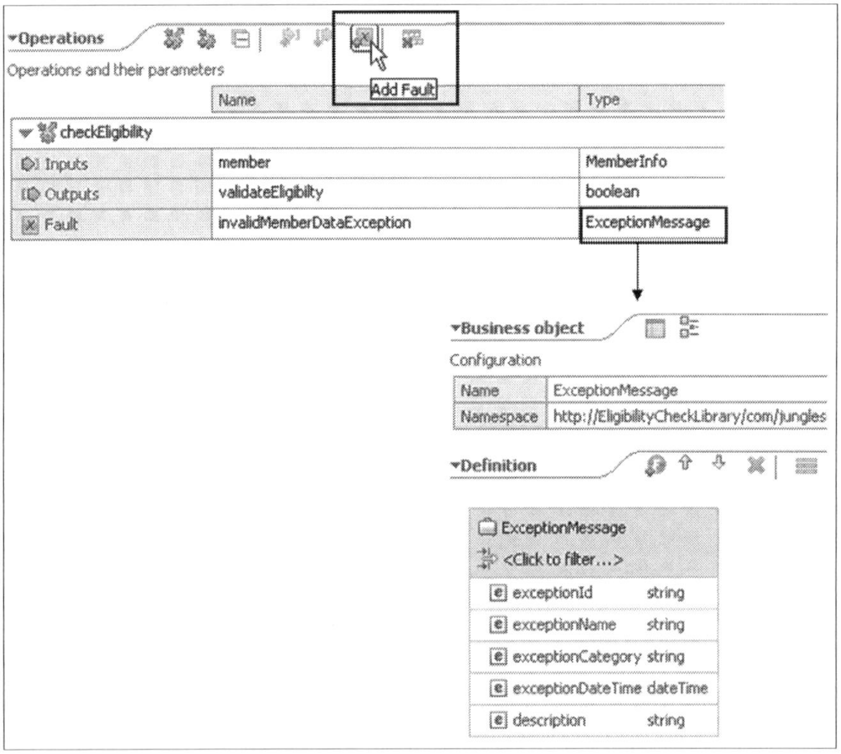

2. To synchronize the **PerformEligibilityCheck** component with the changes made to its interface, open the assembly diagram. Right-click on the **PerformEligibilityCheck** component and select **Synchronize Interfaces and References | Implementation**. All the changes made to the interface will not be reflected in the business process component. Now let's attach fault handlers in various places within the process.

> You can specify fault handlers for Invoke activities, Scope, and also at the global process level in the WID process editor.

3. We will first check for the validity of the incoming member data. We will check for the existence of **FirstName** and **LastName** in the incoming member message and also check if the age is not zero or non-negative. Open the **PerformEligibilityCheck** component using the process editor and add a Choice named **MemberDataCheck** before the **CheckAge** Choice element. Rename the default case element as **MemberDataCorrect**. This will make sure the member data is correct and we will use an XPath expression as follows to evaluate this:

```
string-length($member/FirstName > 0) and
string-length($member/LastName > 0) and
$member/Age > 0 and
not($member/Age < 0)
```

4. If any of the preceding conditions are not met, the element will handle this as an exception condition. We will use an assign statement to populate the right values into a new variable we will create named **Exception** of type **ExceptionMessage**. As we are close to the problem (data validation in this case), as the first line of defense, we will provide enough contextual information as an exception message and allow the client to rectify the condition.

5. Below the other case element, we will add an assign activity to populate the Exception variable. After doing this, the process will look as shown in the following image:

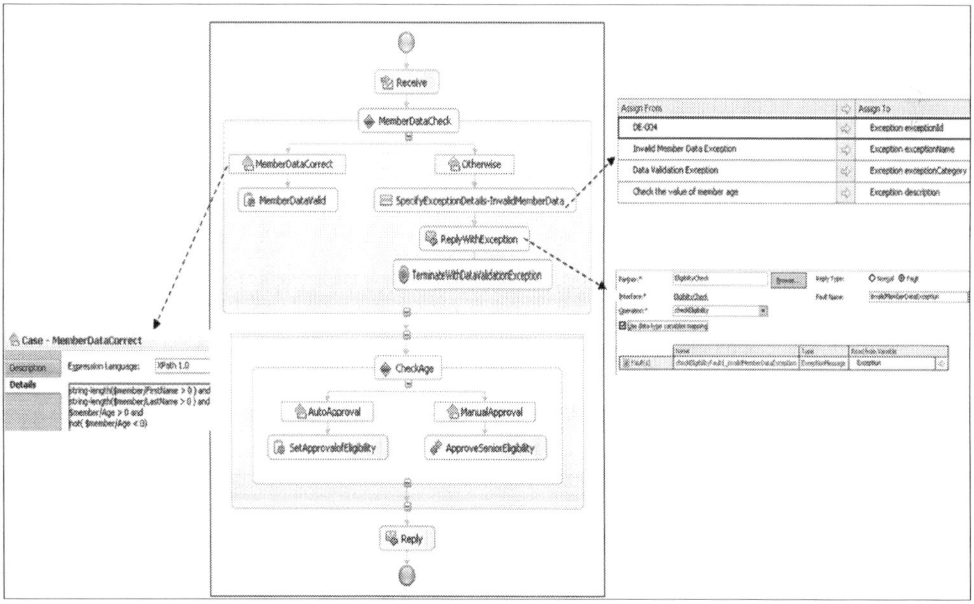

6. Secondly, we will add fault handling to the **ApproveSeniorEligibility** invoke activity. We will define this as an application fault on the invoking WSDL interface. For now, we will use the **invalidMemberDataException** fault defined in the interface. You can also define one more fault to the operation or make the existing fault generic enough to handle all faults. If the exception resulting from the invoke activity is not caught by its fault handler, it uses a handler further up the handler chain.
7. Finally, we will define fault handling at the global process level. Faults progressively propagate from the inner scopes to the enclosing outer scopes until they reach a specific fault handler or reach the application-defined, global process fault handler, as shown in the following image. If you have not defined a global process level handler, the process will fail to complete gracefully. Now the exception handling steps are complete.

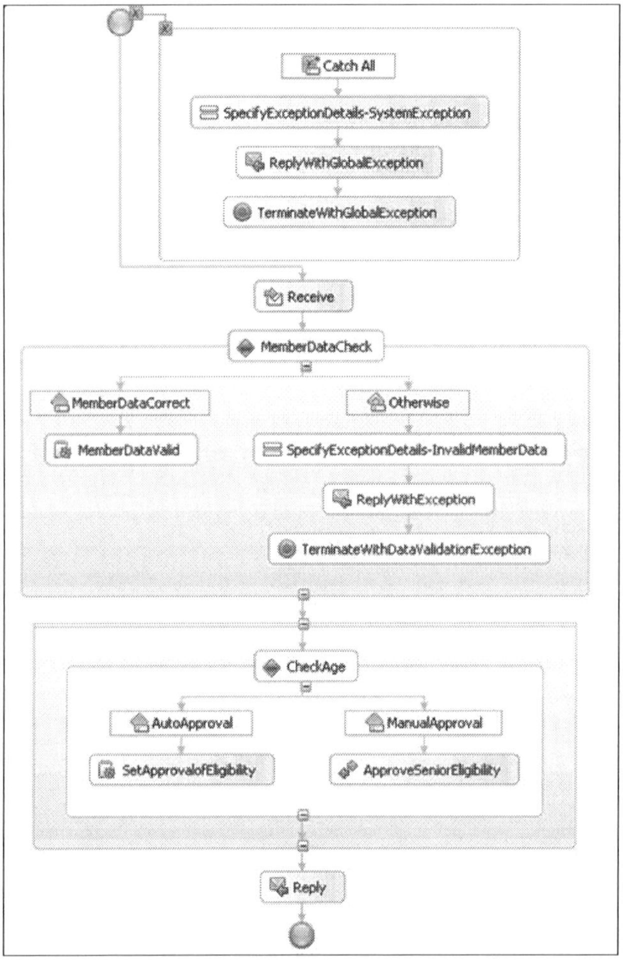

To summarize a few key points about exception handling with BPEL components:

- A well-designed process should consider faults and handle them whenever possible.
- Define user-defined faults to handle all possible application-related exceptions.
- For long-running processes, also consider in addition using the Continue On Error setting on the process to handle unexpected faults administratively.
- Handle exceptions as close to the problem as you can. As a first line of defense, consider the initial requestor. If the caller knows enough to perform a corrective action, you can rectify the condition on the spot. If you propagate an exception far away from the source, it can be difficult to trace the source. Often objects further away from the problem can't make meaningful decisions.
- If an unexpected fault occurs after doing so, the process will change to a stopped state instead of a failed state to do the repair actions.
- Restarting a process instance is similar to starting a process instance for the first time. However, when a process instance is restarted, the process instance ID is known and the input message for the instance is available.

> You can use the "Continue on Error" (IBM extension for fault handling) setting in the process **Properties** | **Defaults** tab. If you set it to:
>
> - **Yes**—the business process creates and throws a fault.
> - **No** (default setting)—the business process stops the activity and creates a task (work item) for the administrator of the business process. The administrator has to take action and the activity can be "fixed" and retried, forced complete, or failed.

Failed Event Manager

Failed Event Manager is a capability provided by WPS to manage and work with failed invocations or process instances. WPS provides a web-based client for working with and resubmitting the failed invocations. This is available through the Administrative console, displays the number of failed events, and provides a number of search capabilities. You can also query for failed events using a variety of criteria such as date, last successful or failed event, exception text, or a combination of these. We will go into detail about the Failed Event Manager in *Chapter 13, Management, Monitoring and Security*.

Relationships

So in simple terms, what are relationships and why do I need to know about them? Fundamentally, a relationship is used to establish associations between business entities. For example, in many integration scenarios, you may need to cross-reference information. Customer Order in one system may be termed as Order in another system. Semantically these mean one and the same. You need to have a mechanism in place that can help you create and maintain cross-reference information between these two systems that store information about customer orders. WPS helps you achieve this capability. So when you enter a customer order in one system and submit it to the second system for processing, you may ask, where is the need for relationships? But when we update our order in the order entry system, we also have to update the order data in system two as well. WPS relationships, along with the relationship service, allow this kind of functionality.

Using Visual Snippets

Though not very relevant to the PerformEligibilityCheck component that we are building now, it is worth spending a few minutes to explain this concept. We have used Visual Snippets quite a bit in Chapter 3 and Chapter 4. So let's try to recollect what we have learned so far. There are two ways to create a snippet:

1. Directly in the business process editor, we can drag-and-drop a Snippet primitive and add our custom Java code in there visually. The following screenshot shows how, within a business process, a visual snippet is used to assign some values and print customized messages to the system logfile:

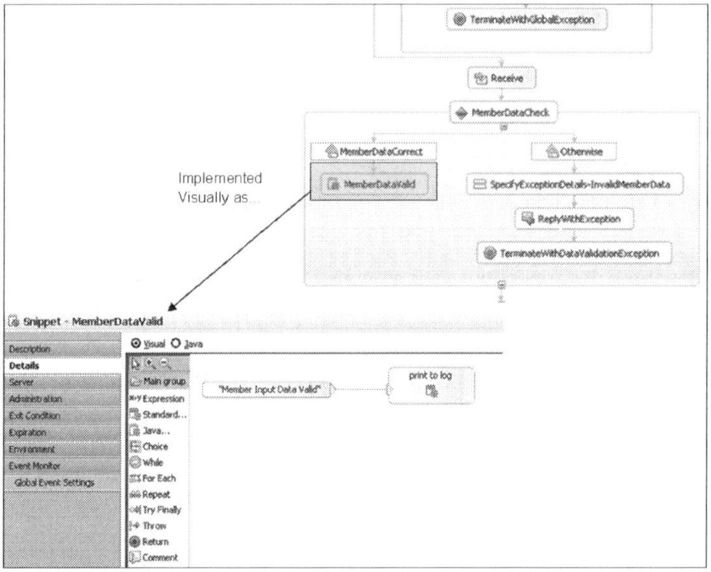

2. The second option is to create a reusable visual snippet that can be shared across the different components in a module. To create a new custom visual snippet, click on the module or the library, select **File** | **New** | **Other**, and find **Custom Visual Snippet** under the **Business Integration** category. After giving a meaningful name to the custom Java code you are writing, the Visual Snippets view will open.

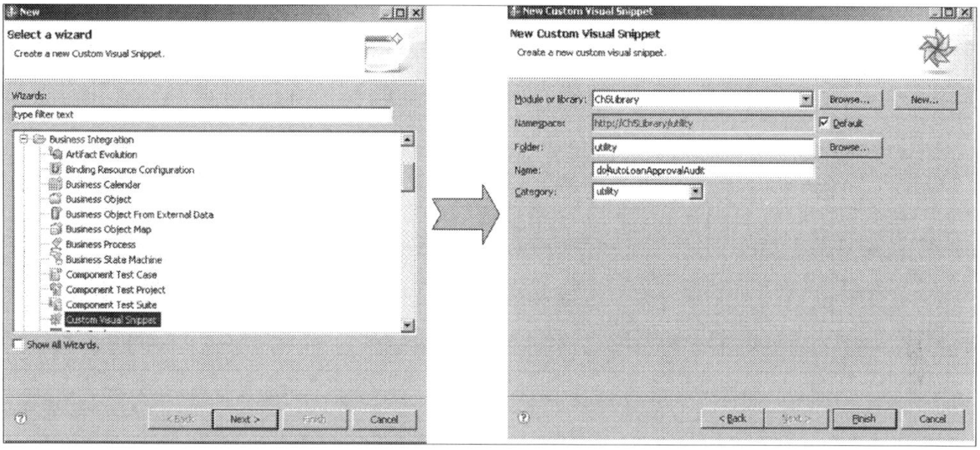

The visual snippet editor has a palette that is divided into several areas. The palette contains several **pre-built and pre-packaged** snippets that are most commonly used and most essential. These constructs can be dropped onto the canvas area. The tray area lists the inputs, outputs, and exceptions for this particular Java snippet. The snippet editor is also used in conjunction with the Properties view to further develop the snippet. The following screenshot shows the various parts of the visual snippet editor, as previously explained:

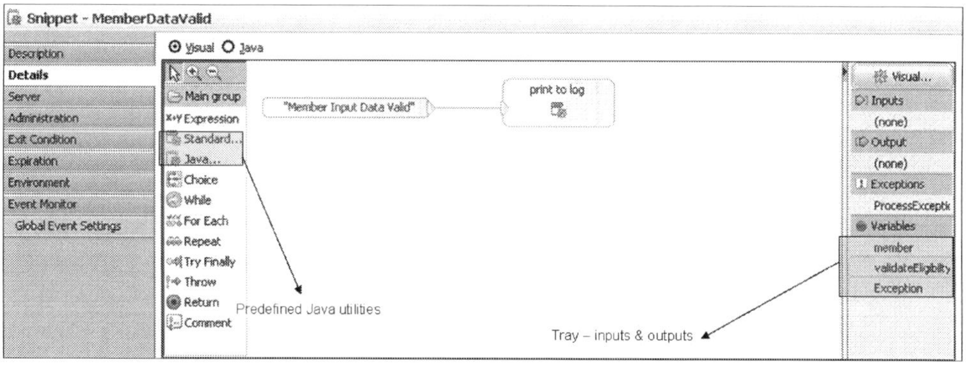

Handling human tasks

We are now left with implementing the final step of the **PerformEligibilityCheck** process component. However, before we begin to implement the human task, it would be good for us to understand what a human task is. A human task component provides you with the ability to integrate human interaction into the business process. This is very essential as most businesses in real life require some form of human intervention like approvers, underwrites, and so on, and therefore make it necessary for SCA to also accommodate human tasks.

The human task component enables coordination of requests that require human intervention and the management of the state of human tasks and work items. A developer can define the following types of human tasks:

- **To-do Task**: This is used to enable service to human interaction. You will be working with this in more detail through our example.
- **Invocation Task**: This is used to enable human to service interaction.
- **Collaboration Task**: This is used to enable human-to-human interaction.

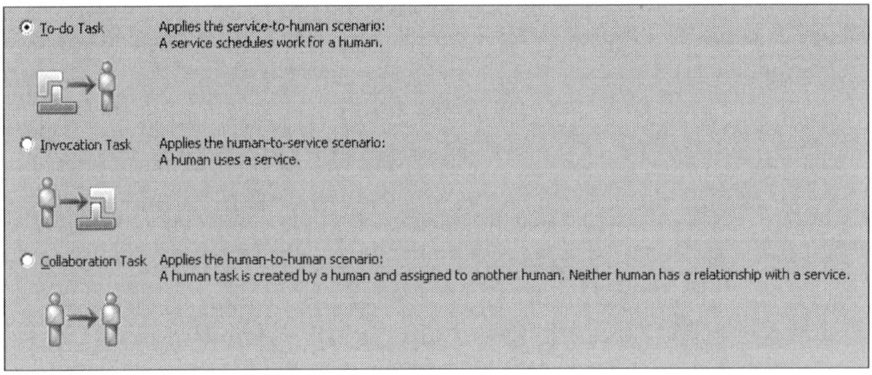

Let's now complete this use case by implementing the Human Task corresponding to the invoke activity in the **PerformEligibilityCheck** process.

1. Right-click on **Integration Logic** in the **Business Projects** window. Select **New | Human Task.** Give the process the name **ApproveEligibility** and folder **com/junglesea/solution/eligibilityCheck/process/ht.** Select **To-do task** and **EligibilityCheck** under existing interfaces. Then select **Single type of human task ownership** and click on the **Finish** button.

> The type of task ownership can be single or parallel. Tasks with single ownership require only one owner and any potential owner can claim the task in the BPC Explorer. Tasks with parallel ownership allow potential owners to work simultaneously on the task. The wizard will automatically select the operation based on the interface selected.

2. In the human task editor window, specify the user interface (UI) as BPC Explorer. Add **User Interface Business Process Choreographer Explorer.** Save the human task using *Ctrl+S*.

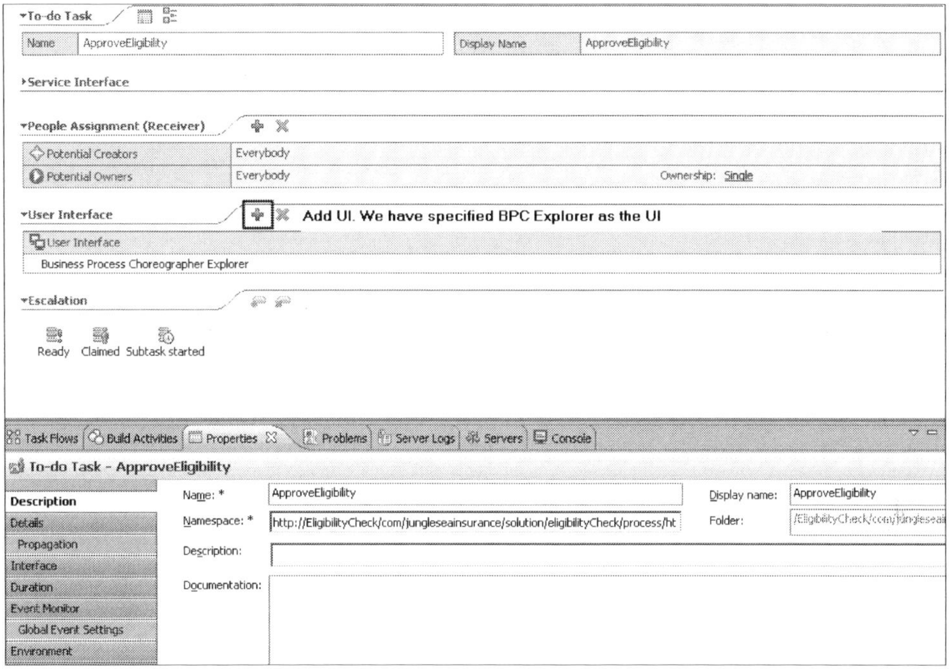

3. Double-click on the **EligibilityCheck** module assembly diagram.
4. Drag the **ApproveEligibility** human task on to the canvas and wire **PerformEligibilityCheck** to **ApproveEligibility**, as shown in the following screenshot.

5. To synchronize the **PerformEligibilityCheck** component with the changes made to its interface, open the assembly diagram, right-click on the **PerformEligibilityCheck** component, and select **Synchronize Interfaces and References | Implementation**. All the changes made to the interface will not be reflected in the business process component.

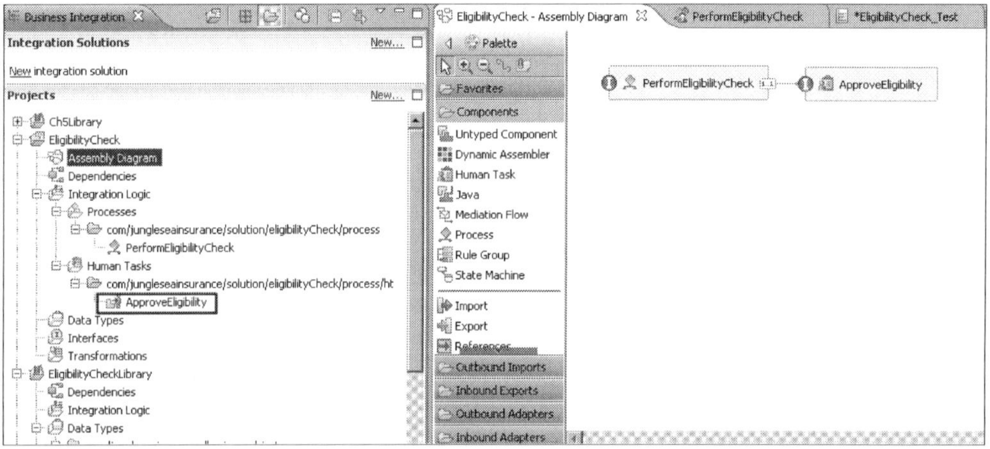

Congratulations! This completes the solution that will satisfy the requirements of the eligibility check use case. The next step is to deploy and test this process. You can deploy this application on the WPS that comes bundled with WID for testing purposes. Here are the steps to follow when deploying the module to the local WPS server:

1. Click on **Servers** tab. Start the WPS server by clicking on green play button, as shown in the following screenshot.
2. Wait for the server to start. This may take a few minutes.
3. Right-click on **WebSphere Process Server v7.0.** Select **Add and Remove Projects.**
4. Select **EligibilityCheckApp | Add | Finish.**

As described in Chapter 3, you will test the process using the Business Process Choreographer Explorer. You will run **PerformEligibilityCheck** to execute this solution, as shown in the following screenshot:

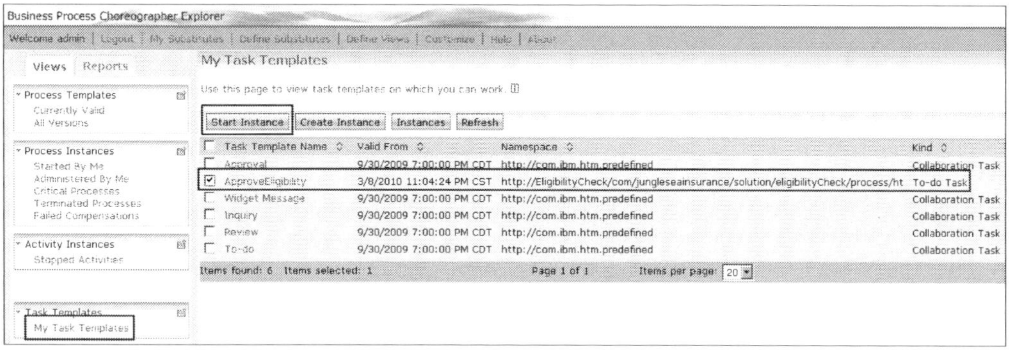

We will run the following test cases to understand the different paths in the business process.

Test Case 1	
Input values	FirstName: Joe LastName: Doe Age: 70
Procedure	• Launch and log in to BPC Explorer • Under **Process Templates** | Select **eligibilityCheckProcess** | Click **Start Instance** • Enter the values as given | Click **Submit** • Wait for a few seconds • Click on **My To-dos** | Select **approveEligibility** | Click **Work On** • **Check validateEligibility** | Click **Complete**
Result	The solution directed the eligibility check request for a member older than 65 years of age for manual approval by a human. Under **My To-dos** in the left column, you will see a task listed for you to approve this request. Select the task, click **Work On**, validate this request, and click **Complete**.

Implementation of Test Case 1 is shown in the following screenshot:

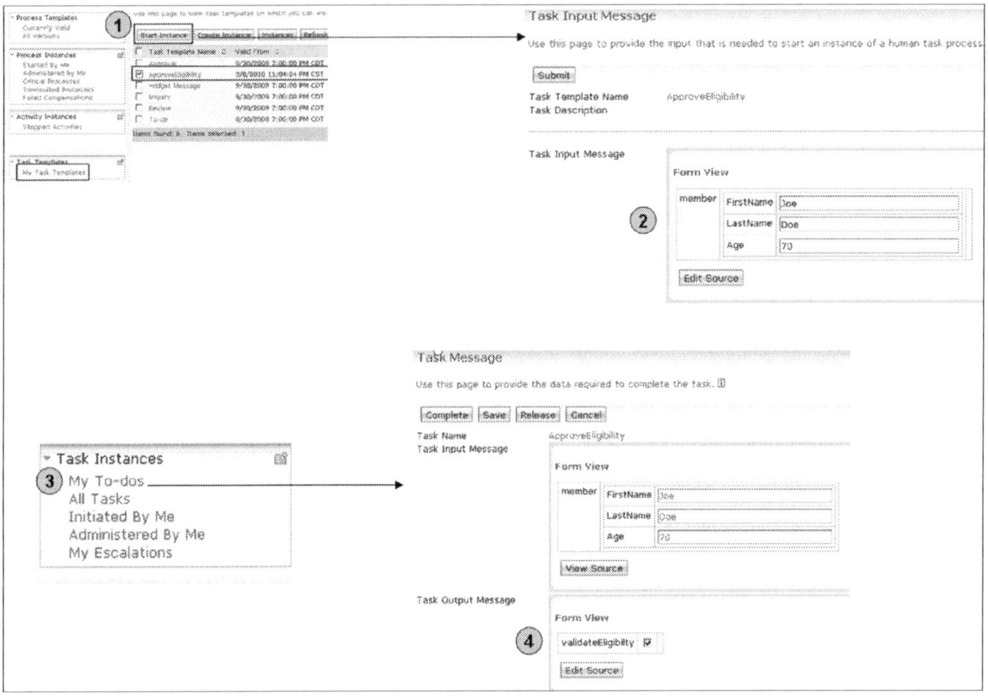

Test Case 2	
Input values	FirstName: Jack LastName: Sparrow Age: 25
Procedure	• Launch and log in to BPC Explorer • Under **Process Templates** | Select **eligibilityCheckProcess** | Click **Start Instance** • Enter the values as given | Click **Submit** Click on **My To-dos**. There should be no tasks listed underneath here.
Result	The solution auto-approved a member eligibility check request for a member younger than 65 years of age. The result will be true.

Test Case 3	
Input values	FirstName: Mary LastName: Thomas Age: 0
Procedure	• From the WID assembly diagram, right-click on the **PerformEligibilityCheck** component, and select **Test Component**. • In the **Unit Test Client** window that launches, specify the right values for the member object. • Press the **start play** icon, as shown in the following screenshot. Specify the server and provide credentials (admin/ admin by default).
Result	Since the age is specified as zero, the exception handler logic kicks in and throws a nice exception message back.

```
<?xml version="1.0" encoding="UTF-8"?>
<invalidMemberDataException
xsi:type="in:ExceptionMessage"
xmlns:xsi="http://www.w3.org/2001/
XMLSchema-instance" xmlns:in="http://
EligibilityCheckLibrary/com/jungleseainsurance/
interfaces">
  <exceptionId>DE-004</exceptionId>
  <exceptionName>Invalid Member Data Exception</
exceptionName>
  <exceptionCategory>Data Validation Exception</
exceptionCategory>
  <description>Check the value of member age</
description>
</invalidMemberDataException>
```

Implementation of Test Case 3 is shown in the following screenshot:

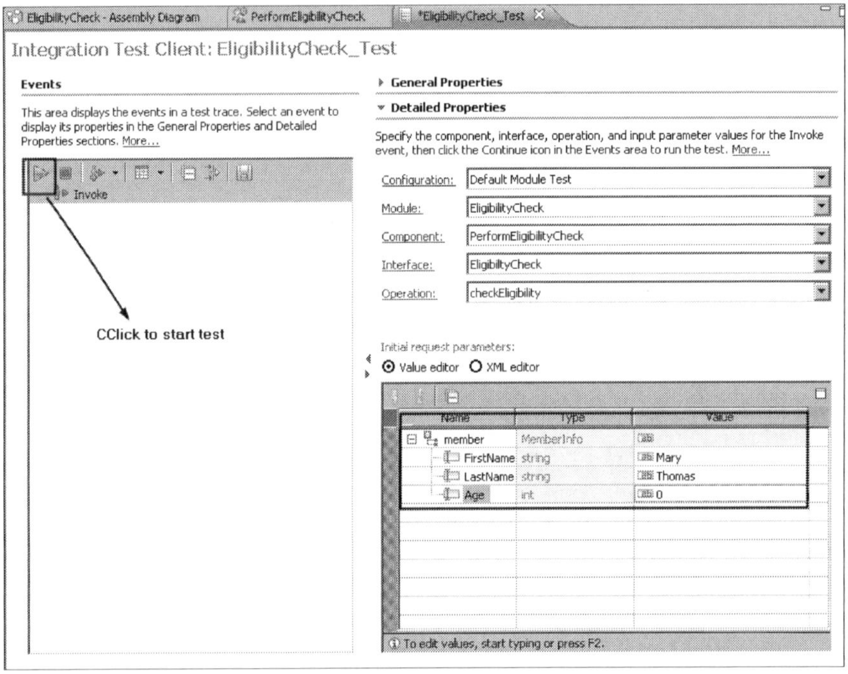

You have just completed working on a very simple business process. However, in real life, the business logic used to make business decisions is much more complex than a simple age check. For example, if the requirement to check eligibility involves complex business logic, and more specifically, if there are opportunities to externalize the decision-making logic, how would you handle this situation? You may have to check eligibility based on many business factors like medical history, weight, salary, and so on. What would happen to your business process then? It would require more complex control and decision-making activities in the business process. As the points of variability increase, it is very natural that the complexity of the process flow being created in the business process module also increases. Therefore, it is a good practice to identify these points of variability well in advance through detailed process modeling techniques and by adopting variability analysis identification techniques. Also, it is wise to decouple business decision making from the business process as far as possible. WID provides several capabilities to make this happen. One such key tool here is business rules.

Using rule groups and rules

Business rules help you abstract points of variability away from the implementation of the business process itself. Business rules are assembled into business rule groups in WID.

Business rules

Let's see some examples of business rules:

- If the applicant is above the age of 25, but younger than 60, married, employed full time, and has a good credit rating, then the applied mortgage rate is 4.5 percent
- If the customer has bought three shoes of the same brand under clearance, then the third pair is free
- If the customer is shopping in Texas, then the applied sales tax is 8.25 percent

Business rules control the behavior of a business process. They tune the business process to handle a given specific set of circumstances more efficiently. Business rules provide business policies and guidelines that can be managed independent of the application. These business rules can be externalized away from a business process, hence making the business processes decoupled and agile when changes are needed to be made to the business rules itself. For example, the sales tax may be increased to 8.35 percent. Therefore, they help reduce the impact of business environment changes on business processes. Furthermore, they can be used to ensure business partners are conforming to their business agreements.

Business Integration perspectives are modified using the web-based business rules manager in the WPS admin console. Business rules are persisted through the WPS database, making them available to all processes running on the server. The main idea behind a rule group is to club rule sets or decision tables together that share a common business purpose. In order to use a rule group, drag the component to your assembly diagram. Similar to other SCA components, you will need to associate an interface that describes the inputs needed to execute the business rules and an output that carries the result of business rules to the process. This component is then wired to the business process and accessed through an **Invoke** activity.

Let's create a simple business rule. Right-click on **EligibilityCheck | Integration Logic | New Rules | Rule Group**. Name it **EligibilityCheckRuleGroup**, under the folder **com/jungleseainsurance/solution/eligibilityCheck/rules**. Specify the interface to be **EligibilityCheck**. Once you press **Finish**, the rule editor will open.

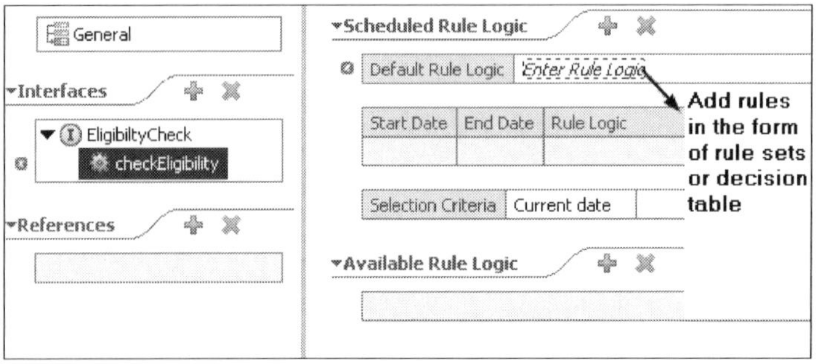

On the left, all the interfaces with their operations and reference interfaces that are associated with or referred to by the business rules are listed. On the right side is the rules logic area, where the rules will be created and configured through easy-to-use visual selections. Very limited programming will be required in this implementation. The rules logic area provides the ability to create rules and also define when they are applicable. Developers are given two options to create rules: Rule Sets and Decision Tables. They are created by clicking on the **Enter Rule Logic** and selecting either rule Set or decision table, as shown in the following screenshot:

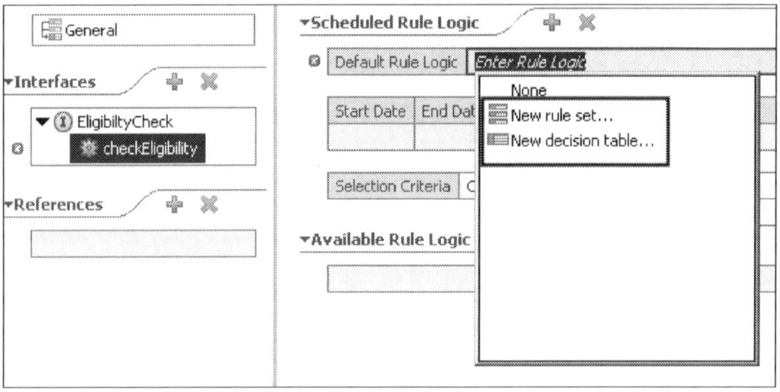

Business rule sets and templates

A rule set is a set of business rules that are applied together. They are typically used when rules need to be expressed in a natural language or if you need to fire multiple rules. These rules are graphically expressed in the form of if-then statements. In the rule set editor, you will define condition and actions that occur if those conditions hold true. The following screenshot shows how we have defined a rule in the rules set editor:

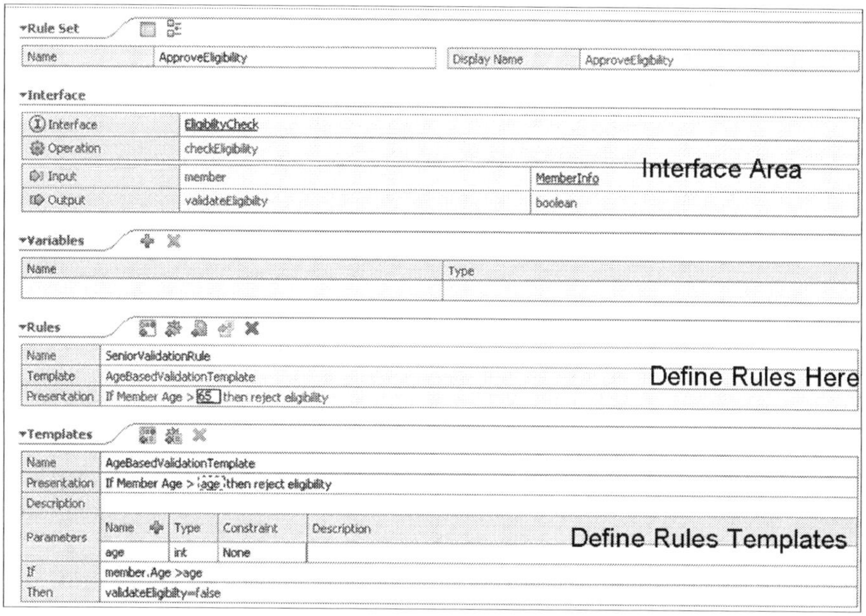

The rule set editor essentially has three main areas that will be used to create a rule set

1. **Interface Area:** This area displays the interface that is currently associated with the rule set.
2. **Variables Area:** This area displays the variables that are and can be used by the business rules to store data, as needed. The tool bar icons provide the ability to add and remove variables.
3. **Rules Set:** This area is used to graphically define the set of business rules that will be exercised when this rule set is invoked. You are given the option to create new `if-then-else` statements or apply rule templates.

In our example, validation rules have been defined to approve the eligibility of an applicant. An action rule is used to initialize the output to true. Then a rule template called **AgeCheck** is used to check if the age of the person is more than 65. If it is, then **validateEligibility** will be set to false. The last rule is added using an `if-then` statement to check the employment status of the applicant.

The toolbar icons in the rules area toolbar perform the following functions:

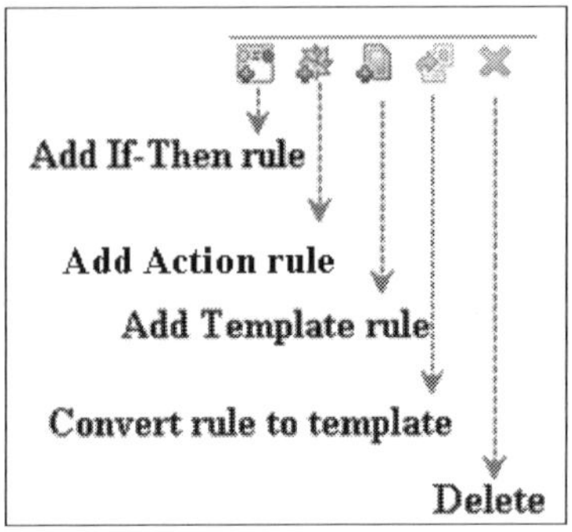

The templates area: This area is used to graphically define templates for a rule set using either `if-then` templates or action templates. The main advantage of templates is that they enable these rules to be edited and changed without requiring the redeployment of these rules. Rules that are in the form of templates can be managed through the web-based Business Rules manager in the WebSphere Process Server Administrative Console. In this way, a developer can expose business rules that can then be managed by business users or analysts in production. The toolbar icons provide the following functionality:

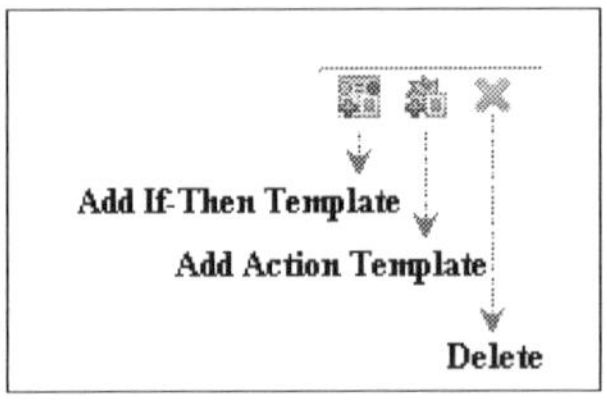

> If a rule template is used in a rule set, then it cannot be deleted. You will need to remove all references to a rule template before it can be deleted.

Decision tables

A decision table is another way of defining business rules that are used when rules need to be expressed in a table format or when the same set of conditions are applied to many rules. It handles multiple rules efficiently, evaluates in a tree structure instead of sequentially, and allows you to enact multiple actions for the one rule that is executed. Let's open the decision table editor to look at it more closely:

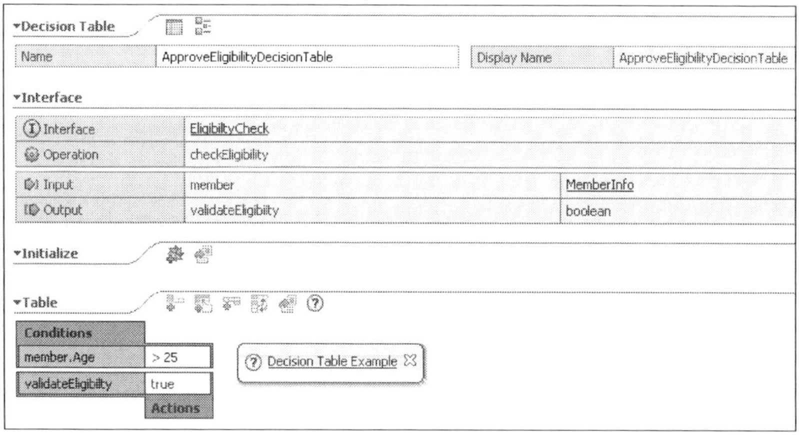

The three main work areas in the decision table editor are as follows:

1. **Interface Area:** This area displays the interface that is currently associated with the rule set.
2. **Initialize Variables Area:** This area is used to initialize variables that are used in the decision table. In our example, here we have initialized **validateEligibilty** to the **Approved** status. The **Convert Rule** or **Table Cell into template** options helps expose this business rule in the web-based Business Rules manager in WebSphere Process Server Administrative Console. This option enables this rule to be maintained by business users and analysts without having to redeploy the application.
3. **Decision Tables:** This area is used to define a tabular format for the business rules based on conditions and associated actions. It provides a rich representation of multiple conditions and fires actions based on them. In the end, only one rule is executed based upon all the conditions that apply.

We enhanced our eligibility check example with the help of decision tables to make different assertions based upon both the applicant's age and employment status. In our example, we are able to have different outcomes for different combinations of the values of age and employment status. This was only possible in a rule set through more complex if-then statements.

Words of wisdom — tips, tricks, suggestions, and pitfalls

- As the complexity of the process flow being created in the business process module increases, it starts dimensioning some of the main advantages of using SOA. Therefore, try as much as possible to decouple business decision making from the business process.
- When your application is dependent on other modules, it is important to ensure that the **Deploy with Module** in the **Dependencies** window is checked so that the dependencies will also be installed together with the module. If this is not done, you may see deployment errors.
- Business rules can only be deployed on the WebSphere Process Server (WPS) and are persisted through the WPS database. This makes them available to all instances running on the server.
- Decision tables are used when rules need to be expressed in a table format or when the same set of conditions are applied to many rules. They handle multiple rules efficiently, evaluate in a tree structure instead of sequentially, and allow you to define multiple actions for different combinations on the conditions. It is important to realize that in a decision table, only one rule is executed based on all the condition that apply.
- Rule sets are used when rules need to be expressed in a natural language or if you need to fire multiple rules. Rule sets are easier to understand than decision tables. These rules are evaluated sequentially, which can be inefficient when there are many rules.
- Using the Business Rule Manager Web tool, one can see rules in a browser. It's an optional install and can be installed by running the `installBRManager.jacl`. The `BRManager.war` is in the `installableApps` directory of the WebSphere Process Server install path. The Business Rule Manager Web tool is a JSP/Servlet based enterprise application that pulls and pushes Business Rules. Users are authenticated using standard WebSphere authentication and security.

Summary

In this chapter, you learned to work hands-on with key and fundamental WID topics. You also learned the various aspects and functions of WPS and WESB that are absolutely and fundamentally essential. The topics covered are Business Process (WS-BPEL), Business Objects, Business Rules, State Machines, Visual Snippets, Compensation, Fault Handling, and Control Structures. Now, you can confidently select the right tool (component) from the toolbox when building applications for WPS.

6

Mediations Fundamentals

This chapter will focus on the fundamentals of mediations within WESB. We have introduced the concept of mediation and its purpose within the Enterprise Service Bus in the previous chapters. This chapter covers more in-depth within the mediation flows and how to implement them. Topics covered include Mediation Flows, Mediation Primitives including Message Logger, Message Filter, Fan In and Fan Out, Adapters and Dynamic routing and so on. This chapter also walks you through each of these aspects, functions, and features with examples so that you can relate to them and their usage applicability. The following mind map outlines this chapter's topics:

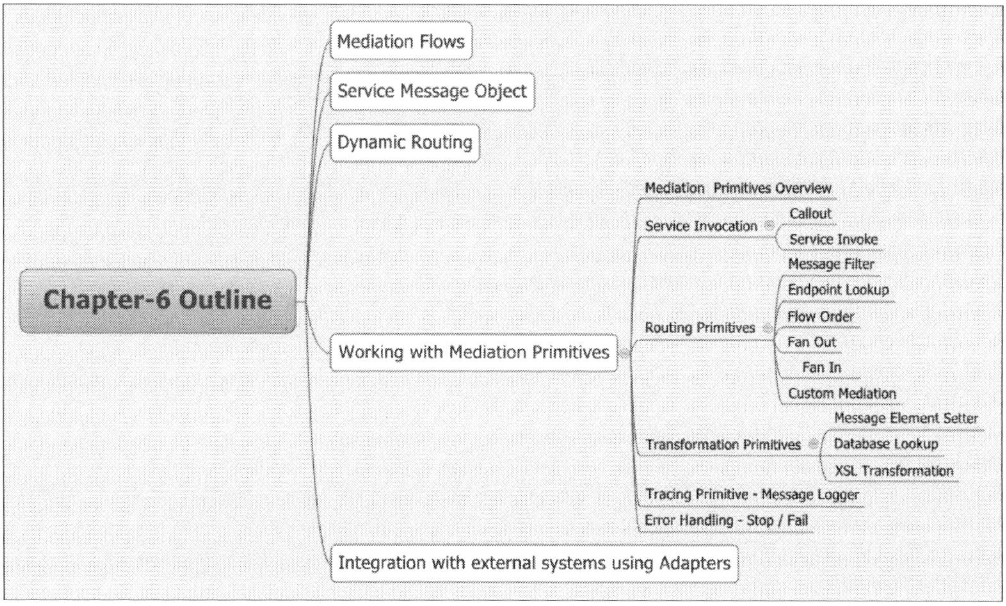

Mediation flows

As discussed in the previous chapters, Enterprise Service Bus (ESB) is a fundamental building block for an SOA. ESB is an architectural integration pattern that provides a flexible infrastructure that enables dynamic and adaptable service integration. In the heart of this infrastructure is the mediation flow component, which provides the mediation logic applied to a message as it flows from a service consumer to a provider. The mediation flows help achieve the service virtualization and connectivity necessary in interactions between service consumer and providers. A mediation flow basically receives an inbound request message from a service consumer. It then operates and processes the message and sends an outbound request message to the service provider. For example, if an order management system (the service provider) requires a specific format for sales order message (say OM-1), and the order entry system (the service consumer) uses a different order message (say OM-2), the mediation flow can transform or map from OM-1 format to OM2 using the XSL Transformation primitive. The mediation flow component is a type of SCA component that is typically used in a mediation module, but can also be used in a module. A mediation flow component contains a source interface and target references similar to other SCA components. The source interface is described using WSDL and must match the WSDL definition of the export to which it is wired. The target references are described using WSDL and must match the WSDL definitions of the imports or Java components to which they are wired.

Within the mediation flow, for the input and output flows, you model the flow logic using **Mediation Primitives**. As described in the following diagram (mind map of a Mediation Primitive), there are many types of mediation primitive available out-of-the-box that provide a predefined functional capability. These mediation primitives can be configured using properties which define how they behave. The overall logic of the flow is defined by wiring these configured Mediation primitives together into a logical flow. The mediation flow component, as shown in the preceding figure, through the Mediation primitives can perform all the ESB functions.

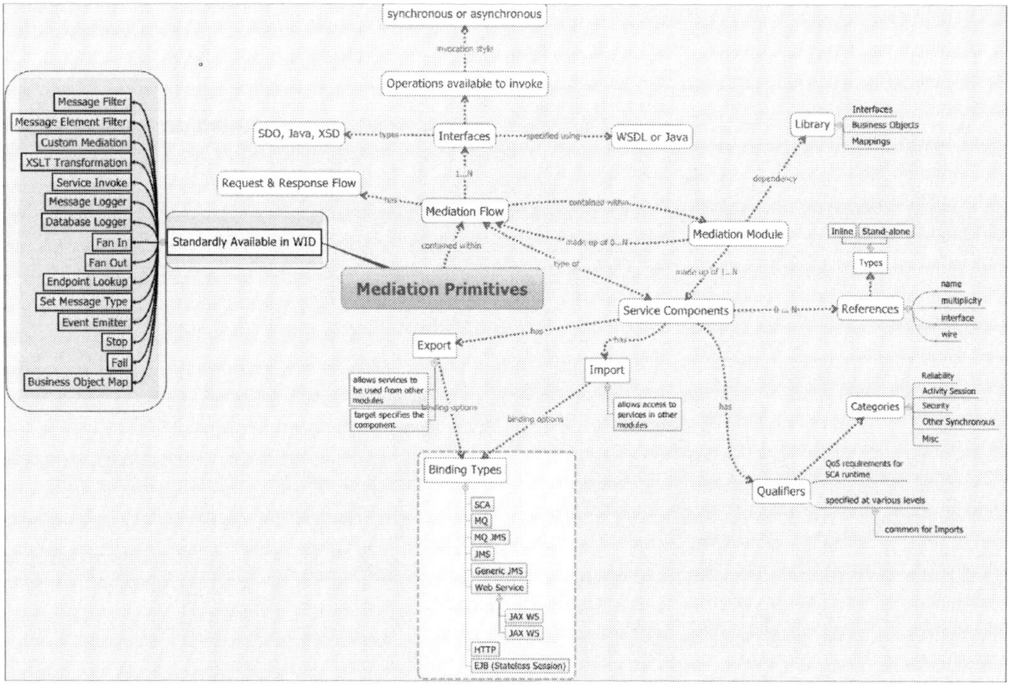

Service Message Object (SMO)

As explained in the previous section, the heart of a mediation module is the mediation flow component, which provides the mediation logic, applied to a message as it flows from a service consumer to a provider. Mediation flows operate on a message between a service consumer and service provider. So how do we represent these messages? Also the messages originating from a service consumer and the eventual messages that land up in a service provider may be in different forms. The service consumer may be a Web Services client, but the eventual service provider may expose its capabilities using JDBC and hence require the data to be in a non-XML format. There is a need to represent the message that flows through the mediation flow and hence the Mediation primitives. And this common representation of a message is what a Service Message Object (SMO) does. SMOs provide a common representation of a message that accounts for differing protocols and differing interfaces, operations, and parameters that the message represents. SMOs are built using Service Data Object (SDO) technology. SDO uses a schema that describes the basic structure of an SMO which is composed of three major sections. The following figure is an SMO whose:

- *body* represents the specific interface, operation and parameters relevant to this message. This represents the payload of a message.

- *headers* section of the message carry the information about the protocol over which the message was sent. SCA binding type determines which headers are populated. (Export for request flows and Import for response flows.)
- *context* section represents data that is important to the internal logic of the flow itself that is passed between Mediation primitives.

The data within an SMO is accessed using SDO, specifically the SDO Data Object, which enables access using XPath, the generic DataObject APIs, and some SMO-specific APIs that are aware of the SMO schema. The following screenshot gives a detailed overview of the structure of an SMO.

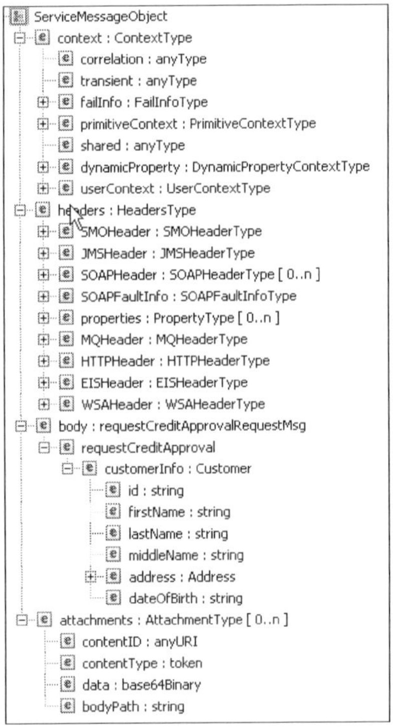

Working with Mediation primitives

Let's implement a simple credit management use case that takes in a credit rating request for a customer and then routes the incoming request message to that customer's residence state credit agency. In this particular example, use Texas Credit Agency, New York Credit Agency, and California Credit Agency as the three supported state agencies.

We will use this example to understand the different mediation flow primitives, get primitives in order to get a more realistic understanding and appreciation for these components.

Please follow the steps to build the application as defined in the use case:

1. Create a library called **Ch6Library** with the following data types as shown in the following screenshot (refer to Chapter 2 for details on creating a library):

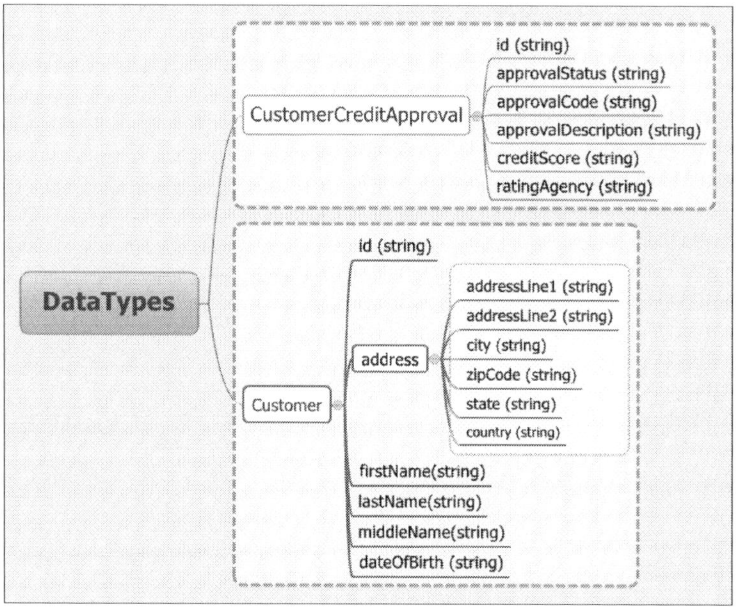

2. Add an interface called **CreditManagement** under folder **com/junglesea/ch6/mediations/interfaces** with a two-way operation **requestCreditApproval** as shown in the following screenshot:

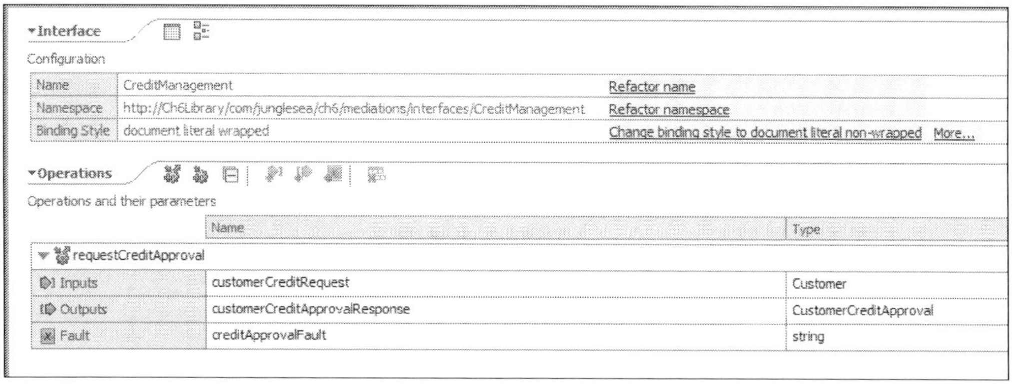

3. Save all your changes.
4. Create three separate modules associated with **Ch6Library** library that represent credit agencies for each of the states—Texas, New York, and California with the names **Ch6_TexasCreditAgency, Ch6_CaliforniaCreditAgency,** and **Ch6_NewYorkCreditAgency** respectively.

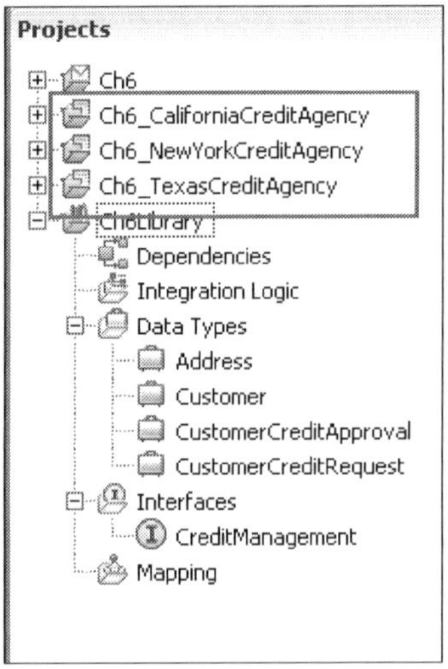

5. To each module add a Java component linked to the **CreditManagement** interface with an SCA binding export as shown in the following screenshot:

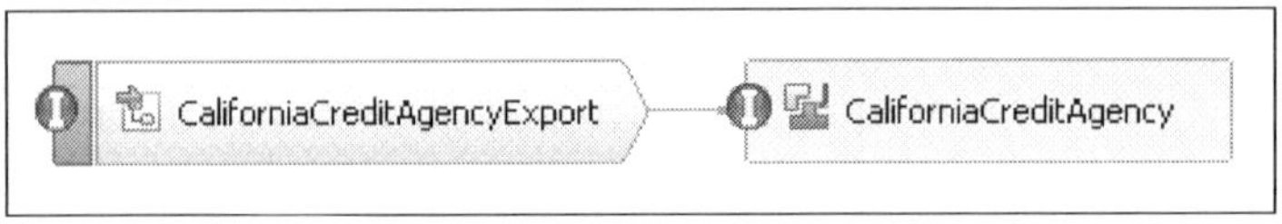

6. Implement each Java component under package **com.junglesea.solutions.creditagency** and replace the `public DataObject requestCreditApproval(DataObject customerInfo) {}` function with the following code:

```
public DataObject requestCreditApproval(DataObject
customerInfo) {
    ServiceManager serviceManager = ServiceManager.INSTANCE;
    BOFactory boFactory = (BOFactory)serviceManager.
locateService("com/ibm/websphere/bo/BOFactory");
    DataObject customerCreditApproval = boFactory.
create("http://Ch6Library","CustomerCreditApproval");
customerCreditApproval.setString("id",customerInfo.
getString("id"));
```

```
    customerCreditApproval.setString("approvalStatus","Approv
ed");
    customerCreditApproval.setString("approvalCode","0000");
    customerCreditApproval.setString("approvalDescription","Cre
dit has been approved");
    customerCreditApproval.setString("creditScore","740");
    customerCreditApproval.setString("ratingAgency","California
Rating Agency");
//For Texas set ratingAgency to "Texas Rating Agency"
//For New York set ratingAgency to "New York Rating Agency"
    return customerCreditApproval;
    }
```

7. You may need to add an import for package **com.ibm.websphere.bo**, as shown in the following screenshot:

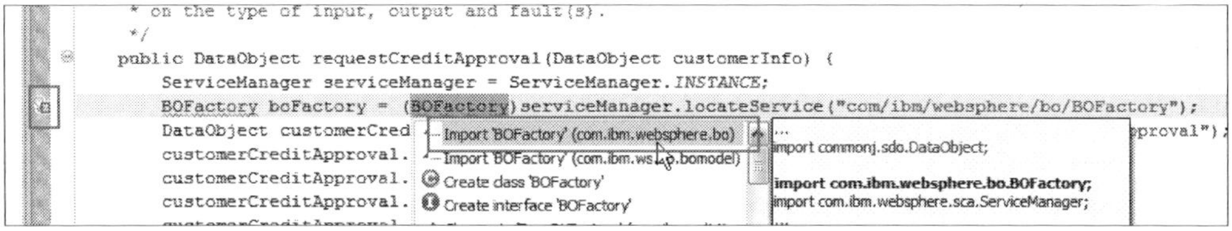

8. Save all your changes.
9. Create a new module called Ch6 associated with Ch6Library library and open the Assembly diagram.
10. On the canvas implement three imports, one for each state's credit agency SCA service and one export linked to **CreditManagement** interface.
11. Drag the Mediation Flow component from the Palette onto the canvas and name it **CreditManagementMediationFlow.** Wire **CreditManagementMediationFlow** between the export and three imports as shown in the following screenshot:

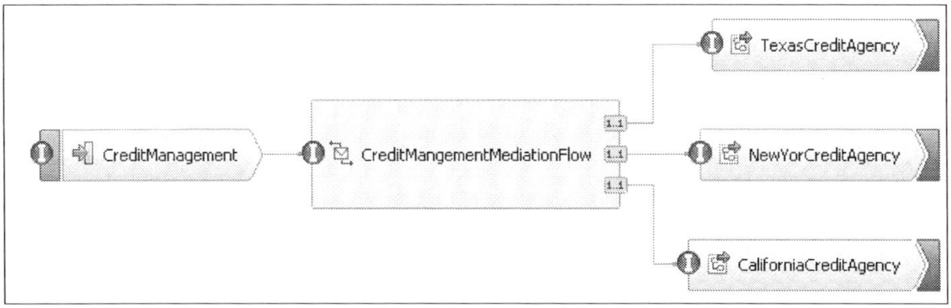

Congratulations! You have now completed setting up the Ch6 module to begin learning about the different Mediation primitives.

In Chapter 4, Mediation Primitives we listed the different categories of the Mediation primitives, the primitives within each category and their specific usage. The following screenshot captures the various categories for us:

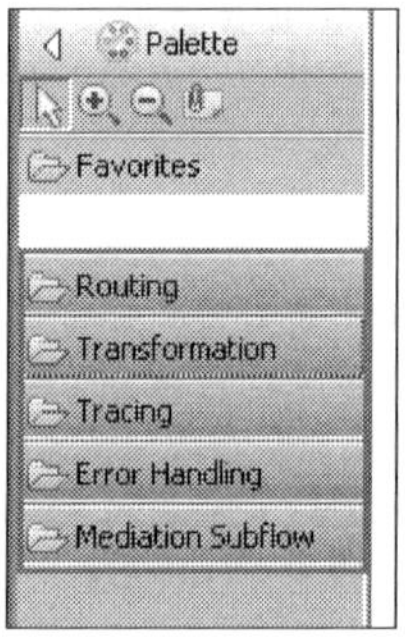

Mediation primitive overview

Before we begin talking about specific mediations primitives let's look at some of the common features of all Mediation primitives starting with the Mediation flow editor.

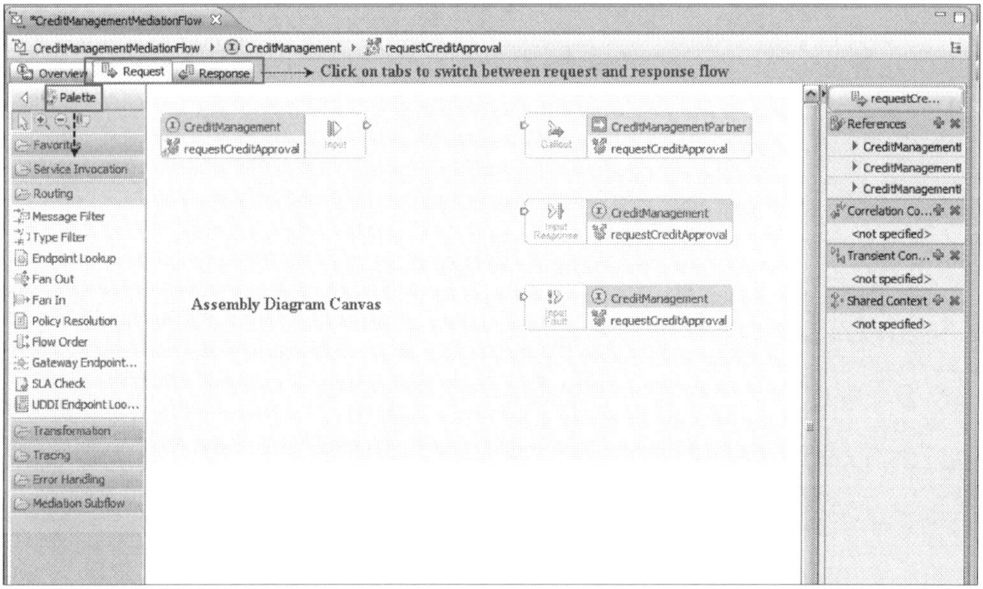

The preceding screenshot gives the layout of the Mediation Flow editor. In this editor you typically define a mediation flow from the operation on the input interface to one or more operations on the output interface. For a particular operation connection, the mediation flow logic for that input operation is shown in the Mediation Flow panel portion of the editor. This panel has two tabs which are used to display the mediation logic for either the request flow or the response flow. Within the mediation flow, various mediation primitives are used and wired together between the nodes to define the logic of the flow.

The Mediation primitives have three terminals namely, the input, output, and fault terminals. The inputs and outputs for Mediation primitives are defined through **terminals.** Terminals denote the messages that flow through the terminal. The message type is defined by the structure of the Service Message Object body that is present in that part of the flow. There is one Input terminal per Mediation primitive except for Fan In primitive and it defines the input message type. A Mediation primitive can have zero, one, two or a variable number of output terminals. The fail terminal is used for exception handling and when the Mediation primitive fails during the processing of a message. The fail terminal is always of the same message type as the input terminal.

The nature of these terminals may differ from primitive to primitive. In the following sections we have provided details for each individual primitive's terminals.

Selecting any specific Mediation primitive in the editor displays the properties for that primitive in the Properties view, which is in the bottom panel. This is where the properties are specified to configure the behavior of the primitive. When you select a particular primitive and look under the **Properties** window you will see four options on the left column menu—**Description**, **Terminal**, **Details**, and **Promotable Properties** as shown in the following screenshot:

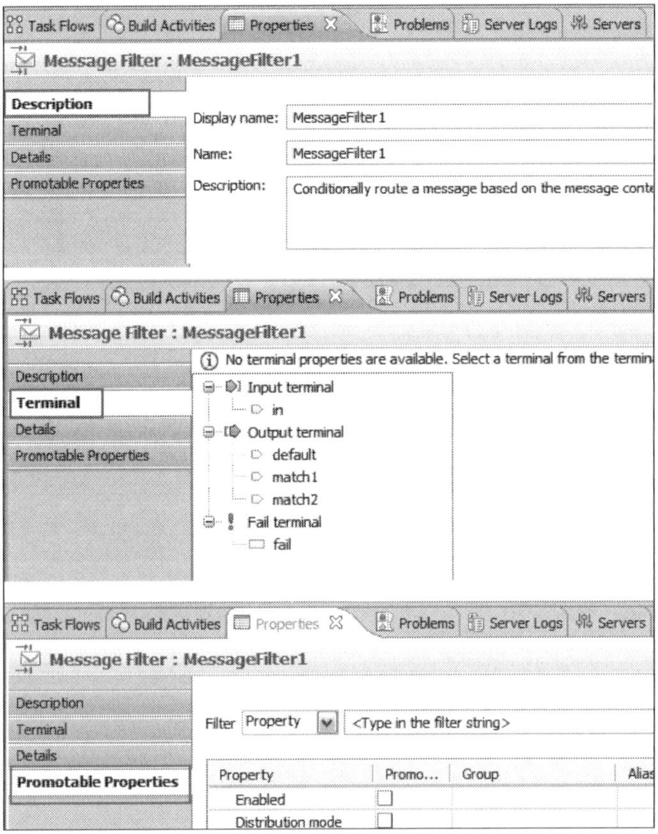

- **Description**: This window provides the option to configure the primitive's display name, name, and description fields.
- **Terminal**: This window provides the option to configure the input, output and fault terminals for the primitive. You also have the ability to add and delete terminals which may differ for each particular primitive.
- **Details**: This window is specific to each primitive and provides options to configure and define the implementation of the primitive.

- **Promotable Properties**: This window provides the options to make the listed properties administrable at runtime. This means that the administrator can change the values of these properties without having to redeploy the application. For more information, go to `http://publib.boulder.ibm.com/infocenter/dmndhelp/v7r0mx/topic/com.ibm.wbit.help.mediation.doc/topics/cpromoted.html`.

Implementation steps common to most Mediation primitives

At high level here are the steps to implement any Mediation primitive:

1. Create a Mediation Flow SCA component in your assembly diagram canvas. Specify an interface for this component and wire it to the target component(s), to which it will have to mediate to from a data and a protocol perspective.
2. Double-click on the mediation flow component to the mediation flow component overview page.
3. Select the operation on source interface and then select the mediation flow template to be used to implement the mediation flow.
4. In the mediation flow editions drag the Mediation primitive from the Palette onto the mediation canvas.
5. Wire the source input terminals to the Mediation primitive and then the mediation primitive to the output terminal and Fail component.
6. Configure the **Properties** and **Promotable Properties** for the Mediation primitive.

Service invocation

We will take a few more commonly-used Mediation primitives, beginning with service invocation Mediation primitives, and describe the different kind of mediations that can be conducted on the incoming message and how to implement each primitive.

Callout

A **callout** node represents an endpoint in the response mediation flow. It is responsible for invoking the target operation with the processed messages.

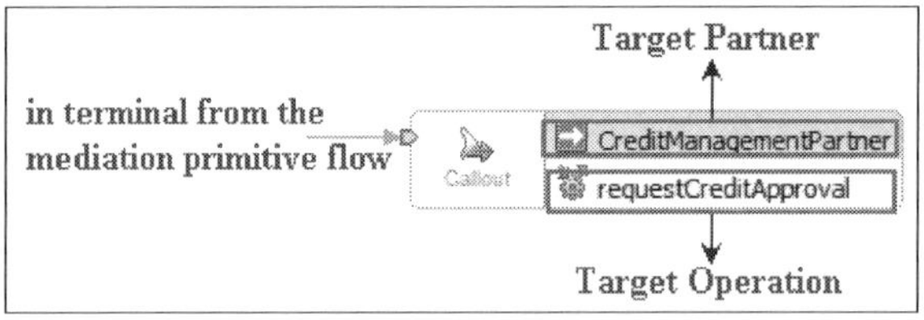

Properties

1. The configuration and properties for the callout node under **Properties | Details** view are shown in the following screenshot:

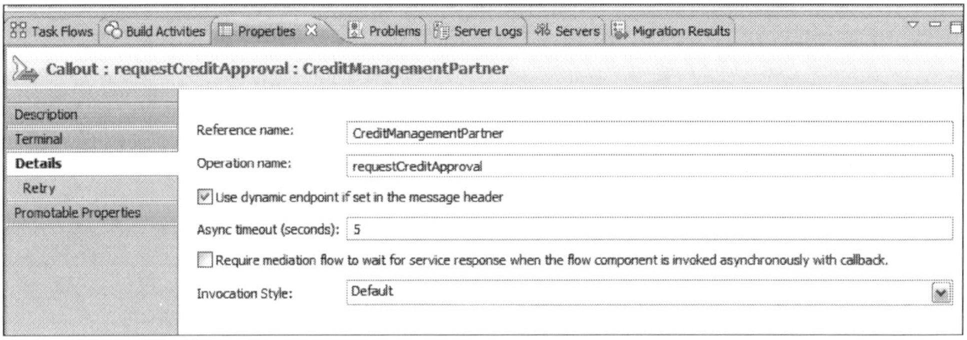

2. The **Details** page lists the **Reference partner** and **Operation name**. These fields are not editable. This page does give you the ability to define the nature of the endpoint invocation. The options available are:
3. Dynamic endpoint provides the option to define the target service endpoint dynamically at runtime. This endpoint can be set in the mediation flow in SMO Header/headers/SMOHeader/Target/address field or in the /headers/SMOHeader/AlternateTarget field. By default this property is selected though if there is no endpoint defined in the SMO Header the static endpoint that the call out is bound with is used.
4. **Invocation Style** provides three options—**Default, Sync,** and **Async**. Default means that the invocation style is determined by other factors such as the invocation style used by the mediation module's export.
5. Listed under **Details** in the left column menu of **Properties** is the **Retry** option which gives the ability to retry a service invocation depending on the kind of fault received from the first invocation.

[For more details about the callout please refer to `http://publib.boulder.ibm.com/infocenter/dmndhelp/v7r0mx/topic/com.ibm.wbit.help.mediation.doc/topics/rcallout.html`]

Example — Callout

Let's begin the implementation of the **CreditManagment** mediation flow we started in the beginning of this section using this primitive.

1. Double-click on **CreditManagementMediationFlow** in the assembly diagram for Ch6 module and implement it under folder **com/junglesea/solutions/mediations/**. This will open the Mediation Flow Overview Editor. Click on the source **requestCreditApproval** operation to bring up the mediation flow templates as shown in the following screenshot:

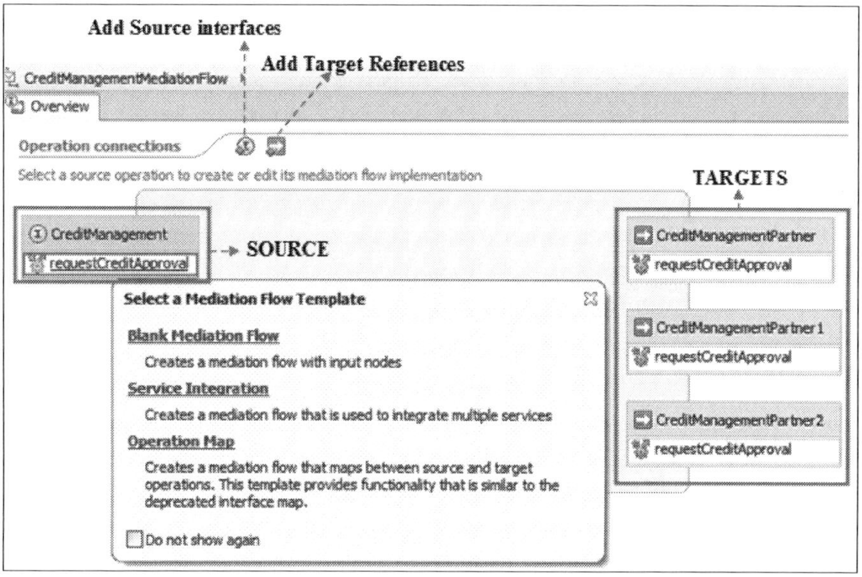

[The mediation flow templates dialog is a usability feature that preconfigures the mediation flow based on your selection that is Blank Mediation flow, Services Integration, and Operation Map. These template flows can also be built later from a blank mediation flow.]

2. In the template selection dialog, choose **Service Integration**.

3. In the service selection dialog, add the target operations **CreditManagementPartner**, **CreditManagementPartner1,** and **CreditManagementPartner2** and click on the **Add button**.
4. This will open the mediation flow editor for **CreditManagementMediationFlow**. Based on your configuration for the service selection the callouts for each of the targets would be predefined in the assembly canvas.

Usage tips

Here are some usage tips that will prove useful as you work with this primitive:

- Dynamic callouts enable the mediation flow to be truly dynamic and not dependent on the static wiring defined in the assembly diagram of the process flow. This is a very useful ability as it allows the mediation flow to change endpoints specific to each transaction handled by it without requiring redeployment.
- The dynamic callout ability is particularly useful with the Endpoint Lookup Mediation primitive that provides access to WebSphere Service Registry and Repository.

Service invoke

This Mediation primitive is used to invoke a reference partner or external service from within the mediation request or response flow. Each primitive is associated with a reference interface. The functionality is similar to the service invoke activity in business process flows. The operation for the interface can be a one-way operation or a request response operation. An invocation call later can be either synchronous or asynchronous.

This primitive can be configured to override the wired target and use a dynamic endpoint at runtime. The terminals of the primitive are shown in the following figure:

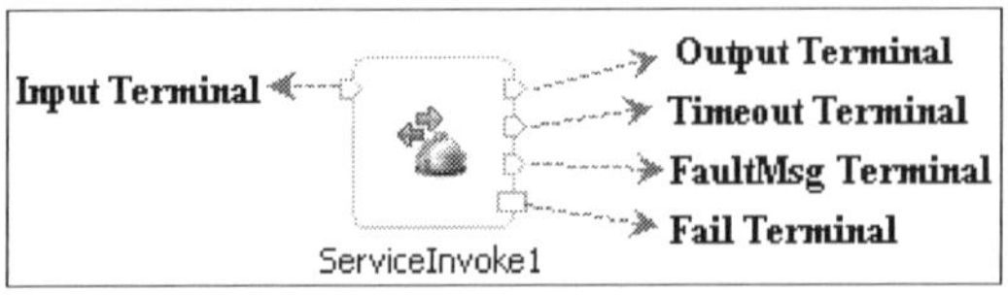

Key use

This Mediation primitive can be used to invoke an external service from within the mediation flow

Properties

1. The configuration and properties view for the service invoke primitive under the **Properties | Details** view are shown in the screenshot below. It shows the various properties and attributes you can specify for the service invoke primitive.

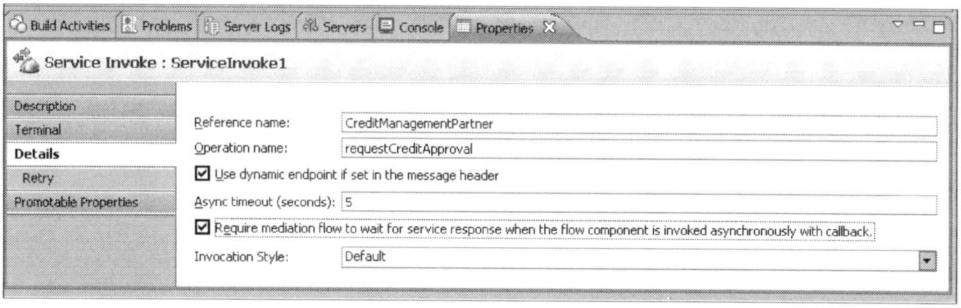

Reference name	This is a read-only field that displays the name of the target reference partner.
Operation name	This is a read-only field that displays the name of the target reference partner operation.
Checkbox—Use dynamic endpoint ...	When checked the service invoke primitive checks the SMO header/Target field for an endpoint reference and, if defined, overrides the wired target reference partner.
Async timeout (seconds)	This used to define the time to wait for an asynchronous operation to respond. If there is no response, the timeout terminal is fired. This is only valid if the Require mediation flow to wait for service response when the flow component is invoked asynchronously with callback is not checked.
Checkbox—Require mediation to wait	Set this property to true to force an asynchronous call to work in a synchronous manner or in a single transaction.
Invocation Style	This lets us set the invocation style to Default, Sync or Asynch. **Default** setting means that the invocation style is determined by other factors like the target.

Usage tips

Here are some usage tips that will prove useful as you work with this primitive:

- When service invoke is used in a synchronous fashion, then the mediation thread is blocked till the service returns.
- When service invoke is used in an asynchronous with deferred response (SCA invokeAsync) fashion, then the mediation thread making the call to continue in parallel until a response is received (SCA invokeResponse) and the maximum wait time is according to the what is defined as a configurable property on the primitive.
- When service invoke is used in an asynchronous with callback (SCA invokeAsyncWithCallback) fashion, the mediation thread will continue in parallel, and the response when it arrives will kick off a new mediation thread.
- The service invocation can be configured to retry an invocation if it fails. You can specify the number of retries or retry count, the time between retries or retry delay, and alternate endpoints if the invocation still fails. These configurations are made under **Properties** | **Details** | **Retry**.
- If a service invoke is configured to invoke a service asynchronously, but is used with a contained sub flow or FanOut/FanIn operation, then at runtime this service call is forced to act in a synchronous fashion.

Routing primitive

The next category of primitives that we will look at is routing primitives which control and manipulate the flow of the message between service requestors and service providers.

Message filter

The message filter primitive helps route incoming messages to one or more selected output terminals based upon user defined criteria. These criteria are simple conditional expressions on the incoming messages that are defined using XPATH expressions. Each expression is then mapped to an output terminal. If an expression holds true then that output terminal is selected.

The selection process behavior can be controlled using the distribution mode:

- **First** distribution mode is used when you want the selection process to complete as soon as it finds the first expression that is true for a particular incoming message and routes the message to that matching output terminal.

- **All** distribution mode is used when you want the all the expressions to be evaluated. The incoming message is then routed to all matching terminals of expressions that are true.

This primitive also gives us the ability to define the default criteria in the event none of the XPath criteria are applicable and a fail terminal to route failure messages.

The terminals of the primitive are shown in the following figure:

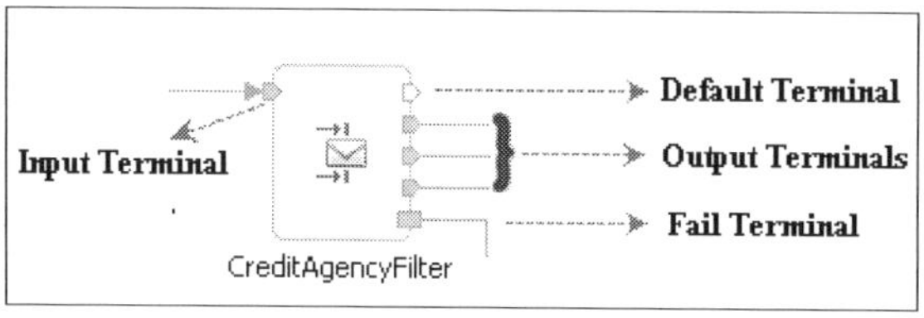

Key uses

Some of the key uses for this primitive are:

- Use cases where different process flow paths need to be taken based on the incoming message.
- To validate incoming messages against certain criteria.
- In combination with other primitives, such as Database Lookup, to implement more complex logic. For example, to get the customer credit score based on the incoming customer info from a database table and then route the message according to that credit score.

Example – Message Filter primitive

Having learned about Mediation Filter primitives, let's begin to implement the request and response flows for this mediation module:

1. From the Palette of the mediation editor drag a **Message Filter** primitive onto the canvas and change **Display Name under Properties** to **CreditAgencyFilter**.
2. Under the **Properties** window for **CreditAgencyFilter,** select **Terminal.** Add **Output Terminal – match2** and **match3.**

3. Wire the primitive to input and target partners, as shown in the following screenshot:

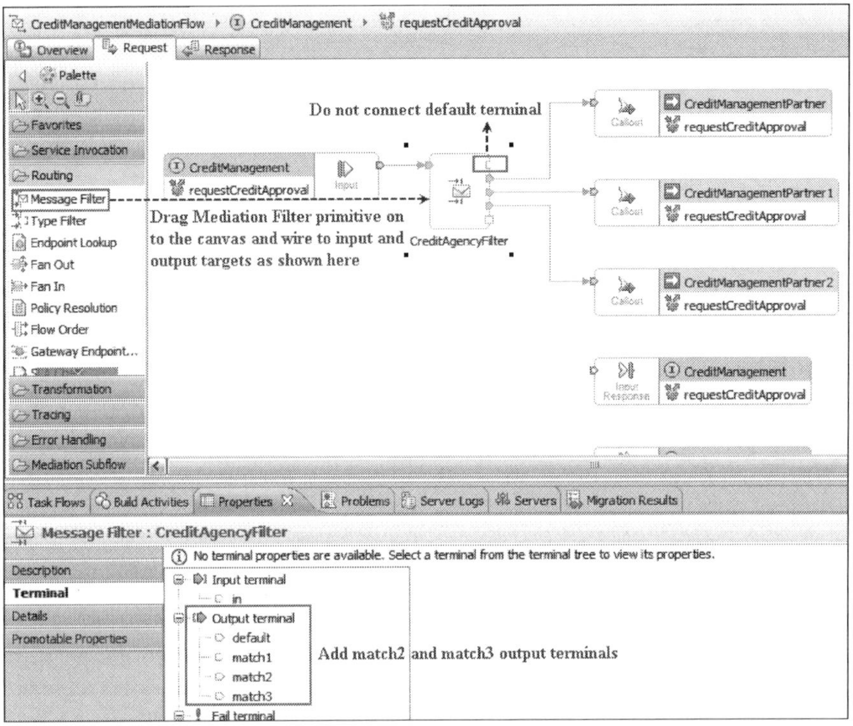

4. The mediation filter primitive has now been deployed. The last step to complete this implementation is to configure this primitive under **Properties | Details** view.

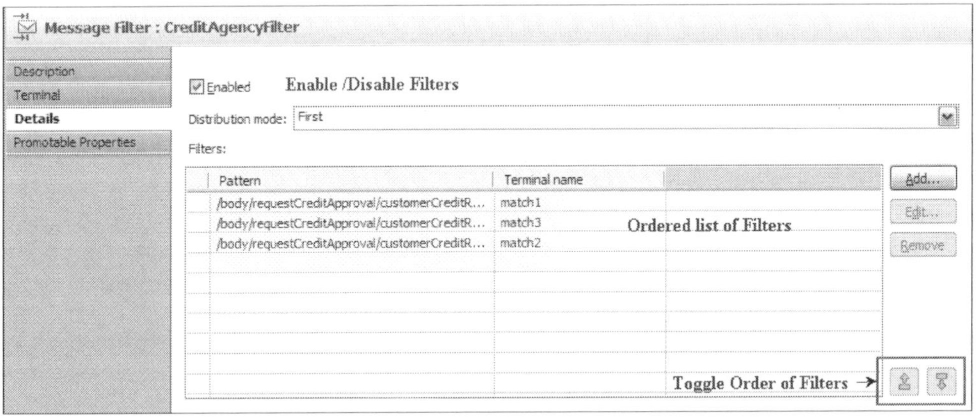

5. Click on the **Add** button to open the XPATH Editor and define an expression **/body/requestCreditApproval/customerCreditRequest/address/state = 'TX'** and match it to **match1,** which is wired to **TexasCreditAgency** import in the assembly diagram. Similarly match:

   `/body/requestCreditApproval/customerCreditRequest/address/state = 'NY'to match2.`

   `/body/requestCreditApproval/customerCreditRequest/address/state = 'CA' to match3.`

> This use case also serves as an introduction to dynamic routing of messages. The endpoint that will be invoked is selected at runtime based on these filters we have applied in the last step. Details on the dynamic routing are provided in the next section.

6. Save all your changes.
7. The last step to complete this implementation is to define the response flow. Click on the **Response** tab and wire the service providers callouts to the input node, as shown in the following screenshot:

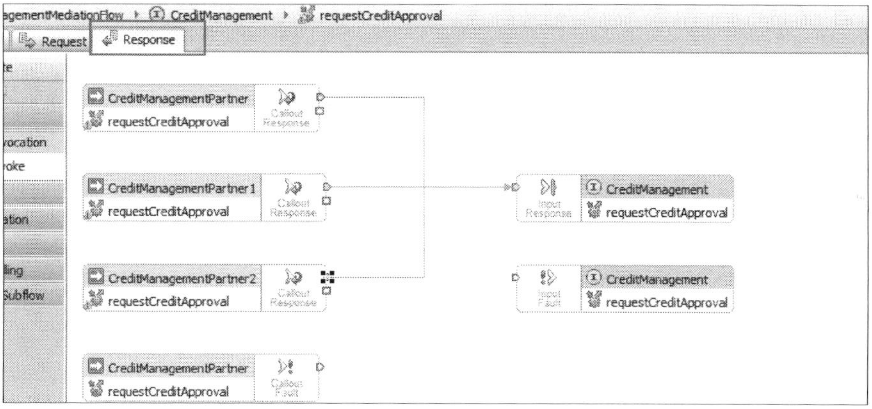

8. Save all your changes.

This completes our implementation of the use case. Now let's test this implementation to ensure that we get the desired results.

Test and execution

In *Chapter 3, Building your Hello Process Project* and *Chapter 4, Building your Hello Mediation Project*, we used the Business Process Choreographer Explorer to test and execute the HelloWorld applications. In this section we shall use the Test Component feature in WID to test the CreditManagement process flow.

1. Under the **Servers** tab, right-click on **WebSphere Process Server v7.0** and select **Add** and **Remove Projects**. In the **Add** and **Remove Projects** dialog box add **Ch6_TexasCreditAgency, Ch6_NewYorkCreditAgency**, and **Ch6_CaliforniaCreditAgency**.
2. Under the **Ch6** module open the Assembly diagram.
3. Right-click on **CreditManagement SCA export** and select **Test Component**.
4. Under the **Value editor,** enter the **state** value as 'NY'.

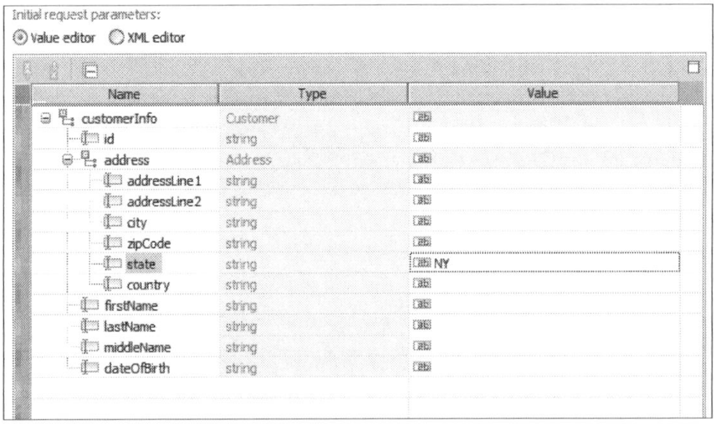

5. On left side click on the green play button under the **Events** section to execute the test as shown in the following screenshot:

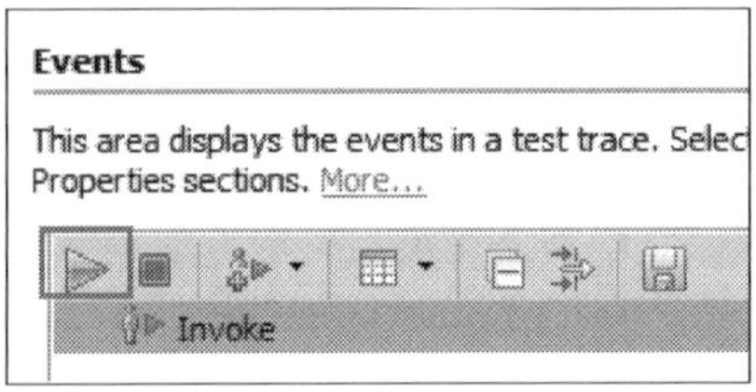

6. In the **Deployment Location** dialog, select **WebSphere Process Server v7.0,** and click on the **Finish button.**
7. Enter administrator user credentials and wait a few minutes for the process flow to deploy and execute.
8. If your setup is correct, then New York Credit Agency endpoint should get invoked, proving the test to be successful, as shown in the following screenshot:

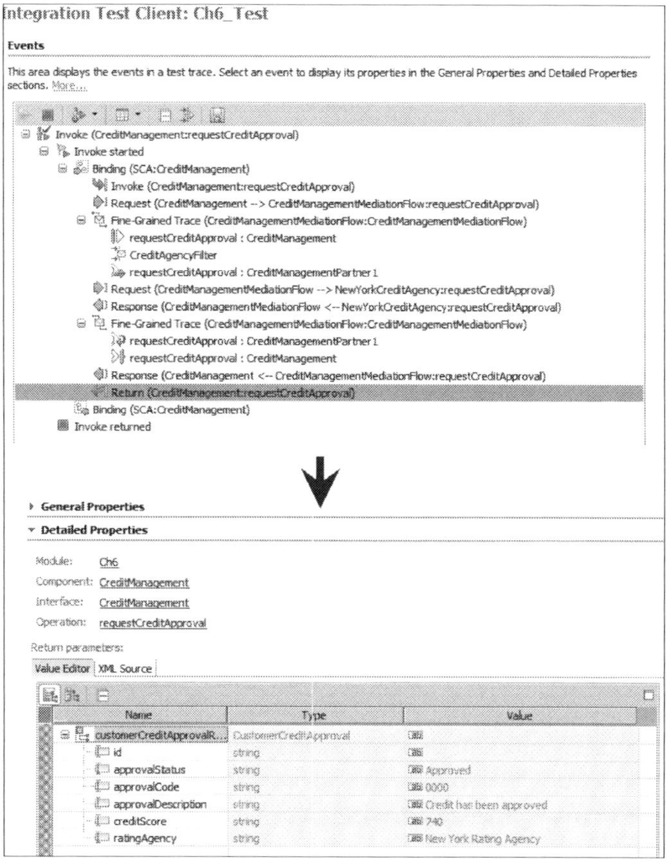

9. Repeat this test to execute the state values TX and CA.

Usage tips

Here are some usage tips that will prove useful as you work with this primitive:

- When using Distribution mode **All** there is the possibility of creating multiple active paths through the flow. This Mediation primitive can only handle one returned response and therefore if multiple responses are returned it will cause exceptions apart from the first returned message. One possible use is for a one-way operation where you need to selectively broadcast to multiple services based on the content of the message.
- It is possible to have multiple filters pointing to the same target. However, they need to be associated with different out terminals or matches on the primitive. These out terminals will then be wired to the same target callout.

Endpoint lookup

This Mediation primitive gives you the ability to use a service registry like WSRR to find service provider endpoints based on a set of selection criteria. The results of the lookup can be set in the service message object header. This can then be used downstream in the mediation flow like in a service invoke primitive.

The primitive has the following terminals:

- **Out Terminal**: Used when one or more endpoint matches are found. This propagates the updated SMO to the target partner
- **No Match Found**: Used when no matching endpoints are found. This propagates the original SMO to the target partner

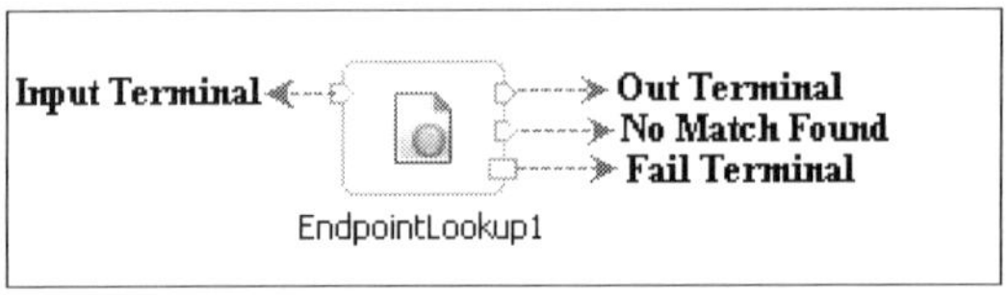

Key uses

This primitive can be used to dynamically route messages to appropriate service endpoints as determined at runtime by user-defined selection criteria.

Properties

1. In **Properties | Details, view configuration explanation for EndPoint Lookup primitive** is detailed in the following screenshot:

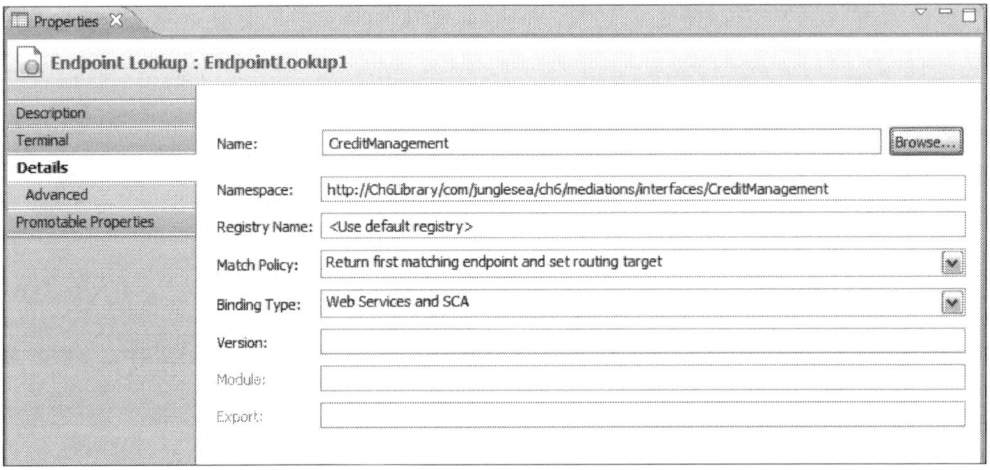

Name	This is the name of the interface selected through the **Browse** button along the Namespace which helps define the Port Type of the endpoints to be selected.
Namespace	This is the namespace associated with the selected interface.
Registry Name	This identifies the registry against which the endpoint lookup will be done.
Match Policy	In event that multiple endpoints are found for your selection criteria, this then tells the system how to manage them. This has the following values: • Return all matching endpoints • Return first matching endpoint and set routing target • Return all matching endpoints and set alternate routing targets • Return endpoint matching latest compatible service version • **Return endpoint matching latest compatible service version** requires Version, Module, and Export fields to be set
Advanced	User defined endpoint selection criteria are configured here.

Usage tips

Extra information on how to set up a WSRR definition can be found at `http://publib.boulder.ibm.com/infocenter/dmndhelp/v6r2mx/topic/com.ibm.websphere.wps.620.doc/tasks/twesb_createwsrrdef.html`.

Flow Order

Flow Order primitives are a new primitive that was introduced in version 7.0. This Mediation primitive helps you define the order in which branches of a mediation flow are executed. This primitive has one **Input** terminal and number of Output terminals as shown in the following screenshot:

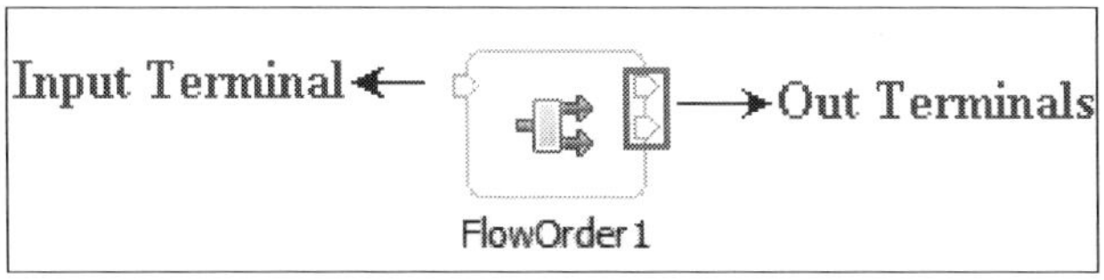

The input message is not modified by this primitive. You may make additional output terminals for each new branch of the flow. The output terminals are fired in the order that they are defined on the primitive, with each branch completing before the next starts. The only exception is in the case of an Asynchronous Service invocation. In this case, the asynchronous service is called but the Flow Order does not wait for the service invocation to complete before moving on to the next branch.

Properties

There are no detail properties or promotable properties for this primitive. Only the Description and Terminals properties are available that work similar to the other primitives.

Usage tips

If an exception is thrown by any of the downstream Mediation primitives and they do not handle it themselves (for example, through their fail terminal), any remaining flow branches are not fired.

Fan Out

This Mediation primitive is used to either broadcast a single input message into different mediations flow paths or to participate in an aggregation scenario in conjunction with the Fan In primitive. The following image provides an overview of this primitive:

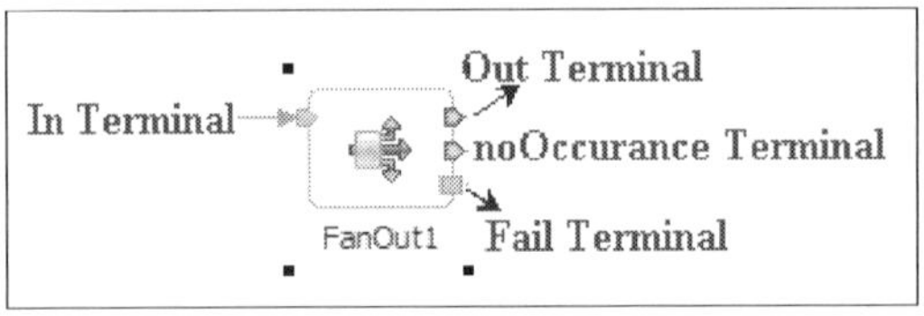

Key use

This primitive can be operated in two different modes:

1. When a single message is sent into different flow paths with changing the original input message the primitive is said to be used in the once mode. In this case, the input message is propagated only once, from the out terminal; this is the default mode.
2. If an input message is broken into different messages based on a repeating element in the input message then the primitive is said to be used in an iterative mode.

Based on these modes the mediation primitive has two key uses. First use is to either send the message once or iteratively across different mediation flow paths which is then aggregated into a single output message using the Fan In primitive. You can think of it as the start and end of a processing loop. The second use is to broadcast a single input message or once over different mediation flow paths. The repeating elements can be, for example, an array of elements.

Implementation steps

Once the Fan Out primitive has been placed on the canvas, based on the common implementation steps defined earlier you need to wire the primitive as follows:

- Wire the source to the input terminal that receives the message.
- Wire the out terminal to one or more flow paths as needed.
- Wire the **noOccurance** terminal to the flow path that should be invoked in the event that there are no instances of the repeating element in the input message. This is only used in the iterative mode.
- Wire the fail terminal to the failover mediation flow path.

The last step is to define the properties for this primitive, as will be explained in the next section.

Properties

The following screenshot is a view of the **Properties** | **Details** page:

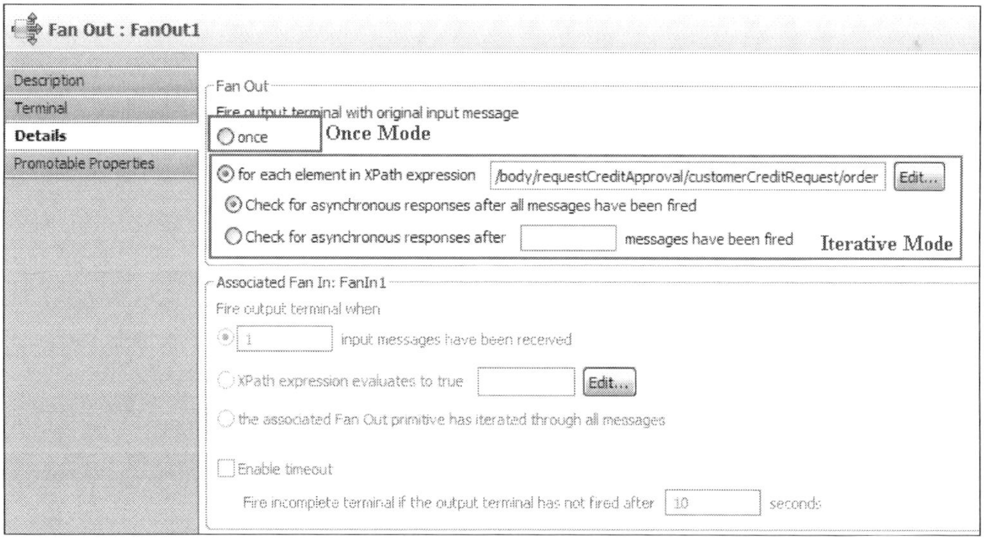

Under the **Properties | Details** tab you have the option to set the Fan Out primitive to once mode or iterative mode. If you select iterative mode then you have the option to set the condition for the iteration which is defined by an XPath expression.

In the event you are asynchronously using service invoke primitives in your mediation flow paths you can control how parallel processes may occur by defining when the asynchronous responses should be checked. This number is called the batch count and it is the only promotable property for this primitive. This batch count has no impact to the number of iterative messages that are fired through the out terminal.

For your reference the detailed properties of the associated Fan In primitive are also displayed in a read-only mode. This helps the developers to ensure that Fan Out and Fan In primitives used in an aggregation scenario complement each other.

Usage tips

Here are some usage tips that will prove useful as you work with this primitive:

- The order in which the flow paths are initiated is indeterminate, and therefore you cannot have dependencies between the flow paths based on the order of processing.
- The FanOut Context in the SMO located under **context/primtiveContext/FanOutContext**, contains the instance of the repeating element in the iterative mode. The body will always contain the original array of the repeating element.
- For the iterative mode, if the XPath expression defines an element which is not repeating then the flow will only be fired once for that element.
- Under **Properties | Details** for the iterative mode, if you select the option that is Check for asynchronous responses after all messages have been fired then the batch count is set to zero.

Fan In

This Mediation primitive is used to aggregate a message from different mediations flow paths that have been initiated by a Fan Out primitive. The following figure provides an overview of this primitive.

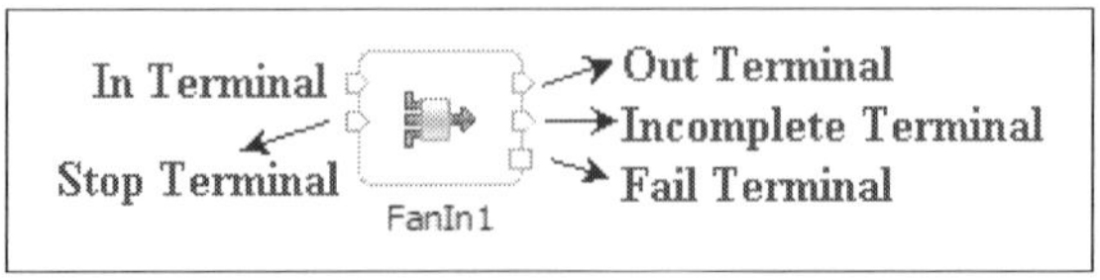

The In terminal receives the input from one or many flow paths that originate from the Fan Out primitive. The stop terminal stops the iterative flow between the Fan Out and Fan In primitive and propagates the message through the incomplete output terminal.

The out terminal propagates the message received by the primitive back to the mediation flow once the completion criteria for the Fan In has been met. The second output terminal is the incomplete terminal which as specified earlier propagates the message that is received through the stop input terminal. It is also used to handle error cases like timeouts and scenarios when the Fan Out primitive iterated through all the messages but the completion criteria on Fan In primitive has not been satisfied.

Key uses

The Fan In primitive provides the point of aggregation in the flow, bringing together multiple flow paths or serving as the endpoint of iteration within a flow. Fan Out primitives have two different modes of operation namely, iteration on and iteration off. In iteration on mode the Fan Out iterates through a repeating element that is contained in the input message. The Fan In receives an input message for each instance of the repeating element. In the iteration off mode the output terminal of the Fan Out is fired once. In this mode, there may be one or more flow paths from the out terminal of the Fan Out which join back together at the Fan In. Each flow path wired to the Fan Out primitive's out terminal is driven sequentially and the Fan In receives the result of each flow path as input.

Implementation steps

Once the Fan In primitive has been placed on the canvas based on the common implementation steps defined earlier you need to wire the primitive as follows:

- Wire the one or multiple mediation flow paths origination from the Fan In terminal to the input terminal that receives the message.
- Wire the out terminal to the target flow path.
- Wire the incomplete terminal to the flow path that should be invoked in the event that there are no instances of the repeating element in the input message. This is only used in the iterative mode.
- Wire the fail terminal to the failover mediation flow path.

The last step is to define the properties for this primitive as explained in the next section.

Properties

Here is a view of the **Properties** | **Details** page:

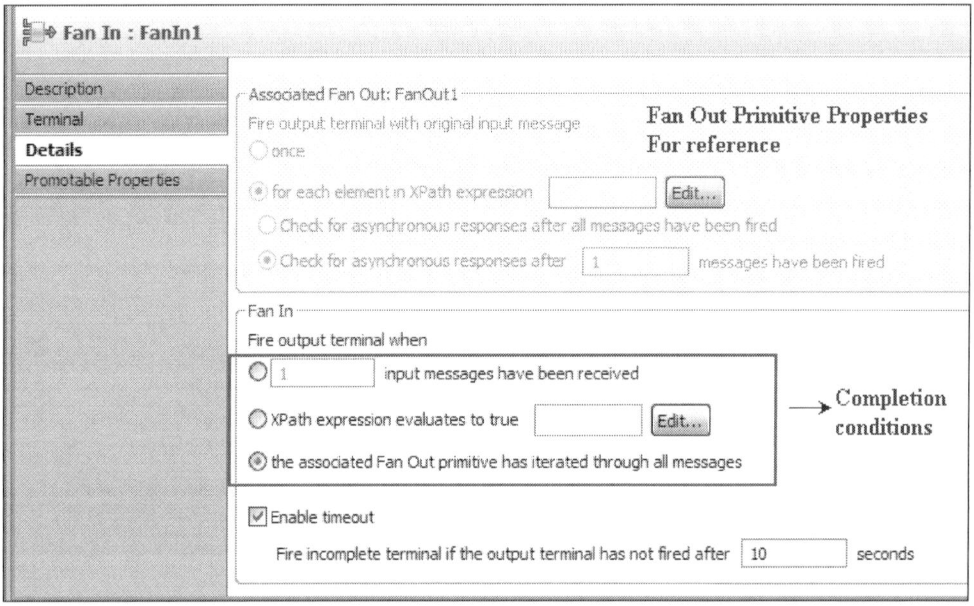

The Fan In primitive provides the following completion conditions for iterations under **Properties** | **Details**:

- Enter the number of input messages to be received before the iteration is complete
- Define an XPath condition that should evaluate to true for the iterations to complete
- Wait till all the Fan Out primitives have iterated through all the defined messages

On the details page you can also set a timeout to define the time when the message once fired from the out terminal of the Fan Out primitive should reach the in terminal of the Fan In primitive.

Usage tips

Here are some usage tips that will prove useful as you work with this primitive:

- The Fan In Mediation primitive cannot be used without the Fan Out Mediation primitive.

- The promotable properties for this primitive are the XPath expression, the count value, and the timeout value. Make sure you promote only those values that are actually being used in the primitive.
- The out terminal of the Fan In primitive is fired only when the completion criteria is met.
- It is possible for the completion criteria to be met before the last message has arrived at the fan in.
- In an iterative mode it is very important to ensure you the constructiuon of the flow between Fan Out and Fan in and the completion criteria complement your Fan In complement each other. If this is not been done correctly you can have error scenarios where the Fan In completion condition gets satisfied and Fan Out has no more messages to send. Therefore, the incomplete terminal of the Fan In is fired.
- The Async Timeout values for the Service Invoke Mediation primitives should not exceed the value of the Timeout property of the aggregation's Fan In.

Transformation primitives

So far, we have looked at Mediation primitives that impact the routing of messages. Next we shall take a closer look at some of the primitives that help transform the incoming messages.

Message element setter

This Mediation primitive gives you the ability to make changes to the message elements within the incoming message payload including add, copy, update, or delete elements. The primitive has the following terminals:

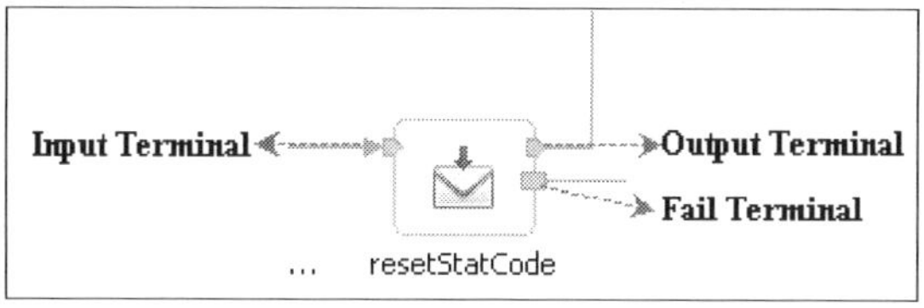

Key use

This primitive is used when there is a need to set, update, or remove message elements in the incoming payload. This can be very useful when used in conjunction with other primitives.

Properties

Select the Message Element Setter primitive and open the **Properties | Details** view page to configure this message primitive. The following screenshot is a walkthrough of the **Properties | Details** page:

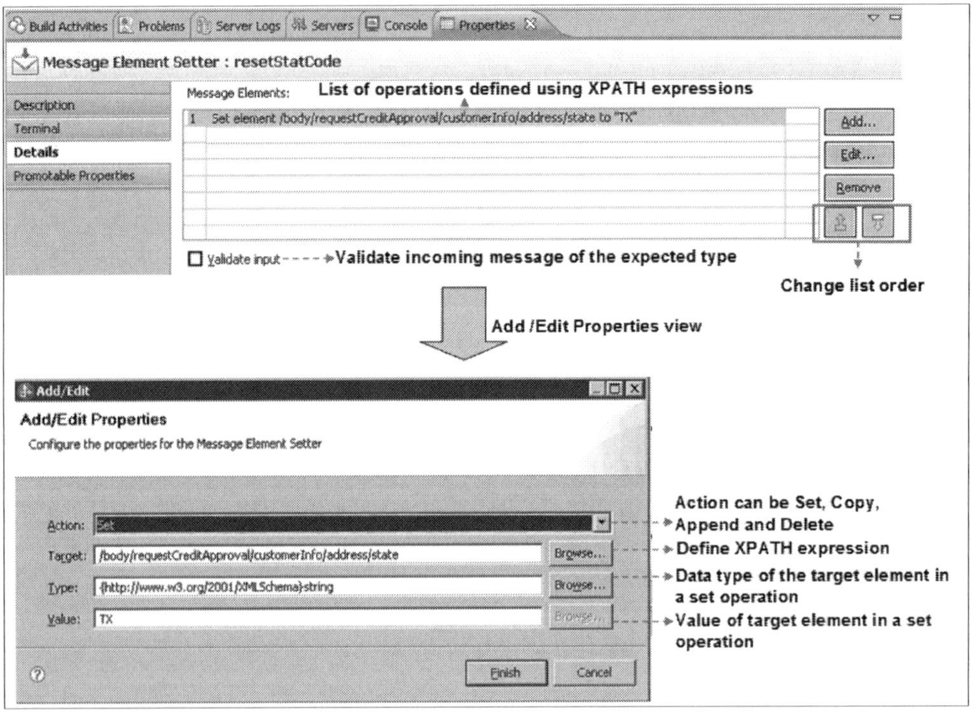

Usage tips

Here are some usage tips that will prove useful as you work with this primitive:

- The primitive cannot be used to change the message type of the incoming message.
- This primitive can be used to copy one part of the incoming SMO to another part as long as the sub trees in consideration have a matching structure.
- The operations are listed in an ordered list. The order of processing can be changed.
- The ordered list of operations is executed in an ordered sequence. It gives the ability to create operations dependent on other operations before them.
- This primitive is more efficient at runtime than XSL transformation and Business Object maps as it does the set operations in place without creating a copy of the SMO.

> A good example for using Fan In and Fan Out in an iterative aggregation scenario is `http://www.ibm.com/developerworks/webservices/library/ws-websphereesb1/`. The version of the product used in the example is 6.1 but the same concepts still apply.

Database Lookup

This Mediation primitive gives you the ability to modify a message with the data retrieved from a user-defined database at runtime. The primitive has the following terminals:

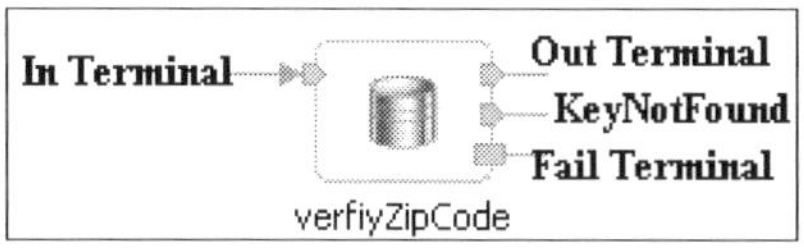

Key uses

This Mediation primitive is useful when you want to add information to a message from a database or you want to verify that the information is valid. In this example we are using this to verify that the zip code is valid.

Implementation steps

1. Drag the Database Lookup primitive from the **Palette | Transformation** primitives onto the mediation flow editor canvas.
2. Wire the source input terminal to the Database Lookup in terminal. Then wire the Database Lookup out terminal to the target partner, wire the key not found terminal to flow that you want to handle that condition with and the fail terminal to a stop or fail primitive. In the following example we have wired the key not found terminal to a Stop primitive.
3. Define the properties for the Database Lookup primitive as explained in the following example.

Example — Database Lookup primitive

Let's extend the credit management use case to update the state value from the client database if the incoming message state field is left blank. To do this you need to look up the database entries and update the state field. This can be done through a Database Lookup primitive.

Before you begin you need to have the following assets and configurations in place:

- A database that holds the client information. For our example we can create a database on DB2 using the following scripts that creates the database ClientDB on the `D:\ drive`:

```
CREATE DATABASE ClientDB AUTOMATIC STORAGE YES  ON '<Add
location>' DBPATH ON 'D:\' USING CODESET IBM-1252 TERRITORY US
COLLATE USING SYSTEM PAGESIZE 4096;
CONNECT TO CLIENTDB;
CREATE TABLE ADMINISTRATOR.CLIENTINFO ( CUSTOMER_ID CHARACTER (10)
NOT NULL , ADDRESSLINE1 CHARACTER (20) , ADDRESSLINE2 CHARACTER
(20) , CITY CHARACTER (10) , ZIPCODE CHARACTER (10) , STATE
CHARACTER (10) , COUNTRY CHARACTER (10) , FIRSTNAME CHARACTER
(10) , LASTNAME CHARACTER (10) , DATEOFBIRTH CHARACTER (10)  ,
CONSTRAINT CC1268155949316 PRIMARY KEY ( CUSTOMER_ID)  ) ;
CONNECT RESET;
```

- Configure a Data Source called jdbc/CustomerDatabase as shown in the following screenshot:

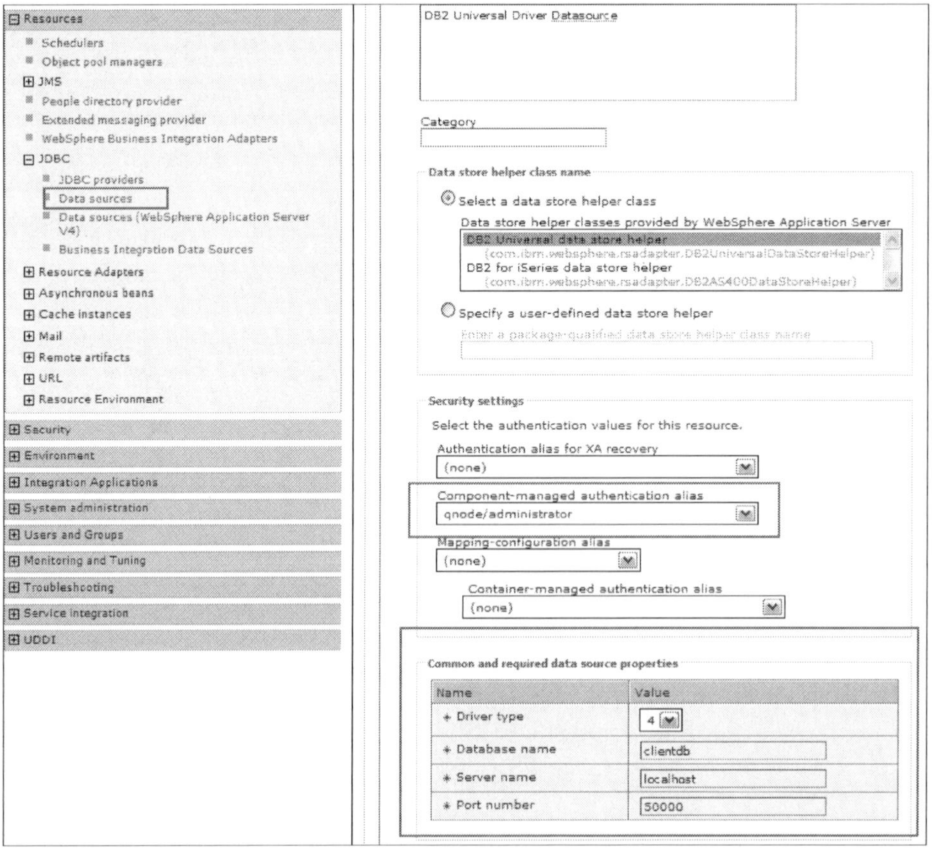

To begin implementing the extension to the credit management use case, first add another Message Filter primitive called **checkStateCode** to filter messages that have their state field empty. The filter map the XPath expression `/body/requestCreditApproval/customerCreditRequest/address/state =''` to `match1`. These filtered messages are then routed to a Database Lookup primitive called **setStateCode** to assign the state code, as shown in the following screenshot:

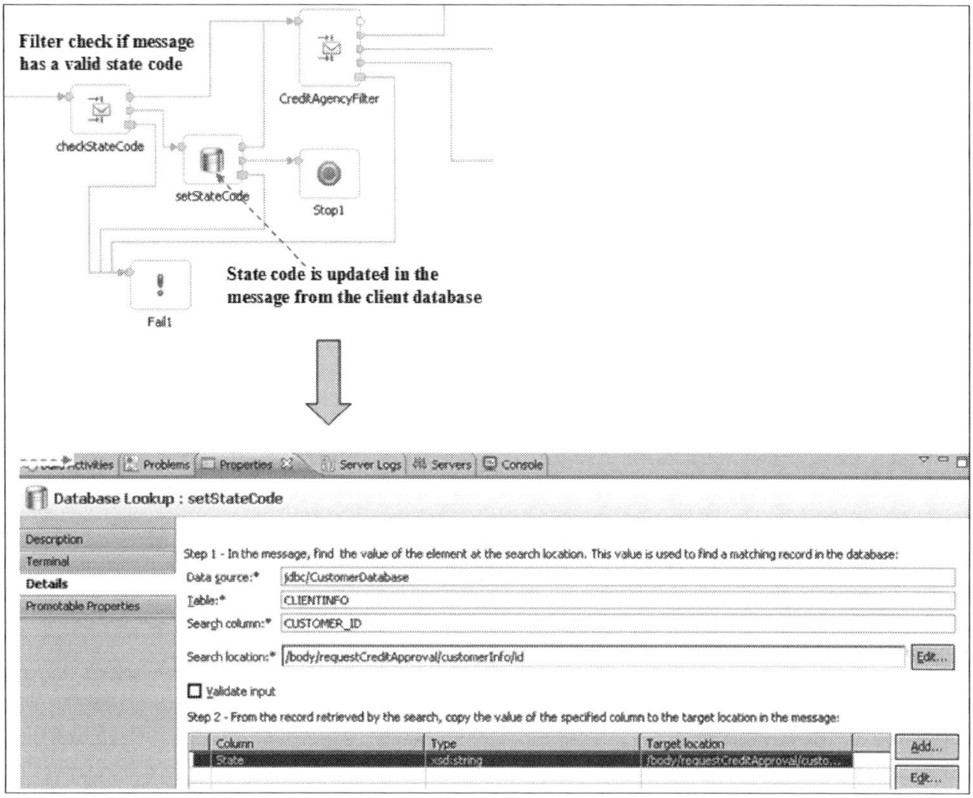

You will need to perform the following steps to configure the Database Lookup primitive:

- Configure the database by specifying the data source on the server, the complete table name with schema (schema.tablename) and the key column for the table. You will also need to identify the message field that holds the key value for that table. In this use case it is the **customer_id**. This will select the row in the database table.
- Next you will identify the column within the row whose value needs to be retrieved and the target field that will be assigned the value. Ensure that the data type is the same for both of these fields.

This will complete the configuration and deployment of the Database Lookup primitive.

Custom Mediation

This primitive gives you the ability to implement your own custom mediation logic that may not be available through the in-built primitives. This logic is implemented using Java through a Visual Snippet editor or Java Snippet editor. You are also given access to complete SMO objects including header information. Therefore you have complete flexibility to implement any mediation logic as needed. The primitive has the following terminals:

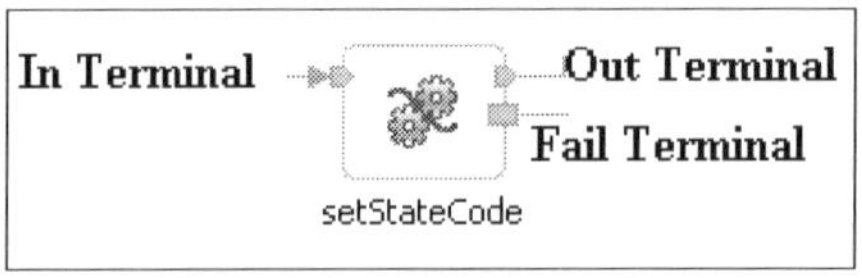

Key use

This primitive is useful if there is a limitation in the available primitives. You can then build your own custom logic in Java in one of the provided editors.

Example — Custom Mediation

We will now implement the use case for the Database Lookup primitive example using the Custom Mediation primitive. From the previous Database Lookup example replace the **Database Lookup** primitive with a **Custom Mediation** primitive and reconnect the wiring shown as follows:

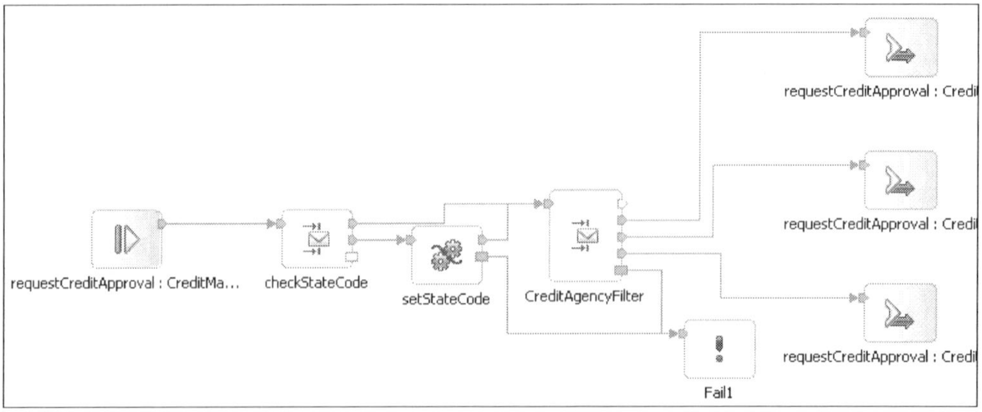

Open the **Properties** | **Details** page to configure this primitive:

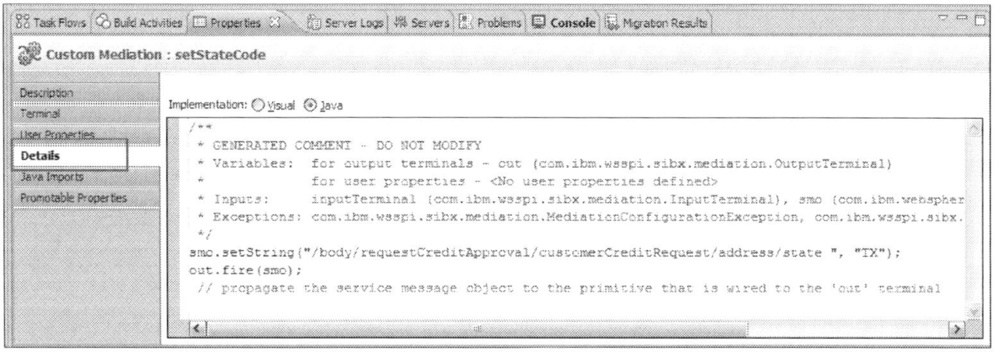

On top there are two options, **Visual** and **Java.** For this example select the **Java** option and add the following code:

```
smo.setString("/body/requestCreditApproval/customerCreditRequest/
address/state ", "TX");
out.fire(smo);
```

In this example, the **Message Filter** primitive **checkStateCode** only routes those messages that do not have the state value already set in them. The **Custom Mediation** primitive **setStateCode** then sets the state value in the SMO to TX through the Java code. In this way the **Database Lookup** primitive capability from the previous example can be simulated, though all state codes will be set hardcoded to TX instead of using the customer ID to get the actual state code for the customer.

In all our examples so far we have only worked with the three states: NY, TX, and CA. What if we need to add another state, say Washington? Also what if the Washington Credit Rating Agency uses a different interface than what we have currently been using?

Let's look at the next Mediation primitive—XSL Transformation primitive—to answer that question.

Usage tips

Here are some usage tips that will prove useful as you work with this primitive:

- You can have more than one input or output terminals with this primitive as needed by the mediation logic
- If you switch between the Visual snippet and the Java Snippet editor, you will lose the work done in the existing snippet editor

XSL Transformation primitive

This primitive gives you the ability to transform data to make it compatible with the receiving or target service. The XSL Transformation primitive, as the name suggests, uses extensible style sheet language transformations for transforming one XML document into another XML document through an XML map. In WebSphere Integration Developer this is done through an XML Map editor. The primitive has the following terminals:

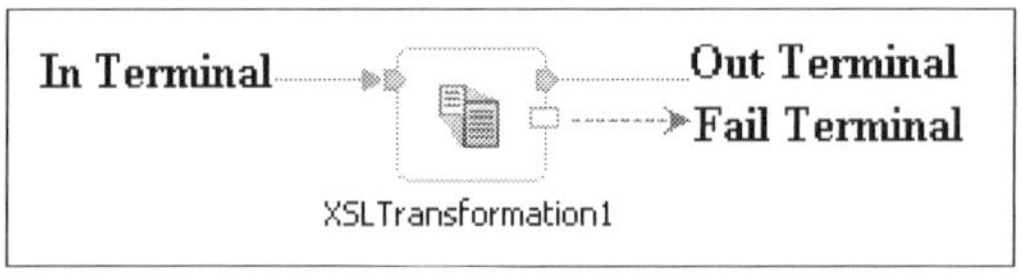

Key use

XSL Transformation primitive is useful to transform the input message to make it compatible with different output message formats. This primitive is also useful if you need to manipulate the message body.

Example — XSL Transformation primitive

We will learn about the implementation and properties of the XSL Transformation primitive through an example. Here we will create a new module to represent the Washington Credit Agency that accepts an input, which has a different schema than the input message **customerCreditRequest**. The first step is to define the Washington Credit Agency as a module.

Create a new interface in the **CH6Library** *under* **com/junglesea/ch6/mediations/interfaces** for the Washington Credit Rating Agency called **WashingtonCreditAgencyService** and configure it as shown in the following screenshot:

Now create a new module called **WashingtonCreditAgency** associated with **CH6Library**. Implement a Java component called **WashingtonCreditAgency** in the assembly diagram that refers to the **WashingtonCreditAgencyService** interface.

Replace the `requestCreditApproval` function with the following:

```
  public DataObject requestCreditApproval(String customerInfo) {
    ServiceManager serviceManager = ServiceManager.INSTANCE;
    BOFactory boFactory = (BOFactory)serviceManager.
locateService("com/ibm/websphere/bo/BOFactory");
    DataObject customerCreditApproval = boFactory.create("http://Ch6Li
brary","CustomerCreditApproval");
    customerCreditApproval.setString("id",customerInfo);
    customerCreditApproval.setString("approvalStatus","Approved");
    customerCreditApproval.setString("approvalCode","0000");
    customerCreditApproval.setString("approvalDescription","Credit has
been approved");
    customerCreditApproval.setString("creditScore","740");
    customerCreditApproval.setString("ratingAgency","Washington Rating
Agency");
    return customerCreditApproval;
  }
```

You may need to add and import the package com.ibm.websphere.bo. Export this component with an SCA export called **WashingtonCreditAgencyExport** as shown below:

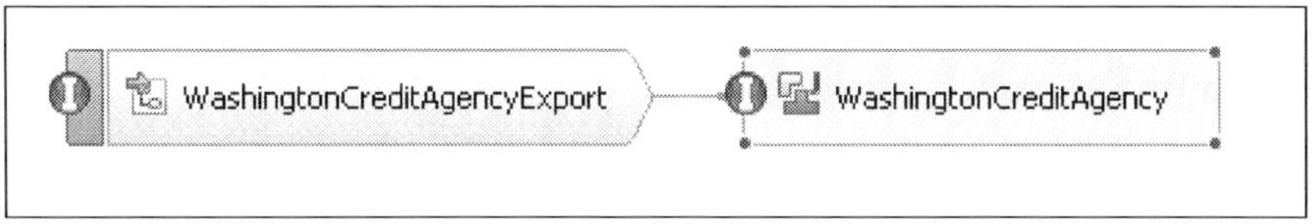

This completes the Washington Credit Agency. Our next step is to add this to an existing example from the Message Filter primitive.

1. Go to **Ch6** module, select **Assembly Diagram** and add the **WashingtonCreditAgencyExport** as an import with SCA binding called **WashingtonCreditAgency**, as shown in the following screenshot:

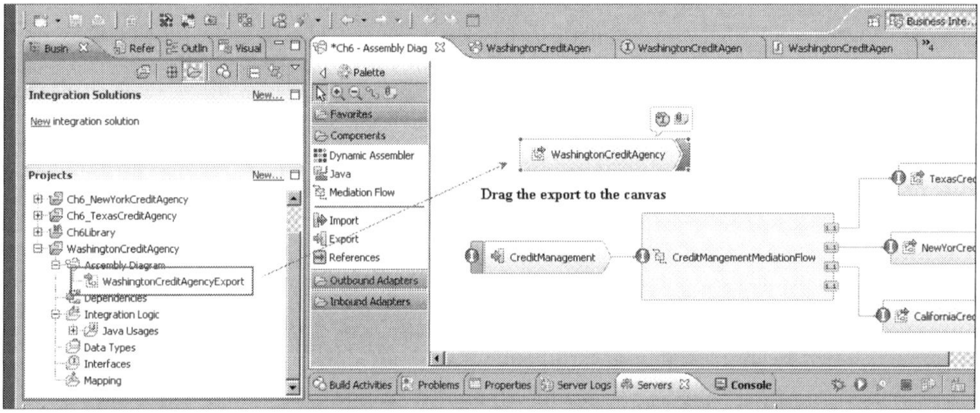

2. Wire existing **CreditMangementMediationFlow** to **the WashingtonCreditAgency** import.
3. Double-click on **CreditMangementMediationFlow** to open the mediation flow.
4. Open the **Overview** tab.
5. Click on the **Add Reference** icon and select **WashingtonCreditAgencyService**.

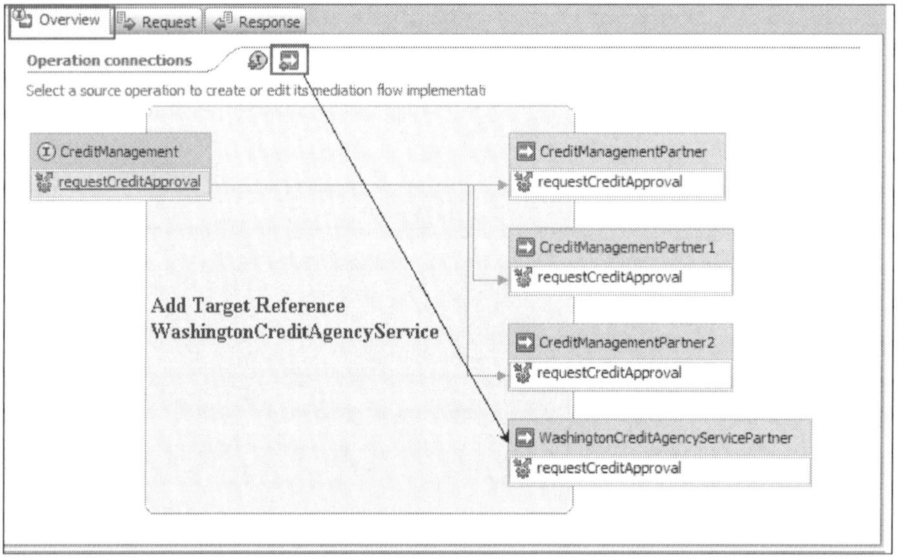

6. Click on the **Request** tab next to the **Overview** tab.
7. Add a callout that references **WashingtonCreditAgencyServicePartner.**
8. Add another output terminal to the **CreditAgencyFilter** primitive and then match it to the following filter:
    - /body/requestCreditApproval/customerCreditRequest/address/state = 'WA'
9. Wire **CreditAgencyFilter** primitive to the **WashingtonCreditAgencyServicePartner** callout.

    The mediation flow editor detects incompatibility in the message formats and pops up a dialog stating **Incompatible Message Types,** as shown in the following screenshot:

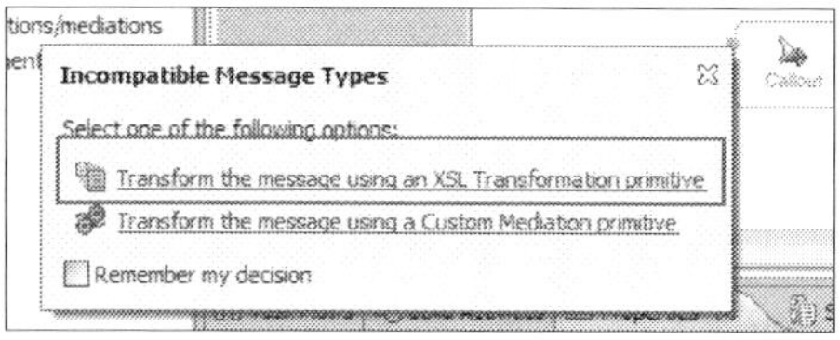

10. Select **Transform the message using an XSL Transformation primitive**.
11. Rename the autogenerated XSL Transformation primitive to **setCustomerInfo.**
12. Save all your changes.
13. Double-click and open the **setCustomerInfo** to bring up the **New XML Map** wizard.
14. Keep the defaults and select **Finish.** This will open the XSL transform map.
15. Expand the left side **requestCreditApproval | customerCreditRequest**.
16. Wire **id** within the **customerCreditRequest** string to the **customerInfo** string within **requestCreditApproval** on the right side, as shown next:

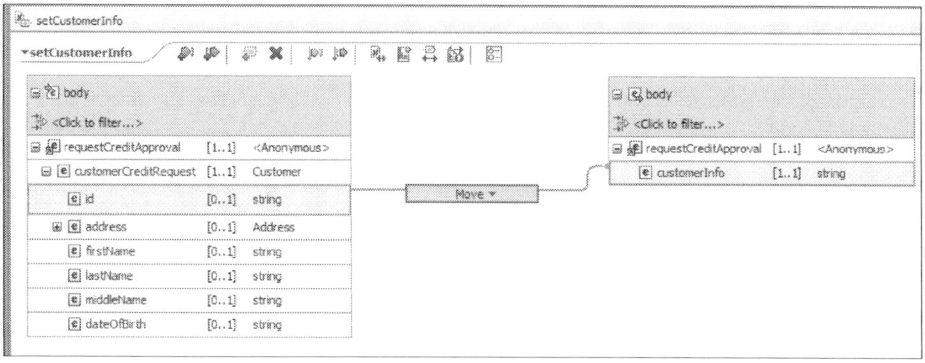

This XSL map will convert the **CreditManagement** input request to the **WashingtonCreditAgencyService** input request. You will need to create an XSL map for the response flow to complete the mediation flow. We recommend that you use the icon to **Map source and target based on name and types** icon from the toolbar on the XSL map to establish the mapping as shown in the following screenshot:

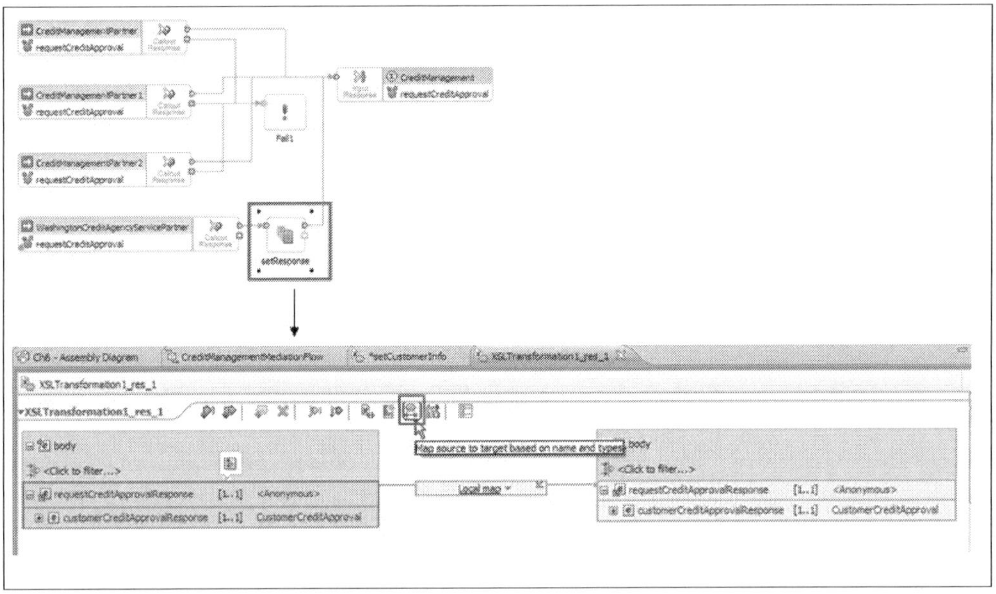

We recommend following the steps described earlier under the Message Filter primitive example to test and execute this example.

Usage tips

Here are some usage tips that will prove useful as you work with this primitive:

- More examples for using XML map editor are available at: `http://publib.boulder.ibm.com/infocenter/dmndhelp/v6r2mx/topic/com.ibm.wbit.620.help.bo.ui.doc/topics/cxmltips.html`
- You can reuse XSL transformation maps

Tracing primitives

The next set of primitives we shall look at are primitives that help in problem determination.

Message Logger

A Message Logger Mediation primitive logs an XML-converted copy of the service message object (SMO) passing through the mediation flow into a relational database or to custom logging medium as defined. By default, this database is defined in the Cloudscape database within the WebSphere ESB Server, but it can be configured to use other relational databases like DB2. The primitive has the following terminals:

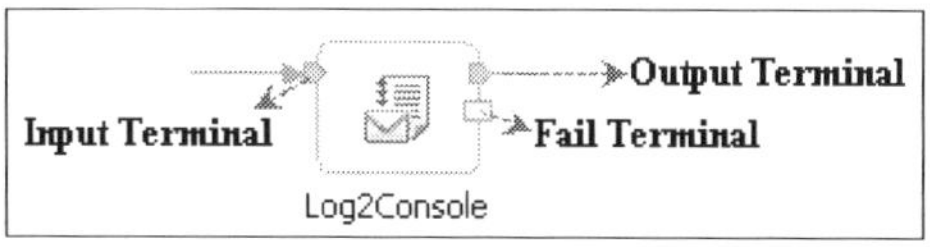

Key use

This primitive is useful for logging, auditing, and debugging purposes to provide more insight into the messages being processed within the process flow.

Implementation steps

Define the properties for the Message Logger primitive. There are two logging types provided by the **Message Logger** primitive:

1. **Database** logging is used to log to a relational database identified by the **data source name.**
2. **Custom** logging is based on the J2SE Java logging APIs which make use of a handler, formatter, and filter.

We will use the example provided later on to help us understand the property configurations and options available.

Usage tips

Here are some usage tips that will prove useful as you work with this primitive:

- You have the flexibility to store the complete or part of the SMO based on the XPath expression defined. The default value is the message payload (/body).
- You have the option to define your own database using the scripts defined under the <WPS_HOME>/util/ESBLoggerMediation/database_type/table.ddl.
- Message Logger uses only one input terminal, one output terminal, and one fail terminal. Furthermore, the source and target partners must have the same message type.

For more information on using the handler, filter, and formatter implementation classes please see: `http://java.sun.com/j2se/1.4.2/docs/api/java/util/logging`.

Example — Message Logger primitive

Add a Message Logger primitive called Log2Console to log incoming messages to the system console of the XSL transformation primitive example we just implemented, as shown in the next screenshot:

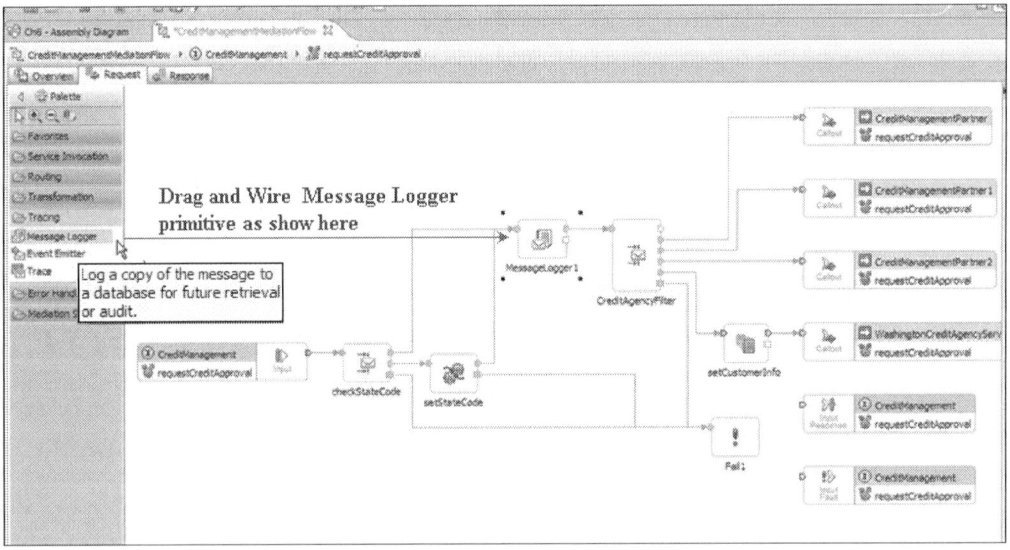

The various configuration options under the **Properties** | **Details** view is shown in the following screenshot:

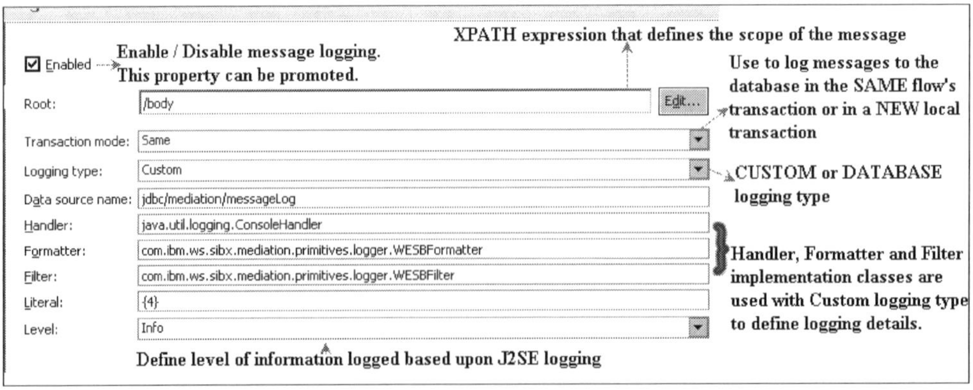

The preceding example used a Custom logging type with a `Java.util.logging.ConsoleHandler` java handler to log messages to the system console, as shown next:

```
[3/11/10 0:42:05:718 CST] 0000009b SystemErr     R 3/11/10 12:42
AM,4BF564F7-0127-4000-E000-1EF0C0A80167,Log2Console,Ch6,<?xml
version="1.0" encoding="UTF-8"?>
<body xsi:type="ma:requestCreditApprovalRequestMsg" xmlns:xsi="http://
www.w3.org/2001/XMLSchema-instance" xmlns:ma="wsdl.http://
Ch6Library/com/junglesea/ch6/mediations/interfaces/CreditManagement"
xmlns:ma_1="http://Ch6Library/com/junglesea/ch6/mediations/interfaces/
CreditManagement">
  <ma_1:requestCreditApproval>
    <customerCreditRequest>
      <id></id>
      <address>
        <addressLine1>Street Car</addressLine1>
        <addressLine2></addressLine2>
        <city>Austin</city>
        <zipCode>78722</zipCode>
        <state>CA</state>
        <country>USA</country>
      </address>
      <firstName>Joe</firstName>
      <lastName>Doe</lastName>
      <middleName></middleName>
      <dateOfBirth>01/01/01</dateOfBirth>
    </customerCreditRequest>
  </ma_1:requestCreditApproval>
</body>
```

Next we will look at the Fail and Stop primitives that are wired to the Fail terminal of other primitives to help handle errors within the mediation flow.

Error Handling — Stop/Fail

These primitives are used in conjunction with other Mediation primitives to handle errors. They propagate the incoming messages and the error messages to the process flow. The Stop primitive is used to terminate the current path in the event of an error. This primitive does not raise an exception or generate any message. The Fail primitive is used to raise an exception and terminate the mediation flow. The Stop and Fail primitives both have an input terminal, but no output or fail terminals.

Key use

These primitives should be used to efficiently handle errors in a predictive and controlled manner with the least impact to your overall process flow.

Implementation steps

The Fail and Stop primitives are wired to the Fail terminal of other primitives to help handle errors within the mediation flow. In the case of the Stop primitive, it can also be wired to an output terminal if you want the flow to terminate at that point.

In the following example, the process flow will be terminated if the zip code is not found in the database. However, if there is a failure in the database invocation, then that is handled by the Fail primitive.

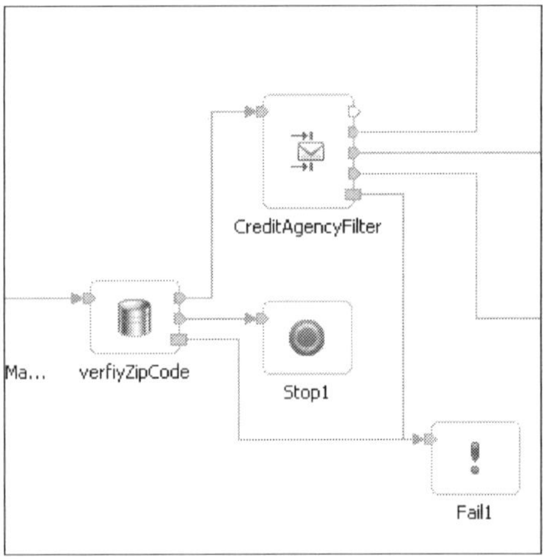

Usage tips

For the Stop primitive, if there are multiple active paths beyond the current path, they would still continue to execute whereas a FAIL primitive will cause all the active paths to fail.

Dynamic routing

Dynamic routing is where the mediation flow itself is dynamic, but all possible endpoints are predefined statically in the module or from an external source at runtime. Dynamic endpoint selection is where the WESB runtime can route messages to an endpoint address identified by a message header element. Based on inspecting the incoming SMO for business data, using a message filter primitive, the message header element can be updated by Mediation primitives in a mediation flow. With these approaches you can change service endpoints (credit providers) without the need to update and redeploy the mediation flow and any business processes that may use the mediation flow exports.

You can configure your mediation flow component to route messages to endpoints that are determined dynamically at runtime. There are basically three ways in which you can achieve dynamic routing and endpoint selection:

- Selecting endpoints using the registry lookup
- Selecting endpoints using a database
- Dynamic routing using dynamic endpoint property

An endpoint in a mediation module can be selected either statically by using an import's binding or dynamically by using an endpoint address identified by a target address element in the message header. This endpoint address can be added to the target address element in the message header by Mediation primitives within a mediation flow. The endpoint address could be updated with information from a registry, a database, or with information from the message itself.

In order for the runtime to implement dynamic routing on a request, the Use dynamic endpoint property of the callout node must be set. When this property is set, the callout will route the message using the endpoint address in the element `/headers/SMOHeader/Target/address` of the message. If there is no endpoint address information in the message header, then a service will be selected statically, if an import is wired to the associated reference of the callout in the mediation flow component. By default, the Use dynamic endpoint property is set, and therefore dynamic routing is enabled. For a summary of this behavior, see the description of the Callout node.

Dynamic endpoint support does not require you to wire a reference to an import. However, if you want to provide default configuration settings for the dynamic endpoint, you can use a wired import. After a reference is wired to an import, the configuration settings of the import apply to all dynamic endpoints using that reference. For example, if you want to influence whether a service is called synchronously or asynchronously, from the callout or Service Invoke primitive, you can specify the Preferred interaction style on the import and wire the reference to this import. Similarly, you can configure the security settings for a web service dynamic endpoint by using a wired import with web service binding.

What is the need for dynamic routing or endpoint selection?

So far, we have seen examples where we route messages in various ways using endpoints defined at integration time. But we also discussed the Endpoint Lookup primitive in Chapter 3. So with WESB you can route messages to endpoints determined, dynamically, at runtime. So why do we need this?

JungleSea deals with many suppliers and partners who want to sell their products using our platform. Depending on the state from which the supplier and partner are based on, the value or quantity of the products that they want to sell, and the size of their company, the credit approval process will be different. Also the type of credit rating agency that will have to be used for verification will depend upon the these factors. Moreover, JungleSea constantly evaluates many credit rating providers and would want to try them out if they turn out to be cost effective. So if such a situation should arise, we don't want to be changing our business processes every single time we adapt to a new credit rating provider based on business factors. So we want to dynamically be able to select the right credit rating provider and invoke their credit approval services. This pattern is commonly referred to as "late binding", which makes the business processes that depend on credit rating susceptible to any changes made by a business to add or retire credit rating providers.

Integration with external systems using adapters

No discussion about mediations fundamentals is complete without talking about Adapters. Let's take closer look at what these are.

What are adapters?

We have, on numerous instances, explained about web services. In a raw sense web services can be treated as adapters. Let's suppose you want to expose a capability or capabilities out of an application such that there is an access point mechanism through which the particular capability can be programmatically invoked. This access point is the adapter. The adapter provides you with not just connectivity to the end application but also with connectivity to access data and perform protocol transformation and any other capabilities including, and not limited to, connection setup and tear down, marshalling and unmarshalling of data, exception handling and so on. The adapter is also referred to as a connector.

Connectors typically tend to enable synchronous connections to applications. Unlike connectors, adapters combine both the target application interface plumbing and also any transport-related functions.

How different are the adapters when compared to mediation flows?

Adapters help you to connect to the backend application. Think of it as a pattern. It not only provides an access point to the end application, but one that can also handle transport or a messaging Business Integration. However, it very rarely has any business functionality within it. What you build using mediation flows are in essence an adapter pattern realization. Mediation flows allow you to define message flows, routing logic and so on, and also invoke the end applications either through an adapter or a web service. Alternatively, you could also invoke the end application's atomic APIs (Custom Primitive), wrap them with a mediation flow, and expose the mediation flow as a service itself.

What are these WebSphere Adapters?

WebSphere Adapters (also referred to as Resource Adapters) enable bidirectional connectivity between end application and various SCA components in WPS/WESB. WebSphere Adapters are compliant with J2EE Connector Architecture (JCA 1.5). WebSphere adapters support outbound and inbound processing for WPS and WESB. **Outbound** processing refers to cases wherein the request data flows from a process or a flow to the end application. In this case, the adapter acts as the connector between the application component and the end application. **Inbound** event processing refers to cases where something starts happening because of an event happening within the end application. In inbound event processing the adapter converts events generated from the end application into business objects and sends the business object to the client application, which could be a process or a flow or a message queue.

There are two types of WebSphere adapters:

- Application
  - These connect to popular packaged applications such as SAP, Siebel, PeopleSoft, JD Edwards and so on
- Technology
  - These provide connectivity to applications and systems that expose their capabilities through such technologies and protocols as relational databases, flat files, email messages, FTP, and so on

WID is the tooling environment for the WebSphere adapters and the runtime environment is WPS or WESB.

What types of adapter come "out-of-the-box" with WPS/WESB?

The following adapters are provided along with the WID installation. You will be able to find it in the assembly diagram under the Palette categorized as Outbound Adapters and Inbound Adapters. You would also find other Application Adapters:

- IBM WebSphere adapter for CICS
- IBM WebSphere adapter for IMS
- IBM WebSphere adapter for iSeries
- IBM WebSphere adapter for JD Edwards EnterpriseOne
- IBM WebSphere adapter for Oracle E-Business Suite
- IBM WebSphere adapter for Siebel Business Applications
- IBM WebSphere adapter for SAP Software
- IBM WebSphere adapter for PeopleSoft
- IBM WebSphere adapter for Siebel
- IBM WebSphere adapter for JDBC
- IBM WebSphere adapter for Email
- IBM WebSphere adapter for Flat Files
- IBM WebSphere adapter for FTP

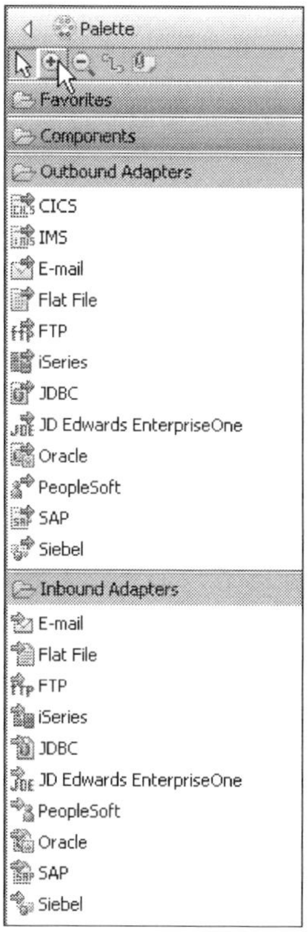

The IBM WebSphere adapter Toolkit provides the development tools, libraries, and sample code to assist you in creating your own JCA resource adapters. Let's leave it at this level.

Summary

This chapter covered an in-depth study of mediation flows, Mediation primitives, and adapters. It walked us through the various aspects and concepts about Mediation primitives and Service Message Objects that are absolutely fundamental and essential. With the help of numerous examples, this chapter described the commonly-used Mediation primitives, which included Message Logger, Message Filter, XSL Transformations, Fan In, and Fan Out. The other topics that this chapter touched upon were Adapters and Dynamic routing. With this information you should now be able to select the right tool (component) from the toolbox when building applications for WESB.

7

Sales Fulfillment Application for JungleSea Inc.

JungleSea has decided to re-engineer their Sales Fulfillment Application. In this chapter, we will first analyze the business requirements and rationalize our thoughts to see if an SOA approach is the right way. Then we will create an SOA-based architecture by:

- Identifying use cases (and scenarios)
- Identifying business processes, variability points, top-down, bottom-up, goal-oriented decomposition to identify the right services
- Identifying external and internal applications to integrate with and services/components
- Laying out the various principles and patterns we will adopt
- Finally, identifying the appropriate WPS and WESB components that will have to be built

By the end of this chapter, the goal is to be ready to walk the talk and be all set for building the various parts of the application that make up the whole.

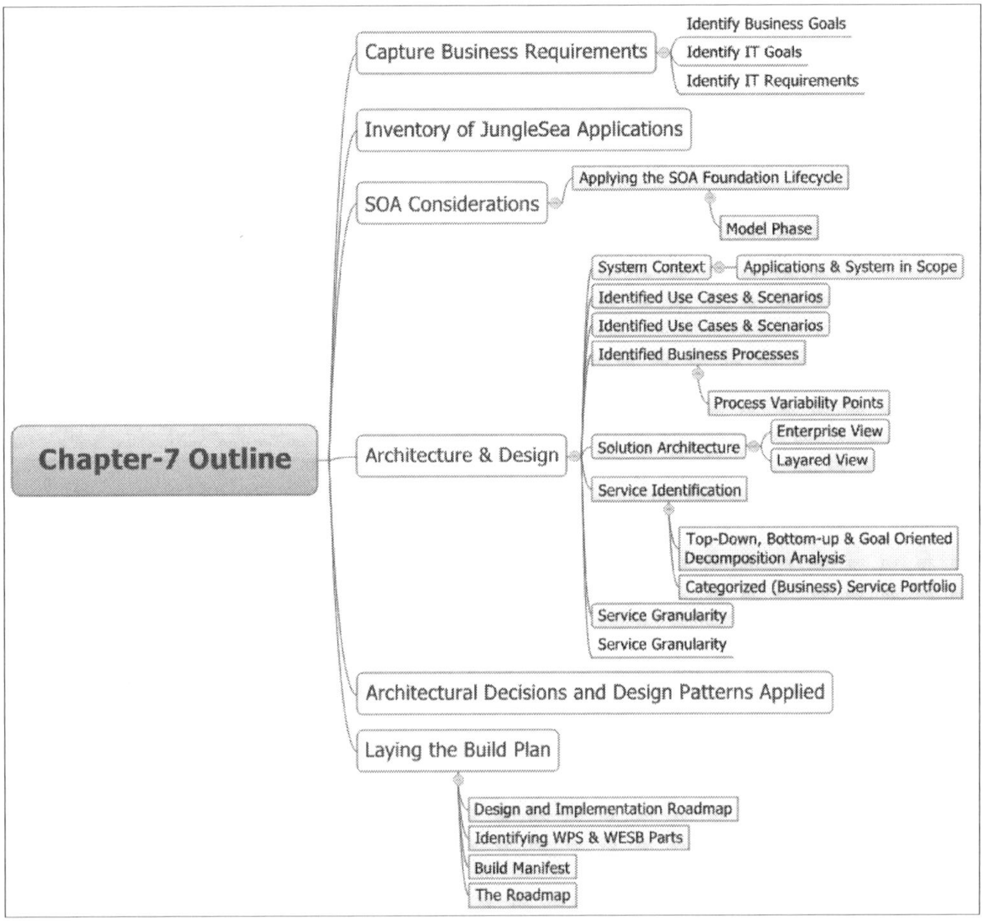

Business requirements

JungleSea Inc. allows its customers to find and discover anything they might want to buy online. Its objective is to bring in as many suppliers and partners as possible into their ecosystem so that they can offer a wide range of products for customers to buy at the lowest possible prices. However, their current IT infrastructure is not agile or responding to the changing needs of their business. Years of stovepipe application development (stovepipe systems so tightly bound together that the individual elements cannot be differentiated, upgraded, or refactored) has created a proliferation of enterprise and regional applications, with little thought given to an integrated enterprise. Some of the shortcomings include:

- Poorly documented sales and order fulfillment business process
- Lack of visibility into the end-to-end sales fulfillment business
- Multiple inventory systems to deal with and more to come in the future
- Customer and order management systems not integrated in real time. As a result, there is manual copying of data (and some ETL (Extract-Transform-Load) batch processes) across systems and fat fingering of data resulting in errors
- Lack of sales order visibility
- Rigid backend systems, with nonstandardized interfaces
- No reuse of any sort
- High costs to maintain and make any changes

Business goals

As a first step, JungleSea Inc.'s business wants to re-engineer its Sales Fulfillment Application such that it becomes more agile and faster responding to its changing needs for bringing more suppliers and partners into its IT ecosystem. For the first phase of the project, the goal would be to improve its telephone (ordering via phone) sales and order fulfillment performance by systematically gathering and processing order data and then driving the fulfillment activities. The business has also understood that automating its existing manual processes will deliver strong tactical and strategic value. In short, JungleSea would like to align its IT resources with their key business priorities, while increasing IT infrastructure flexibility. Some of the key business requirements set forth by the business for the newly re-engineered Sales Fulfillment Application include:

- Accelerate time to market
    - Changing business requirements can be rapidly supported
    - Ability to offer new products quickly
    - Standardized business processes for order fulfillment
- Increase revenue
    - Enabling telesales order fulfillment
    - Ability to scale while streamlining of multi-channel process invocation
    - The process is always executed no matter from where the process is requested. Requests could be triggered from an internal website, from the Internet, or from a company employee meeting a customer face-to-face in an office.

- Ease of use
- Enable seamless order entry through customer data and order data integration
- Action to insight
    - Automatic interaction with people and requesting the right people
    - Notification and escalation (order status, jeopardy, management, workforce, IT)
    - Automated routing of work depending on the business factors (order priority, customer type, region, and so on)
    - Unified access to process-relevant data
    - Business process monitoring and insight into business process execution
    - Ability to handle exception notification and act on them intelligently
- Reduce costs
    - Reduce development costs through reuse and building functionality that makes meaningful sense to the business
    - Reducing system maintenance costs

IT goals

Some of the goals set forth by the IT department while building the Sales Fulfillment Application include:

- Ability to integrate the different backend applications. Connect the various applications within JungleSea—whether they are legacy, package, custom, or external systems—to make the right data available to all of the other layers of the architecture.
- Systems, users, and multi-channels seamlessly integrated to reduce maintenance costs and provide any-to-any linkages.
- Abstraction layer to hide the complexities of interacting with different systems.
- "Abstract" the business process logic from the software application logic.
- Ability to measure business performance down to the task level in the order fulfillment processes through established Key Performance Indicators (KPIs).

- Avoid duplication by identifying SOA services and promoting reuse.
- Ability to cater to various non-functional requirements including security, scalability, reliability, and so on.

IT requirements

Some of the IT requirements set forth by JungleSea Inc.'s enterprise architecture for the new system include:

- The solution will implement SOA regarding the execution of necessary solution integration.
- Establish an "Integration Layer", whose architecture will simplify and speed up all aspects of integration of data and applications as well as to gain flexibility when implementing new systems and services and/or when changing related business processes.
- Proposed Integration Architecture shall employ industry standards, specifications, and proven technologies.
- The Integration Layer should consist of "Business Process Management (BPM)" and "Enterprise Service Bus (ESB)" layers.
- Point-to-point integration between applications should be avoided whenever possible.
- Reuse existing application interfaces as much as possible.
- Identify business-level services and reuse them across the enterprise.
- Business services shall be orchestrated to support end-to-end business processes.
- Service consumers and providers shall communicate through messaging and ESB shall be the messaging backbone.
- ESB shall provide the connectivity, application adapters, routing of messages based on rules, and data transformation engine.
- Use of a Canonical Data Model to be used by business services and business processes.
- Integration Layer to transform from source system format to the Canonical Data Model and from the Canonical Data Model to the target system's format.
- Ability to expose the business processes and business services in multiple protocols (SOAP, XML/HTTP, XML/SOAP over HTTP and/or JMS, Java Message Service (JMS), MQ Series).

Finally, the business and IT departments have jointly decided that IBM's WebSphere Process Server platform (that also includes the WebSphere Enterprise Service Bus) would be the software platform on which the new application would be built.

Existing JungleSea Inc. applications

Having understood the goals and objective, you may ask: I get what we are trying to do here. But what are we up against? What are the existing applications that we will have to deal with and integrate to be able to build this new Sales Fulfillment Application?

To start answering all your questions, first let's list down all the applications (and a brief description) in JungleSea that we will have to deal with for the purpose of building this application. All these applications will form our landscape and will support the application/system requirements for the Sales Fulfillment Application's phase 1 release. Let us organize and categorize the applications based on their business function and capability, hence providing a common frame of reference. By using a common mapping layout and nomenclature, the current and future landscape would be much easier for Junglesea Inc. to understand, both the situation and in describing their current and future needs and intentions. Under each category, there can be one or many physical systems that provide the same capability.

> For the purposes of this book, we are not trying to build the applications that are going to be listed below. These applications, which we assume will exist (again for the purposes of this book), expose capabilities via different methods—EJB's, WebServices, JDBC, and so on. What we want you to understand is, for this book, you can leverage these existing applications, enable the capabilities and functions provided by them as a standardized SOA service, and use these SOA services in the larger context of solution architecture. Again, for the purpose of this book, we will simulate these applications and assume they exist for us.

Customer Information Management

Customer Information Management is an application that allows creation, update, lookup/search, and view of the customer information. Customer information includes, but is not limited to the following:

- Customer name
- Contact persons for this customer
- Customer addresses (residence, shipping, billing, and so on)
- Customer contact phone numbers (home, mobile, fax, and so on)

- Customer organizational hierarchy (relevant for household, business, and corporate customers)
- Customer's existing products/services (linked to Customer Order Management)
- Customer's billing accounts (linked to Billing Account Management)
- Customer's current and past orders (linked to Customer Order Management)

Currently, there is a system named "Green" that provides this capability in JungleSea.

Order Entry

An order entry application allows a customer service representative or a customer to interact with the Sales Fulfillment Application and has the ability to enter and configure orders. We will not be building an order entry UI application for the purpose of this book.

Product Catalog Management

A product catalog provides the ability to create, organize, and maintain products that can be sold to customers in the target market. It provides customers with access to descriptions of the products that you want them to buy. Typical product information may contain the following:

- Products offered
- Product hierarchy
- Product/Customer profile mapping (which type of customers can buy what)
- Availability rules
- Product validity period
- One-time charges (including shipping charges)
- Recurring charges
- Discount information
- Product cost

There is currently a system named "PCS" that provides this capability in JungleSea.

Customer Billing Management

The name says it all. This application is responsible for billing a customer, producing timely and accurate invoices on a variety of media and formats, and also managing changes (change of address) to a billing account to ensure accurate billing. One other key responsibility of this application is to automate and manage the processing of financial transactions affecting the customer's financial account and to provide the capability to view a customer billing account and the financial information to answer a query on a bill.

Currently, a system named "**PayMe**" provides this capability in JungleSea.

Order Management

Order Management applications manage the end-to-end lifecycle of a customer request for products. This includes order establishment (step guiding, data collection, and validation), and order publication as well as order orchestration and overall lifecycle management. The Order Management application also handles order requests to cancel and change existing ordered products. The Order Management applications typically serve all the customer touch points/channels, including call center, retail, self-service, dealers, affiliates, and so on. The order may be initiated by any channel and visible to the other channels if needed. Customer Order Management applications provide the following key functionality:

- Order Establishment
- Order Publication
- Order Orchestration
- Order Lifecycle Management
- Order Status Notification

Though an application exists in JungleSea currently, this will be a spanking brand new application that will be implemented, leveraging the capabilities of WPS especially.

Shipping Management

This application is responsible for shipping a particular order to customer-provided shipping addresses, once the order is fulfilled. Some of the key capabilities provided by this application include:

- Validate and clean shipping addresses
- Ability to print shipping labels
- Generate tracking numbers for shipments
- Calculate and provide shipping rates
- Shipping status information based on tracking number

JungleSea uses two partners, "**Fast**" and "**Rapid**", whose application provides capabilities for Logistics and Shipping management. However, they expose their key capabilities to JungleSea to achieve the above-mentioned capabilities.

Inventory Management

The Inventory System provides real-time management and maintenance of the inventory information for items in JungleSea Inc.'s product catalog. Inventory management applications manage information of all the inventory items used to implement products. Key capabilities provided by this application include:

- Inventory information retrieval
    - Provides information about currently-available items in warehouse and their status
    - Provides information about where the items are available
- Inventory update
    - Updates status of the items in the warehouse

Currently there are two systems named "**Alpha**" and "**Beta**" that provide this capability in JungleSea. Alpha supports JungleSea Inc.'s residential or non-commercial customers, while Beta supports commercial or enterprise customers.

Customer Credit Management

For enterprise customers and for high value orders, JungleSea would like to manage the risk and want to check an incoming order against a customer's credit limit. Due to an insufficient credit limit, the order will be blocked and the credit manager can re-evaluate the customer's credit worthiness.

Currently, an application named "**Equal**" provides information about a customers' credit score. But the other capabilities, including credit limit evaluation and approval by manager, will have to be implemented as a manual approval process in WPS.

Supplier / Partner Management

The Supplier/Partner Management system includes the systems and applications provided to JungleSea by its various partners. The scope of these applications encompass order acceptance, order processing, and related fulfillment activities. Shipping management can be thought of as an extension of this domain.

Currently, an application named "**Moonlight**" exposes the interfaces and operations to JungleSea to perform activities related to supplier/partner order processing and fulfillment.

SOA considerations

To achieve an optimal level of flexibility when adopting an SOA-based approach, you must take into consideration key patterns, principles, and procedures. In this well-written article *Increase flexibility with the Service Integration Maturity Model (SIMM)* by *Ali Arsanjani* and *Kerrie Holley* (`http://www.ibm.com/developerworks/webservices/library/ws-soa-simm/`), there are seven stages of SOA maturity that are described. The path to SOA must consider several typical approaches addressed in the article. SOA adoption is a gradual process. JungleSea Inc. will embark on an SOA journey, in the context of building the Sales Fulfillment Application, by integrating applications using a service-oriented integration (SOI) approach.

JungleSea Inc. hired a consulting service from a top-tier consulting firm and experts in SOA. They found through workshops, maturity assessments, and business value assessment of their current and proposed projects that an SOA approach can potentially reduce three-year costs by 30 percent, accelerate time to value for launch of new products by 60 percent, and reduce risk. They firmly believed that there is a market shift away from traditional IT to adoption of the SOA approach based on open standards and responsibility-driven componentisation. Knowing what has to be built and delivered and having decided that SOA is the right approach, how would JungleSea's implementation team, responsible for designing and implementing the Sales Fulfillment Application, go about and deliver this solution? What steps should they take? What happens in each and every step? Who does what? What are some of the considerations to be taken into account?

Now let's look at various aspects of SOA and the design considerations that the consulting firm has asked the JungleSea implementation team to take into account. These are aspects of SOA that have influence on the design itself. Let's go through some of the most key and common SOA considerations that will have to be taken into account and are essential for JungleSea's implementation team to adopt:

- **Loose coupling**: It represents the binding between the service consumer and the service provider. We would want this to be loose. Loose coupling allows software on each side of the conversation to change without impacting the other, provided that the message schema stays the same. The service consumer should have no knowledge of the technical details of the service provider's implementation, such as the programming language, deployment platform, and so forth. The service consumer typically should invoke the exposed interfaces and hence operations by way of XML-based messages—a request message and the response—rather than through the use of APIs or file formats.
- **Service granularity**: It represents the relative measure of how broad a service must be in order to address the need at hand. The overall quantity of functionality encapsulated by a service determines the service granularity.
    - A fine-grained service typically provides a small unit of functionality or exchanges a small amount of data.
    - In contrast, a coarse-grained service encompasses and abstracts larger chunks of capability within a single interaction.
    - If a service is too coarse, then it will have many operations and hence many service consumers impacting performance.
    - There is no golden standard that determines how granular is coarse-grained or fine-grained.
    - If your application component requirements include microsecond response time, low latency, the ability to handle pass-by-reference semantics, presuming synchronous processing, and being tightly coupled to the caller's execution context (language, QoS, and locality), then your component is fine-grained and should be developed using a fine-grained component model.

> This article provides a good set of guidelines for categorizing software component technology in the context of SOA and how SCA offers a natural model for coarse-grained components.
>
> `http://www.ibm.com/developerworks/webservices/library/ws-soa-granularity/`

- **Well-defined interfaces**: The service interaction must be well-defined and expressed using a WSDL. WSDL does not include any technology details of the implementation of a service. The service consumer neither knows nor cares whether the service is written in Java code, C#, COBOL, or some other programming language.
- **Stateless services**: One of the very key and fundamental principles of SOA is having the services stateless. The services should be independent, self-contained requests and should not rely on the state from one request to another when implemented. Services should not be dependent on the context or state of other services. When state dependencies are required, they are best implemented and defined using business processes.
- **Choreography versus Orchestration**: You will have to carefully make a distinction between choreography and a low-level composition.
    - Choreography is a business process that typically spans domains within an organization; it is stateful, involves human interactions, and invokes one or many services along its path. Use Choreography when absolutely needed and necessary. It is expensive from a performance point of view.
    - Orchestration is a business process that is state free and is typically within a domain. It has ultra fast response times and never has human tasks.
- **Not everything is a service**: You don't have to expose every possible component as a service. The service should make meaningful sense to the larger organization itself. We will go over service identification in detail in the coming sections.
- **Quality of service considerations**: When designing services, you should take into consideration non-functional characteristics such as security, reliability (guaranteed delivery and order of delivery), availability, and response time of services you deploy in order to ensure that they are within the promised range.

Applying the SOA Foundation Lifecycle

So we have the business requirements, IT requirements, and applications in scope, and we listed down the key considerations to be taken into account when adopting an SOA approach. Should we adopt the IBM's SOA foundations life cycle that we explained in Chapter 1, *Introducing IBM BPM and ESB*? If the answer was a "yes", then excellent recollection and presence of mind! SOA is pretty new to JungleSea and hence we need to adopt repeatable and yet proven methods and processes to increase the chances of successful adoption and also deliver the Sales Fulfillment Application. Having a documented process is necessary for SOA governance. Yes we're going to adopt IBM's SOA foundation lifecycle while building this application.

> We would be adopting **Rational Unified Process** (**RUP**) as the design methodology. RUP has been developed over many years based on experience of what works in practice. IBM's Service-Oriented Modeling and Architecture (SOMA) consist of prescriptive tasks that produce SOA-related artifacts by roles within the lifecycle. IBM offers the Rational Unified Process for SOMA as Eclipse plugins. For more information and to download the plugin, visit:
>
> `http://www.ibm.com/developerworks/rational/downloads/06/rmc_soma/`

The IBM SOA Foundation is integrated with open standards based on a set of IBM software, best practices, and patterns. The key elements of the IBM SOA Foundation are the SOA life cycle (model, assemble, deploy, manage), reference architecture, and SOA scenarios. The IBM's SOA foundation lifecycle consists of the following iterative phases:

- **Model**
- **Assemble**
- **Deploy**
- **Manage**
- **Govern** (that spans all phases)

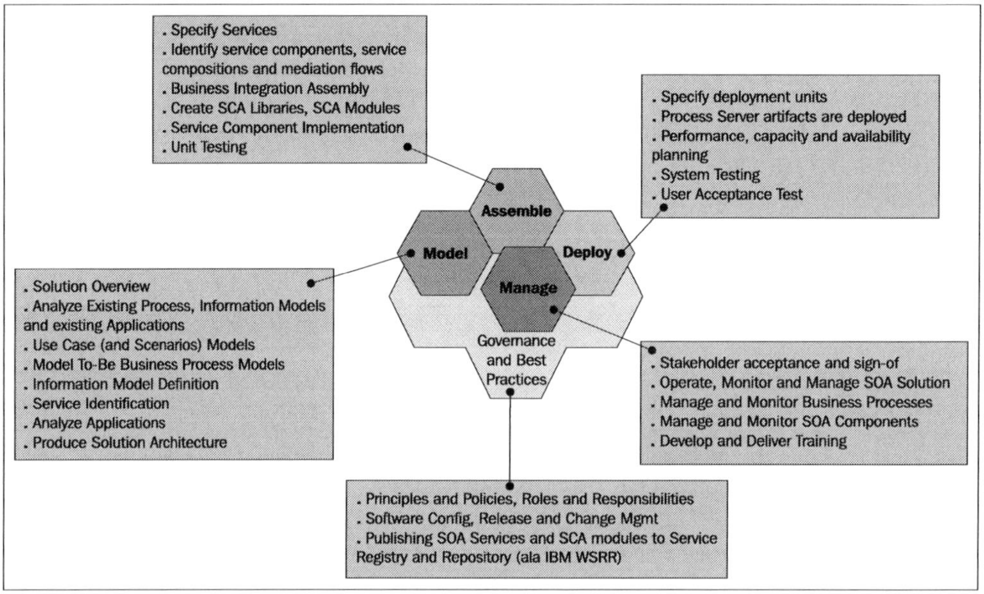

The lifecycle, as shown in the previous figure, outlines the key steps and the key activities that happen in each phase to deliver the solution. Not only that, you can use the business-oriented information to identify, specify, and design the realization of services to build the sales fulfillment system.

Governance and processes are critical to the success of any SOA project. It is an extension of IT governance specifically focused on the lifecycle of services, metadata, and composite applications in an organization's SOA. SOA governance helps address how an organization's IT governance decision rights, policies, and measures need to be modified and augmented for a successful adoption of SOA, thus forming an effective SOA governance model. It provides a framework for the reuse and sharing of services, a key value derived from leveraging SOA.

For further reading on SOA governance, refer to *SOA Governance* by *Todd Biske*.

Architecture and design

Most of us are familiar with the process of building a home, at least at a 50,000 foot level. An architect creates the blueprint—the design plans—and hands it over to the construction engineer. The construction engineer with a project manager devises a plan, procures material, and has things in order to "build" the house. Then they lay out the floor plans, design each room in the house meticulously, and at the same time, take into account architectural considerations and factors. This is not an arbitrary process; it is architecture and is much disciplined.

You can draw a parallel to building IT systems from building houses. Many of the attributes of building architecture are applicable to system architecture. The way you architect and design the IT system determines in a very large way the successful delivery of the IT system. In general, architecture is a set of rules that defines a unified and coherent structure consisting of constituent parts and connections that establish how those parts fit and work together.

An architecture description is a formal description of a system, organized in a way that supports reasoning about the structural properties of the system. It defines the system components or building blocks and provides a plan from which products can be procured and systems developed, which will work together to implement the overall system.

Architecture may be conceptualized from a specific perspective focusing on an aspect or view of its subject. The architecture must define the rules, guidelines, or constraints for creating conformant implementations of the system. While this architecture does not specify the details on any implementation, it does establish guidelines that must be observed in making implementation choices. Now, let's see how we can put together the architecture for the Sales Fulfillment Application, which will serve as the basis for the implementation (that we will do in Chapters *8*, *9*, and *10*).

> At this juncture, JungleSea Inc. had already selected and decided that it will use IBM WebSphere Process Server and IBM WebSphere Enterprise Services Bus as the core platform on which the Sales Fulfillment Application will be built and deployed.

System context

The system context represents the Sales Fulfillment Application system as a single object and identifies all external entities that may interact with a system. Shown in the following figure is the system context diagram which defines the Sales Fulfillment Application system, the existing JungleSea applications it interacts with, and identifies the information and control flows that cross the system boundaries. The system context provides a decomposition of the business context and traceability to the business context information. It helps identify some key architectural artifacts that will be required in order to build the complete solution.

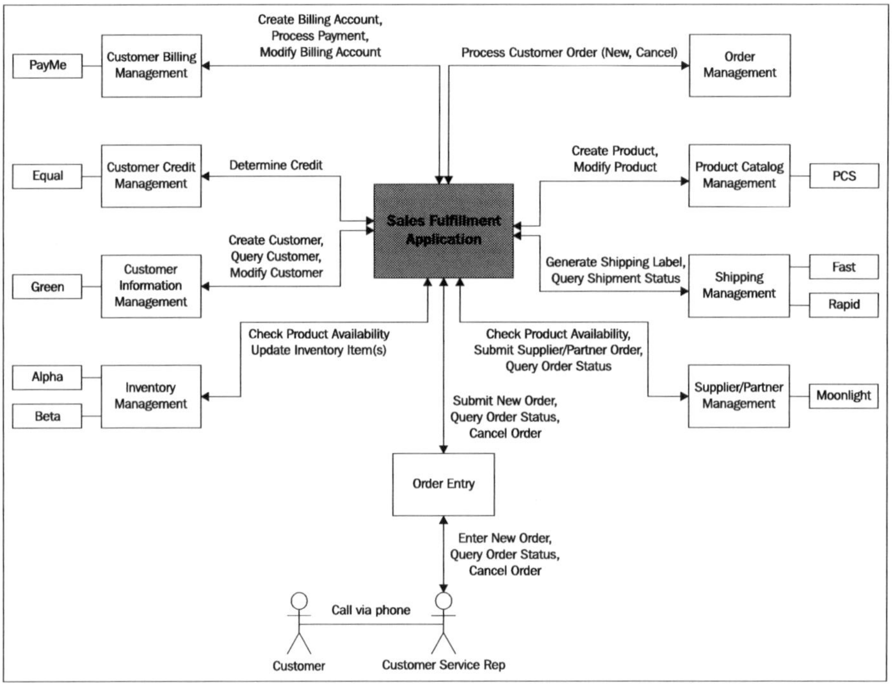

Identified use cases and scenarios

Functional requirements capture the intended behavior of the system. Use cases describe the functional behavior of a system and how it should respond under different circumstances to a request made from a stakeholder/actor. Actors are parties outside the system that interact with the system. A use case is initiated by a user with a particular goal in mind and completes successfully when that goal is satisfied. A use case may have a sequence of steps which are called scenarios. Scenarios are instances of a use case which sum up to become goals. The use case model uses graphical symbols and text primarily to specify how users in specific roles use the system (that is use cases). The use case model acts as the basis for the following:

- Visualizing the overall scope of the system to be built
- Facilitating communication between end users and developers
- Planning and estimation
- Identifying business processes, services, components, and interfaces
- Defining the user interface requirements
- Testing user acceptance
- Creating user guide and documentation

Actors

There are four types of users who will interact with Sales Fulfillment Application System (for release 1):

- Customer Service Representatives (CSR)
    - Initiates orders from customers for products and services
- Supervisor (handles escalation work item)
    - Responsible for overall supervision of order execution and handling escalation
- System Actor
    - This includes
        - Order Entry
        - Order Management
- System Administrator
    - Responsible for configuring and maintaining the system

Customers will not be interacting directly with the system. Instead, they will interact through the CSR.

Use cases

A use case describes "who" can do "what" with the system in question. One or more scenarios may be generated from a use case, corresponding to the details of each possible way of achieving that goal. Shown in the following figure are the identified initial sets of use cases for the Sales Fulfillment Application. These use cases will allow us to capture and specify the Sales Fulfillment Application's behavioral requirements by detailing scenario-driven threads through the functional requirements. The following use cases and scenarios have been identified for the Sales Fulfillment Application organized around business domain areas.

- Customer Domain
    - Process Customer Order
        - Prepare Shipping Label
        - Notify Order Shipment and Completion
        - Approve Order
        - Query Order Status
    - Manage Customer Information
        - Create Customer Profile
        - Update Customer Profile
- Billing Domain
    - Check Customer Credit
    - Process Payment
    - Send Invoice
- Product Domain
    - Manage Product Information
        - Create New Product
        - Update Product Information
    - Manage Inventory
        - Update Inventory Stock
        - Back Order Items
    - Check Product Availability

The use case model we captured previously will help us capture interactions that are not naturally covered by the tasks in the business processes. In a high-level business process, one process task might equate to a number of use cases. In a low-level process, a use case might relate to multiple tasks.

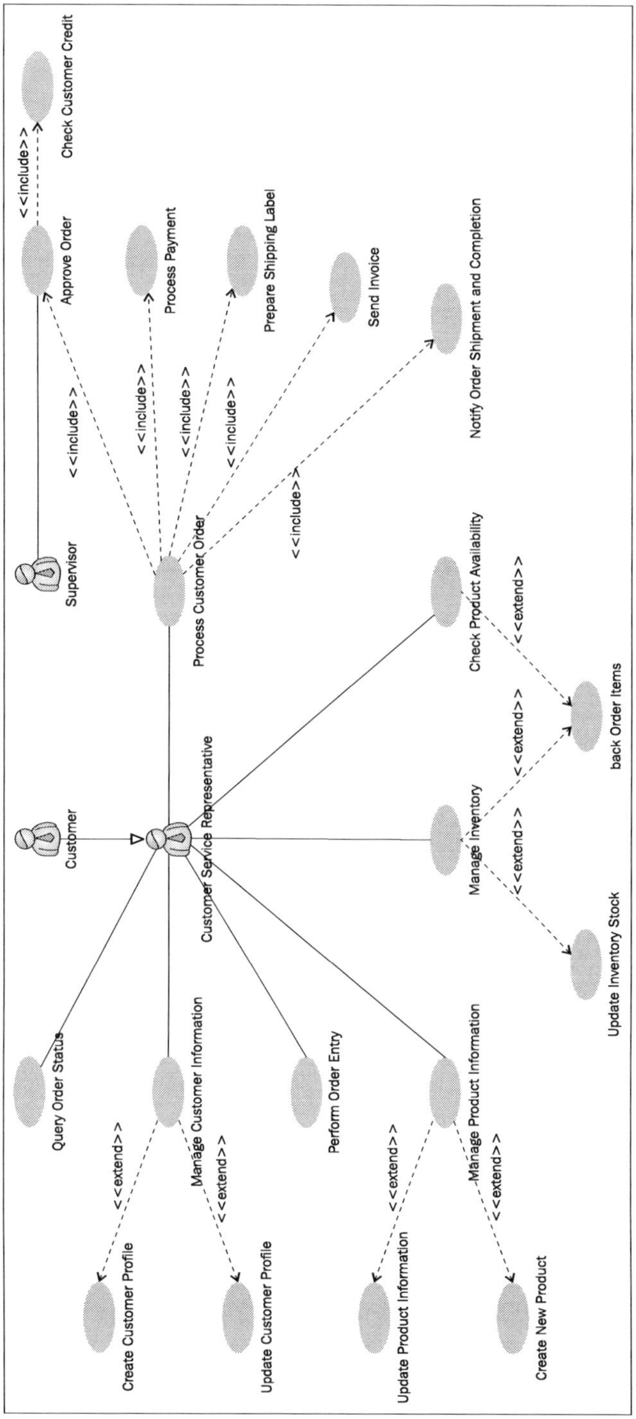
Check Customer Credit
<<include>>
Approve Order
Supervisor
<<include>>
Process Payment
<<include>>
Prepare Shipping Label
<<include>>
Send Invoice
<<include>>
Notify Order Shipment and Completion
<<include>>
Process Customer Order
Customer
Customer Service Representative
Check Product Availability
<<extend>>
back Order Items
<<extend>>
Manage Inventory
<<extend>>
Update Inventory Stock
Query Order Status
Manage Customer Information
<<extend>>
Create Customer Profile
<<extend>>
Update Customer Profile
Perform Order Entry
Manage Product Information
<<extend>>
Update Product Information
<<extend>>
Create New Product

Identified Business Processes

Business process discovery, modeling, and simulation are an art by themselves. They can span several phases and several activities that constitute a single phase. The understanding of the current business processes (if they exist) called AS-IS processes is key. The AS-IS processes are modeled using tools like the WebSphere Business Modeler and then can be simulated to identify possible bottlenecks. The identified bottlenecks can be addressed through business process optimization techniques, and hence making the process more agile and better performing. There is no such thing as "the final version" business processes. Based on real-time process instance metrics including process performance and measurement data (based on the key performance indicators you had define in your process) collected over a period of time, the processes can be optimized to behave appropriately. The result of this optimization is realized as TO-BE business processes. Process simulations can be performed on these TO-BE models also. The outcomes can be validated against the business requirements, both functional and non-functional.

The modeled TO-BE business processes are then realized as a combination of SCA components such as BPEL, state machines, rules, human tasks, and so on, and deployed on the WebSphere Process Server runtime. The processes also typically require business services, atomic services, and components to be realized as mediation flows, adapters, and so on. These again are deployed on the WebSphere Process Server runtime (which includes the WebSphere Enterprise Service Bus).

> WebSphere Business Modeler (which is not in the scope of this book) offers process modeling, simulation, and analysis capabilities to help business users understand, document, and deploy business processes for continuous improvement. It provides the following capabilities:
>
> - Enables business users to design, model, and deploy business processes
> - Advanced simulation capabilities based on modeled and actual data
> - Process optimization by allowing users to visualize and identify bottlenecks and inefficiencies in processes
> - Integration with the IBM WebSphere Process Server through role-based Business Space, a unified end user interface that integrates BPM content for a holistic management of business processes
> - Enables subject matter experts to share models and collaborate to translate business intent into process models using a Web browser with WebSphere Business Compass
>
> The business process modeling is not in the scope of this book. The implementation team obtained the TO-BE process models given to them by JungleSea Inc. business analysts based on the use cases.

The business analysts provided the JungleSea implementation team with the TO-BE business process for the Customer Order Management process. They were modeled using WebSphere Business Modeler and are shown in the figures that we will subsequently look at. The process models capture information that includes:

- Business events or business transactions that start the process
- Applicable business rules that may provide variability to the business process
- Detailed description of task inputs and outputs and data structures
- Task type, for example, human or system
- Applications or roles or resources that enable tasks, for example, applications, data, systems, internal and external services
- Decisions that change the flow of the process
- Conditions that stop the process
- Favorable and unfavorable process outcomes

Business analysts have also captured the strategic business goals and objectives for the TO-BE processes. The KPIs allow you to analyze data to gain business insight into what is happening and what is not. Based on these goals, the following are some of the KPIs that have been defined by the business analysts:

- Number of orders received daily
- Number of orders fulfilled successfully daily, weekly, monthly, and quarterly
- Percentage of orders that cannot be fulfilled due to unavailable inventory
- Orders received by region
- Number of orders canceled by customer
- Number of orders not fulfilled by Supplier-Partner
- Duration required for the human task "Ship Order"

> WebSphere Business Monitor and the WebSphere Monitor Toolkit provide business activity monitoring capabilities that offer real-time insight into the business processes. It provides visualization dashboards (through BusinessSpace, which we will discuss in the forthcoming chapter) such as business process information, human task activities, process diagrams, key performance indicators (KPIs), dimensional views, visualizing a process flow, and so on.

These TO-BE customer order management process models were created by the JungleSea's business analyst. As you can see the process spans end ot end and it covers the various systems or applications depicted as the "swim lanes". The functions or activities that will be performed within or against each of the systems are shown. Taking this process model as one of the inputs we will identify the SOA services and also the integration touch point with the applications that will have to be developed.

The following two figures below have been split up into two to accomodate into a single page and for readability:

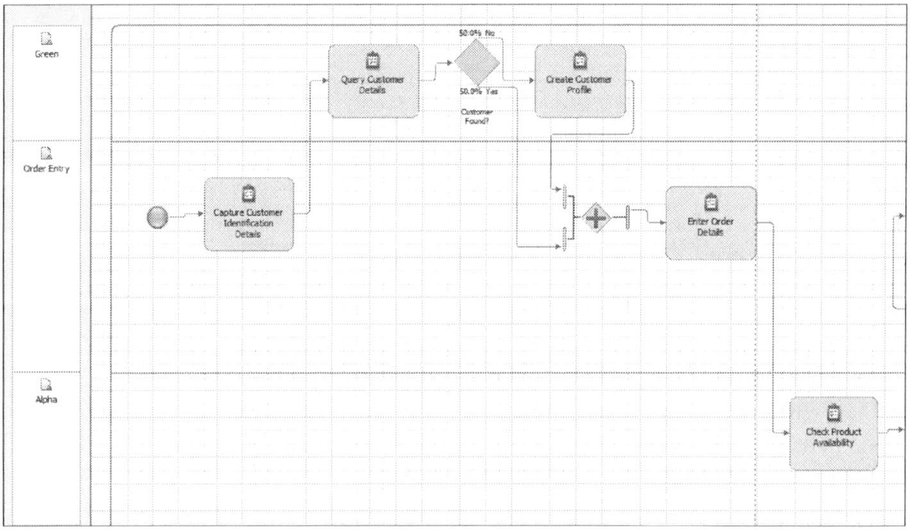

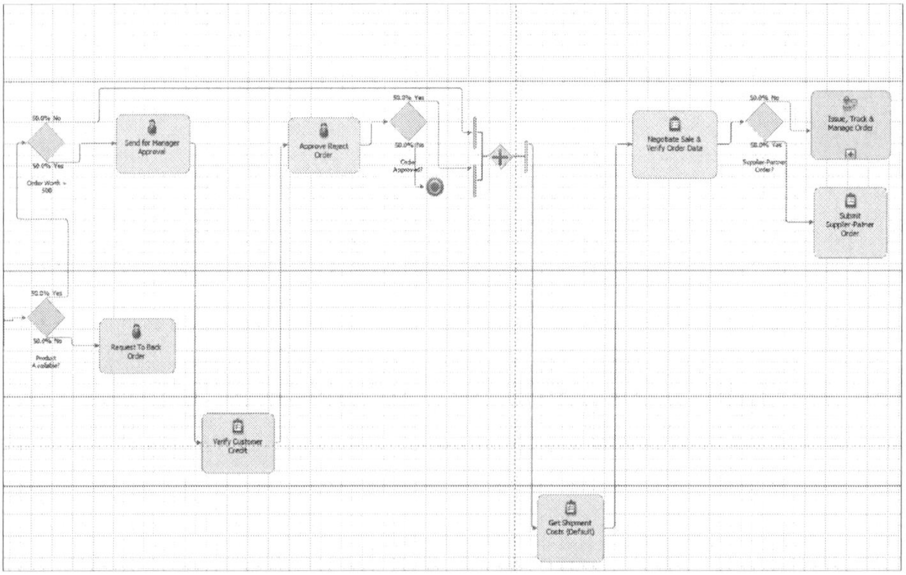

The following figure is the continuation of the TO-BE business process model:

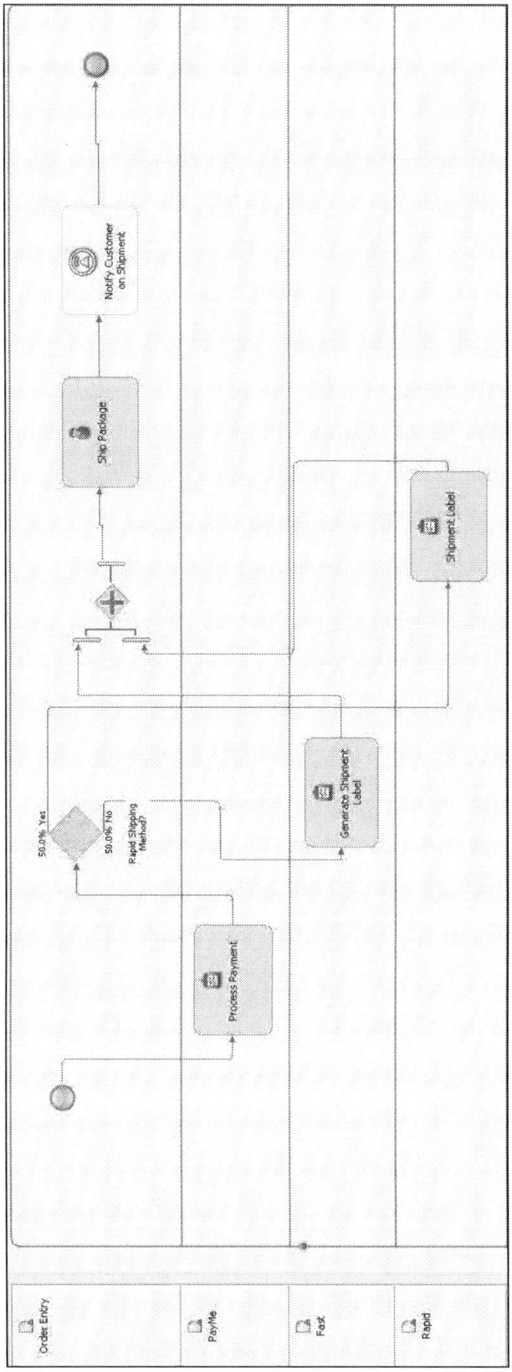

Solution Architecture

When you want to build a house, you start with an architecture that lays out what, why, and how you are going to build. There are several ways to depict the architectural plan through views.

Architecture views are representations of the overall architecture meant to convey meaningful information to one or more stakeholders interested in the system. One of the primary responsibilities of an architect is to develop a set of views that will enable the architecture to be communicated to, and understood by, all the stakeholders, and enable them to verify that the system will address their concerns.

Architecture is usually represented by means of one or more architecture models that together provide a coherent description of the system's architecture. A single, comprehensive model is often too complex to be understood and communicated in its most detailed form, showing all the relationships between the various business and technical components. As with the architecture of a building, it is normally necessary to develop multiple views of the architecture of an information system, to enable the architecture to be communicated to, and understood by, the different stakeholders in the system. For example, just as a building architect might create wiring diagrams, floor plans, and elevations to describe different facets of a building to its different stakeholders (electricians, owners, planning officials), similarly an IT architect might create physical and security views of an IT system for the stakeholders who have concerns related to these aspects.

Our high-level overview of what the solution should be is depicted through the following figure. It's basically a white board sketch of how the various applications involved in the Sales Fulfillment Application would come together and be integrated. It represents the candidate building blocks of the IT system and enterprise architecture. It provides an overview of the main conceptual elements and relationships in architecture, including the candidate internal systems and external systems.

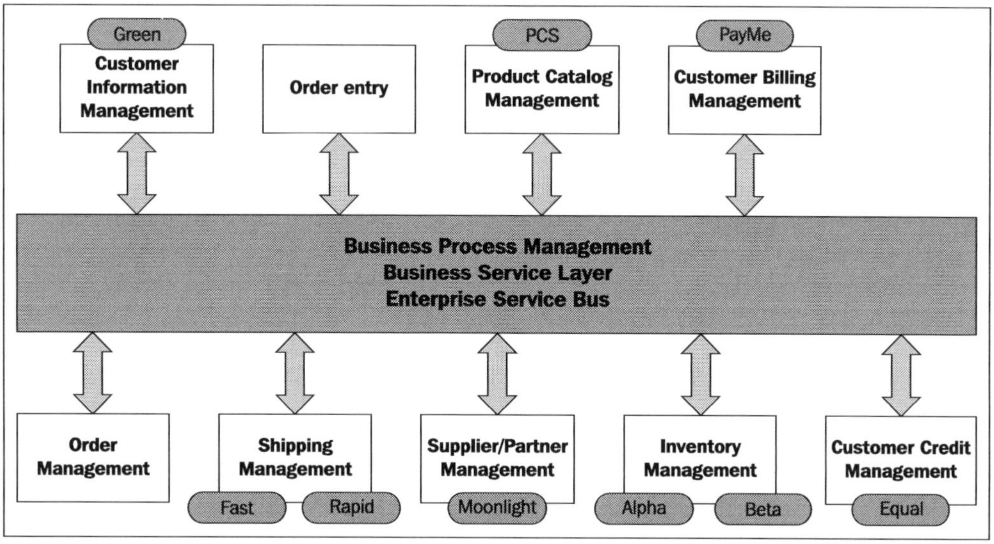

As mentioned earlier, JungleSea Inc. had already selected and decided that it would use IBM WebSphere Process Server and IBM WebSphere Enterprise Services Bus as the core platform on which the Sales Fulfillment Application would be built and deployed. So let's delve into the next level and look at the architecture view from an enterprise level, as shown in the subsequent diagram. This is used to describe the vision of the IT capabilities required by the Sales Fulfillment Application. It identifies from a high-level perspective the capabilities and components that should be deployed to support the solution. It provides an overview of the main capabilities, key elements, and relationships in the architecture, including candidate systems, components, nodes, connections, channels, users, and so on. As you can see in the diagram, the capabilities and components are tiered or compartmentalized based on the IBM SOA Reference Architecture capabilities.

- **Interaction Services** will provide the capabilities required to deliver functions and data that would be required by the Customer Service Representative to interact with the Sales Fulfillment Application.
- **Process Services** provides the capability to define end-to-end business processes and automation of all processes in the system for order handling, human activities, fallout/error handling, notifications, process visualization, monitoring, process data mediation, and storage. This layer is built using IBM's WebSphere Process Server.
- **Business Services** provides the coarse-grained business functions that have a meaningful significance to JungleSea Inc.

- **Access Services** provide the bridging capabilities between the business services interfaces and the end application interfaces through the ESB. This layer will also provide the capability to intercept and modify messages that are passed between the business services and the end JungleSea application service interfaces (providers). Mediation services can be implemented using mediation modules deployed on the WebSphere Enterprise Service Bus or the WebSphere Process Server.

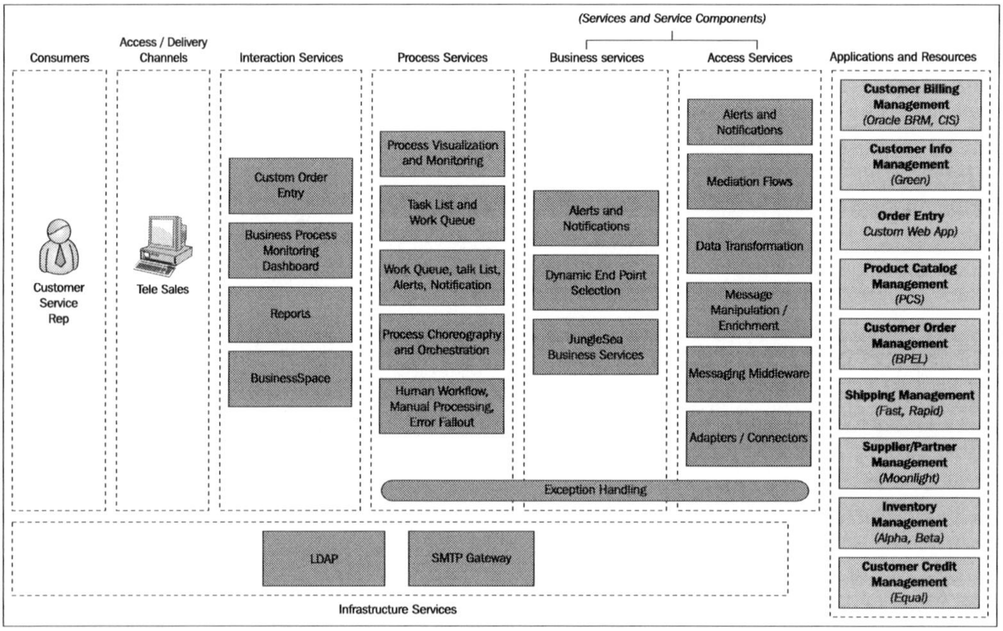

We will create one more view of the solution architecture that will solidify this vision of the solution and communicate the same with the various stakeholders. The figure below depicts the "Sales Fulfillment Application" solution architecture view, based on the IBM SOA Reference Architecture layers (that we discussed in Chapter 1). The layers in this solution stack are designed to reinforce SOA business value. This view certainly influences creation of a component model and operational model (which we will create in the coming section).

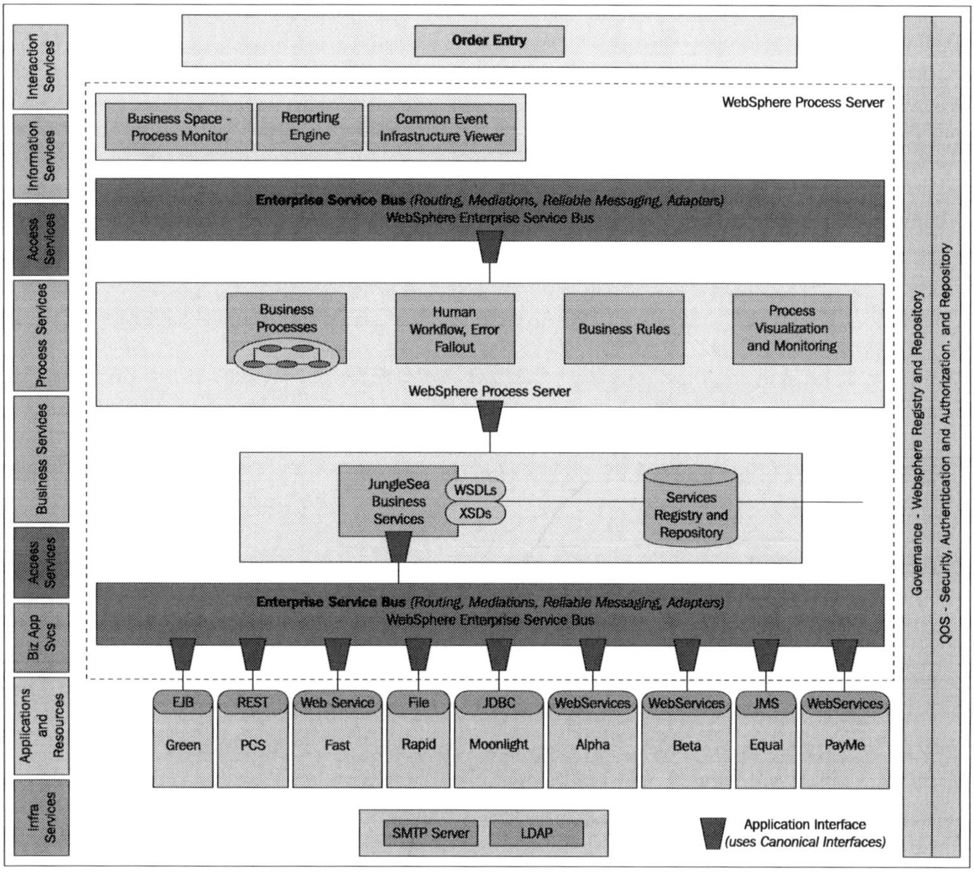

Service identification

In its fundamental essence a service is a logical grouping of service operations with a published interface. We have laid out (as mentioned in the earlier section) the differences between coarse-grained versus fine-grained services and we should identify and expose services that make meaningful sense to the overall organization. **Business services**, which represent a discrete yet coarse-grained business function, can get invoked from business processes and also other mechanisms including portals, client applications, other applications, and so on. Technical (atomic) services, in contrast, are very fine-grained and are typically embedded in the infrastructure that supports these business services. Hence, it's imperative to realize the full transformation potential of SOA and that the right set of business services, and hence operations, are identified and specified.

Shown in the following figure is the relationship between the service granularities and the relevance they have to the business as a whole. So mapping the identified business services to business domains to establish business ownership makes the service discoverable, usable, and gives the promise of SOA. What should these "Business Services" be for JungleSea? What are the criteria for making the distinction between business services and fine-grained technical or atomic services? Let's look at them.

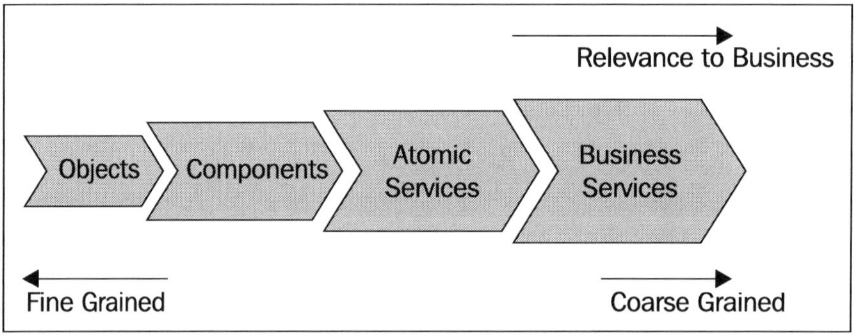

Service granularity

Service granularity, which is a key topic in SOA, is an indication of the level of interaction between a service consumer and a service provider. A fine-grained service typically provides a small unit of functionality or exchanges a small amount of data. In contrast, a coarse-grained service encompasses and abstracts larger chunks of capability within a single interaction. If a service is too coarse, then it will have many operations and hence many service consumers impacting performance. The following figure depicts an example business service, Verify Customer Credit, which in turn is made up of many atomic services and components. The point here is that, Verify Customer Credit is a composite service which can verify the credit for a residential and an enterprise customer, verify the customer data, and also make meaningful sense to JungleSea as an organization.

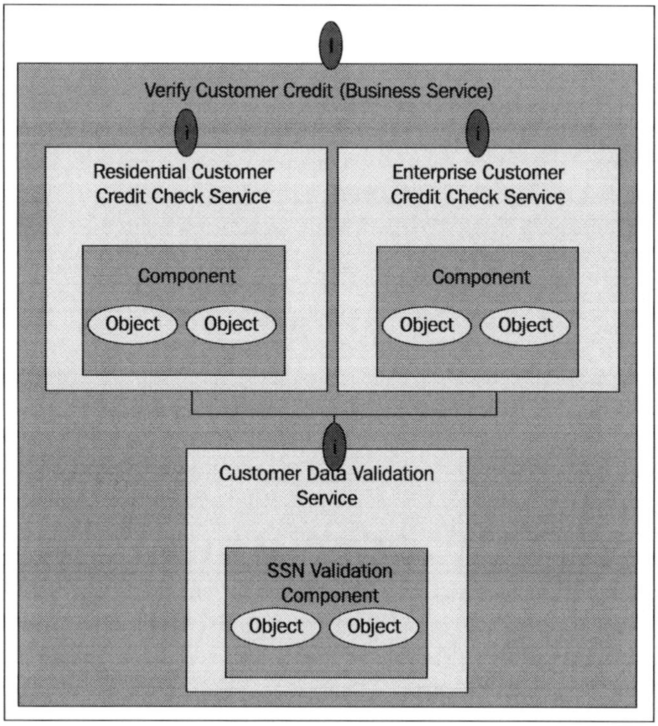

There is no golden standard that determines how granular is coarse-grained or fine-grained. This is where IBM's **Service-Oriented Modeling and Architecture (SOMA)** technique comes handy. SOMA refers to the more general domain of service modeling necessary to design and create SOA.

SOMA covers a broader scope and implements service-oriented analysis and design (SOAD) through the identification, specification, and realization of services, components that realize those services (also known as "service components"), and flows that can be used to compose services. SOMA includes an analysis and design method that extends tradition and introduces new techniques such as goal-service modeling, service model creation, and a service litmus test to help determine the granularity of a service. SOMA identifies services, component boundaries, flows, compositions, and information through complementary techniques, which include domain decomposition, goal-service modeling, and existing asset analysis. Typically, there are three major phases in SOMA:

- service identification
- service specification
- service realization decisions

With respect to service identification, SOMA recommends a three-step approach (one that necessarily does not have to be done in serial).

- Domain decomposition (top-down)
- Goal-service modeling
- Existing system analysis (bottom-up)

> For more information on SOMA, refer to the article on Service-Oriented Modeling and Architecture named *How to identify, specify, and realize services for your SOA* by *Ali Arsanjani*.
>
> `http://www.ibm.com/developerworks/library/ws-soa-design1/`

Top-Down, Bottom-up, and Goal-Oriented Decomposition Analysis

To properly organize the identified business services into the right business domain buckets, JungleSea's business owners along with IT have decided to use the following domain areas:

- Customer Information Management
- Product Catalog Management
- Customer Billing Management
- Shipping Management
- Supplier/Partner Management
- Inventory Management
- Customer Credit Management

The business and IT worked together to define the responsibilities for each of these domains and also at a high-level mentioning what business functions that these domains should provide.

The TO-BE business process gives JungleSea a good starting point to identify what are the business services that will have to be exposed and made available to the business process. The "Customer Order Management Process" business process can be decomposed into tasks. The first business task of business process is named "Query Customer". This task can be realized as a service "Manage Customer Information" business service. Business Services are coarse-grained services, which may encapsulate one or more fine-grained services. Then we identify the service operation from the task, which we will name "queryCustomer". We will define the interface for this service based on a canonical messaging model. So why do we need to use a canonical message model?

The primary goal of creating these business services is to make them reusable and also make them enterprise grade, so that anyone within JungleSea can use them. Reusability implies that a service has a number of different consumers, and the consumers should not be exposed to the (ugly) specifics of the backend applications. A customer, as an entity in one system, may not be the same in a different system. A customer in one system can be treated as person in another system, leading to a semantic mismatch. A canonical model is a well-known pattern that acts as an abstraction layer between the service consumers and providers. This way, any change made to a consumer or a provider will have minimal impact on all of its integration points. The canonical model typically should remain unchanged regardless of what happens inside the service, which in turn, ensures that the contract between the service consumer and the service itself remains unaffected. The maximum possible impact on the service may be the need to change the mappings between internal service data structures and the canonical model. So the business services will transform data from the canonical to the end application data model and vice versa. The business process layer hence will always communicate using the canonical messaging model.

> A very good article on applying the canonical modeling pattern in SOA is provided at the following website:
> `http://www.ibm.com/developerworks/data/library/techarticle/dm-0803sauter/`

Categorized (Business) Service Portfolio

Continuing the same process, we derive the services model and hence identify all the necessary business services or the Categorized Service Portfolio. The Categorized Service Portfolio represents the list of candidate (SOA) business services required for the Sales Fulfillment Application, categorized based on the business application domain they belong to. The following figure shows the identified business services captured as a service model:

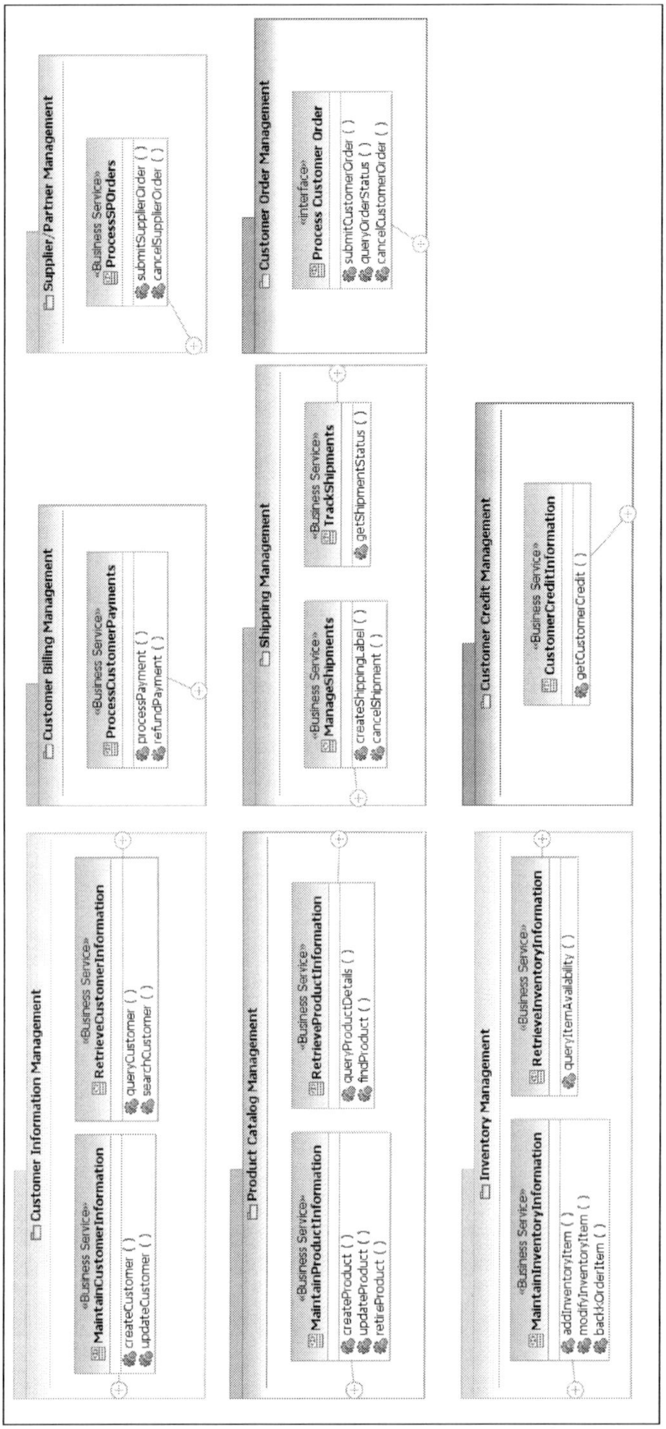
Customer Information Management
«Business Service»
MaintainCustomerInformation
createCustomer ( )
updateCustomer ( )
«Business Service»
RetrieveCustomerInformation
queryCustomer ( )
searchCustomer ( )
Customer Billing Management
«Business Service»
ProcessCustomerPayments
processPayment ( )
refundPayment ( )
Supplier/Partner Management
«Business Service»
ProcessSPOrders
submitSupplierOrder ( )
cancelSupplierOrder ( )
Product Catalog Management
«Business Service»
MaintainProductInformation
createProduct ( )
updateProduct ( )
retireProduct ( )
«Business Service»
RetrieveProductInformation
queryProductDetails ( )
findProduct ( )
Shipping Management
«Business Service»
ManageShipments
createShippingLabel ( )
cancelShipment ( )
«Business Service»
TrackShipments
getShipmentStatus ( )
Customer Order Management
«interface»
Process Customer Order
submitCustomerOrder ( )
queryOrderStatus ( )
cancelCustomerOrder ( )
Inventory Management
«Business Service»
MaintainInventoryInformation
addInventoryItem ( )
modifyInventoryItem ( )
backOrderItem ( )
«Business Service»
RetrieveInventoryInformation
queryItemAvailability ( )
Customer Credit Management
«Business Service»
CustomerCreditInformation
getCustomerCredit ( )

Identified components and services

Having identified the business services, we next need to identify the components and fine-grained services that would make up the business services. A component model helps simplify the process of building and assembling services that are required to build the Sales Fulfillment Application. The implementation specifics of the component itself are left to the developer (remember the core tenet of SCA). A developer may choose to implement base components using BPEL, Mediation Flow, or Java. SOA as a programming model is more fundamentally concerned with component interactions and their integration into new composite components, applications, and solutions.

From a bottom-up perspective, an application named Green provides the customer information management capabilities within JungleSea. It already provides:

Application area	App instance	Interface/Integration options
Customer Information Management	Green	Enterprise Java Beans exposed by the application.
Product Catalog Management	PCS	REST style services to perform CRUD operations.
Customer Billing Management	PayMe	Web Services exposed by the application. Security enabled.
Shipping Management	Fast	Web Services exposed by the application.
	Rapid	File based interface. Shipment labels sent back by email.
Supplier/Partner Management	Moonlight	Integration only through Java Database Connectivity (JDBC) calls.
Inventory Management	Alpha	Web Services exposed by the application.
	Beta	Web Services exposed by the application.
Customer Credit Management	Equal	Capabilities via Java Message Service (JMS) exposed by the application.

As mentioned in the earlier chapter, we are not going to be building the applications and service interfaces exposed by the JungleSea applications listed previously. We assume they exist and we will leverage them to expose them as meaningful business services. In the next chapter, we will discuss briefly the interface specifics of the above applications and also discuss how we will leverage them when implementing the solution.

> SOMA's Service Litmus Test helps verify exposure decisions to avoid misalignment with business, new objectives, or "proliferation of services." Tests for exposure decisions are:
>
> - Business alignment
> - Composability
> - Redundancy elimination
> - Technical feasibility
> - Externalized service description
>
> A variety of factors can affect service exposure decisions, such as the level of capability and maturity that an organization has reached with respect to SOA. The Service Litmus Test is the key criterion recommended for most situations. Nevertheless, an organization that is early in the adoption cycle may want to show a few services as a way to experiment with a technology like Web Services.

Architectural decisions and design patterns applied

One of the key activities as part of architecting any solution is the architectural assumptions, decisions, and constraints around which the solution is designed, implemented, and operated. Typically, a running and live document named "Architectural Decisions" will be maintained through the life of the engagement that delivers the solution. This document lists the key architectural decisions and recommendations adopted by the solution, based on prior experiences and leading practices. It provides a single place to find important architectural decisions and the rationale and justification for which they were made. It not only helps evolve the system in the future but also helps people looking to understand the solution in detail know about the key decisions made. Here are some of the key architectural decisions and patterns that will be adopted for the phase 1 of the Sales Fulfillment Application.

- The solution architecture will be (obviously) based on the principles of SOA, with reusable components that will be choreographed and orchestrated.
- The architecture will aim to eliminate redundant components and services, thereby promoting the ease of maintenance.
- Exposed interfaces and integration options of existing applications and systems will be leveraged and reused to provide the desired functionality as much as possible. Potentially in the future, some of these existing applications may be replaced with off-the-shelf applications. The architecture will have to account for such scenarios.

- Process choreography should be used to implement cross-service component business process logic. WebSphere Process Server in conjunction with WebSphere ESB will be used for integration-intensive BPM.
- Implementation Architecture Layers based on IBM SOA reference architecture will consist of the following layers:
    - Interaction Services
    - Process Services
    - Business Services
    - Access Services
    - Business Application Services
- The data formats used by the services interfaces for the process services and business services (and the northern half of the access services) will be based on a canonical model. As explained earlier, the canonical model is a well-known pattern that acts as an abstraction layer between the service consumers and providers. This way, any changes made to a consumer or a provider will have minimal impact on all of its integration points.
- The canonical model typically should remain unchanged regardless of what happens inside the service, which, in turn, ensures that the contract between the service consumer and the service itself remains unaffected. The maximum possible impact on the service may be the need to change the mappings between internal service data structures and the canonical model. So the business services will transform data from the canonical to the end application data model and vice versa. The business process layer hence will always communicate using the canonical messaging model.
- The architecture hence will adopt Service Component Architecture (SCA) programming model with Service Data Object (SDO) as a standard representation of a message passing between services. When a service is invoked, data objects are passed as an XML document with WSDL when using a web service or as a Java object when using a Java interface. Similar to components, Service Data Objects separate the data object from its implementation.
- The Process Services and Business Services will have its interfaces exposed based on the common messaging model (meaning Generic Business Objects).
- The interfaces for the northern half of the Access Services will be exposed based on the common messaging model (meaning Generic Business Objects). The southern half, which integrates with the backend applications, will transform to and from the application-specific message formats.

- The Access Services will provide the mediation capabilities needed to integrate with the backend applications including protocol transformation, data transformation, and message enrichment capabilities before forwarding the request to the backend applications. This layer will transform the request/response from the common messaging model format to the end application format.
- The Order Entry system (simulator in this case) will invoke business services based on the common messaging model.
- The end-to-end Customer Order Management business process will be wrapped into a business service—Process Customer Order.
- When there is a need for invoking business services from more than one component that belong to different application domains, a business process layer (using a BPEL) will be used to choreograph the interactions. They will not be contained within the business service component itself.
- Use of open standards such as Java, XML, Web Services, WS*, and so on should be considered for building the solution.
- There are several message exchange patterns (as explained in Chapter 1) that can be employed for communicating messages among the service providers and service consumers including:
    - Request/Reply
    - Fire and Forget—single and multiple receivers
    - Publish/Subscribe
    - Notifications
    - Request with Acknowledgement
- There is no golden standard on which message exchange pattern to use and hence the decision to use the appropriate pattern will be on a case-by-case basis.
- For phase 1 of the solution, wherever possible, HTTP will be the protocol used to implement the communication interaction between the service consumers and the service providers.
- In general, the following architectural and design principles will be adopted by the solution:
    - Complexity Hiding—wrapping and encapsulation
    - Ability to interoperate with existing systems in a standardized fashion
    - Component Computing—delivery of functionality as simple, reusable components

 - Component Isolation—components should be loosely coupled to other components
 - Responsibility-driven architecture with each layer being responsible for and performing a distinct role
 - As close as possible proximity placing of processing and data to each other
 - Design for reliability, reusability, and configurability
 - Instrument all components for supporting, monitoring, and configurability
 - Design for audit and logging ability
- All business services will eventually have to be published into a services registry and repository like the WebSphere Service Registry and Repository (WSRR) and thereby enabling service discovery and governance. However, for the first phase of the solution, we will not be using WSRR.

Laying out the build plan

We have done a whole bunch of things so far in this chapter to architect the Sales Fulfillment Application—use cases, system context, solution architecture diagrams, service models or service identification models, architecture and design decisions, and capabilities provided by the end application. Now we are ready to start designing and implementing the solution itself using WID, WPS, and WESB. Before we start identifying the piece meal parts that will make up the solution, let's lay out the plan for designing and implementing the solution. The following figure shows the path to design and implement the Sales Fulfillment Application. The steps, as mentioned in the figure, are very self-explanatory. We will use this as a guide as we proceed into Chapters 8, 9, and 10 and follow them diligently. As we do this in the later chapters, you will be able to understand the individual steps in detail. Later as you complete this book, we hope you can weave these steps into the respective design and delivery methodology that you may follow within your organization.

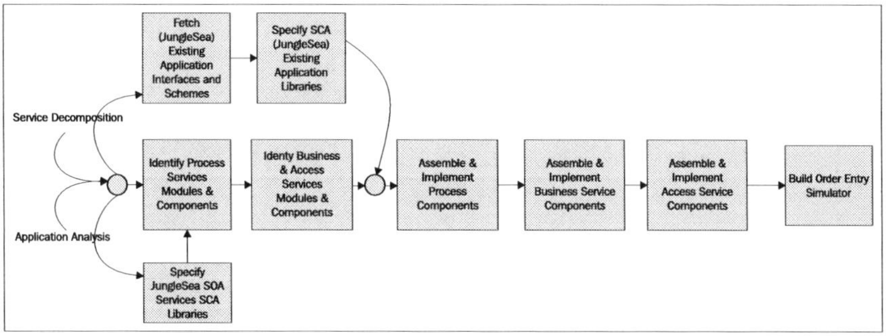

Identifying WPS and WESB parts

How do we identify the different software components (processes, business services, components, and so on) that will have to be implemented or leveraged in order to have a working Sales Fulfillment Application? In Chapter 2 we saw that WID provides a capability called integration solution diagram that organizes and displays how modules, mediation modules, libraries, and other dependent projects connect, in the context of an overall solution. You can certainly use WID to specify the modules, libraries, and components (sans implementation) and visualize the solution. One other way that I recommend is writing them down in a matrix format. You can specify:

- The modules you will have to build
- Components the modules contain
- Component type (Business Process, Mediation Flow, and so on)
- Interface to be used by the component

And organize the above by Process Services, Business Services, and Access Services. One such attempt for the Process Services is shown in the figure below. Process Services provides the capability to define an end-to-end business processes and automation of all processes in the system for order handling, human activities, fallout/error handling, notifications, process visualization, monitoring, process data mediation, and storage. As you can see, we will have to build three major business process components that will choreograph order management activities. These processes will be implemented based on the TO-BE process models identified earlier in the chapter.

	Module Name	Component Name	Component Implmentation Type	Interface
Process Services	ProcessServices-OrderHandling	TrackAndManageCustomerOrder	BPEL (Long Running)	*ProcessCustomerOrder*
		HandleOrderFallout	BPEL (Long Running)	*ManageOrderFallout*
	ProcessServices-CustomerInterfaceManagement	HandleCustomerContactProfile	BPEL (Microflow)	*MaintainCustomerInformation*

The following figure shows the modules, components, component types, and interfaces for the Business Services layer. Business Services provide the coarse-grained business functions that have a meaningful significance to JungleSea Inc. The next identified parts are a direct reflection of the service model we identified earlier in the chapter.

	Module Name	Component Name	Component Implementation Type	Interface
Business Services	BizServices-CustomerBillingMgmt	ProcessCustomerPayments	BPEL (Microflow)	*ProcessCustomerPayments*
	BizServices-CustomerInfoMgmt	MaintainCustomerInformation	BPEL (Microflow)	*MaintainCustomerInformation*
		RetrieveCustomerInformation	BPEL (Microflow)	*RetrieveCustomerInformation*
		HandleCustomerContact	BPEL (Microflow)	*HandleCustomerContact*
	BizServices-SupplierPartnerMgmt	ProcessSPOrders	BPEL (Microflow)	*ProcessSPOrders*
	BizServices-ProductCatalogMgmt	MaintainProductInformation	BPEL (Microflow)	*MaintainProductInformation*
		RetrieveProductInformation	BPEL (Microflow)	*RetrieveProductInformation*
	BizServices-ShippingMgmt	ManageShipments	BPEL (Microflow)	*ManageShipments*
		TrackShipments	BPEL (Microflow)	*TrackShipments*
	BizServices-CustomerOrderMgmt	ProcessCustomerOrder	BPEL (Microflow)	*ProcessCustomerOrder*
		HandleOrderFallout	BPEL (Microflow)	*HandleOrderFallout*
	BizServices-InventoryMgmt	MaintainInventoryInformation	BPEL (Microflow)	*MaintainInventoryInformation*
		RetrieveInventoryInformation	BPEL (Microflow)	*RetrieveInventoryInformation*
	BizServices-CustomerCreditMgmt	CustomerCreditInformation	BPEL (Microflow)	*CustomerCreditInformation*

The following figure shows the modules, components, component type, and interfaces for the Access Services layer. Access Services provide the bridging capabilities between the business services interfaces and the end applications (of JungleSea Inc.) interface through the ESB. This layer will also provide the capability to intercept and modify messages that are passed between the business services and the end JungleSea application service interfaces (providers). We have chosen to implement the mediation services using mediation modules deployed on the WebSphere Enterprise Service Bus or the WebSphere Process Server.

	Module Name	Component Name	Component Implmentation Type	Interface & Operation	End App Exposure Style (Import)
Access Services	AccessServices-Green	Med-CustomerProfile-createCustomerAccount	Mediation Flow	**MFC:** *MaintainCustomerInformation > createCustomer* **Target**: *CustomerProfile > createCustomerAccount*	EJB
		Med-CustomerProfile-modifyCustomerAccount	Mediation Flow	**MFC:** *MaintainCustomerInformation > updateCustomer* **Target**: *CustomerProfile > modifyCustomerAccount*	EJB
		Med-CustomerProfile-findCustomer	BPEL (Microflow)	**MFC:** *RetrieveCustomerInformation> searchCustomer* **Target**: *CustomerProfile > findDetails*	EJB
		Med-CustomerProfile-getCustomerDetails	Mediation Flow	**MFC:** *RetrieveCustomerInformation> queryCustomer* **Target**: *CustomerProfile > getCustomerDetails*	EJB
	AccessServices-PCS	Med-PCSProductCatalog-productSearch	Mediation Flow	**MFC:** *RetrieveProductInformation > queryProductDetails* **Target**: *PCSProductCatalog > productSearch*	REST
	AccessServices-Fast	Med-ShipService-createPendingShipmentRequest	Mediation Flow	**MFC:** *ManageShipments > createShippingLabel* **Target**: *ShipService > createPendingShipmentRequest*	Web Service
		Med-ShipService-queryPendingShipmentStatus	Mediation Flow	**MFC:** *TrackShipments > packageMovementInfo* **Target**: *ShipService > queryPendingShipmentStatus*	Web Service
	AccessServices-Rapid	Med-LabelsAndShipments-prepareShipLabel	Mediation Flow w/ File Adapter	**MFC:** *ManageShipments > createShippingLabel* **Target**: *LabelsAndShipments > prepareShipLabel*	File
		Med-LabelsAndShipments-shipmentStatus	Mediation Flow	**MFC:** *TrackShipments > packageMovementInfo* **Target**: *LabelsAndShipments > shipmentStatus*	Web Service
	AccessServices-Moonlight	Med-ProcessPurchaseOrders-processOrder	Mediation Flow w/ JDBC Adapter	**MFC:** *ProcessSPOrders > submitSupplierOrder* **Target**: *ProcessPurchaseOrders > processOrder*	Database with JDBC
	AccessServices-Alpha	Med-AlphaFBAInventoryPortType-GetInventorySupply	Mediation Flow	**MFC:** *RetrieveInventoryInformation > queryItemAvailability* **Target**: *AlphaFBAInventoryPortType-GetInventorySupply*	Web Service
	AccessServices-Beta	Med-BetaInventoryService-CheckItemAvailability	Mediation Flow	**MFC:** *RetrieveInventoryInformation > queryItemAvailability* **Target**: *BetaInventoryService > CheckItemAvailability*	Web Service
	AccessServices-Equal	Med-EqualCreditPulseSoap-creditPulseByIndividual	Mediation Flow	**MFC:** *CustomerCreditInformation > getCustomerCredit* **Target**: *EqualCreditPulseSoap > creditPulseByIndividual*	JMS
	AccessServices-PayMe	Med-CreditCardService-ccPurchase	Mediation Flow	**MFC:** *ProcessCustomerPayments > processPayment* **Target**: *CreditCardService > ccPurchase*	Web Service
		Med-CreditCardService-ccSettlement	Mediation Flow	**MFC:** *ProcessCustomerPayments > refundPayment* **Target**: *CreditCardService > ccSettlement*	Web Service

For the purpose of the book, we may not implement all the components, as laid out in the previous three figures. We have shown them for completeness sake and what it takes to build an end-to-end solution. For the purposes of this book, we will pick the most essential modules and components that will provide the order management capabilities.

Summary

In this chapter, we guided you through the steps involved in architecting the new Sales Fulfillment Application. We first analyzed the business and IT requirements, identified and laid out the key SOA considerations, and rationalized their thoughts to see if an SOA approach is the right way. Then we showed step-by-step how to create an SOA-based architecture by adopting various principles and patterns; identified use cases (and scenarios) and business processes; laid out the architecture (and expressed using different views), process variability points, top-down, bottom-up, and goal-oriented decomposition to identify the right services; and identified external and internal applications to integrate with and services/components. Finally, we laid out a roadmap or a series of steps we will adopt to design and implement the solution. Then to wrap up, we identified the appropriate WPS and WESB components that will have to be built. By the end of this chapter, the goal is to be ready to walk the talk and be all set for building the various parts of the application that make up the whole.

8
Walk the Talk

So far, we have concentrated on laying the foundation for building SOA solutions in WebSphere Business Process Management. This included understanding concepts of SOA and learning the features and capabilities of the products that help us assemble, implement, deploy, execute, and maintain those solutions. Now has come the time to walk the talk, to get our hands dirty, and to put our knowledge into action.

The next few chapters will build out the pieces and parts of the Sales Fulfillment Application using the various features and capabilities provided by WPS and WESB. The architectural discussions so far have described the business and IT goals and requirements for JungleSea Inc., identified existing application systems, defined actors and use cases, and described business domains, process services, Business Services, and Access Services for the Sales Fulfillment Application. In this chapter, we will begin the process of assembling the SOA solution. The scope of this chapter is to accomplish two very critical steps. The first step towards assembling these components is to catalog their interface and data types in shared libraries that can then be leveraged by the different modules of the Sales Fulfillment Application. The next step will be to visualize the solution from a top-down perspective and identify the process, business, and Access Service layers.

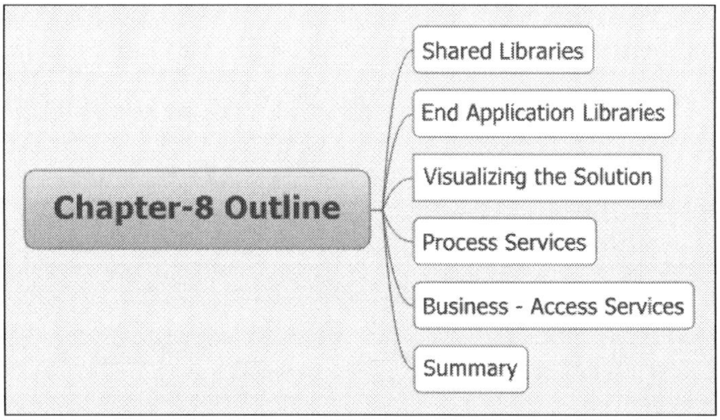

Shared libraries

When services, interfaces, and business objects need to be shared so that resources in several modules can reuse them, it is a best practice in WID to create library modules to catalog them. This is also recommended when interfaces need to be published or consumed by a third party.

Please note that in order for a module to use the assets from a library, it has to be added as a dependent to the module. Libraries should be added by right-clicking the module and selecting Dependency Editor. Shared libraries are included in each module, so if you change any one of the shared libraries, you must republish all the modules that are associated with it.

> A library can have dependent libraries. In this way, one library can use resources from another library without actually duplicating the asset in both the libraries.

There is no rule of thumb on how many libraries to create and what assets should go in which library. For JungleSea Inc., we recommend separating the libraries by business domain and by external business applications integrated in the solution. This helps catalog assets belonging to the same business area or domain together such as Customer Information or Shipping Management. It also helps keep external or third-party assets separate. Therefore, changes in one area do not impact the other areas. Let's look at each separately.

Business Doman Libraries

In the previous chapter, we identified the following business domains:

- Customer Information Management
- Product Catalog Management
- Customer Billing Management
- Shipping Management
- Supplier/Partner Management
- Inventory Management
- Customer Credit Management

The following figure is a reflection of the work flow laid out in *Chapter 7, Sales Fulfilment Application for JungleSea Inc.* and highlights where we are in the flow:

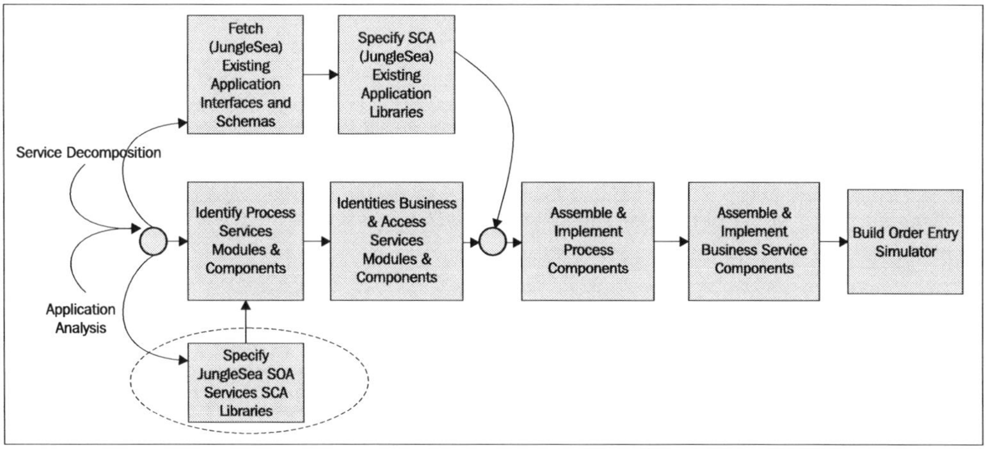

In this step, we will specify the JungleSea SOA service SCA library modules that will hold all the business domain specific assets like Business Objects and interfaces.

Based on the analysis from the previous chapter and the work done by JungleSea Inc. data architects, it has been decided to create the following business domain-specific libraries:

- BillingDomain-v1_0
- CommonDomain-v1_0
- CustomerDomain-v1_0
- ProductDomain-v1_0
- SupplierPartner-v1_0

Creating the Common Domain library

Now let's look at how we accomplish the creation of a typical library module using the Common Domain library as an example.

The Common Domain library contains interfaces and Business Objects that are common to all business areas and external applications. It enables reuse of assets between the different business domains.

You may use these steps to create the remainder of the libraries:

1. In WID, change to the **Business Integration** perspective and right-click under **Projects**. Select **New | Library**. Give the library the name **CommonDomain-v1_0** and click on the **Finish** button. This will create the library in the **Projects** area, as shown in the following screenshot:

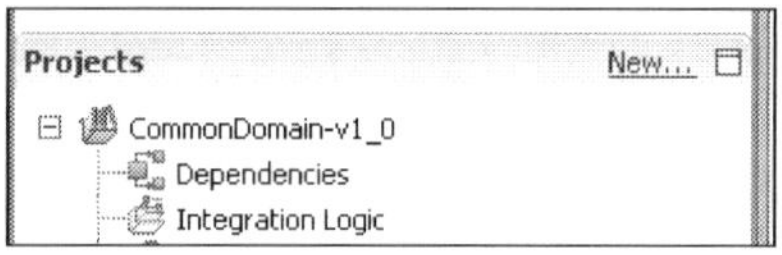

2. Right-click on **CommonDomain-v1_0** and select **New | Business Object**, as shown in the following screenshot:

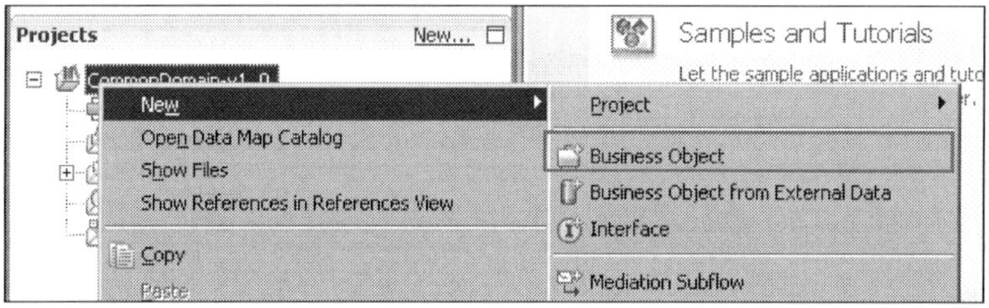

3. In the **Create a Business Object** window enter **Folder** as **com/junglesea/bo**, **Name** as **Acknowledgement**, and click on the **Finish** button.

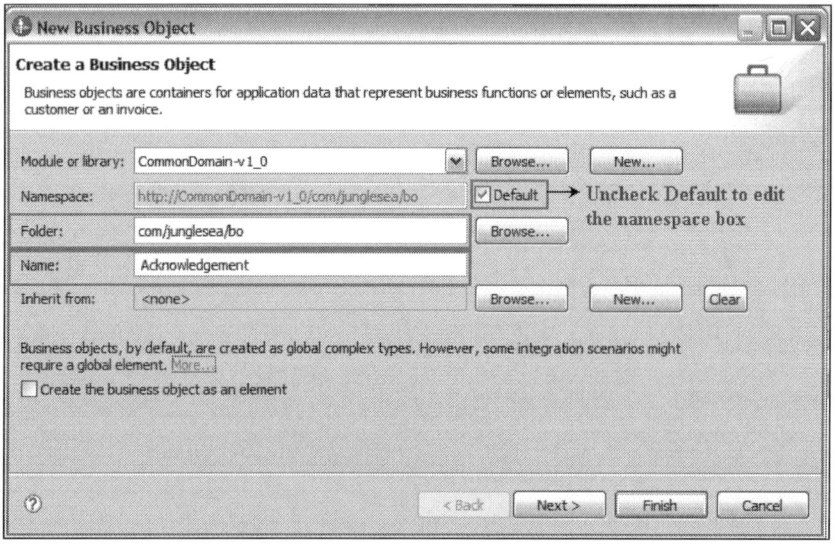

[**Namespace** plays a very important role to define context within which a business object is defined. It is very important to keep the namespace unique. If the same namespace is used between different libraries or modules then business objects of these modules become inaccessible to each other.]

4. For the **Acknowledgement** Business Object, you can create the fields using the add field icon. By default, the **Type** is set to **string**. Click on **string** to change the type as needed.

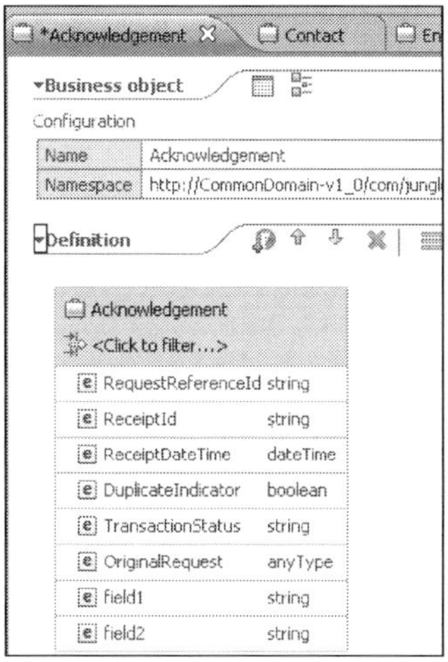

Acknowledgment Business Object (BO) holds the details about the receipt and acknowledgement of a transaction.

5. Repeat steps 3 and 4 to create the following Business Objects and the associated fields.

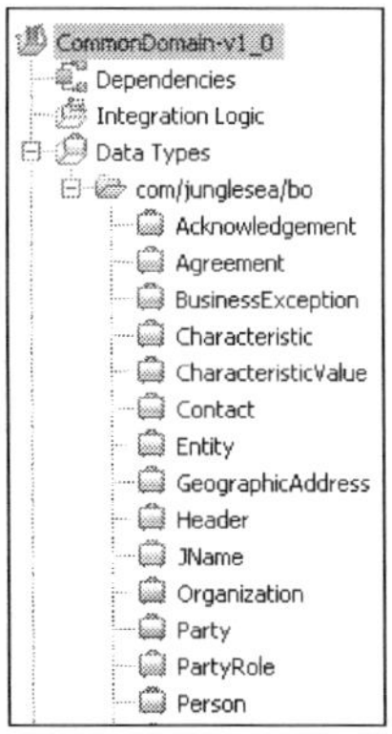

6. Here is the breakdown of the fields associated with each of the Business Objects listed above:

    - **Agreement**: This Business Object will hold the agreement details. Agreement is a type of Business Interaction that represents a contract or arrangement that sets out terms and conditions based on which JungleSea will sell the products and services to its customers.

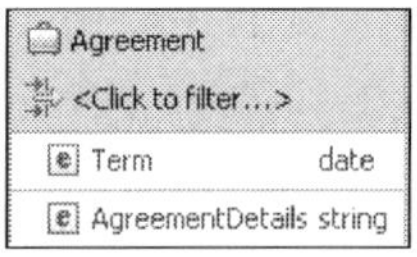

    - **BusinessException**: It represents the business-level exceptions and report details about the error in the Header Business Object.

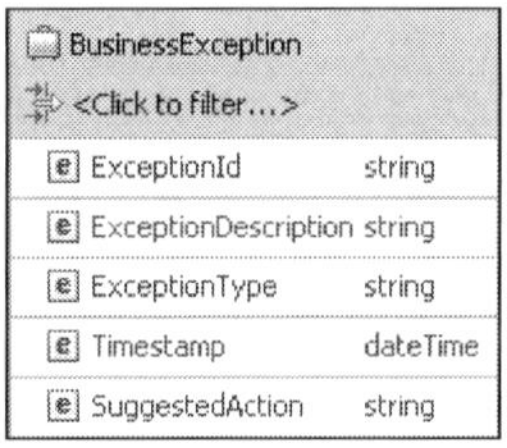

    - **Characteristic**: It represents the essential attributes for a Business Object or an entity (as explained above) that you want to dynamically specify. With JungleSea selling many products, and each having its own set of unique characteristics, to avoid statically defining them as elements, we can dynamically define product characteristics such as weight, color, height, and so on. We dynamically define these as characteristics.

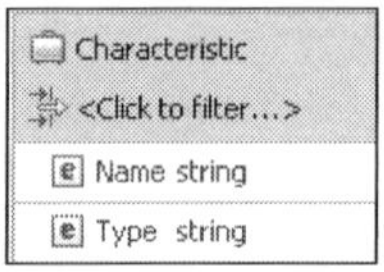

    - **CharactertricValue**: It represents the values of the essential attributes itself.

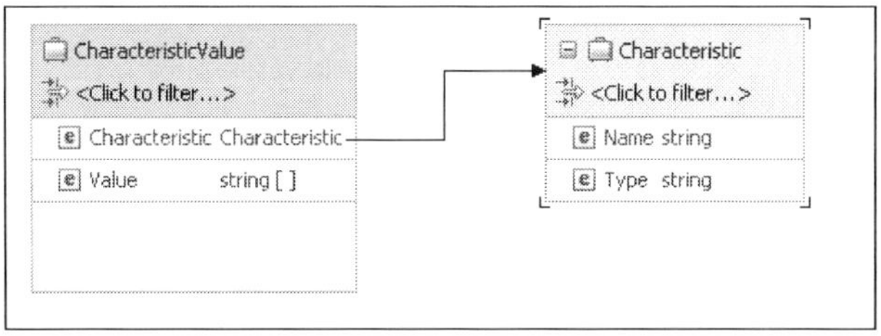

- **Contact**: This object represents all the contact details of the party like the contact person's name, phone, website, and so on.

- **Entity**: It represents classes of objects that play a business function. Entities can be either managed or unmanaged. In the context of the message schemas we have defined, it allows you to dynamically define Business Objects (type objects in OO) on the fly. We use this as a poor man's implementation of the Dynamic Object Model for allowing dynamic typing in XML Schemas. For more information on the Dynamic Object Model, refer to `http://st-www.cs.illinois.edu/users/johnson/papers/dom/DynamicObjectModel.pdf`

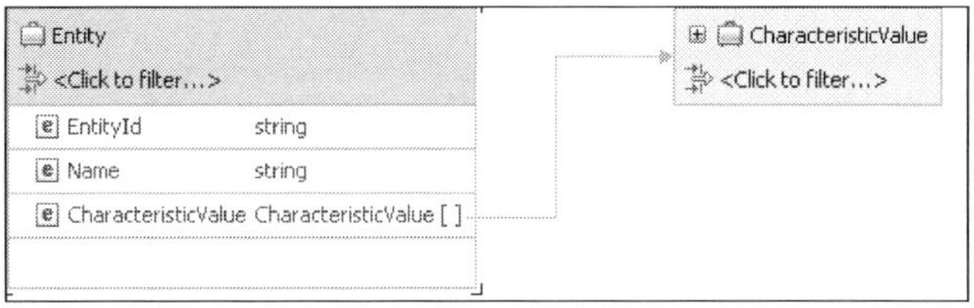

- **GeographyAddress:** This Business Object holds the physical address of the party.

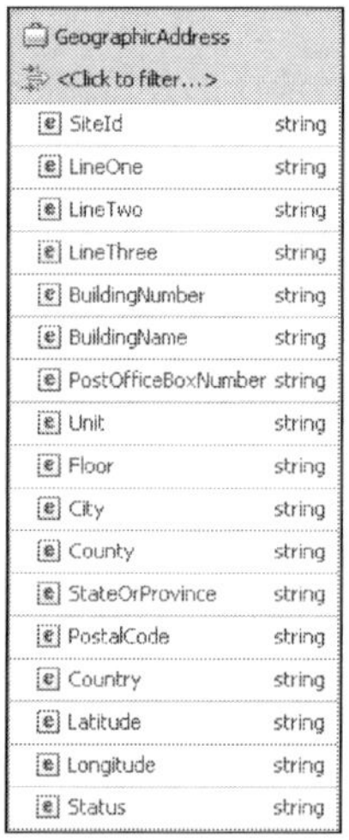

- **Header**: This Business Object is used as part of an every message Business Object definition. It is used to identify the business transaction itself. It's used to carry the metadata about the business transaction and can hold information such as what message type or transaction type is this (Request, Response, or Error), originator identification, unique message ID for the transaction itself, and so on. There may be cases where you will not be using web services and hence non-SOAP messages. In such cases, you can also add message-specific properties that you would not want to pass in the canonical Business Object itself. An example would be, say, you may want to pass the originator's e-mail ID so that you can send notifications back. You can specify this as a message-specific property (as a name value pair) in the **Header** BO.

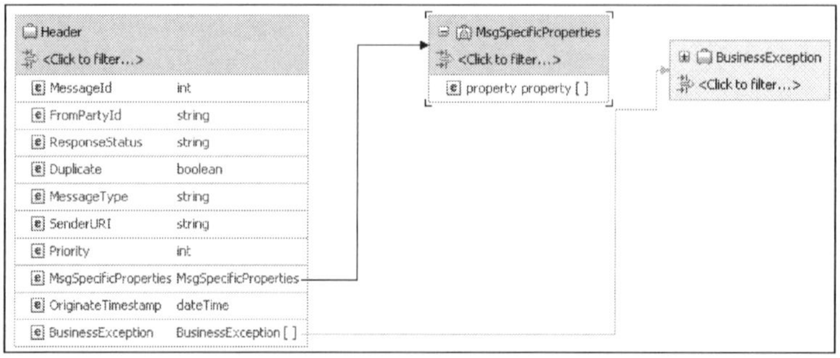

- **JName:** WID does not allow two BOs to have the same BO name. We prefixed the letter "J" to uniquely identify the "Name" object that refers to the name of a party versus the name used in the **Characteristic** BO.

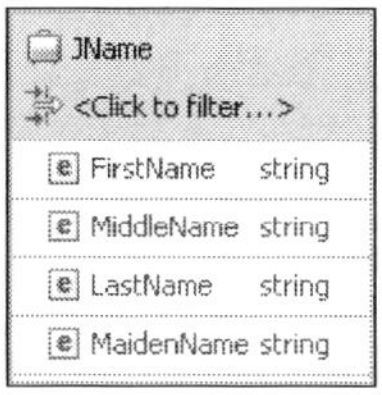

- **Organization**: This Business Object holds the details of the organization. Notice that it contains fields of the type **GeographicAddress** and **Contact** that we created earlier. This is a good example of reusing assets.

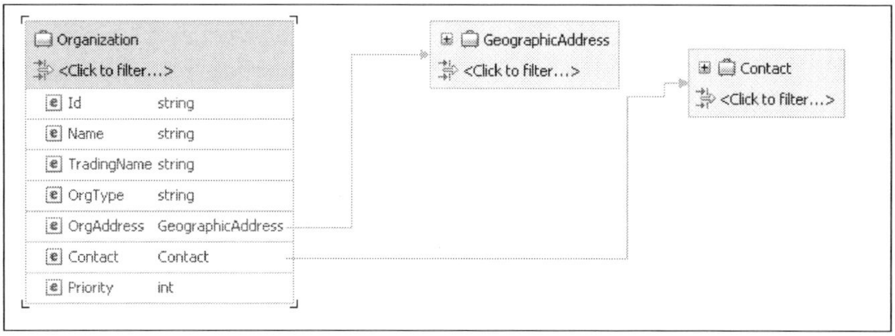

- **Party:** This Business Object defines the type of party and associated details. A party can be one of the following types: **Person, Organization**, or **SupplierPartner**. The party's details are defined accordingly.

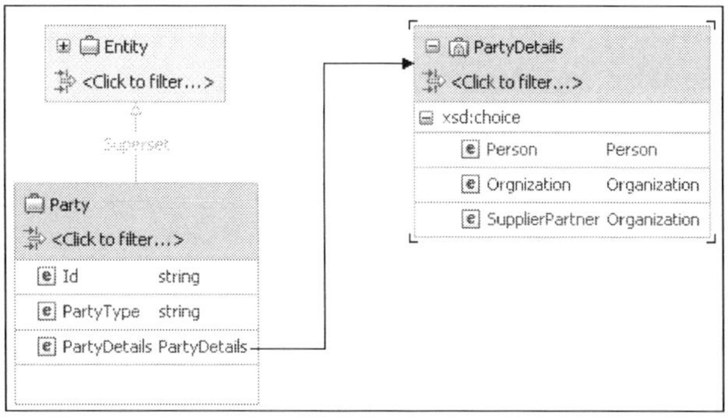

- **PartyRole:** This Business Object holds the **Status** and the **Party** fields.

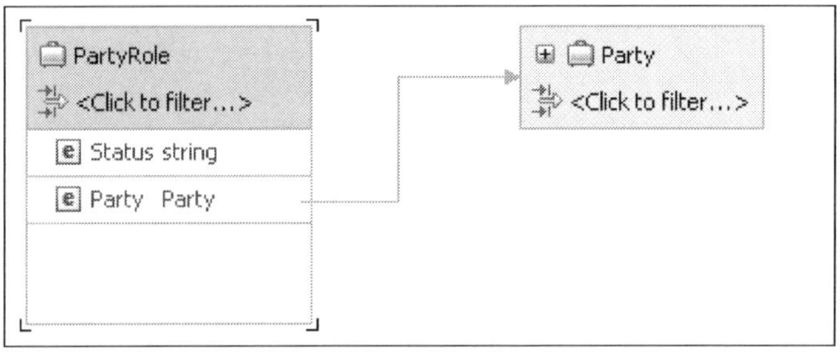

- **Person:** This Business Object holds details about a person like the **Name**, **Gender**, **Contact**, and so on.

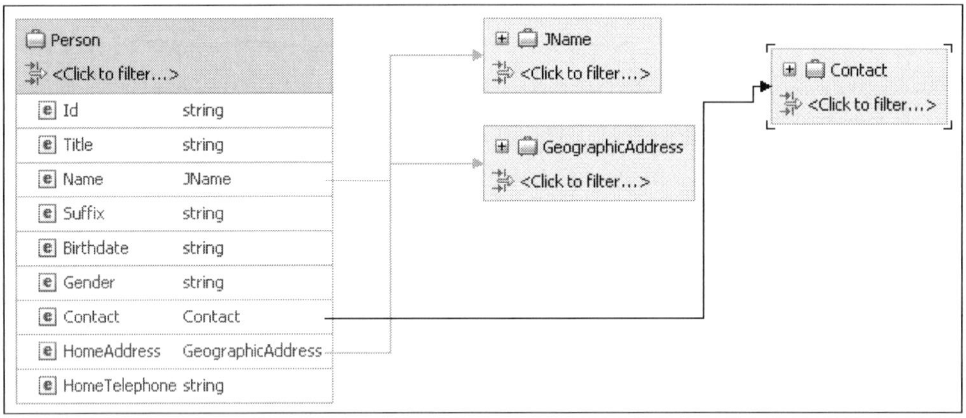

Having created the common domain library, we take a closer look at the remaining business libraries.

BillingDomain-v1_0

Now let's look into the **BillingDomain-v1_0** library, which contains all the interfaces and Business Objects for the applications used in the billing business domain. The following table provides details of this library:

BillingDomain-v1_0		
Interfaces	ProcessCustomerPayments	CustomerCreditInformation
Business Objects	System Business Objects	
	CreditCardDetails	Invoice
	InvoiceCharges	Payment
	PaymentMethod	
	Message Business Objects	
	PaymentMSG	PaymentAcknowledgementMSG

If you notice, we broadly categorized the Business Objects under system and messages Business Objects. System Business Objects are used for the data items that are needed by the application while the message Business Object helps extend the system Business Objects with header or metadata information about that particular Business Object. This gives us the ability to make business decisions in the process using the sent data along with the metadata captured by the message Business Objects.

> Please refer the PI file provided for this chapter to gain details about the fields for each of these Business Objects.

CustomerDomain-v1_0

Next, let's look into the **CustomerDomain-v1_0** library which contains all the interfaces and Business Objects for applications used in the customer business domain. The following table provides details about this library:

CustomerDomain-v1_0		
Interfaces	MaintainCustomerInformation	ProcessCustomerOrder
	RetrieveCustomerInformation	HandleCustomerContact
	ManageOrderFallout	
Business Objects	System Business Objects	
	Customer	CustomerCollection
	CustomerCredit	CustomerAccount
	Order	OrderItem
	OrderStatus	
	Message Business Objects	
	CustomerMSG	CustomerCollectionMSG
	CustomerCreditMSG	CustomerOrderMSG
	CustomerOrderStatusMSG	CustomerCommunucationMSG

ProductDomain-v1_0

Next, let us look into the **ProductDomain-v1_0** library, which contains all the interfaces and Business Objects for applications used in the product business domain. The following table provides details about this library:

ProductDomain-v1_0		
Interfaces	MaintainProductInformation	MaintainInventoryInformation
	RetrieveProductInformation	RetrieveInventoryInformation
Business Objects	System Business Objects	
	Item	Product
	ProductCollection	ProductAgreement
	ProductOffering	
	Message Business Objects	
	InventoryItemMSG	ProductMSG
	ProductCollectionMSG	

SupplierPartner-v1_0

Next, let us look into the **SupplierPartnerDomain-v1_0** library, which contains all the interfaces and Business Objects for applications used in the supplier partner business domain. The following table provides details about this library:

SupplierPartnerDomain-v1_0		
Interfaces	ProcessSPOrders	ManageShipments
		TrackShipments
Business Objects	System Business Objects	
	SupplierPartner	SupplierPartnerOrder
	SupplierPartnerOrderStatus	Shipment
	Message Business Objects	
	SupplierPartnerOrderMSG	ShipmentMSG

This completes the creation of the SOA services SCA libraries.

End Application libraries

We will now refer to the workflow from *Chapter 7, Sales Fulfilment Application for JungleSea Inc.* and look at the next step, as shown in the following diagram:

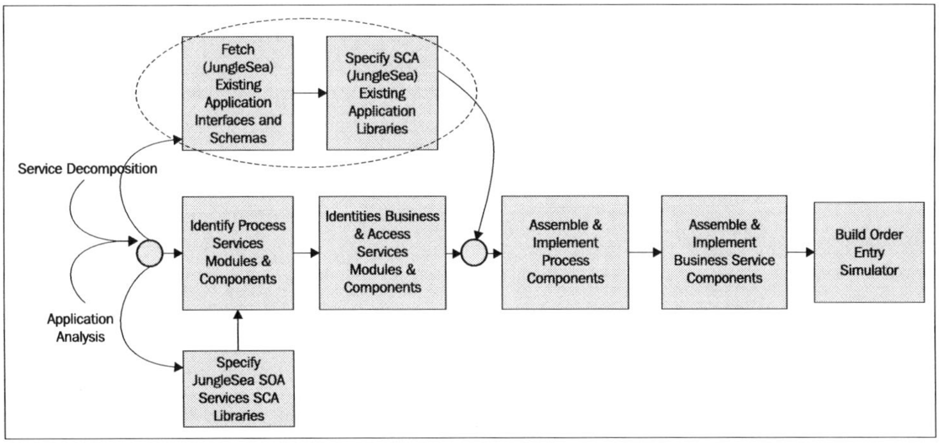

After creating the interfaces and Business Objects for the business domains, we move our attention to the end applications that will be integrated with this SalesFulfilment solution. In this step, we will import or define the interfaces and schemas from the end applications and catalog them under library modules. We recommend creating a library per application in order to maintain flexibility and clarity in our solution. The libraries for the SalesFulfilment solution will be:

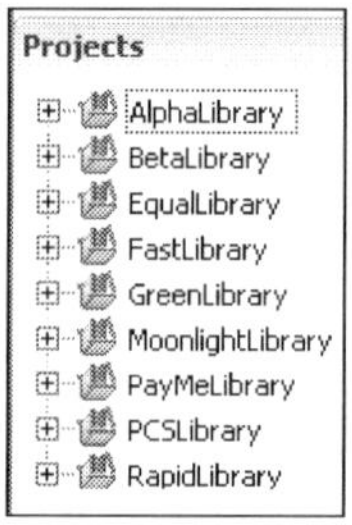

In each of these libraries, we will catalog the interfaces and Business Objects exposed by the respective application. After the completion of this task, we now have all the interfaces we need to build out Sales Fulfillment Application and we begin with the actual assembly of components. However, before doing that, it is important to model the components on paper to a get a clear understanding of what needs to be built. For the purpose of this book, we will provide a top-down visualization of the components. This task also begins the next step in the workflow, as shown in the following diagram:

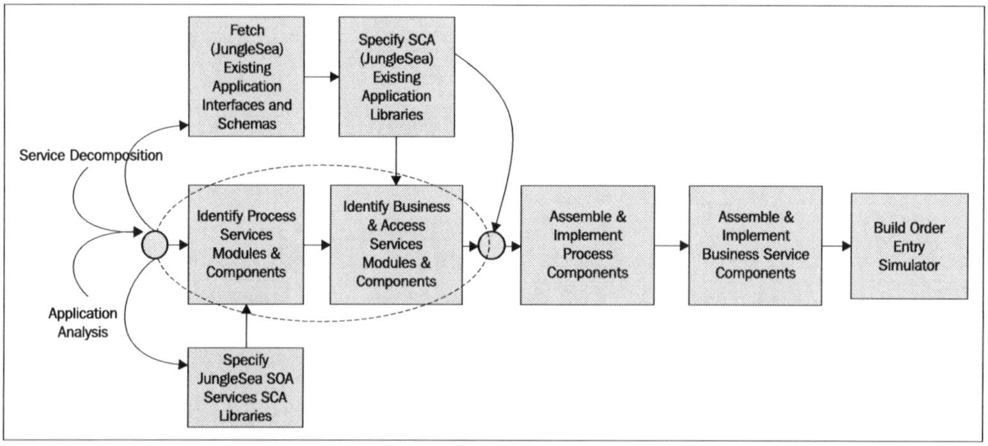

Visualizing the solution

Before we walk down the top-down description of this solution, it is important to revisit *Chapter 7, Sales Fulfilment Application for JungleSea Inc.* for the different tiers of capabilities or services laid out by IBM SOA Reference Architecture:

- Process Services provides the capability to define an end-to-end business processes and automation of all processes in the system for order handling, human activities, fallout/error handling, notifications, process visualization, monitoring, process data mediation, and storage. This layer is built using IBM's WebSphere Process Server.
- Business Services provide the coarse-grained business functions that have a meaningful significance to JungleSea Inc.
- Access Services provide the bridging capabilities between the Business Services interfaces and the end application interface through the ESB. This layer will also provide the capability to intercept and modify messages that are passed between the Business Services and the end JungleSea application service interfaces (providers). Mediation services can be implemented using mediation modules deployed on the WebSphere Enterprise Service Bus or the WebSphere Process Server.
- Business Application Services are the services that are exposed by the end applications that our solution will integrate with.

Assumption: We are assuming that business application services, which are needed by the Sales Fulfilment Application, are available and that the integration and exposure of legacy systems is beyond the scope of this exercise.

These layers are responsible to help abstract and loosely couple the components, so that in the future this solution is extremely flexible, manageable, and adaptable to changes in the business environment with minimum impact to the overall process. Hence these layers become critical to deliver some of the key values of SOA. In the next chapter, we will see how easy it is deliver this abstraction of layers through an SCA platform using tools such as WID and WPS.

Process Services

As identified in the previous chapter, our application consists of two process services—OrderHandling and CustomerInterfaceManagement, as shown in the following figure:

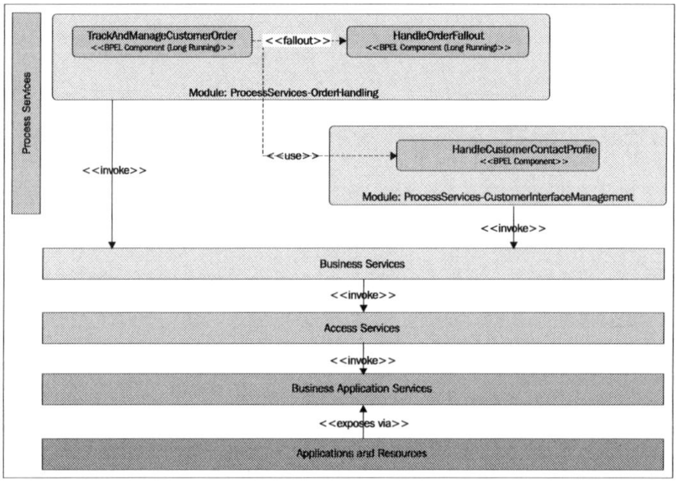

How to read the preceding diagrams:

The outer boxes represent the modules of the process service. The module names represent the actual module name in the Sales Fulfillment Application in WID. The inner boxes with the module box represent the components in the module assembly that make up the module and the << >> signifies the type of implementation used to develop that component. Lastly, << >> on the arrows defines the interrelationships between modules/components/layers and how they are integrated together.

For example, the module ProcessServices-OrderHandling in WID contains two components, namely, TrackAndManageCustomerOrder and HandleOrderFallout, which are both implemented as long running BPEL processes. TrackAndManageCustomerOrder in the event of a fallout invokes HandleOrderFallout to handle the exception.

Under this process layer lies the business and Access Services that support the end-to-end process. It is important to note here that a process service may potentially call one or many process, business, or Access Services as needed. In our application, we will use the TrackAndManageCustomerOrder process service. Likewise, a Business Service may call one or more business or Access Services.

Let's take a closer look at each of these process services, unwrapping each service to expose the underlying business and Access Services associated with them.

Process Service — Order Handling

First we analyze the Order Handling Process Service. The process service modules are created by an assembly of components, which are in turn integrated with Business and Access Services giving the layered SOA solution. The following component layout map provides visibility across these different layers and helps define the depth needed to develop the solution.

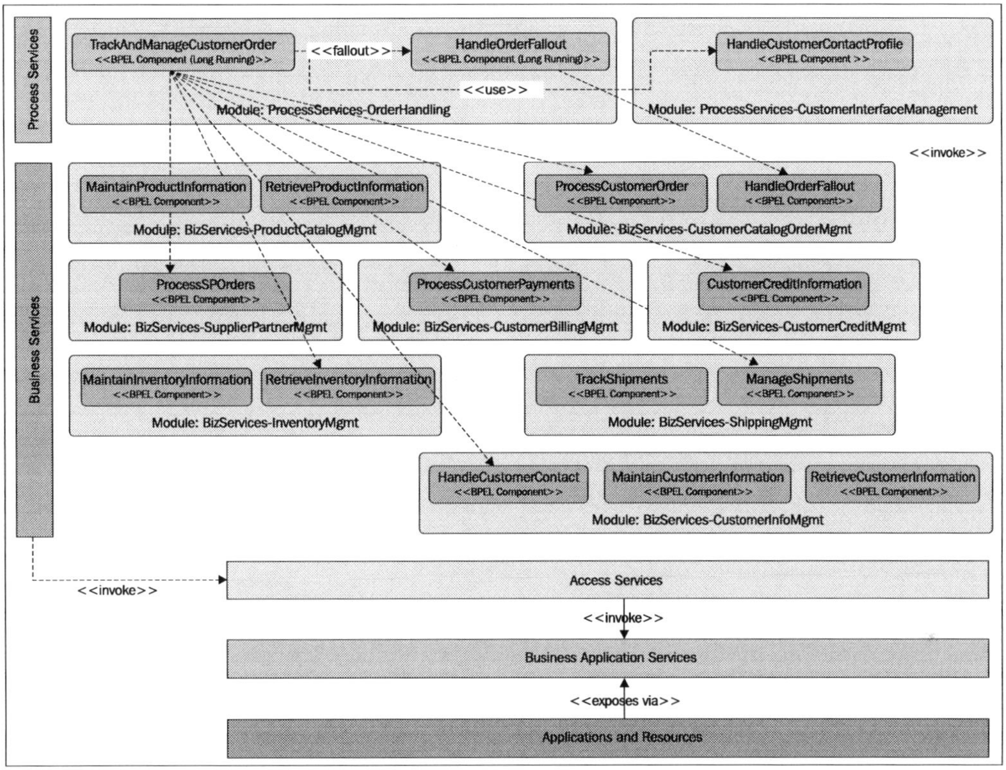

This layout is critical as it provides an end-to-end assembly of the different layers that make the SOA a truly flexible architecture. At each level, the components are linked together independent of the technology they are developed in. This means that the TrackAndManageCustomerOrder process service, which will be implemented as a BPEL process, can easily consume services built using different technologies like mediation flows, web services, and so on. The trick is that each of these services are exposed using a component and interface that hides their actual implementation. In the preceding diagram, the actual WID module represents the outer box and the components that make up that module are represented by the inner box. As we unwrap the Order Handling service, let's take a closer look at these two components—TrackAndManageCustomerOrder and HandleOrderFallout.

Process Service — Order Handling components

In order to understand and develop any component, we need to understand what purpose the component will serve, how it will be used, how it will be developed, and what tooling features can we use to implement it.

TrackAndManageCustomerOrder component has:

- **Purpose**: The main process that processes, manages, and tracks all incoming orders.
- **Implementation type**: BPEL (Long Running Process)
- **Interface name:** ProcessCustomerOrder
- **WPS/WID capabilities**: Human Task

HandleOrderFallout component has:

- **Purpose**: This component handles errors and sends out notifications accordingly
- **Implementation type**: BPEL (Long Running Process)
- **Interface name**: ManageOrderFallout
- **WPS/WID capabilities**: Human Task

The WPS/WID features listed above provide guidance on how the component will eventually be developed. The Business Service and Access Service layers for this service will be unwrapped in the following section.

Process Service — CustomerInterfaceManagement

For this process service, we begin unwrapping by creating a component layout that clearly describes all the layers and the depth of this service through the layers, as shown in the following diagram:

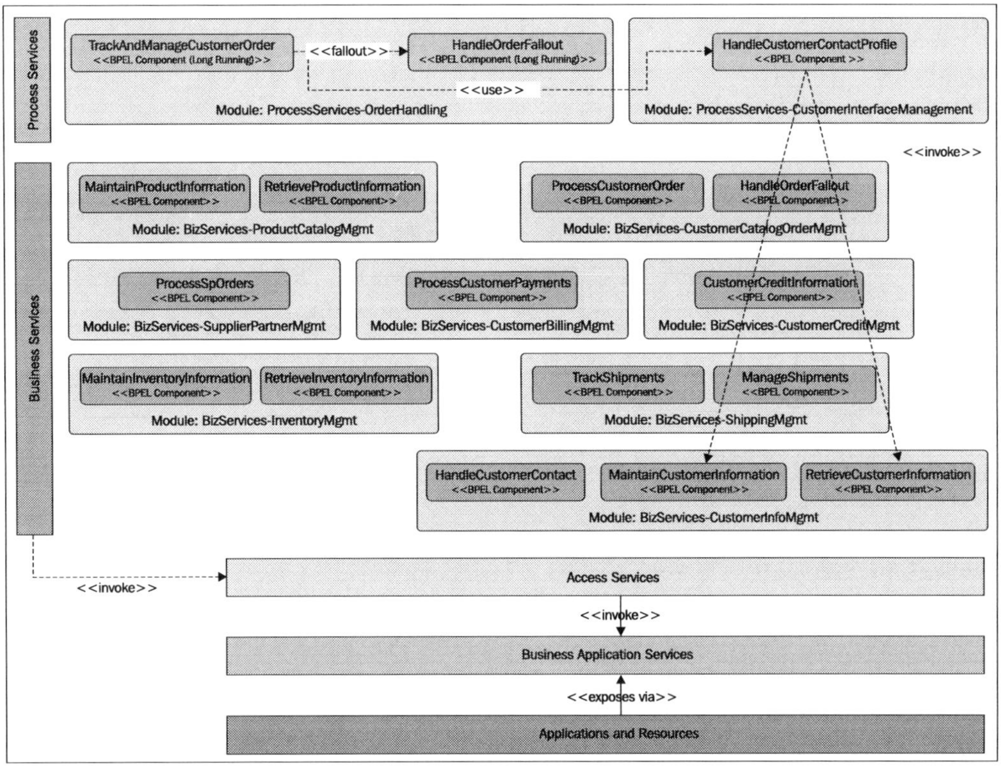

Process Service — CustomerInterfaceManagement components

CustomerInterfaceManagement process contains one component called HandleCustomerContactProfile. Similar to OrderHandling service, the information below provides details about this component that we will need to understand and develop it in WID.

HandleCustomerContactProfile component has:

- **Purpose:** To create and manage customer contact information and notification preferences
- **Implementation type**: BPEL (Long Running Process)
- **Interface name**: HandleCustomerContactProfile
- **WPS/WID capabilities**: Human Task

This completes the unwrapping of the process service layers. We now take the analysis to the next layer, which is the business and Access Service layer.

Business Services and Access Services

Business Services provide the coarse-grained business functions that have a meaningful significance to the enterprise. These coarse-grained services may leverage one more business or Access Service. Access Services provide the bridging capabilities between the Business Services interfaces and the end application interface through the ESB. These capabilities, as explained in the previous chapter, include adapters, mediation flows, and process flows. In this section, we will provide a visualization of the business and Access Service layers. For each Business Service, we will also provide details about purpose, interface, implementation details, and Access Services associated with them.

Business Services for TrackAndManageCustomerOrder component

We begin the analysis with the TrackAndManageCustomerOrder process service component, which is associated with the following Business Services:

- ProductCatalogManagement
- CustomerOrderManagement
- SupplierPartnerManagement
- CustomerBillingManagement
- CustomerCreditManagement
- InventoryManagement
- ShippingManagement
- CustomerInformationManagement

Let's look closely at each of the Business Services and define:

- The component layout map for the Business Service
- Essential information about each of the Business Services, including the WPS/WID features that will be used during implementation
- Essential information about each of the associated Access Services including WPS/WID features that will be used during implementation

Business Service — ProductCatalogMgmt

The ProductCatalogMgmt Component Layout Map is shown in the following diagram:

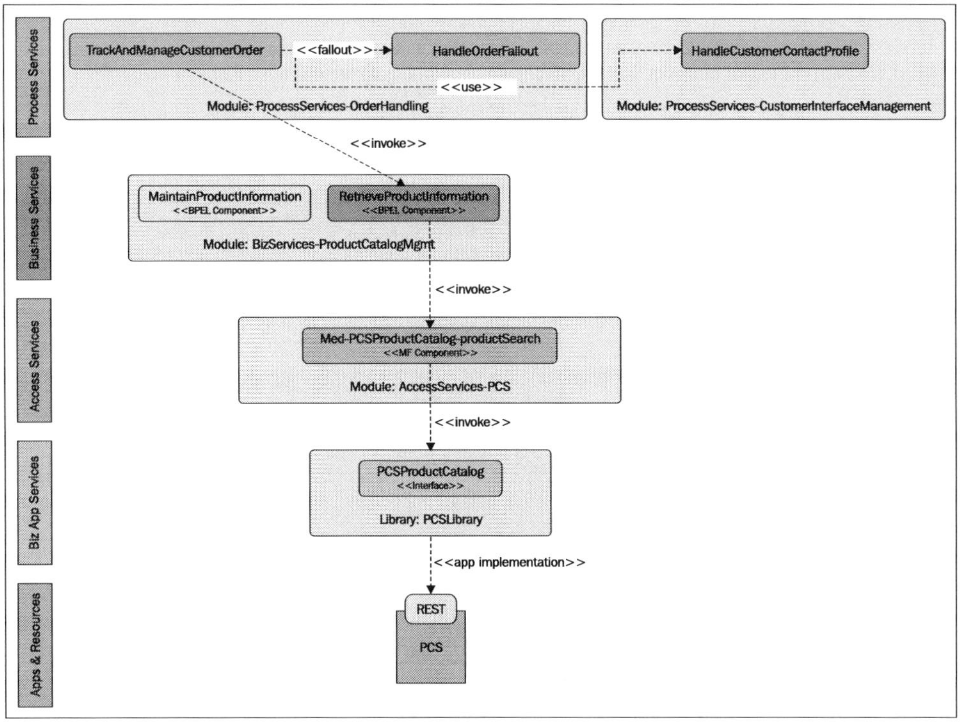

The preceding diagram states that the WID module BizServices—**ProductCatalogMgmt** has two components, namely, **MaintainProductInformation** and **RetrieveProductInformation**. This module invokes AccessServices—**PCS module**, which in turn uses the **PCSProductCatalog** interface from the PCS Library to communicate with PCS backend system.

MaintainProductInformation component has the following features:

- **Purpose:** To add, edit, and delete product information in the product catalog.
- **WPS/WID Implementation**: BPEL implemented through the Process SCA component of type microflow. Microflow means that a process completes from start to finish and that no human interaction is involved.
- **Interface name**: MaintainProductInformation.

RetrieveProductInformation component has the following features:

- **Purpose:** To retrieve product information from the product catalog.
- **WPS/WID Implementation:** BPEL implemented through the Process SCA component of type microflow.
- **Interface name:** RetrieveProductInformation.

Lastly, we need to describe the PCS Access Service:

- **Operation:** productSearch.
- **WPS/WID Implementation**: BPEL implemented through the Process SCA component of type microflow.
- **Interface name**: PCSProductCatalog.

Business Service — InventoryManagement

The InventoryManagement Component Layout Map is shown in the following diagram:

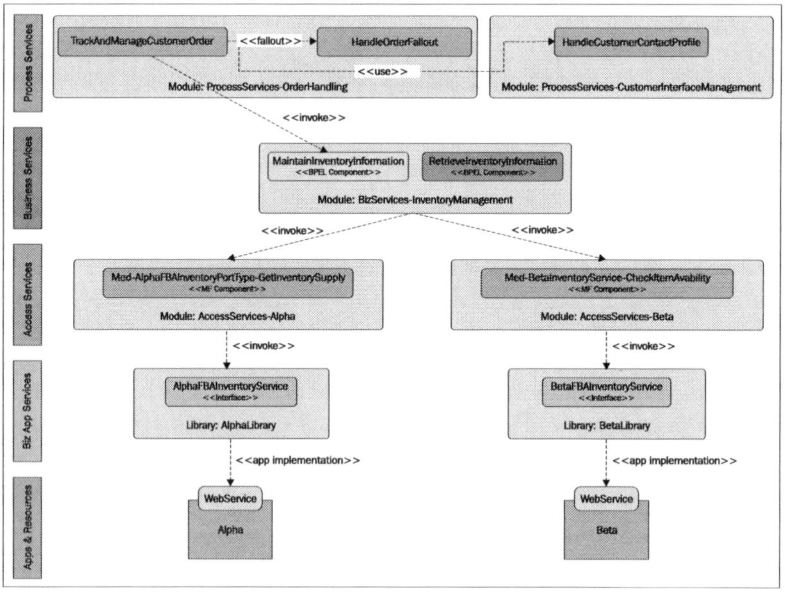

The preceding diagram states that the WID module BizServices—InventoryManagement has two components, namely, MaintainInventoryInformation and RetrieveInventoryInformation. This module invokes Access Service modules called AccessServices—Alpha or Access Services—Beta, which in turn uses the *AlphaFBAInventoryPortType* or *BetaInventoryService* interface from the Alpha or Beta Library to communicate with Alpha or Beta systems respectively.

MaintainInventoryInformation component has the following features:

- **Purpose:** To add, edit, and delete inventory information
- **WPS/WID Implementation:** BPEL implemented through the Process SCA component of type microflow
- **Interface name:** MaintainInventoryInformation

RetrieveInventoryInformation component has the following features:

- **Purpose:** To retrieve inventory information
- **WPS/WID Implementation:** BPEL implemented through the Process SCA component of type microflow
- **Interface name:** RetrieveInventoryInformation

Lastly, we need to define the Access Services. First, let's define the Alpha Access Service:

- **Operation:** GetInventorySupply
- **WPS/WID Implementation:** Mediation Flow
- **Interface name:** AlphaFBAInventoryPortType

Then, let's describe the Beta Access Service:

- **Operation:** CheckItemAvailability
- **WPS/WID Implementation:** Mediation Flow
- **Interface name:** BetaInventoryService

Business Service — CustomerCreditManagement

The CustomerCreditManagement Component Layout Map is shown in the following diagram:

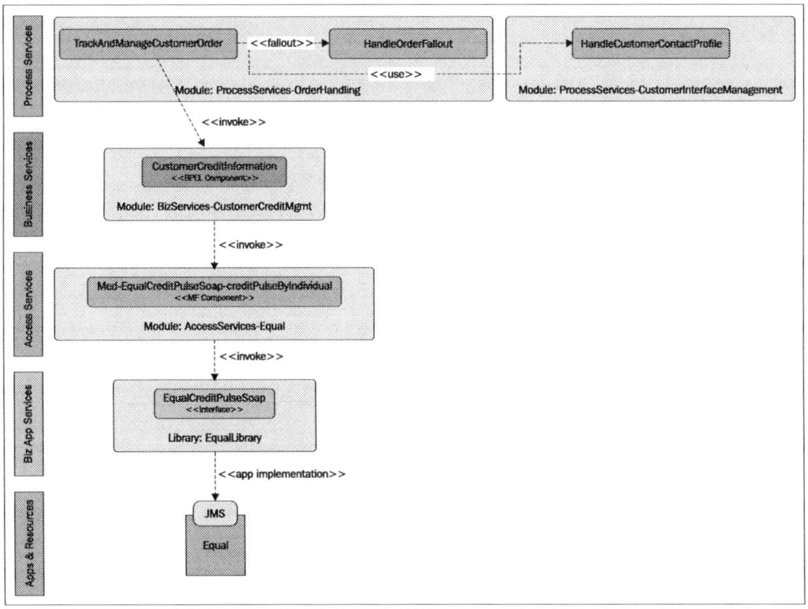

The preceding diagram states that the WID module BizServices—CustomerCreditManagement has one component, namely, CustomerCreditInformation. This module invokes AccessServices—Equal module, which in turn uses the EqualCreditPulseSoap interface from the EqualLibrary to communicate with Equal systems.

The **CustomerCreditInformation** component has the following features:

- **Purpose:** To get credit information for a given customer
- **WPS/WID Implementation:** BPEL implemented through the Process SCA component of type microflow
- **Interface name:** CustomerCreditInformation

Lastly, we need to define the Equal Access Service:

- **Operation:** creditPulseByIndividual
- **WPS/WID Implementation:** MediationFlow
- **Interface name:** EqualCreditPulseSoap

Business Service — SupplierPartnerManagement

The SupplierPartnerManagement Component Layout Map is shown in the following diagram:

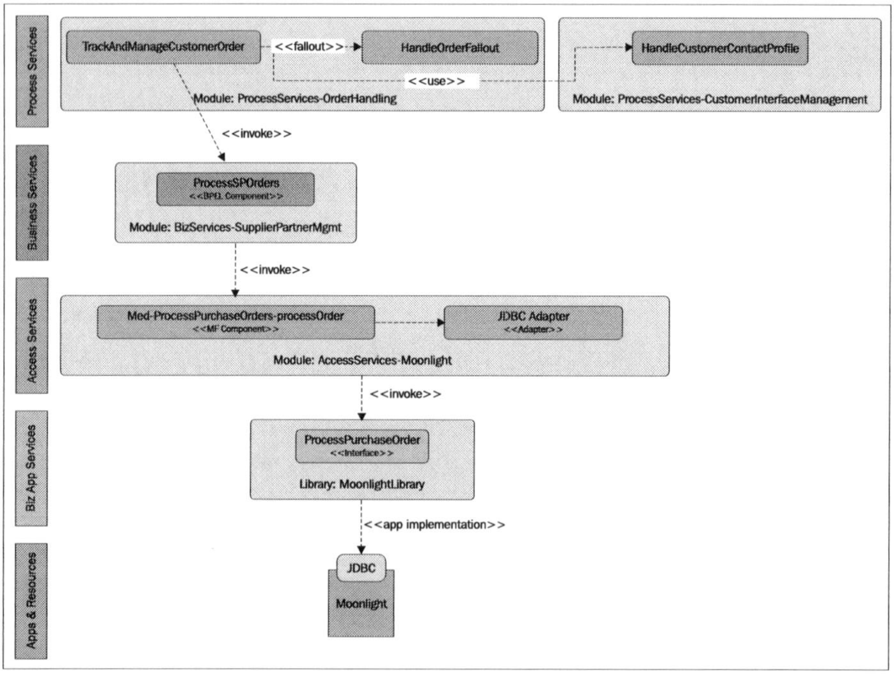

The preceding diagram states that the WID module BizServices—SupplierPartnerManagement has one component, **ProcessSPOrders**. This module invokes AccessServices—Moonlight module, which in turn uses the ProcessPurchaseOrders interface from the Moonlight Library to communicate with Moonlight systems.

The **ProcessSPOrders** component has the following features:

- **Purpose:** To process supplier partner orders
- **WPS/WID Implementation:** BPEL implemented through the Process SCA component of type microflow
- **Interface name:** ProcessSPOrders

Lastly, we need to define the Moonlight Access Service:

- **Operation:** processOrder
- **WPS/WID Implementation:** MediationFlow/JDBC Adapter
- **Interface name:** ProcessPurchaseOrders

Business Service — CustomerBillingManagement

The CustomerBillingManagement Component Layout Map is shown in the following diagram:

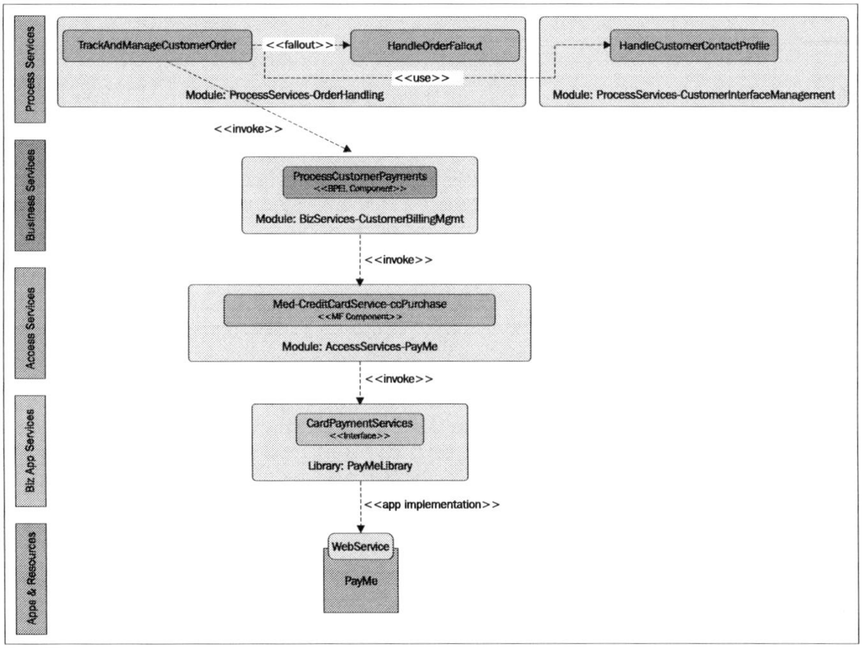

The preceding diagram states that the WID module BizServices—CustomerBillingManagement has one component, **ProcessCustomerPayments**. This module invokes the AccessServices—PayMe module, which in turn uses the *CreditCardService* interface from the PayMeLibrary to communicate with PayMe systeThe **ProcessCustomerPayments** component has the following features:

- **Purpose:** To process customer payments in the desired payment method
- **WPS/WID Implementation:** BPEL implemented through the Process SCA component of type microflow
- **Interface name:** ProcessCustomerPayments

Lastly, we need to define the PayMe Access Service:

- **Operation:** ccPurchase, ccSettlement
- **WPS/WID Implementation:** MediationFlows
- **Interface name:** CreditCardService

Business Service — ShippingManagement

The ShippingManagment Component Layout Map is shown in the following diagram:

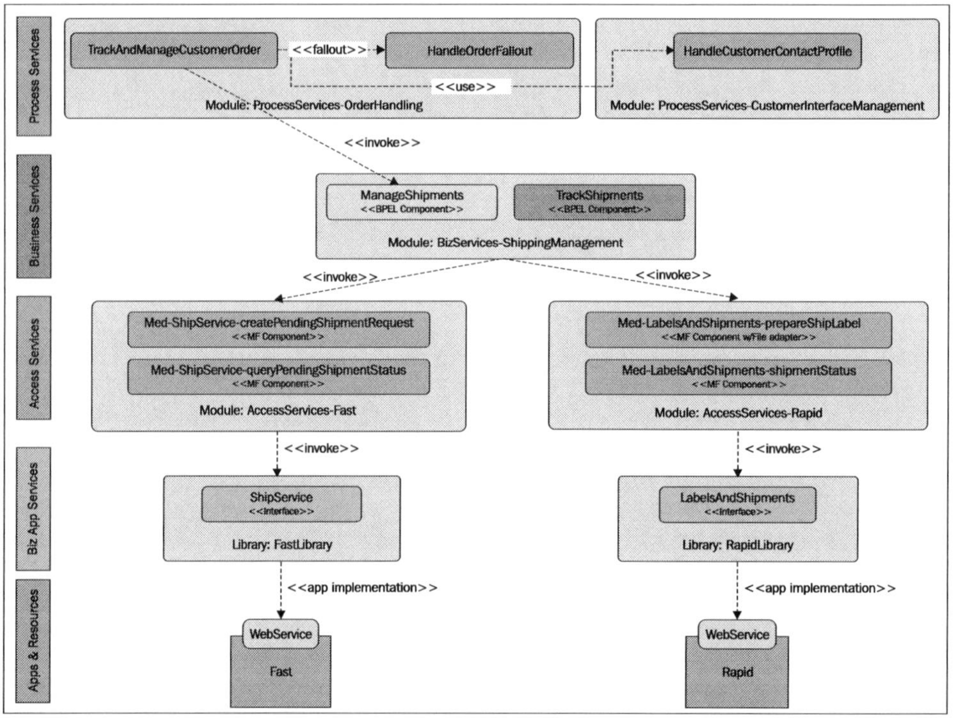

The preceding diagram states that the WID module BizServices—ShippingManagment has two components, namely, ManageShipments and TrackShipments. This module invokes either the AccessServices—Rapid module or the Access Service—Fast. The Access Service then uses the respective interface to communicate with either the Rapid or Fast systems.

The **ManageShipments** component has the following features:

- **Purpose:** To create and manage shipments
- **WPS/WID Implementation:** BPEL implemented through the Process SCA component of type microflow
- **Interface name:** ManageShipments

The TrackShipments component has the following features:

- **Purpose:** To track a shipment
- **WPS/WID Implementation:** BPEL implemented through the Process SCA component of type microflow
- **Interface name:** TrackShipments

Lastly, we need to define the Access Services. First, let's define the Alpha Access Service:

- **Operation:** prepareShipLabel, shipmentStatus
- **WPS/WID Implementation:** Mediation Flow/File Adapter
- **Interface name:** LabelsAndShipments

Then, let's define the Beta Access Service:

- **Operation:** createPendingShipmentRequest, queryPendingShipmentStatus
- **WPS/WID Implementation:** MediationFlow
- **Interface name:** ShipService

Business Service — CustomerOrderManagement

The CustomerOrderManagement Component Layout Map is shown in the following screenshot:

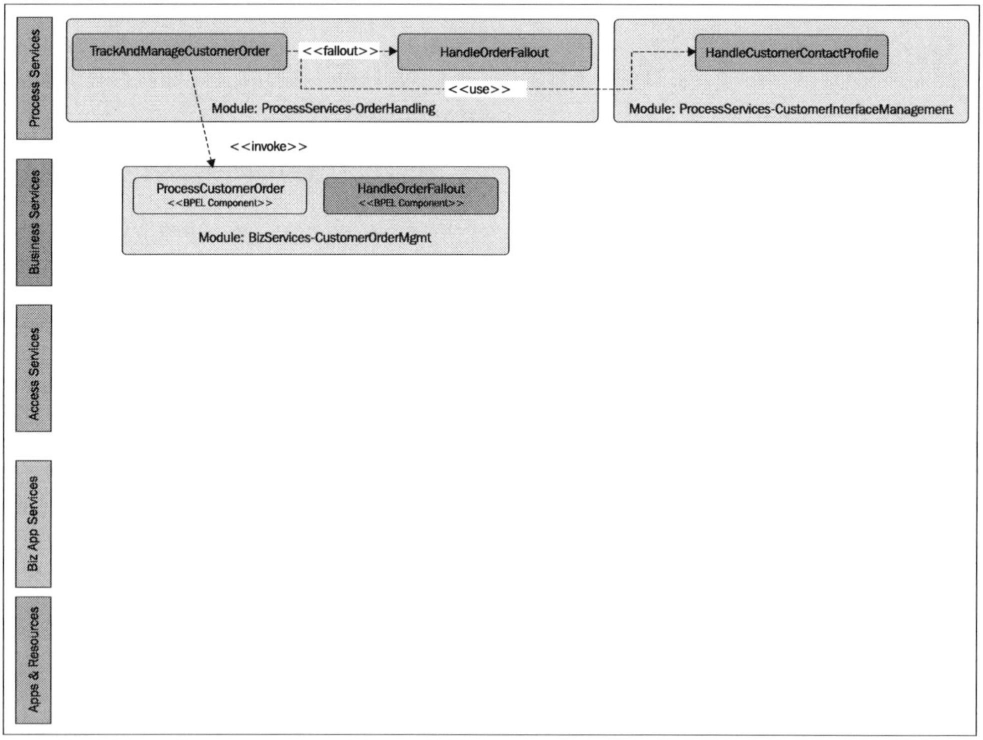

The preceding diagram states that the WID module BizServices–ShippingManagment has one component called ProcessCustomerOrder.

The **ManageShipments** component has the following features:

- **Purpose:** To process customer orders
- **WPS/WID Implementation:** BPEL implemented through the Process SCA component of type microflow
- **Interface name:** ProcessCustomerOrder

Business Service — CustomerInformationManagement

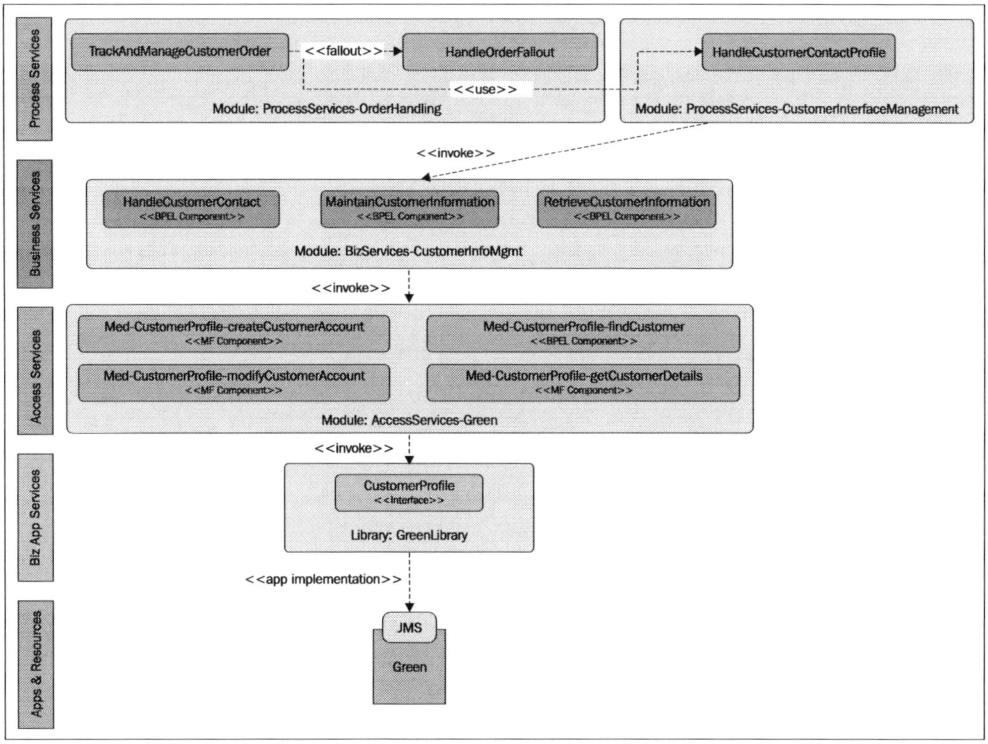

The preceding diagram states that the WID module BizServices—CustomerInformationManagement has two components, namely, MaintainCustomerInformation and RetrieveCustomerInformation. This module invokes the AccessServices—Green module that then uses the *CustomerProfile* interface to communicate with the Green systems.

The **MaintainCustomerInformation** component has the following features:

- **Purpose:** To create and maintain customer information
- **WPS/WID Implementation:** BPEL implemented through the Process SCA component of type microflow
- **Interface name:** MaintainCustomerInformation

The RetrieveCustomerInformation component has the following features:

- **Purpose:** To retrieve customer information
- **WPS/WID Implementation:** BPEL implemented through the Process SCA component of type microflow
- **Interface name:** RetrieveCustomerInformation

Lastly, we need to define the Green Access Service:

- **Operation:** createCustomerAccount, modifyCustomerAccount, findCustomer, and getCustomerDetails
- **WPS/WID Implementation:** Mediation Flow and BPEL
- **Interface name:** CustomerProfile

Summary

This chapter provided details around the assembly phase of the IBM SOA Reference Architecture. We first saw how to assemble components to catalog their interface and data types in shared libraries that can then be leveraged by the different modules of the Sales Fulfillment Application. Then we visualized the solution from a top-down perspective and identified the process, business, and Access Service layers. It started with the creation of shared libraries and then provided a top-down breakup of the process, business, and Access Services that will be developed and assembled for the Sales Fulfillment Application in the later chapters.

9

Building the Order Handling Processes

In this chapter, we will build the Process Services modules—*ProcessServices-OrderHandling* and *ProcessServices-CustomerInterfaceManagement*, and the associated business processes (BPELs) that we identified. As we build these modules incrementally in the respective assembly diagrams, we will initially **import** the **exports** with SCA bindings from the Business Services modules that will have no implementation behind them (we will build the Business Services and Access Services modules in *Chapter 10, Integration with Various Applications*). As we build these BPELs, we will accommodate the business, technical, and Non-Functional Requirements (NFRs), including fault handling, human task management, data mappings, and so on. We will see how they deal with various implementation issues and the design decisions they make appropriately. This chapter will explain the following topics:

- BPEL development steps
- Using business rules in the process
- Implementing human tasks
- Usage of control structures
- Fault handling including compensation
- Discuss about:
    - Correlation sets
    - Event handling
    - XPath
- Testing the end-to-end business processes once the Business Service and Access Service modules have been built

Module assembly

In *Chapter 7, Sales Fulfillment Application for JungleSea Inc.*, we established the workflow we will follow to build the Sales Fulfillment Application. Based on this flow of steps, we will assemble and implement the components that make up the solution. We will perform steps for assembling and implementing the components in the process services layer, as shown in the following figure:

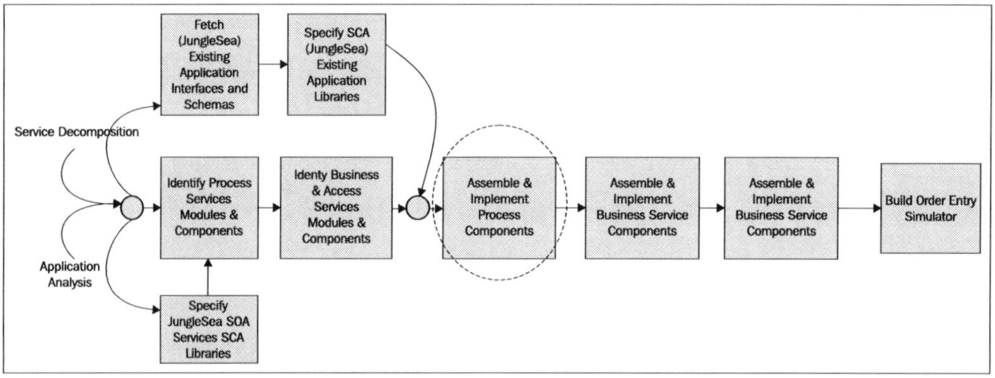

Now let's look at how we can accomplish these steps. The assembly diagram is the visual tool for constructing the modules and mediation modules, defining and assembling SCA artifacts including components, exports, imports, and standalone references, and for wiring them together to build applications/solutions. You can drag-and-drop various components from the palette onto the canvas that you need to have a deployable module. Based on the build manifest we identified in *Chapter 7* and *Chapter 8, Walk the Talk*, we will have to construct the following modules and the associated components:

- ProcessServices-CustomerInterfaceManagement
    - HandleCustomerContactProfile (*Micro-flow BPEL Component*)
- ProcessServices-OrderHandling
    - TrackAndManageCustomerOrder *(Long Running BPEL Component)*
    - HandleOrderFallout *(Long Running BPEL Component)*

[As mentioned in *Chapter 7* you can use the WebSphere Business Modeler (IBM's premier business process modeling and analysis tool for business users) to model business processes using the BPMN notation. These process models can be automatically exported as BPELs for implementation in the WebSphere Process Server when modeled using the WebSphere Process Server Modeling mode. But for the purposes of this book, we will be manually creating the business processes in WID using the process flow editor.]

Steps involved in building business process

The steps involved in building a module with business process components (BPEL) can be listed as follows. We will follow these steps in the later sections for each of the business process components we will have to implement.

[You can use these steps as a reference and as part of your larger development process in the future to implement any business process component.]

- **Import Application libraries and Modules/Simulators:**

  Import the end application interfaces (WSDL) and Business Objects (XSD) into their respective libraries—*GreenLibrary*, *PCSLibrary*, *PayMeLibrary*, *FastLibrary*, *RapidLibrary*, *MoonlightLibrary*, *AlphaLibrary*, *BetaLibrary*, and *EqualLibrary* (these were identified and created in Chapter 8) into your workspace. These libraries will have to be added as dependencies to the module(s) you will be creating. As recommended earlier, these libraries should be version-controlled in a version control system such as CVS or IBM ClearCase.

[Note: As mentioned earlier, for the purposed of this book, we will be simulating the JungleSea end applications, including *Green*, *PCS*, *PayMe*, *Fast*, *Rapid*, *Moonlight*, *Alpha*, *Beta*, *Equal*.]

- **Create and import JungleSea Domain libraries:**

  Import the libraries that contain the interfaces and Business Objects to be used by the business process components. These libraries, namely, *CustomerDomain-v1_0, BillingDomain-v1_0, ProductDomain-v1_0, SupplierPartnerDomain-v1_0,* and *CommonDomain-v1_0* were created in Chapter 8 based on the output of the service decomposition exercise done in Chapter 7.

- **Create and/or import necessary dependent modules:**

  Make sure you have all the necessary Business Service and Access Service modules imported into the workspace. If the necessary modules are not available, create them with components that have no implementation. The business process component will leverage the SCA exports of the corresponding business service component. As we build these modules incrementally, in the respective assembly diagrams, we will initially import the exports with SCA bindings from the Business Services modules that will have no implementation behind them (we will build the Business Services and Access Services modules in Chapter 10).

- **Creating a module:**

  - Create a module by giving it an appropriate name as per the build manifest we identified in Chapter 7 and Chapter 8.
  - Add JungleSea Domain libraries as project dependencies. Double-click on the **Dependencies** node, add the libraries, and save.
  - Create the business process components with an appropriate interface and name them per the build manifest we identified in Chapter 7 and Chapter 8. Right-click on the **Integration Logic** node and select **Business Process**.
  - Choose the appropriate operations on the interface that will start the process. Note that if the selected operations are not starting operations, then the generated business process will contain errors.

- **Module, Assembly, and Wiring:**
    - Drag-and-drop the business process component created in the previous step onto the assembly diagram canvas.
    - External components that a Business Process can invoke are called Partners. In the SCA assembly diagram, visually assemble the module by dragging and dropping the appropriate SCA exports (as imports) from other modules and wiring them to the business process component (created in the earlier step) and from the properties view of the Invoke, select the appropriate operation of the partner.
    - Create a standalone reference on the business process component (if necessary) for the outside world (in our case, the Order Entry web UI) to invoke it. Right-click in the white space in the assembly diagram and select **Add Node | Reference**.
    - Define Quality of Service (QoS) qualifiers such as reliability, transactions, activity session, security, and reliable asynchronous invocation to the business process components and also the interfaces and references (imports).
- **Implement the Business Process component:**
    - In WID, open the business process component and create the basic business process flow using the visual process editor, based on the TO-BE business process model and the detailed design you may have performed (we did not cover this in detail in Chapter 7, but did mention that a detailed design phase automatically follows the modeling and architecture phase).
    - Leverage the "Reference Partners" while building the process flow. Since we imported the necessary business services and wired them to the business process component in the "Module Assembly and Wiring" step, you would be able to see the respective imports as "Reference Partners" in the process editor palette to the right. As mentioned earlier, the business services will have no implementation yet (we will build them in the next chapter), and hence these will be non-working stubs for all practical purposes.
    - Add activities to the business process flow to accomplish individual business tasks that make up the whole goal.

- Add Event Handlers if it is necessary to respond to an external invocation/stimuli with an appropriate defined action.
- Add Java snippets using a (Visual) Snippets task. You can also use XPath to manipulate or iterate a business object using XPath expressions.
- Define local variables as needed by the process to store the messages that are exchanged between itself and its reference and also the data that is used in its business logic. As explained in *Chapter 3, Building your Hello Mediation Project*, a variable belongs to the scope in which it is declared. If it is created in the global process scope, then it is a global variable and thus visible to the process as a whole.
- If the process is long running, you can define Correlation Sets and Correlation for tracking the multiple, long-running exchanges of messages between the business process and its reference partners. Correlation is typically used when a process consists of more than one receive or invoke activity.
- Use control structures for structured activities.
- Wherever appropriate, externalize business logic away from the process component using a business rule component. This will make the business process more dynamic, adaptive, and susceptible to business condition changes.
- Wherever necessary, use human tasks in the process whenever there is a need for input or action from a person or manual approval is needed. Typically, you would integrate WPS to use a user directory for user roles and user definitions. Use collaboration to create enhanced dynamic workflows so that business logic can be adapted at runtime.
- Finally, in the event monitor define events of interest for generation (*Completion forced, Entry, Exit, Expired, Failed, Retry forced, Assigned, Completion forced, Created, De-assigned*, and so on). The event monitor can be opened from the Properties view in many of the editors. At runtime, you can use the Common Base Event browser to view generated CEI events.

- **Implement Fault Handling:**
    - It's a good practice to handle any exceptional conditions and conditions that may affect the normal behavior of a business process. Faults can be classified into three buckets—Business, System, and Standard. While WPS provides the System (propagated by ServiceRuntimeException objects) and Standard faults, you as the implementer of the business process flow, should handle these faults gracefully and throw them back to the consumer with a meaningful business context.
    - The WS-BPEL specifications define a standard set of fault types for common system failures, which WPS has implemented. These built-in fault types are available to you in WID to add them to your business process.
    - There are also non-BPEL standard faults *cannotResolveEndpoint*, *runtimeFailure*, *serviceTerminated*, *splitFailure*, and *timeout* available to you.
    - Use Fault Handlers (Catch and Catch all) and Fault Activities (Compensate, Terminate, Throw, Rethrow) to catch and act on the faults appropriately.
    - Define Fault variables as necessary, as type *BusinessException* defined in the *CommonDomain-v1_0* SCA library.
    - Use Compensation to revert business transactions that have already been committed and will have to be reverted by invoking a balancing operation (for example, deleteCustomer may be the compensating operation for a committed createCustomer).
- **Testing the Business Process**
    - Test the business process end-to-end from a business integration point of view. Create Test Suite and Test Cases, as appropriate.

IBM and WS-BPEL 2.0 standard

As you know, WS-BPEL (or BPEL used interchangeably) provides the ability to express stateful, long-running interactions between Web services. IBM was the author of the original proposal for the BPEL specification, one of the first vendors to support BPEL, and supports WS-BPEL throughout its product, including:

- WebSphere Business Modeler
- WebSphere Integration Developer
- WebSphere Process Server
- WebSphere Business Monitor

The WS-BPEL 2.0 specification can be found at `http://docs.oasis-open.org/wsbpel/2.0/wsbpel-v2.0.html` and was approved in April 2007. IBM is a major contributor to the WS-BPEL 2.0 standard. Diane Jordan from IBM has been the chair of the OASIS technical committee and several others from IBM in the technical committee.

As mentioned earlier in *Chapter 3, Building your Hello Process Project*, WID/WPS does not completely support WS-BPEL 2.0 specifications. Majority of WS-BPEL 2.0 language elements are available in WID/WPS version 7.0. Additional value-add functions in WPS/WID even go beyond the standard.

Building ProcessServices-CustomerInterfaceManagement

As explained in the previous chapter, the purpose of this component is to handle the customer profile. It should check for the existence of a customer, and if not present, create the customer profile. This is a classic example of a composite service, and you may wonder why this is implemented as a business process. In the future, if we have to handle the creation of a billing account as part of a customer profile data, then it essentially leads to a cross-domain service invocation, which rightfully should be choreographed using a business process. When there is a need for invoking business services from more than one component and that belong to different application domains, a business process layer (using a BPEL) will be used to choreograph the interactions. They will not be contained within the business service component itself.

The pseudo logic for this business process component is depicted as an activity diagram, as shown next:

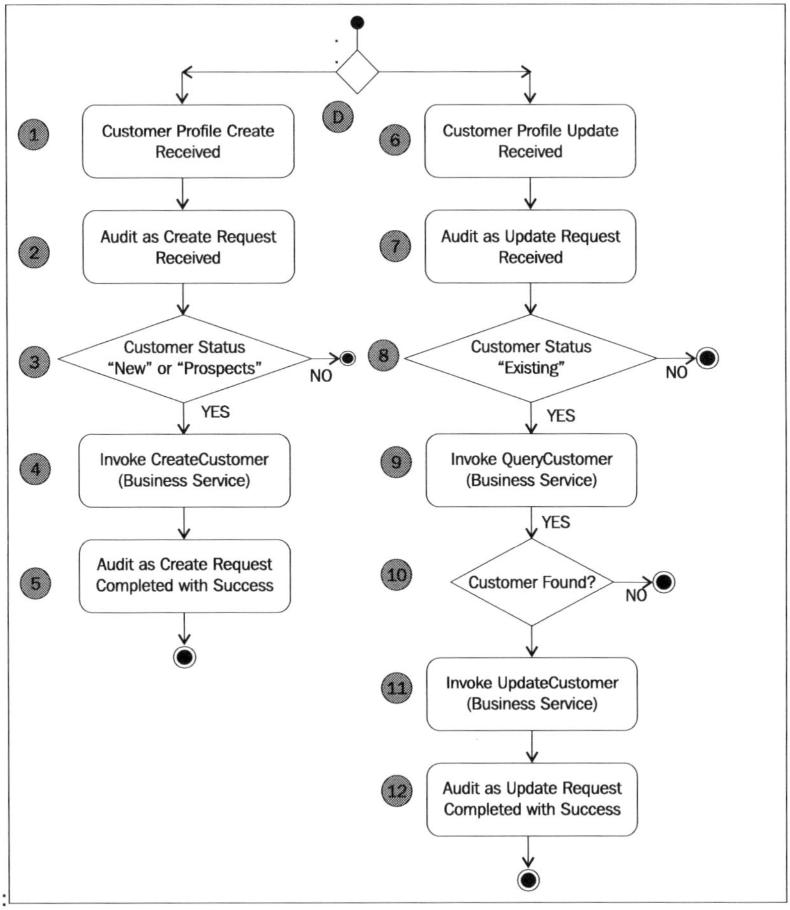

1. Receive a request for the creation of a new customer profile.
2. Audit the fact that a customer create request has been received.
3. Verify that the request (CustomerMSG) has a CustomerStatus value of "Prospect" or "New".
    - If not present, throw a business exception—"Customer Status Invalid" and terminate the process
    - Indicate "Failure" in the ResponseStatus in the Header
    - Log the exception to a file
4. Invoke the business service "MaintainCustomerInformation" on the "createCustomer" operation.

5. On a Successful completion, Audit that the customer creation has been successfully performed.
6. Return CustomerId populated in the response.
7. Indicate "Success" in the ResponseStatus in the Header.
8. On Exception:
    - Indicate "Failure" in the ResponseStatus in the Header
    - Throw a business exception with the relevant message
9. Receive request for updating an existing customer profile.
10. Audit the fact that a customer update request has been received.
11. Verify that the request (CustomerMSG) has the CustomerStatus value of "Existing":
    - If not present, throw a business exception - "Customer Status Missing Invalid" and terminate the process
    - Log exception to file
12. Invoke the business service "RetrieveCustomerInformation" on the "queryCustomer" operation to check to see if the customer already exists and enrich any data, if necessary.
13. If the customer is not found:
    - Indicate "Failure" in the ResponseStatus in the Header
    - Throw a business exception with the relevant message
14. Invoke the business service "MaintainCustomerInformation" on the "updateCustomer" operation.
15. On Successful completion, Audit that the customer update has been successful.
16. Indicate "Success" in the ResponseStatus in the Header.
17. On Exception:
    - Indicate "Failure" in the ResponseStatus in the Header
    - Throw a business exception with the relevant message

Implementing HandleCustomerContactProfile business process component

Let's follow the eight step process to implement the HandleCustomerContactProfile business process component:

> Recollect the key architectural decisions from *Chapter 7, Sales Fulfillment Application for JungleSea Inc.*, which we will have to adopt in the implementation of this business process component:
>
> - The Process Services and Business Services will have their interfaces exposed based on the common messaging model (meaning Generic Business Objects).
> - The data formats used by the service interfaces for the process services and business services (and the northern half of the Access Services) will be based on a canonical model.
> - The business processes will always invoke Business Services to accomplish business functions (as exposed by various applications). The bindings exposed by the Business Service components will be of type SCA.

Importing application libraries and modules/simulators

In the previous chapter, we had created end application libraries by importing the end application interfaces (WSDL) and business objects (XSD) into respective libraries, listed as follows:

- GreenLibrary
- PCSLibrary
- PayMeLibrary
- FastLibrary
- RapidLibrary
- MoonlightLibrary
- AlphaLibrary
- BetaLibrary
- EqualLibrary

These libraries should be in your workspace, as depicted by the following screenshot:

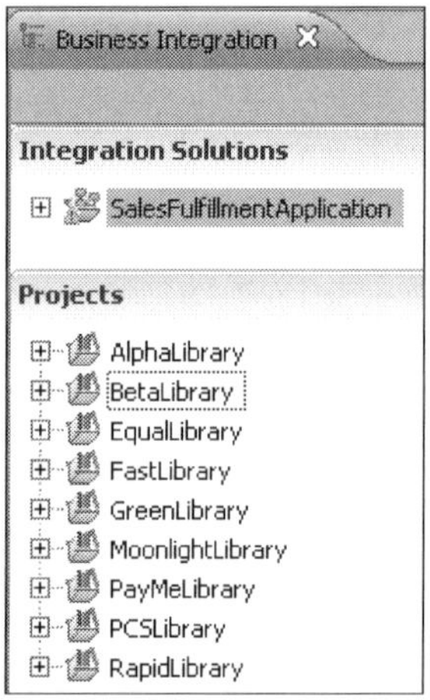

Creating and importing JungleSea domain libraries

In the previous chapter, we created the JungleSea domain interfaces (WSDL) and business objects (XSD) in their respective libraries listed below. These libraries were built based on the service decomposition exercise we explained in Chapter 7:

- CustomerDomain-v1_0
- BillingDomain-v1_0
- ProductDomain-v1_0
- SupplierPartnerDomain-v1_0
- CommonDomain-v1_0

These libraries should be in your workspace, as depicted and highlighted in the following screenshot:

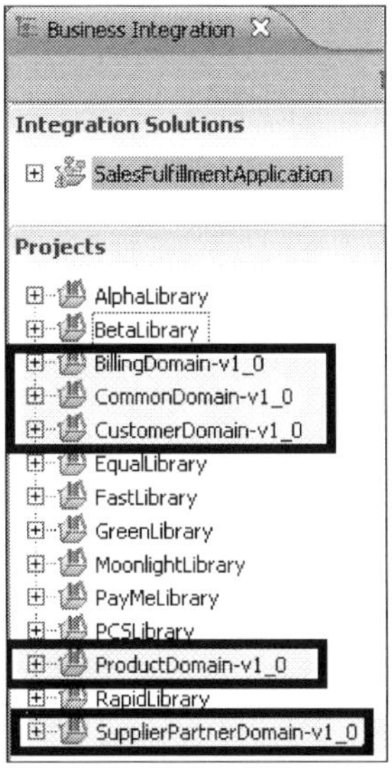

Creating and/or importing necessary dependent modules

In Chapter 8 we had identified what Business Service components would be needed to invoke the HandleCustomerContactProfile business process component to accomplish its goal. The module and the associated components were:

- BizServices-CustomerInfoMgmt (*Module*)
    - HandleCustomerContact (*BPEL Component*)
    - MaintainCustomerInformation (*BPEL Component*)
    - RetrieveCustomerInformation (*BPEL Component*)

1. First we will create modules that will hold all the Business Service components with names and interfaces, as we did in Chapter 8. Create a module by selecting **File | New | Module**, which will open the **New Module** wizard, the first screen of which is shown in the following screenshot. Name the module **BizServices-CustomerInfoMgmt**.

   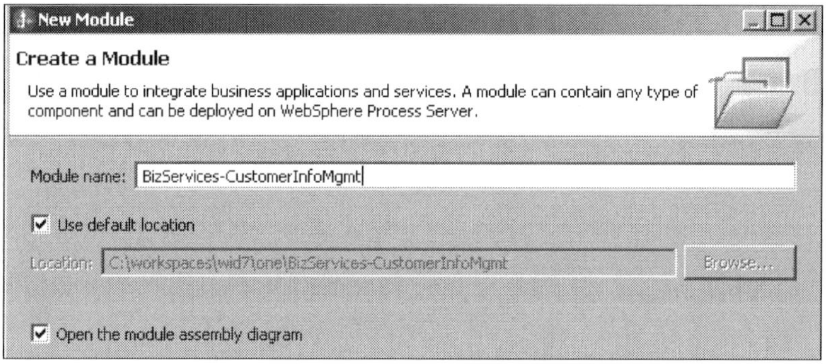

   In the next wizard screen, specify the dependent libraries required by this module, as is shown in the following screenshot, and press **Finish**.
   As you can see, we are not adding any JungleSea application libraries as a dependency. This is the beauty of the layered architecture approach we decided to adopt. The business process is not directly exposed to the end application interfaces (as in point-to-point mode), but instead goes through the Business Services layer

   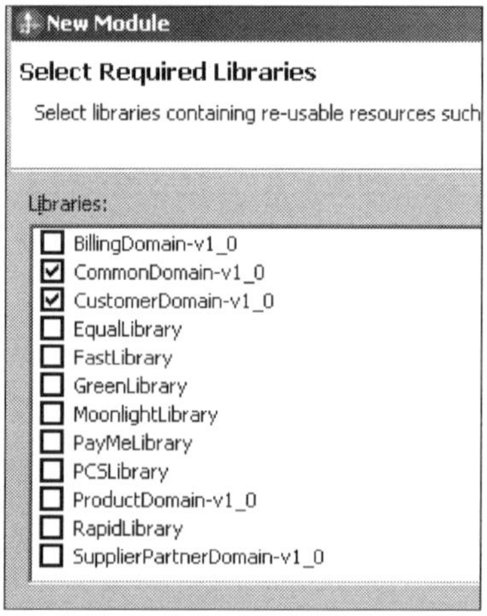

2. The assembly diagram for the module will open (if not, open it). Create a new BPEL (Microflow) component by right-clicking on **BizServices-CustomerInfoMgmt | Integration Logic | New | Business Process**. This will bring up the business process wizard, and you will have to start providing information. In the first screen, as shown in the following screenshot, provide the folder names (which are analogous to packages and become the basis for namespace) **com/junglsea/businessservices** and the name of the first component identified from Chapter 8 as **MaintainCustomerInformation**.

> As you can see from the following screenshot, the Namespace for this component is based on the module name and the folder name we provided. You are free to follow any other naming scheme.

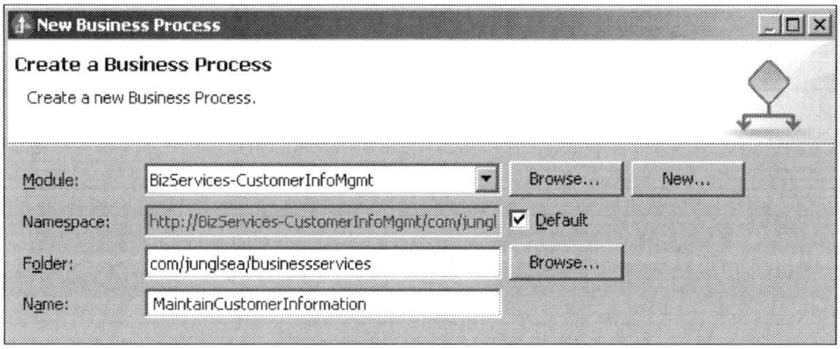

3. Continue with the wizard and specify the type of the business process component to be **Microflow**, as shown in the subsequent screenshot. Since we want the Business Services to be contained within a single transaction, and we want them to be executed very quickly in the runtime environment, we are making it of type Microflow.

Choosing between Long Running Process versus Microflow

A Microflow is contained within a single transaction and is not interruptible. They contain IBM's extensions to the BPEL specifications. A long-running process is typically one that executes over a long period of time and is multi-transactional. Choose the process type to be long running, if it meets any of the following criteria:

- Requires human intervention/contains a human task
- Needs to wait for an event or a notification to proceed
- We do not want any of the IBM extensions enabled for this process
- Need for parallel execution path each run within their own transaction and their transactional behavior must be set to be either commit before or requires own

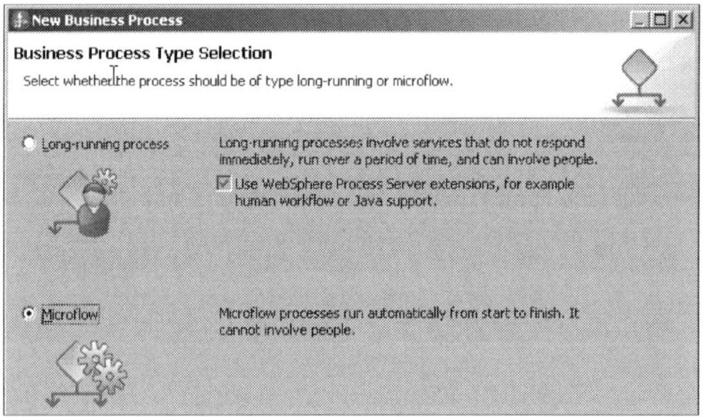

4. Continue with the wizard, and as shown in the following screenshot, select an interface by enabling the **Select an interface** radio button and browsing to the **MaintainCustomerInformation** interface name contained within the CustomerDomain-v1_0 (which we added as a dependent library earlier). As you can see in the following screenshot, we have selected both the operations to be ones that would start the business process, meaning the business process will implement both the operations inside its flow and will choose the right operation based on a "Receive Choice" action. You will have to select all the operations contained in the interface, even if you do not implement any logic for that operation, or else we will end up with BPEL errors.

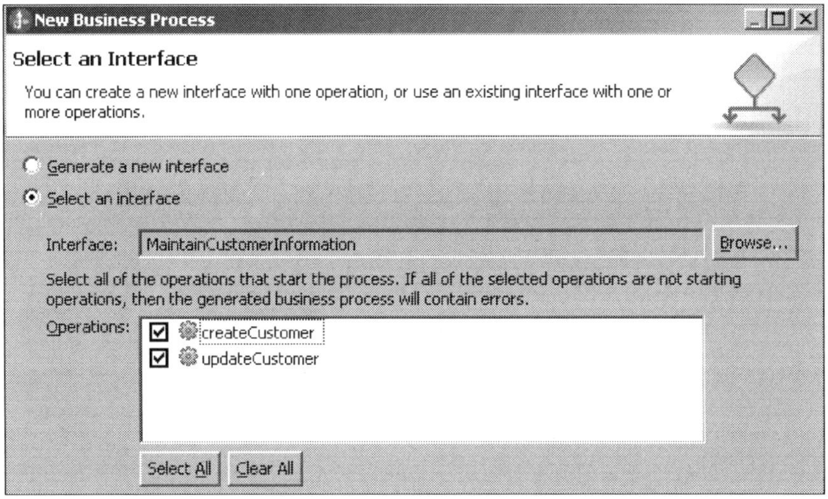

5. Similarly, create the other two Business Services identified for the modules "*RetrieveCustomerInformation*" and "*HandleCustomerContact*", following the same steps, as explained above.
6. Having created all the necessary Business Services (as business process components) drag-and-drop the components under **BizServices-CustomerInfoMgmt | Integration Logic** to the assembly diagram. Right-click on each of the components, and select **Generate Export | SCA Binding**.

> If no binding is specified, an export SCA becomes the default binding.

7. Your assembly diagram, after all the previously-mentioned steps, should look like the following screenshot. The Business Service components have no implementation behind them (we will implement them in Chapter 10), and also, as you can see in the following screenshot, the Business Service components have no imports.

8. Add imports of the "*Access Services*" to the assembly diagram as placeholders. We will NOT specify any bindings on these imports yet, and once we create and implement "Access Services" modules and associated components in *Chapter 10*, we will then revisit this module and specify the bindings. These imports will have the same interface as the business service component.

Recollect the relevant architectural decisions

The interfaces for the northern half of the Access Services will be exposed based on the common messaging model (meaning Generic Business Objects). The southern half, which integrates with the backend applications, will transform to and from the application-specific message formats.

The Access Services will provide the mediation capabilities needed to integrate with the backend applications, including protocol transformation, data transformation, and message enrichment capabilities, before forwarding the request to the backend applications. This layer will transform the request/response from the common messaging model format to the end application format.

9. To create an Import, drag the interface MaintainCustomerInformation CustomerDomain-v1_0 from the library and drop it into the assembly diagram. When prompted, select the **Import with No Binding** option. Now wire the **MaintainCustomerInformation** component with this import by clicking on the Business Service component, and in the right end of the component, you will see an **Add Wire** handle appearing. Connect this to the import. Repeat the same for **RetrieveCustomerInformation** and **HandleCustomerContact** interfaces. Your assembly diagram, after all the previously-mentioned steps, should look like the following screenshot:

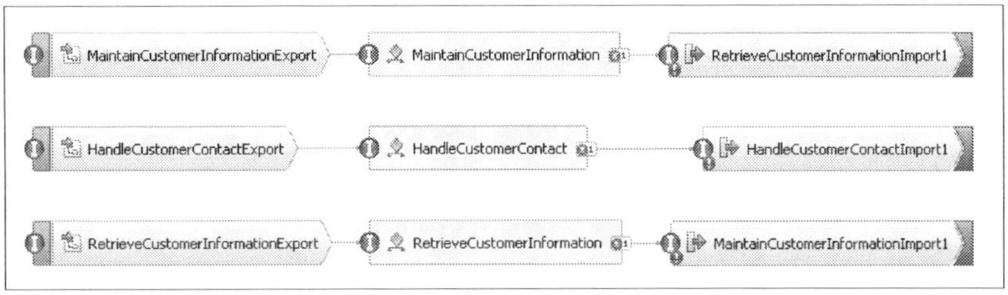

10. Finally, as you can see from the preceding screenshot, errors appear in the Business Service component reference node. This is because the component is not synchronized with the information that an import has been wired. Since we added the Business Service component first and then modified it by adding the imports, the component implementation is no longer synchronized with its component. An error is flagged as a small red x on the component, on the interface, or on a reference. To synchronize the component, right-click on the component, and select **Synchronize Interfaces and References** *to* **Implementation**. Save and build; you will see the errors disappear. Do this for all the components. Your assembly diagram, after following all the preceding steps, should look as shown in the following screenshot:

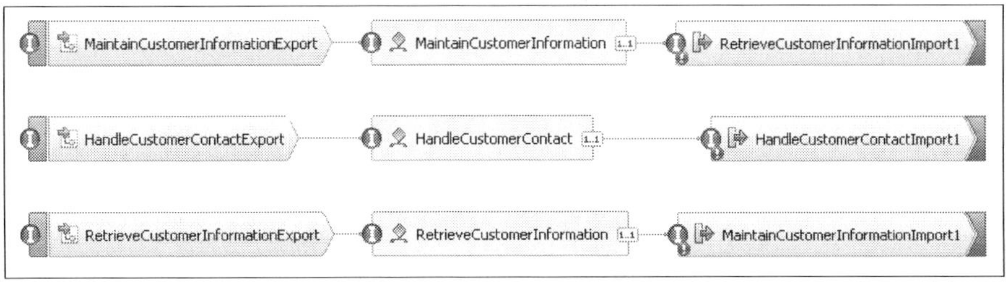

Creating ProcessServices-CustomerInterfaceManagement module

In Chapter 8 we had identified what business process components would be contained within the ProcessServices-CustomerInterfaceManagement module. Recollecting the modules and components—ProcessServices-CustomerInterfaceManagement (Module) and HandleCustomerContactProfile (BPEL Microflow Component). Now let's look at the steps involved in the implementation of this component:

1. Create a module named ProcessServices-CustomerInterfaceManagement.
2. Add the JungleSea domain libraries as dependencies.

Module assembly and wiring

In this step, being true to the SCA specification, we will assemble the components and not worry about its implementation (yet). This is what we do:

1. Create a new BPEL component and provide the folder name com/junglsea/businessprocesses and name of the component as HandleCustomerContactProfile.
2. Select the type of business process to be a **Microflow**.
3. Select the interface to be **MaintainCustomerInformation**, since we are dealing with the maintenance of customer information. Choose to implement all the operations—createCustomer and updateCustomer on the interface, and click on the **Finish** button.
4. Open the Assembly Editor, and drag-and-drop the **HandleCustomerContactProfile** component to the canvas.
5. Drag-and-drop the needed Business Services exports—*MaintainCustomerInformationExport* and *RetrieveCustomerInformationExport* from the *BizServices-CustomerInfoMgmt* module created in step-4 with an SCA binding. After you drop them to the canvas, you will have to change the names of the import to something meaningful—*MaintainCustomerInformationImport* and *RetrieveCustomerInformationImport*. These imports become reference partners in the business process editor.

> To change names of components, it is suggested that you refactor them by right-clicking on the component and selecting **Refactor** | **Rename**.

7. Wire the *HandleCustomerContactProfile* component with the imports, and your assembly editor will look as shown in the following screenshot:

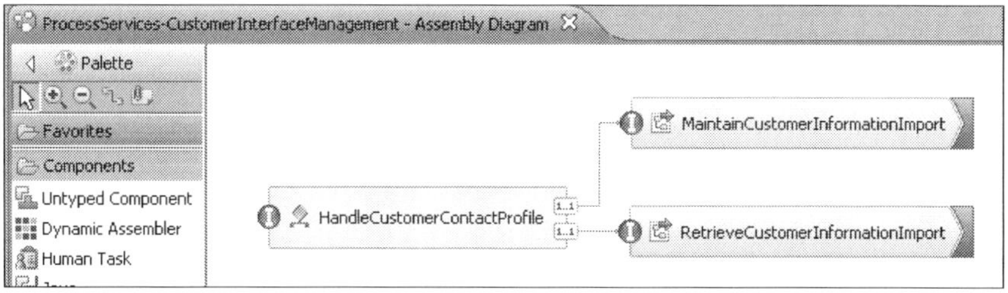

Implementing HandleCustomerContactProfile BPEL component

Now let's look at the steps involved in the implementation of this component:

1. Now we need to implement the sequence of activities that the business process should perform to its intended purpose and goal. For this, we use the business process editor, which will allow you to visually build and manipulate business processes.

> The business process editor (that helps you build a BPEL-based business process visually), as shown in the following screenshot, consists of the following distinct areas/parts in its screen real-estate:
>
> 1. Palette—provides various objects and primitives that can be (dragged and dropped) used in the construction of a business process (or a business state machine).
> 2. Canvas—the white area where you visually assemble objects from the palette to build a business process.
> 3. Action bar—small dialog pop-up that appears when you hover you mouse over certain activities in your business process (for example, when you hover over an invoke activity, you will see an action bar that pops up giving us options to add a fault handler or a compensation handler and so on.
> 4. Tray—displays the interface and reference partners, variables, correlation sets, and correlation properties associated with the business process you are building.
> 5. Properties view—displays properties of any selected object from the canvas or tray.
> 6. Navigation bar—helps you to navigate between different levels in a business process or jump back to the assembly diagram.

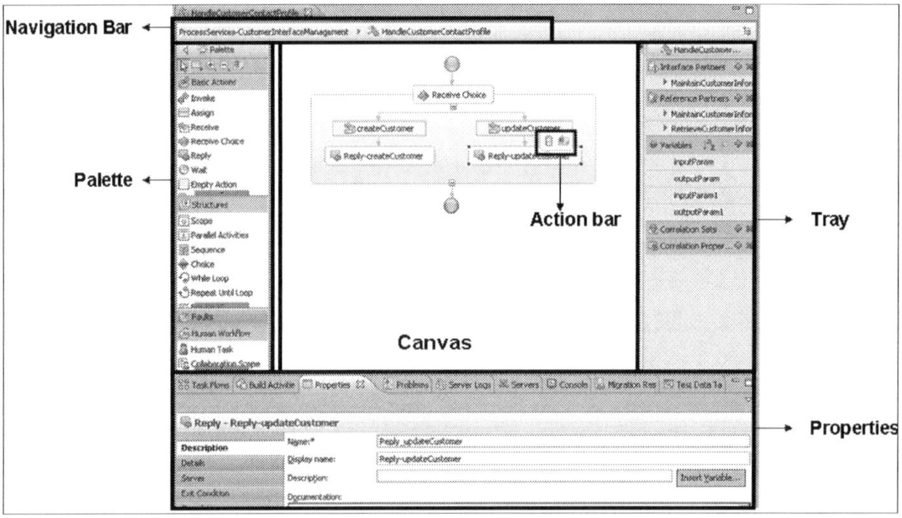

2. Drag-and-drop the "createCustomer" operation from the Reference Partners that you should see in the Tray to the createCustomer branch in the canvas. You'll notice that this would result in an "Invoke" activity that would invoke the import SCA binding of the Business Service—MaintainCustomerInformation. Click on the object and rename the default name "Invoke" to "InvokeCreateCustomer" by changing the Name and Display Name in the properties view.
3. Drag-and-drop the "updateCustomer" operation from the Reference Partners that you should see in the Tray to the updateCustomer branch in the canvas. Click on the object and rename the default name "Invoke" to "InvokeUpdateCustomer", by changing the Name and Display Name in the properties view.
4. Drag-and-drop the "queryCustomer" operation from the Reference Partners that you should see in the Tray to the updateCustomer branch in the canvas. Click on the object and rename the default name "Invoke" to "InvokeQueryCustomer" by changing the Name and Display Name in the properties view. You would be able to see the various properties of these Invoke objects by clicking on the object and viewing the Properties view. After saving, your business process editor should look as shown in the following screenshot. Notice the errors on both the Invoke objects. This is because we have not specified the input and output variables for the Invoke activities.

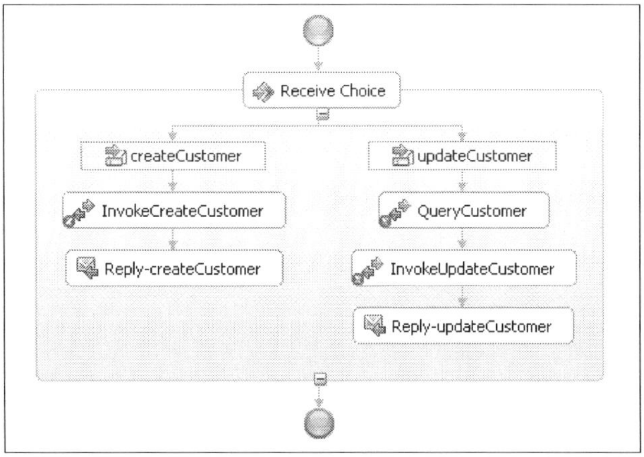

5. Now let's assign variable to these Invokes and also define a few variables. Variables persist the messages that are exchanged between the reference partners in a business process and any data that you manipulate within the business process. The variables have scope, and if they are created in the global process scope, then it is a global variable and available to the process as a whole. Those created within nested scopes are called scoped or local variables, and can only be seen by objects within the scope in which it was created.

> There are two types of variables in WID:
>
> 1. Data type variable that points to a Business Object.
> 2. Interface variable that stores either the input, output, or fault parameter for a particular operation of an interface.
>
> It's much preferable to use the data type variable and it's a must for usage within a business process.

6. Click on the + symbol in the **Variables** area of the tray. A pop-up window will appear; add a new variable named "auditMessage" of type string. Create a variable "businessSvcException" of type BusinessException. Create two more variables, queryCustomerIn and queryCustomerOut of type CustomerMSG.
7. Click on the **InvokeCreateCustomer** object, and in **Details** in the **Properties** view, specify the input and output variables—inputParam and outputParam respectively.
8. Click on the **InvokeUpdateCustomer** object and in **Details** within the **Properties** view, specify the input and output variables—inputParam1 and outputParam1 respectively.

9. Click on the **QueryCustomer** object, and in **Details** within the **Properties** view, specify the input and output variables—queryCustomerIn and queryCustomerOut respectively. Drag-and-drop an **Assign** activity before the queryCustomer call to assign the incoming inputParam1 to queryCustomerIn.
10. Now all Invoke activities have variables specified, so save your process. You will notice that the errors will go away.
11. Before the InvokeCreateCustomer activity, we will have to audit the action, and we will use a Visual Snippet for this. For the purposes of this book, we audit the message to the System out log. Typically, you would use a database to persist audit messages. After doing this, the business process will look as shown in the following screenshot:

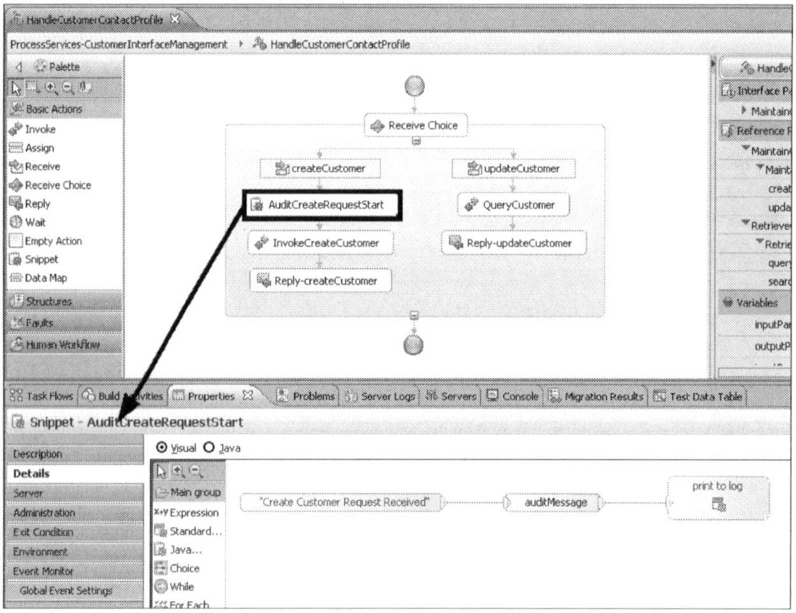

Implementing Fault Handling

1. Add a Fault Handler (named AssignToBusinessException) to the InvokeCreateCustomer activity by selecting it from the Action bar. We will select the fault (named CatchAppFault) to be user-defined WID automatically recognized the fact that we defined a fault to the interface and specified a message type. BPEL allows fault propagation using throw, rethrow, and reply within a fault handler. Throw the exception that will have to be caught by a Catch All element. You can define multiple catch elements in the catch block, each corresponding to a particular exception type (user defined, system and so on).

In cases when the type of fault is unknown, you can use the Catch All element, but you may only define one of these elements per fault handler. It is a recommended best practice to use a Catch All element in the Global Process' fault handler. Add a Catch All element to the fault handler of InvokeCreateCustomer as well.

2. Define a Catch All block with the global scope. You can do this by clicking on the green start object and selecting the Catch All from the Action bar. In the Catch All with the global scope, add a Reply activity object of type Failure, and specify businessSvcException as the reply (fault) parameter.

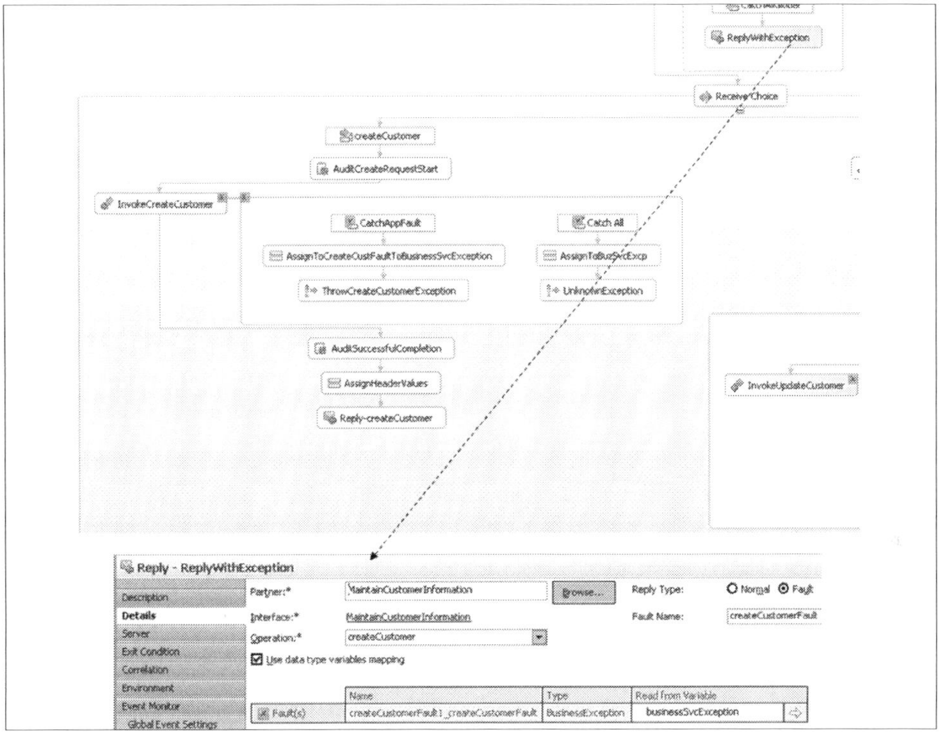

3. Now we will follow the same steps to implement the flow for the updateCustomer path. We will have to check for the existence of a customer before we perform a customer update.

4. Add a Choice activity after the QueryCustomer Invoke call and check if the response came back with valid query customer response. Check the **queryCustomerOut | MessageHeader | InteractionDescription** to check for a **Valid Customer Found** response description as an XPath expression as follows:

```
$queryCustomerOut/MessageHeader/InteractionDescription = 'Valid
Customer Found'
```

5. Move the InvokeUpdateCustomer as an activity to the "CustomerFound" case flow. Add an **Otherwise** case that would throw a business exception back and stop the process execution. You will have to assign meaningful values to the **businessSvcException** variable, and it is shown in the following screenshot. After doing all of this, the business process will look as shown in the following screenshot:

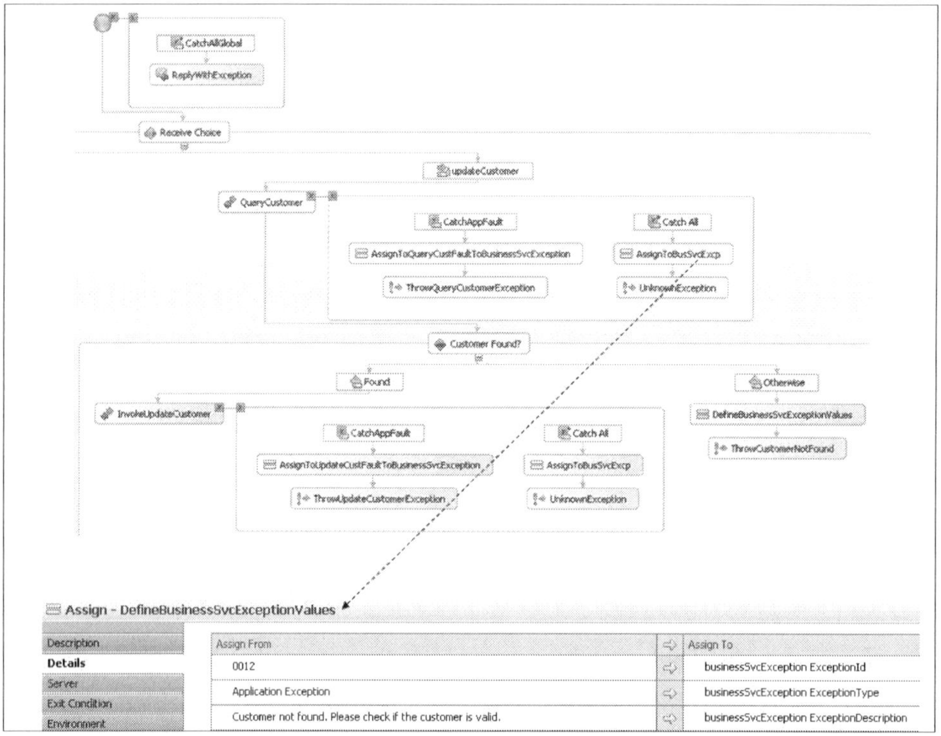

6. To monitor this business process in the event monitor, define some events of interest for generation (Completion forced, Entry, Exit, Expired, Failed, Retry forced, Assigned, Completion forced, Created, De-assigned, and so on). The event monitor can be opened from the **Properties** view in many of the editors. At runtime, you can use the Common Base Event browser to view generated CEI events.

7. Complete the process by adding appropriate Reply activity objects, and before each of the reply activities, have an Assign activity that will assign the right metadata to the message header (remember it had a purpose). After doing all this, the business process will look as shown in the following screenshot:

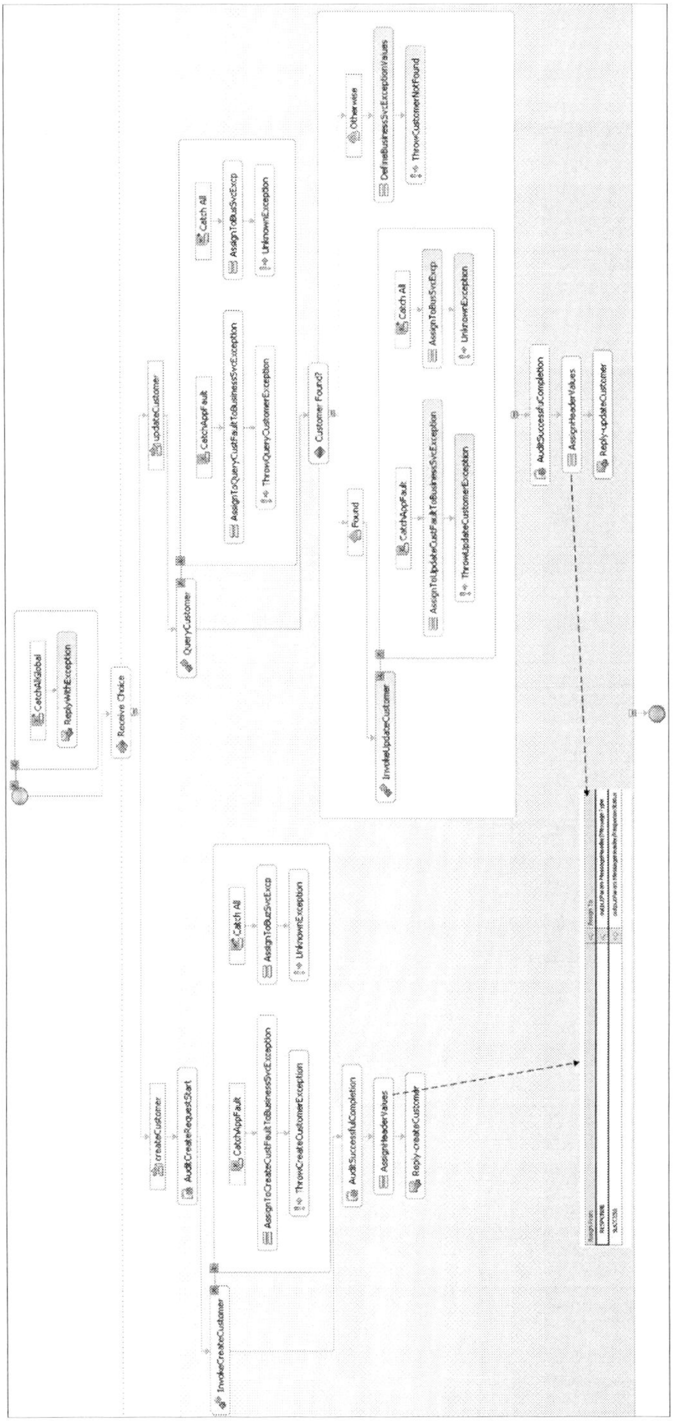
CatchAllGlobal
ReplyWithException
Receive Choice
createCustomer
AuditCreateRequestStart
InvokeCreateCustomer
CatchAppFault
AssignToCreateCustFaultToBusinessSvcException
ThrowCreateCustomerException
Catch All
AssignToBusSvcExcp
UnknownException
AuditSuccessfulCompletion
AssignHeaderValues
Reply-createCustomer
updateCustomer
QueryCustomer
AssignToQueryCustFaultToBusinessSvcException
ThrowQueryCustomerException
Customer Found?
Found
InvokeUpdateCustomer
AssignToUpdateCustFaultToBusinessSvcException
ThrowUpdateCustomerException
Otherwise
DefineBusinessSvcExceptionValues
ThrowCustomerNotFound
Reply-updateCustomer

Testing the business process

Since the Business Service SCA components have been assembled but NOT implemented, we will not test the process in this chapter. When we implement the Business Services in the next chapter, we will use the integration test client to test this business process. If you still try to test the module, you would get an Unknown Exception Occurred message while invoking Create Customer, as per the fault handling logic we had just implemented in the previous steps. The actual Integration Test Client screenshot will look as follows:

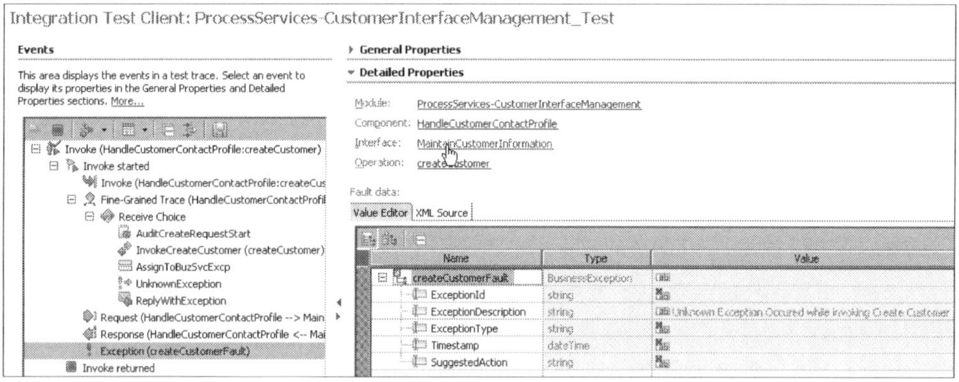

> **Viewing component references**
>
> You can view which activities in the HandleCustomerContactProfile use which particular business object by selecting **Window** | **Show View** | **References**. The **References** view opens in the lower left of the perspective, where you see a graph of all Business Objects used by relevant activities.

Building ProcessServices-OrderHandling

Now by following the same detailed steps, let us also build the other core and yet very important order handling business process. As explained in the previous chapter, the purpose of this component is to accept the configured customers orders for products and deal with activities related to the fulfillment of the order including product availability, credit verification, order issuance, shipment management, processing the payments, and finally through its lifecycle, provide order status and tracking details. This will be implemented as a long-running business process (BPEL) since the process will have several human tasks along its path and will have to wait for responses for certain activities for an extended period of time.

> Since we have explained in the earlier chapter and also in this chapter how to work with the WID business process editor, we will not delve into step-by-step details of how we would build this process like we did with the earlier one. Rather, we would cover the key WID capabilities that are unique to this process including compensation, human task that we will focus on. Please refer to the PI file provided for details around the implementation of this business process.
>
> Moreover, an order handling process would typically cater to New, Modify, and Cancel variations. For the purpose of this book, we will take into consideration and implement only the New case.
>
> Finally, the order fallout handling will be very minimal, and we will cover only the happy path scenario of order processing.

The pseudo-logic for this business process component is depicted as an activity diagram, as shown in the following figure:

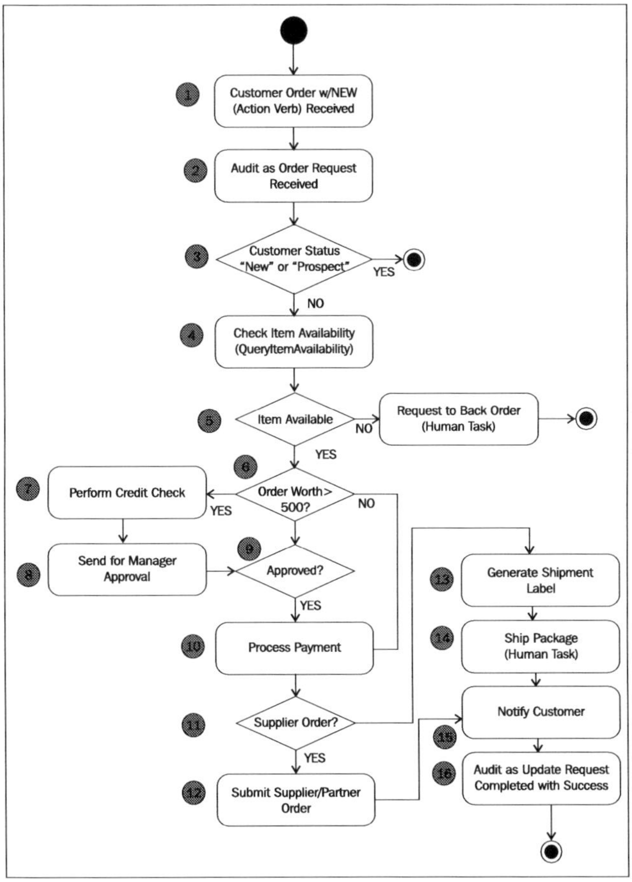

1. Receive the customer request with a NEW order action.
2. Audit the fact that a customer order has been received.
3. Verify that the request (CustomerMSG) does not have a **CustomerStatus** value of **Prospect** or **New**.
4. If present, throw a business exception—**Customer Status Invalid**, and terminate the process.
5. Indicate **Failure** in **ResponseStatus** in the Header.
6. Log exception to file.
7. Check the requested inventory item's(s) availability by invoking the Business Service **RetrieveInventoryInformation** on the **queryItemAvailability** operation.
8. If the item is available, proceed to step 6, or else create a human task to backorder the item(s) and terminate the process.
9. If the Order net work over $500 proceed to steps 7 and 8, or else proceed to step 10.
10. Perform a customer credit check.
11. Send to the manager in order to approve the order.
12. If the order is approved by manager, proceed to step 10.
13. Process the payment for the order based on the payment processing information contained in the order.
14. Check to see if the order has to be fulfilled by a supplier/partner. If so, proceed to step 12. If not, proceed to step 13.
15. Send the order to the right supplier partner for fulfillment and inform the customer.
16. Generate the shipping label for the item(s) contained in the order.
17. Create a human task for the shipment package to be created and shipped.
18. Notify the customer of successful order shipment.
19. Audit the fact that a customer order has been shipped.

Implementing TrackAndManageCustomerOrder business process component

Now perform the following steps to implement this business process component TrackAndManageCustomerOrder, and let's see how we will implement it. First we will import application libraries and modules/simulators, and then create and import JungleSea domain libraries.

Creating and/or importing necessary dependent modules

In Chapter 8 we had identified what Business Service components the *TrackAndManageCustomerOrder* business process component would need to invoke to accomplish its goal. The identified modules and the associated components were as follows:

- BizServices-CustomerBillingMgmt *(Module)*
    - ProcessCustomerPayments (*BPEL Component*)
- BizServices-SupplierPartnerMgmt (*Module*)
    - ProcessSPOrders (*BPEL Component*)
- BizServices-ShippingMgmt (*Module*)
    - ManageShipments (*BPEL Component*)
- BizServices-InventoryMgmt (*Module*)
    - RetrieveInventoryInformation (*BPEL Component*)
- BizServices-CustomerCreditMgmt (*Module*)
    - CustomerCreditInformation (*BPEL Component*)

In the previous section, we have already seen in detail how to assemble these Business Services without any implementation. Please refer to the earlier section and create the modules and components (including the type - BPEL of type microflow) with the names listed as above. As mentioned earlier, we will not be implementing these Business Service components and will do them in Chapter 10. Create a module named ProcessService-OrderHandling, and add the JungleSea domain libraries as dependants.

Module Assembly and Wiring

In this step, being true to the SCA specification, we will assemble the components; don't worry about its implementation (yet). So this is what we do:

1. Create a new BPEL component and provide the folder name "com/junglesea/businessprocesses" and name of the component as "*TrackAndManagerCustomerOrder*".
2. We will make this process long running and will select the "use WPS extensions" since we will have to use human task and Java snippets within the process.
3. The interface for the process will be ProcessCustomerOrder from the CustomerDomain. As mentioned earlier, for the purpose of this book, we will take into consideration and implement only the New order cases. So we will fully implement only the "submitCustomerOrder" operation in the interface (queryOrderStatus and cancelCustomerOrder on the interface, though selected will be left black).
4. Open the Assembly Editor; drag-and-drop the *TrackAndManagerCustomerOrder* component to the canvas.
5. Drag-and-drop the required Business Service exports *ProcessCustomerPaymentsExport*, *ProcessSPOrdersExport*, *ManageShipmentsExport*, *RetrieveInventoryInformationExport*, *CustomerCreditInformationExport*, and *MaintainInventoryInformationExport* from their respective modules (specify the import binding to be SCA). Rename the imports appropriately, and they can be as per the following figure.
6. Wire the *TrackAndManagerCustomerOrder* component with the imports, and your assembly editor will look as shown in the following diagram:

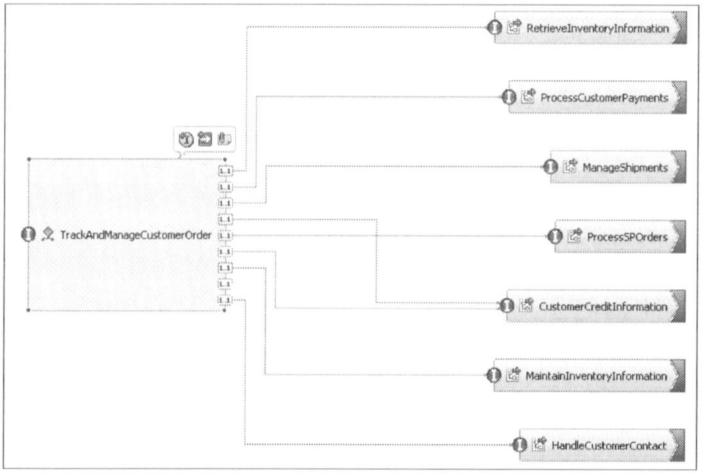

Implementing the business process component

Now let's implement the first business process component, TrackAndManageCustomerOrder, based on the activity diagram we sketched out earlier. The key aspect of this business process is that it handles the entire lifecycle of a customer order and hence may take anywhere from a few minutes to several days to complete. So this is what we will do to implement this component (we will go over some of the key steps only and by this time you should be familiar and conversant with using the WID tooling):

1. *Using ForEach Control Structure*: When we receive the customer order for each.
2. *Process Instance Persistence:* We will now specify how the process instances should be persisted. As shown in the figure below, in the **Details** tab of the process properties (click anywhere in the business process editor whitespace and go to **Properties** | **Details**), relevant only to long-running processes, we will specify that process instances should not be deleted once they have run their course. This will help us to diagnose any problems that may result when a process runs into exceptions and also allows an administrator to restart. If this option is set to **Yes**, then if the process fails, it will not appear as a failed event in the BPC Explorer.

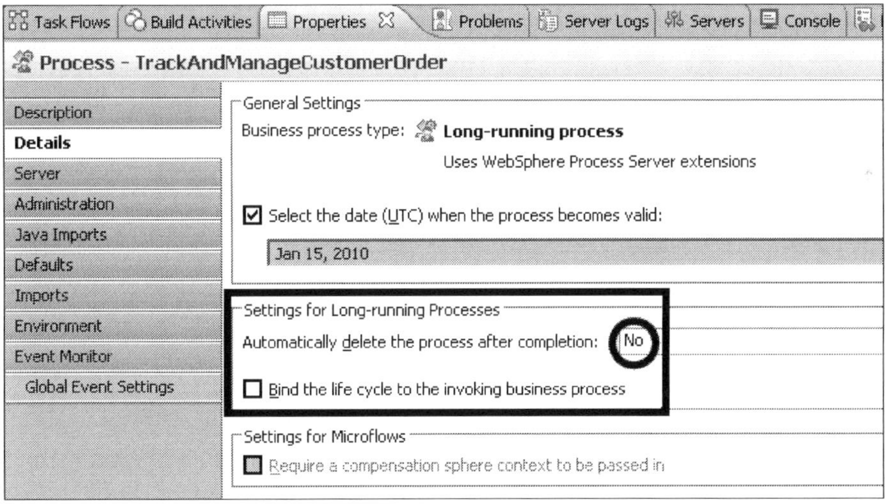

3. *Failed Process Instance Administration*: Now we will specify how to handle the faults that may happen within the order handling process and how to handle the process instances with tasks that include terminating, suspending, resuming, deleting a process instance, or handling faults. Under the **Administration** tab of the process properties, we will define default administration settings for all of the activities within that process. So if any activity within the order handling process fails or has an exception, the user will need administrative rights to recover the process instance.
   As shown in the following screenshot, we will name the administration task **HandleOrderFallout**, which will result in a human task created:

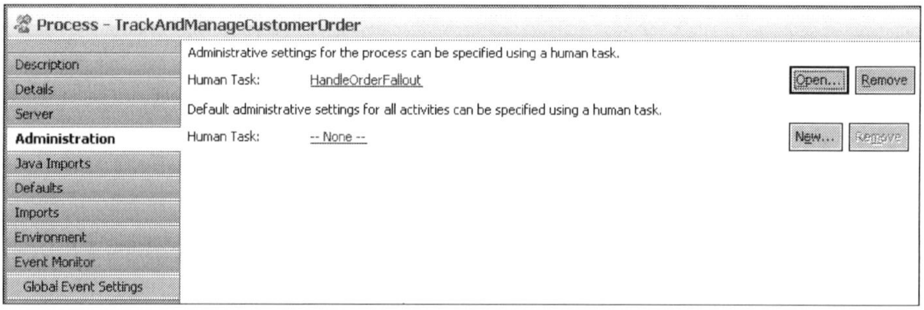

4. *Human Task Escalation:* We will define an escalation for this human task, such that if the process instance is not claimed or addressed within 30 minutes, it will raise an exception e-mail to the "CustomerServiceRepresentative" group. Some of the key properties of this human task are shown in the following screenshot. As shown for the replacement variable, we will set it to be a business process variable and will specify the customer order message as the variable to be inserted into the text of the escalation e-mail.

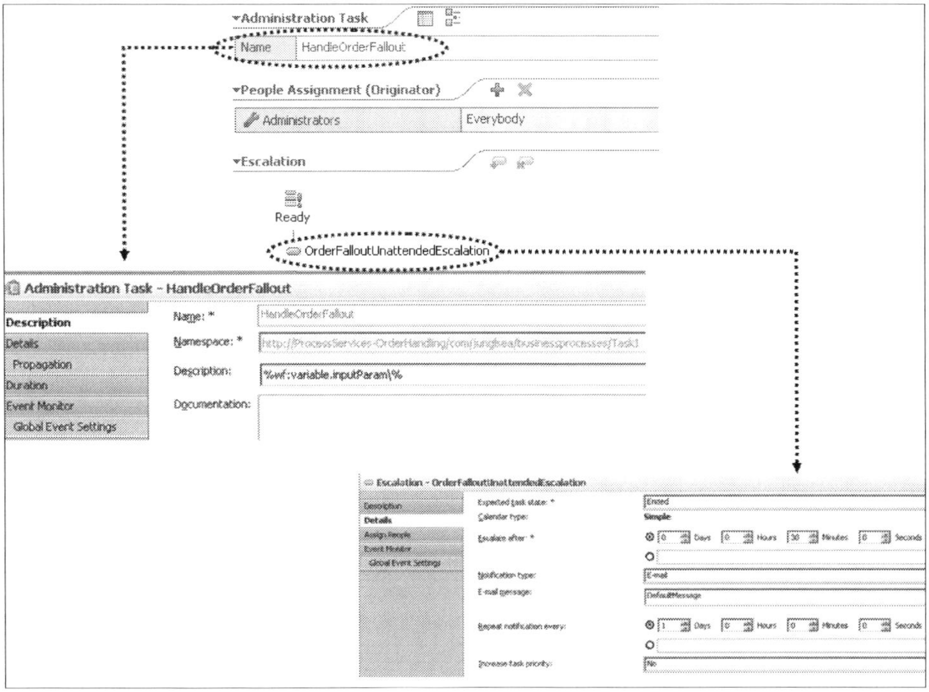

[To create users and groups in WPS, go to **Administrative Console** | **Users** and **Groups**.]

5. *Event Monitoring*: Now let's define the events that would help monitor this process using the Event Monitor from the process Properties. We will select the following individual events in **Properties** | **Event Monitor**: Entry, Exit, Failed, Restarted, and Suspended. Secondly, we will enable the **Enable default events** in **Properties** | **Global Event Settings** | Enable the default events checkbox. To view the CEI events generated, right-click the server and select **Launch** | **Common Base Event Browser**.

> There are three key event-related concepts that you need to understand:
>
> - *Common Event Infrastructure (CEI)*: Infrastructure that provides basic event management services such as event generation, transmission, persistence, and consumption.
> - *Common Base Event (CBE)*: Define an XML-based format for business events, system events, and performance information.
> - *Business events*: Capture and analyze information relevant to a business.
>
> Typically, you would use the WebSphere Business Monitor development toolkit to work with the monitor models that use these events.

6. *Using ForEach Control Structure*: When we receive the customer order, for each of the order items in the customer order we will have to check against the inventory for the item availability. We identified the Business Service RetrieveInventoryInformation. We will use the **ForEach** activity as an iterator that repeats its contained scope activity based on the number of order items in the incoming order message (CustomerOrder/OrderItems). The iteration will be chosen to be performed serially (though it can be performed either serially or in parallel). If an item is not available, we will issue a request to backorder the item through the Business Service MaintainInventoryInformation and backOrderItem operation. The following diagram shows the relevant properties and how the process will look:

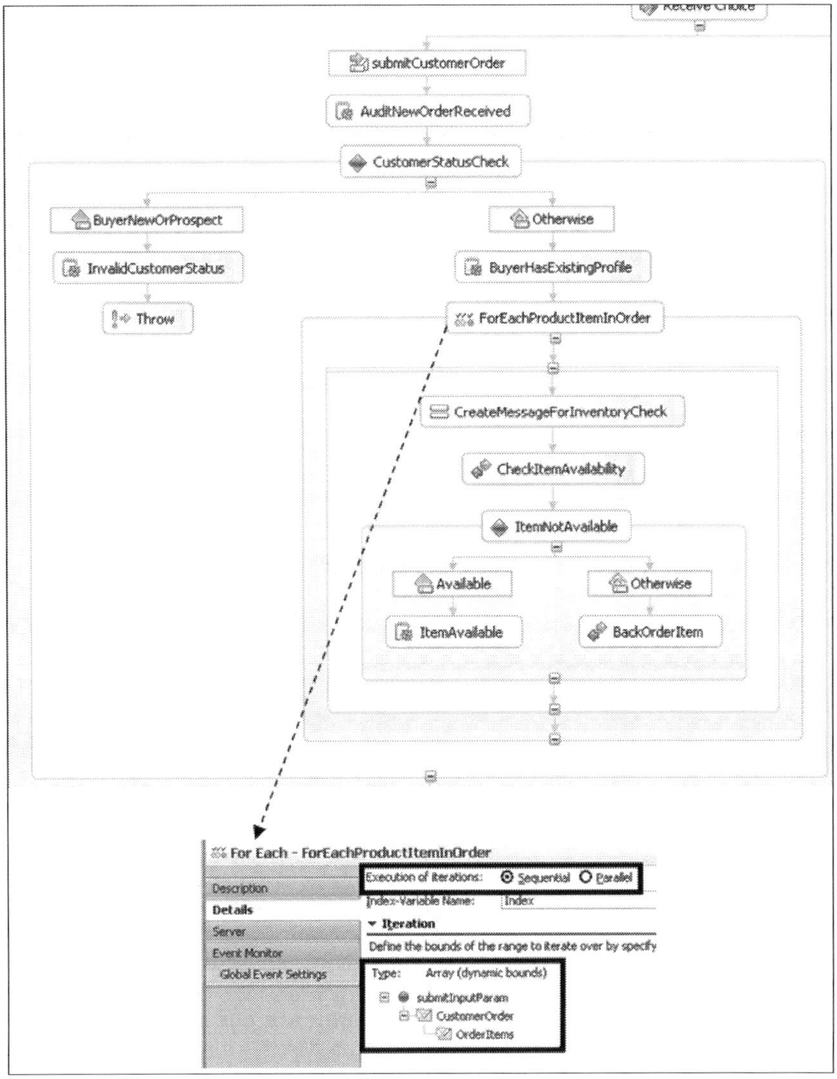

Notice in the assign activity "*CreateMessageForInventoryCheck*", where we will have to iterate an array or product items contained within the customer order within the "ForEach" activity. We have specified that we want the ForEach activity to iterate via the Array (dynamic bounds) option based on the CustomerOrder/OrderItems part that contains an array of items that have been ordered. The ForEach activity will then iterate through the elements of this array.

The index variable's value starts with 1 and is increased on every iteration up to the array's size. The assign activity also reads the right order item values based on the "OrderItemCount" index-variable name, and how it is done is shown in the next screenshot. We will use (per the WS-BPEL 2.0 specification) `bpws:getVariableData('OrderItemCount')` to right address the array element.

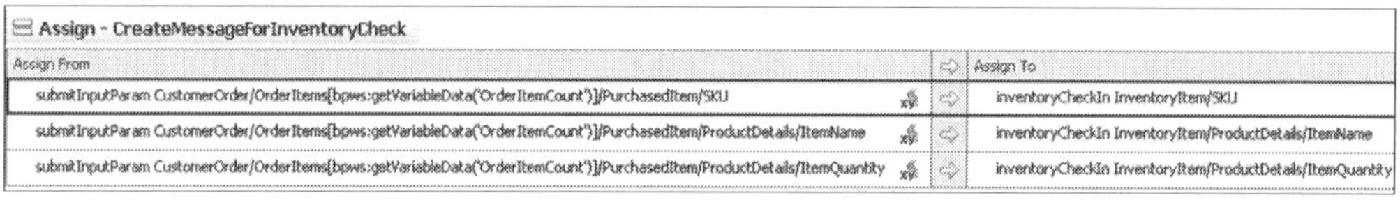

7. *Using Business Rules*: Continuing with the implementation of the business process, we will have to check if the order's total worth is over $500, and if so, initiate a credit check. As this amount of "$500" may change as a business decides, we will business rule to decide if a credit check is needed or not. More specifically, we create a decision table—CreditCheckDecision, within the business rule group OrderManagementRuleGroup; this decision table will be wired to the Business Process. The decision table will look as shown in the next screenshot. Depending on the outcome of the decision table evaluation, and if it evaluates to credit check required, we will invoke a Business Service CustomerCreditInformation, and the response will have to be approved by a manager through a human task.

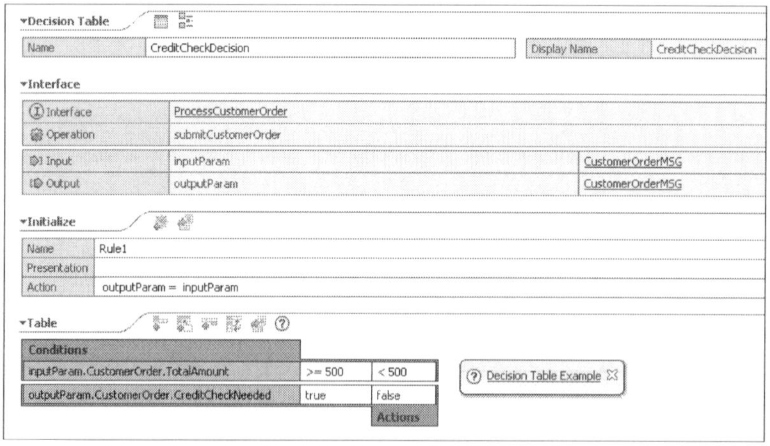

After performing all the preceding steps, the relevant sections in the process will look as shown in the following screenshot:

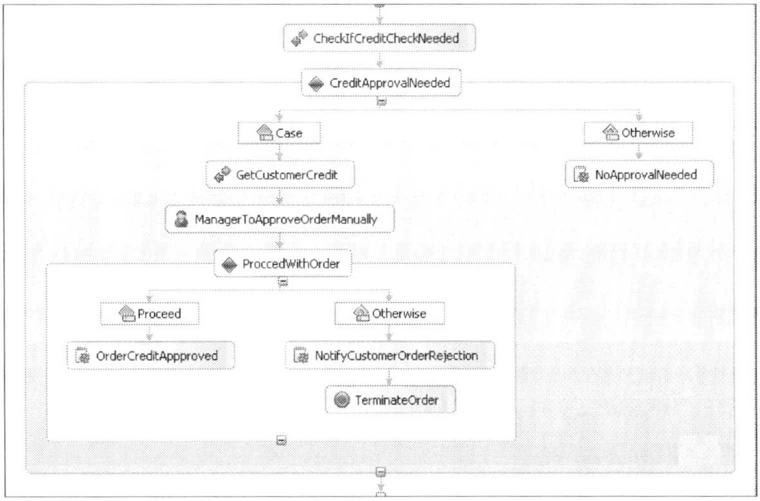

8. *Invoke Expiration:* Next we will have to process the payment for the order using the Business Service, ProcessCustomerPayments, using the operation processPayment. For this activity, as shown in the following screenshot, we will specify expiration (in the **Properties | Expiration**) and enter a duration value of **10 Seconds**, and expiration will occur the moment this period has passed.

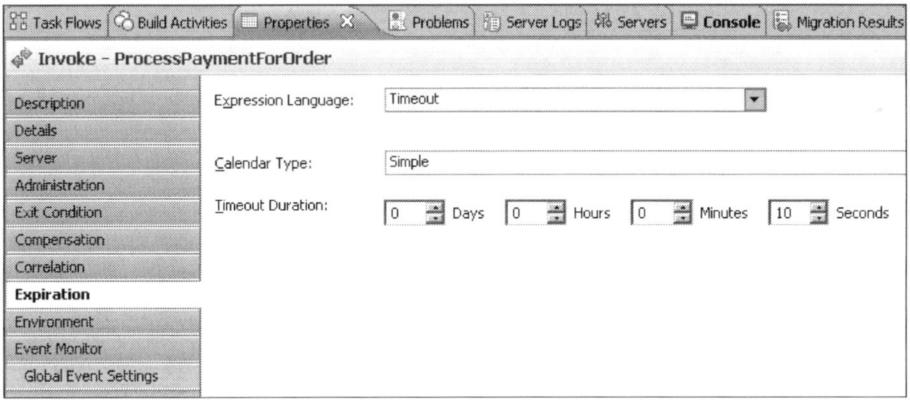

9. *Compensation:* For this activity (scope) will **compensation handler** to specify undo actions—refundPayment in case anything goes wrong. As shown in the following screenshot, the activity within the compensation handler will be an invoke activity of the refundPayment operation, and it will only run when a fault is thrown and after the parent activity has already been committed.

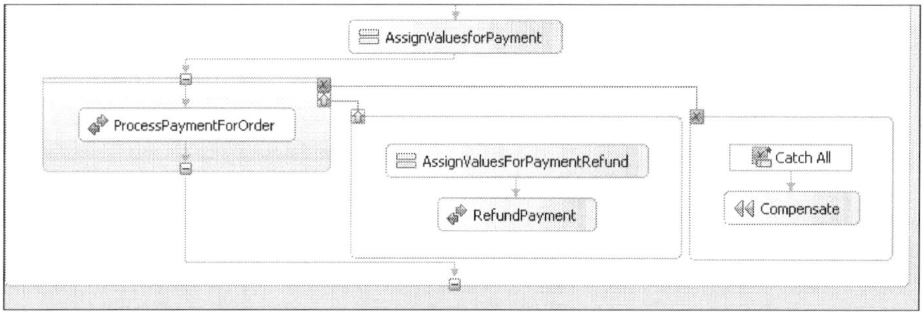

- A compensation handler specifies compensation logic and is typically defined for a scope or an invoke activity and hence callable from a fault handler
- Compensation activity triggers compensation and allows you to trigger compensation handlers
- You cannot define a compensation handler and a compensation action at the same time

Next, we will check if the order has to be sent to a supplier/partner or processed internally. We will check if the incoming order is for a supplier/partner using an XPath expression:

```
$submitInputParam/CustomerOrder/OrderItems/SupplierOrder = 'true'.
```

If found to be `true`, we will invoke the Business Service Process SPOrders on the submitSupplierOrder operation. If not, we will proceed to implement the other activities needed to fulfil the order internally per the activity diagram. After doing all of the above, the relevant section in the process will look as shown in the following screenshot:

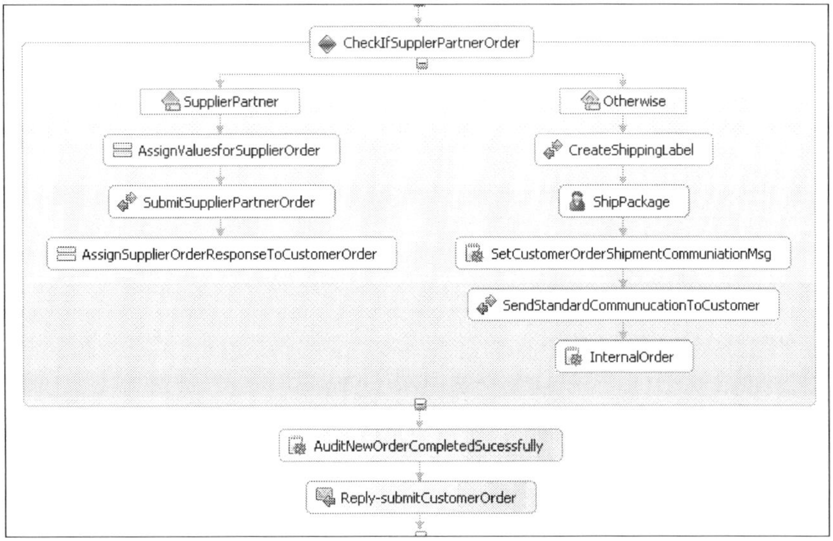

Implementing Fault Handling

As shown in the next screenshot, on the Receive object we will define two more built-in Catch elements. We will name these faults RuntimeFailureExcpetion and TimeoutException respectively. RuntimeFailureExcpetion is thrown when an invoked service returns an SCA ServiceRuntimeException or the execution of a customer code snippet. TimeoutException is thrown when an expiration is specified for an asynchronous service call in a long-running process and a response is not received within the specified time.

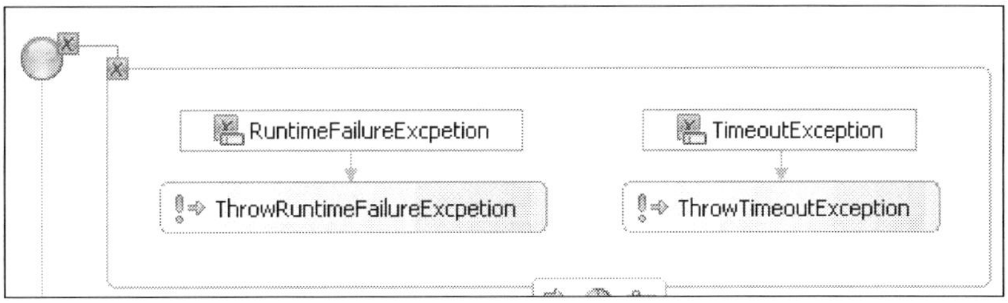

Testing the Business Process

Add all the modules to the WPS unit test server. As the Business Service SCA components have been assembled but not implemented, we will not test the process in this chapter. When we implement the Business Services in the next chapter, we will use the integration test client to test this business process. However, you can simulate the Business Service component and test the module.

Correlation sets in BPEL processes

We have, in this chapter, developed process templates that contain the process definitions for HandleCustomerContactProfile and TrackAndManageCustomerOrder to be deployed and installed in the runtime WPS environment. A process instance is the instantiation of a process template, and its properties are derived from the corresponding process template. A particular process instance completes in all of the following states:

- Last activity completes
- A terminate activity runs
- A fault occurs that is not handled by the process

Instance properties, such as the state of the process instance, are assigned and modified during the lifetime of the process instance. All of these properties are stored in the runtime database. They can be accessed using the Business Process Choreographer database views, such as the PROCESS_INSTANCE view or QUERY_PROPERTY view, or using query tables.

A correlation set allows a BPEL process instance to hold conversations with the reference partners involved in the execution path of the process. Since at any given time, the WPS runtime may have multiple process instances (of the same process template), the correlation sets allow two partners to initialize a business process transaction based on the contents of the message body. Thus a correlation set allows a process instance to hold a conversation with the partner service.

Anatomy of a correlation set

A correlation set for a business process consists of a name and one or more correlation properties. Each correlation property has a name and a type; the type itself is an alias to a specific message part. In our case, by using the TrackAndManageCustomerOrder BPEL, orders for a customer can be submitted for processing. The customer may decide to cancel the order he placed before it reaches the shipment phase. In order for you to do this, you will have to be able to identify your ordering process instance using the order identifier that was used when the order was submitted. In this case, the process would have defined a correlation set (named say "OrderProcessingReference") with a property: "custOrderIdCorrelation".

> For more information on the correlation set, as defined in the WS-BPEL 2.0 specifications, refer to the following link:
> `http://docs.oasis-open.org/wsbpel/2.0/OS/wsbpel-v2.0-OS.html#_Toc164738499`

Where and when to use correlation set:

- Use in invoke, receive, pick, and reply activities to indicate which correlation sets occur in the messages that are sent and received.
- Use if a process consists of more than one receive or pick activity
- The receive or pick activity that initiates a new process instance does not necessarily need a correlation set. The remaining receive or pick activities, however, need a correlation set to uniquely identify the process instance to route the message to.

Using a correlation set

Here are the steps to create a a correlation set and property, as specified in the section above:

1. Open the TrackAndManageCustomerOrder using the business process editor. In the Tray to the right of the business process editor, you will be see options to create Correlation Sets and a Correlation property, as shown in the following screenshot:

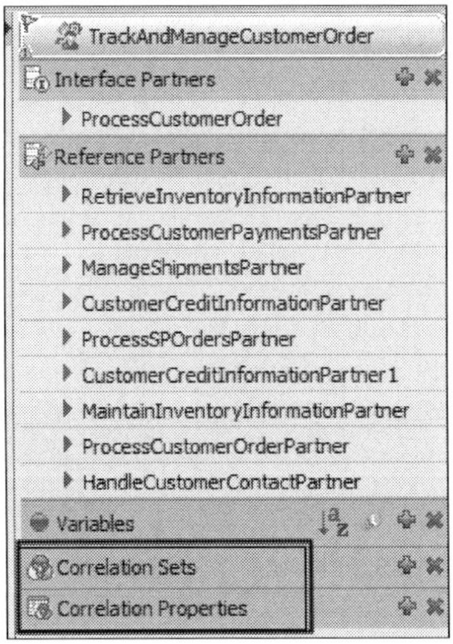

2. In the tray, to create a new correlation set, click the + icon beside **Correlation Sets** and name it "*OrderProcessingReference*".
3. In the tray, to create a new correlation property, click the + icon beside **Correlation Properties**, name it "*custOrderIdCorrelation*", and choose the data type to be string (XSD simple data type).
4. Now create a property alias (that maps to the OrderId in the CustomerOrder. In the **Description** tab for **custOrderIdCorrelation**, select the **submitCustomerOrder** operation in the interface table, and right-click **Add**, which will open the **Create Property Alias** window. As shown in the following screenshot, specify the **OrderId** from the tree and specify that this variable is an input. Repeat the same for the **cancelCustomerOrder** operation.

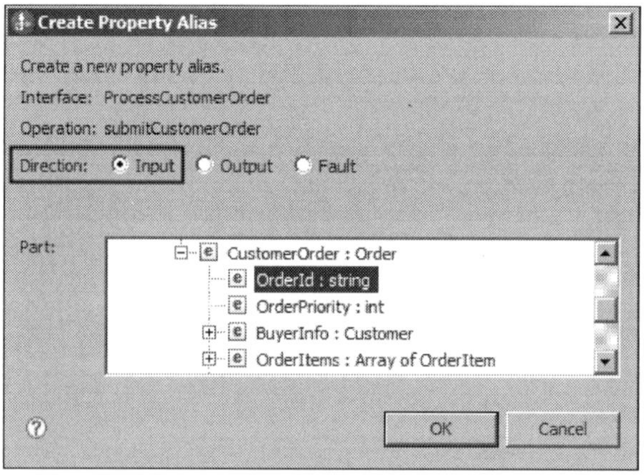

5. In the business process editor, click on the **submitCustomerOrder** receive activity and associate the **OrderProcessingReference** correlation set. To do this, click **Correlation** in the properties area, and click **Add**. The **OrderProcessingReference** will appear by default as it's the only correlation set defined.

> In the **Direction** field, you will notice that "receive" is specified by default. The options available here will depend upon what kind of activity you are configuring. For some activities such as receive, reply, or elements, such as receive, this field is set for you.

6. In the **Initiation** field, select **Yes,** as this will be the first time this correlation set has been executed.

> Select **No** if the correlation set will always be initialized by another activity.
>
> Select **Join** if multiple activities can initialize the correlation set. This is especially useful if you are designing a process with multiple parallel receives and you are not sure which one will get executed first.

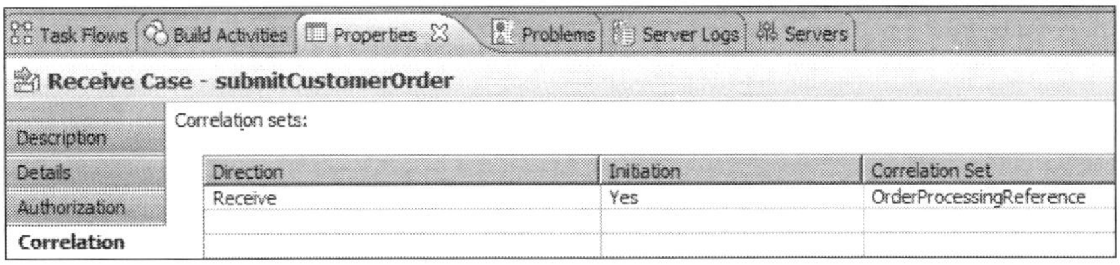

7. Repeat steps 5 and 6 for the submitCustomerOrder receive activity. The only change will be in the **Initiation** field. Select **No** as the correlation set will be initialized by the submitCustomerOrder activity.

Now having implemented the process components, import the project interchange `chap9PI.zip` and view for yourself the processes we implemented in this chapter. Based on what we have done so far, the solution diagram view of the solution we have built is depicted in the following diagram:

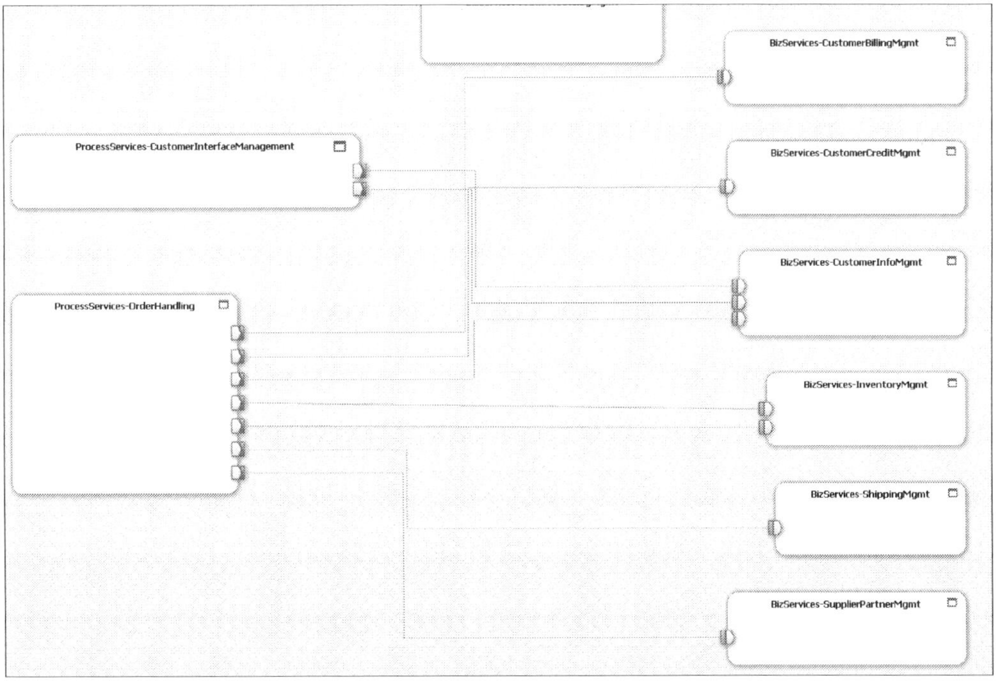

Summary

This chapter guided us through how to build the Process Services modules ProcessServices-OrderHandling and ProcessServices-CustomerInterfaceManagement and the associated businesses processes (BPELs). While we built these BPELs, we accommodated the business, technical, and NFRs including fault handling, human task management, data mappings, and so on. We will see how they deal with various implementation issues and the design decisions they make appropriately. We covered several topics including BPEL development steps, using business rules in the process, implementing human tasks, usage of control structures, fault handling including compensation, correlation sets, and how to test the business processes end-to-end once the Business Service and Access Service modules have been built.

In the next chapter, we will build the Business Services and Access Services modules, and hence perform an end-to-end integration test from these business processes right the way down.

10
Integration with Various Applications

In this chapter, we will implement the Business and Access Services modules associated with Process Services that were developed in the previous chapter. As we implement these modules and the associated components incrementally in the respective assembly diagrams, we will first wire the components and then implement the individual layers—to stay true to the promise of SCA. We will see how to deal with various implementation issues and the design decisions. This chapter contains the following topics:

- Business Service development steps
- Access Service development steps
- Using mediation flows and associated primitives
- Performing data transformations
- Handling exceptions
- Using adapters
    - Flat File adapter
    - JDBC adapter
- Using JMS imports
- Discuss how to test the service components individually
- Discuss how to test the end-to-end process

> We strongly recommend that you import the PI into your WID workspace and use it as a reference when reading this chapter. Also, some of the intricacies which could not be explained in this chapter will be very forthcoming and revealing in the PI itself.

Patterns addressed

In *Chapter1, Introducing IBM, BPM, and ESB*, we discussed briefly about the various design and adoption patterns for BPM- and ESB-based deployments. The Business Services are essentially the business facades to the components (mediation flow components) in the Access Services layer. The Business Services will perform the following functions:

- Perform endpoint selection (essentially the mediation flow in Access Services) based on business and technical context and content
- Check if the preconditions required for invoking the Business Services are met, including any prior state or operations that may have to be completed
- Handle the postconditions including state of the system and the possible error handling conditions and raise them as business exceptions

The Access Services contain the following WESB mediation flow components:

- **Protocol switch/Transformation**: Typically dealing with protocol transformation, for example, receiving a JMS request from a service consumer and going to a service provider who supports MQ
- **Data transformation**: Transform and translate the incoming message from one schema format to the target schema format. May have to perform and apply data validation, integrity, and transformation rules
- **Data enrichment**: Augment or enrich the incoming message payload by fanning-out and fetching data from one to many sources and fanning-in
- **Exception handling**: At the end application layer including timeout, retry, and so on

Module assembly

Based on the flow of steps, we will have to assemble and implement the components that make up the solution. We are in the step of assembling and implementing the components in the Business and Access Services layer, as shown in the following figure:

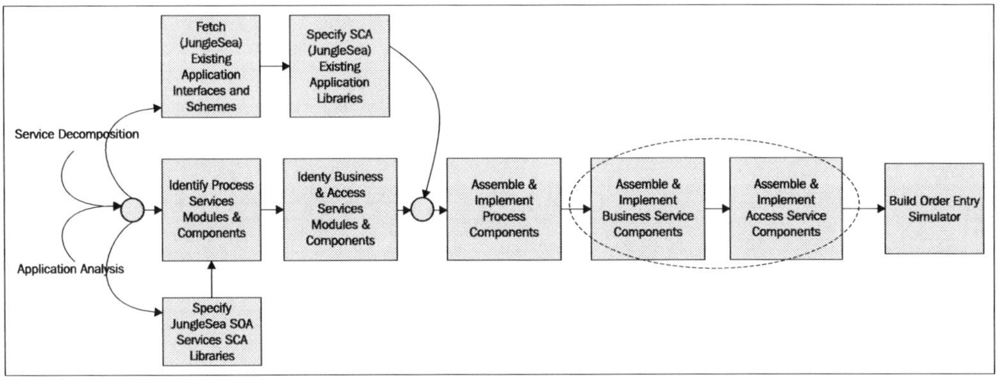

Now let us look at the how we accomplish this step. In *Chapter 9, Building the Order Handling Processes*, we used the assembly diagram to construct the modules, define and assemble SCA components, and to wire these components together to build the process services. This assembly was done in accordance with the build manifest we identified in *Chapter 7,Sales Fulfillment Application for JungleSea Inc.* and *Chapter 8, Walk the Talk* (and relevant to the scope of the business process we built in Chapter 9). In this chapter, we then follow the similar steps to build out the following Business Services and associated Access Services (shown in italics), as mentioned in the following table:

Business Service Module Name	Component Name	*Access Service Module Name*	*Component Name*
BizServices-CustomerBillingMgmt	ProcessCustomerPayments	***AccessServices-PayMe***	*Med-CreditCardService-ccPurchase*
BizServices-CustomerInfoMgmt	MaintainCustomerInformation	***AccessServices-Green***	*Med-CustomerProfile-createCustomerAccount*
	RetrieveCustomerInformation	***AccessServices-Green***	*Med-CustomerProfile-getCustomerDetails*
	HandleCustomerContact	***N/A***	*N/A*
BizServices-SupplierPartnerMgmt	ProcessSPOrders	***AccessServices-Moonlight***	*Med-ProcessPurchaseOrders-processOrder*
BizServices-ShippingMgmt	ManageShipments	***AccessServices-Fast***	*Med-ShipService-createPendingShipmentRequest*
		AccessServices-Rapid	*Med-LabelsAndShipments-prepareShipLabel*
BizServices-InventoryMgmt	RetrieveInventoryInformation	***AccessServices-Alpha***	*Med-AlphaFBAInventoryPortType-GetInventorySupply*
		AccessServices-Beta	*Med-BetaInventoryService-CheckItemAvailability*
	MaintainInventoryInformation	***N/A***	*N/A*
BizServices-CustomerCreditMgmt	CustomerCreditInformation	***AccessServices-Equal***	*Med-EqualCreditPulseSoap-creditPulseByIndividual*

Testing the modules

In the previous chapter, we briefly discussed testing. Now let us look at some of the capabilities provided by WID to test the modules and components and also its simulation capabilities. WID allows you to test the modules by either **unit testing** or **component testing**. WID provides a capability called test suite editor that allows us to create and define test cases for testing the components that you implement in WID. The test cases are comprised one or more operations, and hence you can test the components and interfaces that contain the operations that you want to test. The test suite editor and associated wizards allow you to automate and run tests in the integration test client. Additionally, you can perform batch component testing on either a test environment server or a standalone server by using test scripts or the Web-based Component Test Explorer user interface.

Key concepts

Following are some key concepts related to the integration test client.

Test configurations

Test configurations essentially control the tests you define. You specify, within a configuration, one or many modules to test associated components, references, emulators, and monitors for the wires in the module. Modules within a test configuration are referred to as test configuration modules. To launch the unit test client, you can:

- Right-click on a component and select Test Component from the context menu
- Right-click anywhere in the assembly diagram's whitespace and select Test Module from the context menu

The **Integration Test Client** provides you with a default test configuration, and in most cases, it would do the job of testing your modules and components. You can also edit and customize the default test configuration; for example, when adding emulators for references. Shown in the following screenshot is an example default test configuration that shows up when trying to test the **TrackAndManageCustomerOrder** BPEL component. As you can see, we have not defined any emulators for references (Business Services) or the human tasks.

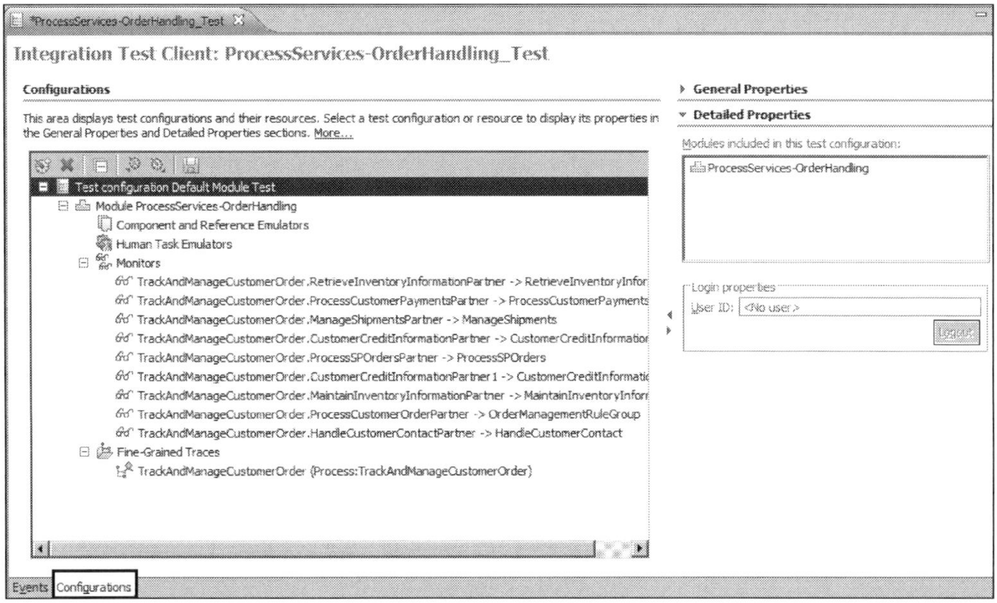

Emulators

In cases where you don't have the imports/references (end application services that you import in the assembly diagram, for example) available or the components implemented, you can use the emulator capability provided in the integration test client. It enables you to emulate the components or the references in your modules by defining them in the test configuration. When you do unit or component testing and when the control flows to an emulated component or reference, the integration test client intercepts the invocation and routes it to the associated emulator. You can define two types of emulators:

1. Manual
    - You specify the response values for the emulated component or reference at runtime
    - During a test, when a manual emulator is encountered, a manual Emulate event is generated, and the test pauses so that you can manually specify the output values or throw an exception for the emulated components or references
    - When testing an entire module, the default test configuration will contain manual emulators for all unimplemented components and unwired references

    - When testing an individual component, or a set of components within a module, the default test configuration will contain manual emulators for any other components that were not selected for testing, regardless of whether they are implemented or not
    - You can remove the manual emulators or redefine them as programmatic emulators

2. Programmatic
    - Values are automatically provided by a Java program contained in a visual snippet or Java snippet

Monitors

Monitors are automatically added to the test configuration for any component wires and exports in the modules of the test configuration, and they show the parameter data in the Events area of the integration test client. These monitors listen for any requests and responses that flow over the wires and exports when you test an operation. If a request is detected, a Request event is generated. And if a response is detected, a Response event is generated. Monitors are automatically added for the wires and components in the test configuration modules. You can also remove the monitors or add additional monitors as required.

Events

When you run a test by invoking an operation or emitting a common base event in the integration test client, several different types of events are generated over the course of the test. These events are either interactive or informative. By default, certain types of events are always generated by the integration test client, such as Return events. However, you can customize test configurations to control whether other types of events are generated, such as monitor Request and Response events.

Unit testing

Using the integration test client, you can unit test your modules and report the results of your test. Unit testing is typically performed on the interface operations within a component. Using the integration test client, you can test:

- An individual component
- A set of interacting components
- An individual module
- A set of interacting modules

Component testing

With component testing, you can sequentially test multiple operations as a group in the integration test client. You can also perform batch component testing on either a test environment server or a standalone server by using test scripts or the user interface of the Web-based Component Test Explorer.

Implementing Business Service and Access Service modules

Now let's get started with the implementation of the Business and Access Service modules. Following are the steps involved in assembling and implementing the Business and Access Service modules and associated components:

> We created the business services modules and components without any implementation in Chapter 9, to be able to complete the implementation of the business processes. We will directly start with the implementation of the business service component.

(These steps are similar to those stated in Chapter 9 which have been repeated for your reference.)

1. **Implement the Business Service component**
   i. In WID, open the business process component and create the basic business process flow using the visual process editor.
   ii. Add activities to the business process flow to accomplish the capability that the Business Service will deliver.
   iii. Add Event Handlers if necessary to respond to external invocation/ stimuli with an appropriately-defined action.
   iv. Add Java snippets using (Visual) Snippets task. You can also use XPath to manipulate or iterate a business object using XPath expressions.
   v. Define local variables as needed by the Business Service to store the messages that are exchanged between itself and its reference and also the data that is used in its business logic.
   vi. Use control structures for structured activities.

vii. Wherever appropriate, externalize business logic away from the component using a business rule component. This will make the Business Service more dynamic, adaptive, and susceptible to business conditions changes.

viii. Finally, in the event monitor define events of interest for generation (*Completion forced*, *Entry*, *Exit*, *Expired*, *Failed*, *Retry forced*, *Assigned*, *Created*, *De-assigned*, and so on). The event monitor can be opened from the Properties view in many of the editors. At runtime, you can use the Common Base Event browser to view generated CEI events.

2. **Implement Fault Handling for the Business Service components**

   It's a good practice to handle any exceptional conditions, and conditions that may affect the normal behavior of a business process. Faults can be classified into three buckets—Business, System, and Standard. While WPS provides the System (propagated by ServiceRuntimeException objects) and Standard faults, you, as the implementer of the business process flow, should handle these faults gracefully and throw them back to the consumer with a meaningful business context.

   The WS-BPEL specifications define a standard set of fault types for common system failures, which WPS has implemented. These built-in fault types are available to you in WID for adding them to your business process.

   There are also non-BPEL standard faults available to you such as *cannotResolveEndpoint*, *runtimeFailure*, *serviceTerminated*, *splitFailure*, and *timeout*.

   i. Use Fault Handlers (*Catch* and *Catch all*) and Fault Activities (*Compensate*, *Terminate*, *Throw*, and *Rethrow*) to catch and act on the faults appropriately.

   ii. Define Fault variables as necessary, as type *BusinessException* defined in the *CommonDomain-v1_0* SCA library.

Next, we will implement the appropriate Access Service component(s) that the Business Service will invoke in order to achieve the business functionality. Following are the steps involved in assembling and implementing the Access Service modules and its associated components:

1. **Create the Access Service module**

   i. Create an Access Service module by giving it an appropriate name, as per the build manifest we identified in Chapter 7, and Chapter 8. (set the folder name to `com/junglesea/accessservices`).

   ii. Add JungleSea Domain Libraries as project dependencies. Double-click on **Dependencies** node, add the libraries, and save.

   iii. Add the appropriate end application library to integrate with the backend applications.

2. **Implement Adapters** (as necessary)

   Adapters help integrate with the various backend applications in cases where the end application does not expose its capabilities in a standardized format.

   The reference partners in the Access Services module can also be imports of adapters that help communicate with backend applications and systems like file systems, databases, SAP, Siebel, FTP, email, and many more, including the option to create your custom adapter.

   i. Add Outbound adapters from communication that need to happen from the service to the end system.

   ii. Add Inbound adapters from communication that need to happen from the end system to the service.

   iii. Mediation flows help transform and process messages appropriately, when communicating with adapters.

   iv. Test the adapters to ensure that they are working as expected.

3. **Access Service module assembly and wiring**

   i. Create a mediation module by giving it an appropriate name, as per the build manifest we identified in Chapter 7, and Chapter 8.

   ii. Drag-and-drop the Access Service components (including mediation flows) with appropriate interfaces, as per the build manifest we identified in Chapter 7 and Chapter 8 on to the assembly diagram canvas.

   iii. In the SCA assembly diagram, visually assemble the module by dragging-and-dropping the appropriate SCA exports (as imports) from the JungleSea application libraries and wiring them to the business process component (created in the earlier step). From the properties view of the Invoke, select the appropriate operation of the partner.

   iv. For mediation flows, generate an export to expose the mediation flow in Access Service to communicate with the Business Service layer invoking them from above. In the SCA assembly diagram, right-click on the mediation flow component, and select Generate Export/Web Service Binding or any other binding as needed.

   v. Define Quality of Service (QoS) qualifiers.

> For more information on quality of service, refer to `http://publib.boulder.ibm.com/infocenter/dmndhelp/v7r0mx/topic/com.ibm.wbit.help.advanced.doc/qos/topics/cpolicies.html`

4. **Implement mediation flows**

> A quick reminder from *Chapter 6, Mediations Fundamentals*— A mediation flow basically receives an inbound request message from a service consumer, operates and processes the message, and then sends an outbound request message to the service provider.

i. In the assembly diagram, double-click on the mediation flow to generate an implementation of the mediation flow. You will be presented with an overview window, which has the input interface with its operations on the left side and the reference partner on the right side.

ii. Select the operation that needs to be worked on and then select what kind of mediation flow template should be generated. The choices are blank, service integration, and operation map. Based on your selection, a canvas is generated to further assemble and define the mediation flow.

> Blank mediation flow generates a mediation assembly canvas with only the input nodes. The target nodes are not defined. Service Integration is used to handle integration between multiple services in the generated mediation flow canvas. The Operation map is used when a mapping needs to be established between a source and a target. Selecting Service Integration or the Operation Map will prompt for further information to efficiently generate the mediation assembly canvas.

iii. Add callouts for any reference partners (including adapters) that are not already defined in the canvas.

iv. Make sure you define both the request and response flows for the mediation.

v. You are given the option on several Mediation primitives to define the messaging process. These primitives have been classified under service invocation, routing, transformation, tracing, error handling, mediation subflow, and fabric. Mediation primitives may also be selected and added under favorites in the palette to ease access to the most commonly-used primitives.

vi. Add routing Mediation primitives to control flow of the message to and from the partners. This includes filtering, endpoint look up, parallel flows, policy resolution, and SLA compliance.

vii. Add XSLT transformation Mediation primitives to transform messages between the input interfaces and the reference partners. This transformation can be done using XSL maps, Business Object maps, and by setting message elements, or message types. There is also the option to perform a database lookup, JMS headers, SOAP headers, MQ headers, and HTTP headers as the message flows between systems.

viii. Add tracing Mediation primitives for increased logging and monitoring purposes.

ix. We recommend adding Error handling primitives to all your flows to ensure that exceptions and errors are efficiently captured and reported up the layers. Message valuators and stop primitives can also be used to help diagnose errors.

x. Test the mediation flow components. Create test suite and test cases as appropriate.

5. **Wiring to Business Services and Access Services**

    i. Drag-and-drop the appropriate Access Service export to the respective Business Service module's assembly diagram.

    ii. Wire the Business Service component with the import.

6. **Testing the Business Service end-to-end**

    i. Deploy all dependent Access Services before executing the end-to-end test.

    ii. The Emulator functionality of the test client can be used to work around or imitate broken or unavailable parts of the assembly diagram like unavailable Access Services.

> A good article on WID-integrated test client is: `http://www.ibm.com/developerworks/websphere/techjournal/0712_gregory/0712_gregory.html`

    iii. Test Business Services components end-to-end all the way to the Access Service.

    iv. Make sure you validate each usage scenario for the Business Service and verify that the information returned is as expected.

> An explanation of assembling each of these Business Services is beyond the scope of this book. We shall look at some key examples that may then be used to develop the remaining components.

Building BizServices-ShippingMgmt module

As explained in the previous chapter, the purpose of this module is to manage shipping-related activities that could supplement the order handling process. In Chapter 7 we learned that JungleSea Inc. works with two partners, namely, "Fast" and "Rapid" for Logistics and Shipping management. These partners have exposed interfaces (Fast through web services, and Rapid through a file interface) to their end applications that will be consumed by the Shipping Management Business Services through Fast Access Service and Rapid Access Service. This is a classic example of a Business Service that exposes a key business function without actually exposing the implementation of the functionality. As there is a need for invoking Access Services from more than one component that belong to different partners, a Business Service layer (using a Microflow BPEL) will be used to choreograph the interactions. The individual Access Services will be implemented as mediation flows leveraging adapters.

The pseudo logic for this Business Service component is depicted as an activity diagram, as shown in the following figure:

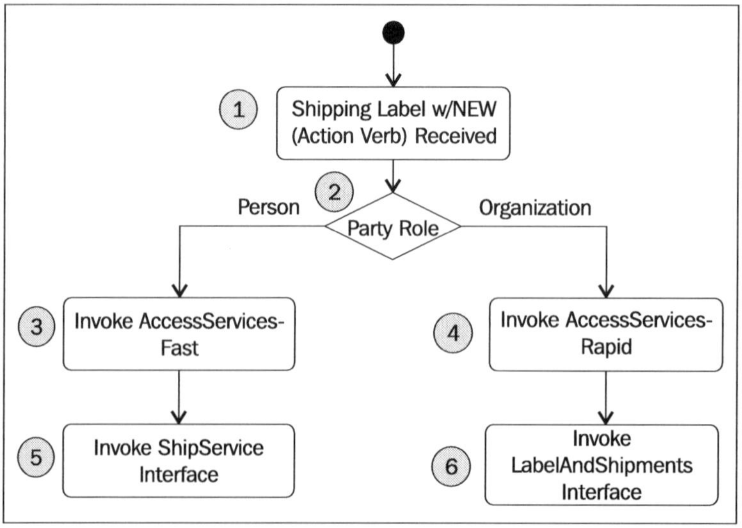

The logic detailed in the previous diagram is as follows:

1. Receive request for the creation of a new shipping label.
2. Check value of the business object Party Role in the request (CustomerOrderMSG).
3. If Party Role is set to Person, invoke `AccessServices-Fast` on operation `CreatePendingShipmentRequest`.
4. If Party Role is set to Organization, invoke `AccessServices-Rapid` on operation `prepareShipLabel` operation.
5. For AccessServices-Fast invoke `ShipService Interface` exposed by the Fast end application.
6. For AccessServices-Rapid invoke `LabelsAndShipments Interface` exposed by the Rapid end application.

Let's follow the steps listed in the beginning of this chapter to implement this Business Service component and the underlying Access Service components. From Chapter 9, you should have all the JungleSea Inc. application- and domain-specific libraries in your workspace as shown in the following screenshot.

Implement the Business Service component

In Chapter 8 we had identified what Access Services components the *ShippingManagement* Business Service module would need to invoke to accomplish its goal. In Chapter 9 we implemented the *ShippingManagement* Business Service module without any implementation. We will implement this component, such that it selects the right Access Service endpoint based on the customer type. This is shown in the following screenshot:

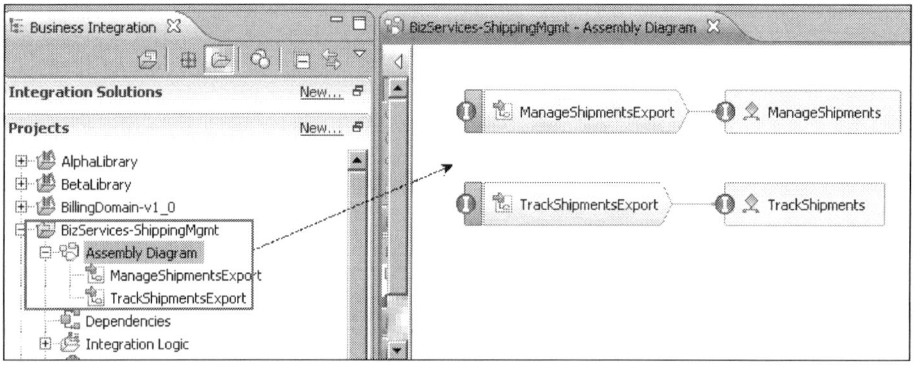

i. In the assembly diagram for **BizServices-ShippingMgmt**, double-click on **ManageShipments** to open the implementation of the business process component.

ii. Under the **createShippingLabel** choice, delete the assign activity.

iii. Drag a **Choice** activity under the **Receive Choice | createShippingLabel** activity, as shown in the following screenshot:

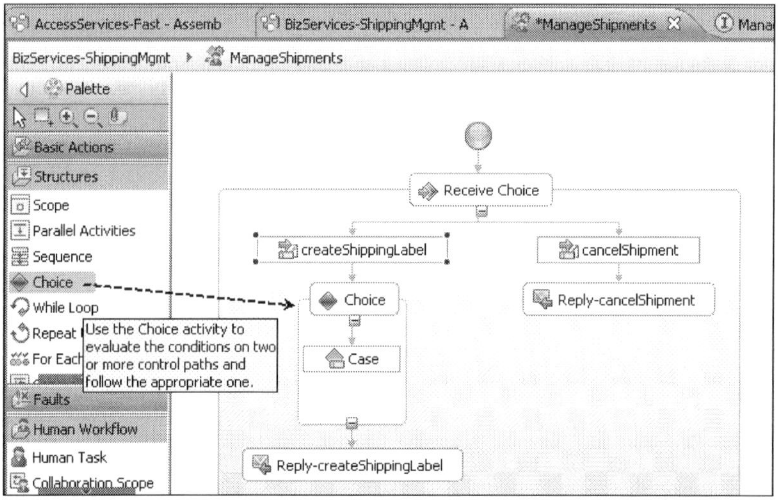

iv. Select the **Choice** activity and change the **Name** and **Display Name** to **PartyRole** under the **Properties** | **Description** tab, as shown in the following screenshot:

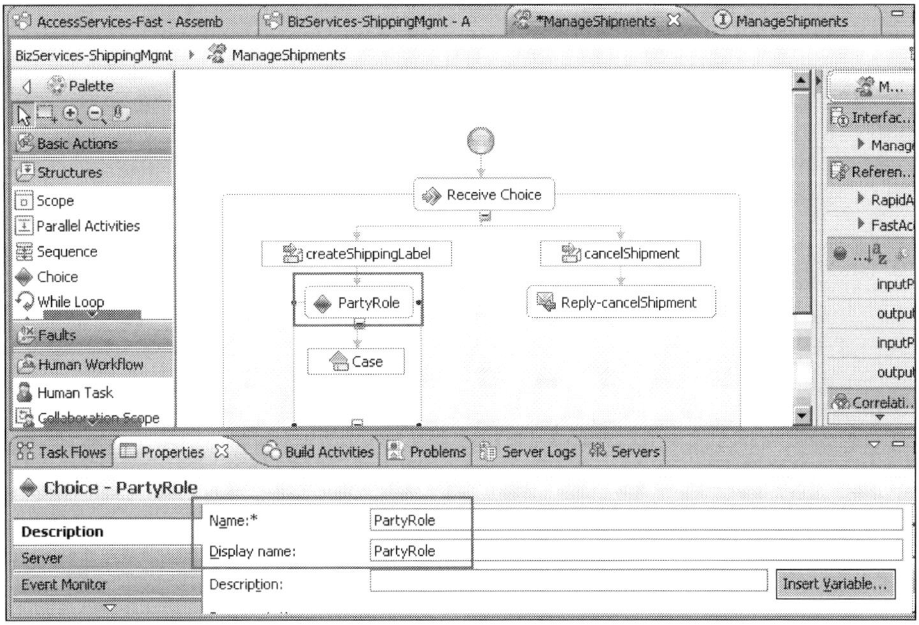

v. Similarly, rename **Case** to **AccessServices-Rapid** in the **Properties** | **Description** tab.

vi. Click on the **Details** tab in **Properties** window for the AccessServices-Rapid case.

vii. Click on **Create a New Condition** and add the condition, as shown in the following screenshot:

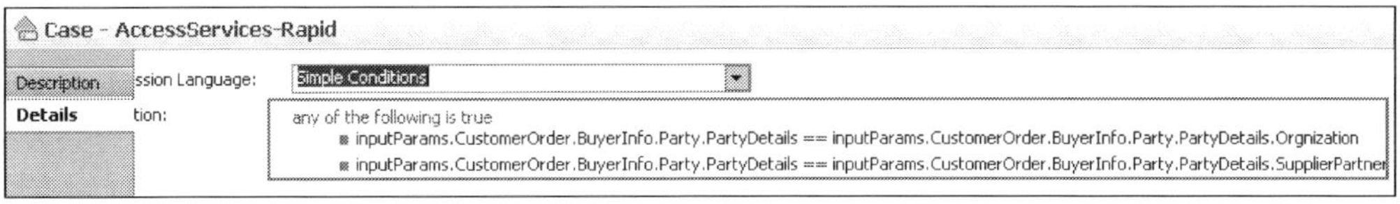

> Both the following are true:
> inputParams.CustomerOrder.BuyerInfo.Party.PartyType == 'Organization'
> inputParams.CustomerOrder.BuyerInfo.Party.PartyType == 'SupplierPartner'

viii. Right-click on choice activity **PartyRole** and select **Add a Case**. Name the choice case "AccessServices-Fast".

ix. Click on the **Details** tab in the Properties window for the AccessServices-Fast case. Click on **Create a New Condition** and add the condition, as shown in the following screenshot:

[inputParams.CustomerOrder.BuyerInfo.Party.PartyType== 'Person']

x. Add an invoke activity for each of these choice activities. We will define these invoke activities in the wiring Business and Access Services step. The completed business process activity should be as shown in the following screenshot:

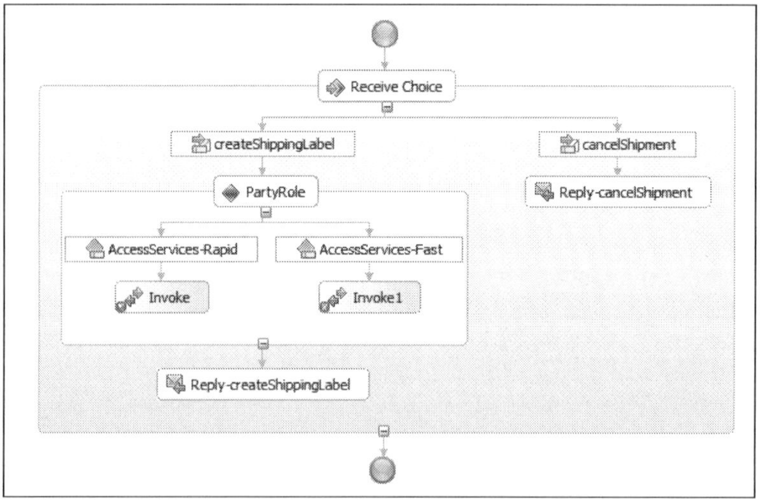

xi. Save all the changes.

Building AccessServices-Rapid module

Following the process just discussed, we begin defining the Rapid Access Service module.

Creating the Access Service module

1. In this step, we will implement the following dependant Access Service modules and the associated components:
    i. AccessServices-Rapid *(Module)*.
    ii. Med-LabelsAndShipments-prepareShipLabel *(Mediation Flow Component w/ email Adapter)*.
    iii. Med-LabelsAndShipments-shipmentStatus *(Mediation Flow Component)*
    iv. AccessServices-Fast *(Module)*.
    v. Med-ShipService-createPendingShipmentRequest *(Mediation Flow Component)*.
    vi. Med-ShipService-queryPendingShipmentStatus *(Mediation Flow Component)*.
2. The previous chapter walked us through (in detail) how to assemble the Business Services without any implementation. Similarly, assemble the Access Services.
    i. First, we will create modules that will hold all the Access Service components with names and interfaces, as discussed in Chapter 8. Create a module by selecting **File** | **New** | **Module**, which will open the New Project wizard, the first screen of which is shown in the following screenshot. Name the module **AccessServices-Rapid**.

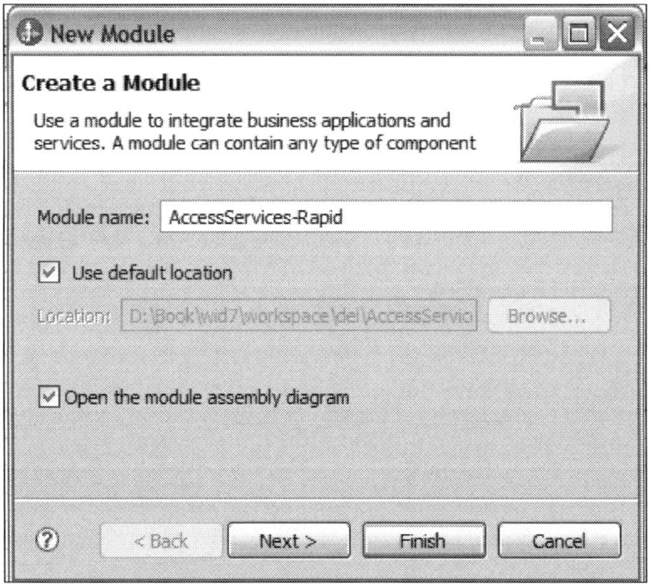

ii. In the next wizard screen, specify the dependent libraries required by this module, which is shown in the following figure, and press **Finish**. As you can see, we are adding JungleSea application libraries as a dependency. If you remember, in the case of Business Services, we did not add any application service library. We are also adding the domain libraries that will be interacting with the applications. Hence, AccessServices-Rapid will have dependency on both SupplierPartnerDomain Library and RapidLibrary. This completes our layered architectural approach and provides the flexibility and independence to the JungleSea Inc. business process from its partner's services and implementation. This also lets JungleSea Inc. add and remove partners with minimum impact to the overall end-to-end process.

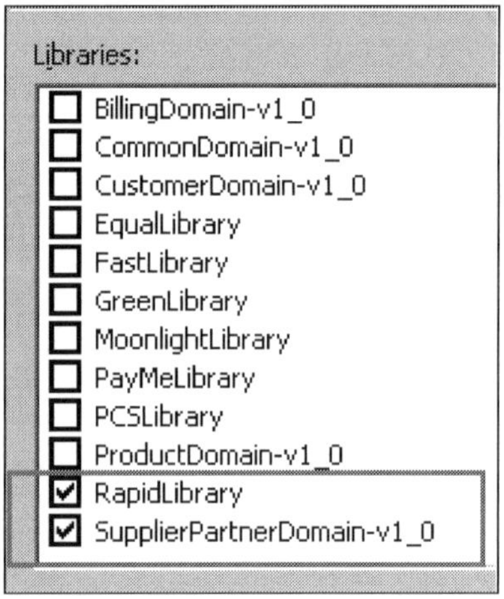

You have completed creating the AccessServices-Rapid. Repeat the same steps a and b and create AccessServices-Fast with dependency on *FastLibrary* and *SupplierPartnerDomain-v1_0.*

Implementing adapters

Following are the steps required for the implementation of adapters:

i. The assembly diagram for the module will open after completing the create wizards. In **Palette**, under **Outbound Adapters**, select **Flat File** adapter, and drag it on the canvas, as shown in the following screenshot:

ii. The **New External Service** wizard should open. Select the **Advance | Create Flat File** service, using the complete wizard, and click on the **Next** button. In next window, leave the default **IBM Websphere Adapter** selected, and click on the **Next** button.

iii. The default Connector file is selected, which is shipped along with WebSphere Integration Developer. Change the name of the Connector project to "OutboundRapidFileAdapter". For the Target server, ensure that "WebSphere Process Server V7.0" is selected and click on the **Next** button.

iv. As shown in the following screenshot, in the Service Configuration Properties, ensure that **Deploy connector project** is set to **With module for use by single application**. Enter the output directory to a predefined location. In the **Data format options**, select **Specify a data format for each operation**. Click on the **Next** button.

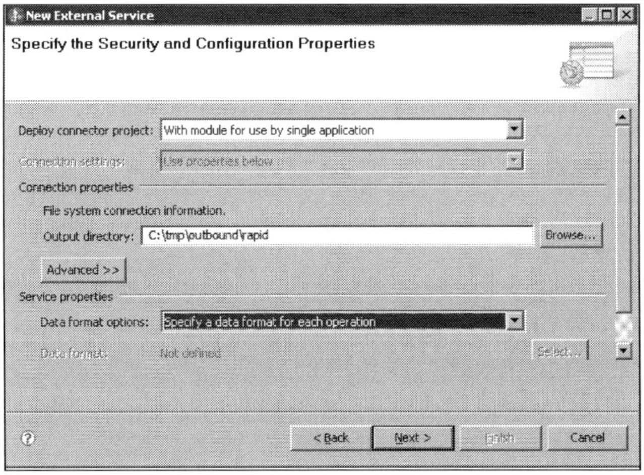

v. We shall now define create and retrieve operations for the file adapter to write and read from the file. As shown in the following screenshot, click **Add...** on the **Add Operation** window. Select **Operation kind | Create** and **Data type for the operation | User-defined type**. Since we only want to do a "create" operation without a response, leave the **Enable response type for the operation** unchecked. Click on the **Next** button.

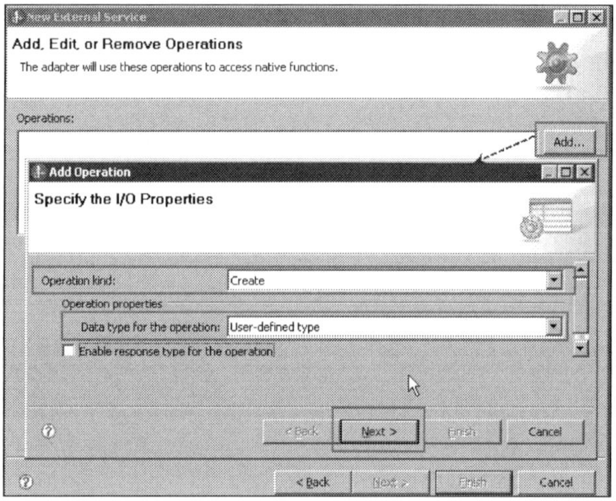

vi. On the **Specify the I/O Properties**, select **Data format options**. Click on **Browse** and select **shipping_label**. Click on the **OK** button. This completes the create operation.

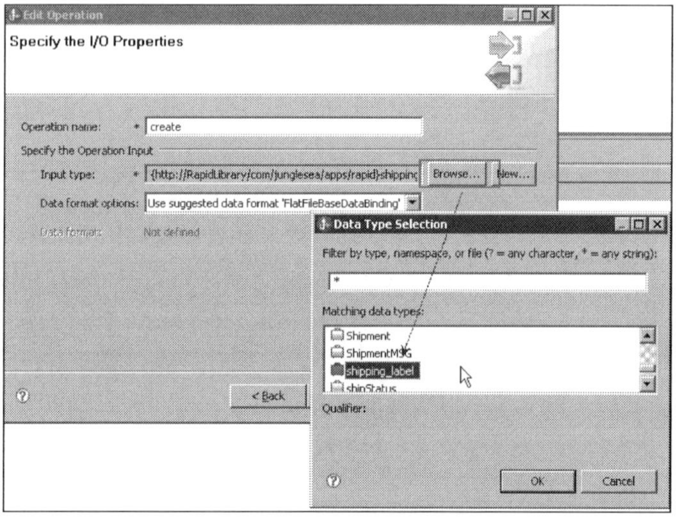

vii. You are now returned **Add, Edit** and **Remove Operations** page. Click on the **Next** button.

viii. On the **Specify the Name and Location** screen, change the default name to **OutboundRapidFlatFileAdapter**. Click on the **Finish** button.

ix. Save all your changes.

The Flat File adapter **OutboundRapidFlatFileAdapter** has now been defined.

Access Service module assembly and wiring

Following are the steps for assembly and wiring:

i. The assembly diagram for the module will open (if not, open it) after completing the adapter wizards. Create a new mediation flow component by right-clicking on **AccessServices-Rapid | Integration Logic** and selecting **New | Mediation Flow**. This will bring up the mediation flow wizard, and you will have to start providing information. In the first screen, as shown in the following image, provide the folder names (which are analogous to packages and become the basis for namespace) **com/junglsea/accessservices** and name the first component identified in Chapter 8 as **Med-LabelsAndShipments-prepareShipLabel**. Click on **Next.**

> As you can see from the following screenshot, the **Namespace** for this component is based on the module name and the folder name we provided. You are free to follow any other naming scheme.

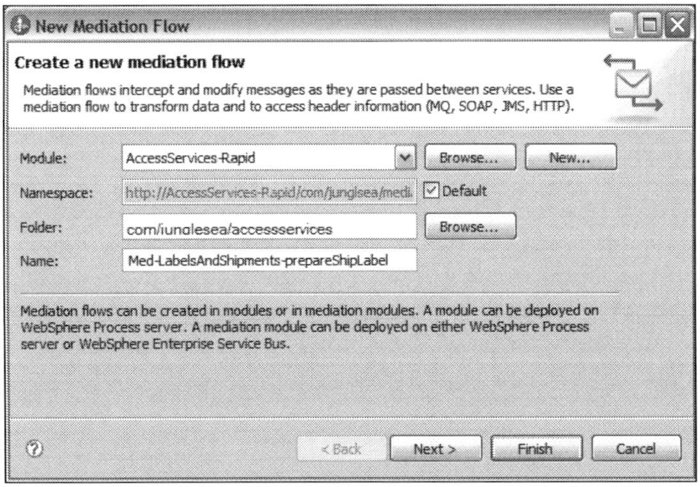

ii. The next wizard screen is the **Add Source Interfaces and Target References**. Specify the **Source interfaces** and **Target references** of the mediation flow component, as shown in the following screenshot. Click on **Finish**. The message from the **ManageShipments** interface will then be routed to the Rapid partner application. The mediation flow will establish communication between the source interface "ManageShipments" and the target reference "OutboundRapidFlatFileAdapterImport". This setup is shown in the following screenshot:

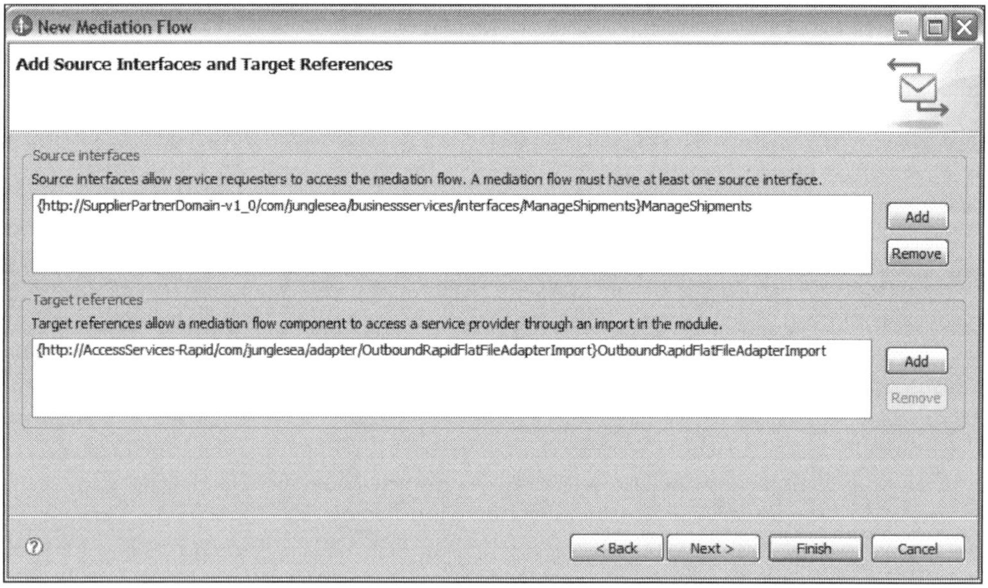

In the event that you are working with multiple developers on this module, click on **Next** and select **Save the mediation flow as multiple files**. In our particular case, we have one developer, so by default WID will generate only one file.

iii. Drag-and-drop the mediation flows components from under **AccessServices-Rapid | Integration Logic** to the assembly diagram. Right-click on each of the components and select **Generate Export | SCA Binding**. Save all your work.

If no binding is specified for an export, SCA becomes the default binding.

iv. Wire the **Med-LabelsAndShipments-prepareShipLabel** to **LabelsAndShipmentsFileAdapter**.

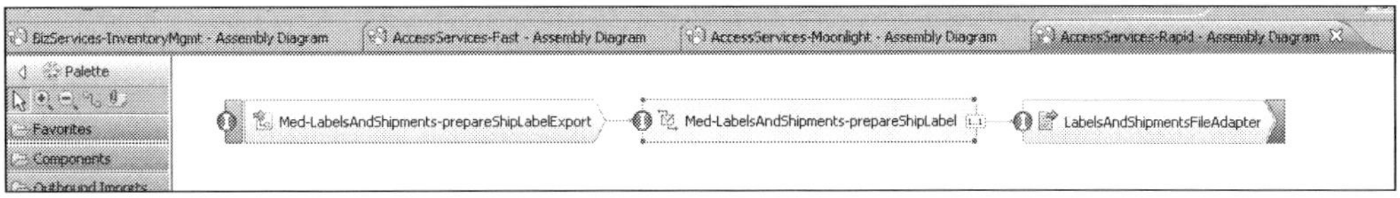

Implementing Mediation Flows

We will now implement Med-LabelsAndShipments-prepareShipLabel mediation flow. This should be used as an example to develop the other mediation flows. Following are the steps involved:

i. Open the **Med-LabelsAndShipments-prepareShipLabel** mediation flow. Click on the **createShippingLabel** operation listed under the **ManageShipments** interface and select **Operation Map**. Select in the **Reference** option **"OutboundRapidFileAdapterPartner"** and click on **OK**. We selected the operation map as we need to map the incoming shipping label request to the Rapid application interface.

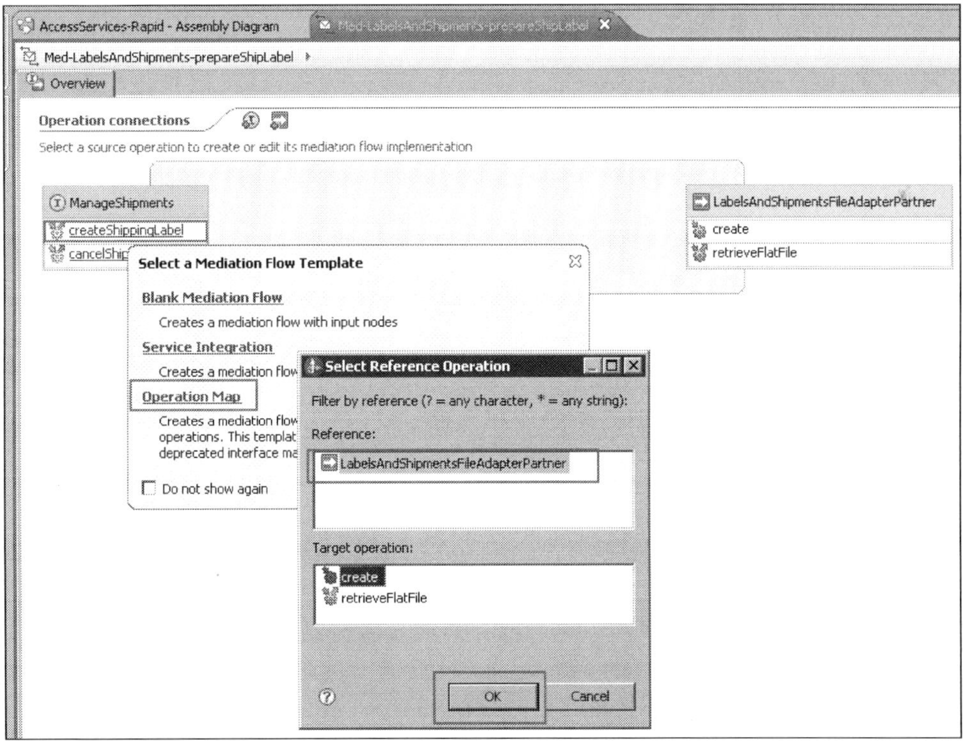

ii. A mediation flow assembly canvas will be generated based on your selections in the last step. Double-click on input_map primitive to open the **New XML Map** wizard. In the window, change **Folder** to **com/junglesea/transforms** and **Name** to **createShippingLabelRequestMsg_2_createRequestMsg**. Check the **Create a sample xml input file for testing the XML Map**. Click **Finish**.

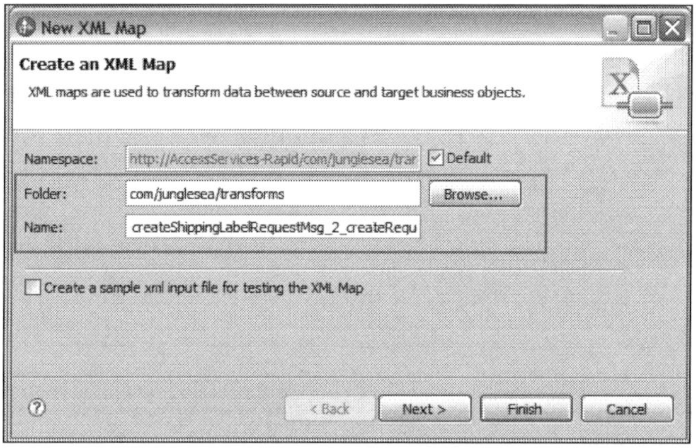

iii. The **CustomerOrdertoShippingLabelMap** window will open. Expand the left- and right-side objects to get a view of the fields, as shown in the following screenshot:

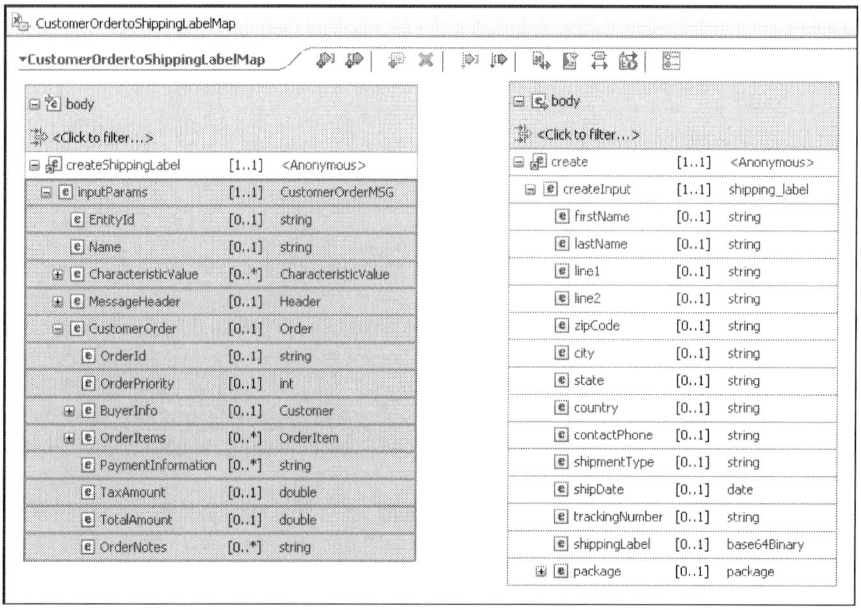

iv. On the XML Map page, you will see three distinct columns—Source, Transform, and Target, as shown in the screenshot below. WID gives a wide range of tools, to map and transform fields between source and target. We shall now take a closer look at some of these options.

v. First, let's begin with **Move**, which moves the value of one field to another field of the same type. The **Move** map is established simply by linking one field to another. In **CustomerOrdertoShippingLabelMap**, let's link **CustomerOrder | BuyerInfo | Party | PartyDetails | Organization | ContactPersonName** to **createInput | firstName** and **CustomerOrder | BuyerInfo | Party | PartyDetails | Organization | Phone** to **createInput | contactPhone**.

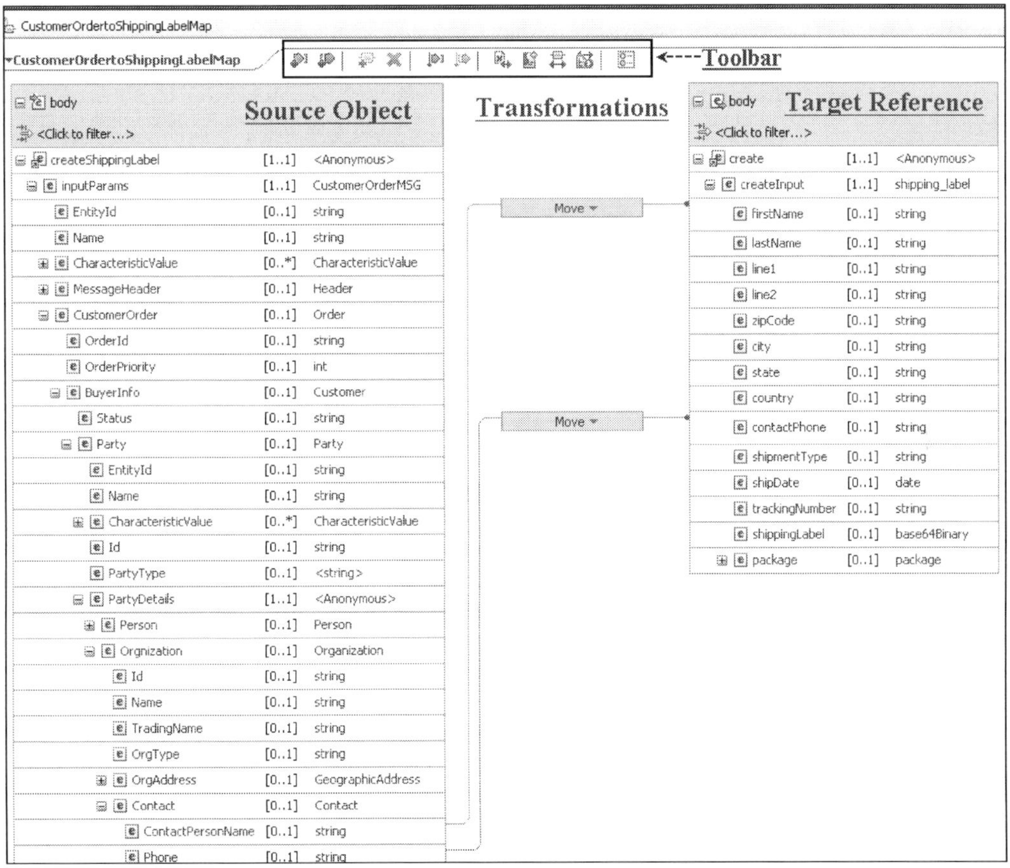

> Toolbar tips:
>
> Map source to target icon in the navigation toolbar creates matches between the source and target elements or attributes that have the same name and type. This may help reduce your development effort.
>
> Test Map is another useful feature used to test the XSL transformation in isolation.

vi. We can further refine our map to set **createInput | FirstName** to **Organization | ContactPersonName** only if **PartyType** field is set to **Organization**. First change **Move** transform to **If** and link **PartyType** to the box. Now select the **If** transform box and set under **Properties | Condition**, as shown in the following screenshot:

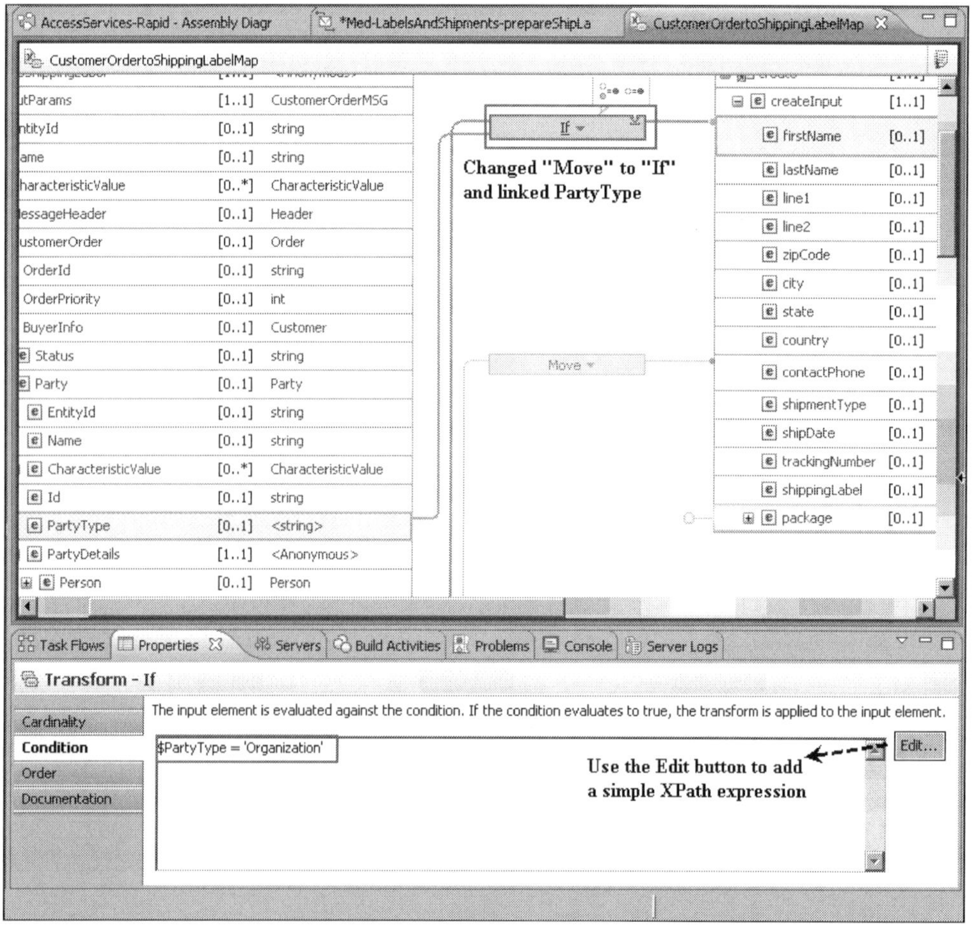

vii. Next, double-click on the **If** transform box. In the transform definition window, link **Organization | ContactPersonName** to **createInput | FirstName**. Return to the main **CustomerOrdertoShippingLabelMap** using the navigation bar, as shown in the following screenshot:

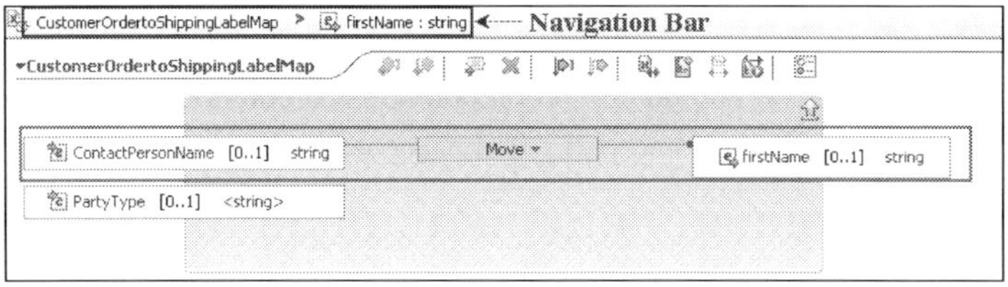

viii. Repeat the steps to add an "Else If" condition to map **SupplierPartner | ContactPersonName** and **Phone** to **createInput | firstName** and **Phone** with **$PartyType = SupplierPartner**.

ix. Establish the following **Move** maps from **CustomerOrder | OrderItems | ShippingAddress** to **shippingLabel**.

ShippingAddress	shippingLabel
LineOne	LineOne
LineTwo	LineTwo
PostalCode	zipCode
City	City
StateOrProvince	State
Country	Country

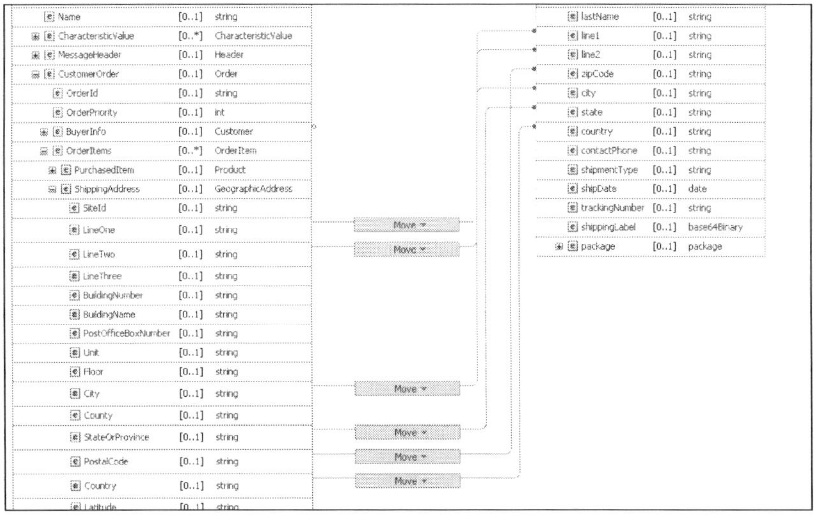

x. The map we created above mapped an array OrderItem to a singleton. Therefore, our next step is establishing the cardinality of the array item that will be used for the map. For the purpose of our example, we are assuming that all items are being shipped to the same person and address on the same date. To establish cardinality, select the **Move** box. Under **Properties | Cardinality**, set the value to **1**, as shown in the following screenshot.

> In case of defining cardinality for arrays in the transformation properties, the index for the first item is 1 and not 0. If you leave the cardinality blank or *, it means all the items.

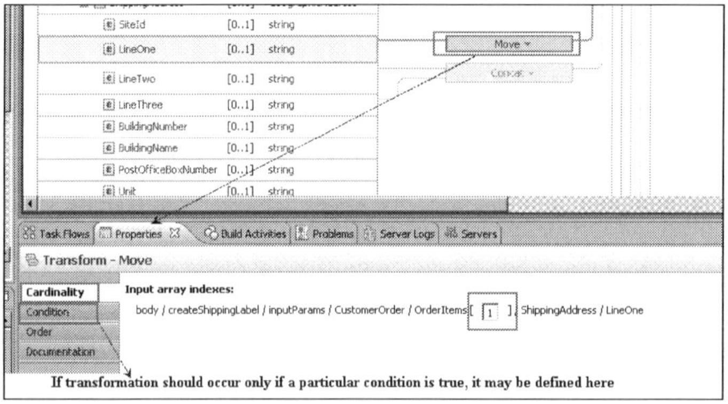

xi. We shall now combine two strings to map to another string using the **Concat** option. We had mapped **CustomerOrder | OrderItem | ShippingAddress | LineTwo** to **ShippingLabel | LineTwo**. Now we will add the content in LineThree to this by linking **LineThree** to the **Move** box. WID will automatically change the operation to **Concat**, as shown in the following screenshot:

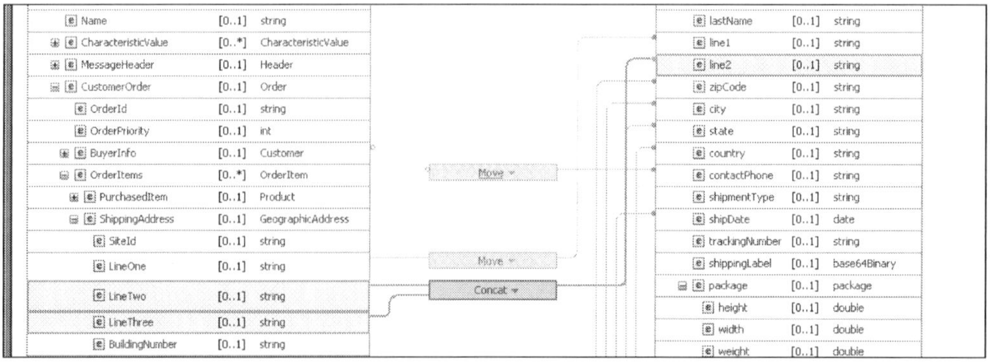

xii. Next, we shall look at Custom XPath. Link **CustomerOrder | OrderItems | PurchasedItem | ProductDetails | ItemQuantity** to **shippingLabel | package | weight**. Link **CustomerOrder | OrderItem | PurchasedItem | ProductDetails | ItemQuantity** to **ShippingLabel | package | ItemWeight** to the **Move transform box**. Now on the **Move transform box**, select **Custom XPath**. Now we need to define the Custom XPath expression. Select the **Custom XPath** under **General** and add **$ItemQuantity*$ItemWeight**.

xiii. The last step to creating this transformation is testing it. Click on the **Test Map** icon in the navigation toolbar. This will generate an input data based on the source schema and an output transformation XML based on the transformation setup. You can then look at the end result, as shown in the following screenshot, and verify if the transformation happened as expected.

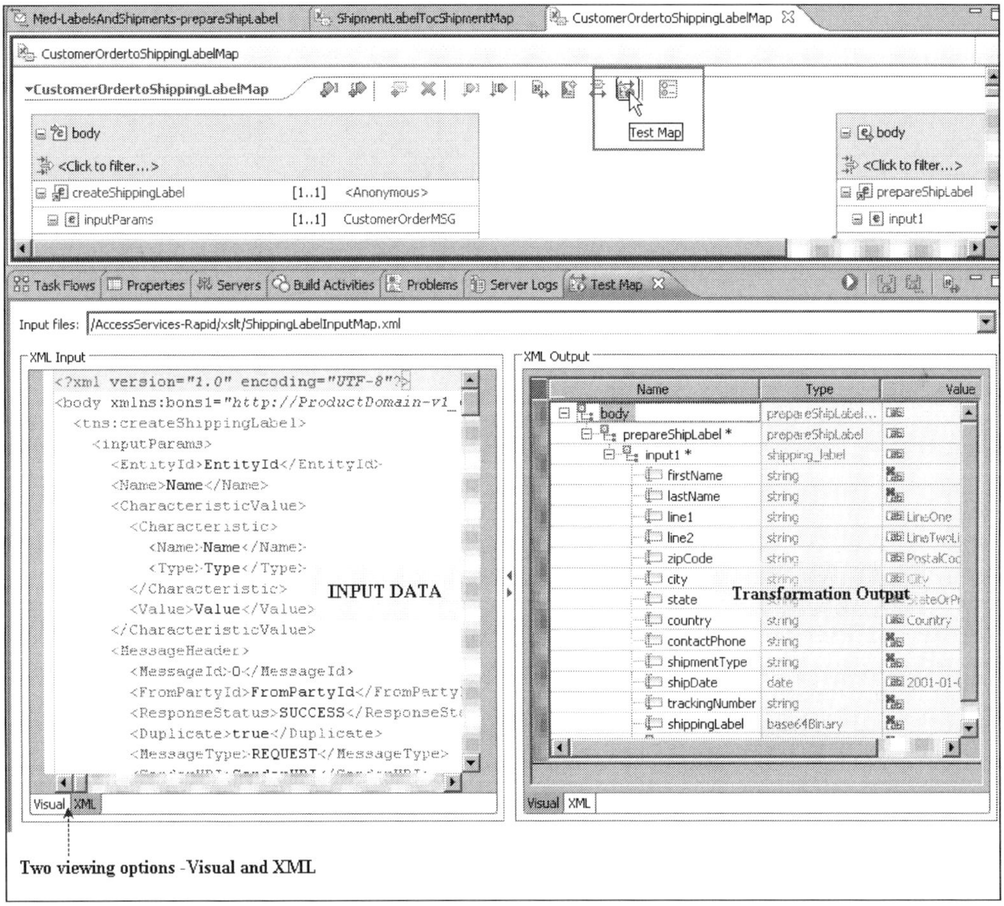

xiv. Return to the **Med-LabelsAndShipments-prepareShipLabel** mediation assembly canvas. Delete the output_map that gets autogenerated in the request canvas.

We have so far submitted a "create shipping label" request. Our next step is to retrieve the label from the file adapter. For this, create an Output Flat File adapter called **RetrieveRapidShippingLabelAdapter** with retrieve operation. Target the adapter to retrieve the shipping label from a predefined location. In our example, we have used **C:\tmp\retrieve\shippinglabel**.

i. Link **Med-LabelsAndShipments-prepareShipLabel** to **RetrieveRapidShippingLabelAdapter**.

ii. Double-click on **Med-LabelsAndShipments-prepareShipLabel**.and add **Med- RetrieveRapidShippingLabelAdapter** as a reference.

iii Click on **createShipLabel** to open the response mediation flow, drag a **Callout** primitive to the canvas, and link it to **retrieve FlatFile** operation under **RetrieveRapidShippingLabelAdapter**.

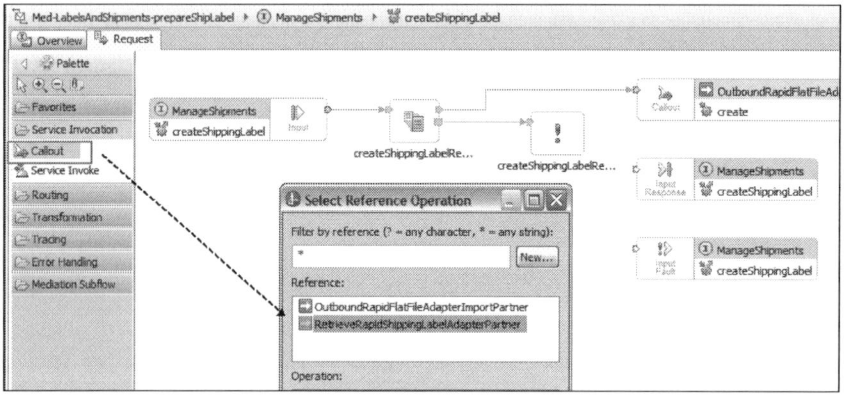

iv. Next add a **Flow Order** primitive. This primitive will help first send a shipping label request and then retrieve the shipping label.

v. Wire the response flow, as shown in the following screenshot:

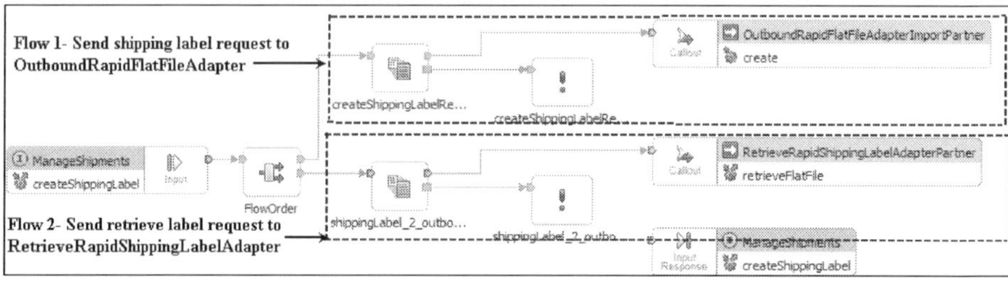

vi. You may use the code example with the book to see this retrieve shipping label request implementation.

vii. Next, we will cover how to read the response from **RetrieveRapidShippingLabelAdapter**.

viii. You will now see a **Response** tab. Click the **Response** tab and wire **retrieveFlatFile** to **createShippingLabel**.

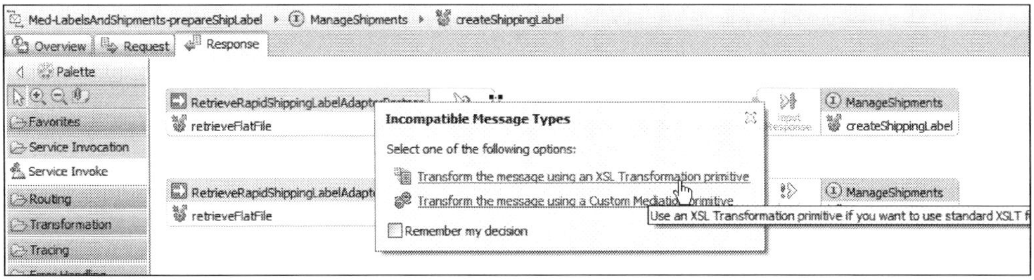

ix. Use the steps defined earlier to implement the **retieveShipmentLabel_2_shipmentLabel** map for the Response mediation flow, as shown in the following screenshot. This completes the creation of the **Med-LabelsAndShipments-prepareShipLabel** mediation flow.

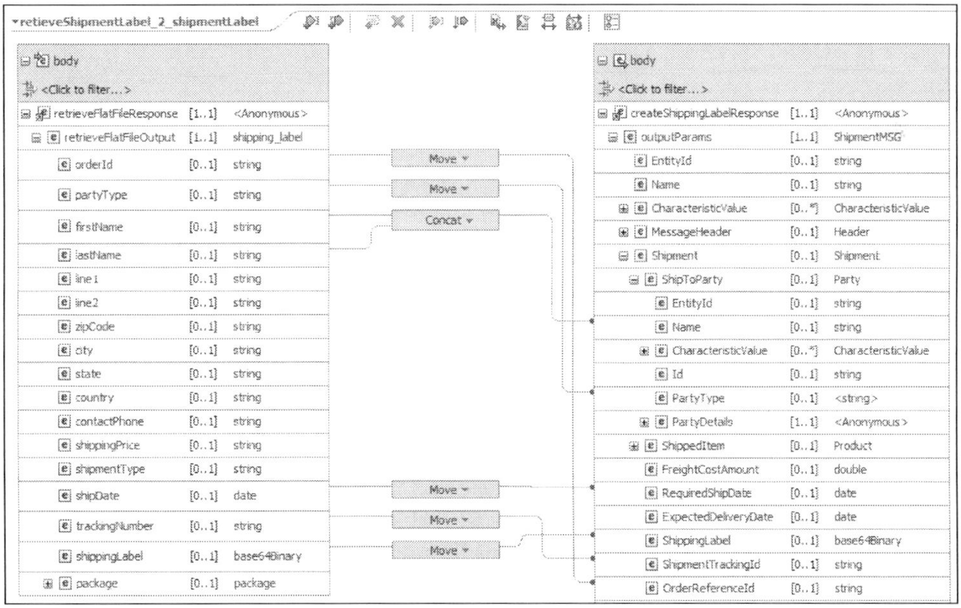

x. Save all your work.

Unit Testing the Mediation Flows

Perform the following steps to unit test the Mediation flows:

i. Open the assembly diagram for AccessServices-Rapid. Right-click on the **Med-LabelsAndShipments-prepareShipLabel** mediation flow and select **Test Component**.

ii. This will open the integration test client. Change the operation to be tested to **createShippingLabel**, as shown in the following screenshot:

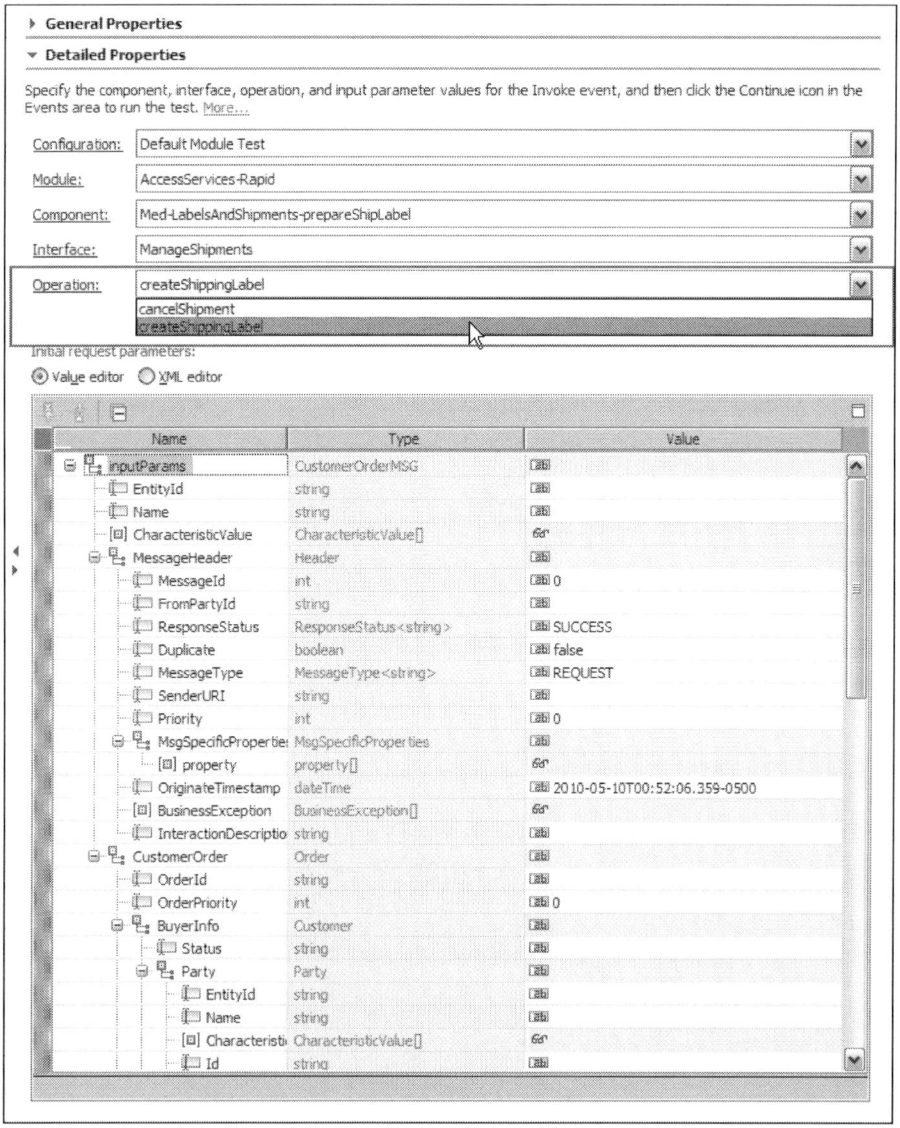

> For more information on the integrated test client, refer to: `http://publib.boulder.ibm.com/infocenter/ieduasst/v1r1m0/topic/com.ibm.iea.wpi_v6/wpswid/6.1/TestingEnvironment/WBIV61_WID_TestingApps/player.html?dmuid=20080419142538867762`

iii. On the right side, right-click on input params in the initial parameters request section. Select **Use Value from Pool** and open **ShippingLabelRequest1.objectpool**.

iv. We have a predefined request to help with testing under the data pool **ShippingLabelRequest1.objectpool**, as shown in the following screenshot:

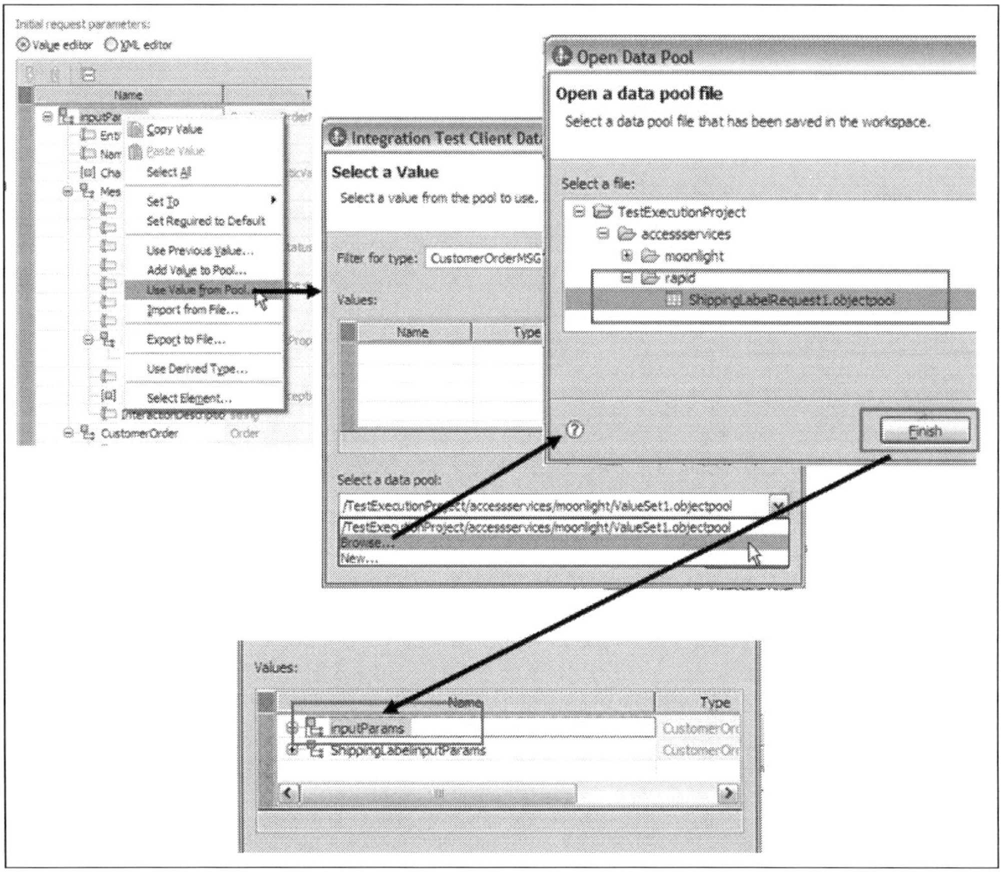

v. Select **inputParams** under VALUES to autopopulate by default the initial parameters for the request. Next click on the green play button to start the transaction.

vi. If you are asked to select a server, then select WebSphere Process Server 7.0 and provide the security credentials.

vii. Verify no expectations are thrown in the execution. Visually view the response values to ensure they are correct, as shown in the following screenshot:

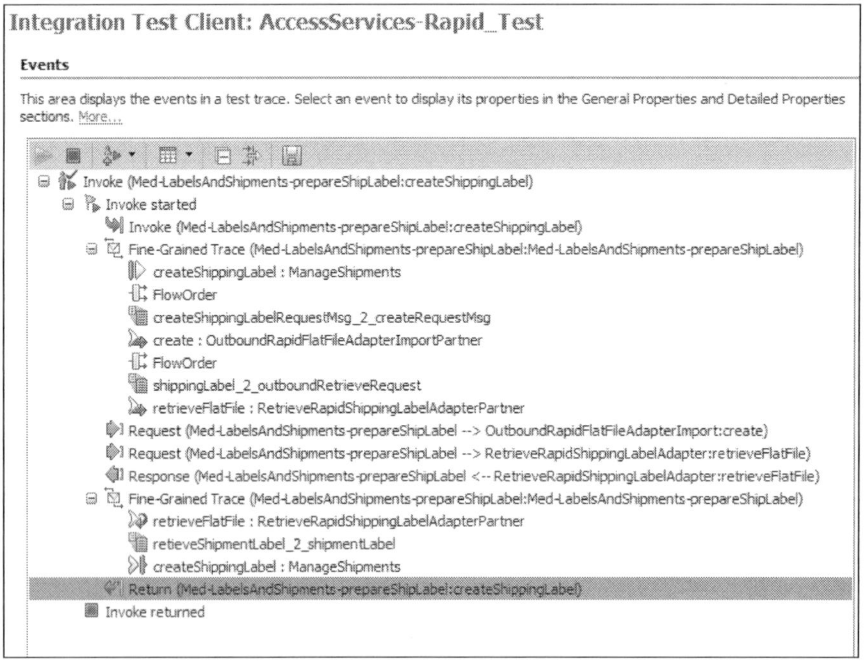

[Implementation of the Fast Access service has not been covered in this book. Please refer to the project interchange (PI) to look at the implementation.]

Wiring Business Services and Access Services

We will now wire the Rapid and Fast Access Services to BizService-ShippingMgmt.

i. Open the BizService-ShippingMgmt assembly diagram.

ii. In the left column in the **Project** section, expand **AccessServices-Rapid | Assembly Diagram** and drag **Med-LabelsAndShipments-prepareShipLabelExport** onto **BizService-ShippingMgmt** canvas. On the **Component Creation** dialog, select **Import with SCA Binding**, as shown in the following screenshot:

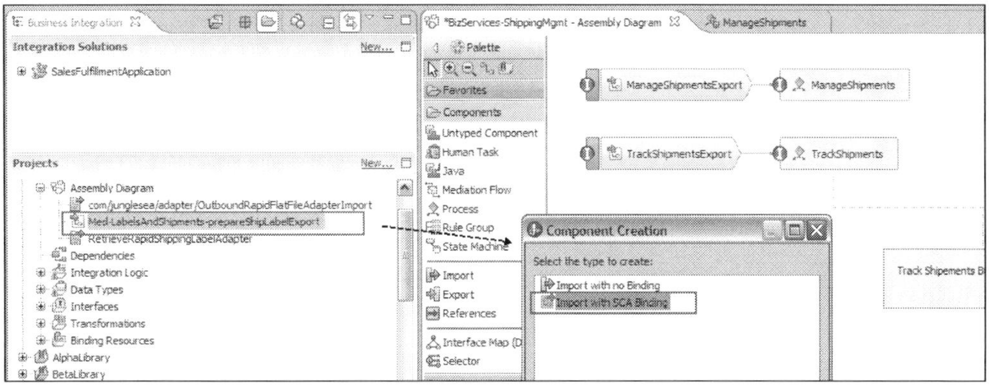

iii. Rename the import to **AccessServices-RapidImport** and wire a **ManageShipments** process component to it.

iv. Similarly, add **AccessServices-FastImport** of **Med-ShipService-createPendingShipmentRequestExport** from **AccessService-Fast** and wire a **ManageShpiments** process component to it, as shown in the following screenshot:

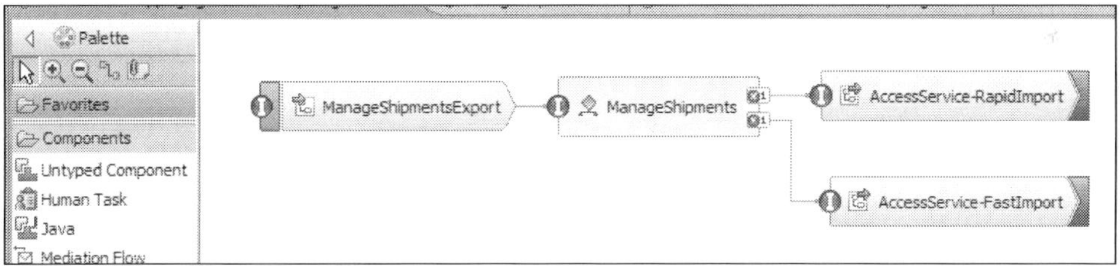

v. Save all your changes.

vi. You may see an error under the Problems tab—The process component file **platform:/resource/BizServices-ShippingMgmt/ManageShipments.component** contains a reference **ManageShipmentsPartner** that does not have a corresponding partnerLink in the process implementation file.

vii. To resolve the issue, right-click on the message and select **QuickFix**. In the QuickFix dialog, select **Synchronize Interfaces and References to Implementation** and click on the **Finish** button, as shown in the following screenshot:

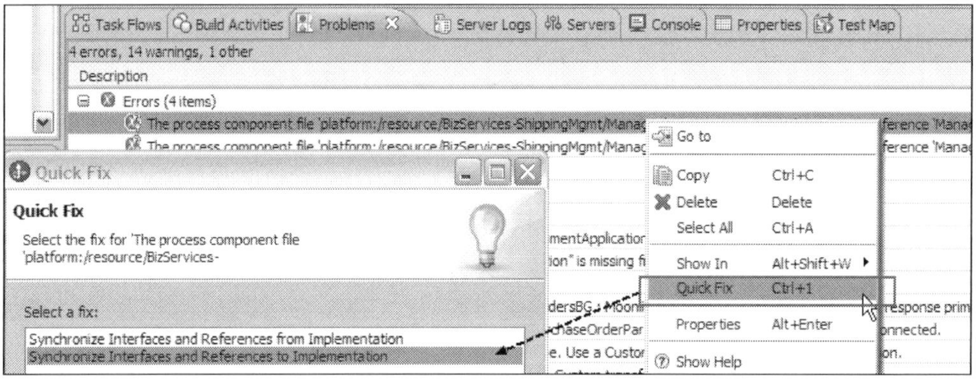

viii. The last step is to link the Access Services to the **ManageShipments** Business Service. Double-click on **ManageShipments BPEL component** to open it.

ix. In process flow, select the **Invoke** activity under choice **AccessService-Rapid**. Open the **Properties | Details** view. Click on **Browse** and select **ManageShipmentsPartner**. Select operation **createShippingLabel**. Define the input and output parameters, as shown in the following screenshot:

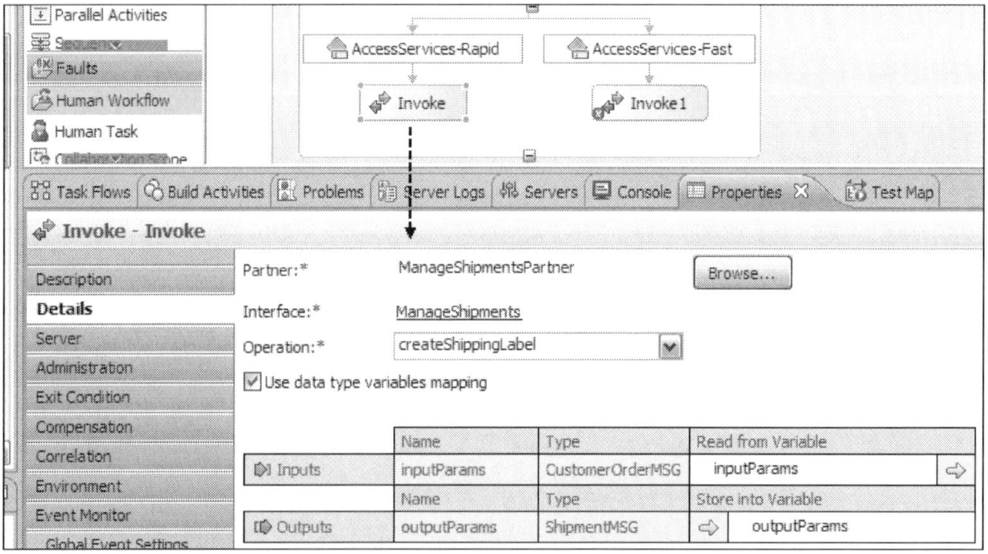

x. Similarly, select the **Invoke1** activity under choice **AccessService-Fast**. Open the **Properties | Details** view. Click on **Browse** and select **ManageShipmentsPartner1**.

xi. Save all your changes.

We have now successfully created a Business Service and the underlying Access Service. Our last step is test it end-to-end.

Testing the Business Service end-to-end

In this exercise, we will only test the **ManageShipments** process flow. However, in actual practice, it is highly recommended to test all possible usage variations of each of the Business Service operation and process flows. We will use the integrated test client to test **BizServices-ShippingMgmt**. These steps are similar to testing the mediation flow.

i. Under the **Servers** view, right-click on **Websphere Process Server** and deploy **AccessService-Fast** and **AccessService-Rapid** through the **Add and Remove Projects** dialog. Wait for the deployment to complete.

ii. Right-click on **ManageShipmentsExport** and select **Test Component**.

iii. Under **Detailed | Properties**, verify that the **createShippingLabel** operation is selected.

iv. Use the data pool to set the initial request parameters. In the code example, we have provided two sets of values—one for Person Party Type and one for Organization Party Type.

v. Run each set of values. Verify that **Person Party Type** invokes the **AccessService-Fast** and **Organization Party Type** invokes **AccessService-Rapid**.

This completes the end-to-end test of **BizServices-ShippingMgmt** for the purposes of this exercise.

> Having walked you through the process of building a Business Service component and Access Service Components (including an adapter), we will breeze through the implementation of the rest of the modules and components. We will stop and spend time wherever there is a concept that needs explanation.

Building BizServices-CustomerCreditMgmt module

Customer credit Business Service allows JungleSea to manage the risk and would want to check an incoming order against a customer's credit limit. Currently, an application named "Equal" provides information about customers' credit score and exposes the capability on a Java Messaging Service (JMS) interface. The response to the credit risk evaluation will have to be approved by the manager, which we implemented in the order handling business process. By all means, we can move that functionality to this component. But adhering to one of the fundamental tenets of SOA, keeping services stateless, we will leave it as it is.

> The steps to implement a Business Service were discussed in the previous sections. We will not repeat those steps, assuming that you will follow them. As explained earlier, we strongly recommend that you import the PI into your WID workspace and use it as a reference. Also, some of the intricacies that could not be explained in this chapter will be very forthcoming and revealing in the PI itself.

Building AccessServices-Equal module

JungleSea Inc.'s Equal application provides the capability to assess the credit (risk) rating for a given customer order. The credit check allows JungleSea to evaluate orders that are over a set limit ($500 for the purposes of this book and determined through a business rule, as discussed in the previous chapter), based on the credit standing of the customer ordering the product(s). This application returns the overall credit score and status for the customer and this order as the response. This credit score will be internally and manually evaluated by a manager/supervisor to approve the order transaction. We will see how we can build the Access Service mediation flow component that would make use of JMS import bindings.

> We will use JMS to access the WebSphere Default Messaging Provider—the Service Integration Bus (SIBus), which is a JMS provider that implements the JMS 1.1 specification. The SIBus is internally used by both WPS and WESB. WPS and WESB use the SCA.SYSTEM (for inter-SCA messaging) and SCA.APPLICATION (for components with JMS bindings) SIBuses. In WID, you will see various message bindings including JMS Binding, Generic JMS binding, MQ binding, and MQ JMS binding.
>
> For the purposes of this book, we will use the JMS binding on the import component to show how we can invoke the Equal application. Again, since we are simulating the JungleSea apps, the Access Service mediation component will make a request to the SIBus queue (which in turn would invoke a method in an Equal application in real life).

On the JMS import binding, you will need to specify a WSDL interface, which will be the interface provided in the EqualLibrary. The data binding specifies the transformation of the data from a Business Object (SDO or SMO), to a native format such as a stream of bytes. The JMS standard defines a Message class (javax.jms.Message), which is the root interface of all JMS messages. It defines the message header, the acknowledge method used for all messages, and properties, but no body (payload). The JMS standard also defines five sub-classes of Message, each of which has a different body type:

- **BytesMessage**: The message body is a byte array.
- **MapMessage**: The message body is set of name/value pairs, which can be addressed by name and where the value is a simple Java type.
- **ObjectMessage**: The message body is a serialized Java Object.
- **StreamMessage**: The message body is a stream (sequence) of simple Java types.
- **TextMessage**: The message body is a Java String.

WID provides six simple JMS data bindings for predefined JMS message body types, one for the Message class and one for each sub-class of Message. Two specialized JMS data bindings also exist, one for Text and one for Object messages. For the purposes of this component, we will stick to the default message type as Byte.

Create Access Service module

Create a mediation module named AccessServices-Equal and add project dependencies to the JungleSea domain libraries—Billing, Product, Customer, and Common and Equal application library.

Access Service module assembly and wiring

Perform the following steps for assembly and wiring:

i. Create a mediation flow component named **Med-EqualCreditPulseSoap-creditPulseByIndividual** and a folder (namespace) as **com/junglesea/accessservices**.

ii. Specify the source interface **CustomerCreditInformation** and target the interface to be **EqualCreditPulseSoap**.

iii. Drag-and-drop this mediation flow component to the assembly diagram.

iv. In the assembly diagram palette, under **Outbound Imports**, select **JMS**, and drag it to the assembly editor.

v. In the **New JMS Import Service** dialog, specify the interface to be **EqualCreditPulseSoap**, and click on the **Next** button.

vi. In the **Configure JMS Import Service** wizard, specify the JMS messaging domain to be **Point-to-Point** and also select configure the new messaging provider resources option. We will use the default data format UTF8XMLDataHandler that serializes a business object into UTF-8 encoded XML data when sending a message. Also, one point to note here is WPS JMS import supports several data format transformations including Atom, Delimited, JAXB, JSON, Simple JMS message data binding, and so on.

vii. When server security is enabled and we will have to specify the user ID and password using the J2EE Connector (J2C) authentication data entries, we will use the **SCA_Auth_Alias**. The configuration dialog will look as shown in the following screenshot.

viii. Complete the wizard by pressing finish and you would find that the JMS binding is created.

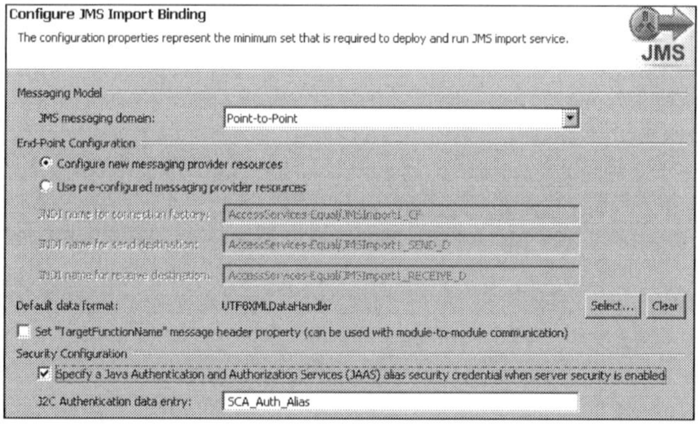

ix. View the JMS import properties, and configure the JMS provider connection information. We will specify the JNDI lookup name under the **End-Point Configuration** tab. For the purposes of this book, we will not specify a JNDI lookup. So the managed connection factory will be created on the server using the properties specified here.

x. The necessary connection properties are completed for you, as shown in the following screenshot:

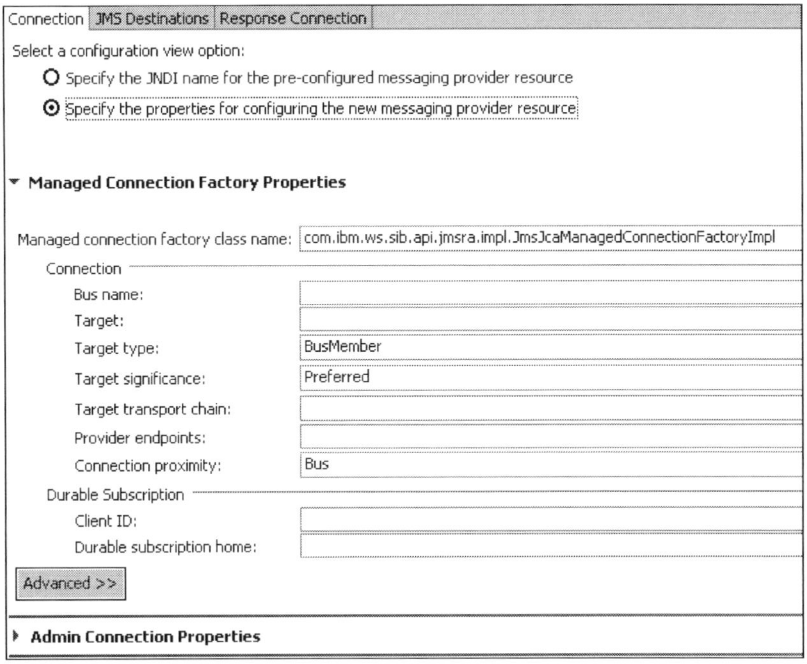

xi. **Advanced** indicates quality of service properties such as persistence properties and if this is a shared property.

xii. **Admin Connection Properties** provides connection pool properties and configuration properties if you would like custom names and values. If you had specified a JNDI name earlier, it is empty since the server is determining connection pooling values.

xiii. In the **JMS destinations** tab, you would be able to see the **JMS queue names** where messages will be sent: **AccessServices-Equal. EqualSubmitOrderQueue_SEND_D**. If you specify nothing in the **Queue Name** or **Topic Space** field, a default value will be created.

xiv. You configure the JMS header properties under the **Method bindings** tab for each method on the interface. For example, we will define a property named **JungleSeaInternal** of Type **java.lang.boolean** and set **Value** to **true**. This will indicate the orders are originating from a JungleSea internal application. This is shown in the following screenshot:

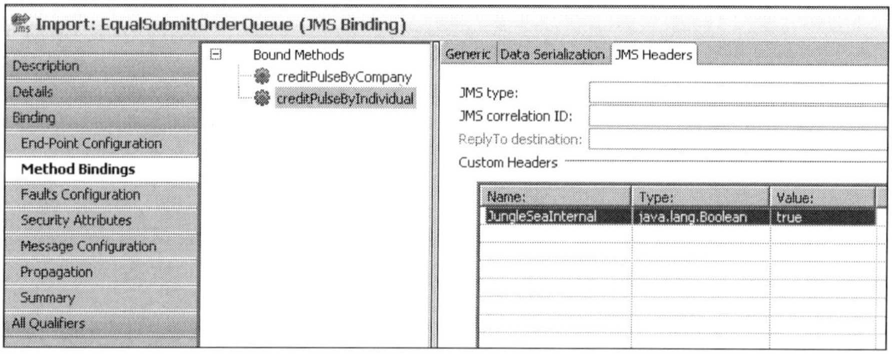

xv. You can view the messages being sent to this queue via the Service Integration Bus Browser available in the Administrative Console of WPS, as shown in the following screenshot:

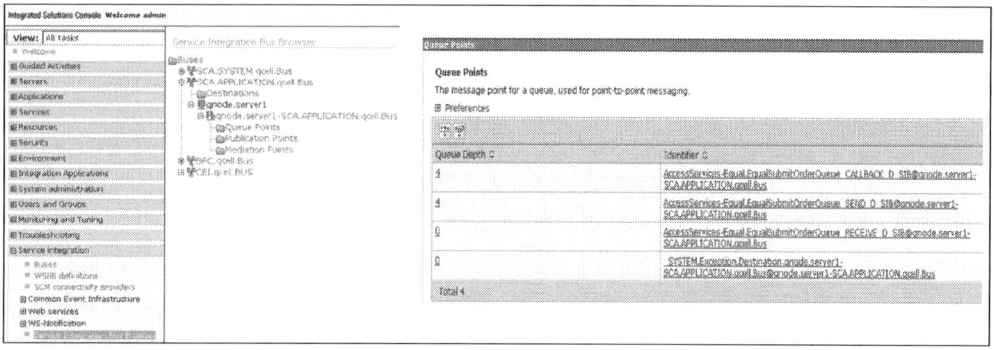

You can use the SIBus Explorer to browse and navigate the SI Bus queues. The tool is available from the following location:

`http://www.alphaworks.ibm.com/tech/sibexplorer`

Implementing Mediation Flows

The implementation of the mediation flow itself will consist of performing a data transformation from the CustomerOrderMSG to company CreditChkRequest in the request flow and vice versa in the response flow. You can look at the project interchange file to see how we implemented the transformations using the XSLT primitive. On the "callout" node in the request flow, we will specify how to handle retry if an exception occurs. We will elaborate on the occurrence of any fault, the retry count should be three times, with a delay of 15 seconds between retries. This configuration will look as shown in the following screenshot:

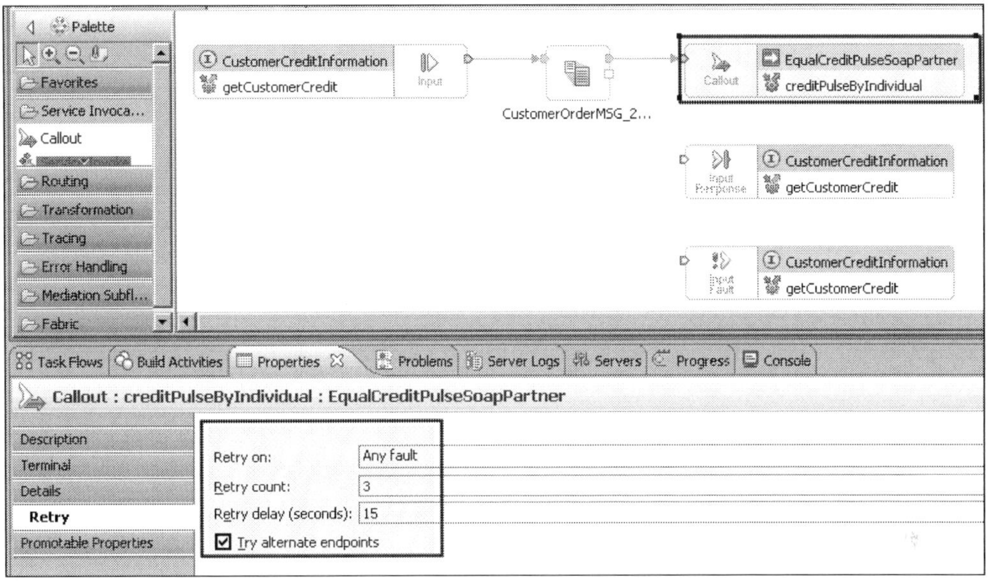

We will also add fault handling to the mediation flow in case the Equal application JMS queues are not accessible. We will use the Fail nodes to specify fault handling logic. This is shown in the following screenshot:

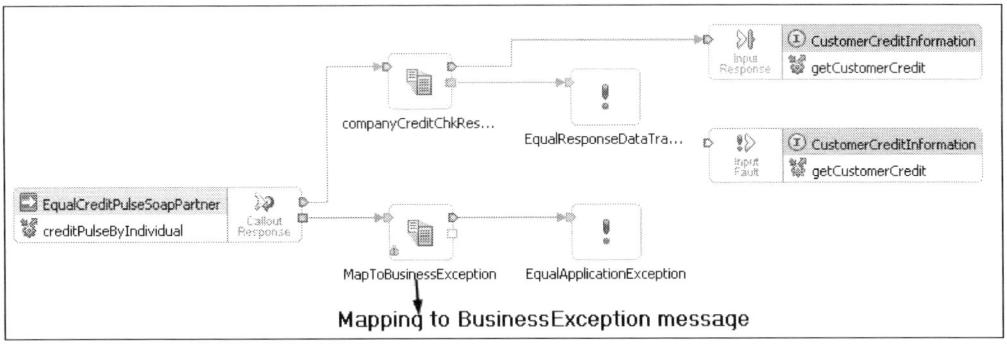

Testing the Mediation Flows

We will use the integration test client to test the mediation flow and see how messages land up in the send queue. We will use IBM's **IBM Client Application Tool for JMS** to read the messages being put on the send queue **AccessServices-Equal/EqualSubmitOrderQueue_SEND_D** by the preceding JMS import binding and put the message back on **AccessServices-Equal/EqualSubmitOrderQueue_RECEIVE_D** receive queue thereby simulating Equal. You can download this tool from:

`http://www.alphaworks.ibm.com/tech/jmstool`

> To read about how to create and configure JMS resources on a SIBus, refer to
> `http://www.ibm.com/developerworks/websphere/techjournal/0504_reinitz/0504_reinitz.html`

One of the test case input XML blurbs used for testing is as follows:

```
<CustomerOrder>
    <OrderId></OrderId>
    <OrderPriority>0</OrderPriority>
    <BuyerInfo>
      <Status>New</Status>
      <Party>
        <EntityId></EntityId>
        <Name></Name>
        <Id></Id>
        <PartyType>Person</PartyType>
        <PartyDetails>
          <Person>
            <Id>12345</Id>
            <Title>Mr</Title>
            <Name>
              <FirstName>Jack</FirstName>
              <MiddleName></MiddleName>
              <LastName>Johnson</LastName>
              <MaidenName></MaidenName>
            </Name>
            <Suffix></Suffix>
            <Birthdate>12/12/1960</Birthdate>
            <Gender>Male</Gender>
            <HomeTelephone>972-000-0000</HomeTelephone>
          </Person>
        </PartyDetails>
```

```
        </Party>
        <CustomerId>11111</CustomerId>
        <CustomerStatus></CustomerStatus>
        <CustomerPriority>0</CustomerPriority>
      </BuyerInfo>
      <TaxAmount>0.0</TaxAmount>
      <TotalAmount>504.0</TotalAmount>
      <CreditCheckNeeded>false</CreditCheckNeeded>
  </CustomerOrder>
```

Wiring to Business Services and Access Services

Finally, create an SCA export for the mediation flow component. Wire the export (as an import) to the **CustomerCreditInformation** Business Service component in **BizServices-CustomerCreditMgmt**. Finish the implementation of the Business Service component, and it will look as shown in the following figure:

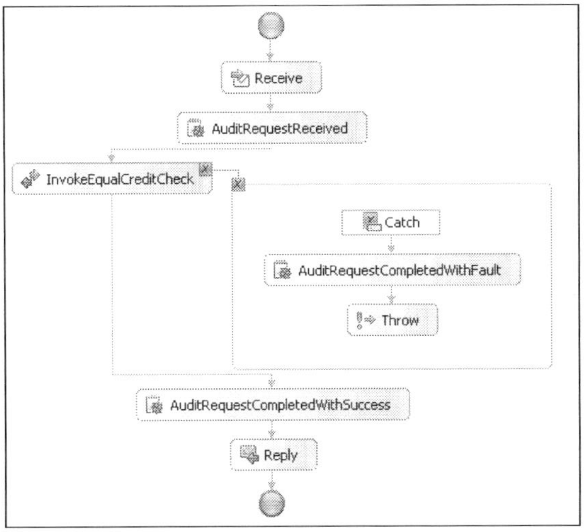

Building BizServices-SupplierPartnerMgmt module

In Chapter 8 we learned that the purpose of BizServices-SupplierPartnerMgmt is to process supplier partner orders. This module invokes **AccessServices-Moonlight** module, which in turn uses the **ProcessPurchaseOrders** interface from the Moonlight Library to communicate with **Moonlight systems.** The steps to implement a Business Service were discussed in the previous sections. We will not repeat those steps and assume that you will follow them.

Building AccessServices-Moonlight module

We also learned from Chapter 8 that the Moonlight Access Service provides the ability to submit orders to the Moonlight partner database. We shall follow the six steps laid out at the start of this chapter to build the **AccessService-Moonlight.**

Create the Access Service module

Create a mediation module named AccessServices-Moonlight with a mediation component called Med-ProcessPurchaseOrders-processOrder. Add project dependencies to the Moonlight application library and SupplierPartnerDomain library. Save all your changes.

Implement JDBC adapter

The Moonlight access server will use a Java database connectivity (JDBC) mechanism to submit an order. WebSphere Integration Developer provides the connectivity with databases through WebSphere Adapters that support JDBC-based connectors. In this section, as we build the Access Service mediation to integrate with Moonlight, we will show how to use (and implement) a JDBC adapter to connect to the Moonlight partner's DB2 v9.5 database called MOONLGT. The authentication alias or data source called jdbc/moonlgt to connect to this database has already been set up in WPS, as shown in the following screenshot. This data source is needed in the creation of the adapter to set the authentication details to connect to the database.

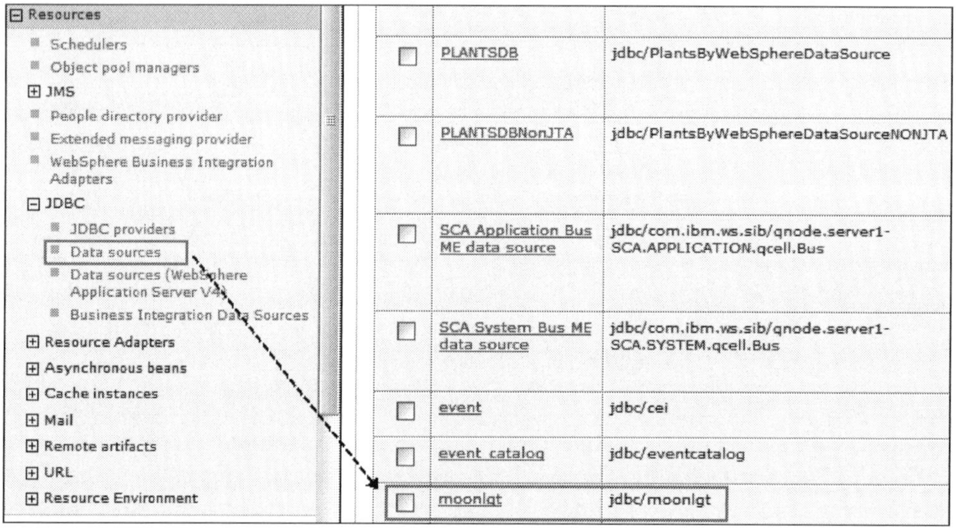

Following are the steps to implement the JDBC adapter:

i. The assembly diagram for the module will open (if not, open it) after completing the create wizards. In the **Palette**, under **Outbound Adapters**, select **JDBC Adapter** and drag it on the canvas, as shown in the following screenshot:

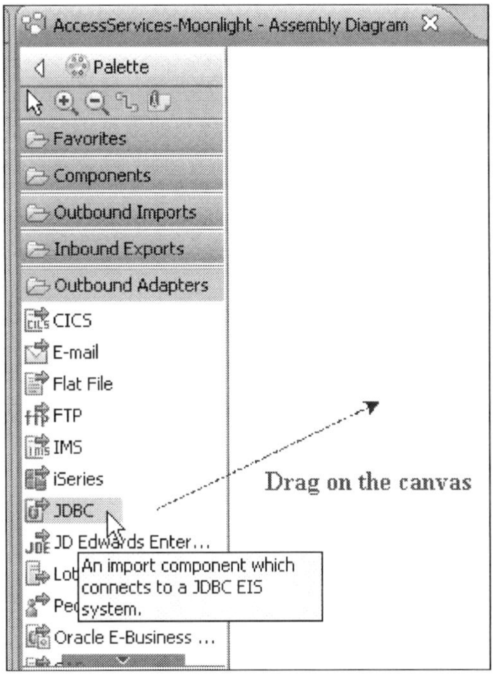

ii. The **New External Service** wizard should open. Leave the default IBM WebSphere Adapter selected and click **Next.**

iii. The default Connector file is selected, which is shipped along with WebSphere Integration Developer. Change the Connector project name to **MoonlightJDBCAdapter**. For a Target server, ensure that the WebSphere Process Server V7.0 is selected and click **Next.**

iv. Specify the location of the JDBC driver JAR files for DB2 server, as shown in the following screenshot. Click **Next**.

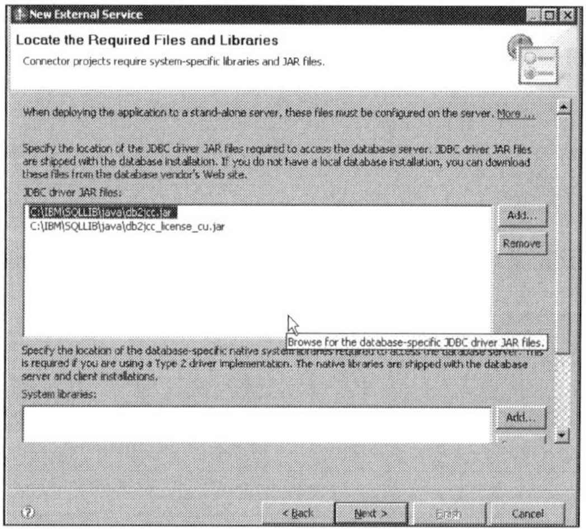

[If you are using Type-2 driver implementation, then you will also have to identify the location of the System Libraries.]

v. In the next window, specify the discovery properties required by the adapter to connect to the database, as shown in the following screenshot. Change the database name to MOONLGT, and add the username and password. Click **Next.**

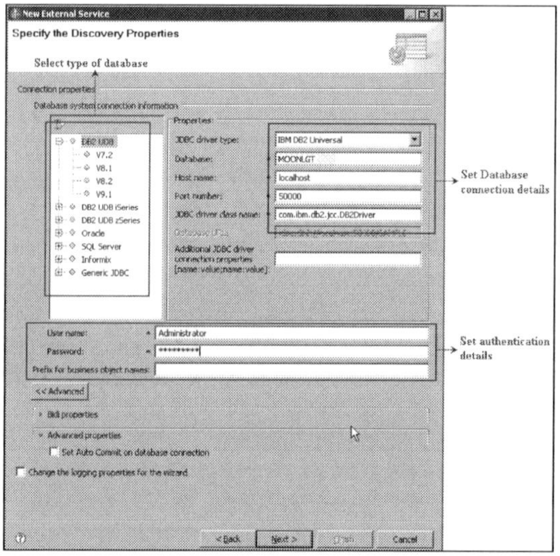

vi. In the next window, you will identify the objects that are needed from the database for the application. You are given the flexibility to change the query to the database as needed. For our purposes, we will leave the default query and click Run Query. From the list of discovered objects, select **ADMINISTRATOR | Tables | SUPPLIERORDER**. In the **Select the primary key ...** window, click **Add** and select **sp_orderin** as the primary key. Click **Next**.

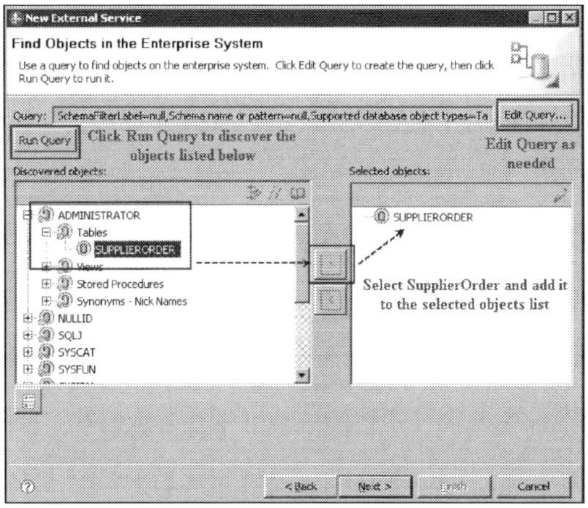

vii. In the next window, define the different operations exposed by the adapter interface to be performed on the database. If you prefer, you may define wrapper objects that are targeted towards specific database objects and functions. Leave the defaults and click **Next**, as shown in the following screenshot:

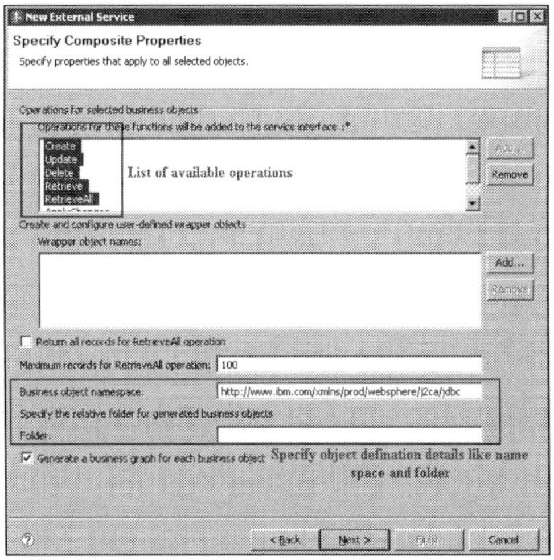

viii. In the next window, define the deployment properties for this adapter. Select **Other** and then specify the JNDI data source previously created in WPS called **jdbc/order**, as shown in the following screenshot. When an adapter is deployed, it will use this data source to connect to the database MOONLGT.

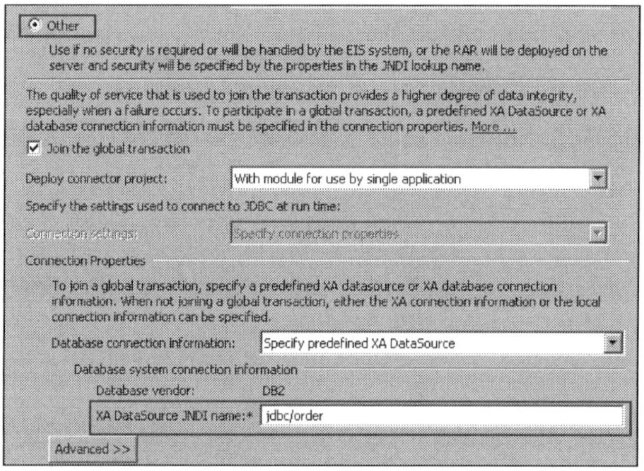

ix. Click on the **Next** button. Change the name on the adapter to **MoonlightJDBCAdapter.**

x. Click **Finish**. This completes the creation of the JDBC adapter to DB2 database called MOONLGT, as shown in the following screenshot:

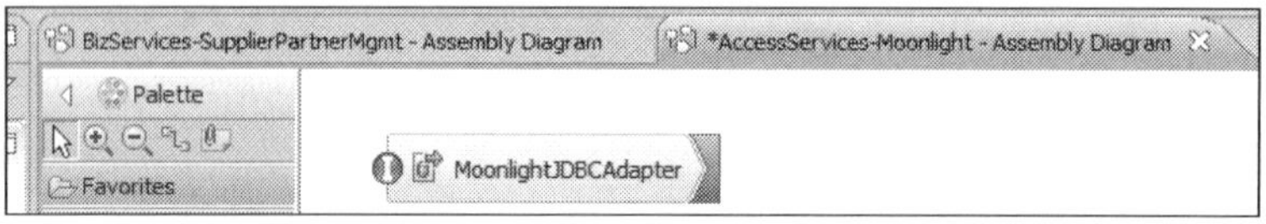

After implementing the adapter, follow the previous example to complete the remaining four steps to implement this Access Service and wire it to the Business Service layer.

Building BizServices-InventoryMgmt module

The Inventory System provides real-time management and maintenance of the inventory information for items in JungleSea Inc.'s product catalog. Currently, there are two systems named "Alpha" and "Beta" that provide this capability in JungleSea and expose the capability in the web service interfaces.

In this example, we will only implement the Information Retrieval operation for residential or non-commercial customers.

> The steps to implement a Business Services were discussed in the previous sections. You may follow those steps to create a business service module BizServices-InventoryMgmt with the process components **MaintainInventoryInformation** and **RetrieveInventoryInformation.**

Building AccessServices-Alpha module

We learned from Chapter 7 that Alpha supports JungleSea Inc.'s residential or non-commercial customers, while Beta supports commercial or enterprise customers. Later on, in Chapter 8 we identified that Alpha and Beta systems expose the backend functionality through a web service interface.

In this example, we shall follow the six steps laid out in the start of this chapter to build the AccessService-Alpha that communicates with a backend Alpha system interface called "AlphaFBAInventoryPortType" in the AlphaLibrary module.

Creating the Access Service module

Perform the following steps in order to create the Access Service module:

i. Create a new module named "AccessServices-Alpha" with library dependencies to the "AlphaLibrary, CommonDomain-v1_0" and "ProductDomain-v1_0" application library.

ii. Save all your changes.

> For this Access Service we do not need to implement an adapter, because the backend systems expose their functionality via web services, which are directly consumable.

Access Service module assembly and wiring

Perform the following steps for assembly and wiring:

i. Create a new mediation flow component called **Med-AlphaFBAInventoryPortType-GetInventorySupply** in the AccessService-Alpha module with source "RetrieveInventoryInformation" interface and target "AlphaFBAInventoryPortType" interface.

ii. Drag the **Med-AlphaFBAInventoryPortType-GetInventorySupply** component onto the **AccessServices-Alpha-Assembly Diagram.**

iii. Right-click on the **Med-AlphaFBAInventoryPortType-GetInventorySupply** component and generate an export with SCA binding.

iv. For the purposes of our example, we have created an **AccessService-AlphaFacade** Java component representing the backend Alpha system exposed by an HTTP export within the AccessService-Alpha module. We replaced the generated CheckItemAvailability method with:

```
public DataObject CheckItemAvailability(DataObject
checkItemAvailability) {
        DataObject itemAvailability = checkItemAvailability;
itemAvailability.setString("ItemAvailabilityType.
AlphaInventoryStatusType.AvailabilityStatus", "Available");
itemAvailability.setDouble("ItemAvailabilityType.
AlphaInventoryStatusType.AvailableQuantity", 10);
        return itemAvailability;
}
```

The following screenshot shows the façade:

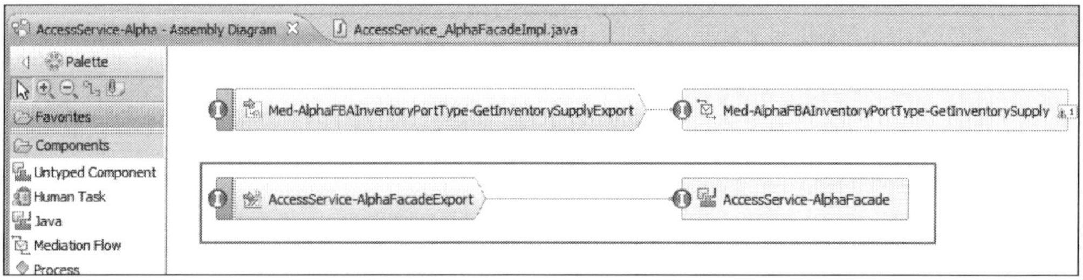

v. Drag an **Import** component from the **Palette** onto the assembly canvas and name it **AccessService-AlphaFacadeImport**. Wire the target of **Med-AlphaFBAInventoryPortType-GetInventorySupply** component to this import.

vi. Save all your changes.

Implement the Mediation module

When you implement the "Med-AlphaFBAInventoryPortType-GetInventorySupply" mediation flow, you need to create two XSLT maps to transform objects from the source "RetrieveInventoryInformation" interface to the target "AlphaFBAInventoryPortType" interface.

Testing the Business Service end-to-end

Use the previous examples to complete the implementation of AccessService-Alpha and test the Business Services. Refer to the PI provided, which contains the completed implementation and corresponding test cases.

Building BizServices-CustomerBillingMgmt module

Customer Billing Management Business Services allows JungleSea to process customer payments including credit card payments. The components in this module invoke the AccessServices-PayMe module, which in turn uses the CreditCardService interface from the PayMeLibrary to communicate with PayMe application. The PayMe application exposes its capabilities via Web Services.

> The steps to implement a Business Service were discussed in the previous sections. We will not repeat those steps and assume that you will follow them, as explained earlier.
>
> The PayMe application exposes its capabilities as Web Services. We will follow the steps that we have followed so far to implement the module and the associated mediation flows.

Building BizServices-CustomerInfoMgmt module

Customer Information Management Business Service allows JungleSea to create, maintain, lookup/search, and view customer information. The application named "Green" exposes its capabilities through Enterprise Java Beans (EJB). We will have to implement the RetrieveCustomerInformation Business Service as a BPEL component.

We will use the EJB import bindings to enable the mediation flow components to invoke services provided by a Green application running on an external Java enterprise application server. In order for you to use the EJB import, you will need the associated EJB client JAR files as dependencies in your module to be able to invoke the remote interface. Once you do this, you can create an EJB import in the assembly diagram. As shown in the following screenshot, from the palette, you can use the Enterprise Java Beans from the Outbound Imports in the WID assembly diagram and specify the remote (or local) interface to import. Once you do this, the rest of the steps are the same as with the other modules.

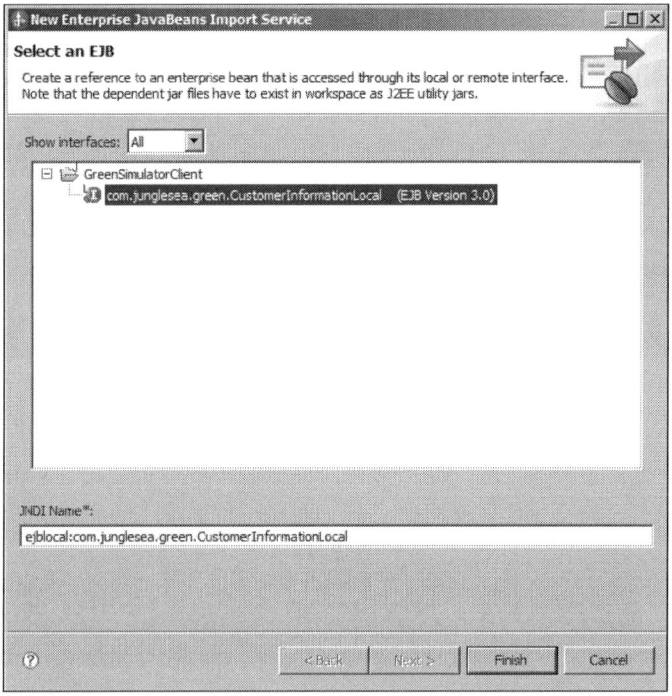

Having implemented all the necessary modules and associated components, the solution diagram view of the solution we have built so far is depicted in the following figure:

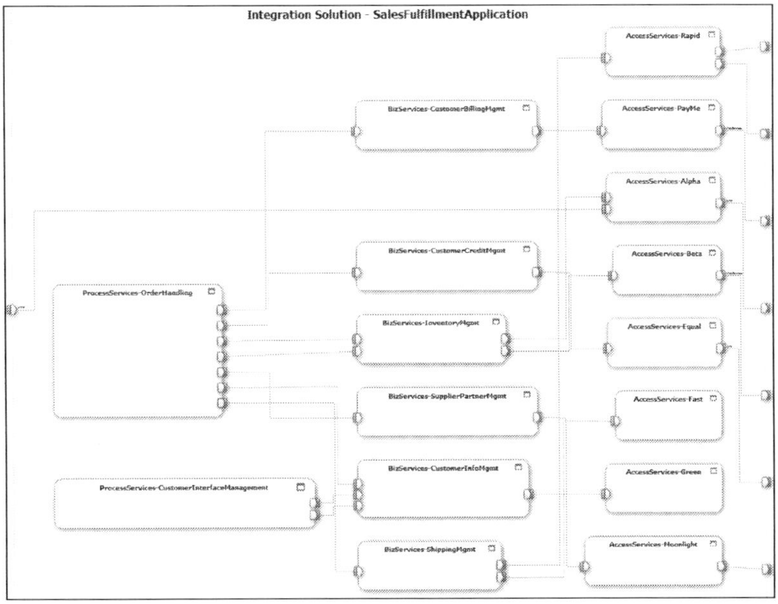

Summary

We did quite a bit in this chapter. We completed the implementation of the first working version of the Sales Fulfillment Application. We had to implement all the Business Service modules (with the associated components) and the corresponding Access Services (with the associated components). We started by explaining the fundamentals behind module testing and the key concepts associated with integration test client. We discussed how to perform unit testing and component testing. We discussed test configurations and the use of emulators in cases where you don't have the imports/references available (end application services that you import in the assembly diagram, for example) or the components implemented. Then we jumped into the implementation of the Business and Access Service modules. We devised a step-by-step method to implement them and unit test them. Along the way for the implementation of each module, we heavily delved and leveraged the capabilities of WPS (Microflow BPEL including exception handling) and WESB (for mediation flows and adapters). We discussed several techniques to adopt when integrating using the JDBC adapter, File adapter, JMS, Web Services, and so on. In the end, we were able to implement all the modules (and associated components) that would be required for the business processes we had built in the previous chapter to work end-to-end. We strongly recommend that you import the PI into your WID workspace and use it as a reference when reading this chapter. Also, some of the intricacies, which could not be explained in this chapter, will be very forthcoming and revealing in the PI itself.

11
Business Space

JungleSea Inc. has now successfully built an SOA-based application that helps give their company a strategic advantage and the business flexibility that they were looking for. The previous chapters also walked through various tools available with WebSphere Business Process Management Systems to integrate this business process with existing applications and legacy systems. Next, we will focus on the frontend of the business process through Business Space. This chapter will provide a description of Business Space and its advantages, walkthrough some basic concepts, detail some common tasks including creating a Business Space, adding widgets, and sharing business spaces. The following mind map lists the topics covered in this chapter:

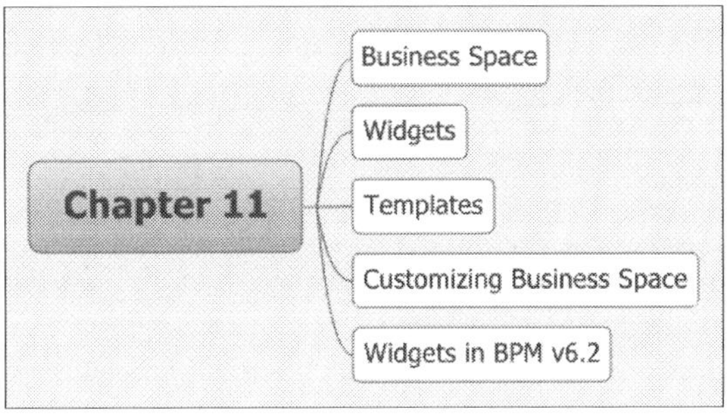

What is Business Space?

Business Space provides an integrated, flexible, and collaborative user interface to monitor and manage BPM solutions that are built using WID and WPS. It is not a separate product, but a face to the different products within the WebSphere Business Process Management portfolio, that enables business users to model business processes, administer common tasks like human task flows, and monitor key performance indicators through a secure browser-based graphical user interface developed on Web 2.0 concepts.

The following diagram provides a comprehensive view of the Business Space within the portfolio:

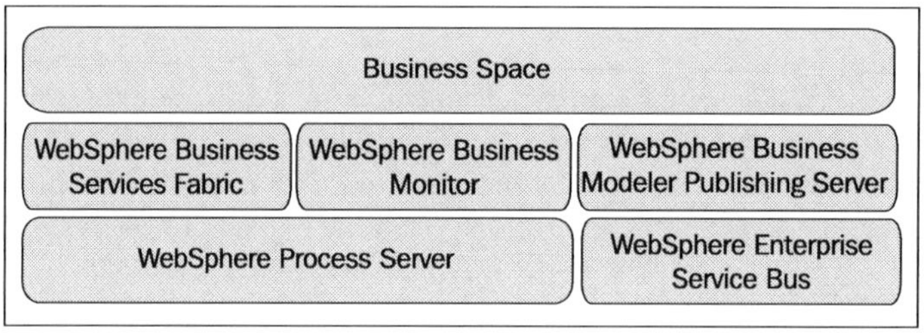

Business Space brings IT closer to business. It helps incorporate business users in the administration, monitoring, and managing of applications. Thus making these activities more solution- and business-centric, and less deployment-centric. It provides a collaboration platform for the creation of agile and rich business process that originate from the business users. This platform allows business and IT to work together to work on processes that solve a business problem.

A business user in Business Space is able to create a mashup called Business Spaces from a combination of different web applications called widgets on a page. This enables the user to have access to all the information the user is most interested in on one unified screen. These widgets can be sourced from different BPM products. For example, on the same page a user can have a Human Task Management widget from WebSphere Process Server and a Monitor widget from WebSphere Business Monitor. Furthermore, a business user can have many of such related pages that serve a business purpose. This collection is called a Business Space. Users are given the ability to create and share pages and spaces with other users—to enable a collaborative environment.

Access to Business Space can be secure and role-based, giving the capability to control access to the spaces, pages, and widgets within. There are four levels of access that can be assigned to users to control what they can do with a page or a space. In this way, different users can be given different levels of access, based on the business role they are fulfilling. These four access levels are described in the following table:

Viewer	View only privileges to the pages and business spaces associated with the user.
Editor	Privileges include: • Add and modify pages in a space. If an editor creates a page, then he/she is the owner of that page only. • Add, configure, and delete widgets in a page. • All viewers access privileges.

Owner	Privileges include: • Delete, transfer ownership, and determine access to the space and individual pages. • Determine level of access, that is, viewer or editor access. • Initial owner of a space or page is the person who created it. • A space owner automatically has owner access to every page in that space. • Has all editor-level privileges.
Super user	Privileges include: • Administrative rights and owner access to all spaces and pages. • Share access to a space or a page with selected users or all users. • Modify pages and templates. • Has all owner level privileges.

Business Spaces

As explained earlier, a Business Space is a collection of related web content, or pages that provide the business users with visibility into their business process and the capability to manage these processes as needed.

Let's open a Business Space page and walkthrough the various sections of the page, as shown in the following screenshot:

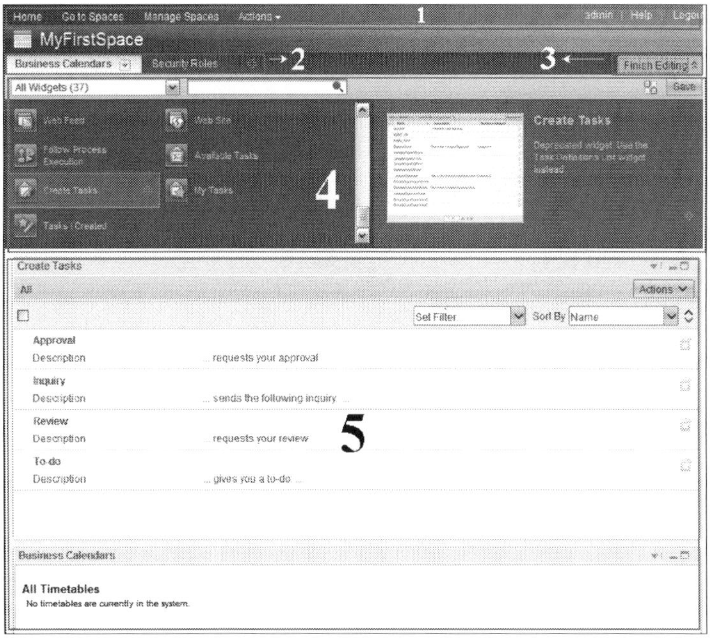

The first section is the menu bar, which gives the user the ability to manage and switch between business spaces. The user can also use this section to access functions like **Help** and **Logout**. The second section lists all the pages that are associated with the current Business Space. The third section toggles the current pages edit mode. In the edit mode, the user can add or remove widgets that have been assigned to them. This is represented by the fourth section in the screenshot. The last section (or the fifth section) is the work area which lists all the widgets associated to the current Business Space page. Next, let's take a closer look at creating a Business Space.

Launching Business Space

There are two ways to access Business Space:

1. Directly through the URL: `http://<Host Name>:< Port Number>/BusinessSpace`, for example, `https://localhost:9448/BusinessSpace`
2. In WebSphere Integration Developer, you can right-click on the server listed in the **Server** tab for the unit test environment (UTE), as shown in the following screenshot:

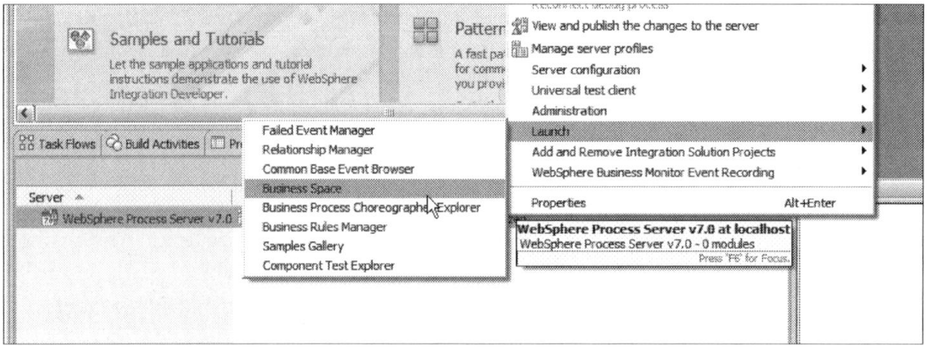

Creating a Business Space

Creating a Business Space is very simple. Execute the following steps:

1. Log in to **Business Space** with a super user role, as shown in the following screenshot:

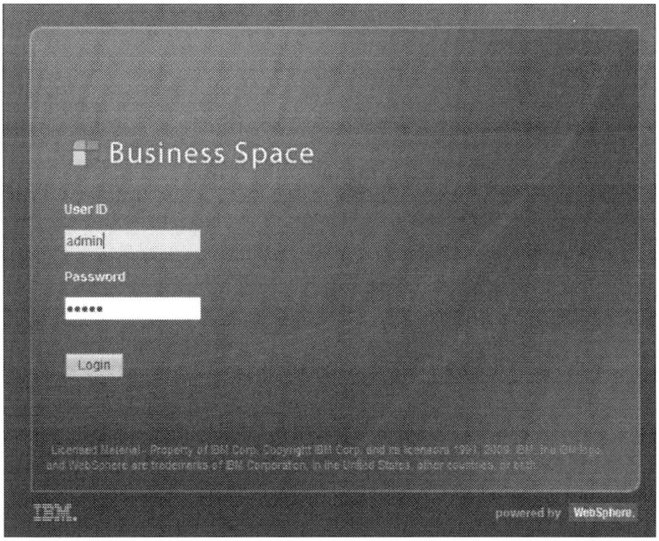

[For more information to assign super user access, go to `http://publib.boulder.ibm.com/infocenter/dmndhelp/v6r2mx/topic/com.ibm.websphere.wbpm.bspace.config.620.doc/doc/tcfg_bsp_superuser.html`]

2. By default, the WPS (WebSphere Process Server) administrator role has this access level to access the **Getting Started** page. Click on **Start**, as shown in the following screenshot:

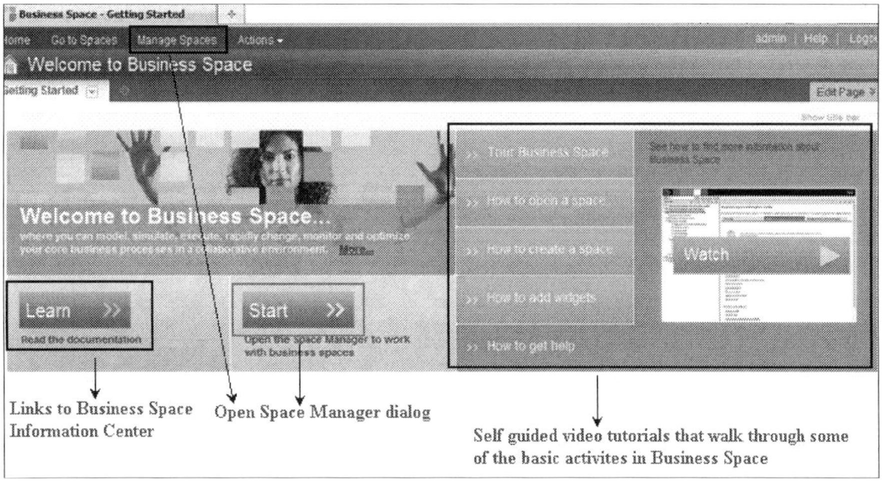

3. This will open the Space Manager dialog. Click on Create a Space icon. This opens the **Create Space** page, as shown in the following screenshot:

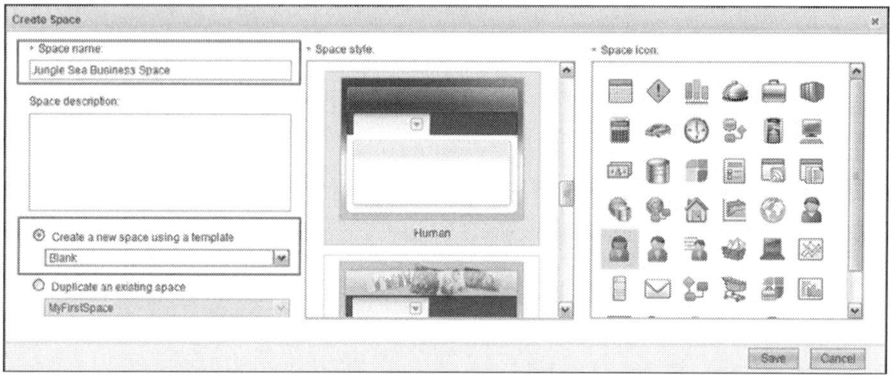

There are three choices available to you to create a new Business Space:

- Create an empty space with no predefined pages or widgets using the **Blank** option, as shown in the previous screenshot
- Create a space from a Business Space template
- Duplicate an existing Business Space

4. Give the Business Space the name **Jungle Sea Business Space**. Optionally you may select a **Space style** or a **Space icon** and click on **Save**, as shown in the previous screenshot.
5. On clicking **Save**, you will see the new Business Space called **Jungle Sea Business Space** listed in available business spaces. Click on **Jungle Sea Business Space** to open the Business Space.

Congratulations! You have created your first space.

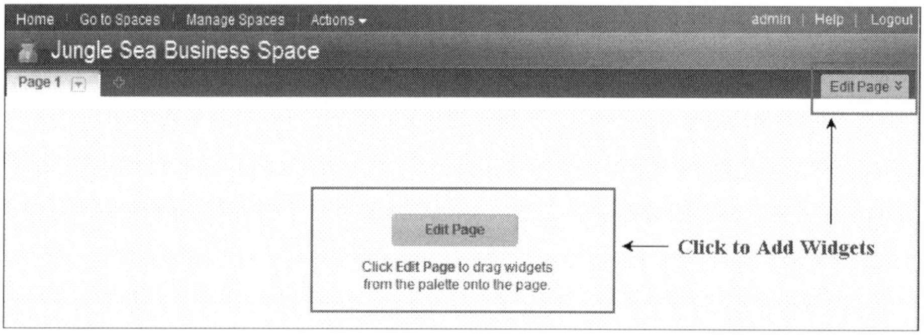

Creating a Business Space template

Business Space templates are shortcuts to create preconfigured Business Spaces that contain preconfigured pages, which in turn contain preconfigured widgets. In version 7.0, you can either have Business Space templates exposed by a product or custom cross-product templates exposed by the Business Space owner/super user. The Space Manager window will list only the product templates for the products that are installed in your environment. Cross-product templates have widgets from more than one product. The Space Manager window lists all of the cross-product templates.

Here are the steps to create a template of the **Jungle Sea Business Space**:

1. In the menu bar, select **Manage Spaces**. This will open the **Space Manager** dialog, as shown in the following screenshot:

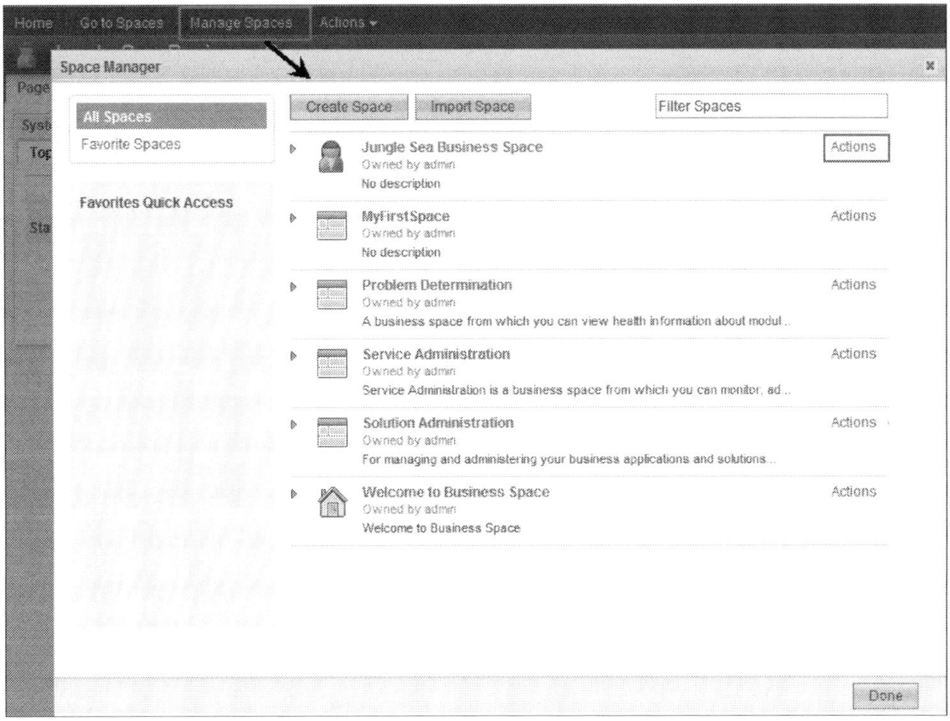

2. Click on the **Actions** link next to **Jungle Sea Business Space** to get a list of options, as shown in the following screenshot:

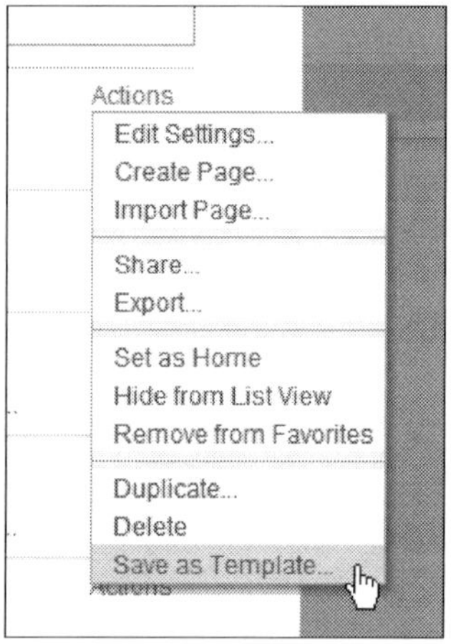

3. In this menu, select **Save as Template....** Another option here is **Share....** which will export a ZIP file of this Business Space, which may then be imported to other Business Space instances.
4. After creating the template, you create a new Business Space based on **Jungle Sea Business Space**, as shown in the following screenshot:

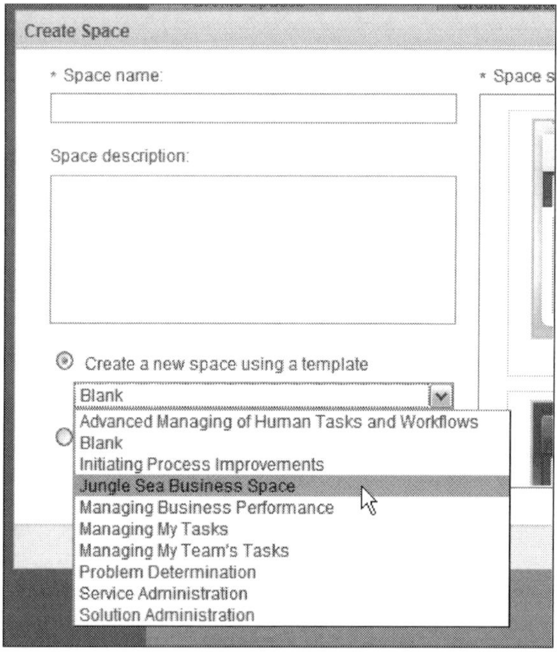

Sharing a Business Space

One of the other options listed in the **Actions** menu, along with **Save as Template...**, is **Share....** This option gives the ability to share a Business Space with other users. As the Business Space owner or super user, you have the option to give views or edit privileges to each user, as shown in the following screenshot:

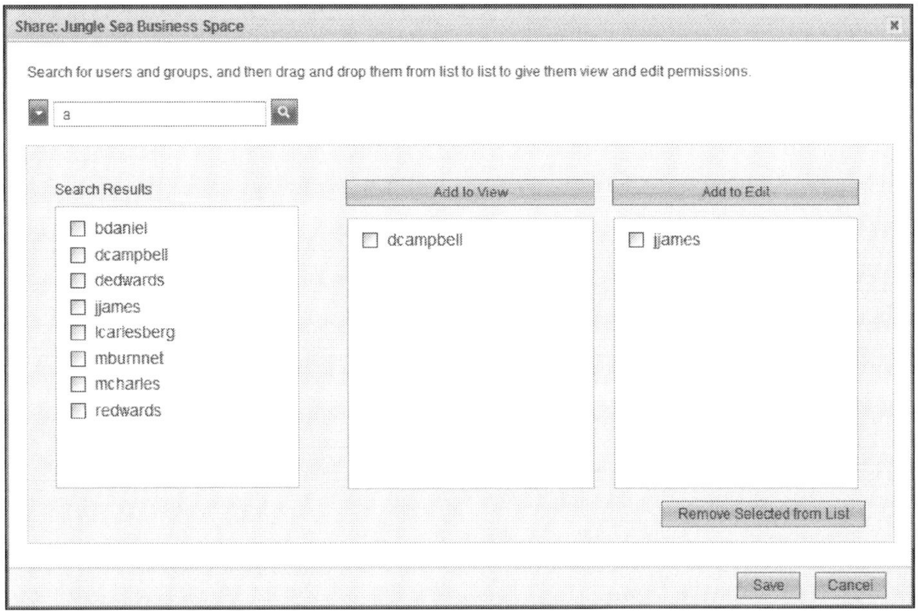

Next, we will add widgets to this space.

Widgets

Widgets are the pluggable user interface components that expose certain capabilities to help business users to model, administer, manage, and monitor business processes and activities with the BPM products. A business user can place many of such widgets to create a mashup of application functionalities from different sources on a single page. Some widgets can also be wired to interact with other widgets to perform more complex tasks beyond the scope of individual widgets.

WebSphere Business Process Management portfolio tools also expose functionalities to business users through widgets. The following table lists widgets of the WebSphere Business Monitor and WebSphere Publishing Server:

WebSphere Business Monitor	WebSphere Publishing Server
Getting Started for Monitor	Getting Started Publishing Server
KPIs	Publishing Server Access
Instances	Inspect Released
Diagrams	Draft Manager
Alerts	Released Manager
Reports	Publishing Server Status
Dimensions	
Human Tasks	
KPI Manager	
Alerts Submission	

Adding widgets to Business Space

To add a widget on a page, click on the **Edit Page** on the **Jungle Sea Business Space**. Select the desired widgets, as shown in the following screenshot:

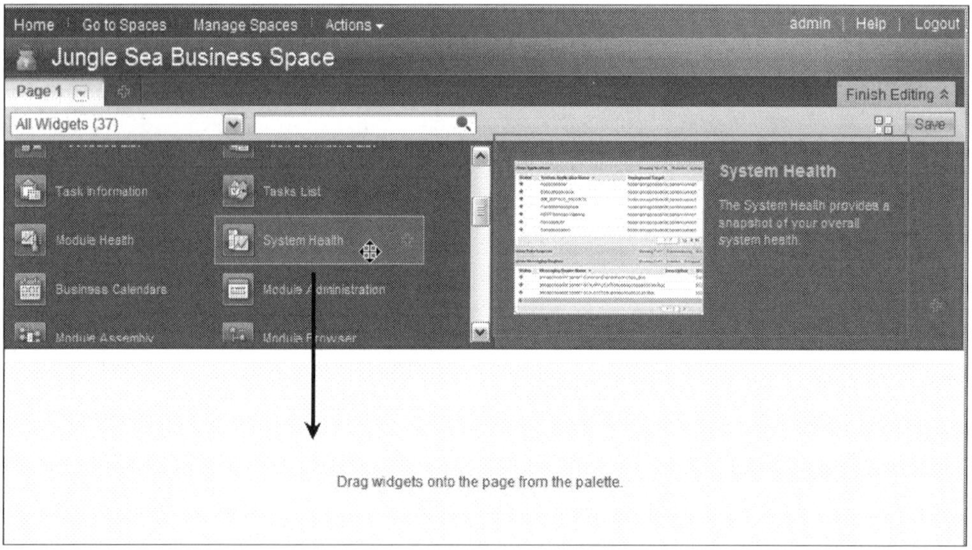

In this example, we will add the **System Health** widget. The right side shows a description of the widget selected. For example, it states: **The System Health provides a snapshot of your overall system health**. Drag the widget onto the canvas, click **Save**, and then **Finish Editing** in the top-right corner.

Congratulations! You have added your first widget. It appears as shown in the following screenshot:

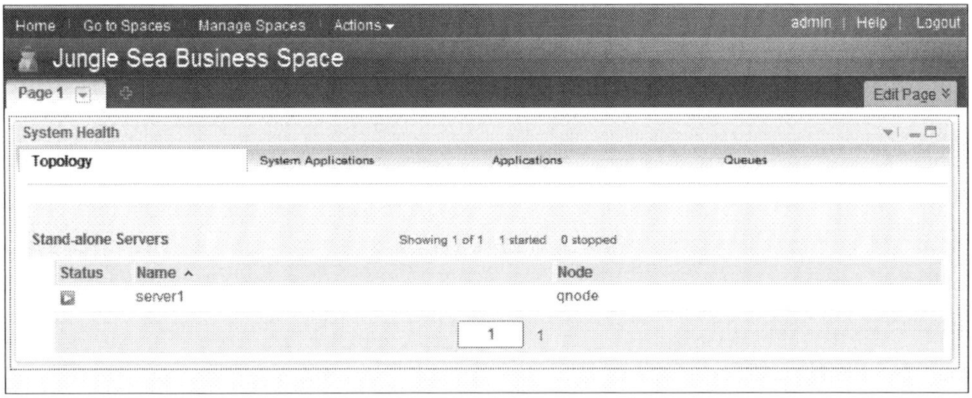

Summary

Business Space serves a very critical function for the WebSphere Business Process Manager portfolio. It provides the much-needed integrated user interface to the products and tools, enabling users to seamlessly administer and manage their solutions. This chapter helped provide an overview of the Business Space and touched upon some of the basic concepts and functionalities to help you get started.

12
Deployment Topologies

JungleSea Inc. has now successfully built the Sales Fulfillment Application using WID, WPS, and WESB. We walked you through the various stages and steps in building the application, and along the path, we explored and used the various capabilities from WID. In this chapter, we will cover some of the fundamental terminologies and concepts behind deployment topologies for WPS/WESB and the types of topologies available—common and advanced, considerations for scalability, failover, and load balancing using clustering. This chapter will cover:

- Deployment topology considerations and the guiding principles for selecting a right topology.
- The clustering and WebSphere Network Deployment fundamentals.
- Guidance on the various WPS and WESB topologies available for you to select for a production environment.
- How the various WPS and WESB components use the infrastructure.
- The "Gold Topology" briefly according to which the Sales Fulfillment Application's deployment topology will be based upon.

The following mind map lists the topics covered in this chapter:

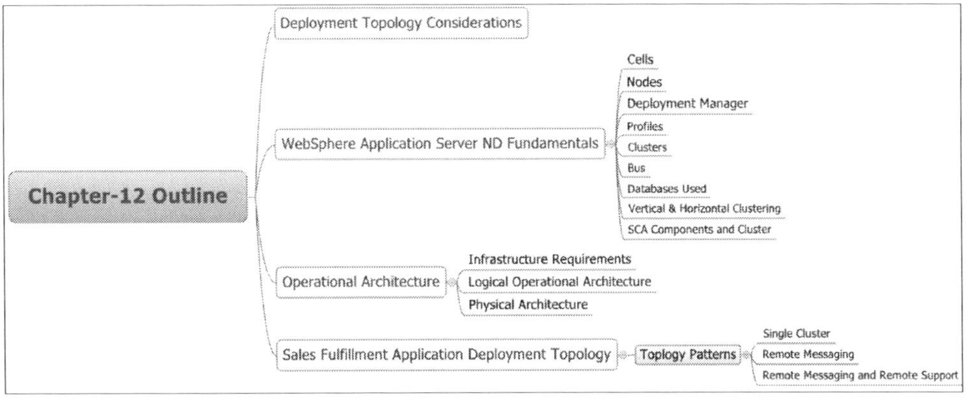

Note that in this chapter, we will not be going into the details of the installation of the clustered topology. It's a separate exercise, and is out of the scope of this book. What we want to convey in this chapter is the fundamental concepts that you need to understand from a WPS/WESB infrastructure point of view.

Deployment topology considerations

So far, you have used WID and the ingratiated WPS/WESB unit test environment to deploy and test the Sales Fulfillment Application. In the unit test environment, all the necessary artifacts were created for you automatically using the embedded Derby database. To deploy the Sales Fulfillment Application into production, you will need a robust deployment environment topology that makes use of a database like IBM DB2. A deployment environment is a collection of configured clusters, servers, and middleware that collaborate to provide an environment to host software modules. The characteristics of a successful deployment topology include:

- **Scalability**: Indicates the ability of a system, subsystem, application, or a deployment environment itself to either handle growing amounts of work in a graceful manner, or to be readily enlarged. You can scale it vertically (or scale up) by adding resources to a single node in a system, typically involving the addition of CPUs or memory to a single computer/system. You can also scale horizontally (or scale out) by adding more nodes to a system, such as adding a new computer/system.
- **Availability**: Indicates the degree to which a system, subsystem, application, or a deployment environment itself is operable and the proportion of time it is in a functioning condition.
- **Recoverability**: The degree to which (measured in time, cost, and people involved) a system, subsystem, application, or deployment environment itself can recover from any failure.
- **Performance**: Characterized by the amount of work accomplished by a system, subsystem, application, or deployment environment itself, compared to the time and resources used. Characteristics based on which performance can be measured or expressed include throughput, utilization, response time, and so on.
- **Maintainability** (applications and the infrastructure itself)**:** Ease with which a system, subsystem, or application can be modified, in order to address enhancements, fix defects, make future maintenance easier, and ease of administration itself.

- **Optimal usage of software license**: Should use an optimal set of software licenses and hence minimize the cost as well as the total cost of ownership.

  Picking the right deployment topology is not only driven by the factors just mentioned, but also (as in our case), SCA modules and components that make up the Sales Fulfillment Application itself. The topology, and hence the system, should tolerate failure and allow for maintenance without the loss of data or loss of service. You also want to make sure that there is room to add processing capacity to grow your systems, in order to meet increased user demand. WebSphere Network Deployment (WAS ND) provides these capabilities and much more.

WebSphere Application Server Network Deployment fundamentals

WebSphere Application Server Network Deployment (WAS ND) is the base foundation platform for the IBM BPM portfolio of products including WPS and WESB. Network deployment provides the scalability, availability, performance, and maintainability that is generally required of a production environment. In network deployment, a group of servers can be used collaboratively to provide workload balancing and failover. The servers are managed centrally, using a single administrative console. Following are some of the key concepts to understand the WPS (and WESB) topologies.

Cells

Cell is a logical grouping of nodes that is centrally managed and has access to shared resources. Nodes within a cell typically run one or more applications that are similar in terms of business requirements or non-functional requirements.

Nodes

Node is a managed container for one or more application servers, for the purpose of configuration and operational management. A node's boundaries are limited to within a machine or a logical partition, commonly called an LPAR (in the case of AIX or z/OS environments) and cannot span beyond those boundaries. Typically, a single node corresponds to a single machine with a distinct IP address. You can have multiple nodes on a single machine. A node consists of a **node agent**, by which the node is controlled, and the application servers hosted on that node.

Deployment manager

Deployment manager manages one or many nodes in a distributed configuration. The deployment manager runs a single application, a web-based configuration frontend, known as the **Integrated Solutions Console** or **Administrative Console** (which we will discuss in detail in *Chapter 13, Management, Monitoring and Security*), through which you can perform nearly all management tasks.

Profiles

Profile defines a unique runtime environment (server), with separate command files, configuration files, and logfiles. Profiles define three different types of environments:

1. **Standalone server**: This server profile does not belong to a cell and runs its own administrative console.
2. **Deployment manager**: This server profile is the central location for managing and administering clusters and servers in a cell.
3. **Managed node**: This server profile has a node agent that manages all the servers on the node. It is usually associated with a deployment manager.

Using profiles, you can have more than one runtime environment on a system without having to install multiple copies of WPS. When you install WPS on a server, the first profile can be automatically created. You later use the **Profile Management Tool (PMT)** or the `manageprofiles` command to create further profiles on the same system, without installing a second copy of the binary files.

Clusters

Cluster is a logical collection of application servers, configured to perform the same task. Clusters are sets of identical servers that are managed together and that participate in workload management. The servers, which are members of a cluster, can be on different host machines. Clusters provide scalability and failover capabilities. A cell can have zero or more clusters, and these clusters can span machines and also different operating systems. The member application servers can be distributed across one or more nodes in any configuration.

Bus

A **Bus** destination is a virtual location within a **Service Integration Bus (SI Bus)**, to which applications attach as producers, consumers, or both, to exchange messages. It is a managed communication mechanism that supports service integration through synchronous and asynchronous messaging. A Bus consists of interconnecting **messaging engines**, which is a component running inside a server that manages messaging resources for members of the Bus. Applications are connected to a messaging engine when they connect to a Bus. WPS makes use of the following SI Buses:

- **SCA System Bus (SCA.SYSTEM Bus)**: Used to host queue destinations for SCA modules. The SCA runtime uses these queue destinations to support asynchronous interactions between components and modules.
- **SCA Application Bus (SCA.APP Bus)**: Supports the asynchronous communication between WebSphere adapters and other SCA components.
- **Common Event Infrastructure Bus (CEI Bus)**: Used to transmit common base events (CBEs) asynchronously to a CEI server.
- **Business Process Choreographer Bus (BPC Bus)**: Used for transmitting messages internally in the Business Flow Manager.

The following figure depicts the key concepts to understand the WPS/WESB topologies, as just explained:

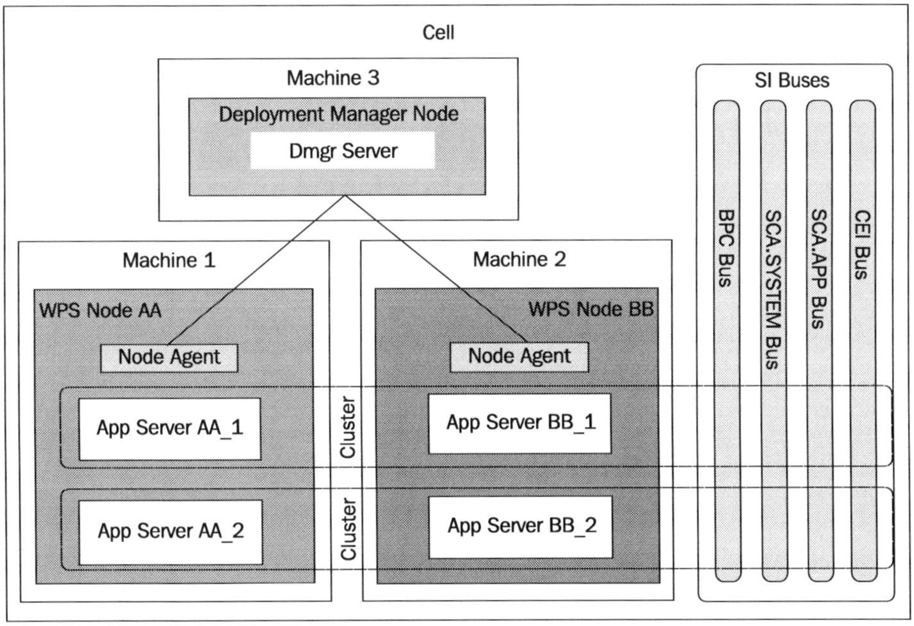

The nodes are separate physical systems (they can also be on the same physical system as virtual machines). The deployment manager node is on a separate machine as well. To host more than one node, the host machine must have ample memory, disk space, and processor capacity. If any one of the servers experiences a problem, and depending on how the system is configured, it will be possible for one of the remaining two to recover the work in progress. To add capacity, more servers can be added directly to the cluster or another machine can be brought online and the new node can be federated into the cell, and more servers can be added to the cluster.

Databases

As mentioned several times, WPS uses multiple databases to hold, store, and track information. It makes use of the following databases:

- **Common database** (**WPRCSDB**): Used as a repository for various components in WPS. It must be created prior to starting WPS and contains information regarding the components.
- **Business Process Choreographer database** (**BPEDB**): Used by the Business Flow Manager and the Human Task Manager. It must be created prior to starting BPC components.
- **Business Process Observer database** (**OBSVRDB**): Used by the BPC Observer application to store event information from the CEI Bus in an event collector table.
- **Messaging engine database** (**MEDB**): Used by the SCA system and application buses, the CEI Bus, and the Business Process Choreographer Bus.
- **Event database** (**EVENT**): This database contains information regarding the Event Service such as Common Based Events.

The following table lists the databases required by individual components in WPS and WESB:

WPS/WESB component	Database
Business Process Choreographer	BPEDB
Business Process Choreographer Explorer reporting function	OBSRVDB
Business Space	WPRCSDB *(common database)*
Common Event Infrastructure	EVENT
Relationships	WPRCSDB *(common database)*
Mediation	WPRCSDB *(common database)*
Recovery	WPRCSDB *(common database)*
Application Scheduler	WPRCSDB *(common database)*
Selectors/Business rules	WPRCSDB *(common database)/ Repository DB*
SIBus	User created when you don't want to use a file store (default) in a network deployment environment
Enterprise Service Bus	EsbLogMedDB, which is the ESB Log Mediation database

Technically, all the database objects required by WPS could be configured in the same database (DB2) or SID (Oracle) so that the different DBs can be tuned and maintained separately. However, it is suggested that you use different DB2 databases and different SIDs. For example, one DB for the common DB, one for all the messaging engine schemas, and one for the BPEDB. This is, however, a DBA strategy and decision.

Vertical clustering

As shown in the following image, multiple application servers (*App Server AA_1*, *App Server AA_2*) can be placed onto the *same* node (*WPS Node AA*). Vertical clustering is used in cases where you would want to increase throughput and provide resiliency if one member of the cluster fails due to an application fault.

> When adopting vertical clustering, and when the hardware hosting, the system fails, you do not get any form of resiliency.

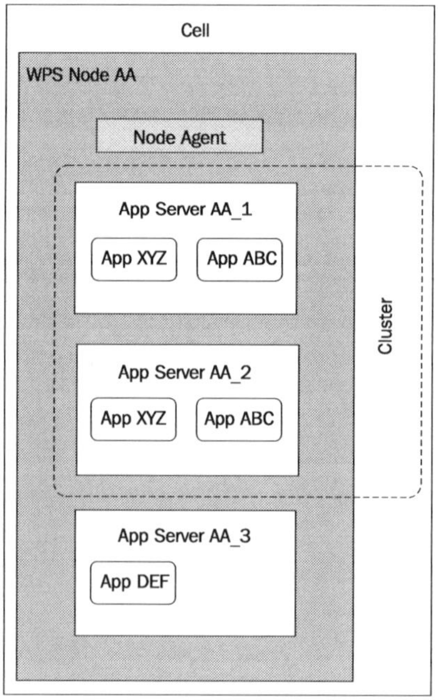

Horizontal clustering

As shown in the following figure, multiple application servers (*App Server AA_1*, *App Server BB_1*, *App Server CC_1*) are distributed *across* nodes (*WPS Node AA*, *WPS Node BB*, *WPS Node CC*) and hence across physical systems. Horizontal clustering is used in cases where you want to increase throughput and provide resiliency if a cluster member fails due to an application fault or if the hardware underpinning of that member's node fails.

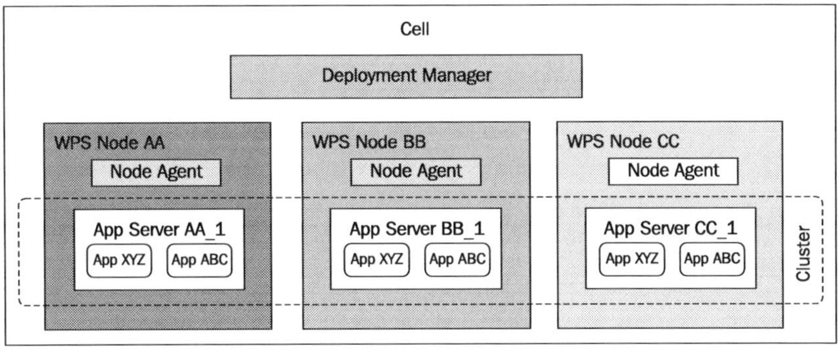

SCA components and cluster

We have used several types of SCA components (BPEL, rules, mediation flows, adapters, and so on) for building the Sales Fulfillment Application. How do each of these components interact with the WPS cluster infrastructure? Let's discuss them briefly:

- BPEL microflow
    - Implements single threaded, synchronous, stateless, transactional service orchestration.
    - BPEDB is used to store the process template, *not* the process instances.
    - In cases when the microflow component is exported as JMS or asynchronous invocation (both of which we don't have in the Sales Fulfillment Application), there is a need for using the messaging infrastructure.
- BPEL long-running process
    - Implements long-running, stateful processes mostly comprised of multiple transactions and of parallel activities.
    - Messaging infrastructure used by default.
    - In addition to the process templates, the state of the process instances is saved in the BPE database. This mechanism also applies to Human Tasks Inline or standalone.
- Mediation flow components
    - Mediations may use messaging resources to store correlation context information.
    - Use the EsbLogMedDB database for the loggers primitive.

- WebSphere adapters
    - Uses the Event DB (on the application).

Operational architecture

Typically, for every solution that is being developed, based on the functional, non-functional, regulatory, and corporate requirements, an appropriate infrastructure model is created. For the Sales Fulfillment Application, an infrastructure work stream is responsible for the design, implementation, and management of facilities, networks, security, general system environments, and the overall IT environment needed to support the application and operations. This work stream is responsible for creating an operational architecture, that is, a representation of how the Sales Fulfillment Application would be made up in terms of a network of computer systems, their associated peripherals, and the systems software, middleware, and application software that they run. The operational model typically consists of the following:

- Logical diagram of the candidate nodes of the architecture and their connectivity
- Description and purpose of each candidate node
- Physical views of the architecture, including a network topology view and a systems management view

> We will not be discussing the current infrastructure topology at JungleSea Inc. It is not relevant to the scope of this book.

Infrastructure requirements

The functional requirements for the solution have been discussed, architected, and implemented in the previous chapters. So we know what the infrastructure should cater to, in terms of accommodating the functional needs of the solution. The non-functional requirements (NFRs) specify the quality criteria or constraints of any system that must be satisfied. These requirements address major operational and functional areas of the system, in order to ensure the robustness of the system. A few core and critical NFRs for the Sales Fulfillment Application are listed below and placed under their relevant categories:

- Performance (including Capacity)
    - Handle at least 2500 orders per day.
    - Handle at least 500 transactions per second.
    - Handle around 500 concurrent users (customer service representatives) actively performing ordering-related activities.
    - Average response time for synchronous invocations (including business processes) should be less than four seconds.
- Scalability
    - The anticipated growth for this application will be in terms of the addition of new channels and hence volume of orders.
    - JungleSea estimates that there will be a 100 to 200 percent growth from inception through the second year of deployment which must be horizontally scalable.
    - In this way, the capacity of the solution should be able to be extended on demand by adding additional node servers as required, without fundamental change to the architecture of the system.
- Availability (including Recoverability and Reliability)
    - The solution must be available no less than 20 hours per day to accommodate customer order requests.
    - The solution availability should be no less than 99.9 percent.
    - Solution should have redundancy capabilities (via clustering).
    - Service shall be restored in conjunction with other similarly prioritized systems in the enterprise. The recovery priority of this set of applications, relative to other business applications, is dependent on the same data center/facility.
    - To accommodate necessary maintenance activities, the solution should accommodate inquiries (customer data, order status, and so on).
- Maintainability (including Flexibility)
    - Support web-based maintenance capabilities to maintain the system and administer it.

- Security
    - Conform to corporate security requirements and practices of JungleSea Inc.
    - Support dual authentication and authorization.
- Manageability
- Environmental
- System Usability

Logical operational architecture

Based on the functional and NFRs, the following figure depicts the logical operational model for the Sales Fulfillment Application. It provides a conceptual overview of the nodes and classifies the software components that run on the node that are grouped into deployment units. Nodes are potential hardware systems, though several nodes may be combined into one physical system. Within each node, as shown in the following figure, the respective software components or deployment units that will run are present.

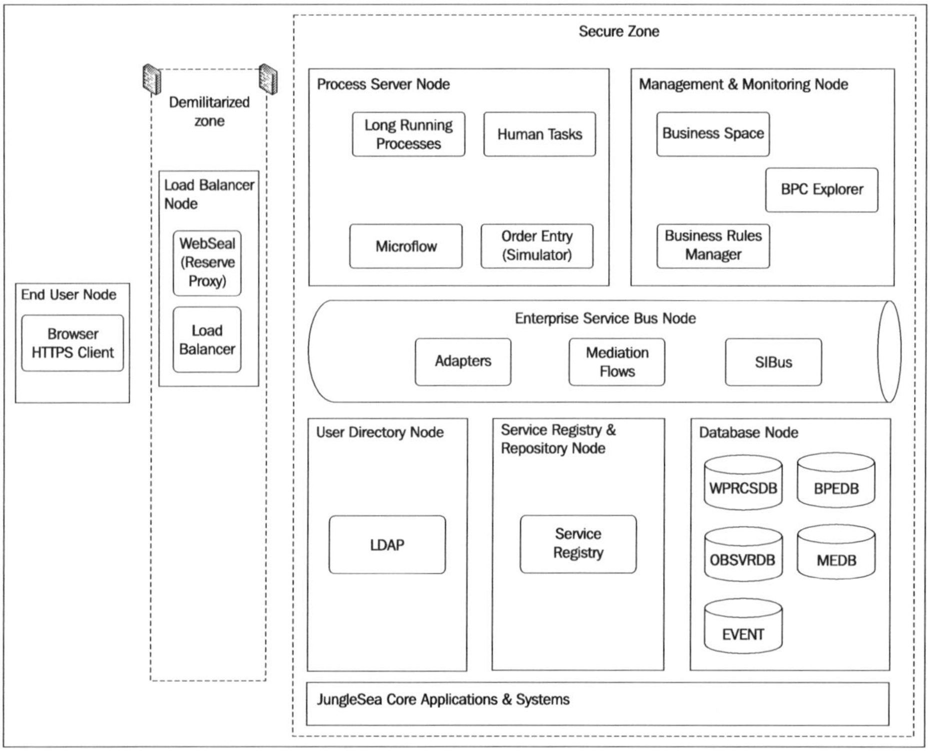

Following is a brief description of each node and what deployment units it contains:

- **End User node**: This node will host the entire End User (CSR) interface to access the order entry (simulator) for the Sales Fulfillment Application.
- **Load Balancer node**: This node will provide the load balancing and act as a security proxy for the web access channel into the Sales Fulfillment Order Entry Application. All web access from the extranet zone should go through this proxy.
- **Process Server node**: It consists of the Process Services and Business Services modules that provide process choreography, orchestration, Business Services, human task management, and business process lifecycle management capabilities.
- **Management and Monitoring node**: This node provides the various units necessary to manage the Sales Fulfillment Application including Business Space, BPC Explorer, and so on. It also provides the monitoring components including dashboards to display business process metrics and also monitoring information about the various components that constitute the Sales Fulfillment Application.
- **Enterprise Service Bus node**: Enables connectivity to various backend applications and also includes the ESB for JungleSea including the Sales Fulfillment Application. It consists of the Access Services mediation modules that contain mediation flow components and adapters to the backend applications.
- **User Directory node**: This node will contain the Lightweight Directory Access Protocol or LDAP server for the whole Sales Fulfillment Application, managing all users' (CSRs, administrators) security-related information. All authentication information will be retrieved from this node, such as username and groups of the user.
- **Service Registry and Repository node**: This node contains the WebSphere Registry and Repository that will help manage and control the lifecycle of the SOA services developed within JungleSea Inc.
- **Database node**: This node consists of all the databases required by the WebSphere Process Server infrastructure. IBM DB2 will be the physical database and will run on top of the Red Hat Enterprise Linux Operating System.

Physical architecture

Having defined the logical operational model (including the nodes and software components within the nodes), we will define the physical architecture for the Sales Fulfillment Application solution. This physical architecture will identify the specific components that will be used in the infrastructure including detailed specifications for each system. This will also include detailed connectivity design and implementation considerations.

The topology and physical distribution of the Sales Fulfillment Application, the definition of the nodes (computer platforms) and network connections, and where and how users and external systems interact with the system being developed. The following figure depicts the different hardware systems that will be used for the Sales Fulfillment Application and what components (or the nodes identified in the logical model above) will be deployed on which server.

As depicted in the following figure, you see that requests are initially directed to an IP sprayer, either the WebSphere Network Dispatcher or some other IP sprayer. The requests are then forwarded to the layer of HTTP web servers (sfsHTTP1 and sfsHTTP2), where the WebSphere plugin evaluates each request and determines whether it should be forwarded on to the WPS layer (*sfsBPM1* and *sfsBPM2*). The information used by the plugin to determine how to route requests to WPS is static this means that the mapping between request URLs and the set of applications deployed on WPS with web services exports that can service those. There is no communication path back from the WPS machines to the Web server plugin.

In the next section, we will see how we will create a clustered deployment topology for the WebSphere Process Server components. As depicted in the following figure, from a WPS/WESB perspective (not counting the DB2 cluster, HTTP server, and the IP sprayer), we will have three physical servers. IBM BladeCenter HS20 is allocated to the solution. Two of the blades, *sfsBPM1* and *sfsBPM2,* (each of which, to start with, will have one logical partition or LPAR, but more partitions or LPARs can be added in the future to support vertical clustering) will be used for hosting the WPS/WESB-related components. The third blade, *sfsBPMManage*, will be used as Deployment Manager. *sfsBPM1* and *sfsBPM2* will be used as a database cluster *jungleDB* (IBM DB2 cluster) server to host the multiple databases. WPS and WESB use multiple to hold, store, and track information.

> We are not addressing the User Directory/LDAP, Service Registry and Repository, Load Balancer, and so on, as part of this book and hence do not discuss their topology. It is assumed they exist and will be leveraged appropriately by WPS components during installation and also at runtime as needed.

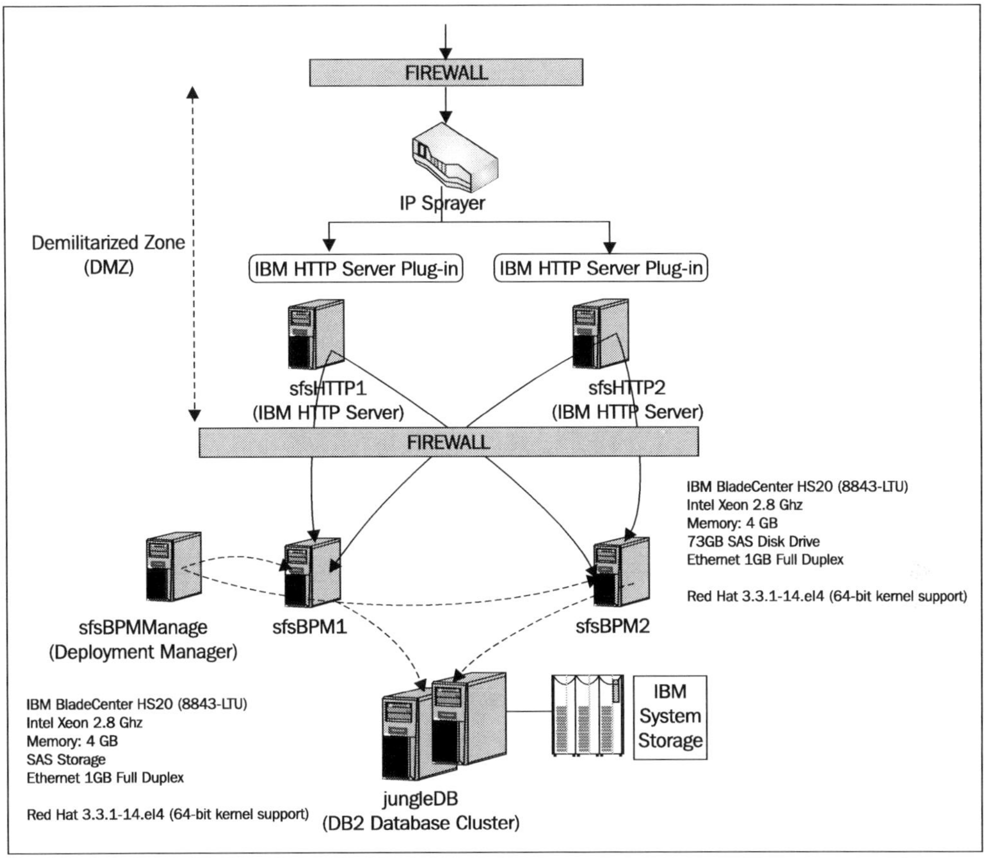

Sales Fulfillment Application deployment topology

As explained earlier, clustering provides scalability and failover capabilities. A cell can have zero or many clusters and can be distributed across one or more nodes in any configuration. For the Sales Fulfillment Application, JungleSea will adopt clustering to not only allow the above-mentioned benefits, but also to allow high throughputs, resiliency, and to provide space for future growth (per the NFRs listed in the earlier section). Typically, the selection of a right deployment topology should be based on the following criteria:

- System resources
- Invocation patterns in the solutions

- Types of business processes implemented
- CEI usage
- Business rules usage
- Future scalability needs
- Administrative effort required

There are several deployment patterns available from IBM, which are also available for WPS. The most common deployment environment patterns include:

- **Single Cluster (bronze)**: This pattern simply consists of *one* cluster for all the functional components. The user applications, messaging infrastructure, CEI, and support applications are all configured in the same cluster. Typically, this topology is used for testing proofs of concept and demonstration environments. Each cluster member is an application deployment target.
- **Remote Messaging (silver)**: This pattern consists of *two* separate clusters, where one cluster will contain the messaging infrastructure (named Messaging) and the other will contain all of the remaining components (named AppTarget). This pattern creates a topology, which is named Loosely Coupled Topology and is typically used for isolated environments.
- **Remote Messaging and Remote Support (gold)**: This pattern contains *three* different clusters and is the preferred topology for production environments.
    - Remote messaging cluster (named Messaging)
    - Support infrastructure cluster (named Support)
    - Application deployment target cluster (named AppTarget)

  The remote messaging and support pattern therefore enables the installation of the best separation-of-concerns topology.

There are several ways to create a WPS deployment environment that is based on one of the above topologies. These patterns are included in the administrative console and also the profile management tool. Generating a deployment environment on the administrative console creates an XML-based representation of the topology that can be exported and imported and reused to create the topology on any number of systems.

> Refer to the following article which discusses in detail building clustered topologies in WPS – *Building clustered topologies in WebSphere Process Server V6.1:*
>
> `http://www.ibm.com/developerworks/websphere/library/techarticles/0803_chilanti/0803_chilanti.html`

A deployment environment is just a description of the topology and does NOT contain or refer to the actual physical resources, such as data sources, JMS queues, SI Buses, and so forth, that constitute the topology itself.

To accommodate the NFRs for the Sales Fulfillment Application we will adopt the **Remote Messaging and Remote Support** topology pattern (**gold topology**), which is the preferred topology for production environments. Not only that, gold topology is the most frequently adopted topology because of the flexibility it offers in terms of its potential for scalability. Shown in the following figure is the "Golden Topology" for the Sales Fulfullment Application deployment topology. As shown, the Sales Fulfillment Application cell (SFSCell01) will contain multiple nodes and the application itself will be deployed in a cluster with cluster members on multiple nodes. We will be using three clusters:

- **Application Cluster** (**SFAGold.AppTarget**): All the SCA applications including the business processes, human tasks, WESB mediations, adapters, and so on. The BPC is configured in the AppTarget cluster, so each cluster member has a business process container and a human task container.
- **Messaging Cluster** (**SFAGold.Messaging**): For the messaging engines that constitute the Service Integration Bus (SIBus) including:
    - SCA.SYSTEM
    - SCA.APPLICATION
    - CEI
    - BPC

  As shown in the figure, the messaging engines are split across the members of the Messaging cluster. SFAGold.Messaging.wpsNode01 cluster member has active SCA.SYSTEM and SCA.APPLICATION messaging engines. SFAGold.Messaging.wpsNode02 cluster member has CEI and BPC messaging engines. By default, each cluster member is capable of running all four of the messaging engines, and the server that starts first will automatically run all four of the engines.
- **Support Cluster** (**SFAGold.Support**): For the WPS supporting applications including:
    - BPC Explorer
    - BPC Observer
    - Business Rules Manager
    - CEI
    - Business Space

> We have discussed security considerations to protect not only the applications and resources deployed on the WPS/WESB server, but also, note the administrative security as such is a larger and wider system administration topic, which is out of the scope of this book.

From a scalability standpoint, the Remote Messaging and Remote Support topology provide the most flexibility. Because each of the distinct functions within WPS is divided among the three clusters, you can pinpoint performance bottlenecks and adjust the cluster size fairly easily. If you need additional CEI processing, you can simply add a node and a cluster member to the support cluster.

Similarly, if you need more processing capability for your business processes or human tasks, you can add additional nodes and members to the application target cluster. This is because expanding the messaging infrastructure beyond three cluster members has no affect on processing capability. The scalability limitations present in the Remote Messaging policy also apply to the Remote Messaging and Remote Support topology. As with the Remote Messaging topology, the Remote Messaging and Remote Support topology provide an ideal environment for long-running business processes, state machines, human tasks, and asynchronous interactions (including JMS and MQ/JMS bindings). Because the application target cluster is only responsible for running your Business Integration applications, performance tuning and diagnostics are much simpler than in the previous topologies, where the application target cluster had additional responsibilities.

The Remote Messaging and Remote Support topology is also ideal for environments that make extensive use of CEI for monitoring and auditing. Separating the support infrastructure into its own cluster provides you with a dedicated set of cluster members for CEI and for the supporting applications like BPC Explorer and Business Space.

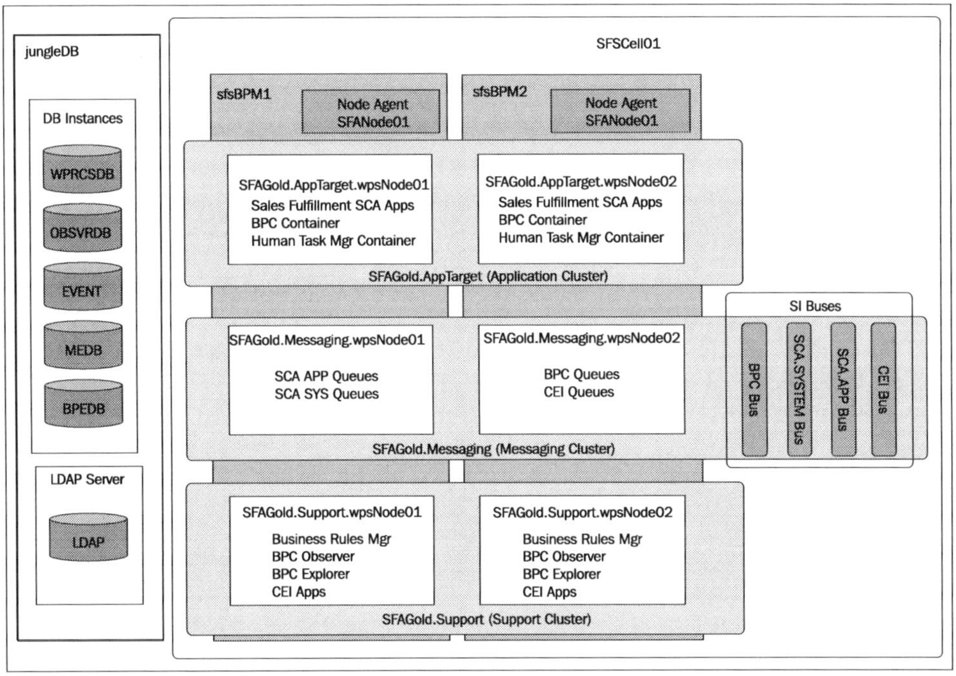

Custom Topologies

Custom topologies allow you to define your own environment, where you may choose not to install certain components due to additional overhead associated or no requirements (CEI and BPC Observer, for example, or if your organization has no need for the CEI). In such cases, you could create a custom topology that removes CEI support and the BPC Observer from your environment. Similarly, if your organization has governance rules that prevent you from taking advantage of the Business Rules Manager, you could remove it from your deployment.

Words of Wisdom

- Here are the steps to start a clustered WPS environment:
    - Start deployment managers: You must start the deployment manager before you can use its administrative console to manage the cell.
    - Start node agents: Must be started before you can start servers on the node. The node agent must be started for the deployment manager to communicate with it.

    - Start the clusters: You can start all the servers in a cluster (cluster members) in one action. When you start a cluster, you automatically enable workload management.

- You can export and import deployment environments from the Admin Console (Integrated Solutions Console, click Server Deployment Environments). The Export button creates a backup of, and Import generates environments based on, previously configured environments.
- The WESB clusters can, in most cases, share the same ME cluster with the WPS cluster. If you have more than two systems/machines/servers, you can better distribute the cluster members. For example, in a four-node environment, two nodes could run WPS and two nodes WESB. The main advantage with this approach is reduction in licensing costs.
- Factors that may indicate you need a topology beyond Gold topology (custom for example):
    - Number of modules
    - Messaging cluster startup
    - Number of mediation modules versus process modules
    - Number of human tasks
- Periodically export the deployment environments and 'version-control' them. This will help you roll back to a previously known working environment in case of a catastrophe. It will also be helpful when you want to promote an environment from one environment to another.
- Recovery of a WPS/WESB cell requires at a minimum recovery of:
    - Databases—take periodic backup databases
    - Transaction logfiles
    - WPS/WESB cell configuration onto a backup cell
- For a complete recovery, you will need:
    - Installation files if you need to reinstall
    - Topology or deployment environment configuration
    - Application modules
    - Runtime data that represents the current state of interaction occurring in WPS at a given time in the databases (such as the BPEDB), messaging engine destinations (ultimately backed by a database), and in the transaction logs.

- After generation of an operational environment, any changes made to a specific resource (for example, a data source) will not be reflected in the deployment environment descriptor.
- Use products like IBM Tivoli Composite Application Manager to monitor the production topology. The most common deployment environment patterns include. For more detailed information on deployment topology for WPS/WESB, refer to this IBM Redbook—*WebSphere Business Process Management V6.2 Production Topologies* — `http://www.redbooks.ibm.com/redbooks/pdfs/sg247732.pdf`.
- For more information on how to operate WPS environments, refer to the following interesting articles:
    - Expanding clustered topologies for WebSphere Process Server and WebSphere Enterprise Service Bus

      `http://www.ibm.com/developerworks/websphere/library/techarticles/0901_herness/0901_herness.html`
    - Operating a WebSphere Process Server environment, Part 1: Overview

      `http://www.ibm.com/developerworks/websphere/library/techarticles/0912_herrmann2/0912_herrmann2.html`
    - Operating a WebSphere Process Server environment, Part 2: Options for maintaining an optimal Business Process Choreographer database size

      `http://www.ibm.com/developerworks/websphere/library/techarticles/0912_herrmann2/0912_herrmann2.html`
    - Asynchronous replication of WebSphere Process Server and WebSphere Enterprise Service Bus for disaster recovery environments

      `http://www.ibm.com/developerworks/websphere/library/techarticles/0809_redlin/0809_redlin.html`

Summary

In this chapter, we started with the fundamental aspects to take into consideration when choosing a deployment topology. Then we discussed the fundamentals behind WebSphere Application Server Network Deployment (WAS ND) which is the base foundation platform for the IBM BPM portfolio of products including WPS and WESB.

We discussed clustering, how to do vertical and horizontal clustering, and briefly looked at the databases used by WPS. Then we created the operational architecture for the Sales Fulfillment Application including the logical and physical architecture. Finally we discussed the several deployment patterns available from IBM and how, from them, we choose the Remote Messaging and Remote Support topology pattern (gold topology) as the production topology.

We discussed the gold topology we created for the Sales Fulfillment Application. Hopefully, by now, you have a fairly decent understanding of the deployment topologies, and we recommend that you refer to the links provided for further detailed reading.

13
Management, Monitoring, and Security

This chapter will cover some of the most essential and common topics related to management, monitoring, security, and administration capabilities and the tools provided by WPS and WESB. Firstly, we will show, in the context of the Sales Fulfillment Application we have built so far, how to administer WPS and WESB using Integrated Solutions Console, Business Space, and Business Process Choreographer Explorer. We will discuss how to enable administrative security, enable application security, and create profiles with security. We will go through the steps involved in installing and deploying the modules.

We will then briefly cover how you can monitor the applications and components on WPS and WESB. We will discuss the various tools and capabilities provided in WID/WPS/WESB to monitor the applications and components. We will discuss service invocation monitoring, business process monitoring, and an explanation of the fundamentals behind Common Event Infrastructure (CEI).

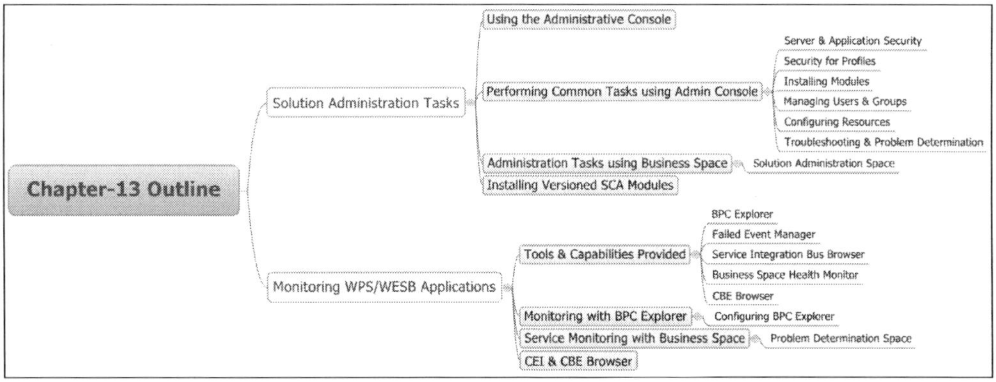

Solution administration tasks

After the Sales Fulfillment Application has been deployed, as described in *Chapter 7, Sales Fulfillment Application for JungleSea Inc.*, we enter the fourth phase of the IBM SOA Architecture—Manage. In this phase, the SOA solution, business process, and related assets are monitored and managed to ensure they continue to deliver the business value they were developed for. Typical solution administration tasks encompass tasks such as deploying modules, enabling and configuring security, viewing and administering modules, configuring resources, monitoring modules, troubleshooting modules, and so on. In order to be able to accomplish these, WPS and WESB provides administrative capabilities to manage and monitor applications running on them. By leveraging these features, system administrators can accomplish common administration tasks such as review logfiles, start/stop servers, install/remove applications, define security settings, and manage integration with other tooling and databases. We shall look at some of these tasks in more detail later on in this chapter. These capabilities are exposed to the system administrators and other interested groups through the **Integrated Solution Console**, also known and used interchangeably as the **Administrative Console** or **Admin Console**.

Using the administrative console

The admin console is the integrated browser-based interface used to administer, manage, and monitor modules, applications, services, and other resources at a cell, node, server, or cluster level. Using the integrated solutions console, you can:

- Deploy the various modules that make up the Sales Fulfillment Application
- Use a common interface to administer the application, which in turn reduces time and expense required for training administrative personnel
- Manage applications, buses, servers, and resources for a standalone server, network deployment cell, manage node, and deployment manager node

> The **wsadmin** tool is a command-line version of the administrative console and can be used to script any activity executed in the administrative console.

You launch the admin console from WID by right-clicking on the **UTE server** and by selecting **Administration | Run administrative console** from the context menu. You can also directly launch it in a web browser by going to the URL `https://<server IP>:<port:>// ibm/console/logon.jsp`. (`https://localhost:9048/ibm/console/logon.jsp`, for example). Administrative console pages are of three types, as shown in the following screenshot:

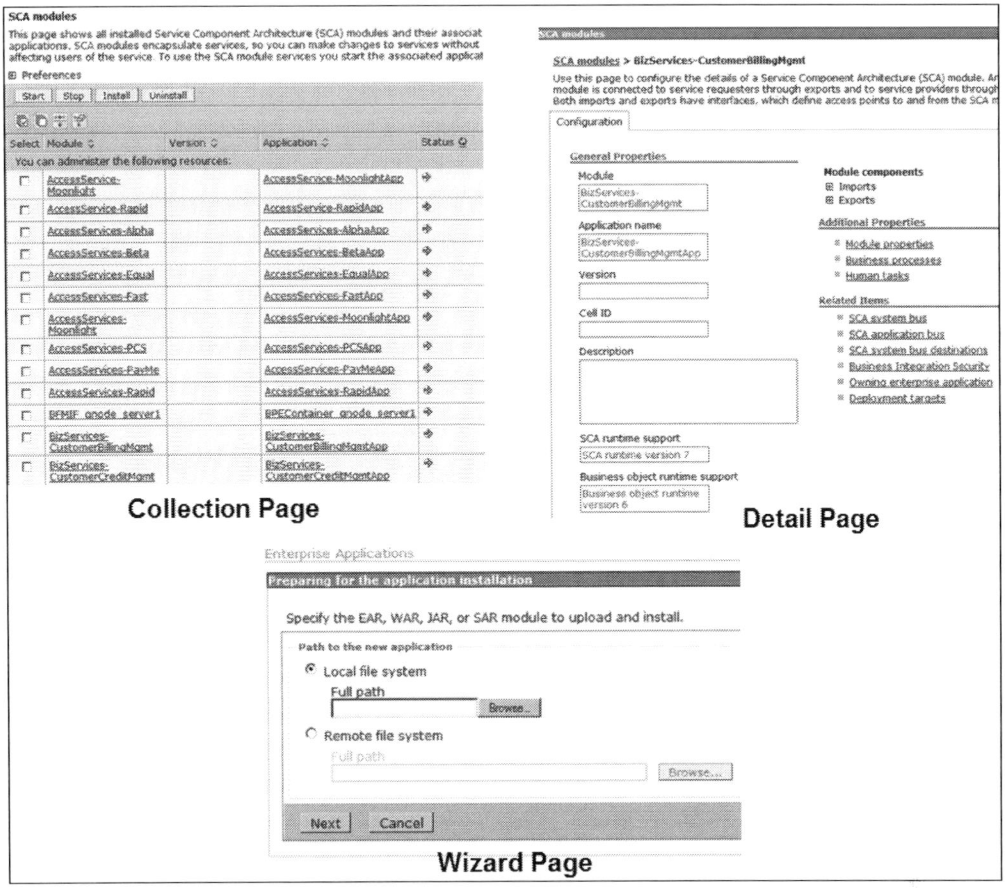

1. **Collection Page**: A **Collection Page** manages a collection of existing administrative objects normally displayed in the form of a table of objects, events, or resources with administrative functionality to control them.
2. **Detail Page**: These are used to view detail and configure objects and resources.
3. **Wizard Page**: These pages help you complete a configuration process comprised of several steps.

Let's take a closer look at the landscape of the admin console. This page essentially has four main areas—**Navigation Tree**, **Work Area**, **Task Bar**, and **Page help**, as shown in the next screenshot:

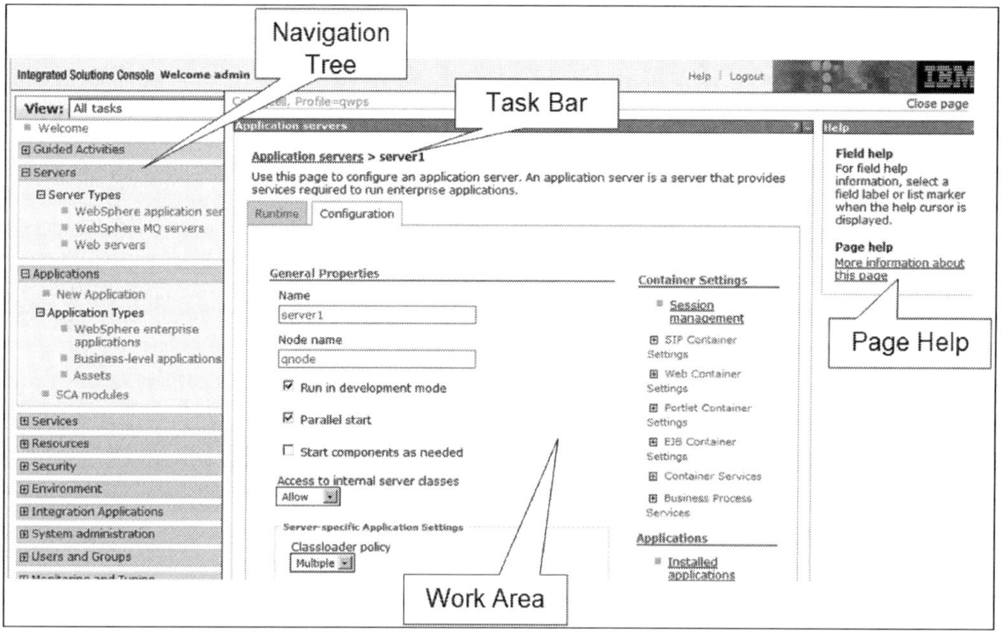

1. **Task Bar**: The **Task Bar** is located at the very top of the console. All tasks like saving changes, logging out, specifying preferences, and accessing product information are provided here.
2. **Work Area**: The **Work Area** is located in the center of the console. It displays the main content of the page where you can create and administer servers, applications, and other resources. You access these pages by clicking the links in the Navigation Tree or by clicking links within the workspace pages themselves.
3. **Page help**: The right side of the workspace provides brief information about each field on the current page, as well as a link to more detailed information in the help browser.
4. **Navigation Tree**: On the left side of the Work Area is the **Navigation Tree**. It provides links to console pages that you use to create and administer servers, applications, and other resources. You can expand or collapse each item in the Navigation Tree using the plus or minus icon respectively or by clicking on the item itself. The various items provided by the Navigation Tree are expanded and shown in the following screenshot:

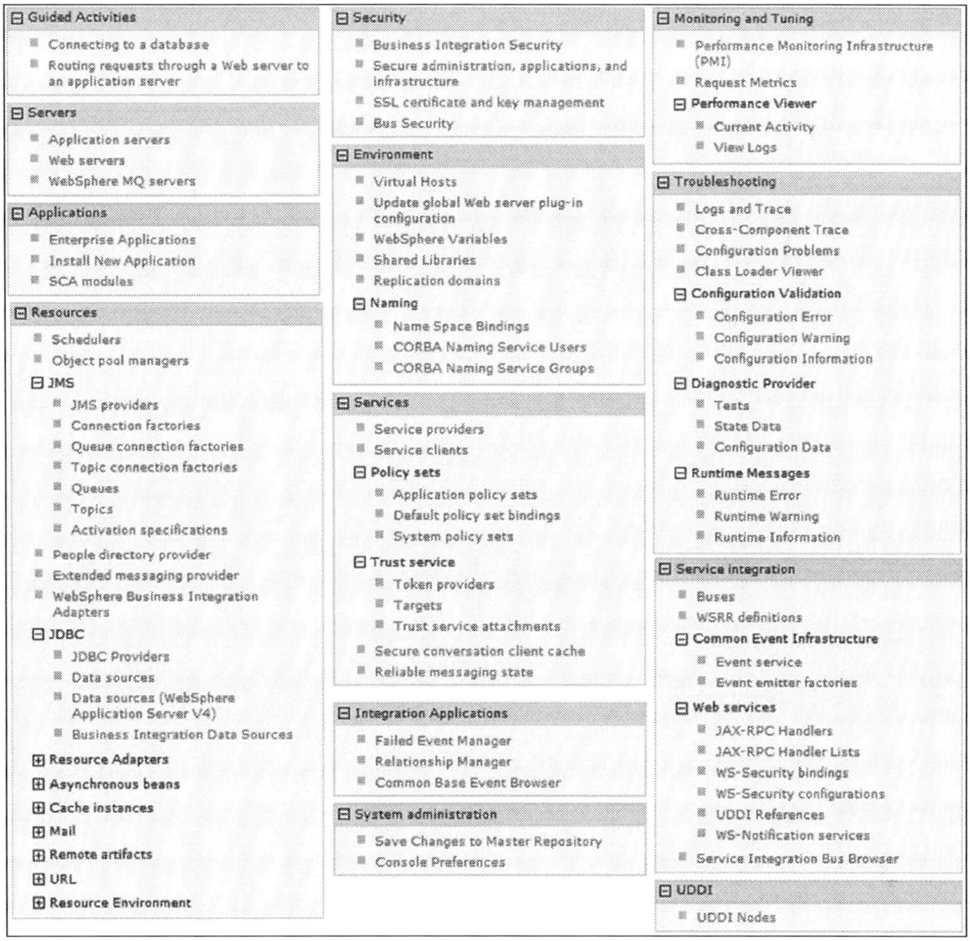

For more details on *Administering WebSphere Process Server*, please refer to this white paper:

ftp://ftp.software.ibm.com/software/websphere/integration/wps/library/pdf620/administering_wpsmp_en.pdf

Performing common tasks using the administrative console

Our next step will be to get our hands dirty and walk through some of the more common tasks that any administrator would need to do using the admin console.

> In the case of clustered WPS/WESB, it is recommended that you ensure the deployment manager is running before you use the widget. In addition, the node agents must be running in order to see the module status in the widget.

Enabling server and application security

Security is an integral part of WPS and is based on the **WebSphere Application Server (WAS)** version security. Security can be established both at a global, administrative, and application level. **Global security** helps provide the basic security for all administrative functions and user applications. During installation of WPS, administrative security is enabled by default and will require you to define a user with an administrative role. If needed, this option can be unchecked to turn **Global security** off but this is not recommended. This can be configured later through administrative console.

Application security helps control and secure identity, access, and data flowing to and from the modules. Application security can be established programmatically or declaratively through the administration console. It should be noted here that administrative security needs to be established before security for applications can be configured.

WPS also helps define security to communicate with external and internal system components like databases, messaging engines, and connection factories.

The **Navigation Tree**, as shown in the following screenshot, provides these options to configure and define security settings for the server and user applications that run on it.

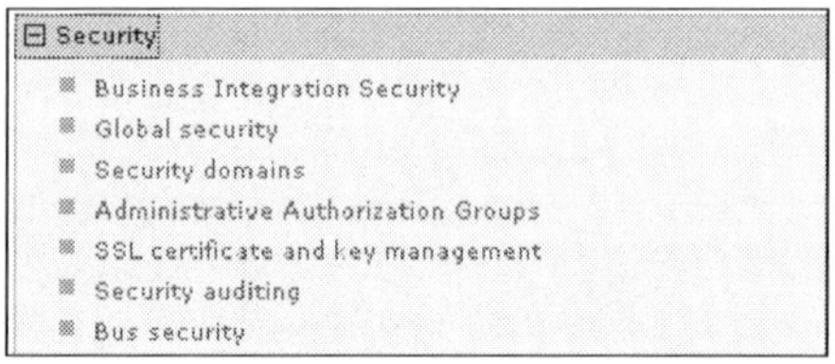

The **Business Integration Security** panel is used to define and manage authentication aliases for various runtime components including the **Business Process Choreographer**, **Common Event Infrastructure**, and **Service Component Architecture**. You are also given the option to define users and groups for the different default roles for **Business Process Choreographer**, as shown in the following screenshot:

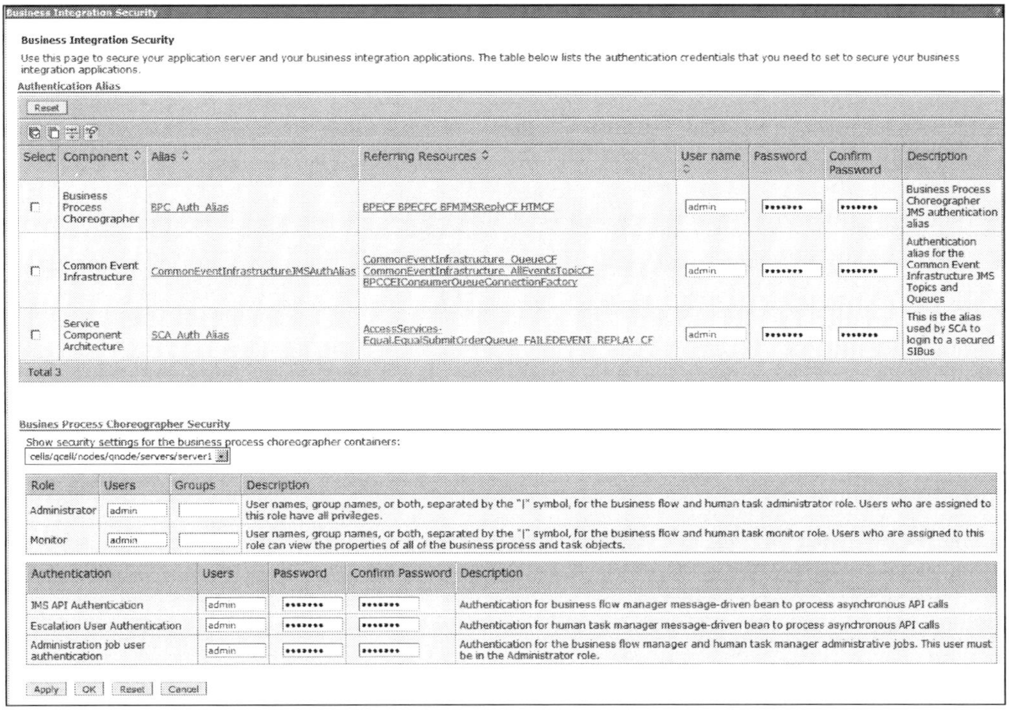

By default, they are all set to the default administrative user.

- The **Global security** panel is used to configure administration and the default application security policy. We shall cover this in more detail under the *Administrative Security procedures* section.
- The **Security domains** panel is a new feature in version 7.0 that allows for greater flexibility in configuring and applying security settings. This is used to manage multiple security domains by providing the ability to create new domains, delete existing domains, or copy domains that can be scoped to an entire cell or a specific server, cluster, or service integration bus. It can also be used to configure separate security configurations for administrative applications, end user applications, and third-party security providers.
- The **Administrative Authorization Groups** panel is used to create and manage the current **Administrative Authorization Groups** available in the cell.
- The **SSL certification and key management** panel is used to manage security for Secure Socket Layer (SSL) and key management, certificates, and notifications.

- The **Security auditing** panel is used to capture and store auditable security events like authentication, authorization, and resource access that can then be presented in a consumable form through user-friendly reports.
- The **Bus security** panel is used to manage security for the Service Integration Buses.

Administrative Security procedures — Enabling administration security at profile creation

When installing WPS or WESB or when creating a new profile in the server, you are given the option to **Enable administrative security**, as shown in the following screenshot:

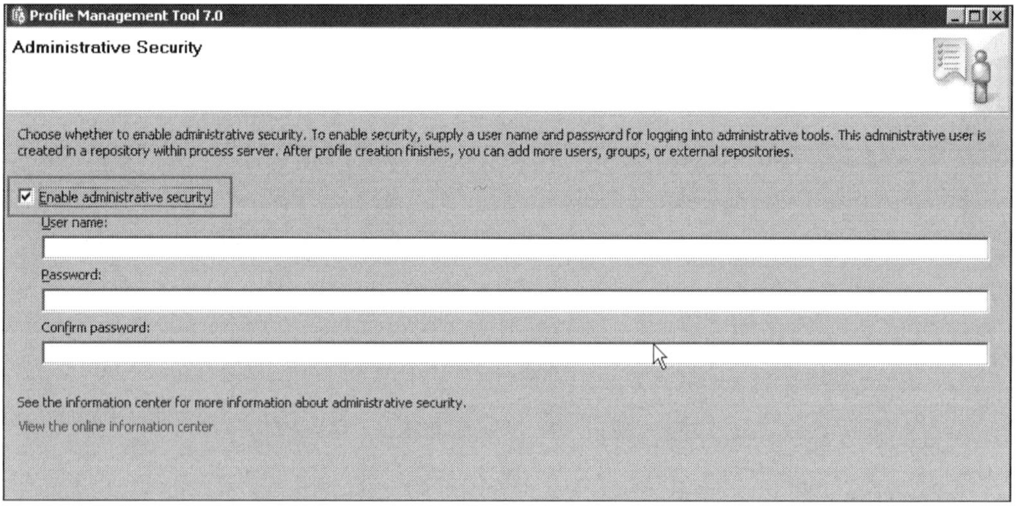

If **Administrative security** is not enabled at installation, it can be established during post installation. Steps to do this have been documented in the *IBM Redbook WebSphere Application Server V7.0 Security Guide* under the *Administration Security* section.

> For further information regarding security, please refer to the *IBM Redbook WebSphere Application Server V7.0 Security Guide*
> `http://www.redbooks.ibm.com/abstracts/sg247660.html?Open`

Installing SCA modules using the admin console

You can use the admin console to deploy an SCA module or a mediation module to the WPS/WESB server. While there is a certain possibility to automate the deployment of these modules using **Jython** or **Java Application Control Language (JACL)** executed using the wsadmin tool, we will see in this section how to use the admin console. To export a module for deploying through the admin console, execute the following steps:

1. In WID, right-click on the module or modules and select **Export**.
2. In the **Export** wizard, choose **Business Integration | Integration modules and libraries**, and proceed with the Wizard by clicking on the **Next** button.
3. Select the appropriate modules in the list.
4. Proceeding with the wizard, select the **Target Directory** where you want to export the `EAR` files.
5. Finally, complete the wizard at the end of which you will find the `EAR` versions of the module(s) that can be deployed on the server.

Once you have exported the module(s) from WID, you will, most likely, want to version control the exported `EAR` file using CVS or ClearCase as part of a software configuration management procedure.

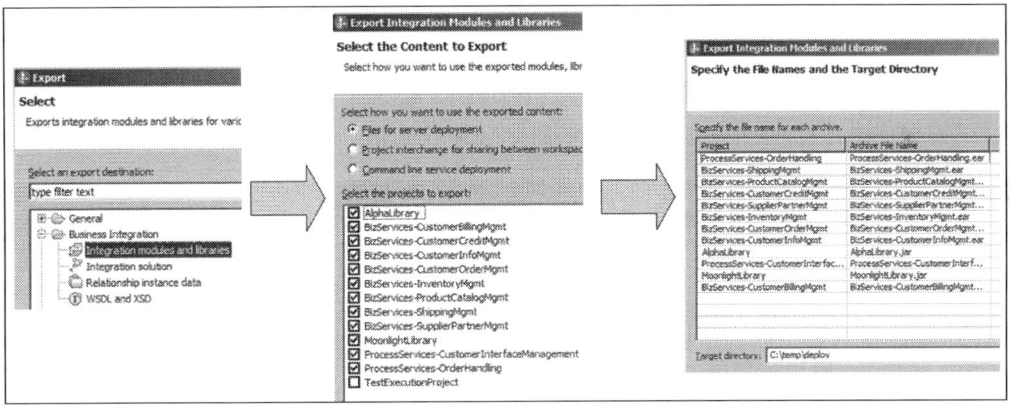

[In WID, the default sharing behavior for modules and libraries is **share-by-copy**.]

By default, when you export a module for deployment from WID, modules bring along with it a copy of the library that contains WSDLs, XSDs, and so on). These shared SCA library projects are exported (as `.jar` files) and each included in an SCA module application enterprise archive (`.ear`) file. When the size of the libraries becomes large, you don't want to do share-by-copy. Sharing these assets by reference can reduce this memory footprint. The solution is to use a WebSphere shared library (SL) instead of the default share-by-copy method.

In the Library Dependency editor, if you look at the **Sharing across Runtime Environments** section, you have two radio button choices:

- **Global** (share-by-reference)
- **Module** (share-by-copy)

If you want the library to be deployed as a shared/global library, select radio button **Global**. You need to do this for each library in the workspace. When you export the module, the libraries will be exported as individual `JARs` and the module `EAR` of course. Please note that if you choose to take the share-by-reference approach, you need to set up the shared libraries. For more information, refer to the following article:

`http://www-01.ibm.com/support/docview.wss?rs=2307anduid=swg21322617`

Now in the admin console, select the **Install New Application** wizard that guides you through the deployment of a new application onto WPS or WESB. Now let us go through the steps involved as follows:

1. In the **Navigation Tree** under **Applications**, click on **Install New Application.**
2. The application `EAR` file that you exported from WID may be on the local file system or at a remote location; specify the location.
3. Select if you want to be prompted for the additional information that is needed in the installation or if you want to view all installation options and procedures. The first choice is quicker than the second.
4. Click on the **Next** button.
5. Follow the required installation steps as directed.
6. Save the installation if everything goes through successfully.
7. Click on **Applications | Enterprise Applications** to list all the installed applications.
8. Locate the application just installed. It has not yet been started.
9. Enable the checkbox next to the application on the table.

10. After installing a module it is not automatically started. The application needs to be started manually using the admin console. Click on the **Start** button, as shown in the following screenshot:

Congratulations! You have completed installing an application module.

> One of the most common question that can be asked after reading the previous section will be, "How can I automate the build process?" Since every customer situation is unique, WPS does not offer out-of-the-box scripts to build and deploy application modules. However, it does provide ANT tasks to do the following:
>
> -`serviceDeploy` to pack and build SCA modules from a `.jar` or `.zip` file that contains service components. For more information, refer to:
>
> `http://publib.boulder.ibm.com/infocenter/dmndhelp/v7r0mx/topic/com.ibm.websphere.wps.doc/doc/rdev_servicedeploy.html`
>
> For more information on how to do these ANT tasks, please refer to the links below:
>
> `http://publib.boulder.ibm.com/infocenter/dmndhelp/v7r0mx/topic/com.ibm.websphere.wps.doc/doc/tdep_usingant.html`
>
> For more information on using JACL scripts, refer to:
>
> `http://www.ibm.com/developerworks/websphere/library/techarticles/0709_maheswaren/0709_maheswaren.html`

Managing Users and Groups

User management is an integral part of deploying and administering any application. It is critical to ensure that the end user is given just the right level of access to serve the business need. In WPS or the WESB admin console, these features are listed under **Users and Groups**, as shown in the following screenshot:

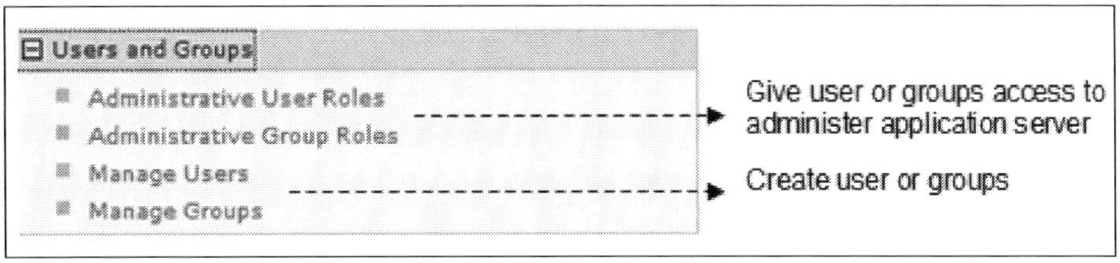

Now let us look at the steps involved in the creation of a new group **Jungle Sea Users** with one user **JoeUser**:

1. Under **Users and Groups** in the **Navigation Tree**, click on **Manage Groups.**
2. Click on the **Create** button.
3. Enter a **group name Jungle Sea Users**, and click on the **Create** button.
4. Click on **Manage Users** under **Users and Groups** in the **Navigation Tree**.
5. Click on the **Create** button.
6. Enter user details, as shown in the following screenshot:

7. Click on the **Group Membership** button.
8. When you return to the **Create a User** page, click on the **Create** button.

Congratulations! You have created a **JungleSea** user group with a user **Joe User**.

Integration with LDAP

WPS or WESB can be easily integrated with your existing LDAP, Federated repository, Local operating system users, or any other customer user registry. These settings are found under **Security | Secure administration, applications, and infrastructure** in the **Navigation Tree**.

For more information, please refer to
`http://publib.boulder.ibm.com/infocenter/dmndhelp/v7r0mx/topic/com.ibm.websphere.bpc.doc/doc/bpc/t4staff_ldap.html`

Configuring Resources

Most production applications in today's world need to leverage resources for security, persistence, integrations, and other operation needs. The various modules and mediation modules we have developed so far make use of a wide range of resources including JMS, JDBC, service integration (destinations), CEI, and so on. To administer these resources, you can use the admin console, commands, and scripting tools. As shown in the following diagram, WPS and WESB provide administrative capabilities to manage these resources under **Resources** in the **Navigation Tree**. Let's take a closer look at some of the more commonly-used applications:

- **JMS** is used to create, configure, and manage JMS providers, queues, topics, connection factories, and activation specifications.
- **JDBC** is used to create, configure, and manage JDBC settings for the applications. The **JDBC providers** object encapsulates the specific JDBC driver implementation class for the data sources that you define and associate with the provider.
- **Mail** is used to create, configure, and manage mail sessions needed for the applications and server.

Start the wsadmin tool to run the following commands.

Some of the common commands to manage and get information about the modules include:

- To list the SCA modules deployed on the server:

  `$AdminTask listSCAModules`
- To display the details of a particular SCA module:

  `$AdminTask showSCAModule {-moduleName moduleName}`

- To display the properties of a particular SCA module:

```
$AdminTask showSCAModuleProperties {-moduleName myModule}
```

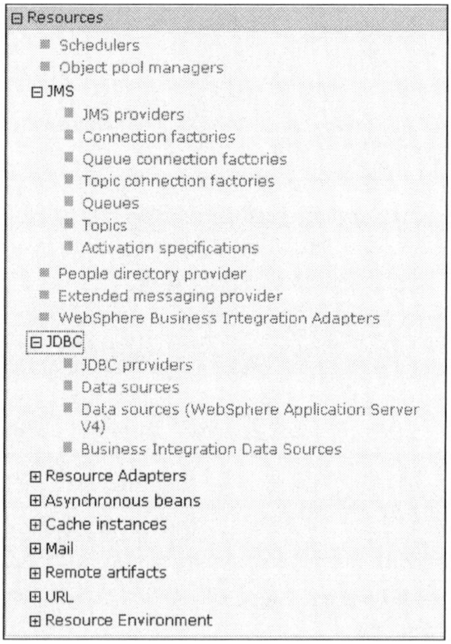

Troubleshooting and Problem Determination

Having deployed the Sales Fulfillment Application, how do we troubleshoot and diagnose it in case of problems? Troubleshooting is one of the critical features needed to diagnose the issues and rectify the problem with as minimum impact as possible. When troubleshooting, you should be asking these questions or items you will have to address:

- What is causing the problem?
- Which part of the application is it occurring in?
- When do the problems appear?—Time of the day, certain scenarios, and so on. What are the symptoms of the problem?
- How can I reproduce the problem?

You need tools that assist you in the troubleshooting process. WPS/WESB and WID include several tools you can use to troubleshoot your applications that you develop and deploy on the server. The admin console provides capabilities for troubleshooting. In the admin console, under the **Troubleshooting** navigation item, you can perform several things to troubleshoot your module(s) if anything goes wrong.

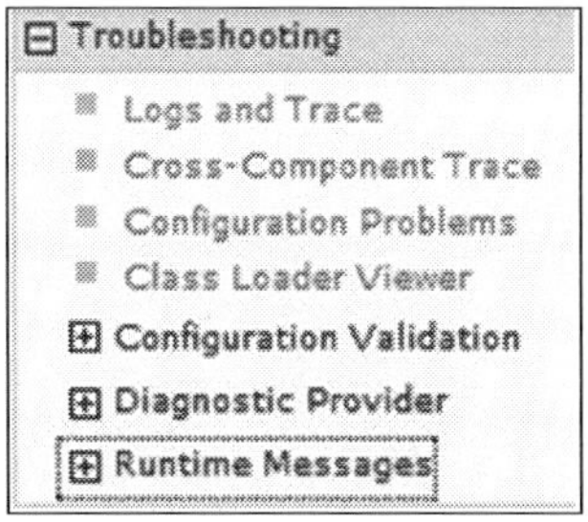

- **Logs and Trace** is used to configure logging and tracing levels for the server logs. These logs can also be viewed through these pages.
- **Cross-Component Trace** allows you to identify data that is captured in the `trace.log`. This data can include error and event information, such as corrupted data or runtime exceptions, captured during SCA processing. The input and output data passing between WPS and WESB components can also be captured and used for determining a problem using WID.
- **Configuration Problems** is used to view and identify issues that may exist in the current configuration.
- **Class Loader Viewer** helps you to troubleshoot issues that may occur with class loaders.
- **Runtime Messages** pages show events published by the application server class including errors, warnings, and information.

The runtime messages that appear in the logs during installation consist of a four- or five-character message prefix, followed by a four- or five-character message number, which is followed by a single-letter message type code (**CWWBS0000E**, **CWWBS0032I**, **CWWBS0059W**, and so on).

- C: Indicates a severe message
- E: Indicates an urgent message
- I: Indicates an informational message
- N: Indicates an error message
- W: Indicates a warning message

You can often resolve the problem by reading the entire message text and the recovery actions that are associated with the message.

> For a complete list of runtime messages, their explanations, and the recommended recovery actions, refer to the following link:
>
> `http://publib.boulder.ibm.com/infocenter/dmndhelp/v7r0mx/topic/com.ibm.websphere.wbpm.messages.doc/doc/welc_ref_msg_wbpm.html`

First Failure Data Capture (**FFDC**) provides the instrumentation for exception handlers (catch blocks) to record exceptions that are thrown by a component. The captured data is saved in a logfile for use in analyzing the problem. These logfiles can be found in your WTE under:

```
%WID7_WTE_HOME%\runtimes\bi_v7\profiles\qwps\logs\ffdc
```

Administration tasks using Business Space

Business Space provides templates that help you administer solutions deployed on WPS and WESB. You can create a **Solution Administration** space in Business Space to manage and administer the Sales Fulfillment Application deployed on WPS and WESB. To create a new space, once you log in to the Business Space, click on the **Actions** | **Create Space** menu option on the top menu. As shown in the following screenshot, this will bring up a wizard where you can specify a name for the space and select **Solution Administration** from the list of available templates. You can also specify a **Space style** and **Space icon** to customize its look and feel.

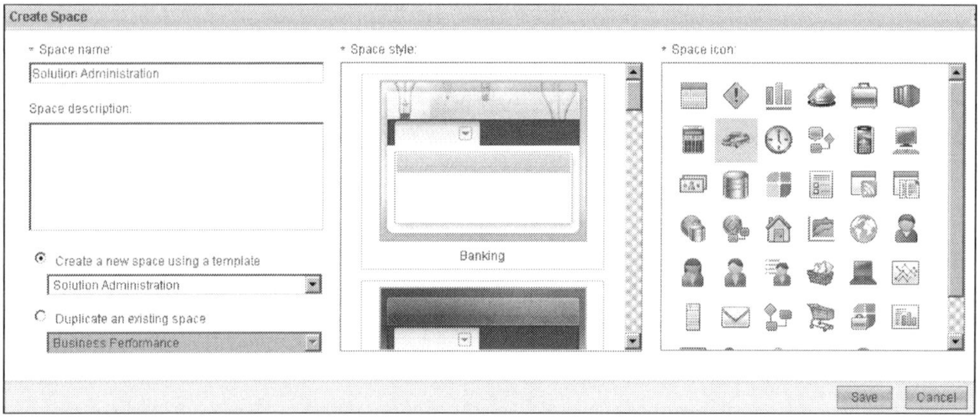

Once you create this **Solution Administration** space, it becomes the container that allows you to browse all the modules deployed on the server through **Module Browser**. When you click on the module name to expand the tree view, as shown in the following screenshot, you will be able to see the following as pertinent to the module:

- Service imports and service exports
    - Click on the **view service import or export name** in **Module Browser** to display its high-level binding endpoint details in the **Module Administration** widget
- Any properties and policies defined for the module
- Business rule groups defined
- Processes and process instances
    - You can view the process instances by clicking on the **process component name** in the **Module Browser** widget, clicking the link to open **Business Process Choreographer Explorer** in a new browser window, and administering the artifact
- Business state machines
- Human tasks
- Business calendars defined
- Security roles defined

> You must have the BPMAdmin or BPMRoleManager authority to assign or modify roles

- Service control points defined

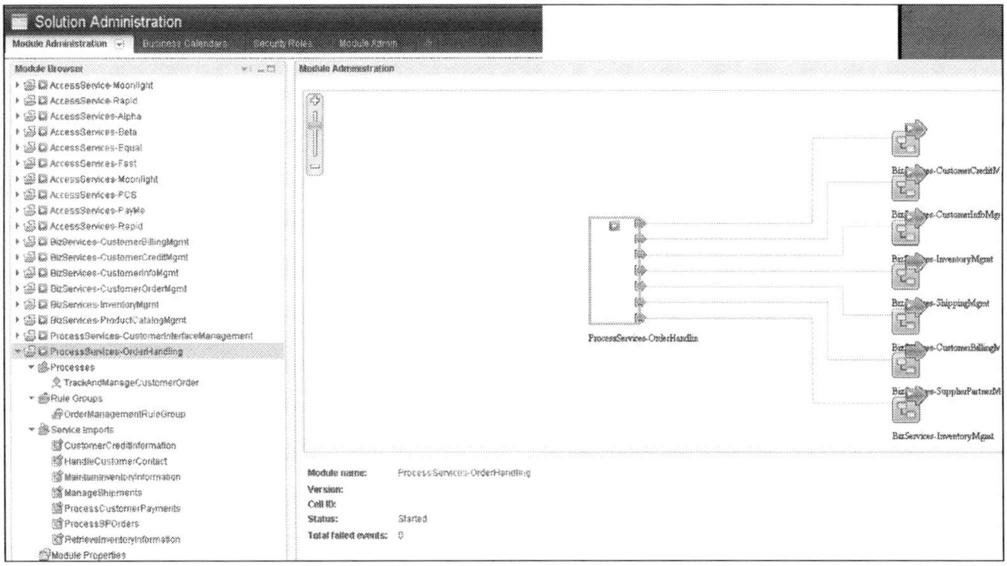

Installing versioned SCA modules

You can deploy a different version of the same SCA module into a server or cell that has a different version of the same module such that both the versions can co-exist on the server or in the cell. To be able to do this, you should make sure that the module is versioned in WID and export it for command-line deployment.

> Refer to this link for more information on how to create versioned modules and libraries:
>
> `http://publib.boulder.ibm.com/infocenter/dmndhelp/v7r0mx/index.jsp?topic=/com.ibm.wbit.help.basics.doc/topics/tcrtvers.html`

Now, next are the high-level steps to follow:

1. Export the versioned module as an installable `EAR` file using `serviceDeploy`. For example, `serviceDeploy BizServices-CustomerBillingMgmt.zip`.
2. Install the module using the admin console by performing the steps mentioned in the earlier sections.
3. If you want to install the versioned module on multiple servers or clusters in a cell, do the following for each module instance you require:
    - Use the `createVersionedSCAModule` command to create an instance of the module

      ```
      createVersionedSCAModule -archiveAbsolutePath input_archive_dir -workingDirectory working_dir -uniqueCellID cell_ID
      ```
    - Install the resulting `EAR` file, as described in Step 2

Monitoring WPS/WESB applications

There is also a need to understand, from a runtime perspective, what is happening within the deployed solution. Some of the common visibility items include:

- Overall System/Server Health—CPU usage, memory usage, IO usage, connection pool, thread pool, event logs, disk space, and so on
- Module Health—Status of modules, failed events, status of process instances, and so on
- Services Health and Performance—Response time, throughput, periodic statistics, failure rates, and so on
- Diagnostic Information—Logs, trace, threads, and so on

- Business Process/Activity Performance—One of the goals of modelling a business process (like what we did in *Chapter 7, Sales Fulfillment Application for JungleSea Inc.*) is to measure the efficiency and the performance of the process itself based on KPIs and other instance metrics

From an overall system monitoring perspective, you need to make sense out of the raw data you are looking at. You need meaningful information and capabilities that give you this information that you are looking for. Also, we need to understand and act on various exceptions that are being thrown by the SCA components and associated escalations, human tasks, compensation, and escalation chains. So from a WID/WPS/WESB point of view, let's look at the tools and capabilities available to get visibility into the solution.

> **WebSphere Business Monitor** and the **WebSphere Monitor Toolkit** provide business activity monitoring capabilities that offer real-time insight into the business processes. It provides visualization dashboards (through Business Space, which we will discuss in forthcoming chapter) such as business process information, human task activities, process diagrams, **Key Performance Indicators** (**KPI**), dimensional views, visualizing a process flow, and so on. These products allow you to monitor the processes that are being executed on WPS and analyze them for further and future tuning. Usage of this product is out of the scope of this book.

Tools and capabilities provided

For the purpose of this book, we will see in this section how to monitor the business processes and the SCA modules and components using BPC Explorer, BPC Observer, Business Space, and CEI Browser.

To monitor the modules including Business Process Components for throughput and performance-related issues, WPS provides the following capabilities:

- **Business Process Choreographer Explorer** (**BPC Explorer**): Used to monitor process instances and also to determine whether you need to take action so that the process can run to completion.
- **Failed Event Manager**: Used to monitor errors in asynchronous communication. If, for example, a message could not be delivered to a target component, the user may use the Failed Event Manager to resubmit this message after either correcting a message payload or after correcting the error.
- **Service Integration Bus Browser**: Used to monitor and administer the SIBus topology underneath WPS.

- **Business Space Health Monitor**: Provides an aggregated and high-level view on application and component health, which are part of WPS.
- **Common Base Event browser (CBE browser)**: To retrieve and view events in the Common Event Infrastructure (CEI) event database.

> You can use Tivoli Performance Viewer to do performance tuning of a Business Process Management production environment. This is a separate product from IBM.

All of the mentioned tools are web-based utilities and can be launched from WID. Right-click on your **Server** | **Launch**. The tool will be launched within WID itself.

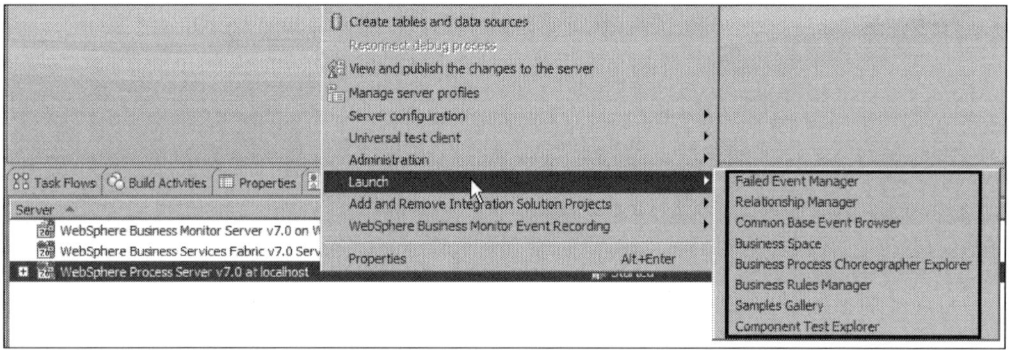

Now let us look at how we use the BPC Explorer, Business Space, and CBE Browser.

Monitoring with BPC Explorer

No discussion around WPS administrative capabilities and features would be complete without BPC Explorer. We briefly touched up on this topic in *Chapter 3, Building your Hello Process Project* and provided an example in *Chapter 5, Business Process Choreography Fundamentals*. BPC Explorer provides a robust runtime environment to manage all aspects of Business Process Execution Language (BPEL). BPC Explorer supports short-running and long-running business processes, as well as synchronous and asynchronous services and human tasks. You can launch BPC Explorer from WID by right-clicking on the UTE server and selecting **Launch** | **Business Process Choreographer Explorer** from the context menu. You can also directly launch it from a web browser and browse to `http://<Server_HostName>:<Server port> / bpc`. If security is enabled, then enter your username and password. Your privileges within the BPC Explorer depend upon authorization granted to the group that you belong to. This has been covered in brief in the previous section under security.

For more information, refer to
`http://publib.boulder.ibm.com/infocenter/dmndhelp/v7r0mx/topic/com.ibm.websphere.bpc.doc/doc/bpc/c7webclt.html`

Once you are logged into BPC Explorer, you can view process templates that you can launch. For example, you can launch an instance of the **HandleCustomerContactProfile** BPEL process, as shown in the following screenshot:

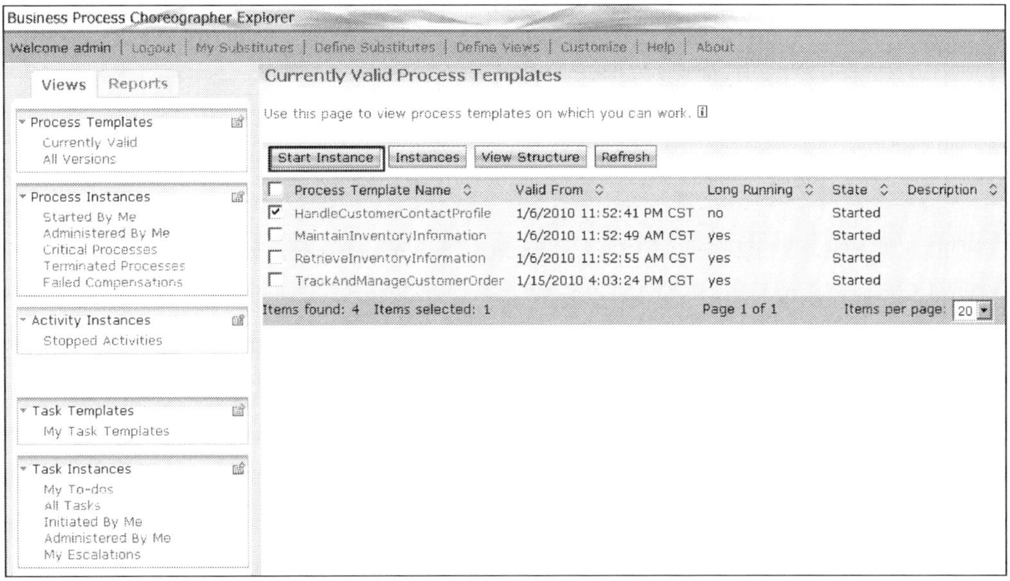

You can also look at the **Process Instance** you started or **Process Instances** that are currently running. For example, the following screenshot shows that a **Process Instance** named **Submit Customer Order for Jack Coxley** of the **TrackAndManageCustomerOrder** BPEL process template is running.

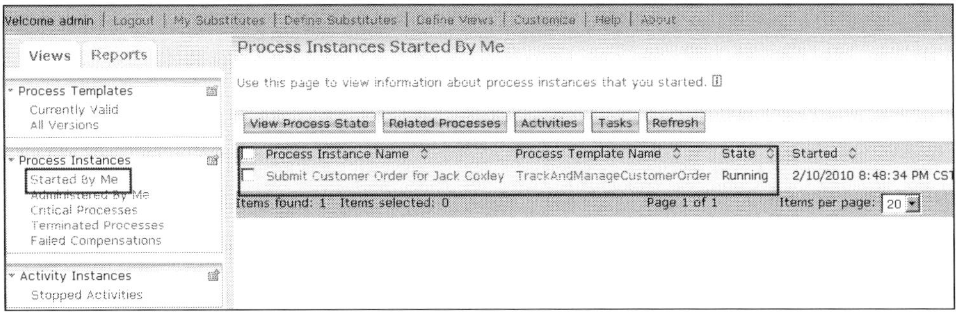

You can click on the **Process Instances** to find out the details behind the instance including who started it, when it was started, process input messages, which step in the process it currently is in, and so on. You can also view the graphical view of the process by clicking on the **View Process State**, and it will display the state of the process, tasks completed, and task currently waiting for/executing marked as green. You can also terminate and suspend **Process Instances** from this view. Under the **Task Instances | My Escalations**, you will be able to see the escalation that belong to you or needs your attention.

Configuring BPC Explorer

In order to use BPC Explorer, it must be first configured under **Servers | Clusters | WebSphere application server clusters | Cluster name** or **Servers | Server Types | WebSphere application servers | Server name**. Then on the **Configuration** tab, in the **Business Integration** section, expand **Business Process Choreographer**, and click **Business Process Choreographer Containers**. Make sure that you restart your server once the configurations have been made.

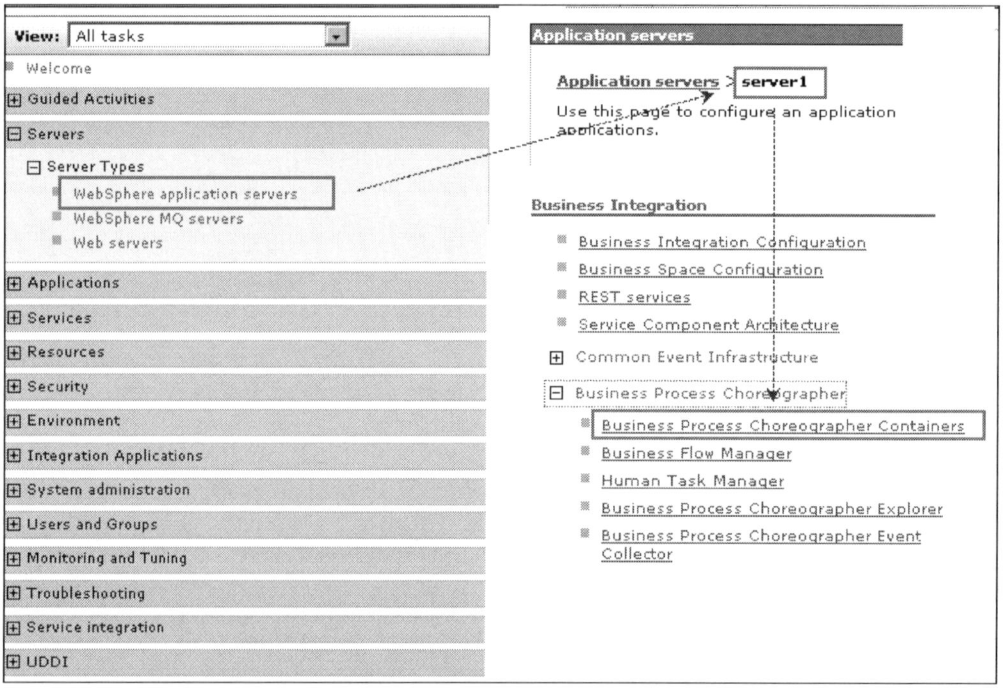

Ensure that the **Business Process Choreographer Containers, Human Task Manager**, and **Business Process Choreographer Explorer** applications are installed on the WPS.

Service Monitoring with Business Space

With the Business Space **Service Monitor** widget, you can measure various performance characteristics of an SCA module including the **Response Time** and request **Throughput**. You choose which specific operations, within a module that is exposed to requestors (SCA exports) and consumed (SCA imports), to monitor.

The widget plots **Response Time** and **Throughput** data on graphs, visually distinguishing those calls that exceed any **Threshold** you have defined. The graphs always show the latest monitoring statistics. However, you can see historical data by increasing the length of time shown on the graphs. With this widget, you can get the following information that can be used to monitor ongoing problems and pinpoint which part of your solution is not responding as expected.

- How much time do specific services require?
- Does service duration degrade over time?
- Service invocation count
- Throughput adherence against the defined values and how much it degrades over time

> Ensure service monitoring is configured and enabled. By default, service monitoring is enabled for servers or clusters created as part of deployment environment and standalone server profiles. If you have created a new server with the admin console, however, you must configure and enable the service monitor before you can use the **Service Monitor** widget. Refer to the following link to see how to do it:
>
> `http://publib.boulder.ibm.com/infocenter/dmndhelp/v7r0mx/topic/com.ibm.websphere.wbpm.bspace.config.doc/doc/tcfg_bsp_servicemon.html`

As shown in the next screenshot, on the **Service Monitor | Edit Settings**, you can specify the operations from the modules you would like to monitor.

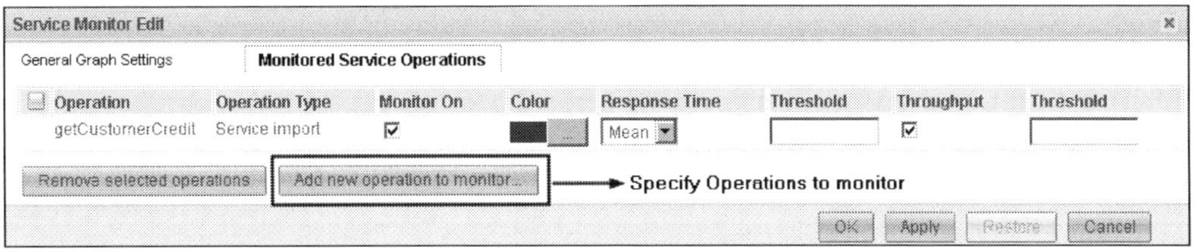

Monitoring with Problem Determination Space

Using the problem determination space in Business Space, you can track the health of the overall system and also the administrative artifacts that comprise a module (queues, messaging engines, data sources, servers, and clusters, to name just a few).

You can do this by creating a space within Business Space using the predetermined problem determination template provided by WPS to monitor the health of your solution. This space has all the necessary widgets needed. As shown in the following screenshot, for a given module, you can find information including which applications are running, topology status, queue depth, messaging engines status, failed events, and so on. You can use this information to determine which part of your solution is not responding and act appropriately.

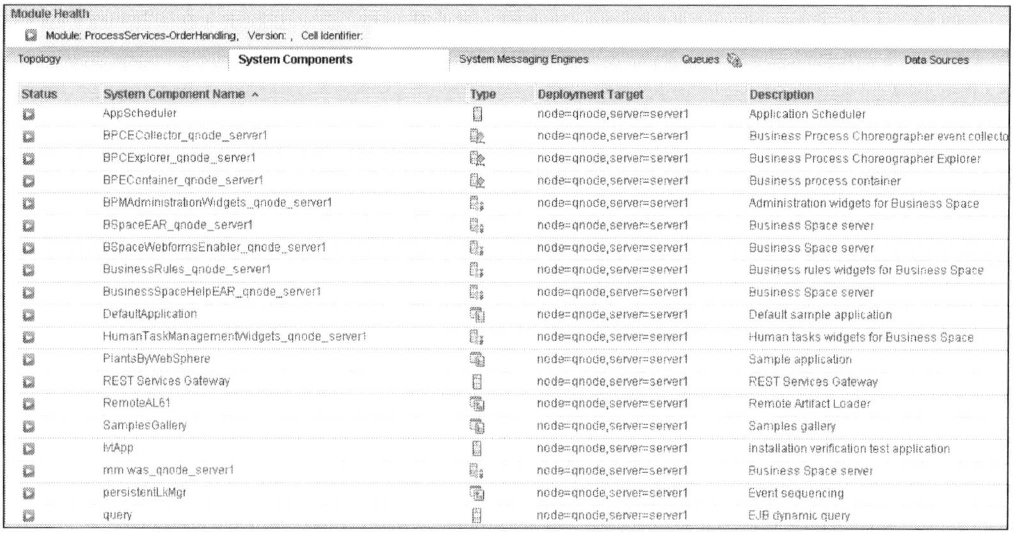

Status	System Component Name	Type	Deployment Target	Description
	AppScheduler		node=qnode,server=server1	Application Scheduler
	BPCECollector_qnode_server1		node=qnode,server=server1	Business Process Choreographer event collecto
	BPCExplorer_qnode_server1		node=qnode,server=server1	Business Process Choreographer Explorer
	BPEContainer_qnode_server1		node=qnode,server=server1	Business process container
	BPMAdministrationWidgets_qnode_server1		node=qnode,server=server1	Administration widgets for Business Space
	BSpaceEAR_qnode_server1		node=qnode,server=server1	Business Space server
	BSpaceWebformsEnabler_qnode_server1		node=qnode,server=server1	Business Space server
	BusinessRules_qnode_server1		node=qnode,server=server1	Business rules widgets for Business Space
	BusinessSpaceHelpEAR_qnode_server1		node=qnode,server=server1	Business Space server
	DefaultApplication		node=qnode,server=server1	Default sample application
	HumanTaskManagementWidgets_qnode_server1		node=qnode,server=server1	Human tasks widgets for Business Space
	PlantsByWebSphere		node=qnode,server=server1	Sample application
	REST Services Gateway		node=qnode,server=server1	REST Services Gateway
	RemoteAL61		node=qnode,server=server1	Remote Artifact Loader
	SamplesGallery		node=qnode,server=server1	Samples gallery
	ivtApp		node=qnode,server=server1	Installation verification test application
	mm.was_qnode_server1		node=qnode,server=server1	Business Space server
	persistentLkMgr		node=qnode,server=server1	Event sequencing
	query		node=qnode,server=server1	EJB dynamic query

Common Event Infrastructure (CEI) and CBE Browser

As briefly explained in *Chapter 1, Introducing IBM BPM and ESB*, Common Event Infrastructure (CEI) provides the foundation architecture for the management and handling of events produced by business processes. Common Base Event (CBE) specification provides the XML-based format for business events, system events, and performance information. When we implemented the **TrackAndManageCustomerOrder** and **HandleCustomerContactProfiles** BPEL processes, we specified events to be monitored. However, in the business process editor and the human task editor, there are **CEI** and **Audit Log** checkboxes that enable you to choose where to log the generated events. If you select the **CEI** checkbox, business events relating to business processes and inline and standalone human tasks will be generated into the **CEI** data store. If you select the **Audit Log** checkbox, the same business events will also be generated as audit events in the process choreographer database.

It is important to note that unlike audit events that are logged in the process choreographer database, CEI events are generally accessible to all components and event consumers. For this reason, unless you have a specific need to work with audit events, it is recommended that you enable the generation and monitoring of CEI events rather than audit events.

You launch the **Common Base Event Browser** from WID by right-clicking on the **UTE server** and selecting **Administration | Common Base Event Browser** from the context menu. From here, you can view the defined events that may include logging, tracing, management, and business events from the event database.

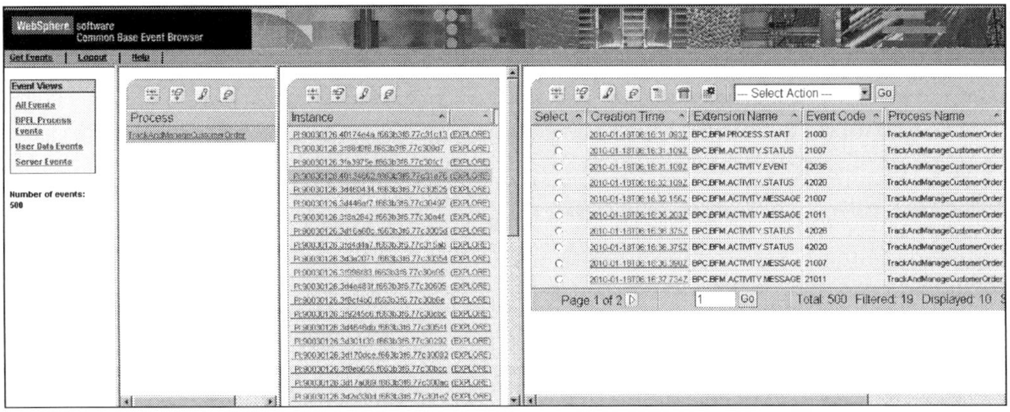

Here is a summary of the tools and capabilities provided by WPS/WESB, other external capabilities/tools that you would need, and what to use from the perspective of visibility.

Tools	Capabilities
Overall System/ Server Health	Standard logs (system out, system error)
	OS/Hardware monitoring software
	Database monitoring software
	JVMPI (Java Virtual Machine Profiler Interface)
	Admin console
	JMX Beans
	ITCAM for WebSphere
	Business Space—problem determination space
Module Health	Common Business Events (CBEs)
	Logging API
	Failed Event Management (FEM)
	BPC Explorer
	Business Space—problem determination space
Services Health and Performance	Logging API (instrumentation)
	Logging and Tracing in the WAS
	Admin console
	Business Space—service monitor space
	ITCAM for SOA
Diagnostic Information	Logging API (instrumentation)
	Logging and tracing in the admin console
	Cross Component Trace (**XCT**). XCT analyzes local or remote logs. XCT defaults to the server console of the running WebSphere Test Environment (WTE).
	First-failure data capture (FFDC)
	IBM Log Analyzer
	IBM Support Assistant
Business Process/Activity Performance	CEI and CBE Browser
	BPC Explorer
	WebSphere Business Monitor

Words of wisdom — tips, tricks, suggestions, and pitfalls

- Make use of IBM Support Assistant (ISA) Lite to quickly collect diagnostic files such as logfiles and configuration files or to run traces. For more information, refer to

  `http://www-01.ibm.com/software/support/isa/download.html`

- Analyze and monitor the WPS/WESB logs (system out, system err) regularly. You can consider using a tool like IBM Log Analyzer. For more information about analyzing the logs, refer to

  `http://www-01.ibm.com/support/docview.wss?uid=swg21330148` or AWStats (`http://awstats.sourceforge.net/`)

- Incorporate Audit (in places where a state change is involved or when identifying and recording the requestor) and Logging (with right levels) to log the detailed information about events, exceptions, warnings, and so on, into a logfile or a queue.
- Use tracing wisely to record any information that could be useful in debugging problems with your code. When you turn diagnostics on, it affects system performance and usability of the logs.
- Avoid using System.out.
- Consider using the in-memory buffer such that trace can be created in memory, and only dumped when required.
- Encourage the use of Cross Component Trace (XCT).
- Consider the Tivoli Composite Application Manager for WebSphere for real-time problem detection, analysis, and repair to help maintain the availability and performance of on demand applications.
- Consider the Tivoli Composite Application Manager for SOA for infrastructure management, which offers integrated management tools that speed and simplify identification and resolution of SOA problems.
- For comprehensive Business Activity Monitoring (BAM), consider using IBM WebSphere Business Monitor

Summary

In this chapter, we discussed how to perform some of the most common solution administration tasks including how to use the admin console and various activities we can perform using it. We discussed how to use the admin console, enable server and application security, install and manage modules, manage users and groups, configure resources, and also troubleshooting. Then we discussed how business space solution and administration space can be used for administering and managing the solution. We briefly discussed about installing versioned SCA modules. Then we moved to discussing how to monitor the applications deployed on WPS/WESB. We saw the different aspects to monitoring, and limited the scope to monitoring the modules deployed on WPS/WESB. We discussed the various tools and capabilities provided in WID/WPS/WESB to monitor the applications and components. We covered how to use BPC Explorer, Business Space, problem determination space, and lastly, an explanation of the fundamentals behind CEI and using the CBE Browser. We hope that by the end of this chapter you have obtained a fairly decent idea of how to manage the WPS/WESB server, applications deployed on it, configuring resources, and monitoring using the various tools provided.

WID, WPS, and WESB Tips, Tricks, and Pointers

After a long journey, we are finally coming to the end of this book. We have successfully built the SOA-based Sales Fulfillment Application, designed a deployment topology for it and also addressed management and monitoring of the same. We addressed several topics, capabilities, and features of WID, WPS, and WESB; however, there are always advanced topics and specific how-tos that you may be interested in. While there are several sources available to go and hunt for this information, what if you had some of the most important ones listed concisely? This chapter will be a random yet useful collection of typical questions, how-tos, and tips on different topics when developing with WID, WPS, and WESB. In this chapter, we will cover some of the most common questions related to:

- WID development tooling and the unit test environment
- Working with Imports/Exports
- Managing and administering the runtime

This chapter is meant to be a quick reference where we scratch the surface of some advanced topics that warrant a book by itself. We aim to provide you with the right pointers so that you can get to the appropriate information and not have to search for it.

Any suggested method to backup WID?

WID as such will have to be backed up using tools like Norton Ghost, which allows you to create full system backups and to restore from system failures. But there may be cases where your WID test environment profiles can get corrupted. The practical suggestion to back WID profiles would be to use the **manageprofiles** utility. The `manageprofiles` command-line tool allows you to not only create a new profile, but also to back up and restore profiles. A profile backup does a file system backup of the entire profile directory (not just the XML configuration) and the profile metadata from the profile registry file. To back up a profile, stop the server to be backed up and issue the following command (by switching to the `<WID_HOME>\runtimes\ bi_v7_stub\bin` folder or `<WPS_HOME>/bin`)

```
manageprofiles(.bat)(.sh) -backupProfile -profileName profile_name
-backupFile backupFile_name -username user_name -password password
```

The following message is displayed:

INSTCONFSUCCESS: Success: The profile backup operation was successful.

Please note that, you must first stop the server and the running processes for the profile that you want to back up. For more information on `manageprofiles`, refer to:

`http://publib.boulder.ibm.com/infocenter/dmndhelp/v7r0mx/topic/com.ibm.websphere.wps.doc/doc/rins_manageprofiles_parms.html`

Restoring a profile from a backup

Backed up profiles can be restored using the `-restoreProfile` option. To restore a profile from a backup, perform the following steps:

1. Make sure the server is stopped.
2. Manually delete the directory for the profile from the filesystem.
3. Run the `-validateAndUpdateRegistry` option of the `manageprofiles` command.

Restore the profile by using the `-restoreProfile` option of the `manageprofiles` command (by switching to the `<WID_HOME>\runtimes\ bi_v7_stub\bin` folder or `<WPS_HOME>/bin`).

```
manageprofiles(.bat)(.sh) -restoreProfile profile_name -backupFile
backupFile_name
```

Increasing WID's heap size

See the following link for more information on this:

`http://wiki.eclipse.org/FAQ_How_do_I_increase_the_heap_size_available_to_Eclipse%3F`

> To interactively update the JVM Maximum Heap Size, please refer to the following blog article:
>
> `http://soatipsntricks.wordpress.com/2006/11/14/interactively-update-the-jvm-maximum-heap-size/`

How to add projects and libraries as dependencies in WID?

1. Right-click on the project for which you would want to add dependent libraries or other projects and choose the **Dependency Editor**. The **Unresolved Projects** section will show which are the unresolved projects or libraries that you may be missing.
2. Add the relevant Libraries (under the **Libraries** section), **Java** or **J2EE** projects (under **Java** or **J2EE** sections respectively), as shown in the following screenshot:

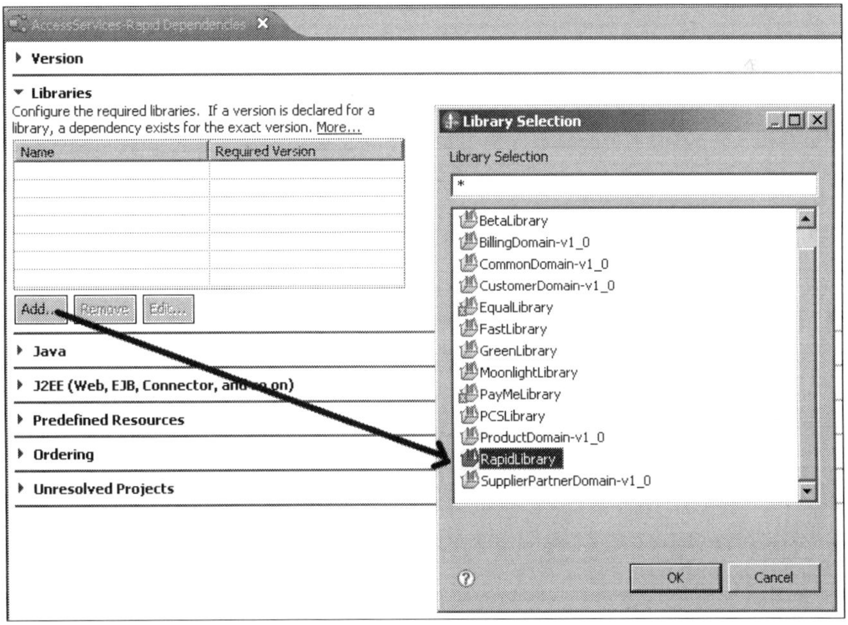

How to reset a profile within WID?

Sometimes it may be necessary and required to reset a profile within WID—especially after applying a fix pack on the unit test server. Resetting a profile is equivalent to the deletion and (re)creation of the profile. To reset a profile, right-click on the desired server from within the **Servers** view and select **Manage Server Profiles**. This will bring up the **Manage the Server Profiles** window from which you can choose to reset the selected server, as shown and highlighted in the following screenshot:

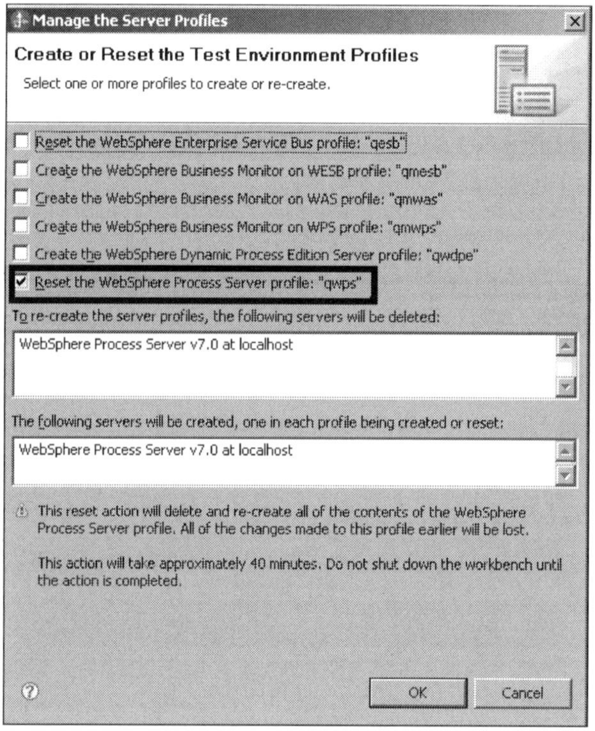

How to change the level of Web Services Interoperability (WS-I) compliance?

In WID, go to **Preferences** | **Service Policies** to set the level of WS-I compliance. For each of the profiles listed, you can select from three levels of compliance with WS-I specifications:

1. Require WS-I compliance—this level prevents you until the WSDL or Web Service is complaint with WS-I specification.
2. Suggest WS-I compliance—this level allows you to create a non-compliant WSDL or Web service, but provides a visible warning stating how the service is non-compliant.
3. Ignore WS-I compliance—as the name states, this option does not notify you of non-compliance.

How to change the type of your business process?

If you want to change a business process component from type **Long-running** to a **Microflow** (or vice versa), click on an empty area of the business process editor canvas, click the **Details** tab in the **Properties** area, and click the **Refactor to Microflow** link (as shown in the following screenshot).

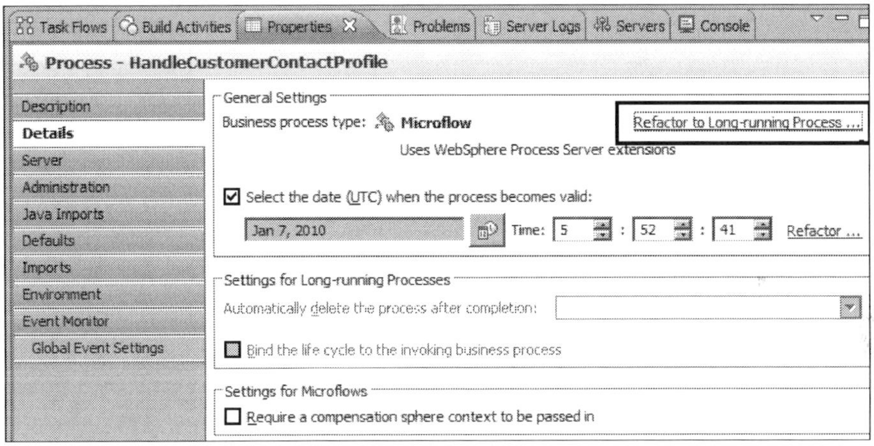

How to get the list of ports the server uses for connections?

To view the communication ports for a server, you can use the admin console. In the admin console, click **Servers** | **Application Servers** | **<server_name>** | **Communications** | **Ports**. This page displays only when you are working with ports for application servers.

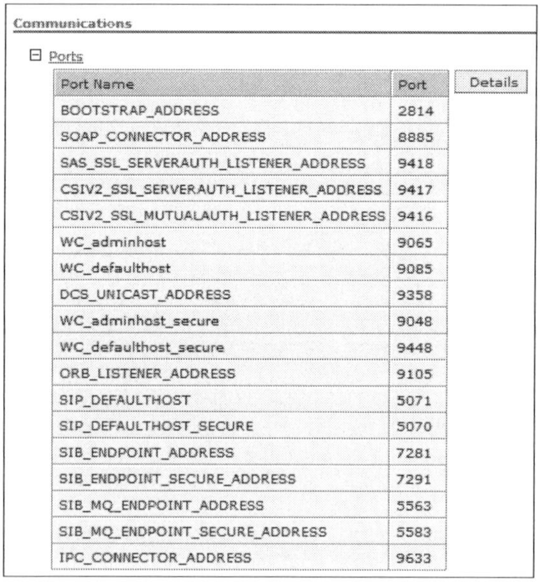
Communications

Ports

Port Name	Port
BOOTSTRAP_ADDRESS	2814
SOAP_CONNECTOR_ADDRESS	8885
SAS_SSL_SERVERAUTH_LISTENER_ADDRESS	9418
CSIV2_SSL_SERVERAUTH_LISTENER_ADDRESS	9417
CSIV2_SSL_MUTUALAUTH_LISTENER_ADDRESS	9416
WC_adminhost	9065
WC_defaulthost	9085
DCS_UNICAST_ADDRESS	9358
WC_adminhost_secure	9048
WC_defaulthost_secure	9448
ORB_LISTENER_ADDRESS	9105
SIP_DEFAULTHOST	5071
SIP_DEFAULTHOST_SECURE	5070
SIB_ENDPOINT_ADDRESS	7281
SIB_ENDPOINT_SECURE_ADDRESS	7291
SIB_MQ_ENDPOINT_ADDRESS	5563
SIB_MQ_ENDPOINT_SECURE_ADDRESS	5583
IPC_CONNECTOR_ADDRESS	9633

Details

Various tools and associated URLs that we should be aware of and bookmark

WPS provides several administrative and management tools. Here is a concise list of the tools and URLs you need to be aware of:

Integrated Solutions Console or admin console	https://<server IP>:<port:>/admin (For example, https://localhost:9048/admin)
Business Space	https://<server IP>:<port>/BusinessSpace (For example, https://localhost:9448/BusinessSpace)
Business Process Choreographer Explorer	https://<server IP>:<port>/bpc (For example, https://localhost:9448/bpc/)
Common Base Event Browser	https://<server IP>:<port>/ibm/console/cbebrowser (For example, https://localhost:9048/ibm/console/cbebrowser)
Business Rules Manager	https://<server IP>:<port>/br (For example, https://localhost:9448/br/)
Failed Event Manager	https://<server IP>:<port:>/admin (For example, https://localhost:9048/admin)

All of the preceding tools are web-based utilities and can be launched from WID. Right-click on your **Server** | **Launch**. The tool will be launched within WID itself.

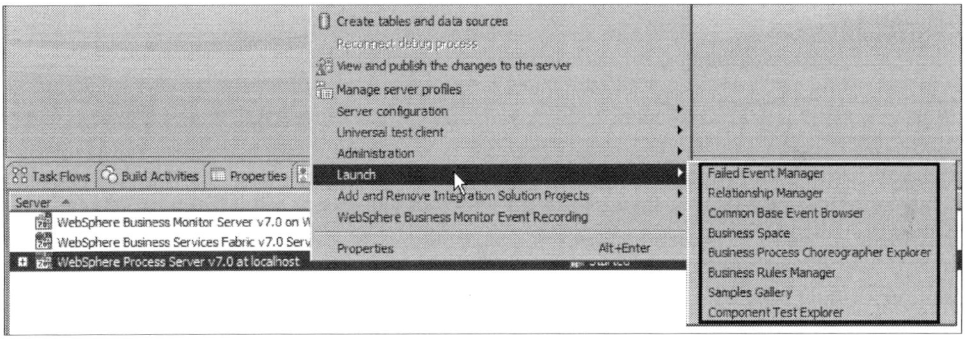

Checking the version of the WPS or WESB server

1. Open the admin console with a browser. The default URL of the admin console is typically https://localhost:9048/admin. Your URL will depend on how many profiles you created post the WID installation.
2. From the welcome screen, click on the **WebSphere Process Server** hyperlink, which will display the server version level, as shown in the following screenshot:

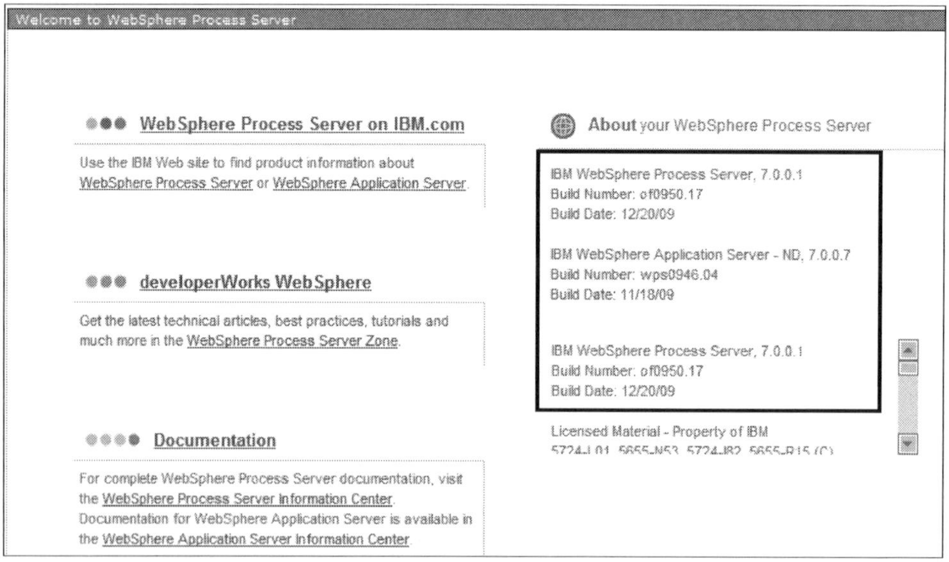

How to list all defined profiles on a WPS server?

Using the command (from <WID_HOME>\runtimes\ bi_v7_stub\bin or <WPS INSTALL ROOT>/bin folder) will give you the list of existing profiles.

```
manageprofiles -listProfiles
```

What is the difference between backing up admin configuration and profile backup?

WPS or WESB server represents their administrative configurations as XML files. Typically, you should regularly back up these configuration files using `backupConfig` and `restoreConfig` commands. Also when restoring the configuration, you will have to make sure the level of the release, including fixes, matches the release to which you are restoring exactly.

The `manageprofiles` command-line tool allows you to not only create a new profile, but also to back up and restore profiles. A profile backup does a filesystem backup of the entire profile directory (not just the XML configuration) and the profile metadata from the profile registry file. The server to be backed up has to be stopped prior to backup using the `manageprofiles` command. For example, usage of this command would be:

```
manageprofiles(.bat)(.sh) -backupProfile -profileName profile_name
-backupFile backupFile_name
```

The administrator user ID and password to log in to the administrative console

The administrator user ID is defined and set by the WebSphere system administrator. The username used is typically admin and the default password (unless changed during installation time) is admin.

The recommended WPS deployment topology

Every client, every solution, and every application built using WPS/WESB is different. No two solutions will be the same for the most part. Hence the selection of deployment topology is dependent on various factors including non-functional requirements, functional requirements, and so on. We discussed these in detail in *Chapter 12, Deployment Topologies*. But for the most part a Gold Topology—Remote Messaging and Remote Support is recommended.

Turning off IBM-specific BPEL Extension

As explained in the earlier chapters, when building a business process (BPEL), the business process type by itself can either be a **Microflow** or a **Long-running process**. A **Microflow** contains IBM's extension to the BPEL specifications. If you do not want to use these IBM extensions, then you cannot make the process a microflow. You can enable the extensions by clearing the **Disable WebSphere Process Server BPEL extensions** checkbox on the **Details** tab of such a process. When you do so, you will be warned that this step cannot be undone. If you proceed, then the **Refactor to Microflow** link is displayed on the **Details** tab and can be used to convert the process to a **Microflow**.

Deploying modules with libraries by reference

By default, when you export a module for deployment from WID, modules bring along a copy of the library. If the library is used as a dependency in different modules, each of these modules will contain a copy of the library. In the Library Dependency editor, if you look at the **Sharing across Runtime Environments** section, you have two radio buttons to choose from:

1. **Global** (by reference)
2. **Module** (by copy)

If you want the library to be deployed as a shared/global library, select the first radio button. You need to do this for each library in the workspace. When you export the module, the libraries will be exported as individual `JAR` files and the module as `EAR`, of course. Please note if you choose the first option, you need to set up the shared libraries. Refer to this link:

`http://www-01.ibm.com/support/docview.wss?rs=2307&uid=swg21322617`

How to create versioned modules and libraries?

Versioning allows you to identify snapshots in the lifecycle of a solution, service, or component in the runtime environment, and to be able to concurrently run multiple snapshots at the same time in a runtime environment. So what can be versioned in WID, WPS, and WESB?

- A module can have a version number.
- SCA export bindings in a module. SCA bindings inherit their version information from the module they are associated with.
- SCA imports can specify a target version number.

> SCA import/export bindings are the only bindings that are version-aware.

- Library can be versioned. Modules that use a library have a dependency on a specific version of that library, and libraries can also have dependencies on specific versions of other libraries.
- Business processes.
- Human tasks.
- State machines.

Versioning allows you to simultaneously deploy multiple versions of an SCA module to the same deployment environment. For example, if you have updated the **TrackAndManageCustomerOrder** business process, you can modify this process without modifying its consumers. The existing consumers will be able to seamlessly pick up the newest version of the process the moment it becomes effective. You can also have several versions of the same process co-exist on the server so that long-running processes can complete without interruption.

You can create versioned modules and libraries in WID, and these versions are for use on the server at runtime, not for distinguishing levels of completion in a development environment. By default, versioning is not enabled in WID.

> Enabling versioning on the module or library results in a new side file containing the version metadata—`sca.module.attributes` or `sca.library.attributes`.

In WID, to enable versioning so that all newly-created modules and libraries have versioning by default, go to **Window Preferences** | **Business Integration** | **Module And Library Versions** and select the **IBM Supplied Version Scheme** from the drop-down list. Note that you can also choose the **IBM Supplied Version Scheme** from the Dependency editor, as outlined in the following steps.

In WID, to enable versioning on an existing module or library, open the particular module's or library's Dependency editor and expand the **Version** section. As shown in the following screenshot, click on the drop-down arrow, select **IBM Supplied Version Scheme**, and enter a version number for the module or library as required (the default scheme uses three numbers for version, release, and modification).

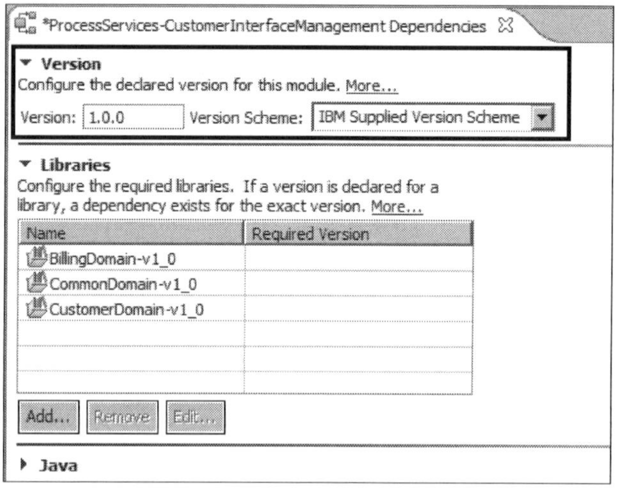

Exporting a versioned SCA Module from WID for server deployment

A versioned SCA module must be exported from WID specifying **Command line service deployment**. Exporting as `EAR` will result in a non-version-aware `EAR`, just as if you had not enabled versioning. To export a module:

Right-click on it, and select **Export** | **Business Integration** | **Integration modules and libraries**. Proceed with the wizard by clicking on the **Next** button.

1. Select the appropriate modules in the list.
2. Choose the **Command line service deployment** option.

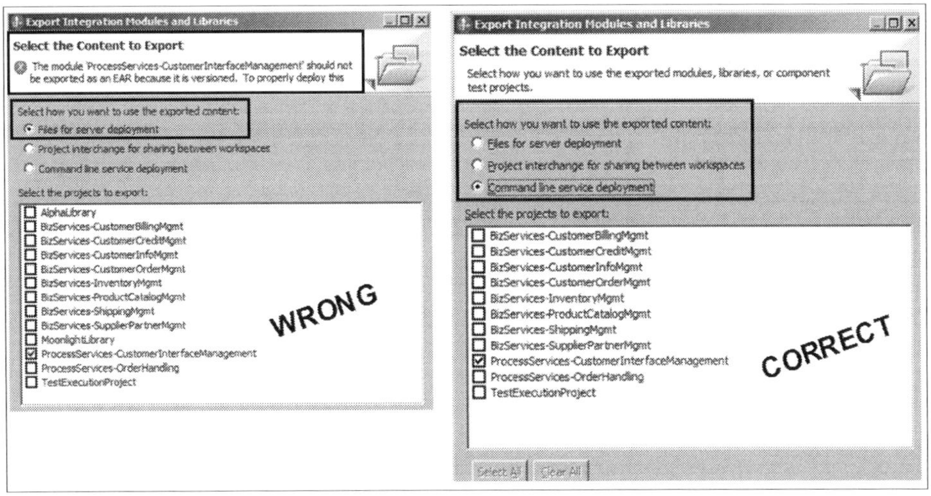

3. Select the target directory where you want to export the `EAR` files and complete the wizard.

Some considerations or practices to adopt when dealing with versioned modules

Versioning scheme is: version.release.modification (such as, 1.0.0).

1. The initial version of a module has a default value of **1.0.0**. Do not change this if not necessary.
2. Version all libraries.
3. Every version of the module should be version controlled in CVS or IBM ClearCase.
4. Versioning scheme is: version.release.modification (such as, 1.0.0).
    - Update version value when:
        - Changes are incompatible with the prior version.
        - Examples can be interface and/or operation signature changed, operation removed from interface, added a required attribute to a BO, and so on.
    - Update release value when:
        - Changes being made are compatible with the prior version.
        - Examples can be operation added to interface or optional attribute added to BO.

- Update modification value when:
    - Changes being made are internal changes only.
    - Examples include changes that have no effect on the interface, operation, or BO, performance improvements in code, and implementation changes that are internal only.

5. WID WTE is not version-aware. Remove the module from the WTE before working with another version of the module with the same WTE (server) instance.
6. Non-SCA import/export bindings are not version-aware, so must be changed manually. So when using JMS/MQ bindings, the queue names must be unique between SCA module versions. When using SOAP HTTP bindings, endpoint names must be unique between SCA module versions.
7. If the module contains BPEL processes that use late binding, you need to update the **validFrom** value. If the module contains BPEL processes that do not use late binding, you need to rename and refactor the process component. For BPEL-based components (processes, state machines), the BPEL database uses the component name and **validFrom** value as the unique key. To avoid conflicts, the combination of these two parts must be unique among module versions. If the process is not using late binding, the component name alone is the unique key.

   For more information on module versioning in WPS, refer to

   `http://publib.boulder.ibm.com/infocenter/dmndhelp/v7r0mx/topic/com.ibm.wbit.help.basics.doc/newapp/topics/tcrtvers.html`

Recommended practices when working in a team environment or when performing team programming

WID provides the capability for a team of developers to develop applications in a team environment and share resources with a central repository.

Using the plugins provided by WID, you can connect to software configuration management repositories like CVS, Rational ClearCase, or other repositories. While the Business Integration perspective and view provides a logical view of the resources within a module, mediation module, and library, the physical files and artifacts themselves can be stored in a repository such as CVS or ClearCase. Some of the recommended practices to adopt when working in a team environment include:

1. Before starting work on any module, synchronize with the repository.
2. When you have completed the implementation of a particular component and are ready to check in the module (or library), synchronize with the repository first and accept all incoming changes. Make sure that there are no conflicts. Update and commit changes. Give verbose comments to what were the changes/additions/fixes addressed and so on.
3. If you want to tag versions to a module or library, you can use the following versioning scheme: version.release.modification (such as, 1.0.0).
4. If you check out any tagged version, you will have to switch back to the HEAD trunk to conduct normal business with WID.
5. Avoid concurrent development and merge scenarios `http://publib.boulder.ibm.com/infocenter/dmndhelp/v6r2mx/topic/com.ibm.wbit.620.help.addev.doc/topics/cshare.html`.
6. Work in the Business Integration view where possible.
7. After moving to a new workspace, be cautious of adding new files to source control.
8. Derived flag can be lost after importing the files into a new workspace (`https://bugs.eclipse.org/bugs/show_bug.cgi?id=150578`).

Performing team programming with CVS

Refer to the following link:

`http://publib.boulder.ibm.com/infocenter/dmndhelp/v7r0mx/topic/org.eclipse.platform.doc.user/concepts/concepts-26.htm`

Stopping and starting process templates with the admin console

You can use the admin console to start and stop each installed process template individually. These will be in cases where you do not want to allow anyone to create any process instances of a particular process template. Here are the steps to stop/start a process template:

1. Log in into the admin console.
2. Navigate to the module that contains the process template—**Applications | SCA modules | module_name**.
3. In the **Configuration** page and under **Additional Properties**, click on **Business processes** and **process template**.
4. Stop/Start the **process template**.

tranLog

WPS and WESB uses the transaction log, and the tranlog directory contains all the files that hold the record details of transactions that are managed by WAS (which is the underlying transaction manager for WPS). Deleting the transaction logfile can cause inconsistencies in active BPEL processes that participate in a transaction. The case is the same for a development environment also.

See the following link for more information:

`http://www-01.ibm.com/support/docview.wss?rs=2307&uid=swg21316028`

Enabling and disabling Cross-Component Trace settings

Cross-Component Tracing allows you to identify the `trace.log` data that is associated with modules and components. The data can include error and event information, such as corrupted data or runtime exceptions, captured during SCA processing. The input and output data passing between components can also be captured and used for problem determination in WID. See the following link for more information on how to use it:

`http://publib.boulder.ibm.com/infocenter/ieduasst/v1r1m0/topic/com.ibm.iea.wpi_v6/wpswid/6.2/WID/WBPMv62_WID_Cross-ComponentTraceLab.pdf`

Use of global variables in a forEach within a BPEL process

In a business process, a forEach activity is very useful in cases where you want to interact with a set of partners in parallel, and the partners are dynamically determined at runtime. When using forEach in its parallel mode, be very careful when changing variables that are global (created outside the scope of the forEach). There is no semantics of what order parallel branches get executed in. What this means in reality is that when the parallel branches of the forEach execute, if they are assigned to global variables, there is no definition of which order those assignments will get executed in.

With scope isolation, WS-BPEL 2.0 allows you to control the access of global data. If a scope's isolated attribute is set to 'yes', then it is guaranteed that there will be no concurrent access to the global data that the scope is referencing while the scope executes. For a very informative article on the usage of the forEach activity, available attributes, and typical usage patterns with code snippets, please refer to the following article:

```
http://www-01.ibm.com/support/docview.wss?rs=2307&context=SSQH9M&uid=
swg27011753
```

Enabling event monitoring in WID

In *Chapter 9, Building the Order Handling Processes*, we discussed and demonstrated how to use the event monitor to enable (or disable) event generation and monitoring. The event monitor is accessible from the properties page of the assembly editor and the business process editor. You should ensure that you have configured WPS/WESB to support the monitoring and logging of business process and human task events. Refer to the following link for more information:

```
http://publib.boulder.ibm.com/infocenter/dmndhelp/v6rxmx/index.
jsp?topic=/com.ibm.wbit.help.cei.ui.doc/topics/tprep.html
```

Using DynaCache to improve the performance of your WPS or WESB solution?

Refer to the following URL:

```
http://www.ibm.com/developerworks/websphere/tutorials/0912_telerman/
index.html
```

What is the difference between Shared context, Correlation context, and Transient context? When to use which?

	Definition	When to use?
Shared context	Thread-based memory location shared across all instances of the SMO running within the same thread for the request or response flow.	Used typically in a fan-out/fan-in aggregation to temporarily store service responses.
Correlation context	Used when Mediation primitives want to pass values from the request flow to the response flow.	Used to pass values from the request message onto the response.
Transient context	Used for passing values between Mediation primitives within the current flow—either the request flow or the response flow. The transient context cannot link requests and responses and hence cannot be used across.	Used when you want to save an input message before a service invokes call (within a request or response flow). After the service invoke call, the next primitive can create another message by combining the service invoke response and the original message stored in the transient context.

What is WID history logging?

History logging is primarily meant to aid debugging during development and also help IBM support people when working on issues. It's a capability that is configurable in WID (turned on by default) whose intent is to gather, at a coarse level, just enough information so that we can have a good idea of the steps that a user took that led to an error. Rotating logs are written in the user's workspace `.metadata` directory and are named `widHistory_n.log`. These logs are viewable in the **Server Logs** view within WID by navigating to the workspace and loading the logfiles from the workspace `.metadata` directory. To view the configurable properties, open **WID** | **Preferences** | **Business Integration** | **Logging and Tracing**, as shown in the following screenshot:

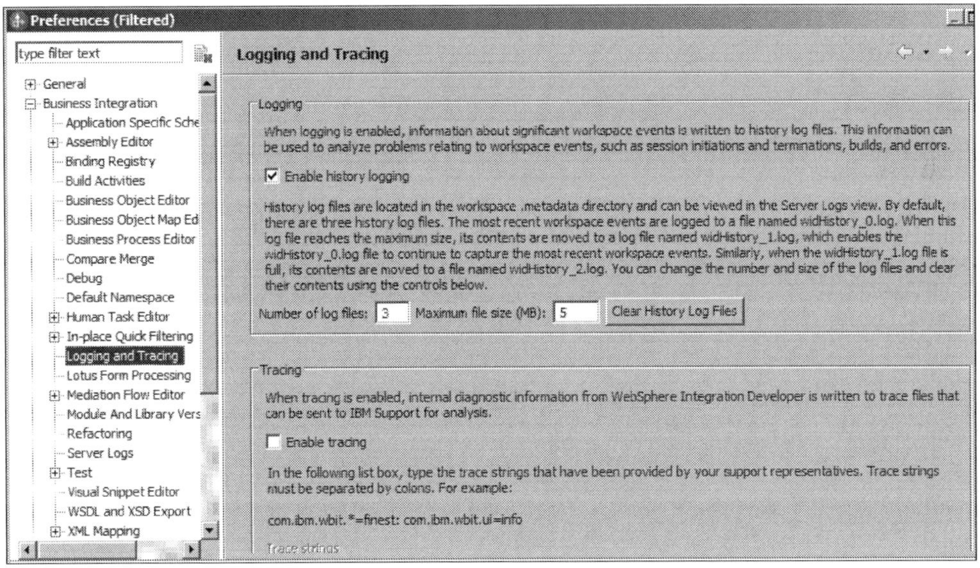

There are various aspects that get logged in the history logs and are viewable through the WID **Server Logs** view. As shown in the following screenshot, when a history log is loaded, the aspects name appears in the content area, and these names can be filtered using the content filter of the **Server Logs** view. These include:

- **GeneralUI**—shows WID start/end, view, or if editor is opened/activated/closed.
- **BUILD**—shows build-related activities (incremental and clean).
- **REFACTOR**—shows refactoring start/stop and what is being refactored.

- **SERVER**—shows server initialization, state change for server and module on a server start, details about port, connection information, modules deployed to server, and so on.
- **PUBLISH**—shows publish start/stop, publish type, and type of publish (added, changed, removed), and publish time.
- **INTEGRATED TEST CLIENT**—shows server starts, modules added and published to the server, waits for modules to start, and how a server start or publish originated.
- **MIGRATE**—shows files migrated to WID.
- **FROM_ECLIPSE_ERROR_LOG**—shows errors that appear in the Eclipse error log, that is, the **Error Log** view. These errors indicate the workspace state when the error occurred.

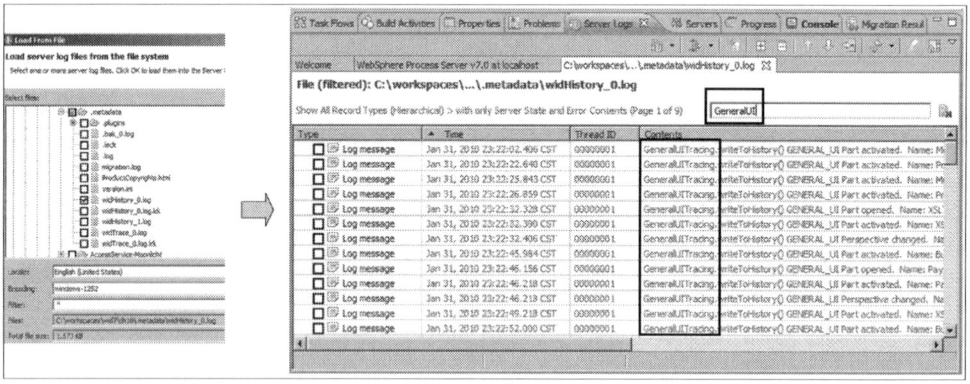

WID Tracing

Tracing in WID is switched off by default. Rotating logs are written in the user's workspace `.metadata` directory and are named `widTrace_n.log`. These files are viewable through the WID **Server Logs** view. You can turn it on and must specify components that should be traced. You must specify the Trace string and example including:

```
com.ibm.*=finest would trace all.
com.ibm.wbit.*=finest: com.ibm.wbit.ui=info
```

Tracing levels can be one of fine, finer, finest, info, warning, or error. Any changes made are immediate—no need to restart WID.

BPEL or Mediation Flows — which and when to choose?

For a detailed write up, refer to:

`http://www.ibm.com/developerworks/websphere/library/techarticles/0803_fasbinder2/0803_fasbinder2.html`

Some common business process implementation types and when to use them

Some of the common implementation types of business process that can be implemented using WPS include:

- GUI-intensive process:
    - Navigational flow and data aggregation is controlled from a user interface layer rather than in a BPEL process in WPS.
    - WPS not involved in process navigation, but may be used to provide swiftly-responding synchronous services.
    - Use for cases where a GUI application performs the process orchestration or control.
- Synchronous transactional process:
    - A slight extension to the GUI intensive process type. A collection of short-running BPEL processes provide real-time responses to graphical user interfaces or for transactional sub-processes.
    - Transactional and therefore must complete within the global timeout. No state is persisted by the process.
    - Errors are typically translated for clarity and then passed back to the caller.
    - Use for cases when you need high performance and the caller needs a response immediately.

- Asynchronously initiated transactional process:
    - Caller transaction is minimal and just makes a request but does not wait for a response. Process is assured to occur at a later time in a separate transaction.
    - The caller seeks feedback through notifications or e-mail.
    - Error handling more complex than a simple synchronous transactional process, since the caller is no longer present to take action.
    - Used for cases when you need high performance and a caller does not need a response immediately, but only an acknowledgement.
- Briefly persisted process:
    - A special use of a long-running process where the process completes relatively swiftly. Process lifespan is deliberately short (seconds, maybe minutes), such that process versioning issues can be avoided.
    - The process must be designed to complete in a timely fashion, so no human tasks are allowed and error handling actions should be passed and pushed out of the process (may not receive in-process events).
    - Allows parallel processing, so good for aggregation. This is one of the most common motivations for this usage type.
    - Careful thought must be put to the the error handling implications of this multi-transactional scenario.
    - A synchronous transactional process is always preferable, if at all possible. For briefly persisted processes, persistence adds a significant overhead and the error handling is much more complex.
    - Used for cases where the process will take a long time (more than the runtime transaction timeout) and a process instance can be flushed through to enable simple maintenance.
- Versioned long-lived process:
    - It is a true long-running process that will last a relatively long time (days, weeks, and so on). Process instances will always be present in the systems such that the complex issues of process versioning must be taken into account.

  - Can contain human tasks and complex error handling such as compensation.
  - May receive in-process events which need to contain sufficient information to be correlated with the existing process instance.
  - Invocation typically does not provide a response and late-binding techniques need to be well understood.
  - Activities can be set to wait for manual intervention on error.
  - Use for cases where the process will take a long time (more than the runtime transaction timeout) and process contains external system interactions.
- Task-based process:
  - Used to balance multiple tasks between a number of different users, possibly in different teams/departments.
  - Necessitates long-lived processes, and hence must consider process versioning issues.
  - Allows progressive automation of tasks.
  - This is a very broad category still and can be broken into four sub-types:
    - Structured Workflow
    - Case Handling
    - User Modeled
    - Pageflow
  - Used for cases where the process will take a long time (more than the runtime transaction timeout) and contains human interactions.

Seeing WPS data in a Derby DB

Refer to:

`http://www.ibm.com/developerworks/forums/servlet/JiveServlet/download/820-204851-14082706-321856/How_to_see_WPS_data_in_a_Derby_DB.pdf`

Miscellaneous Snippet Topics

- The Requires Own option on a BPEL activity is used to prevent a retry of the previous activities in case of an error.
- When a business process calls a one-way service asynchronously, a failed event is generated in case of a runtime exception in the called component.
- To restrict who can start a business process when using the BusinessFlowManager API to start the process, add a human task assigned to the designated group of potential starters on the Authorization tab of the respective receive activity.

In a long-running BPEL, you will uncheck the **Enable persistence and queries of business relevant data** flag on an Invoke activity to improve performance by avoiding activity-related data from being persisted to the database.

A notification event handler plugin within a human task is executed during an escalation.

- In a long-running process when you need more than one person involved from a human task perspective, you can use ad-hoc follow-on tasks.
- XPath to access an HTTP SOAP header in a mediation flow/headers/SOAPHeader.
- When the call out Response node's fail terminal is not wired and an unmodeled fault is received, a mediation runtime exception will occur.
- To interact with third-party messaging middleware use the "Generic JMS" binding.
- Typically, you would choose to implement a JCA adapter rather than a Web Service (to an enterprise application) when the end application does not support transactions but a composite application requires assured delivery on all calls to the application.
- Use a receive choice with a timeout element when a long-running business process needs further input from the client for a specified time, and if that time has passed without further user input, default processing should start.

Overriding a Web Service endpoint in a mediation flow

In a mediation flow component, say you have a Web Service import that invokes an external application; you may want to override it because of several reasons (endpoint URL changed, shift to a makeshift endpoint, and so on). While the right solution is to use a service registry like WSRR or use an endpoint lookup primitive, there are ways to override. See the following article for more information.

```
http://soatipsntricks.wordpress.com/2010/01/12/overriding-a-web-
service-endpoint-in-websphere-esb/
```

What is deferred parsing in the context of WESB?

Certain types of mediations have been optimized for WESB and deliver improved performance. This specialized optimization can be regarded as a kind of fast path through the code and is in addition to any general optimization of the WebSphere ESB mediation code. The optimization is known as **deferred parsing**. As the name implies, parsing the message can be deferred until absolutely required, and in several cases, parsing can be avoided altogether.

Some performance tips and considerations

While the question is a simple one, the answer itself is not. Every customer is unique including the physical topology, network topology, requirements, needs, and other application and hardware that make up the ecosystem. Performance tuning is a personalized exercise that is done uniquely with and for the customer. As mentioned several times, WPS and WESB are built on the core capabilities of the WebSphere Application Server infrastructure. Hence solutions built using WPS and WESB also benefit from tuning, configuration, and best practices information for WAS and the corresponding platform JVMs. However, having said this, here are some tips, considerations, and areas to look into for performance improvements:

- Use Microflows wherever possible instead of long-running processes.
- Use a high-performance disk subsystem.

- Use DB2 instead of the default Derby DBMS. DB2 is a high-performing, industrial strength database designed to handle high levels of throughput and concurrency, scale well, and deliver excellent response time.
- Disable tracing and monitoring; use this wisely.
- Configure thread and connection pools to enable sufficient concurrency.
- Avoid unnecessary usages of asynchronous invocations.
- Use events (CBE) with judgment, since it uses a persistence mechanism.
- BPC DB2 Database Tuning:
    - Avoid RUNSTATS on empty tables.
    - Separate the logfiles from the data, put them on their own volumes.
    - Large enough space allocation for logfiles and the log buffer.
    - Make the buffer pool big enough to avoid disk I/O.
    - Set only the monitor switches that are really needed to on.
    - Update optimizer statistics (RUNSTATS) to avoid deadlocks.
- The throughput of the services you build on WPS and WESB will be limited by the external applications and services it will have to invoke which may have a lowest throughput capacity. Design your system taking into consideration these bottlenecks.
- For large object (over 5 MB in general) processing consider batch patterns by splitting the large objects as multiple small objects.
- Consider moving to a 64-bit mode (for server runtime) for applications that are well behaved and liveset exceeds 32-bit memory limitations.
- Cache results of `ServiceManager.locateService()` in your Java code.
- Use synchronous SCA bindings across local modules, since this binding has been optimized for module locality and will outperform other bindings.
- Do not apply a QoS qualifier at the interface level if it is not needed for all operations of the interface.
- When designing long-running business process components, ensure that callers of a two-way (request/response) interface do not use synchronous semantics, as this ties up the caller's resources (thread, transaction, and so on) until the process completes. Instead, such processes should either be invoked asynchronously, or through a one-way synchronous call, where no response is expected.
- Minimize number and size of BPEL variables declared and business objects because each commit saves modified variables to the database.

- The throughput is inversely related to the number of transaction boundaries traversed in the scenario, so fewer transactions are faster.
- In an SCA assembly, we recommend using the SCA transactional qualifiers to reduce transaction boundaries. For any pair of components where this is desired, we recommend using the following golden path:
    - `SuspendTransaction=false`, for the calling component's reference
    - `joinTransaction=true`, for the called component's interface
    - `Transaction=any|global`, for both components implementation
- Components and modules can be wired to each other either synchronously or asynchronously. The choice of interaction style, especially choosing an asynchronous style, can have a profound impact on performance. Use asynchronous style only when needed. Set the preferred interaction style to Sync whenever possible.
- Avoid asynchronous invocation of synchronous services in a fan-out/fan-in block.
- There are three categories of Mediation primitives in WebSphere ESB that benefit to a greater or lesser degree from these internal optimizations:
    - Category 1 (greatest benefit):
        - Route on message header (message filter primitive)
        - XSLT primitive (transforming on /body as the root)
        - Endpoint Lookup without XPath user properties
        - Event emitter (CBE header only)
    - Category 2 (medium benefit):
        - Route on message body (message filter primitive)
    - Category 3 (lowest benefit):
        - Custom Mediation
        - Database lookup
        - Message Element Setter
        - Business Object (BO) mapper
        - Fan-out
        - Fan-in

    - Set message type
    - Message Logger
    - Event Emitter (except for CBE header only)
    - Endpoint Lookup utilising XPath user properties
    - XSLT Primitive (with a non /body root)
- XSLT and BO Maps—In a mediation flow that is eligible for deferred parsing, the XSLT primitive gives better performance than the BO Map primitive. However, in a mediation flow where the message is already being parsed, the BO Map primitive gives better performance than the XSLT primitive. Note that if you are transforming from the `root` (/), then the Business Object map will always perform better.
- Do not run the production server in development mode or with development profile.
- Do not use the UTE for performance measurement.
- Use query tables to optimize query response time.
- Place database logfiles on a fast disk subsystem.
- WID performance considerations:
    - Opt for a faster and high speed disk drive
    - Defragment the drive periodically
    - Make use of shared libraries in order to reduce memory consumption

The difference between testing a module and testing a component

A module, as you know, consists of one or more components and a component may call other components or imports. When you do **Test Component** (by right-clicking on the component) the integration test client tests only the component that was selected. The other components, imports, and exports are emulated, which means that you need to enter values that you want the components, imports, and exports to return.

If a user selects **Test Module**, the integration test client will automatically emulate anything that can't be called including unimplemented components, imports with no bindings, and references that aren't wired.

What are the best forums to get help in WID, WPS, and WESB?

The following IBM developerWorks forums are an excellent place to get help and discuss topics:

- WebSphere Process Server

  `http://www.ibm.com/developerworks/forums/forum.jspa?forumID=820`

- WebSphere Enterprise Service Bus

  `http://www.ibm.com/developerworks/forums/forum.jspa?forumID=1672`

- WebSphere Integration Developer

  `http://www.ibm.com/developerworks/forums/forum.jspa?forumID=821`

- Business Processes with BPEL4WS

  `http://www.ibm.com/developerworks/forums/forum.jspa?forumID=167`

- SOA Tips and tricks

  `http://soatipsntricks.wordpress.com/`

Where can I listen or read up on advanced presentations and Webcasts?

Refer to the following Technical Exchange Webcasts:

`http://www-01.ibm.com/software/websphere/support/supp_tech.html`

What are some useful pointers to articles, IBM redbooks, and other sources for advanced topics related to WID, WPS, and WESB?

WID-related:

- Featured documents for WebSphere Integration Developer

  `http://www-01.ibm.com/support/docview.wss?uid=swg27009453`Service

Component Architecture:

- WebSphere Process Server invocation styles

  http://www.ibm.com/developerworks/websphere/library/techarticles/0811_chacko/0811_chacko.html

- Asynchronous processing in WebSphere Process Server

  http://www.ibm.com/developerworks/websphere/library/techarticles/0904_fong/0904_fong.html

- Exploring WebSphere Process Server transactionality

  http://www.ibm.com/developerworks/websphere/library/techarticles/0906_fasbinder/0906_fasbinder.html

- Webcast replay: Transactions in WebSphere Process Server

  http://www-01.ibm.com/support/docview.wss?uid=swg27017626

- Event sequencing using WebSphere Process Server

  http://www.ibm.com/developerworks/websphere/library/techarticles/0910_wadley/0910_wadley.html

- Developing integration solutions with WebSphere Process Server relationships

  http://www.ibm.com/developerworks/websphere/techjournal/0802_busjaeger/0802_busjaeger.html

Data Translation, mapping, and relationships:

- XML mapping in WebSphere Integration Developer V6.1.2, Part 1: Using the XML Mapping Editor to develop maps

  http://www.ibm.com/developerworks/websphere/library/techarticles/0811_rice/0811_rice.html

- XML mapping in WebSphere Integration Developer V6.1.2, Part 2: Working with complex XML strcuctures

  http://www.ibm.com/developerworks/websphere/library/techarticles/0812_rice/0812_rice.html

- Validating business objects in WebSphere Process Server

  http://www.ibm.com/developerworks/websphere/library/techarticles/0907_xie/0907_xie.html

Human tasks and Business Calendar:

- Human-Centric Business Process Management with WebSphere Process Server V6

  http://www.redbooks.ibm.com/abstracts/sg247477.html?Open

- WebSphere Process Server 6.2: Dynamic Human Workflows—Introduction and Best Practices

  http://www-01.ibm.com/support/docview.wss?uid=swg27016314

- Using WebSphere Process Server business calendars in business processes

  http://www.ibm.com/developerworks/websphere/library/techarticles/0903_khangaonkar/0903_khangaonkar.html

Business rules:

- Extending the power of the WebSphere Process Server business rules component

  http://www.ibm.com/developerworks/websphere/library/techarticles/0905_dinardo/0905_dinardo.html

Business Space and user interfaces:

- Customizing HTML-Dojo forms for Business Space powered by WebSphere

  http://www.ibm.com/developerworks/websphere/techjournal/0810_kreis/0810_kreis.html

- Developing custom widgets using DOJO, Part 1: Generating Dojo markup using a generic markup handler

  http://www.ibm.com/developerworks/websphere/library/techarticles/0912_khanna/0912_khanna.html

- Developing custom widgets for Business Space using Dojo, Part 2: Creating a Dojo DataGrid component using a generic grid handler

  http://www.ibm.com/developerworks/websphere/library/techarticles/1001_khanna/1001_khanna.html

Exception handling:

- IBM WebSphere Process Server Best Practices in Error Prevention Strategies and Solution Recovery

  http://www.redbooks.ibm.com/abstracts/REDP4466.html

- Exception handling in WebSphere Process Server and WebSphere Enterprise Service Bus

  http://www.ibm.com/developerworks/websphere/library/techarticles/0705_fong/0705_fong.html

- Error handling in WebSphere Process Server, Part 1: Developing an error handling strategy

  http://www.ibm.com/developerworks/websphere/library/techarticles/0810_chacko/0810_chacko.html

- BPEL fault handling in WebSphere Integration Developer and WebSphere Process Server

  http://www.ibm.com/developerworks/websphere/library/techarticles/0704_desai/0704_desai.html

Versioning:

- Versioning and dynamicity with WebSphere Process Server

  http://www.ibm.com/developerworks/websphere/library/techarticles/0602_brown/0602_brown.html

- Versioning and dynamicity, Part 1: Creating multiple versions of a business process with WebSphere Process Server

  http://www.ibm.com/developerworks/websphere/library/techarticles/0802_fasbinder/0802_fasbinder.html

- Versioning and dynamicity, Part 2: Applying versioning and process dynamicity using WebSphere Process Server V6.1

  http://www.ibm.com/developerworks/websphere/library/techarticles/0803_fasbinder/0803_fasbinder.html

- Versioning business processes and human tasks in WebSphere Process Server

  http://www.ibm.com/developerworks/websphere/library/techarticles/0808_smolny/0808_smolny.html

Security:

- WebSphere Process Server security overview

  http://www-128.ibm.com/developerworks/websphere/library/techarticles/0602_khangaonkar/0602_khangaonkar.html

Common Event Infrastructure:

- Use Common Event Infrastructure for business-level logging to improve business processes

  http://www-128.ibm.com/developerworks/websphere/library/techarticles/0512_becker/0512_becker.html

Administration and deployment topologies:

- WebSphere Business Process Management V7.0 Production Topologies

  `http://www.redbooks.ibm.com/redpieces/abstracts/sg247854.html?Open`

- Webcast replay: Best Practices for Clustering WebSphere Process Server v6.0.2

  `http://www-01.ibm.com/support/docview.wss?uid=swg27010103`

- Operating a WebSphere Process Server environment, Part 1: Overview

  `http://www.ibm.com/developerworks/websphere/library/techarticles/0912_herrmann1/0912_herrmann1.html`

- Operating a WebSphere Process Server environment, Part 2: Options for maintaining an optimal Business Process Choreographer database size

  `http://www.ibm.com/developerworks/websphere/library/techarticles/0912_herrmann2/0912_herrmann2.html`

- Operating a WebSphere Process Server environment, Part 3: Setup, configuration, and maintenance of the WebSphere Process Server Business Process Choreographer database

  `http://www.ibm.com/developerworks/websphere/library/techarticles/0912_grundler/0912_grundler.html`

Testing:

- Test-driven development in an SOA environment, Part 1: Testing data maps

  `http://www.ibm.com/developerworks/websphere/techjournal/0807_vines/0807_vines.html`

- Test-driven development in an SOA environment, Part 2: Continuous integration with WebSphere Process Server

  `http://www.ibm.com/developerworks/websphere/techjournal/0812_vines/0812_vines.html`

- Taking component testing to the next level in WebSphere Integration Developer

  `http://www.ibm.com/developerworks/websphere/library/techarticles/0806_gregory/0806_gregory.html`

Performance tuning:

- WebSphere Business Process Management V7 Performance Tuning

  `http://www.redbooks.ibm.com/redbooks.nsf/RedpieceAbstracts/redp4664.html?Open`

- Performance Tuning Worksheet for Business Process Choreographer

  `http://www-01.ibm.com/support/docview.wss?uid=swg27011121`

- Database Planning, Performance Tuning and Maintenance for Business Process Choreographer

  `http://www-01.ibm.com/support/docview.wss?uid=swg21419235`

- Endurance testing with WebSphere Process Server V6.1

  `http://www.ibm.com/developerworks/websphere/library/techarticles/0810_gunasekaran/0810_gunasekaran.html`

Problem determination and troubleshooting:

- Problem determination in WebSphere Process Server

  `http://www-128.ibm.com/developerworks/websphere/library/techarticles/0601_tung/0601_tung.html`

WESB- and Messaging-related:

- Developing custom mediations for WebSphere Enterprise Service Bus

  `http://www-128.ibm.com/developerworks/websphere/library/techarticles/0601_daniels/0601_daniels.html`

- IBM WebSphere Developer Technical Journal: Building a powerful, reliable SOA with JMS and WebSphere ESB, Part 1

  `http://www-128.ibm.com/developerworks/websphere/techjournal/0602_tost/0602_tost.html`

- IBM WebSphere Developer Technical Journal: Building a powerful, reliable SOA with JMS and WebSphere ESB, Part 2

  `http://www-128.ibm.com/developerworks/websphere/techjournal/0603_tost/0603_tost.html`

- Designing ESB mediations for deployment to WebSphere Enterprise Service Bus

  `http://www.ibm.com/developerworks/websphere/library/techarticles/0812_chinoda/0812_chinoda.html`

- IBM WebSphere Developer Technical Journal: Building a powerful, reliable SOA with JMS and WebSphere ESB, Part 3

  `http://www-128.ibm.com/developerworks/websphere/techjournal/0604_tost/0604_tost.html`

Advanced Solution Design:

- Workflow Patterns

  http://is.tm.tue.nl/research/patterns/download/wfs-pat-2002.pdf

- Pattern Based Analysis of BPEL4WS

  http://is.tm.tue.nl/research/patterns/download/qut_bpel_rep.pdf

- IBM Advantage for Service Maturity Model Standards

  http://www.ibm.com/developerworks/webservices/library/ws-OSIMM/index.html

- Solution design in WebSphere Process Server, Part 1: What do solutions look like in WebSphere Process Server?

  http://www.ibm.com/developerworks/websphere/library/techarticles/0904_clark/0904_clark.html

- Solution design in WebSphere Process Server and WebSphere ESB, Part 2: Designing an ESB Gateway in WebSphere Process Server and WebSphere ESB

  http://www.ibm.com/developerworks/websphere/library/techarticles/0908_clark/0908_clark.html

Index

Symbols

A

B

C

D

E

N

O

P

Q

R

S

T

U

V

W

X

[PACKT] enterprise
professional expertise distilled
PUBLISHING

Thank you for buying

Application Development for IBM WebSphere Process Server 7 and Enterprise Service Bus 7

About Packt Publishing

Packt, pronounced 'packed', published its first book "Mastering phpMyAdmin for Effective MySQL Management" in April 2004 and subsequently continued to specialize in publishing highly focused books on specific technologies and solutions.

Our books and publications share the experiences of your fellow IT professionals in adapting and customizing today's systems, applications, and frameworks. Our solution based books give you the knowledge and power to customize the software and technologies you're using to get the job done. Packt books are more specific and less general than the IT books you have seen in the past. Our unique business model allows us to bring you more focused information, giving you more of what you need to know, and less of what you don't.

Packt is a modern, yet unique publishing company, which focuses on producing quality, cutting-edge books for communities of developers, administrators, and newbies alike. For more information, please visit our website: `www.packtpub.com`.

About Packt Enterprise

In 2010, Packt launched two new brands, Packt Enterprise and Packt Open Source, in order to continue its focus on specialization. This book is part of the Packt Enterprise brand, home to books published on enterprise software – software created by major vendors, including (but not limited to) IBM, Microsoft and Oracle, often for use in other corporations. Its titles will offer information relevant to a range of users of this software, including administrators, developers, architects, and end users.

Writing for Packt

We welcome all inquiries from people who are interested in authoring. Book proposals should be sent to author@packtpub.com. If your book idea is still at an early stage and you would like to discuss it first before writing a formal book proposal, contact us; one of our commissioning editors will get in touch with you.

We're not just looking for published authors; if you have strong technical skills but no writing experience, our experienced editors can help you develop a writing career, or simply get some additional reward for your expertise.

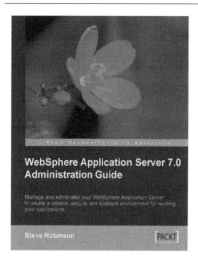

[PACKT] enterprise
PUBLISHING
professional expertise distilled

Middleware Management with Oracle Enterprise Manager Grid Control 10g R5

ISBN: 978-1-847198-34-1 Paperback: 350 pages

Monitor, diagnose, and maximize the system performance of Oracle Fusion Middleware solutions

1. Manage your Oracle Fusion Middleware and non-Oracle middleware applications effectively and efficiently using Oracle Enterprise Manager Grid Conrol
2. Implement proactive monitoring to maximize application performance

---

JDBC 4.0 and Oracle JDeveloper for J2EE Development

ISBN: 978-1-847194-30-5 Paperback: 444 pages

A J2EE developer's guide to using Oracle JDeveloper's integrated database features to build data-driven applications

1. Develop your Java applications using JDBC and Oracle JDeveloper
2. Explore the new features of JDBC 4.0
3. Use JDBC and the data tools in Oracle JDeveloper
4. Configure JDBC with various application servers

Please check **www.PacktPub.com** for information on our titles

[PACKT] enterprise
professional expertise distilled
PUBLISHING

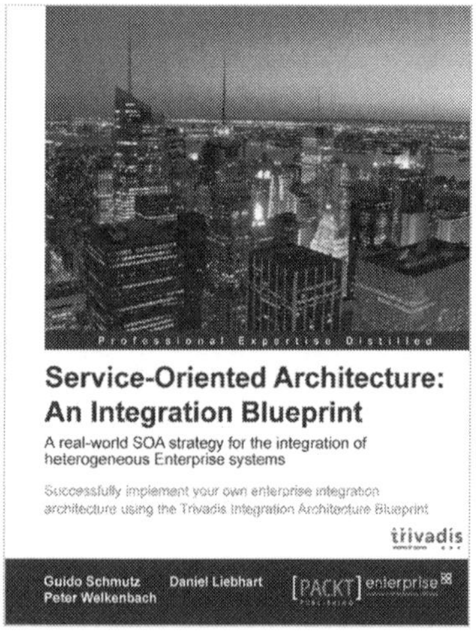

Service Oriented Architecture: An Integration Blueprint

ISBN: 978-1-849681-04-9 Paperback: 240 pages

Successfully implement your own enterprise integration architecture using the Trivadis Integration Architecture Blueprint

1. Discover and understand the structure of existing application landscapes from an integration perspective
2. Get to grips with fundamental integration concepts and terminology while learning about architecture variants
3. Map and compare a variety of different vendor platforms to the blueprint

---

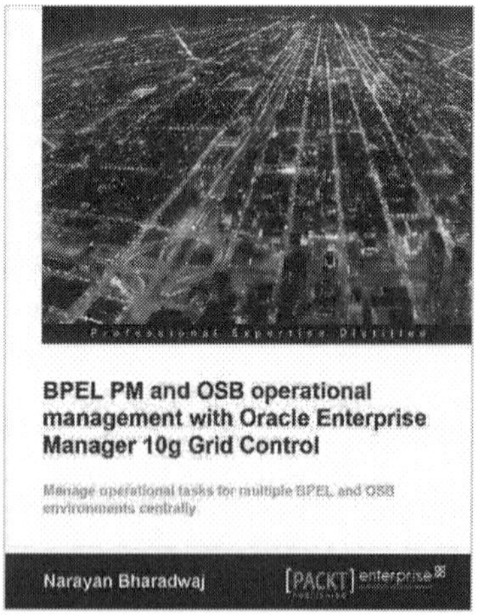

BPEL PM and OSB operational management with Oracle Enterprise Manager 10g Grid Control

ISBN: 978-1-847197-74-0 Paperback: 300 pages

Manage the operational tasks for multiple BPEL and OSB environments centrally

1. Monitor and manage all components of your SOA environment from a central location
2. Save time and increase efficiency by automating all the day-to-day operational tasks associated with the SOA environment
3. Packed with real-world use cases and detailed explanations

Please check **www.PacktPub.com** for information on our titles

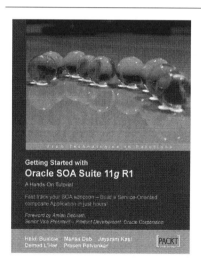

8623644R0

Made in the USA
Lexington, KY
18 February 2011

Lloyd B Olson

PUBLICATIONS OF THE NATIONAL BUREAU OF ECONOMIC RESEARCH, INCORPORATED

No. 10

BUSINESS CYCLES

The Problem and Its Setting

National Bureau of Economic Research, Inc.

Incorporated under the Membership Corporation Laws of the State of New York, January 29, 1920

ITS ORGANIZATION AND PURPOSES

THE National Bureau of Economic Research was organized in 1920 in response to a growing demand for exact and impartial determinations of facts bearing on economic, social, and industrial problems.

It seeks not only to find facts and make them known, but to determine them in such manner and under such supervision as to make its findings carry conviction to Liberal and Conservative alike.

Entire control of the Bureau is vested in a Board of twenty-one directors, representing universities, learned and scientific societies, financial, industrial, agricultural, commercial, labor, and technical organizations.

Rigid provisions in the Charter and By-Laws guard the Bureau from becoming a source of profit to its members, directors, or officers and from becoming an agency for propaganda. No report of the Research Staff may be published without the approval of the Directors and any Director who dissents from any finding approved by a majority of the Board may have such dissent published with the majority report.

The members of the Board of Directors are as follows:

BUSINESS CYCLES

The Problem and Its Setting

By

WESLEY C. MITCHELL

DIRECTOR OF RESEARCH
IN THE
NATIONAL BUREAU OF ECONOMIC RESEARCH

WITH A FOREWORD BY
EDWIN F. GAY
DIRECTOR OF RESEARCH

NEW YORK
NATIONAL BUREAU OF ECONOMIC RESEARCH, INC.
1928

First Printing, July, 1927
Second Printing, August, 1927
Third Printing, November, 1927
Fourth Printing, March, 1928

Printed in the United States of America by
J. J. LITTLE AND IVES COMPANY, NEW YORK

FOREWORD

There is printed with this volume a resolution on the relation of the directors of the National Bureau of Economic Research to the economic work of the Bureau. Since the establishment of the National Bureau it has been the practice to submit for the approval of the Board of Directors or their executive committee all proposals for new work to be undertaken by the staff, and reports on work in progress have been made regularly to the executive committee and to the annual meeting of the Board. The completed studies in draft form have been circulated for staff criticism and amendment and then have been sent by the directors of research to all the members of the Board. Only when the study had been approved in writing by a majority of the Board could it be released for publication, and dissenting views, if not accepted by the staff, were published with the book. The new resolution defines more precisely the steps in this procedure, by requiring a preliminary written statement of principles and methods and a synopsis to accompany the final manuscript. It states accurately the responsibility of the Board. It also fixes a time-limit on its voting.

The action of the Board implies a recognition of the success of the National Bureau's plan for securing from men of every divergent opinions a guarantee of the impartiality of its findings. Some friends of the enterprise feared at the outset that the plan might prove to be unworkable—for opposite reasons. Either, they said, the disagreements would be so serious as to embarass the staff and impede publication, or it would be found impossible to induce busy men to give the time necessary for such scientific jury-service. But such men have been found, and their differences have been a source of strength instead of embarrassment. In practice, it is true, some members of the Board have occasionally given their approval after merely cursory examination of the work submitted to them. It is for the alleviation of conscience in such cases that the briefer synopsis is to be provided and that the last clause of the sixth paragraph of the resolution has been inserted. But the responsibility of the Board toward the public is obviously too great and too keenly realized to permit any relaxation

in the established custom. The majority of the members of the Board will in the future, as in the past, continue to read and criticize the manuscripts, often bulky, which are submitted by the staff of the National Bureau. Our jurymen, fairly representative of the various currents of thought in American economic life, have effectively manifested their desire, not to accommodate their opinions, but to seek a common basis of agreed facts. Since the staff of the National Bureau is animated by the same purpose, it has welcomed gratefully the criticism and coöperation of its governing Board, and it counts on the continuation of a relationship, unique in scientific research, which the new and more precise regulations promise to make even closer and more helpful.

It happens that Professor Mitchell's book, "Business Cycles, The Problem and Its Setting," is the first to which the new regulations apply. Since, therefore, it carries the first publication of the Board's resolution, it has seemed desirable to make this accompanying explanation. The coincidence, fortunately, gives me an opportunity to express on behalf of the National Bureau our lively satisfaction in presenting the first section of Professor Mitchell's work, which will give on its completion a rewriting, based on new and fuller statistical material, of his book on "Business Cycles," published in 1913. The National Bureau had already, in 1921, requested Professor Mitchell to undertake, with the assistance of its available resources, a comprehensive analysis of business cycles, when Mr. Hoover turned to it for aid in the work of the President's Commission on Unemployment. The Bureau's staff, under Professor Mitchell's direction, produced the report on "Business Cycles and Unemployment" which appeared as volume IV of the National Bureau's publications and was also issued by the Commission. The National Bureau was glad to make in this way its contribution, then especially timely, to that diffusion of knowledge which is essential if the severity of recurring business cycles is to be mitigated. But since its original undertaking, however much stimulated by the economic situation of 1921, was motivated primarily by scientific interest, it was also glad in 1923 to turn to the patient labor of fact collection and analysis. The first of the series of studies of business cycles, Dr. Thorp's "Business Annals," was published last year. The present volume will be followed by the publication, in successive installments, of an exceptionally complete collection of statistical material,

now being utilized by Professor Mitchell in the preparation of the final section of his work.

Just as the estimating of the national income, which had been the first and remains the continuing task of the National Bureau, led to the need of inquiry into the causes of fluctuations in that income, and thus to the related study of business cycles, so Professor Mitchell's interest in business cycles was closely linked with his earlier investigation of prices and monetary instability. His book of 1908 on "Gold Prices and Wages under the Greenback Standard" was thus the forerunner of his "Business Cycles" of 1913 and of his fresh attack upon the problem which he has undertaken with the National Bureau of Economic Research. Two decades of a life-time, so consistently employed, approach, in statistical parlance, to the dignity of a "trend," and there are many, in addition to the professional statisticians, who will watch with keen interest this particular curve of development.

EDWIN F. GAY.

RESOLUTION

ON THE RELATION OF THE DIRECTORS TO THE ECONOMIC WORK OF THE BUREAU

1—The object of the Bureau is to ascertain and to present to the public important economic facts and the interpretation thereof in a scientific and impartial manner, free from bias and propaganda. The Board of Directors is charged with the responsibility of ensuring and guaranteeing to the public that the work of the Bureau is carried out in strict conformity with this object.

2—The Directors shall appoint one or more directors of research chosen upon considerations of integrity, ability, character, and freedom from prejudice, who shall undertake to conduct economic researches in conformity with the principles of the Bureau.

3—The director or directors of research shall submit to the members of the Board, or to its executive committee when such is constituted and to which authority has been delegated by the Board, proposals in respect to researches to be instituted; and no research shall be instituted without the approval of the Board, or of its executive committee.

4—Following approval by the Board, or its executive committee, of a research proposed, the director or directors of research shall as soon as possible submit to the members of the Board, by written communication, a statement of the principles to be pursued in the study of the problem and the methods to be employed; and the director or directors of research shall not proceed to investigate, study, and report in detail, until the plan so outlined has been approved by the board or the executive committee thereof.

5—Before the publication of the results of any inquiry the director or directors of research shall submit to the Board a synopsis of such results, drawing attention to the main conclusions reached, the major problems encountered, and the solutions adopted, the nature of the sources from which the basic facts have been derived, and such other information as in their opinion shall have a material bearing on the validity of the conclusions and their suitability for publication in accordance with the principles of the Bureau.

6—A copy of any manuscript proposed to be published shall also be submitted to each member of the Board, and every member shall be entitled, if publication be approved, to have published also a memorandum of any dissent or reservation he may express, together with a brief statement of his reasons therefore, should he so desire. The publication of a volume does not, however, imply that each member of the Board of Directors has read the manuscript and passed upon its validity in every detail.

7—The results of any inquiry shall not be published except with the approval of at least a majority of the entire Board and a two-thirds majority of all those members of the Board who shall have voted on the proposal within the time fixed for the receipt of votes on the publication proposed; such limit shall be 45 days from the date of the submission of the synopsis and manuscript of the proposed publication, except that the Board may extend the limit in its absolute discretion, and shall upon the request of any member extend the limit for a period not exceeding 30 days.

8—A copy of this memorandum shall, unless otherwise determined by the Board, be printed in each copy of every work published by the Bureau.

PREFACE

Much has been learned about business cycles since 1913, when my first book on that problem was published. Economic theorists have been studying the phenomena with increasing energy and thoroughness—Albert Aftalion and Jean Lescure in France; Mentor Bouniatian and S. A. Pervushin in Russia; Gustav Cassel in Sweden; John Maurice Clark, William T. Foster, Waddill Catchings, Alvin H. Hansen, and Henry L. Moore in America; R. H. Hawtrey, John A. Hobson, A. C. Pigou, and Dennis H. Robertson in England; Emil Lederer, Joseph Schumpeter and Arthur Spiethoff in Germany, to name but a few. Economic statisticians have made rapid progress in analyzing time series—witness the accomplishment of Warren M. Persons and his many co-workers here and abroad. Most important of all in promise for the future, the leading commercial nations are learning to keep more adequate records of their economic activities. Of the extraordinary business fluctuations through which the world has been passing of late, we have fuller knowledge than of any earlier cycles.

For perhaps ten years my unwieldy quarto has been out of print. At least as long it has been out of date. Nor could it be brought abreast of current research by mere revision. It became plain that if I could add anything of value to the work in process it would be only by writing a new book. But single-handed, I could not manage the wealth of new materials, or apply the improved methods of statistical analysis. From this quandary I was rescued by the National Bureau of Economic Research, which offered to collect and analyze the data I needed, and to supply the gaps in my equipment.

Despite the National Bureau's efficient aid, my resurvey of the field is taking more time than the first survey took. This work has been my chief concern since 1923, yet only one volume is ready for publication. It deals, as the sub-title indicates, with "The Problem and its Setting." A second volume on "The Rhythm of Business Activity" will follow as soon as I can finish it.

The present treatise resembles its forerunner in general plan. But the statistical data prove so extensive that they must be pub-

lished separately in a series of volumes, instead of being included as before with the theoretical discussion. There is the more reason for this change in that the National Bureau's collection of tables promises to be a source book of great value to many workers concerned with other problems than business cycles. Also, the collection of annals, which in the earlier treatise covered only four countries and 23 years, has grown into a survey embracing 17 countries and extending back to 1790 in the United States and England. That collection, made by Dr. Willard L. Thorp, has already appeared in print.

I have not been able to devise a new way of conducting the inquiry which seemed better than the way followed in 1913. My earlier impressions that business cycles consist of exceedingly complex interactions among a considerable number of economic processes, that to gain insight into these interactions one must combine historical studies with quantitative and qualitative analysis, that the phenomena are peculiar to a certain form of economic organization, and that understanding of this scheme of institutions is prerequisite to an understanding of cyclical fluctuations—these impressions have been confirmed by my efforts to treat the subject in a simpler fashion. Hence the new version is not shorter or easier than its predecessor. Much to my regret, it makes even heavier demands upon a reader's time and effort.

From the Staff and the Directors of the National Bureau of Economic Research I have had most generous help. Among the staff members Drs. Frederick C. Mills, Willford I. King, Willard L. Thorp and Simon S. Kuznets have put their technical skill freely at my disposal. Among the Directors, Professor Allyn A. Young and Colonel Malcolm C. Rorty have made especially searching criticisms of the first draft. Dr. Edwin F. Gay, Director of Research, has been my mainstay for counsel from the beginning of the undertaking. Several other friends have read parts of the manuscript and suggested improvements—Messrs. Carl Snyder and Karl Karsten, Professors Walter F. Willcox, Warren M. Persons, Vladimir G. Simkhovitch, and James W. Angell. The Harvard Committee on Economic Research through its chairman Professor Charles J. Bullock, the American Telephone and Telegraph Company through its statistician Mr. Seymour L. Andrew, Sir William Beveridge, Mr. Snyder, and Dr. Dorothy S. Thomas have kindly consented to the free use I have made of their contributions. Miss Edith Handler of the National

Bureau has made most of the charts. My secretary, Miss Catherine Lochhead, has shared in the labors of proof reading and indexing.

To all these men and women, and to the many co-workers by whose criticisms and constructive suggestions I have sought to profit, my hearty thanks are due.

WESLEY C. MITCHELL.

New York City, June 1st, 1927.

CONTENTS

LIST OF TABLES

LIST OF CHARTS

BUSINESS CYCLES

CHAPTER I.

THE PROCESSES INVOLVED IN BUSINESS CYCLES.

I. The Plan of Attack.

As knowledge of business cycles grows, more effort is required to master it. Formerly, an attack upon the problem required no special preparations. Early writers upon "commercial crises" could assume that they and their readers were familiar with the phenomena to be explained and the methods to be used. They felt no need of collecting statistics, of compiling business annals, of comparing the amplitude and the timing of cyclical fluctuations in different activities, of developing and defining technical concepts. After the briefest of introductions, they plunged into a discussion of the cause of crises, and worked such evidence as they cited into their argumentation. In consequence, their discussions had an agreeable directness, which our generation may envy, but cannot wisely imitate.

Elaborate preparations have become necessary, not because the direct attacks upon the problem proved futile, but because they won so many and such different results. Every investigator of the cause of commercial crises seemed to make out a case for the hypothesis he favored. In trying to prove their divergent explanations correct, successive theorists did prove that business cycles were more intricate phenomena than any of them had surmised. These cycles turned out to be complexes, made up of divergent fluctuations in many processes. Familiarity with the phenomena to be explained came to mean familiarity with the interrelations among cyclical fluctuations in the production of raw materials, industrial equipment and consumers' goods; in the volume of savings and investments; in the promotion of new enterprises, in banking, in the disbursement of incomes to individuals and the spending of incomes, in prices, costs, profits and the emotional aberrations of business judgments. However

conversant he may be with practical affairs and economic theory, no competent investigator now supposes that he can explain the fluctuations of these interrelated factors on the basis of his general knowledge.

This lesson from experience in making theories of business cycles has been confirmed in recent years by work with statistics. Serried tables of figures, and charts drawn from them, have made our knowledge of cyclical fluctuations much more definite. Year by year the range covered by statistical compilations has grown wider, the accuracy of reporting has improved, and the technical methods of analysis have become more refined and more powerful. But we have no statistical evidence of business cycles as wholes. What the data show us are the fluctuations of particular processes—producing pig iron, transporting freight, clearing bank checks, selling goods by mail, declaring dividends, and so on. And these fluctuations differ widely. In certain cases we assemble or average the data for various processes, and say that we have "indexes" of cyclical fluctuations in wholesale prices, physical production, the volume of trade, or even "general business conditions." Yet the most inclusive indexes we can make fall far short of showing all that we mean by business cycles. The more intensively we work, the more we realize that this term is a synthetic product of the imagination—a product whose history is characteristic of our ways of learning. Overtaken by a series of strange experiences our predecessors leaped to a broad conception, gave it a name, and began to invent explanations, as if they knew what their words meant. But in the process of explaining they demonstrated how inadequate their knowledge was. From their work we can learn much; the first lesson is that we must find out more about the facts before we can choose among the old explanations, or improve upon them.

An inquiry into business cycles, then, cannot wisely begin by defining the general concept, and proceed systematically to take up one part of the whole after another. It should begin rather with the individual processes which can be studied objectively, seeking to find what these processes are, how they affect each other, and what sort of whole they make up.

The best way to learn what processes are involved in business cycles is to profit by the discoveries of earlier workers. Most of these men found the clue to business cycles in the recurrent fluctuations of some single economic process. All together they may not have

covered the whole field. But in no other way can we get so comprehensive a view of business cycles, or such vivid insight into their complexities, as by following a series of persuasive demonstrations that each one of a dozen different processes reveals the factor of crucial importance.

It is not advisable to attack the statistical data until we have made this survey of theories. For while the statistics will come to seem scanty as our demands develop, they are sufficiently abundant and diverse, susceptible of enough transformations and combinations, to make hopeless a purely empirical investigation. At every turn, we shall need working hypotheses to guide our selection of data, and to suggest ways of analyzing and combining them. Our survey of theories will provide us with the most promising hypotheses which have been invented. Not until we are thus equipped can we begin constructive work upon the problem of business cycles, confident that we are not overlooking elements already proved to be important.

II. The Discovery of the Problem.

Serious efforts to explain business crises and depressions began amid the violent fluctuations in trade which followed the Napoleonic Wars. For a century or more Western Europe had been experiencing at intervals speculative manias, glutted markets, and epidemics of bankruptcy. The Mississippi Bubble and the South Sea Scheme which had burst in France and England in 1720, and the commercial crises of 1763, 1772, 1783 and 1793, not to mention less notable cases, had excited much discussion.[1] But the eighteenth-century writers dealt mainly with the dramatic surface events; concerning the underlying causes they developed no arresting ideas. By 1815 progressive changes in economic organization were forcing the problem to the fore, and men were better equipped to attack it. The Physiocrats and Adam Smith had made political economy a branch of philosophy, if not of science, and when the wars ended Ricardo was recasting the theory into the form which is still dominant.

It was not the orthodox economists, however, who gave the problem of crises and depressions its place in economics, but sceptics who had profited by and then reacted against their teachings. From Adam Smith to Mill, and even to Alfred Marshall, the classical mas-

[1] See Mentor Bouniatian, *Studien zur Theorie und Geschichte der Wirtschaftskrisen. II Geschichte der Handelskrisen in England, 1640-1840.* Munich, 1908.

ters have paid but incidental attention to the rhythmical oscillations of trade in their systematic treatises. They have been concerned primarily to elucidate principles which hold "in the long run," or apply to the "normal state." To them crises and depressions have been of secondary interest—proper subjects for special study or occasional reference, but not among the central problems of economic theory.[2] To force into prominence the fact that economic activities are subject to recurring phases of contraction and expansion was the work primarily of men who were critics, not merely of orthodox economics, but also of modern society—men such as Sismondi and Rodbertus.

J. C. L. Simonde de Sismondi was an Italian Swiss who had early become enamored of Adam Smith's doctrines and expounded them for continental readers in a treatise *De la Richesse Commerciale.* After publishing this book in 1803, Sismondi had turned to medieval research and won European celebrity as the historian of the Italian Republics. Then an invitation from the Scotch physicist, Sir David Brewster, to write an article on "Political Economy" for the new *Edinburgh Encyclopædia,* recalled him to his first theme in 1818.

The time was one of widespread distress. As Napoleon's fall drew near, English manufacturers and merchants, anticipating the reopening of hungry continental markets, accumulated large stores of goods for export. Waterloo was fought in June, 1815. There followed several months of brisk trade and optimistic speculation. But before the year was out it became clear that European consumers lacked the means to buy freely. Heavy consignments of British goods overstocked the markets and many of the consignors went bankrupt. The year after Waterloo was one of distress from beginning to end. Recovery began in the spring of 1817 and made rapid progress, so that 1818 showed great industrial activity. But in 1819 fresh difficulties occurred, and depression returned to last through 1820. Not

[2] Thus Adam Smith mentions the "knavery and extravagance" of the South Sea Company's "stock-jobbing projects," (*Wealth of Nations,* Cannan's ed., vol. ii, p. 236); Ricardo speaks of "revulsions in trade" accompanying the outbreaks or the ending of great wars (*Principles of Political Economy,* Gonner's ed., pp. 250, 251); Mill discusses "commercial crises" in his chapters on the Rate of Interest and on the Tendency of Profits to a Minimum, besides mentioning them incidentally in several other passages (*Principles of Political Economy,* Ashley's ed., pp. 561, 641, 644, 651, 709, 734-735, 845); Marshall puts a book on "Fluctuations of Industry, Trade and Credit," not into his *Principles of Economics,* but into his volume on *Money, Credit and Commerce,* London, 1923, pp. 234-263.

until 1821 did a sustained revival begin,—and the prosperity which presently reigned ended in the panic of December, 1825.[3]

Sismondi had accepted Brewster's invitation readily, thinking he had merely to write a brief exposition of "principles universally admitted." But as he studied current developments he was assailed by doubts concerning the theories he had accepted from Adam Smith.

> I was deeply affected, (he wrote), by the commercial crisis which Europe had experienced of late, by the cruel sufferings of the industrial workers which I had witnessed in Italy, Switzerland and France, and which all reports showed to have been at least as severe in England, in Germany and in Belgium.

The case of England was to him particularly significant—that "surprising country which seemed to be undergoing a great experiment for the instruction of the rest of the world." If the land of the economists, the land where the doctrine of economic liberty had freest sway in government, the land where the new methods of machine production had scored their greatest triumphs—if that land was plunged in want by the return of peace, must there not be something wrong in the philosophy of *laissez faire?* When everyone was free to produce as much as he could, it seemed that no one could buy what he needed to consume. How could this be? Sismondi set himself to solve the problem. The result was his *Nouveaux Principes d'Économie Politique,* published in 1819.[4]

We should not expect the first efforts to explain so complicated a phenomenon as a business crisis to be free from crudities. Nor was Sismondi fully equipped to solve the problem he had posed; though an excellent observer, he lacked analytic finesse. Yet he made several suggestions, ill coördinated with each other, which were developed and combated by later writers, and which continue to play rôles of importance in theories now current.

One of these suggestions is that commercial organization is at fault. The business man, as Sismondi phrases it, caters to a "metaphysical public"—customers whose numbers, tastes, consumption and purchasing power are all unknown to him, and all variable. The only guide he has in planning how much to produce is prices. By

[3] See the conspectus of English business annals in Chapter IV below, or better the chapter on England in *Business Annals,* by Willard L. Thorp, National Bureau of Economic Research, 1926.

[4] See the prefaces to the first and second editions. The latter appeared in 1827

comparing present prices with costs, he decides whether to increase or restrict his output in the near future.

> Unfortunately this comparison is made by all the producers at the same time . . . and all of them together, ignorant of how much their competitors will undertake, nearly always exceed the limit which they had in view.[5]

A second suggestion is that in periods of industrial activity the income available for buying consumers' goods falls short of the value of the goods sent to market. This idea sounds modern, but Sismondi's supporting analysis offered a broad target to his detractors. The purchasing power available to absorb the produce of any year, he stoutly contended, is the aggregate income of the preceding year—a notion probably suggested by his life among the peasants of Italy. When capacity to produce is increasing rapidly through the introduction of machinery, the markets must become glutted frequently. For the faster the increase in production, the wider will be the gap between last year's income and this year's output.[6]

Still a third suggestion embodies in quaint form the "over-saving" theory of crises. In opulent nations, production often goes astray because its volume is determined by the abundance of capital seeking investment rather than by the demand of consumers. Of course the latter demand is the only safe guide; the fact that merchants and manufacturers have money to invest in new ventures does not guarantee a market for their wares.[7]

Sismondi laid most stress, however, upon an idea often repeated but never clearly worked out in his book: the fundamental cause of crises is inequality in the distribution of incomes.

> It is a serious error into which most of the modern economists have fallen to represent consumption as a power without limits, always ready to devour an infinite output. . . . The needs of the laboring man are narrowly limited of necessity.

The masses do not wish luxuries so much as they wish respite from toil. But when methods of production are improved, our economic institutions, instead of giving the workers leisure, keep them busy as long as ever and increase the volume of products offered for sale.

[5] *Nouveaux Principes*, 2d ed., I, 325-330.
[6] The same, I, 106, 121-124.
[7] The same, I, 367-368.

Who is to buy? After food, clothing and housing on a meager scale have been provided for the wage-earners, the chief market for further goods is the market for luxuries. The desire for such goods is indeed without limit. But the increase of trade in luxuries puts a nation's industry in a precarious position. Domestic consumers of luxuries prefer foreign wares, and domestic producers must seek foreign outlets. Recent experience of unsalable consignments all over the globe has shown the English how undependable is the export trade. Everyone would be better off if the workers had incomes sufficient to give the home demand a broad base.[8]

III. The Multiplying Solutions.

In a generation addicted to economic speculation, events which affected so many fortunes as did the vicissitudes of trade were certain to be explained in different ways. Sismondi was but the most suggestive among a numerous company of writers, most of whom had their own explanations to offer and their own remedies to urge. Nor did the differences of opinion grow less with the passing of time. On the contrary, as later crises brought new men and new materials into the discussion, the explanations multiplied. Gradually the plausible views became standardized into several types of theory, each represented in the growing literature by a number of variants. Before the end of the nineteenth century there had accumulated a body of observations and speculations sufficient to justify the writing of histories of the theories of crises.[1]

A simple form of the "over-production" or "under-consumption" theory was widely held. Through the adoption of modern machinery, it was said, the power of society to produce has outgrown its power to consume. Hence the periodical occurrence of "general gluts"—paradoxical episodes in which superabundance causes want. Unable to

[8] The same, I, 75-78, 357-372. The best modern account of Sismondi's views is given by Albert Aftalion, *L'Oeuvre Économique de Simonde de Sismondi,* Paris, 1899.

[1] The most elaborate of these histories is Eugen von Bergmann's *Die Wirtschaftskrisen: Geschichte der nationalökonomischen Krisentheorien,* Stuttgart, 1895. The best accounts in English and French are Edward D. Jones' *Economic Crises,* New York, 1900, and Jean Lescure's *Des Crises Générales et Périodiques de Surproduction,* 3rd ed., Paris, 1923, pp. 313-412.

See also Harry E. Miller's paper on "Earlier Theories of Crises and Cycles in the United States." *Quarterly Journal of Economics,* February, 1924 (xxxviii, pp. 294-329), and Adolf Löwe's review of recent German contributions, "Der gegenwärtige Stand der Konjunkturforschung in Deutschland," in *Festgabe für Lujo Brentano,* Munich and Leipzig, 1925, vol. ii, pp. 329-377.

sell their increasing output of goods at remunerative prices, employers are forced to close their factories and turn away their hands—a remedy which aggravates the disease by reducing yet further the community's power to purchase for consumption.

To most of the classical economists, the theory of general overproduction was a heresy, which they sought to extirpate by demonstrating that the supply of goods of one sort necessarily constitutes demand for goods of other sorts.[2] But maladjusted production they allowed to be possible, and their brief references to crises usually aimed to show how production becomes maladjusted through the sinking of capital in unremunerative investments. They often held that such misuse of capital was one result of "the tendency of profits to a minimum." When the current rate of profits has fallen to an unaccustomed level, the less sagacious capitalists become dissatisfied and embark on ill-considered schemes. There result the production of goods for which no market can be found, business failures, and loss of confidence—in short, a crisis which extends over all lines of trade.

Another group of writers, among whom Schäffle was prominent, accepted ill-adjusted production as the cause of crises; but accounted for it by the complexity of modern business organization—the first of Sismondi's suggestions. Not only are manufacturers compelled to produce goods months in advance for markets whose changes they cannot forecast, but investors are compelled years in advance to put their funds into enterprises the need of which is uncertain. A close adjustment of supply to demand cannot be maintained. Mistakes are inevitable, and should be ascribed less to bad judgment than to the planlessness of capitalistic production.

The most vigorous attempt to prove that crises are a chronic disease of capitalism, however, was that made by Rodbertus and elaborated by Karl Marx. The germ of this theory also is found in Sismondi and Robert Owen. Wages form but a fraction of the value of the product and increase less rapidly than power to produce. Since the masses dependent upon wages constitute the bulk of the population, it follows that consumers' demand cannot keep pace

[2] Upon this point, as upon many others, Malthus dissented from the "orthodox" opinion. See his *Principles of Political Economy*, 1st ed., London, 1820, 351-375; 2d ed., London, 1836, 314-330. Mill admitted that "there may really be, though only while the crisis lasts, an extreme depression of general prices, from what may be indiscriminately called a glut of commodities or a dearth of money. But (he added) it is a great error to suppose, with Sismondi, that a commercial crisis is the effect of a general excess of production. It is simply the consequence of an excess of speculative purchases." *Principles of Political Economy*, Ashley's ed., p. 561.

with current supply in seasons when factories are running at full blast. Meanwhile the capitalist-employers are investing their current savings in new productive enterprises, which presently add their quotas to the goods seeking sale. This process of over-stocking the market runs cumulatively until the time comes when the patent impossibility of selling goods at a profit, or even at cost, brings on a crisis.[3]

A wider acceptance was accorded to the "inflation" theory. An increase in gold, in irredeemable paper money, in bank notes, or in deposit currency was held to start an advance in prices. The latter in turn stimulates business to great activity, which runs to extremes in reckless investments and foolish speculation, and ends in a crash of credit and widespread bankruptcy.

The "psychological" type of explanation was elaborated in John Mills' paper "On Credit Cycles and the Origin of Commercial Panics," published in 1867.[4] On this view the fundamental cause of crises lies less in the character or abuse of economic institutions, than in the emotional aberrations to which business judgments are subject. Fair trade breeds optimism, optimism breeds recklessness, recklessness breeds disaster. In their turn, the disasters of a crises breed pessimism and pessimism breeds stagnation. From depression business picks up only when men's spirits recover on finding that matters have gone less badly than they had feared.

As John Mills sought the fundamental cause of commercial fluctuations in psychology, so W. Stanley Jevons sought it in physics. His theory that the activity of solar radiation controls mundane weather, weather controls crops, and crops control business conditions, was first announced in 1875.

Finally, some economists, for example Wilhelm Roscher, despaired of finding any theory which would account for all crises in the same way. To these men a crisis is an "abnormal" event produced by some "disturbing cause," such as the introduction of revolutionary inventions, the development of new transportation lines, wars, the return of peace, tariff revisions, monetary changes, crop failures, changes in fashion, and the like. This view assumes that the equilibrium of economic processes has become so delicate that it may be upset by untoward conjunctures of the most dissimilar kinds, and

[3] For a recent statement of the Marxian theory of crises by a sympathetic interpreter, see Otto Leichter, "Zur Analyse der Weltwirtschaftskrise," in *Der lebendige Marxismus, Festgabe zum 70. Geburtstage von Karl Kautsky,* Jena, 1924, pp. 45-100.

[4] *Transactions of the Manchester Statistical Society,* 1867-68, pp. 5-40.

points to the conclusion that each crisis has its own special cause which must be sought among the events of the preceding year or two.

While all these speculations and others unmentioned concerning the cause of crises and depressions were being debated, some progress was made toward more exact observation and description of the phenomena. The most distinguished pioneer in work of this sort was Clement Juglar, whose elaborate treatise *Des Crises Commerciales et de leur Retour Périodique* was published in 1860 and again in 1889. Max Wirth emphasized the international character of the major crises in his *Geschichte der Handelskrisen* (Frankfort a, M. 1858; 4th ed., 1890), Tugan-Baranovski made an intensive study of English crises in the nineteenth century,[5] and numerous observers wrote pamphlets or books on single crises.

In this descriptive work, much freer use was generally made of statistical materials than in the theoretical essays. As the century wore on, the data available concerning prices, currency, banking, interest rates, foreign trade, production and employment grew wider in range, more reliable, and more precise. Meanwhile statisticians like Jevons and Edgeworth were developing a better technique for wresting significant conclusions from masses of seemingly chaotic data. But the use of these methods in theoretical inquiries was slow to develop.

The most fundamental change to which the use of statistics contributed was a change in the conception of the problem to be solved. The earlier writers had sought for the cause merely of crises, or of crises and depressions. It is true that a wider view had been suggested occasionally. In 1833, an English journalist, John Wade, remarked casually that

> The commercial cycle is ordinarily completed in five or seven years, within which terms it will be found, by reference to our commercial history during the last seventy years, alternate periods of prosperity and depression have been experienced.[6]

Presently this idea of cyclical oscillations was amplified by more influential writers—Lord Overstone, Hyde Clark, William Langton.

[5] Published first in Russian (1894), then in German (1901) and finally in French under the title *Les Crises Industrielles en Angleterre* (Paris, 1913).

[6] John Wade, *History of the Middle and Working Classes*, 2d ed., London, 1834, p. 211.

John Mills, Condy Raguet and Amasa Walker: [7] it was indeed implied in the numerous discussions of the "periodicity of crises." One could talk about credit cycles and "periodic" crises, however, without devoting much attention to business revivals after depression, or the process by which revivals grow into prosperity. But one could scarcely use time series, showing the fluctuations of activity year after year, without seeing that the developments in the non-crisis periods offered quite as much a problem as did the crises themselves. Thus the use of statistics hastened the time when economists passed on from the theory of crises to the theory of business cycles. Clement Juglar's great "book of facts" made clear the need of the step.[8]

So bald a statement as the preceding falls far short of doing justice to the nineteenth century writers; but it suffices to indicate the foundations upon which our contemporaries have built their more elaborate theories. The latter conserve all of permanent value which the older economists achieved, and contain in addition certain fresh contributions to the subject. Accordingly, a more detailed account of the leading explanations which have been offered recently will put us in possession of the ideas most likely to prove useful in further work.

IV. The Theories Now Current.

Recent writers upon business cycles differ from one another less in principle than in emphasis. Everyone who studies the problem with care must realize that many processes are involved in the alternations of prosperity and depression. But each investigator decides for himself the question: What among these many processes is the prime mover in producing cyclical oscillations, and what processes merely adapt themselves as best may be to changes produced elsewhere?

[7] Lord Overstone's statement may be quoted:

"The history of what we are in the habit of calling the 'state of trade' is an instructive lesson. We find it subject to various conditions which are periodically returning; it revolves apparently in an established cycle. First, we find it in a state of quiescence,—next improvement,—growing confidence,—prosperity,—excitement,—overtrading,—convulsion,—pressure,—stagnation,—distress,—ending again in quiescence." *Reflections suggested by a perusal of Mr. J. Horsley Palmers' pamphlet on the Causes and Consequences of the Pressure on the Money Market.* By Samuel Jones Loyd, London, 1837.

On the American observations, see Harry E. Miller, "Earlier Theories of Crises and Cycles in the United States," *Quarterly Journal of Economics,* February, 1924, vol. xxxviii, p. 300.

[8] *Des Crises Commerciales,* 2d ed., Paris, 1889, chapter i and *passim.*

Each gives chief attention to the one or more factors which he believes to play the chief causal rôle; but many writers also show how the changes produced by their chosen causes affect other processes, and in so doing they are likely to find use for the work of men whose distribution of emphasis differs from their own.

Among the factors to which the leading rôle in causing business cycles has been assigned by competent inquirers within the past decade are the weather, the uncertainty which beclouds all plans that stretch into the future, the emotional aberrations to which business decisions are subject, the innovations characteristic of modern society, the "progressive" character of our age, the magnitude of savings, the construction of industrial equipment, "generalized over-production," the operations of banks, the flow of money incomes, and the conduct of business for profits. Each of these explanations merits attention from those who seek to understand business cycles; for each should throw light upon some feature or aspect of these complex phenomena.

We need not, however, review the full analysis of the writers by whose ideas we seek to profit. That would be the task of a treatise upon theories of business cycles. This book deals with the cycles themselves, and to it the theories are tools to be used in constructive work. The following pages, therefore, aim merely to borrow from the recent books and articles upon business cycles those suggestions which promise to enlarge our understanding of the problem as a whole.

1. The Weather.

Most elegant among current explanations of business cycles are the meteorological theories.

In 1801 Sir William Herschel suggested that changes in sun-spots may affect the weather, hence crops, and hence prices.[1] This idea, coupled with Schwabe's discovery (recognized by the Royal Astronomical Society in 1857) that sun-spots are cyclical, fascinated the speculative mind of W. Stanley Jevons, and led him to the hypothesis that business cycles are caused by solar cycles. To test this notion, Jevons studied the records of English trade from 1721 to

[1] Observations tending to investigate the nature of the Sun in order to find the Causes or Symptoms of its variable Emission of Light and Heat; with Remarks on the Use that may possibly be drawn from Solar Observations. *Philosophical Transactions of the Royal Society of London*, 1801, vol. xci, pp. 265-318.

1878 to see how closely the two cycles agreed with each other. He concluded that there had been 16 crises in this period of 157 years. Thus he obtained an average length of 10.466 years for the commercial cycle, which agreed almost exactly with the length then assigned to the sun-spot cycle, 10.45 years. Jevons declared himself

> perfectly convinced that these decennial crises do depend upon meteorological variations of like period, which again depend, in all probability upon cosmical variations of which we have evidence in the frequency of sunspots, auroras, and magnetic perturbations.[2]

Unfortunately for this theory, since 1878 astronomers have revised their computations of the sun-spot cycle (the average now commonly accepted is 11 + years),[3] and commercial cycles have departed still further from the decennial norm. Hence in 1909, Jevons' son, Professor Herbert Stanley Jevons, suggested a modification of the solar hypothesis. He believed that meteorologists had demonstrated the existence of a 3½ year period in solar radiation and in barometric pressure. By analyzing agricultural data he found evidence of a 3½ year periodicity in crop yields also. Trade cycles, he held, are either 7 or 10½ years in length. He tied these two results together by observing that a single period of good crops does not suffice to produce an unhealthy boom in business, but that two or at most three such periods following each other will do so. In this revised form, he concluded that his father's meteorological theory of the business cycle remains valid.[4]

Since Professor Jevons had relied largely upon American data to establish his weather cycle of 3½ years, surprise was felt when Professor Henry L. Moore announced in 1914 that harmonic analysis of rainfall data from the grain areas of Ohio and Illinois shows the existence of a 33-year and an 8-year cycle. His supplemental computations showed high coefficients of correlation between crop yields per acre and other indices of business conditions, such as wholesale

[2] Jev[illegible]ading papers on this topic, dating from 1875 to 1882, are reprinted in his *Investigations in Currency and Finance*, edited by H. S. Foxwell, London, 1884, pp. 194-243. The passage quoted is on pp. 235, 236. Jevons' first investigation, by a different method, will be referred to in Chapter IV, section iv, 1, below.

[3] Sir William H. Beveridge, "Wheat Prices and Rainfall in Western Europe," *Journal of the Royal Statistical Society*, May, 1922, vol. lxxxv, pp. 434-437.

[4] See "The Causes of Unemployment: III, Trade Fluctuations and Solar Activity," *Contemporary Review*, August, 1909, vol. xcvi, pp. 165 ff. Reprinted with added preface and summary, as *The Sun's Heat and Trade Activity*, London, 1910.

prices and pig-iron production. Professor Moore formulated his conclusions in the following "law":

> The weather conditions represented by the rainfall in the central part of the United States, and probably in other continental areas, pass through cycles of approximately thirty-three years and eight years in duration, causing like cycles in the yield per acre of the crops; these cycles of crops constitute the natural, material current which drags upon its surface the lagging, rhythmically changing values and prices with which the economist is more immediately concerned.[5]

Later, Professor Moore extended his investigations to other parts of the United States, to England and to France, finding confirmation for his 8-year, but seemingly not for his 33-year cycle. He also suggested an astronomical cause for this dominant weather cycle more daring than the sunspot theory. At intervals of 8 years Venus comes directly into the path of solar radiations to the earth. Its magnetic field, thinks Professor Moore, may affect the stream of electrons flowing from the sun and so produce an effect on earthly magnetism and weather.[6]

To complete the record of divergencies among the economists who have utilized meteorological data, it must be added that Sir William H. Beveridge has applied harmonic analysis to European wheat prices for the three centuries from 1545 to 1844, and found evidence that there are, not one or two, but many cycles in the weather. Of these cycles a few of the best accredited have lengths (1) of 5.1 and 35.5 years (shown by harmonic analysis and confirmed by independent meteorological data), and (2) of 5.671, 9.750, 12.840, 19.900, 54.000 and possibly 68.000 years (clearly shown by harmonic analysis, but not yet confirmed by meteorological observations). There is no 8-year period in the cycles for which Sir William Beveridge finds the strongest evidence. But a period of 8.050 years occurs in his third group, for which there is "some, but not first-rate, evidence both in wheat prices and in meteorology."

Sir William's conclusion is that,

> Somewhere or other in the solar system there are periodic movements affecting our weather and crops, 10 or 20 or more

[5] *Economic Cycles: Their Law and Cause.* New York, 1914, p. 149.

[6] These later investigations are summed up in Professor Moore's volume, *Generating Economic Cycles,* New York, 1923.

> in number, far more regular than had ever been believed, possibly approaching in some cases the regularity and persistence of free orbital motion, subject in other cases to sudden birth and death. These movements may be of one type, or of several types; they may be in the sun or the planets or the moon; in the earth or in the air or water upon its surface.[7]

A novel variant of the weather theories was propounded by Professor Ellsworth Huntington in 1919. Starting to collect statistical evidence of the effect of business conditions upon health, Huntington convinced himself that "Health is a *cause* far more than an effect" of economic conditions.

> The statistics from 1870 to the Great War show that a high death rate regularly *precedes* hard times, while a low death rate precedes prosperity.

He also found that his death-rate curve, when inverted, agreed well with the fluctuations of school attendance one year later, New York bank clearings three years later, wholesale prices and National Bank deposits four years later, and immigration five years later.

> Business cycles (Professor Huntington concluded) appear to depend largely on the mental attitude of the community, . . . the mental attitude depends on health . . . and health depends largely upon the weather.[8]

Professor Werner Sombart's theory of the dissimilarity in the rhythm of production of organic and inorganic goods may be regarded as a view intermediate between the preceding group of theories which trace business cycles to physical causes and the following groups which trace them to economic factors. He points out that the inorganic industries, typified by the steel trade, can expand enormously within a brief period without being seriously hampered by scarcity of raw materials. The organic industries, typified by cotton-spinning, on the contrary are always in precarious dependence upon the year's harvests. In the organic industries, one may say, the condition of business is determined largely by the yield of raw materials; in the inorganic industries, the condition of business itself determines how

[7] Sir William H. Beveridge, "Wheat Prices and Rainfall in Western Europe," *Journal of the Royal Statistical Society,* May, 1922, vol. lxxxv, pp. 412-459. The quotation is from p. 452.

[8] Ellsworth Huntington, *World-Power and Evolution.* New Haven, 1919, chapters ii-iv. The passages cited are on pp. 29 and 42.

much of the raw materials shall be produced. In a period of prosperity, the organic industries dependent upon uncertain harvests for their supplies may be unable to keep pace with the inorganic trades, which are being rapidly expanded by heavy investments of capital. There results a disturbance of the proportion which must be maintained in the production of the two types of goods, if the current supplies of both types are to find a profitable market. The modern crisis, therefore, is at bottom the result of a clash between the workings of physical and economic processes.[9]

2. Uncertainty.

Of the theories which trace business cycles to economic rather than physical conditions, the simplest is that which develops Sismondi's indictment of prices as guides to production. A fresh statement of this familiar idea is given by Dr. Charles O. Hardy of the Institute of Economics in his book on *Risk and Risk-Bearing.*

The business man's "principal devices for securing a balanced output," Dr. Hardy points out, "are prices and advance orders." Both are fallible guides.

> Prices and orders give information concerning the prospective state of demand compared with the known facts of present and future supply, but they give no clue to the changes in supply which they are themselves likely to cause.

This situation results in "a tendency to alternations of over- and under-production." When prices and orders indicate an expansion of demand,

> the tendency is for an increasing number of persons to try to take advantage of the situation, each more or less in ignorance of the other's plans, and no force intervenes to check the continued increase of production till it reflects itself in declining orders and falling prices. By that time, however, investments have been made, contracts let, and operations started which will result in further augmentation of the supply. Time is required to check this increase in the volume of production, and during this time production outruns consumption unless

[9] See Werner Sombart, "Die Störungen im deutschen Wirtschaftsleben während der Jahre 1900 ff." *Schriften des Vereins für Socialpolitik,* September, 1903, vol. cxiii, pp. 130-133.

consumption is stimulated by unprofitably low prices. Moreover, just as was the case on the upswing, the indications that production is being overdone result in curtailment of operations by independent producers in ignorance of each other's intentions, and this tendency continues till output is decreased to a rate below that which is economically justified.

Speculative purchases and sales form a quite independent cause of cyclical fluctuations in business, reënforcing the first cause. For the speculators must base their judgments on substantially the same data as the producers. Hence their operations grow rapidly in prosperity and shrink rapidly in depression.

The effect of this tendency to mass movements of buying and selling is greatly to accentuate the effect of the producers' uncertainty concerning one another's plans. . . . For an increase in middlemen's stocks gives the producers *twice* a false index of the amount of production which is economically justifiable. When the increase in buying takes place it swells the volume of orders and creates a false appearance of expansion in the market, and whenever the excess stock is utilized it again gives a false indication, this time of contraction in the market.

At bottom, then, business cycles result from

uncertainty, chiefly uncertainty on the part of producers and middlemen concerning the conditions that will prevail in the market when they are ready to dispose of their goods.[1]

3. The Emotional Factor in Business Decisions.

Everyone recognizes the uncertainties with which business men must contend in planning their operations; but most writers on business cycles hold that uncertainty merely provides opportunity for the working of other factors to which they attach greater significance. One of these factors is the "psychological," or more accurately, the emotional influences which warp business judgment. The best exposition along this line is that given by Professor A. C. Pigou of Cambridge University. In his opinion "the movement of business confi-

[1] Charles O. Hardy, *Risk and Risk-Bearing,* Chicago, 1923, chapter v. The passages quoted are on pp. 72-75.

Dr. Hardy's exposition may be regarded as an elaborated form of "the competition theory" set forth by Sir William H. Beveridge in *Unemployment, a Problem of Industry,* London, 1908, 2d ed., 1910, chapter iv.

dence" is "the dominant cause of the rhythmic fluctuations that are experienced in industry": "optimistic error and pessimistic error, when discovered, give birth to one another in an endless chain."

After stating the conditions which make it difficult to avoid errors in planning production, Professor Pigou attacks the problem why the majority of these errors run in the same direction, instead of cancelling each other. It is at this point that his explanation diverges from the path that contents Dr. Hardy. While the latter relies upon the similarity of the price and order data used by producers and by speculators to account for the similarity of their errors, Professor Pigou has recourse to waves of elation and discouragement which sweep over the business community.

> Let us suppose the business world to be in a neutral position, not suffering from either type of error. On this situation there supervenes some real cause for increase in the demand for business activity.

Then, because business men cannot foresee the results which will be produced by their own and other men's response to the stimulus, errors of the optimistic type will begin to be made. But why should these errors multiply so rapidly and grow so huge?

> When an error of optimism has been generated, (Professor Pigou answers) it tends to spread and grow, as a result of reactions between different parts of the business community. This comes about through two principal influences. First, experience suggests that, apart altogether from the financial ties by which different business men are bound together, there exists among them a certain measure of psychological interdependence. A change of tone in one part of the business world diffuses itself, in a quite unreasoning manner, over other and wholly disconnected parts. . . . Secondly . . . an error of optimism on the part of one group of business men itself creates a justification for some improved expectation on the part of other groups.

Thus the optimistic error once born grows in scope and magnitude.

But since the prosperity has been built largely upon error, a day of reckoning must come. This day does not dawn until after a time long enough to construct new industrial equipment on a large scale, to bring the products of the new equipment to market, and to find that they cannot be disposed of promptly at profitable prices. Then

the past miscalculation becomes patent—patent to creditors as well as to debtors, and the creditors apply pressure for repayment. Thus prosperity ends in a crisis. The error of optimism dies in the crisis, but in dying it

> gives birth to an error of pessimism. This new error is born, not an infant, but a giant; for an industrial boom has necessarily been a period of strong emotional excitement, and an excited man passes from one form of excitement to another more rapidly than he passes to quiescence.

Under the influence of the new error, business is unduly depressed. For a time there is relatively slow extension of facilities for production. In consequence,

> a general shortage of a number of important commodities gradually makes itself apparent, and those persons who have them to sell are seen to be earning a good real return. Thereupon, certain of the bolder spirits in industry see an opportunity and seize it.

Business begins to pick up slowly and gradually.

> The first year or two, say, is taken up with a wholly justified expansion. But, after the first year or two, further expansion represents, not a correction of the past error, but the creation of a new one.

And the new error grows until it has betrayed business men into courses which end in a fresh crisis.[1]

Professor Pigou represents waves of elation and depression as arising from changes in the business situation, changes which are magnified into business cycles by the emotions they excite. Dr. Maurice Beck Hexter, Director of the Federated Jewish Charities of Boston, has thrown out the suggestion that these waves of feeling have an origin independent of the business world.

By an elaborate statistical analysis of vital and economic data, Dr. Hexter has reached the conclusion that

[1] A. C. Pigou, *The Economics of Welfare,* 1st ed., London, 1920, Part vi, chapter vi. The quotations are from pp. 833, 839, 840, 843 and 844. In companion chapters, Professor Pigou shows how the results of the "dominant cause" are modified by other factors, such as harvest fluctuations, and the workings of the monetary system. Professor Pigou has dropped this discussion from his second edition, hoping to incorporate it "in the next year or two" in "a study of industrial fluctuations." See preface of the 2d ed., 1924.

. . . fluctuations in conceptions *precede* fluctuations in wholesale prices by about eight months; fluctuations in the birth-rate *precede* fluctuations in unemployment by about seventeen months . . . fluctuations in the death-rate *precede* fluctuations in wholesale prices about seventeen months; and . . . fluctuations in the death-rate *precede* fluctuations in unemployment by about ten months.

A causal explanation of these relations is suggested by the powerful emotional reactions excited in men by the death of friends and the prospect of having children. Dr. Hexter argues thus:

Business enterprise is the application of mental effort to the transformation of our physical environment. Anything which affects the emotions of men must necessarily affect their ability to make decisions, anticipate decisions, or postpone decisions. If these times of postponed decisions or accelerated judgments or stimulated efforts are not isolated, but, on the contrary, run in wave-like movements, we think that there may be something to (*sic*) the suggestion that varying birth-rates and fluctuating death-rates can and do affect business cycles. The errors of optimism and the errors of pessimism may be closely connected with these variations in human emotions. It may very well be that these waves of emotion which run through society from time to time are very closely related to these variations in births and deaths.[2]

It will be noticed that Dr. Hexter's hypothesis is related to Professor Huntington's quite as closely as to Professor Pigou's. But Hexter differs from Huntington in that he does not seek to connect fluctuations in vital statistics with fluctuations in the weather.

4. Innovations, Promotion, Progress.

Professor Joseph Schumpeter of Bonn holds that to explain business cycles by errors bred of uncertainty and nourished by mass psychology is superficial. That errors are made, that they wax with prosperity, and that they play a considerable rôle in the cycle he admits; but, he adds, crises and depressions would continue to run their round if miscalculation were eliminated.

The fundamental cause of business fluctuations Schumpeter finds

[2] Maurice B. Hexter, *Social Consequences of Business Cycles*. Boston and New York, 1925, Part ii. The quotations are from pp. 169, 174 and 175.

in the innovations made from time to time by the relatively small number of exceptionally energetic business men—their practical applications of scientific discoveries and mechanical inventions, their development of new forms of industrial and commercial organization, their introduction of unfamiliar products, their conquests of new markets, exploitation of new resources, shiftings of trade routes, and the like. Changes of this sort, when made on a large scale, alter the data on which the mass of routine business men have based their plans. These plans doubtless involve a certain element of error; but business innovations produce a far graver situation.

Somehow, all enterprises must adapt themselves to the novel conditions now confronting them, or go to the wall. Considerable numbers do fail. A far larger number manage to work out new plans based on the new data concerning prices, costs, methods and markets. But this process of feeling out the novel conditions and making adjustments to them takes time. While the readjusting is under way, the making of innovations slows down; even the most restless of enterprisers cannot get the capital and coöperation required to carry out their schemes. This is the period of depression. It lasts until the readjustments have gone far enough to produce a fairly stable condition of affairs, stable enough to let men regain confidence in the future.

But the very restoration of quasi-stability makes it possible for the disturbers of the business peace to resume operations on a large scale. By borrowing for their new projects the innovators raise interest rates; by investing capital they raise the prices of industrial equipment and increase payroll disbursements. There follows an increase of demand and a rise in the prices of consumers' goods. The general activity thus initiated brings prosperity to the mass of enterprises—and stimulates further innovations. Prosperity continues until the unsettling consequences of the business changes begin to appear *en masse* in the shape of large supplies flooding the market, high costs of materials and labor, shifting of demand to new products, the supersession of old sources of production by new sources, and so on. Then comes a new crisis and a new period of readjustments.

To complete this theory it is necessary to show why innovations themselves come in waves. Schumpeter explains that the combination of capacities required for conceiving new undertakings and carrying them through all obstacles and hazards is rare among men; but that when a few highly endowed individuals have achieved success,

their example makes the way easier for a crowd of imitators. The rising prices, the increasing demand, the spread of optimism make borrowers more eager and lenders less cautious. Men who do not have the capacity to originate new schemes may have the wit to profit by and even improve upon the work of the pioneers. So, once started, a wave of innovation gains momentum—until it is checked by the consequences which it produces.[1]

The "promotion theory" of business cycles, developed by Professor Minnie T. England of the University of Nebraska, rests upon the same foundations as Schumpeter's theory of innovations. While less complete in its formal logic, Mrs. England's exposition runs in more realistic terms and cites more evidence. It should be studied by those who feel that Schumpeter's sketch lacks substance.[2]

While Mrs. England represents promoters and Professor Schumpeter represents a less specialized group of innovators as responsible for business crises, Dr. Emanuel H. Vogel, late of Vienna University, lays the responsibility upon "progress" at large.

In his eyes, crises are accidents which are bound to happen every now and then in a growing society based on private enterprise. For when such a society is expanding year after year, prosperity requires the maintenance of an economic equilibrium which is itself moving. The rates at which the important industries are growing must be kept in adjustment to each other; so also must the rates at which the incomes of all classes of the people and their consumption of goods are growing.

Such a consummation of adjustment, Dr. Vogel argues, is thinkable only in a society whose changes are always in the same direction and at the same pace. It is not thinkable in a society whose fortunes are represented by an ascending saw-toothed curve. We know that expansion at a constant rate never continues unbroken long at a

[1] Dr. Schumpeter's first version of this theory was published in May, 1910: "Ueber das Wesen der Wirtschaftskrisen," *Zeitschrift für Volkswirtschaft, Sozialpolitik und Verwaltung*, vol. xix, p. 271. Successive revisions appear in his *Theorie der wirtschaftlichen Entwicklung*, Leipzig, 1912, chapter vi; "Die Wellenbewegung des Wirtschaftslebens," *Archiv für Sozialwissenschaft und Sozialpolitik*, July, 1914, vol. xxxix, pp. 1-32, and in the second edition of his *Theorie der wirtschaftlichen Entwicklung*, Munich and Leipzig, 1926, chapter vi. This latest version includes replies to several critics of the theory, and is written in the most emphatic tone.

[2] See "Fisher's Theory of Crises," *Quarterly Journal of Economics*, November, 1912, vol. xxvii, pp. 95-106; "Promotion as the Cause of Crises," the same, August, 1915, vol. xxix, pp. 631-641; "Economic Crises," *Journal of Political Economy*, April, 1913, vol. xxi. pp. 345-354; "An Analysis of the Crisis Cycle," the same, October, 1913, vol. xxi, pp. 712-734.

time; every community experiences setbacks which check its economic progress. Unfavorable political events, mistaken forecasts of the future, the disturbances caused by improvements in technical methods, discoveries of new sources of supply, alterations in consumers' tastes, suggest how various are the factors which are changing the pace of growth and occasionally causing shrinkage.

Irregularities of change, then, are rooted deep in modern economic organization. And to these irregularities it is quite impossible that all the different rates of growth should adjust themselves promptly and in such a way as to maintain among themselves a moving equilibrium. A serious rupture of equilibrium produces an economic crisis followed by a period of declining activity. Gradually men work out a fresh series of adjustments, equilibrium is re-established, and progress resumes its course until something new happens to which the rates of growth cannot adjust themselves without losing adjustment to each other.[3]

5. The Processes of Saving and Investing.

One of the explanations of crises most in favor among business men is that they are caused by "scarcity of capital." Investments during prosperity are so heavy that the supply of loan funds is gradually exhausted. When this stage is reached, borrowers are unable to complete their financing and the boom ends in a crisis. This idea has been elaborated by Professor Michel Tugan-Baranovski, whose Russian treatise of 1894 has been repeatedly revised and translated into French and German.

It is necessary to distinguish, Tugan-Baranovski begins, between loan funds and capital invested in production. The loan fund is the aggregate of savings made by individuals belonging to all classes, and by business enterprises. During depressions the savings of business enterprises, business men, stockholders and wage-earners decline. But there is an important class of savers whose incomes are little affected by depression—landlords, bond-holders, salaried officials; indeed their savings are augmented by the lower cost of living. Thus saving continues on a large scale during depression, and (the vital point) if the aggregate declines below the records of prosperity, it certainly declines less than does investing. Hence depression brings

[3] *Die Theorie des volkswirtschaftlichen Entwickelungsprozesses und das Krisenproblem.* By Dr. Emanuel Hugo Vogel. Vienna and Leipzig, 1917.

the gradual accumulation of a huge uninvested fund of loan capital. Evidence of this accumulation appears in the swollen bank reserves and in the low rates of interest and bank discount.

Of course, the reason why these savings are not invested as they are made is found in the disorganized state of business. Few business men wish to borrow on a large scale during depression. But let savers become eager enough to get their funds into profitable use, let the rates of interest which they will accept drop low enough, the dam behind which the loan fund has been accumulating will give way, and money will begin to flow into investment.

When this time comes the huge purchases made with borrowed loan funds bring prosperity. Stimulated by its own effects, investment keeps expanding and presently attains a scale so large as to exceed current savings. Hence the uninvested loan fund is gradually exhausted. When the point of exhaustion is neared, available capital becomes so scarce that pending plans for further business extensions cannot be financed. Interest rates rise to prohibitive levels, bank reserves drop to the danger point, the makers of industrial equipment get no new orders, and prosperity ends in a crisis.[1]

While giving the preceding account of the process by which crises are bred periodically, Tugan-Baranovski holds that the alternate accumulation and exhaustion of the loan fund could not occur were income more evenly distributed.

> It is the inadequate remuneration of labor . . . which is the fundamental cause of the rapid accumulation of social capital, which in its turn provokes crises.[2]

This is the idea which an English publicist, Mr. John A. Hobson, has developed into the theory that business cycles are due to "over-saving" —a theory quite different from Tugan-Baranovski's.

Mr. Hobson holds that at any given time

> there is an exact proportion of the current income which, in accordance with existing arts of production and existing foresight, is required to set up new capital so as to make provision for the maximum consumption throughout the near future.

[1] The latest exposition known to me is the French edition of Tugan-Baranovski's treatise, *Les Crises Industrielles en Angleterre*, traduit par Joseph Schapiro (Bibliothèque Internationale d'Économie Politique), Paris, 1913. See especially Part II.

[2] The same, p. 279.

If in a period of prosperity, the rate of consumption should rise *pari passu* with the rate of production, there is no inherent reason why the prosperity might not continue indefinitely. But in modern societies, a large portion of the wealth produced belongs to a small class. In active times their incomes rise more rapidly than their consumption, and the surplus income is perforce saved. There results for the community as a whole a slight deficiency of spending and a corresponding excess of saving. The wealthy class seeks to invest its new savings in productive enterprises—thereby increasing the supply of goods and also increasing the incomes from which further savings will be made. This process runs cumulatively during the years of prosperity until finally the markets become congested with goods which cannot be sold at a profit. Then prices fall, liquidation ensues, capital is written down, and the incomes of the wealthy class are so reduced that savings fall below the proper proportion to spending.

During the period of depression, the glut of goods weighing upon the market is gradually worked off and the prospect of profitable investment slowly returns. Savings rise again to the right proportion to spending and good times prevail for a season. But after a while the chronic impulse toward over-saving becomes fully operative once more; soon or late it begets another congestion of the markets, and this congestion begets another depression.

Proximately then, the cause of alternating prosperity and depression is the tendency toward over-saving; ultimately it is the existence of the surplus incomes which lead to over-saving.[1]

[1] Mr. Hobson has presented his theory in several books, but most fully in *The Industrial System,* London, 1909, chapters iii and xviii, and in *Economics of Unemployment,* London, 1922. The passage quoted is from p. 53 of the earlier volume.

Another form of the savings theory is presented by Mr. N. Johannsen. The act of saving by itself, means the withdrawal of purchasing power from the market, and so always tends to produce business depression. But when the sums saved are promptly invested "in the creation of new productive capital," the deficiency of purchasing power is offset, and the community's wealth is increased. No such offsetting occurs, however, when savings are used to buy property from embarrassed owners, or loaned to people in distress. Those who get the money expend it; but their expenditures merely offset their own losses, and the withdrawal of purchasing power caused by the act of saving is not compensated for. Whether saving tends to sustain prosperity or to cause depression thus "depends upon the manner of investment." "Impair savings," as Mr. Johannsen calls savings which are not used to create new capital, "always hurt business, and if sufficiently large, they cause a general depression." See N. Johannsen, *A Neglected Point in Connection with Crises,* New York, 1908, and *Business Depressions: Their Cause. A Discovery in Economics,* Stapleton, New York, 1925.

Dr. Rudolf Stucken of the University of Kiel argues in a somewhat similar vein that, if a period of expansion in business activity is checked for any reason, savings will not be invested in productive enterprises, but used to repay bank loans. The immediate result is to reduce the purchasing power offered for goods below the current supply seeking sale, and so to convert the check upon expansion into a contraction.

6. Construction Work.

Among the numerous theorists who have been influenced by Tugan-Baranovski are writers who have sought to show what his

But the reduction of bank loans, and the concomitant reduction of demand liabilities enables the banks to increase their credit advances to business men liberally when a revival begins, and thus to convert revival into prosperity. See Rudolf Stucken, *Theorie der Konjunkturschwankungen,* Jena, 1926.

While Mr. D. H. Robertson cannot be classified with the savings theorists, since he believes that other factors have a leading share in producing cyclical oscillations in trade, the most notable feature of his recent book on *Banking Policy and the Price Level,* (London, 1926), is an analysis of the role played by savings in "trade cycles." For this analysis he invents a curious terminology.

> "The essence of the activity of providing capital" is "Lacking." "A man is lacking if during a given period he consumes less than the value of his current economic output. . . . The amount of Lacking done in a given period may be measured by the volume of consumable goods lacked. . . . The things in the provision of which Lacking eventuates I propose to call Capital. . . . Long Lacking is directed towards providing society with the use . . . of the fixed and durable instruments of production: Short Lacking towards" providing society with the use of circulating capital, which, like fixed capital, consists of commodities. (Pp. 40-42.)

Equipped with these definitions, Mr. Robertson argues:

> "From our present point of view, the fundamental feature of the upward swing of a trade cycle is a large and discontinuous increase in the demand for Short Lacking, occurring as the essential preliminary to an expansion of output . . . the supply of (Spontaneous) Short Lacking is not sufficiently elastic to cope with such pronounced and discontinuous increases in demand, and . . . the responsibility for meeting them rests almost entirely upon the banking-system (Pp. 71, 72) . . . Now the banking-system can, of course, only 'provide' . . . Short Lacking . . . by extorting it from the general public through the multiplication of currency." (Pp. 88, 89.)

The meaning seems to be that current output cannot be expanded freely in a period of prosperity unless there has been an increase in the commodities whic constitute circulating capital; that these commodities cannot be provided in sufficien quantity unless the general public is prevented from increasing its consumption as fas as output rises, and that the banks put the necessary brake upon consumption by rais-ing prices through an increase of the currency.

Mr. Robertson holds that most periods of prosperity bring also a rapid increas in the demand for fixed capital, and therefore for the Long Lacking which provides it Part of this demand is met by investors, but part falls on the banks. The latte can provide Long Lacking only by the means which they use to provide Short Lacking that is, they must extort Long Lacking from the public by expanding the currenc and raising prices. (Pp. 84-89).

But the rise of prices through which the banks extort Lacking, Short and Long, fro the public increases the money value of the circulating and fixed capital required b business enterprises, and therefore makes necessary a greater rise of prices. Obviousl a self-inflating process of this sort cannot be sustained indefinitely. To keep the proces under control, the banks raise interest rates, sell government securities, and, at nee limit new money loans. Despite the skill which modern banking-systems have ac quired in promoting equilibrium between the demand for and supply of Lackin many crises are still characterized by what is popularly called "an acute shortag of capital," and what is properly called "a deficiency in the activity Lacking." (P 79, 90).

I offer this interpretation of Mr. Robertson's analysis with a diffidence whic readers of his book will understand. It is certainly incomplete; I hope it is not wron

analysis of savings means in terms of production. By so doing they have shifted the emphasis from over-saving to over-production of one type of goods in comparison with another type. This variant of business-cycle theory is represented in Germany by Professor Arthur Spiethoff of the University of Berlin;[1] but it will suffice to cite the less technical exposition given by Mr. George H. Hull, an American business man.

High prices of construction, runs Hull's thesis, is the hitherto "unknown cause of the mysterious depressions" from which the industrial nations suffer. The greater part of modern trade fluctuates within relatively narrow limits. Agriculture provides the necessities of life, commerce distributes them, and finance adjusts the bills. The volume of all this business is fairly constant, because the demand for necessities is incapable of sudden expansion or contraction. Industry, on the contrary, may expand or contract indefinitely, especially that part of industry devoted to construction work. For the sources of booms and depressions, therefore, we must look to the enterprises which build and equip houses, stores, factories, railways, docks, and the like.

Of the huge total of construction, which Mr. Hull believes to make "say 77 per cent of all industrial products of the nation" after "deducting land and the necessities of life," about two-thirds, even in the busiest of years, consists of repairs, replacements, and such extensions as are required by the growth of population. This portion of construction is necessary and must be executed every year. But the remaining portion is "optional construction," and is undertaken or not according as investors see a liberal or a meager profit in providing new building and equipment.

When the costs of construction fall low enough to arouse "the bargain-counter instinct," many of the "far-seeing ones who hold the purse-strings of the country" let heavy contracts, and their example is followed by the less shrewd. The addition of this new business to the volume of "necessity construction" and the provision of consumers' goods, creates a boom. But, after a year or two, con-

[1] Professor Spiethoff published his analysis in a series of articles in Schmoller's *Jahrbuch für Gesetzgebung,* 1902, pp. 721-759; 1903, pp. 670-708; 1909, pp. 445-467, 927-951, 1417-1437. See also Spiethoff's article "Krisen" in the 4th edition of the *Handwörterbuch der Staatswissenschaften,* Jena, 1925, vol. vi, pp. 8-91. Mr. Dennis H. Robertson has developed a theory of "constructional relapse" which runs on similar lines. See *A Study of Industrial Fluctuation,* London, 1915, pp. 170-198.

A summary of Spiethoff's theory may be found in the earlier edition of this book, pp. 10, 11.

tractors discover that their order books call for more work than they can get labor and materials to finish within the contract time. When this oversold condition of the contracting trades is realized, the prices of labor and raw materials rise rapidly. The estimated cost of construction on new contracts then becomes excessive. Shrewd investors therefore begin to postpone the execution of their plans for extending permanent equipment, and the letting of fresh contracts declines apace. While the contractors are gradually completing work on their old orders, all the enterprises making iron, steel, lumber, cement, brick, stone, etc., begin to suffer a serious shrinkage of new business. Just as the execution of the large contracts for "optional construction," let in the low-price period, brought on prosperity, so the smallness of such contracts, let in the high-price period, now brings on depression. Then the costs of construction work fall until they arouse "the bargain-counter instinct" of investors once more, and the cycle begins afresh.[2]

Colonel Malcolm C. Rorty has suggested that the over-construction theory should be expanded into an "over-commitment" theory, and strengthened by analysis of financial processes. At an early stage in many periods of prosperity, he points out, simultaneous over-commitments to business extensions and new ventures are made in most, if not in all, branches of industry. Each such commitment involves the creation, through credit extensions, of new purchasing power. Since the additional purchasing power is not offset promptly by a corresponding increase in production, prices rise. This process of extending commitments, expanding credit and raising prices continues until it is checked by shortage of credit facilities, or until prices have reached a level at which experienced business men see danger in making further additions to their stocks of goods. Then comes a contraction of purchases, and a crisis.

Such are the essential features of a typical boom and crisis, arising from causes inherent in the business organization. But Colonel Rorty adds that we have cycles of two other types. The milder periods of prosperity and recession arise from mere current readjustments of production, distribution and consumption. Still other cycles arise primarily from non-business causes, such as wars. Admitting that sometimes it is difficult to decide to which of these three types a

[2] George H. Hull, *Industrial Depressions,* New York, 1911. The passages quoted are from pp. 103-107.

given case belongs, Colonel Rorty holds that this classification clarifies the problem, and explains why no one theory accounts in satisfactory fashion for all cycles.[3]

7. Generalized Over-Production.

The emphasis which Spiethoff and Hull put upon the difference between the rôles played by industrial equipment and consumers' goods in business cycles has become a commonplace in later writings. Two theorists in particular have developed this idea, and in developing it have reached results which differ sharply from those of Tugan-Baranovski and Hull. Against the first they contend that there is and can be no accumulation of uninvested loan-capital; against the second they contend that crises result from a general, not a partial over-production of goods, and that the seat of difficulty is in the industries making consumers' goods rather than in those making industrial equipment. Mentor Bouniatian, professor at the Polytechnic Institute of Tiflis was perhaps the earlier to publish; but the clearer exposition has been supplied by Albert Aftalion, professor at the University of Paris.[1]

When the price level rises after a period of depression—why it should rise will appear later—business men see that current demand for consumers' goods is larger than current supply at the old prices. To secure their shares of the good profits in prospect, manufacturers enlarge the volume of their orders for industrial equipment. These orders increase employment, thus stimulate consumers' demand, and so encourage the placing of still larger orders for equipment.

To construct the equipment which is typical of modern industry, however, requires months and often years. Hence a considerable time must pass before notable additions can be made to the current supply

[3] See M. C. Rorty, *Some Problems in Current Economics,* Chicago, 1922, pp. 73-84, and the report of Colonel Rorty's address to the National Founders Association, in *The Iron Age,* November 25, 1926, pp. 1478-1482.

[1] On the relations between the ideas of these two writers see the preface of *Les Crises Économiques,* par Mentor Bouniatian, Traduit du Russe, (Moscow, 1915) par J. Bernard (Bibliothèque Internationale d'Économie Politique), Paris, 1922. Bouniatian's first book on the subject was *Wirtschaftskrisen und Ueberkapitalisation,* Munich, 1908. Aftalion published first a series of articles on "La réalite des surproductions générales" in the *Révue d'Économie Politique,* 1908-09 (vol. xxii, pp. 696-706; vol. xxiii, pp. 81-117, 201-229, 241-259); then an *Essai d'une théorie des crises générales et périodiques,* Paris, 1909, and finally a treatise, *Les Crises périodiques de Surproduction,* 2 vols., Paris, 1913.

of consumers' goods. During this "period of gestation," [2] the supply of consumers' goods continues inadequate, prices keep advancing, employment grows fuller, large incomes are disbursed and prosperity reigns.

After prosperity has grown at an increasing pace for some time, however, large quantities of new equipment are ready for use and the current supply of consumers' goods is augmented. Then trouble begins. For, according to "the laws of value," these increments added to the supply of consumers' goods cannot be sold at prices such as have recently prevailed. When the supply of any commodity increases, the wants satisfied by consuming new increments are less intense than the marginal wants recently satisfied. The later days of prosperity are therefore characterized by a decline in the marginal utility of consumers' goods. This decline brings with it a reduction in the prices consumers are willing to pay—a fall which is rendered greater by the concomitant rise in the marginal utility of money, caused by the increasing demands upon the circulating medium made by active trade. Presently it becomes clear that general over-production prevails. The fall of prices extends from one field to another and prosperity ends in a crisis.

General over-production accompanied by a declining price level lasts for a year or so after the crisis, because the new equipment has cost so much money that it must be kept running, if that is anywise possible. Indeed, over-production increases for a time, since part of the equipment ordered in the latter part of the boom is not finished until after the crisis, and when it is delivered it must be made to give some return upon the capital locked up in it. The fall of prices is now opposed by a decline in the marginal utility of money, which is less needed in depression; but the decline in the marginal utility of consumers' goods more than offsets this factor.

Recovery from depression comes after three or four years, because, while prices are falling, there is little inducement to order new equipment. It is true that some new orders are placed even in th

[2] The phrase is borrowed from Mr. D. H. Robertson, who has developed this poir more fully than Aftalion or Bouniatian. In particular Mr. Robertson suggests that th recurrence of business cycles may be due in large part to the more or less simultaneo wearing-out and re-ordering of large masses of equipment made in an earlier period prosperity. See *A Study of Industrial Fluctuation,* pp. 13-25, London, 1915.

Professor Pigou, who also makes much of the "period of gestation," ventures th statement that "ten years seem to be, not merely the average, but also the marked predominant" length of life of machinery. *The Economics of Welfare,* 1st ed., pp. 82 830, 841-848.

worst of times; but the volume shrinks greatly in comparison with that of the preceding period of prosperity. Meanwhile the demand for consumers' goods continues to grow, though at a slightly slower pace than in prosperity. Let this situation persist for a few years, and gradually the current demand for consumers' goods at the low prices which depression causes will come to exceed current supply. When this happens, prices turn upward again. Then business men seek to increase their output and begin ordering equipment more freely. But while their orders are being executed, the current supply of consumers' goods becomes scantier in comparison with the growing demand, prices rise further, and another period of prosperity dawns.

8. Banking Operations.

All the explanations summarized in the preceding sections take for granted that the processes which they trace run in communities equipped with modern monetary and banking systems. From their viewpoints, however, money and bank credit are simply mechanisms through which the economic forces causing business cycles work their effects. At most these theories admit that the monetary mechanism accentuates the wave movements which are started by more fundamental factors.[1] The explanations which make business cycles a direct consequence of banking operations therefore constitute a distinct variety of cycle theories.

No one has contented himself with a briefer statement of the reason for adopting this type of explanation than Professor Alvin H. Hansen of the University of Minnesota.

> Demand, (he argues), is based on purchasing power. The source of purchasing power is income, and the source of income is the production of material goods and services. . . . In short, goods and services are exchanged against goods and services. On this basis one would expect production to run an even course, and not to run in cycles. And indeed in the barter economy there were no business cycles.

But how does the rise of money economy produce cyclical oscillations? Under modern conditions, Professor Hansen answers,

[1] See, for example, Professor Pigou's chapter on "Accentuation of Wave Movements due to the Working of the Monetary System." *The Economics of Welfare*, 1st ed., pp. 849-864, and Mr. Robertson's chapter on "The Wage and Money Systems," *A Study of Industrial Fluctuation*, pp. 206-238.

> The nominal purchasing power obtaining in any society at any given moment may be measured substantially by the amount of money in hand-to-hand circulation and the volume of bank credit in the form of deposit currency.

The amount of purchasing power, and therefore of demand, made available by the banks is limited

> by two things: first, by the quantity of reserves; second, by the desirability of converting personal credit into bank credit, and this depends upon the discount rate and the profitableness of the employment of capital in industry.

Plainly neither these limits themselves nor the closeness with which they are approached is fixed; hence the purchasing power which the banks provide can fluctuate through a wide range.

When the banks increase nominal purchasing power by granting more credit, they add to the circulating media.

> The effect is an increase in prices and therefore no increase in real purchasing power. The nominal incomes of people generally are as before, but their real purchasing power is reduced because of the increase in prices. The issuance of bank credit simply redistributes purchasing power, reducing the real purchasing power of income receivers generally, and increasing the purchasing power of entrepreneurs able to secure bank credit. It is this redistribution of purchasing power, accomplished through the instrumentality of banking institutions, that changes demand, upsets prices, affects the profit margin, and therefore production. Here, in short, may be found the fundamental cause of the business cycle.

To complete the theory, it is neccssary to follow the round of events:

> When accumulated stocks have run out, when costs are falling, when labor is easily obtainable, when loanable funds are plentiful and interest rates run low, then prospects for profit-making are bright and entrepreneurs apply for bank credit. The issuance of bank credit increases the purchasing power of entrepreneurs. The result is increased bidding for raw materials, capital equipment, construction work, etc., with a consequent increase in prices.

The business men, who profit by the increased demand, in their turn apply for bank loans and so the process runs expansively for a time.

"This upward movement comes to a close only when bank credit can no longer be further extended, for the reason that it has already reached the limit of banking safety." But this limit can hardly be reached without being overrun; for the activity of trade causes more money to be drawn into hand-to-hand circulation, at the expense of bank reserves. "It therefore becomes necessary not merely to stop the expansion of bank credit, but actually to reduce the outstanding volume." The resulting contraction causes prices to fall, the volume of business to shrink, and the demand for bank credit itself to slacken —once more a self-propagating process.

> But as the upward movement culminated because of the strain placed upon bank reserves through an undue extension of bank credit, so the downward movement comes to a close because of the great accumulation of bank reserves due to the reduction of outstanding bank credit and the return of money from hand-to-hand circulation following the decline of prices. This continued accumulation of reserves leads bankers progressively to lower discount rates to a point low enough to make the employment of bank credit again profitable. New securities are freely issued, bank loans are readily obtainable, and the purchasing power of business enterprises increases. Thus the upward swing returns and the cycle repeats itself.[2]

Like Professor Hansen, Mr. R. G. Hawtrey of the British Treasury thinks he has "proved that there is an inherent tendency toward fluctuations in the banking institutions which prevail in the world as it is." But Hawtrey lays more stress than Hansen upon the importance of changes in discount rates.

"An expansion of trade occurs," Mr. Hawtrey explains, "when the amount of credit money in existence is less than the bankers think prudent, having regard to their holdings of cash, and they lower the rate of interest in order to encourage borrowing." This reduction in the cost of loans starts a long train of consequences: dealers give larger orders to producers, producers increase output and raise prices, employment becomes fuller and wages rise, the increase of incomes augments retail demand, the prosperous business classes borrow more

[2] *Cycles of Prosperity and Depression in the United States, Great Britain and Germany,* by Alvin H. Hansen (University of Wisconsin Studies in the Social Sciences and History, No. 5). Madison, 1921. The quotations are from pp. 104-108.

freely—and so on progressively, until the banks, having lent all the credit they think prudent,

> no longer need to keep down the rate of interest. The rate of interest is then raised to the "profit rate," and the inducement (for dealers) to increase stocks of goods is removed.

Trade expansion is followed by trade depression, because the high rates of interest tempt the banks to lend as much as possible. For a time they can expand loans without losing much cash; but when the lagging rise of wage rates gets under way, bank reserves are reduced. Further, high prices are likely to stimulate imports, check exports and so cause an outflow of gold from the country enjoying prosperity. When their reserves decline appreciably, the banks are forced to contract outstanding loans. For this purpose they raise the rate of interest still further and withdraw funds loaned on the investment market. Then securities fall and dealers in commodities seek to reduce stocks on which the carrying charge has become heavy. They give fewer orders to producers, producers decrease output and cut down their working forces; retail demand falls off; stocks threaten to become redundant again because of fewer sales, and the process starts all over again. During this period of depression business men need less credit and the reduced wage disbursements allow cash to accumulate in the banks. Thus the banks win back to an easy condition, and "no longer need to keep up the rate of interest." By the fall in interest rates the way is prepared for a new expansion of trade.[3]

[3] *Good and Bad Trade. An Inquiry into the Causes of Trade Fluctuations,* by R. G. Hawtrey, London, 1913. The quotations are from pp. 3, 199, 268 and 269.

In a later volume, Mr. Hawtrey seems to have changed his fundamental thesis somewhat. "Far from causing the cyclical fluctuations," he says on p. 425 of *Currency and Credit* (2d ed., London, 1923), "a banking system diminishes their violence and facilitates their control." The "instability of credit" is due "not so much to the banker as to the merchant and the promoter." (p. 423). But he adds, "though credit institutions are not themselves the cause of this phenomenon, yet where such institutions exist it is through them that the fluctuations take effect." (p. 425). For present purposes, it is Mr. Hawtrey's analysis of the process by which cyclical fluctuations come to pass in modern communities, rather than his brief discussion of their causes, which is helpful. To this analysis he adheres in *Currency and Credit* (see p. 130 and chapters ix, x), with minor modifications, of which I have incorporated the most important into my summary made from his *Good and Bad Trade.*

Mr. Hawtrey's theory has much in common with views formerly held by Professor Irving Fisher. But there is a significant difference. Professor Fisher built upon what he believed to be a statistically demonstrated fact that changes in interest rates lag behind price movements. This lag increases the profits of business borrowers when prices are rising and stimulates activity. When prices are falling, the lagging of interest rates reduces profits and augments depression. Mr. Hawtrey, on the other hand, repre-

9. Production and the Flow of Money Incomes.

In a sense, all of the theories so far reviewed are ways of explaining why the people of a country sometimes cannot or will not buy at profitable prices all they produce; or, what comes to the same thing, why they produce more than they can sell. But the most direct way of solving the problem when stated in this way has still to be noticed. It consists in giving new reasons for Sismondi's contention that in periods of activity money incomes lag behind the money value of the goods produced.

The suggestion of Mr. R. E. May introduces the subtle recent theories which follow this line. May builds upon two corner stones: (1) in a modern industrial community wages form by far the largest of the income streams, (2) wages increase less rapidly in prosperity than the aggregate value of goods produced. Thus the purchasing power of the most important class of consumers fails to keep pace with the volume of goods seeking sale. Let the resulting excess of dollar supply over dollar demand accumulate for a year or two, and it is inevitable that the market for consumers' goods will be glutted. Then come a crisis and depression which restore the body economic to health, by forcing down prices to the point where the wage-earning consumers can buy what is offered. And Mr. May

sents changes in bank-discount rates as themselves the active force in initiating trade fluctuations, with their concomitant price fluctuations.

For Professor Fisher's theory, see *The Purchasing Power of Money,* New York, 1911, chapters iv and xi, sections 15-17; and "Gold Depreciation and Interest Rates," *Moody's Magazine,* 1909, pp. 110-114 (a summary statement). As late as December, 1923, Fisher still suspected "that the principal force affecting the cycle is the *real* rate of interest, the sum of the *money* rate of interest and the rate of appreciation (positive or negative) of the purchasing power of the dollar." (See "The Business Cycle Largely a 'Dance of the Dollar'," *Journal of the American Statistical Association,* vol. xviii, p. 1024). Recently, however, Professor Fisher has come to believe that "the" business cycle is a myth. Fluctuations in "trade," (which remain genuine in his eyes), are due primarily to "price-change"; but the next most important influence "is probably that of the rate of interest." See "Our Unstable Dollar and the So-called Business Cycle," *Journal of the American Statistical Association,* June, 1925, vol. xx, pp. 191, 198.

Professor Wilhelm Röpke of Jena has suggested an interesting combination of the savings and the banking theories of business cycles. The "real cyclical bacillus" he finds in periodic variations in the ratio between accumulation and consumption, which cannot be altered much without producing serious disturbances in the process of exchange. But these periodic variations in the ratio between accumulation and consumption are due in large part to periodic changes in the volume of credit—changes which appear in discrepancies between the real and the nominal rates of interest, in the liquidity of the credit-granting banks, and in their operating policies. See his paper on "Kredit und Konjunktur," in *Jahrbücher für Nationalökonomie und Statistik,* March-April, 1926, vol. cxxiv, pp. 243-285.

follows the logic of his diagnosis to the point of recommending a legal limitation of profits, in order that producers may be forced to reduce selling prices as they increase output.[1]

A more adequate development of this theme has been provided by Professor Emil Lederer of Heidelberg.

Depression is characterized, he begins, by a decline in physical production and in prices. Though general, the price decline is not uniform. The prices which constitute the incomes of the propertied and salaried classes shrink but little. Nor do wage cuts and unemployment reduce the money incomes of the working masses so much as the cost of living falls. Farmers, also, as a rule lose less than they gain by the price movements. Thus, the discrepancies characteristic of the decline in prices enable consumers to buy perhaps a larger physical quantity of commodities, certainly a larger quota of the current output. Business profits, on the other hand, fall heavily, just because wages, rent and interest charges lag behind the decline of selling prices. The unprofitableness of business, and the consequent reduction of savings check the expansion of industrial equipment. But the increasing purchasing power of the majority of income receivers gradually absorbs whatever stocks of consumers' goods were carried over from the prosperous phase of the cycle in addition to the reduced current output, and so produces a condition which favors a resumption of activity.

A business revival, as it gets under way, reverses the trend of prices. Rising prices and the growing volume of trade call for larger payments. To a limited extent, the increase in payments can be effected by quickening the circulation of money and credit, which had become sluggish during depression. Further expansion may be provided for by additions to the gold supply. Seldom, however, are these resources adequate to the need. Broadly speaking, periods of prosperity are made possible only by "additional credit"—that is, purchasing power, provided chiefly by banks, which is not based upon previous production.

Supported by "additional credit," the advance of prices gains momentum as activity waxes. But the advance is no less unequal than the decline had been. The prices which make up the incomes of the propertied, the salaried, and the wage-earning classes lag

[1] R. E. May, *Das Grundgesetz der Wirtschaftskrisen und ihr Vorbeugensmittel im Zeitalter des Monopols,* Berlin, 1902.

behind the prices of commodities. Hence the buying power of these classes is reduced, or, at least, fails to keep pace with the expansion of output. Meanwhile the lagging of those prices which constitute costs to business enterprises behind the prices which constitute receipts is enhancing profits. Larger profits lead to larger savings, larger investments in industrial equipment, and, when this equipment is ready for use, to larger supplies of consumers' goods, for which the demand is growing less rapidly, if not actually shrinking. Under such circumstances a crisis is inevitable, and a crisis reverses the trend of prices once more, starting the processes with which the analysis began.

According to Lederer, then, the most important cause of business cycles lies in the inequalities characteristic of price movements—inequalities which alter the distribution of purchasing power among income classes, the demand for different types of products, the rate at which industrial equipment grows, and the trend of price movements themselves. "Disproportionality of production" is as characteristic of business fluctuations as "disproportionality of income"; but the two developments have quite different effects. Over-production of certain goods in comparison with others leads to price changes, which affect profits, force alterations in production schedules, and so restore proper balance. "Disproportionality of incomes" is not self-rectifying; its consequences cumulate until they reach the critical point at which they convert depression into prosperity, or prosperity into depression.[2]

Like Professor Lederer, Messrs. Catchings, Foster and Hastings of the Pollak Foundation for Economic Research hold that prosperity is checked by the failure of consumers' incomes to keep pace with the output of consumers' goods. But the Pollak group give an explanation of this deficiency of consumer buying which differs from Lederer's theory of the inequalities in the rates at which different prices advance.

To keep business active, the Pollak theory begins, consumers must receive and spend incomes equal to the full value, at current retail prices, of the consumers' goods sent to market. Were industry confined to providing consumers' goods, this requirement would mean (1) that the total selling value of all products must be paid out

[2] Emil Lederer, "Konjunktur und Krisen," *Grundriss der Sozialökonomik*, Part iv, Section i, Tübingen, 1925, pp. 354-413.

promptly by business enterprises as costs (that is, as wages, salaries, rent, interest, taxes, etc.) or as dividends; (2) that all the money received by individuals must be paid back promptly to business enterprises for their products.

In the real world, of course, many business enterprises make goods which are not offered to consumers, and in so doing disburse incomes to individuals. It may seem that these disbursements, plus the incomes disbursed by industries making consumers' goods, must exceed the value of consumers' goods sent to market. But in so far as producers' goods are raw materials or supplies used up currently in contributing toward the making of consumers' goods, their full selling prices must be charged into the prices of the latter products, and the incomes disbursed for making the materials and supplies can do no more than equal this element in the prices of consumers' goods. There remain some things which consumers are not called upon to buy on completion; for example, public works and industrial equipment. Incomes disbursed in making such goods add to consumer purchasing power without adding an equivalent supply of consumers' goods. In periods of active construction, income payments on this account, plus the payment of wages before products are sent to market, for a time provide consumers with incomes exceeding the supplies of consumers' goods then on sale. Such a situation, however, soon produces consequences which end it. Prices of consumers' goods rise, that rise stimulates production at once, and the difficulty reappears of maintaining consumer purchasing power adequate to absorb the larger output at the higher price level. The difficulty is further accentuated as soon as the new industrial equipment on which men have been working begins adding its quota, directly or indirectly, to the consumers' goods flowing to market.

Thus "overproduction—a supply in excess of demand—is a purely monetary phenomenon," and, as such, might be prevented by monetary adjustments.

> If corporations went on forever increasing their output, and, in the process, expanding the volume of money in circulation *at a sufficient rate,* and if the flow of the output to the markets sufficiently lagged behind the flow of the new money as wages to consumers, consumers might continue to buy all that the markets actually offered. Such an expansion of money, however, does not long take place. Business men always fear a slump in demand; and when they doubt the capacity of con-

sumers to buy current output, they have no incentive for increasing output—no motive for using bank loans for that purpose.

But why should not business enterprises pay out the full values received for their products, and thus prevent a deficiency of consumer purchasing power? Because under modern conditions, a thriving enterprise must provide for expansion, and the safest way to finance expansion is "to plough part of the profits into the business." Messrs. Foster and Catchings believe that, on the average, American corporations do not disburse as dividends much over half of their profits. Nor would the situation necessarily be better if corporations paid out all their profits as dividends, and financed their extensions by selling stock to their shareholders. For in that case, consumers would divert income which is needed to sustain the demand for consumers' goods into demand for equipment, in order to make still more consumers' goods in the future. Even as matters stand, consumers are continually saving current income, for reasons as sound as those which justify the financial conservatism of corporations. And their savings are as much responsible for the deficient demand for consumers' goods as is the dividend policy of business enterprises.

To sum up:

> Progress toward greater total production and resultant higher standards of living is retarded because consumer buying does not keep pace with production. Consumer buying lags behind for two reasons: first, because, on account of corporate savings industry does not disburse to consumers enough money to buy the goods produced, without a fall in the price-level; second, because consumers, under the necessity of saving, cannot spend even as much money as they receive. Partly on account of these savings, there is not an even flow of money from producer to consumer, and from consumer back to producer. Furthermore, the savings of corporations and individuals are not used to purchase the goods already in the markets, but to bring about the production of more goods. The expansion of the volume of money does not fully make up the deficit, for money is expanded mainly to facilitate production, and the product must be sold to consumers for more money than the expansion has provided. Consequently we make progress only while we are filling the shelves with goods which must either remain on the shelves as stock in trade or be sold at a loss,

> and while we are building more industrial equipment than we can use. Inadequacy of consumer income is, therefore, the main reason, though not the only reason, why we do not long continue to produce the wealth which natural resources, capital facilities, improvements in the arts and the self-interest of employers and employees would otherwise enable us to produce. Chiefly because of shortage of consumer demand, both capital and labor restrict output, and nations engage in those struggles for outside markets and spheres of commercial influence which are the chief causes of war.[3]

While the Pollak group were developing their theory of business cycles in this country, Mr. P. W. Martin of the International Labour Office was working on similar lines in Switzerland. Martin holds that the factor which ends phases of prosperity, and, he adds, the factor which keeps production even in prosperous years far below its attainable levels, is the impossibility of selling what we desire to produce. In turn, the lack of markets is due to lack of "buying power." But Martin differs from Foster and Catchings in paying slight attention to the distinction, which they stress, between consumers' and producers' goods. To maintain prosperity, it is quite as necessary to have an adequate market for industrial equipment as for clothing. And Martin ascribes the deficiency of buying power, not to saving by corporations and individuals, but to the need of larger "liquid capital" which prosperity brings. His summary runs:

> So long as the community's buying power is used exclusively to pay for goods, the price system works. But from time to time industry must increase its liquid capital. This means that part of the community's buying power, which is needed to pay for goods if equilibrium between the flow of buying power and the flow of prices is to be maintained, goes instead

[3] A brief sketch of this theory was given in 1923 by William T. Foster and Waddill Catchings in chapter xx of *Money* (No. 2 of the Publications of the Pollak Foundation for Economic Research). A more elaborate exposition was worked out by Hudson B. Hastings in *Costs and Profits* (No. 3 of the same series), 1923. A later and somewhat different statement is found in Foster and Catchings, *Profits* (No. 8 of the Pollak series), 1925. The quotations are from p. 320 of *Profits* and pp. 16, 17, 28, and 29 of "The Dilemma of Thrift," a summary of their theory by Foster and Catchings, reprinted from the *Atlantic Monthly,* April, 1926. *Business Without a Buyer,* Foster and Catchings' latest exposition, appeared after this chapter had been set up. (No. 10 of the Pollak series).

The Pollak theory relates to crises rather than to business cycles: it does not explain how activity revives after depression, or how revival grows into prosperity.

to induce the production of more goods for sale. As a consequence, goods are produced for which no buying power exists.

This "flaw in the price system" can be remedied by supplying buyers with money enough to purchase what is offered for sale.

The first step will be for the Government, acting in agreement with the banks, to increase buying power how, when, where and to what extent the best available information shows to be advisable, until unemployment is reduced to its minimum. From that time on the Government and the banks will endeavour to adjust the additions to the community's buying power so that it shall always be exactly sufficient to provide an adequate market for the goods offered for sale. Their guide in this will be the price level. If the price level falls, the natural indicator of a lack of markets, they will pump in additional buying power until the lack of markets is completely obviated (as shown by the price level regaining its former position). If prices rise, the signal of inflation, additions to buying power will be made more slowly (if necessary buying power will be drained out even), until the price level is brought back to "normal," until, that is to say, all symptoms of inflation have been totally eliminated. These measures will be applied by special offices using the best knowledge and most scientific instruments available. Supporting their efforts at every turn will be the automatic action of the psychological factor in industry, tending to be, not as now, an inflationary agency during prosperity, a depressing agency during depression, but an automatic stabiliser of both prices and markets.[4]

Still another variation upon the income theme has been composed by Dean Arthur B. Adams of the University of Oklahoma. An increase in the buying of consumers' goods may lead to recovery from depression; but it cannot initiate a period of prosperity. For business in consumers' goods cannot give rise to money incomes which exceed the sales value of the current output, and prosperity requires that consumers be able to buy an increasing output at rising prices. Therefore, it is an error to think that "recovery generates a period of

[4] See P. W. Martin, *The Flaw in the Price System,* London, 1924, and *The Limited Market,* London, 1926. The quotations are from the later book, pp. 53, 54, 69, 70.

The theory expounded by Major C. H. Douglas of the Royal Air Force in a series of books seems to be an adumbration of the ideas worked out by the Pollak Foundation group and by Mr. Martin. See, for example, Major Douglas' volumes, *Credit Power and Democracy,* London, 1921, and *Social Credit,* London, 1924.

prosperity," or that "business is always going through some phase of a business cycle." The end of one cycle is sometimes separated from the beginning of the next by a prolonged period of "oscillating equilibrium." A new cycle does not start until something happens to give consumers incomes exceeding the value of the consumers' goods on sale. The factor which most often plays this rôle is "rapid expansion of capital equipment," financed by expansion of bank credit. Periods of prosperity, initiated by such developments, grow more intense for a time, but are finally terminated by the following "forces," working singly or together: (1) the output of consumers' goods eventually overtakes and exceeds the volume of consumers' incomes, (2) costs of production per unit eventually rise faster than selling prices, (3) the banks eventually reach the limit of their ability to increase loans.[5]

10. The Rôle Played by Profit-Making

There remain the theories which explain business cycles by the fact that the producing, transporting and distributing of goods are conducted mainly by business enterprises which aim at making money. Of course the theories already reviewed take the quest of profits for granted; but they treat business enterprise as an organization through which more fundamental forces operate. The distinguishing characteristic of the theories now to be noticed is that they represent the alternations of prosperity and depression as arising from certain technical exigencies of profit-making itself. This view was developed in 1904 by Dr. Thorstein Veblen, of the New School for Social Research, and in 1906 by Professor Jean Lescure of the University of Bordeaux.[1]

Dr. Veblen begins his discussion of "the theory of modern welfare" by pointing out that prosperity, crisis, and depression

> are primarily phenomena of price disturbance, . . . They affect industry because industry is managed on a business footing, in terms of price and for the sake of profits.

A period of prosperity is ushered in by a rise of prices, caused, for example, by an increased supply of gold, or by heavy government

[5] See A. B. Adams, *Economics of Business Cycles,* New York, 1925.

[1] *The Theory of Business Enterprise,* New York, 1904, chapter vii; *Des Crises Générales et Périodiques de Surproduction,* Paris, 1906, 3rd ed., 1923. A summary of Lescure's version is given in the first edition of the present book, p. 13.

purchases. This rise affects first some one industry or line of business, which responds with a burst of activity and increased investment by business men eager to exploit the profitable field. Partly by actual increase of demand, partly by lively anticipation of future increases, aggressive business enterprise extends its ventures and pushes up prices in remoter branches of trade.

Now the growing demand and enhanced prices increase the prospective profits of the business enterprises in each trade as they reach it. Larger prospective profits lead to higher market capitalization of the business enterprises, and, of course, higher market capitalization means an increased value of the properties as collateral security. Thus the way is paved for the marked extension of credit on which the active trade is largely dependent.

This sequence of growing demand, rising prices, increasing expectations of profit, swelling capitalization of business enterprises, and expanding credit keeps repeating itself on an ever growing scale so long as its basis lasts—an anticipated increase in demand or selling prices greater than the anticipated increase in costs. But eventually the process undermines its basis. For the expense of doing business rises with the increasing cost of labor, and with the gradual extension of the advance in prices to all the commodities which business enterprises buy. In the end, these costs gain so much upon prospective selling prices as to narrow the anticipated margins of profit. Then the enhanced market capitalization of the business enterprises begins to seem excessive. Consequently, the security behind the loans which have been granted shrinks in the estimation of the business community, and ceases to be regarded as an adequate guarantee of repayment. The confident tone of business expectations which characterized the period of prosperity yields to nervousness. To bring on a general crisis, it needs but that some considerable creditor should conclude that the present earning capacity of his debtors no longer warrants the capitalization upon which their collateral is appraised. When this happens liquidation begins, extending from one industry to another and converting prosperity into depression.

Veblen differs from most writers in holding that, once begun, business depression tends to perpetuate itself, instead of tending to produce a resumption of activity. The financial reorganization of embarrassed enterprises reduces their fixed charges, and turns the weakest competitors into the most dangerous. Yet more important is the unceasing advance in technical perfection which characterizes

modern machine industry, and which enables the new plants which are built from time to time to start with a marked initial advantage in equipment over their partially antiquated predecessors.[2] The difficulty of earning a fair profit without submitting to a reduction of capitalization is made chronic by these conditions. Hence periods of prosperity are taking on the character of episodes, initiated by some extraordinary increase in the demand for goods, and running out presently into the normal state of depression through the sequence of events which has been recited.

To Veblen, then, the important factor in determining the character of a business period is the relation between current capitalization and anticipated earning capacity. When prospective profits rise, business has a season of prosperity, during which capitalization expands rapidly. But rising costs always undermine the basis for anticipating high profits and then capitalization is left higher than prospective profits warrant. The latter situation characterizes depression.

The "profits theory" of business cycles has been accepted, or independently arrived at, by several writers since the publication of Veblen's and Lescure's books. These recent versions differ from the earlier models and from each other in the emphasis which they put upon various factors affecting profits. Thus Professor Gustav Cassel of the University of Stockholm ascribes especial importance to the fluctuations in both interest rates and construction work.[3] Mr. F. Lavington of the University of Cambridge, following Professor Pigou, emphasizes fluctuations in business confidence.[4] Major J. R. Bellerby of the International Labour Office stresses the expansion of the currency as a factor in breeding booms, and the reduction of surplus stocks of commodities and the artificial support of consumers' demand as factors in starting revivals of activity.[5] Professor John Maurice Clark of Columbia University has fitted into the profits theory his acute analysis of the relation between the orders for new industrial equipment and the *rate* of growth or shrinkage in the demand for

[2] Dr. Robert Liefmann suggests that this factor, the introduction of technical improvements in production and the consequent "scrapping" of equipment not yet amortized, is the most fundamental cause of crises. See his *Grundsätze der Volkswirtschaftslehre,* 2nd ed., Stuttgart and Berlin, 1922, vol. ii, pp. 840, 841.

[3] *The Theory of Social Economy,* New York, 1924, Fourth Book. (First published in Leipzig, 1918, *Theoretische Sozialökonomie.*)

[4] *The Trade Cycle, an Account of the Causes Producing Rhythmical Changes in the Activity of Business.* London, 1922.

[5] *The Controlling Factor in Trade Cycles.* Reprinted with additions from the *Economic Journal,* September, 1923, vol. xxxiii, pp. 305-331.

finished products.[6] Finally, Mr. Lawrence K. Frank has given a "behavioristic" interpretation of business cycles which has so definite a bearing upon current statistical work that it must be summarized.

> The 'cause' (Mr. Frank remarks), if we wish to use that term, of business cycles . . . is to be found in the habits and customs (institutions) of men which make up the money economy, with its money and credit, prices, private property, buying and selling, and so on, all loaded, so to speak, on the industrial process.

This institutional situation gives rise to alternations of "over-buying" and "under-buying" by business men in this way: In a depression retail purchases of consumers' goods do not shrink greatly, certainly not so much as the current production of these goods shrinks. Hence depression sees a gradual dwindling of current stocks of finished goods, and also a dwindling of the stocks of materials carried by producers. Given that situation, it is merely a question of time when retail merchants will find their assortments growing meager and will be forced to increase their current orders for goods, even though their current sales remain constant or contract slowly. When this time does come, production of consumers' goods will pick up a bit. Before long, the producers from whom the retailers or wholesalers bought will exhaust their supplies of materials and must increase the orders they place with other producers. So an increase of buying, started by retail merchants, spreads from group to group, and grows as it spreads.

Each business man, as he sees his sales increasing, thinks it well to acquire a larger stock of the goods he sells or uses. "Moreover, speculator-traders place orders for future delivery and begin to accumulate stocks." The consequence is that rates of production are increased. Statistical evidence seems to show that this acceleration of production becomes more rapid as it travels back from consumers' goods through semi-finished commodities to raw materials and industrial equipment. But just as retail trade did not shrink greatly during the depression, so now it does not expand greatly during prosperity. Presently the rate of production exceeds the rate of

[6] *Studies in the Economics of Overhead Costs,* Chicago, 1923, chapter xix. See also Professor Clark's paper, "Business Acceleration and the Law of Demand: A Technical Factor in Economic Cycles." *Journal of Political Economy,* March, 1917, vol. xxv, pp. 217-235.

consumption, and so produces an accumulation of stocks which grows larger as long as the processes in question continue.

But these accumulations are limited by storage capacity and the willingness of banks to lock up their funds in doubtfully liquid loans. As these limits are approached, purchases decline. Then the stocks of commodities are discovered to be overlarge for the reduced volume of sales. To reduce stocks, men fill their current orders from goods on hand and curtail production or orders from producers. Current production then falls below current consumption. The business groups which have accumulated the largest stocks—those furthest from the retailers—will almost stop buying.

> Hence the rates of production in the several stages will decrease progressively faster going backward to raw materials, until the end of the ensuing depression brings a revival again.[7]

To this exposition of Mr. Frank's, Dr. Thomas Warner Mitchell of the Federal Trade Commission has made an important addition by explaining how fluctuations in demand are amplified as they run back through the channels of trade from consumers to producers of raw materials. His explanation runs as follows:

> (1) Because of the length, in time, of the whole production process from the natural resources to the ultimate consumer, and the length of time required for selecting and training personnel in building up a production organization, production rates that have fallen below demand rates cannot quickly be augmented to equal the demand rates, but require many months to be so augmented. (2) There is deception and illusion all along the line as to the real extent of demand, due to over-ordering by customers. (3) The illusion is accentuated under our atomistic competitive system by counting the same demand several times over as it is presented to different atoms in the industrial organization. All three operate together to produce a grossly exaggerated measurement of demand in the boom period, followed automatically by a crisis and by a gross under-measurement of demand during the crisis and depres-

[7] "A Theory of Business Cycles," by Lawrence K. Frank, *Quarterly Journal of Economics,* August, 1923, vol. xxxvii, pp. 625-642.

Before Mr. Frank wrote, Mr. Henry S. Dennison had sketched a similar theory. See "Management and the Business Cycle," *Journal of the American Statistical Association,* March, 1922, vol. xviii, pp. 20-31. Dr. Simon S. Kuznets enriches the analysis and shows its statistical support in his volume on *Cyclical Fluctuations, Retail and Wholesale Trade, United States, 1919-1925,* New York, 1926.

sion; and that followed automatically, in turn, by another boom. Consumers' psychology, manifested in the form of resistance to the rising cost of living and a slowing-up of their demand near the end of a boom period, accentuates the effect of the superabundance with which the merchants' orders for goods are eventually filled, and materially assists in precipitating a crisis. The cyclical movement, once started, tends to complete and repeat itself automatically and perpetually.[8]

V. Plans for Further Work.

1. Problems Raised by the Diversity of Explanations.

We began the preceding survey of current theories to find what economic activities are involved in business cycles, and to get working hypotheses for use in a fresh attack upon the problem. It may seem that we have been too successful: we have found so many processes involved and have collected so many explanations that the materials threaten to be confusing rather than illuminating. What we sought was aid toward solving one problem: we now find on our hands a new puzzle—to determine the relations among a lot of theories. What explanations are incompatible with each other, what are complementary? Each theory taken by itself seems plausible; but how can we work with so many hypotheses? Is it necessary to test each hypothesis in turn? Must we plan an eclectic theory, selecting useful elements from several different writers? Or can we find some way of developing a thoroughly unified explanation of business cycles, and yet incorporate the seemingly diverse hypotheses with which we have become acquainted?[1]

[8] "Competitive Illusion as a Cause of Business Cycles," *Quarterly Journal of Economics,* August, 1924, vol. xxxviii, pp. 631-652.

[1] The humorous reader is invited to observe at this point what care has been taken to economize his effort. In place of ten types of theories in some twenty variant forms, twice or five times that number might have been put forward as having claims on his attention. A look at the table of contents in von Bergman's *Geschichte der Nationalökonomischen Krisentheorien* (Stuttgart, 1895), or at the catalogue of any large library of books on economics will show how much literature has been omitted. The list of theories reviewed above is a most exclusive list, admitting only (with one diverting exception) those explanations which can show the best of credentials.

Among the recent books passed over for one reason or another are the following:

Ludwig Pohle, *Bevölkerungsbewegung, Kapitalbildung und periodische Wirtschaftskrisen.* Göttingen, 1902.

Pierre Vialles, *La Consommation et les Crises Économiques.* Paris, 1903.

Hugo Bilgram and Louis E. Levy, *The Cause of Business Depressions.* Philadelphia, 1914.

Daniel Bellet, *Crises Économiques,* Paris, 1918.

Wilhelm Röpke, *Die Konjunktur.* Jena, 1922.

Embarrassing as the multiplicity of explanations may seem at this stage, it is an embarrassment which must be faced, because it arises from the complexity of the problem itself. Everyone who has had practical experience in business knows that business is affected by numberless factors physical, psychological, political, economic or social in origin; local, national or world-wide in scope; obvious or obscure in character and working; temporary or enduring in effect. And everyone who has studied economics realizes that business activity depends upon the smoothly coördinated functioning of many processes, the extraction or growing of raw materials; the fabricating, distributing, transporting and consuming of goods; the paying and spending of money incomes; the saving and investing of capital; the granting and canceling of credits. Any of these factors or any of these processes can be made to yield a plausible theory of business cycles, provided some investigator can show that it is an independent source of recurrent fluctuations in the activity of trade. And that is what each of our theorists believes himself to have done with reference to the factor of his choice. Nor can we be sure in advance that any one of them is wrong.

An easy affirmation that business cycles are exceedingly complex phenomena is not an adequate preparation for constructive work. To plan this work wisely we need to know what the complexities are. Such knowledge we get in the most convincing way from the conclusions reached by earlier investigators. It is for this reason that study of current theories forms the best introduction to the subject, at its present stage of development. Knowing what we now do, we should be effectually guarded against the besetting sin of theorists in this

Hugh W. Sanford, *The Business of Life*, New York, 1924. Vol. i, pp. 1-222.
Paul Mombert, *Einführung in das Studium der Konjunktur*. Leipzig, 1925.

Moreover, several important contributions have been mentioned but incidentally, because they stress the joint importance of two or more processes which are exploited separately in other writings. Comprehensiveness of view is certainly no defect; but the complexity of business cycles can be exhibited most effectively by following many leaders, each of whom focuses attention upon some single process and represents all other developments as subordinate to, or as contributing to, his chosen chain of cause and effect. If this chapter were intended to evaluate recent studies of business cycles, the following books would have conspicuous places:

Dennis H. Robertson, *A Study of Industrial Fluctuation*, London, 1915; *Banking Policy and the Price Level*, London, 1926.
Gustav Cassel, *The Theory of Social Economy*, Translated by Joseph McCabe, New York, 1924. (First published in German, Leipzig, 1918.)
John Maurice Clark, *The Economics of Overhead Costs*, Chicago, 1923.
Arthur Spiethoff, "Krisen," *Handwörterbuch der Staatswissenschaften*, 4th ed., Jena, 1925. Vol. vi, pp. 8-91.
Simon S. Kuznets, *Cyclical Fluctuations*, New York, 1926.

field—neglecting phenomena which do not fit neatly into preconceived schemes.

Realizing how many lines of analysis we must be ready to test and perhaps to accept, we cannot regard the planning of our work as an easy, or a brief task. We must provide a place for every line of analysis which may prove important in the sequel, and yet not lose our way in a maze of interactions. How to draw up such a plan is our next concern.

2. A Classification of the Theories.

As the first step in this systematic planning of our work, we must set our collection of working hypotheses in order. The exposition given above proceeds as far as feasible from the simpler to the more intricate theories. Now we can rearrange the theories on logical lines, according to the processes which they stress.

First, the different theories may be classified as physical, emotional and institutional explanations.[1] The large third class may then be subdivided into (1) theories which find the source of fluctuations in institutional change, and (2) theories which find the source of fluctuations in the functioning of institutions in their present form. Finally, the last named group may be further divided into four or five species according to the economic processes in which fluctuations are held to start: namely, theories concerned with (1) the quest of profits, (2) the flow of incomes from business enterprises to indi-

[1] Compare E. M. Patterson, "The Theories Advanced in Explanation of Economic Crises," *Annals of the American Academy of Political and Social Science,* May, 1915, vol. lix, pp. 133-147.

Since this chapter was written, Professor Warren M. Persons has published a classification of "theories of business fluctuations" which resembles the present classification of theories of business cycles. See *Quarterly Journal of Economics,* November, 1926, vol. xli, pp. 94-128.

Persons' classification is the first stage of a critical examination of "the theories of business fluctuations." My classification is the first stage of a constructive study of business cycles. Persons is interested primarily in the causes of business fluctuations stressed by different writers: I am interested primarily in those parts of a theory which offer working hypotheses which I can use. This difference between our aims leads us at times to classify the same writer under quite different heads. To give a single example: Professor Persons ranks Dr. Veblen among those who emphasize "factors other than economic institutions," because Veblen holds that revivals "are pretty uniformly traceable to specific causes extraneous to the process of industrial business proper." However, Persons notes that Veblen's analysis of prosperity, crisis, and depression runs in terms of economic activities. For my purposes, it is this analysis which is most significant in Veblen's theory. I therefore rank Veblen among the writers who treat business cycles in terms of institutional factors, and merely mention his view that some "disturbing cause" from outside the system of business dealings is necessary to revive activity after a depression. (See above section iv, 10).

viduals and frcm individuals back to business enterprises, (3) the balance between rates of production and of consumption at large, (4) the special balance between personal consumption and the production of industrial equipment (the under- and over-savings, as well as the construction theories), and (5) the functioning of the banks in relation to the rest of the community.

For ready reference from time to time, it will be convenient to have this classification, with some elaboration of detail, set out in tabular form.

A Classification of Current Theories of Business Cycles.

I. Theories which trace business cycles to *physical* processes

1. Three-and-a-half-year cycles of solar radiation produce similar cycles of crop yields, and so seven- or ten-year cycles of business activity. H. S. Jevons.
2. Eight-year periods in the conjunction of Venus produce similar cycles in mundane weather, crop yields, and business. Henry L. Moore.
3. Weather cycles affect health, health affects mental attitudes, and mental attitudes affect business. Ellsworth Huntington.

A theory intermediate between the groups stressing physical and institutional processes.

Industries which depend upon organic, and industries which depend upon inorganic materials have unlike rhythms. The resulting disturbances and restorations of balance produce business cycles. Werner Sombart.

II. Theories which trace business cycles to *emotional* processes

1. "Optimistic error and pessimistic error, when discovered, give birth to one another in an endless chain." A. C. Pigou.
2. The fluctuations of birth rates and death rates are chiefly responsible for mass alternations of optimism and pessimism, and thus indirectly responsible for alternations of prosperity and depression. M. B. Hexter.

III. Theories which trace business cycles to *institutional* processes

1. Cycles arise from the change of institutions.
   (1) Social progress is by nature jerky: changes in its pace and direction produce disturbances from time to time in the moving equilibrium of economic processes. Emanuel H. Vogel.
   (2) Innovations come in waves, and initiate periods of activity followed by crises and depressions. Joseph Schumpeter, Minnie T. England.

2. Cycles arise from the functioning of existing institutions.
   (1) From the technical exigencies of money-making:
   Fluctuations in prospective profits cause fluctuations in business capitalization and confidence; the latter in turn give rise to new fluctuations in prospective profits. Thorstein Veblen, Jean Lescure.
   The money economy leads to fluctuations in mercantile orders, manufacturing and the production of raw materials which are progressively larger than the fluctuations in consumers' purchases, upon which all business depends, directly or indirectly, for its market. Henry S. Dennison, Lawrence K. Frank, Simon S. Kuznets.
   The reason why the aforesaid fluctuations grow wide as one passes from consumer demand toward the production of raw materials lies in the competitive illusion to which our business system gives rise. Thomas W. Mitchell.
   (2) From lack of equilibrium in the processes of disbursing and spending incomes and of producing values:
   Incomes paid to wage earners lag behind changes in the money value of goods produced, thus making consumers' demand alternately larger and smaller than current supply. R. E. May.
   Inequalities in the rates at which prices rise and fall cause consumers' incomes to lag behind the output of consumers' goods in prosperity, and to exceed that output in depression. Emil Lederer.
   Incomes disbursed by business enterprises to individuals are alternately less and more than the full value of the goods produced for sale; the fluctuations thus initiated are enhanced by the savings of individuals. Waddill Catchings, William T. Foster and Hudson B. Hastings.
   Prosperity requires an increase of liquid capital, which can be provided only out of funds which must be spent for consumers' goods if prosperity is to continue. Recovery comes because depression checks the growth of liquid capital. P. W. Martin.
   Consumers' incomes can be made to exceed the value output of consumers' goods only by expansion of capital equipment, financed by expansion of bank credit. But this condition, which characterizes prosperity, works its own undoing. A. B. Adams.
   (3) From lack of equilibrium in the process of producing and consuming goods in general:
   Waves of general over-production result from "the well-nigh

universal fact of industrial competition." Sir William H. Beveridge.

The uncertainty involved in all business planning leads to alternate over- and under-production of goods. Charles O. Hardy.

Good trade leads to rapid increase in industrial equipment and later in output, and finally to a decline in the marginal demand prices for consumers' goods. A depression follows in which the growth of industrial equipment and output is checked. The marginal demand prices for consumers' goods finally rise again, and a new period of activity begins. Albert Aftalion, Mentor Bouniatian.

(4) From lack of equilibrium in the processes of consuming, saving, and investing capital in new construction:

In prosperity the demand for capital exceeds current savings; the resulting scarcity of capital brings on a crisis. In depression, investment falls below current savings; free capital accumulates until investing becomes aggressive once more and starts a new period of activity. Michel Tugan-Baranovski.

Large incomes, which grow rapidly in prosperity, lead to over-saving and over-investment in new plants, so that supply exceeds current demand. Depression follows, in which the large incomes are reduced, and over-saving ceases, so that consumption catches up with output and starts a revival. John A. Hobson.

Crises are caused by over-production of industrial equipment and concomitant under-production of the goods necessary to use that equipment. Arthur Spiethoff.

Relatively slight changes in demand for consumers' goods and in costs of construction cause far more violent changes in the volume of construction work: the latter changes react to heighten and propagate changes in the demand for consumers' goods. George H. Hull.

Over-commitments to business extensions of all sorts involve additions to purchasing power not counterbalanced by increased production. Prices rise until they reach a level at which men see danger in adding to their stocks. Then purchasing contracts and a crisis comes. Malcom C. Rorty.

(5) From the processes of banking:

Banks increase the purchasing power of business men, when prospects are favorable, by lending credit; the activity thus stimulated grows cumulatively until the banks are forced to restrict advances. Then comes a crisis and depression,

during which idle funds accumulate in the banks and enable them to start a new movement of expansion. Alvin H. Hansen.

When banks have large reserves they reduce discount rates, and thus encourage borrowing and business expansion, which grows cumulatively until the banks find that larger cash requirements are impairing their reserves. Then banks raise discount rates, restrict loans and thus reduce business activity. Funds again accumulate in the banks because cash requirements are now smaller, and the cycle starts afresh. R. G. Hawtrey.

The exceedingly condensed summaries in this table do no more than suggest the central theses maintained by the writers named. One who has not read the books drawn upon, or at least read the preceding section on "Current Theories of Business Cycles," will find the entries scarcely intelligible and may well distrust his own guesses at their meaning. Of course the classification provides no single niche for men like Mr. Robertson, Mr. Lavington, Professor Cassel, Professor J. M. Clark and Major Bellerby who make large use of several different causes of fluctuations. Nor does the table show the effective supplementary use made by many writers of ideas other than their leading theses.

3. The Necessity for Making Measurements.

Regarding the technical methods to be used in the investigation one broad conclusion is already clear. The conception of business cycles as congeries of changes in numerous processes running abreast or following each other—a conception made vivid by the review of current theories—shows the need of quantitative knowledge. What is the relative importance of the factors represented as causes of fluctuations? What is the relative amplitude of the fluctuations characteristic of these factors and of the effects which they are said to produce? In what sequence do the fluctuations appear and at what intervals of time? These are but samples of the quantitative problems which become crucial in an effort either to test a given theory or to do constructive work. Such problems can be solved only by appeal to statistics.

Indeed, our best chance of improving upon the work of earlier writers lies in this direction. Because each year as it passes extends

the record for study, because of the widening scope of statistical compilations and the progressive refinement of statistical technique, the latest investigator has a quasi-mechanical advantage over his predecessors, plus the advantage of profiting by his predecessors' ideas. Nor is this advantage of more precise knowledge limited to recent cycles. To-day we have better data concerning the trade fluctuations after the Napoleonic Wars than were available to Sismondi, or Jevons, or Tugan-Baranovski. Obviously we should exploit this advantage to the full, not forgetting that the figures are of little use except as they are illuminated by theory.

4. Causal Theory and Analytic Description.

The next step in planning our work is to drag into the light for inspection the tangled problem of cause and effect which most of the theorists have tried to solve.

The usual aim of writers upon business cycles is to show where and how wave movements start—that is, to discover "the cause" of business cycles. A second aim, followed in the full-length discussions, is to show how the original wave movement spreads from its source over all the processes of industry, commerce, and finance. This spread is also treated in terms of cause and effect, but the causal relations grow intricate. The first effects become causes producing new effects, which act as new causes, and so on. Often the analysis moves consciously in a circle or a spiral; the final effects reënforce the first cause, or after a lapse of time start the first cause into activity again, or even produce the first cause afresh.[1]

This broadening of business-cycle theories from the effort to discover causes into an effort to explain the full round of events is demanded by both our scientific and our practical interests. But as our knowledge grows wider and more intimate, our attitude toward the discussion of causes undergoes a subtle change. When we have accounted in casual terms for each stage in a lengthy series of actions and reactions, we find that our analysis deals with many causes, each one of which is logically indispensable to the theory we have elaborated. On reflection, we see the application to our work of the old contention that the idea of causation has pragmatic, rather than

[1] Of course there is nothing "vicious" in a circle of this sort. The argument is not circular in the sense of depending upon itself, but in the sense of following a process which is conceived to be rhythmical.

scientific, warrant. All the conditions which are indispensable to produce a certain result stand on much the same footing from the viewpoint of science. But there may be practical reasons why, from the many conditions indispensable to produce certain results, we should single out some one or more for special attention, and call them "the cause" or "the causes." We stand a better chance of making a wise selection of factors for special attention, however, if we have already gained a scientific understanding of the process as a whole.

In the progress of knowledge, causal explanations are commonly an early stage in the advance toward analytic description. The more complete the theory of any subject becomes in content, the more mathematical in form, the less it invokes causation. In business-cycle theory, the transformation from causal explanations into analytic description is being hastened by free use of statistical materials and methods. What time series can be made to show are functional relationships. We are always reading something into statistics, when we assert that the process represented by one series exercises a causal influence upon the process represented by a second series. Yet a stiff refusal to employ causal expressions in the detail of our investigation might often hamper us. In the present stage of our knowledge, we can probably make more rapid progress toward attaining insight into business cycles, by using the thought-forms of daily life than by trying to express ideas at which we are grasping in the form which may ultimately prevail.

5. History and Theory.

A few business-cycle theorists not only work forward from "the cause" of wave movements to its effects, but also work backward from "the cause" to its cause. As already noted, Professor Tugan-Baranovski, after expounding his theory of the alternate accumulation and exhaustion of uninvested loan funds, adds,

> . . . it is the inadequate remuneration of labor, and the consequent misery of the working classes, that is the fundamental cause of the rapid accumulation of social capital which provokes crises.[1]

Similarly, Professor Aftalion, after tracing the origin and development of general over-production through two volumes, remarks at the end,

[1] *Les Crises Industrielles en Angleterre*, p. 279.

> It is to the conditions established by the capitalist technique of production that we must attribute the great difficulty of avoiding error. It is this technique, after all, which must bear the responsibility for the appearance of over-production.[2]

And Mr. Frank, after exploiting the difference in the rhythms of consumption and production, concludes by saying,

> The 'cause,' if we wish to use that term, of business cycles . . . is to be found in the habits and customs (institutions) of men which make up the money economy . . .[3]

Presumably, this contention, that business cycles arise from that peculiar form of economic organization which has come to prevail in England within the last two centuries, and over much of the world in more recent times, would be admitted by most theorists. On this view, of course, the cause of business cycles lies enmeshed among the causes that produced modern money economy, or capitalism.

Needless to say, our theorists have not followed the logical implications of this historical perspective. No one writes an economic history of mankind as a prolegomenon to a theory of business cycles. The current practice is to take the existing scheme of institutions for granted, and to show how cyclical oscillations come to pass under this régime.

Nor do our theorists treat business cycles as episodes each of which is to be fully accounted for on historical grounds. On the contrary, they consciously endeavor to abstract from the peculiarities of particular cycles, in order that they may arrive at a clearer understanding of the generic features. The statistical investigator does the best he can to segregate the cyclical oscillations in his time series from all complicating features, and for this purpose he has developed an elaborate technique.[4] The man of speculative temper does his abstracting in bolder fashion. Surveying the phenomena of concrete experience, he seeks to fasten on the factors of chief moment, and to isolate these factors in his thoughts. By a series of imaginary experiments, he develops a synthetic account of cyclical oscillations which contains enough of reality to be enlightening and not so much as to be confusing.

[2] *Les Crises Périodiques de Surproduction*, vol. ii, pp. 359, 360.
[3] "A Theory of Business Cycles," *Quarterly Journal of Economics*, August, 1923, vol. xxxvii, p. 639.
[4] See Chapter III below.

Of course, there is no logical opposition between the theoretical and the historical viewpoints, any more than there is opposition between causation and analytic description. On the contrary, history and theory supplement each other. The theorist who wishes to analyze the workings of current economic institutions needs a vivid, objective view of their characteristics. That view he can obtain most effectively by a study of their evolution. Nor is current history less important to him than history of the past. It is only by historical observations that he can determine what features of business cycles are common and what are occasional, a matter upon which he should satisfy himself before he devises his imaginary experiments. So, too, the statistical worker appeals to history for help in performing the most difficult of his technical tasks—separating "irregular" from cyclical fluctuations. And by whatever methods a theorist works, he may—and should—check his explanations by seeing how far they account for the cycles of history.

Several distinguished theorists have prepared themselves for explaining cyclical phenomena by elaborate historical investigations. For example, Tugan-Baranovski wrote the history of English crises from 1825 to 1910; Bouniatian carried the account back to 1640; Lescure begins his treatise with a history of French, German, English, and American crises from 1810 to 1922.[5] Doubtless many theorists, without making first-hand historical researches for themselves, have studied such historical accounts. To follow the precedent is an obvious piece of common sense. Indeed, we should strive to achieve a closer blending than our predecessors have accomplished of the data and the suggestions afforded by history with the hypotheses suggested by economic theory. The statistical series we shall analyze are fragments of the historical record. The business annals summarized in a later chapter are a condensed account of cyclical fluctuations in numerous countries at different stages of development. These collections of historical materials, and economic history in its more elaborate form, we can use to exhibit the general characteristics of modern economic organization, to aid in determining what features are common to business cycles at large, to suggest hypotheses, and to test our conclusions.

[5] See M. Tugan-Baranovski, *Les Crises Industrielles en Angleterre*, Paris, 1913, Part i; M. Bouniatian, *Geschichte der Handelskrisen in England, 1640-1840*, Munich, 1908; J. Lescure, *Des Crises Générales et Périodiques de Surproduction*, 3d ed., Paris, 1923, pp. 3-312.

6. The Framework of the Investigation.

Another step in planning our work is to decide whether we shall use a framework provided by the theories we have reviewed, or a framework provided by the subject matter.

It is possible to take up the theories one by one, make a critical examination of the evidence offered in support of each, at need devise new tests, and treat conclusions regarding the validity of each theory as our main objective. It is also possible to take up the successive phases of business cycles one by one, collect facts regarding periods of prosperity, crisis, depression and revival in different countries at different times, use the theories to suggest facts which should be gathered and relations looked for, and make conclusions regarding the fluctuations our main objective, treating verdicts upon the theories as by-products to be turned out when convenient.

Between these two procedures it is easy to choose. What we want is insight into the facts. We care about the theories only as aids toward attaining such insight. The plan of testing theories would indeed lead to work with the facts, but in an artificial order, and one involving much repetition. At best it would turn into a study of one or two processes at a time in successive phases of the cycle, whereas we are concerned primarily with these phases, and wish to discover the relations among different processes which give each phase its character and at the same time transform it into the following phase.[1]

But if we are to use the phases of business cycles as a framework, we run grave risk of getting hopelessly confused in a maze of interacting processes. That danger the review of current theories has made startlingly clear. The physical processes of making and consuming goods of numberless kinds, the business processes of buying and selling, the flow of money incomes to and from individuals, the circulation of money and credit, borrowing and lending, saving and investing must all be watched in relation to each other—and each of these processes is itself a complex of variables.

To guard against losing our way in this tangle, we must get as clear a view as possible of the organic relations among these various

[1] There is the less need for making a critical study of the several theories because Professor Warren M. Persons has promised to perform that arduous task. See the first paper in the series, "Theories of Business Fluctuations," *Quarterly Journal of Economics*, November, 1926, vol. xli, pp. 94-128.

processes before we begin to study their fluctuations from phase to phase of the cycle. That is, we must survey that form of economic organization which has come to prevail in all "advanced" communities as if it were a curiosity instead of our familiar environment. In particular, we must get what light existing statistics shed upon the relative magnitude of those factors which our survey of current theories has pointed out as playing important rôles in business cycles.[2]

[2] In his recent critique of current German studies of business cycles, Dr. Adolf Löwe makes the following comment upon the treatment of facts and theory in my earlier book upon business cycles:

> As in all social-economic work, so in our narrower field, the analysis of facts forms the second chapter of an exposition. It must be preceded by a chapter on the theory of business cycles. Such is always the order in truth, even though the first chapter remains unwritten, and though (worse still) the writer is not conscious that his mind harbors a theory. For it is theory which provides the principles by which the irreproducible fullness of reality can be set in order; it is theory which formulates the questions which the facts must answer. (See "Der gegenwärtige Stand der Konjunkturforschung in Deutschland," in *Die Wirtschaftwissenschaft nach dem Kriege, Festgabe für Lujo Brentano*. Munich and Leipzig, 1925, vol. ii, p. 367. I have translated freely in an effort to preserve the vigor of the original.)

I cannot claim to heed Dr. Löwe's counsel in the present volume, unless my vague impressions concerning what phenomena should be looked into deserve to be called a theory. Of course Chapter I does treat theories of business cycles, but it uses these theories to reveal certain facts—that is, to show how many processes run side by side in cyclical fluctuations. In the light of these results, I pass on in Chapter II to discuss modern economic organization, in Chapter III to treat statistical problems, and in Chapter IV to draw conclusions from business annals, all before I undertake in Chapter V to formulate a definite conception of business cycles. As for a theory of the subject, that is deferred to Volume II. This order seems to me more likely to lead to the discovery of new truth than a treatment which begins with a "theory" and then looks for "facts."

Dr. Löwe's view of the relations between facts and theory in scientific work is a common one. But it seems to me over-schematic. Against the statement, "One cannot set economic facts in order unless one has a theory" (I should prefer to say "hypothesis"), can be put the statement, "One cannot form an economic theory unless one knows some facts." And both these statements overlook the fact that the two categories are not mutually exclusive. The theories with which science works cannot be conceived as existing apart from the facts of human experience, and men can apprehend facts only in terms of the notions with which their minds are furnished. The more thoughtfully one considers the relations between these two phases of knowing, the less separable they become. Even on the basis of the crude usage which contrasts fact and theory, it is futile to debate which of the two comes first in the history of the race, in the life of an individual, in the growth of a science, or in the progress of an investigation. What is clear is that in scientific work these two blends, knowledge of fact and theoretical conceptions, keep stimulating, extending and enriching each other. An investigator who starts with what purports to be an exposition of theory is tacitly using the facts by which the ideas have been molded. And one who starts with what purports to be an exposition of facts, is tacitly using the theoretical conceptions by which facts have been apprehended. Whether it is better to begin a particular task by elaborating upon the theoretical conceptions employed, saying little about the facts for the moment; or to begin by elaborating upon the facts, saying little about theories for the moment, depends upon the problem in hand and upon the contribution which the investigator hopes to make toward its solution. In an investigation of moment, both

This survey is the most important step in preparing for the constructive work we hope to accomplish. To it is devoted the next chapter.

the theory and the facts are elaborated at various stages of the proceedings, each by the aid of the other, and later workers start with a fact-theory blend improved by the new contribution.

CHAPTER II.

ECONOMIC ORGANIZATION AND BUSINESS CYCLES.

I. The Historical Connection Between Business Cycles and the Use of Money.

1. A Preliminary Statement.

That business cycles occur only in communities having a distinctively modern type of economic organization is explicitly recognized by several of the writers cited in Chapter I, and is implied by all who trace these cycles to institutional factors of recent development. Even the theories which resort to physical causes need not be taken as dissenting opinions. Whatever cycles occur in the weather produce cycles in economic activities only where economic activities are organized upon a business basis.

This dependence of business cycles upon a particular scheme of institutions must be a fact of the highest theoretical significance. But what we can learn from it will depend upon our understanding of the institutional scheme in question. Modern economic organization is so bewildering a complex that it explains nothing. Before we can make the historical connection illuminate our problem, we must find some way of breaking the complex into comprehensible elements, related to each other in a comprehensible fashion. Is there not, then, some feature of the economic organization found in all communities subject to business cycles, which will help us to plan our inquiry into the various processes marked for investigation in the first chapter?

Two suggestions are provided by Chapter I. Many economists have held that crises and depressions are a result of "capitalism," or, as others phrase it, "a disease of capitalism." A few recent writers have preferred to say that business cycles are produced by "money economy."[1] Neither of these statements professes to be a theory of business cycles. But both statements suggest working programs

[1] For illustrative citations, see the section of Chapter I called "Causal Theory and Analytic Description."

which we might follow. Can we organize our inquiry into the various processes involved in business cycles more efficiently if we relate these processes to "capitalism," or if we relate them to "money economy"?

The view which will be developed here runs as follows: The feature of modern economic organization which throws most light upon business cycles is that economic activities are now carried on mainly by making and spending money. This condition is characteristic of capitalism; but that term puts its stress upon other features of the present scheme of institutions—such as the ownership of the means of production—features of primary importance in certain problems, and not to be neglected here, but features of less service in the effort to understand alternations of business prosperity and depression than the feature stressed by the term "money economy." Accordingly, we shall seek a less ambiguous term for this concept, analyze its meaning, and use it in exploring the maze of processes which we have found to be involved in business cycles.

One reason why the connection between business cycles and pecuniary organization was long overlooked is that the difference between the use of money in communities which do not and in communities which do suffer from business cycles is a difference in degree, not a difference in kind. Economists accustomed to depend upon what Alfred Marshall called "qualitative analysis" were prone to overlook the significance of differences in degree, and to concentrate attention upon differences in kind, or what they took to be such. Capitalism seemed to many men in the nineteenth century, men not versed in economic history, a new portent in economic life. They fastened upon it as an explanation of many phenomena which seemed to them equally new—commercial crises among others.

As will be shown below, the coming of business cycles is a gradual development. It can be explained only by some change which proceeds by degrees. Communities slowly become subject to recurrent alternations of prosperity and depression as a large proportion of the people begin to rely upon making and spending money in a large proportion of their activities. We lack the data which might enable us to assign a critical point, or a critical range, in the growth of money economy at which business cycles appear. But we can tell in what period the critical range was reached in various countries.[2]

[2] Capitalism also developed gradually, and, so far as that goes, might serve as well to explain the coming of business cycles as does the cumulative growth of pecuniary

Just because its development has been so gradual, "money economy" has many meanings. It calls to mind certain features in the dissimilar economic organizations of states which have flourished at various times through several thousand years of history. A term which can be taken to cover all the successive stages in a long and checkered evolution is not an apt term to characterize the peculiarities of the latest stage in the series. To suggest the differentiating features of that highly developed form of money economy within which business cycles occur, we shall do well to use words which have modern associations in our minds. Perhaps the combination "profits economy" or "business economy" is most suggestive and least misleading. The second of these terms will be used in this discussion, but with frequent reminders that what seems to count in producing business cycles is the common practice of money-making and money-spending by the population as a whole, not merely by a limited class of business men.

2. The Meaning of "Business Economy."

To repeat: we do not say that a business economy has developed in any community until most of its economic activities have taken on the form of making and spending money. That way of organizing production, distribution and consumption is the matter of importance —not the use of money as a medium of exchange.[1]

Instead of making the goods their families need, men "make" money, and with their money incomes buy for their own use goods made by unknown hands. The exceptions to this rule presented by the domestic work of housewives, by the consumption of their own produce by farmers, by the raising of vegetables in family gardens,

organization. As said above, the reason for organizing the present inquiry around the use of money, rather than around the ownership of the means of production, is that the former plan puts the problems to be faced in a way which makes them more open to attack. Of course no contention of this sort can be justified in advance. It must stand or fall by the results to which it leads.

[1] One of the objections to the term "money economy" is that it is often contrasted with a "credit economy." Thus Bruno Hildebrand, who seems to have introduced the terms, distinguished three stages of economic development: *Naturalwirtschaft, Geldwirtschaft,* and *Kreditwirtschaft* (*Jahrbücher für Nationalökonomie und Statistik,* vol. ii, pp. 1-24). But Hildebrand's stages have not proved of much use either in economic history or in economic theory, and his term *Geldwirtschaft* seems now to be used in Germany much as "business economy" is used here. In this sense, of course, the predominant use of credit instruments in effecting payments is merely one feature of a highly developed money economy.

and by agricultural leases for shares of the crops, are continuations of an earlier order, in which most families subsisted chiefly upon goods produced by their own efforts and themselves consumed most of what they produced.

It is characteristic of the dominating rôle played by money in economic planning that the nation collects hardly any data concerning these surviving elements of "real" income which families produce for themselves. Housewives form by far the largest occupation group, outnumbering farmers three to one, and the group whose work affects welfare most intimately. Yet the census of occupations does not count the number of housewives working at home. Enumerators are instructed to include only "gainful occupations," those from which people get money incomes. When the National Bureau of Economic Research made its first studies of income, it could do no more than estimate the number of housewives, and apply to this number the average wages of a group of paid workers consisting mainly of women who do some of the multifarious tasks of the housewife. The rough results thus obtained ran above 18 billion dollars in 1919, more than a quarter of the total money income. But the whole procedure was so conjectural that the National Bureau did not venture to add the housewife item to its other figures.[2]

The other elements of family-produced income can be priced without hesitation, because they consist of goods such as pass through the markets. Yet we know their magnitude but vaguely. In 1914, Mr. W. C. Funk of the Department of Agriculture made a careful study of the incomes of 483 farm families, and estimated the value of their own produce which these families consumed.[3] With the aid of Funk's data, Dr. W. I. King has figured that the non-monetary income of American farmers amounted to nearly 2 billion dollars in 1913 and nearly 4½ billions in 1920—say 6 per cent of the national income in the latter year. Much smaller values, not reaching half a billion, are produced for their own consumption by urban and village

[2] See *Income in the United States*, by the Staff of the National Bureau of Economic Research, New York, 1921, vol. i, pp. 57-60.

[3] See United States Department of Agriculture, *Farmers' Bulletin* No. 635, December, 1914. More recently Messrs. L. M. Bean and O. C. Stine of the United States Bureau of Agricultural Economics have estimated that the income "consumed on farms for family living" has varied between 21.6 per cent of "operators' *gross* income from agricultural production" in 1919-20 and 27.6 per cent in 1921-22. "Income from Agricultural Production," *The Annals of the American Academy of Political and Social Science*. January, 1925, vol. cxvii, p. 33.

families which cultivate kitchen gardens, or keep cows, pigs and poultry.[4]

Finally, as the most important survival of exchange by barter, it may be noted that rather more than a quarter of the 6,450,000 farms in the United States were cultivated in 1920 by tenants who paid as rent a share in the produce.[5]

Despite the considerable importance of these continuations of an earlier order, the economic comfort or misery of a family now depends more upon its ability to command an adequate money income and upon its pecuniary thrift, than upon its efficiency in making useful goods and its skill in husbanding supplies. Even in years when crops are short and mills are idle, the family with money need not be uncomfortable. The family without money leads a wretched life even in years of abundance.[6]

To the family, then, prosperity and depression appear less as problems of the adequacy of the goods produced by itself or by the community as a whole, than as problems of the adequacy of its money income. To the nation, the making of money is important in a way quite different. Comfort and misery do not depend upon the aggregate of money incomes received by its citizens; they depend upon the abundance of useful goods. Efficiency in producing goods is important to an individual chiefly because of its bearing on his ability to make money; money-making is important to a nation chiefly because of its bearing upon efficiency in production. Natural resources, mechanical equipment, workmanlike skill, and scientific technique are factors of fundamental importance under any form of organization. But where business economy prevails natural resources are not developed, mechanical equipment is not utilized, workmanlike skill

[4] See *Income in the United States,* vol. ii, p. 231. There are other items of income, particularly, the rental value of owned homes and the use of other consumption goods such as furniture, which do not figure in the money income and outgo of a family each year. But most of these goods have been bought for money in the past, and the real income derived from them cannot be regarded as produced by the recipients. The estimate of the non-monetary income of farmers given in the text does not include the rental value of farm homes.

[5] *Fourteenth Census of the United States,* Agriculture, Washington, 1922, vol. v. p. 124.

[6] Compare Dr. Robert L. Hale's statement: "All incomes, in the last analysis, whether derived from ownership of property or from personal services, are not 'products' created by the recipients; they are payments derived from the rest of the community by the exertion of some sort of pressure. To say this is not to condemn the exertion of such pressure; it is the only means a man has under present arrangements, and perhaps under any workable scheme of things, for keeping alive." "Economic Theory and the Statesman," *The Trend of Economics,* edited by R. G. Tugwell, New York, 1924, p. 216.

is not exercised, scientific discoveries are not applied, unless conditions are such as to promise a money profit to those who direct production.

The elaborate coöperative processes by which a nation's people provide for the meeting of each other's needs are thus brought into dependence upon factors which have but an indirect connection with the material conditions of well-being—factors which determine the prospects of making money.

3. The Evolution of Business Economy.

To grasp the rôle played in our lives by this form of organization is difficult, because we who have grown up in a business economy have had our minds molded by it. In studying the institution as it now exists, we are practicing a sort of introspection into our own mental processes. To get an objective view of the present situation, our best course is to trace the stages by which the uses of money have grown. What is so familiar and organic a whole to us that we hardly see the need of analyzing it, will dissolve into thought-suggesting parts as we note how our race has slowly evolved one element in the complex after another.

The faltering first steps toward the use of money were taken in those dim stretches of time when men were beginning to exchange gifts and then to barter for the sake of goods, to evolve the concept of ownership, to express values in a common denominator, to use some commodity as currency, to hold markets, to develop specialized occupations, and to mix trading as a business with cattle lifting, man stealing and town sacking. Of all these slow developments what little information is available comes mainly from anthropologists and archæologists and is loosely tied together by conjecture.

When written history begins in Babylonia and Egypt, in China and India, in Europe, in Mexico and Peru, it shows us a more advanced stage. Men are using copper, silver or gold as currency; they are making contracts involving the future; they are buying and selling, borrowing and lending on a considerable scale; they are keeping rude accounts. Very slowly these practices diffuse from the centers of cultural achievement, and quite as slowly the shifting cultural centers score advances. The epochal invention of coinage was probably made in western Asia Minor about 700 B. C., and was carried by Phœnician traders round the Mediterranean world.

Having passed through these earlier stages, the uses of money entered a phase of rapid development in Phœnicia, Carthage, and Greece and upon a still more notable expansion in Rome. Money changing, letters of exchange, simple banking, production of staple goods on a large scale for a wide market, speculation, business enterprises not only in trading, but also in mining and manufacturing, became common. Large fortunes were built up by private people and invested for profit. Despite the prevalence of slavery, many men worked for wages. It was, indeed, a business-like society that flourished under the Pax Romana.

But with the disintegration of Roman culture, pecuniary organization declined as decisively as any other phase of civilization. In economic, as in political life, a sharp contrast appeared between East and West. Over those parts of the empire which were later to assume leadership in culture, central authority dissolved into a shifting multitude of local controls; petty warfare became a chronic misery; the admirable Roman roads fell into disrepair; commerce shrank to a dribble of luxuries for the powerful and a local exchange of indispensables like iron, salt and tar for the commonalty; manufacturing for a wide market almost disappeared; coinage became scanty, irregular, and incredibly confused; the use of money was superseded in large part by the payment of feudal and manorial dues in personal services and commodities. The vast majority of the population lived in village communities, each of which produced most of the things its low standard of living required, and consumed most of its own products. Even the kings and other magnates spent much of their time moving about from one manor to another, eating up the local produce on the spot. All the more elaborate achievements of pecuniary organization had to be won over again.

Quite different was the situation in the area dominated by Constantinople. There the money economy suffered no such eclipse as in western and northern Europe. Gold coinage, a banking system, manufacturing on a considerable scale, a commerce which tapped the Orient on one side and the western Mediterranean on the other side were maintained and in some respects elaborated. It was due largely to this continuation that the reëstablishment of money economy in western and northern Europe was a far more rapid process than its original growth, requiring scarcely a thousand years. What the Byzantines had conserved they, and the Saracens, passed on. After the sack of Constantinople by crusaders and Venetians in 1204, and

more decisively after the capture of Constantinople by the Ottoman Turks in 1453, commercial leadership passed to the Italian cities. Many merchants emigrated to Venice, Amalfi, Genoa, and other towns, carrying with them their capital, as well as their skill in commerce and finance. A vigorous development of money economy began in the lands bordering the western Mediterranean and spread by degrees to northern countries.

The stages of this revival are imperfectly known, though they have been lived through so recently. Economic history is a young specialty, and the men devoted to it have not been fully alert to the importance of pecuniary institutions. Nor do the surviving materials on which their work is based pay much attention to the homely details of the life of the peasant, the craftsman and the merchant, except as these humble people had relations with their lords. Yet enough is known, particularly regarding England, to reveal the broad features of the story.

In economic development, the leaders were successively the Italian cities, Spain, Southern Germany, France and the Low Countries. England lagged behind until the 18th century, when London finally displaced Amsterdam as the greatest financial center, and the English began to live by making and spending money incomes as generally as the Dutch. In a history of money economy, English developments would form but one strand in a complicated fabric—a strand which does not fairly represent the whole. But the very slowness of English developments serves the present purpose. For that purpose is not to sketch the history of pecuniary organization as a whole; but to make clear the complex character of the institutions which we are wont to take as a simple matter of course. Also, the English have peculiar interest for us, because, when they finally took the lead, pecuniary organization was just reaching that stage which ushers in the business cycles of our historical record.

Even in Anglo-Saxon times, the English kings were finding that the use of money was a more efficient method of administration than levying upon commodities and requiring feudal services. They early began to commute the duties in kind upon exports and imports, for example, so many tuns of wine or bales of wool in a cargo, into money payments, and to collect in money as much of the internal taxes, fines, and dues as their officers could. The Danegeld, for instance, was levied and paid in silver. The Anglo-Saxon kings struck a cur-

rency of silver pennies based on the Carolingian pound. (It was not until 1343 that gold coins were issued in England and the gold standard was not established until nearly 400 years more had passed.) Besides taxing, the English kings borrowed on a considerable scale from religious establishments, from the Jews until their expulsion in 1290, and later from Italian merchants and bankers who did business in London.

Another great step in pecuniary organization was taken when the kings began to replace the unreliable feudal levies with paid professional soldiers. This change involved commuting the tenant's obligation to render military service in person with his retainers at his back into money payments by the tenant-in-chief and his knights. And a similar change was effected gradually in the management of the crown lands. On royal manors the villeins were allowed to commute their dues in labor and commodities into sums of money which constituted a revenue the king could use where convenient.

Meanwhile the reorganization of life among the common people on the basis of buying and selling was proceeding spontaneously in the towns. Here the differentiation of crafts could develop only so fast as the exchanging of products increased. As they devoted more and more time to their specialties, the master craftsmen had to buy their raw materials and most of the food for their families, apprentices and in-working journeymen. The towns were also the centers of what foreign or inter-regional trade was carried on, and the volume of such trade grew unsteadily larger with each generation. Thus the towns came to be "islands of money economy" in a sea of customary duties and rights—*foci* from which organization on a monetary basis diffused itself gradually over the countryside.

In the rural districts the epochal change was the extension of commutation into money rents of the week-work, boon-work and commodity payments required of the masses of villeins and cotters. From the manors held by the crown and the great religious houses, this change spread slowly and unevenly to manors held by lesser magnates. The process was piecemeal, marked by pauses and spurts, but cumulative. It was accompanied by the rise of estate management for revenue, instead of for subsistence. More slowly still the masses of the peasantry moved, or were shoved, into a new manner of life. Holdings of scattered strips in the common fields were amalgamated into blocks. The waste lands, the commons and the common fields themselves were enclosed. On many manors, the old three-

field system of cultivation was abandoned in favor of the more lucrative grazing of sheep for the export commodity, wool, and later for methods involving more use of fertilizers and the rotation of crops.[1] Specialization in animal husbandry and crops increased. Those of the old population who could not master the new arts of making and living on money, sank to the position of wage-workers on the land, or drifted away to the towns. The more adaptable men turned into business-like farmers, paying money rents, using hired laborers and selling most of their produce. So slow and so uneven was the process of transformation that over much of England these changes were still going on in the 18th and early 19th centuries. Perhaps four-fifths of English acreage was enclosed after 1760.

Even by the 16th century, however, the uses of money had developed far enough in England to make the inflow of Mexican and Peruvian silver from Spain produce grave social results. The "price revolution" of the 16th and 17th centuries reduced the value of the money payments into which many dues had been commuted and so forced a reorganization of estate management upon many reluctant landlords. On the other hand, it gave increased opportunities for profit by dealings between the districts where silver was abundant and the districts where it was scanty. Thus the new supplies of the precious metals (for presently gold began to come in considerable volume from the Brazilian placers) gave a powerful impetus to commercial enterprise. England, which had been mainly a self-contained agricultural state, entered upon a career of colonizing, developed a mercantile marine, and in the 18th century became the foremost commercial power.

As commerce increased, financial organization became more elaborate. Lending at interest, which had been permitted only under conditions carefully stipulated by the Church, became a legalized practice as the benefits of investment of capital grew clearer. Presently banking arose in England. During the 17th century the London goldsmiths, whose business with precious metals made strong boxes necessary, were resorted to more and more frequently by merchants and other wealthy men for the safekeeping of moneys. The goldsmiths who accepted deposits found that they were never required to

[1] Dr. Harriett Bradley in *The Enclosures in England,* New York, 1918, cites evidence to show that wool growing became more profitable than wheat raising only on lands whose fertility had been depleted by long continued cropping. The price of wool was low in comparison with the price of wheat during the enclosure period of the 15th and 16th centuries. See chapter ii, and pp. 97-100.

pay back more than a fraction of the total in any day or week. They could make profits by lending part of the sums in their hands. To increase the funds which they could lend, they presently began to pay interest upon deposits. Soon they discovered that it was as easy to lend their promises to pay as it was to lend coin. Goldsmiths' notes became familiar currency among well-to-do people, and London had a flourishing set of banks of deposit, lending, and issue some decades before the Bank of England was established in 1694.

With the increased scale and growing intricacy of business dealings, there was need for more accurate bookkeeping. On large estates the stewards had perforce kept simple accounts of the work done and the commodities received from the numerous tenantry. Doubtless merchants and many craftsmen had made more elaborate records of their transactions. But the mystery of double-entry bookkeeping—an Italian invention first published in 1494—was both a marked technical advance in itself and an incitement to the further improvements which led to modern accounting. That mystery the mercantile classes of England began to acquire in the 16th century.

Commerce came home to the mass of English people while it was extending to the ends of the earth. The periodical markets and fairs, which made such a picturesque feature of medieval life, became inadequate to meet the needs as communities became less self-sufficient. Weekly markets became common, then daily markets, then retail shops. By 1700 not only London but also several other towns had a variety of shops doing business with a wide clientele.

Lagging not very far behind the development of new economic practices came their recognition and enforcement at law. Through their dealings with foreign traders abroad and at home, English merchants early became acquainted with the law merchant—a highly developed commercial code which had grown up during the Middle Ages in the great continental fairs. In his *Legal Foundations of Capitalism,* Professor John R. Commons has shown how the English judges gradually reshaped the old feudal conceptions of suzerainty to fit the nascent conception of private property in land; how side by side with the law of prerogative they built up the common law to regulate the relations among individuals; how they legitimized property in promises to pay, in good will, in going concerns. The great development of mercantile law by Chief Justice Mansfield came in the middle of the 18th century.

Trade, and to a less extent mining and colonial schemes, had been

the favorite field of what business enterprise appeared in the 16th and 17th centuries. Manufacturing, banking and insurance were added to this list in the 17th and 18th centuries. Capitalistic organization of various industries, as opposed to the earlier craft organization, developed with the widening of markets, and the consequent opportunity for mass production and standardization of products. Thus it antedated the "Great Inventions" by two or three generations. But the introduction of power machinery and the building of factories quickened and broadened the process. Adam Smith could take it for granted that a capitalist employer was the typical figure in industry, just as he took it for granted that a capitalist farmer paying money rent was the typical figure in agriculture. The proportion of men working on their own account shrank in all fields of enterprise, as did the number who consumed their own products, while the proportion of men working for wages increased.

As the scale of business undertakings grew, the one-man enterprise, and even the partnership, became inadequate. Large and hazardous ventures in foreign trade were carried on in the 15th and 16th centuries commonly by "regulated companies" enjoying certain privileges conferred by government, but composed of merchants each of whom traded on his own account. In the latter half of the 16th century, the joint-stock form of organization began its conquering career in England with the Russia Company and the Adventurers to Africa. The Bank of England (preceded by several continental institutions) adapted this form to banking and it spread slowly to other fields. But in 1776 Adam Smith argued that, in most lines of business, the joint-stock company was necessarily less efficient than the simpler organization in which one man or a few partners were giving strict attention to their personal interests. The enlarged capital needs of factories, however, the coming of railroads and the rapid growth in the volume of business, so altered the situation that within a century after the *Wealth of Nations* was published the joint-stock company in some of its proliferating variants became the dominating form of business organization outside of farming, retail trade, and the professions. The spread of this form was much more rapid after 1862, when Parliament accepted the principle of limited liability of stock holders.

An investment market evolved with the growth of capital. Stockbrokers had long been known in London before the great outburst of speculation in the shares of the South Sea Company in 1720. The

development of their business owed much to the rise of high-grade investments, particularly the manifold forms of government obligations. In 1773 the London brokers organized the Stock Exchange, and so had the financial machinery ready to handle the great increase of investment and speculative transactions in securities which came with the Napoleonic Wars, the spreading of joint-stock companies, and the building of railways. These facilities gave a stronger impetus and a wider scope to two processes already familiar to Englishmen. A new leisure class of people who had inherited "money" developed in each generation from the families of successful business men, and the old leisure class of landowners could strengthen their position by participating silently in business ventures or by intermarrying with the new rich.

When European settlers came to America they brought with them the monetary usages of their various home countries in the 17th century. But under the rough conditions of frontier life the colonists suffered a temporary recession to simpler forms of organization. They were short of coin and had to use commodity currencies at times—tobacco, wampum, beaver skins. They had to live more of their own, somewhat after the fashion of medieval villagers; the differentiation of occupations was simpler; financial machinery was scarcely needed and scarcely existed; the chief business of life was to get enough food and clothing, to build houses and clear land, to keep off the Indians.

This recession was relatively short-lived on the Atlantic seaboard, but it remained characteristic of life on the westward-moving frontier as long as the frontier lasted. Always the fur traders, the trappers and hunters, the early settlers, had to get or make much of what they consumed, though they could draw upon trading posts for their arms, tools and firewater, and barter or sell such of their products as were easily transportable. Even the more thickly-settled Eastern colonies, despite their rapid progress in economic matters, continued to lag behind England in the drastic thoroughness with which they practiced monetary habits, and the refinement with which they developed financial organization. It was not until late in the nineteenth century that the United States drew fairly abreast of the mother country in this respect. Even to-day our farming is not quite so business-like as the English, except for our large-scale ventures in coöperative marketing of agricultural products. Our investors have not evolved or borrowed all of the British institutions to look after their interests

our foreign financial connections are less perfect, and our technique in foreign trade is inferior. But on the other hand, retail trade on the whole is more highly organized than in England, and our industrial corporations probably excel the English not only in the scale of their operations but also in systematic organization.

This sketch is all too brief and too simple to give an adequate impression of the way in which the developing uses of money have altered the life of mankind, and how they have fitted into the growth of other institutions, checking some and stimulating others. Still less does it show how the development of monetary practices in England was related to the larger growth in Europe. But with all its omissions, the sketch suggests how "fearfully and wonderfully made" is the complex of pecuniary practices which seems to us so natural. The commutation of feudal dues into money payments, the corresponding commutation of labor and commodity rents into money, the development of crafts with exchange of products, the rise of towns as trading centers, the invention of banking, the growth of retail shops, the excogitation of business law, the organization of joint-stock companies and their rise to dominance in most fields of business enterprise, the adoption of accounting as the technique for controlling economic ventures, the evolution of special organizations to provide for investment and speculation, the differentiation of the whole population into those who live on wages, on profits, on income from investments, or on an income which combines these types, the shifting of power from men of prowess or high birth to men of great wealth or marked business ability, the discomforting of those whose talents are not such as to command considerable incomes in a money-making world—all these developments have combined to produce the current form of business economy. Nor can we assume that this current stage is the final pattern. On the contrary, it is probable that pecuniary institutions are now changing as rapidly as at any period of their long history.[2]

[2] Although the literature of money is reputed to be more extensive than that upon any other branch of economics, we have no comprehensive treatise upon the development of pecuniary institutions. In default of adequate guidance, I have had to compose the best sketch I could by piecing together bits drawn from many sources. To give a list of the books used would take much space and render little help to anyone acquainted with economic history. My heaviest obligations are to Dr. Edwin F. Gay who made many critical and constructive suggestions concerning my first draft.

I hope that better equipped investigators will presently take up the study of this subject, which is as fascinating as it is important, and which promises large returns to

4. When Business Cycles First Appear.

It is not until the uses of money have reached an advanced stage in a country that its economic vicissitudes take on the character of business cycles.

This remark does not mean that the economic life of communities with simpler organization is free from crises, or from alternations of good and bad times. On the contrary, life seems to have been more precarious, economic fortune more fluctuating, in a medieval town than in a modern city. But until a large part of a population is living by getting and spending money incomes, producing wares on a considerable scale for wide markets, using credit devices, organizing in business enterprises with relatively few employers and many employees, the economic fluctuations which occur do not have the characteristics of business cycles described in the preceding chapter.

If the coming of business cycles depends upon the gradual development of a specific form of economic organization, it must be difficult to date their first appearance in any country with precision. And so it is. To take the best explored case: Dr. William Robert Scott of St. Andrews has made a minute study of British business records in manuscripts, official reports, books, pamphlets and newspapers from the middle of the 16th century to 1720. From these materials he has compiled a summary showing the periods of good and bad trade and of crisis during the 163 years he has covered. The table on pages 76 and 77 gives Scott's list of crises, and his "remarks" concerning each. In a few cases where his entries are very brief, I have added in brackets explanations drawn from his text. Also, I have inserted a column showing the number of years from the beginning of one crisis to the beginning of the next.

With Dr. Scott's remarks upon English crises from 1558 to 1720, we may compare Dr. Willard L. Thorp's concise descriptions of English crises from 1793 to 1925, published in the National Bureau's volume of *Business Annals*. Several differences appear.

competent workers. Anyone who contemplates an investigation will find that Georg Simmel's *Philosophie des Geldes* (2d ed., Leipzig, 1907) is a most suggestive book to read before plunging into the historical sources. An interesting sidelight upon developments in Europe is thrown by a forthcoming monograph in the Columbia University Studies in History, Economics and Public Law: *The Penetration of Money Economy in Japan and its Effects upon Social and Political Institutions,* by Matsuyo Takizawa.

A List of Crises in England from 1558 to 1720

From William R. Scott, *The Constitution and Finance of English, Scottish and Irish Joint-Stock Companies to 1720*, vol. i, Cambridge, 1912, pp. 465–467.

"Serious crises" are marked with an asterisk

The "number of years between crises" is counted from the beginning of one crisis to the beginning of the next.

Dates of Crises	No. of Years between Crises	Remarks
1558–9	..	Famine 1556–8.
1560	2	English bills refused abroad [because of the financial difficulties of Government].
1563 (Aug.) to 1564 (Aug.) *	3	Plague (the number of deaths said to be 20,000), interruption of trade with Flanders, famine.
1569 (Jan.) to 1574 *	6	Seizures of English goods in Flanders, January, 1569, followed by failures. Norfolk's insurrection, December, 1569, followed by failures. Bad harvests from 1571 to 1574. It is slightly uncertain whether the years 1570–4 should be classed as a part of the crisis or of the subsequent depression.
1586–7 *	17	Babington plot, failures, bad harvest, 1587.
1596–7 *	10	Famine, 1595–8.
1603 *	7	Plague, deaths in London, 30,561.
1616–17	13	Crisis in cloth trade [disorganized by manipulations of James I].
1620–5 *	4	Effects of crisis in cloth trade, Dutch competition in foreign trade, default of East India and Russia companies, bad harvests, plague, deaths in London, 35,403.
1630 *	10	Famine, tonnage dispute, plague, deaths in London, 1,317.
1636–7	6	Depression through the monopolies of Charles I, plague, deaths in London, 10,400.
1640 *	4	Seizure of bullion by Charles I. (July), of pepper (Aug.), plague, deaths 1,450.
1646–9 *	6	Exhaustion of the country through the Civil War, great dearth, high taxation.
1652–4	6	Losses of shipping in the Dutch War, possibly too effects of the Navigation Act.
1659–60	7	Losses in Spanish War, especially in cloth trade, strain of continued high taxation.
1664 (Winter) to 1667 (July)*	5	Dutch War, plague (deaths 68,596), Great Fire, Dutch fleet in the Thames, 1667. Run on bankers.
1672 *	8	Stop of the Exchequer, failure of bankers.
1678	6	Prohibition of trade with France, expectation of war with Holland, run on bankers.
1682	4	Run on bankers occasioned by state of home politics foreign trade little affected.

A LIST OF CRISES IN ENGLAND FROM 1558 TO 1720—*Continued*

Dates of Crises	No. of Years between Crises	Remarks
1686	4	Depression in cloth trade, failure of Corporation bank [1685, on news of Monmouth's rebellion], foreign trade still fairly prosperous.
1688	2	Revolution—run on bankers.
1696–7 *	8	The financial strain of the war, exaggerated ideas of the nature of credit, bad harvests, suspension of cash payments by Bank of England, failure of Land bank schemes.
1701 (Feb.) *	5	Tension between East India companies, political situation, run on banks and consequent failures.
1704 (Oct.) to 1708 (Feb.) *	3	Losses in the war, financial strain, tension between England and Scotland, fears of a French invasion, run on Bank of England.
1710–11 (Winter)	6	Financial strain of the war, change of ministry.
1714 (Jan. to April)	4	Fears as to the succession, reported death of Anne, run on Bank of England.
1715 (Oct.)	1	Rebellion.
1717 (Jan. to March)	2	Walpole's conversion scheme.
1718 (Oct.)	1	Fears of an invasion.
1720 (Sept.) *	2	Panic, following the collapse of speculation [South Sea Bubble].

(1) Dr. Scott connects almost all of the early crises with famines, outbreaks of the plague, wars, civil disorders, irregularities of public finance, or high-handed acts of Government. Dr. Thorp notes the occurrence of bad harvests, epidemics, wars, political unrest, and changes in public policy from time to time in 1790-1925, and now and then suggests a connection between such events and a crisis. But disasters of non-business origin, which occupy the foreground in Dr. Scott's remarks, recede into the background of Dr. Thorp's account. They continue to influence economic activities; but the sources which Dr. Thorp condenses put developments within the world of business foremost among the factors responsible for crises.

It may be that, because of shortcomings in his sources, Dr. Scott over-stresses the influence of "disturbing causes." He has checked contemporary opinions by actual business records and by such statistics as he could find. But these materials are less abundant in his period than they have since become, and he must depend in part upon commentators who were prone to hold Government or nature responsible for whatever went amiss. To make sure that our con-

clusions concerning the character of earlier and of later English crises are not warped by differences between the economic insight of observers in 1558-1720 and of observers in 1790-1926, we may note further contrasts between the pictures drawn by Scott and Thorp.

(2) Dr. Scott represents a fifth of his crises as lasting three years or more—1569-74, 1620-25, 1646-49, 1652-54, 1664-67, and 1704-08. Since periods of "depressed trade" are entered in a separate column of Scott's summary, the implication is that trade continued to be not merely dull, but seriously disturbed during the periods cited. Reference to the fuller accounts given in Scott's earlier chapters justifies this interpretation. In Thorp's annals, it is difficult to find a parallel to these long crises.

(3) In modern business cycles, the crisis or recession follows a period of prosperity. It still happens occasionally, that a season of acute strain, such as Dr. Scott presumably would enter as a crisis, occurs in a period of depression. The most striking recent instance is the trouble caused by the outbreak of war in 1914—an episode which Dr. Thorp does not list as a crisis, just because it came in the trough of a cycle which had culminated in 1913.[1] In Scott's summary, no less than 12 out of 30 crises listed were preceded by periods, not of prosperity, but of "depressed trade."

Of course, this difference between the earlier and the later crises is connected with that first noted. It confirms Scott's conclusion concerning the dominant rôle played in business fluctuations of 16th- to 18th-century England by non-business factors. Crises which are due primarily to such economic processes as are considered in Chapter I can occur only after prosperity has produced certain stresses within the business system. Crises which are dominated by events of a non-business character can occur equally well in any phase of a cycle. Whether crises due to wars, famines, epidemics, or the like will occur more often when trade is good or when trade is poor, must depend in the long run upon the relative number of fat and lean years. The number of crises listed by Scott as following years of depressed trade is greater than the ratio of lean years to fat years would lead one to expect.[2]

[1] For other cases of financial strain occurring during depressions, see below, Chapter IV, section iii, 4.

[2] As closely as I can reckon from Scott's table, the periods of good trade in 1558-1720 covered about 64 years, the periods of depressed trade about 38 years. On this basis, the crises breaking out when trade is good should have exceeded in number the crises breaking out when trade was bad by 1.8: 1. The actual excess was not over 1.5: 1.

This computation cannot be made with precision. Scott does not report the con-

(4) Dr. Scott calls attention to the fact that

> a time of good trade tended to persist, once it had set in, with a long interval between crises, while in the converse case the interval between them was reduced. For instance, in the eleven good years from 1575 to 1585, there was, as far as is known, no crisis, again in seventeen prosperous years (1603 to 1620), there was only one, whereas in an equal number of bad years (1586 to 1603) there were three, and again from 1696 to 1708, there were only four years free from very great disturbances of trade.[3]

Modern business history does not run in such considerable stretches of good times free from crises, serious or mild, and of bad times in which serious crises crowd one another. The longest period of prosperity revealed in Thorp's English annals for 1793-1920 lasted only four years. Nowadays it is periods of depression which "tend to persist"—if that expression is permissible at all. Yet the longest English depression in our record lasted less than six years.[4]

(5) The intervals between the beginnings of crises in Scott's list and the intervals between recessions (which include both mild and severe crises) in Thorp's annals give similar averages: 5.6 years in 1558-1720, 5.8 years in 1793-1920. But the intervals are decidedly more irregular in the earlier period. They run from 1 to 17 years in Scott's list, from 2 to 10 years in Thorp's. The coefficient of variation—perhaps the best measure of variability for this comparison—is 63 per cent in the one case and 39 per cent in the other.[5]

(6) In a business cycle, the order of events is crisis, depression, revival, prosperity, and another crisis (or recession). That Scott does not enter revivals separately in his summary means little; for scant attention has commonly been given to that least dramatic phase of the recurrence. But it is significant that in only 5 cases out of his 29 does Scott report a crisis as followed by depression, prosperity

dition of trade preceding the first of his crises, 1558-9; he does not always show the month or quarter of a year when business conditions changed; there are several intervals scattered through his summary, totaling some 7½ years, for which he makes no report.

The time covered by Scott's 30 crises is 49 years—more than all his periods of depressed trade put together.

[3] W. R. Scott, *Constitution and Finance of English, Scottish and Irish Joint-Stock Companies to 1720,* vol. i, Cambridge, 1912, p. 470.

[4] Chapter IV, section iv, below, "The Duration of Business Cycles."

[5] The coefficient of variation in a statistical array is the standard deviation expressed as a percentage of the arithmetic mean. On the standard deviation see Chapter III, section v, 1, "The Amplitude of Cyclical-Irregular Fluctuations."

and another crisis, in the modern order. Eleven of his intervals between crises contain no period of "good trade"; 12 intervals contain no period of depression; one interval runs: crisis, "good trade," "depressed trade," crisis. No reasonable discount for the stereotyping influence which the concept of business cycles exercises upon the minds of modern business annalists will reduce the record of English business since 1790 to such irregularity of sequence as Dr. Scott records.

It seems clear, then, that the English crises of 1558-1720 were not business crises of the modern type, and that the intervals between these crises were not occupied by business cycles.[6]

Were Dr. Scott's investigations carried backward in time, they would doubtless continue to show frequent crises of a sort as far as records of business transactions could be followed in England. And since England lagged behind other countries in developing business traffic, crises of the type Scott describes must run back to earlier times in the Low Countries, France, Southern Germany, and the Italian towns.[7] Still earlier chapters in the same story appear in the economic histories of Constantinople, of Rome, of Athens. Indeed, we may feel sure that crises, in the sense of serious trade disturbances, are just as old as trade itself. They must have been familiar phenomena in ancient Babylonia and ancient Egypt. But if the crises of 17th- and even 18th-century England differed from the crises of 19th- and 20th-century England as much as Dr. Scott's results suggest, it seems most improbable that the crises of earlier date in any country resembled recent crises closely. Such accounts as I have read of early crises strengthen the inferential doubt. In certain respects interest-

[6] In view of the differences pointed out in the text, it is not surprising that Dr. Scott finds the modern theories of crises inapplicable to his period. "Occurrence of the unforeseen" is the explanation which best fits the facts in his opinion.

> It is when the forecast of the majority of traders is in error that a crisis results. The cause of the miscalculation may lie either mainly in the men who judge or in the events to be judged. . . . At later periods the importance of man's judgment and calculation becomes marked in the period of speculative activity which precedes a crisis. But, prior to the development of banking, such intense activity is scarcely to be expected. . . . Analyzing the crises up to 1720 . . . it will be seen that, owing to defective intelligence in the form of news or to bad government, the objective aspect tends to predominate.

See *Joint-Stock Companies,* vol. i, pp. 469-471.

[7] For example, the second volume of Richard Ehrenberg's *Das Zeitalter der Fugger* gives a most interesting account of the great 16th century crises in Antwerp and Lyons, precipitated by the debt repudiations of the Spanish, French and Austrian monarchs. Not less vivid is Alfred Doren's history of the checkered fortunes of business in Florence at the height of her prosperity in the 13th and 14th centuries. *Studien aus der Florentiner Wirtschaftsgeschichte,* Stuttgart, 1901; *Entwicklung und Organisation der Florentiner Zünfte in 13. und 14. Jahrhundert,* 1896.

ing parallels can be drawn between the business difficulties with which we are familiar, and the business difficulties of which we read in early modern times, in the Middle Ages, or even in classical antiquity. But the differences are striking—most obviously, the difference in the rôle played by events of a non-business type.

The difficulty of deciding when the transition from crises dominated by crop failures, epidemics, wars, public finance and political struggles, to recurrent cycles dominated by business processes took place in England is increased by a gap in our detailed knowledge. There is no adequate record for the years between 1720, when Dr. Scott stops, and 1790, when Dr. Thorp begins. Jevons' list of English crises in the 18th century is too meager and too uncertain to be of much service.[8] The chief study of later date, Mentor Bouniatian's *Geschichte der Handelskrisen in England, 1640-1840,* is based on no such thorough examination of the original sources as Scott made, and mentions only the most impressive cases.[9] Possibly a close year-by-year record of developments would give a more modern impression than does an account limited to half-a-dozen dramatic episodes. That must remain uncertain until some thorough investigator closes the gap between Scott and Thorp. Meanwhile, we have Bouniatian's opinion that no crisis of really modern type can be found before the close of the 18th century.

According to this authority, the next memorable crisis after 1720 occurred in 1745, when the Pretender with his Highlanders got within 120 miles of London. The end of the Seven Years War was followed in 1763 by lively speculation and collapse. Again in 1772, England and Scotland suffered a banking crash after a period of wild speculation—a crash which extended next year to Holland, Hamburg and other continental centers of trade. Six years later, losses brought on by war with the American colonies caused serious difficulties in England. When the war ended in 1783, peace once more gave rise to a sudden expansion of business, and expansion led to a crisis. Finally, in 1793, came what Bouniatian ventures to call the first of England's great industrial crises, followed by depression in general business.[10]

[8] "The Periodicity of Commercial Crises and Its Physical Explanation," 1878. See W. S. Jevons, *Investigations in Currency and Finance,* London, 1884, pp. 207-215.

[9] Bouniatian's book was published at Munich in 1908. During the period treated by both Bouniatian and Scott (1640-1720), the former includes only five crises, the latter nineteen.

[10] Bouniatian, as cited above, p. 171.

As further evidence of the historical connection between business cycles and an advanced stage of pecuniary organization, I may refer to the National Bureau's collection of *Business Annals* at large. These annals show that in the countries which lag furthest behind in pecuniary organization—China, India, Brazil, South Africa, Russia—the vicissitudes of economic life have least of business character. Droughts and floods, epidemics among men and cattle, or civil disorder are responsible for a large part of the economic troubles which are recorded. Indeed, Thorp's record for China in 1890-1925 is curiously like Scott's record for England in, say, 1558-1660. Such misfortunes have consequences more serious in the less business-like communities than similar events have in western Europe or in North America. But, mingling with these phenomena of the natural economy, we find even in China indications that the nascent business activities of the people are subject to fluctuations arising from other sources. The merchants of the coast cities, at least, have their share of troubles with fluctuating commodity prices and exchange rates; some producers find the export demand for their produce falling and rising with conditions in other countries; the banks feel the reaction of developments in Lombard and Wall Streets. Thus the beginnings of business cycles in the laggard countries appear largely as reflections of the cycles in more advanced countries, and are perhaps overemphasized by foreign observers. But these beginnings promise to grow in significance as the backward lands organize a larger and larger part of their economic life on the basis of making and spending money incomes.

II. The Modern Organization for Making Money.

1. The Money-Making Population.

Table 1, compiled from the Fourteenth Census eked out by an estimate, shows broadly how the American people use their time.

Children under ten years of age form more than a fifth of the population. Their chief business is to develop into future citizens; for the time being they must be cared for and trained by adults in the family and the school. Any contributions they may make toward the community's support are incidental.

Leaving out this group of young children, the census indicates that 95 people in the hundred are either getting educated, or are

contributing to the country's real income. The money makers form 50 per cent of this group, the home makers form 27 per cent, the students form 17 per cent, and those not accounted for in the table form 5 per cent.

The 4,610,000 persons not accounted for include some 400,000 children over 9 neither at school nor at work, a much larger number of the infirm in body or mind,[1] the "leisure class" among the rich and among the poor, those reported as following disreputable occupations, together with workers concerning whom the enumerators learned nothing but their names and residences.

TABLE 1

A Conspectus of the Population of the United States in 1920

	Total Number	Attending School	Keeping House (estimated)	Gainful Workers	Not accounted for, 10 years of age and over
Totals	105,700,000	21,800,000	22,500,000	41,600,000	4,610,000
Under 10 years of age					
Under 5 years	11,600,000				
5–9 years	11,400,000	7,800,000			
10–19 years of age					
10–14 years	10,600,000	9,800,000		600,000	200,000
15–19 years	9,400,000	3,700,000	1,100,000	4,400,000	200,000
20–64 years of age					
Males	29,800,000	280,000		28,300,000	1,220,000
Females	28,000,000	210,000	20,100,000	6,600,000	1,090,000
Over 64 years of age					
Males	2,500,000			1,500,000	1,000,000
Females	2,400,000		1,300,000	200,000	900,000
In Percentages of the Total Population					
Totals	100.0%	20.6%	21.3%	39.4%	4.4%
Under 10 years of age					
Under 5 years	11.0				
5–9 years	10.8	7.4			

[1] "The Department of Commerce announces that on or about January 1, 1923, there were 893,679 persons confined in Federal, state, city, county and private institutions for defectives, dependents, criminals, and juvenile delinquents, hospitals for mentally diseased, institutions for feebleminded and epileptics, homes for adults and dependent or neglected children, institutions for juvenile delinquents, penal institutions and almshouses." Of this total 229,780 were children. Needless to say a large, though unknown, number of the infirm in body or mind are cared for by their families and do not appear in a census of institutions. The quotation is from an official press release of July 14, 1924.

TABLE 1 — *Continued*

A CONSPECTUS OF THE POPULATION OF THE UNITED STATES IN 1920

	Total Number	Attending School	Keeping House (estimated)	Gainful Workers	Not accounted for, 10 years of age and over
10–19 years of age					
10–14 years	10.0	9.3		.6	.2
15–19 years	8.9	3.5	1.0	4.2	.2
20–64 years of age					
Males	28.2	.3		26.8	1.2
Females	26.5	.2	19.0	6.2	1.0
Over 64 years of age					
Males	2.4			1.4	.9
Females	2.3		1.2	.2	.9
In Percentages of the Age and Sex Classes					
Under 10 years of age					
Under 5 years	100.0				
5–9 years	100.0	68.4			
10–19 years					
10–14 years	100.0	92.4		5.7	1.9
15–19 years	100.0	39.4	11.7	46.8	2.1
20–64 years of age					
Males	100.0	.9		95.0	4.1
Females	100.0	.7	71.8	23.6	3.9
Over 64 years of age					
Males	100.0			60.0	40.0
Females	100.0		54.2	8.3	37.5
In Percentages of the Occupation Classes					
Totals	100.0%	100.0%	100.0%	100.0%	100.0%
Under 10 years of age					
Under 5 years	11.0				
5–9 years	10.8	35.8			
10–19 years of age					
10–14 years	10.0	45.0		1.4	4.3
15–19 years	8.9	17.0	4.9	10.6	4.3
20–64 years of age					
Males	28.2	1.3		68.0	26.5
Females	26.5	1.0	89.3	15.9	23.6
Over 64 years of age					
Males	2.4			3.6	21.7
Females	2.3		5.8	.5	19.5

Persons of unknown age are included in the group 20–64 years of age.
Notes on Table 1 continued on page 85.

The 14,000,000 students 10 years of age and over are made up mainly of children under 15. About that age half or more of the children drop out of school and begin earning money or helping with housework. Less than half a million persons over 19 years are reported as attending school, and not a few of them are also doing other work.

The 22,500,000 housewives are mainly women in the middle years of life; but there seem to be over a million girls and a somewhat larger number of elderly women who devote themselves primarily to maintaining homes for their families.

Finally, the 41,600,000 money earners include nearly half of the children between 15 and 19 years, not quite a quarter of the women of 20-64, nearly all of the men within these ages, more than half of the older men and a small part of the older women. Arranged in another way, the data show that of the gainful workers 12 per cent are under 20 years, 16 per cent are adult women, and 72 per cent are adult men.

Our concern, as students of business cycles, is mainly with this group of money makers. But we must not conceive the money makers as "supporting" the whole population; housewives contribute a large slice of real income. For the matter of that, the work young people do in school is of vital concern to economic welfare in the long run. And as consumers, the whole population comes into our reckoning.

Notes on Table 1 continued:

The number of women entered as "keeping house" without pay is based on estimates kindly made at the writer's request by Dr. Alba M. Edwards of the Bureau of the Census and by Dr. Ralph G. Hurlin of the Russell Sage Foundation. One of Dr. Edwards' methods, utilizing various population returns, yielded 23,000,000 housewives; the second, starting with the number of "homes" reported by the census, deducting for institutions enumerated as homes, and for family homes maintained by single men, paid housekeepers and by women having gainful occupations, and adding for homes managed by two women, yielded 22,300,000 housewives. Dr. Hurlin also tried two ways of approximating the number of unpaid housewives. His first method was to estimate the number of women occupied in other ways; by elimination, there seemed to be some 21,900,000 housewives. A second method, which Dr. Hurlin prefers, applies the American ratio of private to census families in 1900 and the British ratio of private families to "all occupiers" in 1911 to the 1920 count of homes, and after deductions for homes not managed by unpaid women, yields 22,500,000 housewives. The round figure adopted in the table is a little higher than the mean of these four estimates.

Some persons are reported both as attending school and as having gainful occupations. These cases are counted twice in the table. Their number is not known; but probably is not large enough to affect the results seriously. The gainfully-occupied women who also keep house are not counted as housekeepers.

The gainful workers include persons temporarily unemployed, and inmates of institutions who have specific work to perform. They do not include people of independent means who report no regular money-making occupation.

2. The Business Enterprise.

In spending money, the family is still the dominant unit of organization. But as the dominant unit of organization for making money, the family has been definitely superseded by the business enterprise, except perhaps in farming, petty trade, and the professions. The business enterprise commonly draws its members from several or many families, paying each individual a money income, and welding them into a new unit organized to make profits.

A business enterprise is an organization which seeks to realize pecuniary profits upon an investment of capital, by a series of transactions concerned with the purchase and sale of goods in terms of money.[1] The goods dealt in may be commodities of any vendible kind from coal to newspapers; they may be services, such as transportation, storage, or technical advice; they may be rights, such as bank credit, securities, or insurance against specified risks. The enterprise may "produce," or fabricate, or store, or transport, or distribute, or merely hold the title to the goods in which it deals.

3. The Size of Business Enterprises and Business Cycles.

Business enterprises of a highly organized type have come to occupy almost the whole field in railway and marine transportation. They dominate mining, lumbering, construction work, warehousing, most branches of manufacturing, the public utilities not managed by government, wholesale trade, insurance, banking and finance at large. They play an important, if not a controlling, rôle in retail trade, journalism, market gardening, fishing, hotel keeping, and various amusement trades. They are invading dairying, fruit raising, general farming, and the learned professions—engineering, architecture, law, education, medicine.

Of course, everyone who is working on his own account—the peddler, the cobbler, the farmer, the doctor and lawyer, the boarding-house keeper, the newsboy—may be regarded as running a business enterprise. All these people, and those whom they suggest, get their money incomes by buying and selling goods, or by selling their services to numerous buyers. But there are broad differences between the

[1] Compare Werner Sombart, *Der Moderne Kapitalismus*, 1st ed., Leipzig, 1902, vol. i, p. 195.

industries dominated by small-scale and those dominated by large-scale enterprises. In commercial alertness and business method, in complexity of organization, in dependence upon the money market, the typical farm, repair shop, neighborhood store, and boarding house are in a different class from the enterprises typical of mining, manufacturing, commerce and finance. Most professional men engaged in private practice hold, what some business men deny, that there is also a significant difference between professional and commercial aims.

In the study of business cycles, this uneven development of business enterprise in various fields is important. It is within the circle of full-fledged business enterprise that the alternations of prosperity and depression appear most clearly and produce their most striking effects. All of the authorities whose theories were reviewed in Chapter I seem to agree tacitly, if not explicitly, upon this fundamental point. They deal primarily with processes that run their rounds within the centers of commerce, industry, construction work, transportation, and finance. Farming, the professions, personal service, repair work, and petty trade are in the background of the picture. Even the writers who regard changes in crop yields as the cause of business fluctuations are no real exception; for while they hold that cyclical fluctuations arise in agriculture, they recognize that these fluctuations manifest themselves chiefly in commercial dealings, manufacturing activity, transportation, and financial operations.

Statistical evidence for this view that business cycles are primarily phenomena of large-scale enterprise was provided incidentally in 1923 by one of the investigations made by the National Bureau of Economic Research for the President's Conference on Unemployment. The pertinent results are assembled in Table 2. While the figures in this table are estimates based upon rather slender samples; while they refer to but one cycle in one country, and cover but one aspect of business—shrinkage in the hours worked by employees in depression—they give the most comprehensive statistical view yet presented of the relation between scale of organization and degree of cyclical fluctuations.

Two conclusions are indicated by the table. (1) When arranged according to the severity of the decline in employment after the crisis of 1920, the leading industries form three groups. Manufacturing, railroading, mining, and construction work were most disastrously affected by the depression. A second group, in which the shrinkage

of employment was far less serious, but substantial, included finance, wholesale trade, and transportation other than by railroad. These two groups of industries constitute the sphere of business par excellence. The remaining industries, among them agriculture and retailing, are characterized by small-scale organization, or by the prominence of non-commercial aims, or by both features. These industries

TABLE 2

Cyclical Decline in the Volume of Employment Offered by Different Industries, and by Establishments of Different Sizes, from the Peak of Prosperity in 1920 to the Trough of Depression in 1921–22.

	All establishments Per cent decline	Establishments with 0–20 employees Per cent decline	Establishments with 21–100 employees Per cent decline	Establishments with over 100 employees Per cent decline
All Industries	16.50	3.08	13.84	28.23
All Factories	29.97	8.21	19.21	38.56
Steam Railways	29.68	[a]	[a]	29.68
Extraction of Minerals	29.66	[a]	[a]	30.18
Building and Construction	18.92	14.66	[a]	[a]
Finance	7.14	0.00	0.00	25.58
Transportation other than railways	6.77	3.72	9.80	8.17
Wholesale Trade	5.64	0.00	12.31	7.77
Public and Professional Service	4.57	[a]	[a]	[a]
Domestic and Personal Service	4.11	5.40	4.48	3.92
Agriculture	3.18	2.15	[a]	[a]
Retail Trade	2.75	1.31	4.66	10.84
Hand Trades other than Building	0.00	2.11	4.67	[a]

[a] Reports received from less than 20 enterprises.

The comparisons are based upon quarterly reports from 9,289 enterprises, and cover the full years 1920 and 1921, and the first three months of 1922.

Adapted from Willford I. King, *Employment, Hours and Earnings in Prosperity and Depression. United States, 1920–1922.* National Bureau of Economic Research, New York, 2d ed., 1923, pp. 55–58, 60. (I have corrected a misprint in the source.)

reduced the amount of employment offered but slightly. (2) The correspondence between scale of organization and violence of fluctuations holds not merely among industries as wholes, but also among the establishments within an industry. As a rule, large establishments were more affected by the depression than medium-sized establishments, and the latter were more affected than small establishments.

These conclusions cannot be regarded as definitely proven, until they have stood the test of further investigations. They harmonize, however, not only with the assumptions of theoretical writers, but

also with what is known about the fluctuations of prices, production, stocks, and the like in different industries. At a later stage, these fluctuations will be analyzed at length. In the meantime it is important to inquire what proportion of economic activity is exposed to a large business-cycle hazard and what part to a slight one.

Well over one-half of all employees in the United States seem to depend for work upon manufacturing, mining, railroading and building and construction, the industries in which the cyclical oscillations appear to be most violent.[1] Within these industries probably three-fourths or more of the employees are in concerns which have over 100 hands—the subdivision most exposed to the business-cycle hazard.[2] The middle group of industries shown in Table 2 has a much smaller body of employees, perhaps as much as one-tenth, perhaps as little as one-twentieth of the total. There remain in the industries least exposed to cyclical fluctuations something like a third or two-fifths of all wage and salary earners. And a large majority of these workers are employed in the smallest and least-affected class of enterprises.[3]

Very different is the distribution of men working on their own account. Estimates based upon the 1920 census of occupations indicate that the number of such persons in the United States was a little more than 10,000,000.[4] Certainly less than one-tenth, perhaps not

[1] See Dr. King's estimate of the number of employees working in various industries in 1920, *Employment, Hours and Earnings*, p. 20.

[2] The Fourteenth Census gives definite data for manufactures, mines, and quarries, which may be summarized thus:

MANUFACTURING ESTABLISHMENTS AND MINES AND QUARRIES: CLASSIFIED ACCORDING TO NUMBER OF EMPLOYEES: UNITED STATES, 1919

Number of Employees per Establishment	Manufacturing Establishments		Mines and Quarries	
	Per cent of Number	Per cent of Total Employees	Per cent of Number	Per cent of Total Employees
20 or less	81	10	73	6
21–100	13	19	17	18
Over 100	6	71	10	76
	100	100	100	100
Actual numbers	290,000	9,096,000	21,300	982,000

Compiled from *Fourteenth Census of the United States*, vols. viii, *Manufactures*, p. 90, and xi, *Mines and Quarries*, p. 31.

All the operating railroads, of course, employ more than 100 men. Concerning building and construction, the data are meager; but Dr. King has made a very rough estimate that in 1920, not quite one-third of the employees were working for concerns having more than 100 persons on the payrolls. See *Employment, Hours and Earnings*, p. 20.

[3] Once more see Dr. King's estimates on p. 20 of *Employment, Hours and Earnings*.

[4] See the three estimates compared by Dr. Leo Wolman in *The Growth of American Trade Unions, 1880-1923*. New York, National Bureau of Economic Research, 1924, pp.

one-twentieth, of these enterprisers [5] were in those branches of business most exposed to the business-cycle hazard. About nine-tenths, on the other hand, were in the least exposed group of industries,—farming, retail trade, and professional, domestic and personal service.[6]

4. Economic Resources and the National Dividend.

Of the vast array of natural resources and man-made equipment used by our 41,600,000 money-earners and our 22,500,000 housewives—to keep the 1920 census figures of Table 1—many writers upon business cycles have emphasized one category, and taken the others for granted. Hobson's theory of over-savings and over-investment in industrial equipment, Tugan-Baranovski's theory of the alternate accumulation and exhaustion of loan-funds, Hull's theory of the changing costs of construction work, the numerous theories which stress the effects of extending plant capacity, Foster and Catchings' theory of the inability of consumers to buy the goods offered them, all build in one way or another upon a contrast between the process of supplying current income and the process of increasing the appliances for future production.[1]

To lay a factual basis for testing these views, we should find out what we can about the relative magnitude of (1) the value of the equipment with which the population works, (2) the income produced, and (3) the annual additions made to working equipment out of income. The present section deals with the first two magnitudes; a later section will deal with savings.

For summaries of the resources which the population uses in its work, we must turn to inventories of the national wealth. Two esti-

78-81. Mr. Carl Hookstadt's figures cited here are raised well above 10,000,000 by including 1,850,119 "home farm laborers" with the employers. *Monthly Labor Review*, July, 1923, vol. xvii, p. 2, footnote.

[5] Of the various aliases under which the man who is doing business on his own account passes in current economic literature (entrepreneur, undertaker, capitalist-employer, business man), the name enterpriser seems least objectionable. It is an old English word, recently brought back into current use at almost the same time by Professors Frank A. Fetter (*Principles of Economics*, New York, 1904), and H. Stanley Jevons (*Essays on Economics*, London, 1905).

[6] Compare the estimates given by Dr. W. I. King in the first chapter of Dr. Maurice Leven's *Distribution of Income by States*, New York, National Bureau of Economic Research, 1925, and by Dr. Leo Wolman in his monograph cited above, p. 77.

[1] See the references to the writers named in Chapter I, section iv. Among the men who assign much importance to the construction of additional equipment are Veblen, Spiethoff, Bouniatian, Aftalion, J. M. Clark, Robertson, Cassel, and A. B. Adams.

mates for the United States as of December 31, 1922, have recently been made by the Bureau of the Census and the Federal Trade Commission. Both organizations recognize that their results are rough approximations at best. The concept "national wealth" is so vague that statisticians differ about the items to be included, and about the proper methods of ascertaining values. Also, the data with which they must work leave much to be desired in comprehensiveness and accuracy. Under such circumstances, it is not to be expected that different estimates will agree closely, or that any estimate can command full confidence. The Federal Trade Commission's total for 1922 is some 10 per cent greater than that of the Census, primarily because the Commission includes "land and improvements in streets and public roads," which the Census omits, and because the Commission values "public service enterprises" at 46 billion dollars, while the Census values them at 35 billions.[2] But the 10 per cent difference between the two totals does not represent the margin of uncertainty surrounding both results. Accordingly, I shall use the figures only in the broadest fashion to indicate the great classes of resources with which the population works, the order of magnitude among these classes, and the relative value of man-made equipment and of annual income.

[2] See *Estimated National Wealth,* Bureau of the Census, Washington, 1925; *National Wealth and Income, A Report by the Federal Trade Commission* (Senate Document No. 126, 69th Congress, 1st session), Washington, 1926. The Federal Trade Commission's estimate is rather a reworking of and supplement to the basic Census figures than an independent investigation of the whole field.

With these official estimates compare the inventory of "Physical Property in the United States" in 1920, made by Dr. Walter Renton Ingalls, *Wealth and Income of the American People,* 2d ed., York, Pennsylvania, 1923, p. 79. Dr. Ingalls' total of 273 billion dollars is 18 per cent less than the Census total and 29 per cent less than the Federal Trade Commission total. These differences are smaller than one would expect in view of the facts that (1) Ingalls' estimates are for 1920, the Census and Commission estimates for the end of 1922; (2) Ingalls used 1913 values, so far as possible, the Census and Commission tried to use current values; (3) Ingalls made relatively freer use of estimates as contrasted with enumerations, than did the Census and Commission. (For example, to arrive at the value of manufacturing machinery, Ingalls estimated that 7,750,000 workers used plant of average cost of $2,000 per worker, while the Census summed up many thousands of reports from manufacturing enterprises concerning the value of their machinery.) On the other hand, it should be noted (1) that the period 1920-22 included a severe crisis and depression, during which the increase of wealth was retarded; (2) that the money values of real estate, buildings, heavy machinery, and the like were far less affected by price fluctuations than our current index numbers might lead one to think, and that none of the estimators can hold rigorously to values of a given date; (3) that several of the items must be guessed at, and it may make little difference (as in the machinery item) whether the guess is based on elaborate study of a sample, or on the estimate of an expert who has had long experience in valuation work. Needless to say, in some items the percentage differences among the three estimates are far larger than the differences among the three totals. But it is not feasible to enter into details in this place.

Since our national inventories refer to the end of 1922, it seems well to compare them with the mean income of the two calendar years, 1922 and 1923. For national income in these years, we have three estimates, one made by the Federal Trade Commission, one made by Dr. W. R. Ingalls, and preliminary figures made by Dr. W. I. King for the National Bureau of Economic Research. These estimates are not strictly comparable; for the Federal Trade Commission and Dr. Ingalls omit two items which Dr. King includes—the rental value of homes occupied by their owners and interest upon the value of consumers' goods owned by families. Since the inventories we are using include both family dwellings and personal effects as considerable items of national wealth, consistency requires that we include the services rendered by these goods in the income estimates which we compare with the wealth estimates. This consideration points to the use of King's figures. But King's figures for 1922-23 are preliminary estimates, while the Federal Trade Commission's figures are the result of elaborate investigation. It seems best, therefore, to use the Commission's estimate as basic, but to add King's figures for the two items in question. This procedure gives 70 billion dollars as the average income for 1922-23.[3]

We may begin our canvass of economic resources with an item on which no one can set a price—the knowledge which enables men to use other resources as they now do. What count here are not merely the engineering applications of modern science, but also the organiz-

[3] For the three estimates, see Walter Renton Ingalls, "An Estimate of National Income for 1925," *The Annalist,* September 24, 1926, p. 395, and the National Bureau's *News-Bulletin,* February, 1927.

The figures for 1922-23 are as follows:

Estimates of National Income in the United States
In billions of Dollars.

	Ingalls	National Bureau	Federal Trade Commission
1922	60.5	65.6*	61.7
1923	71.9	76.8*	69.8

* Preliminary estimates, subject to revision.

King's estimates for the two items omitted by the other authorities are, in billions of dollars:

	Rental value of homes occupied by owners.	Interest upon value of consumers' goods owned by consumers.
1922	1.8	2.6
1923	1.9	2.8

The addition of these items to the Federal Trade Commission estimates brings their average for 1922-23 within 1¼ per cent of King's corresponding figure (70.3 billions in one case and 71.2 billions in the other).

ing capacity of business men, the skill of mechanics, the ability of housewives as both managers and manual workers—indeed the whole mass of commonplace and of specialized knowledge which enables people to work in disciplined harmony for each other and to make use of each others' products.

In a discussion of secular trends in economic life, past or future, this resource would take first place. Man's ability to multiply and to raise his standard of living, in a world where many natural resources appear to be exhaustible, depends upon the progress of his knowledge. In treating business cycles we need not face this issue at large. Yet several of the working hypotheses which other investigators have suggested show that we cannot set knowledge aside as a factor of no concern to us. Vogel, Schumpeter, Mrs. England, and Cassel regard business cycles as by-products of progress in the arts of production and of business organization.[4]

Though we cannot value the inestimable, we can make contact between the maintenance cost of knowledge and our measuring stick, the national income. Knowledge is one of the resources which must be continuously renewed. According to the occupation tables, one money-earner in every fifty is a school or college teacher, and according to the Educational Finance Inquiry one fiftieth of our national income is spent upon schools.[5] But these figures give a most inadequate impression of the effort we make as a nation to educate ourselves. The census figures of Table 1 show that more than a fifth of the total population are attending school. For every two persons earning money, one person is studying. The discount upon this comparison for the brevity and irregularity of school attendance by many children is partly offset by the irregularity of the work done by many adults. It is a common aim of state laws to give every child eight or nine years of schooling. There must be several millions of Americans who have spent fifteen years or more primarily in study.[6] Nine years make a fifth, and fifteen years make a third of an active working life of 45 years. And besides the years we devote to formal training, each

[4] See Chapter I, section iv.

[5] Mabel Newcomer, *Financial Statistics of Public Education in the United States*, (Educational Finance Inquiry, vol. vi) New York, 1924, pp. 11-29.

Dr. Newcomer estimates the governmental expenditures upon schools (1.220 million dollars in 1920) at 1.6 per cent of the national income in 1910, 2.0 per cent in 1915, and 1.7 per cent in 1920. No one knows how large are the educational expenditures of endowments and private schools. I take one-fiftieth of the national income to indicate merely the order of magnitude of the money outlay upon this item.

[6] Table I shows that in 1920, 490,000 persons over 19 years of age were reported as "attending school."

of us spends much time in learning and in teaching others how to do specific jobs at home or where we are employed.

To all this effort spent upon imparting our inherited store of knowledge must be added a further item, much smaller in amount, but doubtless involving a direct money outlay of hundreds of millions annually upon efforts to improve and extend knowledge. Here belongs all the energy put into research proper, and the endless experimenting with new devices and methods for doing the world's work.[7]

To come to the tangible resources: (1) In the national inventories for 1922, an item of nearly 40 billion dollars is entered as "furniture and personal effects." If we add a rough figure for pleasure automobiles, this item rises to 42 or 43 billions—say two-thirds of one year's national income.

How rapidly the goods in question are worn out and replaced on the average, we do not know. But family budgets throw some light on that problem. In 1924, the Federal Bureau of Labor Statistics published tables summarizing the expenditures of over 12,000 white families living in 92 industrial centers, and having incomes which averaged about $1,500. Of their total outlays, 23 per cent was spent for clothing, furniture, furnishings, and miscellaneous items which can be classified as "personal effects." [8] The representative value of these figures is open to question. Negro and farm families probably spend a smaller proportion of their money for clothing and personal effects than do white urban families; but well-to-do families probably spend more than wage-earners.[9] Also, the period covered by the Bureau of Labor Statistics' budgets—mainly the calendar year 1918—was peculiar in several ways. Hence we cannot trust wholly the

[7] Secretary Hoover has recently ventured the following estimates:

"We are spending in industry, in government, national and local, probably $200,000,000 a year in search for applications of scientific knowledge—with perhaps 30,000 men engaged in the work . . . the whole sum which we have available to support pure science research is less than $10,000,000 a year, with probably less than 4,000 men engaged in it, most of them dividing their time between it and teaching."

Herbert Hoover, "The Nation and Science," *Science,* January 14, 1927, vol. lxv, pp. 26, 27.

[8] See "The Cost of Living in the United States," *Bulletin of the U. S. Bureau of Labor Statistics,* No. 357, p. 5, and last section of Table G. The largest miscellaneous item is "automobiles, motor cycles, bicycles." The budgets were collected in 1918-19, from places scattered over 42 states.

[9] In the Bureau of Labor Statistics' table the percentages of outlay for clothing, furniture and furnishings, and miscellaneous objects all rise with family income. Also see the table on p. 26 of the National Bureau's report on *Income in the Various States,* 1925. These figures, compiled by Dr. King, indicate that expenditures on automobiles

conclusions that upwards of a quarter of family income is spent for quasi-durable consumers' commodities, and that the stock of these commodities on hand is between two and three years' purchases. But such are the indications of what data we have.

(2) At all times there is a huge stream of raw materials, partially-fabricated products and finished goods flowing through the country's industrial and commercial enterprises on its way toward family or business consumers. The 1922 inventories value this flow at about 36 billion dollars. That sum is equivalent to half of the national income in the year concerned, and is not much smaller than the value assigned to the furniture and personal effects owned by families.

The contrast drawn by writers like Henry S. Dennison, Lawrence K. Frank, T. W. Mitchell, and Simon S. Kuznets between the fairly even pace of consumer purchasing and the fluctuating course of production suggests that the volume of merchandise and materials on hand, on wheels, and in process, undergoes large changes. The rough comparison which the national inventories let us make between the value of "products, merchandise, etc." at a given time and the national income for one year indicates that a check upon production need not check consumption at once. But we need more continuous, specific, and reliable data than an occasional inventory can give. Fortunately, we have a clear view of the flow of goods in at least one industry.

By checking the input of copper by smelters against the deliveries of copper by refiners, the American Bureau of Metal Statistics is able to make a continuous record of the flow of copper through the metallurgical system. This record commands the confidence even of its compilers—a virtue rare in industrial statistics. The reports show for the first of each month the quantity of copper at five successive stages of its trip toward consumers—blister at smelteries, blister in transit, blister at refineries, metal in process of being refined, and refined copper on hand at refineries. The total tonnage reported at these five stages month by month varies considerably—for example, it shrank in 1922 from 427,000 tons at the beginning of the year to 344,000 tons at the close. The general level of the tonnage in this flow is about one-third to one-half of the annual output of virgin copper.

(including tires), books, clothing, diamonds, furs, house furnishings, and pianos made up about 28 per cent of the outlays of urban employees, 29 per cent of the outlays of families spending $5,000 annually, and 32 per cent of the outlays of families spending $25,000 annually.

All this refers solely to the metallurgical system, which is construed as ending at the exit gates of the refineries. After passing through these gates into the manufacturing system, copper travels to mills wherein by itself, or as brass, bronze, or nickel silver, it is made into sheets, rod, wire, tubing, or castings. From the mills, basic fabricated products go partly into direct consumption (for example, electrical transmission wire), but more largely to other manufacturers who make finished goods, such as electrical motors and automobiles. Many products (for example, hardware and house fittings) pass from secondary manufacturers through jobbers to the shelves of retailers. A complete report would show copper in transit, in stock, in process, and ready for delivery at each of these supplemental stages before it passes into actual use in a myriad of forms. Moreover, in the manufacturing processes a considerable proportion of the copper worked up passes into scrap, turnings, borings, etc. This scrap is reworked, so that an appreciable fraction of our copper is continuously going round and round in the manufacturing system. It is computed that in 1923 the quantity of such scrap was about one-third of the manufacture, which would mean a lockup of about four months' supply in this form alone, in addition to the lockup of from three months' to six months' supply in the metallurgical system. The copper in transit, in processes, and in stock in the manufacturing and distributing systems, for which there is no statistical accounting, should be added. The director of the American Bureau of Metal Statistics, Dr. W. R. Ingalls, believes that "the normal stock of copper in the United States is equivalent to something between six months' and twelve months' production, and more nearly the latter than the former." [10]

How representative the copper industry is in this respect, we shall not know until other industries develop similar statistical services. Meantime, we may take this case as illustrating, though not as measuring, a feature of economic activity too often overlooked.

(3) Business-cycle theorists have concentrated their attention primarily upon the next item—movable equipment—though its value in the inventory is a little smaller than the value of "furniture and personal effects," and only a little larger than the value put on "products, merchandise, etc." As movable equipment we count some 16 billion dollars worth of manufacturing machinery, tools, and im-

[10] See W. R. Ingalls, *Wealth and Income of the American People,* 2d ed., 1923, p. 150. It is to Dr. Ingalls that I am indebted for information concerning the work of the American Bureau of Metal Statistics.

plements; 11 to 14 billions of public service equipment (apart from improvements upon land); 6 billions of live stock; 2½ billions of farm implements and machinery, and 1 or 2 billion dollars worth of motor trucks and cars used wholly or largely for business. The total runs to about 37 billion dollars according to the Census, and to about 40 billions according to the Federal Trade Commission—somewhat over half of one year's national income.

(4) The value of "improvements upon land," including much besides buildings, is a highly conjectural figure.[11] Doubtless we are safe in accepting the conclusion that this item is much larger than any of the preceding, and is every year larger than the current national income. The Census figures give a total of 89 billion dollars; the Commission figures mount to 108 billions.

(5) The value of land itself is estimated by the Census method at 112 billion dollars in 1922, and by the Commission method at 122 billions. With these imposing sums we have little concern. Land values are unquestionably influenced by changes in business activity, and excited real-estate speculation is a familiar feature of "booms." But what men get out of land year by year, and what improvements they make upon it, are matters of greater moment in the study of business cycles than are the money values imputed to land.

One point, however, we should notice. On the face of the returns, agriculture is capitalized at a higher figure than manufacturing. According to Dr. King's figures, by 1920 the number of money-earners who depended upon manufactures for their living had become decidedly larger than the number who depended upon agriculture—11,500,000 persons against 8,900,000.[12] Of machinery and implements, the factory workers used in 1922 a value six times that of the farm workers—15.8 billion dollars against 2.6 billions. Adding 5.8 billions for live stock still leaves the farm workers with far less movable equipment. But the value assigned to farm real estate is more than double that assigned to the real estate used in manufacturing—53 billion dollars against 24 billions. Of course, the farm is a home as well as an income-making enterprise; but even if we subtract a fifth from the real-estate value of farms to cover this item, we have left a difference of 17 or 18 billions between agricultural and manufacturing real estate—more than enough to offset the excess in the value of

[11] On its derivation, see the Federal Trade Commission's report on *National Wealth and Income,* pp. 31-34.

[12] See his introduction to *Income in the Various States,* National Bureau of Economic Research, 1925, pp. 21 and 23.

movable equipment used in manufacturing.[13] Of the real estate used in these two great branches of industry, it is safe to assume that improvements constitute a larger percentage in manufacturing than in farming. Thus the high capitalization of agriculture is due wholly to the greater value imputed to land itself. If we could separate the value of all man-made equipment (including live stock) from the value of natural resources, we would find that the average factory worker uses a far larger stock of the first in his work than does the average farm worker, but that the nominal value of the average farm worker's total equipment is the greater.

(6) Finally, our inventories include a small item, 4.3 billion dollars, representing the value of gold and silver coins and bullion. From the national viewpoint, this resource must be regarded as part of the permanent equipment for production. But it is a peculiar type of equipment. It renders its service as it changes ownership, or as it lies in vaults as a "reserve" supporting a larger volume of credit currency. It is one of the most durable man-made resources, so that the supply consists mainly of past accumulations. The changes in any country's stock during a year are usually due more to a redistribution of the world stock than to fresh production minus wastage. Both the redistribution and the annual production of the precious metals bear upon price fluctuations. That fact secures this item, small as it is in comparison with other resources, a leading place in studies of business fluctuations.

The chief conclusion to be drawn from this survey of economic resources is that the physical, man-made equipment with which the American population works represents a value equivalent to between three and four years' effort of its money-earners. Barring land, the

[13] The estimates used are given in a footnote on p. 29 of the Federal Trade Commission's report on *National Wealth and Income*. Even the 1920 Census figure of 44 billion dollars for the "capital" of manufacturing establishments—a figure against which the Bureau of the Census itself warns us—falls far short of the value of farm property minus an allowance for farm homes. A third figure showing the "estimated value of wealth used in *corporate* business" by manufacturing industries (33.7 billions of dollars) is derived by the Commission from tax reports made to the Bureau of Internal Revenue (see p. 135 of *National Wealth and Income*). According to the Census of Manufactures in 1920, incorporated enterprises produced 87.7 per cent of the total value of manufactured goods. If we apply this ratio to the above estimate of "the value of wealth used" by manufacturing corporations, we get some 38 billion dollars as "the value of wealth used" by all manufacturing enterprises. That figure agrees fairly well with the estimates used in the text (15.8 billion dollars worth of movable equipment, plus 24 billion dollars worth of real estate).

The estimate of the value of farm real estate in 1922 (53 billions) was made by the Department of Agriculture.

Bureau of the Census values our tangible man-made resources at 209 billion dollars in 1922. The Federal Trade Commission puts the figure at 231 billions.[14] To raise the first estimate to three times the national income of 1922-23, we should have to add to it a billion dollars. To raise the second estimate to four times the national income we should have to add 49 billions. But though our conclusion is protected by these margins (one of which is narrow), we should view it as no more than a rough approximation based upon imperfect data.[15]

[14] A tabular recapitulation of the figures may be useful. I have rearranged the items to serve the present purpose, but have not altered the figures. The slight discrepancies between the totals entered and the sums of the items are due to the dropping of fractions.

ESTIMATES OF THE NATIONAL WEALTH OF THE UNITED STATES IN 1922
In billions of dollars

		Census		Federal Trade Commission
Land		112		122
Improvements on land		89		108
Movable equipment				
Live stock	5.8		5.8	
Farm implements and machinery	2.6		2.6	
Manufacturing implements and machinery	15.8		15.8	
Public service equipment	10.6		13.6	
Motor cars and trucks	2.0		2.0	
		37		40
Products and merchandise		36		36
Furniture and personal effects (including automobiles)		42		42
Gold and silver coin and bullion		4		4
Total man-made equipment		209		231
Grand Total		321		353

For more detailed estimates, see the Federal Trade Commission's report on *National Wealth and Income*, 1926, pp. 28 and 34.

[15] One would expect to find the accumulated stock of wealth larger in proportion to current income in western Europe than in the United States. This surmise is supported by computations based on the data collected by Sir Josiah Stamp in "The Wealth and Income of the Chief Powers," *Journal of the Royal Statistical Society*, July, 1919, vol. lxxxii, pp. 441–493. From Sir Josiah's summary table (p. 491) and from land values given in his text (pp. 455, 467 and 475), the best figures I can make run as follows:

RATIO OF ONE YEAR'S NATIONAL INCOME TO:

		National Wealth	National Wealth minus value of land
United Kingdom	1914	1:6.4	1:5.9
Germany	1914	1:7.7	1:6.1
France	1914	1:8.0	1:5.9
Australia	1914	1:5.9	....
United States	1914	1:5.8	....
United States	1922–23	1:5.0	1:3.3

Although the results answer expectations, and although I have included only the countries for which tolerably good estimates of wealth and income are available, the comparison is hazardous. In particular, it seems that the valuation of lands must be

The possession of this equipment gives a modern community not only vastly enhanced power of producing income, but also power to consume for a time more than it produces. Even a private family can fall back at need upon its store of "furniture and private effects" —a store which our estimates make equal to nearly two-thirds of a year's income on the average. They can suspend renewals and repairs upon such goods, and even turn some goods into food at a pinch—though seldom without heavy loss. A farmer can sell part of his live stock, let his buildings run down, and make shift with his old implements—not to speak of depleting the fertility of his land. A business enterprise can pursue the same policy—particularly it can reduce its inventories of materials, products or merchandise on hand. Of course, neglect of maintenance usually incurs heavy economic penalties; but there are times when families and business men have no choice in the matter. They must live "on their fat" for a while.

Nor is that all. While current net additions to man-made equipment are probably smaller in value one year with another than are current renewals, these additions can be nearly suspended at need, and made in large volume when conditions are favorable. In practice, the fluctuations in extension and betterment work doubtless have far larger amplitudes than the fluctuations in repairs and renewals. Added to the latter, they make the cyclical swings in production considerably greater than the cyclical swings in consumption.

What the present section adds to common knowledge is that, in dealing with business cycles, (1) attention should be paid to several types of resources besides buildings, machinery, and public-utility equipment, (2) account should be taken of fluctuations in outlay upon maintenance, as well as of fluctuations in outlay upon extensions, and (3) the value of all tangible man-made resources in use at a given time seems in the United States to be less than four times the value of one year's national income, as that income is usually reckoned.

5. The Interdependence of Business Enterprises.

Every business enterprise for which a set of books is kept may be treated as an independent unit. Indeed, the Bureau of the Census

made on different principles in the four countries for which figures are given. On the face of the figures, land values make 8 per cent of total wealth in the United Kingdom, 21 per cent in Germany, 26 per cent in France, and 35 per cent in the United States. Probably the ratios of income to total wealth are less reliable approximations than the ratios of income to wealth minus land values.

accepts this test of separate bookkeeping as its chief criterion in deciding how many "establishments" to recognize in its enumerations of mines, factories and farms. Yet all business enterprises are so bound to each other by industrial, commercial, and financial ties that none can prosper and none can suffer without affecting others.

As an industrial plant handling commodities, the typical enterprise is one wheel in a great machine. Our wants are supplied by series of nominally independent plants which pass on goods to each other in succession. One series, for example, embraces wheat farms, elevators, railways, flour mills, wholesale dealers in provisions, bakeries, and retail distributors. Each set of members in such a series is dependent upon the preceding set for its chief supplies and upon the succeeding set for its chief vent. The wheat, as grain, flour and bread, flows through the successive sets of enterprises in an unceasing stream, though the volume of flow is far from steady.

Further, no industrial series is self-sufficing. Each set of enterprises in the example, from farms to retail shops, is dependent upon other industrial series for buildings, machinery, fuel, office supplies, transportation, insurance, professional services, and sundries. An especially intimate dependence exists between all other industrial enterprises and the railways. Coal mining and the steel trade also serve almost all industrial enterprises in one way or another. So far, indeed, have industrial differentiation and integration been carried that "the whole concert of industrial operations is to be taken as a machine process, made up of interlocking detailed processes, rather than as a multiplicity of mechanical appliances each doing its particular work in severalty." [1]

To the public the unbroken flow of goods from plant to plant until they finally reach consumers is the matter of prime concern. But business men are concerned more with the commercial than with the industrial aspects of this flow. The movement of goods through successive sets of enterprises which form industrial series, and between enterprises which belong to different industries, is maintained by purchase and sale. Hence the commercial bonds which unite business enterprises to one another in varying degrees of intimacy. Each enterprise is affected by the fortunes of its customers, its competitors, and the purveyors of its supplies.

[1] Thorstein Veblen, *Theory of Business Enterprise,* New York, 1904, p. 7.

Financial interdependence is in part but a third aspect of these industrial-commercial bonds. Complicated relationships of creditor and debtor arise from the purchase and sale of goods upon credit, and make the disaster of one enterprise a menace to many. On this financial side of their operations, the banks bear a relation to all other enterprises not unlike that which the railways bear on the industrial side; for most enterprises need bank credit not less than they need freight service. As a serious congestion of railway traffic applies the brake to industrial operations, so any hampering of banking operations applies the brake to business dealings.

There is a further set of financial bonds which need not run parallel with industrial-commercial relationships. The corporate form of business organization facilitates the acquisition of common ownership in enterprises nominally independent of each other. The same capitalist or group of capitalists often owns a large or even a controlling interest in companies doing different kinds of business, or the same kind in different places. Thus the selling agent may acquire an interest in the factory whose output he handles; the manufacturer may open his own retail stores, or buy stock in a competing company, or secure his raw materials by taking over timber lands or mines; the large capitalist may invest in steel and real estate, in railways and banks, in newspapers and hotels, in mines and moving pictures. Thus also we have our chain shops, chain banks, chain newspapers, chain theaters, chain lumberyards, and the like. Often the financial bond is made less personal, but more direct, by one corporation holding stock in tributary or even in rival companies.

How dominant the corporate form of organization has become in certain fields, the census shows. In 1920 corporations owned 32 per cent of American manufacturing establishments, employed 87 per cent of the wage-earners and turned out 88 per cent of the value produced. In mining, corporations were even more important, owning 51 per cent of the mines, employing 94 per cent of the men, and producing 94 per cent of the product.[2] Of course in railway transportation corporations cover the whole field, and they probably do more than half of the business in all branches characterized by large-scale organization. In 1920, 345,600 corporations filed tax returns showing an aggregate gross income of some $126,000,000,000.[3] Even

[2] *Fourteenth Census of the United States,* vol. viii, *Manufactures,* p. 119, and vol. xi, *Mines and Quarries,* p. 29.

[3] *Statistics of Income from Returns of Net Income for 1920.* United States Internal Revenue, p. 61. The gross income of all corporations has been increased as suggested on

in agriculture, retail trade, domestic, personal and professional service, corporations cut an appreciable figure.[4]

The tangle of financial relationships among business enterprises which has arisen from the prevalence of corporate organization is so complicated that it never has been, and perhaps cannot be, adequately represented in figures. Many corporations are owned, in whole or in large part, by some parent company or holding concern. In other cases, formerly independent enterprises have cemented a financial alliance by exchanging stocks. In still other cases, two or more companies are owned largely by a common group of stockholders. Some of these financial bonds are close and permanent, others are loose and shifting. The reasons for the financial alliance, whatever its form, are sometimes far from obvious—business makes strange bed fellows as well as politics.[5] The alliance may be used to safeguard the interests of all the participants, or it may result from and be used to enhance the power and profit of some preponderating interest. Under the corporate form of organization an investor may reduce his risks by spreading his holdings among numerous enterprises and industries; a corporation may enlist the interest of thousands of customers or employees in its welfare by seeking a wide distribution of its shares; a group of financiers which has won prestige may control the use of business capital far larger than its members own; unscrupulous managers may run an enterprise primarily for their personal advantage through stock-exchange operations in its securities or through corrupt bargains with other concerns in which they hold shares. These are indeed but suggestive examples of the many opportunities, wholesome or injurious, which the rise of joint-stock companies has brought to the denizens of a business economy.

The one fact of commanding importance for the present purpose which emerges from this tangle of relationships and opportunities is that interlocking ownership organizes many nominally independent enterprises into communities of interest. While such bonds are far less comprehensive than the industrial-commercial-credit bonds which

p. 8 of this document, to correct the incomplete returns of railroad and other public utility corporations.

[4] The number of corporations reporting in these fields were as follows: farming, 12,376; retail trade, not including department stores, 50,604; domestic service, 7,298; amusements, 5,258; professional and other service, 10,510. See as above, pp. 62-69.

[5] Compare the diverse reasons found by Dr. Willard L. Thorp for the formation of "central-office concerns"—groups of industrial establishments operated from a single office. *The Integration of Industrial Operation*, Census Monographs, iii, Washington, 1924, pp. 159-265.

embrace practically all enterprises, they are important, both because they affect particularly the largest corporations, and because they give to close-knit groups enhanced strategic influence upon business activity as a whole.

Besides the close bonds based upon commercial dealings, credit arrangements and ownership, there are looser ties which make the fortunes of business enterprises interdependent.

(1) Business enterprises must buy what they need in a common market, and compete against each other for possession of the common stock of the numerous goods which almost every enterprise requires. Among these goods we must list not only railway transportation, coal, steel and bank credit, but also many other widely used commodities, investment funds, land, common labor, and certain highly skilled services, for example, those of business executives, salesmen, engineers, lawyers, and accountants. When business is slack this interrelation through dependence upon a common source of supply is scarcely noticed; but at the peak of an intense boom its importance becomes manifest.

(2) Business enterprises must also sell in a common market, bidding against each other for the money of customers. This tie becomes closest in periods of depression. It is not simply that the clothier feels the competition of his trade rival, but also that the clothing industry feels the competition of the automobile industry, theaters fear the inroads of motion pictures and radios upon their market, insurance companies find their claims upon family incomes endangered by the claims of landlords, labor unions and the makers of automatic machines contest for the same work, and so on.

(3) If in these two respects the relations of business enterprises are competitive, it is not less true that business enterprises draw their support from one another. All business depends in the last resort upon the demands of personal consumers—even the enterprises which make products like mining machinery or bank equipment. And the bulk of the incomes which enable consumers to buy are incomes disbursed by business enterprises as wages, rents, interest or profits. Any serious reduction in the flow of incomes from business enterprises to consumers reacts promptly upon the concerns which provide consumers' goods and through them upon the concerns which cater to business needs.

All the interrelations among business enterprises here spoken of are matters of common knowledge. But since the study of business cycles is concerned with the spreading of given changes from their points of origin, it is well to note explicitly the variety of the bonds which unite all the enterprises of a country into a loose system. For these bonds are also channels through which the quickening or slackening of activity in one part of a business economy spreads to other parts.

6. Profits as the Clue to Business Fluctuations.

Not less important for the present purpose than the interrelations among all business enterprises, is the relation between the making of goods and the making of money within each enterprise. A business enterprise can serve the community by making goods only on condition that, over a period of years, its operations yield a profit.[1]

The subordination of service to money-making is not grounded in the mercenary motives of business men, but is one of the necessary results of pecuniary organization. A business man may be as public spirited or as scientifically minded as any one in the community, he may get his personal satisfaction chiefly from the contribution his enterprise renders to human well-being; yet he must so order affairs that his receipts exceed his expenses, or he will be put out of business and lose his chance to render service. Probably in the long run scrupulous maintenance of quality of output, avoidance of all misrepresentation, fairness in dealing with customers, liberal treatment of employees, and similar policies conducive to well-being are more profitable in dollars and cents than are sharp practices. Probably the man who thinks of little else than the money he is making on each deal is less likely to achieve large business success than the man who thinks much about the wants of others and how they can be satisfied. But the fact remains that the survival or extinction of a business enterprise or policy is determined by a financial test. Only Government and philanthropy can provide services which do not

[1] Of course there are ways of making money which contribute nothing toward human welfare, and ways which are detrimental to welfare. Business men themselves, social reformers, legislators, and the courts are continually striving to check abuses as they develop, or as they are recognized, by amending the rules of the business game. In this process of modifying the business economy, the results of economic analysis play a rôle. But in trying to understand how business cycles develop, it is confusing to mix considerations of welfare with considerations of process.

pay. In business the useful goods produced by an enterprise are not the ends of endeavor, but the means toward earning profits. And the business economy ruthlessly enforces that subordination.

The profits which count in determining solvency are not merely the profits or losses realized in the recent past, but also the profits anticipated in the near future. Indeed, business looks forward more than it looks backward. Even a concern which has been losing money for several years is likely to get the financial support required for continued operations, if its principals and backers believe that its fortunes will mend. And anticipated profits play the decisive rôle in fixing the direction to be taken by business expansion. It is the enterprises with faith in their future which finance extensions out of their own funds or out of funds borrowed from investors. Among the new ventures continually being organized by promoters, it is the ones which people with money to invest think likely to prove most profitable that get beyond the paper stage.[2] Finally, it is at those stages of business cycles when the profits anticipated from such operations are most attractive that extensions of old and launchings of new enterprises reach their highest points.

It follows that an account of economic fluctuations in a business economy must deal primarily with business conditions—with the pecuniary aspect of economic activity. This conclusion runs counter to one of the traditions of economic theory. Most economists have explicitly subordinated the pecuniary aspect of behavior, on the ground that money is merely a symbol the use of which makes no difference save one of convenience, so long as the monetary system is not in disorder.[3] The classical masters and the masters of utility analysis thought that they were delving deeper into the secrets of behavior when, with scarcely a glance at the "money surface of things," they took up the labor and commodities, or the sacrifices and utilities, which they held to be the controlling factors. When followed in the present field of study, this practice diverts attention

[2] Men can often be induced to put money into ventures in public welfare which promise only a meager return—for example, model tenements or liberty bonds;—but such mixing of philanthropy or patriotism with business is limited in scale, except in great national crises.

[3] Compare John Stuart Mill's dicta to this effect, *Principles of Political Economy*, book iii, chapter vii (Ashley's edition, 1909, pp. 483-488). See also Wesley C. Mitchell, "The Rôle of Money in Economic Theory," *American Economic Review*, Supplement, March, 1916, vol. vi, pp. 140-161.

from the way in which business cycles come about, and concentrates attention upon alleged non-business causes of fluctuation.

Of course, business prospects are continually being influenced by changes in crops, and in methods of manufacturing, storing, shipping and distributing goods—as well as by changes in politics, fashion, education, recreation, and health. But it is only as these changes affect the prospects of making money that they affect business activity. To take profits as the leading clue to business cycles does not rule out in advance causes of fluctuation which arise from non-business sources; what it does is to focus attention upon the process through which any cause that stimulates or retards activity in a business economy must exercise its influence. And that is a desirable result. For it is only by study of the processes concerned that we stand much chance of discovering how recurrent business fluctuations come about.

7. Factors Affecting Business Profits.

Economic activity in a money-making world, then, depends upon the factors which affect present or prospective profits. Profits are made by connected series of purchases and sales of goods—whether in merchandising or manufacturing, mining or farming, railroading or insurance. Accordingly, the margins between the prices at which goods can be bought and products sold are one fundamental condition of business activity. Closely connected with price margins is the second fundamental condition—the present and prospective volume of transactions.

Just as the ever-recurring changes in prices affect business activity and through it the volume of goods produced and distributed, so do changes in the volume of business react upon prices. A period of expansion starts an interminable series of readjustments in the prices of various goods. These readjustments in their turn alter the pecuniary prospects of the business enterprises which buy or sell the commodities affected and lead to new changes in the volume of trade. As the latter changes take place, the whole process keeps starting over again. Prices once more undergo an uneven readjustment, prospects of profits become brighter or darker, the volume of transactions expands or contracts, prices feel the reflex influences of the new situation—and so on without end.

III. The System of Prices.

The prices ruling at any moment for the infinite variety of commodities, services, and rights which are being bought and sold constitute a system in the full meaning of that term. That is, the prices paid for goods of all sorts are so related to each other as to make a regular and connected whole. Our knowledge of these relations is curiously inexact, for a matter so important and so open to investigation.[1] What follows is merely a sketch designed to indicate the organic character of the relationships among different parts of the system of prices.

1. The Prices of Consumers' Commodities.

The prices which retail merchants charge for consumers' commodities afford the best starting-point for a survey of this system.

For most commodities in a given market at a given time, there is not a single retail price, but a variety of retail prices. It is only by an elaborate policy devised for the purpose, that a uniform price can be maintained, and the frequent infractions of price-maintenance schemes attest the strength of the commercial forces which make for price variety. Yet the differences among the prices charged for the same article by various shops are kept within fairly definite limits. For inexpensive articles, the differences may form a large percentage of the mean price, but they seldom amount to many cents. For costly articles, the differences may amount to many dollars, but they seldom form a large percentage of the mean. In other words, though the retail prices at which a given article is sold by different shops on the same day in the same town are not identical in the majority of cases, they are closely related to each other.

A much looser, but still significant, bond connects the retail prices charged for goods of unlike kinds. An advance in the price of any commodity usually diverts a part of the demand for it to other commodities which can be used as substitutes in certain of its uses, and thus creates business conditions which favor an advance in the price of the substitutes.

[1] At the present time, the National Bureau of Economic Research is carrying on certain studies in this neglected field. The investigator in charge, Dr. Frederick C. Mills, hopes to have his first results ready for submission to the directors with a view to publication before the end of 1927.

Retail prices are also related to the prices for the same goods which shopkeepers pay to wholesale merchants and the latter to manufacturers. In most cases, the wholesale prices for a given article, also constitute arrays rather than single quotations. The series of successively smaller prices for the same commodities in different hands often has more or less than three members, because of the intervention of more than one wholesaler or jobber, or of an importer in the traffic, or because of direct selling by manufacturers to retailers or even to consumers.

There is wide diversity in the margins between the successive prices in these series. The margins are generally wider in retail than in wholesale trade; wider in "charge-and-deliver" than in "cash-and-carry" shops; wider on goods limited in sale, slow in turnover, perishable, sold in small lots, requiring a large assortment, subject to changes in fashion or season, than on durable, standardized staples handled in bulk.[1] A manufacturer who sells directly to consumers must charge a wider margin than does any one of the several dealers who commonly intervene. Perhaps also the margins average wider when a large advertiser or quasi-monopolist dominates a trade than under conditions of keen competition; that is not certain, for competition may be carried to a pitch which leaves each enterprise with so small a volume of business, or with such heavy selling expenses, that wide margins between buying and selling prices are made necessary for all concerned. It is notorious that wide margins do not always mean large profits.

These diversities in the margins are themselves established and kept tolerably regular by the quest of profits. Controlled in this way, the margins between the successive prices in the series for each kind of consumers' commodities form a feasible basis for making money out of the process of supplying the community with the goods it uses.

[1] Recent investigations by the Bureau of Agricultural Economics and the Port of New York Authority have shown that the factor of chief moment in fixing retailers' margins upon perishable food products is the average size of the package sold. Seemingly, the retailer must impose a service charge, which varies little from the mean, 10 cents, upon every package handed to a customer. On goods usually sold in small lots, for example fresh onions, this service charge constitutes a much larger percentage advance upon the jobbers' price, than on goods (like potatoes) sold in larger lots. Perhaps this generalization will be found to apply to many other branches of retailing.

See Dr. Charles E. Artman, *Food Costs and City Consumers* (Columbia Studies in History, Economics and Public Law, No. 280), New York, 1926, chapter iii.

2. The Prices of Producers' Goods in Relation to the Prices of Consumers' Commodities.

The business enterprises engaged in squeezing money profits out of these price margins are seldom, if ever, able to keep the whole differences between their selling and buying prices. From retailers back to manufacturers, unless they are operating on a minute scale, they must purchase various commodities, services and rights for the efficient conduct of their business. For such producers' goods they have to pay out prices which commonly absorb the greater part of the price margins on the consumers' commodities in which they deal. The most important classes of these producers' goods are raw materials and such current supplies as coal and stationery, buildings with proper machinery or other equipment, manual and clerical labor, loans, leases, transportation, advertising and insurance.

To all business enterprises, the prices which they pay for these producers' goods are important factors in fixing the margins between the buying and selling prices of the commodities in which they deal. But, save in the case of transportation and certain kinds of labor, men who handle a variety of goods require elaborate accounting systems to connect the prices which constitute costs with the margins upon which they sell particular goods. For the cost prices of producers' goods are paid for the advantage of the enterprise as a whole, and the accruing benefits extend to many transactions and often cover a long time.

3. The Prices of Producers' Goods in Relation to Antecedent Prices.

With the exception of labor, producers' goods are provided, like consumers' commodities, chiefly by business enterprises, large or small, operating on the basis of margins between buying and selling prices. Hence the price of any given producers' good is related not only to the prices of the consumers' commodities to the production or distribution of which it must finally contribute in some way, but also to the prices of the various other producers' goods employed in its own manufacture and distribution. Thus the prices of producers' goods do not end the series of price relationships; at most they begin new series of relationships, which run backward with countless rami-

fications and never reach definite stopping points. Even the prices of raw materials in the hands of first "producers" are related systematically to the prices of the labor, current supplies, machinery, buildings, land, loans, leases, and so on, which the farmers, miners, quarrymen, lumbermen, and fishermen employ.

Concerning the prices of such producers' goods as consist of material commodities no more need be said. And most of the less tangible services—loans, advertising, transportation, insurance—require but a word. They are the subjects of an organized business traffic, in which price margins play the same rôle as in the buying and selling of commodities. Therefore, the prices charged by the bank, the advertising agency, the railway and the insurance company, are systematically related both to the prices which these enterprises must pay for their own producers' goods, and to the prices of the wares dealt in by the enterprises which borrow money, use publicity, ship goods and carry insurance.

The prices of labor—manual, clerical, professional and managerial—may seem to bring the series to a definite stop, at least along one line. For men do not have a business attitude toward the production of their own energy, and not wholly a business attitude toward the acquisition of their own training. But the prices which wage- and salary-earners can command are indubitably connected with the prices of the consumers' goods which established habit has made into standards of living for the classes to which they belong, as well as with the prices of the goods they help to make. Along this line, therefore, analysis of the interrelations among prices brings us, not to a full stop, but back to our starting point—the prices of consumers' commodities.

4. The Prices of Business Enterprises.

Connected with the prices of consumers' commodities, of raw materials, and of other producers' commodities or services, are the prices of business enterprises.

Occasionally, established business enterprises are sold outright as going concerns. Promoters are also constantly offering for sale new business organizations or reorganizations of old enterprises. But far the most numerous transactions of this type are dealings in the shares of corporations.

Closely associated with the prices of such shares are the prices of

corporate notes, bonds and debentures. Theoretically, a sharp line may be drawn between ownership of common stock in an enterprise (carrying no right except to vote at its meetings, and to share in its dividends, if any), and ownership of its mortgage-assured bonds. But many types of securities have been invented intermediate between these extremes—stocks "preferred" in various ways, convertible bonds, voting bonds, bonds secured by second or third mortgages, and so on through a long list. All of these securities carry an interest in the corporation with them, some risk, and the possibility of having to assume control under certain contingencies. Indeed, the common stocks of some corporations are rated a safer investment than the first-mortgage bonds of others. An effort to classify all these securities on logical lines would involve much elaboration. In a summary view of the system of prices it is permissible to pass over such details and treat the traffic in corporate securities of all kinds under one head.

That the prices of whole business enterprises, of shares in them, and of their promises to pay are intimately related to the prices already discussed, is clear. For the value of an enterprise is determined primarily by capitalizing its present and prospective profits. Profits depend primarily upon price margins times the volume of business transacted. The rate of interest at which prospective profits are capitalized is determined by the going price for the use of investment loan funds, and as such is related to the whole complex of prices which affect the investment markets.

5. The Prices of Services to Persons.

There remains one other grand division of the system of prices—a division which has much in common with the price of consumers' commodities on the one hand, and with the prices of personal services to business enterprises on the other hand. It consists of the prices of the heterogeneous services which are rendered to persons. Here belong the prices of domestic service, medical attendance, most life insurance, much instruction, some legal advice, many forms of recreation, passenger transportation, hotel accommodation, and so on.

In part, this field is cultivated by large-scale business enterprises, conducted methodically for the profit to be made out of price margins. Hotels, amusement places, travel bureaus, life-insurance companies, standardize their goods, watch their operating expenses, and com-

pete for custom on a price basis in much the same way as department stores. But in other parts of the field, business traffic can scarcely be said to exist. Contacts are made and maintained largely on a personal basis, the services are not and often cannot be standardized, the sellers often deprecate commercial motives, and prices are often varied according to the individual buyer's capacity to pay. Consumers do not shop about for the services of family lawyers, doctors, or even cooks, as they shop for shoes. Hence, the prices of non-business services to persons form the most loosely organized and irregular division of the system of prices.

6. The Interrelations Among Prices.

The aim of this classification of prices is not to set up different categories, but rather to emphasize the relations which bind all prices together and make of them one system. The close relations (1) between the prices of consumers' commodities in the hands of retailers, wholesalers and manufacturers; (2) between these prices and those of producers' goods, whether used directly or indirectly in making consumers' commodities, and (3) between the buying and selling prices in any branch of trade and the prices of securities of the business enterprises engaged in it, are sufficiently clear, and enough has been said about (4) the looser bonds which unite the prices of services to persons with the larger field of business dealings. But several other lines of relationship should be called to attention.

(5) On the side of demand, almost every good has its possible substitutes in some or in all of its uses. Through the shiftings of demand among commodities thus made possible, changes in the price of one commodity are passed on to the prices of its substitutes, from the latter to the prices of their substitutes, and so on. An initial price change usually—though not always—becomes smaller as it spreads out over these widening circles.

(6) Similarly, on the side of supply, almost every good has genetic relationships with other goods, made from the same materials, or supplied by the same set of enterprises. Along these genetic lines also, price changes radiate from the points of disturbance over a wide field. Particularly important because particularly wide are the genetic relationships arising from the use of certain producers' goods in many lines of business. Land, loan funds and transportation most of all; with somewhat less universality, coal, steel, certain types of

labor, and insurance enter into the cost of most commodities. Accordingly, a changed price established for one of these well-nigh universal producers' goods in any important use will extend to a wide variety of other uses, and may produce further price changes without assignable limit.

(7) Closely connected with this genetic relationship through common producers' goods, is the relationship through business competition, both actual and potential. Price margins which make one trade decidedly more or less profitable, all things considered, than other trades in the same market area cannot long continue in the lines of business which anyone controlling capital really can "break into" if he so desires. For, after a time which varies with technical and business conditions in the trade which is out of step, the influx or efflux of capital changes the supply of commodities in question and brings the price margins into closer adjustment with those prevailing in other trades.

This familiar proposition does not mean that competition tends to bring the price margins on which all goods are handled to a common level. On the contrary, the tendency is to make these margins differ from each other,—differ in whatever way is necessary to keep the prospects of return to capital and enterprise, everything considered and over whatever periods men think of in planning their ventures, so nearly alike that no one of the lines open to investment seems much more attractive to the average enterpriser than its alternatives.

Nor does this proposition imply that there is a tendency toward an equality of profits in business. Whatever such tendency exists is limited to equalizing the prospective opportunities for making profits on fresh investments. In every branch of business followed by numerous enterprises, and in every year, experience shows a marked diversity of returns, running from liberal profit percentages to substantial losses. There seems to be no tendency for these divergencies to disappear, except perhaps when a trade becomes concentrated in the hands of very few concerns. Where there are many concerns, the tendency toward equalizing the prices of similar producers' goods and similar products—and in the given market areas this tendency is real—makes profits depend upon the skill of managements and the particular circumstances under which each management operates. Since neither skill nor circumstances are uniform, the differences in profit rates which they produce tend to recur indefinitely.

(8) Present prices are affected by prices of the recent past and also by the anticipated prices of the near future. Indeed, present prices are determined largely by past bargains, many of which established time contracts still in operation. Over a wider field, our ideas of what is a "fair price" to ask come from past experience to affect present and future conduct. Thus the price system has no definable limits in time. No analysis can get back to the earliest term in the endless series of bargains which helped to make the prices of to-day, nor can anyone say how much influence is exerted to-day by the anticipations of what prices will be to-morrow, or how many to-morrows are taken into business reckonings.

(9) Nor has the price system any logical beginning or end. At whatever point analysis may begin tracing the interlocking links of the price chain, to that point will it come round again if it proceeds far enough. The above analysis, for example, started from the prices of consumers' commodities at retail. These prices are paid out of personal incomes. But personal incomes are themselves aggregates of prices received for labor, for the use of loan funds, or for the use of rented property; or they are aggregates of the net price differences which yield profits.

Thus all the prices in a business economy are continually influencing one another. To account for any one item in the system, one must invoke the whole. Realization of that fact has made economic theorists dissatisfied with efforts to explain the prices of particular goods in terms of their respective costs, or utilities, or supply and demand. In 1874 Léon Walras showed how any number of prices can be conceived as simultaneously determined, under certain imaginary conditions. Mathematical economists are now seeking to make his method of approach (the use of several sets of simultaneous equations equal in number to the number of the "unknowns") applicable to real life.[1] These efforts may provide students of business cycles with a better technique than they now possess for treating the problem of price changes. But even as matters stand, we can trace the main channels through which price fluctuations propagate themselves by using statistical data in ways suggested by the preceding analysis.

[1] See Walras, *Éléments d'Économie Politique Pure,* 1874; 4th ed., Lausaunne and Paris, 1900; Gustav Cassel, *Theory of Social Economy,* New York, 1924; Henry L. Moore, "A Theory of Economic Oscillations," *Quarterly Journal of Economics,* November, 1926, vol. xli, pp. 1-29.

Among writers who make no use of mathematical symbols, Herbert J. Davenport has faced the mutual interdependence of all prices perhaps more frankly than anyone else. See his *Economics of Enterprise,* New York, 1913.

7. The Rôle of Prices in Economic Life.

Prices, then, form a system—a highly complex system of many parts connected with one another in divers ways, a system infinitely flexible in details yet with a fairly stable equilibrium among its parts, a system like a living organism in its capacity to repair the serious disorders into which it recurrently falls.

So much for the structure of the system of prices; concerning its functions in economic life a few words must be added. The system of prices is our mechanism for regulating the process of producing, and distributing goods. Prices make possible the elaborate exchanges, and the consequent specialization and coöperation in production which characterize the present age, and so are one of the factors contributing to its relative comfort. They are the means by which all consumers in concert make known what goods the community wants and in what quantities; the signs which enable all business enterprises in concert to come as near as they do toward achieving a satisfactory allocation of productive energies amidst the million channels into which these energies might flow. Prices are the source from which family income is derived, and the means by which goods are obtained for family consumption; for both income and cost of living—the jaws of the vise in which the family feels itself squeezed—are aggregates of prices. Prices also render possible the rational control of economic activity by accounting; for accounting is based upon the plan of representing all the unlike commodities, services and rights with which an enterprise is concerned as buyer or seller in terms of a money price. Most important of all for the present purpose, the margins between different prices within the system hold out that prospect of money profit, which is the motive power that drives our business world.

IV. The Monetary Mechanism.

Monetary and banking systems are such obvious features of the business economy that they require little attention here. It is well, however, to state the sense in which certain terms will be used, to note the relative magnitude of important variables, and to indicate the bearings of a famous controversy upon the problem of business cycles.

1. Ambiguity of the Terms "Money" and "Currency."

Business men, economists at large, and writers upon business cycles in particular, use the word money in a confusing variety of meanings. The variants important here are illustrated by Professor Irving Fisher on the one side and by Messrs. Foster and Catchings on the other. Fisher defines money as "what is *generally* acceptable in exchange for goods," thus distinguishing money from bank deposits subject to check. "Currency" is Fisher's broad term for all the common media of exchange. On the contrary, Foster and Catchings use the word money in the broad sense assigned by Fisher to currency, and the word currency in the narrow sense assigned by Fisher to money.[1]

Needless to say, both of these opposing usages can be defended by abundant precedents, drawn from the world of books and from the world of affairs. To follow either usage, however, is to invite misunderstanding by those accustomed to the other. Care in stating definitions in one chapter and consistency in adhering to them in later passages may be a logical defense against the misinterpretations of readers who have "skipped" or forgotten the formal definitions; but it is better to give no opening for mistake when that is feasible. The shortest unambiguous term for what Fisher calls money and what Foster and Catchings call currency seems to be "coin and paper money." We must choose between the unattractive alternatives of using some such cumbrous expression or of facilitating misunderstanding. Of these two evils, the latter seems the greater.

Accordingly, in the chapters which follow, the terms "coin and paper money" and "deposit currency" will be used. All the common means of making monetary payments taken together will be called the "circulating medium."

2. The Relative Importance of Checks and of Coin and Paper Money in Making Payments.

Our knowledge on this head has not been advanced materially since 1909, when Professor (now President) David Kinley of the University of Illinois superintended an investigation made by the Comptroller of the Currency for the National Monetary Commis-

[1] See Irving Fisher, *The Purchasing Power of Money*, New York, 1911, pp. 8-13; W. T. Foster and Waddill Catchings, *Money*, Boston and New York, 1923, pp. 17-18.

sion. The Comptroller secured reports from some 11,500 banks of all kinds concerning the character of the funds deposited with them on Tuesday, March 16, 1909, by retail merchants, wholesale merchants, and customers of other occupations. From these returns, supplemented by estimates of deposits in the non-reporting banks and vaguer approximations to the transactions of people without bank accounts, Kinley concluded that we may "safely accept an average of 80 to 85 per cent as the probable percentage of business in this country done by check." In wholesale trade the percentage was above 90, in the business of non-mercantile depositors it was "close up to that of the wholesale trade," in retail trade it was 50 to 60 per cent, and even of the pay rolls made up by banks 30 per cent were in checks. On comparing the 1909 returns with those secured in a similar investigation which he had supervised in 1896, Kinley also concluded "that the percentage of the volume of ordinary payments made by check has been increasing somewhat." [1]

Of course estimates based upon the transactions of a single day are especially unsatisfactory to students of business cycles, since they are much concerned with the magnitude of seasonal, cyclical, secular and random fluctuations in business processes. Probably the percentage of payments made by checks is higher on dates when rents, salaries, dividends, bond coupons, and income taxes are being paid in large amounts than on a mid-month day, like March 16th. Full records over a period of years might show fairly regular seasonal variations in the percentage, corresponding in timing to the seasonal variations in bank clearings. There may also be cyclical fluctuations in the relative use of checks and coin or paper money, as well as a rising secular trend for the first and a declining secular trend for the second. But all this is surmise. What we know with certainty is that the great bulk of payments in the United States is made with checks. Probably coin and paper money do not more than a tenth or at most a fifth of the "money work." The figure intermediate between these limits, 15 per cent, seems to fit well with the run of the estimates presented in the following sections.

[1] David Kinley, *The Use of Credit Instruments in Payments in the United States.* National Monetary Commission. 61st Congress, 2d session, Senate Document 399, Washington, 1910, pp. 197-201. (The critical reader may be warned that the percentage of pay rolls in checks is misstated on p. 200; the correct figures are given on p. 103). Kinley gives percentages for checks on p. 198 which run somewhat higher than his final conclusions quoted above. It is these higher figures which Professor Irving Fisher uses in his *Purchasing Power of Money,* revised ed., p. 491, to support his own estimate that 91 per cent of all business in 1909 was done with checks.

3. The Elasticity of the Circulating Medium.

How far the money mechanism responds to the changing requirements of business from phase to phase of a cycle, and how far the money mechanism may start, augment or limit business fluctuations, are among the problems raised in Chapter I. Presumably, these problems have no single solution, since so much depends upon what the changing requirements of business are, upon how the money mechanism is arranged, and upon the skill with which it is managed. All three conditions differ from country to country, and in any one country they may differ from time to time. Close attention must be paid to this factor in business cycles later on. At present it will suffice to show that the currency which the business community provides for itself through the banks rises and falls with the activity of trade more regularly than coin and paper money provided through government agencies.

The fluctuations in the amount of gold in monetary use in any country during a given year depend mainly upon (1) the current output of such gold mines as it possesses, (2) the country's gain or loss of gold by international shipments, and (3) the quantity of gold which goes into industrial uses. No one of these factors can be depended upon to increase the supply of gold currency when trade is brisk, or to diminish the supply when trade is dull.

(1) Changes in gold production are controlled mainly by the discovery and exhaustion of deposits, by improvements in the arts of mining and metallurgy which make it possible to work lower grade ores at a profit, and by conditions which facilitate or hinder industrial operations in the mining districts. None of these factors are organically related to business fluctuations. Of secondary importance are financial conditions which affect the raising of capital for investment in gold mining, and price conditions which affect the cost of operating mines. Prosperity facilitates the raising of capital, but increases operating costs. In turn, high operating costs give mining engineers a stronger incentive to develop improved methods of work, and thus may lead presently to increased output. All in all, one would not expect a close correspondence between business cycles and gold production, and when one examines the statistics over a period of years this negative expectation seems to accord with experience.

Over periods much longer than those typical of business cycles,

however, there seems to be an organic relation between gold production and the rate of economic expansion. The periods of large additions to the world's gold supply have been accompanied or followed by periods in which the prosperous phases of business cycles have been relatively long and intense and the depressed phases have been relatively short. The reverse also seems true: periods of declining gold production have been accompanied or followed by periods in which the phases of prosperity have been relatively short and the phases of depression relatively long. Thus the fluctuations of gold output are important in the study of business cycles; but important as a part of the economic environment in which cycles run their course, rather than as part of the cycles themselves. But this relationship we can study to better advantage after we have won such insight as we can into the character of cyclical fluctuations.

(2) The industrial demand for gold is decidedly sensitive to business conditions; it rises in prosperity and falls in depression. Since the general level around which this percentage fluctuates seems to approximate a quarter of the annual output, and since the plus and minus departures from this average are considerable, we have here a not unimportant factor of "perverse elasticity" in the monetary supply of gold.

(3) The amount of gold shipped into and out of any country in the course of a year is the net resultant of a multitude of factors. Among the more important are the relative magnitudes of payments and receipts on merchandise account, freight account, travelers' account, migration account, and banking account. While every one of these items may be directly affected by the state of trade in the country in question, it is hard in most cases to be sure whether the state of trade will affect the credit side more than the debit side of that item. Moreover, the problem is never limited to the influence exercised by the state of trade in any one country; it includes also the influence exercised by the state of trade in every one of the other countries with which the first has extensive dealings. Of especial importance to the Western world is the highly variable flow of gold to the Orient, especially to British India—a flow which depends less upon business conditions in the West than upon conditions in the East. The net resultants of all these complicated factors, as summed up by official statistics, show that no simple conclusion can be drawn concerning the relation between international gold movements and business conditions, except in severe crises.

The exception is important. In times of peace, any nation menaced by a credit collapse has usually been able to secure within a few weeks a large inflow of gold from the "free gold market" of London, or, in recent years, New York. International business has developed a rudimentary centralized gold reserve, which any commercial nation can draw upon, after negotiation and somewhat tardily, to meet emergencies. Perhaps this constitutes the world's most considerable achievement toward adjusting the supply of gold currency to the demands of business.

As for government paper money, it is notorious that the large changes in issues are controlled by the exigencies of public finance. Paper standards occur as episodes in monetary history. The suspensions of specie payment, by which they are ushered in, are usually forced by wars, political revolutions, or national bankruptcies. A return to specie payments becomes an aim of fiscal policy after the emergency has passed, though an aim which is often pursued in a wavering and dilatory fashion. Of course, the developments which lead to suspensions, the depreciation of the monetary unit which usually follows suspensions, and the appreciation which usually precedes resumption, all influence the activity of trade. But these influences, like the influence exerted by marked changes in the rate of gold production, must be classed among the "disturbing causes," by which theorists explain the divergencies characteristic of different business cycles.

Government paper money as an element of monetary systems having a metallic standard is seldom controlled in such a way as to make its volume regularly responsive to changing needs. But much as the gold supply of a country has often been increased in severe crises by huge importations, so governments have sometimes aided business in emergencies by increasing their paper issues, or by shifting paper money from the public treasury to the banks.

The broad conclusion from the preceding analysis is that, except in severe crises, business must depend primarily upon bank notes, checking deposits, and bills of exchange to keep the supply of the circulating medium adjusted to its changing pace.

This adjustment is made possible within certain limits by the fact that bank notes are issued and bank deposits created chiefly by the granting of bank loans, while bank notes are retired and bank deposits are canceled chiefly by the repayment of bank loans. The

drawing of a check against his deposit by the customer of a bank no more reduces the volume of deposit currency than the payment of a bank note by one man to another reduces the volume of notes in circulation. In both cases a part of the circulating medium is merely transferred from one holder to another—unless the check or note is used to repay bank loans. Now a period of prosperity, during which production expands, prices rise, and profits swell, increases the money value of the security upon which banks make their loans, and so provides a basis for the increase of bank currency which is required by trade. A period of depression, on the contrary, diminishes the business demands for bank loans, and through their repayment contracts the volume of notes and deposit currency as the requirements for means of payment decline. The qualifications to which these sweeping statements must be subjected in later chapters prevent the adjustment of bank currency to the needs of business from being always prompt and precise; but the broad contrast between the responsiveness to changes in business activity of bank currency and the unresponsiveness of coin and government notes remains valid.

Of course, the limits within which bank notes, checking deposits, and bills of exchange can be thus adjusted to the changing volume of trade depend upon the organization and management of a country's banking system. Mistakes in adjustment disastrous to business can be made within these limits, as well as by failure to heed them. Hence we may expect to find that the development of banking legislation and of banking practice has played an important rôle in the history of every country's business cycles.

4. The Velocity of Circulation.

Fluctuations in the activity of business lead to changes not only in the volume of deposit currency and bank notes, but also in the average rate at which all forms of circulating media pass from hand to hand. An increase in the volume of payments can be effected in either of these ways, and in practice is usually effected both by an expansion in the quantity of bank currency and by a quicker turnover of coin, paper money and deposits. Changes in the velocity of circulation are not limited by technical factors as are changes in the quantity of the circulating medium. Broadly speaking, anyone in receipt of current funds can spend them again as quickly or as slowly as suits him. But like most phenomena produced by the actions

of millions of men, the average velocity of circulation is markedly regular in its changes.

It is only of late that we have attained even rough measurements of this factor in business processes. In 1907 Professor E. W. Kemmerer summed up a few preceding studies and made the best estimate of velocity which the data then permitted. Kinley's study of credit instruments for the National Monetary Commission enabled Irving Fisher in 1911 to improve upon Kemmerer's results. In turn, certain recent investigations of the Federal Reserve Bank of New York have made it possible for Dr. W. Randolph Burgess to supersede Professor Fisher's figures.[1]

The New York Reserve Bank has collected monthly data concerning the volume of individual demand deposits and the debits to individual accounts in the banks of eight cities, ranging in size from New York to Syracuse and in location from Boston to San Francisco. The data, beginning in January, 1919, and extending by months to February, 1923, when they were analyzed by Dr. Burgess, covered somewhat more than one full business cycle, and so gave a basis for approximating not only the mean velocity of bank deposits but also the variations about the mean.

Dr. Burgess found that there is a close relationship between the amount of bank deposits in a city and the rapidity of their turnover. In New York the velocities ran six to eight times as high as in Syracuse. Between these extremes, the velocities in other towns (excepting Albany) varied so neatly with the volume of deposits that it seemed justifiable to use this relationship as a basis for estimating the average velocity of deposits in the United States. Computations following the line thus suggested indicated that a reasonable estimate would place the velocity of circulation for the country as a whole at a rate somewhere between 25 and 35 times a year, and probably under rather than over 30.

Not less important for our purpose than the general average reached by Dr. Burgess, are the seasonal and cyclical variations which he found to characterize deposit velocities. The seasonal swings ranged from 12 per cent of the annual mean in San Francisco and 14 per cent in Chicago to 29 per cent in Boston and 31 per cent in Albany. After these seasonal changes had been eliminated from the

[1] See E. W. Kemmerer, *Money and Credit Instruments in their Relation to General Prices,* New York, 1907, pp. 108-119; Irving Fisher, *The Purchasing Power of Money,* New York, 1911, pp. 441-477; W. Randolph Burgess, "The Velocity of Bank Deposits," *Journal of the American Statistical Association,* June, 1923, vol. xviii, pp. 727-740.

series, the cyclical swings remaining were even larger. They ranged from 22 per cent of the average value for the whole period in Chicago, and 26 per cent in San Francisco to 63 per cent in Syracuse and 68 per cent in Albany. New York, which is often thought of as subject to exceedingly wide seasonal and cyclical variations in all financial matters, was near the center of the range in both the seasonal and cyclical array.[2]

Certain of Dr. Burgess' results can be tested by using other recent data. The Federal Reserve Board now compiles the total "debits to individual accounts" in the banks of many cities. These figures come far closer to showing the volume of payments made by check in the United States than do any earlier data:—among other advantages, debits include the millions of checks which are deposited in the banks against which they are drawn, and which therefore do not pass through a clearing house. By careful analysis of these returns from 240 cities in 1922, Mr. Carl Snyder has shown that the total debits for the whole country in that year were about 534 billion dollars. This is probably a close approximation as such matters go; for the actually recorded amounts not only cover banks holding more than

[2] The leading results of this important paper may be presented in tabular form as follows:

VELOCITY OF BANK DEPOSITS, JANUARY, 1919, TO FEBRUARY, 1923

	New York	Albany	Buffalo	Rochester	Syracuse	Boston	Chicago	San Francisco
Original data								
Average	73.7	29.9	19.7	20.2	9.9	34.1	46.1	39.9
Maximum	91.3	49.0	25.1	23.6	15.3	47.6	51.5	44.9
Minimum	62.1	21.6	16.1	16.7	7.0	24.7	38.4	34.0
Range	29.2	27.4	9.0	6.9	8.3	22.9	13.1	10.9
Range as per cent of average	39.6	91.6	45.7	34.2	83.8	67.2	28.4	27.3
Seasonal Fluctuations								
Average month	100	100	100	100	100	100	100	100
Maximum	112	117	112	109	113	113	106	106
Minimum	91	86	92	92	89	84	92	94
Range	21	31	20	17	24	29	14	12
Cyclical Fluctuations (Seasonals eliminated)								
Average	73.7	29.9	19.8	20.2	9.9	34.1	46.0	40.0
Maximum	84.8	43.0	26.1	22.8	13.5	42.1	52.0	45.9
Minimum	63.4	22.7	16.3	16.9	7.3	29.0	41.7	35.5
Range, per cent of average	29.0	67.9	50.0	29.2	62.6	38.4	22.4	26.9

W. Randolph Burgess, "Velocity of Bank Deposits," *Journal of the American Statistical Association*, June, 1923, vol. xviii, pp. 727–740.

All of the velocities in this table are computed on a yearly basis.

four-fifths of the total deposits, but also afford a good basis for making estimates for the missing banks.[3] If we had equally trustworthy figures of the average volume of deposit currency to compare with this total, we could compute its velocity of circulation with confidence. Once a year the Comptroller of the Currency does compile a nearly complete table of deposits in all kinds of banks in the country; but the portion of these deposits subject to check is not stated for all kinds of banks and must be estimated in part. Then these partially estimated figures for June 30th must be made into annual averages as well as may be by using an index based upon a comparison between the individual deposits of the National Banks on June 30th and the average of such deposits in the five (or four) reports to the Comptroller. Figures made in this fashion must be accepted as subject to a margin of uncertainty; but an error of a billion dollars one way or the other would not make 5 per cent of the total. Indeed, this method of approximating the velocity of deposit currency involves less estimating than Dr. Burgess' more elaborate method, which builds upon returns that are more precise, but include only 8 cities.

Table 3 shows that the results to which this method leads agree well with Dr. Burgess' conclusion that the average turnover of deposit currency for the country as a whole is somewhere between 25 and 35 times a year, and probably under rather than over 30. In view of its firmer foundation, this estimate has better claim to acceptance than the pioneer figures of Professor Irving Fisher, who had set the velocity of bank deposit currency at nearly 37 in 1896, 53 in 1909 and 96 in 1918.[4] The table also confirms the conclusion that the velocity of deposit currency rises and falls with business activity, though of of course these annual figures do not move through nearly so wide a range as the data which Dr. Burgess presents by months.

If 80-85 per cent of the country's payments are made with checks, if the volume of checking deposits rises and falls with the activity of trade, and if the circulation of these deposits is quickened in prosperity and retarded in depression, it may seem that the money

[3] Compare Carl Snyder, "A New Index of the General Price Level from 1875," *Journal of the American Statistical Association,* June, 1924, vol. xix, pp. 189, 190.

[4] See his *Purchasing Power of Money,* New York, 1911, p. 304, and "The Equation of Exchange for 1918," *American Economic Review,* June, 1919, vol. ix, p. 407. Even before the Federal Reserve Bank data on bank-deposit velocity were gathered, Professor Fisher had become skeptical of his own values, at least for years far from his basing points, 1896 and 1909. See the article just cited.

TABLE 3

THE VELOCITY OF DEPOSIT CURRENCY, ESTIMATED FROM TOTAL PAYMENTS BY CHECK AND AVERAGE DEPOSITS SUBJECT TO CHECK

The United States, 1919–1926

	Estimated Volume of Payments made by Check Billions of Dollars	Estimated Average Volume of Deposits Subject to Check Billions of Dollars (As of July 1st)	Estimated Average Velocity of Deposits
1919	546.8	18.99	28.8
1920	587.7	21.08	27.9
1921	484.0	19.63	24.7
1922	533.9	20.47	26.1
1923	570.3	22.11	25.8
1924	600.1	23.53	25.5
1925	653.4	25.98	25.1
1926	695.3	25.57	27.2

NOTE: The data used in this table were supplied by Mr. Carl Snyder of the Federal Reserve Bank of New York. For the 1922 estimate of payments by check, see text. The figures in other years for the country outside of New York were made from the 1922 estimate by means of an index based upon debits in 140 cities. Mr. Snyder believes that the margin of error in these estimates may be 10 per cent.

economy has developed a mechanism adequate to the changing requirements made upon it from phase to phase of business cycles. Whether this impression is sound depends, of course, upon the relative magnitudes involved. And these magnitudes vary from cycle to cycle and from country to country. Here, then, is another problem which we must treat on a quantitative basis, with the expectation that the results will not be the same in all cases, or in all phases of the cycle.

While the payments made in coin and paper money seem not to exceed one-tenth or one-fifth of the total, these payments must be made, and they cannot be made in checks without a mass change in monetary habits and arrangements. The velocity of coin and paper money is, therefore, a highly important variable. Concerning its average magnitude and its limits of fluctuation scarcely anything has been learned since 1911 when Professor Fisher was studying the equation of exchange. His final result for 1909 was that coin and paper money changed hands against goods on the average 21.1 times, as compared with 52.8 times for deposit currency.[5] Our next problem is whether the first of these figures is as far out of the way as later data show the second to be.

[5] *The Purchasing Power of Money,* p. 304.

Professor Fisher's method of approximating the velocity of coin and paper money involved (1) an estimate of the amount of coin and paper money flowing into and out of the banks in a year—an estimate built up from the deposits made in a part of the banks in one day; (2) an estimate of the sums withdrawn from the banks which are paid to non-depositors, and (3) estimates of the average number of times the cash received by depositors and by non-depositors exchanges against goods before it is redeposited in banks. Fisher's final picture of the circulation in 1909 is as follows:

Coin and paper money withdrawn from banks	Use made of the funds withdrawn	Average circulation of the funds withdrawn before they are redeposited	Volume of payments made outside of banks by coin and paper money
8 billions	Paid to depositors	Once	8 billions
12 "	Paid to non-depositors	Twice	24 "
1 "	Paid to non-depositors	Three times	3 "
21 billions			35 billions

To get the average velocity of coin and paper money in this year, he divided this total of 35 billions by his estimate of the amount of money in circulation, 1.63 billions, and thus got 21.5—a figure which he scaled down in the final adjustments to 21.1.[6]

Little confidence can be felt in results resting upon so many conjectural estimates. And the best test that we can make by the use of later data, while somewhat less conjectural, yields but vague results. As said above, Mr. Snyder has shown that the check payments in the United States in 1922 totaled about 534 billion dollars. If we accept Kinley's estimates that payments made by check constitute 80-85 per cent of all payments, then we must put the payments made by coin and paper money in 1922 at from 94 to 133 billions. If, as Professor Fisher thinks proper, we take at least 90 per cent as the proportion of payments by check, the payments in coin and paper money shrink to 59 billions. The average amount of money in circulation that year outside of the treasury and the banks was 3.67 billion dollars.[7] Division gives the average velocity of coin and paper money

[6] For the details of this elaborate computation, see *The Purchasing Power of Money*, pp. 448-477.

[7] On the assumption that the coin and paper money in all commercial banks on June 30th, bore the same ratio to the average for the year as is borne by the coin and paper money outside the Treasury and the Federal Reserve System to the average for the year.

in 1922 as 16, 26, or 36 times, according as we take 90, 85, or 80 as the percentage of payments by check. Professor Fisher's figures—21.1 in 1909 and 30 in 1918—fall within this range. There seems to be no such difference as he surmised between the velocity of deposit currency and of paper money and coin. The middle figure in the range, 26, seems the most plausible. It coincides with the velocity of deposit currency in 1922 shown by Table 3. But of course this is a most uncertain guess. Whatever figure we accept as representing the average velocity of coin and paper money, we may suppose that the annual rate rises and falls with the activity of trade, though probably in less degree than the velocity of bank deposits.

5. The Quantity Theory and Business Cycles.

So far we have been concerned with the way in which the circulating medium responds to the changes which business cycles bring in the volume of trade. We cannot leave this topic, however, without noting the contention that fluctuations in the quantity of the circulating medium are causes of price changes and so of business cycles, rather than adaptations to the needs of business. This view is most picturesquely put in the title of one of Professor Fisher's recent articles, "The Business Cycle Largely 'A Dance of the Dollar.'"[1]

The problem can best be presented by using the equation of exchange as formulated by Fisher: $MV + M'V' = PT$. M stands for the quantity of coin and paper money in circulation and M′ for the amount of deposits subject to check. V and V′ are the respective velocities at which these media are exchanged for goods. P represents the price level and T the physical volume of goods exchanged. Thus the equation means that the total volume of payments made in coin, paper money and checks in a given time equals the money value of the goods bought and sold.

For the moment we are not concerned with the conditions under which this equation is valid, but with the causal relationship among the several magnitudes represented in the equation. Professor Fisher holds that

> *The price level is normally the one absolutely passive element in the equation of exchange.* It is controlled solely by the

[1] See *Journal of the American Statistical Association,* December, 1923, vol. xviii, pp. 1024-1028.

> other elements and the causes antecedent to them, but exerts no control over them.[2]

In this proposition the word "normally" is important: for Professor Fisher admits that *"to a limited extent during transition periods, or during a passing season* (e.g. *the fall*)" the "price level is an independent cause of changes" in other magnitudes in the equation.[3]

What, then, are "transition periods," and what fraction do they make of time? Professor Fisher's answer begins as follows:

> The change which constitutes a transition may be a change in the quantity of money, or in any other factor of the equation of exchange, or in all.[4]

The discussion of transition periods, thus introduced, gives him occasion to expound a theory of "credit cycles," which stresses the lag in the adjustment of interest rates to changes in the price level. And

[2] *The Purchasing Power of Money*, p. 172. Italics as in original.

Through a most ingenious statistical study, of which some account will be given in the next chapter, Professor Fisher has recently come to the "conclusion that changes in price level almost completely explain fluctuations in trade, for the period 1915-23," and that they "dominate" fluctuations in trade from 1877 to 1924. See "Our Unstable Dollar and the So-called Business Cycle," *Journal of the American Statistical Association*, June, 1925, vol. xx, pp. 191 and 201.

Without inquiring for the moment into the significance of Professor Fisher's statistical researches, it is pertinent to ask whether his two conclusions (1) that the price level is normally "absolutely passive" and "exerts no control over" other elements in the equation of exchange, and (2) that changes in the price level "dominate" fluctuations in the volume of trade, are consistent with each other.

The two conclusions can be reconciled formally by putting a strict construction upon the word "normal." My understanding is that Professor Fisher draws a sharp line between what is normally true and what is historically true. What is normally true is that which would happen under certain hypothetical conditions which are never fulfilled absolutely. What is historically true is that which actually happens under conditions which combine the factors represented in the theorist's imaginary case with a continually changing host of other factors. Hence relations which hold normally may never be realized historically.

Granted the logical validity of this distinction, the question remains how an investigator should choose the hypothetical conditions to be assumed in his theorizing. One who is interested in pure theory for its own sake may choose any hypothetical conditions which provide the basis of an interesting argument, whether that argument will illuminate experience or not. But I take it Professor Fisher is not interested in pure theory for its own sake; he desires that his theorizing shall give insight into actual experience. On this interpretation, it seems doubtful whether hypothetical assumptions are well chosen for his purposes when they lead to conclusions concerning what is normally true which run counter over long periods to the results of his statistical studies of historical processes. By altering the assumptions underlying his theorizing about the relations among the factors in the equation of exchange, Professor Fisher might draw a different set of conclusions concerning what is normally true which would harmonize better with his version of historical truth.

[3] *The Purchasing Power of Money*, p. 169. Italics as in the original.

[4] The same, p. 55.

while he is dealing with this subject, Professor Fisher observes that "periods of transition are the rule and those of equilibrium the exception." [5]

On this showing, there seems to be no reason from the viewpoint of a quantity theorist, why a student of business cycles should treat the price level as a "passive element" in the equation of exchange. His business is with "transition periods," these periods are "the rule," and during them the price level may be "an independent cause of changes" in other factors of the equation of exchange. Thus, the quantity theory interposes no bar to following any leads which the analysis of business dealings may suggest.

We cannot rest content, however, with so negative a conclusion. What we need is insight into the relations between changes in prices and changes in the circulating medium under modern business conditions. Our best chance of getting such insight is to follow the process of determining prices, transferring goods, and making payments.

The three quantities represented in the equation of exchange as simultaneous—payments, prices, and physical volume of trade—are in fact three stages through which business transactions pass in time. When a sale is made, the parties agree, tacitly or explicitly, upon the price, upon the quantity of goods to be transferred, upon the date of delivery, and upon the date when payment is due. In retail trade, all three stages are frequently completed in a few minutes—the customer assents to the price, receives his bundle, and pays cash. But delivery is deferred when consumers' goods are made to order, and payment is often deferred to the end of the month, or spread over several months on some "installment plan." In wholesale trade, weeks or months commonly elapse between the date when a sale is made at an agreed-upon price, the date when the goods are delivered to the buyer, and the still later date when the seller receives a check. In other types of business the time relations between the three stages present a wide variety, ranging from prepayment for goods to be delivered in the future to long deferred payments for goods delivered in the past. How long are the average lags of deliveries behind price agreements, and of payments behind deliveries; how these lags vary from trade to trade, from district to district and from period to period, are matters about which little is known; but that such lags play a prominent rôle in business planning is certain. Time is therefore a

[5] The same, p. 71.

factor which cannot be disregarded in studying the relations between prices and the circulating medium.

In terms of the equation of exchange, these observations mean that of the payments (MV + M′V′) made to-day, the bulk are payments for goods transferred (T) some time ago, at prices (P) most of which were agreed upon still earlier; a considerable fraction are payments for goods transferred to-day at prices now agreed upon; a minute fraction are payments for goods which will be transferred later. Similarly, of the goods transferred (T) to-day, a few have been paid for in advance, more are paid for now, but the bulk will be paid for in the future. Once more, of the prices (P) agreed upon to-day, a part are paid at once, but a larger part will be paid in weeks, months, and years to come.

Though merely a suggestion of the complications of business practice, what has been said suffices to show that on every business day the payments then made, the transfers then effected, and the prices then agreed upon refer to three different aggregates of transactions. In other words, the day-by-day relations between MV + M′V′ and PT are indeterminate—the payments made to-day are most unlikely to equal the prices quoted to-day multiplied by the goods exchanged to-day.[6] The only way to maintain the equation for such brief intervals is to interpret the PT of a given day as meaning the exchanges for which payments are then being made, instead of the current exchanges and prices. But on that interpretation, the relation between the time intervals covered by the two parts of the equation becomes indeterminate. An expression which shows nothing about time gives slight help toward solving problems in which time relations are important.

Quite different is the position when we test the equation of exchange as summarizing the transactions of a large community for some such interval as a year—the longer the interval, the better for the equation. On that basis, we can say both that the payments, prices and transfers represented all refer to approximately the same period of time, and that the two sides of the equation are nearly equal in fact. To be concrete, the payments made each year in the United

[6] Indeed, on a day-to-day basis the expression PT is nonsense; for only a part of the goods which change hands on a given day change hands at the prices which are current on that day—the P's then quoted refer in large part to T's which will come later. Also the expression MV + M′V′ may have a different interpretation on a day-to-day basis from that assigned it on an annual basis. Of course, the equation was not made to represent the transactions of a single day, and its inadequacy for that purpose is not surprising.

States are mainly payments for goods transferred within that year at prices then current. Some tranfers and some payments are made under price agreements entered into before January 1st; some price agreements are made before December 31st in transactions which are not completed by transfers and payments until the following year or later. But the difference between these two "carry overs" is small in comparison with the aggregate volume of transactions completed within the year.

So much seems clear. The critical question is: What period of time should we consider in trying to discover the relations between prices and the circulating medium? If we consider periods of a year's duration, we shall have the equation of exchange to aid us. But we cannot follow business processes in annual summations. To learn how changes in prices, physical volume of trade, and dollar volume of payments are related to each other, we must watch these changes going on as they go on in every hour of every business day. Accordingly we must concentrate attention upon what happens in, or rather through, brief intervals of time. If an analysis of the day-by-day processes of agreeing upon prices, transferring goods, and making payments is sound, we can be sure that it will prove consistent with the relations which the equation of exchange reveals over longer periods.

Consider, then, a business man buying raw materials or goods for resale—one of those commercial transactions which reach a money total far exceeding the volume of retail trade. How are such a man's decisions regarding prices related to the quantity of coin, paper money and deposit currency in his possession?

The one definite remark we can make in answer is that, if our business man must pay in cash and cannot borrow, the means of payment in his possession set an upper limit upon the dollar volume of his purchases. Note that the price he can offer per unit is not limited, unless the price of a single unit would exhaust his funds. Nor is the number of units he can buy limited, with the same exception. The limit is imposed not upon prices as such, nor upon physical volume of trade as such, but upon prices times physical volume. Below this limit, even our cash-paying, non-borrowing business man has free play for judgment concerning what price to pay and how much to buy. His range of discretion is further enlarged by the factor of time. He can increase or diminish the scale of his purchases according as he thinks prices will rise or fall in the near future; he need not

spend his funds as he receives them, but can buy on a hand-to-mouth schedule for a while and wait for a favorable opportunity to make a large purchase. Yet we must note, also, what our business man is not likely to forget, that the more goods he can buy and sell at given margins the more money he will make. Thus he has a standing incentive to expand his transactions to the limit set by his circumstances. These limiting circumstances are numerous and shifting; but among them the amount of his funds is a factor of the first rank under the conditions we are discussing.

Of course, these conditions are not typical; nearly every business man can both buy on time and borrow. That fact makes the relations between prices and the quantity of the circulating medium still more elastic. The upper limit upon an individual's purchasing power is set by the funds in his hands plus the credit he can get from sellers and banks. The credit he can get depends not merely on his financial position at a given moment, but also on his financial prospects over a period which varies considerably from case to case, and on the financial position and prospects of those from whom he seeks credit. Thus the consideration of an individual business man's ability to buy widens out into consideration of the business community's ability to provide him with the means to pay.

If the financial positions and prospects of both seekers and grantors of credit are important factors in determining the purchasing power of business men, then the problem of prices and the circulating medium will change its complexion as these positions and prospects shift. For the business community as a whole, we know that the financial position and prospect changes from phase to phase of business cycles. Therefore in dealing with the problem of prices and the circulating medium, we must not merely consider brief intervals of time, but must recognize also that what is true of one brief interval may be false of another. What present knowledge enables us to do is to discuss the problem with reference to intervals characterized by business depression, revival, prosperity, and recession. Of the facts required for such a discussion, the more important have been suggested by the preceding sections, or by the "banking theories" of business cycles summarized in Chapter I.

During a period of depression, the quantity of coin and paper money which was in hand-to-hand use toward the close of the preceding period of prosperity, exceeds current requirements. The velocity

of circulation declines; "idle money" accumulates in the banks, swelling their cash reserves; if the bank-note currency is elastic, it is contracted; if business remains more active in other countries, gold is likely to be exported. What happens to coin and paper money happens also to deposit currency and to commercial credits. Business men turn over their funds less rapidly, require less working capital, repay part of their bank loans (despite the lower discount rates), and reduce their accounts payable. The reduction of bank loans commonly exceeds the net flow of idle cash to the banks, so that deposits subject to check decline somewhat. Accordingly, the limit upon coin and paper money in circulation is fixed, not by the monetary stock and bank-note policy, but by the current demands of trade. Similarly, the limit upon deposit currency is fixed, not by what the banks can provide, but by what business men care to use. In Professor Fisher's terms, the fall of prices and the concomitant shrinkage in the physical volume of trade are, for the time being, the "active" factors in the equation of exchange. To the conditions which they produce, the monetary and banking factors adjust themselves in whatever way the organization of the monetary and banking systems permits.

These banking and monetary adjustments to business depression are among the developments which facilitate a revival of activity. The low discount rates, the reserve lending-power of the banks, the redundant quantity of coin and paper money, the low velocities of circulation mean that an increase in business transactions will encounter no check from the inadequacy of the circulating medium. Business men who see a prospect of profit in enlarging their purchases have no difficulty in securing means of payment if their bankers share their confidence. The physical volume of trade and prices can enter an ascending spiral, every increase in the one promoting an increase in the other. As the dollar volume of business expands, a new series of adjustments is worked out in the distribution of coin and paper money between the banks and the public, in the issue of bank notes, perhaps in the international distribution of gold, certainly in the volume of deposits subject to check, and in the velocities of circulation. Monetary and banking conditions may be said to "permit" these developments, and even to "favor" them; but the "active" rôle is still played by prices and the physical volume of trade.

Not until the dollar volume of business has grown so large that it taxes the elasticity of the monetary and banking system, do the

monetary factors in the equation of exchange begin to dominate business transactions. That point is sure to be reached in business cycles, however, provided some non-monetary factor does not put an earlier close upon the expansion of trade. Even in the centers of finance, the velocity of circulation cannot be increased indefinitely. There is little assurance that the monetary stock of gold will grow with the need of bank reserves, and there is full assurance that prosperity will draw an increasing quantity of coin and paper money into hand-to-hand circulation. If bank reserves do not decline, at least they fail to expand as rapidly as do demand liabilities. There are limits, more or less definite, fixed partly by law, partly by practical experience, upon the minimum ratios between bank reserves on the one hand and bank notes and deposits on the other hand. When these minima are approached, bankers must check the expansion of loans. On the development of such conditions it ceases to be true that the business man can count upon obtaining funds to finance what promise to be profitable transactions. It then becomes true that both prices and the physical volume of trade are "passive" factors, controlled for the time being by monetary and banking conditions. And this domination becomes more absolute if the stringency develops into a financial panic, and many business men fear lest they cannot obtain funds to meet their maturing obligations.

In numerous business cycles, we shall find that prosperity wanes from other causes before the dollar volume of trade has attained dimensions which overtax the monetary and banking systems. Many recessions show slight traces of monetary stringency. Thus the periods when monetary and banking factors dominate prices and the physical volume of trade are brief, and they recur less regularly than the periods of depression, revival, and moderate prosperity, when prices and the physical volume of trade play the "active" rôles. Nevertheless, the intervals of monetary domination have had critical importance in the history of prices.[7] How that has come about may be stated in terms of the foregoing analysis, though not without some repetition.

The net shifts of price levels between two dates separated by decades depend upon the relative duration of the several intervening periods of prosperity and the corresponding periods of depression,

[7] This whole discussion relates to metallic-standard monetary systems, supplemented by banks of deposit and issue. Inconvertible paper-money standards present certain special problems which it is not necessary to consider here.

together with the rates at which prices rise in the first set of periods and fall in the second set. Hence, a factor which helps to lengthen the prosperous periods of successive cycles, to shorten the periods of monetary stringency, and to provide financial conditions which favor early revivals, tends to give the undulating curve of prices a rising secular trend. Under gold-standard monetary systems, an increase in the current output of gold is such a factor. A large flow of gold into bank reserves and general circulation postpones the time when an expansion in the pecuniary volume of trade will overtax the monetary and banking resources for making payments. When a monetary stringency does occur, such a flow brings quicker relief, and hastens the day when a revival of activity becomes financially possible. A dwindling of the current additions to the monetary stock of gold has the opposite effects, and tends to give the undulating course of prices a declining secular trend. We now have index numbers of wholesale prices covering some century and a half in countries which most of that time have had gold standards. The correspondence between the secular trends of these index numbers and the secular trends of gold production has been fairly close. When the world output of gold has been increasing rapidly, or has been fluctuating about a high level, prices have moved up and down with the alternations of business prosperity and depression; but they have risen more than they have fallen. When the annual output of gold has declined, remained on a relatively low level, or increased slowly, prices have continued their cyclical oscillations; but the declines have exceeded the advances.[8]

To sum up: the lag of deliveries behind price agreements, and of payments behind deliveries, gives business men time to arrange the financing of their transactions. In periods of depression, revival, moderate prosperity, and even mild recession, the man who buys skillfully knows that the possession of goods which can be sold at a profit will help him to borrow part of the funds wherewith to make pay-

[8] To enter into further details concerning this well-known correspondence would divert attention from what is at present the main issue. Yet it may be noted that there are grounds for hoping that men may free themselves from dependence upon fortuitous changes in the annual output of gold by more skillful management of their monetary and banking systems. Whether such policies as have recently been adopted by the Federal Reserve Banks of the United States to prevent a huge supply of gold from producing such an inflation of prices as might have been expected from historical precedents can be generally applied and further developed is a matter for the future to determine. Seen in historical perspective, these experiments appear as the current stage in that long and gradual process by which men are learning to keep money, the good servant, from becoming at times a bad master.

ment. It is the current and prospective money value of merchandise that counts to the credit man. Thus an increase of P, which swells the value of inventories, becomes a basis for an increase of M′, and of that part of M which consists of bank notes. An increase of T (physical volume of trade) plays the same rôle, unless it is offset by a decline of prices. Usually, though not always, these two factors rise and decline together—a close study of their shifting relations from phase to phase of business cycles is one of the leading problems for later chapters. When the pecuniary volume of business expands, it not only swells the volume of credit currency, but also quickens the velocities of circulation. Thus, most of the time, P and T are the "active" factors in the equation of exchange; they bring about changes in M′, V and V′; to a less extent they affect even M.

Modern monetary and banking systems provide a considerable measure of elasticity in all the factors which affect payments, except gold and certain types of government paper money. Gold is particularly important because under monetary systems of the approved type it provides the critical reserve for M′. The free movements of P and T are confined within the range provided by this elasticity. When the pecuniary volume of trade has reached limits which tax $MV + M'V'$, then monetary and banking factors assume the "active" rôle, and force a reduction in PT. Not every business cycle reaches a pitch of intensity which brings on a financial stringency. But in the past that point has been reached with regularity sufficient to let the secular trends of gold production control the secular trends of wholesale prices.

These conclusions may be repeated in slightly different form: Because of the lag of deliveries behind price-agreements and of payments behind deliveries, the payments made on a given day are most unlikely to equal the prices then current times the transfers then in process. But in buying goods, business men must plan to pay for them by the dates set by trade practices or formal contract. This means that the equation of exchange, which, as commonly interpreted, does not hold for short periods, is substantially valid for periods such as a year or more. Nor does it matter whether the years be years of depression or prosperity, crisis or revival, save that the proportion of bad debts may become appreciable in a year of severe crisis. All the time, business men have an incentive to buy as many goods as they can resell at a profit, and to charge prices as high as the traffic will bear. In depression, revival, moderate pros-

perity and mild recessions, the effective limit upon their transactions is set by commercial demand. Monetary and banking conditions would permit a larger volume of business. But in intense booms, the commercial demand may become so active that transactions reach the limit set by the monetary and banking systems. Over long periods of time, prices and the physical volume of trade have tended to expand up to these limits—not steadily, but in recurrent spurts of activity. And that fact has given changes in the annual output of gold a dominant influence upon the secular trends of wholesale prices, and seemingly some influence upon the secular trends of the physical volume of trade.

Time, then, is of the utmost consequence in considering the relations between prices and "the quantity of money." Relations which hold in long periods do not hold in short ones. Nor are all short periods alike; what is true in certain phases of business cycles is not true in all phases. Yet most of the seemingly contradictory statements which fill the long controversy over this problem can be reconciled when put in their proper relation to time. For example, I do not think that anything said here is incompatible with Professor Fisher's exposition of the causal relations between the factors in his equation of exchange, provided his term "normally" is not taken in the sense of usually. Nor is the present discussion inconsistent with the celebrated theorem: "Other things being equal, prices vary directly as the quantity of money in circulation." That theorem is formally valid. Equally valid are a number of other theorems similar in form: for example: "Other things being equal, the quantity of the circulating medium varies directly as prices:" "Other things being equal, the quantity of the circulating medium varies directly as the physical volume of trade." Any of these propositions can be developed into an adequate theory of the "relations between money and prices" by analyzing the "other things" which are supposed to remain equal. Yet it is an awkward way of working to start with a proposition which suggests so limited a view of the problem, and it is misleading to end with a proposition which contains so limited a version of the truth. The orthodox formulation of the quantity theory owes its prominence to the fact that economists have given most attention to the long-period relations between gold-supply and prices at wholesale. For that particular problem, the proposition "other things being equal, prices vary directly as the quantity of money in

circulation" is both valid and important. But for the periods with which the theory of business cycles is concerned, we need a far more discriminating statement of the relations among prices, the physical volume of trade, the quantity and the velocity of the circulating medium—a statement which takes into account changes in these relations produced by depression, revival, prosperity and recession.[9]

V. The Flow of Money Payments.

1. Production and Purchasing Power.

To make the business economy function smoothly, it is necessary not only that the volume and velocity of the circulating medium shall respond to the changing pace of business, but also that coin, paper money, and deposit currency shall keep flowing through the hands of business enterprises and individuals in exchange for goods. The flow, moreover, must be kept adjusted to the counterflow of goods offered for sale, in detail as well as in gross. If the dollar volume of any kind of goods flowing to market exceeds the flow of purchasing power which the prospective buyers are receiving and expending for that kind of goods, business troubles result—troubles that are trifling or grave as the quantities involved are small or large.

As we saw in Chapter I, two sets of theorists have found an explanation of cyclical fluctuations in this feature of the business economy. The Pollak Foundation group contend that in prosperity the flow of money incomes to consumers, and from consumers to the sellers of consumers' goods, lags behind the dollar volume of the consumers' goods poured into the markets. Mr. P. W. Martin holds a similar thesis with regard to money incomes at large and goods of all kinds. The over-production theorists look at the process from the other side; they offer a variety of reasons why the flow of goods to market exceeds the markets' ability or willingness to buy at profitable prices. To make use of these hypotheses in interpreting business

[9] Much the best survey of the literature concerning the quantity theory of the value of money known to me is given by Professor James W. Angell's recent treatise on *The Theory of International Prices,* Cambridge (Massachusetts), 1926. Although he shows that attention has frequently been called to the factor of time in discussions of the relations between money and prices, Angell notes that writers upon monetary theory have neglected the problems presented to them by cyclical fluctuations in trade. (See pp. 127, 134, 181.) The leading exception is Mr. R. G. Hawtrey, whose *Currency and Credit* (2d ed., London, 1923) deals acutely with the topic. Writers upon business cycles have done little to supply what the monetary theorists have omitted.

activities we need to know the basic facts about the flow of purchasing power.

Our knowledge on this head is just beginning to attain quantitative form. Every year, the volume of monetary payments vastly exceeds the money value of the goods produced—that is a matter of course. Some progress has been made toward tracing and measuring the currents which are parts of this general circulation. One current of especial importance is the disbursement of money incomes to consumers and the spending of these incomes by consumers. Large as it is, this current is but a minor part of the total circulation of purchasing power. Much greater are the payments made by business enterprises to each other, as they pass products through the successive links of the chains which connect producers of raw materials with retail shops, or with final business buyers. Even the "savings" of individuals and business enterprises are almost all paid out for goods in some form, constituting another current of strategic interest. There are also the payments from one individual to another for personal service, and the payments involved in collecting government revenues and making government disbursements. Finally, not only current products and services, but also a portion of the accumulated property rights in real estate, business enterprises, government loans and the like change hands each year. So huge is the aggregate value of these properties, that a shift of ownership in a minor fraction creates a current of payments running in the tens of billions of dollars.

2. The Flow of Money Incomes to Individuals.

The magnitude we have now to measure as best we may—incomes received by individuals in money—is considerably smaller than the country's income as estimated by the National Bureau of Economic Research. It does not include the value of their own produce consumed by farm families; commodity income from family gardens, poultry and cows; the rental value of homes occupied by their owners, or any allowance for the use of household furnishings and personal effects. As estimated by Dr. King, these items have an aggregate value which ranges from nearly 7 to slightly over 8 billion dollars per annum in 1919-26. By subtracting the sums in question from the corresponding estimates of current income, we get estimates of income received in money. Table 4 shows these results, together

with King's estimates of total payments to employees as wages, salaries, pensions, compensation for injuries, and the like. It should be noted that all the figures for 1922-26 are preliminary, and subject to revision on the basis of a more detailed analysis of the underlying data, which is now being made in the National Bureau.

TABLE 4

ESTIMATES OF INCOME RECEIVED IN MONEY BY INDIVIDUALS
UNITED STATES, 1919–1926

	Total Income Received in Money Billions of Dollars	Payments to Employees Billions of Dollars	Percentage of Total Paid to Employees
1919	59.9	34.8	58 per cent
1920	65.9	41.6	63 " "
1921	55.4	34.7	63 " "
1922	58.9 *	35.3 *	60 * " "
1923	69.7 *	39.4 *	57 * " "
1924	72.0 *	39.6 *	55 * " "
1925	78.9 *	43.0 *	54 * " "
1926	82.1 *	44.5 *	54 * " "

* Provisional figures, subject to change.
All the entries are estimates made by the National Bureau of Economic Research under the supervision of Dr. Willford I. King.

According to these estimates, payments to employees must be by far the largest of the income streams. Supplementary studies of the National Bureau indicate that salaries of officials average between 7 and 9 per cent of total payrolls in the highly organized branches of trade (where they are most important), and probably less than 3 per cent of all income received in money.[1] Even if we subtract such salaries from payrolls, the remainder exceeds all the other money-income streams put together. Another conclusion of importance for students of business cycles is that the ratio of wages and salaries to total income paid in money rises decidedly in depression and declines in prosperity.

A less comprehensive, but more detailed, view of the relative magnitude of the several money-income streams can be had from the statistical reports of the Tax Division of the Bureau of Internal Revenue. Table 5 summarizes the pertinent data. Of course these figures must be considered critically. (1) They include less than half of the aggregate money incomes of individuals, according to

[1] See *Income in the United States,* vol. i, p. 99, National Bureau of Economic Research, 1921.

the estimates of the National Bureau, mainly, though by no means solely because tens of millions of small incomes are exempt from the tax, and are not reported to the federal authorities. (2) Since these small incomes are composed largely of wages, the percentages of wages and salaries in Table 5 run somewhat lower than in Table 4, though not so much lower as one might expect. (3) Relatively few farmers and other small business men report. The deficiency in profits which results is believed to be offset in part by the inclusion under this head of considerable interest payments. (4) Interest is rather low, not only for the reason just suggested, but also because interest upon the large sum of tax-exempt bonds is not reported fully. (5) Finally, efforts to avoid and to evade taxation distort the

TABLE 5

PERSONAL INCOMES REPORTED TO THE UNITED STATES BUREAU OF INTERNAL REVENUE, CLASSIFIED BY SOURCES

1919–1924

	1919	*1920*	*1921*	*1922*	*1923*	*1924*
Billions of Dollars						
Total	22.4	26.7	23.3	24.9	29.3	29.6
Salaries, wages, commissions, bonuses, directors' fees, etc.	10.8	15.3	13.8	13.7	14.2	13.6
Business, trade, commerce, partnerships, farming, and profits from incidental sales of property	6.7	5.9	4.2	5.3	7.6	8.0
Dividends	2.5	2.7	2.5	2.7	3.1	3.3
Rents and royalties	1.0	1.0	1.2	1.2	1.8	2.0
Interest, investment, and fiduciary income	1.5	1.7	1.7	2.0	2.6	2.6
Percentages of the Total						
	1919	*1920*	*1921*	*1922*	*1923*	*1924*
Total	100	100	100	100	100	100
Salaries, wages, commissions, bonuses, directors' fees, etc.	48	57	59	55	49	49
Business, trade, commerce, partnerships, farming, and profits from incidental sales of property	30	22	18	21	26	27
Dividends	11	10	11	11	11	11
Rents and royalties	4	4	5	5	6	7
Interest, investment, and fiduciary income	7	6	7	8	9	9

Compiled from *Statistics of Income from Returns of Net Income for 1924*, Washington, 1926, pp. 8, 32–33.

income returns to an unknown extent, and one which may vary appreciably with changes in tax rates, efficiency of administration, and perhaps with business conditions.

Even in incomes large enough to be subject to the federal tax, wages and salaries average slightly more than half of the total one year with another. Profits come second, despite the omission of nearly 99 per cent of the farmers, and equal or exceed dividends, rent and interest added together in the years of business activity. Interest payments are smaller than dividends, but that appearance may be due to a difference in the degrees of under-reporting. Finally, of the commonly recognized sources of incomes, rent is the smallest according to these figures.

A second question can be answered in general terms by rearranging the data in Table 5: How are the money incomes of individuals from different sources affected by business cycles? If we reduce the yearly figures for the various income streams to relatives based upon their respective average values, and also compute the percentage change from one year to the next, we can see which streams have been fairly steady and which have been highly variable. Table 6 serves this purpose.

In view of the extraordinary price gyrations of 1919-21, the figures in Table 6 have no claim to stand as typical of the changes in money incomes which accompany the business cycles of less disturbed times. A supplementary table covering pre-war years would be useful; but the data for making estimates of money income command less confidence prior to 1914 than the data for recent years, and the latter require confirmation. Under these circumstances, we must make the most of the fact that a case which magnifies the changes has its advantages.

When an individual is considering the investment of his funds, he thinks of bonds as yielding a fixed rate of interest (in dollars), and of stocks as yielding dividends which may change in any quarter year. If he buys real estate, he may be expecting an income fixed by a long lease as rigidly as interest on a bond; or he may be expecting an income subject to many fluctuations—all depends upon the character of the property he acquires. If he goes into business on his own account, he expects a higher average return upon his investment than he could get from income yielding bonds, stocks or

TABLE 6

RELATIVE VARIABILITY OF THE FLOW OF MONEY INCOMES FROM DIFFERENT SOURCES
UNITED STATES, 1919–1924

Based upon Table 5

Percentages of the Average Values during the Period Covered

	Average Values in Billions of Dollars	Percentages of the Average Values					
		1919	*1920*	*1921*	*1922*	*1923*	*1924*
Total	26.0	86	103	90	96	113	114
Salaries, wages, commissions, etc.	13.6	80	113	102	101	105	100
Business, trade, profits on sales of property, etc.	6.3	107	94	67	84	121	127
Dividends	2.8	89	96	89	96	111	118
Rents and royalties	1.4	73	73	88	88	132	146
Interest, investment, and fiduciary income	2.0	74	85	85	99	129	129

Percentage Rise (+) or Fall (−) from Value in Preceding Year

	1919–1920	*1920–1921*	*1921–1922*	*1922–1923*	*1923–1924*
Total	+19%	−13%	+7%	+18%	+1%
Salaries, wages, commissions, etc.	+42	−10	−1	+4	−4
Business, trade, profits on sales of property, etc.	−12	−29	+26	+43	+ 5
Dividends	+ 8	− 7	+ 8	+15	+ 6
Rents and royalties	0	+20	0	+50	+11
Interest, investment, and fiduciary income	+13	0	+18	+30	0
Total income from dividends, rents, and interest	+ 8	0	+ 9	+27	+ 5

The percentages have been computed from figures carried to more places than are shown here.

real estate; but he must expect that his profits will vary widely from year to year.

These expectations regarding the relative steadiness of incomes from interest, dividends, rents, and profits are based upon the returns per dollar invested in different ways. That is not what Table 6 shows. It purports to give changes in the total incomes received under various captions by all individuals who report to the Internal Revenue. The total receipts are affected each year by the investment of new funds in bonds, stocks, real estate, and business. More than

that, the tax returns include "investment income" and "fiduciary income" with interest, they include royalties with rents, and they include gains from the shifting of investments with business profits. Hence differences between prevailing opinions regarding the relative steadiness of returns upon investments of the various sorts on the one hand, and the conclusions suggested by the totals on the other hand, need not be taken as discrediting either the opinions or the statistics. In studying the flow of incomes to individuals, we are concerned with the total payments, rather than with the returns per dollar invested.

(1) Profits appear to be, as one expects, much the most variable type of income. They fall nearly 30 per cent in one year and increase over 40 per cent in another year. (2) Rents and royalties rank next in average variations; but these figures may not be representative, because, during the years covered, rents seem to have been undergoing a belated adjustment to the change in the general level of prices brought about by the war. They make spasmodic advances in 1921, 1923 and 1924, while in two other years they show no change. (3) Interest, investment and fiduciary income varies much more than one would expect. All the changes are increases. Even in the severe depression of 1921, interest receipts did not fall off. (4) Dividends, while moving up or down every year, proved decidedly the stablest type of money income in this period. That is, the changes, though frequent, were small in comparison with the maximum changes in the other types of income. Particularly striking, and particularly important for our problem, is the contrast between the extreme variability of profits and the relative steadiness of dividends. Nor does Table 6 bring out this contrast in full. The profits there shown are the profits of individuals and partnerships, while dividends are paid by corporations. If we subtract the deficits reported each year to the Internal Revenue by the corporations which lost money from the profits reported by the corporations which made money, we get net corporate incomes of 8.4 billion dollars in 1919, 5.9 billions in 1920, 0.5 billions in 1921, 4.8 billions in 1922, 6.3 billions in 1923 and 5.4 billions in 1924.[2] Dividends reported by individual taxpayers were far less than net corporate incomes as computed here in the relatively good business years, and far more than net corporate incomes in 1921.

[2] See the appropriate text tables in the official *Statistics of Income* for these years.

While the differences in variability of dividends, interest, and rent are interesting, they are not of great importance to us. Most men of property diversify their investments, holding some bonds, some stocks, and perhaps some real estate. Hence the changes in the money incomes of the investing classes are best ascertained by adding together interest, dividends and rents. On so doing we get an income stream whose average volume (according to the Internal Revenue figures) is about equal to the volume of profits, but which varies not much more than dividends. This is the flow which we should compare with profits on the one hand and wages on the other.

That comparison indicates that the largest of the income streams, payments to employees, as wages, salaries, commissions, bonuses, pensions, and the like, was decidedly less variable than profits in 1919-24, and decidedly more variable than income from investments in securities and real estate. More precise statements would have little meaning, because we know that our data are open to question and that the period covered is peculiar. But it seems improbable that the variations of wages and salaries in this period were more exaggerated than the variations of interest and rents. Thus the conclusion is probably valid that the largest of the money-income streams are also the most variable in flow. According to Table 6, wages, salaries and profits, added together, make over three-quarters of taxable income; of total income received in money they probably make four-fifths. And their aggregate volume may change by 15, or 20 per cent, or, in extreme cases even more, in a single year.

3. The Outflow of Personal Incomes.

All business enterprises disburse money incomes directly to individuals; but only a few classes of enterprises share directly in the reflow of purchasing power from individuals. By far the greatest collectors of consumers' funds are the retail merchants. A much smaller stream flows to the landlords, who may or may not be business enterprises, and still smaller streams to enterprises which render personal services of various descriptions, and to public utilities.

Our most detailed information on this head comes from the analysis of family expenditures. In 1918-19 the United States Bureau of Labor Statistics collected budgets from over 12,000 families. On rearranging the data according to channels of expenditure, we get the following results:

TABLE 7

CHANNELS THROUGH WHICH FAMILY EXPENDITURES FLOW. BASED UPON BUDGETS OF 12,096 AMERICAN FAMILIES IN 1918–19, COLLECTED BY THE U. S. BUREAU OF LABOR STATISTICS.

	Average Expenditures	Percentage of Total
Payments made to		
Retail shops	$994.37	66.1
Service agencies (insurance, laundry, amusement, etc.)	83.03	5.5
Public utilities	56.07	3.7
	$1,133.47	75.3
Landlords	186.55	12.4
Professional men (doctors, dentists, nurses, etc.)	43.42	2.9
Organizations (churches, trade unions, lodges, etc.)	18.22	1.2
Servants	4.01	.3
Government (postage, taxes)	3.62	.2
Undistributed ("patriotic," gifts, vacations, etc.)	36.98	2.5
Surplus	78.93	5.2
Total	$1,505.20	100.0

Compiled from *Cost of Living in the United States,* Bulletin of the U. S. Bureau of Labor Statistics, No. 357, Washington, 1924.

While these data are doubtless representative of the important class whose expenditures the Bureau of Labor Statistics wished to cover (white families in industrial centers, depending mainly upon wages or small salaries), they are certainly not representative of the population as a whole. The budgets collected by Dr. King for the income studies of the National Bureau indicate that, as incomes increase, families devote larger percentages of their expenditures to housing, to domestic service, to travel and amusement, and smaller percentages to purchases from retail shops and public utilities. The expenditures of farmers probably follow still a different pattern, but the data available do not suffice to show details.[1] In short we lack budgets representative of the population as a whole.

We can, however, get at the point most important for us—the proportion of money income spent at retail shops by the population as a whole—in a different way. Mr. Lawrence B. Mann, formerly of the Federal Reserve system, Professor Paul H. Nystrom of the Retail

[1] See the weights used in making index numbers of the prices of consumers' goods bought by families which expend $25,000 per year and $5,000 per year; by families of urban employees, and by farm families; introduction to *Income in the Various States,* National Bureau of Economic Research, 1925. These figures do not profess to be complete budgets; but they do cover the main heads of family expenditure, and justify the statements made in the text.

Research Bureau, and the Federal Trade Commission have made estimates of the money volume of retail trade in the United States, estimates which we can compare with the estimates of money income made by the National Bureau. The results, given in Table 8, show what the preceding paragraph makes one expect—that the proportion of money income which flows to the retail shops is somewhat smaller in the case of the whole population than in the case of urban wage earners.

TABLE 8

ESTIMATED PROPORTION OF INCOME RECEIVED IN MONEY SPENT IN RETAIL SHOPS

UNITED STATES, 1919-23

	Estimated Income Received in Money	Estimated Volume of Retail Trade		Percentage of Money Income Spent in Retail Shops	
		Billions of Dollars		Per Cent	
	Billions of Dollars From Table 4	Nystrom-Mann	Federal Trade Commission	Nystrom-Mann	Federal Trade Commission
1919..........	59.9	32.6	34.8	54	58
1920..........	65.9	38.3	38.3	58	58
1921..........	55.4	33.6	30.7	61	55
1922..........	58.9 *	33.5	32.5	57	55
1923..........	69.7 *	35.0	38.2	50	55

* Provisional figures, subject to change.

NOTE: I have taken Paul H. Nystrom's figure for 1923 (35 billion dollars) as basic, and used Lawrence B. Mann's figures for 1919–22 as an index for carrying the series backward. The connecting link is an estimate, which Professor Nystrom made at my request, that the volume of retail trade was 4 or 5 per cent larger in 1923 than in 1922. See Mann, "The Importance of Retail Trade in the United States," *American Economic Review*, December, 1923, vol. xiii, pp. 609–617; Nystrom, "An Estimate of the Volume of Retail Trade in the United States," *Harvard Business Review*, January, 1925, vol. iii, pp. 150–159.

The Federal Trade Commission's estimate is part of their report upon *National Wealth and Income*, Senate Document No. 126, 69th Congress, 1st Session, Washington, 1926, pp. 306–313.

Of the three estimates, Professor Nystrom's seems to rest upon the broadest study of the relevant materials. The Federal Trade Commission figures are built up by a bold combination of various bits of evidence which may not be an adequate foundation for the superstructure. It seems improbable that the percentage of money income spent at retail shops fell off in the bad year 1921, as the Commission figures indicate. An increase in this percentage, such as Mann's estimates show, is more plausible.

The general conclusions which seem justified by the data may be put in this form: (1) More than half of the money incomes received by individuals flow back to the world of business through retail merchants, (2) probably this proportion rises somewhat in dull times,

(3) other business enterprises, such as public utilities and service agencies, collect probably less than a tenth of the money income, (4) more than a quarter, perhaps nearly a third, is paid to landlords (some of whom are corporations), professional men, voluntary organizations, servants, and the government, or is invested as savings.

4. The Flow of Payments Among Business Enterprises.

Business-cycle theorists have concerned themselves more with the circuit flow of payments from business enterprises to consumers and from consumers back to business enterprises than with the flow of payments from one enterprise to another. Yet the latter flow is certainly several times as great as the former. In preceding sections we have obtained rough estimates for recent years of the payments made by check in the United States, of the volume of money income, and of the volume of retail trade. These figures, supplemented by a new (and hazardous) estimate of payments made in coin and paper money, are assembled for comparison in Table 9.

Inspection of these figures may inspire more confidence in their accuracy than is merited. The percentage relationships among the quantities are fairly stable; but such is likely to be the case when one expresses any set of figures as percentages of much larger sums. A considerable margin of uncertainty surrounds every series in the table—a margin which is broadest in the estimates of payments made in coin and paper money. Yet the estimates are probably trustworthy concerning the order of magnitude of the three quantities, and that is the point at issue.

On the face of the figures, retail sales account for not much more than one-twentieth of the aggregate volume of payments, and the payment of money incomes to individuals for about one-tenth. Even the round-flow of money incomes to individuals and from individuals seems to make only a fifth of the aggregate payments in average business years. While these rather precise ratios may be faulty, it seems certain that the payments arising from other business transactions are several times the volume of payments involved in receiving and spending personal incomes.

All business is said to depend in the last resort upon consumers' demand, and the statement is doubtless valid in a broad sense. Yet there is no mystery in the fact that retail trade itself is but a small

TABLE 9

Comparison of the Estimated Volume of Payments, Income Received in Money, and Volume of Retail Sales

United States, 1919 to 1923 or 1926

	Estimated Volume of Payments in Checks	Estimated Volume of Payments in Coin and Paper Money	Estimated Volume of Payments Total	Estimated Incomes Received in Money	Estimated Retail Sales	Percentages of the Estimated Total Volume of Payments: Income Received in Money	Percentages of the Estimated Total Volume of Payments: Retail Sales
	Billions of Dollars	Billions of Dollars	Billions of Dollars	Billions of Dollars	Billions of Dollars	Per Cent	Per Cent
1919.......	547	106	653	59.9	32.6	9.2	5.0
1920.......	588	121	709	65.9	38.3	9.3	5.4
1921.......	484	97	581	55.4	33.6	9.5	5.8
1922.......	534	93	627	58.9 *	33.5	9.4	5.3
1923.......	570	102	672	69.7 *	35.0	10.4	5.2
1924.......	600	98	698	72.0 *		10.3	
1925.......	653	95	748	78.9 *		10.5	
1926.......	695	105	800	82.1 *		10.3	

* Preliminary estimates, subject to revision.

The estimated payments in checks are taken from Table 3.

The estimated payments in coin and paper money are computed by assuming that the average volume of these media outside of the Treasury and the banks has the same velocity of circulation each year as is shown by the estimates of deposit velocity in Table 3. This assumption is as plausible as any other, but it may be considerably in error. The results it yields happen to agree with the view that 85 per cent of American payments are made in checks. That is, sums of the above estimates for 8 years make the payments in coin and paper money 14.9 per cent of the grand totals. On Mr. Carl Snyder's advice, I have used the official statements of coin and paper money in circulation, except in 1919 and 1920. Adjustments of the official figures for certain bank holdings of coin and paper money give respectively 3.67 and 4.33 billion dollars in these two years.

The estimated incomes received in money are taken from Table 4.

The estimated retail sales are the Nystrom-Mann figures from Table 8.

fraction of business. In most cases the components of the goods which the consumer finally buys have been bought and sold several times over by wholesale merchants, jobbers, manufacturers, and producers of raw materials. These successive turnovers much more than counterbalance the higher prices which consumers pay.[1] Then there

[1] Kinley found the deposits of wholesalers to be more than twice the deposits of retail dealers—$124,824,000 against $60,447,000 on March 16, 1909. He also found that "all other deposits" were upwards of three times the volume of retail and wholesale deposits added together—$502,817,000. *The Use of Credit Instruments in Payments in the United States* (Senate Document No. 399, 61st Congress, 2d session). Washington, 1910; pp. 85, 133, 171.

Building upon admittedly questionable taxation returns from Pennsylvania, the Federal Trade Commission estimates the dollar volume of wholesale trade at 63.22 per cent of the dollar volume of retail trade in 1923. Presumably this estimate takes account only of the sales by wholesale merchants to retailers. See *National Wealth and Income,* 69th Congress, 1st Session, Senate Document No. 126, pp. 308, 314, 315.

are all the incidental payments involved in running an enterprise which deals in consumers' goods, from freight and insurance to repairs and credit transactions. Next we must add in the business in producers' goods, including the construction of industrial equipment. Changes in the ownership of securities and real estate call for another vast sum of payments. So also does the investment of fresh savings, and the making and repaying of loans. These items are not independent of each other—for example, the investing of fresh savings is largely the paying for new industrial equipment—and we cannot measure them as yet. But the list, though incomplete, shows that there is no reason to discredit the conclusions drawn from Table 9.

For the smooth working of the business economy it is as necessary that the immensely larger flow of payments among business enterprises shall be maintained as it is necessary that the smaller flow of payments from consumers to retail merchants shall continue unchecked. The strategic importance of the two flows, however, cannot be judged from their relative volumes. Indeed, the greater the volume of all business payments in comparison with the volume of retail trade, the more delicate may become the equilibrium, if all types of business are really concerned indirectly with satisfying personal wants. Here we have developed yet another problem which we must face when we come to study the interrelations among the processes of business expansion and contraction.

5. Saving and Spending.

We commonly think of spending money and saving money as activities the opposite of each other. But every kind of saving except actual hoarding involves spending. In the business economy, indeed, the process of saving is one current in the flow of money payments.

This process, also, has been made to yield theories of business cycles. Professor Tugan-Baranovski contends that crises come because people do not save enough money to meet the huge capital requirements of prosperity. Professor Spiethoff holds that crises come because people put their savings into too much industrial equipment and not enough consumption goods. Mr. Hobson says simply that, when incomes expand in prosperity, rich people save too much, and by their investments in productive enterprises overstock the markets with wares.

Data concerning saving are among the most difficult of economic

records to obtain with precision. The very word "saving" has half a dozen different meanings. The most ingenious effort so far made to surmount these difficulties, conceptual and statistical, is that of Dr. Willford I. King. Taking as his basic data the doubtful census returns of wealth, and subtracting or adding the estimated foreign debits or credits of the country, Dr. King finds a total increase of wealth between 1909 and 1918 of 122 billion dollars. But correction for price fluctuations reduces that huge sum to 46 billions. These savings equal 14 per cent, or one-seventh of the estimated income of the country during this nine-year period. We might doubt this result because of the admitted inaccuracies of the census data, inaccuracies which may or may not be sufficiently different in the reports for 1909 and 1918 to make the estimate of increase in wealth far wrong. But Dr. King has made a second, quite independent, estimate which confirms the first. He has computed the percentage of increase in all the important items of wealth for which he could get reliable data in physical units over the same years, and found that the average increase was even higher than his first method indicated. He concludes, accordingly, that "The normal fraction of the national income saved is about one-seventh."

If this percentage seems large, it must be remembered (1) that about 40 per cent of the country's savings are made by business enterprises, through the retention and reinvestment of profits which might otherwise have been distributed to individuals, and (2) that about 9 per cent more seems to consist in the accumulation of larger stocks of clothing, personal ornaments, furniture, and automobiles. Thus only half of the total corresponds to what many have in mind when they speak of the savings of people. Finally it should be said that defects of the data lead Dr. King to present his results as rough approximations, which require confirmation or revision in the light of later and fuller statistics. Certainly his estimate covers an exceptional period; in 1916 Dr. King finds that savings jumped to twice the pre-war average even after he had allowed for the rise of prices, and in 1918 he finds that the war wastes more than offset savings. While these exceptional cases tend to cancel each other, there is small assurance that ten years of post-war experience will yield averages agreeing closely with 1910-18.

Little can be gained by attempting to refine upon rough approximations; but it must be pointed out that Dr. King's average of 14 per cent of income saved means 14 per cent of income as estimated by

the National Bureau in its first report. If the savings were compared with money income, the percentage would run somewhat higher. On the other hand, Dr. King quite properly treats an increase in the stock of durable consumption goods as savings. But we have just been considering what part of money incomes is spent in buying goods at retail, without reference to the problem of saving. Subtracting the increase of consumption goods (9 per cent of savings, according to Dr. King), would make the savings which flow into revenue-producing investments a lower percentage of money income. In view of the partial offsetting of these two items, we have no clear reason for saying that the proportion of money income invested to produce income is greater or less than one-seventh.

On the basis of Dr. King's estimates, it seems that on the average employees "save" about 5 per cent of their annual wages and salaries; farmers, together with owners of farm lands and mortgages, "save" about 12 per cent of their net income from agriculture; other business men "save" about 33 per cent of their annual incomes. That is, these classes spend the respective percentages of their income in ways which increase their stocks of semi-durable consumption goods, or better their equipment for making money, or buy securities which enable some enterpriser to better his equipment, or acquire revenue-bringing claims against other people. Of the total savings in his period Dr. King attributes 20 per cent to employees, 12 per cent to the agricultural interest, and 68 per cent to business men and property owners in non-agricultural lines. Two-fifths of all the saving is done directly by business enterprises, without the funds ever passing into the hands of individuals. Dr. King also finds, and this point is of especial interest here, that "the volume of saving by business concerns varies directly with the waves of business activity," but that "the extent of private saving is much less closely correlated with the economic cycle." [1]

Another study of American savings, made on a different plan by Dr. Walter Renton Ingalls, confirms King's chief results. Using the National Bureau's and his own estimates of national income from 1912 to 1922 on the one side, and on the other side David Friday's and his own estimates of savings, Dr. Ingalls computes that, before the war, savings made about 15 per cent of annual income, one year

[1] Willford I. King, "The Net Volume of Saving in the United States," *Journal of the American Statistical Association,* September and December, 1922, vol. xviii, pp. 305-323 and 455-470.

with another. This percentage agrees closely with Dr. King's fraction —one-seventh. Again like King, Dr. Ingalls finds that nominal savings were greatly enhanced by the war, but that the war savings were mostly spent in destroying lives and property, or lost in the post-war readjustments. Finally, in 1920-22, Dr. Ingalls thinks that savings shrank to about half their pre-war proportion—say 7 or 8 per cent of the national income.[2] Of course, a marked decline of savings in a three-year period which includes a great crisis followed by a severe depression is not out of line with Dr. King's results.

Both of these investigations indicate that saving, whether measured in dollars or in percentages of national income, belongs among the highly variable factors in our problem. Any average which we may take to represent the general run of affairs will differ widely from the figures for years of great prosperity and deep depression. Yet we must use some average in order to compare current savings with the accumulations of the past. If we take Ingalls' pre-war estimate of 15 per cent, or King's estimate of one-seventh, as a fair average of the part of income saved annually, and if we accept the estimate presented in an earlier section that the value of man-made equipment possessed by our people is equal to the national income of three or four years, it follows that, in the United States, the man-made equipment on hand represents a value equivalent to the average savings of between 20 and 30 current years.[3]

VI. The Guidance of Economic Activity.

1. The Problem of Adjusting Supply to Demand in a Business Economy.

The discussion of the flow of money payments in the preceding section provides a basis for treating one aspect of the protean problem of supply and demand in a business economy. Another aspect of this problem must now be faced—the difficulty of keeping the rate at

[2] See W. R. Ingalls, *Wealth and Income of the American People,* 2d ed., York, Pennsylvania, 1923, pp. 202-204, 252-254, and *Current Economic Affairs,* 1924, pp. 82, 152.

[3] Professor Cassel believes that in Sweden annual savings average approximately one-fifth of national income, and that national income averages approximately one-seventh of national wealth. I judge that the estimate of wealth used includes the value of land. On this basis, the accumulated wealth of Sweden equals the average savings of some 35 years. The National Defense Commission estimated the average annual increase of wealth in 1885-1908 at 3.18 per cent. See Gustav Cassel, *Theoretische Sozialökonomie,* 3d ed., Erlangen and Leipzig, 1923, p. 52.

which each kind of goods is being produced adjusted to the rate at which each kind is being bought.

Within the hundred years since Sismondi wrote about the uncertainties of catering to a "metaphysical public," this problem has been growing ever more intricate. Factory production has taken over one household industry after another, market areas have widened, the variety of products has multiplied, industrial equipment has become more elaborate and more specialized. On one side of the market stand the millions of money-income receivers, who provide for most of their families' want by buying goods which others make. On the other side stand these same millions with their diversified capabilities as workers, their diversified properties in natural resources and industrial equipment, and their fluid investment funds, seeking the most profitable markets for all these productive energies. The buyers of goods and the sellers of goods are the same persons; but this identity does not enable them to keep their efforts as producers, organized in business enterprises, adjusted to their wants as consumers, organized in families.

So pervasive is this problem in a business economy and so constant its pressure, that generation by generation a large part of the routine shrewdness and a large part of the innovating energy of business men are absorbed in keeping abreast of it. Many-sided progress has been achieved in the course of this effort. Communication has become incomparably more rapid within the century, and made to yield vastly better reports of demand in widely separate markets. Improvements in transportation have rendered possible a more satisfactory distribution of supplies. The collection and analysis of commercial statistics are beginning to aid the distribution of goods through time, as the telegraph, railway and steamship aid distribution in space. Trade associations make competition less blind, and industrial integration makes planning of production more systematic. Insurance has expanded to equalize the burden of carrying a vast variety of economic risks. The standardization of goods, which comes with mass production, partially offsets the diversification of products. One use of advertising is to control demand for goods, so far as may be. Combined with all these technical improvements, is the day-by-day effort of every responsible business man to follow current demand with vigilance, to take advantage of every favorable change, to guard against every decline, with all the skill which mother wit and practical experience can muster.

Yet it is not certain that those efforts all put together have gained upon the growing difficulties of the problem. For, on the side of business administration itself, there are forces which keep the markets from attaining equilibrium. So long as free enterprise prevails on a competitive basis, there cannot be a stable adjustment of supply to demand. As Dr. Schumpeter has pointed out, every business innovation disturbs the preceding basis of adjustment.[1] New products and new styles or brands of old goods, new sources of supply, new methods of production, even new competitors turning out familiar goods by familiar methods, keep forcing changes in the production and marketing schedules of established houses. And there is no evidence that the current of business innovations is becoming less swift.

In the trades which cater to personal needs, the trend seems to be toward offering to consumers an ever wider variety of wares and services ready for immediate delivery. Trade goes largely, perhaps increasingly, to enterprises which enable consumers to buy "what they want when they want it." To make such buying possible, some business enterprise must provide goods in anticipation of the demand. If the manufacturer does not make to stock, then the wholesale merchant or the retailer must assume the hazard.

Nor is the case widely different in trades which make goods only to order. There the business enterprise must provide facilities for executing orders before it can get them. Inventory hazards may be reduced; but not the larger and longer hazards upon investment of capital and time. Business men who embark in any productive enterprise, investors who advance capital, and wage-earners who learn trades are all taking a chance that the demand for their services at a satisfactory price will prove less than the supply they offer. This hazard is faced even in an enterprise which has a complete monopoly of its special field.

"Uncertainty," to use Dr. Hardy's term, is thus an all-pervading phase of every business undertaking.[2] Its tap root is uncertainty concerning what people will buy at what prices. Its lateral roots are uncertainty what competitors, direct and indirect, will sell at what prices; uncertainty what supplies of all the needed kinds can be bought at what prices, and uncertainty what will happen within the enterprise, or within its business connection, to affect its profits.

[1] See Chapter I, section iv, 4.

[2] See Chapter I, section iv, 2. On the distinction between risk and uncertainty, see Frank H. Knight, *Risk, Uncertainty and Profit,* Boston, 1921.

The fruits of uncertainty appear in the emotional aberrations of business judgments and competitive illusions, by which Professor Pigou and Dr. T. W. Mitchell explain business cycles.[3] And under the pressure of uncertainty men have evolved that elaborate co-operative system of guiding economic activity, which we have next to consider.

2. The Rôle Played by Business Managements.

The most active rôle in determining what use shall be made of the country's natural resources, industrial equipment, investment funds, brains and brawn is played by business men.

When the earliest theories of crises were being formulated, economists could assume that there stood at the head of the typical business enterprise a capitalist-employer, who provided a large part of the invested funds, carried the brunt of the hazard, performed the "work of superintendence," and pocketed the profits. Millions of enterprisers of this versatile type are still in business; but they are most numerous in industries where the scale of organization has remained what it was in the days of Sismondi and Ricardo. These are industries in which the business-cycle hazard is small.[1] In the industries dominated by large-scale organization, the single capitalist-employer has ceased to be typical; though in mining, manufacturing, and construction work such men can be counted by the tens or the hundreds of thousands. In this field which particularly concerns us, because of the wide oscillations in business activity to which it is subject, quite a different form of business leadership has evolved.

The corporations, which now handle the bulk of large-scale business, are usually owned by a miscellaneous and shifting body of stockholders. The funds required for fixed investment are provided in some measure by these owners, but in large part by bondholders, who may or may not own shares as well as bonds. The immediate pecuniary hazards are borne by the shareholders; but ordinarily under provisions which limit their liability to loss of the sums which they have put into their shares, and under conditions which enable them to throw a large part of the business-cycle hazard upon the employees. The work of management is largely dissociated from ownership and financial responsibility. The stockholders delegate the super-

[3] See Chapter I, section iv, 3 and 10.
[1] See above in this chapter, section ii, 3.

vision of the corporation's affairs to a committee—the directors—and the directors turn over the task of administration to a set of general officers. The latter are paid fixed salaries, though they may receive in addition a percentage of the profits, or hold stock in their own right.

In such an organization it is difficult to find anyone who corresponds closely to the capitalist-employer. Certainly stockholders who take no part in managing the corporation beyond sending in their proxies to be voted at the annual meeting, do not fill the bill. Neither do directors who confine such attention as they may give the corporation's affairs to passing on questions of general policy, selecting officers, criticizing or approving reports, and the like. Finally, the general officers, dependent on the directors, remunerated largely if not wholly by salaries, and practicing among themselves an elaborate division of labor, have no such discretion and carry no such responsibility as the capitalist-employer. The latter, in fine, has been replaced by a "management," which includes the more active directors and high officials, often with the addition of one or two financial advisers, legal counsel, and large stockholders. Practically, it is this group which decides what the corporation shall do.

There are, however, many small and a few large corporations in which a single person dominates affairs. The stockholders elect his candidates to office, the directors defer to his judgment, the officials act as his agents. His position may be entrenched by outright ownership of a majority of the voting shares, or it may rest upon his influence with those who "own the control." In these "one-man" corporations, the theoretical division of responsibility and function becomes a legal fiction. Yet the position of such a captain of industry usually differs from the position of the old capitalist-employer, in that he furnishes a smaller proportion of the capital, assumes a smaller proportion of the detailed labor of superintendence, and shares the uncertainties and the profits with more associates. Instead of restricting, these limitations enhance his power; they mean that the individual who controls a corporation can determine the use of a mass of property and labor vastly greater than his own capital would permit.

Thus, while the corporate form of organization has produced a division of the leadership of business enterprises among several parties at interest, it has made possible greater centralization of power. The captains of finance and industry wield an influence increased by the

capital which their prestige attracts from thousands of investors, and sometimes augmented still further by working alliances among themselves.

Another development to be noted is the partial differentiation of a class of enterprisers who play an exceptionally active rôle in guiding economic activity—promoters. The promoter's special province is to find and bring to the attention of investors new opportunities for making money; new natural resources to be exploited, new processes to be developed, new products to be manufactured, new organizations of existing business enterprises to be arranged. But the typical promoter is merely an explorer who points out the way for fresh advances of the army of industry. When an enterprise of his imagination has been organized and begun operations, the promoter seldom retains the leadership for long. As permanent officers, men of more cautious temper and more systematic habits commonly take command.

3. The Rôle Played by Technical Experts.

The "labor of superintendence" which men like Richard Arkwright and Robert Owen undertook in the early nineteenth century involved oversight of industrial, as well as commercial and financial, plans and operations. But under the impetus of scientific discoveries and mechanical inventions, the technique of industrial processes rapidly became so elaborate that this combination of functions ceased to be feasible. A few, very few, men possessed the versatility and the energy to keep abreast both of the increasingly exacting business problems and of the increasingly exacting industrial problems. Almost with the start of the Industrial Revolution, there began a division of labor between the men skilled in designing and operating machinery, and the men skilled in dealing with the markets for wares and money. While the old capitalist-employer has evolved on the one side into a business management, he has evolved on the other side into a set of technical experts.

As early as the middle of the 18th century, the civil engineers in England had branched off from the military engineers. The civil engineers were concerned mainly with the construction of roads, bridges, aqueducts, canals, harbors, docks and lighthouses. From this parent stock, there were differentiated successively the mechanical, mining, marine, sanitary, gas, chemical, and electrical engineers. By applying the results and the methods of modern science to the

everyday work of the world, these men led that rapid advance in the making of goods which characterizes the present age. They became the chief directors of productive energies, on the technical side.

The prompt rise of the engineering professions must be ascribed to the relatively advanced stage of physical science, and the obvious advantage of applying its discoveries to industry. The social sciences lag far behind mechanics, chemistry and electro-physics in certainty and precision, and hence in the practical usefulness of the knowledge they convey. But in recent years they too have begun to yield results applicable to practice. At least as rapidly as they have grown ripe for the task, these sciences have been put to work by new groups of experts, who are gradually gaining something of the self-confidence and the recognition enjoyed for decades by engineers. Personnel managers are being trained to select and deal with employees, to study the requirements of different jobs, and to supervise working conditions, with the double object of increasing output and diminishing friction. Marketing—the art of winning and keeping customers—is becoming a field for specialists in advertising and selling. Business statisticians give advice on many phases of planning and current operations. "Scientific management" calls for a combination of so many kinds of expertness that perhaps it will contribute to the growth of half-a-dozen professions rather than one. Indeed, these developments are all so recent, so much in process, that one can be sure of little except that new professions are growing up which offer guidance to economic activity based on the still modest achievements of the social disciplines.

Thus a business management is now able to command supposedly expert advice in the direction of its affairs, not only from its old counsellors in law and accounting, but also from a bewildering array of talent versed in the sciences of nature and man. Perhaps the time is coming when the chief function of the business executive will be deciding whose advice to ask and what advice to accept, what experts to enroll in his staff and what to consult on occasion. If the multiplication of technical professions continues, that function itself may evolve into a profession.

In 1923, the National Industrial Conference Board made an effort to estimate the number of men in the United States who can fairly be "included in the category of those who plan, supervise and administer the business of the nation." As such it counted

major officials, managers, superintendents, technical engineers, designers, draftsmen, inventors, architects, chemists, assayers, metallurgists, and auditors, together with one-quarter of the number of foremen, overseers and inspectors in agriculture, mining, construction, trade, transportation and public service.

Even with this liberal definition of business and industrial guides, the Board found, on analyzing the census data for 1920, that only a million and a half persons could be included. This number is much smaller than the number of men engaged in business on their own account—some 10,000,000.[1] But the proportion of all persons having gainful occupations who are "administrators, supervisors and technical experts" has been rising steadily each decade; it stood at 1.25 per cent in 1870 and 3.80 per cent in 1920. And this percentage is decidedly higher in the large-scale industries subject to a considerable business-cycle hazard, than in small-scale industries like agriculture.[2]

While the technical experts who build upon the natural sciences know most about the making of goods and the technical experts who build upon social sciences are coming to know most about the managing of men, they remain for the most part merely advisers to the

[1] See above, section ii, 3.
[2] The chief results of this report are shown in the following table:

THE GAINFULLY OCCUPIED COMPARED WITH ADMINISTRATORS, SUPERVISORS AND TECHNICAL EXPERTS

THE UNITED STATES, 1920

	Total Persons Gainfully Occupied Thousands	Administrators, Supervisors, and Technical Experts Thousands	Percentage
Agriculture and animal husbandry	10,953	200[a]	1.83
Extraction of minerals	1,090	44	4.00
Manufacturing and mechanical industries	12,819	600	4.68
Transportation	3,064	105	3.42
Trade	4,243	229	5.39
Public service	770	34	4.41
Professional service	2,144	265[b]	12.36
Domestic and personal service	3,405	5	.14
Clerical occupations	3,127	30	.95
Total	41,614	1,510	3.63

[a] Rough approximation.
[b] Includes engineers and other technical persons.
See *Engineering Education and American Industry,* Special Report No. 25, National Industrial Conference Board, New York, 1923, p. 6.

captains of industry. Higher authority belongs to the business men. That is an inevitable result of economic organization on the basis of money economy in its present form. For the crucial factor in deciding the fate of a business enterprise is not the perfection of its mechanical processes, the excellence of its personnel work, or even the cleverness of its selling methods. All such excellencies contribute toward business success, and it is on this ground that the technical professions get their chance to share in the guidance of economic activity. But the final test is the ability of an enterprise as a whole to make profits. This fact entrenches the business men in their position as the authoritative leaders of the industrial army.

4. The Rôle Played by Lenders.

Business managements, however, must often submit their decisions to review by a higher court. Most enterprises need to borrow, and this fact gives the lenders an effective veto power over proposals which do not meet their approval.

Whenever an enterpriser applies to an individual capitalist to take an interest in some project, to a bank to discount his notes, or to the investing public to buy bonds, he must satisfy the lenders of his ability to pay the interest and to safeguard the principal. Even when the applicant can provide collateral security for the loan, and obviously when he cannot, the lender's decision depends largely upon his own judgment regarding the business prospects of the intended venture. To aid their officers in forming intelligent decisions, banks require applicants for loans to make statements of their financial position. In addition, the banks and the houses which grant mercantile credits subscribe to commercial agencies and maintain credit departments of their own, to collect and analyze information about the business prospects of their customers. Similarly, corporations which offer bonds or stocks for sale furnish circulars setting forth their financial records, the purposes for which money is being raised, and the anticipated profitableness of the extensions in view. Affidavits from certified public accountants, legal counsel, and consulting engineers are often appended to lend these statements greater force. Credit men perform a technical function for large lenders similar to the function performed by engineers for industrial companies.

This review of the projects of enterprises by lenders, then, is no perfunctory affair. Nor is its practical influence upon the guidance of

economic activity slight. There are always being launched more schemes than can be financed with the available funds. In rejecting some and accepting other schemes, the men of money are taking an important, though not a conspicuous, part in determining how labor shall be employed, what products shall be made, and what localities built up.

Not all lenders, however, are able to make intelligent decisions. The great mass of small investors, and not a few of the large, lack the experience, or ability, or time to discriminate wisely between profitable and unprofitable schemes. Many such folk put their funds into savings banks, rely upon the advice of friends who are better equipped, consult with their banks and lawyers, study the financial press, employ investment counsel, or follow what they suppose to be the lead of some conspicuous figure in high finance. Investors who lack independent judgment are peculiarly subject to the influence of feeling in the matters where feeling is a dangerous guide. The alternating waves of confidence and timidity which sweep over the market for securities are among the most characteristic phenomena of business cycles. Even those who are relied upon for advice are not wholly immune from the emotional contagion. Thus the guidance of economic activity by the investing class is only in part an intelligent review of plans by competent experts.

A more vigorous and more intelligent leadership is exercised by the larger capitalists. They excel the investing public not only in means of securing information and in business sagacity, but also in the efficiency with which they follow up their investments. The greatest lenders become perforce much more than lenders. Over the enterprises in which their fortunes and their prestige are at stake they keep close watch. On the highest levels of business success, indeed, the functions of the investor and the enterpriser merge into each other.

5. The Rôle Played by Consumers.

The court of last resort in deciding what goods shall be made is the whole body of consumers with money incomes to spend.

Since retail merchants, public utilities, personal service agencies, and professional men strive to supply what the public will buy, this rule applies immediately to the production of goods which gratify personal wants. Less strictly, the rule applies also to the production

of the materials from which consumers' goods are made, to the production of all producers' goods used in making consumers' goods, and even to the production of producers' goods used in making producers' goods. But the farther the remove from personal wants, the less is the control of consumers over demand and the larger the element of business discretion. Business managements and their technical advisers have considerable leeway in choosing what locations, what materials, what equipment and what services they shall use in production, and in what proportions they shall combine the several factors. Nor is the timing of business purchases rigidly bound by the timing of consumers' purchases. Thus the accurate form of statement is: production is guided by forecasts of what consumers will buy, supplemented by judgments concerning profitable methods of providing both consumers' goods and the endless variety of producers' goods which modern technique requires.

What proportion of current effort goes directly to the making of consumers' goods, and so falls most strictly under the rule of consumers' demand, we do not know. Of course, the preceding estimate that some such fraction as one-seventh of the total money income of the American people is "saved" on the average does not mean that six-sevenths of productive effort is spent directly upon consumers' goods. Still less does the estimate that the receipt of money incomes constitutes only a tenth of business transactions mean that nine-tenths of productive effort goes into making producers' goods. But where between these wide limits consumers' control fades into a mere sphere of influence we have no means of telling. The one certainty is that the development of modern technique directs an even larger amount of energy to the production of goods for making goods, and to the training of men to plan and supervise the directly productive efforts of other men.[1]

Even within the range where their control is most direct, consumers exert their authority as guides of production in a passive fashion. Usually they reveal what they want made only by buying briskly certain of the finished goods offered them, and by buying

[1] Mr. H. Gordon Hayes has estimated from the American Census of Occupations that about a quarter of "gainfully occupied" persons are engaged in the production of "durable goods"—including "all household furnishings and all household equipment that is made of wood or metal." He also estimates that about 4.25 per cent of the gainfully occupied are engaged in the construction and repair of factory buildings, machinery, railway roadway and rolling stock, and agricultural implements. "Production After the War," *Journal of Political Economy*, December, 1918, vol. xxvi, pp. 941-951.

other goods slowly. Producers follow the leads thus given as closely as they can, but also endeavor to stimulate demand and to direct it into profitable channels. Indeed, it seems that consumers often learn what they want by looking over the wares displayed in the shops. People are conscious of the general character of their needs, rather than of the specific goods which they desire. To decide precisely what foods, garments, furnishings, ornaments, or amusements one will buy is a difficult task. The picture given by so many economic treatises of buyers coming to market with their minds already made up about what goods they wish, and what price they are willing to pay at need for successive units of each kind, is an undeserved compliment to the mental energy of mankind. Even to canvass the market's offerings thoroughly takes more time and thought than the average shopper will devote to the task. So people follow an easier course, buying what they have bought before, what they see others using, or what advertisements and salesmen urge them to buy. The psychological categories important to the understanding of consumers' demand are habit, imitation and suggestion—not reflective choice. In particular, new products are seldom called for by consumers conscious of ungratified wants; they are pushed upon consumers by business enterprises, which often spend large sums in "educating the market," or "creating demand."

One reason why spending money is a backward art in comparison with making money was suggested early in this chapter;—the family continues to be the dominant unit of organization for spending money, whereas for making money the family has been superseded largely by a more highly organized unit. The housewife, who does a large fraction of the world's shopping, is not selected for her efficiency as a manager, is not dismissed for inefficiency, and has small chance of extending her sway over other households if she proves capable. She must buy so many different kinds of goods that she cannot become a good judge of qualities and prices, like the buyers for business houses. She is usually a manual laborer in several crafts, as well as a manager—a combination of functions not conducive to efficiency. From the sciences of most importance to consumption, physiology and psychology, she cannot get as much practical help as the business man can get from the more mature sciences of physics and chemistry. Above all, she cannot systematize all her planning on the basis of accounting like the business man; for while the dollar is a satisfactory unit for reckoning profits as well as costs, it is not a satisfactory unit

for expressing family welfare. Under these conditions, it is not surprising that what the world has learned in the art of consumption has been due less to the initiative of consumers, than to the initiative of producers striving to win a market for their wares.[2]

Yet with all their puzzles, consumers are in a strong market position. Their formal freedom to spend their money incomes as they like, combined with their massive inertia, keeps producers under pressure to solicit custom, to teach the public to want more goods and new goods. This task of stimulating demand is never done; for the march of technical improvement is ever increasing our capacity to produce, and before we have learned to distribute and to use what has just been added to our output, new advances have been scored. Hence the chronic complaint of business men that our industries are "over-built." The classical economists had logic of a sort on their side when they argued that general over-production is impossible in an exchange economy, because a supply of one kind of goods constitutes demand for goods of other kinds. But keener insight was revealed by Sismondi, and by Malthus who said,

> That an efficient taste for luxuries and conveniences, that is, such a taste as will properly stimulate industry, instead of being ready to appear at the moment it is required, is a plant of slow growth, the history of human society sufficiently shows.[3]

If anyone falters at reviewing the evidence which Malthus airily cites, he can try the conclusion by work-a-day business experience. Testimony abounds that the crucial difficulty in modern business lies in the "selling end," and the sincerity of this opinion is attested by the rapidly-increasing volume of selling costs.[4]

This pressure passively put by consumers upon producers is relaxed occasionally by the wasteful consumption of wars, and more frequently in booms, when the volume of demand is speciously magni-

[2] Compare Wesley C. Mitchell, "The Backward Art of Spending Money," *American Economic Review*, June, 1912, vol. ii, pp. 269-281; Henry Harap, *The Education of the Consumer*, New York, 1924 (a demonstration of how much a consumer needs to know), and Hazel Kyrk, *A Theory of Consumption*, Boston, 1923 (a demonstration that the economic theory of consumption is as laggard as the practice).

[3] T. R. Malthus, *Principles of Political Economy*, 2d ed., London, 1836, p. 321. For Sismondi's similar views, see above, Chapter I, section ii.

[4] For an effective presentation of the sellers' problem in modern business by an economist who has had practical experience, see George Binney Dibblee, *The Laws of Supply and Demand*, London, 1912, chapters x-xv.

fied for a while by business illusions. But most of the time the pressure is felt to be severe by the bulk of business enterprises. And that fact keeps consumers' demand the final arbiter of production, both in amount and in kind.

Back of consumers' demand, of course, stands the congeries of factors which control the distribution of income and the habits of spending. But this remark means merely that society's ways to-day are conditioned by its ways yesterday, coupled with its inability to make quick adjustments to altered conditions. To follow this fascinating line of analysis further would not be irrelevant, but the bare suggestion must suffice.

6. The Rôle Played by Government.

Concomitantly with the growth of money economy in Europe after the Middle Ages, the rôle which Government played in guiding economic activity became less active. The time had been when all men believed that the state should direct and regulate the economic life of its people for the good of the commonweal, quite as much as it should provide for the common defense. But as money economy extended, it began to appear that the merchant and the craftsman, in order to make money for themselves, must provide goods which the public wanted, and that in competing with each other for trade these private agents would keep down prices. The economic theory of *laissez faire,* as expounded by the Physiocrats, Adam Smith and the classical school, was an intellectual reflection of these accumulating facts of experience. By rationalizing the policy of private initiative in search of profits, which had developed spontaneously within the old scheme of governmental control, the economists expedited the transition in progress. Matters moved so fast, indeed, that the beginnings of reaction against extreme *laissez faire* appeared within the generation of Ricardo. The unrestricted pursuit of profits led at certain points to shocking ills, which Parliament intervened to check. England, and after her the world, in the fumbling fashion characteristic of social experimentation, presently attacked the problem of finding in detail what part of economic activity is best left to the guidance of business managements, and what part is best directed by the state. With that problem the leading nations are wrestling to-day as vigorously as ever. They seem to be no nearer a uniform and

satisfactory solution than they were in the transition days of Adam Smith; for, though progress is doubtless made, the problem keeps developing new difficulties.

Of course, the great argument for confiding economic activity to the Government's guidance is that Government aims at promoting public welfare, while business enterprises must make money. Government can consider what needs it is most important to satisfy and can assess the cost upon those most able to bear it; whereas business enterprises must consider what demands it is profitable to meet, and cannot serve those who cannot pay. Were that the whole story, Government would to-day play a more active rôle in economic life than it played in the era of Mercantilism. But most people prefer to buy what they like, rather than to pay for what the authorities think ought to be produced. And most men are skeptical of Government's efficiency in pursuing its aims. Hence the scope of Government activities varies from country to country and from time to time with changes in public opinion—not to say public sentiment—on these fundamental issues.

At present Government in the United States, including the federal, state and local authorities, constitutes one of the leading branches of production. Government owns a huge amount of property, employs about 9 per cent of all wage- and salary-earners, and pays about 8 per cent of the current income of individuals. These are post-war figures.[1]

The few services which are almost everywhere performed by Government are services in which management for profit is deemed incompatible with public welfare. Schools run for profit would not teach the children of the very poor; sanitary bureaus run for profit could not force their services upon communities which need attention. The longer list of services which in some places are assumed by Government and in others left to business enterprises fall mainly into four classes: undertakings like water supply, street cars, and railways which are most economically managed as monopolies, and are therefore open to the suspicion of practicing extortion; undertakings like the management of forests, in which the community is interested in conserving sources of supply over a longer period than competing business enterprises find it profitable to regard; undertakings like the

[1] The percentage for incomes is an average for the years 1919-21. The percentage for employees refers to 1921. Both figures are drawn from Dr. King's estimates. See his introductory chapter to Dr. Leven's *Income in the Various States*, National Bureau of Economic Research, New York, 1925.

improvements of rivers and harbors, the reclamation of waste lands, and the buildings of canals in which the prospects of profits are not sufficiently bright to attract the requisite amount of private capital; and undertakings like the salt, tobacco, mining and lottery monopolies of Europe, which are frankly exploited by Government for the sake of raising revenue.

Over a far wider field, Government affects the guidance of economic activity by trying to prevent the pursuit of private profit from clashing with public welfare. Factories are required to adopt expensive safeguards for the benefit of their employees or patrons; they are forbidden to employ the cheap labor of young children, to keep women at work more than eight hours a day, and so on, with many variations from country to country and state to state. Certain products are often forbidden, such as impure foods and drugs. So too, in this country, are business practices restrictive of competition.

Most economic regulations of Government are negative in character; but Governments sometimes attempt to direct business enterprise into undertakings which are believed by the majority of the moment to be socially advantageous, though unprofitable without assistance from the state. Protective tariffs upon imports, bounties upon the production of sugar, and ship subsidies are examples in point. In other cases, the Government provides producers with expert technical advice—exporters and farmers, for example.

Still more in general, the whole plan of raising public revenues and apportioning public expenditures, the methods of providing for the public defense and maintaining domestic order, the monetary system and even the form of political institutions, in short, everything Government is and does, influences the direction of economic activity. For the business economy is so flexible a form of organization that the prospects of profits, and therefore the direction of economic activity by private initiative, are affected by a thousand acts of Government done for other than economic ends. Indeed, it is mainly as a "disturbing factor" that Government figures in the theory of business cycles. Its own economic operations are perhaps freer from cyclical fluctuations than those of any industry.

7. The Alleged "Planlessness" of Production.

With technical experts to plan the processes of production, business experts to guide the making of money, lenders to review all

projects requiring large investments, Government to care for the public welfare, and with the whole buying public as a final arbiter, it may seem as if the business economy provides a staff and a procedure adequate to the task of directing economic activity, vast and intricate as that task is.

This impression is strengthened by observing that each class of guides is spurred to efficiency by hope of gain, and deterred from recklessness by fear of loss. The engineer who blunders is discharged, the enterpriser who blunders goes into bankruptcy, the lender who blunders loses his money, and even the administration which blunders may lose office—though that is less sure. Thus the guides who misdirect the industrial army are always being eliminated from the number of those who lead. On the other hand, those who succeed are always being promoted to posts of wider power.

Nor does all this apply merely to the leaders of economic activity. In theory, every adult is free to choose whatever lawful ways of making a money income he thinks wise, and to change as often as he likes. Thus every worker is supposed to have a modest share in directing production. In practice, of course, the range of occupations for which anyone can qualify is limited both by his native capacity and by his opportunities to get the requisite training and social connection. But the pressure which the business economy applies to the rank and file of the industrial army to develop efficiency in working and spending money is certainly not less severe than the pressure it applies to the captains. The older writers who expounded the philosophy of individualism emphasized the need of such pressure to make men work and save, at the same time as they argued that each man is the best judge of his own interests. Later writers, who credit men with less rationality than was the fashion a century ago, hold that economic individualism, involved in the current money economy, is a safeguard against failures to recognize where self-interest lies. Professor John Maurice Clark's remark on this head is whimsical only in part:

> Individualism may be regarded, not so much as the system calculated to get the utmost out of a people of extremely high intelligence, as the system in which human stupidity can do the least harm.[1]

[1] "The Socializing of Economics" in *The Trend of Economics*, edited by R. G. Tugwell, New York, 1924, p. 97.

With this powerful stimulation of individual efficiency, the business economy unites an opportunity for coöperation on a grand scale. By paying money prices, the leaders can enlist the aid of laborers who contribute work of all kinds, of expert advisers who contribute special knowledge, of landlords who contribute the uses of their property, and of investors who contribute the uses of their funds. And all these classes can be made to work in disciplined order toward the execution of a single plan. The fusing of incitements to individual efficiency with opportunity for wide coöperation is the great merit of the business economy.

That men like making and spending money as a way of organizing economic activity on the whole better than any other system they have yet practiced on a large scale, is indicated by history. The first section of this chapter suggests that the business economy grew out of the preferences of millions of men in successive generations in all quarters of the world. The medieval king and his tenants, the lord of the manor and his serfs, seem all to have gained by substituting monetary payments for the rendering of personal services. No one forced the housewife to give up making her own bread and her candles; no one forced the frontiersman to buy clothing in place of dressing in buckskin. It was because they preferred the new way of providing for their wants when the opportunity to choose was presented, that consumers patronized the retail shop selling factory products. So, too, banking could develop only as great numbers of people year after year found it useful. Not that the growth of money economy has involved no coercion, loss, and injustice—witness, for example, the tragic side of the enclosures which made possible farming for profit, the sufferings of peasants who could not learn the art of living on money, the oppressions exercised by money lenders, and the tragic struggle of the hand-loom weavers against the power loom. But broadly speaking, it seems clear that this feature of culture could have attained such general acceptance by the most advanced peoples of the world after so thorough a trial only because it seemed to meet their needs more adequately than the other forms of economic organization with which they have had experience.

Nevertheless, the business economy has obvious limitations as a system of organizing economic effort for the satisfaction of wants—limitations which must be noticed because they bear on the problem of business cycles.

1. The business economy provides for effective coördination of effort within each business enterprise, but not for effective coördination of effort among independent enterprises.

The two schemes of coördination differ in almost all respects. Coördination within an enterprise is the result of careful planning by experts; coördination among independent enterprises cannot be said to be planned at all; rather is it the unplanned result of natural selection in a struggle for business survival. Coördination within an enterprise has a definite aim—the making of profits; coördination among independent enterprises is limited by the conflicting aims of the several units. Coördination within an enterprise is maintained by a single authority possessed of power to carry its plans into effect; coördination among independent enterprises depends on many different authorities which have no power to enforce a common program, except so far as one can persuade or coerce others. As a result of these conditions, coördination within an enterprise is characterized by economy of effort; coördination among independent enterprises by waste.

In detail, then, economic activity is planned and directed with skill; but in the large there is neither general plan nor central direction. The charge that "capitalistic production is planless" therefore contains both an important element of truth and a large element of error. Apart from the transient programs of economic mobilization adopted under stress of war, civilized nations have not yet developed systematic plans for the sustenance of their populations; they continue to rely on the badly coördinated efforts of private initiative. Marked progress has been made, however, in the skill with which the latter efforts are directed, and also in the scale on which they are organized. The growth in the size of business enterprises controlled by a single management is a gain, because it increases the portion of the field in which close coördination of effort is feasible.

2. But the managerial skill of business enterprises is devoted to making money. If the test of efficiency in the direction of economic activity be that of determining what needs are most important for the common welfare and satisfying them in the most economical manner, the present system is subject to a further criticism. For, in nations where a few have incomes sufficient to gratify trifling whims and where many cannot buy things required to maintain their own efficiency or to give proper training to their children, it can hardly be argued that the goods which pay best are the goods most needed.

It is no fault of the individual business leaders that they take prospective profits as their own guide. On the contrary, they are compelled to do so; for the men who mix too much philanthropy with business soon cease to be leaders. But a system of economic organization which forces men to accept so technical an aim as pecuniary profit cannot guide their efforts with certainty toward their own ideals of public welfare. And Government can remedy this defect only in part.

3. Even from the point of view of business, prospective profit is an uncertain, flickering light. For profits depend upon two variables—on margins between selling and buying prices and on the volume of trade—related to each other in unstable fashion, and each subject to perturbations from a multitude of unpredictable causes. That the system of prices has its own order is clear; but it is not less clear that this order fails to afford certainty of business success. Men of long experience and proved sagacity often find their calculations of profit upset by conjunctures which they could not anticipate. Thus the business economy confuses the guidance of economic activity by interjecting a large element of uncertainty into business ventures.

4. The hazards to be assumed grow greater with the extent of the market and with the time which elapses between the initiation and the fruition of an enterprise. But the progress of industrial technique is steadily widening markets, and requiring heavier investments of capital for future production. Hence the share in economic leadership which falls to lenders, that of reviewing the various chances offered them for investment, presents increasing difficulties. And, as has been shown, a large proportion of these lenders, particularly of the lenders on long time, lack the capacity and training for the successful performance of such work.

These defects in the system of guiding economic activity and the bewildering complexity of the task itself allow the processes of economic life to fall into those recurrent disorders which constitute crises and depressions. To recognize this fact, however, is but the beginning of wisdom. Much patient analysis is required to discover just how these disorders arise, and why, instead of becoming chronic, they lead after a time to the return of prosperity.

VII. International Differences in Economic Organization.

1. The Uneven Development of Business Economy.

All the highly civilized nations of the world to-day have substantially the same form of economic organization. The business economy, sketched in this chapter with particular reference to the United States, prevails in Great Britain, France, Belgium, the Netherlands, Switzerland, the Scandinavian countries, Germany, Austria, and the great British colonies with white populations. A somewhat less mature stage of the money economy has been reached by the other European countries, by the Spanish- and Portuguese-speaking peoples of South America, and by the European colonists in South Africa. A still less mature stage prevails in the Orient, aside from Japan.[1]

In no country is the development of the business economy uniform over all sections. Everywhere the city dwellers carry on more of their activities by making and spending money incomes than the country folk. Nearly every country, even in the Orient, has its centers of large-scale industry and trade, and every country has its areas where production is organized rather on a family basis than on the basis of full-fledged business enterprises.

This uneven development of business economy influences the course run by business cycles in different parts of the world. It has been shown that alternations of prosperity and depression occur with increasing regularity as business economy extends in scope, and seem to arise more from economic processes and less from political or physical events.[2] It will be shown in the fourth chapter that the business cycles of countries which have highly developed business economies correspond to each other in timing and intensity rather closely; between countries where pecuniary organization is less mature the correspondence is distinctly less close. Finally, within every large country, there are measurable differences in the timing and the intensity of cyclical fluctuations in different sections—differences which appear to correlate with the differences in thoroughness of pecuniary organization.

[1] These statements are based upon rather vague and general impressions. Perhaps the grouping suggested is not quite fair in all cases; certainly it is subject to revision as conditions develop in the countries which we now count laggard.

[2] See section i, 4, of this chapter.

The history of the past two hundred years suggests that the international and sectional differences in economic organization are gradually becoming less. In all quarters of the globe business economy has been gaining ground. But the approach toward uniformity is slow, not only because the laggard peoples learn new habits deliberately, but also because the advanced peoples keep elaborating their pecuniary institutions. For as long a time as we can envisage, differences will maintain themselves on a scale sufficient to prevent business cycles from reaching in all quarters of the world even the measure of uniformity which they now possess among the central European nations, Great Britain, Canada and the United States.

2. The Proportion of the Workers Engaged in Farming.

A second set of conditions which make business cycles differ from country to country is found in the character of the occupations followed by their peoples. Of course, all the major industries are represented in every large population; but the proportions of the people engaged in agriculture, manufacturing, mining, transportation, trade, and the professions, vary widely. Because of the divergencies noted above in the business-cycle hazards to which various industries are subject,[1] it is pertinent to make international comparisons of occupation groups.

Unfortunately, occupations are classified in such unlike ways by different countries that close comparisons are out of the question. But the point of most importance—the percentage of male workers engaged in farming[2]—can be ascertained roughly for the countries whose business annals will be presented in a later chapter. The figures are given in Table 10. While the foreign data have been rearranged to fit the American census classification as nearly as may be, the percentages can be trusted only as showing the existence of very wide differences in dependence upon agriculture, and, by inference, upon other industries, particularly manufacturing.

England and Wales here stand in a class by themselves, with only one-ninth of their workers on farms. This does not mean that business cycles in England are more exempt from agricultural influences than business cycles in the European countries or the United

[1] See section ii, 3, of this chapter.

[2] Much better figures can be found for men than for women in several of the countries included.

States which have from a quarter to a third of their men in the fields, but that the harvests which affect English cycles are the harvests in

TABLE 10

PROPORTION OF GAINFULLY EMPLOYED MALES ENGAGED IN AGRICULTURAL PURSUITS IN VARIOUS COUNTRIES

Country	Date	Per Cent in Agriculture
China	1911	75.0[a]
India	1911	71.4
Russia	1897	61.6[b]
Japan	1908	58.5[c]
Union of South Africa	1911	55.4
Italy	1911	53.8[d]
Sweden	1910	49.1[e]
Austria	1910	45.5
Brazil	1920	45.0[d]
Canada	1911	41.0[f]
France	1911	40.0
United States	1910	35.8[f]
Argentina	1914	30.0[g]
Netherlands	1909	29.4
Australia	1911	29.0[h]
Germany	1907	28.3
England and Wales	1911	11.0[f]

NOTES:

[a] Estimated. See *China Year Book*, 1916, p. 3; *Journal of the American Asiatic Association*, 1911, vol. xi, p. 203; *Statesman's Year Book*, 1923, p. 771.

[b] Data for the entire Empire, including Siberia and the Caucasus.

[c] Percentage represents the proportion of all households engaged in agriculture to the total number.

[d] Males over 10 years of age.

[e] Males over 15 years of age.

[f] Males 10 years of age and over.

[g] Occupation data do not include workers in occupations not sufficiently specified, such as day-laborers, which tends to lower the percentage of agriculturally employed. The surprisingly low percentage is somewhat substantiated by the fact that 55 per cent of the population is classed as urban. A considerable part of the town and city dwellers consists of landlords and their dependents.

[h] "Exclusive of full-blooded aboriginals."

Compiled by Willard L. Thorp from censuses or official year books of the several countries, except in the cases of China and Russia. For the Chinese sources, see above note ([a]). The Russian data were obtained from the French population census of 1911, I, part iii, p. 176.

The occupation data in the various censuses have been regrouped to conform as nearly as may be to the category in the United States *Census of Occupations*, 1910, entitled "Agriculture, Forestry and Animal Husbandry," not including fishermen and oystermen. In order to make the records as comparable as possible, the data were taken from the census nearest to 1910 for each country.

the countries from which England buys the bulk of her foodstuffs and to which she sells the bulk of her exports.

At the other extreme are the great Oriental populations of China and India, followed by the Russian Empire and Japan. Several of the European countries in the list depend more upon farming than does the United States. More surprising are the low percentages for Argentina and Australia. Defects in the original data (particularly from Argentina, which omits from her occupation tables workers whose trades are not definitely specified) may be partly responsible for this result; but few North Americans realize how large a proportion of the people in these two southern lands live in cities.

3. Enterprise and Thrift.

Observers generally agree upon two temperamental differences which are revealed in the business behavior of the foremost commercial nations. The French are held to show less business enterprise than the Americans (who are inclined to credit themselves with preeminence in this quality), or the English, or the Germans. Their railways could not be built without a state guarantee of dividends; their merchant marine relies upon bounties; their great credit companies, founded largely to aid in establishing new enterprises, have gone over mainly to the less hazardous business of accepting deposits and handling investments for customers; their private banks are concerned chiefly with transactions in foreign exchange and short-time credits. The Frenchman seems to have no great fondness for the game of business. He aims to secure a competency by the thrifty conduct of his affairs along conservative lines, then to retire and invest his accumulations in *rentes*. It may be largely for this reason that the cyclical fluctuations in French business are relatively narrow in scope, and seldom marked by severe crises.[1]

On the other hand, the French are believed to surpass Americans, English, and even Germans in thrift. In the years preceding the war, France seemed to be displacing England as the world's greatest lender. The relative lack of domestic business enterprise, combined with an enormous aggregate of small savings, provided each year hundreds of millions of francs which sought investment in foreign securities. And in the selection of their investments the French preferred what they believed to be a conservative policy. Occasionally they might buy freely of speculative stocks, like "Kaffirs"; but the bulk of their sav-

[1] Compare K. Wiedenfeld, "Das Persönliche im Modernen Unternehmertum," *Schmoller's Jahrbuch für Gesetzgebung*, 1910, pp. 229-233,

ings went into government obligations, high-grade railway and industrial bonds, or into shares long established as dividend payers.[2]

It would be easy to elaborate by pointing out various contrasts between the business traits commonly believed to characterize the North and the South Americans, the Japanese and the Chinese, or the Russians and the Scandinavians. Nor can it be doubted that whatever differences exist among national temperaments have their bearing upon the whole economic life of the peoples in question. But such elaboration would not sensibly promote the present inquiry. For, after showing in the fourth chapter what relations exist among business cycles in different parts of the world, we shall concentrate attention upon the United States, England, France, and Germany. And about the differences in their business traits what has been said will suffice.

4. Monetary and Banking Systems.

Before the Great War it was thought that all the commercial nations of the world would soon have monetary systems of the same type. One country after another had gone over to the single gold standard, with supplementary use of silver coins, and of paper money issued by the Government, by the banks, or both. China was the greatest nation remaining on the silver basis; there were no bimetallic standards, and irredeemable paper standards seemed to be rare episodes. While the war produced wild confusion in monetary systems and forced many of the European nations to suspend specie payments, it now seems probable that within a few years the earlier uniformity will be restored in large measure. If so, the old facility of international transactions will return, and the financial bonds which connect the business fortunes of the great commercial nations will become closer than they have been since 1914—unless non-business forces again intervene to prevent.

Banking systems, also, had been growing more alike before the war, as various countries strove to adapt features which had succeeded elsewhere to their peculiar needs. The last great step in this direction was the establishing of the Federal Reserve System by the

[2] Compare, for example, A. Neymarch, *French Savings and Their Influence*, pp. 163-181; publications of the National Monetary Commission (Senate Document No. 494, 61st Congress, 2d Session).

United States in 1914—a measure which introduced a modified form of centralization into a system theretofore composed of some 29,000 independent banks. But banking systems and banking usages had never attained such similarity as characterized monetary systems. The difference of chief moment to the student of business cycles is between the preponderant use of bank checks in making payments among the Anglo-Saxon communities, and the relatively slight use of checks in other countries. But it should also be recalled that outside of Europe, North America and Australia, the use of banking facilities is confined mainly to the commercial centers and so touches the bulk of the people only by indirection.

5. Government's Share in Directing Economic Activity.

Finally, there are considerable differences even among those modern nations whose pecuniary institutions are most alike, in the share which central and local Governments take in directing economic activities.

Partly because of limitations placed by constitutional law upon the powers of Government, partly it would seem because of a temperamental restiveness under control, Americans have made fewer and less bold experiments in municipal operation of public utilities, or in state operation of railways, telegraphs, telephones, mines, and the like, than have the Germans, French, or British. Perhaps, however, this difference is growing less decade by decade. Certainly, the rise of public commissions as agencies for regulating privately-owned enterprises has given the federal, state and municipal Governments of the Union a share in directing several branches of business.

While later chapters will show that all the international differences in economic organization and practice which have been pointed out possess some significance, by far the most important is the uneven development of business economy. There are, indeed, close organic relations between this uneven development and the proportion of men engaged in agriculture, the prevalence of an enterprising spirit in business affairs, the use of banking facilities, and perhaps even the share which Government takes in directing economic activity. Yet all these differences together account only for a part of the divergencies which the fourth chapter will show among the business annals of various countries. Another part must be ascribed to factors of a

political or physical type. About the relative importance of the forces which produce divergencies among business cycles, however, and about their interactions, our knowledge is meager. Perhaps we are overlooking forces which will some day be found to play dominating rôles. But the way to hasten the day of fuller understanding is to make the best use we can of our present insights, imperfect though they are.

VIII. Conclusion.

1. The *Raison d'Etre* of Chapter II.

Taken one at a time, most of the theories of business cycles reviewed in Chapter I seem plausible, not to say convincing. Certainly each theory, this time without exception, illuminates some angle of the problem. Taken all together, the theories render a different service—one which is welcome only to the man who has the courage and time to enter upon a thorough investigation. They show that business cycles are congeries of diverse fluctuations in numerous processes—physical, psychological, and economic. Indeed, upon reflection the theories figure less as rival explanations of a single phenomenon than as complementary explanations of closely related phenomena. The processes with which they severally deal are all characteristic features of the whole. These processes not only run side by side, but also influence and (except for the weather) are influenced by each other. Thus the diversity of explanations, which at first seems confusing, becomes an aid toward envisaging the complex character of the problem.

Complexity is no proof of multiplicity of causes. Perhaps some single factor is responsible for all the phenomena. An acceptable explanation of this simple type would constitute the ideal theory of business cycles from the practical, as well as from the scientific, viewpoint. But if there be one cause of business cycles, we cannot make sure of its adequacy as an explanation without knowing what are the phenomena to be explained, and how the single cause produces its complex effects, direct and indirect. Neither on the single-cause hypothesis, nor on the hypothesis of multiple causes, are we equipped to deal with the problem of causation until we have learned what are the processes characteristic of business cycles, and how these processes are related to one another. Chapter I indicated what the leading proc-

esses are. The way to discover their relations is to study the development and the functioning of the economic organization within which business cycles run their courses. Hence the sketch of the business economy drawn in this chapter.

Few writers upon business cycles deem such an introduction necessary. None of them question that most processes of modern life, social and political as well as economic, have some share in the alternations of prosperity and depression. But most investigators take the complexities for granted, credit themselves and their readers with a knowledge of economic organization sufficient for their purpose, and concentrate upon demonstrating the source from which comes the dominant impetus to cyclical fluctuations. A theorist who has satisfied himself upon that central issue is prone to adduce only the evidence and arguments which seem to prove his explanation, spending little time upon processes which adjust themselves to his ruling cause. A skillful exposition of this type is likely to convince the reader also, unless he is acquainted with one or several equally confident demonstrations that some other cause is primarily responsible. In the latter case, the reader must give up the puzzle, or choose among the explanations on inadequate grounds, or study for himself the interrelations among the processes exploited by his various authorities.

Our debt to men who have written, and even thought, in this summary fashion is heavy. It profits us less to dwell upon their lack of circumspection than to dwell upon their positive achievements. When the problem of business cycles was first attacked it was inevitable that the hypotheses offered would be inadequately worked out. The complexities of the problem, the possibility of making numerous hypotheses, had to be discovered. Contemporaries who still follow out a single line of causation without careful examination of other lines, may seem a trifle quaint; yet they too may add new discoveries to the growing stock of knowledge, or new ideas on which to work. We must choose, however, between following their methods and making use of their results. If we see a promise of usefulness in the seemingly divergent conclusions reached by several different groups of investigators, we must set about our own constructive work with more care than our guides deemed necessary.

2. A Summary.

Now that the sketch of economic organization is completed, we may sum up the leading results in form for future use.

Business cycles do not become a prominent feature of economic experience in any community until a large proportion of its members have begun to live by making and spending money incomes. On the other hand, such cycles seem to appear in all countries when economic activity becomes organized predominantly in this fashion. These observations suggest that there is an organic connection between that elaborate form of economic organization which we may call "business economy," and recurrent cycles of prosperity and depression.

As a money economy attains high development, consumption continues to be carried on mainly by families; but production comes to be carried on mainly by a new unit—the business enterprise. Further, there is evidence that business cycles are most pronounced in those industries which are dominated by full-fledged business enterprises, and that within these industries they affect large enterprises more seriously than small ones.

According to the best available estimates, the man-made equipment which American workers now use has an aggregate value of not far from three years' current income. This equipment includes not only buildings, transportation systems, factories, and implements of all kinds, but also roads, the products and merchandise on their way toward consumers, and the personal effects owned by individuals. The possession of this stock of accumulated wealth makes it possible for the population to consume for a time more than it is producing. Every year the population eats about the same amount of food per capita; but the expenditure upon maintaining and extending the equipment used for business purposes need not be, and in practice is not, kept so nearly uniform. Thus modern industrial methods and modern business organization in combination open the door to wide cyclical fluctuations in at least one important field of economic activity.

To prosper, even to survive, business enterprises must make profits —not every year, but on the average. Hence the making of profits is of necessity the controlling aim of business management. The industrial processes which enterprises carry on in producing, transporting, storing, and distributing goods are means toward this end.

In other phrases: industry is subordinated to business, the making of goods to the making of money.

Yet the quantity of goods handled within a given period is a matter of primary concern, even from the strictest business viewpoint. Profits are the difference between the prices which an enterprise pays for all the things it must buy, and the prices which the enterprise receives for all the things it sells. Thus profits depend upon the physical volume of goods bought and sold, as well as upon the margins between buying and selling prices.

The prices of the innumerable kinds of goods made and consumed in a business economy constitute an orderly system. The active agency in maintaining the relations among the various parts of this system is the quest for profits itself. Business men are ever looking for opportunities which promise a large volume of trade at wide price margins. Where the margins seem wide and demand active, new enterprisers crowd in if they can, and their competition presently raises buying and lowers selling prices. When margins seem narrow, new investments are avoided, and such of the old investments as can be withdrawn are shifted to more promising fields. In consequence, buying prices are likely to fall and selling prices to rise. The result of these shiftings of investment, which are always in progress, is not to make uniform the percentage margins on which all classes of goods are handled; but so to adjust buying and selling prices that the net price margins, together with the volume of trade which can be handled with a given investment, will hold out similar prospects of profits in all branches of business open to newcomers. This uniformity never is attained in fact; but the plus and minus departures from the prevailing level of prospective profits are the guides which business men try to follow in planning investments.

In our analysis of business cycles, then, we must recognize that profit making is the central process among the congeries that constitute the activities of a business economy. Weather conditions count in so far as they affect profits, so do emotional aberrations, so do the production and consumption of consumers' goods, and so do a thousand other factors. On the other hand, the prospects of making profits react upon all these other processes, in so far as they are affected by human behavior. Even the factors which we classify as political or social rather than economic are influenced in varying measure by the profitableness of business. But, of course, attention must be concentrated upon the relations among the processes which

are of outstanding importance as affecting and affected by prospective profits. In this chapter, an effort is made to get as good estimates as possible of the relative magnitude of a few fundamental factors.

The elaborate exchanges required by the system of "production for the use of others and acquisition for the use of self" are managed in relatively small part by the use of coin and paper money, and mainly by the use of credit instruments. In the United States it seems that something like 85 per cent of payments are made by check. Deposit currency is adapted to the varying activity of business, because both its volume and its rate of turnover rise and fall with prosperity and depression.

The goods produced by business enterprises are distributed among the community by the continual paying and spending of money incomes. Of the several income streams, wages and salaries is much the largest, averaging over one-half of total money income. Profits ranks second, and is approximately equal to dividends, interest, and rents put together. From the money incomes received by individuals, upwards of 60 per cent seems to be spent at retail shops in average years; the rest is distributed among various channels, of which rent is the most important.

It is characteristic of the business economy that the process of providing goods to meet human needs gives rise to business transactions which far exceed current income. Recent data indicate that the total volume of payments in the United States is perhaps ten times the aggregate money incomes of all individuals, or five times the transactions involved in both receiving and spending personal incomes.

A not inconsiderable fraction of current income is "saved" every year—that is, expended in ways which increase the community's stock of fairly durable consumers' goods or increase its capacity to produce future income. The best available estimate for the United States, which is none too certain, makes this fraction average about one-seventh of current income. Two-fifths of the saving is done not by individuals, but by business enterprises. The indications are that the accumulated wealth of the United States (excluding the value of land) is equal to the savings of some 20 to 30 years.

An economic organization which distributes incomes in money, and lets the recipients spend the money in any way they like, makes extremely difficult the task of adjusting the supply of each kind of goods to the profit-paying demand for it. To cope with this task of directing production in detail, the business economy has evolved

an elaborate system. Business managements play the most active rôle in guiding production; but they have the assistance of technical experts of various sorts, and they must submit most of their important projects to review by lenders of credit or investment funds. In the last resort consumers determine what shall be made, by buying certain products freely and others sparingly; their choices, however, can be and are influenced in considerable measure by business enterprises, and business managements decide the technical question what producers' goods, direct and indirect, they had best use in making consumers' commodities.

As the money economy developed in Europe, the share which Government took in guiding economic activity gradually shrank. The turning point seems to have come in the 17th century in England, early in the 18th century in France and late in the 18th century in Germany. Governments now render certain services which the community will not confide to commercial exploitation—a list that varies considerably from place to place—and for the rest endeavor to check methods of making money which are deemed incompatible with public welfare. Aside from schemes of economic mobilization during wars, no country has developed a comprehensive plan for the direction of its economic energies. The scheme of guidance by business managements, technical experts, lenders, and consumers, which has been evolved in the later stages of the money economy, is confined within the limits of single business enterprises, or groups of enterprises dominated by a common control. The relations among the undertakings of independent money-makers are not planned, but are established and altered by the mutual competition of these enterprises—in which anyone who can command the necessary capital is free to join, and in which some enterprisers win more or less monopolistic advantages. Business cycles are among the unplanned results of this scheme of organization.

Business economy nowadays prevails in much the same form among the nations in which Euro-American culture is highly developed. It seems also to be making headway in other countries; but in the Orient, aside from Japan, and in less civilized regions, it has not reached the point at which business cycles attain marked significance. Even among the great commercial nations there are minor differences in economic organization, respecting such matters as the percentage of the population engaged in farming, the relative development of thrift and enterprise, monetary and banking habits,

and the economic policy of Government. These differences combine with a multitude of non-economic factors to prevent the business cycles of any two countries from being precisely alike.

3. The Conception of Equilibrium.

To repeat once more: by showing that business cycles are intricate complexes made up of diverse fluctuations in numerous activities, Chapter I forced us to seek some orderly scheme for conceiving the relations of these processes to each other. The scheme which Chapter II presents centers on the pursuit of money profits. All the "causes" of business cycles stressed by the theories reviewed owe whatever influence they exert upon economic activity to their bearing upon profits, and the like must hold concerning any other "causes" which future investigation reveals. Thus we have a pattern to follow in future chapters, a pattern which should enable us to discuss the wide diversity of processes involved in business cycles without falling into confusion.

A further device for keeping order in the discussion is to treat the detailed problems marked out by our pattern as having all the same form—problems of equilibrium. The conception that business cycles consist in rhythmical ruptures and restorations of balance in some fundamental process is explicitly presented by several of the theories reviewed, and may be read into others. Can we make use of this idea?

Doubtless it was a mechanical analogy which gave its vogue to the notion of economic equilibria. Everyone admits that analogies, though often most suggestive in scientific inquiries, are dangerous guides. The usefulness of the analogy in question was greatest and its dangers least when economists were treating what they called "static" problems. Such problems can be given a quasi-mechanical character, for they are not taken from life, but made in an inquirer's head to suit his purposes, and mechanical analogies are appropriate to mechanical problems. But the problems of business cycles are the opposite of "static." If we are to conceive of them in terms of an equilibrium of mechanical forces, we must conceive of an equilibrium among numerous forces which are constantly changing, changing at different rates, and influencing one another as they change. Perhaps an ingenious person who thought the game worth while might design a mechanical contrivance which would work somewhat after the fashion of cyclical business fluctuations. If he did so, however, most

economists would find his machine so difficult to understand, and the real similarity of its operations to business processes so uncertain, that they would leave its intricacies to the pleased contemplation of the inventor.

Yet there is a different conception of equilibrium which may help us—the equilibrium of a balance sheet, or better, of an income and expenditures statement. Such a statement has nothing to do with mechanical forces, and that is a safeguard against false analogies. It deals with pecuniary quantities, and they are genuine elements in our problem. It sums up the results of numerous processes which concern us, through periods of time which we can divide according to their business characteristics. More than that, the statements for successive periods of time link into each other, as they should do for our purposes. The statement for one period shows what has happened to certain items included in its predecessor, and shows also certain items the disposition of which will appear in its successor. Finally, the balance which is struck is really a device for finding how much the expenditures and the receipts are out of balance. The difference between these two aggregates of items is put down on the income side as profit or loss, a positive or a negative sum. That feature, too, serves our needs. We have no more warrant for assuming in advance that business processes "tend" to maintain an equilibrium than to assume that they "tend" to get out of balance. What we need when we employ the concept of equilibrium, is a device for showing the relations between the aggregates which stand opposite each other in various processes, as expenditures and receipts stand opposite each other in bookkeeping. Having found equality, or having found one set of items in excess of the other, our problem is to trace the consequences. It is not a foregone conclusion that these consequences will always be of the sort which tend to restore a balance, any more than losses suffered by a business enterprise one year tend to give it profits in the year following. Yet we know that the modern business system does not function smoothly when the aggregates of the opposing items in certain pairs get too much out of balance.

To indicate the uses of this conception of equilibrium in discussing business cycles is to review again the leading conclusions of the present chapter. The central proposition is the one to which the statement of receipts and expenditures applies directly: business enterprises cannot "carry on" unless in the long run their incomes exceed their outlays by a satisfactory margin of profits. In order that this relation

(which the bookkeeper expresses as a balance) may be maintained, an indefinite number of other changing aggregates must be kept in due relation to each other. For example, the selling prices of each of the million kinds of goods produced and sold must be adjusted severally to their costs of production. So, too, the physical quantities of each kind of goods turned out must be adjusted severally to the physical quantities that can be sold. That payments may be made, the quantity and turnover of coin, paper money, and deposit currency must be adjusted to the pecuniary volume of trade, or the pecuniary volume of trade to the circulating medium. Also, the means of payment must be disbursed to buyers as money incomes, or as loans, in proportions duly adjusted to the value of goods sent to market. To provide for expansion of industrial equipment, a portion of the income and loans must be saved and invested, but that proportion must not be excessive.

So we might go on indefinitely, translating perhaps all of the theories of business cycles into terms of equilibrium. Clearly that form of statement has advantages, and may be resorted to freely without danger, if we remember that the equilibria in mind are akin to the balances of bookkeeping rather than to the equilibria of mechanics. Our balances take place in time, over periods which vary from case to case, and which are seldom definite. The balances need not be exact; business plans seek to provide liberal factors of safety; if results fall out in the neighborhood of expectations, all is well. When balances fail persistently by wide margins for a considerable period of time, men can restore them in many cases by writing certain constituents up or writing them down. For business balances usually combine both estimates of certain values and records of certain transactions; they look to the future as well as the past; they are used to control plans quite as much as to register results; their reliability depends upon judgments not less than on arithmetic.

CHAPTER III.

THE CONTRIBUTION OF STATISTICS.[1]

I. The Current Distinction Between Theoretical and Statistical Work.

The review of current theories in Chapter I barely mentions the type of work upon business cycles which is most characteristic of the present and seems most promising for the future—analysis of statistical data. A few of the theorists—notably Henry L. Moore—make skilled and elaborate use of quantitative methods, and almost all cite statistical evidence upon occasion. But most theories of business cycles are still built up by methods which would have seemed familiar to Sismondi and Ricardo.

On the other hand, there has recently appeared a group of business-cycle statisticians who as yet have sought, not to construct general theories, but to establish more precisely the facts concerning cyclical fluctuations in particular economic processes. By their detailed researches, the statistical workers are building up a literature more like the current literature of the natural sciences than like that of economic theory. It contains few treatises, but a multitude of technical papers; it is mathematical in form and empirical in spirit; it deals with restricted problems, lays stress upon measurements, and aspires to prediction.

Between these two groups of workers, the theorists and the statisticians, there has been less communion than their mutual interests require. Many of the statisticians pay little heed to current theories of business cycles, and many of the theorists make little use of statistical methods. A similar divergence of outlook, associated with a similar division of labor, seems not uncommon in modern science. Experimentalists and pure theorists often have difficulty in understanding each other; but in the long run each group provides grist for the other's mill, and scientific progress is a joint product of the

[1] In writing this chapter, I have had generous help from the Staff of the National Bureau, particularly from Dr. Frederick C. Mills, and from the Directors, particularly from Professor Allyn A. Young.

two lines of attack upon the unknown. Such must prove to be the case in work upon business cycles.

Statistical analysis affords the surest means of determining the relations among and the relative importance of the numerous factors stressed by business-cycle theories. In turn, rational hypotheses are the best guides of statistical research, and theoretical significance is the ultimate test of statistical results. Aside from the limitations of investigators or of their resources, the line commonly drawn between statistical and theoretical work has no justification.

II. Development of the Statistical Approach.

1. Why the Early Writers Upon Business Cycles Made Slight Use of Statistics.

A promising beginning of statistical work upon social problems had been made in England by contemporaries of Sir Isaac Newton. The most conspicuous figure in the group, Sir William Petty, dealt with "Political Arithmetick," sought to express himself in "Terms of *Number, Weight,* or *Measure,*" and to "bottom" his discourses upon quantitative "Observations or Positions" which are "either true, or not apparently false . . . and if they are false, not so false as to destroy the Argument they are brought for."[1] But political arithmetic had not prospered greatly. "Observations . . . expressed by *Number, Weight,* or *Measure*" were scarce, and the "Positions," "either true, or not apparently false," upon which Petty's followers bottomed their discourses sometimes led to contradictory conclusions. While Adam Smith was writing the *Wealth of Nations,* Dr. Richard Price was proving that the population of England and Wales had decreased near a quarter since the Revolution, and Arthur Young was proving that the population had increased. It is not surprising that Adam Smith had "no great faith in political arithmetic," and made sparing use of it in expounding "the obvious and simple system of natural liberty."[2]

Yet it is an exaggeration to picture the generation which developed the first theories of business cycles as virtually destitute of

[1] From the preface to *Political Arithmetick,* 1690. See *The Economic Writings of Sir William Petty,* edited by Charles H. Hull. Cambridge, 1899; vol. i, pp. 244, 245.

[2] *The Wealth of Nations,* Cannan's edition, vol. ii. pp. 36 and 184.

significant statistics. One has but to look into such volumes as George Chalmers' *Estimate of the Comparative Strength of Great Britain*, 1782, Sir Frederick M. Eden's *State of the Poor*, 1797, the second edition of Malthus' *Essay on the Principle of Population*, 1803, or Thomas Tooke's *Thoughts and Details on the High and Low Prices of the Last Thirty Years*, 1823, to assure himself that men who had an aptitude for that type of inquiry could gather and use critically a considerable quantity of data covering a considerable range of problems. And the books mentioned are but prominent examples of a type of work which was rapidly increasing in volume, improving in quality, and gaining public support. In 1801 the first census of Great Britain was taken, and in 1832 a Statistical Department was added to the Board of Trade. How voluminous and how varied were the statistical materials which had been quietly accumulating in official sources between these two dates was shown in 1833, when John Marshall published his quarto *Digest of all the Accounts Relating to the Population, Productions, Revenues, Financial Operations, Manufactures, Shipping, Colonies, Commerce, etc., etc., of the United Kingdom, diffused through more than 600 volumes of Journals, Reports, and Papers presented to Parliament during the last Thirty-five Years.*

It is also a mistake to think of the early nineteenth century as altogether lacking in statistical technique. In *Chronicon Preciosum*, published in 1707 and more than once reprinted, Bishop Fleetwood had shown how to treat changes in the purchasing power of money on a quantitative basis. A definite plan for making index numbers of prices had been put before the Royal Society by Sir George Schuckburg-Evelyn in 1798.[3] William Playfair had used graphic methods of presenting time series in the successive editions of his *Commercial and Political Atlas, representing, by Means of Stained Copper-plate Charts, the Progress of the Commerce, Revenues, Expenditures, and Debts of England, during the whole of the Eighteenth Century* (1786, 1787, and 1801). Joseph Fourier had developed harmonic analysis in a memoir crowned by the *Academie des Sciences* in 1812.[4] Most important of all, Laplace had published his *Essai Philosophique sur les Probabilités* in 1814. In this charming essay, the most celebrated mathematician of the age summed up the analytic methods de-

[3] "An Account of Some Endeavors to Ascertain a Standard of Weight and Measure," *Philosophical Transactions of the Royal Society of London*, 1798. Part I, art. viii, pp. 132-186, especially pp. 175, 176.

[4] *Théorie des mouvements de la chaleur dans les corps solides.*

veloped by his predecessors and himself, and proposed their use in dealing with social problems.

> Let us apply to the political and social sciences (he wrote) the method founded upon observations and calculus, a method which has served us so well in the natural sciences.

And to that end, Laplace urged that the compilation of social statistics be made systematic. It is highly important to keep in every branch of

> public administration an accurate record of the effects produced by the various measures taken, which are so many experiments tried on a large scale by governments.[5]

Thus it is an over-simple explanation to ascribe the neglect of measurements by early business-cycle theorists wholly to the lack of pertinent data or to the immaturity of statistical technique. Had they taken the line suggested by Laplace, these writers might have used and added to the available data; they might have learned and developed the analytic methods which had been suggested. But like other economists of the day, most writers upon crises had an easier, a quicker, and, as it seemed to them, a more effective method of working. Observers had no trouble in conceiving plausible explanations of crises, and they could rapidly expand their conjectures into imposing theories by selecting from the facts generally known those which accorded with their leading ideas. In this way they avoided a host of doubts and difficulties which would crop up if they tried to bottom their work upon the stubborn data of statistics. With the contemporary writers of economic treatises, they might admit, when discussing problems of method, that their "deductive" reasoning required "inductive verification"; but they somewhat easily excused themselves from going through the second and more arduous operation.[6] Perhaps still more important is the fact that writers who practiced the "deductive" method were apt to formulate their problems in ways which raised obstacles to "inductive verification,"—obstacles

[5] *Essai Philosophique,* 6th ed., Paris, 1840, p. 135.

[6] Note, for example, the difference between the procedure which John Stuart Mill recommended in his *System of Logic,* 1843, and the procedure which he practiced in *The Principles of Political Economy,* 1848. In but few chapters does Mill really carry out the "concrete-deductive method."

which might have been avoided by a different approach.[7] Statistical method could not develop its full efficiency so long as it was called in only at the end of an inquiry, and asked to answer questions it had no share in framing.

2. The Growth of Statistical Technique.

The mathematical statisticians of the early 19th century did not enter the economic field. The social phenomena to which Laplace applied the theory of probabilities in his *Essai Philosophique* were such matters as the credibility of the evidence given by witnesses, the decisions of assemblies, mortality, and the average duration of marriages. Adolphe Quetelet dealt with physical, intellectual and moral qualities in his two volumes *Sur l'Homme,* 1835. Henry Thomas Buckle sought to introduce statistical method into historical research, holding in his *History of Civilization in England* (1857 and 1861) that human actions are ruled by laws as fixed and regular as those which govern the physical world; but that these laws can be discovered only by a survey of the facts so comprehensive that disturbing factors will cancel one another. Meanwhile, the chief contributions to statistical technique continued to come from mathematicians proper. Gauss published the method of least squares in 1823. In 1837, Poisson made the theory of probability more applicable to social problems by showing how the curve of distribution is modified

[7] Consider Ricardo's contention that it is impossible to determine "the value of a currency" by its "relation, not to one, but to the mass of commodities."

"To suppose that such a test would be of use in practice," Ricardo argued, "arises from a misconception of the difference between price and value.

"The price of a commodity is its exchangeable value in money only.

"The value of a commodity is estimated by the quantity of other things generally for which it will exchange.

"The price of a commodity may rise while its value falls, and *vice versa.* A hat may rise from twenty to thirty shillings in price, but thirty shillings may not procure as much tea, sugar, coffee, and all other things, as twenty shillings did before, consequently a hat cannot procure so much. The hat, then, has fallen in value, though it has increased in price.

"Nothing is so easy to ascertain as a variation of price (*sic*), nothing so difficult as a variation of value; indeed, without an invariable measure of value, and none such exists, it is impossible to ascertain it with any certainty or precision." ("Proposals for an Economical and Secure Currency," 2d ed., 1816. Ricardo's *Works,* edited by J. R. McCulloch, p. 401.)

Nowadays, economists apply to money Ricardo's definition, "The value of a commodity is estimated by the quantity of other things generally for which it will exchange," and proceed to the construction of price indexes. Then they can compare the price fluctuations of single commodities with this general index, and approximate Ricardo's conception of measuring variations in value, without having an "invariable measure of value."

by dropping the assumption of equal *a priori* probabilities at every trial, and directed attention to "the law of great numbers."

The only economist concerned with the theoretical uses of statistics in this period was Augustin Cournot. In considering the old problem of variations in value, he made a casual suggestion that "Here, as in astronomy, it is necessary to recognize *secular* variations, which are independent of *periodic* variations." More important was Cournot's discussion of demand curves. While his own dealings with this subject were confined to mathematical analysis "by means of an indeterminate symbol," he emphasized the need of statistical inquiry into the relations between demand (D) and price (p). In this connection, he suggested the technique by which statistical laws defining the relationships between economic variables may be discovered.

> Since so many moral causes capable of neither enumeration nor measurement affect the law of demand (he wrote), it is plain that we should no more expect the law to be expressible by an algebraic formula than the law of mortality, and all the laws whose determination enters into the field of statistics, or what is called social arithmetic. Observation must therefore be depended on for furnishing the means of drawing up between proper limits a table of the corresponding values of D and p; after which, by the well-known methods of interpolation or by graphic processes, an empiric formula or a curve can be made to represent the function in question; and the solution of problems can be pushed as far as numerical applications.[1]

Yet Cournot made no use of statistical data in his *Theory of Wealth*, and in his *Exposition de la Théorie des Chances et des Probabilités* (published in 1843), he did not apply the theory to a much wider range of social problems than Laplace had considered in 1814. It was left for W. Stanley Jevons to give the first powerful impetus to statistical work in economic theory.[2]

[1] *Researches into the Mathematical Principles of the Theory of Wealth.* Translated by Nathaniel T. Bacon. New York, 1897, pp. 25, 47-49, and 53, 54. Originally published in 1838.

[2] In 1833 the British Association for the Advancement of Science had set up a Statistical Section, and a Statistical Society had been formed in Manchester. But both organizations sought to avoid discussions of the theoretical implications of their data. "Several men of eminence in statistics chafed at being thus relegated to the position of 'hewers and drawers for political economy and philosophy,' so they joined in promoting the Statistical Society of London, now the Royal Statistical Society, with the view of providing therein a wider scope for their inquiries. Their hopes were frustrated, for a time at least, by the same spirit of caution which dictated the limitations imposed upon

While still a student in the University of London, Jevons began studying "periodic commercial fluctuations"—or, as we now say, "seasonal variations." He passed on quickly to an investigation of the changes in the "value of gold" which had followed the Californian and Australian discoveries.

> It has been abundantly shown by Quetelet and others (he remarked), that many subjects of this nature are so hopelessly intricate, that we can only attack them by the use of averages, and by trusting to probabilities.

To ascertain what changes had occurred in the "value of gold," Jevons made index numbers of the wholesale prices of 39 commodities by years from 1845 to 1862. He discussed the best type of average to use; tested his results by taking a larger sample of 118 commodities, and invoked the theory of probabilities to find the cause of the advance in prices, computing that

> the odds are 10,000 to 1 against a series of disconnected and casual circumstances having caused the rise of prices—one in the case of one commodity, another in the case of another—instead of some general cause acting over them all.[3]

And we may regard Jevons' book on *The Coal Question* (1865) as an important contribution to the study of secular trends.

The theory and the use of index numbers made slow progress for a generation after Jevons' pioneer work in 1863. But in 1887 Professor F. Y. Edgeworth began his long series of distinguished contributions to the problem, and about the same time Adolf Soetbeer, Augustus Sauerbeck, and Roland P. Falkner began providing index

the earlier institutions." For their *Journal* expressed its policy by the self-denying motto, *Aliis exterendum,* which was not dropped until about 1857, although the society had re-defined its aims in a wider style by 1840.

See Sir Athelstane Baines, "The History and Development of Statistics in Great Britain and Ireland," in *The History of Statistics,* edited by John Koren (Seventy-fifth anniversary volume of the American Statistical Association), New York, 1918, pp. 385, 386.

[3] *On the Study of Periodic Commercial Fluctuations,* 1862; *A Serious Fall in the Value of Gold Ascertained,* 1863; *The Depreciation of Gold,* 1869. Reprinted in *Investigations in Currency and Finance,* by W. Stanley Jevons, London, 1884. The quotations are from the paper of 1869, pp. 155-157 of the *Investigations.*

Later writers have questioned the applicability of the theory of probability to index numbers. For citations and discussion of the problem, see Professor F. Y. Edgeworth, "The Element of Probability in Index Numbers," *Journal of the Royal Statistical Society,* July, 1925, Vol. 88, pp. 557-575.

numbers for England, Germany and the United States.[4] Thereafter this bit of statistical technique rapidly became current among economists, though skepticism concerning the trustworthiness of the results lingered long in certain quarters.

As slow in winning general recognition was the contribution of another economist—Wilhelm Lexis. Approaching the theory of probability from the statistical side, Lexis showed in a series of investigations that the birth rates of different populations are not distributed around their mean values in accordance with the so-called "normal curve," and developed a mathematical-statistical explanation of the divergencies. Thus the way was opened for the empirical study of actual distributions—a type of work which spread gradually from vital statistics into other fields.[5]

The theoretical justification for applying the theory of probability to economic data at large was worked out mainly by Professor Edgeworth. In 1885 he directed attention to the fact that

> the distribution of averages will be approximately normal even though the distribution of the items composing the averages deviate considerably from normal.

Later he showed that the observations subjected to the probability analysis

> need not be perfectly independent of each other, "it suffices that there should be a considerable amount of independence"; that they need not be of the same order of magnitude, "it suffices that no two or three preponderate"; that the condition for the absence of systematic errors is not necessary, "it suffices that the center of gravity for the series of observations

[4] Edgeworth's early contributions were published in the *Reports of the British Association for the Advancement of Science,* 1887, 1888, 1889 and 1890 (reprinted in *Papers Relating to Political Economy,* by F. Y. Edgeworth, London, 1925, vol. i, pp. 195-343). Soetbeer's index numbers appeared first in 1885, Sauerbeck's first in 1886, and Falkner's in 1893. For more explicit references, see "Index Numbers of Wholesale Prices in the United States and Foreign Countries," *Bulletin of the United States Bureau of Labor Statistics,* No. 284, October, 1921.

[5] See Wilhelm Lexis, *Die französischen Ausfuhrprämien in Zusammenhange mit der Tarifgeschichte und der Handelsentwicklung Frankreichs seit der Restauration,* Bonn, 1870; *Zur Theorie der Massenerscheinungen in der menschlichen Gesellschaft,* Freiburg, 1877; *Abhandlungen zur Theorie der Bevölkerungs- und Moralstatistik,* Jena, 1903. Eugen Altschul gives an interesting account of Lexis' later views concerning the application of statistical method to social problems in a paper on "Konjunkturtheorie und Konjunkturstatistik," *Archiv für Sozialwissenschaft und Sozialpolitik,* January, 1926, vol. lv, pp. 77-82.

indefinitely prolonged should coincide with the true point which forms the quaesitum." [6]

Another technical contribution for which the economists presently found use was the theory of correlation. Invented by Sir Francis Galton as a method of studying the inheritance of characteristics, it was developed in the early 1890's by Professors Karl Pearson, F. Y. Edgeworth and G. Udny Yule, and later applied to measuring the relationship between paired items in time series.[7]

3. The Accumulation of Statistical Data.

The cumulative growth of statistical technique adapted to the treatment of economic problems in the second half of the 19th century was paralleled by a cumulative growth of statistical data. The impetus toward the collection of statistics came from practical activities rather than from scientific inquiries. Most of the ever-shifting issues in the political life of modern nations have had their economic aspects. Those who urged or those who opposed "reforms," and often both parties, sought to strengthen their cases by instituting special inquiries to show the extent of the evils to be remedied, or of the evils which the proposed remedies would produce. And as changes were made in public policy, administrative agencies were set up which had to keep continuous records not unlike those for which Laplace had called in 1814.

Thus the history of statistics in every country bears the impress of its social struggles. The United States owes its relatively abundant statistics of money and banking to the currency problems which the country has faced in different forms from the days of Alexander Hamilton to the days of the Federal Reserve Board. The relative backwardness of vital statistics in the United States arises from the fact that the population problem has been less pressing in this country than elsewhere. Our statistics of immigration and emigration remained meager until the country became exercised about the millions of newcomers from Southern Europe. So, too, our statistics of income

[6] Warren M. Persons, "Statistics and Economic Theory," *Review of Economic Statistics,* July, 1925, vol. vii, pp. 185-186.

This paper contains the best account known to me of the development of statistical methods now utilized by economists. I have drawn upon it freely.

[7] See Galton's *Natural Inheritance,* 1889, and, for later contributions, Karl Pearson, "Notes on the History of Correlation," *Biometrica,* October, 1920.

were vastly improved by the adoption of the federal income tax. Doubtless one might cite similar examples for any other country.

While Governments were being forced by practical exigencies to increase the scope of their statistical work decade after decade, private business was expanding its quota of statistics. On this side, also, practical needs dominated. The closer integration of business activities, the increasing dependence of every section and industry upon other sections and industries, created a widespread interest in business news. Reports of transactions and prices upon the stock and produce exchanges, reports of money-market conditions, bank clearings, security issues, bankruptcies and the like were wanted by a wide public, and numerous agencies collaborated to meet the demand. Trade journals found that statistical data of technical interest to their clientele attracted subscribers. Later, many trade associations began offering statistical service to their members.

In the various branches of economic activity, the progress toward making an adequate statistical record was influenced by the relative ease of collecting data. Highly organized central markets, like the produce and stock exchanges, made the statistician's task relatively simple. In the commodity field, price quotations were easier to get than production statistics, wholesale prices were easier to get than retail prices, and market prices were easier to get than contract prices. On the side of production, it was easier to compile reports for the highly standardized raw materials like coal, petroleum, and agricultural produce, or for partially fabricated materials like pig iron, spelter and cotton sheetings, than for the vast variety of finished goods like machinery, clothing and household supplies. In comparison with production, transportation presents a comparatively simple problem. On the contrary, statistics of stocks on hand, of orders booked, of mercantile operations, of costs and of profits have been very difficult to obtain.

Though the obstacles in the way of collecting adequate data remain formidable, economic evolution is facilitating the task. The organization of workers in trade unions gave the first opening for collecting significant and regular statistics of unemployment, while the concentration of an increasing proportion of employees in large establishments facilitated the collection of the more significant data concerning numbers on payrolls. The rise of department and chain stores made it feasible to gather the first reliable data concerning retail sales. Obviously, the trend toward standardization of technical

processes and of products favors the statistician. So does the trend toward the standardization of accounting methods, a trend which is most marked in such fields as banking, railway transportation, and public utilities, where financial reports must be submitted on official forms to government bureaus. The trend toward publicity of corporate accounts, observable in business circles, promises to give us in the future more accurate knowledge of costs and profits. In the not distant future we may know more about the arcana of business than Sismondi's generation knew about market prices. A policy which combines standardization with publicity is favored by modern methods of producing by automatic machinery, selling by national advertising, and financing by appeal to a large circle of investors. Standardization and publicity give the statistician what he wants.[1]

4. The Present Situation.

Thus it happened that by the time writers upon business cycles began to make systematic use of statistics—say in the decade beginning in 1900—they could utilize many methods already developed by mathematicians, anthropometrists, biologists and economists, and many data already collected by public and private agencies. As their work progressed, these men encountered problems which required special adaptations of the methods used in other fields and problems which required data not yet collected. Yet so well had the way been paved for them that they could make rapid progress toward establishing the study of business cycles upon a quantitative basis.

To analyze time series was the central problem. First, the recurrent cyclical fluctuations had to be isolated so far as possible from the other fluctuations to which time series are subject. Second, the relationships among the cyclical fluctuations of many different series had to be ascertained.

Jevons had made a beginning upon the first task by his studies of what are now called seasonal variations, a beginning which George Clare had continued in his brief treatise upon the London money

[1] The details concerning the increase of statistical data since the opening of the 19th century are far too intricate to sketch. Perhaps the best general view of developments on this side is given by the volume published by the American Statistical Association in commemoration of its 75th Anniversary: *The History of Statistics, Their Development and Progress in Many Countries,* Collected and edited by John Koren, New York, 1918.

A more detailed view of the British, French, German and American data relevant to business cycles is afforded by the collection of statistics which the National Bureau of Economic Research has made in preparation for the present book and which the Bureau hopes to publish.

market.[1] Another step was taken by J. H. Poynting and R. H. Hooker, who attacked the problem of determining secular trends, using for that purpose moving averages.[2] The second task, finding the relationships among quantities varying in time, was undertaken by Professor G. Udny Yule in 1899 and Mr. Hooker in 1901, both of whom applied Pearson's methods of correlation to economic data.[3]

In 1902, Dr. John Pease Norton combined and improved upon these various methods in his *Statistical Studies in the New York Money Market*.[4] Norton measured secular trends by fitting exponential curves to his data; he considered the dispersion as well as the averages of seasonal variations, taken as percentages of his trends; he used lines of regression as well as coefficients of correlation in examining the relations among his variables. Another notable step was taken by Professor Henry L. Moore, who in 1914 applied harmonic analysis to time series.[5] The following year, Professor Warren M. Persons made the first of his business barometers,[6] and in 1917 the Harvard Committee on Economic Research enabled him to begin a more elaborate analysis of economic statistics than had been possible for any of his predecessors. By establishing the *Review of Economic Statistics* in January, 1919, this committee provided an organ devoted primarily to the quantitative study of business cycles. The models which Persons and his colleagues have set in this journal have been studied and imitated widely, not only in the United States, but also in Europe.

This list of men who shared in adapting statistical methods to the analysis of economic time series is far from complete; it mentions only a few of the most noteworthy contributors. Still less justice can be done to recent work. Of late the number of economic statisti-

[1] *A Money-Market Primer and Key to the Exchanges*, London, 1891; 2d ed., 1903.

[2] See J. H. Poynting, "A Comparison of the Fluctuations in the Price of Wheat and in the Cotton and Silk Imports into Great Britain," *Journal of the Royal Statistical Society*, 1884, vol. xlvii, pp. 34-64; R. H. Hooker, "On the Correlation of the Marriage-rate with Trade," the same, 1901, vol. lxiv, pp. 485-492. A sketch of the progressive improvements in ascertaining secular trends will be given in Dr. Simon S. Kuznets' forthcoming monograph on that subject.

[3] Hooker as cited in preceding note; Yule, "An Investigation into the Causes of Changes in Pauperism in England," *Journal of the Royal Statistical Society*, 1899, vol. lxii, p. 249 *f.*

[4] Published for the Department of Social Sciences, Yale University; New York, 1902.

[5] *Economic Cycles: Their Law and Cause*, New York, 1914.

[6] "Construction of a Business Barometer Based upon Annual Data" (presented in part to a meeting of the American Statistical Association, August 11, 1915), *American Economic Review*, December, 1916, vol. vi, pp. 739-769. See a supplemental paper "On the Variate Difference Correlation Method and Curve-fitting." *Publications of the American Statistical Association*, June, 1917, vol. xv, pp. 602-642.

cians has grown rapidly. Efforts to improve the technique in detail, and efforts to win fresh knowledge by more intensive and more extensive analysis are being made constantly. In later sections I must attempt a critical summary of the constructive achievements of the whole campaign. Here it suffices to remark that recent contributions are to be found in the *Journal of the American Statistical Association,* the *Review of Economic Statistics,* the *Harvard Business Review,* the *Journal of the Royal Statistical Society,* and less frequently in the journals devoted to economics at large.

On the side of data, the Department of Commerce has rendered valuable service by extending the collection of statistics into fresh fields, and by establishing the *Survey of Current Business* in 1921. In this source are assembled most of the current series, old and new, collected by public or private agencies, which are useful to students of business cycles. Of scarcely less interest are the *Federal Reserve Bulletin* and the bulletins issued by the several Reserve Banks. Many of the most significant series, or indexes made from them, are regularly published in "adjusted" form by the *Review of Economic Statistics.*

As the preceding references indicate, the statistical study of business cycles has had its headquarters in the United States. This country continued to suffer from severe crises for a generation after they had been transformed into mild recessions in Europe and Canada. Thus the problem was especially intriguing to Americans. Further, Americans had rather fuller statistics to work with than were available in any other country, partly because of the prominence of economic issues in American politics, partly because of the highly standardized character of American products. The development was much stimulated and colored by a widespread demand for business forecasts. To improve the statistical technique of forecasting was Professor Persons' chief aim, and the hope of finding trustworthy indexes to the future has animated and secured financial support for many ingenious investigations.

Since the war, interest both scientific and practical in this type of work has been spreading to other countries. Since 1921, the *Economic Bulletin of the Conjuncture Institute,* edited by Professor N. D. Kondratieff, has been compiling, analyzing and interpreting Russian data. In Great Britain, the London and Cambridge Economic Service, cooperating with the Harvard University Committee on Economic Re-

search, began the publication of a *Monthly Bulletin* in 1923. The Institute of Statistics of the University of Paris has a similar plan of coöperation with the Harvard group, and publishes *Indices du Mouvement Général des Affaires en France et en Divers Pays.* Germany has an Institut für Konjunkturforschung under the direction of Dr. Ernst Wagemann, which began publishing *Vierteljahrshefte zur Konjunkturforschung* in January, 1926. Two Institutes of Statistics connected with the Universities of Padua and of Rome have joined forces to publish *Indici del Movimento Economico Italiano* under the direction of a Committee presided over by Professor Corrado Gini. The League of Nations has appointed a "Committee of Experts on Economic Barometers," Professor A. W. Flux, chairman, which held its first meeting at Geneva in December, 1926. Finally, in January, 1927, an Oesterreichisches Institut für Konjunkturforschung was organized in Vienna, with a scientific staff directed by Dr. F. A. von Hayek.

The present chapter aims neither to give a full exposition of the statistical methods which have been applied to the study of business cycles—that would fill a volume and exceed my competence,— nor to show what the statisticians have contributed toward our knowledge of cyclical fluctuations—that will be attempted in a second book. It aims rather to show what problems the statistical workers have attacked, how far they have pushed their researches, and what light they shed upon the character of business cycles.

III. The Analysis of Time Series.

1. The Quality and Quantity of Economic Statistics.

A biologist or anthropologist working upon statistical problems is often able to collect his own data by measuring material in his laboratory. Such measurements can be made to fit the requirements of the problem, and their accuracy can be controlled within assignable limits. A meteorologist is dependent upon data collected mainly by other observers; but these observers are men with at least a modicum of training, using scientific apparatus, and working under scientific direction. The quantitative worker upon economic problems is less fortunate in respect to his raw materials. Seldom can he make in his statistical laboratory a significant collection of measurements. He deals not with "material," but with the behavior of

men, and that behavior must be observed and recorded "in the field." Because his phenomena are highly variable, he usually needs a large array of cases, more than he can collect by himself or through the trained assistants at his disposal. Forced to rely upon observations made by others, he must often adapt his problem to the data, when he wishes to adapt his data to the problem.

Economic statistics are usually a by-product of governmental or business administration, collected in a form, at intervals, and by methods determined by some statute, official ruling, or business practice. Even when a public bureau plans a statistical inquiry with an eye to the scientific use of the results—and that happens with increasing frequency—it is usually necessary to fit the results for a variety of uses, and hence not feasible to adapt them precisely to any specific use. Finally, the accuracy attainable in most economic measurements leaves much to be desired. Often the data consist of estimates or rough approximations, and when precision is attainable with reference to the items counted there may be grave uncertainty regarding the representative character of the sample.

It is sometimes suggested that what economic statistics lack in quality they make up in quantity. There are grounds for arguing that a large number of observations compensates for lack of precision in each single observation, and the volume of economic statistics is certainly imposing—it is even intimidating at first sight. But on closer inspection the mass proves to consist less of a multiplication of independent observations upon particular phenomena, than of observations upon a vast variety of phenomena, and of the infinite detail in which certain processes must be observed.

To take the last point first: A student of business cycles is concerned largely with aggregates, for example, bank clearings in the United States, the wheat crops of the world, pig-iron output. On each of these topics and a hundred like them he can find a huge quantity of figures. But the mass is not for all his purposes a large number of observations upon one variable; it consists of many separate items which must be added to get one series of totals. The investigator is glad to have the figures in detail, for he may find occasion to examine the fluctuations (say) of wheat yields in different countries. But he has only one or two estimates for each country each year. Another type of problem is exemplified by efforts to measure changes in the "level" of wholesale or retail prices. Again a huge quantity of raw data is available—the prices of particular commodities, in particular

markets, at particular dates. In Professor Edgeworth's phrase, the task is

> to extricate from fallible observations a mean apt to represent the "general trend of prices." [1]

But the investigator has to take the changes between every pair of dates in every country or smaller area as a separate problem, and for no such problem is his number of "fallible observations" very large. The War Industries Board's index number of wholesale prices in 1913-18 included nearly 1500 commodities; but that collection was a *tour de force,* and the largest of the currently published series cover only some 400 commodities, while in many cases the commodities quoted number less than 50.[2]

Hardly less responsible for the bulkiness of economic statistics is the variety of activities covered. Every new attempt to systematize business operations—and such attempts seem endless—involves the making of new records, more and more of which emerge from bookkeeping into statistics. Only a tiny fraction of the records kept appears in published tables; yet in a country like the United States that fraction spreads over a bewildering diversity of processes. Nor can students of business cycles be sure that they are safe in ignoring any section of the record. Certainly they are concerned with the production, exchange, transportation, and distribution of commodities; with wages, rents, interest rates, profits, bond yields, and dividends; with family incomes and expenditures; with prices of all sorts, financial operations, savings, orders, bankruptcies, the launching of new enterprises, patents, construction work, banking in its various aspects, unemployment, migration, imports, exports, and tax receipts. In many cases they need detailed data for particular industries or localities. And they cannot properly neglect pertinent figures from any country which collects them. Even the fact that certain series show slight traces of cyclical fluctuations hardly lessens their task; for that fact may be highly significant in a general view of the problem. They

[1] F. Y. Edgeworth, *Papers Relating to Political Economy,* London, 1925, vol. i, p. 405.

[2] See *History of Prices during the War, Summary,* by Wesley C. Mitchell, (War Industries Board Price Bulletin, No. 1) Washington, 1919, p. 5. For the number of commodities contained in the leading wholesale price indexes of various countries at present, see *Institut International de Statistique, Bulletin Mensuel.* The issue for October, 1925, for example, pp. 76, 77, credits the United States Bureau of Labor Statistics with quoting 404 commodities, and the Canadian Department of Labour with quoting 271. Most of the series for the 31 countries represented are made from quotations for less than 100 commodities.

It may be noted that the question, "What shall be counted a distinct commodity in a price index?" is difficult to answer.

cannot even confine their researches within the field of economic statistics. Hypotheses concerning the causes of business cycles carry them back into meteorological data, morbidity rates, and what not, while interest in the consequences of business cycles carries them forward into the fields of vital statistics, criminal statistics, statistics of dependency, philanthropy, poor relief. And the more they learn about the problem, the wider grows the range of data which they deem it pertinent to study.

As an investigator gets deeper into a quantitative analysis of business cycles, his first impression that the statistical data to be dealt with are embarrassingly abundant turns into a conviction that they are painfully inadequate. Each business cycle becomes to him one case, one chance for observation. His method is to make measured observations upon as many cases as he can, and to draw such generalizations from the array of observations as his skill permits. For a very few of the recent cycles in the United States he finds data which allow him to observe with varying degrees of precision a good many of the processes involved. But seldom do the observations of a given process show marked uniformity from case to case. Hence the investigator becomes eager to increase the number of his cases. But as he passes from recent cycles in the United States to earlier cycles, or as he passes from American to European cycles, he finds the supply of statistics rapidly diminishing, and his doubts increasing about the trustworthiness of what statistics there are. In the end he must content himself with such data as practical needs or accident have preserved, make the best use of what he finds, and hope that his efforts may at least help toward getting for his successors better figures than are available to him.

If such an investigator does not give up the effort to frame a general theory of business cycles, he at least gives up the effort to base his theory wholly upon measurements. What statistical results he does attain, he presents as tentative. These results he prefaces, strings together, interprets, and supplements with analysis based upon non-quantitative observations.

2. Time Series in Their Raw State.

Since business cycles follow one another in time, the statistical data of chief concern to us are time series—data which show the

value of some variable at successive points, or during successive periods, of time. Occasionally surveys showing the magnitude of some factor, or the distribution of certain phenomena at a given moment are drawn upon, but the analysis of time series remains the outstanding task.

These time series have many forms:—prices, aggregate money values, physical quantities (in units of number, weight, length, area, volume, energy), percentages of a total which changes with time, percentages of a total at some past date, ratios to some other quantity, and so on. The intervals vary from the day, week or month to the year or the decade. Many such series cover but a year or two, some have been kept in fairly uniform fashion for a generation, a very few quasi-continuous series run back or can be pieced back, for a century, two centuries, or even more.[1] Some series are available in comparable form for several different countries—for example, wheat production, coal and iron output, discount rates;—some are available only for one country—for example, the valuable German series showing receipts from the tax on bills of exchange, the American data concerning retail sales, the British statistics of outdoor relief. It is indeed a most miscellaneous collection which the investigator of business cycles must use as his raw materials.

A few of the series which such an investigator uses report the variations in factors which are indivisible units in the business situation. For example, the official minimum discount rate of the Bank of England is a single figure, known with precision for every week through long years. Many different matters have been weighed by the bank's directors in deciding upon the rate announced each Thursday; but once announced there is no analyzing the rate into constituent parts. Most time series, however, are aggregates, or averages, which the investigator can, and frequently should, analyze. For example, if bank clearings in the United States fall five per cent between July and August, it may be that in a majority of the clearing houses transactions increased; and in the minority of towns where transactions shrank, the declines may have varied from a fraction of one per cent to half the July volume. Similarly, an index number of

[1] For example, Sir William H. Beveridge has compiled an index number of "Wheat Prices in Western and Central Europe" by years for the whole period, 1500-1869. See his paper on "Weather and Harvest Cycles," *Economic Journal*, December, 1921, vol. xxxi, pp. 449-451. I understand that he has now secured data which will enable him to carry this table much further back than 1500.

wholesale prices shows for each date merely the net resultant of most diverse changes in the prices of individual commodities—changes which nearly always run the gamut from a considerable decline to a considerable rise.[2] In thinking graphically of price changes we should

[2] By way of illustration consider the following charts of price changes. The first chart (adapted from the *Bulletin of the U. S. Bureau of Labor Statistics,* No. 284) shows the mixture of diversity and concentration in the fluctuations of the wholesale prices of the commodities included in the B.L.S. index number, by years, from 1891 to 1919. Each year the fluctuations are ranked in order of their magnitude, and then divided into ten groups containing equal numbers of commodities. The dividing points, called decils, and the extreme fluctuations of each year are represented on the chart by dots. By an arbitrary convention the 11 dots for each year are connected by slanting lines with the middle point of the distribution of the preceding year. The vertical scale is logarithmic. While the chart gives a lively impression of the variety of price changes

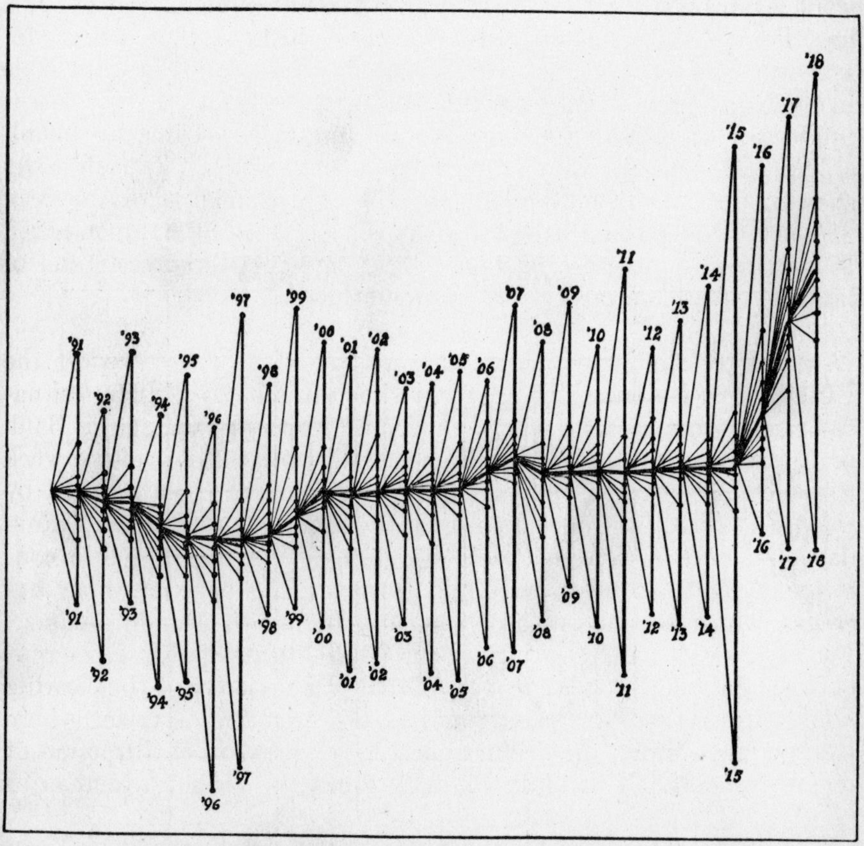

occurring every year, it over-simplifies the situation by picturing the annual changes as all starting from the same point. A chart which did not over-simplify some aspect of the changes would be a hopeless tangle of lines.

The second chart (adapted from *History of Prices during the War, Summary,* War

think, not of the movements of a single curve, such as represents adequately the Bank of England rate, but of a broad, irregular band, within which many lines are moving, some up, some down, some horizontally—lines which are rather far apart near the edges of the band but thickly congregated near the middle, and which keep crossing each other as they shift their relative positions.

It is true that an investigator often writes of series like bank clearings or price indexes as if they represented magnitudes not less definite than the Bank of England rate. Doubtless there are problems which justify the practice—problems in which the one matter of significance is the net resultant of a complicated mass of movements. Yet such problems are rare, and it is always wise to ask explicitly whether the hypothesis in use does not require that notice be taken of the diversity

Industries Board Price Bulletin, No. 1) is another device for illustrating the diversity and concentration of price changes. It shows the distribution of the relative prices of 1437 commodities in 1918, computed on the base average prices, July, 1913, to June, 1914 equal 100. Here the horizontal scale is logarithmic. The chart shows, for example, that one commodity fell 64 per cent in price from the pre-war level to 1918, another commodity rose 2,991 per cent, but that nearly 600 commodities (over two-fifths) were concentrated in the range of 50 to 109 per cent advance.

1918 DISTRIBUTION OF 1437 COMMODITIES
ACCORDING TO THE MAGNITUDE OF THEIR RELATIVE PRICES

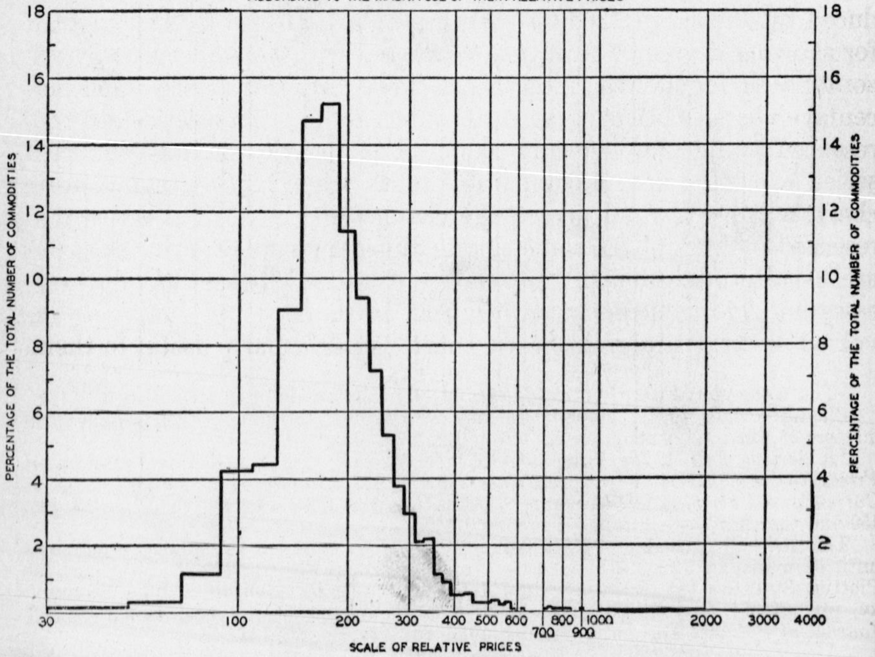

of movements which are hidden in the simple-seeming aggregates or averages. Certainly we do not get the full benefit of the statistical approach to the study of business cycles, unless we keep in mind the range and variety of the changes which most of our time series represent.

The first step toward using any series is usually to represent the figures by a line drawn on a chart. The invention of this device in 1786 is claimed by William Playfair, who set forth its advantages as follows:

> As the eye is the best judge of proportion, being able to estimate it with more quickness and accuracy than any other of our organs, it follows, that wherever *relative quantities* are in question, a gradual increase or decrease of any . . . value is to be stated, this mode of representing it is peculiarly applicable; it gives a simple, accurate, and permanent idea, by giving form and shape to a number of separate ideas, which are otherwise abstract and unconnected.[3]

A variant of Playfair's method of charting time series was introduced by Jevons in 1863-65—the use of a logarithmic vertical scale for showing degree of variation, combined with an arithmetical horizontal scale for showing intervals of time.[4] By this device equal percentage changes occuring at equal intervals in a time series are represented by lines of the same slope. Further, two or more different series, expressed in non-comparable units, when plotted upon a ratio chart, will have equal percentage changes in the several series represented by lines of the same slope. Since students of business cycles are usually interested in the relative changes which economic processes undergo recurrently, rather than in the absolute quantities involved in the changes, the "ratio chart" is particularly useful to them.

[3] *The Commercial and Political Atlas,* 3d ed., London, 1801, p. x.

Playfair's claim to be "actually the first who applied the principles of geometry to matters of Finance" is made on pp. viii and ix.

[4] *A Serious Fall in the Value of Gold Ascertained* (1863), and *The Variation of Prices, and the Value of Currency since 1782* (1865). Reprinted in *Investigations in Currency and Finance,* by W. Stanley Jevons, London, 1884. See especially pp. 53, 128, 150 and the charts which follow pp. 56 and 150.

This method of making charts did not come into common use among economists until its merits had been explained by Professors Irving Fisher, "The 'Ratio' Chart for Plotting Statistics," *Publications of the American Statistical Association,* June, 1917, vol. xv, pp. 577-601, and James A. Field, "Some Advantages of the Logarithmic Scale," *Journal of Political Economy,* October, 1917, vol. xxv, pp. 805-841.

To illustrate the materials and problems before us, samples of the time series most useful in studying business cycles are given in Chart 1.[5] These series run in units of long tons of pig iron, pounds of copper, percentages of the constantly changing membership of British trade unions, bushels of wheat, miles of railway track, percentages of the average prices of commodities in 1867-77, billions of dollars, and percentages which the interest received forms of the changing purchase price of bonds. The vertical logarithmic scale of the chart makes comparable the percentage fluctuations in all these different quantities. The only bar to close comparison is that some of the series give data only by years, while others give data by quarters or months.

Looked at broadly, the curves show striking differences. American pig-iron output, copper output and wheat crops present one type of changes. The characteristic of this type is its upward trend, more rapid in the two metal curves than in the other, and frequently broken in all three curves by brief reactions. Bank clearings give a similar picture from 1875 to 1914; but the great inflation of the war period introduced a sudden change of trend less marked in the series representing physical production unmixed with prices. American railway building presents a second type of changes. After rising to a peak in the 1880's, it declined unsteadily to a level comparable with that of the 1850's. A third type, characterized by several changes in the direction of movement, is presented by British prices at wholesale. They rise from the 1850's to 1873, fall from 1873 to 1896, rise from 1896 to 1913 at a rate then thought rapid, accelerate their rise in 1914 to 1920, and later fall precipitously. The bond-yield curve also shows several changes in trend; but changes less marked than those of the price curve. Finally, the British unemployment percentages fluctuate about the same general level through the whole 70 years for which they have been compiled.

Except in the unemployment series and perhaps that showing railway construction, these long-period shiftings of level, or "secular trends" as they are technically called, are the most conspicuous features of the chart. But the conspicuous feature of the unemployment

[5] The numerical data used in drawing the charts in this volume are taken, with a few exceptions noted in the proper connection, from the collection of statistical materials which the National Bureau of Economic Research is making and hopes to publish in the near future. Since that collection will have a full index, and will state the original sources from which all the series are obtained as well as the methods of compilation, it seems needless to publish the tables here.

CHART 1.

SAMPLE TIME SERIES PLOTTED ON A LOGARITHMIC VERTICAL SCALE.

Only the Relative Slope, Not the Vertical Position, of These Curves Is Significant.

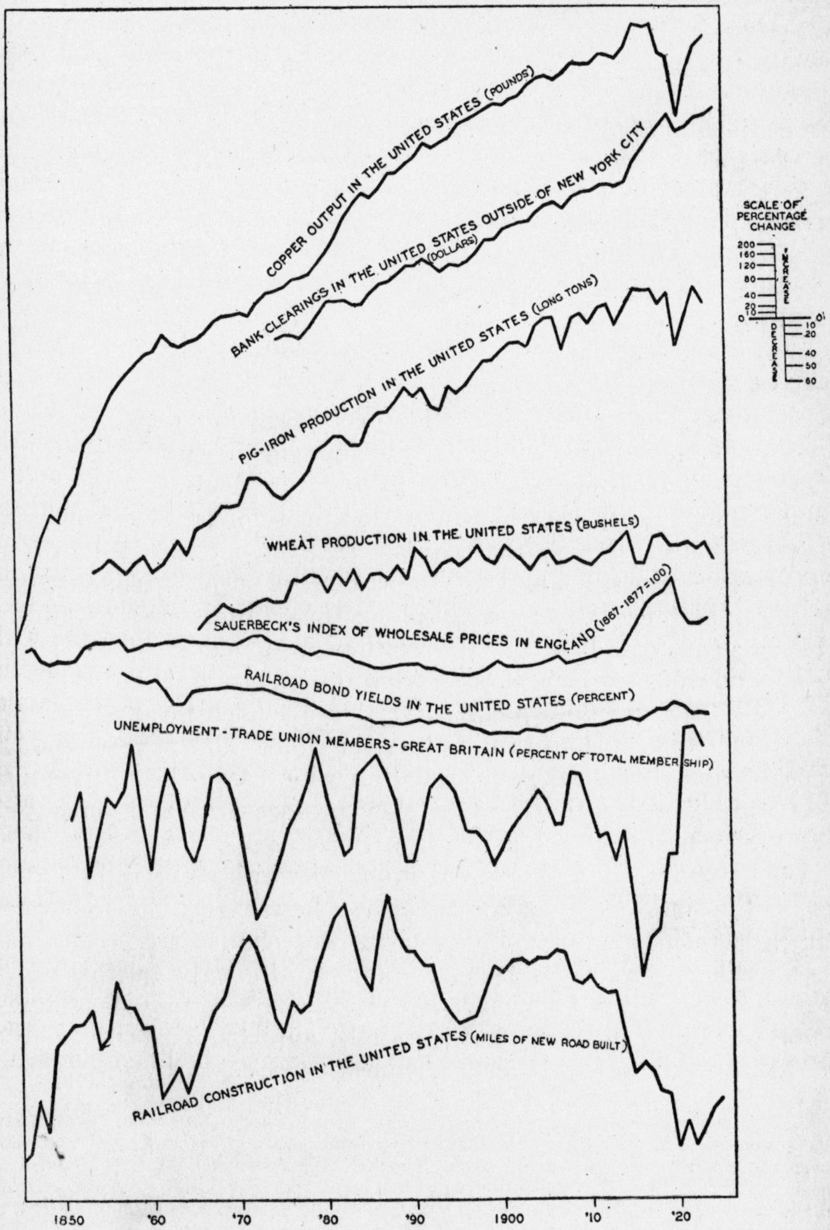

curve is its wavelike movement about a nearly constant level. Of course, these wave-like movements, or "cyclical fluctuations," are the center of our interest. Are they present in the other cases? Traces of them may be seen in all the curves, except perhaps the curve for wheat crops, where the fluctuations seem capricious. But in all the curves, including that for unemployment, the cyclical fluctuations are obscured by intermixture with changes of other sorts. Accordingly, the first problem faced by the student of business cycles in the statistical analysis of time series is whether he can develop a technique which will enable him to isolate the cyclical fluctuations for intensive observation and measurement.

The clarity of the cyclical fluctuations in the unemployment curve suggests the idea of seeking to reduce the secular trends in the other curves to horizontal lines. Can that be done?

Were that accomplished, would the cyclical fluctuations be isolated? Closer examination of the unemployment curve itself raises doubt. The percentage of men out of work in England seems to be greater almost every year in winter than in summer, whether times are good or bad, though that characteristic is not revealed by the annual figures used in Chart 1. Indications of such "seasonal variations" can be traced in a monthly plot of many time series. Can the presence or absence of seasonal variations in a time series be determined, and can they be separated from the cyclical fluctuations?

Finally, the unemployment curve shows sudden breaks now and then, which appear as interruptions in the course which the combined cyclical-seasonal changes seem to be following. Can these "irregular fluctuations" be identified? Can they be measured and separated from the cyclical fluctuations?

Such is the conventional list of problems which statistical investigators of business cycles have attacked. These workers have devised many ingenious methods of measuring and eliminating from time series secular trends and seasonal variations. In dealing with irregular perturbations they have made less progress. One group has sought to find periodic fluctuations in the data by applying harmonic analysis. Much of the work is highly technical. Consequently the following survey of what has been done can be neither brief nor easy.

3. The Problem of Secular Trends

Secular trends of time series have been computed mainly by men who were concerned to get rid of them. Just as economic theorists

have paid slight attention to the "other things" in their problems which they suppose to "remain the same," so the economic statisticians have paid slight attention to their trends beyond converting them into horizontal lines. Hence little is yet known about the trends themselves, their characteristics, similarities, and differences. Even their relations to cyclical fluctuations have been little considered. Here lies in obscurity a heap of problems, waiting for properly equipped investigators to exploit.[1]

(1) The Empirical Approach to the Problem.

The procedure adopted in ascertaining secular trends is usually empirical in high degree. Starting with a time series plotted to a convenient scale on a chart, the statistician seeks to find for that one series, within the period covered by his data, the line which best represents the "long-time tendencies" shown by the plotted curve. In cases like that presented by British wholesale prices in Chart 1, he splits the whole period into sections, and seeks to find lines of secular trend for each section separately, or else to find a function which changes direction in the manner of the data.

The technical process usually consists in (1) fitting a "mathematical curve" (for example, a straight line or a third-degree parabola) to the data, or to the logarithms of the data, by the method of least squares or of moments; (2) computing moving or progressive arithmetic means or moving medians, including in the averages whatever number of items seems to give satisfactory results; (3) first computing moving averages and then fitting trend lines to the results; (4) drawing a free-hand curve through the data representing the investigator's impression, formed from careful study, of the long-time tendency; or (5) using ratios between the paired items of series which are believed to have substantially the same secular trends.[1]

[1] So far as I know, the only one working upon secular trends as a problem in its own right is Dr. Simon S. Kuznets, one of the Research Fellows of the Social Science Research Council. Dr. Kuznets has generously allowed me to profit by his results in advance of publication.

[1] Technical directions for computing secular trends by the commoner methods are given in most of the recent textbooks of economic statistics. For example, see Frederick C. Mills, *Statistical Methods,* New York, 1924, chap. vii, W. L. Crum and A. C. Patton, *Economic Statistics,* Chicago, 1925, chap. xx, or Edmund E. Day, *Statistical Analysis,* New York, 1925, chap. xvii.

Among the recent contributions to the subject are Warren M. Persons, "Indices of Business Conditions," *Review of Economic Statistics,* January, 1919, Preliminary vol. i, pp. 8-18; and the following papers in the *Journal of the American Statistical Associa-*

When a secular trend has been fitted by any of these methods or their variants, how can the agreement between the line of trend and the plotted data be determined?

It might be thought that a trend can be tested by breaking a series into two parts, computing trends for the separate sections and seeing whether they agree. But lack of agreement would not prove that the trend for either section of the data was wrong for the period it covered. Secular trends are "subject to change without notice," and it is a common experience that a line which gives an excellent fit to the data for one period ceases to fit well when carried backward in time, or projected for a few years. Thus the failure of a trend fitted now to mark the line followed by developments in the near future need not mean that to-day's work is wrong. Perhaps our successor who computes a new trend for the longer series of data available to him will not be able to improve upon our fit for the period we analyzed.

Then why not break long series into relatively brief segments and compute the secular trends for each separately? That is a device to which the statistical student of business cycles resorts at need; but to go far in that direction is to give up the problem of secular trends rather than to solve it. Unless it is possible to find trends which are satisfactory throughout long periods—long in comparison with business cycles—the distinction between secular and cyclical fluctuations is blurred and the whole analysis loses its point. Just how far the process of subdividing periods for the computation of trends shall be carried is a question to be decided by the character of each series and the uses to which the results are to be put.

There is, indeed, no single criterion for determining "goodness of fit." A mathematical test can be applied only in certain cases. Provided one is choosing between two lines of trend whose equations contain the same number of constants, one can compare the standard deviations of the actual values from the trend lines. A test of wider application is to consider the "reasonableness" of the values shown by projecting trend lines into the future, and to choose lines which

tion: W. L. Crum, "The Determination of Secular Trend," June, 1922, vol. xviii, pp. 210-215, and "The Least Squares Criterion of Trend Lines," June, 1925, vol. xx, pp. 211-222; Holbrook Working, "The Determination of Secular Trend Reconsidered," December, 1922, vol. xviii, pp. 497-502; Willford I. King, "Principles Underlying the Isolation of Cycles and Trends," December, 1924, vol. xix, pp. 468-475; Lincoln W. Hall, "A Moving Secular Trend and Moving Integration," March, 1925, vol. xx, pp. 13-24; Olin Ingraham, "The Refinement of Time Series," June, 1925, vol. xx, pp. 231-233.

indicate results judged to be probable. In forecasting work this test is important for projections within the period to which the forecast applies. For the rest, statisticians fall back upon a visual comparison between the actual values and the trend lines within the time limits of the data. Their confidence in a fitted curve seems to be greater the simpler is its equation and the longer the period within which it gives a reasonable fit. But published expressions of opinion show that a fit which seems good to one man would be called poor by another. Personal equations play a large rôle in such judgments.

Nor is there any general method of deciding in advance what one among the several ways of determining trends will yield the best fit to a given time series, according to these rather indefinite criteria. In the same piece of work, an investigator may fit a straight line to one series and a parabola to a second, compute three-year moving medians of a third and seven-year moving arithmetic means of a fourth, run a free-hand curve through a fifth, use ratios to some other series for a sixth, and devise some novel method for a seventh. He may even use two or three unlike methods of determining the trend in different sections of the same series. Nor will he hesitate to compare the deviations of the actual data from the trends measured in these different ways, if he believes that each of the trend lines expresses the long-time tendency of its data better than would one of the other devices.

Each method has technical advantages, which should be considered with reference to the problem presented by each investigation. Subsequent uses of the data may make it desirable to have a trend which can be expressed by a simple equation, as can curves of known properties. The purpose in view may, or may not, make it important to reject curves which, though they may fit the data admirably for a long period in the past, would indicate results deemed absurd in the future. Ease of construction counts in favor of free-hand curves, and ratios to other series. Of course, the last device is of limited use, for it can be employed only when two series are found which seem to have nearly the same trend. Moving averages are controlled by the data as free-hand curves are not, and this independence of the investigator's personal equation gives comfort to many minds. In business-cycle work, moving averages will yield a satisfactory line of trend, if the trend is linear, if the period of the average corresponds to the duration of the cycles, and if the cycles are regular both in duration and intensity. These conditions are seldom strictly

satisfied. If the true trend is a convex curve, a moving average lies above the curve, and so produces errors in the cyclical deviations, the magnitude of which increases with the convexity of the curve and the period of the moving average. If the true trend is concave, errors of opposite sign result. Finally, moving averages seldom yield trends that look satisfactory unless they are centered, and such averages cannot be kept up to date except by the hazardous practice of estimating figures for future years.[2] The advantage claimed for combining moving averages with curve fitting is that it minimizes the influence of the extreme years, which "may represent either the accident of the particular phase of the business cycle with which the series begins or ends, or a change in the real secular trend." [3] Free-hand curves, drawn with care, are preferred by some statisticians of wide experience, not merely because they are easier to make than any other trend lines, but also because they meet the test of visual comparison with the plotted data quite as well as the more pretentious mathematical constructions.

To illustrate the results obtained by applying different methods, Chart 2 has been made. The first section of the chart shows several different trends fitted to a single series—pig-iron production in the United States; the second section shows the application of the same method to several different series, and the third section shows different methods applied to different series.

Having ascertained the secular trend of a time series, the investigator's next step is "to eliminate the trend" from the original data.[4] To that end he finds the numerical value represented by the trend line at each successive interval of time, through computation or by readings from the scale of his chart, and then determines the plus and minus deviations of the actual data from those values in actual amounts or in percentages.[5] Finally, he draws a new chart in which he represents the secular trend by a horizontal line, and the devia-

[2] For example, the trend figure for 1927 in a seven-years' moving average, centered, is computed by adding actual and estimated data for 1924-30 and dividing by seven.

[3] Olin Ingraham, "The Refinement of Time Series," *Journal of the American Statistical Association*, June, 1925, vol. xx, p. 233.

[4] Frequently this elimination is postponed until the seasonal variations have been computed. But of that later.

[5] Professor Allyn A. Young has called attention to the fact that the cyclical deviations from a secular trend are likely to be least trustworthy toward the extremities of the period for which the trend is fitted. Further, it is at the extremities that the differences among the various curves which may be employed as trends commonly become most marked. See "An Analysis of Bank Statistics for the United States," *Review of Economic Statistics*, January, 1925, vol. vii, p. 28.

CHART 2.

Examples of Secular Trends of Time Series Fitted by Various Methods.

Section 1.

Different Trends Fitted to the Same Series. Pig-Iron Production in the United States.

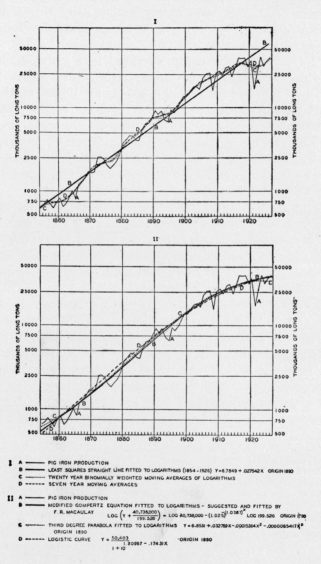

I

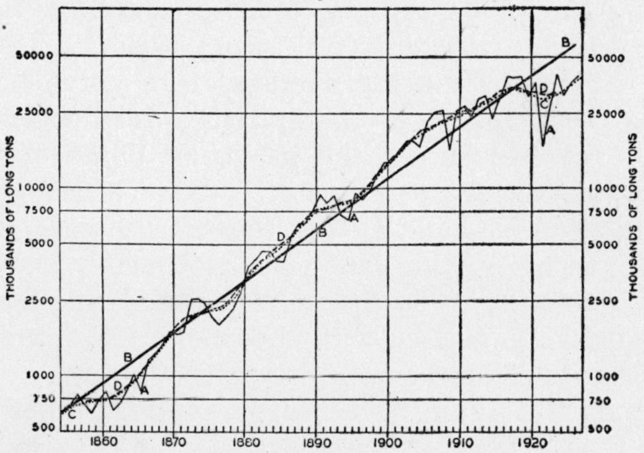

II

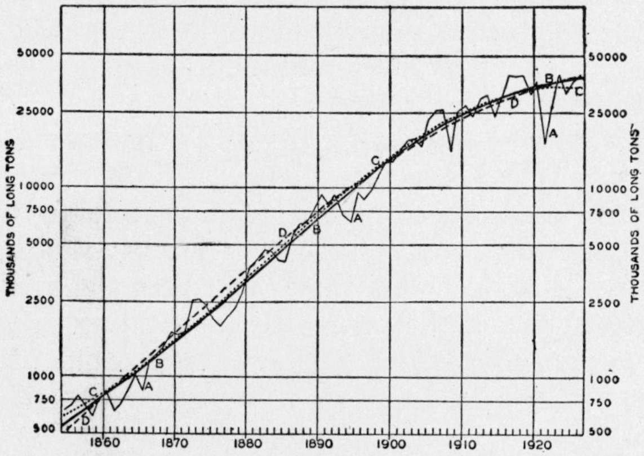

I
A ——— PIG IRON PRODUCTION
B ——— LEAST SQUARES STRAIGHT LINE FITTED TO LOGARITHMS (1854 - 1926) $Y = 6.7849 + .027542X$ ORIGIN 1890
C .... TWENTY YEAR BINOMIALLY WEIGHTED MOVING AVERAGES OF LOGARITHMS
D - - - - - SEVEN YEAR MOVING AVERAGES

II
A ——— PIG IRON PRODUCTION
B ——— MODIFIED GOMPERTZ EQUATION FITTED TO LOGARITHMS - SUGGESTED AND FITTED BY F. R. MACAULAY $\text{LOG}\left(Y + \frac{40{,}738{,}000}{199.526}\right) = \text{LOG } 40{,}738{,}000 - (1.025)^{-(1.0387)^{X}} \text{ LOG } 199.526$ ORIGIN 1790
C -........ THIRD DEGREE PARABOLA FITTED TO LOGARITHMS $Y = 6.8531 + .032789X - .0015364X^2 - .0000065417X^3$ ORIGIN 1890
D - - - - - LOGISTIC CURVE $Y = \frac{50{,}403}{1 + 10^{1.80987 - .17431X}}$ ORIGIN 1860

CHART 2 (*Continued*).

Examples of Secular Trends of Time Series Fitted by Various Methods.

Section 2.

The Same Method Applied to Different American Series. Straight-Line Trends from the *Review of Economic Statistics*.

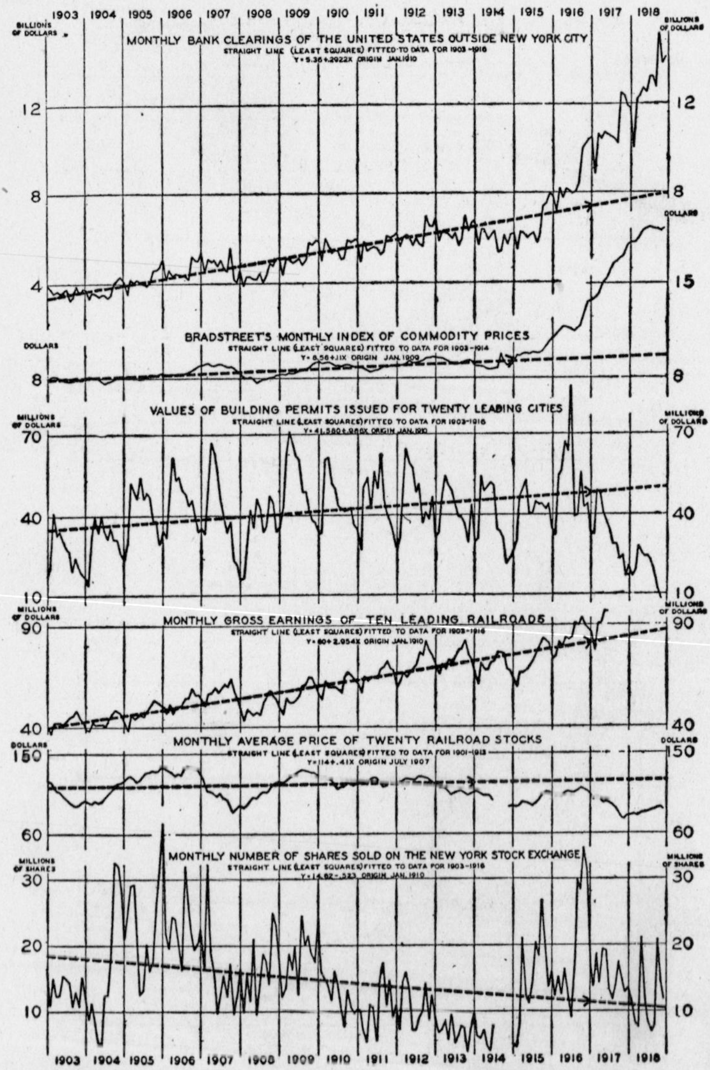

CHART 2 (*Continued*).

Examples of Secular Trends of Time Series Fitted by Various Methods.

Section 3.

Different Methods Applied to Different Series.

I

SAUERBECK'S INDEX OF BRITISH WHOLESALE PRICES (1867-1877=100) WITH TREND FITTED BY STRAIGHT LINES (LEAST SQUARES) TO LOGARITHMS, BY PERIODS

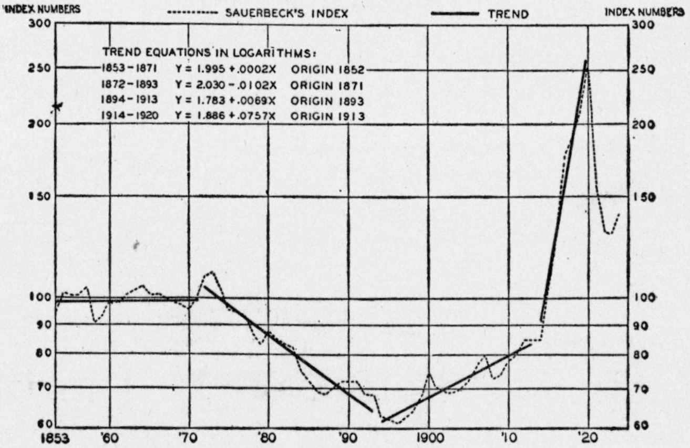

II

RAILROAD BOND YIELDS, UNITED STATES, WITH TREND FITTED BY A TWENTY YEAR BINOMIALLY WEIGHTED MOVING AVERAGE CENTERED OPPOSITE THE ELEVENTH YEAR (F.R.MACAULAY)

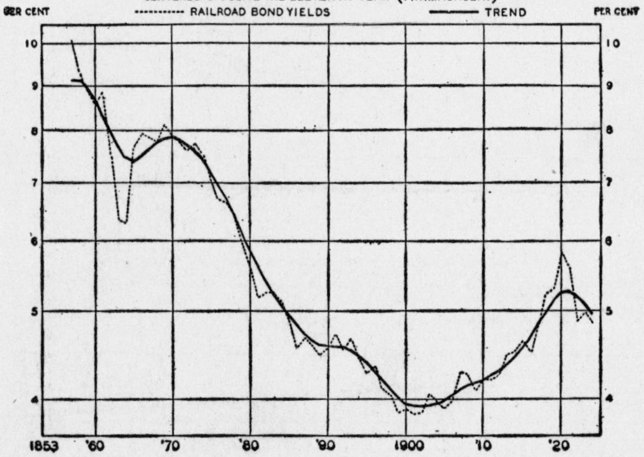

CHART 2 (*Continued*).

EXAMPLES OF SECULAR TRENDS OF TIME SERIES FITTED BY VARIOUS METHODS.

Section 3 (*Continued*).

Different Methods Applied to Different Series.

III

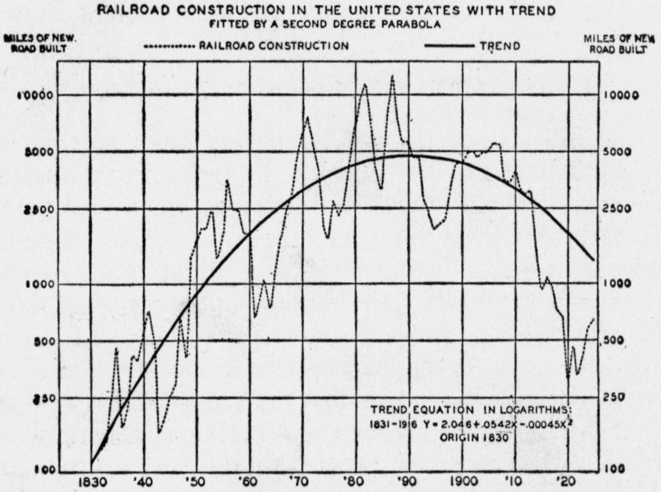

IV

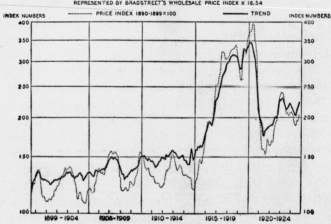

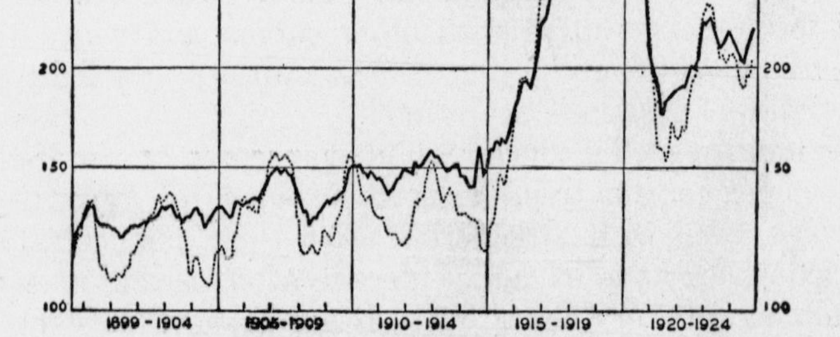

tions by a curve which fluctuates about the horizontal. Several examples of such construction are given in Chart 3.

When a statistical inquirer into business cycles has reached this point in his work, he commonly goes on at once to ascertain the seasonal variations left in his curve of deviations from the trend, or to use the deviations as they stand. But preoccupation with theory requires us to pause here, and to look at the problem from another angle.

(2) The Interpretation of Secular Trends.

What meanings have the secular trends fitted to time series by empirical methods? As Dr. Kuznets remarks, every mathematical curve used as a trend has definite implications, whether the statistician notices them or not. To take the simplest example: a straight line sloping upward implies future increase without limit. Its constant rate of increase per unit of time implies that the size of the variable at one moment does not affect the size of the increment between that moment and the next. Its percentage rate of increase diminishes along a hyperbolic curve. When we find that a straight line trend fits a given series well, do we accept these mathematical implications as characteristic of the economic process represented by the data? Are successful fits of mathematical curves discoveries in economics?

These questions suggest another way of treating the whole problem of secular trends. We form various hypotheses concerning the long-time tendencies of economic developments in population, production, transportation, exchange, and the like. These hypotheses are derived from and linked to causal explanations; but ordinary reasoning does not enable us to test them adequately. Can we choose curves whose mathematical implications correspond to our causal hypotheses, fit them to time series, perhaps modify the hypotheses in the light of the first results, experiment with other curves, and when finally we have secured good fits argue that we have thrown new light upon the characteristics of economic evolution?

A step toward such a conception is represented by the frequent interpretation of certain trend lines as showing the "growth factor." Statisticians dwell with satisfaction upon their demonstrations that certain industries have expanded decade after decade at a substantially uniform rate, or at a rate which has changed in some uniform way. They take almost as much pleasure in contemplating the somewhat similar rates at which different industries have grown in given

CHART 3.

Samples of Time Series Plotted as Deviations from Secular Trends Represented by Horizontal Lines.

(Selected from Chart 2).

RAILROAD BOND YIELDS - UNITED STATES

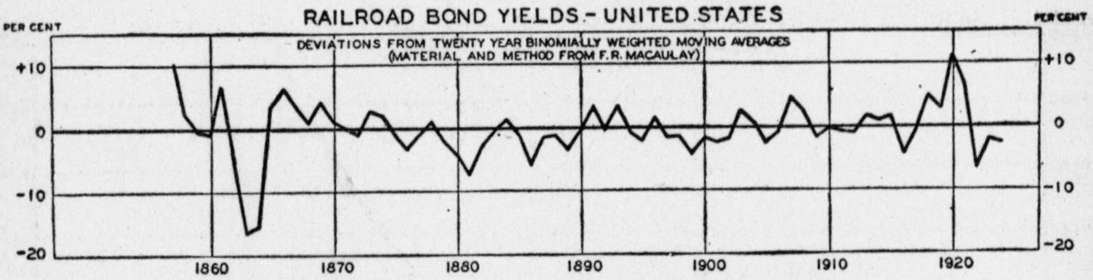

SAUERBECK'S INDEX OF WHOLESALE PRICES IN ENGLAND

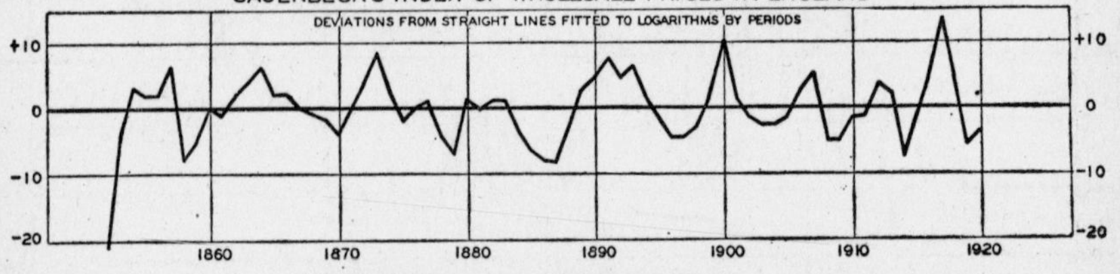

PIG-IRON PRODUCTION IN THE UNITED STATES

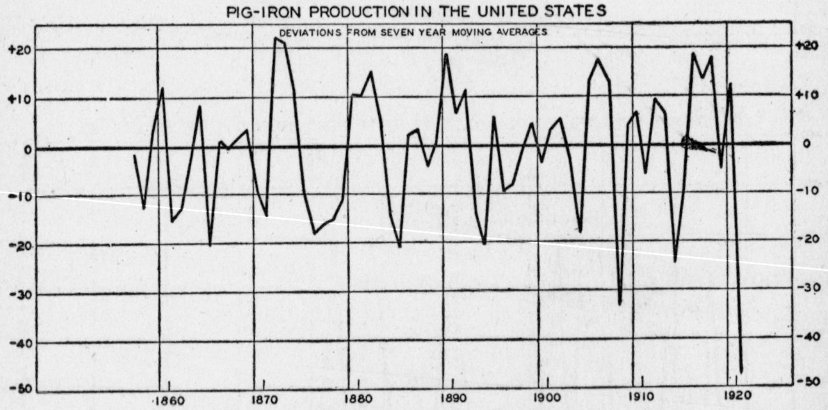

PRICE INDEX OF BUSINESS CYCLES, UNITED STATES: 1890-1899=100

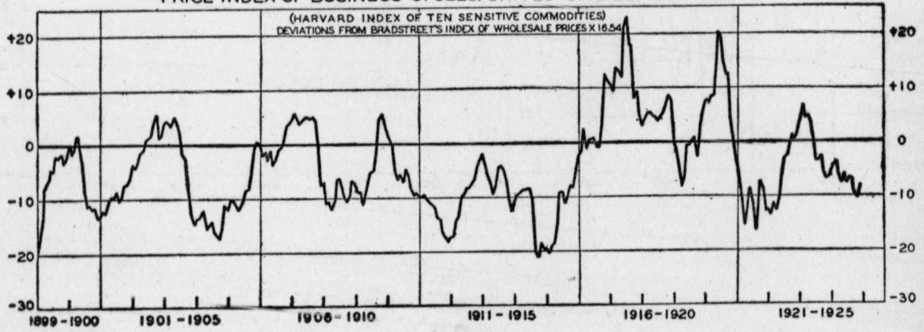

CHART 3 (*Continued*).

EXAMPLES OF TIME SERIES PLOTTED AS DEVIATIONS FROM SECULAR TRENDS REPRESENTED BY HORIZONTAL LINES.

(Vertical Scale—¼ of scale on opposite page).

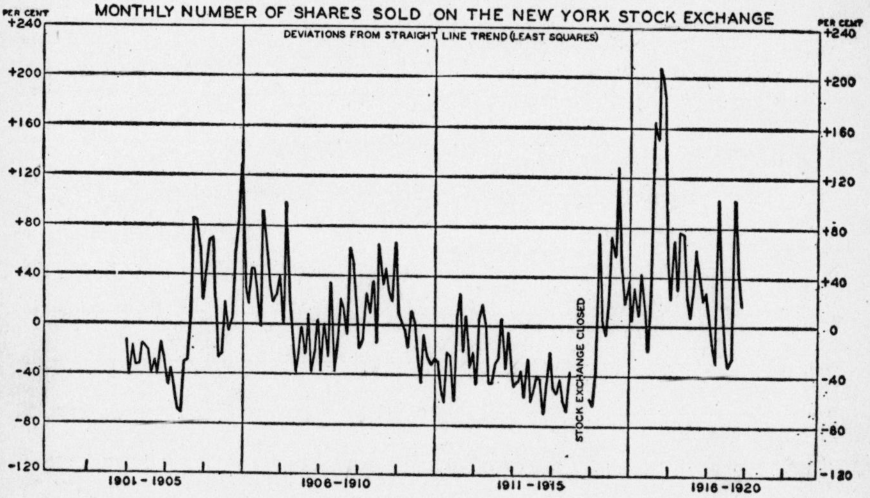

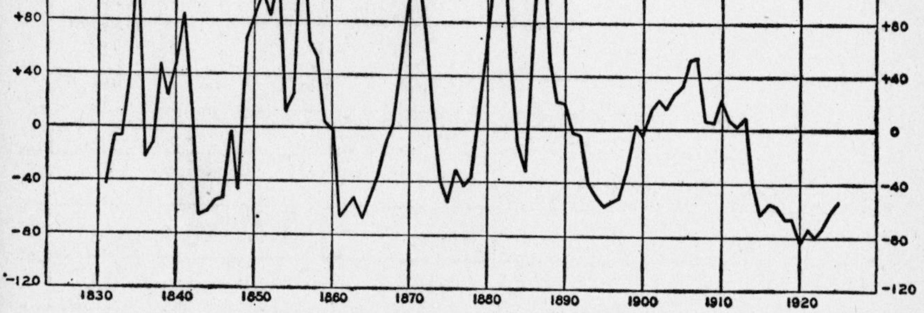

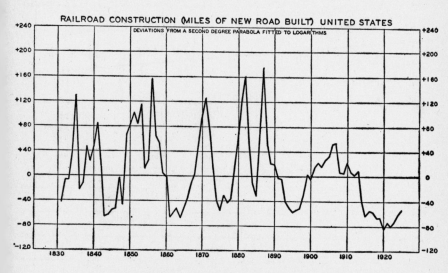

periods and countries. Nor are they at a loss for explanations of these uniformities. In view of the increase in population characteristic of the great commercial nations, and of the advance in industrial technique, it seems scarcely fanciful to think of modern society as "tending" to produce an ever larger supply of goods for the satisfaction of its wants. On this basis, cyclical fluctuations appear as alternating accelerations and retardations in the pace of a more fundamental process. Secular trends, in short, are taken to measure economic progress generation by generation.

A bold speculation of this sort has been ventured by Mr. Raymond B. Prescott. He suggests that perhaps "all industries, whose growth depends directly or indirectly upon the ability of the people to consume their products," pass through similar phases in the course of their development. Four stages seem to be common:

1. Period of experimentation.
2. Period of growth into the social fabric.
3. Through the point where the growth increases, but at a diminishing rate.
4. Period of stability.

On this basis, Mr. Prescott suggests that the secular trends of all such industries may be represented by a single type of curve—that yielded by the Gompertz equation.

> Every country (he adds) may have a different rate of growth, and so may every industry, because no two industries have the same combination of influences. They will trace the same type of curve, however, even though the rate of growth is different.[1]

[1] "Law of Growth in Forecasting Demand," *Journal of the American Statistical Association,* December, 1922, vol. xviii, pp. 471-479.

To illustrate his suggestion, Mr. Prescott publishes the following copyrighted diagram, of which the caption is significant.

CURVE OF PROGRESS OR LAW OF GROWTH (R. B. PRESCOTT)

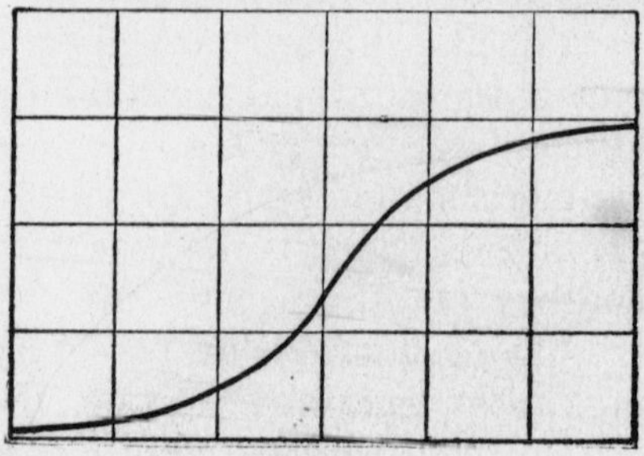

Dr. Simon S. Kuznets, who has fitted more Gompertz or "logistic" curves (with three constants) to economic series than anyone else known to me, finds that the Gompertz curve gives good fits to a number of series, but that in more cases he gets good fits by using the three-constant "logistic curve." The important properties of this curve are: (1) Finite limits, zero and an upper value to which the curve is asymptotic. (2) The rate of increase per unit of time is directly proportioned to the size of the variable at a given point, multiplied by the distance between that point and the upper limit. This implies that (say) the output of an industry grows in physical units at a rate which increases from the start to the point of inflection of the curve, and then decreases gradually to zero as the curve approaches its upper asymptote. (3) The percentage rate of increase declines steadily from the beginning. These three characteristics, Dr. Kuznets supposes, appear in the history of the many economic processes, whose long-time statistical record is well described by a logistic curve.

The use of logistic and Gompertz curves is not limited to describing the secular trends of growing industries. They can be adapted also to the conditions of industries with a shrinking output. Such industries are not unimportant, even in a highly prosperous country like the United States. Conspicuous examples are canal traffic, gold mining, shipbuilding, bicycle manufacturing, and lumbering. Indeed, a declining phase may be anticipated for most industries, if we define an industry somewhat strictly in terms of its specific output and its geographical location. The cause of the decline may be competition from some other industry (for example, canals *versus* railways, bicycles *versus* automobiles); the depletion of natural resources (for example, lumbering and gold mining), or the approximate satisfaction, at least for a time, of a non-recurrent need (for example, railway building). In adapting his analysis to such cases, Dr. Kuznets takes the maximum output reached by the industry as the upper limit of the variable, and supposes a decline toward zero along an inverted logistic curve. By introducing an additional constant into his equations at need, he is able to secure satisfactory fits.

There remain numerous time series to which the idea of growth and decay is not applicable. Such is the case with all series of prices whether of commodities or other goods, and with many series of ratios, such as interest rates, bond yields, percentages of bank reserves to deposits, marriage rates, and credit ratios. Some of these series

are highly important in the study of business cycles. It is a simple task to find empirical trend lines which fit the data reasonably well. For example, in Chart 1 the British unemployment series suggests the use of a horizontal line, and the British index of wholesale prices suggests a series of oblique lines which meet each other at certain well-known dates. But it is exceedingly difficult to rationalize the procedure, as one can in devising trends for quantities which grow or decay. Yet it may be that certain recent investigations are laying foundations on which can be built a rational analysis even of changing price trends.

(3) The Hypotheses of "Secondary Trends" and of "Long Waves"

In studying the relations between the data points of his industrial series, and the logistic or Gompertz trend lines he had fitted, Dr. Kuznets observed that the annual deviations tended to have positive values during the periods when wholesale-price indexes followed rising trends, and to have negative values when the trend of the price indexes was declining. Of course, this observation seems to be a statistical version of the familiar statement that a long-period rise of wholesale prices stimulates, and that a long-period fall of wholesale prices retards, industrial progress. But Kuznets went further, extending his analysis to the wholesale prices of various great staples. In dealing with these series he had to use empirical trends. Again he found that the annual deviations swerved upward from their long-period trends when the general level of wholesale prices was rising, and swerved downward when the general level of prices was sagging.

To test these observations, Kuznets removed the cyclical fluctuations of the annual deviations from the primary trends so far as possible by taking moving averages with periods slightly longer than business cycles, and measured the duration of the swerves, which he called "secondary trends." He found that the swerves averaged a little shorter in the production series than in the corresponding price series—about 11 years in the one case and about 12 years in the other. Doubling these periods to get the full period from crest to crest, or trough to trough, of these fluctuations, he concluded that the average duration since say the middle of the 19th century has been a little less than 25 years.

Dr. Kuznets inclines to treat these secondary trends as a distinct species of business fluctuations, intermediate between the much

longer primary trends and the much shorter business cycles. To account for them he thinks economists must develop a special theory. His tentative explanation combines emphasis upon factors of a non-business origin with emphasis upon the fact that certain cyclical developments in business activities have effects which persist from one cycle to the next.

In 1913, a Dutch economist, J. van Gelderen, called attention to what he named "large cycles" in economic development, covering about 60 years. A compatriot, S. de Wolff, confirmed van Gelderen's results in 1924 by the use of more technical statistical analysis. Meanwhile the Russian investigator, N. D. Kondratieff, had developed the same idea independently in 1922. Not content with his first results, Kondratieff collected and analyzed all the time series he could find which covered long periods. The results of his work, which agree substantially with those of van Gelderen and de Wolff, were published in Russian in 1925 and summarized in a German article of last December.[1]

Kondratieff starts with the "long waves" of British wholesale price indexes; the rise from 1789 to 1814, the fall to 1849, the rise to 1873, the fall to 1896, the rise to 1920. Similar waves appear in the interest yields upon French *rentes* and British consols; also in French and English wages. Turning to series which show aggregate values or physical quantities, Kondratieff adjusted them to his needs by reducing the original data to a per-capita basis, fitting mathematical trend lines, computing deviations from the trends, and smoothing the deviations with 9-year moving averages. Such smoothed deviations show "long waves" in French imports, exports, and total foreign trade; British exports; French savings-bank balances; the portfolio of the Bank of France; coal production (or consumption) in France, England, the United States, Germany, and the world; iron production in England, the United States, and the world; lead production in England; and the area planted to oats in France and to cotton in the United States. On the other hand, "long waves" are not found in

[1] See Van Gelderen (using the pen-name "J. Fedder"), "Springvloed Beschouwingen over industrielle ontwikkeling en prijsbeweging," *De Nieuwe Tijd,* 1913, pp. 253-277, 369-384, 445-464; de Wolff, "Prosperitäts- und Depressionsperioden," in *Der lebendige Marxismus, Festgabe zum 70. Geburtstage von Karl Kautsky,* Jena, 1924, pp. 13-43; Kondratieff, *The World Economy and its Conjunctures during and after the War* (in Russian), Moscow, 1922; "The Problem of Economic Conditions," *Monthly Economic Bulletin of the Conjuncture Institute,* 1925, Supplement, pp. 28-79 (in Russian); "Die langen Wellen der Konjunktur," *Archiv für Sozialwissenschaft und Sozialpolitik,* December, 1926, vol. lvi, pp. 573-609.

French cotton consumption, American wool and sugar production, or "in the movement of certain other elements."

Surveying the whole body of his results, Kondratieff concludes that the western world has seen two-and-a-half "long waves" since the closing years of the 18th century.[2] The turning points are as follows:

	Trough of the wave	Crest of the wave	Trough of the wave	Approximate duration
1st long wave.......	Late 1780's or early 1790's	1810–17	1844–51	50–60 years
2nd long wave.......	1844–51	1870–75	1890–96	40–50 years
3rd long wave.......	1890–96	1914–20	.....	....

While Kondratieff believes that his statistical results make the existence of "long waves" highly probable, he offers no hypothesis to account for them. But he does regard these waves as cyclical phenomena, and believes that they arise from causes inherent in "capitalistic economy"—not from accident. Like van Gelderen and de Wolff, he rejects the easy explanation that the "long waves" in prices, and hence in other processes, are due to accidental discoveries of gold deposits combined with improvements in mining and metallurgical methods. To these economists it seems more probable that the business conditions characteristic of the ebbing of a "long wave" offer strong incentives to prospecting for new gold deposits and to improving the technical processes of exploiting known deposits. Thus the ebbing of a "long wave" tends to produce effects which favor a rise in prices and a mounting wave. *Vice versa,* the business conditions which characterize the rising of a "long wave" tend to make gold production unprofitable, hence to check the output, to stop the rise of prices, and so to reverse the direction of the whole movement once more. In other words, they treat the long-period swings in gold output as themselves an organic part of the 40-50-60-year cycles. But

[2] De Wolff suggests that each half of the long waves is composed of 2½ smaller cycles, and that the latter cycles are growing briefer according to this schedule:

10 years	10 years	10 years
9 "	9 "	9 "
8 "	8 "	8 "
7 "		

Beginning with 1825 (de Wolff's starting point), this scheme works out as follows:

		Beginning	Duration in years	Ending
1st cycle	Declining phase..........	1825	10+10+5=25	1850
2nd "	Ascending "	1850	5+ 9+9=23	1873
	Declining "	1873	9+ 8+4=21	1894
3rd "	Ascending "	1894	4+ 8+7=19	1913

See *Der lebendige Marxismus*, pp. 37, 38.

Kondratieff, at least, does not regard this suggestion as an adequate theory of the mechanism by which long cycles are alternately initiated and ended.

Until some adequate reason has been shown why we should expect more or less regular recurrences of "long waves" in economic activities, we shall have nothing beyond empirical evidence concerning their existence. We may admit the probable validity of Kondratieff's statistical argument that two-and-a-half "long waves" have occurred in various economic processes since the end of the 18th century, and yet hold open the question whether the series will be continued. Two-and-a-half recurrences do not suffice to establish empirically a presumption that any feature of modern history will repeat itself.

Another uncertainty is presented by the difference in order of magnitude between the duration of the "long waves" found by van Gelderen, de Wolff and Kondratieff, and the duration of the "secondary trends" found by Kuznets. It may be that the difference in the results is due to differences in methods of fitting trends, and computing and smoothing deviations. Or perhaps the European investigators, looking for replicas of the major swings of wholesale prices, paid slight attention to swerves which attract notice in a less preoccupied mind. Or it may be that there really are two sets of long-term fluctuations in economic activities, one of which averages double the duration of the second. Further research is needed to settle these issues.

But whether there be two sets of long-term fluctuations or only one set, whether (if there be but one set) the typical length is about a quarter or about half a century, and whether these fluctuations are merely historical episodes of considerable interest or an inherent characteristic of "capitalist economy," the investigations of van Gelderen, de Wolff, Kondratieff and Kuznets open an alluring perspective of future work. Starting with the study of commercial crises, the realistic students of economic activities have discovered successively several types of fluctuations which, at least for more than a century, appear to have been recurrent—the seasonal variations to which Jevons directed attention in his youth, the inter-crisis cycles of Juglar and others, the shorter business cycles of later writers, the secular trends of empirical statisticians, the 22-24-year "secondary trends" of Kuznets, and "long waves." Of course, some of these discoveries may prove to be invalid; but, on the other hand, recurrences of other periods may be revealed Sismondi's problem was merely to explain

crises: now the problem is to ascertain how many types of fluctuations are intermixed in economic experience, to differentiate these types from each other, to measure the wave-length of each type and to ascertain its regularity of recurrence, finally to construct a theory which will account adequately for all the types of fluctuations and make clear their relations to each other. As treatises upon crises, or crises and depressions, are giving place to treatises upon business cycles, so the latter may in turn give place to treatises upon economic oscillations.

While the time for undertakings of such scope has not quite come, we should keep constantly in mind the probable interconnection between business cycles and the less-studied fluctuations of shorter or longer duration. One connection is clear. Our writers on secular trends confirm an old contention when they point out that during the ebbing phase of a "long wave" years of depression predominate in the inter-crisis cycles, while during the mounting phase of a "long wave" years of prosperity predominate.[3]

We stand to learn more about economic oscillations at large and about business cycles in particular, if we approach the problem of trends as theorists, than if we confine ourselves to strictly empirical work. The trends which promise the most important additions to our knowledge are those which correspond to rational hypotheses, although they may not "fit the data" so well as empirical constructions which are difficult to interpret. For it may prove possible to integrate the rational hypotheses which yield instructive trends with the theory of business cycles.

(4) Conclusion.

The upshot of this discussion is that lines of secular trend show the effects of causes which, though subject to change at any moment, have influenced an economic process in some regular, or regularly changing, way through periods of time long in comparison with business cycles. What these causes have been, and whether they are still in operation, are matters for further inquiry. The empirical inquirer measures something which he knows merely as secular trend; that something is a set of net resultants; he may or we may not try to find out to what that something is due.

If we embark upon a search for causes of secular trends, we must

[3] See, for example, Kondratieff's article cited above, *Archiv für Sozialwissenschaft und Sozialpolitik,* December, 1926, vol. lvi, p. 591.

expect to find not one cause peculiar to each series, but a peculiar combination of a multitude of interrelated causes. These causes may be classified as (1) causes related to changes in the number of population, (2) causes related to the economic efficiency of the population—its age, constitution, health, education, technical knowledge and equipment, methods of coöperation, methods of settling conflicts of interest, and many other matters; (3) causes related to the quantity and quality of the natural resources exploited by the population.

Not only the second, but also the first and the third of these categories consists of a complex of factors which sustain all sorts of relations to each other. Even kinds of causes which the classification separates are interacting. The growth of population is influenced by changes in industrial technique and in natural resources; the growth of population also influences the development of technique and of resources; finally, changes in technique produce changes in resources (the iron-ore ranges and water powers of North America did not exist for the red men), and changes in resources are ever stimulating changes in technique. All of which means that we must think of every type of economic activity in a country as conditioned by a concert of fundamental factors, albeit a concert in which the ranking of the factors differs endlessly from case to case.

Another approach may make the conclusion clearer and more significant. There are secular causes which affect many economic activities in much the same way, for example, changes in gold output, depletion of soil fertility. There are secular causes which affect economic activities in different ways: the extension of the railway net over the United States checked canal building, diminished river traffic, and led to the abandonment of many eastern farms; but it stimulated the settlement of western lands, built up interior cities, and fostered the expansion of the coal and steel trades. There are secular causes whose direct effects are confined mainly to some single line of activity: —a series of inventions which cheapens the cost of producing some article of secondary importance is an example. Those secular causes which influence many activities in much the same way produce a measure of likeness among the secular trends of different time series. Those secular causes which influence various activities in opposite ways, and those secular causes whose perceptible influence is limited in scope introduce diversities in secular trends. There can scarcely be any time series whose trend is not a joint product of factors which tend toward uniformity and factors which tend toward diversity.

The most valuable contributions toward an understanding of the trends empirically established by statisticians have been made by the economic historians. These workers have studied in detail such great movements as the Agricultural and the Industrial Revolutions, the evolution of capitalism, the world-spread of the European races, the discovery, utilization and impairment of natural resources. They have sought not merely to record but also to explain these long-period changes in human affairs, using such statistics as they could gather and such hypotheses as their materials suggested. But they have been kept so busy mastering a vast mass of materials that they have not yet begun a systematic attack upon the problem of secular trends. Nor have they equipped themselves with the statistical technique needed for the most effective use of numerical data.

Economic theorists also have shown some interest in secular trends, but their contributions have been speculations concerning the future, rather than analysis of the past. The "pure" economic theory of recent years has dealt mainly with "static" problems, from which secular changes are barred. Economic "dynamics" has been regarded as more treacherous ground, and the mischances of eminent men who have walked thereon by the light of theory have been discouraging. Ricardo, for example, expected that mankind would be forced to resort to ever poorer soils and ever more intensive cultivation to get food for their increasing numbers; that in consequence real wages would remain at best constant, profits would decline unsteadily, and rents rise until "almost the whole produce of the country, after paying the laborers, will be the property of the owners of land and the receivers of tithes and taxes."[1] Of the numerous speculations of this type, those of Karl Marx are of especial interest here, because they include the increasing frequency and increasing severity of business crises among the secular trends which are to usher in the socialistic state.[2]

It is no wonder that a field which requires the fusion of statistical technique with historical learning and theoretical finesse has not yet

[1] *Principles of Political Economy,* ed. by C. K. Gonner, London, 1891, p. 99.

[2] Marx's theory of crises runs through all three volumes of *Capital,* not to speak of his other writings. For a brief statement of the rôle of crises in the scheme of economic revolution, see the preface which he wrote in 1873 for the first volume of *Capital* (English translation by Moore and Aveling, Chicago, 1915, p. 26.)

John R. Commons, H. L. McCracken, and W. B. Zeuch have made a systematic study of the ideas concerning secular trends propounded by economic theorists. They hold that the conceptions of trends and business cycles have been derived from the theories of value entertained by the writers they discuss and from the types of organization these writers had in mind. See "Secular Trends and Business Cycles: a Classification of Theories," *Review of Economic Statistics,* Preliminary vol. iv, pp. 244-263.

been explored. Yet the time may be near when the problem of secular trends will have as definite a standing in economic research, attract as many investigators, and yield as interesting results as the problem of business cycles. In the meanwhile, students of the latter problem suffer the grave disadvantage of having to deal with a factor which is both important and obscure. They cannot anticipate the results of researches not yet made; they cannot make adequate studies of secular trends as an incident in their studies of cyclical fluctuations, and they cannot let the problem alone.

One set of questions is particularly insistent. Is there a definite relation between secular trends and cyclical fluctuations? Are activities characterized by a rapidly rising trend subject to more frequent, or more violent, cycles than activities whose trend is nearer the horizontal? And more at large, can the trends of time series, after they have been measured, be discarded as of no further interest? Or must the trends themselves be brought into the explanations of cyclical fluctuations, as is suggested by those theories which connect business cycles with "progress"? [3] Are the trends themselves generated by cyclical fluctuations, as Mr. Lawrence K. Frank has argued? [4] While these questions arise at this point, they cannot be answered by any process short of considering the pertinent evidence in detail. But the mere fact that such problems must be faced by the business-cycle theorist suffices to show that he cannot imitate the business-cycle statistician in merely eliminating secular trends.

4. The Problem of Seasonal Variations.

Chart 4, drawn on a larger scale than the charts illustrating secular trends, shows how time series differ in respect to seasonal variations. As in Chart 1, the data are plotted in their original form, in order to make clear the varied difficulties which confront the statistician who is trying to isolate cyclical fluctuations.

There are series in the chart which undergo seasonal changes each year of much the same sort, and of an amplitude so large as to obscure the cyclical fluctuations, if not the secular trends. There are series in which the seasonal variations, while fairly regular, are not wide. There are others which suggest the presence of seasonal factors

[3] Compare Chapter I, section iv, 4.

[4] See Mr. Frank's paper, "Long-Term Price Trends," *Journal of the American Statistical Association,* September, 1923, vol. xviii, pp. 904-908.

CHART 4.

A Collection of Time Series to Illustrate Differences in Seasonal Variations.

GROUP I-LARGE AND REGULAR SEASONAL VARIATIONS

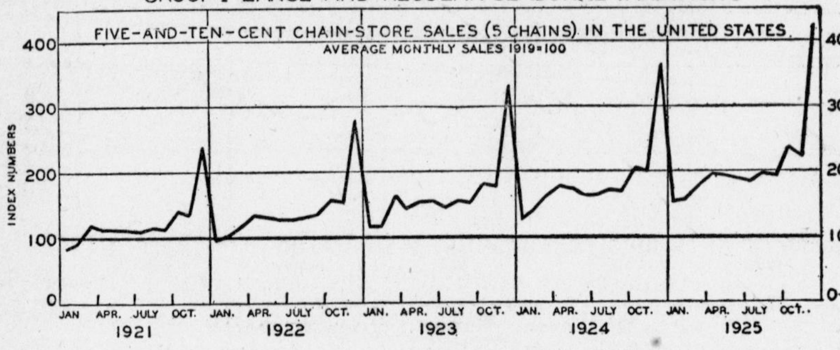

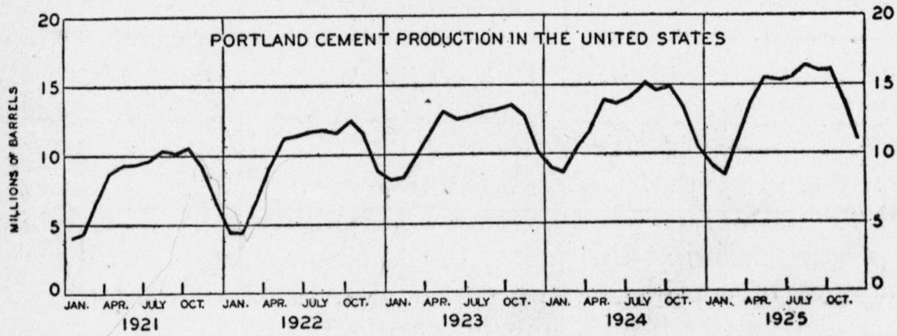

GROUP II- SMALL AND FAIRLY REGULAR SEASONAL VARIATIONS

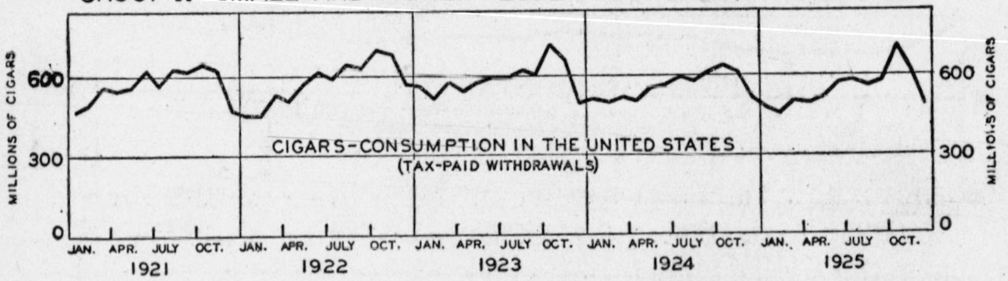

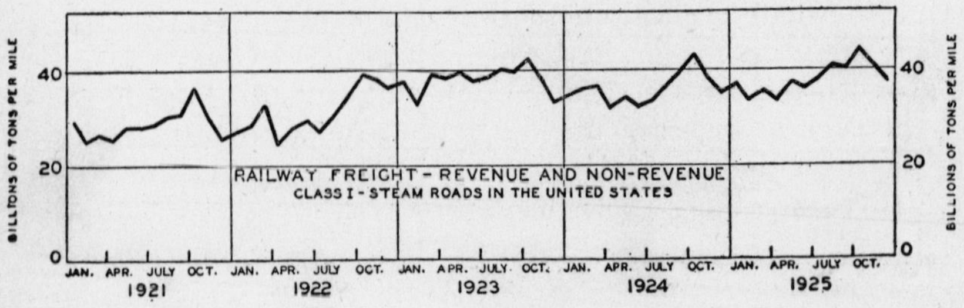

CHART 4 (*Continued*)

A COLLECTION OF TIME SERIES TO ILLUSTRATE DIFFERENCES IN SEASONAL VARIATIONS.

GROUP III – RATHER IRREGULAR SEASONAL VARIATIONS

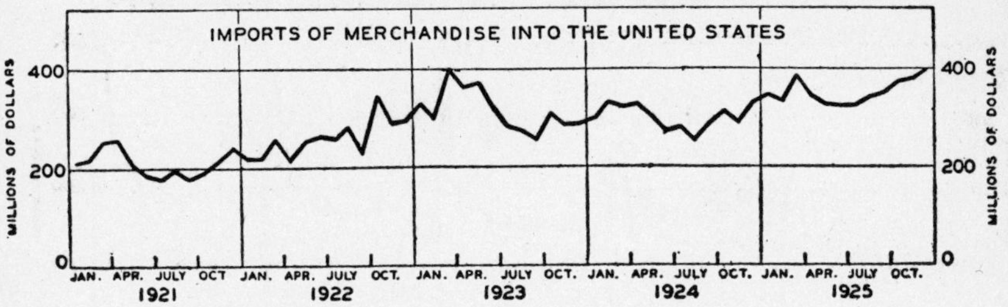

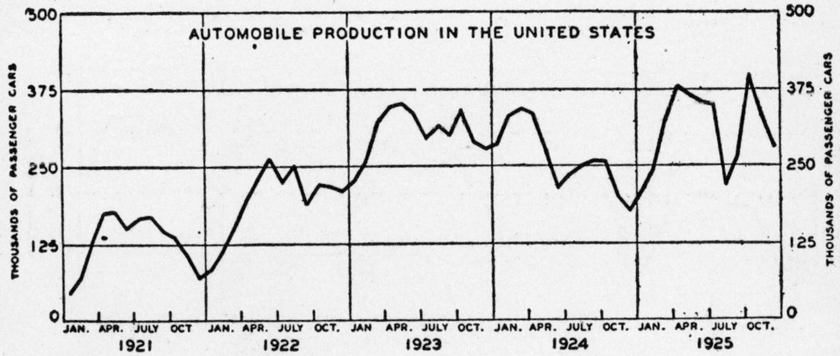

GROUP IV – NO PERCEPTIBLE SEASONAL VARIATIONS.

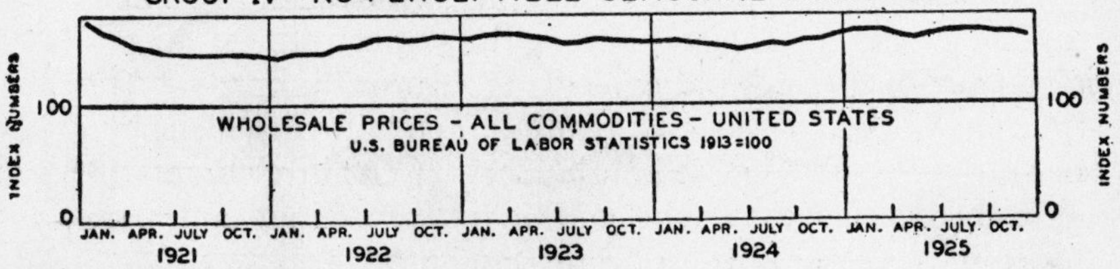

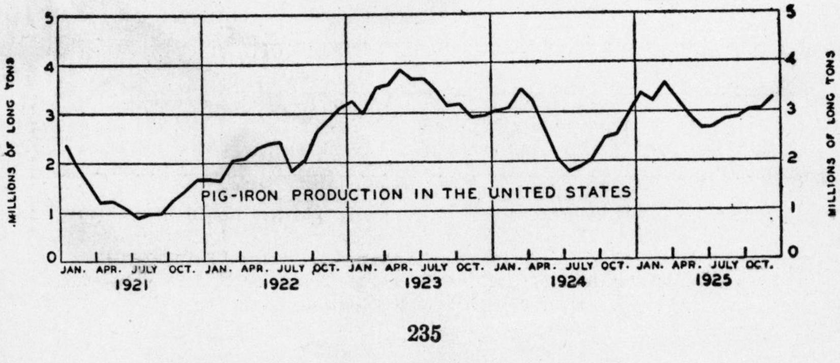

rather irregular in themselves, or so combined with changing conditions of other types as to produce rather irregular results. Finally, there are series in which it is difficult on inspection, or even on analysis, to detect any semblance of regularity in the month to month movements of different years.

To isolate cyclical fluctuations for close study, we should be able to determine in doubtful cases the presence or absence of seasonal variations, to measure their amplitudes where found, and finally to get rid of them when we wish. How to accomplish all this is a problem which the business-cycle statisticians have attacked with vigor.[1] Business-cycle theorists, on the contrary, have paid little attention to these short-period oscillations—an omission which it is unwise to imitate.

(1) The Causes and Pervasiveness of Seasonal Variations.

Two types of seasons produce annually recurring variations in economic activities—those which are due to climates and those which are due to conventions. Upon some activities these seasons act directly, upon others indirectly.

(1) In the temperate zones at least, where lie the areas of chief concern to us, climatic seasons control the growth of crops and of such animal products as wool. They exercise a marked influence upon the current supply of many other animal products, such as fish, milk, poultry and eggs. In varying degree they affect almost all processes carried on out-of-doors, building, logging, transportation, road making, construction work at large. They are a factor in the efficiency or the cost of many processes carried on indoors. Certainly climatic seasons influence the death rate; doubtless they influence morbidity rates and so affect almost all activities in some measure.[1]

Upon the demand for certain types of goods, the effect of climatic seasons is not less clear than its effects upon certain types of produc-

[1] The earliest studies of seasonal variations known to Jevons were made in 1854 to 1856 by J. W. Gilbert (bank-note circulation, *Statistical Journal*, vol. xvii, pp. 289-321, and vol. xix, pp. 144-168) and Charles Babbage (bank clearings, the same, vol. xix, p. 28). Jevons began his own economic studies with a paper, "On the Study of Periodic Commercial Fluctuations," which he sent to the meeting of the British Association in 1862. In 1866 he read a much more elaborate paper, "On the Frequent Autumnal Pressure in the Money Market," to the Statistical Society of London. See *Investigations in Currency and Finance*, by W. S. Jevons, London, 1884, pp. 1-12, and 160-193.

[1] On the seasonal variations of the death rate, see Maurice B. Hexter, *Social Consequences of Business Cycles*, Boston and New York, 1925, pp. 55-57.

tion. The sort of clothing we wear, our sports, the amount of fuel we use, undergo radical changes from winter to summer.

Market supply is kept far steadier than the rate at which goods subject to strong seasonal influences are produced. This steadiness is a triumph of economic planning. It is won by arranging compensatory seasonal variations in the activities which intervene between producing and consuming. The processes of preserving, storing, transporting and distributing goods are purposely made to vary in such a way that a highly unstable rate of production is converted into a fairly even rate of market supply, or into a rate of market supply which varies with seasonal changes in demand. Some efforts are made to counteract also the variations in demand produced by climatic seasons. For example, a seasonal change is made in the price of coal to stimulate buying during the summer, and most seasonal goods can be had cheaper in their "off seasons." Thus the effects of climatic seasons are extended by man's contrivance over a wide variety of economic processes.

(2) Conventional seasons have many origins—ancient religious observances, folk customs, fashions, business practices, statute law.

The most pervasive of all the seasonal variations in time series is due to the calendar. February is nearly 10 per cent shorter than January, except in leap years when it is about 6 per cent shorter, and April is nearly 3 per cent shorter than March. Series of monthly aggregates are thus made to show a spurious seasonal variation—spurious in the sense that it bears no relation to the current rate of activity. And this spurious variation is made irregular from year to year by the different ways in which Sundays and holidays are divided among the months.

Many of the conventional seasons have considerable effects on economic behavior. We can count on active retail buying before Christmas, on the Thanksgiving demand for turkeys, on the July demand for fireworks, on the preparations for June weddings, on heavy dividend and interest payments at the beginning of each quarter, on an increase of bankruptcies in January, and so on. One of these conventional seasons is especially troublesome to statisticians, because it is movable. Easter may come as early as March 22d or as late as April 25th. Seasonal variations in series affected by Easter buying are decidedly different in the March and the April years.

From the activities directly affected by climatic or conventional seasons, acting separately or in unison, seasonal influences radiate to

all other activities, probably without exception. In part these radiations are due to the conscious efforts already spoken of to counteract seasonal changes in demand or supply; in part they are unplanned consequences of these changes. For example, the fact that American crops are harvested largely in the autumn gives rise to a seasonal demand for currency in the farming districts, to seasonal changes in interest rates (and sometimes stock prices) in the financial centers, to seasonal changes in railway traffic, to seasonal changes in farmers' receipts, to seasonal changes in their payments to creditors, to seasonal changes in the business of country merchants, and to seasonal changes in wage disbursements. So, too, the expectation of heavy buying by consumers in the holiday season leads retailers to increase their stocks at earlier dates. In turn, the prospect of these large orders injects still earlier seasonal variations into manufacturing, into the demand for raw materials, into employment, and into wage payments, thus tending to produce secondary seasonal variations in retail buying itself.

It seems probable that these reflex effects of the primary seasonal disturbances grow smaller in most cases as they radiate to other processes. For example, manufacturers of goods for which the demand is largely concentrated in a few weeks seek to spread the production over a longer period. It is far less costly to provide a moderate equipment which can be used continuously in making a year's supply of goods than to provide a large equipment which must stand idle most of the time in order to produce a year's supply in a rush. Of course the ideal of continuous production is seldom attained in seasonal trades; but the business motives for stabilizing operations are clear enough and strong enough to moderate the effect of seasonal factors in a notable degree.[2]

Not less important, is the fact that both the original and the derived impulses toward seasonal activity are well scattered over the months of the year. For example, coal mining and logging grow brisk while construction work is falling off and farming requires fewer hands. In Great Britain employment reaches its maximum in

[2] Dr. N. I. Stone has pointed out that efforts to stabilize operations usually begin with seasonal variations, and later may or may not extend to cyclical variations. See his chapter on "Methods of Stabilizing Production of Textiles, Clothing, and Novelties," in *Business Cycles and Unemployment*, National Bureau of Economic Research, 1923, pp. 116-133.

References to the rapidly growing literature upon methods of mitigating seasonal and cyclical variations may be found in the bibliography given by Lewisohn, Draper, Commons and Lescohier in *Can Business Prevent Unemployment?* New York, 1925, pp. 217-226, and in the footnotes of H. Feldman's *The Regularization of Employment*, New York, 1925.

March for shipbuilding; in April and May for the furnishing trades; in June and July for engineering; in August for building; in September for iron mining and iron and steel making; in November for tin-plate and sheet-steel work, the miscellaneous metal trades, and printing; in December for coal mining.[3] This diversity of dates makes the business of a country as a whole far steadier from month to month than are most of the component parts. As the seasonal impulses produced by any factor radiate from the center of disturbance, they encounter the radiating effects of the seasonal variations which have occurred or are expected in other factors. If some time series, like the Bureau of Labor Statistics index number of prices at wholesale or stock prices, seem to be nearly or quite free from seasonal variations, it is presumably because they are affected by many different seasonal influences which cancel one another.

Reflection upon the causes which we assign for seasonal movements suggests that few of them will produce precisely the same effects year after year. An exceptionally cold winter will increase the seasonal swing in coal consumption, in the sale of woolen underwear, and in construction work. The conventional seasons which have not a fixed date in the calendar—particularly Easter—are responsible for other deviations from the seasonal pattern. In careful work, the months with five Sundays must be treated differently from months with four Sundays. And even the conventions tied to fixed dates—like holiday shopping and January and July interest payments—produce different effects when they occur in combination with different phases of business cycles. Over long periods, also, changes in industrial technique, communication, transportation, and business organization alter seasonal oscillations. The autumnal drain upon the money markets for moving the crops, for example, has become decidedly less of a bugbear to operators on the New York Stock Exchange than it was before the organization of the Federal Reserve System. Hence statisticians who break long time series into briefer periods often find that the seasonal variations of the parts differ appreciably. Chart 5 gives two examples of this sort, one taken from

[3] See A. L. Bowley and K. C. Smith, "Seasonal Variations in Finance, Prices and Industry," *London and Cambridge Economic Service,* Special Memorandum, No. 7, July, 1924, pp. 14, 15. The seasonal variations are derived from data for the years 1900-1913.

CHART 5.

EXAMPLES OF SEASONAL VARIATIONS WHICH HAVE CHANGED IN THE COURSE OF TIME.

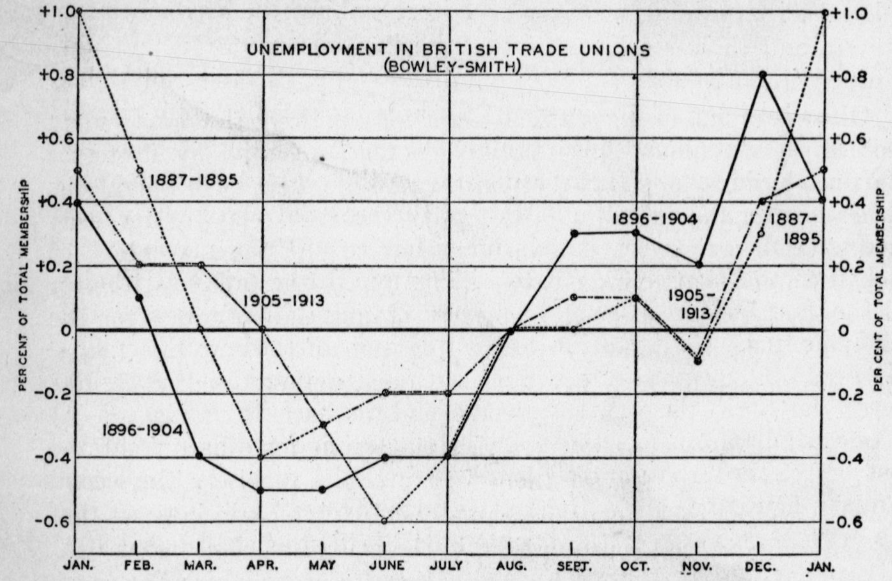

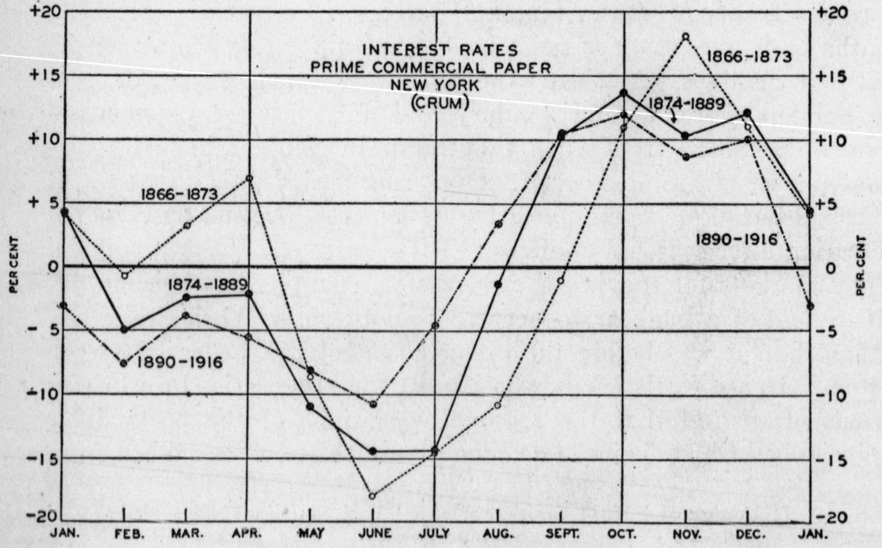

the British unemployment data, the other from interest rates on prime commercial paper in the New York market.[4]

(2) Methods of Measuring Average Seasonal Variations.

Of ways of measuring seasonal variations, perhaps the most widely used is the ingenious "link-relative" method invented by Professor Warren M. Persons. This method requires six successive operations upon the original data. (1) Compute the link relatives for each successive month (week or quarter), that is, find the percentage of each item to the preceding item. (2) Arrange the link relatives for all the Januaries in a frequency table. Make similar tables for the other months. (3) Find the median in each of these twelve tables. (4) Forge the medians into a chain with January represented by 100. Carry the chain through the twelve months back to January. (5) If, as usually happens, the second January figure differs from the first one, adjust the figures for all the months to make the second January figure 100. (6) Readjust all the figures once more so that the arithmetic mean of the twelve monthly figures shall equal 100.[1]

[4] See the paper of Messrs. Bowley and Smith cited above, and W. L. Crum, "Cycles of Rates on Commercial Paper", *Review of Economic Statistics*, January, 1923, Preliminary vol. v, p. 29.

The data from which Chart 5 is drawn are as follows:

	Seasonal Variations of					
	Percentage of Members Unemployed in British Trade Unions			Interest Rates on Prime Commercial Paper in New York		
	1887–95	1896–1904	1905–13	1866–73	1874–89	1890–1916
January	+1.0	+.4	+.5	+ 4.1	+ 4.4	− 3.0
February	+ .5	+.1	+.2	− .7	− 4.9	− 7.6
March	0	−.4	+.2	+ 3.2	− 2.4	− 3.9
April	− .4	−.5	0	+ 6.9	− 2.3	− 5.6
May	− .3	−.5	−.3	− 8.7	−11.0	− 8.1
June	− .6	−.4	−.2	−18.0	−14.4	−10.8
July	− .4	−.4	−.2	−14.6	−14.3	− 4.6
August	0	0	0	−10.9	− 1.4	+ 3.3
September	0	+.3	+.1	− 1.1	+10.2	+10.5
October	+ .1	+.3	+.1	+10.9	+13.6	+11.8
November	− .1	+.2	−.1	+18.0	+10.3	+ 8.6
December	+ .3	+.8	+.4	+11.1	+12.1	+10.0

[1] For examples of this method see Professor Persons' papers in the *Review of Economic Statistics*, particularly Preliminary volume i. Later expositions are given by Professor Persons in "Correlation of Time Series," *Journal of the American Statistical Association*, June, 1923, vol. xviii, pp. 713-726, and in his contribution to the *Handbook of Mathematical Statistics*, edited by H. L. Rietz, Boston, 1924, chapter x.

A technical improvement upon Persons' method has been suggested by Professor W. L. Crum. Instead of using the medians given by the frequency tables, take "the

It will be noticed that Professor Persons measures the seasonal variation of a series before he has computed its secular trend. It is primarily because of the trend that his second January figure usually differs from the first, and that his fifth step has to be taken. Dr. William L. Hart has argued that it is better first to determine the trend of a series by whatever method is most appropriate; second to eliminate the trend, by subtracting the magnitude it indicates from the original item for each month, and then to compute the arithmetic means of all the Januaries, all the Februaries, etc., as shown by the data in this corrected form.[2]

Several statisticians have pointed out that Dr. Hart's method of "monthly means" does not guard against the influence upon the seasonal index of extreme and irregular deviations.[3] As a remedy for this defect, Dr. Lincoln W. Hall and Miss Helen D. Falkner proposed what the latter calls the "ratio-to-ordinate" method. Like Dr. Hart, they start by determining the secular trend. Next they compute the percentage of each original item to the corresponding value given by the trend line, make frequency tables of these percentages for each month, select from the frequency tables a typical value (usually the mean of a middle group of items), and finally adjust the twelve typical values so that their average for the year is 100.[4]

Still another method, devised by Dr. Fred R. Macaulay, is to make 12-months moving averages of the original items centered at the seventh month, compute the ratio of the original item for each month to its moving-average value, find medians of these ratios for

mean of a middle group of items (two or four if the series contains an even number of items, three if an odd number)." "Use of the Median in Determining Seasonal Variation," *Journal of the American Statistical Association*, March, 1923, vol. xviii, pp. 607-614.

Criticisms of this method may be found in several of the papers presently to be cited, and on p. 26 of the paper by Bowley and Smith cited above. "It is very doubtful . . .," say these writers, "whether the comparison of each month with the preceding is as appropriate for the measurement of seasonal influence as the comparison of each month with the position determined by the general average or by the line of trend." They regard Professor Persons' method as "specially suitable for correcting records for seasonal variation" (since it reveals irregularities in the frequency tables), but hold that the most accurate method of "measuring the seasonal effects" is to use deviations from a 12-months moving average.

[2] William L. Hart, "The Method of Monthly Means for Determination of a Seasonal Variation," *Journal of the American Statistical Association*, September, 1922, vol. xviii, pp. 341-349.

[3] See, for example, W. M. Persons in the *Handbook of Mathematical Statistics*, edited by H. L. Rietz, pp. 155-158.

[4] See Lincoln W. Hall, "Seasonal Variation as a Relative of Secular Trend," *Journal of the American Statistical Association*, June, 1924, vol. xix, pp. 155-166, and Helen D. Falkner, "The Measurement of Seasonal Variation," in the same issue, pp. 167-179.

all the Januaries, Februaries, etc., and convert the medians into percentages which total 1200 for the year.[5]

Choice among these methods is to be guided, of course, by the characteristics of the series to be dealt with and the specific purpose in view. As Messrs. Bowley and Smith point out in their systematic discussion of the problem, the first question to be asked is whether the seasonal variation of any month from the annual average is more appropriately considered as a given amount, or as a given proportion. For example, do the October imports of wheat into England tend to be 50,000 tons more than the average of all months, or do they tend to be 11 per cent above the average? If greater regularity is secured by considering amounts, then seasonal variations should be expressed in percentages borne by the absolute difference between the average amount in each month shown by the data (in their original form or adjusted for trend) and the arithmetic mean for the whole year. If greater regularity is secured by considering proportions, then seasonal variations should be computed from ratios, and geometric means should be used. A second question to be considered in either case is whether the series shows an upward or downward trend. If not, the absolute differences or the relative differences may be computed directly from the original data. If there is a trend to be eliminated, that can be accomplished by using moving averages or by fitting curves, and the absolute or relative differences ascertained from the data corrected for trend. Thus Bowley and Smith discuss and use in different series six methods—three based on amounts and three on proportions, one of each set without correction for trend, one with the trend removed by moving averages, and one with the trend removed by the method of least squares. Of these methods they think the two which use moving averages are the most accurate, though the most laborious. In a few cases they make use also of Persons' link-relative method.[6]

(3) Efforts to Measure Changing Seasonal Variations.

In all the preceding methods the object is to find one set of monthly figures which measures the average seasonal influence. Oc-

[5] See "Index of Production in Selected Basic Industries," *Federal Reserve Bulletin*, December, 1922, vol. iii, pp. 1414, 1415.

[6] A. L. Bowley and K. C. Smith, "Seasonal Variations in Finance, Prices and Industry," *London and Cambridge Economic Service*, Special Memorandum, No. 7, July, 1924.

casionally statisticians who use one of these methods notice that the seasonal fluctuations of their series seem to undergo a change between the beginning and the end of their period. They may then break the whole period into two or more parts, and compute fixed seasonals for each segment in the fashion of Chart 5. A more ambitious plan, that of measuring seasonal variations as they change from one year to the next, has been suggested by Dr. Willford I. King. His successive steps are as follows: (1) Plot the data. (2) Draw a free hand curve through the data representing the cyclical fluctuations. (3) Read from this "preliminary cycle curve" the numerical values which it indicates each month, and (4) divide the actual data by these values. The quotients give the first approximation to the seasonal variations. (5) Smooth out the irregularities of this rough approximation by using 9-period moving averages of all the Januaries, all the Februaries, etc. Plot the results and smooth out the small irregularities which may still remain. (6) Adjust the results so that the sum of the twelve seasonal indexes for each year shall equal 1200.[1]

Dr. King's effort to take account of the changes which seasonal variations undergo from time to time has commended itself to other statisticians; but his method has been questioned because of the free play given to the investigator's personal equation.[2] Dr. W. L. Crum has devised a method of showing progressive changes in seasonal variations which is not open to this objection. The essential feature of his plan is to find the secular trend of all the January items in a series, all the February items, and so on, and to use the ordinates of these 12 monthly trends as the basis for determining the seasonal variations in each successive year.[3]

This method is designed primarily to yield "seasonal *standards* applicable to the study of current phenomena." It applies to series

[1] Willford I. King, "An Improved Method for Measuring the Seasonal Factor," *Journal of the American Statistical Association,* September, 1924, vol. xix, pp. 301-313.

[2] Compare O. Gressens, "On the Measurement of Seasonal Variations," *Journal of the American Statistical Association,* June, 1925, vol. xx, p. 205.

[3] The details of this method differ according as the investigator works with link relatives or with monthly means of the data. See W. L. Crum, "Progressive Variation in Seasonality," *Journal of the American Statistical Association,* March, 1925, vol. xx, pp. 48-64. As Dr. Crum points out, similar suggestions have been made by Dr. E. C. Snow, "Trade Forecasting and Prices," *Journal of the Royal Statistical Society,* May, 1923, vol. lxxxvi, p. 334, and by Mr. Harold Flynn, quoted in *The Problem of Business Forecasting,* Boston and New York, 1924, p. 104.

For an interesting application of the method, see Edwin Frickey, "Bank Clearings Outside New York City, 1875-1914," *Review of Economic Statistics,* October, 1925, vol. vii, pp. 258-262. Mr. Frickey found seasonal variations in the terminal years of a period by fitting straight line trends to link relatives for each month, and then made progressively changing seasonals for the intervening years by straight line interpolations.

whose seasonal variations change slowly and progressively for considerable periods.[4] But it does not take account of yearly changes in seasonal factors, such as are produced, say, by warm and cold winters, or by March and April Easters. Mr. O. Gressens has proposed a method which will show changes of the latter type. He computes the ratio of a variable each month to the average monthly value for its year, corrects these monthly ratios when necessary for the trend within the year, smooths them by the use of moving averages, moderates any widely divergent items which may remain, and adjusts his ratios for each year so that their sum shall be 1200. This method he believes to have the merits of Dr. King's procedure, and to be "mechanically more definite." [5]

(4) Conclusion.

The preceding review shows how much labor statisticians have devoted to the measurement of seasonal variations. That problem has an interest of its own, apart from its bearing upon the isolating of cyclical fluctuations. Efforts to mitigate seasonal reductions in employment, and to reduce costs of production by "budgeting" production and marketing are stimulated and made more effective by knowledge of the magnitude and regularity of the seasonal variations in the numerous activities which have to be considered in laying plans. Happily for us, it is often possible to turn results worked out for practical ends to theoretical uses.

A few illustrations of seasonal variations, as measured by statistical investigators have already been given in Chart 5. Additional illustrations are presented in Chart 6, which shows the same method applied to different series, and Chart 7, which shows various methods applied to the same or different series.

Non-technical readers who feel a bit confused by the variety of methods which have been sketched may take comfort in Chart 7. It illustrates a remark made by Messrs. Bowley and Smith. Having experimented with different ways of measuring seasonal variations perhaps more elaborately than any other investigators, they observe

[4] W. L. Crum, as cited, pp. 60, 61.

[5] O. Gressens, "On the Measurement of Seasonal Variation," *Journal of the American Statistical Association,* June, 1925, vol. xx, pp. 203-210.

Dr. King, on the other hand, points out that it is difficult to apply either Crum's or Gressens' method to time series in which the seasonal variations are relatively slight and the cyclical fluctuations relatively violent.

CHART 6.

INDEXES OF SEASONAL VARIATIONS.

Made by the moving-average-median method (F. R. Macaulay).

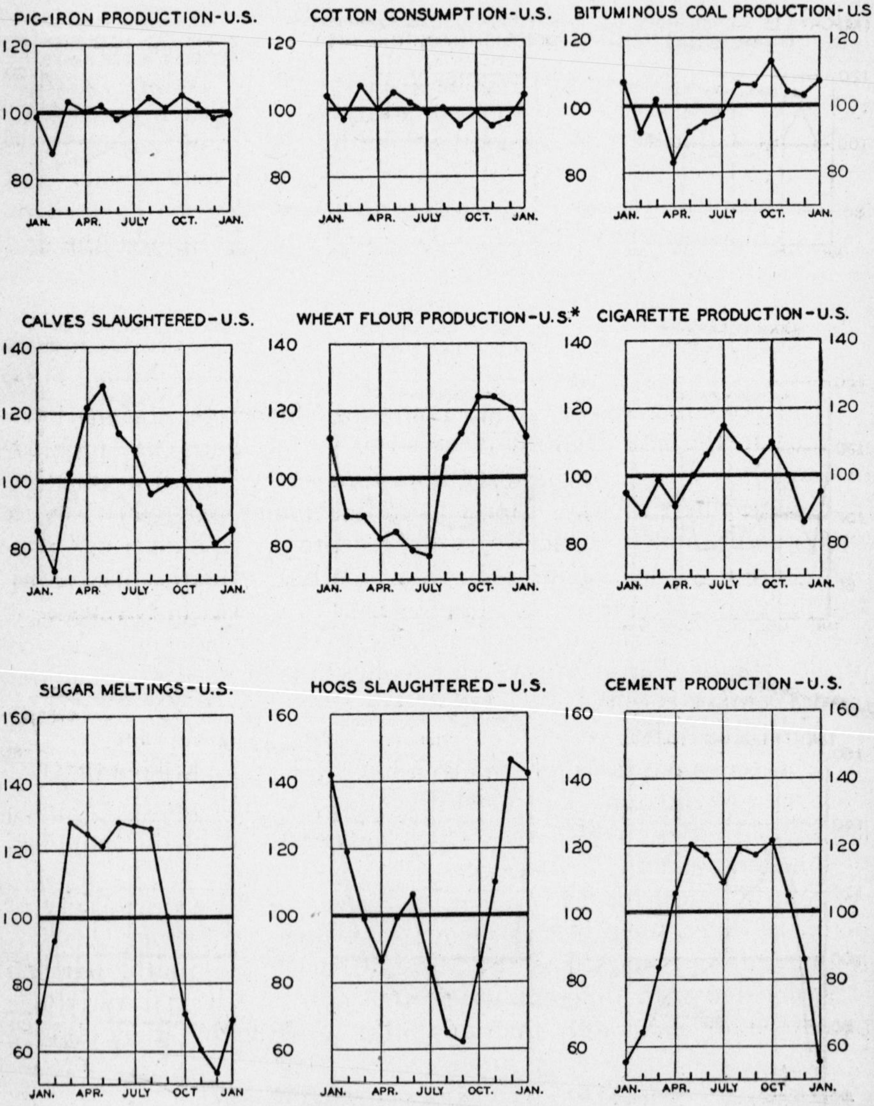

COMPUTATION BASED ON DATA FROM JAN. 1913 TO DEC. 1921
*COMPUTATION BASED ON DATA FROM JAN. 1914 TO DEC. 1921

CHART 6 (*Continued*).

INDEXES OF SEASONAL VARIATIONS.

Made by the link-relative method (W. M. Persons).

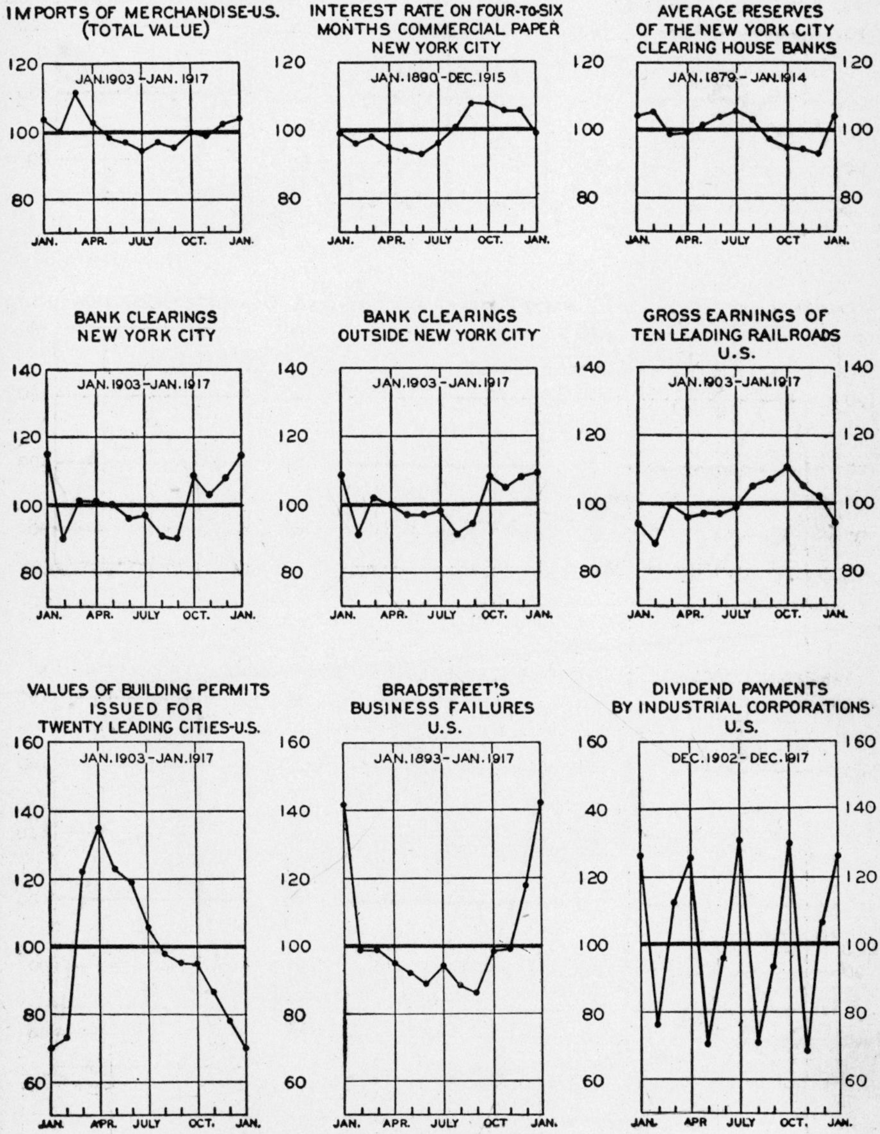

CHART 7.

Indexes of Seasonal Variations Made by Various Methods.

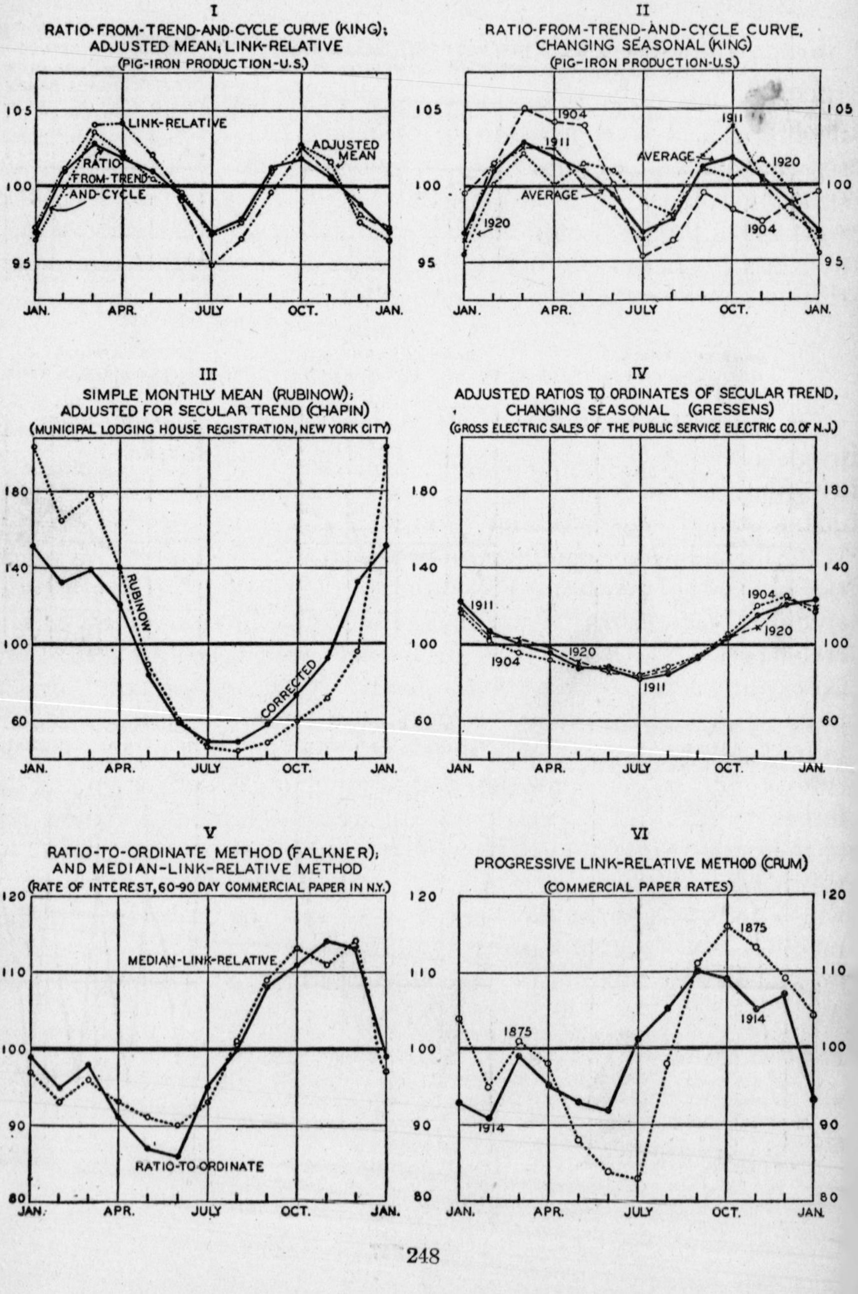

that "in fact, these methods give nearly identical results in most cases." [1]

5. The Problem of Irregular Fluctuations.

While less progress has been made in dealing with the irregular fluctuations of time series than in dealing with secular trends and seasonal variations, we are not at liberty to dismiss this topic quite so summarily as do most statisticians. The conceptual difficulties with which the problem bristles are significant for the theory of business cycles. In considering them, we shall find ourselves confronting certain issues fundamental to our further work.

(1) The Concept of Irregular Fluctuations.

So far as known, all social time series without exception present irregularities of contour in their raw state. Statisticians take these irregularities for granted without attempting to define them, as they define secular trends, seasonal variations, and cyclical fluctuations.[1] What little they say upon the subject concerns the causes of irregularities in particular series. For example, they point out that wars or civil insurrections may disturb many economic processes for a considerable period. Less serious disturbances may be caused by such events as earthquakes, conflagrations, floods, droughts, epidemics, insect pests, strikes and lockouts, railway embargoes, inventions, changes in trade routes, discoveries of fresh resources, changes in laws, judicial rulings, and so on through an interminable list. Nor should we forget the effects of changes in the method of compiling statistics, and of inaccurate reporting. The addition of a new town to the list for which bank clearings are published, the disruption of a trade union which had made unemployment returns, changes in the lists of commodities used in a price index, the failure of customs-house clerks to include all July invoices in their July statement of imports, revisions

[1] "Seasonal Variations in Finance, Prices and Industry," *London and Cambridge Economic Service,* July, 1924, Special Memorandum, No. 7, p. 3.

[1] The nearest approach to a definition has been made by Professor Edmund E. Day, who proposes to divide irregular fluctuations into two classes—namely,

"Episodic movements due to specific causes, ordinarily reflected in sharp, pronounced breaks in the record of the variable. . . .

"Fortuitous or accidental movements, of unknown origin, quite irregular in character, but involving only minor disturbances of the general course of the variable."

See Day's *Statistical Analysis,* New York, 1925, pp. 285, 302-306, and 310-312.

in the estimates of monetary stocks to take account of losses, reclassifications of railroad freight, errors in addition, misprints—a thousand such matters may produce purely artificial irregularities in time series.

The idea suggested by this practice of listing causes is that we may classify as an irregular fluctuation any movement of a curve which we do not ascribe to secular, seasonal or cyclical changes. If we had clean-cutting methods of ascertaining what changes in our curves are due to these three sets of factors, the treatment of irregular fluctuations as residuals would be satisfactory. On that basis we might rationalize our procedure as follows: The activities represented by a time series are influenced every day by a host of factors which are not secular, cyclical, or seasonal in character. Most of these random factors are known vaguely, if at all. But the theory of probabilities justifies the assumption that the random factors acting at a given moment cancel one another when they are very numerous, independent in origin, and of the same order of magnitude. Indeed, Professor Edgeworth has shown that these strict conditions may be relaxed:—there will be much canceling if the random factors are not few, if there is a considerable measure of independence among them, and if no two or three preponderate over the rest.[2] It often happens, however, that even the relaxed conditions are not complied with. At any time a group of mutually related factors may dominate the complex, or one or two factors far more powerful than the other random influences may crop up. Under such circumstances, the random factors cease to cancel one another, even roughly. Instead, they produce a large or small deviation from the undulating curve marked out by the secular trend, seasonal variations, and cyclical fluctuations in combination. It is deviations caused by such failure of mutual canceling of the random factors which we call irregular fluctuations.

One doubt concerning this conception can be met by an extension of the argument. As we saw in the last section, some of the causes of seasonal variations vary from year to year. Likewise all secular trends are admitted to be subject to change without notice, and those trends which are ascribed to growth may be inconstant by nature for aught we know. Finally, among the numerous causes of cyclical fluctuations reviewed in the first chapter, there is not one which we should expect to produce perfectly regular cycles. Thus, once we

[2] Compare section ii, 2, above.

adopt the current practice of the statisticians and start discussing irregular fluctuations in terms of their causes, we seem forced to admit that irregularities may occur in the movements which we classify as secular, cyclical and seasonal. In other words, an attempt to treat secular, seasonal and cyclical changes as regular runs counter to much that we know and more that we suspect.

This conclusion may be admitted, and treated as a reason, not for abandoning the classification of fluctuations in time series into the regular and the irregular, but for making it more rigorous. That is, we may conceive the causes of seasonal, secular, and cyclical changes as so many complexes, each made up of one or more causes which act regularly according to some "law," and of random factors which more or less often fail to cancel each other. Then we may throw the irregularities which are connected with the seasons, with the factor of growth, and with business cycles into the same box as the irregularities which we ascribe to wars, earthquakes, epidemics and misprints. In contrast to this heterogeneous collection of irregularities, we have left secular trends which, if not constant, change in some regular way, seasonal variations which, if not uniform, change in some regular way, and what one who took this view would probably call "normal" cycles.

From the theoretical viewpoint this conception seems clear, whatever difficulties might be encountered in applying it to time series. But is it the conception with which business-cycle statisticians work? Perhaps such an idea is implicit in the application of periodogram analysis to time series.[3] Perhaps there are champions of the "40-month cycle" who would accept the notion.[4] The majority of the business-cycle statisticians, however, find certain features of the idea ill adapted to their needs.

The men who analyze time series primarily with an eye to forecasting the future commonly accept the notion of regular trends and seasonal variations. They need standards by which they can test current developments and on which they can base reasoned expectations. Such standards they can make with trends and seasonals which change according to some rule, but not with irregular seasonals and trends. The forecasters believe themselves justified by the past behavior of many time series in setting up the standard trends and

[3] See the remarks on periodogram analysis at the end of the next section.
[4] See below, section vi, 3, (6) "The Duration of Business Cycles."

seasonals they need, and judging what departures from these standards seem probable in the near future. For while they admit that actual trends have altered and actual seasonals have differed in the past, they seldom find these changes very sudden, or very great. But when they come to cyclical fluctuations, they find less warrant in the past behavior of time series for setting up similar standards. The past changes in these fluctuations have been so sudden, so frequent, and so considerable as to make the notion of a "normal cycle" inappropriate. Not feeling justified in imposing a "normal cycle" upon their data, they have no means of distinguishing the regular from the irregular changes in cycles, as they distinguish the regular from the irregular changes in trends and seasonal variations. Nor can they distinguish clearly between the cyclical fluctuations and the irregular fluctuations of a non-cyclical character. All they can do is to note occasional marked departures from the course of events which it seemed reasonable to expect, and to search through descriptive materials for plausible explanations of these gross irregularities.[5]

The statistical analysts who are not attempting to make business forecasts hesitate to accept even the idea of "normal" trends and seasonals. As shown above, they have suggested methods for measuring seasonal variations which change from year to year. Also, secular trends pursue a meandering course when made by the use of free-hand curves or moving averages; they become unsteadier still when obtained by taking ratios to items in other series. Such methods absorb into the seasonals and trends of time series a part of the movements which the methods commonly practiced by forecasters intermingle with the cyclical fluctuations. But even when changing seasonal variations and meandering trends have been eliminated, the residuals show many irregularities.

(2) Irregular Fluctuations in the Theory of Business Cycles.

No method seems to have been devised for segregating and eliminating from the cyclical fluctuations the irregularities not absorbed in seasonals and trends. The nearest approach to such a method is to distribute the irregular fluctuations by the use of moving averages or free-hand curves. Such operations do not show what the cyclical fluctuations would have been in the absence of irregular fluctuations;

[5] Compare Warren M. Persons, "Indices of Business Conditions," *Review of Economic Statistics,* January, 1919, Preliminary vol. i, pp. 33-35.

they merely show the combined cyclical and irregular fluctuations distributed in a new way among the months which are averaged together. And of course we cannot find out what the irregular fluctuations really were by subtracting the successive values of such a smoothed curve from the corresponding original items.

Yet Professor Persons has obtained one result of much theoretical interest by an operation of this character. Taking the value of building permits granted in twenty American cities in the 156 months of 1903-16 (a series in which the irregular fluctuations are marked), he subjected the original data to the following operations: (1) He eliminated the secular trend and the seasonal variations by his favorite methods. The residuals showed the cyclical and irregular fluctuations of the series in combination. (2) He computed the percentages which the twelve months moving averages make of the corresponding ordinates of the secular trend. This process (by averaging) presumably eliminates the irregular variations and seasonal variations, and (by taking ratios) the secular trend; but it does not eliminate the cycles. (3) He subtracted the items found in (2) above from the items described in (1). The irregular variations were present in (1) but not in (2). The resulting differences were, presumably, approximations to the irregular fluctuations. (4) He made the differences thus ascertained into a frequency table. . . . From the data in this table, he drew a rectangular diagram. Finally, to this diagram he fitted a normal curve. From the closeness with which the normal curve fitted the data, Professor Persons concluded that "the distribution of the irregular fluctuations of building permits is normal." [1]

May we not draw a further conclusion? If the irregularities of economic time series over a considerable period are distributed in the same way that errors of observation are distributed, can we not take the combined cyclical and irregular fluctuations of a time series without regard to the temporal order of their occurrence, interpret each fluctuation as one observation upon the behavior of the cyclical factors distorted in some measure by an error, and base our results upon averages drawn with due caution from the array of observations? The confidence we can put in such averages will depend of course upon the number of observations which each time series yields, and upon the way in which the observations in each array are distributed about their central tendency. This procedure is certainly less hazard-

[1] Warren M. Persons, "An Index of General Business Conditions," *Review of Economic Statistics*, April, 1919, Preliminary vol. 1, pp. 137-139.

ous than the attempt to decide what part of a given change in any time series should be ascribed to the failure of random factors to cancel each other. It enables us to utilize all the available statistics, and it gives some basis for judging the probable reliability of the inferences we may draw from them.[2]

In Chapter V, this suggestion will be elaborated, with the aid of the more adequate materials which will then be in hand. Of course, there is no thought of returning to the idea of a "normal cycle." For between the conception of an average empirically determined from the study of statistical arrays, and the conception of "normal" phenomena employed by economic theorists there is a vital difference. The theorist's normal is that which complies with certain conditions which he has laid down. It may approximate average experience, or it may be far removed from the facts of life—all depends upon the manner in which the theorist has chosen the ground for his argument. Even when the two agree closely, they remain conceptually unlike. To speak of average conditions as "normal" is to introduce needless confusion.[3]

In our dealings with irregular fluctuations as theorists, we are confronted again by the problem mentioned at the end of the section

[2] It may be asked: If Professor Persons is justified in computing the irregular fluctuations of building permits in order to find how they are distributed about their central tendency, would he not be justified in eliminating these irregular fluctuations from the residuals left by taking out the trend and the seasonal variations? Would he not thus isolate the cyclical fluctuations? And might not his methods, with this development, be applied freely to other time series?

The reason why statisticians hesitate to follow this obvious line is that in dealing with cycles they cannot accept the rough approximations to irregular fluctuations which will serve in testing the types of distribution to which the latter conform. With 156 irregularities in his frequency table, Professor Persons can suppose that the imperfections of his measurements of irregularities will cancel each other in large degree. He could not make such an assumption regarding the irregular fluctuations which accompanied any specific business cycle. In trying to get a curve representing a succession of cycles, it is small comfort to say that a distortion at one point in one cycle, caused by inaccurate measurement of irregular fluctuations, is probably matched by a distortion of the opposite sort at some unknown point in the same, or another cycle.

The only way in which we can invoke the canceling of random effects in eliminating irregular fluctuations from cyclical fluctuations is the way suggested in the text: namely, by collecting numerous cases showing cyclical and irregular fluctuations in combination, and ascertaining the central tendencies of these arrays.

[3] There is, however, one accredited use of this term in statistics, illustrated in the preceding quotation from Professor Persons: namely, the "normal curve of error" and "normal" distributions, that is, distributions which are described approximately by the "normal" curve. As pointed out by Professor Karl Pearson, who first applied the term "normal" to the curve developed by Laplace and Gauss, the choice was not a happy one. (See Karl Pearson, *Biometrica,* October, 1920, p. 25.) But the usage is so firmly established by this time that more confusion might be caused by departing from than by conforming to it.

upon secular trends. While we desire to discriminate as clearly as we can between the irregular and the cyclical fluctuations of time series, we cannot discard irregular fluctuations offhand as irrelevant to the understanding of business cycles. By doing so we should be tacitly rejecting without investigation some of the working hypotheses presented in Chapter I. Dr. Veblen, for example, holds that in the period from, say, 1816 to 1873 liquidation was "apparently always brought on by some extraneous disturbance," whereas since the 1870's seasons of prosperity "are pretty uniformly traceable to specific causes extraneous to the process of industrial business proper." [4] So also, Professors Arthur B. Adams of Oklahoma and S. A. Pervushin of Moscow argue at length that revival cannot blossom into full prosperity without the aid of some favoring cause which the revival itself does not generate.[5] Several other authorities assign an important though less systematic rôle to "disturbing circumstances" as factors in shaping the course of business cycles. In view of these considered opinions we cannot take it for granted that irregular fluctuations are to be eliminated from our theorizing, much as we should like to eliminate them from our curves. Even statistical elimination is desirable only in the sense that we should like to isolate the irregular as well as the cyclical fluctuations, in order to study intensively both types of changes.

6. The Problem of Isolating Cyclical Fluctuations.

From what has been said regarding the other types of changes found in time series, it is clear that the ambition to isolate cyclical fluctuations has not been attained. Our review of methods of computing secular trends and seasonal variations showed that even for these movements we have approximations rather than measures. Our discussion of irregular fluctuations showed that no statistician ventures to do more than smooth our irregularities in his curves by using moving averages or free-hand constructions. Inability to measure the net effects of secular, seasonal, and random factors separately, or in combination, means that we cannot isolate the cyclical fluctuations of time series by eliminating the three other sets of changes recog-

[4] Thorstein Veblen, *Theory of Business Enterprise,* New York, 1904, pp. 249-255.

[5] Arthur B. Adams, *Economics of Business Cycles,* New York, 1925, pp. 111-158; S. A. Pervushin, *The Business Conjuncture,* Moscow, 1925, pp. 54-61. I am indebted to Dr. Simon S. Kuznets for a synopsis of Professor Pervushin's discussion.

nized by our classification. And no one has yet devised a satisfactory method of measuring the cyclical fluctuations directly.[1]

What we can get from the statisticians, then, are the residual fluctuations of many American and some foreign time series after the secular trends and the seasonal variations (determined by some variant of the methods described above) have been eliminated. The process of eliminating these two types of movements consists in computing, or reading from a chart, the values which the trend, corrected for seasonal variations, would have at successive intervals of time, and then subtracting these values from the corresponding items of the original data, or expressing the deviations of the original data from the corrected trend in percentages.[2]

Chart 8 gives three examples of the results obtained in this way. To apply what has just been said to the chart: the deviations of the

[1] It is true that in his plan for ascertaining seasonal variations which change from year to year, Dr. King draws a "preliminary cycle curve" directly from the raw data—"a free-hand curve representing what was assumed to be the course of the cycle." But neither this curve, nor the "final cycle curve" which Dr. King gets after eliminating his varying seasonal indexes, purports to separate the cyclical from the secular and irregular changes. "An Improved Method for Measuring the Seasonal Factor," *Journal of the American Statistical Association,* September, 1924, vol. xix, pp. 301-313.

[2] To illustrate: Suppose that we have obtained the following results by analyzing a series showing the production of commodity X by months.

Ordinate of secular trend January, 1926, 900 tons.
Monthly increment of secular trend, 5 tons.
Seasonal variations expressed as percentages of mean monthly production:

January	90
February	100
March	110
April	80

Suppose also that the production reported in the opening months of 1926 runs as follows:

January	800 tons
February	1000 tons
March	1100 tons
April	700 tons

Then we can make the following computations:

1926	Ordinates of secular trend		Seasonal variations		Trend adjusted for seasonal variations	Original data
January	900 tons	×	.90	=	810 tons	800 tons
February	905 "	×	1.00	=	905 "	1000 "
March	910 "	×	1.10	=	1001 "	1100 "
April	915 "	×	.80	=	732 "	700 "

Results after eliminating the secular trend corrected for seasonal variations.

1926	In tons	In percentages of adjusted trend
January	−10 tons	99
February	+95 "	110
March	+99 "	110
April	−32 "	96

curves from their base lines do not show the cyclical fluctuations of the series included. What they do show are the cyclical fluctuations combined with the irregular fluctuations, among which are included the deviations of the actual seasonal and secular changes from the curves chosen to represent them.

Thus statistical technique in its present state enables us to picture cyclical fluctuations only in a distorting combination with irregular fluctuations which we cannot measure. It seems legitimate to believe that the cyclical factor or factors operate with greater regularity than the curves suggest. But we are not entitled to believe that, were the effects of all non-cyclical factors excluded, the deviation and amplitude of all cyclical fluctuations would be uniform. For cyclical factors influencing time series may vary from year to year, as many of the seasonal factors vary. Just as our conviction that many seasonal variations are not uniform from year to year rests upon what we know about their causes, so the opinions we may finally form concerning the uniformity or variability of cyclical fluctuations must be based upon what we can learn about their causes, rather than upon study of such curves as are presented in Chart 8.

Graphically we can represent these successive steps by the following segments of charts:

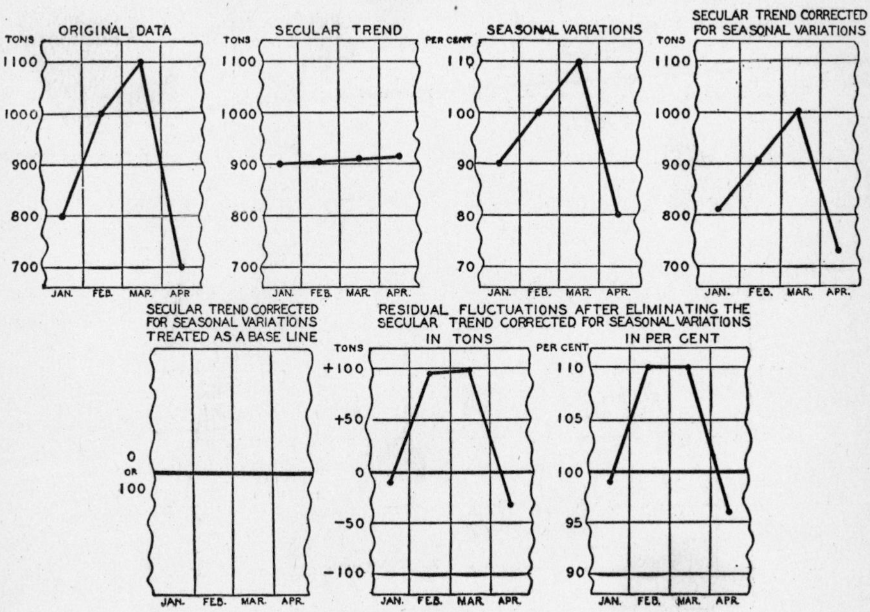

Although the statistical segregation of the factors influencing time series stops short of our desires, a comparison of the refined curves of Chart 8 with the "raw-data" curves of Chart 1 shows that the cyclical

CHART 8.

RESIDUAL FLUCTUATIONS OF TIME SERIES AFTER ELIMINATION OF SECULAR TRENDS AND SEASONAL VARIATIONS.

Percentage deviations of original items from secular trend corrected for seasonal variations.

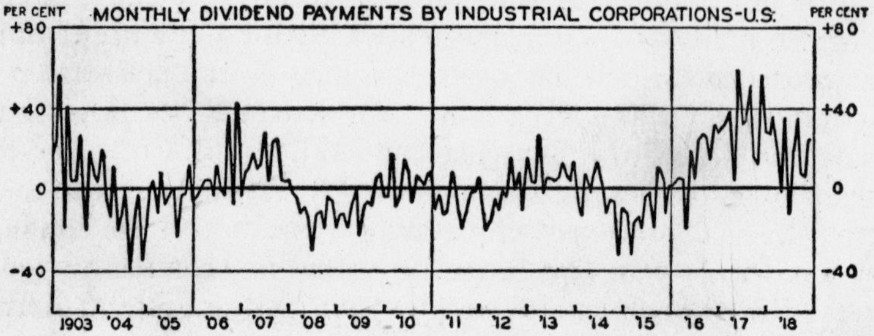

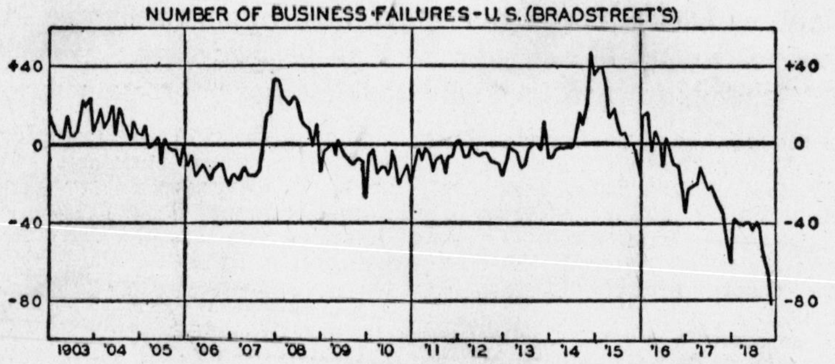

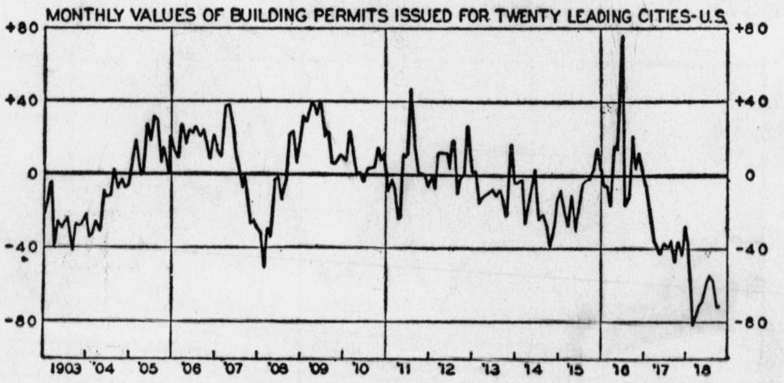

fluctuations stand out more clearly after the statistical trends and seasonal variations have been eliminated, however roughly. We shall therefore make such use as we can of these eliminations in our further work; but instead of ignoring trends and seasonals we shall study them both in their original combinations with cyclical and irregular fluctuations, and in their segregated form.

To readers trained in the natural sciences, it may seem that periodogram analysis should be substituted for the cumbersome and inexact procedure which has been described as the standard method of determining cyclical fluctuations. A few economists, notably Henry L. Moore, Sir William H. Beveridge, and William L. Crum, have made significant experiments with this method.[3] It yields excellent results in many physical processes which show strictly periodic fluctuations of a symmetrical type, and it should reveal any similar periodicities which exist in economic time series. Nor is the method limited to the discovery of simple movements. A periodogram analysis may indicate the existence of several or many periodicities, which when combined with each other give a curve so complicated that the uninitiated reader would not suppose it to be made up of periodic elements.[4] Perhaps it will be found that many of the time series used

[3] For explanations of this rather elaborate method of analysis, and illustrative results, see H. L. Moore, *Economic Cycles: Their Law and Cause,* New York, 1914, and *Generating Economic Cycles,* New York, 1923; Sir W. H. Beveridge, "Wheat Prices and Rainfall in Western Europe," *Journal of the Royal Statistical Society,* May, 1922, vol. lxxxv, pp. 412-459; W. L. Crum, "Cycles of Rates on Commercial Paper," *Review of Economic Statistics,* January, 1923, Preliminary vol. v, pp. 17-29, and "Periodogram Analysis," chapter xi in *Handbook of Mathematical Statistics,* edited by H. L. Rietz, Boston, 1924.

[4] For an example, see the "synthetic curve" made by adding eleven cycles of different lengths, in Beveridge's paper referred to above. (Opposite p. 453.) A section of this curve is reproduced here.

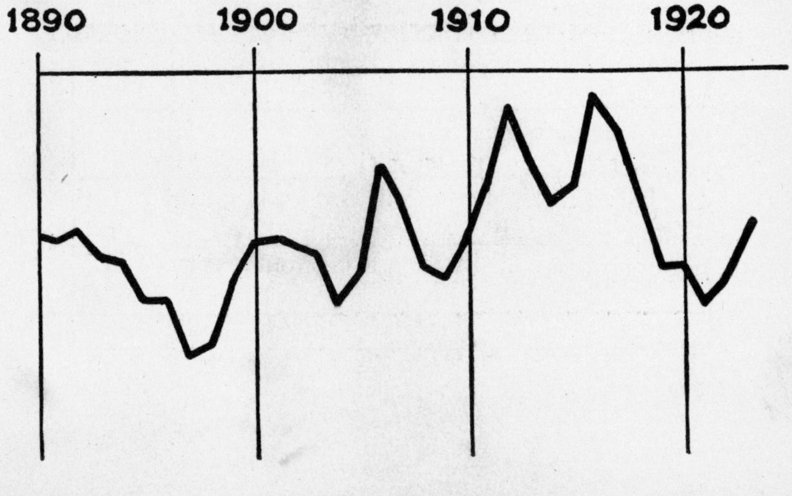

by the business-cycle statisticians can be usefully described by "synthetic curves" formed by adding together several periodic fluctuations which differ in length.

But the systematic application of periodogram analysis to economic series encounters serious obstacles. Comparatively few of the series which we wish to utilize have been maintained over a period long enough to yield satisfactory results when treated in this way. To establish the rather brief cycles in which the business-cycle statistician is most interested, it is necessary to have monthly, or at least quarterly, data, and long series of that character are few. When materials are available in this form, the seasonal variations and the irregular fluctuations so characteristic of economic processes tend to blur the periodograms. To leave out the periods in which irregular fluctuations seem to alter the cyclical movement limits the data available for study still more narrowly, and gives the investigator's personal judgment a considerable influence. To eliminate secular trends and seasonals before applying periodogram analysis is often necessary, but it may bias the results.[5] There remain two doubts more fundamental. Can we assume that the cyclical fluctuations of economic processes are, or tend to be, strictly periodic? If there are tendencies toward periodic fluctuations in given processes at a given point in economic evolution, do such tendencies maintain themselves under changing conditions over a period long enough to be revealed by periodogram analysis?

The most obvious of these obstacles to the systematic use of the periodogram method in business-cycle work—the brevity of the majority of the series which must be analyzed—presumably will shrink with the lapse of time. If the future is less checkered by catastrophes than the past has been, the troubles caused by irregular fluctuations will diminish also. The doubts now harbored about the propriety of adjusting series to get rid of trends and seasonal variations before beginning periodogram analysis may be set at rest by further work. Fuller knowledge may make us readier to accept the working hypothesis that there are true periodicities of various lengths in economic processes, and that these periodicities maintain themselves for long periods of time. Certainly we cannot say that periodogram analysis will not play a large rôle in future economic work. But it seems

[5] Compare Sir W. H. Beveridge's remarks upon this point in the article cited above, pp. 414-415.

equally certain that we cannot yet make it the standard procedure for studying cyclical fluctuations.[6]

IV. On Measuring the Relationships Among Time Series.

While the isolating of cyclical-irregular fluctuations is the end of one set of statistical efforts, it is the beginning of a new set. As we look at Chart 8, we grow eager to attack the problems it presents. The curves resemble each other in that all show at least the major fluctuations in business conditions which occurred during the periods they cover. But this resemblance, though clearer than in Chart 1, before the secular trends and seasonal variations had been eliminated, is still overlaid by striking and persistent differences. If a larger collection is taken than that offered by Chart 8, it is found that the waves in the several curves differ widely in amplitude. They differ also in timing; that is, the crests and troughs come several months later in some curves than in others. They differ finally in shape—some curves have roughly symmetrical waves, others suggest a very choppy sea. What use can we make of these results?

One course is to compile a general index of business cycles from as large and varied a collection of curves as we can assemble, all of them in the form illustrated by Chart 8. If that is our next step, ought we reduce the varying amplitudes of the cyclical-irregular fluctuations characteristic of different series to a common scale? Ought we try to get rid also of the differences in timing, and in shape? Or are the differences in amplitude, timing, and perhaps shape, matters which we do not wish to get rid of, but rather to investigate and use in framing a theory of business cycles? Do we, indeed, wish to make a general index of business cycles? Shall we not gain more by

[6] Colonel M. C. Rorty adds the following comment:

"The harmonic analysis can fairly safely be used to segregate periodicities which are known to be compounded in any series of observations; but I do not believe it can be trusted to establish the existence of periodicities as to the reality of which there is no other definite evidence. The fundamental defect in the harmonic analysis is that it will resolve any ordinary business time series into definite regular periodicities, regardless of whether any real periodicities exist or not. The probability that such resolution has any real meaning would seem to be infinitesimal when the number of cycles subjected to analysis is small and the number of periodicities required for, say, a 90% resolution of the time series exceeds two. Furthermore, when the element of lag is introduced, the value of the harmonic analysis becomes still more tenuous. I doubt whether it is possible to set up a complete and direct mathematical test of the method. Probably the best indirect proof of the lack of value of the harmonic analysis is to create an artificial time series by throwing dice and then analyze this series with and without assumptions as to lag."

concentrating attention upon the fluctuations of particular processes, bringing back into the discussion even the secular trends and the seasonal variations which we have eliminated?

These rhetorical questions suggest their own answers. If we are to make the most of the statistical contribution to business cycles, we must learn all that we can by studying time series separately and studying them with reference to all their characteristics; we must also learn all that we can by studying them in combination, or rather in varying combinations.

For either purpose we need a special technique. Whether we set about comparing the fluctuations of different series, or combining different series into general indexes, we must have some standard method of measuring the relationships among the fluctuations. Such a method has been devised, and we have merely to note how carefully it must be used. But attempts to apply the method lead us on to a subtler problem which statisticians are but beginning to grasp: Precisely what relations among the fluctuations of time series do we wish to measure?

1. The Correlation of Time Series and Its Pitfalls.

Inspection of such curves as are shown in Charts 1 to 8 suggests various conclusions regarding their relationships. But experience has shown that conclusions reached by visual study are strongly biased by the investigator's personal equation. Everyone is likely to see in the curves what he looks for, and not to see relations of which he has no image in his "mind's eye." Moreover, visual comparisons are influenced much more by the conspicuous turning points in the curves—the peaks and the troughs—than by the intermediate segments. Finally, the conclusions yielded by such comparisons are at best vague, and quite incapable of numerical expression. Statisticians have therefore sought some method of measuring the relationships among the fluctuations of time series—particularly among their cyclical-irregular fluctuations—which will be objective, precise, and which will allow due influence to every segment of the curves compared.

Such a method they have found in the correlation calculus invented by Sir Francis Galton for the study of inheritance, developed by Karl Pearson, F. Y. Edgeworth, and G. Udny Yule, and applied to time series by J. Pease Norton and others. The coefficient of

correlation expresses the relationship between two series on a scale which runs from + 1.00 (signifying perfect positive agreement), through 0 (meaning no agreement), to — 1.00 (signifying perfect inverse agreement).[1] In adapting this device to measuring the relationship between two time series, the temporal order of the items must of course be kept—a fact which renders the theory of probabilities inapplicable to the data and to the interpretation of the results.[2] Comparisons are made between the deviations of each successive pair of items from the arithmetic means of their respective series. Thus every item in each series has its influence upon the result, and this result is a mathematically precise average, unaffected (so far as the computation is concerned) by the personal equation of the investigator.

Yet the use of coefficients of correlation does not substitute mathematics for personal judgment, or make less necessary the visual study of charts. Just as the representative value of an arithmetic mean must be judged by the distribution of the array from which it is computed, so the significance of a coefficient of correlation must be judged by critical study of the materials combined in getting it.

This critical study should begin with the original data. When secular trends and seasonal variations have been eliminated in order to correlate the cyclical-irregular fluctuations of two series, the "fit" of the two trend lines requires close scrutiny.[3] For in this operation the correlation coefficient averages the relationship between two sets of cyclical-irregular deviations from two trends, and it will show close agreement between the two sets of deviations if the two trend lines misfit their data in similar fashion. One might expect similarity in misfits to be a rare occurrence. On the contrary, it happens often, and the "spurious correlation" it produces vitiates numerous

[1] Compare Warren M. Persons' chapter on "Correlation of Time Series" in the *Handbook of Mathematical Statistics*, edited by H. L. Rietz, Boston, 1924, pp. 160-165. Directions for computing coefficients of correlation can be found in almost all recent textbooks of statistics. For a fuller treatment see A. A. Tschuprow, *Grundbegriffe und Grundprobleme der Korrelationstheorie*, Leipzig & Berlin, 1925.

[2] Hence the significance of the "probable error" of a coefficient of correlation between two time series is not known. It certainly does not represent, as in other applications, an equal chance that a second computation, based upon a different sample, would deviate from the coefficient first found by no more than the limits which the probable error sets. See Persons, as above, pp. 162-163.

[3] There is, indeed, little point in correlating two time series from which the trends have not been eliminated, except when both trends can be representd by horizontal straight lines. For the results will show primarily the relations of the trends themselves—an aim which can be attained less ambiguously by simpler devices. Compare F. C. Mills, *Statistical Methods*, New York, 1924, pp. 410-412.

investigations in the business-cycle field. Similar misfits of trend lines are especially likely to occur in correlating

> economic series covering both the period of declining prices previous to 1897 and the period of rising prices following that year. Nearly all economic series dip below the linear trend in the nineties so that a correlation coefficient between their deviations would indicate that fact rather than the general correspondence of their fluctuations.[4]

Since there is seldom an objective criterion for determining the goodness of a trend line's fit, there is seldom an objective criterion for determining the representative value of a coefficient of correlation between two sets of deviations from two trends. All that correlation coefficients can do for us is to make more precise the comparisons which are warranted by careful study of the original data, the fit of the trends, and the character of the deviations.

There is another source of error in interpreting coefficients of correlation which statisticians are prone to overlook. The time relations between the cyclical-irregular fluctuations of economic processes may shift from phase to phase of business cycles. For example, the production of industrial equipment may lag behind the production of consumers' goods during the phase of recuperation after a depression, and yet decline earlier than the production of consumers' goods when prosperity begins to wane. Again, New York clearings have usually begun to decline after periods of prosperity some months before outside clearings drop; in the opposite phase of recovery the New York clearings show no such lead.[5] When such changes in timing occur, a coefficient of correlation gives an average relationship which not only has little significance, but may actually put the investigator off a promising trail. The only safeguard against being misled in this way is to study charts with close attention to the regularity with which fluctuations in one curve precede or follow fluctuations in the second. This warning is needed, because the chief use of coefficients of correlation in business-cycle work has been to determine the lag of one series in relation to another.[6]

[4] W. M. Persons, in *Mathematical Handbook of Statistics,* p. 164, note.

[5] See section v, 2 below, "The Time Sequence of Cyclical-Irregular Fluctuations."

[6] See Professor Allyn A. Young's discussion of the interpretation of correlation coefficients in his introduction to *Social Consequences of Business Cycles,* by M. B. Hexter, Boston and New York, 1925.

2. Transformations of Time Series in the Investigation of Their Relationships.

When economists began to study time series they took the data in their original form, whatever that happened to be. The difficulty of incommensurable units—for example gold production in million ounces and bank discount rates in percentages—could be met by drawing charts on which two arbitrarily adjusted scales were laid off. A neater shift was to turn the original data into the form of "relatives," with 100 to represent the values of both variables in some period chosen as the base. Another plan was to chart the logarithms of the two series. Still another was to drop the original data and compare the percentage differences between the successive items in each series.

Once started upon this career of transforming time series into new shapes for comparison, statisticians have before them a limitless field for the exercise of ingenuity. They are beginning to think of the original data, coming to them in a shape determined largely by administrative convenience, as concealing uniformities which it is theirs to uncover. With more emphasis upon statistical technique than upon rational hypothesis, they are experimenting with all sorts of data, recast in all sorts of ways. Starting with two series having little resemblance in their original shape, they can often transmute one series into "something new and strange," which agrees closely with the other series. In work of this type, they rely upon the coefficient of correlation to test the degree of relationship between the successive transformations.

Two recent examples of such researches may be cited. (1) Mr. Karl G. Karsten has studied the relations between the American data for freight-car surplus and shortage and for interest rates on 60-90 day commercial paper in New York. Between the two series in their original form there appeared to be no correspondence, for the coefficient of correlation was nearly zero (+.02). By making the freight-car data lag behind interest rates eight months, Mr. Karsten got a coefficient of +.402. By cumulating the deviations of the freight-car data from their trend, he obtained a curve which gave a coefficient of +.914 when correlated with the interest curve. By using logarithms of interest rates, he raised the coefficient to +.926, and by omitting the nine months, March to November, 1918, when interest rates were purposefully kept from rising above six per cent,

he obtained a coefficient of +.950 between the cumulatives of car shortages and the moving annual averages of interest rates.[1]

(2) Professor Irving Fisher has studied the relation between wholesale-price fluctuations in the United States and the volume of trade. Starting with the Bureau of Labor Statistics index of wholesale prices and Persons' index of the physical volume of trade by months from August, 1915, to March, 1923, he smoothed the latter by a moving average, and found a correlation coefficient between the two series of +.54. Then Fisher turned the price index into figures which showed the rapidity of change in prices, gave this derivative series a seven-months lead over the trade index, and got a coefficient of +.727. Next he made an elaborate set of experiments in distributing this fixed lag over varying numbers of months weighted in different ways "according to the principles of probability." He finally found a scheme of distributing the lag which raised his coefficient to +.941.[2]

These interesting experiments may be the beginning of a long series of efforts to obtain high coefficients of correlation between various pairs of time series by casting them into new forms. Work of this sort is fascinating to the statistical technician. While very expensive, because of the endless experimental computations required, the possibility of finding marketable forecasting series may enable investigators to secure the necessary funds. And such work may yield results of theoretical interest as well as practical value. But it may also lead to grave mistakes, unless soberly controlled.

The proposition may be ventured that a competent statistician, with sufficient clerical assistance and time at his command, can take almost any pair of time series for a given period and work them into forms which will yield coefficients of correlation exceeding ±.9. It has long been known that a mathematician can fit a curve to any time series which will pass through every point of the data. Performances of the latter sort have no significance, however, unless the mathematically computed curve continues to agree with the data when projected beyond the period for which it is fitted. So work of the sort which Mr. Karsten and Professor Fisher have shown how to do must be judged, not by the coefficients of correlation obtained within the periods for which they have manipulated the data, but by

[1] See Karl G. Karsten, "The Theory of Quadrature in Economics," *Journal of the American Statistical Association,* March, 1924, vol. xix, pp. 14-29.

[2] Irving Fisher, "Our Unstable Dollar and the So-called Business Cycle," *Journal of the American Statistical Association,* June, 1925, vol. xx, pp. 179-202. The method devised for distributing the lag will be described below in section v, 2.

the coefficients which they get in earlier or later periods to which their formulas may be applied. Mr. Karsten points out that his coefficient of correlation between adjusted cumulatives of freight-car shortage and the logarithms of the moving average of interest rates sinks from +.95 in 1915-23 to +.856 in 1907-14. Similarly Professor Fisher shows that his coefficient between the rate of change in prices with a distributed lag and the physical volume of trade sinks from +.941 in 1915-23, to +.58 in 1877-99, to +.67 in 1903-15, and to +.78 in 1923-24.[3] Controlled by such tests, the methods of Karsten and Fisher, or rather an endless variety of methods not less intricate, may be applied to the study of the relations among time series *ad libitum* without scruple—provided investigators are chary of interpreting their coefficients as demonstrating causal connections.

This caution is important. Statisticians know that such an average of relationships between paired items of two time series as the coefficient of correlation yields does not prove that the changes in one of the series produce the changes in the second series, even when the latter series has been made to lag in the pairing of dates. Careful workers bear this fact in mind. Mr. Karsten, for example, though he obtained a high coefficient of correlation between his two series for years preceding his trial period, did not suggest that the number of idle freight cars is controlled by interest rates in New York. Nor would a coefficient of correlation, however high, warrant such an inference, unless independent evidence of causal connection could be adduced. Professor Fisher has reason to believe that the rate of change in prices influences the physical volume of trade, and gives a causal interpretation to his results.[4] But even in Professor Fisher's position an investigator should be cautious. It is not unlikely that by taking equal pains another worker studying the relations between the physical volume of trade and (say) reserve ratios, interest rates, profits, or payroll disbursements within Professor Fisher's period might get very high coefficients of correlation, and argue that he too had found "an almost complete explanation of fluctuations in the volume of trade,"—or several "almost complete" explanations.[5]

[3] See the two papers cited above, pp. 23 (Karsten) and 201 (Fisher).

[4] Something will be said about the causal relationship later in the present chapter (see footnote on p. 286); but the problem will be treated more fully in the second volume.

[5] Compare Professor Fisher's conclusion, "These correlations are so high as to leave little or no doubt that changes in the price level afford an almost complete explanation of fluctuations in the volume of trade for the above period beginning in 1915 and ending in 1923. . . . With a correlation of nearly 100 per cent between trade and projected price-change, there is little left to explain." As cited above, p. 191.

While we cannot account for more than 100 per cent of the variations in one time series by any combination of causal relationships, it is not absurd to have several coefficients of correlation adding up to more than 1.00 between a given series and a number of other series which are regarded as exercising a causal influence over the first. Were such a set of results before us, we should have two quite different lines of explanation. The more obvious explanation is that the several variables correlated with the series whose fluctuations we are trying to account for are not independent of each other. In other words, the same causal influences are represented in two or more of the variables. There is much overlapping of this sort among economic time series. The second explanation is that in a theoretically perfect case of causal explanation by the joint action of two or more strictly independent factors, the two or more coefficients of correlation between the various series which represent causes and the one series which represents effects will add up to more than 1.00. Coefficients of correlation are not percentages, though the fact that they run on a scale from — 1.00 to + 1.00 has seemed to Professor Fisher sufficient warrant for calling them percentages. In the perfect case of exhaustive explanation referred to, it is not the several coefficients which equal 1.00 but the sum of their squares.[6] In con-

[6] To illustrate by Fisher's case: Waiving all question about the significance of a relation made to fit one period which does not maintain itself in other periods, let us accept his coefficient of "94 per cent" between price-change with a distributed lag and the volume of trade in 1915-23, and ask what part of the fluctuations in trade is left unaccounted for. The answer is not given by the formula 100 per cent — 94 per cent = 6 per cent; but by the formula $k^2 + r^2 = 1$, in which k stands for the "coefficient of alienation" and r for the coefficient of correlation. The coefficient of alienation measures the lack of agreement between two variables, as the coefficient of correlation measures the degrees of relationship. Substituting .94 for r in the equation, we get $k^2 = 1 - .8836 = .1164$, and $k = .34$. Of course, the coefficient of alienation is no more a percentage than the coefficient of correlation. We must not add 94 per cent and 34 per cent, concluding that we have accounted for 128 per cent of the variability of trade! But we may add $.94^2$ and $.34^2$, and say that their sum, 1.00, represents a theoretically complete explanation. If we insist upon using a percentage scale it should be that of the squared coefficients: $.8836 + .1156 = 1.00$.

Similarly with the results which Professor Fisher gets on applying his method of connecting price-change with volume of trade in other periods than 1915-23. The significance of his correlation of "58 per cent" in 1879-99 is to be judged from the equation $.58^2 + .82^2 = .3364 + .6724 = 1$; the significance of his correlation of "67 per cent" in 1903-15 is to be judged from the equation $.67^2 + .74^2 = .4489 + .5476 = 1$; and the significance of his coefficient of "78 per cent" in 1923-24 is to be judged from the equation $.78^2 + .63^2 = .6084 + .3969 = 1$.

Though calling his coefficients of correlation percentages, Professor Fisher does not commit the error of saying that a coefficient of "94 per cent" explains all but 6 per cent of the variations of the series which lags; he says merely that this coefficient affords "an almost complete explanation." (See preceding note.)

On the coefficient of alienation and its uses, see Truman L. Kelley, *Statistical Method,* New York, 1923, pp. 173, 174.

sidering how much significance attaches to a given coefficient of correlation, therefore, one should take the square of that coefficient, rather than the coefficient itself, as indicating the degree of relationship between the two variables, and compare with it the square of the "coefficient of alienation" as indicating the lack of relationship. And one should always remember that coefficients of correlation, however high, do not suffice to establish relationships of cause and effect.

3. Conclusion

All these cautions about the interpretation of results do not mean that one should hesitate to turn any series into a form which will agree better than the original figures with some variable one wishes to explain. On the contrary, search for relationships which are hidden by the form in which series happen to be compiled is one of the most promising, though one of the most arduous, lines of statistical research. Simple transformations into relatives, logarithms, and first differences have long been practiced with general approval; more elaborate transformations need no justification beyond fruitfulness.

Some hidden relationships between time series may be discovered by accident or by strictly empirical work. But the search is most likely to prosper if guided by rational hypotheses. These hypotheses usually occur to our minds in terms of cause and effect. What we know from non-statistical sources about business processes may suggest that the activities represented by one time series lead to consequences shown by one or more other series. Before plunging into the computations which such a notion suggests, it is wise to think out the hypothesis with care. Precisely what feature of the first series is causally important—the actual magnitudes as reported, the changes in these magnitudes from date to date, the percentage rates of change, the accumulated changes, the excess beyond some critical range, the ratio of the causal factor to some other variable, or what? Similarly: upon what feature of the series regarded as showing effects is the causal effect exercised? The suggestions just listed are possible answers to this question also. Is the relationship direct, or inverse? Is the effect immediate or postponed? Is the effect cumulative? Does the effect change with the phases of business cycles? All these matters, and in many cases others, should be considered. Often it is only by trial computations that one can decide the issues raised; but they are best raised before computations are begun, and then thought out again in the light of what the computations suggest.

In judging the relationship between any two series, how low a coefficient of correlation should one accept as "significant"? That is a question which statisticians often raise, but to which they do not give categorical answers, because much depends upon the character of the data and the purpose in view. When the aim is merely to find whether two phenomena are unrelated to each other, or related in some degree, interest centers less in the absolute size of the coefficient obtained, than in its size compared with that of its standard (or probable) error. Provided a coefficient is several times its standard error, a figure in the forties, or even in the twenties, suffices to show the existence of some relationship. But when the coefficient of correlation is used in estimating the value of one variable from given values of other variables—the problem usually met in correlating time series—a much higher standard must be set. Coefficients ranging from .40 to .50, which often pleased earlier students of cyclical fluctuations, and even coefficients of .60 to .70, are not very imposing when squared, as they should be in thinking about their significance for making such estimates. In many cases a result of this order is best taken as a sign that the investigator has found a promising trail, but is not close to his goal. A reconsideration of the causal relationships involved, and further experimental computations, may lead to much higher coefficients. An expert in research of this type becomes exacting; Mr. Karsten, for example, remarks: "in my own forecasting work I do not consider of much value a coefficient below .90." [1]

V. The Amplitude and the Timing of Cyclical-Irregular Fluctuations in Different Processes.

From the preceding discussion of methods of analyzing time series and their relations we score two gains. One is understanding of and ability to use the results reached by other investigators. The second is guidance in analytic work of our own.

Anyone who takes the statistical approach to business cycles develops a longing to assemble all the pertinent series and analyze them afresh upon some consistent plan, which shall incorporate the best ideas of his predecessors with improvements of his own. But, as must be clear by this time, the analysis of time series is a laborious

[1] Karl G. Karsten, "The Harvard Business Indexes—A New Interpretation," *Journal of the American Statistical Association*, December, 1926, vol. xxi, p. 409.

and expensive process, only less expensive and laborious than compiling the original data. Moreover, the changes made in results by alterations in method are often slight. Hence every investigator does well to go as far as he can in utilizing the results obtained by others, even when these results are not precisely adapted to his needs. Limits are set upon such borrowings by radical differences in methods, in periods covered, and in data treated. When he approaches these limits, the investigator must give up the quantitative approach for the qualitative, or he must undertake the heavy burden of making statistical analyses for himself.

On three topics of great interest we can learn much by the simple process of assembling and comparing the results reached by others: the relative amplitude of the cyclical-irregular fluctuations characteristic of different economic activities, the temporal order in which different activities increase or diminish, and the way in which series differing in amplitude and timing can be combined to throw light upon the cyclical movement as a whole.

1. The Amplitude of Cyclical-Irregular Fluctuations.

While Chart 8 makes it plain that economic processes differ widely in the amplitude of their cyclical-irregular fluctuations, it leaves us with rather vague impressions, and we want measurements. A considerable variety of such measurements, however, lies ready to hand. Analytic statisticians often compute the standard deviations of the cyclical-irregular fluctuations of their time series expressed as percentages of the ordinates of secular trend corrected for seasonal changes.[1] These standard deviations may be used as measures of the average amplitude of cyclical variations in the economic processes concerned, if certain precautions are observed. Technical defects in the method of fitting trends and ascertaining seasonals affect the percentage magnitudes of the cyclical-irregular deviations, and therefore of their standard deviations. Differences in the periods covered also may influence the results; for the cyclical-irregular fluctuations of a given time series are likely to vary somewhat from decade to decade, even in percentage form. Still further doubts are raised by

[1] The standard deviation of a statistical series, conventionally represented by sigma (σ), is computed by taking the arithmetic mean, finding the deviation of each item from this mean, squaring the deviations, adding the squares, dividing the sum by the number of items, and extracting the square root of the quotient. All modern text-books of statistics discuss this device.

differences in the form of the original data analyzed, of which more presently. But if we make a considerable collection of standard deviations computed in similar ways for various periods and countries, confine our observations to broad differences, and avoid some obvious pitfalls, we can reach conclusions of importance.

In computing the standard deviations which we shall borrow, the aim of statisticians has usually been to get similar units in terms of which they can express the cyclical-irregular fluctuations of their time series, in order to make these fluctuations more comparable. Logically, the procedure is analogous to expressing the prices of the different commodities used in constructing an index number as relatives of the actual quotations for each commodity at some base period. Our aim is different. Several of the theories of business cycles reviewed in Chapter I, notably those of Mr. Lawrence K. Frank and Dr. T. W. Mitchell, rely largely upon differences in the amplitude of the cyclical fluctuations characteristic of different processes to explain the origin or the propagation of cyclical impulses. Like certain other features of time series which give trouble to statisticians, these differences of amplitude may give help to the theorist. At least we must learn what we can about them.

In Table 11 there are assembled several collections of standard deviations of cyclical-irregular fluctuations measured by percentage deviations from ordinates of secular trend corrected, when necessary, for seasonal variations. The rather miscellaneous array is classified first by countries, secondly by periods, and thirdly by the magnitude of the standard deviations themselves.

A glance over the various sections of the table shows that economic activities are characterized by marked differences in the amplitude of their cyclical-irregular fluctuations. In part these differences are due to the form in which the original data are gathered. The most notable case is the extreme variability of employment, which is represented in sections H, I and J of the table by percentages of reporting trade-union membership unemployed at successive periods. If the same data were converted into percentages employed, the standard deviations would be greatly reduced. Again, the standard deviations of the British series showing the market values of certain types of securities outstanding are not strictly comparable with the standard deviations of American series showing the average market prices of similar types of securities. Once more, standard deviations computed from data in monthly, quarterly, and annual form are not

strictly comparable. Finally, there are differences of business usage between the United States, Great Britain and Germany which interfere with the comparison of, say, bank clearings, bank loans, and discount rates in the three countries. Most of our comparisons must be limited to items within a given section of the table.

Observing these restrictions does not much reduce the spread of the standard deviations; for the differences between economic processes in the same country and period are much wider than the differences between analogous processes in different countries and periods. In several sections of the table, the standard deviations run from 2 or 3 per cent of the ordinates of secular trend to 30, 40, 50 or 60 per cent. Even in closely related processes, like various banking operations, wholesale and retail trade, the prices of different types of securities, the more variable series of cyclical irregular fluctuations have standard deviations which are two or three times the standard deviations of the stabler series. This table is the statistical justification for the remark made in Chapter I, that we must conceive of business cycles as congeries of cyclical fluctuations in different processes which have widely different amplitudes.

TABLE 11

Relative Amplitude of the Cyclical-Irregular Fluctuations of Various Economic Processes

A. American Series, 1860, 1862 or 1866 to 1880

Standard deviations, arranged in order of magnitude, of the relative deviations of the original data from lines of secular trend, corrected when necessary for seasonal variations.
Compiled from the Appendix to Persons, Tuttle and Frickey, "Business and Financial Conditions following the Civil War in the United States," *Review of Economic Statistics*, Preliminary vol. ii, Supplement, July, 1920.

	Standard Deviations
Call-loan rate on the New York Stock Exchange, monthly, 1866–80	38.7
Clearings of the New York City banks, monthly, 1862–80	24.8
Interest rates on prime commercial paper, New York City, monthly, 1866–80	23.12
Interest rates on prime commercial paper, Boston, monthly, 1860–80	23.0
Yield of U. S. Government 6's of 1881, monthly, 1862–80	21.4
Price of ten common railroad stocks, monthly, 1866–80	18.1
Reserves of all National Banks, 5 calls yearly, 1866–80	11.7
Ratio of reserves to deposits, New York clearing-house banks, monthly 1866–80	9.6
Loans and deposits of all National Banks, 5 calls yearly, 1866–80	8.9
Loans of New York clearing-house banks, monthly, 1866–80	6.85
Wholesale price index (W. C. Mitchell), quarterly, 1860–80	5.63

TABLE 11—*Continued*

RELATIVE AMPLITUDE OF THE CYCLICAL-IRREGULAR FLUCTUATIONS OF VARIOUS ECONOMIC PROCESSES

B. American Series, 1903–14 or 1903–18, by Months

Standard deviations, arranged in order of magnitude, of the relative deviations of the original data from lines of secular trend corrected for seasonal variation.

Compiled from articles by Warren M. Persons, *Review of Economic Statistics*, Preliminary vol. i, pp. 36 and 191.

	Standard Deviations
Shares traded on the New York Stock Exchange	49.6
Unfilled orders of the U. S. Steel Corporation (quarterly before 1910)	32.3
Value of building permits issued for 20 American cities	20.4
Bank clearings in New York City	20.3
Interest rates on 60– to 90–day paper in New York City	19.66
Production of pig iron	19.15
Interest rates on 4– to 6–months paper in New York City	16.46
Average price of 12 industrial stocks	15.03
Dividend payments by industrial corporations	14.96
Number of business failures (Bradstreet's)	13.55
Imports of merchandise	11.91
Reserves of the New York clearing-house banks	10.83
Average price of 20 railroad stocks	10.18
Bank clearings outside of New York City	8.62
Deposits of New York clearing-house banks	8.20
Gross earnings of 10 leading railroads	6.07
Loans of New York clearing-house banks	5.37
Bradstreet's wholesale-price index	3.68
Interest yield on 10 railroad bonds	2.82
Bureau of Labor Statistics wholesale-price index	2.60

C. American Series, 1879–96 and 1897–1913

Standard deviations, arranged in order of magnitude, of the relative deviations of the original data from lines of secular trend, corrected when necessary for seasonal variations.

From Warren M. Persons, "An Index of General Business Conditions, 1875–1913," *Review of Economic Statistics*, January, 1927, vol. ix, p. 28.

	Standard Deviations	
	1879–1896	1897–1913
New York bank clearings	24.55	18.21
Interest rates on prime commercial paper, New York	21.71 *	17.53 *
Pig-iron production	19.30	15.65
Industrial stock prices	14.11	15.07
Bank clearings outside New York City	12.03	7.98
Average of industrial and railroad stock prices	11.91	11.94
Railroad stock prices	10.89	10.12
Wholesale commodity prices (J. L. Snider's series)	7.78	3.77
Loan-deposit ratios of New York clearing-house banks	5.93	3.19
Loan-liability ratios of National Banks outside New York City.	2.22	1.84

* Computed from percentage deviations from 5 per cent, adjusted for seasonal variations.

TABLE 11—*Continued*

RELATIVE AMPLITUDE OF THE CYCLICAL-IRREGULAR FLUCTUATIONS OF VARIOUS ECONOMIC PROCESSES

D. American National Banking Series, 1901–14, by 5 "calls" yearly

Standard deviations of percentage deviations from trend, corrected for seasonal variation.

From Allyn A. Young, "An Analysis of Bank Statistics for the United States," *Review of Economic Statistics*, January and April, 1925, vol. vii, pp. 36 and 101–104.

	Standard Deviations				
	New York City	Outside New York City	Boston	Chicago	San Francisco
Lawful money held.....	11.62	4.25			
Net deposits..........	9.64	3.41			
Investments...........	9.59	4.59			
Individual deposits.....	9.12	3.14	5.51	5.40	17.2
Loans and discounts...	6.80	2.96	3.84	4.02	17.0

	Individual deposits less clearing-house exchanges	Loans and discounts	Investments, except securities against notes and U. S. deposits
Pacific states..........................	7.09	7.96	7.29
Southern states.......................	5.49	5.06	7.16
Western states.........................	5.36	4.92	3.62
New England states..................	2.98	1.98	7.55
Eastern states, excluding New York City.	2.34	2.77	4.19
Middle Western states.................	2.30	2.62	6.97
Money in National Banks..............		5.9	
Money in circulation not in banks.......		3.74	

E. Velocity of Bank Deposits in American Cities, by Months, 1919–February, 1923

Standard deviations of the monthly velocity after adjustment for seasonal variation.

From W. Randolph Burgess, "Velocity of Bank Deposits," *Journal of the American Statistical Association*, June, 1923, vol. xviii, p. 738.

	Standard Deviations		Standard Deviations
New York City....................	5.98	Chicago.................	2.79
Syracuse..........................	4.74	San Francisco............	2.23
Albany..........................	4.36	Buffalo..................	1.79
Boston..........................	3.64	Rochester...............	1.22

TABLE 11—*Continued*

RELATIVE AMPLITUDE OF THE CYCLICAL-IRREGULAR FLUCTUATIONS OF VARIOUS ECONOMIC PROCESSES

F. American Series Showing Volume of Wholesale and Retail Trade by Months 1919–192

Standard deviations of percentage deviations from secular trends corrected for seasonal variations.

From Simon S. Kuznets, *Cyclical Fluctuations: Retail and Wholesale Trade*, pp. 37, 41, 102, 114.

	Standard Deviations Retail Sales	Standard Deviations Wholesale Sales
Mail-order houses	16.4	....
Music-store chains	11.8	....
Dry goods	11.5	16.5
Grocery-store chains	10.6	14.4
Shoe-store chains	9.6	18.1
Tobacco- and cigar-store chains	7.9	....
Candy-store chains	7.9	14.7
Department stores	6.3	15.8
Five- and ten-cent store chains	5.1	....
Drug-store chains	4.4	6.2
Hardware	....	13.4
General index	....	14.8

Series "Deflated" by Dividiug Dollar Volume of Sales by Appropriate Index Number of Prices

	Standard Deviations		
	Retail Trade	Wholesale Trade	Production
Shoe-store chains	9.9	14.6	19.3
Department store chains	6.3	....	....
Grocery-store chains	4.5	7.6	10.8
Dry Goods	...	13.3	....
Hardware	....	10.0	
Drugs	....	5.1	
General index	....	6.7	

G. British Series, by Quarters, before 1850

Standard deviations, arranged in order of magnitude, of the percentage deviations from the line of secular trend, adjusted when necessary for seasonal variations.

From Norman J. Silberling, "British Prices and British Cycles, 1779–1850," *Review of Economic Statistics*, October, 1923, Preliminary vol. v, Supplement 2, pp. 254–257.

	Standard Deviations
Quarterly average market rate of discount in London, best bills, 1824–1850	30.3
General commodity prices at wholesale, by quarters, 1779–1850	5.3

TABLE 11—*Continued*

RELATIVE AMPLITUDE OF THE CYCLICAL-IRREGULAR FLUCTUATIONS OF VARIOUS ECONOMIC PROCESSES

H. British Series, by Quarters, 1903–June 30, 1914

Standard deviations of the percentage deviations from secular trends.

Compiled from Persons, Silberling, and Berridge, "An Index of British Economic Conditions," *Review of Economic Statistics*, Preliminary vol. iv, Supplement 2, June, 1922, p. 189.

	Standard Deviations
Stores of Cleveland pig-iron in public warehouses	64.8
Percentage unemployed in all trades	43.8
Discount rate on 3–months paper in London	27.2
London bank clearings on stock-settling days	13.3
Exports of iron and steel (quantities)	13.2
Number of blast furnaces in blast	8.1
Exports of British produce (values)	7.50
Imports of raw materials, excluding cotton (values)	7.41
Bank clearings in 5 provincial cities	5.99
Sauerbeck Statist index number of wholesale prices of "all materials"	5.68
Market value of securities yielding variable incomes, Bankers' Magazine	4.3
Market value of selected British railway ordinary stocks	3.62
County bank clearings through London	3.34
Market value of local-government bonds	2.14

I. British Series, by Years, various dates—1913

Standard deviations of the percentage deviations from secular trends.

From Dorothy S. Thomas, *Social Aspects of the Business Cycle*, London, 1925, pp. 187, 200, 203 and 211.

	Standard Deviations
Percentage unemployed, "all trades," 1860–1913	54.6
Emigrants of British origin leaving U. K. for U. S. A., 1870–1913	21.3
Total emigrants of British origin from U. K., 1862–1913	19.1
Casual pauperism, 1883–1913	10.5
Production of pig iron, U. K., 1865–1913	8.77
Exports of British produce, 1854–1913	8.08
Sauerbeck's index number, wholesale prices of "all materials," 1854–1913.	7.40
Indoor pauperism, 1857–1913	6.45
Provincial bank clearings, 1887–1913	5.25
Outdoor pauperism, 1857–1913	4.33
Per-capita consumption of spirits, 1856–1913	4.08
Per-capita consumption of beer, 1856–1913	3.83
Production of coal, 1865–1913	3.59
Railway freight traffic receipts, 1881–1913	2.69

TABLE 11—*Continued*

RELATIVE AMPLITUDE OF THE CYCLICAL-IRREGULAR FLUCTUATIONS OF VARIOUS ECONOMIC PROCESSES

J. British Series, by Quarters, various dates to 1914

Standard deviations of the percentage deviations from secular trend corrected for seasonal variations.

From Dorothy S. Thomas, unpublished data.

	Standard Deviations
Unemployed iron founders, 1855–1914	60.52
Unemployment, "all trades," 1887–1914	45.20
Value of total exports of British produce, 1855–1914	9.25
Sauerbeck's wholesale-price index number, "all materials," 1885–1914	6.44
Blast furnaces in blast, 1897–1914	6.30
Provincial bank clearings (Manchester and Birmingham), 1887–1914	6.03
Railway freight traffic receipts, 1881–1914	3.93

K. German series by Quarters or Months, various dates to 1913–14

Standard deviations, arranged in order of magnitude, of the percentage deviations from lines of secular trend adjusted when necessary for seasonal variations.

Compiled from Emerson W. Axe and Harold M. Flinn, "An Index of General Business Conditions for Germany, 1898–1914," *Review of Economic Statistics*, October, 1925, vol. vii, p. 287.

	Standard Deviations
Market discount rates in Berlin, 1868–1914	27.90
Discounts and advances of the Reichsbank, 1872–1914	10.65
Ten-commodity price index of business cycles, 1898–1913	9.43
Index of stock prices on the Berlin Bourse, 1900–1914	8.45
Receipts from the *Wechselstempelsteuer*, 1900–1913	7.66
Value of commodities imported into Germany, 1892–1914	7.06
German bank clearings, 1898–1914	6.83
German pig-iron production, 1882–1914	6.64
Value of commodities exported from Germany, 1892–1914	5.53
Males enrolled in employees' insurance plan, 1904–1913	3.32
Monthly quotation of German *Reichsanleihung*, 1899–1914	2.36

Proceeding to particulars, we may set out certain conclusions which the figures suggest in quasi-tabular form. Regarding the volume of trade and production, the table indicates that

Retail trade shows fluctuations of smaller amplitude than wholesale trade in the same commodities.

Wholesale trade shows fluctuations of smaller amplitude than production of the same commodities, so far as our very limited evidence goes.

Judged by bank clearings, the volume of payments made in the great financial centers is far more variable than the volume of payments made in smaller towns.

The volume of foreign trade seems to be subject to wider fluctuations than domestic business outside the financial centers.

The volume of construction work in the United States, as shown by building permits, varies about as much as New York clearings.

Regarding prices we have no standard deviations for retail index numbers, which would presumably be small; but it does appear that

The cyclical-irregular fluctuations of wholesale-price index numbers have low standard deviations when many commodities are included, and moderate standard deviations (approaching 10.0) only when the indexes are made on purpose to exhibit cyclical fluctuations in a clear light. The "general level of wholesale prices" is one of the relatively stable factors in business, when monetary systems are not subject to grave disturbances, such as those caused by paper standards and great wars.

Stock prices are highly variable as compared with wholesale commodity prices, at least in the United States. (The British and German materials in the table do not admit of satisfactory comparisons with other series.)

Bond prices are even more stable than wholesale commodity prices, if we exclude the bonds of debtors whose credit is doubtful.

Regarding interest rates on short loans in the financial centers, for which alone the table gives data, we find that

The standard deviations are always rather high.[1] They range from 16.5 to 38.7. The London and Berlin rates in 1903-14

[1] It does not follow that the interest rates paid by most commercial borrowers are subject to wide variations. See Carl Snyder, "The Influence of the Interest Rate on the Business Cycle," *American Economic Review*, December, 1925, vol. xv, pp. 684-699.

fluctuate even more than the New York rates, a statistical result which may or may not be significant.

Regarding banking operations we have relatively full results for the National Banks as a whole, and by sections of the United States.

In all the operations for which the standard deviations of cyclical-irregular fluctuations have been computed, the New York figures are more than double the "outside" figures.

As among different operations, lending seems to be the least variable. The most variable item outside New York is the volume of investments; in New York it is the amount of lawful money held.

Another conclusion of theoretical importance is that the volume of coin and paper money held by the banks has larger standard deviations than the volume of coin and paper money in the hands of the public.

2. The Time Sequence of Cyclical-Irregular Fluctuations.

When several time series from which the secular trends and the seasonal variations have been eliminated are plotted by months one above another on the same time scale for a considerable period, the business cycles of that period can usually be traced in most if not all of the curves. But it is highly improbable that all the curves will reach the crests and troughs of their successive cycles in the same months. As a rule the crests and the troughs of the various curves are distributed over periods of several months—often over periods of more than a year.

Closer inspection shows that the order in which the curves reach their crests and decline, or reach their troughs and rise, presents that mixture of uniformity and differences with which economic statistics commonly confront us. The crests of a given curve may precede those of a second curve in some cycles and follow those of the latter curve in other cycles. But other comparisons show tolerably regular time relations over long periods. That is, the cyclical changes in certain economic processes appear to lead or lag behind the corresponding changes in certain other economic processes by intervals of time which are fairly constant.

This feature of the behavior of time series has been turned to account by statisticians interested in business forecasting. Indeed, it forms the corner-stone of several forecasting systems. If certain changes in banking operations regularly preceded certain other changes in discount rates by a regular interval, the latter changes could be foretold as soon as the former changes had been reported. Further, if an invariable series of such time relations between the cyclical fluctuations of different economic processes could be discovered, and if this series returned upon itself in the sense that the last set of changes in one cycle preceded the first set of changes in the next cycle by a regular interval, then business forecasting could be raised to a quasi-mechanical level. Needless to say, no such chain of events with links of unchanging length has been discovered. Perhaps no statistician has expected to find such a chain. But it has been a leading aim of statistical research to determine the time sequence in which important series pass through the successive phases of business cycles, to find cases in which this sequence is fairly regular, and in such cases to measure the average intervals by which certain series or groups of series lead or lag behind others.

The standard procedure in studying the time relationships among cyclical-irregular fluctuations is to start by plotting each series to be studied on a strip of translucent paper laid off with a uniform time scale. Any one of these strips can then be placed above any other and shifted to right or left until that position is found which seems to make the two series of cyclical-irregular fluctuations match best with each other. This matching may be closest when the same dates on the two strips are put together, or it may be closest when one series is made to lag behind the other by several months, by a year, or even more. Sometimes the best matching can be determined with confidence; sometimes it is so uncertain that two trained observers will differ in their opinions.

To test the conclusions suggested by this simple procedure, and to decide the doubtful cases, which are numerous, the statisticians resort to a more objective method. They compute several coefficients of correlation between two series, pairing the items in different ways. For example, if visual comparison of the curves suggests that the cyclical fluctuations of series A agree best with those of series B when A lags two months behind B, the investigator may compute (say) seven coefficients between the two series, one coefficient when

TABLE 12

TIME SEQUENCE IN THE CYCLICAL-IRREGULAR FLUCTUATIONS OF VARIOUS ECONOMIC SERIES

A. American Series, by Months, January, 1903–July, 1914

Compiled from Warren M. Persons, "An Index of General Business Conditions," *Review of Economic Statistics*, April, 1919, Preliminary vol. i, pp. 129, 182.

All the series included in each group have maximum coefficients of inter-correlation when concurrent months are paired, and these coefficients are of significant size. The coefficients are computed from cyclical-irregular fluctuations after elimination of secular trends, and, when necessary, of seasonal variations.

Groups based upon Time Sequence of Cyclical-Irregular Fluctuations	Comparison with Bradstreet's price index: Lead or lag in months	Coefficient of correlation
I Series which precede other groups in time sequence		
Yield of 10 railroad bonds	leads 10	− .72
Price of 20 railroad stocks	leads 10	+ .76
Price of industrial stocks	leads 10	+ .63
II Series which lag behind Group I by 2–4 months		
Shares traded in the N. Y. Stock Exchange	leads 12	+ .44
Value of building permits in 20 American cities	leads 6	+ .61
New York bank clearings	leads 6	+ .60
III Series which lag behind Group II by 2–4 months		
Production of pig iron	leads 2	+ .75
Bank clearings outside of New York City	leads 2	+ .70
Imports of merchandise	leads 2	+ .77
Business failures	leads 2	− .67
IV Series which lag behind Group III by 2–4 months		
Bradstreet's index of wholesale prices	concurrent	+1.00
Bureau of Labor Statistics index of wholesale prices	concurrent	....
Gross earnings of railroads	concurrent	+ .77
Reserves of New York City banks	lags 2	− .78
V Series which lag behind Group IV by 4–6 months		
Dividend payments	concurrent	+ .65
Loans of New York City banks	lags 4	− .67
Rate on 4- to 6-months paper	lags 4	+ .80

the Augusts in series A are paired with the Junes in series B, the Septembers in A with the Julys in B, the Octobers with the Augusts, and so on; a second coefficient when the Julys in A are paired with the Junes in B, etc.; a third when the Junes in A are paired with the Junes in B, etc.; a fourth pairing Mays in A with Junes in B, etc.; a fifth, sixth, and seventh when the Septembers, Octobers and Novembers in A are paired successively with the Junes in B. When all these coefficients have been computed, the investigator concludes that the closest time relationship between the cyclical-irregular fluctuations in the two series is that indicated by the highest of the co-

TABLE 12—*Continued*

TIME SEQUENCE IN THE CYCLICAL-IRREGULAR FLUCTUATIONS OF VARIOUS ECONOMIC SERIES

B. American Series, by Months, January, 1902, to December, 1908

Compiled from Alvin H. Hansen, *Cycles of Prosperity and Depression in the United States, Great Britain and Germany*, Madison, Wisconsin, 1921, pp. 26, 30, 33, 38, 39

Groups based upon Time-Sequence of Fluctuations	Comparison with Series Chosen as Standard for the Group: Lead or lag in months	Coefficient of correlation
I Banking Group which precedes other groups in timing		
Cash reserves of N. Y. Clearing-house banks—*Standard*	concurrent	+1.000
Call-loan rates, New York	concurrent	− .477
Deposits N. Y. Clearing-house banks	concurrent	+ .956
Loans N. Y. Clearing-house banks	concurrent	+ .889
* Commercial paper rates New York	lags 3	− .686
II Investment Group, lags 12 months behind Banking Group		
* Prices of 10 railroad bonds	leads 2	+ .808
Liabilities of business failures	leads 1	− .542
Prices of 10 investment stocks. *Standard*	concurrent	+1.000
Prices of 40 common stocks	concurrent	+ .904
Shares traded on New York Stock Exchange	concurrent	+ .580
* Total bank clearings in the U. S.	lags 3	+ .557
* Building permits in 20 American cities	lags 3	+ .482
* Railroad net earnings	lags 6	+ .473
III Industrial Group, lags 8 months behind Investment Group		
* Railroad net earnings	leads 4	+ .756
* Unemployment (Hornell Hart)	leads 3	− .719
Pig iron production	leads 1	+ .797
Imports of merchandise	leads 1	+ .905
Bureau of Labor Statistics index of wholesale prices. *Standard*	concurrent	+1.000
Railroad gross earnings	concurrent	+ .857
Immigration	concurrent	+ .696
* Exports of merchandise	lags 4	+ .758
Commercial paper rates (see Group I) compared with Industrial Group	lags 5	+ .688

* Series omitted from Group indexes because of lead or lag.

efficients. If the coefficient is highest when the Septembers in A are paired with the Junes in B, the investigator will say that series A lags behind series B by three months; if the coefficient is highest when the Mays in A are compared with the Junes in B, he will say that

series A leads series B by one month; if the coefficient is highest when the Junes in both series are paired, he will say that the two series fluctuate synchronously.

Table 12 shows two sets of results reached in this way by Professors Warren M. Persons and Alvin H. Hansen. Both these men publish the coefficients for several monthly pairings of each set of series, but only the maximum coefficients which they take to indicate leads or lags are entered in the table. Often the maximum coefficients are but little greater than those for a somewhat longer or shorter lead or lag. This fact raises a problem which requires illustration and discussion.

A rather elaborate illustration may be borrowed from Dr. Frederick C. Mills, who has worked out not less than twelve coefficients of correlation for different monthly pairings of an index of prices of industrial stocks and the index of "general business activity" compiled by the statistical division of the American Telephone and Telegraph Company. Dr. Mills gives these twelve coefficients for two separate periods and shows that the results differ considerably—a point to which we shall presently recur. The point of immediate interest is that in both periods the coefficients are much alike for no less than five different pairings. In the first period, with stock prices leading "general business" by 3, 4, 5, 6, and 7 months the coefficients

TABLE 13

COEFFICIENTS OF CORRELATION BETWEEN THE CYCLICAL-IRREGULAR FLUCTUATIONS OF INDUSTRIAL STOCK PRICES AND AN INDEX OF "GENERAL BUSINESS"

Based upon American data, by Months, 1903–14, and 1919–23
From Frederick C. Mills, *Statistical Methods*, New York, 1924, pp. 424 and 426

	Coefficient of correlation 1903–14	1919–23
Stock prices concurrent with business index	+.55	+.75
Stock prices preceding general business by 1 mo.	+.65	+.83
" " " " " " 2 mos.	+.70	+.87
" " " " " " 3 "	+.73	+.88
" " " " " " 4 "	+.76	+.85
" " " " " " 5 "	+.76	+.82
" " " " " " 6 "	+.76	+.77
" " " " " " 7 "	+.74	+.72
" " " " " " 8 "	+.71	+.66
" " " " " " 9 "	+.67	+.57
" " " " " " 10 "	+.61	+.46
" " " " " " 11 "	+.54	+.33

range between +.73 and +.76. In the second period, the coefficients range between +.82 and +.88, when stock prices lead by 1, 2, 3, 4, and 5 months.

Whenever a close relation like this is found between the coefficients computed for several different pairings, the statement that one series lags behind another by some definite interval, such as five months, hardly suggests the facts, and may suggest quite false ideas. The definite lag should be thought of as the central tendency of an elaborate array of time relations between the fluctuations of two variables. When we speak of a lag of say five months we should accustom ourselves to bear in mind the other intervals which may show agreements nearly as close. And when, as sometimes happens, the array of coefficients for lags of different length shows no central tendency, but varies in an irregular fashion, we should be extremely cautious about saying that there is a definite lag.

The importance of the full array of time relations becomes clearer when we consider the causal interpretation of leads and lags. A theorist in thinking about the relations between changes in the price and changes in the production of a commodity does not suppose that an increase in prices made in January will affect production in just one future month, say June. On the contrary, he supposes that the January increase will begin to influence production policies, and perhaps actual output, as soon as it is announced, which may be in advance of the actual change in prices; or, rather, as soon as it is anticipated, which may be in advance of the announcement. The increase in prices actually made in January may have influenced production in the preceding December. Nor is the influence of the price change upon output likely to exhaust itself quickly; it may grow stronger for several months, reach a maximum, and then gradually decline. Conversely, the price influences upon the production of a given month, say, June, are not the result of changes made in some one preceding month, say, January; but the net resultant of price changes made in many preceding months, combined perhaps with price changes which are anticipated in the months to follow—changes which may not take place. Finally, the theorist does not trace the causal relationship in one direction only. He realizes that production reacts upon prices. The January change in prices, of which we have spoken, was probably influenced by the production of many months which preceded, and by anticipation of the production in months still to come.

So complicated a set of causal interrelationships can hardly be followed by statistical methods. But Professor Irving Fisher has shown how to take one step in advance by replacing a fixed lag with a lag which is distributed over many months. On comparing the rate of change from month to month in the wholesale-price index of the Bureau of Labor Statistics with Professor Persons' index of the physical volume of trade from August, 1915, to March, 1923, Fisher found that the usual methods gave the highest coefficient of correlation (+.727) for a lag of seven months in volume of trade. Six and eight months, however, gave coefficients nearly as high (+.719 and +.715). Giving a causal interpretation to the relation between price change and volume of trade, Fisher conceived the hypothesis that the effects of a given price change in one month upon volume of trade are distributed over succeeding months in accordance with the probability curve. He set himself to find out by experiment just what probability distribution of the price changes over time gives the index that correlates best with the volume of trade. As the result of many trials, he concluded that the best fit is obtained when the price changes are distributed along a "normal" curve having a logarithmic time axis, a mode lagging 9½ months behind the change in prices, and "probable error points" lagging about 5 and 18 months. When the price changes of 1915-23 were redistributed in this way, the coefficient of correlation between the new index and the volume of trade index proved to be +.941.[1]

[1] Irving Fisher, "Our Unstable Dollar and the So-called Business Cycle," *Journal of the American Statistical Association,* June, 1925, vol. xx, pp. 179-203.

Our present concern is with the method of treating lags which Professor Fisher has devised; not with the time relations between fluctuations in prices and "trade." But we should note that statisticians interested in the latter problem have questioned the comparability of the two series which Fisher uses, and the interpretation which he gives of the results.

Mr. Carl Snyder points out that the index of physical volume of trade which Fisher borrows from Persons represents essentially fluctuations in basic industrial activity, while his price index is very heavily weighted by agricultural prices. That is, Fisher compares the price changes of one list of commodities with the trade in a decidedly different list.

Dr. Willford I. King suggests that the lag may be explained as follows: wholesale prices are made when orders are placed or contracts drawn; goods are manufactured at a later date; shipments and transfers come later still. Price indexes are based upon current quotations. Volume of trade indexes are based mainly upon manufacturing output and deliveries. Thus volume-of-trade indexes are "post-dated" in comparison with the price indexes. If we could take both price and volume-of-trade records at the same stage of given transactions—that is, if we could take volume of transactions entered into at the time prices are made, or if we could take the prices at which current output and deliveries are being made—the relations between changes in prices and changes in volume of trade might appear in a new light. As matters stand, what is more natural than that the changes in a price index should precede in date the changes in a trade index? But does this lead due to post-dating justify the conclusion that price change causes changes in volume of trade?

As Professor Fisher suggests, the principle involved in this study of time relationship "would seem to be a general and useful one." In practical application to any case, however, the method is exceedingly laborious and costly, because there is no way of determining, except by actual computation, precisely what form of the probability distribution applied to the curve which leads will turn it into the form which correlates best with the curve which lags. Until some far quicker way of distributing lags is devised, the method will have but limited use.[2]

The problem still remains of treating statistically the influence of the variable which lags upon the variable which leads. To apply this remark to Professor Fisher's problem: economic theory suggests that changes in the physical volume of trade react upon prices. Can this reaction be demonstrated and measured by the use of time series? So far as the writer knows, no statistician has attacked this problem. It would be interesting to see what results could be obtained, for example, by treating the volume-of-trade index, or some derivative of it, as the variable which leads, and the price-change index, or some derivative of it, as the variable which lags, presumably choosing a period in which monetary disturbances were less extraordinary than in the years which Professor Fisher took as the base for his experiments. If a significant relation were shown to exist not only between price-change and volume of trade, but also between changes in volume of trade and subsequent changes in prices, the statistician would have come nearer presenting the complicated relations which the theorist contemplates as real.

Time sequence among the cyclical-irregular fluctuations of different series is no more constant than are secular trends or seasonal variations. One illustration of change has already been given in

[2] Professor Fisher himself suggests a "short cut."

"By this method the influence of any given price-change is assumed to begin at a maximum immediately (i.e., at the very next month or quarter following the given price-change), and then to taper off by equal reductions for each successive interval of time. . . . By having only *one* parameter to vary . . . the labor is reduced by at least four-fifths. The only variable becomes the number of months in which the influence tapers off to zero."

This short method yielded somewhat higher coefficients of correlation than the long method in all cases which Fisher worked out in both ways. For example, in 1915-23, the short method, with a tapering off period of 25 months, when compared with the physical volume of trade, gave a coefficient of +.95, against +.94 for the long method. On Professor Fisher's own logic, the short method seems to be better as well as shorter. But, though taking only one-fifth as much time as the long method, it is still laborious. See the paper referred to above, p. 198, note.

Table 13. While the period covered by the second column of that table (1919-23) is too brief to yield final conclusions,

> The results indicate that since the war the movements of general business have followed more closely behind stock-price movements than during the pre-war days. A maximum correlation is secured when stock prices precede the business index by 3 months (instead of 4-6 months as in 1903-14).[3]

So, too, Professor Persons found that the time sequences shown in section A of Table 12 were not maintained in 1914-18.

> The systematic relation of the fluctuations which held during the pre-war period was shattered by the outbreak of war.[4]

Apart from such catastrophic events, the improvement of communication and transportation speeds up many effects which economic processes exert upon each other. Statistically this quickening means a gradual reduction of the intervals by which certain time series lag behind others, as well as a shifting of seasonal variations.

A formal discrepancy between the two parts of Table 12 may have troubled the reader's mind. According to Professor Persons, in 1903-14 New York City bank loans and deposits belonged in the group of series which fluctuated last in the sequence, while the reserves of these banks belonged in the group which was next to the last. On the contrary, according to Professor Hansen, in 1902-08 these three banking series belong in the group which preceded all other groups in the time sequence. To reconcile these opposing results is easy on the theory that business fluctuations have the character of recurrent cycles. One can break into a round of events which keeps repeating itself in time at any point and follow the sequence back to its starting point. A second investigator can follow the sequence equally well by starting where the first man stopped. Our two authorities have merely chosen different starting points for their analyses of time sequence. By linking Professor Persons' last group to his first, one gets Professor Hansen's start; by linking Hansen's last group to his first, one gets Persons' ending.

Another point which requires notice here has already been mentioned in discussing the correlation of time series; [5] but it is so im-

[3] Frederick C. Mills, *Statistical Methods,* New York, 1924, p. 426.
[4] Warren M. Persons, "An Index of General Business Conditions," *Review of Economic Statistics,* April, 1919, Preliminary vol. i, p. 116.
[5] See section iv, i, above.

portant and so seldom attended to that repetition is in order. The time sequence of two series sometimes changes from phase to phase of business cycles. For example, one series may lead a second in reviving after depression, but lag behind the second in declining after prosperity. In such cases a coefficient of correlation computed in the usual fashion will conceal in an average two opposite sequences which may be highly significant. To guard against such misfortunes, the computation of coefficients of correlation to determine time relations should always be preceded by close study of the plotted curves to see whether the sequence of fluctuations changes during the cycles. If such changes do occur it may be feasible to compute separate coefficients for the periods of revival and recession, of prosperity and depression.

Finally, we should recall in connection with the study of time sequences what was said in the preceding section about hunting for the particular phase of one economic process which affects a second process, and for the particular phase of the second process which experiences the causal effects of the first. Economic theorists, like economic statisticians, have been prone to argue from chronological priority to causal relationship, without intensive analysis of the way in which the causal influence is exerted. To illustrate the danger of drawing hasty conclusions: A decline in one activity generally precedes, and so seems to cause, a decline in a second activity; but changes in the volume of the first activity may be controlled by changes in the rate of growth in the second. In that case, throwing the second time series into the form of first derivatives will show that changes in its rate of growth regularly precede the changes observed in the first series, and reverse the inference concerning cause and effect. No feature of business cycles presents more misleading cues than does the apparent chronological order among the cyclical fluctuations of different processes, and no other feature requires from the investigator a finer blend of theoretical insight with statistical skill.[6]

[6] A concrete example may make clearer the type of issues involved in such work. Mr. Karl G. Karsten's paper, "The Harvard Business Indexes—A New Interpretation," (*Journal of the American Statistical Association*, December, 1926) will serve.

The Harvard indexes in question, more fully described in the next section, are represented by three curves: Curve A showing changes in speculation; Curve B showing changes in general business, and Curve C showing changes in discount rates. Index A moves first. Index B, lagging six months behind A, shows a coefficient of correlation with A of +.77 in the pre-war period and of +.73 in the post-war period. Index C, lagging four months behind B, shows a coefficient of correlation with B of +.80 in the pre-war period and (according to Karsten) of +.36 in the post-war period.

Mr. Karsten develops a new set of working hypotheses concerning the causal rela-

VI. Indexes of Business Conditions.

So far we have been dealing with the statistical analysis of time series taken one at a time, or with statistical comparisons of time series taken in pairs. In ascertaining secular trends and seasonal variations, in isolating cyclical-irregular fluctuations, in turning series into new forms, and in computing the standard deviations of cyclical-irregular fluctuations, the investigator treats each series by itself. In computing coefficients of correlation, and in studying leads and lags, he works with two series at a time.

The chief value of statistical methods and results for the theory of business cycles lies in these intensive studies of the fluctuations of particular processes and of their relations to each other. But the theorist can profit also by a further stage in the statistician's program —the effort to combine time series representing different economic processes into general indexes of business conditions. If such indexes can really be made, they should help to solve many theoretical problems.

To find what the indexes of general business mean, what they do and do not tell about business cycles, it is necessary to examine the

tionships among the activities represented by these indexes. (1) He supposes changes in the security prices of Curve A to be determined primarily by the amount of "money" which in dull times flows out of business into the stock market for investment, and which in brisk times is withdrawn from the stock market for business use. (2) What counts in this causal relationship is not the volume of money flowing into or out of the stock market in a given month, but the fund accumulated in the stock market by the net influx and efflux of past months—just as the amount of a bank deposit account is determined by cumulated withdrawals and deposits over a period. (3) On this hypothesis, the movements of Index B should lead the movements of Index A, not lag behind the latter, as the Harvard interpretation holds. (4) Also, the causal relation between general business and speculation is inverse. Dull business tends to produce stock-market activity; active business to produce stock market dullness. (5) Discount rates are controlled by the cumulated demand for loan funds from both general business and the securities market. The volume of the former demand exceeds that of the latter, perhaps by three to one.

Computations which Mr. Karsten made to test these hypotheses show that the cumulation of Index B, inverted, and given a lead of two and one-half months over Index A, yields coefficients of correlation with A of +.94 in the pre-war period and of +.96 in the post-war period. Similarly, by cumulating Indexes A and B, weighted one and three respectively, Karsten gets an index which yields coefficients of +.85 and +.94 when correlated with Index C in the pre-war and post-war periods.

Since these coefficients are on a decidedly higher level than those obtained by the Harvard Committee of Economic Research, Mr. Karsten argues that his interpretation of the causal and chronological relationships among the three Harvard indexes has more theoretical justification and affords a better basis for forecasting than the Harvard interpretation.

That Mr. Karsten's results cannot be regarded as definitely established until they have been subjected to critical examination, makes his paper all the better as an illustration of the argument in the text.

leading specimens, beginning with simple devices and advancing toward more elaborate constructions.

1. A Collection of Indexes of Business Conditions.

(1) Beveridge's Chart of "The Pulse of the Nation," Great Britain, 1856-1907.

Sir William H. Beveridge's chart of "The Pulse of the Nation," made in 1908 and reproduced on the next page, was one of the early efforts to present graphically that "remarkable phenomenon . . . the . . . cyclical fluctuation of industrial activity." Seven important variables are represented:—foreign trade, the bank rate, employment, marriage rate, indoor pauperism, consumption of beer, and capital of new companies registered. Sir William puts the trade-union employment returns in the central position, but he reverses the figures,

> so as to represent an unemployed percentage of 2.5 as an employed percentage of 97.5 and so on. Lines drawn through the successive lowest points of this curve—1868, 1879, 1885, 1894, 1904—cut it up into waves of unequal length, representing successive industrial cycles. The crest of each wave is at about 98; the depressions are anywhere between 89 and 94. The point of the chart is this, that the same lines cut up every one of the other curves into corresponding waves.[1]

No adjustments are practiced upon the data beyond reducing all the series, except the percentage figures, to a per-capita basis. Of course there are differences in the movements of the seven curves; but these differences are matters of detail, and Sir William concludes his picture of business cycles by remarking,

> It would be possible to extend almost indefinitely the . . . review of economic statistics and almost everywhere to meet the same familiar phenomenon. . . . It is hardly too much to say that, apart from the death rate, the only prominent social and economic records in which the pulsation of the nation's aggregate activities cannot be traced as a significant factor, whether cause or symptom, are the price of Consols and the price of wheat.[2]

[1] Sir William H. Beveridge, *Unemployment, a Problem of Industry*, 2d ed., London, 1910, p. 41.

[2] The same, pp. 50, 51.

CHART 9.

SIR WILLIAM H. BEVERIDGE'S CHART OF "THE PULSE OF THE NATION."

GREAT BRITAIN, BY YEARS, 1856-1907.

(Reproduced from the chart in *Unemployment, a Problem of Industry*, 2d ed., London, p. 44.)

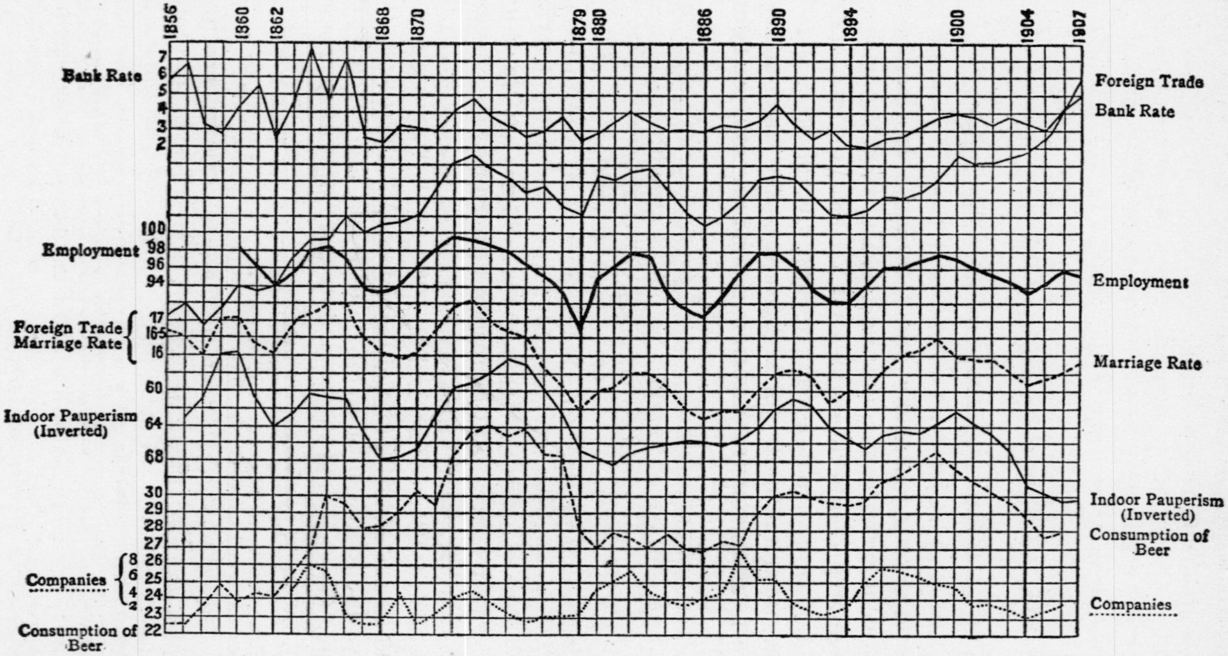

The scales at the left-hand side indicate respectively the actual Bank Rate of discount per cent., the percentage of trade union members not returned as unemployed, the number of marriages in England and Wales per 1000 of the population, the number of indoor paupers in England and Wales per 10,000 of the population, the gallons of beer consumed, and the nominal capital of new companies registered, in pounds, per head of the population. No scale is given for the Foreign Trade Curve. Unless the contrary is stated, all figures apply to United Kingdom generally.

With such a picture before them and with such materials to handle, statisticians wished to get results better adapted to analytic work than a collection of separate curves. Index numbers which reduce the price fluctuations of many commodities to a single series, raised the question whether it is possible to get a single curve to represent business cycles. And since business cycles cover but a few years, the year seemed too large a unit of measurement.

(2) Persons' "Index of General Business Conditions," United States, 1903-14.

By developing a more elaborate technique, Professor Warren M. Persons was able to draw a simpler chart of business cycles in 1919. He first isolated the cyclical-irregular fluctuations in a considerable number of time series in monthly form by the methods described above, and expressed these fluctuations as percentage deviations from the ordinates of secular trend corrected for seasonal variations. Since these deviations presented wide differences of amplitude from series to series, differences which seemed irrelevant for his purposes, Persons next reduced the cyclical-irregular fluctuations of each series to terms of their standard deviation. Then he made elaborate studies of the timing of the fluctuations of his various series expressed in this form, using coefficients of correlation to determine what series varied concurrently, what series lagged behind others, and how long were the lags. Finally, he averaged together the series which varied concurrently. In this way Persons reduced thirteen series to three indexes which he presented as "The Index of General Business Conditions." One index he called an "index of speculation," the second "an index of physical productivity and commodity prices combined," the third "an index of the financial situation in New York." [1]

[1] Warren M. Persons, "An Index of General Business Conditions," *Review of Economic Statistics,* April, 1919, Preliminary vol. i, pp. 111-114.

The series combined to make the three curves are as follows:

Index of speculation: yields of ten railroad bonds, prices of industrial stocks, prices of twenty railroad bonds, bank clearings in New York City.

Index of physical productivity and commodity prices: pig-iron production, outside clearings, Bradstreet's price index, Bureau of Labor Statistics price index, reserves of New York City banks.

Index of the financial situation in New York: rate on 4 to 6 months paper, rate on 60 to 90 day paper, loans of New York City banks, deposits of New York City banks.

For the revised form of this chart used for the post-war period, 1919 to date, see W. L. Crum, "The Interpretation of the Index of General Business Conditions," *Review of Economic Statistics,* Supplement, 1925, vol. vii, p. 226.

Recently Professor Persons has made a similar three-curve index which covers a much longer period than his first one. See his article, "An Index of General Business Conditions, 1875-1913," *Review of Economic Statistics,* January, 1927, vol. ix, pp. 20-29.

Although Persons called his chart "The Index of General Business Conditions," his aim was less to picture business cycles graphically, than to provide a basis for forecasting business changes. The merit of his index for this purpose was that, during the pre-war period, the cyclical fluctuations of the index of speculation systematically preceded in time those of the index of physical productivity and commodity prices, and that the cyclical fluctuations of the latter index systematically preceded those of the index of financial conditions.[2]

CHART 10.

PERSONS' "INDEX OF GENERAL BUSINESS CONDITIONS."

BI-MONTHLY AVERAGES, 1903 TO JUNE, 1914.

From *Review of Economic Statistics,* April, 1919, Preliminary vol. i, pp. 112-113.

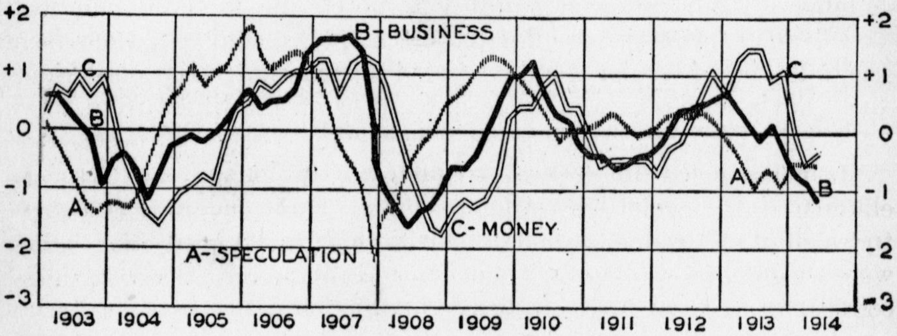

(3) The American Telephone and Telegraph Company's "Index of General Business Compared with Normal," United States, 1877 to date.

Later investigators have used Professor Persons' technique to combine numerous time series into a single index of business conditions. Of such constructions the one which covers the longest period of American business is the chart of "General Business Compared with Normal," 1877 to date, made by the statistical division of the American Telephone and Telegraph Company. In carrying their chart back to 1877 by months, the statisticians of the telephone company had to use such data as they could find. From 1877 to 1884 pig-iron output was the only series available. In 1885, bank clearings outside New York City and blast-furnace capacity were added. In 1892 Brad-

[2] See Professor Persons' paper, cited above, p. 114. Persons' latest statements concerning these lags are quoted below in this section, 2, (4) "Forecasting Sequences."

street's wholesale price index came in. Further changes were made in 1903, 1909, 1913, 1919 and 1921; but the compilers believed that

> Variation in the number of series used and in weights is of little importance, since all the series move together in the business cycle.[1]

Finally in April, 1922, it was decided to drop all data which contained a price factor, and to add several series of recent origin. As Colonel M. C. Rorty explained in publishing the chart,

> . . . it includes no measure of agricultural activity or retail trade, except as such items are indirectly reflected in freight movements and bank clearings, and it includes only a very limited list of non-agricultural raw materials. It is, therefore, primarily a measure of manufacturing activity and the physical movements of commodities. Nevertheless, with all these limitations, it represents, perhaps, as serviceable an approach as can be made to a single "all purpose" business index.[2]

In making this index, secular trends and seasonal variations were eliminated, the cyclical-irregular fluctuations were expressed as multiples of their standard deviations, in this form the several series were weighted according to their values as representatives of business conditions, and weighted totals were cast.

(4) Snyder's "Index of the Volume of Trade," United States, 1919-25.

While the telephone company's statisticians desired to cover as long a period as is feasible in their index, in the first of his indexes Mr. Carl Snyder of the Federal Reserve Bank of New York sought to cover a brief period as thoroughly as possible. For the years 1919 to 1923 Snyder was able to find no less than 56 series in monthly form

[1] *Method of Construction of "General Business" Curve.* American Telephone and Telegraph Company, Office of the Chief Statistician. New York, July 8, 1921, p. 3. (Manuscript.)

[2] M. C. Rorty, "The Statistical Control of Business Activities," *Harvard Business Review*, January, 1923, vol. i, pp. 159, 160. After the revisions of 1922 the items included in the index, and their weights, were as follows:

	Weight		Weight
Pig-iron production	20	Cotton consumption	10
Unfilled orders, U. S. Steel Corporation	10	Activity of wool machinery	10
Freight-car demand	10	Paper production	10
Car loadings	5	Lumber production	5
Net freight ton miles	5	Leather production	5
Coal production	5	Power production	5

which reflected some aspect of the fluctuations in the volume of trade. These series he arranged in 28 groups, which he classified in turn under five general heads, namely: productive activity, primary distribution, distribution to consumers, general business, and financial

CHART 11.

The American Telephone and Telegraph Company's Index of "General Business Compared with Normal."

By Months, 1877 to Date.

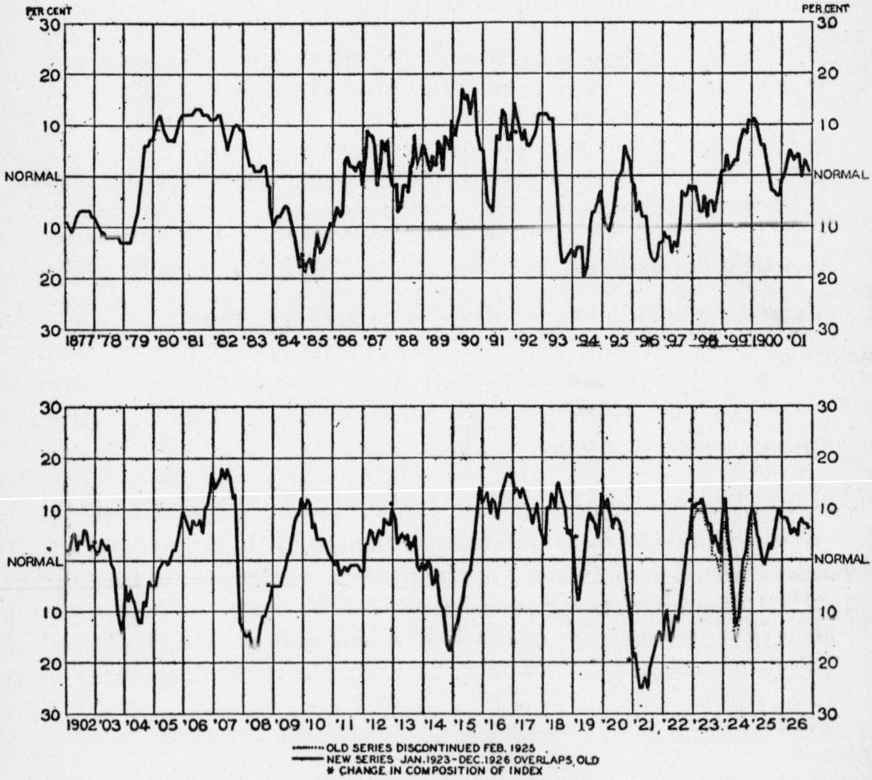

business. In working up his materials, Mr. Snyder divided the series expressed in dollars by appropriate index numbers of prices to eliminate the wild price perturbations of his period, computed secular trends and seasonal variations where necessary, expressed the cyclical-irregular fluctuations as percentages of the trends, and weighted each series according to the importance of the element which it represents

in the country's trade. He did not reduce the percentage deviations from trends to multiples of their standard deviations; but averaged them as they stood. For each of his five general heads and for each of his 28 groups Mr. Snyder computed an index, which can be compared with his index for all of the series. Chart 12 gives his leading results as revised and extended to 1925.[1]

(5) Persons' "Index of Trade," United States, 1903-25.

Valuable for comparison both with the American Telephone and Telegraph Company's index, which covers so many years, and with Snyder's index, which covers so many processes, is the "Index of Trade" which Warren Persons made in 1923. This series is

> designed to give a view of the combined fluctuations of trade, transportation, manufacturing activity and industrial employment in the United States, month by month, since 1903.

[1] Carl Snyder, "A New Index of the Volume of Trade," *Journal of the American Statistical Association,* December, 1923, vol. xviii, pp. 949–963, and "The Revised Index of the Volume of Trade," the same, September, 1925, vol. xx, pp. 397–404.

The 28 series or groups of series included in the revised form of the index and their weights are as follows:

	Weights		Weights
Productive Activity		Distribution to Consumers	
Producers' goods	9%	Department store sales	8%
Consumers' goods	8	Chain store sales	3
Employment	6	Chain grocery sales	6
Motor vehicles	2	Mail order sales	3
Building permits	4	Life insurance written	2
		Real estate transfers	2
	29	Advertising	2
Primary Distribution			
Merchandise car loadings	5		26
Other car loadings	2		
Wholesale trade	8	Financial Business	
Exports	3	New securities issued	2
Imports	2	Stock sales	2
Cereal exports	1	Grain sales	1
Panama Canal	1	Cotton sales	1
	22		6
General Business			
Debits outside N. Y.	8		100
Debits in N. Y.	5		
Postal receipts	1		
Electrical power	2		
Series not published	1		
	17		

Since this chapter was written, Mr. Snyder has assembled in a book his various studies in this field: *Business Cycles and Business Measurements,* New York, 1927.

CHART 12.

Carl Snyder's Index of the Volume of Trade

United States, by Months, 1919–April, 1925.

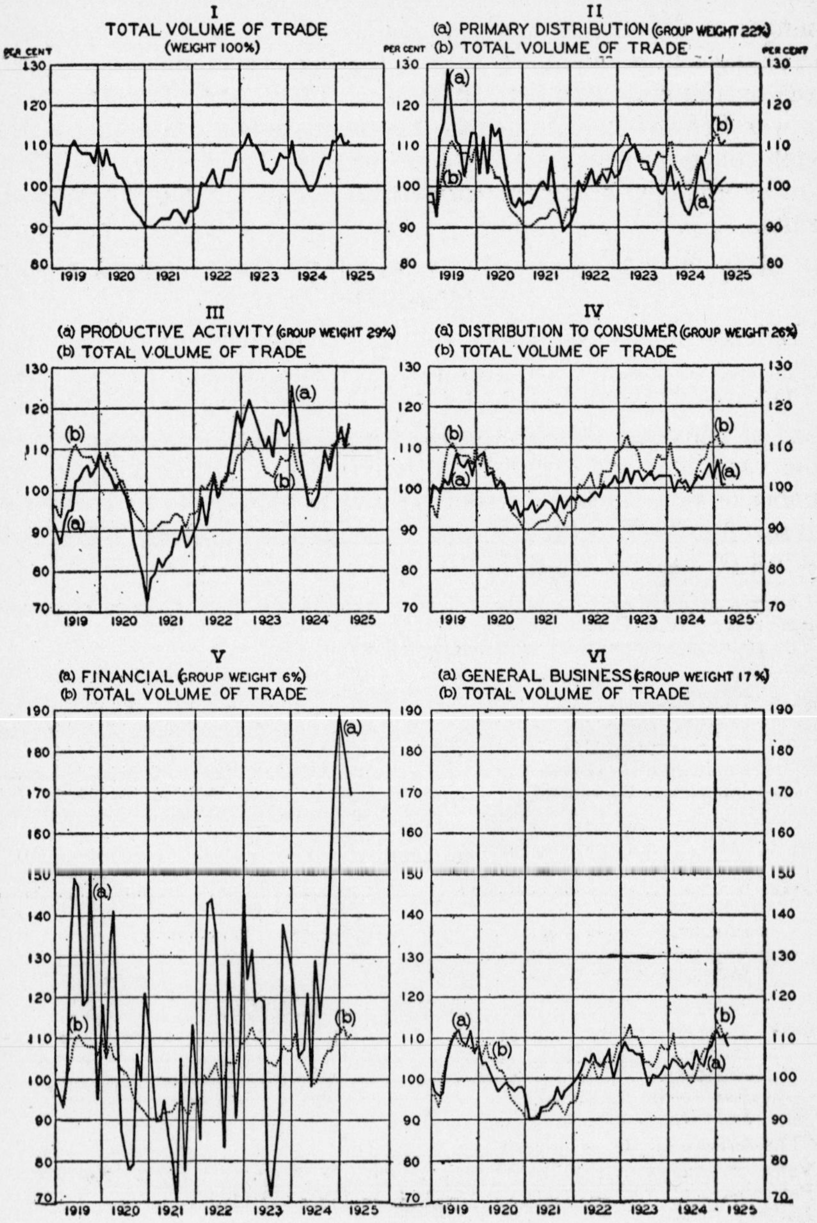

The technical methods employed are modifications of those used in constructing the three-curve "Index of General Business Conditions." Changes in the materials available for different parts of his period, and changes in economic conditions led Persons to make his index in three overlapping segments, 1903-15, 1915-19, and 1919-23. Before the war Persons thought it safe to use materials containing a price factor (outside clearings and values of imports); but from 1915 onward he excluded all series expressed in dollars.[1] Chart 13 shows his results.

(6) Miss Thomas' Quarterly Index of "British Business Cycles," 1855-1914.

Indexes of business cycles similar in character to the American series reviewed above are available for Great Britain and Germany.

The British index made by Dr. Dorothy Swaine Thomas, is a mean of percentage deviations from secular trends corrected for seasonal variations and expressed in units of standard deviations. The number of series included rises from two in 1855-80 to six in 1887-96, and seven in 1897 to 1914. Chart 14 shows the quarterly averages for the full 60 years covered.[1]

[1] Warren M. Persons, "An Index of Trade for the United States," *Review of Economic Statistics*, April, 1923, Preliminary vol. v, pp. 71–78.
The materials and methods used were as follows:

	Series used		Character of average
1903–15:	Bank clearings outside New York Imports of merchandise Gross earnings of leading railroads Production of pig iron Industrial employment		Simple arithmetic means of the percentage deviations from ordinates of secular trend corrected for seasonal variations, expressed in terms of standard deviations. The averages were multiplied by 8.62, the standard deviation of outside clearings.
		Weights	
1915–19:	Net ton-miles of freight carried by railroads	2	Weighted arithmetic means of percentage deviations from linear trends corrected for seasonal variations.
	Production of pig iron	1	
	Raw cotton consumed	1	
	Industrial employment	2	
		Weights	
1919–23:	Total railroad car loadings	6	Weighted arithmetic means of percentage deviations from linear trends corrected for seasonal variations.
	Production of pig iron	1	
	Production of steel ingots	1	
	Raw cotton consumed	1	
	Industrial employment	3	

[1] The series used are as follows:

Value of total exports of British produce, average of monthly items, 1855-1914.
Percentages of iron founders unemployed, inverted, 1855-1914.
Railway freight traffic receipts, 1881-1914.

(Continued on p. 302.)

CHART 13.

PERSONS' INDEX OF TRADE.
United States, by Months, 1903-26.

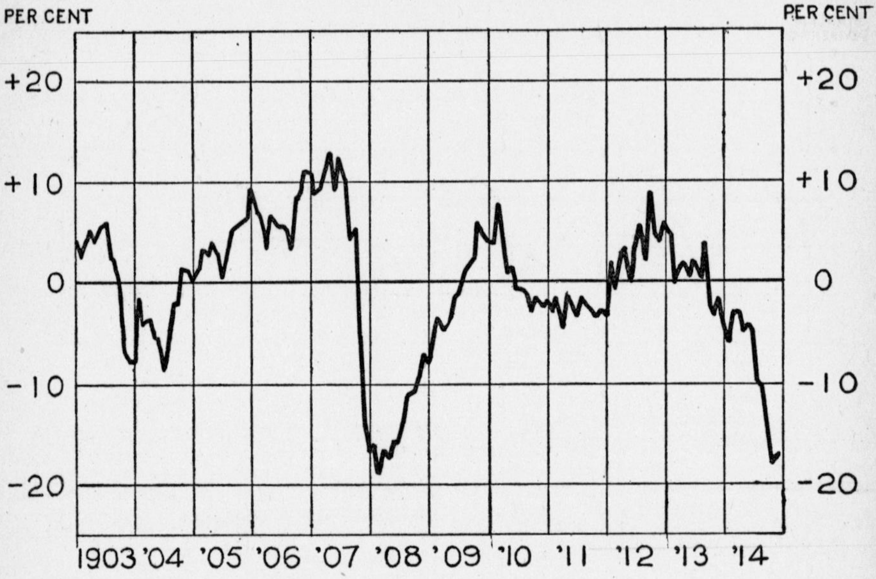

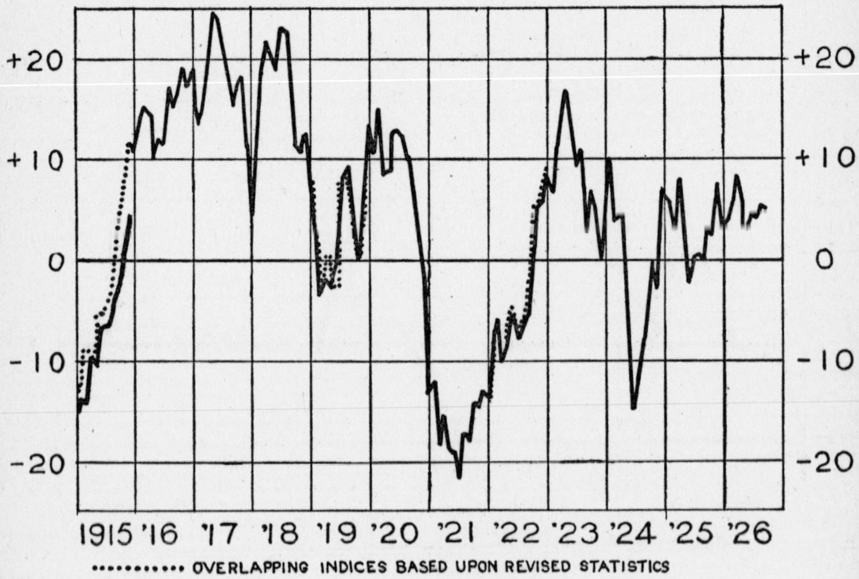

CHART 14.

MISS THOMAS' INDEX OF "BRITISH BUSINESS CYCLES."

By Quarters, 1855 to June, 1914.

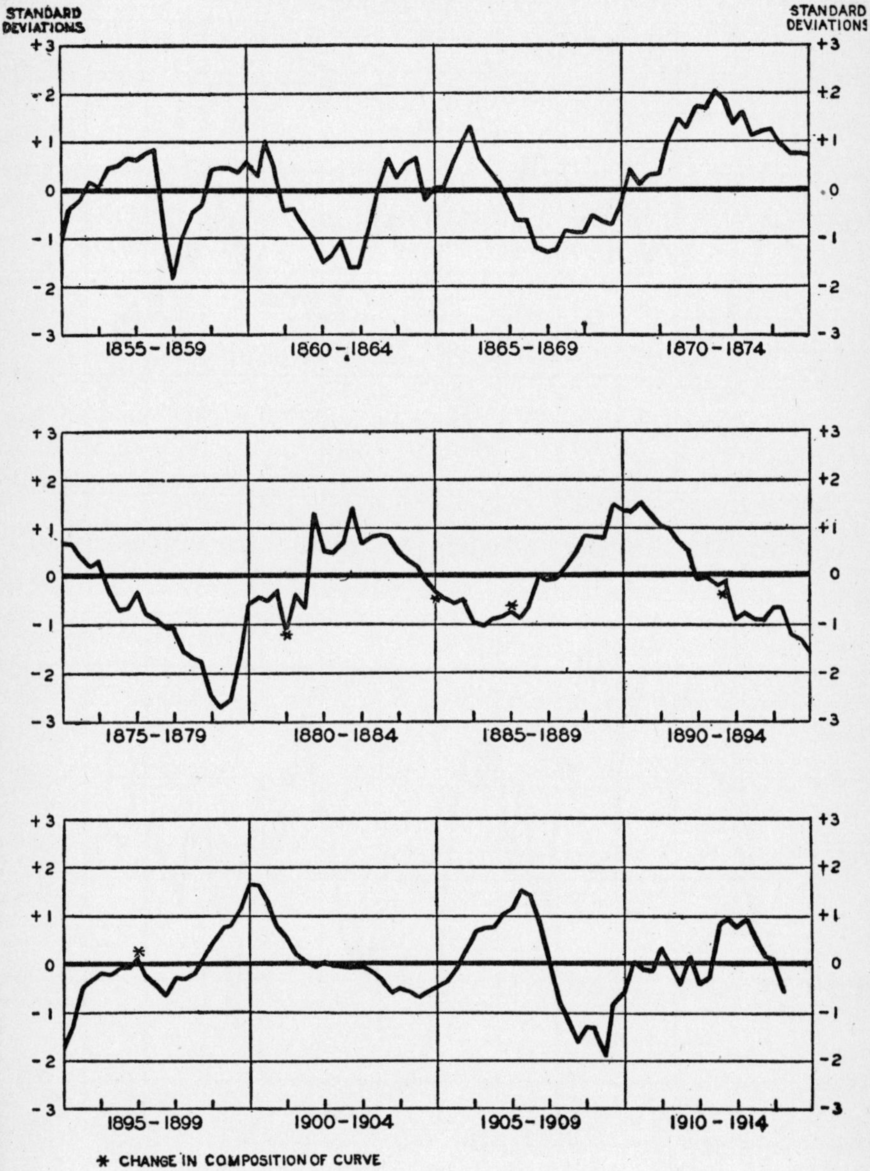

(7) Axe and Flinn's "Index of General Business Conditions for Germany, 1898-1914."

This is a three-curve index, covering the years 1898 to June, 1914, bi-monthly, corresponding in character to Persons' "Index of General Business Conditions in the United States" (number 2 above). It was made by Emerson Wirt Axe and Harold M. Flinn from nine series chosen to represent the fluctuations of "speculation," "business," and "money." The results are averages of percentage deviations from secular trends corrected for seasonal variations and expressed in units of standard deviations. In time sequence the speculation index precedes the business index, and the latter precedes the money-market index—relations corresponding to those found by Persons in America.[1] The three curves are shown in Chart 15.

(8) Annual Indexes of Business Cycles.

In addition to the monthly, bi-monthly, and quarterly indexes of business cycles made by averaging the cyclical-irregular fluctuations of more or less numerous series, several indexes have been made by similar methods from annual data. The most valuable of these series are:

Sauerbeck's wholesale price index, "all materials," 1885-1914.
Provincial bank clearings, Manchester and Birmingham, 1887-1914.
Percentage unemployed,—"all trades," 1887-1914.
Blast furnaces in blast, averages of monthly items, 1897-1914.

Dr. Thomas kindly put her quarterly index at the disposal of the National Bureau in advance of its publication. ("An Index of British Business Cycles," *Journal of the American Statistical Association,* March, 1926, vol. xxi, pp. 60-63). A chart of all the seven series which compose the index forms the frontispiece of her *Social Aspects of the Business Cycle*, London, 1925.

Another "Index of British Economic Conditions," covering the years 1902-14 by quarters, has been made by W. M. Persons, Norman J. Silberling, and W. A. Berridge. It is a three-curve construction, corresponding to number 2 above and to number 7 below. See *Review of Economic Statistics,* Preliminary vol. iv, Supplement, June, 1922, pp. 158-189.

[1] Emerson Wirt Axe and Harold M. Flinn, "An Index of General Business Conditions for Germany, 1898-1914," *Review of Economic Statistics,* October, 1925, vol. vii, pp. 263-287.

The series used in making the three curves of the index are:

Speculation:	Industrial stock prices.
Business:	10-commodity price index, averaged with a volume of business index, made from the following series:
	Pig-iron production.
	Domestic-bill tax receipts.
	Value of merchandise exports.
	Value of merchandise imports.
Money:	Berlin open-market discount rates.
	Discounts and advances of the Reichsbank.
	Bond prices.

CHART 15.

AXE AND FLINN'S "INDEX OF GENERAL BUSINESS CONDITIONS FOR GERMANY."

I.

The Adjusted Index of German Economic Conditions, A—Speculation, B—Business, and C—Money: Bi-Monthly, 1898-1914.

(Cycles).

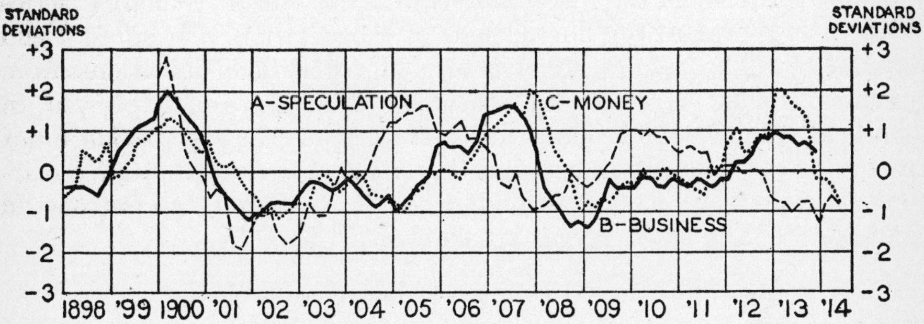

II.

Volume of Business Activity: Monthly, 1898-1914.

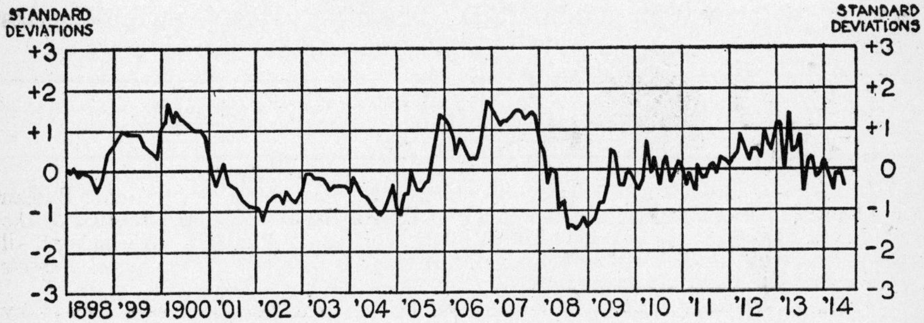

An index of business cycles in the United States, 1870-1920, compiled by William F. Ogburn and Dorothy S. Thomas. Based upon 9 series.

An index of business cycles in Great Britain, 1854-1913, compiled by Dorothy S. Thomas. Based upon 7 series.

"Industrial Composites" for Great Britain, Germany and Italy, 1870-1913, compiled by Harry Jerome. Based upon 5, 4 and 2 series respectively.[1]

[1] For detailed methods of construction and results see Ogburn and Thomas, "The Influence of the Business Cycle on Certain Social Conditions," *Journal of the American Statistical Association,* September, 1922, vol. xviii, pp. 324-340. Reprinted, without the tables, in the book next cited, pp. 53-77. Thomas, *Social Aspects of the Business Cycle,* London, 1925, pp. 12-19, and 166-188. Jerome, *Migration and Business Cycles,* National Bureau of Economic Research, New York, 1926, p. 175.

While annual indexes are well adapted to certain uses, and while they may be employed in business-cycle work when data for briefer intervals cannot be had, they frequently give misleading indications of the trend of developments. When business activity declines rapidly in one year from a high to a low point, and recuperates less rapidly in the next year, annual averages may betray an investigator into thinking of the first year as fairly prosperous and the second year as very dull. Thus cyclical fluctuations get not merely obscured but actually distorted in the annual indexes. And of course no satisfactory measurement of periods so short as business cycles can be made with a unit so large as 12 months. Hence the annual business indexes may be passed by without more ado.

(9) Snyder's "Clearings Index of Business," United States, 1875-1924.

There remain the "single-factor" indexes, that is, the indexes made by treating some time series showing the fluctuations of an economic process which is affected by so many types of business activity as to become itself more or less representative of the general trend. The statistical case for accepting such an index has been presented by Mr. Carl Snyder.

After making his comprehensive "Index of the Physical Volume of Trade" in 1919-23 (number 4 above), Snyder sought some method of getting comparable results for earlier years. He thought that the record of bank clearings outside of New York, which can be followed by months back to 1875, might serve as a basis, provided he could eliminate the influence of price fluctuations. Of course the volume of clearings is affected by changes in the prices of all the goods men pay for in checks—commodities at wholesale and retail, securities, real estate, labor, and so on. For the chief categories of prices, Mr. Snyder could find, or make, fairly good index numbers. The problem was how to weight the several indexes so that they would yield an index of "the general price level," which could be used to transform clearings into a record of changes in the physical volume of goods exchanged. His criterion was that the best scheme of weights would be the one which, when applied to "outside debits," would yield the curve agreeing most closely with his comprehensive index of trade in 1919-23. After much experimenting, he concluded that the best results were given by weighting his index of commodity prices at wholesale by 2, his "composite of wage payments" by 3.5,

his series showing "elements in the cost of living" by 3.5, his index of rents by 1, and by omitting security prices.[1]

Finding that "outside debits" divided by an "index of the general price level," made on this plan, gave a curve which agreed closely with the "index of the volume of trade" in 1919-23, Mr. Snyder felt justified in switching from "outside debits" to "outside clearings," and carrying his computations backward for 45 years. The construction of the index of the general price level by months for so long a period involved a bold use of scanty data. Even wholesale price indexes are not available on a monthly basis before 1900, and the records of living costs, wages, salaries, and rents are meager indeed. But Mr. Snyder drove through his computations with the best materials he could gather, interpolated freely, and published his index for every month from 1875 to 1924.[2]

With his price index in hand, Snyder compiled the record of outside clearings from *The Public* and the *Commercial and Financial Chronicle,* and divided the total for each month by the corresponding item in the price index. To the resulting series, which he interpreted as showing fluctuations in the physical volume of trade, he fitted a parabolic trend. The percentage deviations from the trend, corrected for seasonal variations, and smoothed by a three-months moving average, constitute the "Clearings Index of Business," which is presented in Chart 16.[3]

(10) Frickey's Index of Outside Clearings, United States, 1875-1914.

On the same chart is presented a second index of outside clearings made upon a different plan by Mr. Edwin Frickey. Believing that, in the period before 1903, the introduction of new clearing houses at irregular dates appreciably distorted the series, Frickey decided to base his index upon the clearings in seven cities for which substantially complete figures can be had monthly since 1875, and which in the test period 1903-14 give totals agreeing closely in their cyclical-irregular fluctuations with the aggregates for all clearing houses outside of New York. The cities selected are Baltimore, Chicago, Cincinnati, Cleveland, Philadelphia, Pittsburgh, and San Francisco.

[1] It may be noted that these weights differ widely from those which our data concerning the volume of wholesale and retail trade, and wage payments would suggest. See Chapter II, section v.

[2] Carl Snyder, "A New Index of the General Price Level from 1875," *Journal of the American Statistical Association,* June, 1924, vol. xix, pp. 189-195.

[3] Carl Snyder, "A New Clearings Index of Business for Fifty Years," *Journal of the American Statistical Association,* September, 1924, vol. xix, pp. 329-335.

CHART 16.

SNYDER'S "CLEARINGS INDEX OF BUSINESS" AND FRICKEY'S "INDEX OF OUTSIDE CLEARINGS."
United States, by Months, 1875-1926 and 1875-1914.

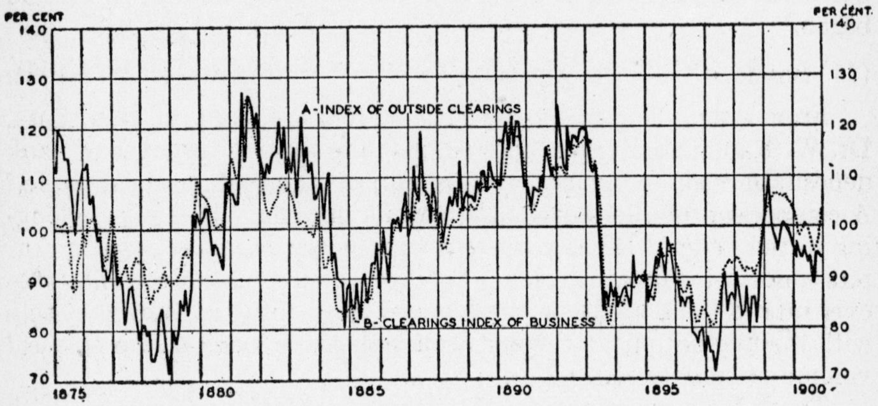

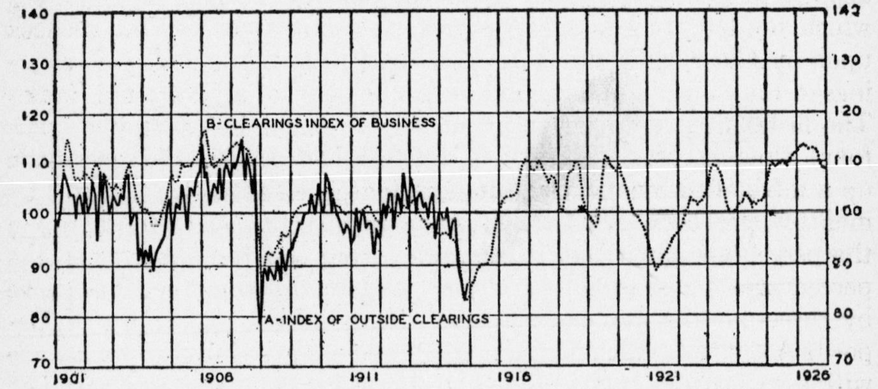

A—Frickey's "Index of Outside Clearings" (Aggregate Bank Clearings for 7 Selected Cities): Relatives to ordinates of trend, adjusted for seasonal variations.

B—Snyder's "Clearings Index of Business" (Bank Clearings Outside New York City, 1875-1918; Debits Outside New York City, 1919-1926): Three-months' moving averages of relatives to ordinates of trend, adjusted for seasonal variations and price changes.

*** Change in composition of index.**

Casting up their total clearings each month, Mr. Frickey fitted a line of secular trend, made corrections for seasonal variations, and found the percentage deviations from the moving base thus obtained. Unlike Mr. Snyder, he attempted no correction for changes in prices; but broke off his index in 1914, just before the great price revolution began.[1]

(11) Snyder's "Index of Deposits Activity," United States, 1875-1924.

From data collected by the Federal Reserve Bank of New York, Dr. W. Randolph Burgess showed that the rate of turnover of bank deposits in eight reporting cities is subject to a wide cyclical swing.[1] A comparison of the individual deposits in about 760 banks belonging to the Federal Reserve System with clearings in 141 leading centers confirmed this conclusion. Further, the fluctuations in the turnover rate of the deposits in these banks, duly adjusted, agreed closely with the fluctuations of Snyder's comprehensive index of the physical volume of trade in 1919-23.

These facts suggested to Mr. Snyder that the velocity of bank deposits constitutes another index of business conditions, an index which he determined to carry back by months to 1875 as a check upon his Clearings Index. As data Snyder used the total bank clearings of the country, and the individual deposits of all National Banks. The latter figures are given at slightly irregular intervals five (now four) times a year. Resorting to interpolation, Mr. Snyder made up a table of individual deposits by months, divided these figures by monthly clearings, used seven-year moving averages as a trend, found the percentage deviations of his ratios from this trend, corrected the percentages for seasonal variations, and finally smoothed his curve by three-months moving averages. Thus he got an "Index of Deposits Activity," which he thought showed a gratifying correspondence with his Clearings Index. The two curves are compared in Chart 17.[2]

2. A Critique of the Indexes of Business Conditions.

Before making use of the indexes assembled in the preceding section, we must examine them critically.

[1] Edwin Frickey, "Bank Clearings Outside New York City, 1875-1914," *Review of Economic Statistics,* October, 1925, vol. vii, pp. 252-262.

[1] See above, Chapter II, section iv, 4.

[2] Carl Snyder, "A New Index of Business Activity," *Journal of the American Statistical Association,* March, 1924, vol. xix, pp. 36-41, and "Deposits Activity as a Measure of Business Activity," *Review of Economic Statistics,* October, 1924, vol. vi, pp. 253-259.

CHART 17.

SNYDER'S "INDEX OF DEPOSITS ACTIVITY" COMPARED WITH HIS "CLEARINGS INDEX OF BUSINESS."

United States, by Months, 1875-1926.

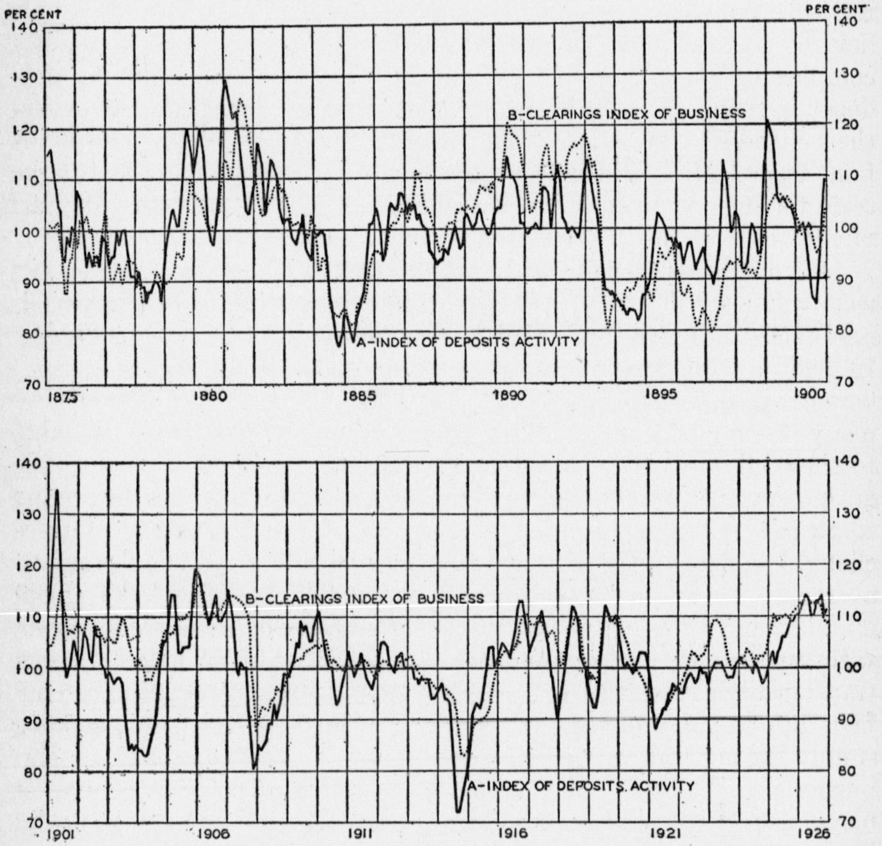

A—Index of Deposits Activity: three-months' moving averages adjusted for seasonal variations and moving average trend.

B—Clearings Index of Business (bank clearings outside New York City, 1875-1918; debits outside New York City, 1919-1926): three-months' moving averages of deviations from trend, adjusted for seasonal variations and price changes.

At the outset, it should be noted that none of the indexes give, or are meant to give, an adequate picture of business cycles. For, as has been said several times, business cycles are congeries of cyclical fluctuations in a large number of economic activities, fluctuations which differ widely in amplitude and considerably in timing. Such intricate phenomena cannot be presented adequately by any simple device. A real chart of one business cycle would be a hopelessly complex tangle of hundreds of curves. Doubtless the shading produced in such a chart by the concentration of lines in certain areas and their dispersion in others would give an interesting total effect. A faint impression of this effect may be gathered by plotting on a large scale for one cycle the 27 series, or groups of series, which Mr. Carl Snyder uses in the construction of his volume-of-trade index.

Anyone who dwells upon the intricacies of Chart 18, made in this way, will grant not only that the business indexes fail to picture business cycles, but also that faithful pictures would be of doubtful value. In dealing with price fluctuations we have learned to use index numbers which represent in a single time series the net resultants of very many dissimilar changes. These price indexes are far from adequate to show all we need to know about price fluctuations; but they are an indispensable tool even to those investigators who are beginning to go back of them in order to study the successive arrays of price changes which the index numbers condense into a single set of averages. Business fluctuations are far more complicated than price fluctuations; for they include the latter as just one strand interwoven with fluctuations in employment, incomes, consumption, production, transportation, commerce, and finance. Precisely because the full facts are so complicated, we need a device, or devices, for showing simply the general drift of all the changes. Such "indexes of general business conditions" may mislead us, of course, just as price indexes may mislead the unwary; but they may also prove a most useful instrument for gaining clear insights, if we remember their limitations. They will not enable us to dispense with more elaborate studies of the interrelationships among particular series, but they should supplement and summarize what we can learn by more intensive analysis.

Do the existing indexes meet our need? Do they show the general drift of business cycles accurately? How can they be improved?

It may seem that the neatest way to treat indexes of business conditions is to define the purpose they serve, to show what materials and methods are appropriate to that purpose, and to evaluate

CHART 18.

ONE BUSINESS CYCLE, UNITED STATES, 1919-21, SHOWN BY A PLOT OF 27 OF ITS COMPONENTS.

Twelve of the Components Used in Snyder's Volume-of-Trade Index to Represent *Productive Activity* and *Primary Distribution.*

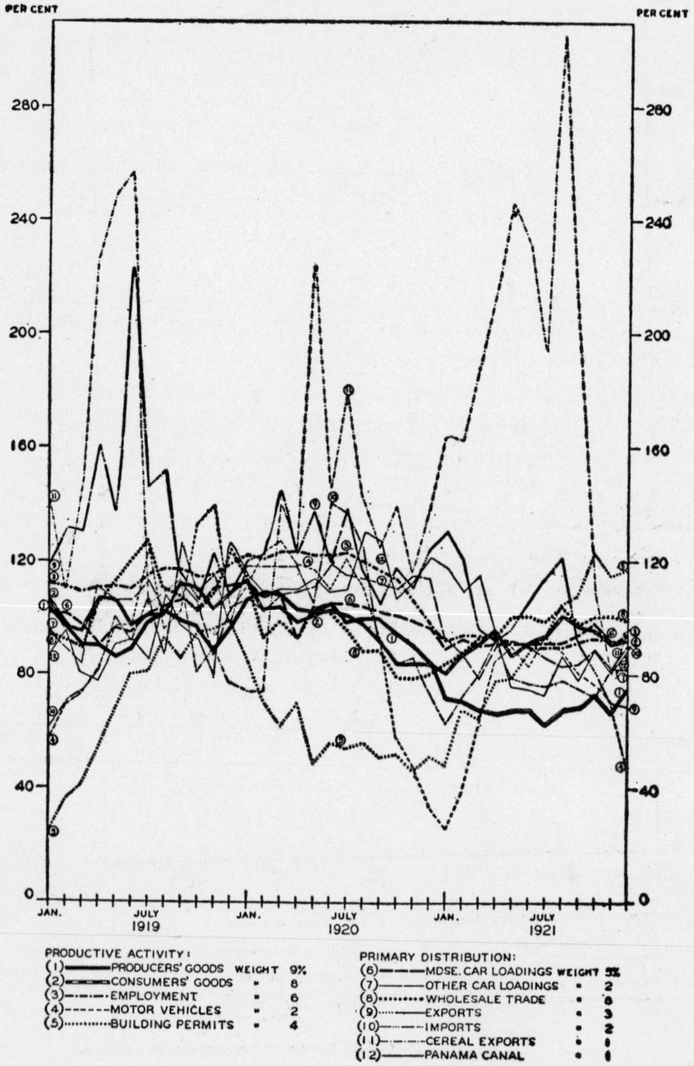

CHART 18 (*Continued*).

ONE BUSINESS CYCLE, UNITED STATES, 1919-1921, SHOWN BY A PLOT OF 27 OF ITS COMPONENTS.

Fifteen of the Components Used in Snyder's Volume-of-Trade Index to Represent *Distribution to Consumers, Finance,* and *General Business.*

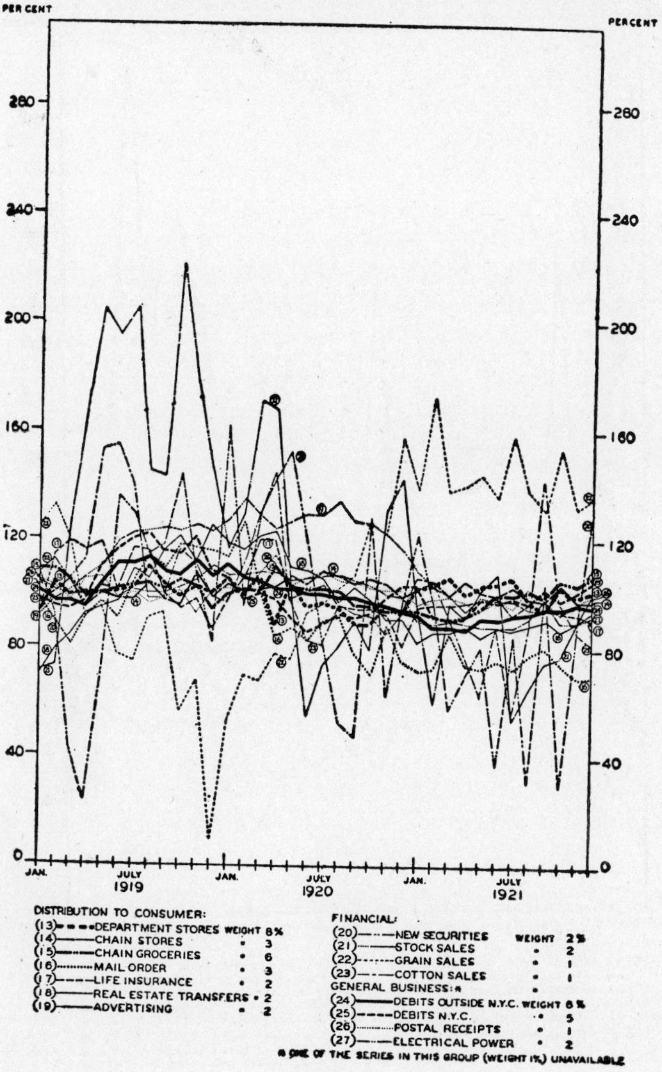

the existing indexes by the canons thus provided. But that procedure assumes some single purpose to be served by business-cycle indexes, a purpose so definite that it dictates an ideal set of materials and an ideal set of methods. This assumption is no more valid in our field than in the better-explored field of wholesale-price indexes. Certainly the purposes for which the statisticians whose indexes we have reviewed designed their series were not all the same, and certainly there is a use to which every one of their series can be put.

We can accomplish more by reversing the procedure. Instead of starting with some single purpose to be served and criticizing the existing indexes for their ill adaptation to this use, we shall start with the materials and methods employed in making the existing indexes, and consider what the results mean and to what uses they may be put. Constructive suggestions of practical value in future work are more likely to come out of a discussion which regards divergent purposes and limited data than out of a speculation spun from some definition.

Round the technique of making index numbers of prices an extensive literature has grown up. This literature warns us that we are entering a field where none but statistical experts feel comfortable. On the making of business indexes there has been but little critical discussion so far, unless we put under that head the preliminary processes of eliminating secular trends and seasonal variations. Our problem stands now much as the price-index problem stood in Jevons' youth. Having little to guide me, I cannot go far, and I may readily go wrong.

√ The chief conclusion to which analysis leads is that the various methods used in making indexes of business conditions produce, not rival measures of the same variable, but indexes of different variables. If we can become clear just what the variable is which each index relates to, we can tell for what uses the several indexes are adapted.

(1) Indexes of the Pecuniary Volume of Business.

Of the variables to which the indexes relate, the most comprehensive, and yet the simplest, is the pecuniary volume of business transactions. We conceive of it as the aggregate made up of all the values exchanged in a country month by month—not merely commodities in the usual sense, but also real estate, securities, funds

loaned and repaid, interest, rents, services of all sorts from manual labor to professional advice, transportation, storage, publicity—to repeat, every good exchanged for a price, counted at every exchange.

The only *measure* of this variable is its own aggregate value. In the United States we now have data which enable us to fix the order of magnitude attained by the dollar volume of payments, and even to venture rough estimates of how many billions it comes to. Such estimates, indeed, have already been given on an annual basis in Chapter II.[1]

To these rough estimates we might add a monthly *index* of changes in the dollar volume of payments, built up from series showing bank debits, retail sales, payroll disbursements, amusement receipts, and the like. We could argue that such series, when properly selected and combined with an eye to their relative importance and to overlaps, give partial totals whose monthly variations probably represent approximately the variations in the aggregate volume.

If we felt sufficient confidence in the figures to elaborate still further, we might tie the monthly index to the annual estimates of the aggregate volume of payments, and say that we were approximating the monthly aggregates. Finally, we might eliminate the secular trend and seasonal variations of our series, if we had data for a sufficient period, and present the results in billions of dollars or in percentages, as showing the cyclical-irregular fluctuations of the pecuniary volume of transactions.

Only one of the business indexes reviewed above relates directly to this variable—Mr. Frickey's series for bank clearings in seven American cities from 1875 to 1914. In technical parlance, however, Frickey's results are not index numbers, but a series of relatives computed on a moving base (each month the ordinate of secular trend, adjusted for seasonal variation, equals 100). Mr. Frickey calls them "a continuous monthly index of business activity as indicated by the fluctuations of bank clearings." [2] The only form of business activity which bank clearings show directly, is the amount of payments made.

Doubtless, this partial record of payments is the best single indicator of the pecuniary volume of trade for the years before bank debits were compiled. But we are not sure whether bank clearings,

[1] See Table 9 above, Chapter II, section v, 4, "The Flow of Payments Among Business Enterprises."

[2] Edwin Frickey, "Bank Clearings Outside New York City, 1875-1914," *Review of Economic Statistics,* October, 1925, vol. vii, p. 252.

even with New York City omitted, give a just impression of the amplitude of the cyclical-irregular fluctuations in the aggregate of payments. For the fluctuations of clearings probably have a larger amplitude than the fluctuations of payments in coin and paper money. And it must be recalled that the volume of payments made does not parallel closely the dollar volume of goods exchanged day by day. Many of the checks cleared are "cash" payments for goods just bought; a few are advance payments for goods to be received in the future, but the majority are payments for goods received some time in the past.[3] Much business is done three times over so to speak, advance orders are placed, or contracts for future performances are made; somewhat later the goods ordered are shipped or the contract work is performed; later still the payments are made. When borrowed funds are used, the scheme is still more complicated, and the pecuniary volume of exchanging growing out of a given operation is enhanced by the making and repaying of loans. We have little information about the volume of the several types of operations, or about the average lags of deliveries behind orders, and of payments behind deliveries. An ideally complete index of pecuniary transactions would have at least three curves, one showing commitments entered into each month, one showing current transfers of goods in dollar values, and one showing payments. The third curve is the only one we can draw with any confidence. But it is important to remember that the two curves we cannot draw represent actual processes of great moment, which certainly differ in timing, and probably differ in amplitude of fluctuation from the process typified by bank clearings.

The reason why few investigators have dealt with the pecuniary volume of trade must be that they have believed other aspects of business activity to be more significant. Almost all of the business indexes have been compiled since the price revolution of the war produced violent oscillations in the pecuniary volume of trade. Even Mr. Frickey, it will be noticed, did not think it worth while to continue his series beyond 1914. While economists have been deeply interested in measuring price changes, they have sought to measure the reaction of prices, not on the amount of exchanging done in dollars, but on the physical volume of goods exchanged.

[3] Compare Chapter II, section iv, 5, above; "The Quantity Theory and Business Cycles."

dexes of the Physical Volume of Trade or of Production.

e pecuniary volume of trade, the physical volume of trade is a definite quantity. It consists of all the goods exchanged in a country, during specified intervals, reckoned in physical units—hours of labor, cubic feet of buildings occupied under leases, numbers of securities transferred, ton miles of freight carried one mile, lines of advertising printed, and so on. Conceivably one might make an inventory of the goods exchanged each month, expressed in such units. But to make from the inventories totals which could be compared month by month, it is necessary to assign each good a money price. If the prices are kept fixed month after month, the aggregates, though expressed in billions of dollars, will show changes in the physical volume of trade weighted by dollar values.

While we lack data to approximate even roughly the physical inventories of goods exchanged annually in the United States, we might build up from series now published an aggregative index of the physical volume of trade which would possess much interest. Such an index would correspond in character to the U. S. Bureau of Labor Statistics index number of wholesale prices. That price index shows changing prices weighted by fixed physical quantities; the volume-of-trade index would show changing physical quantities weighted by fixed prices. With this series in hand, we might eliminate the secular trend and seasonal variations (if any), and thus get an index of the cyclical-irregular fluctuations in the physical volume of trade, expressed in dollars, or converted into ratios of the adjusted trend values.

The current indexes of the cyclical-irregular fluctuations in the physical volume of trade are not made on this simple plan. Instead of starting with an index of the volume of trade and ascertaining its trend, the compilers ascertain the trend of each time series separately, turn the original data into relatives of their trends, weight these relatives, and compute their arithmetic means. Snyder's index of the volume of trade in 1919-25, and the two later segments of Persons' index of the volume of trade (the segments for 1915-19, and 1919-23) are made in this way. Thus they are not quite what their names suggest, indexes of the volume of trade, but weighted arithmetic means of the percentage deviations of certain time series from their adjusted trends. Their analogues among price indexes would be a new type:—weighted arithmetic means of relative prices, com-

puted on the base: ordinates of secular trends, corrected for seasonal variations, equal 100.

It is now generally recognized that weighted arithmetic means of relatives are less desirable price indexes for most uses than relatives made from aggregates of actual prices weighted by physical quantities.[1] If we wish to make an index of changes in the physical volume of trade, we can apply this conclusion with confidence, and say that the aggregative form of index is more serviceable, on the whole, than the weighted mean of relative quantities. But does it follow that an index of the cyclical-irregular fluctuations in the volume of trade is better made by the aggregative method than by weighting and averaging the relatives of the constituent series?

It is clear from their formulas that the two methods do not yield identical results.[2] In seeking to choose between them we get

[1] Of course, the averages of relatives have their advantages; but I think the conclusion stated in the text is valid.

On the relative merits of different forms of price indexes, see Irving Fisher, *The Making of Index Numbers,* Boston and New York, 1922, and Truman L. Kelley, *Statistical Method,* New York, 1924, chapter xiii. A summary of the chief findings is given by Frederick C. Mills, *Statistical Methods,* New York, 1924, pp. 207-221.

[2] The formula for an index of deviations from a secular trend made by the aggregative method, may be written:

$$\frac{\Sigma q_1 \, p_w}{T_1} \qquad (1)$$

Here q_1 represents the quantities of the goods exchanged in time "1"; p_w represents the fixed prices used as weights, and T_1 represents the adjusted ordinate of the secular trend of $\Sigma q \, p_w$ in time 1. We may regard this trend as itself the aggregate of the trends of the constituent series, each weighted by its appropriate price, provided that the trends fitted to all the constituent series and to the aggregate are straight lines, or (perhaps) if some single type of curve other than a straight line is fitted throughout. Then the formula becomes:

$$\frac{\Sigma q_1 \, p_w}{\Sigma t_1 \, p_w} \qquad (2)$$

The formula for a similar index made by averaging relatives weighted by fixed values (v_w) is:

$$\frac{\Sigma\left(\frac{q_1}{t_1}\right) v_w}{\Sigma v_w} \qquad (3)$$

But the values used as weights are products of quantities and prices. Therefore we may replace v_w by $q_w p_w$ and write:

$$\frac{\Sigma\left(\frac{q_1}{t_1}\right) q_w p_w}{\Sigma q_w p_w} \qquad (4)$$

If $q_w = t_1$, formula (4) reduces to formula (1). That is, the two methods yield identical results only when the quantities used in the value-weights applied to the rela-

little help from the discussions of price indexes, for they deal with the problem of comparing the relative values of the same variables in different periods, and our problem is to compare two values of the same variable at the same periods—the values shown by averaging deviations from the adjusted trends of the individual series and the values shown by computing deviations from the adjusted trend of the group aggregate.[3] But by falling back upon broader considerations we can justify a choice. Ease of computation, and, what is more important, ease of comprehension, speak for the aggregative method. That method requires the computation of but one trend and one set of seasonal variations, while the method of averaging relatives requires the computation of as many trends and sets of seasonals as there are component series. An aggregative index of physical volume of trade is relatively easy to conceive; so are its trend, its seasonal variations, and the deviations from its trend adjusted for seasonals. When one tries to think what reality is represented by a weighted average of many sets of deviations made in this way, the conception grows more complicated. Finally, we have need of an index of the physical volume of trade, as well as need of an index of its cyclical-irregular fluctuations. The method of aggregates gives us the first index as well as the second. The average of relatives gives us the second index, but not the first, though in compensation it offers the cyclical-irregular fluctuations of all the component series, for which we can find use. An ideal procedure would be to deal with our quantity series as the federal Bureau of Labor Statistics deals with price series—make the general index from weighted aggregates, but also publish relatives for each series separately, and, of course, add indexes

tives equal the adjusted ordinate of secular trend at the time for which the computation is made. This coincidence may well happen once in a period for which two indexes are made from identical materials by the two methods; but it is most unlikely to happen twice.

When the trend-lines used do not make the ordinates of the trend of the aggregate equal to the sum of the ordinates of the trends of the constituent series, there is no assurance that the two methods will give identical results. This is the commoner case in statistical practice. But the differences between the two sets of results may be small.

[3] For example, in our problem the time bias of arithmetic means of relative prices and of various systems of weighting does not enter. Nor is the "circular test" applicable in the usual way, if at all. The "factor reversal" test can be used, but it is inconclusive, because neither method can pass it. Kelley's test of reliability is pertinent: one might divide a body of data into two samples, compute indexes for both samples by both methods, and see which pair of indexes showed the higher coefficient of correlation. But the test would be laborious, and trial with one set of data might not prove conclusive.

Mathematical statisticians have in this problem a promising field for work.

of the cyclical-irregular deviations from adjusted trends both for the aggregates and for all the components.[4]

The practice of expressing cyclical-irregular fluctuations in terms of their standard deviations is not proper in making volume-of-trade indexes. For differences in the amplitude of these variations are present in the inventories to which such indexes relate. To cover up the differences by reducing the fluctuations of all the series used to a common scale, is to make measurement of changes in the aggregate volume impossible. A series constructed in this way may have some interest as indicating the time at which cyclical-irregular fluctuations have occurred, and as indicating the relative amplitude of successive cycles as pictured by the series in question, so long as it is made of uniform materials; but it is of little value for comparing the amplitude of fluctuations in the physical volume of trade with that of fluctuations in production, employment, prices, or any other variable.

To get reliable indexes of the physical volume of trade and of its cyclical-irregular fluctuations we need representative samples drawn from all parts of the field. Even for recent years in the United States, the materials are not ample. The trading done by farmers is most inadequately covered. There is reason to suspect that the best

[4] The only practical test of the agreement between the two methods of which I know is the following:

In making his "index of physical production for all manufacture" in the United States by years since 1899, Dean Edmund E. Day started with 33 time series showing the output of various types of goods. These series he arranged in 10 industrial groups.

(1) For each group he made an "unadjusted index" by reducing the annual items of the component series to relatives on the base, production in 1909 equals 100, weighting these relatives, computing geometric means, and making certain corrections on the basis of Census data which do not now concern us. Next he weighted the 10 group indexes, and used their geometric means as an "unadjusted index of physical production for manufacture."

(2) To measure the cyclical fluctuations of manufacturing, Day returned to his 33 original series, fitted a trend line to each, expressed the actual figures as percentages of the corresponding trend values, weighted these relatives, computed averages (this time arithmetic) for each of the 10 industries, then weighted these group averages, and finally took their arithmetic means as his "adjusted index."

Day found two objections to the latter procedure. The determination of the lines of secular trend for the 33 original series involved difficult choices of period and line. The computations were laborious. For both reasons he sought a simpler method.

(3) This method was to fit a trend line directly to the "unadjusted index," and turn its annual values into percentages of the corresponding ordinates of this trend. The differences between the results of methods (2) and (3) in the 21 years 1899-1919 did not exceed three points in the percentage scale in any year. Dean Day concluded that the "case for the simpler method of getting the adjusted index is conclusive." I should be inclined to argue that the simpler method is preferable on logical grounds, as well as on practical grounds.

See Edmund E. Day, "An Index of the Physical Volume of Production," *Review of Economic Statistics*, November and December, 1920, Preliminary vol. ii, pp. 310, 311, 332-337, 362-365.

totals we can now make show variations somewhat in excess of the truth; for the types of trading not represented at all, particularly the retail sales of the great mass of small, independent shops, are probably rather steady. By long odds the most comprehensive index we have is Snyder's series for 1919-25.

When compilers go back to pre-war years, they are forced to resort to one of two undesirable shifts. Either they must change the composition of their indexes from time to time, accepting less satisfactory and smaller samples as they work backward, or they must use materials which do not show the physical volume of trade. Mr. Snyder chose the latter alternative in making his "clearings index of business." Instead of treating bank clearings outside of New York City as a sample of fluctuations in the pecuniary volume of transactions, Snyder sought to transmute these dollars figures into a physical-volume index. Of course, it is always questionable how accurately division of such data by a price index really shows the corresponding changes in physical quantities. Mr. Snyder was able to test his procedure more adequately than is often possible in such cases, by making sure that his price index when applied to outside bank debits in 1919-23 gave results which fitted closely his physical-volume index. Yet a doubt remains whether a "deflating series" adjusted to bank debits in the period of violent price fluctuations just after the war is well adapted to deflating bank clearings for distant years, when prices were relatively stable. And at best, clearings is only one sample of volume of trade—though the best single sample.[5]

What has been said about methods of making indexes of the physical volume of trade and its cyclical-irregular fluctuations applies also to indexes of physical production. Production is not limited to the output of tangible commodities; it includes such services as fabrication, transportation, storage, and distribution, which suggests that production indexes should be made on a "value-added" basis. For example, if we have data showing retail sales of shoes in pairs and dollars, wholesale sales, and manufacture in the same double form, leather used by shoemakers in physical units and value, and hides and skins tanned into shoe leather, we can include the output of all these agencies in an index of physical production. Starting with the

[5] These doubts about the reliability of long-period indexes made from changing materials or by deflating clearings are shared by the compilers. It is necessary to note them, but it is also just to add that the criticisms apply to the data, and not to the men who have sought to learn all they can from what records the past provides.

pairs of shoes sold at retail, we can weight the service of the shopkeepers by the average value which they add to the wholesale price, and work back in this way to the fresh hides. Of course, to make the result show changes in physical production, we must keep constant the "values added" which we use as weights. Constructed in this way from exhaustive data, production indexes would cover most of the transactions included in the volume-of-trade indexes; but the weights of the two indexes would differ widely. For example, in a trade index the retail sales of shoes in pairs would be multiplied by the full retail price, instead of by the retailers' margin. Both indexes would run in billions of dollars, but the trade index would show many more billions. There would also be differences in timing. In a trade index the aim is to record exchanges when they are made; in a production index the aim is to record productive services when they are rendered. Manufacturers make goods before they exchange them, and merchants render their productive service to the community from the time they buy goods to the time they deliver packages to the ultimate consumer. These time relations are of great moment in the theory of business cycles.

As we should like three indexes of the pecuniary volume of trade showing commitments entered into, goods transferred, and payments made, so we should like three indexes of production in physical terms, —one showing goods ordered, one showing productive services rendered, and one showing goods delivered. To complete our modest requirements, add that these three indexes should be made to show separately for each industry the operations of retail dealers, wholesale merchants, manufacturers of consumers' and producers' goods, producers of raw materials, and builders of industrial equipment. In all this work adequate samples should be used, the aggregative method followed, and the cyclical-irregular fluctuations taken in their original amplitudes, not in units of their standard deviations.

(3) Indexes of "General Business Conditions."

Most of the indexes under review relate neither to the pecuniary nor to the physical volume of trade, but to the "general condition of business." This concept is much less definite than the others. It corresponds to no sum in dollars, to no inventory of goods, to nothing we can count. By nature it is not an aggregate amount, but a synthesis of relatives. We can say that retail sales in dollars are larger now than they were last month or last year, that the percentage of

unemployment is less, that more tons of steel are being produced, railway traffic is heavier, prices are higher, "money is tighter," and so on. Or we can compare each of these variables with the standard we have made from its secular trends and seasonal variations. But when we combine these series we are not measuring any quantity, or the variations in any quantity. We are merely summarizing our observations upon the values of certain variables from time to time in terms of other values of the same variables. And these variables in their original form are largely incommensurable, or rather are divided among incommensurable groups, prices, physical quantities of many sorts, values, ratios.

Of course, there is no technical difficulty in combining or averaging time series of any sort when they are expressed as relatives, percentage deviations from trends, or multiples of standard deviations. Combinations of incommensurable series are frequently made in the business indexes. The American Telephone and Telegraph Company's index for a time included Bradstreet's price series, the production of pig iron in tons, and bank clearings outside of New York, though it is now made of more homogeneous materials. Persons also used these three series, among others, in making one of the curves in his "Index of General Business Conditions." In her British index, Miss Thomas went even further; she combined unemployment percentages with series expressed in price relatives, physical units, and pounds sterling.

In defense of this practice, it can be urged that the phenomena of business cycles include changes in prices, physical quantities, pecuniary volumes, and ratios—for example, the ratio of bank reserves to demand liabilities. Not only do these four types of variables coexist; they also act and react upon one another. When the statistician combines measurements of the changes in these variables, he is merely trying to represent in one series of figures the net resultants of changes which are genuine and which do interact. Anyone who can conceive of business cycles as congeries of fluctuations in many processes should be able to grasp what is meant by an index made from sample fluctuations. It is true that indexes confined to one type of changes, such as prices, pecuniary volume of trade, or physical production, have a more definite meaning. But what they gain in definiteness they lose in breadth. No business index deserves the term "general" unless it includes samples of the various types of business activities.

By considering the method of weighting the series used in a "general business" index, we can put this elusive problem in the clearest light. Conceivably, a logical basis for weighting even the series which belong to incommensurable groups might be found in the relation which every business series bears to the pecuniary volume of trade.[1] But do we wish such a scheme of weights? Certainly we do not make an index of general business conditions as an indirect way of showing fluctuations in the pecuniary volume of business transactions. As said above, the condition of business is not itself an aggregate of goods or of values, and the components we use in making an index do not derive their importance from the influence they exercise upon anything which can be counted. But to what other criterion can we appeal to make sure that every series we use shall have due chance to influence the results?

In practice, statisticians have not lingered long upon this question. They usually proceed promptly to turn the original data into percentage deviations from their adjusted secular trends, to express each set of deviations in units of its standard deviation, and to take arithmetic means of the series in this form. Sometimes they apply rough weights, but more often not.[2] Reduction of the several sets of deviations to multiples of their own standard deviations is itself a scheme of weighting which gives each series a chance to influence the results in proportion to its variability in terms of its standard deviation; applying different weights to these multiples gives each series an in-

[1] Many series are fractions of that aggregate—bank debits, railway receipts, payroll disbursements, import and export values, and the like. Price data become fractions of the aggregate when multiplied by physical volume of trade; physical-volume and production data become similar fractions when multiplied by prices. A place can be made even for the ratios:—unemployment percentages, for instance, can be related to payroll disbursements, and bank-reserve ratios to the volume of financial transactions. The elaboration of a scheme of weights upon this basis would require much ingenuity, and many conjectural estimates. Not only are there gaps in the data, but there is also much overlapping to be allowed for, particularly between bank debits and other factors. Yet the task is not an impossible one.

[2] For example, for some time the American Telephone and Telegraph Company's "General Business Curve" was made from the following series and weights:

	Weights
Outside clearings	25
Pig-iron production	20
Railroad traffic	15
Failures (number)	10
Copper production	5
Cotton consumption	10
Coal production	5
Commodity prices	10
	100

fluence upon the results proportioned to the investigator's rating of its relative importance. That is, the original differences among the series as components of averages are wiped out, and new differences are written in. No single criterion of the importance of the several series is set up; but statisticians easily agree upon the more important and less important business indicators in any list of series, and agree also that the rankings within these groups must be rather arbitrary. In some lists they judge that even weighting is quite as good as differential weighting.

Of course such general agreement upon schemes of weights for practical use is not a satisfactory solution of the problem how to make an index of general business conditions; but it is the nearest approach to a solution which has been worked out. The need of further methodological research at this point is pressing.

Indexes made in the way described are clearly more representative of general business conditions when they are based upon large and varied lists of series than when the lists are small or one-sided. The rule is sometimes laid down that only series in which the cyclical-irregular fluctuations are synchronous should be included. This rule is proper if the compiler wishes merely to exhibit the cyclical element in business changes; it is not proper if he wishes an index of general business conditions. For we have seen how considerably and how systematically the cyclical-irregular fluctuations of certain processes lag behind those of other processes. To exclude any series from the index merely because it differs in timing from others, and therefore blurs the cycles, is to distort the general business index in the interests of symmetry. The only way to observe the rule and remain faithful to fact is to give up the plan of making a single index, and follow Persons in making a three-, possibly a four-, or a five-curve index, including as many trustworthy series as possible, but throwing them into groups on the basis of synchronous fluctuations. It is not consonant with the aim of representing general business conditions to exclude even series which show no cyclical characteristics.

Granted that general-business indexes combining the changes in many economic activities are not irrational, the question remains, What are they good for? One use at least can be claimed for them. So long as such a series is made from uniform materials by uniform methods, it enables one to compare successive cycles with respect to duration, amplitude and the character of their several phases. The

wider the range of materials included and the longer the period covered, the more significant these comparisons become. For intensive theoretical work they are of slight value. As said before, they do not measure any magnitude. And their value for the extensive work to which they are adapted is compromised by the small number and changing character of the data available for the long periods which they should cover.[3]

(4) Forecasting Sequences.

While the three-curve charts which Professor Persons and his co-workers have made for the United States, Great Britain and Germany are called "Indexes of General Business Conditions," they are made primarily as forecasting sequences. That is, the series used in each curve were chosen for the regularity with which their cyclical-irregular fluctuations are synchronized, and for the regularity with which their cyclical-irregular fluctuations precede or follow those of the series used in the other curves. Such constructions are to be judged on principles somewhat different from those laid down concerning general business indexes proper.

[3] Dr. Frederick C. Mills points out that when standard deviations are used as units in which to measure cyclical deviations from trend lines, they cannot be interpreted in the usual fashion. The standard deviation of a "normal distribution" has a precise meaning; we know what percentage of the total number of cases in such a distribution will deviate from the mean by more (or less) than any given multiple of the standard deviation; we know also what the odds are that a given deviation from the mean will be exceeded by a random observation. These precise rules of the normal distribution apply approximately to a wider variety of actual distributions. But they are frequently violated by the distribution of deviations of time series from their secular trends.

(1) A deviation equal to 6 standard deviations below the mean would occur in a normal frequency distribution once in 1,000,000,000 times. Deviations of that order occur not infrequently among deviations from a secular trend, in consequence of such disturbances as strikes, railway embargoes, wars, panics.

(2) Such extraordinary deviations are particularly common among deviations measured from projected trends. For example, in the publications of the Harvard Committee on Economic Research we find the Bureau of Labor Statistics index number of prices at wholesale represented by a positive deviation of 15.5 times the standard deviation in February, 1920, and Bradstreet's price index represented by a negative deviation of 10.6 times the standard deviation in July, 1921. Deviations reaching or exceeding 4.5 times the standard deviation are somewhat common in this valuable source. In a normal distribution, a deviation of this size occurs three times in a million.

(3) Since these extreme deviations are commoner in some series than in others, we do not quite get away from the danger of distorting our averages by using the standard deviations of the series as units.

In short, Professor Warren M. Persons' argument concerning the non-applicability of the concept of the probable error to time series seems to apply to the use of the standard deviation for measuring departures from a projected trend, if not to its use in measuring departures from a fitted trend. (For the argument see above section iv, 1, "The Correlation of Time Series and Its Pitfalls," note 2.)

A forecasting sequence cannot be expected to utilize all the materials which are available for making a general business index, and which should be included in the latter to render it "general." Comparatively few of the series lead or lag behind others with sufficient regularity to give reliable forecasts. But it may be argued that slenderness of materials is no defect in a forecasting sequence; it is better to limit the series rigidly to those showing the closest approach to perfect regularity of sequence than to gain comprehensiveness at the cost of uncertainty. If it does not matter what is to be forecasted, this view is valid. Strictly speaking, all that can be inferred from a three-curve chart is the movements of the particular series represented by the curves which lag. Both for practical and for theoretical purposes the whole operation is highly important or a curiosity, according as the curves whose movements are forecasted represent activities of large or of slight significance.

As for technical methods, the only criterion applicable to the making of forecasting sequences is supplied by the results. The original data can be made into aggregates, treated as relatives to some base period, computed as deviations from adjusted trends, expressed in units of their standard deviations, or thrown into any other form which brings out most clearly the regularity of the time sequences. The methods developed by Professor Persons serve well, and have been accepted as models by many other investigators.

The chief difficulty in applying these methods lies in securing indexes which maintain fairly regular relationships in the timing of their movements. For the period 1903 to 1914, Professor Persons finds:

> first, that the cyclical fluctuations of curve B, business, lagged eight months, on the average, after those of curve A, speculation; second, that the cyclical fluctuations of curve C, money rates, lagged four months, on the average, after those of curve B, business, and third, that the cyclical fluctuations of curve C, money rates, lagged twelve months, on the average, after those of curve A, speculation.

To complete the full round of events, it is necessary to ascertain the average period by which the movements of curve A, speculation, in one cycle, lag behind the movements of curve C, money rates, in the preceding cycle. Supplemental computations made for the purpose show

that the interval of lag of speculation after money rates was extremely variable and averaged 6-12 months. . . .[1]

All these averages are ascertained by finding the period of lag which yields the highest coefficient of correlation between the indexes paired. The maximum coefficients are not exceedingly high. They run for curves B and A +.81; for curves C and B +.83; for curves C and A +.74; for curves A and C —.67. Moreover, every pairing shows one or two other lags with coefficients nearly equal to the maximum.[2] Of course, this means that the time relationships among the three indexes of the Harvard sequence are not sufficiently regular to afford an assured mechanical forecast of the successive movements which occur within a cycle and which form the transition from one cycle to the next. What is claimed for the sequence is that,

> Although the *lag*—the time by which the movements of one curve lag behind those of another—is not invariable in length, it is much more nearly uniform than is the length of the cycle itself. Furthermore, variations in the duration of lag can in a measure be foreseen by a careful examination of the relations subsisting between the curves at the time of forecast.[3]

3. What the Indexes of Business Conditions Show About Business Cycles.

A classification of certain business indexes according to the economic processes to which they relate will summarize the preceding

[1] See Warren M. Persons and Edwin Frickey, "Money Rates and Security Prices," *Review of Economic Statistics*, January, 1926, vol. viii, pp. 30 and 32.

[2] The full array of coefficients given by Professor Persons in the article quoted (pp 30 and 32) is as follows:

Coefficients of Correlation between Curves A, B, and C, of the Index of General Business Conditions. Bi-monthly, 1903–June, 1914

Curves Correlated	Lag in Months 0	2	4	6	8	10	12	14	16
B follows A........	..	..	.72	.80	.81	.76	..	..	..
C " B........	..	.75	.83	.81	.70	..	..	..	..
C " A........	..	..	..	..	..	.69	.74	.71	.62
A " C........	−.29	−.44	−.58	−.63	−.67	−.65	−.62	..	..

Somewhat different results concerning the lags between curves A and B, A and C, and B and C of the "revised index," are given by Professor W. L. Crum, in "The Pre-War Indexes of General Business Conditions," *Review of Economic Statistics*, January, 1924, vol. vi, p. 19. But since Professor Persons uses the results obtained from the old index in the latest issue I have seen, I follow his example. See W. M. Persons, "An Index of General Business Conditions, 1875–1913," *Review of Economic Statistics*, January, 1927, vol. ix, p. 26.

[3] W. L. Crum, "The Interpretation of the Index of General Business Conditions," *Review of Economic Statistics*, Supplement, September, 1925, vol. vii, p. 223.

critique in part, and prepare for the following constructive comparisons. The indexes selected all refer to the same country, cover relatively long periods by months, and present their results in readily comparable form.

Index Relating to the Pecuniary Volume of Transactions.

Edwin Frickey's "Index of Outside Clearings," United States, 1875-1914.

Relatives (not strictly an index) of bank clearings in seven cities (used as a sample of all clearings outside of New York), computed on the base, monthly ordinate of secular trend, adjusted for seasonal variation, equals 100.

The transactions which give rise to the drawing of checks cover many types of economic relations, but small transactions in general and rural transactions in particular are under-represented. The exclusion of New York City reduces the representation of financial and of speculative transactions. In time, the clearings of a particular day cover transactions ranging from the re-payment of debts incurred years before to the advance of funds to be returned years later. On the average, clearings probably lag some weeks behind the exchange of goods to which they relate.

Indexes Relating to the Physical Volume of Trade.

Carl Snyder's "Clearings Index of Business," United States, 1875-1924.

Relatives (not strictly an index) of all outside clearings, "deflated" by an index of the "general price level," computed on the base, monthly ordinate of secular trend equals 100, corrected for seasonal variations, and smoothed by a three-months moving average.

What is said above concerning the activities represented by outside clearings applies here. It is, of course, questionable how far an aggregate in dollars can be made to show fluctuations in physical volume through division by a price index.

Warren M. Persons' "Index of Trade," United States, 1903-23.

First segment, 1903-15.

A mixed index of physical and pecuniary volume of trade.

Simple arithmetic means of relatives of seven series computed on the base, monthly ordinate of secular trend, corrected for seasonal variations, equals 100, expressed in multiples of their several standard deviations. The arithmetic means are multiplied by the standard deviation of outside clearings (8.62).

Second and third segments, 1915-19 and 1919-23.

Indexes of physical volume only.

Weighted arithemtic means of relatives of four (1915-19) and of five (1919-23) series, computed on the base, monthly ordinate of linear trend, corrected for seasonal variation, equals 100.

Indexes Relating to General Business Conditions.

American Telephone and Telegraph Company's index of "General Business Compared with Normal," United States, 1877-1925.

From 1877 to 1884, when pig-iron output is the only series used, this index relates to physical volume of production. From 1922, when all "dollar series" are dropped, to date, it relates to physical volume of production and of trade. In the intervening years, 1885-1921, it relates to "general business conditions."

Weighted arithmetic means of relatives computed on the base, monthly ordinate of secular trend, corrected for seasonal variations, equals 100, expressed in multiples of standard deviations. The arithmetic means are finally put into percentage form through multiplying by 10 (the approximate weighted average of the standard deviations of the constituent series in percentages).

Carl Snyder's "Index of Deposits Activity," United States, 1875 to 1924.

Relatives (not strictly an index) of the ratios of individual deposits in all National Banks to total clearings, computed on the base, monthly ordinate of secular trend equals 100, corrected for seasonal variations, and smoothed by three-months moving averages.

This interesting series is best classed as relating to general business conditions. The inclusion of New York City clearings (as well as New York City deposits) gives dealings in securities far more weight in this series than they have in Frickey's and Snyder's relatives of outside clearings.

None of the series here described is comprehensive enough to pass as an index of business cycles. Each series relates to but one or a few economic activities, and these activities differ widely. In every case the representative character of the data used is open to question, and the methods of isolating cyclical-irregular fluctuations lack precision. Two series change character from period to period. Three series are relatives measuring the fluctuations of a variable about its adjusted trend; two series show arithmetic means of such relatives reduced to units of their standard deviations. By no means uniform materials, one would say.

If these series made by different hands, with different methods, from different data, to show different things, agree with each other in large measure, it must be that business cycles manifest themselves

in much the same way over a wide variety of economic activities, that these fluctuations are recorded with reasonable accuracy in numerous time series, and that the diversities of method make no great difference in the results. So far as the series differ, we may infer that variety of method does make some difference in the results; that the data are unreliable in different ways; or that the activities to which the series relate have characteristically different fluctuations. Perhaps all these explanations, and others too, are applicable to every difference.

Thus in comparing the five indexes of business conditions in the United States which cover by months the longest periods of time, we shall be testing the underlying statistics, testing the methods of isolating cyclical-irregular fluctuations, and testing the hypothesis that similar cycles occur in different economic activities. Of course, we should prefer to test these matters separately, but must content ourselves with testing them in combination. Further, we shall be testing in one country for about 50 years the regularity of business cycles in respect to duration and amplitude.

(1) The "Saw-Tooth" Contour of the Business Indexes.

All five of our indexes present business cycles, not as sweeping smoothly upward from depressions to a single peak of prosperity and then declining steadily to a new trough, but as moving in a jerky fashion. Even the two curves which Snyder smoothed by moving averages are made up of serrated segments.

Counting shows that the indexes change direction on the average every three months, every two months, or even oftener.[1] We cannot

[1] The following table gives details.

FREQUENCY OF CHANGES IN DIRECTION OF THE CURVES TRACED BY FIVE MONTHLY INDEXES OF BUSINESS CONDITIONS IN THE UNITED STATES, 1877–1922

1877–1922	Number of Times Curves Change Direction: From rise to fall or from fall to rise	From rise or fall to horizontal, or *vice versa*	Total changes of direction	No. of months covered	Proportion of months in which curves change direction
A. T. and T. Index.......	178	134	312	550	57%
Frickey's Clearings Index*	222	59	281	456	62
Snyder's Clearings Index..	103	87	190	552	34
Snyder's Deposits Index..	127	141	268	552	49
1903–1922					
Persons' Trade Index.....	95	61	156	238	66
A. T. and T. Index......	91	39	130	240	54
Frickey's Clearings Index*	69	18	87	144	60
Snyder's Clearings Index..	36	86	121	240	50
Snyder's Deposits Index..	47	69	116	240	48

* To 1914 only.

be sure that these frequent minor irregularities are due wholly to the failure of random influences to cancel each other. They may be due in part to the averaging together of series which differ in timing. And perhaps the cyclical movements themselves keep producing and overcoming small checks.

Reversals of direction are more frequent near the climax of prosperity and in the trough of depression than during the transitions between these extreme states. Charts 11 to 17 suggest that business has a ceiling and a floor, both somewhat elastic or irregular. Between these limiting planes it can glide up or down on a slant rather smoothly. But when business nears the ceiling or the floor it bumps up and down in a jerky fashion for a while before it goes off on the next glide.

(2) Month-to-Month Changes.

A second resemblance among the five indexes concerns the amplitude of their month-to-month changes. The "points" in which the monthly changes are expressed are relatives to ordinates of secular trend, averages of such relatives reduced to percentage form, or averages of such relatives multiplied by the standard deviations of "outside" clearings. In practice, the scales cover similar ranges.

Chart 19 shows the distribution of these monthly changes in percentages of the total number of cases covered by each series.[1]

[1] The data from which the chart is drawn are as follows:

FREQUENCY DISTRIBUTION OF THE MONTH-TO-MONTH CHANGES IN FIVE INDEXES OF BUSINESS ACTIVITY

Unit in each case is one point in the scale of deviations from adjusted trends. These scales differ somewhat from each other. See text.

Percentage Basis

Direction and magnitude of month-to-month changes	A. T. and T. Index 1877–1925	Frickey's Clearings Index 1875–1914	Snyder's Clearings Index 1875–1923	Snyder's Deposits Index 1875–1923	Persons' Index of Trade 1903–1924
+17		.2			
+16		.2			
+15		.2			
+14		.2			
+13		.6			
+12		.2		.2	
+11				.5	
+10	.2	.6			
+ 9		.8		.3	.4
+ 8	.3	1.9	.2	1.2	.7
+ 7	.8	1.7		1.7	1.5
+ 6	1.2	4.0	.5	1.9	1.5

As economic data go, these distributions are remarkably symmetrical and show a high degree of concentration around their central tendencies, most marked in Snyder's Clearings Index and least marked in Frickey's series. The difference between the two clearings indexes in this respect is probably due to the facts (1) that Snyder smoothed his index by a three-months moving average, thus reducing the amplitude of the extreme movements and increasing the number of minor movements, and (2) that Frickey used data from only seven cities, while Snyder took all outside clearings. In each case, the distribution is slightly elongated toward the left; that is, the most violent declines exceed the most considerable advances. The abrupt declines

---

FREQUENCY DISTRIBUTION OF THE MONTH-TO-MONTH CHANGES IN FIVE INDEXES OF BUSINESS ACTIVITY

Direction and magnitude of month-to-month changes	A. T. and T. Index 1877–1925	Frickey's Clearings Index 1875–1914	Snyder's Clearings Index 1875–1923	Snyder's Deposits Index 1875–1923	Persons' Index of Trade 1903–1924
+ 5	3.2	5.2	1.7	2.2	2.7
+ 4	3.6	5.0	2.2	4.1	6.1
+ 3	7.2	7.7	6.2	6.1	7.6
+ 2	12.8	10.5	10.4	11.3	12.2
+ 1	14.3	7.3	18.3	11.6	13.3
0	17.5	8.8	24.0	13.8	13.3
− 1	13.5	7.3	16.9	15.0	11.8
− 2	9.0	7.3	8.5	9.9	7.6
− 3	6.5	8.4	6.0	8.2	6.5
− 4	3.7	5.0	2.1	4.6	6.1
− 5	2.6	4.6	.9	3.1	2.7
− 6	1.7	4.4	.9	1.5	1.9
− 7	.5	2.5	.3	1.0	.4
− 8	.8	1.3	.5	.7	2.3
− 9	.2	2.1	.2	.7	.4
−10		1.0		.2	.4
−11	.2	.2			
−12		.2	.2		.7
−13					
−14		.2			
−15				.2	
−16					
−17	.2				
−18					
−19		.2			
....					
−27		.2			
	100.0	100.0	100.0	100.0	100.0

\+ Indicates a rise.
− Indicates a fall.

CHART 19.

FREQUENCY DISTRIBUTION OF MONTH-TO-MONTH CHANGES IN FIVE INDEXES OF BUSINESS ACTIVITY.

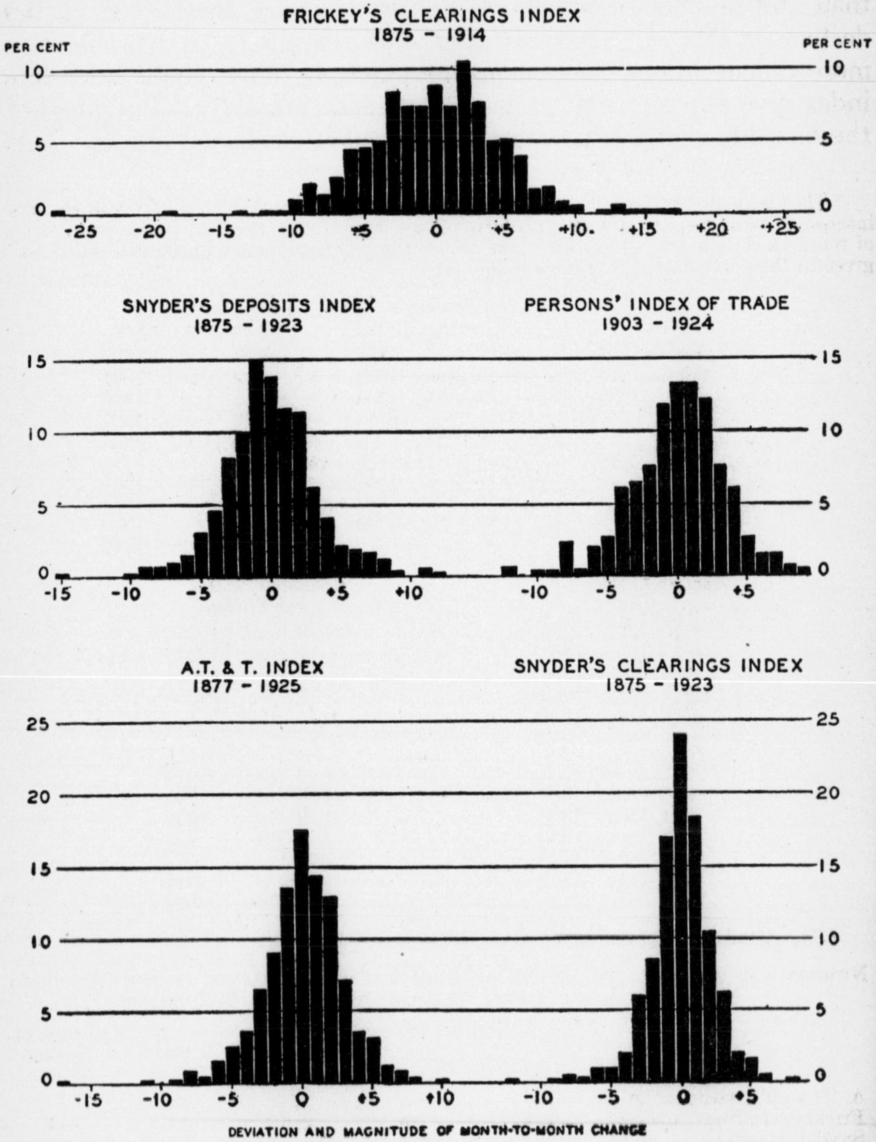

usually occur in crises; the greatest gains occur in periods of revival, or come in other phases of the cycle as reactions after sudden drops.[2] Except in Snyder's deposits index, the number of declines is smaller than the number of advances, but the average magnitude of the declines is greater.[3] Business contraction seems to be a briefer and more violent process than business expansion. Why Snyder's deposits index give opposite indications will appear presently. But most of the monthly changes in both directions have small amplitudes. Less

[2] The dates of the largest month-to-month changes in each of the series have some interest. As above, + indicates an advance, − a decline. Readers whose recollection of business chronology is hazy may care to use the "Conspectus of Business Conditions," given in the next chapter to interpret this table.

A. T. and T. Index	Frickey's Clearings Index	Snyder's Clearings Index
−17 Nov., 1907	−27 Nov., 1907	−12 Aug., 1893
−11 Aug., 1893	−19 June, 1884	− 9 March 1884
− 9 Nov., 1890	−14 July, 1881	− 8 Sept., 1876
		− 8 Nov., 1907
		− 8 Dec., 1907
+10 June, 1886	+17 Nov., 1880	+ 8 June, 1881
+ 8 July, 1891	+16 June, 1881	+ 6 Nov., 1875
+ 8 Aug., 1894	+15 Oct., 1875	+ 6 Nov., 1879
		+ 6 May, 1890

Snyder's Deposits Index	Persons' Index of Trade
−15 July, 1901	−12 Jan., 1921
−10 June, 1901	−12 June, 1924
− 9 Aug., 1875	−10 Nov., 1907
− 9 June, 1880	− 9 Dec., 1907
− 9 May, 1907	
− 9 Sept., 1914	
+12 April, 1901	+ 9 March, 1918
+11 Dec., 1880	+ 8 July, 1919
+11 Dec., 1898	+ 8 Nov., 1922
+11 Dec., 1900	+ 7 Feb., 1904
+ 9 Feb., 1876	+ 7 Oct., 1912
+ 9 July, 1897	+ 7 Dec., 1919
	+ 7 Dec., 1924

[3] The details are as follows:

Number and Average Magnitude of Advances and Declines in the Month-to-Month Changes in Five Indexes of Business Conditions

	Number of cases of			Average magnitude of	
	Advance	No Change	Decline	Advance Points	Decline Points
A. T. and T. business index	256	103	228	2.5	2.7
Frickey, clearings	222	42	215	4.0	4.2
Snyder, clearings	231	141	213	2.0	2.2
Snyder, deposits	241	81	264	3.0	2.8
Persons, trade	121	35	107	2.8	3.3

than half exceed two points in the scales used, except in Frickey's index, and, with the same exception, only a tenth exceed five points.[4]

(3) On Identifying Business Cycles by Use of the Business Indexes.

The irregularities of contour in the business indexes cause considerable difficulty when one tries to count the number of business cycles in a given period. The memorable cycles which culminated in 1882, in 1893, in 1907, in 1917, and in 1920 stand out clearly in all our curves. But in all the curves there are stretches when the cyclical fluctuations are less easy to identify; for example, the later 1880's, the middle 1890's, the early 1900's, the years 1910-13, and 1923-24. While the five monthly indexes agree in presenting this contrast between major and minor fluctuations, it would be hard from study of the curves to lay down rules for determining precisely what movements of an index shall be counted a business cycle. In the less pronounced cycles, the period of greatest activity occasionally (2 times out of 56) remains below the base line in some one of the indexes. In other cycles, the period of least activity occasionally (2 times out of 55) remains above the base line in some index. Often there are double or triple peaks, and double or triple troughs. At times one suspects that irregular fluctuations are dominating the cyclical factors. Nor is the duration of business cycles uniform enough to be used as a criterion in doubtful cases. But one who studies all five curves with care can draw up a list of business cycles which anyone else can identify with confidence in every curve.

Such a list is best made by noting the successive turning points in the business indexes. One may count either the successive crests, or the successive troughs of the waves. These two ways of reckoning usually give different measurements of duration for particular cycles; but the average duration over a period of considerable length must

[4] Once more the details are of interest:

PERCENTAGES OF THE MONTH-TO-MONTH CHANGES IN FIVE INDEXES OF BUSINESS CONDITIONS WHICH FALL WITHIN CERTAIN LIMITS

	± 1 point	± 2 points	± 5 points	± 10 points
A. T. and T. business index.	45.3%	67.1%	93.9%	99.6%
Frickey's clearings index.	23.4	41.2	77.1	97.4
Snyder's clearings index.	59.2	78.1	97.2	99.8
Snyder's deposits index.	40.4	61.6	89.9	99.1
Persons' trade index.	38.4	85.2	89.9	99.4

come out nearly the same whether one counts from trough to trough or from crest to crest.

Table 14 shows that 13 business cycles occurred in the United

TABLE 14

Dates of the Troughs and the Crests of American Business Cycles in 1878–1924 According to Five Monthly Indexes of Business Activity

	A. T. and T. business index	Frickey's clearings index	Snyder's clearings index	Snyder's deposits index	Persons' trade index
Trough....	Dec. '78– Apr. '79	Dec. '78	May '78	June and Dec. '78	
Crest......	June-Aug. '81	June '81	Aug. '81	Feb. '81	
Trough....	Feb., May '85	Nov. '84	Apr. '85	Nov. '84	
Crest......	March '87	June '87	June '87	Nov., Dec. '86	
Trough....	March '88	March '88	March '88	Feb. '88	
Crest......	May, Oct. '90	July '90	July '90	June '90	
Trough....	May '91	March '91	March '91	Jan., Feb. '91	
Crest......	Feb. '92	June '92 Jan. '93	Jan. '93	Feb. '93	
Trough....	June '94	Aug. '93	Oct. '93	Oct. '94	
Crest......	Oct. '95	Oct. '95	Dec. '95	June '95	
Trough....	Oct. '96	May '97	Mar. '97	Apr. '97	
Crest......	Dec. '99 Feb. '00	March '99	June '99	Feb. '99	
Trough....	Nov., Dec. '00	Sept. '00	Sept. '00	Sept. '00	
Crest......	Sept. '02	May '01 Sept. '02 July '03	June '01	Apr. '01 May '01	
Trough....	Dec. '03	May '04	July '04	Apr., May '04	July '04
Crest......	May, July '07	May '07	Feb. '06	Jan. '06	May '07
Trough....	May, June '08	Dec. '07	Jan. '08	Dec. '07	March '08
Crest......	Jan., March '10	March '10	Apr. '10	Feb. '10	March '10
Trough....	April '11	Oct. '11	Dec. '11	Sept. '10	April '11
Crest......	Jan. '13	Oct. '12	Feb. '13	March., Apr. '12	Oct. '12
Trough....	Dec. '14	Nov. '14	Dec. '14	Sept., Oct. '14	Nov. '14
Crest......	Nov. '16 Jan. '17		Dec. '16 Jan. '17	Oct., Nov. '16	May '17
Trough....	March '19		March '19	March '19	June '19
Crest......	Jan. '20		Aug., Sept. '19	July '19	March '20
Trough....	Apr., May, July '21		March '21	Mar., July '21	July '21
Crest......	May '23		May '23	March '23	May '23
Trough....	June '24				June '24

States between 1878 and 1923. Each of these cycles is traced by each of our indexes. The table gives the dates both of the crests and the troughs, as they appear in the several curves. Closer agreement

among the dates could be secured by smoothing out their serrations with free-hand curves, and making a single crest and trough for each successive cycle. That process is legitimate; but it is well to show how frequent are the multiple peaks.

(4) Time Relationships Among the Business Indexes.

Of the several comparisons which Table 14 suggests, the simplest concerns the time sequence in which the five indexes reach their turning points. For this purpose, we need to replace the multiple peaks and troughs by single dates. The method followed is arbitrary and does nothing to lessen the differences among the curves: we place the crest midway between the months showing the highest points revealed by a given wave of activity, and date the troughs in corresponding fashion.[1] With this simplification, we can manage the data easily.

On no occasion do all of our indexes reach the crest or the trough of a given wave in the same month. Four times three out of four series then available agree; [2] but there is always one series which leads or lags behind the others by a month or more. Seemingly, we should think, not of turning points in business cycles, but of turning periods. As a rule, these turning periods are relatively long in the violent cycles and relatively short in the mild cycles. If we count from the date when the first of our indexes turns a given corner to the date when the last one turns the same corner, we get periods which run from one month in the trough of 1888, or two months in the trough of 1914 and in the crests of 1890, 1910, and 1923, to 14 months in the trough of 1893-94, 15 months in the trough of 1910-11, 16 months in the crests of 1901-02, and 17 months in the crest of 1906-07. On the average these turning periods are longer at the crest (8.0 months) than in the troughs (6.1 months).

Snyder's deposits index is the first to reach the crest 12 times out of 13 (the exception occurred in 1892-93). It also leads 8 times out of 13 in reaching the troughs. It will be recalled that this index is made by dividing individual deposits in all National Banks into total clearings. Of total clearings, the New York City figures make

[1] If there is a double crest in two adjacent months (for example, October and November, 1916), we choose the later month to avoid fractions. Similarly, in dealing with a double crest in May and October, 1890, we put the single crest in August, instead of July. There are 23 double or multiple crests or troughs among 111 turning points in Table 14.

[2] These dates are March, 1888, September, 1900, March, 1919, and May, 1923.

roughly half, and the New York City figures are influenced largely by the current volume of transactions on the Stock Exchange. In the other indexes this type of business activity counts for little. We may infer, then, that the pecuniary volume of trading in stocks almost always reaches its peak and begins to decline in a business cycle, before other types of business have culminated. With decidedly less regularity, trading in stocks also precedes other types of business in recovering from a depression.

As for the other indexes, their average order in reaching peaks and troughs is (2) Snyder's clearings index, (3) Frickey's clearings index, (4) the American Telephone and Telegraph Company's general business index, and (5) Person's index of trade. In each of these cases the lags average longer at the crests than in the troughs.[3]

(5) Duration of Periods of Expansion and Contraction.

Since all five indexes never reach the crests or the troughs of cyclical waves at the same time, and since neither the time sequences among the indexes nor the lags are constant, we find considerable differences among our measurements of the duration of periods of rising and declining activity. Table 15 presents the details.

Here we have a double complexity—five different measures of phenomena which themselves vary widely from case to case. But when we strike averages we approach uniformity. According to four of the indexes, periods of business expansion have lasted about two years on the average (23-25 months); while periods of business contraction have averaged little more than a year and a half (18, 18, 19 and 21 months according to the several indexes). That the longest periods of decline are greater than the longest periods of advance makes this average the more striking. It links with what has already been said about the greater number and smaller average value of the upward month-to-month changes. The average (and the modal) American cycle seems to be made up of two unequal segments, a two-year period of gradually increasing activity, and a period, four to six months shorter, of less gradually shrinking activity.

[3] The average lags of the several indexes behind the leaders are as follows:

	A. T. and T.	Frickey	Snyder clearings	Snyder deposits	Persons
In troughs	3.7 mo.	3.2 mo.	3.0 mo.	2.4 mo.	4.2 mo.
At crests	5.8 "	6.1 "	4.2 "	0.9 "	6.5 "
Number of cases	26	21	26	26	12

TABLE 15

Duration of Alternate Periods of Business Expansion and Business Contraction in the United States, 1878–1923, According to Five Indexes of Business Activity.

Based upon Table 14

Business Cycles of		A. T. and T. business index Months Rise	A. T. and T. business index Months Fall	Frickey's clearings index Months Rise	Frickey's clearings index Months Fall	Snyder's clearings index Months Rise	Snyder's clearings index Months Fall	Snyder's deposits index Months Rise	Snyder's deposits index Months Fall	Persons' trade index Months Rise	Persons' trade index Months Fall
1878–85	Rise.........	29		30		39		29			
	Fall..........		45		41		44		45		
1885–88	Rise.........	23		31		26		25			
	Fall..........		12		9		9		14		
1888–91	Rise.........	29		28		28		28			
	Fall..........		9		8		8		8		
1891–94	Rise.........	9		19		22		24			
	Fall..........		28		10		9		20		
1894–97	Rise.........	16		26		26		8			
	Fall..........		12		19		15		22		
1897–00	Rise.........	39		22		27		22			
	Fall..........		11		18		15		19		
1900–04	Rise.........	21		22		9		8			
	Fall..........		15		22		37		36		
1904–08	Rise.........	42		36		19		20		34	
	Fall..........		12		7		23		23		10
1908–11	Rise.........	20		27		27		26		24	
	Fall..........		14		19		20		7		13
1911–14	Rise.........	21		12		14		19		18	
	Fall..........		23		25		22		30		25
1914–19	Rise.........	24				25		25		30	
	Fall..........		27				26		28		25
1919–21	Rise.........	10				6		4		9	
	Fall..........		16				18		22		16
1921–23	Rise.........	24				26		22		22	
Maximum	Rise.......	42		36		39		29		34	
	Fall........		45		41		44		45		25
Minimum	Rise.......	9		12		6		4		9	
	Fall........		9		7		8		7		10
Average	Rise.......	24		25		23		20		23	
	Fall........		19		18		21		23		18

Snyder's deposits index gives a different result. As it almost always leads the other indexes in attaining the crest of a business wave, and less uniformly leads them in reaching the trough, so it makes the periods of increasing activity relatively brief, and the periods of declining activity relatively long. Combined with what we know of its composition and its month-to-month changes, this suggests (though it does not prove) that the cycles in financial activity differ from those characteristic of general business in being made up of a shorter section of relatively rapid advance, and a longer section of decline.

All that has just been said applies strictly to the five indexes under consideration, for one country, in the years 1878-1923. Whether the generalizations are applicable to other indexes, other countries, and other periods remains an open question. In view of the diversity of the items which enter into the averages, we cannot judge the representative value of the averages themselves until a wider array of data is available. In the meanwhile, we may note that in respect to variability, our measures of the durations of business cycles compare not unfavorably with the measures made of many other social phenomena. The period of decline in business cycles is decidedly more variable in duration than the period of advance; the latter period in turn is appreciably more variable in duration than are whole cycles. For the latter measurements our materials show a coefficient of variation of 29.4 per cent.[1]

(6) The Duration of Business Cycles.

In Table 16 the lengths of the American cycles of 1878-1925 are measured by adding together first each period of advance and its subsequent period of decline, secondly each period of decline and its subsequent period of advance. From what we have already seen about the variability of these periods, it is clear that the two ways of measuring seldom give identical results. No reason appears for regarding one set of measurements as more significant than the other.

[1] Using all of the observations given in Table 15, we get the following coefficients of variation (that is, standard deviations as percentages of the corresponding arithmetic means):

	Number of observations	Mean duration	Standard deviation	Coefficient of variation
Period of advance..........	55	22.75 mo.	8.34 mo.	36.7%
Period of decline...........	51	19.82 "	10.10 "	51.0%
Whole cycles..............	101	42.02 "	12.37 "	29.4%

Further, our five indexes often given five different measurements for a given cycle counted in the same way. The differences range from

TABLE 16

Duration of Business Cycles in the United States, 1878–1925, According to Five Indexes of Business Activity

Based upon Table 15

		A. T. and T. business index Months		Frickey's clearings index Months		Snyder's clearings index Months		Snyder's deposits index Months		Persons' trade index Months	
		T–T	C–C	T–T	C–C	T–T	C–C	T–T	C–C	T–T	C–C
Trough-trough	1878–85	74		71		83		74			
Crest-crest	1881–87		68		72		70		70		
Trough-trough	1885–88	35		40		35		39			
Crest-crest	1887–90		41		37		37		42		
Trough-trough	1888–91	38		36		36		36			
Crest-crest	1890–92		18		27		30		32		
Trough-trough	1891–94	37		29		31		44			
Crest-crest	1892–95		44		36		35		28		
Trough-trough	1894–97	28		45		41		30			
Crest-crest	1895–99		51		41		42		44		
Trough-trough	1897–00	50		40		42		41			
Crest-crest	1899–02		32		40		24		27		
Trough-trough	1900–04	36		44		46		44			
Crest-crest	1902–07		57		58		56		56		
Trough-trough	1904–08	54		43		42		43		44	
Crest-crest	1907–10		32		34		50		49		34
Trough-trough	1908–11	34		46		47		33		37	
Crest-crest	1910–12		35		31		34		26		31
Trough-trough	1911–14	44		37		36		49		43	
Crest-crest	1912–17		47				47		55		55
Trough-trough	1914–19	51				51		53		55	
Crest-crest	1917–20		37				32		32		34
Trough-trough	1919–21	26				24		26		25	
Crest-crest	1920–23		40				44		44		38
Trough-trough	Maximum	74		71		83		74		55	
Crest-crest	"		68		72		70		70		55
Trough-trough	Minimum	26		29		24		26		25	
Crest-crest	"		18		27		24		26		31
Trough-trough	Average	42		43		43		43		41	
Crest-crest	"		42		42		42		42		38

2 to 18 months, and average nearly 10 months. Yet even a period of about 45 years is long enough to make the average length of busi-

ness cycles come out nearly the same whatever index is used, and whether the measurements are taken from crest to crest or from trough to trough. The eight averages covering this period all come out 42 or 43 months. Even Persons' index, which overs only 20 years, gives averages of 38 months from crest to crest and 41 months from trough to trough.

Once more we must note the limited scope of the data under analysis and question the representative value of the averages. But these are the most precise measurements of the duration of business cycles we can get for the present; they refer to the country and the period which interests us most, and they come from five different sources. We may therefore consider the distribution of the measurements in some detail. We shall treat each measurement given by each series for each cycle, whether taken from crest to crest or from trough to trough, as one observation upon the duration of business cycles.

The 101 observations which this procedure lets us count are scattered over a range which runs from 18 to 83 months.[1] Half of the

[1] The full arrays, tabulated from Table 16, may be given.

Observations upon the Duration of Business Cycles in the United States, 1878–1923, Made from Five Indexes of Business Activity

Duration in Months	Number of Cases: Trough to Trough	Number of Cases: Crest to Crest	Total	Duration in Months	Number of Cases: Trough to Trough	Number of Cases: Crest to Crest	Total
18		1	1	45	1		1
24	1	1	2	46	2		2
25	1		1	47	1	2	3
26	2	1	3	49	1	1	2
27		2	2	50	1	1	2
28	1	1	2	51	2	1	3
29	1		1	53	1		1
30	1	1	2	54	1		1
31	1	2	3	55	1	2	3
32		5	5	56		2	2
33	1		1	57		1	1
34	1	4	5	58		1	1
35	2	2	4	68		1	1
36	5	1	6	70		2	2
37	3	3	6	71	1		1
38	1	1	2	72		1	1
39	1		1	74	2		2
40	2	2	4	83	1		1
41	2	2	4		—	—	—
42	2	2	4		51	50	101
43	3		3				
44	5	4	9				

(Note continued on p. 342.)

observations, however, are concentrated between 34 and 47 months, an interval of little more than a year.

As often happens in dealing with a frequency table, we get more significant results by grouping the intervals. Here we may combine months into quarters. This we can do in three ways, treating each month as the end, the middle, or the beginning of a quarter. Thus our time scales might be based upon any of these groupings:

1st grouping	2d grouping	3d grouping
22–24 mo.	23–25 mo.	24–26 mo.
25–27 "	26–28 "	27–29 "
28–30 "	29–31 "	30–32 "
etc.	etc.	etc.

These three groupings give appreciably different distributions, as the following figures show:

	Crude Primary Mode	Crude Secondary Mode
1st grouping (22–24 mo., etc.)	15 observations at 34–36 mo.	13 observations at 43–45 mo.
2d " (23–25 " ")	16 observations at 35–37 mo.	12 observations at 44–46 mo.
3d " (24–26 " ")	16 observations at 42–44 mo.	14 observations at 36–38 mo.

Such shifting in the positions of the crude mode as the grouping of the months is altered from one arbitrary scheme to another, makes us wish for an average of the three groupings. In averaging, we can once more arrange the items in three ways, putting (say) the 26-28 month interval first in a combination with 27-29, and 28-30 months; second in a combination with 25-27 and 27-29 months; or last in a combination with 24-26 months and 25-27 months. As before, we have no reason for preferring any of these arrangements to the others. We may therefore use an average of all three. That plan will give as our final distribution of the 101 observations a distribution in which the class-frequencies are weighted averages of the frequencies secured in nine different groupings of the observations. The central

---

Two measures of the central tendencies of the arrays may be added.

	Observations taken From trough to trough	From crest to crest	In both ways
Arithmetic means	42.5 months	41.5 months	42.0 months
Quartile	36	32	34
Median	41	39	40
Quartile	46	49	47

points of the intervals used are 16 months, 19 months, 22 months, etc.[2]

Chart 20, in which the results appear, shows that all our averaging of different arrangements does not completely smooth out the irregularities. The two modes persist in the intervals centering on 37 and 43 months. They are separated by a lower point at 40 months, which happens to be the median of the series.

The conclusion is clear that within the period and country represented by our indexes, business cycles, while varying in length from a year and a half to nearly seven years, have a modal length in the neighborhood of three to three and one half years. They are far from uniform in duration, but their durations are distributed about a well marked central tendency in a tolerably regular fashion. This distribution differs from the type described by the "normal curve" in being prolonged toward the upper end of the time scale somewhat farther than toward the lower end.

There we may leave the topic for the present, planning to return to it in the next chapter, when we shall have for analysis observations upon a larger number of business cycles, over a longer period, and from seventeen countries instead of one.

(7) The Amplitude of Business Cycles.

All our indexes measure the amplitude of business fluctuations in percentage deviations from base lines, which represent the loci of the ordinates of secular trend corrected for seasonal variation.[1] We have noted certain technical differences in methods of construction, but have found that the average magnitudes of the published figures are of the same order in all the indexes. The greatest differences, indeed, are between two indexes which are alike in method of construction—Snyder's series for clearings and for deposits.

Table 17 assembles all the measurements of extreme deviations from the base line at the troughs and crests of successive business

[2] Under this plan, the average for the interval centering on 19 months, for example, is made from the observations for 16-18 months weighted 1, the observations for 17-19 months weighted 2, the observations for 18-20 months weighted 3, the observations for 19-21 months weighted 2, and the observations for 20-22 months weighted 1. By months, this arrangement weights the observation at 16 months 1, at 17 months 3, at 18 months 6, at 19 months 7, at 20 months 6, at 21 months 3, and at 22 months 1.

[1] For the present purpose, Snyder's practice of eliminating the seasonal variations *after* the deviations from secular trends have been computed is not an important departure from the methods followed by Persons, Frickey, and the statisticians of the American Telephone and Telegraph Company.

cycles, and Table 18 shows the magnitude of the successive swings from trough to crest and from crest to trough.

CHART 20.

FREQUENCY DISTRIBUTION OF 101 OBSERVATIONS UPON THE DURATION OF BUSINESS CYCLES: UNITED STATES, 1878-1923.

Based upon Table 16.

Averages obtained by combining several different groupings of the observations. See text.

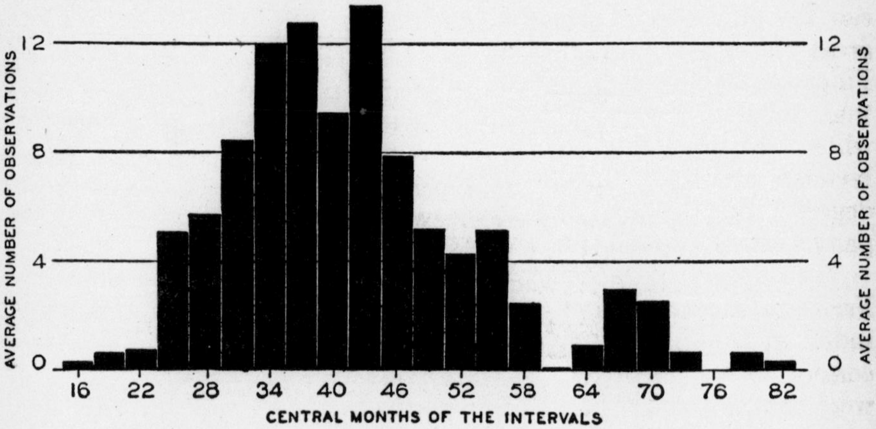

NUMERICAL VALUES

Central Months of the intervals	Average Number of observations	Central months of the intervals	Average Number of observations
16	.3	52	4.2
19	.7	55	5.1
22	.8	58	2.4
25	5.0	61	.1
28	5.7	64	.9
31	8.4	67	2.9
34	11.9	70	2.5
37	12.7	73	.7
49	9.4	76	. .
43	13.3	79	.7
46	7.8	82	.3
49	5.1		
			100.9

The highest pitch of prosperity in the whole period covered was attained in 1881 according to Frickey's and Snyder's clearings indexes, in 1901 according to Snyder's deposits index, in 1907 according

to the American Telephone and Telegraph Company's index, and in 1917 according to Persons' index (which does not go back of 1903). These differences are not to be regarded as discrepancies, but rather as probably reliable indications that the processes to which the indexes specifically relate really attained their highest levels above their base lines in different cycles.

The most interesting case is the maximum shown by Snyder's deposits index in 1901,—a moderate crest according to the two clearings indexes, and the lowest crest in the list according to the American Telephone and Telegraph Company's series. That year saw the great "Northern Pacific corner" on the New York Stock Exchange. Financial activity in New York did perhaps rise higher above its trend then than at any other time between 1878 and 1923. The series which is much influenced by New York City clearings reflects this feverish activity. Outside clearings were stimulated in moderate degree. But "general business," as shown by the telephone company's series, expanded only a little.

The deepest depressions occurred in 1878 and 1896 according to Frickey's index, in 1894 and 1896 according to Snyder's clearings index, in 1914 according to Snyder's deposits index, and in 1921 according to the telephone company's and Persons' indexes. All these were unquestionably periods of extreme hardship, and the differences among the several indexes concerning their relative severity need give us no concern.

The periods of maximum and minimum advance and decline in business activity according to the five indexes are best presented in tabular form. The greatest "boom" in the whole period was that which followed the prolonged period of depression in the 1870's if we consider outside clearings, that which culminated in the Northern Pacific corner of 1901 if we give metropolitan clearings their share in the national total, and that which accompanied or followed the World War if we take the trade indexes. Similarly the most catastrophic declines were those which followed on the greatest booms; for even Snyder's deposits index makes the drop of 1881-1884 slightly larger than that following the Northern Pacific corner. The mildest periods of expansion, on the other hand, were those which culminated in 1895, 1902, and 1912-13, while the mildest depressions came in 1886-88, 1900, and 1910-11. The decline in 1895-97 was also slight; but that was because the preceding period of activity was mild, not because the depression lacked severity. All this is quite consistent

with what is known from other sources concerning the major and minor business cycles of the period.

TABLE 17

PERCENTAGE DEVIATIONS FROM THEIR BASE LINES OF FIVE INDEXES OF BUSINESS ACTIVITY AT THE CRESTS AND TROUGHS OF SUCCESSIVE BUSINESS CYCLES, UNITED STATES: 1878–1923.

		A. T. and T. business index		Frickey's clearings index		Snyder's clearings index		Snyder's deposits index		Persons' trade index	
		Trough	Crest	Trough	Crest	Trough	Crest	Trough	Crest	Trough	Crest
'78	Trough.....	−13		−29		−14		−14			
'81	Crest.......		+13		+27		+26		+30		
'84–'85	Trough......	−19		−20		−19		−23			
'86–'87	Crest.......		+ 9		+19		+11		+ 7		
'88	Trough......	− 7		− 3		− 4		− 7			
'90	Crest.......		+17		+22		+21		+14		
'91	Trough......	− 7		+ 4		+ 3		− 1			
'92–'93	Crest.......		+14		+20		+18		+13		
'93–'94	Trough......	−20		−17		−20		−18			
'95	Crest.......		+ 6		− 2		− 3		+ 3		
'96–'97	Trough......	−17		−29		−20		−11			
'99	Crest.......		+11		+10		+ 7		+21		
'00	Trough......	− 4		−11		− 5		−15			
'01–'02	Crest.......		+ 6		+ 8		+15		+34		
'03–'04	Trough......	−14		−11		− 2		−17		− 9	
'06–'07	Crest.......		+18		+15		+16		+19		+13
'07–'08	Trough......	−17		−22		−12		−20		−19	
'10	Crest.......		+12		+ 8		+ 6		+11		+ 8
'10–'11	Trough......	− 3		− 8		− 2		− 7		− 4	
'12–'13	Crest.......		+10		+ 8		+ 3		+ 5		+ 9
'14	Trough......	−18		−17		−17		−28		−18	
'16–'17	Crest.......		+17				+10		+13		+25
'19	Trough......	− 8				− 2		− 6		− 3	
'19–'20	Crest.......		+13				+ 9		+11		+15
'21	Trough......	−25				−10		− 7		−22	
'23	Crest.......		+10				+11		+ 6		+17
Minimum..........		− 3	+ 6	+ 4	− 2	+ 3	− 3	− 1	+ 3	− 3	+ 8
Maximum..........		−25	+18	−29	+27	−20	+26	−28	+34	−22	+25
Average...........		−13.2	+12.0	−14.8	+13.5	− 9.5	+11.5	−13.4	+14.4	−12.5	+14.5

By far the most important difference among the indexes is that Snyder's clearings series, and less clearly Frickey's companion piece,

suggest that business cycles have been growing progressively milder decade by decade, whereas the other indexes show no such cheering

TABLE 18

Amplitude of the Rise from Trough to Crest and of the Decline from Crest to Trough in the American Business Cycles of 1878–1923 as Shown by Five Indexes of Business Activity.

	A. T. and T. business index		Frickey's clearings index		Snyder's clearings index		Snyder's deposits index		Persons' trade index	
	Rise	Fall	Rise	Fall	Rise	Fall	Rise	Fall	Rise	Fall
Rise 1878–'81	26		56		40		44			
Fall 1881–'84, '85		32		47		45		53		
Rise 1884, '85–'86, '87	28		39		30		30			
Fall 1886, '87–'88		16		22		15		14		
Rise 1888–'90	24		25		25		21			
Fall 1890–'91		24		18		18		15		
Rise 1891–'92, '93	21		16		15		14			
Fall 1892, '93–'93, '94		34		37		38		31		
Rise 1893, '94–'95	26		15		17		21			
Fall 1895–'96, '97		23		27		17		14		
Rise 1896, '97–'99	28		39		27		32			
Fall 1899–'00		15		21		12		36		
Rise 1900–'01, '02	10		19		20		49			
Fall 1901, '02–'03, '04		20		19		17		51		
Rise 1903, '04–'06, '07	32		26		18		36		22	
Fall 1906, '07–'07, '08		35		37		28		39		32
Rise 1907, '08–'10	29		30		18		31		27	
Fall 1910–'11		15		16		8		18		12
Rise 1911–'12, '13	13		16		5		12		13	
Fall 1912, '13–'14		28		25		20		33		27
Rise 1914–'16, '17	35				27		41		43	
Fall 1916, '17–'19		25				12		19		28
Rise 1919–'19, '20	21				11		17		18	
Fall 1919, '20–'21		38				19		18		37
Rise 1921–'23	35				21		13		39	
Minima	10	15	15	16	5	8	12	14	13	12
Maxima	35	38	56	47	40	45	49	53	43	37
Average rise	25		28		21		28		27	
Average fall		25		27		21		28		27

drift. If we confine attention to the most violent cycles of 1878-1923 (including the cycle of 1900-04 in Snyder's deposits index), and com-

TABLE 19

DATES OF THE MOST AND THE LEAST VIOLENT CYCLICAL FLUCTUATIONS IN AMERICAN BUSINESS, 1878–1923, ACCORDING TO FIVE INDEXES OF BUSINESS ACTIVITY

	A. T. and T. business index	Frickey's clearings index	Snyder's clearings index	Snyder's deposits index	Persons' trade index
Greatest rise...	1914–17 1921–23	1878–81	1878–81	1900–01	1914–17
Greatest fall...	1920–21	1881–84	1881–85	1881–84	1920–21
Smallest rise...	1900–02	1893–95	1911–13	1910–12	1911–12
Smallest fall....	1899–00 1910–11	1910–11	1910–11	1886–88 1895–97	1910–11

bine the points of rise and fall shown in Table 18, we get the following results:

TABLE 20

AMPLITUDE OF COMBINED RISE AND FALL IN VIOLENT BUSINESS CYCLES, ACCORDING TO FIVE INDEXES OF BUSINESS ACTIVITY

Based upon Table 18

Business Cycles of	A. T. and T. business index	Frickey's clearings index	Snyder's clearings index	Snyder's deposits index	Persons' trade index
1878–85..........	58	103	85	97	
1891–94..........	55	53	53	45	
1900–04..........	..	..	..	100	
1904–08..........	67	63	46	75	54
1914–19..........	60		39	60	71
1919–21..........	59		30	35	55

On the face of the returns we must conclude that, since the early 1880's, the cyclical fluctuations of outside clearings have been greatly reduced; but that the lessened fluctuations of outside clearings have not led to greater stability in other types of business.[2] It does not necessarily follow, however, that business processes of any one of the many types which affect outside clearings have become more stable. In the periods covered by Snyder's and Frickey's indexes, checks have come into wider use in retail trade, and in paying rents, salaries, and even wages. Transactions of this type have cyclical-irregular fluctuations of notably smaller amplitude than the wholesale transactions which have long been settled with checks. Further, Mr. Snyder's series, which includes all outside clearings, tends to become stabler

[2] It may be remarked that the evidence of the A. T. and T. index on this point cannot be thrown out because of the many changes in the series used in making it. For these changes have been mainly of a sort which tend to render the averages less variable.

from the addition of new clearing houses to the list. In view of these considerations and of the contrary evidence borne by other business indexes, it is rash to say that business cycles are growing milder because the cyclical fluctuations of outside clearings are less now than they were some 40 years ago. The severity of the crisis of 1920 and the depression of 1921 is attested by abundant evidence.

By way of summary we may assemble our 111 observations upon the extreme amplitudes of the crests and troughs of business cycles in another frequency table.[3] Again the question arises how the observations made at successive points shall be grouped to bring out their significance. Taking a span of 5 points in the scale of deviations, I have made groups centered around deviations of 0, 5, 10 . . . points; 1, 6, 11 . . . points; 2, 7, 12 . . . points; 3, 8, 13 . . . points; and 4, 9, 14 . . . points. In all of these groupings, the distributions of the maximum deviations at the troughs of cycles show two crude modes. One or both of these modes shift their locations and their relative prominence on every change in the groupings of the observations. On the other hand, all 5 of the distributions of the maximum deviations at the crests of cycles rise step by step to a

[3] The full array is as follows:

Scale of deviations from base lines in Points		Number of Observations		Scale of deviations from base lines in Points		Number of Observations	
Troughs	Crests	Troughs	Crests	Troughs	Crests	Troughs	Crests
+ 4	− 4	1		−16	+16		1
+ 3	− 3	1	1	−17	+17	6	3
+ 2	− 2		1	−18	+18	3	2
+ 1	− 1			−19	+19	3	2
0	0			−20	+20	5	1
− 1	+ 1	1		−21	+21		2
− 2	+ 2	3		−22	+22	2	1
− 3	+ 3	3	2	−23	+23	1	
− 4	+ 4	3		−24	+24		
− 5	+ 5	1	1	−25	+25	1	1
− 6	+ 6	1	4	−26	+26		1
− 7	+ 7	5	2	−27	+27		1
− 8	+ 8	2	4	−28	+28	1	
− 9	+ 9	1	3	−29	+29	2	
−10	+10	1	4	−30	+30		1
−11	+11	3	5	−31	+31		
−12	+12	1	1	−32	+32		
−13	+13	1	5	−33	+33		
−14	+14	3	2	−34	+34		1
−15	+15	1	3				
					Totals	56	55

single mode and decline again step by step. Only once is this mode shifted to a new position by altering the groupings. If the observations analyzed are representative, the crests of business cycles are more regularly distributed about their central tendency than are the troughs.

On adding together the groupings for troughs and crests, we get five total distributions which are not quite so regular as the distributions of the crests, but decidedly more regular than the distributions of the troughs. In two cases there are two crude modes separated by a lower interval; in one case two adjacent intervals show the same maximum figure; in the other two cases there is a single mode coinciding in position with the mode of the distribution of crests.

Perhaps the best way to establish the broad characteristics of these distributions is to strike averages of all five groupings. Table 21 shows the results of that operation. The number of observations recorded at each point in the scale of deviations from the trend lines of the series appear five times in as many different combinations. In dividing these interlocking combinations for averaging I have used a scale which centers the successive groups around deviations from the trends of 2 points, 7 points, 12 points, etc. Since two troughs are found slightly above and two crests slightly below the trend lines, the first group in the scale centers around + 8 for the troughs and — 3 for the crests.

It will be seen that the double mode persists in the averaged distribution of the troughs. The primary mode is in the group centering about 17 per cent below the trend lines, the secondary mode in the group centering about minus 7 per cent. The intermediate interval, 12 per cent, is the point of greatest concentration of the crests. The distribution which combines crests and troughs has almost equal values at 7, 12 and 17 per cent deviations from trend values.

On the whole, there is no clear evidence of the existence of two distinct types of business cycles—major and minor, or violent and mild—in these observations concerning extreme deviations from the trends. Of course there are major business cycles and minor ones, just as there are tall men and short men in every race; but when all the deviations at the crests and troughs of business cycles are put together they suggest a homogeneous group of phenomena rather than a mixture of two species. Yet the volume of data is not sufficient to close the question.

TABLE 21

FREQUENCY DISTRIBUTIONS OF 111 OBSERVATIONS UPON THE AMPLITUDE OF THE PERCENTAGE DEVIATIONS OF FIVE BUSINESS INDEXES FROM THEIR RESPECTIVE TRENDS AT THE TROUGHS AND CRESTS OF AMERICAN BUSINESS CYCLES: 1878–1923.

Data from Table 17

Averages of five groupings of the observations. See text

Scales of Percentage Deviations		Number of Observations					
Central points of the groups averaged		Actual Numbers			Percentages of Totals		
Troughs	Crests	Troughs	Crests	Both	Troughs	Crests	Both
+ 8	− 8	0.2	. . .	0.2	0.4	. . .	0.2
+ 3	− 3	2.0	1.8	3.8	3.6	3.3	3.4
− 2	+ 2	8.6	3.0	11.6	15.4	5.5	10.5
− 7	+ 7	11.4	13.8	25.2	20.4	25.1	22.7
−12	+12	7.8	16.0	23.8	13.9	29.1	21.4
−17	+17	14.2	11.0	25.2	25.4	20.0	22.7
−22	+22	8.0	5.0	13.0	14.3	9.1	11.7
−27	+27	2.8	2.8	5.6	5.0	5.1	5.0
−32	+32	1.0	1.2	2.2	1.8	2.2	2.0
−37	+37	. . .	0.4	0.4	. . .	0.7	0.4
	Totals	56.0	55.0	111.0	100.2	100.1	100.0

	Arithmetic Means	Medians	Standard deviations	Coefficients of variation
Troughs........	12.6	13.5	7.88	63%
Crests..........	13.0	12.0	7.54	58%
Both...........	12.8	12.7	7.92	52%

FREQUENCY DIAGRAMS
PERCENTAGE BASIS

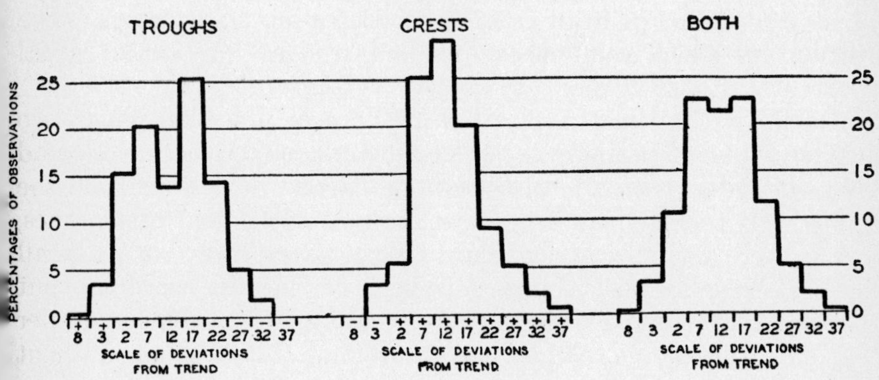

Additional evidence upon this important point can be obtained by analyzing in similar fashion the figures given in Table 18 concerning the percentage amplitude of the swings from crest to trough, and from trough to crest of successive cycles. Of course, the same materials underlie this table and the one we have just been using; but the deviations, instead of being taken always with reference to the base lines, are combined in two new ways: first a deviation in a trough is added (without regard to signs) to the next deviation at a crest; then the latter deviation is added to that at the following trough, and so on. Such re-groupings of data are most useful in trying to determine whether multiple modes reveal features which are accidental or characteristic of the series in which they occur.

Again I have used a span of 5 points; centered my groups successively around movements of 2, 7, 12 . . ., 3, 8, 13 . . ., 4, 9, 14 . . ., 5, 10, 15 . . ., and 6, 11, 16 . . . per cent of trend values, and finally averaged all the groupings together. Double modes appear in most of the groupings; but they shift location as the groupings change, and they dwindle when the five groupings are combined in a general average.

Thus Table 22, which presents the final outcome of these operations, confirms the impression made by Table 21. The diagram for the declines from crest to trough shows a slight secondary mode at 34 per cent separated from the primary mode by a wider interval than appeared in Table 21, while the diagram for the advances from trough to crest shows almost equal frequencies at 19 and 29 per cent, and a slight increase from 34 to 39 per cent. But the diagram which includes both declines and advances rises rapidly to a single mode and then falls gradually step by step with one slight arrest in the descent. On the whole our frequency distributions of the amplitudes of cyclical fluctuations are somewhat more regular than our distributions of their durations, and afford even less basis for supposing that there are two or more distinct species of business cycles.

That business cycles bring enormous economic losses upon a country is clear from this study of their amplitudes. Reckoned in percentages of ordinates of secular trend, the declines from the crests to the troughs of business cycles in the United States from 1878 to 1923 averaged more than a fifth in Snyder's clearings index, and more than a quarter in all the other series. The grand average of all the observations is 25.5 per cent. In extreme cases, these declines exceeded

TABLE 22

Frequency Distributions of 106 Observations, Made from Five Indexes of Business Conditions, upon the Amplitude of the Rise from Trough to Crest and the Decline from Crest to Trough in American Business Cycles, 1878–1923, Reckoned in Percentages of Trend Values.

Data from Table 18

Averages of five groupings of the observations. See text

Scale of percentage rise or decline	Number of Observations					
	Actual Numbers			Percentages of Totals		
Central points of the groups averaged	Decline	Rise	Both	Decline	Rise	Both
4	0.2	0.8	1.0	0.4	1.5	0.9
9	2.0	2.6	4.6	3.9	4.7	4.3
14	9.8	8.8	18.6	19.2	16.0	17.5
19	11.8	10.0	21.8	23.1	18.2	20.6
24	6.2	8.8	15.0	12.2	16.0	14.1
29	5.6	9.8	15.4	11.0	17.8	14.5
34	6.4	4.4	10.8	12.5	8.0	10.2
39	5.0	5.4	10.4	9.8	9.8	9.8
44	1.2	2.4	3.6	2.4	4.4	3.4
49	1.6	1.0	2.6	3.1	1.8	2.5
54	1.2	0.6	1.8	2.4	1.1	1.7
59	...	0.4	0.4	...	0.7	0.4
Totals	51.0	55.0	106.0	100.0	100.0	99.9

	Arithmetic means	Medians	Standard deviations	Coefficients of variation
Decline.........	25.5	23	10.99	43%
Rise............	25.6	25	10.97	43%
Both...........	25.5	24.2	10.89	43%

FREQUENCY DIAGRAMS
PERCENTAGE BASIS

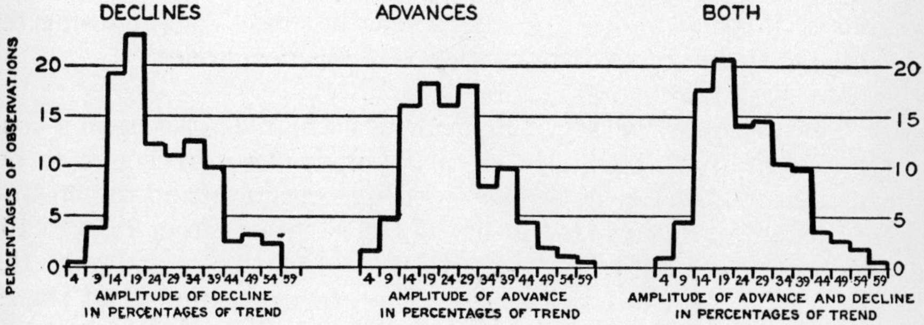

35, 45, and even 50 per cent of the levels indicated by the trends. Perhaps the data from which these indexes are made overweight the activities which are particularly susceptible to the business-cycle hazard; that is another question which requires the study of elaborate evidence which would be confusing here. But one might make large reductions on this score and still leave a huge charge against depressions, without counting the lasting impairment of efficiency produced by business demoralization and unemployment.

(8) The Distinctive Character of Each Business Cycle.

As one analyzes successive business cycles in various ways, one finds evidence, even in the bleak statistical records here used, that each cycle has special characteristics of its own, or rather a special combination of characteristics. More intensive study carried over a wider range in time and space would strengthen this impression. Strictly speaking, every business cycle is a unique historical episode, differing in significant ways from all its predecessors, and never to be repeated in the future. Of course, the theory of business cycles aims primarily to find generalizations which can be applied to all cases. But it is wise for those on theory bent to realize clearly the multi-faceted variability of their cases. Such knowledge may even help them in the process of establishing generalizations. For one who is familiar with the idiosyncrasies of particular cycles will sometimes see that a given rule does apply to cases which at first sight seem to form exceptions. Both as a contribution to our general understanding of business cycles and as an aid to our later inquiries, we may note briefly some of the salient characteristics of the American cycles of 1878 to 1923.

(1) The cycle of 1878-85 followed an exceptionally long and exceptionally severe period of depression. When it finally started, revival was rapid; prosperity was sustained at a high level for an unusually long time; the recession was gentle, and the decline long drawn out. The only season of acute financial strain in this cycle came, not at the downward turning point, but late in the decline—the so-called "crisis of 1884."

(2) While the period of expansion was decidedly shorter than the period of contraction in the cycle of 1878-85, the reverse was true in the cycle of 1885-88. Again the recession was mild, there was no period of acute financial stress, and the depression was not severe.

(3) In the cycle of 1888-91 prosperity attained a higher pitch than in its predecessor, though not so high as in 1881. The recession of 1890 was accompanied by more financial strain than occurred in 1882 or 1887; but the difficulties seem to have been due largely to foreign influences connected with the collapse of Baring Brothers in London. The period of decline was even briefer and milder than in the preceding cycle, being cut short by an unusual harvest situation. The world crop of wheat was poor in 1891, the American crop abundant. Hence our farmers sold a large amount of grain at prices high for that period. Their prosperity, shared by the "granger" railroads and distributors in the agricultural districts, contributed powerfully to an early resumption of activity.

(4) The next period of expansion, 1891-93, was briefer than any of its predecessors shown by our indexes. It was terminated by the great panic of 1893, one of the longest and severest crises in American business history. While this business wave had not risen to a high crest, its trough was very low.

(5) We may call the fluctuations of 1894-97 a submerged cycle. Although the amplitudes of the rise and the decline were not far from the average amplitudes shown by Table 18, the preceding and the following troughs were so low that the crest of the wave did not quite reach the base line in two of our indexes, and barely rose above the base line in two others.

(6) Rising slowly from the low point of 1897, business had not attained a very high level when it was interrupted by the mild reaction of 1900. As in 1890, foreign difficulties seem to have been largely responsible for the recession. The period of contraction was both brief and mild.

(7) The cycle of 1900-04 contained the Northern Pacific corner of 1901, and the peculiar "rich-man's panic" of 1903. In financial circles the fluctuations were of great amplitude, as Snyder's deposits index shows. But business of other sorts was affected relatively little. The American Telephone and Telegraph Company's index makes this cycle the mildest in our list, while Snyder's deposits index makes it the most intense.

(8) Perhaps better than any other case in our period, the fluctuations of 1904-08 answer to the generalized conception of a business cycle presented in the theoretical treatises. From the depression of 1904, business made a fine recovery in 1905, maintained a high pitch of prosperity for some two years, passed through a severe crisis in the

autumn of 1907, and plunged into a new depression in 1908. All the familiar phenomena appeared in standard succession and sharply defined.

(9) and (10) The next two cycles (1908-11 and 1911-14), on the other hand, were mild affairs. While the revival from the depression of 1908 was vigorous, it did not lead to a boom; the recession in 1910 was not sharp, the depression of 1911 was not severe, and the succeeding period of expansion of 1912-13 was terminated early by another mild recession. But the depression which closed the second of these cycles gained dramatic intensity when it was accentuated by the outbreak of war at the end of July, 1914.

(11) Of course the war-time cycle of 1914-18 was distinguished by unusual features—extraordinary price fluctuations, a not less extraordinary shift in the character of production, extreme scarcity of labor, abundance of loan funds, and, toward the end, by government intervention in business on an unprecedented scale.

(12) Hardly less exceptional was the first post-war cycle of 1918-21. After the brief and mild depression ushered in by the Armistice of November, 1918, business started on a boom so sudden that the period which can be labeled "revival" was very brief. Again the price fluctuations were extremely violent. The crisis was of exceptional severity so far as industry was concerned, and, while the Federal Reserve System bore the financial strain with marked success, the subsequent depression was one of the worst in American experience. Yet one who realizes how profoundly economic activities in the United States were affected by the great war, from the time when its sudden onset shattered confidence to the time when industry won back to a peace basis, must wonder that it altered the usual round of business cycles so little. A person who did not know when the great war occurred, could not date it from inspection of our five business indexes, though it would stand out clearly in indexes made largely from price series.

(13) During the cycle of 1921-24, American business gradually returned to more settled conditions. While price fluctuations continued greater than they had been from 1878 to 1914, the price system attained a new equilibrium. After a rather slow recovery from the depression of 1921, business had a short period of almost feverish activity early in 1923, suffered a check, recovered in the opening months of 1924, and then entered upon a sharper decline.

(14) From this trough in the middle of 1924 we may date the

beginning of the cycle in the later stages of which this account is written.

VII. The Need of Combining Theory, Statistics, and History.

From the outset of this inquiry into business cycles, the need of statistical work has been clear. The first demonstration came from a quarter which few might expect—a review of theories made on non-statistical lines. By showing how many processes are involved in business cycles, these theories raised a series of essentially quantitative problems. Which of the causes of cyclical fluctuations stressed by different theorists are the most important? How considerable are the effects produced by these causes, directly and indirectly? What changes occur simultaneously? In what sequence, and after what intervals do other changes follow? How regular are cyclical fluctuations? All these are obviously questions which call for measured observations—very many measured observations upon diverse processes, systematically made in numerous markets over long series of years—in short, the type of observations which constitute statistics. Indeed, the idea suggested itself at the close of Chapter I, that the whole inquiry might shift from a search for causes conducted in the light of common reason to a quasi-mathematical study of the interrelations among a number of complex variables.

Again in Chapter II, when discussing the economic organization within which business cycles run their course, we found ourselves facing quantitative issues at every turn. From the section which dealt with the proportions of "real" income which families produce for themselves and the proportions which they buy with money, to the section on international differences of organization, we had to answer as best we could questions of how much and how often.

But now that in the present chapter we have surveyed the statistical materials and methods of particular concern to students of business cycles, we see that there are grave limitations upon the help we can expect from this source. Rapid progress has been made by the last generation in gathering and in utilizing statistical data; yet we are far from the goal of establishing the study of business cycles upon a strictly statistical basis.

On the technical side, our methods of determining both the secular trends and the seasonal variations of time series are rough. So far, no one has segregated irregular from cyclical fluctuations. While a

method of approximating that result was suggested above and will be elaborated in Chapter V, it yields only averages, and is applicable only to series which cover a considerable number of cycles. Neither the visual study of charts nor the coefficient of correlation are wholly satisfactory methods of determining the relationships among fluctuations. In precisely what forms series should be expressed to bring out their most significant relationships is a problem which statisticians have posed rather than solved. Little systematic work has been done toward measuring the amplitude of the cyclical-irregular fluctuations characteristic of different processes. More attention has been given to the problems of time sequence, but the results are neither comprehensive nor secure. Finally, we have no index numbers of business cycles, nor any definite program for making them. As substitutes we must use a somewhat haphazard collection of indexes relating to such processes as happen to have been recorded in statistical form for considerable periods.

Yet graver limitations are imposed by the paucity of statistical materials. Of the various processes which the theories reviewed in Chapter I represent as of crucial importance, we have satisfactory data concerning not one. Wholesale prices, foreign trade, banking, railway transportation, the metropolitan money and securities markets are the fields best covered in the United States; but the investigator who works on any of these subjects develops many problems for which he cannot get solutions from his data. About profits, savings, advance orders and other future commitments, the production of consumers' goods and industrial equipment, the amount of income disbursed to consumers and their spending, our information is fragmentary. In certain respects other countries offer better data than the United States—the British unemployment returns, and the German receipts from the tax on domestic bills of exchange are examples; but broadly speaking the foreign records are more deficient than our own.

To overcome this handicap so far as possible, the National Bureau of Economic Research has made a systematic collection of economic and social statistics for the United States, Great Britain, France and Germany, which it hopes to publish in the near future for the benefit of all workers in the social sciences. Each series is described, annotated, and presented by months or quarters, if possible, for the full period since its start. The collection covers in considerable detail all types of economic activity, and the leading indicia of social changes.

By enlisting the coöperation of foreign experts, the compilers, Dr. Willard L. Thorp and Mr. Harold Villard, hope to keep errors of omission and commission to a minimum. In addition, the National Bureau is compiling various new series of data which throw light upon salient aspects of business cycles. Dr. Frederick R. Macaulay's studies of bond yields and interest rates since 1857, Dr. Harry Jerome's monograph upon *Migration and Business Cycles,* Dr. Leo Wolman's critical investigations of the labor market, Dr. Frederick C. Mills' intensive work upon the interrelations among price fluctuations, and Dr. Simon S. Kuznets' study of secular trends all promise contributions of importance. Incidental use can be made also of our earlier studies of unemployment, and of Dr. Willford I. King's continuing estimates of income. By utilizing the general collection of statistics, together with the special studies made by the National Bureau and other agencies, we shall be doing what we can to give our inquiry a secure foundation of measurements.

One other source we have, intermediate between statistics and casual observation. This is the collection of *Business Annals,* recently published by the National Bureau. Diligent ransacking and critical comparison of many reports, periodicals, and pamphlets enabled Dr. Thorp to trace the course of business cycles over a longer period and a wider area than is covered by any but the most meager statistics. From his systematic records we can learn certain broad facts about the characteristics of recent cycles in countries of varying culture, and of early cycles in the countries which concern us most. These annals give the best opportunity for studying the international relationships of business fluctuations. They enable us even to make crude measurements of the duration of business cycles, which by covering many more cases supplement and broaden the conclusions drawn above from the business indexes. Exploiting this fresh source is our next task.

Just as a review of theories of business cycles made us see the need of statistics, so our review of statistics makes us see the need of economic history. Of course our historical survey must be condensed, like our summary of theories. When that survey has been completed, we shall not dwell upon the limitations of business annals —they will be obvious.

It is wise to face the shortcomings of each of these approaches to one problem—the theoretical, the statistical, and the historical. But critical though we must be of all our materials and methods, we can

put the criticisms to constructive uses. What has just been said concerning the limitations of statistics should not check, but guide our dealings with tables and charts. The diversity of theories sketched in Chapter I, all plausible and each claiming to reveal the cause of most importance, seemed rather disconcerting. But from each explanation we may get some suggestion of value, and certainly neither our statistics nor our condensed business histories will enable us to do without much reasoning of the sort relied upon by economic theorists. To win as much knowledge as we can of business cycles, we must combine all that we can learn from theory, statistics, and history.

CHAPTER IV.

THE CONTRIBUTION OF BUSINESS ANNALS.

I. The National Bureau's Collection of Business Annals.

Several of the theorists whose writings were laid under contribution in Chapter I—notably Tugan-Baranovski, Bouniatian and Lescure—have devoted much attention to the history of crises and depressions. Similarly, some of the statisticians referred to in Chapter III—for example, Warren M. Persons and his colleagues—have supplemented their time series on occasion by preparing annual summaries of business conditions. But the histories have dealt largely with what was common in the episodes treated, and the summaries have been confined to rather brief periods in a few countries. For theoretical uses, there is needed a systematic record of cyclical alternations of prosperity and depression, covering all countries in which the phenomena have appeared, and designed to make clear the recurrent features of the alternations. If the view taken in Chapter II of the circumstances under which business cycles occur is valid, it may not be impracticable to make a modest descriptive record of this sort which approximates completeness.

While the National Bureau of Economic Research has not been able to perform this whole task, it has sought to form a larger collection of what we may call "business annals" than has been available hitherto. Dr. Willard L. Thorp, who directed the work of compilation, ransacked the rich resources of the New York Public Library for official documents, reports, pamphlets, periodicals, and books dealing systematically or incidentally with business conditions in various countries. The generous coöperation of several foreign scholars brought additional materials and special knowledge to the work.[1] For every year and every country covered, the plan required a digest

[1] Professor Albert Aftalion of Paris reviewed the French annals, Dr. Robert R. Kuczynski of Berlin the German annals, Dr. F. A. von Hayek of Vienna the Austrian annals, Dr. Robert F. Foerster the Italian annals, Dr. E. H. D. Arndt of Transvaal University the South African annals, and Drs. N. D. Kondratieff, A. L. Vainstein and M. B. Ignatieff of the Conjuncture Institute, Moscow, the Russian annals.

of contemporary opinions concerning (1) industrial, commercial and labor conditions, (2) conditions in the markets for loans, securities, and foreign exchange, (3) agricultural production and prices, and (4) non-economic occurrences, such as political events, epidemics, floods or earthquakes, which seem to have influenced business appreciably. From such information as he could gather upon these four heads, Dr. Thorp formed his own opinion concerning the phase of the business cycle through which the country in question was passing each year, and expressed his opinion in a brief caption.

Annals of this sort for the United States have been carried back to 1790, the first year after the adoption of the Constitution. To make possible international comparisons from the beginning of the American record, English annals have been compiled for the same 136 years. Lack of accessible sources, or lack of economic unity, made it difficult to go back of 1840 in France, 1853 in Germany, and 1867 in Austria. To show the geographical spread of business fluctuations in recent times, several other countries were added to the five covered in the long-period studies. With 1890 as the starting-point in all cases, Italy, the Netherlands, Sweden, and Russia were chosen to show diversified conditions in Europe. Next, three great English-speaking colonies on three continents were taken—Canada, Australia, and South Africa. To represent South America, Argentina and Brazil seemed fittest. Finally the foremost Oriental civilizations were included—British India, Japan and China. Needless to say, the sample might well have been enlarged, both by carrying the annals back to earlier dates in several of the nations covered, and by including at least a dozen other countries. The National Bureau hopes that what it lacked means to accomplish may be done by men who have access to the fullest records available for the periods and the countries it has omitted.

Limited as it is in scope, our collection of annals attained proportions and a promise of usefulness which called for independent publication. In the present book, we can use the volume of *Business Annals* much as we use the coördinate statistical series.[2]

[2] See *Business Annals,* by Willard Long Thorp, Publications of the National Bureau of Economic Research, No. 8, New York, 1926.

The present chapter consists mainly of the "Introduction" which I contributed to Dr. Thorp's book, with such omissions, emendations, and additions as are suggested by its relation to earlier chapters, or by sober second thoughts. Once more I may thank the National Bureau's staff, especially Dr. Frederick C. Mills and Dr. Thorp, for much help in analyzing the material contained in the annals.

II. The Trustworthiness of Business Annals.

1. Sources and Methods of Compilation.

The materials with which compilers of business annals work lack the objectivity, as well as the formal precision, of statistics. A man's opinion concerning the fortunes of business in a given year is affected by his personal interests, his training, his opportunities for making observations himself and collecting the observations of others, his aptitude for generalizing, and the care with which he studies his evidence.

One who begins sampling contemporary opinions concerning business conditions in any country with this reflection in mind, will be impressed less by the differences among the conclusions reached by various observers than by their consensus. In the majority of years, business developments are dominated by a trend so clear that it impresses every thoughtful observer, whatever his personal equation may be. Of course, there are years in the record of every country when such is not the case. When the investigator finds serious discrepancies among his sources, he must sometimes ascribe them to bias or incompetence on the part of one or more writers; but more often he discovers that the writers who seem to disagree referred to different industries or different sections of a country—industries or sections which had divergent fortunes.

As the activities of a people get more definitely organized on the basis of business economy, the sources of information concerning business become more numerous, more reliable, and more alike in tenor. On the one hand, different industries and different sections of the country are tied more closely together, so that prosperity or depression in one affects more, and is more affected by, prosperity or depression in others. We shall have occasion to observe, for example, that the American annals reveal greater similarity of fortunes in the opening years of the 20th century than in the closing years of the 18th century. On the other hand, business reporting becomes a profession, and undergoes a development comparable in character to the contemporary development in gathering statistics. Indeed, these two developments foster one another. Since about the middle of the 19th century in England and the United States, and since later dates in other countries, there have been established an increasing

number of periodicals which report business developments weekly or monthly to critical circles of subscribers. Government agencies, especially the consular offices, render similar services to the whole business public. In recent years, it is possible to find for all the countries included in our annals several sources of information, domestic or foreign, which can be checked against each other. In default of local periodicals, British, French and American consular reports can be drawn upon for information concerning trade in every quarter of the world. And besides the reports made at regular intervals for every country, there is a much longer list of pamphlets and books which throw light upon business affairs at different times. The bibliography appended to Dr. Thorp's report shows how numerous and how varied are the sources upon which a diligent compiler of business annals can draw.

In proportion as his sources multiply, an alert compiler, like an alert historian, realizes that his own work has its subjective side. The few sentences he writes to summarize the mass of material are colored by his personal equation, compounded of his preconceptions, his knowledge and his ignorance, his technical training, and all the other characteristics which enter subtly into his appreciation of various bits of evidence. From the same set of sources, no two compilers will make quite the same summaries. In most years, the differences will be slight in comparison with the similarities; but in the years when business conditions as seen by contemporaries are confused, two compilers may get appreciably different impressions concerning the situation as a whole.

Perhaps the gravest danger lurking in the statistical treatment of social problems is that, once data have been compiled into neatly published tables, the figures gain a pontifical authority over many minds. Field statisticians who provide the original data usually retain a prudent skepticism concerning the representative value of the precise-seeming results toward which they have contributed. But "arm-chair statisticians," who have never filled in a questionnaire from interviews, deciphered a factory payroll, audited the accounts of a business enterprise, or assessed the value of a stock of merchandise, are prone to put unmerited confidence in tables they wish to analyze. Business annals have not yet won undeserved credit. But it is not premature to point out that the crisp phrases, in which a compiler of annals sets down his conclusions for country after country and year after year, are as much subject to a margin of error as are

statistical summaries. The compiler, like the statistical field worker, is sure that the width of this margin varies from entry to entry; but, again like the field statistician, he cannot feel much confidence in his own estimate of his probable error.

2. A Comparison of Business Annals and Business Indexes.

Fortunately, there is a way of testing two samples of the National Bureau's annals objectively. As seen in the preceding chapter, we have statistical indexes of business conditions in the United States and England which cover considerable periods. If these series deserve their name, the fluctuations which they show in economic activity and the business changes which our annals describe may be expected to run similar courses.

While Dr. Thorp and his assistants have made some use of statistical tables in compiling their annals, and while the writers whose observations constitute their sources have done likewise, it is by no means a foregone conclusion that the annals and the indexes of business activity will agree closely. For the data used in making the indexes cover a much narrower range of economic activities than are represented in the annual business reviews of such sources as consular reports, the London *Economist,* Raffalovich's *Marché Financier,* or the *Financial Review.* Moreover, in so far as consuls, or editors, or our own compilers have used statistics in drawing their conclusions, they have used the data in unadjusted, or but slightly altered form. The statisticians who make business indexes, on the other hand, subject their data to the elaborate series of transformations described in Chapter III. They compute and eliminate secular trends; often they eliminate also seasonal variations; in some cases they seek to eliminate the effects of price fluctuations. When they are combining several series, they may reduce the fluctuations of each to units of its standard deviation, and "weight" their averages as best they can. As a final step they often "smooth" their curves. All these operations are quite different from those which a financial editor performs when he passes through his mind reports from many cities and many industries, and sets down his broad conclusion concerning the course of business as a whole. The statistical operations are more objective and more precise; but they deal with more limited data, and deal with them in a more circumscribed and mechanical fashion.

To all acquainted with the making of the two types of summaries, it will be clear that a comparison between the annals of business and the statistical indexes of business activity is quite as much a test of the latter as of the former. The makers of the statistical indexes are usually careful to point out the limitations of their results, and eager to compare them with the results of other investigations. They recognize (1) that the original data are subject to varying margins of error; (2) that the technical methods of eliminating secular trends, seasonal fluctuations, and the effects of price variations are far from perfect; (3) that the residuals left in time series by these eliminations contain not merely the cyclical fluctuations, but also the effects of random factors peculiar to the series used. Even if a statistician had relatively abundant raw materials to work up, he would not claim that his results formed a strictly accurate record of changes in business conditions. In his eyes the best results he can get remain approximations, limited by the errors of the underlying data and the uncertainties of his technical methods.

But the most serious limitation is that the statistician who seeks to cover a considerable period can find but few time series fit for his purpose. The indexes of general business or volume of trade which run back of the great war must be made on one of two plans. Either they must be records of a single type of activity—like Mr. Carl Snyder's "clearings index of business"—or they must be made by averaging the fluctuations of groups of series which themselves change from time to time—like the American Telephone and Telegraph Company's "index of general business conditions," or Professor Warren M. Persons' "index of trade."

Now, no single type of transactions—not even such an inclusive type as the volume of checks cleared in all reporting towns outside of New York—can be taken to represent all the important phases of business activity. The payments made by check in the towns which have no clearing houses, and the payments made in coin and paper money may undergo fluctuations which differ in amplitude and timing from the fluctuations of clearings. That is merely a doubt concerning the faithfulness with which clearings represent changes in total payments. Far more important is the certainty that the volume of payments made by check within a given period undergoes fluctuations materially different from the fluctuations which are taking place in the volume of goods produced, shipped, or consumed, and different

from the fluctuations in employment, the disbursing of income, and the purchasing of consumers' goods. Yet the latter processes are quite as much a part of business as is paying bills by check.

The indexes made by averaging the fluctuations of several series represent a wider range of activities. But the activities which can be included are those for which a statistical record happens to have been made for a relatively long period—not the activities which a statistician would choose were he planning an index. Moreover, the changes in the lists of series which are available for successive decades raise grave questions about the comparability of the results for the earlier and the later years covered. Finally, there are puzzling questions about the interpretation of a composite made by averaging the fluctuations of series so different as (say) price indexes, values of goods imported, and tons of pig iron produced.

What we have in our business annals and our indexes of general business conditions, then, are different approaches to the problem of recording the fluctuations of economic activities—approaches each of which has its uncertainties as well as its merits. We cannot expect them to agree perfectly. When they disagree we cannot say that the discrepancy necessarily means error in one or all; it may mean merely that the different activities reflected by the various approaches really did not change in quite the same way. But if we find a general consilience among the results we shall feel increased confidence in the reliability of both approaches, and may regard the occasional discrepancies as presenting genuine problems from the study of which fresh knowledge may be gained.

The charts which follow offer as graphic a comparison as can well be made between our annals and the leading American and British indexes of general trade which cover considerable periods. In the column for each year is entered a brief characterization of business conditions drawn from the annals, and above are plotted the index curves.[1] The curves show cyclical fluctuations above and below the moving base traced by the monthly ordinates of the secular trends of

[1] For the methods followed in making the two American indexes used in Chart 21, see M. C. Rorty, "The Statistical Control of Business Activities," *Harvard Business Review,* January, 1923, vol. 1, pp. 154-166, and Carl Snyder, "A New Clearings Index of Business for Fifty Years," *Journal of the American Statistical Association,* September, 1924, vol. xix, pp. 329-335.

For the recent items in the two series, we are indebted respectively to Mr. Seymour L. Andrew, Chief Statistician of the American Telephone and Telegraph Company, and to Mr. Snyder of the Federal Reserve Bank of New York.

CHART 21. Business Fluctuations in the United States, as shown by the Annals and by Two Statistical Indexes, 1875-1925.

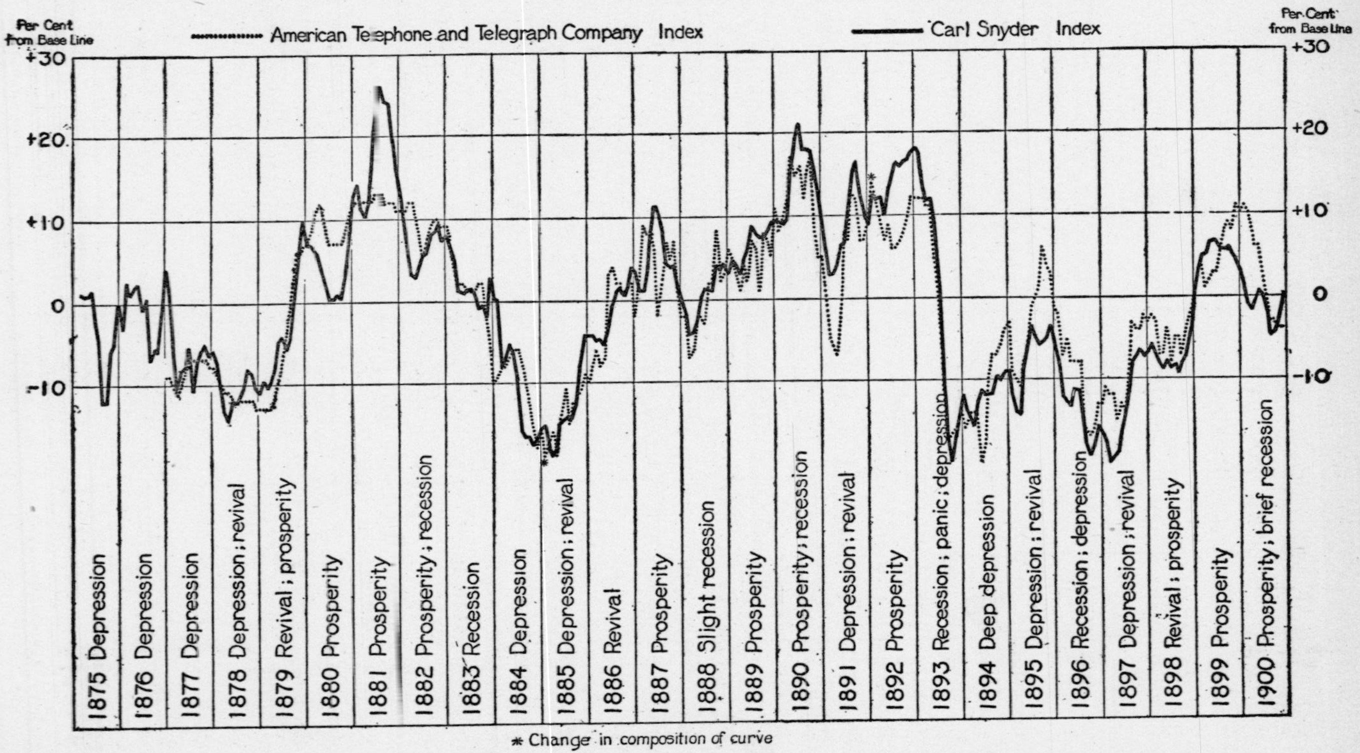

CHART 21. Business Fluctuations in the United States, as shown by the Annals and by Two Statistical Indexes, 1875-1925.—(*Continued*)

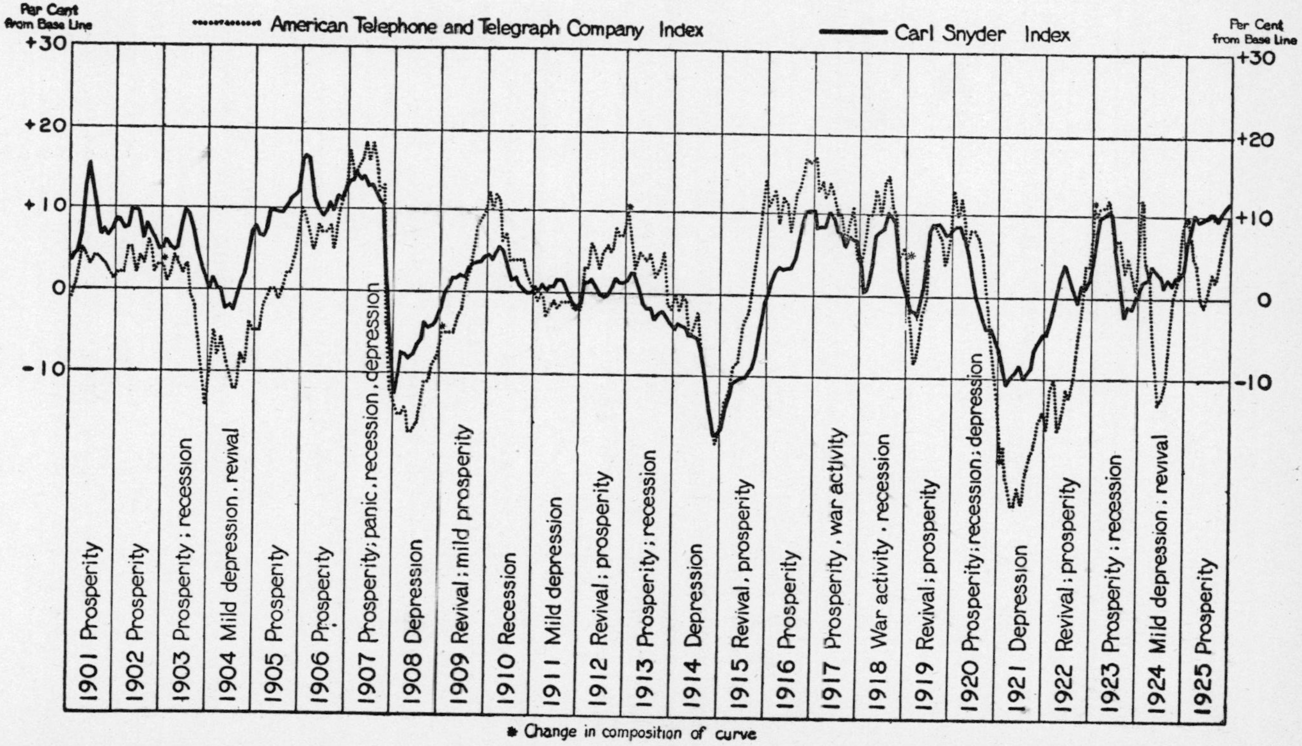

the time series used (corrected when necessary for seasonal variations). Since these ordinates are assigned the value of zero or 100 in the computations, they fall in the chart upon a horizontal line, which may be called the base.

In studying the charts, we must bear in mind that they do not do full justice either to the statistical method of presenting changes in business or to the annals. It is a commonplace that no statistical average represents adequately the array of data from which it is computed. Just so, the catchwords used to summarize the annals do not represent adequately Dr. Thorp's records. Much more than the charts show can be learned by examining the series combined to make the indexes of business conditions, and by reading the fuller form of the annals. In confining our comparison to the most abstract and symbolic summaries of the two sets of materials, we are imposing a severe test of conformity.

On the American chart the correspondence between the annals and the two statistical indexes is very close. Indeed, there are no serious discrepancies. To be more specific, the annals show 13 business recessions, mild or severe, between 1875 and 1924. Every one of these recessions is marked in both of the statistical indexes by a decline in the curve. These declines are slight in the recessions which the annals describe as mild, and abrupt in the recessions which the annals (in their fuller form) describe as crises or panics.[2] Further, the two curves give joint evidence of no recessions other than those mentioned by the annals. Similarly with other phases of the successive cycles. When the annals report revivals the curves ascend; when the annals report prosperity the curves fluctuate on levels decidedly higher than in the preceding or following depressions; when the annals report depressions the curves are relatively low.

The chief difference between the two records is that the annals show but vaguely and irregularly the degrees of prosperity and depression attained in successive cycles, whereas the curves necessarily deviate from the horizontal base by definite distances. Finally, there are indications in the American chart that business commentators are influenced in their use of the terms prosperity and depression by recent experience. From such subjective waverings, the statistical indexes are exempt. But this point comes out more clearly in the British chart, and will be discussed in that connection.

[2] On the use of these three terms in the annals to suggest the varying character of the transitions from prosperity to depression, see below, section iii, 4, "Crises" and "Recessions."

For opportunity to compare the British annals with a British index, the National Bureau is indebted to Dr. Dorothy Swaine Thomas, who generously put at our disposal before publication a series showing changes in business conditions from 1855 to 1913 by quarters.[3] This index, like the American Telephone and Telegraph Company's index for the United States, is a composite made from a list of series which reflect various types of economic activity. Since these materials have grown more abundant with the years, Dr. Thomas' index represents British business as a whole more faithfully in the later decades than in the earlier ones. But of course the introduction of a new series with a numerical value different from the average of the other components of the index produces changes which may not correspond with the changes in business conditions.

On the whole, the correspondence between the British annals and the British index is close, though not so close as in the American comparison. Dr. Thomas' curve usually rises when the annals report revival, stands high when the annals report prosperity, sinks when the annals report recession, and runs on a low level when the annals report depression. But there are exceptions to the rule which require comment.

(1) Judging from the curve, one would expect the annals to report a recession of British business in 1860-61. These years present an unusually mixed state of affairs. As a result of the American Civil War, the cotton textile industry suffered severely from scarcity of raw material. But reports from other trades do not indicate that there was a general recession of activity. On the contrary, most industries seem to have been very active. In the fuller form of the annals these facts are succinctly stated. For his two-word summary Dr. Thorp could find no phrase which seemed more accurate than "uneven prosperity," a phrase which he uses in all cases when most industries are thriving, but one or more important trades are depressed by special circumstances. The statistics available to Dr. Thomas for the 1860's are data in which the cotton industry counts heavily. Hence her curve drops abruptly. Most of the other English series covering these years which the National Bureau has collected confirm the index rather than the business commentators. In our later statistical work we shall have to recognize the cycles which the consensus of statistical evidence shows. But it would be conceal-

[3] See "An Index of British Business Cycles," by Dorothy S. Thomas, *Journal of the American Statistical Association,* March, 1926, vol. xxi, pp. 60-63.

CHART 22. Business Fluctuations in England, as shown by the Annals and Dr. Dorothy S. Thomas' "Quarterly Index of British Cycles," 1855-1914.

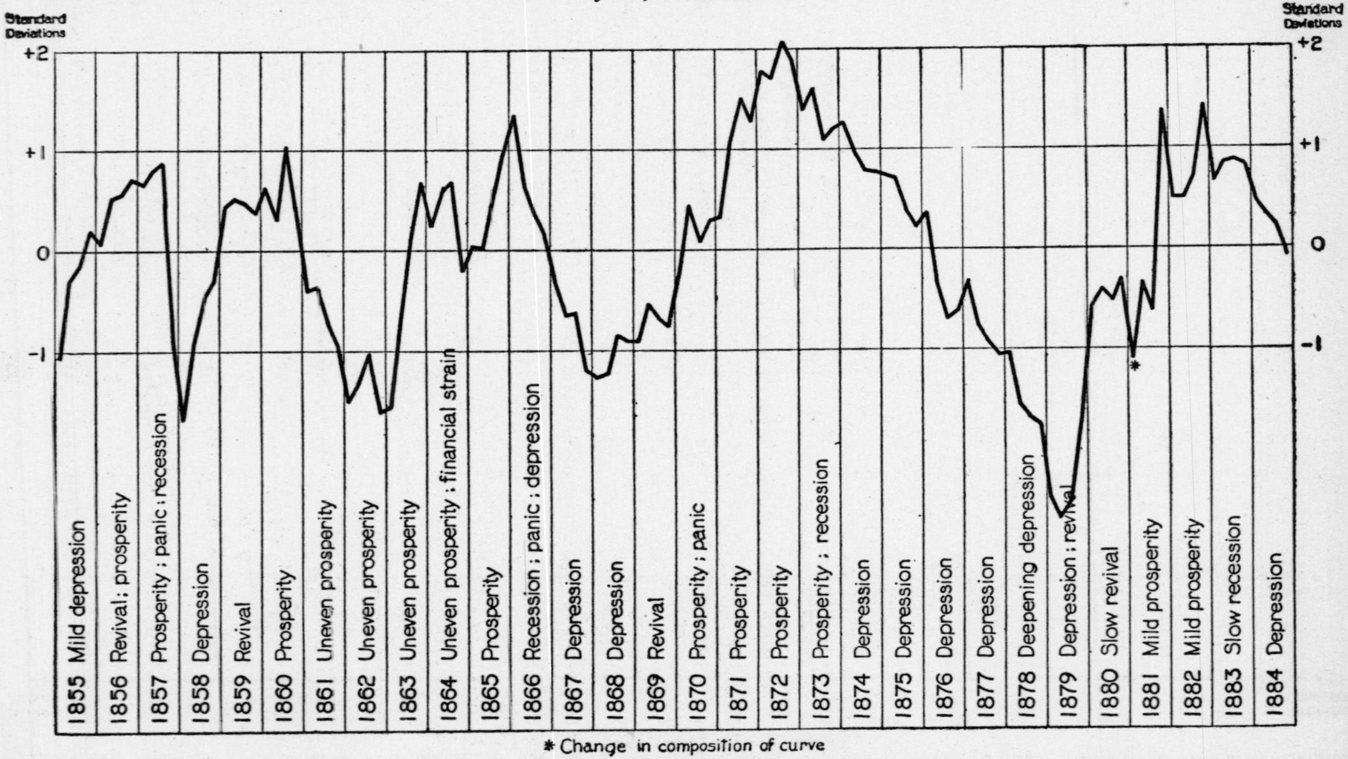

CHART 22. Business Fluctuations in England, as shown by the Annals and Dr. Dorothy S. Thomas' "Quarterly Index of British Cycles," 1855-1914.—(*Continued*)

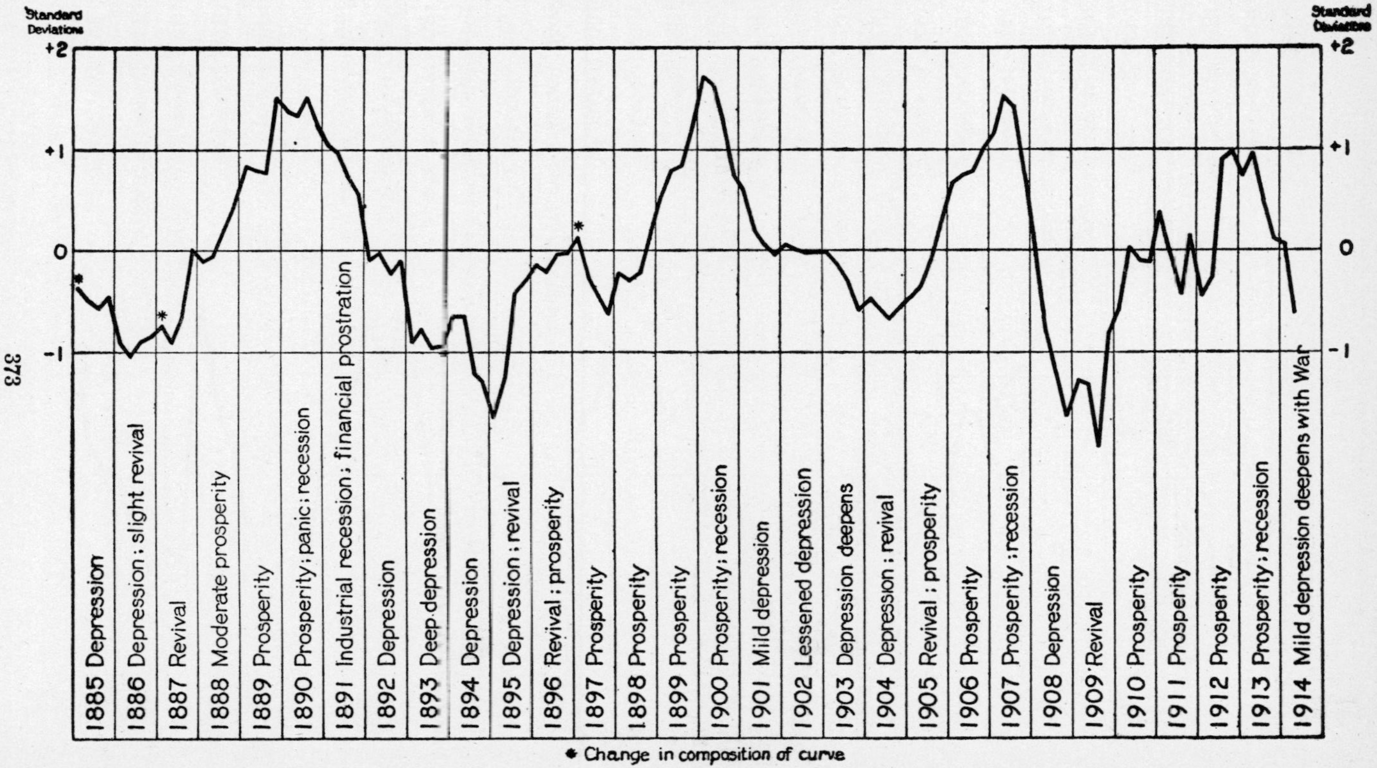

ing, rather than overcoming, a difficulty to make our interpretation of contemporary opinions fit the surviving figures.

(2) In 1874-75 the annals report depression while Dr. Thomas' curve, though declining, is still above the base line. In 1881, 1897-98 and 1910-11 the annals report "mild prosperity" or "prosperity," while Dr. Thomas' curve is slightly below or but slightly above the base line. Perhaps these differences between the statistical record and the annals are due in part to defects in the data at Dr. Thomas' disposal, or to the technical difficulties of eliminating secular trends. But it is probable that they indicate one of the defects characteristic of business annals. In judging current business conditions, everyone is influenced by comparisons with recent experience. When business has been notably good for several years, as it had been in England during the early 1870's, and then grows slack, a commentator will say that business is depressed, though the volume of trade still remains large. Similarly, after business has passed through a period of hard times, commentators are likely to hail as prosperity any substantial increase of activity. In short, men's judgments upon business conditions belong among the social phenomena which are influenced by business cycles. As a summary of current opinion about the state of trade, our annals reflect these subjective changes in the use of terms.

The preceding comparisons cover periods and countries in which business reporting is well developed. Presumably the annals for earlier years in the United States and England, and the annals for countries with a less integrated organization, contain a wider margin of error. But usually there is such a consensus of judgment among the sources as to leave little doubt about the general tenor of affairs. In years when differences of opinion appear among contemporary writers, Dr. Thorp has consulted every source available to him and has weighed the evidence with care. He has endeavored also to use the technical terms employed in characterizing different states of business as consistently as possible. Yet the results are subject to emendation, and readers who discover errors of any sort are urged to let the National Bureau of Economic Research benefit by their acumen.

Despite the difficulties dwelt upon in the preceding chapter, the most satisfactory materials for studying business cycles are statistical data—not mere business indexes, like those shown in the preceding

charts, but series showing month by month the fluctuations of many types of economic activity. But we have found that the periods and the places for which such data can be had in abundance are few. Hence we have been forced to recognize that narrow limits of time and of space are drawn around the quantitative study of business fluctuations. We cannot trace back business cycles to their beginnings in any country of Europe by the aid of figures. Nor can we trace in figures the spread of business cycles to countries which are just beginning to standardize their economic life on the European pattern. For the compilation of abundant statistics of business activities does not begin in any country until the business activities themselves have become highly organized. That comes later than business cycles.

According to the logic of the statistical method, this limitation of the number of cycles for which data have been preserved is most serious. The statistician's art, as practiced in the social sciences, consists in establishing generalizations about variable phenomena by the analysis of an array of cases. When his cases are few, no elaboration of technique can enable the statistician to generalize with security. Business cycles are both highly complex and highly variable phenomena, and statistical inferences concerning them must be taken as tentative until the number of cases available for analysis has grown decidedly larger than at present.

Under these circumstances it is well to learn all that we can from the annals of business. In countries like the United States and England these annals cover at least twice as many cycles as are covered by more than a few statistical series. In countries where statistics are in their infancy, the annals give us some insight into the course of developments. Precision, of course, cannot be had from descriptive accounts; but the annals speak in terms of more and less, they mark off turning points in business trends, they compare in general terms the contemporary fortunes of different countries. Taken, not as a rival, but as a supplement of statistical analysis, an attempt to find the characteristics of business cycles as shown by the longer and wider record of the annals has its value. Indeed, as was said near the close of the preceding chapter, there are certain fundamental problems concerning business cycles which can be answered more certainly by studying the annals than by analyzing the statistics now available.

III. The Cyclical Character of Business Fluctuations.

1. The "Normal State of Trade" a Figment.

The broadest conclusion established by the long and wide experience covered by the annals is that there is no "normal state of trade." The phrase is common both in treatises upon economic theory and in the talk of business men. Yet the historical record shows no reality corresponding to this figment of the imagination.

If "normal" is interpreted to mean usual, prevailing, that which exists in the absence of grave "disturbing causes," the annals show that the only normal condition is a state of change—which is not what the phrase means to those who use it. From England in 1790 to China in 1925, from Sweden to Australia, the tables reveal incessant fluctuations. Frequently the word "prosperity" is used in the annals of some country for several years in succession. But "depression" occurs in series perhaps as often. And in a less condensed summary both of these catchwords would be qualified always, as they often are qualified even in these tables, by adjectives indicating that the prosperity or depression is waxing or waning.

If "normal" means, not that which usually does prevail, but that which we think should prevail, it is equally a figment—though one of a useful kind. There are good reasons for trying to decide what phase of business cycles is most conducive to social welfare; for seeking ways to make that phase last longer and to mitigate departures from it. But when such is the meaning in mind, a less ambiguous word than "normal" should be used.

Of course, the economic theorist's "normal state," that which corresponds to the conditions assumed for purposes of analysis, is not to be looked for in an historical record. Nor can we take for granted the existence of a moving "normal state of trade," of such a nature that departures from it tend to correct themselves. That idea, if needed, can be less ambiguously expressed in terms of economic equilibria.

An additional source of confusion and therefore an additional reason for avoiding the word is supplied by the slipshod practice of business-cycle statisticians, who sometimes write "normal" when they mean a long-period average, and sometimes write "normal" when they mean the course marked by the ordinates of a secular trend.

2. Use of the Term "Cycles."

While the annals show that business is subject to continual fluctuations, they also show that in no country are the alternations of expansion and contraction highly regular. Is it justifiable, then, to speak of these fluctuations as business "cycles"?

That of course is a question regarding the proper use of a technical term. In 1922, President John C. Merriam of the Carnegie Institution called "A Conference on Cycles," in which representatives of several sciences discussed the cyclical phenomena with which they deal. To prevent misunderstandings the conferees needed a definition of cycles applicable alike in meteorology, botany, geology, paleontology, astronomy, geography and economics. Subsequent discussion showed that the definition given by the first speaker, Dr. F. E. Clements, commended itself to the others.

> In general scientific use (said Dr. Clements) the word (cycle) denotes a recurrence of different phases of plus and minus departures, which are often susceptible of exact measurement. It has no necessary relation to a definite time interval, though this is frequently a characteristic of astronomical cycles. Apart from the familiar cycles of the day, the lunar month, and the year, the one best known is the sun-spot recurrence, to which the term cycle is almost universally applied. This furnishes convincing evidence that the significance of the term resides in the fact of recurrence rather than in that of the time interval, since the sun-spot cycle has varied in length from 7 to 17 years since 1788, while the minimum-maximum phase has ranged from 3 to 5 years and the maximum-minimum phase from 6 to 8 years since 1833. In consequence, it seems desirable to use cycle as the inclusive term for all recurrences that lend themselves to measurement, and period or periodicity for those with a definite time interval, recognizing, however, that there is no fixed line between the two.[1]

Now our annals show beyond doubt "a recurrence of different phases" in business activity, and these recurrences "lend themselves to measurement." Hence we have ample warrant in the usages of other sciences than economics for applying the term "cycles" to

[1] "Report of a Conference on Cycles," *The Geographical Review*, Special Supplement, October, 1923, vol. xiii, pp. 657, 658.

business fluctuations. But the term "periodicity" we should not use with reference to business cycles, or with reference to crises. For the time intervals between crises are far from regular. They vary, as will appear presently, even more than the length of sun-spot cycles.

3. The Phases of Business Cycles.

The different phases which recur in business activity are sometimes treated as only two—depression and prosperity. More often there are said to be three phases which recur in the order prosperity, crisis, depression.[1] But if the transition from prosperity to depression is recognized as a separate phase, it seems logical to give similar recognition to the transition from depression to prosperity. Then we have a four-phase cycle of prosperity, crisis, depression, and revival.[2] Professor Warren M. Persons goes further still. By dividing the transition from prosperity to depression into "financial strain" and "industrial crisis," he gets five phases.[3]

This process of subdivision can be carried further indefinitely as statistics with brief time intervals become more abundant. And as knowledge of the subject grows and its practical applications become more important, there may be call for such refinements. As matters stand, however, four phases satisfy the needs of systematic inquiry. The separation of the phase of "financial strain" from that of "industrial crisis" rests on logical quite as much as upon chronological grounds, and is somewhat confusing in a cycle of recurrence in time. Cases will be cited presently of financial strain occurring at other stages of the cycle than the transition from prosperity to depression, and industrial reactions frequently occur when it is difficult to find any trace of preceding financial strain, for example, in the United States in 1923. But we are trenching upon a topic which requires separate treatment.

4. "Crises" and "Recessions."

Two quite distinct conceptions of business crises are current in recent books. Professor Aftalion, for example, defines the crisis as

[1] Compare for example, Dr. E. H. Vogel's description of a cycle, *Die Theorie des volkswirtschaftlichen Entwickelungsprozesses und das Krisenproblem*, Vienna, 1917, pp. 31, 32.

[2] These four phases were recognized and separately described as long ago as 1867 by John Mills, "On Credit Cycles, and the Origin of Commercial Panics," *Transactions of the Manchester Statistical Society*, 1867-68, pp. 5-40.

[3] See Professor Persons' numerous articles in the *Review of Economic Statistics*, and his *Measuring and Forecasting General Business Conditions*, New York, 1920, p. 34.

"the point of intersection . . . at which prosperity passes over into depression." [1] Professor Bouniatian, to give a corresponding example of the second usage, applies the term "to an organic disturbance of economic life, bringing upon a large number of enterprisers loss of fortune and income or complete economic ruin." [2]

From this difference of definition there follow differences in the lists of crises recognized in various books, and hence differences in the average intervals asserted to lie between crises. Professor Lescure, who antedated Aftalion in defining crisis as the point of intersection between prosperity and depression, includes the crisis of 1913 in his historical section. But Bouniatian admits no crisis between 1907 and 1920, and quite consistently; for, as Lescure himself explains, there was no epidemic of bankruptcies in 1913.[3] Tugan-Baranovski goes even further than Bouniatian in stressing the violence of crises, and consequently in shortening his list of crisis dates. A crisis "breaks out like a tempest" in the midst of prosperity, "bringing bankruptcies, unemployment, misery, etc." With this conception in mind, he quite rightly says that England escaped a crisis in 1873, in 1882, in 1890, in 1900 and in 1907—though the "industrial cycle" shows itself in the evolution of English business in these later times "with the same neatness and clarity as before." [4]

Which of these two conceptions of the crisis fits better in a discussion of business cycles is easy to decide. What concerns such a discussion is the recurrence of certain phases of business activity. The transition from prosperity to depression is one of the regularly recurring phases, whether it is marked by "an organic disturbance of economic life," in Bouniatian's phrase, or whether financial strain is conspicuous by its absence.

But while there is no doubt about the reality of these transitions, there is grave doubt whether the word crisis should be retained to describe them. For with that word there is associated in the public mind, as in the minds of writers like Bouniatian and Tugan-Baranovski, the idea of financial strain. When such strain is scarcely perceptible, it is confusing to call the transition a crisis. Close study of the annals shows that transitions free from strain are frequent—

[1] Albert Aftalion, *Les Crises Périodiques de Surproduction,* Paris, 1913, vol. i, Preface, p. vi.

[2] Mentor Bouniatian, *Les Crises Économiques,* Paris, 1922, p. 31.

[3] Lescure, *Des Crises Générales et Périodiques de Surproduction,* 3rd ed., Paris, 1923, pp. 2 and 238-253; Bouniatian, as cited above, pp. 43, 44.

[4] Michel Tugan-Baranovski, *Les Crises Industrielles en Angleterre,* Paris, 1913, pp. 34, 150, 152, 166, 167, 174.

perhaps more frequent than violent transitions. And there are cheering indications that the preponderance of mild transitions is growing greater.

To make the confusion worse, the annals report numerous cases of financial strain, not at the moment when prosperity is passing into depression, but in other phases of the cycle. "Financial stringency" and "bourse panics" are common phenomena in "booms," often occurring a year or two before the phase of expansion in general business ends Less remembered, but not less important, are the cases of financial strain coming in periods of depression. To cite a dozen examples, the annals make such reports for France in 1861, Germany in 1877, England in 1878, Argentina in 1891, Australia and Russia in 1892, Italy and the Netherlands in 1893, the United States in 1896 (as well as in 1819 and 1884), South Africa in 1898, Japan in 1901, and China in 1912. Often the sources from which the annals are drawn use the words "crisis" or "panic" in describing these episodes of depression, and sometimes they use "crisis" as equivalent to depression itself.

"Crisis," then, is a poor term to use in describing one of the four phases of business cycles. If it is to be retained, it must be defined in the colorless fashion of Lescure and Aftalion—as the mere point of intersection between prosperity and depression. But sad experience shows how much misunderstanding comes from the effort to use familiar words in new technical senses. Scientific writers can hardly expect that readers will purge their minds of old associations and form new ones at a terminologist's bidding.

One remedy for the ambiguity of "crisis" is to apply a qualifying adjective whenever the word is used. Thus Mr. Joseph Kitchin distinguishes between major and minor crises. But his major crises are in some cases such mild transitions that many writers refuse to call them crises at all. Such is the case with the American crises of 1882 and 1899 (1900 is a better date), and the English crisis of 1913, all of which Mr. Kitchin labels "major."[5] Thus his conception of a major crisis is even more confusing to non-technical readers than the use of the unqualified term. If the ambiguity is to be remedied by applying adjectives, it seems best to use a pair that bear directly upon the ambiguous point. Thus the common expressions "mild crisis" and "severe crisis" are clear in intent and safe

[5] See the "Dates of Major Crises" in Mr. Kitchin's paper, "Cycles and Trends in Economic Factors," *Review of Economic Statistics*, January, 1923, Prel. vol. v, pp. 10-16.

to use in descriptive work, such as business annals, provided there are not too many cases on the borderline between mildness and severity.

But no set of adjectives can make "crisis" a suitable name for the fourth phase of business cycles. Hardly can one say "depression, revival, prosperity, mild or severe crisis." The choice lies between retaining "crisis" defined in an unfamiliar way, or replacing it by some word corresponding to "revival," which is used to designate the upward turn of the cycle. This second alternative seems the lesser evil, especially in view of the fact that our theoretical and practical interests lie increasingly in those mild transitions from prosperity to depression which have been little attended to by theorists.

In this discussion, accordingly, business cycles are treated as having four phases—depression, revival, prosperity and recession. The word "crisis" is not dropped, but is used like the words "panic" or "boom" to indicate degrees of intensity. Every business cycle includes a phase of recession; this recession may or may not be marked by a crisis; the crisis, if there is one, may or may not degenerate into a panic. All the old and most of the recent books on the subject deal chiefly with crises, panics and severe depressions; these annals endeavor to show also the mild recessions and the periods of dull business.

We have, indeed, gone far—we hope not too far—in calling attention to the mild recessions. Our aim has been to include all cases in which the evidence indicates a general slackening of activity, even though the slackening lasted but a few months, and did not reach grave proportions. Cases in point may be found in the American annals for 1888, 1900 and 1923. Other illustrations are Italy in 1900, England in 1803 and 1854, and the brief reaction in the majority of our 17 countries after the Armistice of 1918. On the other hand, we have tried not to include cases in which only a few branches of business suffered a setback—such as the English case of 1860-61 already referred to, or the financial difficulties caused in London by the outbreak of war between France and Prussia in 1870.

5. "Prosperity" and "Depression."

A somewhat different criticism may be made of the terms used for two other phases of business cycles. In comparing the annals with business indexes, we had occasion to note that the words "pros-

perity" and "depression" are themselves subject to cyclical fluctuations in meaning. Their significance is relative rather than fixed. The more active phase of a given cycle is called prosperous, and the less active phase is called depressed, though both phases may be very mild. We must not suppose that business conditions are almost identical in the prosperous phases of successive cycles, even in the same country—or in the depressed phases.

This relativity of meaning appeared in the review of business indexes in Chapter III, though little was said about it at the time. The crests of business cycles sometimes reach but a little way above the base lines of the index charts. On rare occasions they remain below these lines. The like is true, *mutatis mutandis,* of the troughs. Statistically, prosperity and depression are variables, distributed in a fairly regular fashion over a considerable range.[1]

Perhaps we might develop quantitative definitions for prosperity and depression by saying, for example, that business is prosperous when certain indexes have attained a given percentage height above their corrected trends. The time may come when that shift in practice will appear both feasible and desirable. Or we might substitute for the words in question other terms whose relativity of meaning is patent. For example, we might speak of the phase of business expansion and the phase of business contraction, or of the phase of rising and declining activity. Of course these two proposals are quite compatible with each other. But our business indexes are not yet sufficiently perfect, and they do not yet cover a sufficient range of times and places, to afford satisfactory measurements of degree of prosperity and depression. The second proposal presents no such difficulties, and is often followed in this discussion. Yet the misunderstandings to which the words in question may give rise seem scarcely grave enough to justify discarding them entirely. Few people are likely to think of prosperity and depression as definite states. When their application to business cycles involves a serious stretching of the vague popular usage, a reminder of their technical meaning may be sufficient safeguard.

6. The Uniformity and the Variability of Business Cycles.

Recurrence of depression, revival, prosperity and recession, time after time in land after land, may be the chief conclusion drawn from

[1] See Chapter III, section vi, 3 (3) "On Identifying Business Cycles by the Use of the Business Indexes," and (7) "The Amplitudes of Business Cycles."

the experience packed into our annals; but a second conclusion is that no two recurrences in all the array seem precisely alike. Business cycles differ in their duration as wholes and in the relative duration of their component phases; they differ in industrial and geographical scope; they differ in intensity; they differ in the features which attain prominence; they differ in the quickness and the uniformity with which they sweep from one country to another.

This mixture of uniformity and variability in business cycles may seem disconcerting when stated so baldly. But we confront a similar mixture of fundamental similarity and detailed differences when we visualize men's faces, or consider their characters, or study any social phenomena. In all such cases, variability presents conceptual difficulties not to be glossed over, and difficulties of explanation not surmounted as yet. But uncounted ages ago men found that they could think of pines despite difference in the size, shape, location, color, roughness, and hardness of particular specimens; they could think of trees despite the differences among pines, maples and palms, and the difficulty of delimiting trees from shrubs. And within the past hundred years men have developed a technique for studying variations about a central tendency, a technique which reveals the existence of formerly unsuspected uniformities among variations themselves.

Differences among business cycles, then, afford no reason for doubting that these cycles constitute a valid species of phenomena. But the existence of such differences should put us on our guard against using concepts and methods of analysis appropriate only in work where differences among individuals of a given species either do not exist or can be precisely defined (as in geometry), or are not significant for the problems under consideration (as in certain branches of physics and chemistry). The student of business cycles should picture their characteristic differences as clearly as may be, measure them with what precision he can, and find how these differences are distributed around their central tendencies. While the annals are not quantitative in form, they can be used to some extent in treating this statistical problem.

IV. The Duration of Business Cycles.

1. Current Estimates of Average Length.

The differences among business cycles which have attracted most attention are differences in duration. Quite naturally, the discoverers

of the recurrence overstressed its uniformity in this respect as in others. Influenced by the dominant type of economic theory, these discoverers thought of a "normal" cycle and so simplified their problem—a practice still common. To cite an extreme example: in 1867 John Mills described the "credit cycle" as lasting ten years—three years of declining trade, three years of increasing trade, three years of over-excited trade, and one year of crisis.[1] Even the early statistical workers yielded to the lure of "normality." They were eager to establish the "periodicity of crises," which was suggested by such crisis dates as 1815, 1825, 1836, 1847, 1857 and 1866. This desire warped their selection and treatment of data. Jevons had an admirably candid mind; yet in 1875, when the sun-spot cycle was supposed to last 11.1 years, he was able to get from Thorold Rogers' *History of Agriculture and Prices in England* a period of 11 years in price fluctuations, and when the sun-spot cycle was revised to 10.45 years he was able to make the average interval between English crises 10.466 years.[2] To get this later result, Jevons purposely left out from his list of crises "a great commercial collapse in 1810-11 (which will not fit into the decennial series)"; he also omitted the crisis of 1873, and inserted a crisis in 1878, which other writers do not find.[3]

Jevons' way of reckoning the length of cycles by the intervals between crises, and of counting as crises periods of financial strain coming after booms, or recessions followed by long depressions, is still common among theoretical writers. The results they get are not in close agreement. Tugan-Baranovski takes 7 to 11 years as the limits of variation in the length of cycles and 10 years as the average duration. Bouniatian says that "under normal conditions" cycles last from 9 to 11 years, but adds that there is "a tendency toward a normal period of about 10 years." Cassel takes 1873, 1882, 1890, 1900, and 1907 as crisis years in Europe, and 1873, 1882, 1893, 1903, and 1907 as crisis years in the United States. Cassel himself strikes no average, but his dates give limits of 4 to 11 years and an average of 8½ years. Lavington accepts 8 years as the average duration.

[1] "On Credit Cycles and the Origin of Commercial Panics," *Transactions of the Manchester Statistical Society,* 1867–68, pp. 5-40. Compare the diagram of a cycle which Jevons gives in his *Primer of Political Economy,* New York, 1882, p. 121.

[2] Jevons withdrew his first paper from publication when he discovered "that periods of 3, 5, 7, 9, or even 13 years would agree with Professor Rogers' data just as well as a period of 11 years." See his *Investigations in Currency and Finance,* London, 1884, pp. 207, 225.

[3] See the three papers on crises reprinted in Jevons' *Investigations in Currency and Finance,* especially pp. 200-203, 225, 233.

Slightly different is the method of reckoning cycles by the intervals between depressions. Otto C. Lightner records 18 depressions in American business from 1808 to 1921, not counting "minor" cases, with intervals ranging from 3 to 12 years and averaging 6⅔ years. George H. Hull, denying that depressions are periodic, counts 17 "industrial crises" in the United States from 1814 to 1907. His dates differ somewhat from Lightner's, having intervals ranging from 1 to 11 years, and averaging a little less than 6 years apart.

With these results may be given two others of the same order of magnitude, but reached by quite different methods. Pigou, using British unemployment returns and measuring intervals between both the crests and the troughs of the industrial waves, gets a trifle less than 8 years as his average length. Henry L. Moore also gets 8 years as the standard length both of "generating" and of "derived economic cycles," but gets it from periodogram analysis of time-series.[4]

Other statistical workers have recently reached quite different conclusions. Thus Professor W. L. Crum made a periodogram analysis of monthly interest rates upon commercial paper in New York from 1866 to 1922 and found (somewhat doubtful) evidence of a period of 39-40 months in their fluctuations. At the same time Mr. Joseph Kitchin, after analyzing bank clearings, interest rates, and wholesale prices in Great Britain and the United States from 1890 to 1922, suggested that the cyclical fluctuations of trade are composed of minor cycles averaging 40 months in length, and major cycles, which are aggregates of two or less often, of three minor cycles.[5] Since the publication of these two papers in January, 1923, "the 40-month cycle" has enjoyed a considerable vogue among statisticians. Forty months is also the median value of the observations upon the duration of American cycles in 1878-1923, derived in Chapter III from five indexes of business conditions, while the mean value is 42 months.

[4] See M. Tugan-Baranovski, *Les Crises Industrielles en Angleterre,* 1913, pp. 247, 248; M. Bouniatian, *Les Crises Économiques,* 1922, p. 42; G. Cassel, *The Theory of Social Economy,* 1924, p. 508; A. Aftalion, *Les Crises Périodiques de Surproduction,* 1913, vol. i, pp. 8-14; F. Lavington, *The Trade Cycle,* 1922, p. 14; O. C. Lightner, *History of Business Depressions,* 1922, table of contents; G. H. Hull, *Industrial Depressions,* 1911, pp. 54-57, and the chronological table, pp. 50, 51; A. C. Pigou, *The Economics of Welfare,* 1920, p. 804; Henry L. Moore, *Generating Economic Cycles,* 1923, pp. 15, 64.

[5] See W. L. Crum, "Cycles of Rates on Commercial Paper," *Review of Economic Statistics,* January, 1923, preliminary vol. v, pp. 17-28; Joseph Kitchin, "Cycles and Trends in Economic Factors," the same, pp. 10-16.

2. Measurements Based upon the Annals.

It is not necessary to examine narrowly the discrepancies among the results obtained by measuring the intervals between years of crisis or years of depression. They run back partly to differences in the countries and the periods covered, and partly to differences of opinion concerning the severity which entitles a particular disturbance to be called a true crisis or depression. Granted each author his own conception of what constitutes a cycle, his measurements are presumably correct for the land and period covered. By using the present annals, anyone so disposed might validate, and anyone so disposed might question any of the averages and limits of variations which have been derived in this way.

But anyone who reads the annals closely, whatever the definition of crisis in his mind, will see that there is grave question regarding the unity of many of the 6-, or 8-, or 10-year cycles. Take as the simplest example Professor Cassel's list of crisis years in the United States: 1873, 1882, 1893, 1903 and 1907. Perhaps one may argue that the annals justify these dates from Cassel's viewpoint, though it is not clear why he should omit 1888 if he includes 1903. But the important point is that the cycle from 1882 to 1893 was punctuated by the recessions of 1888 and 1890, and that the cycle from 1893 to 1903 was punctuated by recessions both in 1896 and in 1900.

Now, the differences of opinion concerning the length of American cycles in this period turn less on the facts of business expansion and contraction than on what movements of expansion and contraction should be selected for treatment as business cycles. The older writers fastened upon the salient phenomena—severe crises and the rather long intervals between them—as requiring explanation. This tradition still rules in theoretical treatises. But as knowledge of business cycles grows, and as men seek to use this knowledge more effectively in interpreting current developments month by month, a more intensive treatment becomes both feasible and useful. Without denying the graver importance of the wider swings, we find ourselves involved much of the time in dealing with fluctuations of less amplitude, fluctuations which the theorists have passed over lightly. The same developments which make it wise to substitute the concept of recession for the concept of crisis make it wise to recognize the shorter segments into which the long swings are frequently divisible.

This change reduces the typical duration of American cycles to roughly one-half of the estimate commonest among theoretical writers.

By way of illustration, we may compile from the American annals a list of recessions in the United States since 1790. In this list the recessions are characterized by phrases which indicate their severity, and leading features. Financial troubles occurring in the middle of depressions are not counted as recessions, but cases of this sort which have commonly been listed as crises are noted in the table. In the early years the business fortunes of the northern states alone are followed; sometimes conditions were quite different in the agricultural south and west. Since the annals seldom permit a precise dating of recessions, the duration of successive cycles is reckoned to the nearest whole year.

TABLE 23

Business Recessions in the United States and Approximate Duration of Business Cycles, 1790–1925

		Duration of Cycles in Years
1796 *	Financial crisis, spring	
1802	Recession early in year	6
1807 *	Recession late in year	6
1812	Brief recession, June, War with England	5
1815 *	Crisis, March, following peace	3
1822	Mild recession, May	7
1825 *	Panic, autumn	3
1828	Recession, summer	3
1833	Recession, panic, autumn	5
1837 *	Panic, spring	4
1839 *	Panic, October	3
1845	Brief recession, May	6
1846	Mild recession early in year, War with Mexico	1
1847 *	Recession, financial panic, November	2
1853	Recession, last quarter	6
1857 *	Recession, late spring, panic in August	4
1860	Recession late in year, prospect of Civil War	3
1865	Recession, second quarter, close of Civil War	5
1870	Recession, January	5
1873 *	Violent panic, September	4
1882	Recession late in year, financial panic in 1884 *	9
1888	Slight recession, early in year	5
1890	Financial crisis, autumn	3
1893 *	Severe panic, May	2
1896	Recession early in year, financial stringency	3
1900	Brief and slight recession, spring	4
1903 *	Financial strain, spring	3
1907 *	Severe crisis, autumn	4
1910	Mild recession, January	2
1913 *	Recession, summer	3
1918	Recession after Armistice, November	5
1920 *	Severe crisis, May	2
1923	Mild recession, summer	3

* The dates thus marked show the commonly accepted crisis years. Other dates frequently listed are 1819, a case of financial strain in a business depression, and 1890. The "rich man's panic" of 1903 is omitted in some lists.

To show the usual way of reckoning the length of cycles, the commonly accepted dates of crises in the United States are marked with asterisks. Anyone who checks these dates against those given in other books will find different ways of counting; for example, 1837-1839 is sometimes put down as a single crisis. But, taking the dates as marked, we have 14 cycles between 1796 and 1920, ranging from about 2 years (1837-39) to about 16 years (1857-1873) in length, and averaging 8 6/7 years. We can raise this average by omitting or combining some of the crises counted here, or reduce it by counting some of the other recessions as crises. At best there is a considerable margin for admissible difference of opinion.

When we drop the effort to discriminate the degrees of severity among crises and count all recessions, this margin of uncertainty becomes narrower, though it does not vanish. It is easier to recognize a change of direction in business movements than it is to determine how serious a change for the worse has been. Yet, another compiler drawing off a list of recessions from the most detailed form of our annals might give a slightly different set of dates, and one who made a fresh set of annals from the original sources might increase these differences somewhat. The broad results, however, seem well assured.

Counting business cycles now as the intervals between recessions, noting the quarters in which the turns came, and reckoning to the nearest whole year, we get the following results:

1	cycle	about	1	year	long	(1845-46)
4	cycles	"	2	years	"	
10	"	"	3	"	"	
5	"	"	4	"	"	
6	"	"	5	"	"	
4	"	"	6	"	"	
1	"	"	7	"	"	(1815-1822)
0	"	"	8	"	"	
1	"	"	9	"	"	(1873-1882)

In all we have 32 cycles in 127 years, which yields an average length of not quite 4 years. The commonest length is about three years; and two-thirds of the cases fall within the limits of three to five years.

These results may be compared with similar summaries from the other country for which we have annals covering 136 years. The dates given in Bouniatian's list of English crises are starred to

show the conventional view of cycle chronology. His 16 dates mark off 15 cycles in the 127 years from 1793 to 1920—an average length of almost 8½ years. If 1913 be added to the list of crises and it seems to belong there quite as much as certain dates which Bouniatian admits as turning points unaccompanied by severe financial strain, there are 16 cycles, ranging in length from about 4 to about 13 years, and averaging not quite 8 years.

Of the cycles marked off by recessions, 22 are shown. Perhaps we should add recessions in 1814 after the first abdication of Napoleon, in 1861 when the American Civil War upset the cotton trade, in 1864 when financial strain was marked, in 1870 when the Franco-Prussian War brought confusion to the financial markets, in 1897 and 1911 when the rising tides of activity were checked. But in none of these cases does the evidence of contemporary business reports indicate a general slackening of trade. Even if these cases were counted, it would still appear that English business has experienced fewer recessions than American business during the same period of four generations. Hence English cycles have been longer on the average than American cycles. Taking the dates entered in the table we get an average duration of 5¾ years in England against 4 years in the United States.

But these averages are even less a guide to business forecasting in England than in America. It is difficult to find any regular order in the lengths of the successive cycles in either Table 23 or Table 24. When we tabulate the frequency of English cycles according to duration we find less concentration at the mode than in the corresponding American table. From 1793-1920 there were

2	cycles	about	2	years	long	(1829-31, and 1918-20)
1	"	"	3	"	"	(1807-10)
5	"	"	4	"	"	
2	"	"	5	"	"	
4	"	"	6	"	"	
2	"	"	7	"	"	
3	"	"	8	"	"	
1	"	"	9	"	"	(1873-83)
2	"	"	10	"	"	(1837-47, and 1890-1900)

Four-year cycles are most common in England, three-year cycles in the United States. One-half of the English cases are 4-6 years in

length, while two-thirds of the American cases are grouped at 3-5 years.

TABLE 24

BUSINESS RECESSIONS IN ENGLAND AND APPROXIMATE DURATION OF BUSINESS CYCLES, 1790–1925

		Duration of Cycles in years
1793	Recession, February, following financial pressure in 1792 *	
1797 *	Panic, February	4
1803	Recession, May, renewal of war	6
1807	Mild recession	4
1810 *	Severe crisis, July	3
1815 *	Crisis, autumn, following end of war	5
1819 *	Recession, early spring	4
1825 *	Recession, spring, followed by financial panic	6
1829	Recession, first quarter	4
1831	Recession	2
1837	Recession early in year, following financial panic in 1836 *	6
1847 *	Financial panic, April, recession, summer	10
1854	Recession, January, Crimean War	7
1857 *	Financial panic, November	4
1866 *	Severe financial crisis, first quarter, Overend-Gurney failure	8
1873 *	Recession late in year	8
1883	Slow recession, early in year, perhaps beginning in 1882 *	9
1890 *	Recession following financial crisis in November	8
1900 *	Recession, summer	10
1907 *	Recession, autumn, financial stringency	7
1913	Recession, last quarter	6
1918	Recession on Armistice, November	5
1920 *	Severe crisis, second quarter	2

* The dates thus marked show the crises recognized by Mentor Bouniatian, *Les Crises Économiques,* Paris, 1922, p. 43. Most authorities would include 1913, also, on the same grounds that lead Bouniatian to list crises in 1882 and 1900, although these years were not marked by severe financial strain.

On applying the same methods of analysis to the three other countries for which we have annals running back to the 1860's, 1850's, and 1840's, we find that in average duration their cycles are intermediate between the English and the American patterns. The average length works out as follows:

1838-1920—82 years

France, 15 cycles, average length 5½ years.

England, (1837-1920), 12 cycles, average length nearly 7 years.

United States, (1837-1920), 22 cycles, average length 3¾ years.

1848-1925—77 years

- Germany, 15 cycles, average length 5 years.
- England (1847-1920), 11 cycles, average length 6⅔ years.
- United States (1847-1923), 19 cycles, average length 4 years.

1866-1922—56 years

- Austria, 10 cycles, average length 5.6 years.
- England (1866-1920), 8 cycles, average length 6¾ years.
- United States (1865-1923), 15 cycles, average length not quite 4 years.

3. Frequency Distributions of the Measurements Based upon the Annals.

A systematic summary of our evidence concerning the duration of business cycles is provided by the following exhibits. Table 25 is a companion piece to Tables 23 and 24. It shows the dates of recessions in fifteen countries as accurately as Dr. Thorp can determine them from the annals, and shows also the approximate duration of successive cycles reckoned to the nearest whole year. Chart 23 is a graphic version of Tables 23, 24, and 25. It uses lines of varying length to show the duration of business cycles in each of our countries, in chronological order.

TABLE 25

Dates of Business Recessions in Fifteen Countries: Various Years to 1925

		Duration of Cycles in years
France		
1838		
1847	early	9
1854	March	7
1857	autumn	3
1860	autumn	3
1867	early	6
1870	July	3
1873	early	3
1876	early	3
1882	early	6
1890	early	8
1900	late summer	11
1908	early	7
1913	early summer	5
1918	November	5
1920	summer	2
Germany		
1848		
1857	autumn	9
1866	June	9
1870	July	4
1873	autumn	3
1878	early	4
1880	early	2
1882	summer	3
1890	early	8
1900	August	10
1904	summer	4
1907	summer	3
1913	summer	6
1918	November	5
1922	summer	4
1925	summer	3

TABLE 25—(*Continued*)

DATES OF BUSINESS RECESSIONS IN FIFTEEN COUNTRIES

Austria

		Duration of Cycles in years
1866		
1869	late	3
1873	summer	4
1884	early	11
1892	early	8
1894	early	2
1900	early	6
1908	early	8
1912	autumn	5
1918	October	6
1922	autumn	4

Russia

		Duration of Cycles in years
1891	early	
1899	third quarter	8
1904	February	5
1908	early	4
1914	early	6
1917	March	3
1923	October	7
1925	late	2

Sweden

		Duration of Cycles in years
1892	early	
1901	early	9
1907	late autumn	7
1913	autumn	6
1917	....	4
1920	summer	3

Netherlands

		Duration of Cycles in years
1891	early	
1901	early	10
1907	autumn	7
1913	late	6
1917	early	3
1920	autumn	4

Italy

		Duration of Cycles in years
1888	early	
1900	spring	12
1907	last quarter	8
1913	second half	6
1918	October	5
1920	early	1

Argentina

		Duration of Cycles in years
1890	first quarter	
1892	autumn	3
1900	early	7
1908	early	8
1911	early	3
1913	early	2
1920	December	8

Brazil

		Duration of Cycles in years
1889	November	
1896	early	6
1900	autumn	5
1907	autumn	7
1912	late	5
1918	November	6
1920	autumn	2
1924	second half	4

Canada

		Duration of Cycles in years
1888		
1893	early	5
1900	autumn	7
1907	autumn	7
1913	second half	6
1918	November	5
1920	autumn	2
1924	spring	4

South Africa

		Duration of Cycles in years
1890	September	
1895	autumn	5
1899	October	4
1903	early	3
1913	....	10
1918	late	5
1920	autumn	2

Australia

		Duration of Cycles in years
1890	January	
1901	January	11
1908	January	7
1913	January	5
1914	autumn	2
1920	November	6
1924	January	3

India

		Duration of Cycles in years
1889		
1896	summer	7
1900	summer	4
1907	autumn	7
1914	August	7
1918	November	4
1920	May	2

Japan

		Duration of Cycles in years
1890	January	
1894	August	5
1897	autumn	3
1905	September	8
1907	spring	2
1914	spring	7
1918	November	5
1920	March	1

China

		Duration of Cycles in years
1888		
1897	....	9
1900	May	3
1906	....	6
1910	....	4
1920	midyear	10

Chart 23. Approximate Duration of Business Cycles, arranged in Chronological Sequence.

White inset figures indicate approximate duration in years.

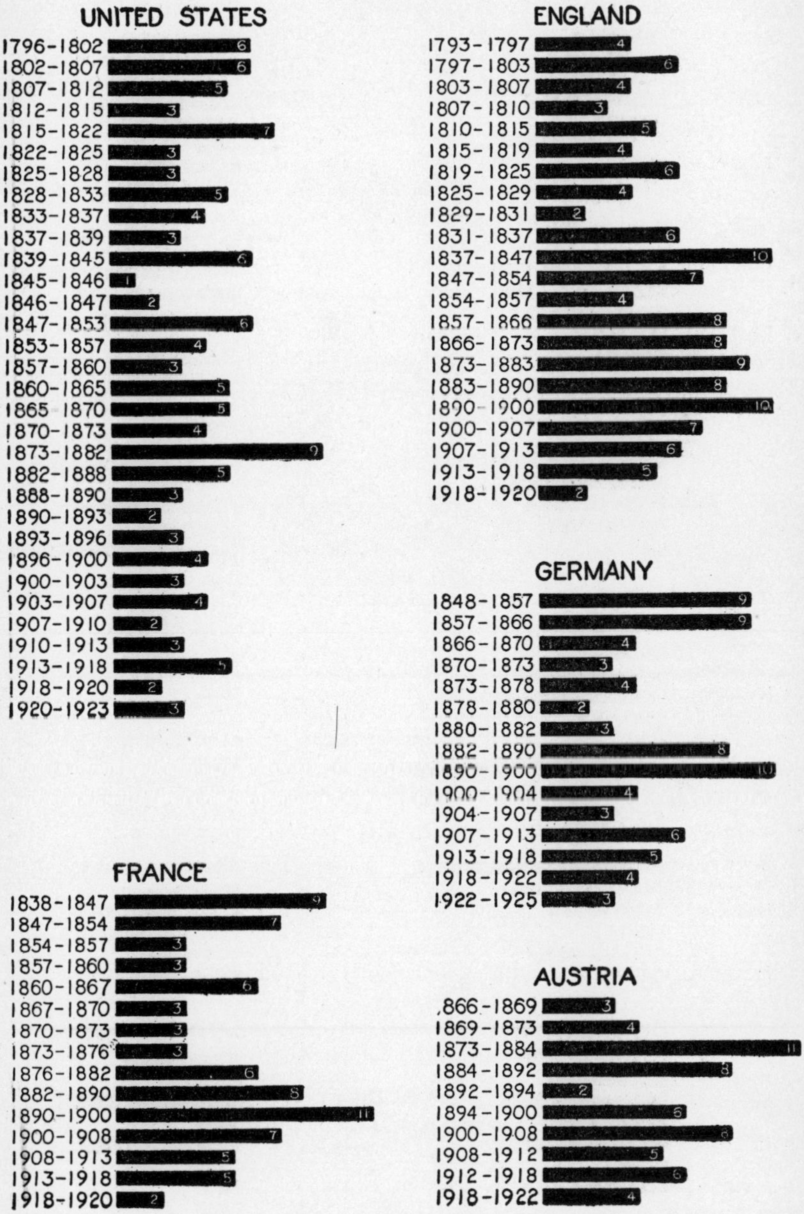

CHART 23. Approximate Duration of Business Cycles, arranged in Chronological Sequence—*Continued.*

White inset figures indicate approximate duration in years.

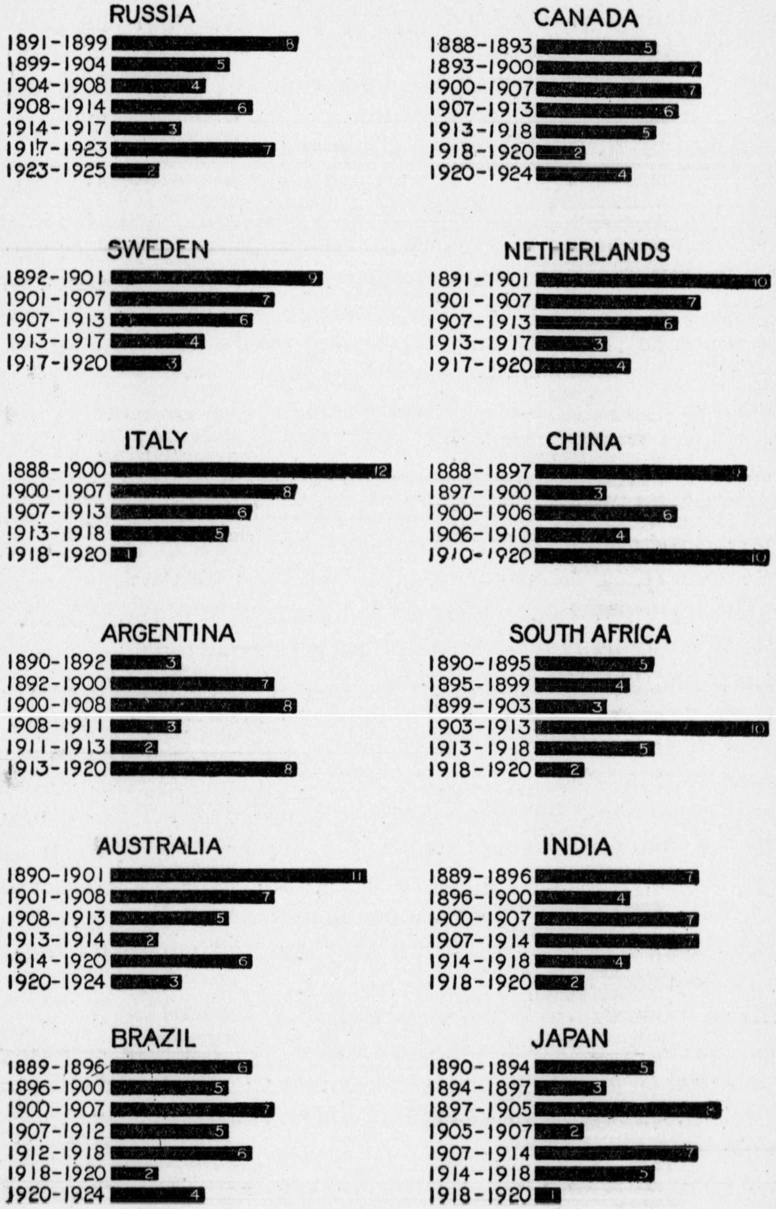

We can treat the observations upon the duration of business cycles assembled in this table and chart as the data of an historical inquiry, or as the data of a theoretical problem. In the first case we ask: What has been the duration of business cycles in the countries and during the periods for which we have annals? In the second case we ask: What expectations regarding the duration of business cycles are justified by the sample observations in hand?

As historical data, our observations probably contain inaccuracies. Conceiving a business recession as a decline in economic activity which follows a period of expansion and spreads over most of a country's industries, we have sought to find and date every recession which occurred in certain countries during certain periods. On the basis of these recession dates, we have measured the duration of successive cycles to the nearest whole year. Finally, we have struck averages from these measurements. Mistakes may have occurred in any of these steps. We may have omitted some recessions; we may have included some cases which do not fit our definition of recessions; we may have blundered in measuring or averaging. But so long as we are trying merely to report what has taken place in the past, these doubts concerning the accuracy of our work are all that need concern us. The historical record is fixed; it has its unique features and interest; in studying it we can indulge in no speculations.

A subtler problem and doubts of another order are presented when we treat our observations as data for drawing theoretical conclusions regarding the duration of business cycles at large. For this purpose, we must ask, not merely whether our observations are historically dependable, but also whether they constitute a representative sample of the phenomena measured. Are the observations sufficiently numerous? Are they sufficiently independent of each other? Ought we to discard the observations upon cycles which we think have been cut short or prolonged by factors which have no organic relation to business activity?

In the sense in which the term is used here—recurrences of prosperity, recession, depression and revival in the business activities of countries taken as units—the total number of past business cycles may well be less than a thousand. For business cycles are phenomena peculiar to a certain form of economic organization which has been dominant even in Western Europe for less than two centuries, and for briefer periods in other regions. And the average cycle has lasted

five years, if we may trust our data. Of the whole number of cases to date, the 166 cycles we have measured form a significant fraction. By compiling business annals for Norway, Belgium, Switzerland, Denmark, Spain, New Zealand and Chile we could probably get additional observations as satisfactory as some of those already included. Perhaps we could trace business cycles in Greece, Egypt, Turkey, some of the Balkan States, possibly Mexico, and additional countries in Spanish America. Doubtless we might carry our observations further back in most of the seventeen countries which we have studied. But after we had pushed our investigations everywhere into the twilight zone where business cycles are doubtfully recognizable, we should still be dealing with relatively small numbers. A strict standard would bar out not only most of the extensions suggested, but also some of the cases we now include. It is not certain that the Chinese fluctuations should be treated as business cycles proper. At best, they represent conditions only in the coast cities having a large foreign trade. Also, our early American observations are open to question, even on the understanding that they refer only to the most highly organized of the thirteen original states.

The observations are not all independent of each other. We shall see presently that the duration of business cycles in every country influences, and is influenced by, the duration of business cycles in other countries. Moreover, the non-business factors which affect the duration of business cycles often produce uniform results in several countries. To cite one example: 7 of our 17 countries had a two-year cycle at the end of the World War. One hundred and sixty-six observations, many of which come in clusters, are likely to show a less regular distribution around their central tendency than would 166 observations strictly independent of each other.

If we wish to find out what we can about the probable duration of future business cycles, we should discard observations upon cycles whose duration has been determined by factors of a kind not likely to be influential in the future. If the data for any country show unequivocal evidence of a change in the length of cycles, the later data are likely to be a safer guide to expectations than the earlier data, or the full array. But we have no warrant for discarding cases in which cycles seem to have been cut short or prolonged by wars, civil disorders, exceptional harvest conditions, or any other factor, unless we believe that such "disturbing circumstances" will not recur

in the future as in the past. Even the man who has supposed that business cycles "tend" to have some standard period will probably conclude upon studying the present charts that he had better take the data as they come.

In fine, our observations form a fairly satisfactory basis for studying the duration of business cycles. Like all observations, their accuracy is open to question; but they have been made with care and their number is sufficient to allow errors to offset each other in some measure. We should be glad to have a larger sample; but the present one constitutes an appreciable fraction of its "universe." We need not reject any of the observations on the ground that the duration of certain cycles has been affected by "disturbing circumstances"; for we are interested in actual cycles in the actual world where "disturbing circumstances" are always present. We might expect a more regular distribution if all our observations were strictly independent of each other. But once again, as the world is constituted, interdependence in duration is characteristic of business cycles in different countries. A complete array of measurements for all past cycles would resemble our sample in this respect, and future cycles seem likely to show increasing interdependence in duration. Perhaps we should conceive of our distributions as made from a number of independent measurements smaller than the nominal count, but with the use of "weights" which total 166. Many cycles are weighted by one, while other cycles, which began and ended on the same dates in countries with close business relations, or dominated by the same non-business factors, are weighted by numbers running as high as seven.

To put our data in shape for analysis, we must disregard the chronological sequence of cycles of varying length, shown in Chart 23, and rearrange all the cases in frequency tables of the sort already given for American and English cycles—tables which show the number of cycles of each recorded duration. That step is taken in Table 26. But the tabulations by separate countries have slight significance except for England and the United States, because the number of cases is small (5-15 cycles). Hence Table 27 is made from Table 26, by combining the observations from single countries into various groups. To facilitate comparisons among the two dozen distributions here shown, all the samples are put in percentages. Chart 24 is a graphic form of these percentage distributions.

TABLE 26.

FREQUENCY DISTRIBUTION OF BUSINESS CYCLES ACCORDING TO DURATION IN YEARS

Data from Seventeen Countries. Various Dates to 1925.
Based upon Tables 23, 24 and 25.

Duration in Years	England 1793–1920	France 1838–1920	Germany 1848–1925	Austria 1866–1922	Italy 1888–1920	Netherlands 1891–1920	Sweden 1892–1920	Russia 1891–1925
1 year	..	..	..	..	1	..	..	..
2 years	2	1	1	1	..	..	..	1
3 "	1	5	4	1	..	1	1	1
4 "	5	..	4	2	..	1	1	1
5 "	2	2	1	1	1	..	..	1
6 "	4	2	1	2	1	1	1	1
7 "	2	2	..	..	..	1	1	1
8 "	3	1	1	2	1	..	..	1
9 "	1	1	2	..	..	..	1	..
10 "	2	..	1	..	..	1	..	..
11 "	..	1	..	1	..	..	..	..
12 "	..	..	..	..	1	..	..	..
Total number	22	15	15	10	5	5	5	7
Average duration in years	5.8	5.5	5.1	5.6	6.4	5.8	5.6	4.9

Duration in years	United States 1796–1923	Canada 1888–1924	Australia 1890–1924	South Africa 1890–1920	Argentina 1890–1920	Brazil 1889–1924	India 1889–1920	Japan 1890–1920	China 1888–1920
1 year	1	..	..	..	..	..	..	1	..
2 years	4	1	1	1	1	1	1	1	..
3 "	10	..	1	1	2	..	..	1	1
4 "	5	1	..	1	..	1	2	..	1
5 "	6	2	1	2	..	2	..	2	..
6 "	4	1	1	..	..	2	..	..	1
7 "	1	2	1	..	1	1	3	1	..
8 "	..	..	..	..	2	..	..	1	..
9 "	1	..	..	..	..	..	..	..	1
10 "	..	..	..	1	..	..	..	..	1
11 "	..	..	1	..	..	..	..	..	..
Total number	32	7	6	6	6	7	6	7	5
Average duration in years	4.0	5.1	5.7	5.0	5.0	5.0	5.2	4.3	6.4

TABLE 27.

FREQUENCY DISTRIBUTION OF BUSINESS CYCLES ACCORDING TO APPROXIMATE DURATION IN YEARS: BY COUNTRIES, GROUPS OF COUNTRIES AND PERIODS

(Based upon Table 26)

Duration in Years	United States		England		United States and England		United States, England, France, Germany and Austria						Duration in Years
							Before 1873		After 1873		Full Period		
	Number	Per Cent	Number	Per Cent	Number	Per Cent	Number	Per Cent	Number	Per Cent	Number	Per Cent	
1	1	3.1	..	...	1	1.9	1	2.1	..	...	1	1.1	1
2	4	12.5	2	9.1	6	11.1	2	4.3	7	14.9	9	9.6	2
3	10	31.2	1	4.5	11	20.4	12	25.5	9	19.1	21	22.4	3
4	5	15.6	5	22.7	10	18.5	10	21.3	6	12.8	16	17.0	4
5	6	18.8	2	9.1	8	14.8	5	10.6	7	14.9	12	12.8	5
6	4	12.5	4	18.2	8	14.8	8	17.0	5	10.6	13	13.8	6
7	1	3.1	2	9.1	3	5.6	3	6.4	2	4.3	5	5.3	7
8	..	...	3	13.6	3	5.6	2	4.3	5	10.6	7	7.4	8
9	1	3.1	1	4.5	2	3.7	3	6.4	2	4.3	5	5.3	9
10	..	...	2	9.1	2	3.7	1	2.1	2	4.3	3	3.2	10
11	..	...	..	...	..	...	..	...	2	4.3	2	2.1	11
Totals	32	100.0	22	100.0	54	100.0	47	100.0	47	100.0	94	100.0	Totals

Duration in Years	Countries with close business relations[1]		Countries relatively independent of each other[2]		Countries with average duration of 5.5 years or more[3]		Countries with average duration of 5.2 years or less[4]				Countries with average duration of 5.0 to 5.7[5] years		Duration in Years
							Excluding United States		Including United States				
	Number	Per Cent	Number	Per Cent	Number	Per Cent	Number	Per Cent	Number	Per Cent	Number	Per Cent	
1	..	...	1	2.6	1	1.4	1	1.6	2	2.2	..	...	1
2	4	10.3	5	13.2	5	6.9	8	13.1	12	12.9	11	10.5	2
3	7	18.0	5	13.2	11	15.4	9	14.8	19	20.4	16	15.2	3
4	6	15.4	8	21.0	10	13.7	10	16.4	15	16.1	17	16.2	4
5	4	10.3	6	15.8	7	9.6	10	16.4	16	17.2	13	12.4	5
6	5	12.8	6	15.8	13	17.8	5	8.2	9	9.7	14	13.3	6
7	2	5.1	3	7.9	7	9.6	9	14.8	10	10.8	13	12.4	7
8	6	15.4	2	5.3	7	9.6	5	8.2	5	5.4	9	8.6	8
9	1	2.6	1	2.6	4	5.5	2	3.3	3	3.2	5	4.8	9
10	2	5.1	1	2.6	4	5.5	2	3.3	2	2.2	4	3.8	10
11	2	5.1	..	...	3	4.1	..	...	..	...	3	2.9	11
12	..	...	..	...	1	1.4	..	...	..	...	..	...	12
Totals	39	100.0	38	100.0	73	100.0	61	100.0	93	100.0	105	100.0	Totals

TABLE 27

FREQUENCY DISTRIBUTION OF BUSINESS CYCLES ACCORDING TO APPROXIMATE DURATION IN YEARS: BY COUNTRIES, GROUPS OF COUNTRIES AND PERIODS—(*Continued*)

Duration in Years	Eight European Countries		Nine Non-European Countries		Five English-Speaking Countries[1]		Twelve Non-English-Speaking Countries		All Countries except United States		All Countries		Duration in Years
	Number	Per Cent	Number	Per Cent	Number	Per Cent	Number	Per Cent	Number	Per Cent	Number	Per Cent	
1	1	1.2	2	2.4	1	1.4	2	2.2	2	1.5	3	1.8	1
2	6	7.1	11	13.4	9	12.5	8	8.6	13	9.7	17	10.2	2
3	14	16.7	16	19.5	13	17.8	17	18.3	20	14.9	30	18.1	3
4	14	16.7	11	13.4	12	16.4	13	14.0	20	14.9	25	15.1	4
5	8	9.5	15	18.3	13	17.8	10	10.8	17	12.7	23	13.9	5
6	13	15.5	9	11.0	10	13.7	12	12.9	18	13.4	22	13.3	6
7	7	8.3	10	12.2	6	8.2	11	11.8	16	11.9	17	10.2	7
8	9	10.7	3	3.7	3	4.1	9	9.7	12	9.0	12	7.2	8
9	5	6.0	2	2.4	2	2.7	5	5.4	6	4.5	7	4.2	9
10	4	4.8	2	2.4	3	4.1	3	3.2	6	4.5	6	3.6	10
11	2	2.4	1	1.2	1	1.4	2	2.2	3	2.2	3	1.8	11
12	1	1.2	..	...	..	...	1	1.1	1	0.7	1	0.6	12
Totals	84	100.0	82	100.0	73	100.0	93	100.0	134	100.0	166	100.0	Totals

RECENT CYCLES ONLY: ABOUT 1890 TO 1925

Duration in Years	European and Non-European Countries				Industrial and Non-Industrial Countries				Totals excluding and including United States				Duration in Years
	Eight European Countries		Eight Non-European Countries[2]		Seven Industrial Countries[3]		Ten Non-Industrial Countries[4]		Excluding United States		Including United States		
	Number	Per Cent	Number	Per Cent	Number	Per Cent	Number	Per Cent	Number	Per Cent	Number	Per Cent	
1	1	2.2	1	2.0	..	...	2	3.2	2	2.1	2	1.9	1
2	3	6.7	7	14.0	5	11.6	8	12.9	10	10.5	13	12.4	2
3	6	13.3	6	12.0	9	20.9	7	11.3	12	12.6	16	15.2	3
4	7	15.6	6	12.0	8	18.6	7	11.3	13	13.7	15	14.3	4
5	6	13.3	9	18.0	5	11.6	11	17.7	15	15.8	16	15.2	5
6	8	17.8	5	10.0	6	14.0	7	11.3	13	13.7	13	12.4	6
7	5	11.1	9	18.0	4	9.3	10	16.1	14	14.7	14	13.3	7
8	3	6.7	3	6.0	1	2.3	5	8.1	6	6.3	6	5.7	8
9	1	2.2	1	2.0	1	2.3	1	1.6	2	2.1	2	1.9	9
10	3	6.7	2	4.0	3	7.0	2	3.2	5	5.3	5	4.8	10
11	1	2.2	1	2.0	1	2.3	1	1.6	2	2.1	2	1.9	11
12	1	2.2	..	...	..	...	1	1.6	1	1.1	1	1.0	12
Totals	45	100.0	50	100.0	43	100.0	62	100.0	95	100.0	105	100.0	Totals

[1] England, United States, Canada, Australia, South Africa.
[2] Not including United States.
[3] England, France, Germany, Austria, Netherlands, Sweden, United States.
[4] All other countries included in *Annals*.

The first six figures in the chart deal with the five countries for which we have annals covering relatively long periods. The peculiarities of the American distribution stand out clearly—the pronounced mode, almost a "spike," at three years, and the relatively slight dispersion, indicated by a standard deviation and a coefficient of variation which are respectively the lowest and next the lowest in the list. In the English distribution, there is a curious predominance of cycles lasting 2, 4, 6, 8 and 10 years over cycles lasting 3, 5, 7 and 9 years. In view of the small number of observations (only 22), it is uncertain whether this feature is significant. However that may be, the irregularities in the American and English distributions compensate each other for the most part, so that Figure C is more regular than either of the arrays from which it is made.

Next, the French, German and Austrian observations are combined with the English and American. Advantage is taken of the larger number of cases to compare earlier with later cycles. By using 1873 as the dividing point, we get two groups each of which contains 47 observations. From 1873 to the end of the late war, the business fortunes of these countries, particularly of the European countries, ran more similar courses than in earlier years. That is, the observations in the later period are less independent of each other than the earlier observations—a fact which may explain the lesser regularity of Figure E as compared with Figure D. As a test of this suggestion we have made a distribution of the cycles in the four countries in our list which seem to have the closest business ties with each other for the period in which we have annals for all four. The results, shown in Figure G, constitute one of the least regular distributions in the whole twenty-four. As a companion piece we have made up a random group of similar size from observations which must be nearly independent of each other, taking English cycles in 1793-1825, American cycles in 1825-57, German cycles in 1857-90, Canadian cycles in 1888-1924, and Russian cycles in 1891-1925. In this comparison the 38 independent observations (Figure H) yield a much more regular distribution than the 39 observations which are inter-correlated with each other. Indeed, the contrast in regularity is more striking than we would expect from other comparisons of the sort.

There follow ten figures in which all of the observations are broken into parts on the basis of four criteria. First, the countries are grouped according to the average duration of their business

Chart 24. Percentage Distribution of Business Cycles in Various Countries and Various Periods According to their Approximate Duration in Years.

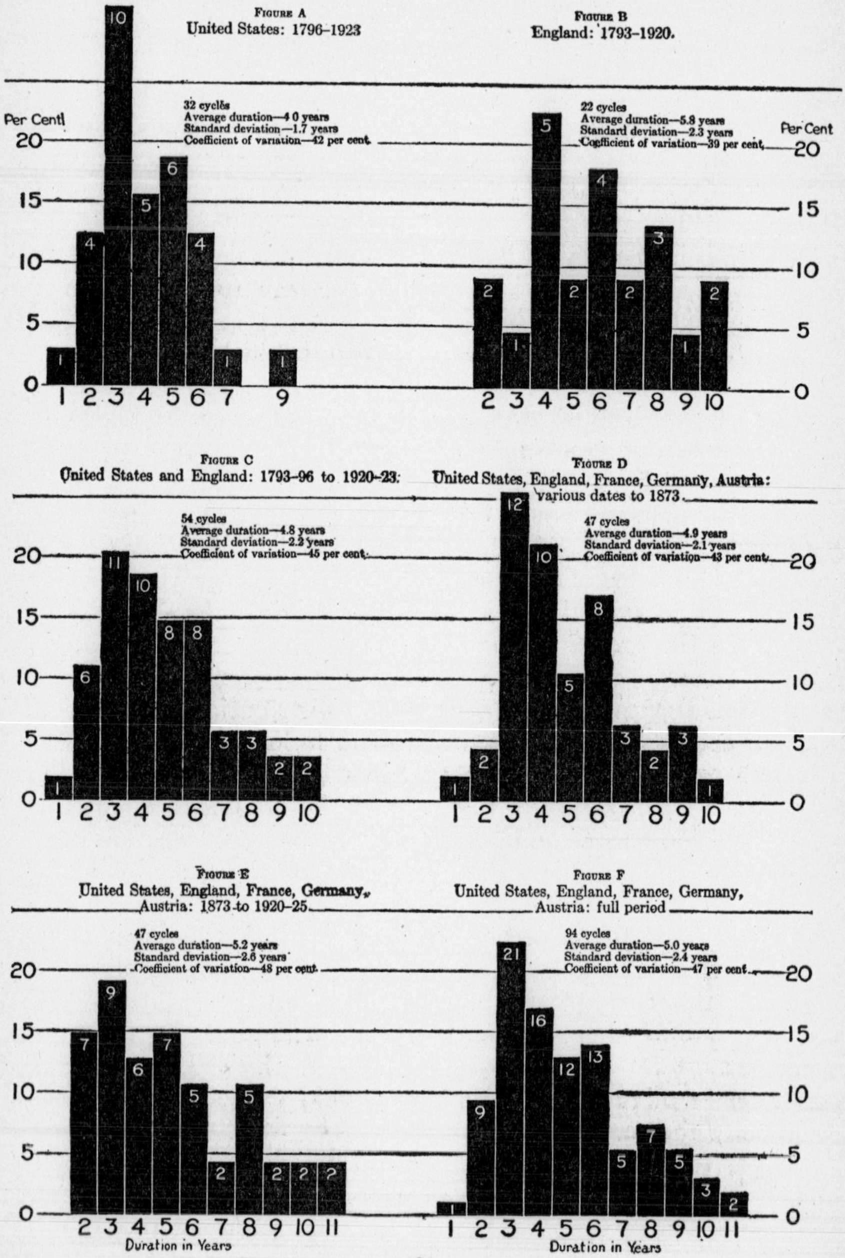

CHART 24. Percentage Distribution of Business Cycles in Various Countries and Various Periods According to their Approximate Duration in Years.—(*Continued*)

FIGURE G

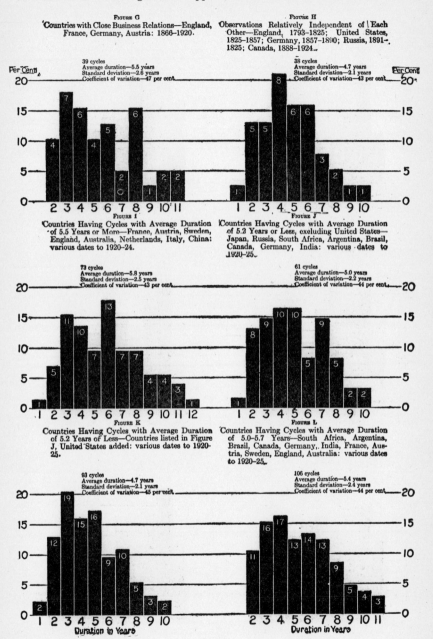

Countries with Close Business Relations—England, France, Germany, Austria: 1866–1920.

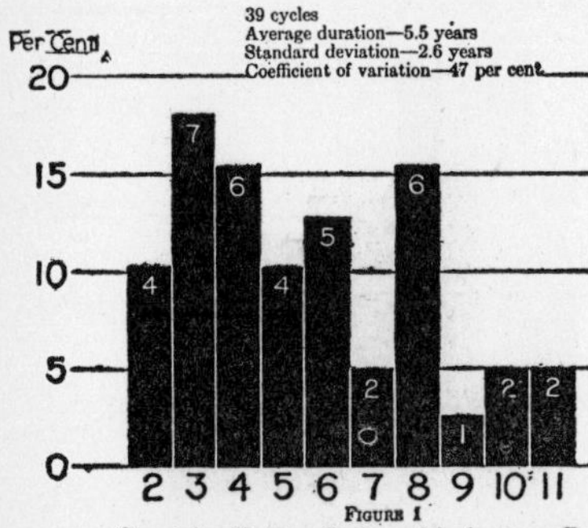

FIGURE H

Observations Relatively Independent of Each Other—England, 1793–1825; United States, 1825–1857; Germany, 1857–1890; Russia, 1891–1825; Canada, 1888–1924.

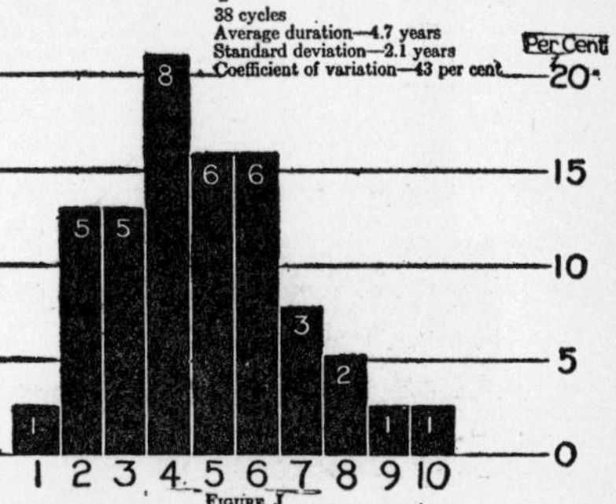

FIGURE I

Countries Having Cycles with Average Duration of 5.5 Years or More—France, Austria, Sweden, England, Australia, Netherlands, Italy, China: various dates to 1920–24.

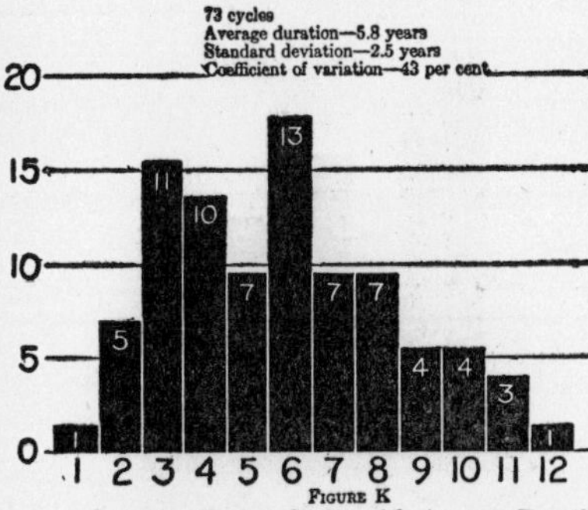

FIGURE J

Countries Having Cycles with Average Duration of 5.2 Years or Less, excluding United States—Japan, Russia, South Africa, Argentina, Brazil, Canada, Germany, India: various dates to 1920–25.

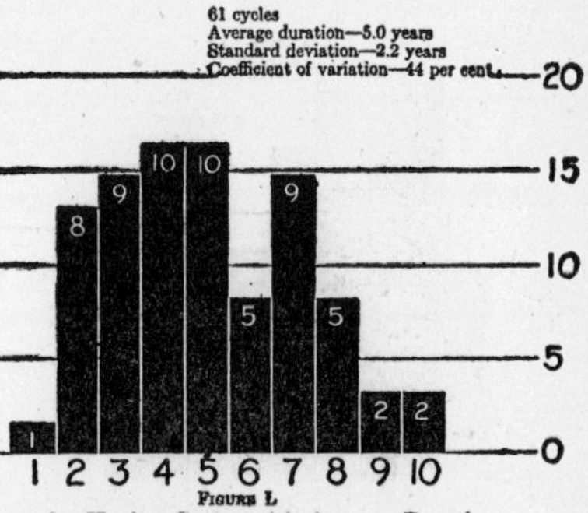

FIGURE K

Countries Having Cycles with Average Duration of 5.2 Years or Less—Countries listed in Figure J, United States added: various dates to 1920-25.

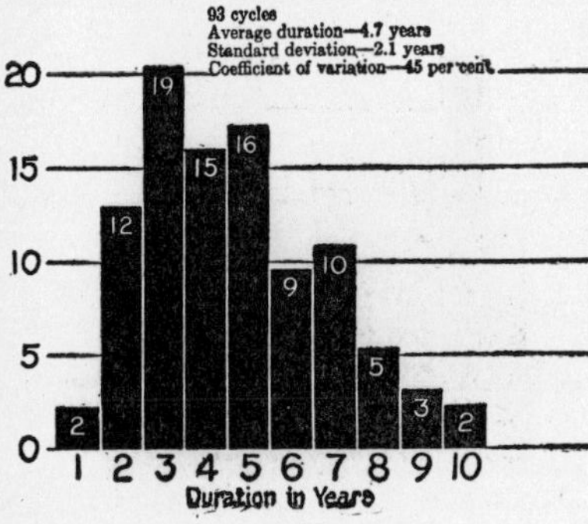

FIGURE L

Countries Having Cycles with Average Duration of 5.0–5.7 Years—South Africa, Argentina, Brazil, Canada, Germany, India, France, Austria, Sweden, England, Australia: various dates to 1920–25.

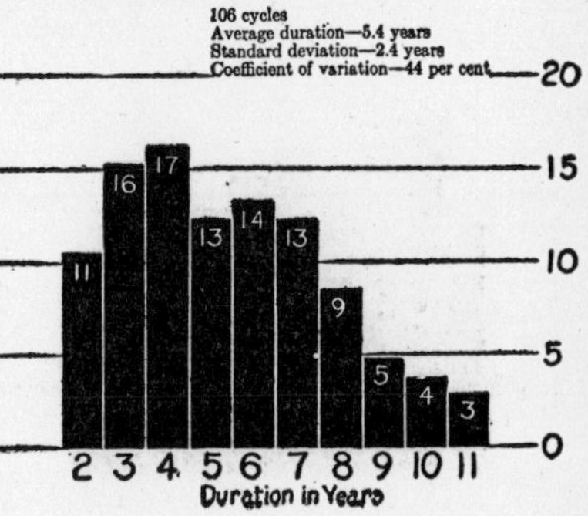

CHART 24. Percentage Distribution of Business Cycles in Various Countries and Various Periods According to their Approximate Duration in Years.—(*Continued*)

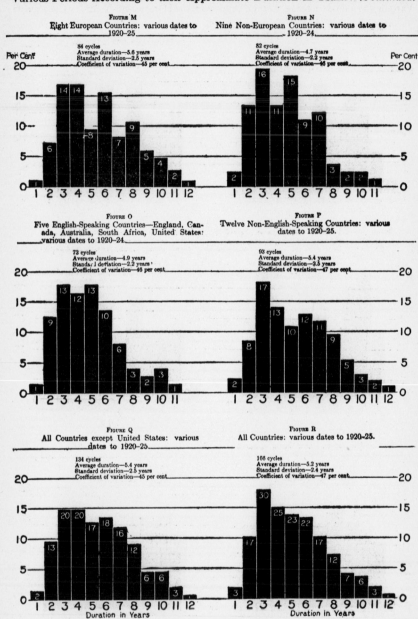

FIGURE M

Eight European Countries: various dates to 1920–25.

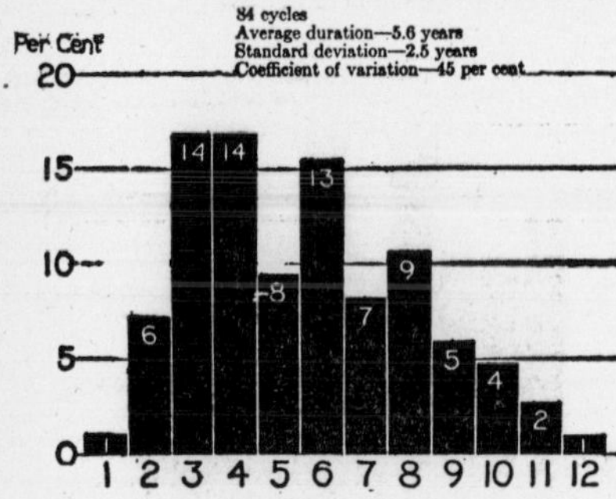

FIGURE N

Nine Non-European Countries: various dates to 1920–24.

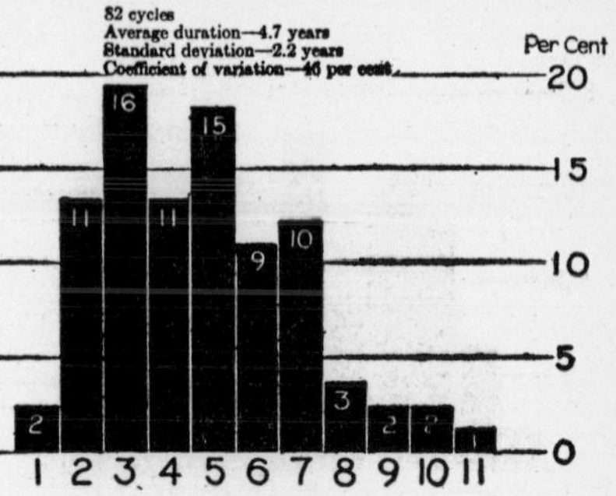

FIGURE O

Five English-Speaking Countries—England, Canada, Australia, South Africa, United States: various dates to 1920–24.

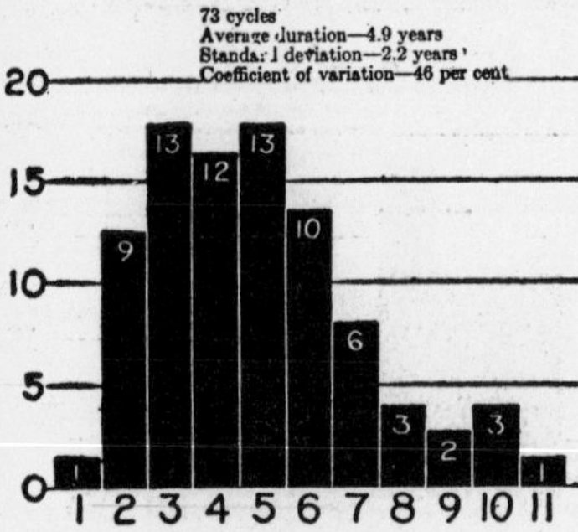

FIGURE P

Twelve Non-English-Speaking Countries: various dates to 1920–25.

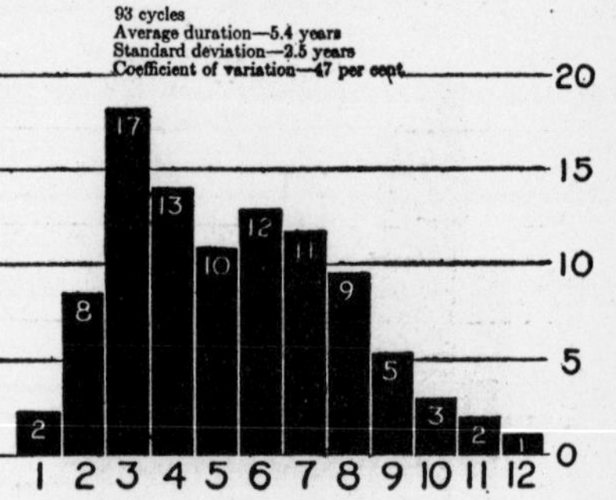

FIGURE Q

All Countries except United States: various dates to 1920–25.

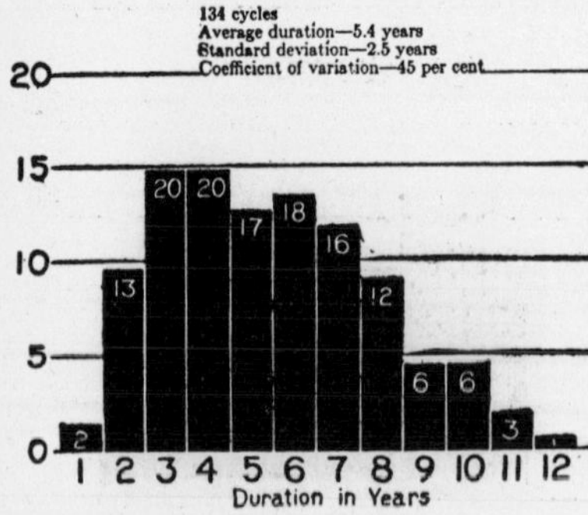

FIGURE R

All Countries: various dates to 1920–25.

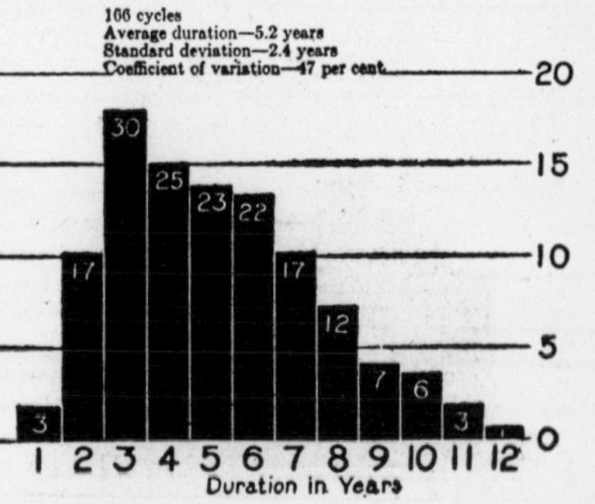

CHART 24. Percentage Distribution of Business Cycles in Various Countries and Various Periods According to their Approximate Duration in Years.—(*Continued*)

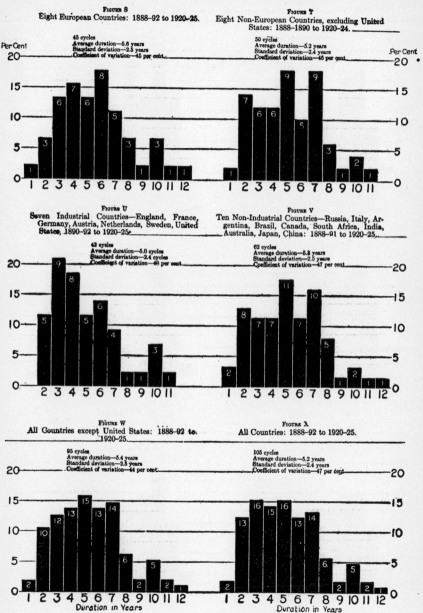

FIGURE S
Eight European Countries: 1888–92 to 1920–25.

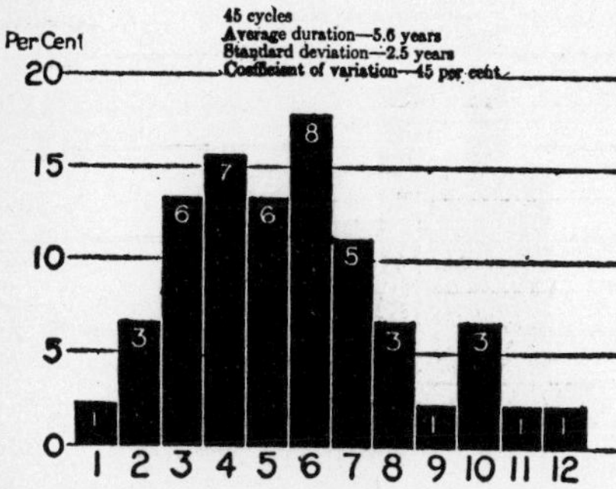

FIGURE T
Eight Non-European Countries, excluding United States: 1888–1890 to 1920–24.

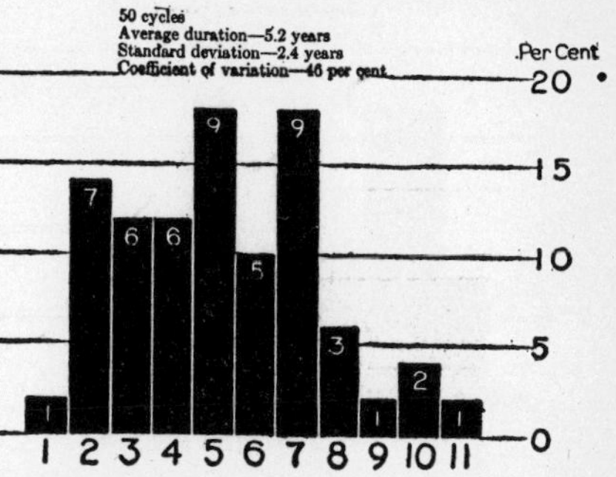

FIGURE U
Seven Industrial Countries—England, France, Germany, Austria, Netherlands, Sweden, United States, 1890–92 to 1920–25.

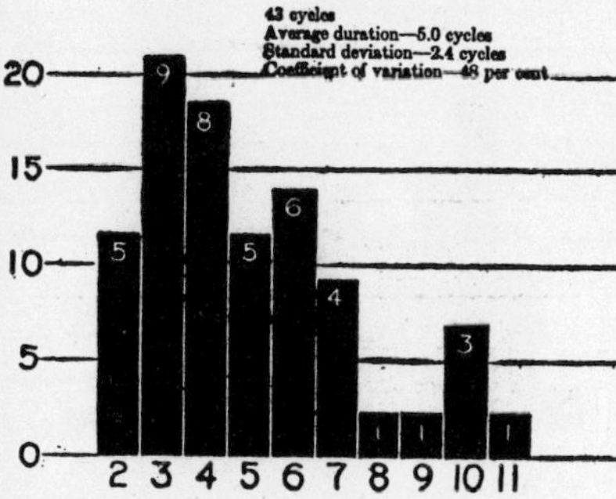

FIGURE V
Ten Non-Industrial Countries—Russia, Italy, Argentina, Brazil, Canada, South Africa, India, Australia, Japan, China: 1888–91 to 1920–25.

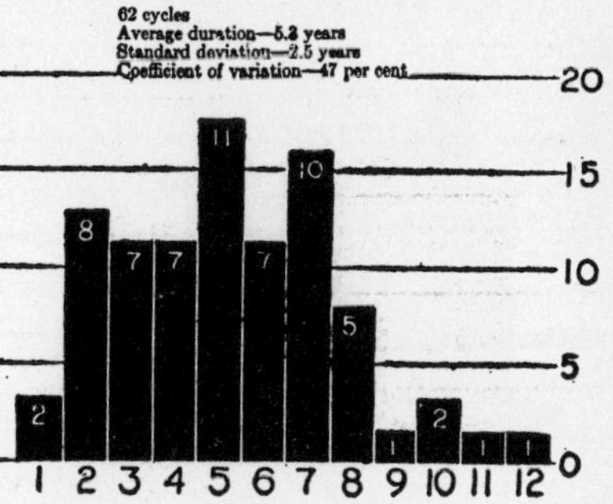

FIGURE W
All Countries except United States: 1888–92 to 1920–25.

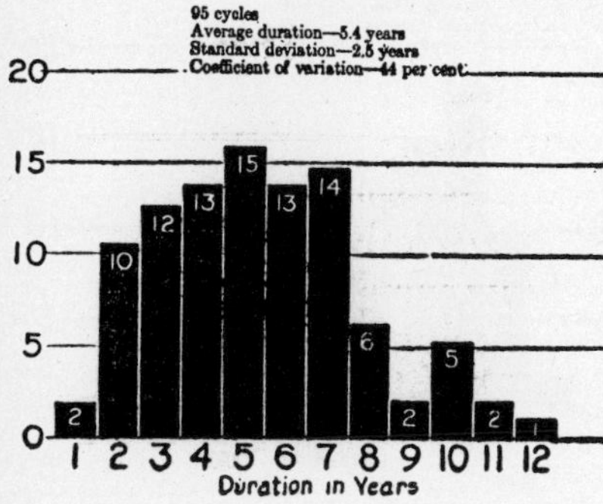

FIGURE X
All Countries: 1888–92 to 1920–25.

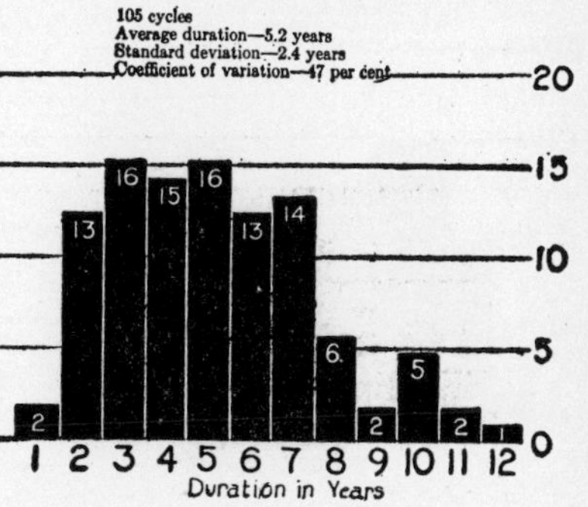

cycles as given in our annals. Figure I shows the observations from countries with relatively long cycles, Figures J and K the observations from countries with relatively short cycles (excluding and including the United States), and Figure L the observations from countries with cycles of medium length. The latter group contains part of the observations used in Figure I and part of those used in Figure J. Second, the European and non-European observations are presented separately in Figures M and N. Third, the observations from five English-speaking and twelve non-English-speaking countries are shown. Fourth, Figure Q gives all the non-American observations for comparison with the American distribution of Figure A. Figure R sums up the whole body of data.

The final section of the chart is confined to recent cycles—those occurring since about 1890. Again the data are divided into groups: observations from European and non-European countries, from industrial and non-industrial countries; from all countries except and all including the United States.

When we review the whole array of distributions, we see that the diagrams and the differences among the diagrams are of a sort common in studies of social phenomena. As usually happens in such work, the small samples, especially when they contain inter-correlated observations, are rather irregular. But with increase in the size of the samples and in the independence of the observations, the distributions grow fairly regular, though not symmetrical.

The materials appear to be fairly homogeneous, with the important exception already noted—the distribution of American business cycles in respect to length differs from the distribution of cycles in other countries. This difference stands out most sharply in the contrast between Figures A and Q. It is responsible for the double modes, separated by a lower point, in Figures O and X, and for the relatively high coefficients of variation in most of the groups combining American and foreign observations. In the samples drawn solely from foreign countries, the diagrams usually have a rounded top quite unlike the spike of Figure A. Combining the American with foreign observations generally produces an unambiguous mode at three years, but twice (Figures O and X) it produces the double mode already spoken of.

Barring out the twelve distributions into which American observations enter does not reduce the variety in the position of the crude

modes. Two of the remaining dozen figures have modes at three years (G and P); two at three and four years (M and Q); and eight at 4, 5, or 6 years, if we may include here one double mode at 5 and 7 years (Figure T). By way of generalization we can hardly be more specific than to say that two-thirds of the foreign cycles are concentrated in the interval three to seven years.

All of the distributions have rather high coefficients of variation. In other words, the observations do not cluster closely around their averages. These coefficients are least in the two distributions confined to single countries (Figures A and B), and greatest in the distributions made from American, British, French, German and Austrian observations since 1873 (Figure E). But the difference between the lowest and highest coefficients (39 and 48 per cent) is not great, and 14 of the 24 round off at 45, 46 or 47 per cent.

All the distributions are skewed positively. The range runs farther above the arithmetic mean than below it in every case, and in every case but Figure T the range also runs farther above the crude mode than below it. Moreover, the crude mode is less than the arithmetic mean in 16 cases, about equal to it in 7 cases, and clearly higher than the mean only in Figure T. One of the most significant distributions, Figure W, which includes all cycles since about 1890 in countries other than the United States, approaches symmetry; but the very broadest groups, Figures X (all recent cycles), Q (all foreign cycles), and R (all cycles) are decidedly, though not extremely, skewed.

Before attempting to interpret these frequency distributions, it is advisable to consider the relative duration of periods of prosperity and depression, the bearing of long-period trends of wholesale prices and secular changes in cycle lengths.

4. The Relative Duration of Prosperity and Depression.

Dr. Thorp has made a special study of the annals to determine as accurately as possible how many months of the record for each country can be classed as prosperous and how many as depressed. Needless to say, this task involved the continuous exercise of personal judgment.

As pointed out in the comparison between the annals and certain statistical indexes of business activity, contemporary observers are always influenced by recent experience in their use of the terms de-

pression and prosperity. Hence, no rigid criterion of what constitutes business prosperity and depression can be evolved from, or read into, our sources. But that fact does not obstruct, it really facilitates, the task in hand. For we seek to compare the duration of the prosperous phase with that of the depressed phase within each cycle treated as a unit. That the prosperous phases of successive cycles in the same country and of synchronous cycles in different countries attain different degrees of intensity is a matter of deep interest, both practically and theoretically; but it is beside the present point.

Dr. Thorp's chief difficulty was that his sources seldom date the transitions from one phase of a cycle to the next phase. In trying to supply that omission in every case, he had to rely upon indications which are often faint. In detail his decisions must be subject to a wider margin of error than his measurements of the durations of whole cycles, since the recessions on which the latter measurements are based, are the phases which have attracted most attention. Hence it will be advisable to confine ourselves to his averages covering several or many cycles, and to draw only broad conclusions.

Table 28 shows the form and drift of Dr. Thorp's tabulations. It

TABLE 28

RELATIVE DURATION OF DIFFERENT PHASES OF BUSINESS CYCLES IN SEVENTEEN COUNTRIES, 1890–1925

	Months	Percentages
Months of prosperity	2,888	39.3
Months of recession and revival	1,756	23.9
Months of depression	2,700	36.8
Total	7,344	100.0

Years of prosperity per year of depression: 1.07.

appears that the phases of recession and revival put together make up rather less than one-quarter of the duration of recent cycles. But in view of the difficulty of saying just when revival has blossomed into prosperity, and just when recession has merged into depression, this conclusion should not be stressed heavily. However, if these decisions can be made on a substantially consistent basis, the comparison between the relative duration of the prosperous and depressed phases of the cycles will not be compromised.[1] What the table indicates is that in this period of 36 years the prosperous

[1] Chart 27, below, shows for every cycle the quarters and years which Dr. Thorp has taken as marking off revival and recession.

phases averaged somewhat longer than the depressed phases. A similar conclusion was drawn from American business indexes in Chapter III. Business contraction was found to be "a briefer and more violent process than business expansion." A crude average of over 50 measurements of the duration of the ascending phase of the cycles since 1878 gives 23 months. The corresponding average for the descending phase is about 19 months.[2]

Similar averages showing the relative duration of prosperity and depression for particular countries and periods are given in Table 29. To get comparable results it has been necessary both to take periods which comprise whole cycles, and to make these periods as nearly synchronous as may be. For the results in any one country vary considerably from one period to another. For example, the English and American averages come out in three different periods as follows:

		Years of Prosperity per Year of Depression			Years of Prosperity per Year of Depression
England	1790–1925.........	1.11	United States	1790–1925....	1.50
	1890–1913.........	1.24		1890–1913....	1.57
	1890–1920.........	1.71		1890–1923....	1.79

As a guide to future expectations, the averages which include the years of the great war seem less significant than the averages which we have for longer periods of time in five countries, or than the averages for 17 countries in the period from about 1890 to 1913.

The wide differences between the averages for the countries at the the bottom and the top of the list in Table 29 show how much business conditions are affected by political turmoil and stability. Brazil, China, Russia and South Africa had grave troubles in the period for which we have compiled their annals, and Austria suffered from her proximity to the Balkan volcanoes. The other figures speak for themselves. But we should remember that the figures for each country speak that country's language. Swedish prosperity may differ from Canadian prosperity—the comparison made is between the prosperous and the depressed phases of Swedish cycles in one case, and between the prosperous and the depressed phases of Canadian cycles in the other case. It is risky to say that one of these countries has been more prosperous than the other, even in the period here covered. And it

[2] See Chapter III, section vi, (2) "Month-to-Month Changes," and (5) "Duration of Periods of Expansion and Contraction."

is easy to conceive that any country might change its ranking in such a list radically within a decade or two.

TABLE 29.

Relative Duration of the Prosperous and Depressed Phases in the Business Cycles of Seventeen Countries during Various Periods

	Period	Years of Prosperity per Year of Depression
United States	1790–1925	1.50
England	1790–1925	1.11
France	1840–1925	1.18
Germany	1853–1925	1.18
Austria	1866–1925	0.70

	Period	Years of Prosperity per Year of Depression	Period	Years of Prosperity per Year of Depression
Canada	1888–1924	1.86	1888–1913	2.08
United States	1890–1923	1.79	1890–1913	1.57
England	1890–1920	1.71	1890–1913	1.24
France	1890–1920	1.70	1890–1913	1.47
Australia	1890–1920	1.69	1890–1913	1.37
Sweden	1892–1920	1.67	1892–1913	1.89
Netherlands	1891–1920	1.61	1891–1913	1.59
India	1889–1920	1.43	1889–1914	1.26
Argentina	1890–1920	1.07	1890–1913	1.06
Japan	1890–1920	1.05	1890–1914	.75
Germany	1890–1925	1.03	1890–1913	1.14
Italy	1888–1920	.98	1888–1913	.90
South Africa	1890–1920	.89	1890–1913	.66
Russia	1891–1925	.81	1891–1914	1.09
China	1888–1920	.65	1888–1910	.57
Austria	1892–1922	.63	1892–1912	.73
Brazil	1889–1924	.45	1889–1912	.29
Seventeen Countries		1.14		1.08

One of the main reasons why these ratios of years of prosperity to years of depression are unstable is revealed by a further analysis of the long records for England and the United States. From various index numbers of prices, it is known that the long-period trend of the wholesale price level changed direction four times in the 130 years, 1790 to 1920. The turning points came at nearly the same dates in this country and England, save that our greenback prices reached their highest point just before the end of the Civil War in

1865, whereas in gold-standard nations prices continued to rise until 1873. Thus we have in both countries five periods of alternately declining and advancing price trends. From 1790 to 1814 wholesale prices rose unsteadily; from 1814 to 1849 they declined unsteadily; from 1849 to 1865 in the United States and to 1873 in England they rose unsteadily; from 1865 in the United States and 1873 in England they declined unsteadily until 1896; from 1896 to 1920 they rose unsteadily. For the periods thus marked off, Dr. Thorp has obtained the following ratios of years of prosperity to years of depression:

TABLE 30.

RELATIVE DURATION OF THE PROSPEROUS AND THE DEPRESSED PHASES OF BUSINESS CYCLES IN PERIODS OF RISING AND DECLINING TRENDS OF WHOLESALE PRICES: ENGLAND AND THE UNITED STATES, 1790–1925

England	Years of Prosperity per Year of Depression	United States	Years of Prosperity per Year of Depression
1790–1815 Prices rising	1.0	1790–1815 Prices rising	2.6
1815–1849 Prices falling	.9	1815–1849 Prices falling	.8
1849–1873 Prices rising	3.3	1849–1865 Prices rising	2.9
1873–1896 Prices falling	.4	1865–1896 Prices falling	.9
1896–1920 Prices rising	2.7	1896–1920 Prices rising	3.1

These results are so uniform and so striking as to leave little doubt that the secular trend of the wholesale price level is a factor of great moment in determining the characteristics of business cycles. That is no novel conclusion; but Dr. Thorp's data lend it new force and precision.

A final point established by study of the relative duration of the prosperous and the depressed phases of business cycles is that the very long cycles usually owe their length primarily to prolongation of depression. Among the 166 cycles we have measured there are 17 which lasted 9 years or more. The average of all our observations, it will be remembered, is 5.2 years. Dr. Thorp has made a special examination of these long cycles to determine when the revivals occurred, and how long were the periods of declining and of increasing activity. His results appear in Table 31.

Whereas the most inclusive average in Table 29 gives a ratio of 1.14 years of prosperity per year of depression, the present table gives a ratio of 0.79. In 11 of the 17 cycles the phase of depression

is longer than the phase of prosperity. The longest period of prosperity found is 72 months; the longest periods of depression run 72, 76 and 100 months. Finally, the average phase of depression in these long cycles is nearly a year longer than the average phase of prosperity.

TABLE 31.

RELATIVE DURATION OF PHASES OF DEPRESSION AND PHASES OF PROSPERITY IN BUSINESS CYCLES LASTING NINE YEARS OR MORE

Length in Years	Country	Periods Covered by the Cycles	Year of Revival	Months of Depression	Months of Prosperity
12	Italy	1888, early–1900, early	1897	100	30
11	France	1890, early–1900, late	1895	60	42
11	Austria	1873–1884	1880	72	36
11	Australia	1890–1901	1896	62	48
10	England	1837, early–1847, April	1843	68	44
10	England	1890, Nov.–1900	1895	42	48
10	Germany	1890, early–1900, summer	1894, late	44	51
10	Netherlands	1891–1901	1896	48	48
10	South Africa	1903–1913	1909	60	36
10	China	1910–1920	1916	60	48
9	United States	1873–1882	1878	57	42
9	England	1873, late–1883, early	1880	69	24
9	France	1838–1847	1840	24	72
9	Germany	1848–1857	1853	54	42
9	Germany	1857–1866	1860	18	66
9	Sweden	1892–1901	1895	30	60
9	China	1888–1897	1895	76	12
			Total	944	749
			Average	55	44

Years of prosperity per year of depression: 0.79.

5. SECULAR CHANGES IN THE AVERAGE DURATION OF BUSINESS CYCLES.

Another matter which demands attention is the differences between the average duration of business cycles in various countries revealed by Table 26. In particular, why do American cycles average only 4 years in length, while English cycles during the same period average nearly 5 years and 10 months?

A possible clew to this puzzle is suggested by the hypothesis, developed in Chapter II, that business cycles are associated with a particular form of economic organization, here called "business economy."

If that hypothesis be valid, the characteristics of business cycles may be expected to change as economic organization develops. We have historical evidence to support this supposition in respect to at least one characteristic: violent panics are giving way to recessions. May not the average intervals between recessions also vary from generation to generation?

In the introduction to *Business Annals* I noted that secular changes in duration have occurred in certain countries for which Dr. Thorp has compiled annals covering an extended period. But I failed to develop the full significance of the data. Dr. Frederick C. Mills of the National Bureau's staff has made a more extended study of the problem, and suggested a tentative explanation, not only of the secular changes which he finds in the average duration of business cycles in the United States, England, France, and Germany, but also of the differences in the average length of business cycles in our 17 countries.[1]

Dr. Mills formulates his hypothesis as follows:

> . . . the duration of business cycles in a given country is a function of the stage of industrial development which that country has attained. More specifically: When the modern type of economic organization is in the initial stage of development, the average duration of business cycles is relatively long. During the stage of rapid growth, when modern types of business enterprise and modern forms of industrial organization are being applied extensively, business cycles are of relatively short average duration. With the decline in the rate of economic change and the attainment of comparative stability, business cycles increase again in length.

To test this hypothesis adequately Dr. Mills recognizes that he needs, not only a larger body of observations, but also an "objective criterion for distinguishing the stages in a country's industrial development, or for classifying countries according to their present state of development." On the view developed in this book, the factor in economic organization critically important for the understanding of business cycles is not the "stage of industrial development" as such, but the proportion of the people who are depending mainly upon making and spending money incomes, and the proportion of total business that is done by large-scale enterprises. Needless to say, we

[1] "An Hypothesis concerning the Duration of Business Cycles," *Journal of the American Statistical Association*, December, 1926, vol. xxi, pp. 447-457.

have neither an "index of industrialization," nor an index of business economy. Under these circumstances, Dr. Mills is forced to make a somewhat arbitrary division of Dr. Thorp's materials into the periods suggested by his hypothesis—a division based partly on the evidence of the annals themselves and partly on other information. Thus he takes the early stage of industrialization in the United States to last from the beginning of the annals to 1822, since which time the country has been in the stage of rapid economic transition. In England he supposes that the first stage had been passed before our annals begin, that the second stage extended from 1793 to 1831, and the third from 1831 to date. The countries which he assigns to this third stage of decreasing rate of progress are England since 1831, France since 1876, Austria since 1873, the Netherlands and Sweden since the beginning of their annals in 1890. Germany he puts into the first stage until 1866, and into the second stage since then.[2]

[2] Mills' full classification of the materials is as follows:

A. Countries in the early stages of industrialization:

United States	to 1822	(Annals begin 1796)*
Germany	to 1866	" " 1848
Italy	to 1907	" " 1888
Canada	to 1913	" " 1888
Australia	to 1913	" " 1890
South Africa	to 1913	" " 1890
China	to date	" " 1888
India	to date	" " 1889
Russia	to date	" " 1891
Argentina	to date	" " 1890
Brazil	to date	" " 1889

B. Countries in the stage of rapid economic transition:

England	to 1831	(Annals begin 1793)
United States	1822 to date	
France	to 1876	" " 1838
Germany	1866 to date	
Austria	to 1873	" " 1866
Italy	1907 to date	
Canada	1913 to date	
Australia	1913 to date	
South Africa	1913 to date	
Japan	to date	" " 1890

C. Countries in which the transition is going forward at a decreasing rate:

England	1831 to date	
France	1876 to date	
Austria	1873 to date	
Netherlands	to date	(Annals begin 1891)
Sweden	to date	" " 1892

* The dates given as marking the beginning of the *Annals* are the dates of the first recorded recessions. In cases where the beginning of a stage is not defined in the above table, that stage is assumed to date from a period prior to the beginning of the *Annals*.

On this basis, Dr. Mills gets the following results:

	Early stages of industrialization	Stage of rapid economic transition	Stage of relative economic stability
Number of observations.........	51 cycles	77 cycles	38 cycles
Mean duration..................	5.86 years	4.09 years	6.39 years
Standard deviation..............	2.41 "	1.88 "	2.42 "

He computes that differences as great as those between the averages of the first and second periods and between the averages of the second and third periods would arise as the result of sampling fluctuations about one time out of 50,000 and 1,000,000 trials respectively. The explanation for the relatively short duration of American cycles suggested by these results is "an exceptional prolongation of the period of industrial transition in this country."

There can be little doubt that the average duration of business cycles has undergone secular changes in the countries for which Thorp has compiled the longest records. If our annals are valid, this conclusion is definitely established for England, and made highly probable for France and the United States. Mills gives the following averages for periods which differ in the case of one country from those used in his systematic classification of all the materials:

England	1793–1831	9 cycles	Average	duration	4.22	years
"	1831–1920	13 "	"	"	6.85	"
France	1854–1876	6 "	"	"	3.67	"
"	1876–1920	7 "	"	"	6.32	"
United States	1796–1822	5 "	"	"	5.20	"
" "	1822–1860	11 "	"	"	3.50	"
" "	1860–1888	5 "	"	"	5.50	"
" "	1888–1923	11 "	"	"	3.20	"

Thus English and French cycles have grown shorter, while American cycles have gone through a curious double swing, first decreasing in length, then increasing, then decreasing again.

But, granting the statistical significance of these averages, and their value as a summary of past experience, what theoretical importance can we attach to them? From the empirical viewpoint they show the existence of secular trends in the duration of business cycles. We have seen that purely empirical trends can be used only in the most tentative fashion as a basis for forming future expectations, or as

a basis for giving explanations. But if trends can be developed from rational hypotheses, they become far more useful. Thus we come back to a critical consideration of the evidence for Mills' hypothesis concerning the connection between the average duration of business cycles and the state of industrialization.

It is doubtful if any half-dozen economic historians, given Mills' necessarily vague definitions of three stages of industrialization, and asked to date the close of each stage in the 17 countries for which we have business annals, would undertake the task, or find themselves in substantial agreement if they did. It is easy to question many of the dates assigned by Mills, and hard either to establish or to disprove their validity. To canvass the pertinent evidence in detail would be an enormous task, and would lead to no conclusive result unless prefaced, first by a more precise statement of the hypothesis than Mills has given, and second by the development of objective standards by which to rate the significance of what facts might be established.

Our best hope for further light upon the hypothesis which Mills makes so interesting lies in further analytic work upon secular trends in economic history. Few problems are more fascinating, more important, or more neglected than the rates at which economic development proceeds in successive generations and in different countries. It is conceivable that men who combine the requisite statistical technique with the requisite historical knowledge can develop effective methods of utilizing the scattered figures which survive in little known sources, and the abundant descriptive materials, in such fashion as to show at least the broad stages in the recent economic development of the leading commercial nations. If they do, sidelights upon changes in various characteristics of business cycles will be a not unimportant gain from their labors.

6. Conclusions.

1. Our measurements of the intervals between recessions do not bear precisely upon the obsolescent debate concerning the periodicity of crises. But measurements made from the annals upon the old plan would be as fatal to the hypothesis of periodicity as the measurements which I prefer. Indeed, counting from crisis to crisis would make the limits within which cycles vary even wider than does counting from recession to recession. The longest cycle shown by the annals

—the Italian case of 1888-1900—would be extended from 12 to 19 years if we skipped the mild recession of 1900 and passed on to the crisis of 1907. Perhaps still longer cycles might be found, were this method of counting systematically applied to all countries. Nor could the extension of the range in one direction be compensated by reduction at the other end of the scale. The shortest cycle could not be prolonged beyond two or three years, except by such violent procedures as telescoping the American panics of 1837 and 1839 into a single crisis.

Nor can I confirm the ingenious suggestion made by Professor H. S. Jevons and Mr. Joseph Kitchin, that long cycles are multiples of two or three short ones.[1] Were such the case, and were the short cycles 3⅓ or 3½ years long as these writers suppose, one would expect our frequency diagrams to show modes, primary or secondary, at 3, 7, and 10, or 11 years. None of them do so. There are diagrams with modes, pronounced or faint, at 3 and 7 years, and 4 and 8 years. But there are also diagrams with modes, pronounced or faint, at 3 and 4 years; 3 and 5 years; 3 and 6 years; 3 and 8 years; 3, 4, 6, and 8 years; 3, 5, and 7 years; 3, 5, and 10 years; 3, 6, and 10 years; 4 and 5 years; 4 and 6 years; 5 and 7 years, etc. More significant is the fact that as the size of the samples increases the minor modes tend to disappear, instead of tending to grow clearer. In the most inclusive sample of all (Figure R of Chart 24), there are no secondary modes.

While few if any recent writers maintain the hypothesis of periodicity in any form, many of them do give some average figure to represent the duration typical of business cycles. Such averages are adequate for certain purposes. But the present results show that no average can suggest the facts about the duration of cycles which are most significant for theory and practice.

2. If there is any regularity in the sequence of cycles of different lengths, I have failed to find it. Chart 23, which represents the duration of cycles taken in chronological order, shows the hazard of attempting to forecast how long the next cycle will last in any of our countries. Neither modal length, nor the duration of the preceding cycle is a safe guide.

3. A semblance of regularity does appear, however, when we disregard chronological sequence and group our observations in fre-

[1] See Herbert Stanley Jevons, *The Sun's Heat and Solar Activity,* London, 1910, and Joseph Kitchin, "Cycles and Trends in Economic Factors," *Review of Economic Statistics,* January, 1923, Preliminary vol. v, pp. 10-16.

quency tables. And the regularity becomes more marked as the size of the sample increases, that is, as the number of independent observations upon the duration of business cycles becomes greater.

The regularity which emerges, consists, not in the preponderance of cycles of any given duration, but in the way in which cycles of different durations group themselves about their central tendency. The distribution is of a type found in many studies of biological and social phenomena. It is not symmetrical, but skewed positively. In all the groups into which we have divided the observations for analysis, the range runs farther above than below the arithmetic mean, and in two-thirds of the groups the crude mode is less than the arithmetic mean.

4. American cycles have a shorter average duration than those of any other country studied. The averages of 32 American and of 134 foreign measurements are 4.0 and 5.4 years respectively. The shortest average duration found in any foreign country is 4.3 years in Japan, where 7 cycles occurred in approximately the period covered by 10 American cycles. The American distribution shows a pronounced mode at 3 years; the most inclusive of the foreign distributions shows a rounded top with equal numbers of cases at 3 and 4 years, and no marked decline in numbers before 8 years.

5. Secular changes in the average duration of business cycles can be traced in countries for which business annals have been compiled for long periods. In England and France the duration has increased; in the United States the duration averaged 5.2 years in 1796-1822, 3.5 years in 1822-60, 5.5 years in 1860-88, and 3.2 years in 1888-1923. This fact makes it difficult to adapt the physical-cause theories of economic fluctuations to business cycles.

The most interesting hypothesis concerning these changes in secular length, and concerning the differences in the average duration of cycles in different countries at a given period, is that offered by Dr. Frederick C. Mills, who suggests tentatively that business cycles tend to be relatively long in a country during the early stages of industrialization, relatively short during the stage of rapid economic transition, and relatively long again when the rate of transition decreases.

6. While our frequency distributions lack the symmetry of the Gaussian normal curve, their form suggests fitting "a logarithmic normal curve; that is a Gaussian curve in which the successive units [standard deviations] of the horizontal scale are readjusted to dis-

tances having a constant ratio rather than a constant difference."[2] This experiment has been tried upon Figure R of Chart 24—the distribution which includes all of our 166 observations. Chart 25 shows that the fit of the logarithmic normal curve to the data is on the whole rather close.[3]

CHART 25. Logarithmic Normal Curve Fitted by Davies' Method to the Frequency Distribution of 166 Observations upon the Duration of Business Cycles.

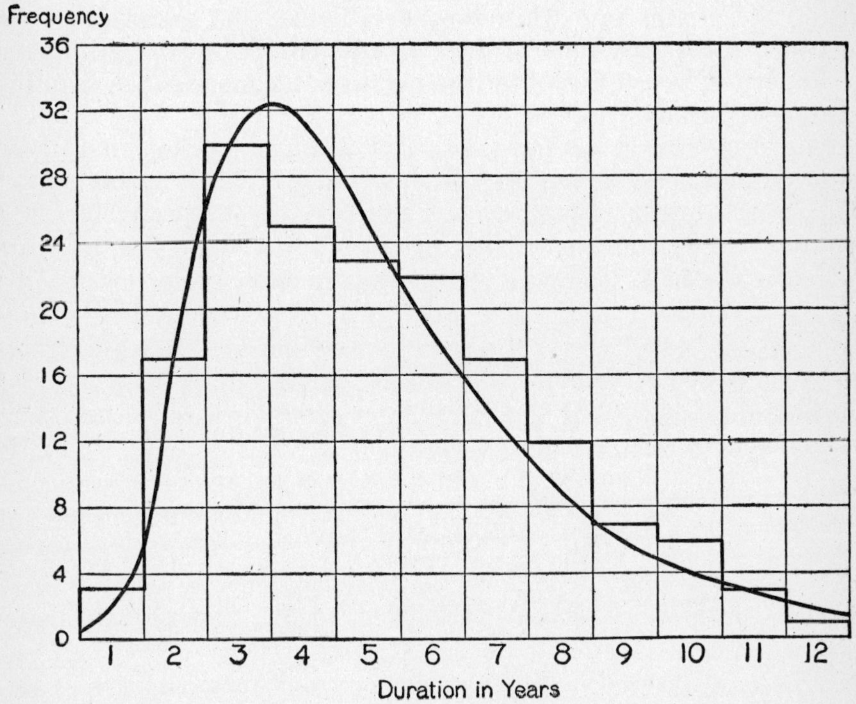

From this fact we infer that, like other biological and social phenomena whose distributions are well described by some form of the normal curve, the durations of business cycles may be regarded as the net resultants of a multitude of factors which are largely inde-

[2] See George R. Davies, "The Logarithmic Curve of Distribution," *Journal of the American Statistical Association,* December, 1925, vol. xx, pp. 467-480. Dr. Thorp has adopted Professor Davies' method in making the chart on this page.

[3] When the cycles now running in our 17 countries are ended, the new batch of observations promises to modify the distribution of Chart 25 somewhat. Five years have already elapsed since the latest recession in three of our countries, and six years in seven countries.

pendent of each other. If there is any dominant factor or set of factors, which tends to produce cycles of uniform duration, its influence is greatly modified by a host of other factors combined in ways which vary endlessly. This conclusion has an important bearing upon the theory of business cycles and the methods by which that theory may be improved.[4]

7. Regarding the relative duration of the several phases which make up business cycles, the annals yield certain fragmentary, but significant, results.

As we interpret them on the basis of current business reports, the phases of recession and revival are relatively brief.[5] Put together, they account for only one-quarter of the duration of business cycles on the average. Of the remaining three-quarters, the prosperous phase occupies a somewhat longer time than the phase of depression. But the ratio of months of prosperity to months of depression varies widely from country to country, and within any country it varies widely from cycle to cycle. Consequently, the average ratios ap-

[4] Dr. Oskar Morgenstern has kindly allowed me to read the manuscript of a paper on "Internationale vergleichende Konjunkturforschung" (soon to appear in the *Zeitschrift für die gesammte Staatswissenschaft*), in which he questions the propriety of my averaging together measurements of the duration of business cycles which have occurred in communities of widely different economic organization. As Dr. Morgenstern points out, the hypothesis that there is an intimate connection between the form of economic organization and business cycles implies that radical differences in economic organization are associated with corresponding differences in cyclical fluctuations. Since I work with the hypothesis in question, am I justified in assembling in a single array measurements of cycles in communities so unlike in organization as contemporary England and China, or the United States of the 20th and of the 18th centuries?

As said in the text, I take the Chinese reports to represent conditions in the coast cities only. Similarly, in dealing with the earlier American annals, I use only the reports from the northern and eastern states, paying no attention to the reports from the southern states and western settlements, which are frequently quite different in tenor. There is evidence that business economy, as defined in Chapter II, had become established (though not highly developed) by 1790 from Pennsylvania to Massachusetts, and by 1890 in the coast cities of China. If that opinion is valid, I seem justified in treating the fluctuations of economic fortune experienced by these two communities as business cycles.

Granted so much, is not something to be learned by studying the available measurements of these highly variable phenomena as a whole, as well as in a variety of small groups? Of course, it would be easy to over-stress the significance of my grand average of the duration of business cycles. I do not attach much importance to the arithmetic mean of the total array; but I do think the distribution of the observations around their central tendency is a matter of much theoretical interest.

Finally, I agree with Dr. Morgenstern that the relation between the duration of business cycles and changes in the form of economic organization was not adequately treated in my introduction to Thorp's *Business Annals*. Since that book was published, Mills' hypothesis has put the problem in a clearer form, and indicated how much work may be required to reach a satisfactory solution.

[5] When it is necessary to define revivals and recessions as the periods within which all of the statistical series in a large collection turn up or turn down, these two phases become relatively long. But more of that matter in the volume to follow.

proach stability only when long periods of time and many countries are included. Perhaps the most significant figures are those for the United States and England in 1790-1925, and for all our 17 countries in 1890-1913. These three results come out respectively 1.50, 1.11 and 1.08 years of prosperity per year of depression.

Both the English and the American records indicate that the relative duration of the prosperous and depressed phases of business cycles is dominated by the secular trend of wholesale prices. In the three periods of rising price trends since 1790, the prosperous phases of the cycles have been prolonged and the depressed phases have been relatively brief. In the three periods of declining price trends, the prosperous phases of the cycles have been relatively brief and the depressed phases prolonged. While the observations upon which these conclusions rest are subject to a margin of uncertainty in every cycle considered, random errors could hardly produce such uniform results as we find.

Finally, it appears that the depressed phases of business cycles are susceptible of greater prolongation than the prosperous phases. Whereas our averages including many cycles all show a slight preponderance of years of prosperity over years of depression, our long cycles as a group show a marked preponderance of years of depression over years of prosperity.

In weighing the conclusions drawn in this section, one should bear in mind certain features of the data and methods used.

No selection or "adjustment" has been practiced upon the observations. The "abnormal cases"—if that phrase has an intelligible meaning—are included with the "normal." Every reader of the annals will note how frequently foreign wars and domestic turmoil, harvest fluctuations, epidemics, floods and earthquakes have checked or reënforced the tides of business activity. A tendency toward alternations of prosperity and depression must have considerable constancy and energy to stamp its pattern upon economic history in a world where other factors of most unequal power are constantly present, and where one or other of these factors, singly or in combination, rises to dominance at irregular intervals.

Our measurements are based solely upon the intervals between recessions. It would be desirable to check the results by a second set, based on the intervals between revivals. We have not attempted

such a check, because business commentators have paid less attention to the upward than to the downward turning points of business cycles. The materials for making the second set of measurements are less full and reliable than the materials we have exploited. If a second set as satisfactory as the first could be made, the frequency distributions it yielded would doubtless differ in numberless details from the frequency distributions here presented. But we have no reason to believe that the broad conclusions suggested by the new frequency distributions would run counter to the conclusions we have drawn.

The year is too large a unit for measuring business cycles. Our results have the crudity of an effort to ascertain the stature distribution of men, women and children from measurements made in feet. In statistical work with time series, it is often possible to substitute the more appropriate unit of a month. But such investigations of business fluctuations are confined to those narrow limits of time, place, and type of business for which elaborate numerical data have been collected.

The best we could do when we were seeking to determine the duration of business cycles by using monthly statistics was to make numerous measurements of a dozen cases in one country. Five business indexes, covering by months part or all of the last half century in the United States, together with the plan of counting durations both from crest to crest and from trough to trough, enabled us to accumulate 101 observations upon the lengths of what the annals represent as 12 cycles (or 12½ if we start with the trough of 1878). That the results obtained in this way agree with the results obtained from the same period of the annals appears from Chart 21. For that chart shows that the most significant of the statistical indexes which run back to 1875 give the same recession dates as do the annals.

It may be worth while, however, to compare the 101 statistical measurements of the 12½ cycles of 1878 to 1923 with the 32 measurements of 32 cycles made from the annals of 1796 to 1923. To that end, we may condense the quarterly figures made from the statistical observations which ran originally by months, into yearly figures, assigning each quarter to that year into which it presumably would fall were the reckoning made from annals. For example, we count the cycles lasting approximately two years as those included in the four quarters centering on 19, 22, 25 and 28 months—that is, the quarters which run from 1½ years to 2 years and five months. Chart 26 gives the results.

CHART 26

PERCENTAGE DISTRIBUTION OF MEASUREMENTS OF THE DURATION OF BUSINESS CYCLES IN THE UNITED STATES BASED UPON BUSINESS INDEXES, 1875–1925, AND BUSINESS ANNALS, 1790–1925.

By using 5 business indexes, and counting intervals both from trough to trough and crest to crest of the cycles, 101 measurements were made of the duration of 12½ cycles. The measurements, originally expressed in months, were grouped first by quarters, and later by years. See Table 16, Chart 20, and context in Chapter III.

The Annals yield a single set of measurements of the duration of 32 cycles. See Table 27.

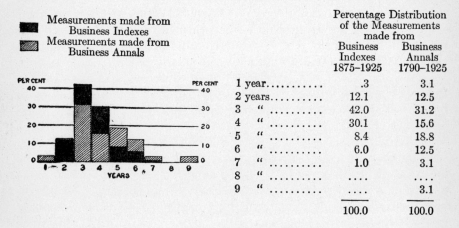

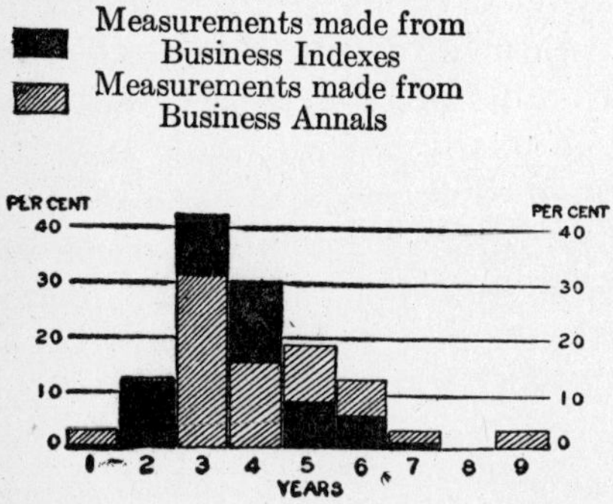

	Percentage Distribution of the Measurements made from Business Indexes 1875–1925	Business Annals 1790–1925
1 year..........	.3	3.1
2 years..........	12.1	12.5
3 "	42.0	31.2
4 "	30.1	15.6
5 "	8.4	18.8
6 "	6.0	12.5
7 "	1.0	3.1
8 "	....	....
9 "	....	3.1
	100.0	100.0

The similarity of the two figures on this chart is patent. If the measurements based on statistics show an even greater concentration at three years than do the measurements made from the annals (42 per cent of the observations as compared with 31 per cent), it is because of the difference in the years covered by the two sets of data. If we take only that part of the annals covered by the business indexes, we find 5 of the 12 cycles lasting 3 years, and 5 is 42 per cent of 12. Similar explanations apply to the other differences between the two figures:—for example, the lack of very short and very long cycles in 1875-1925 as compared with 1790-1925, accounts for the margins between the lines at 1 and 9 years.

In view of the agreement between the two sets of measurements, it seems safe to say (1) that if our business indexes extended back to 1790, they would show less concentration of cycles at 3 years, and a wider spread in the measurements; (2) that if we could elaborate the measurements made from the annals, by counting in months, and reckoning duration not merely from recession to recession, but also

from revival to revival, we should find the modal length to be more than 36 months, as Chart 20 indicates, though less than three and a half years.

V. International Relationships Among Business Cycles.

1. A Conspectus of Business Conditions in Different Countries.

Opinions differ widely concerning the relations between the economic fortunes of different countries. One prevalent view, often implied in discussions of public policy though seldom avowed openly, is that competition for foreign markets and foreign investments makes one nation's gain another nation's loss. A second view is that small countries with a vast commerce—England, the Netherlands, Belgium, Sweden and Norway—experience prosperity or depression as world business quickens or slackens; but that nations with a continental spread need feel slight concern about foreign factors—to them internal development is of overshadowing importance. There is still a third view, that business enterprise has been silently establishing a "world economy," a "commercial league of nations," in which all the members prosper or suffer together.

Needless to say, the annals do not give clear proof or disproof of any of these contentions. But they do indicate a trend in the direction of "world economy."

To facilitate international comparisons of economic fortunes, the annals of all the countries studied have been compressed into a single table. This conspectus begins with the United States and England in 1790, adds France in 1840, Germany in 1853, Austria in 1867, and 12 other countries in 1890. For the last generation it affords a fair view of world experience. The entries have the bleakness of statistical averages; they do not indicate the complexity of conditions prevailing every year within each country. For most purposes the fuller form of the annals given in Dr. Thorp's book should be used rather than the conspectus. But it is only as we concentrate in each country upon the net resultant of its diverse conditions that we can gain a clear view of the international similarities and diversities. Even the conspectus is not simple enough to tell its own story; it needs to be analyzed and summarized, as the reader who looks it over will agree.

TABLE 32

CONSPECTUS OF BUSINESS FLUCTUATIONS IN VARIOUS COUNTRIES

	1790	1791	1792	1793
United States	Revival; prosperity	Prosperity	Prosperity; financial distress	Prosperity
England	Moderate prosperity	Prosperity	Prosperity; financial strain	Recession; panic; depression
	1794	**1795**	**1796**	**1797**
United States	Uneven prosperity	Prosperity	Recession; depression	Depression; panic
England	Depression	Revival	Uneven prosperity	Recession; panic; depression
	1798	**1799**	**1800**	**1801**
United States	Depression	Revival	Prosperity	Mild prosperity
England	Depression	Depression	Depression	Depression; revival
	1802	**1803**	**1804**	**1805**
United States	Recession	Mild depression	Revival	Prosperity
England	Prosperity	Prosperity; recession	Mild depression	Revival
	1806	**1807**	**1808**	**1809**
United States	Prosperity	Prosperity; recession	Depression	Depression
England	Prosperity	Recession	Mild depression	Revival; prosperity
	1810	**1811**	**1812**	**1813**
United States	Revival	Moderate prosperity	Brief recession; uneven prosperity	Prosperity
England	Prosperity; recession	Deep depression	Revival	Prosperity
	1814	**1815**	**1816**	**1817**
United States	Prosperity; financial distress	Prosperity; panic; recession	Depression	Mild depression
England	Uneven prosperity	Boom; recession	Deep depression	Depression; revival
	1818	**1819**	**1820**	**1821**
United States	Mild depression	Severe depression; financial panic	Depression	Depression; revival
England	Prosperity	Recession; depression	Depression; slight revival	Slow revival

TABLE 32—(*Continued*)

CONSPECTUS OF BUSINESS FLUCTUATIONS IN VARIOUS COUNTRIES

	1822	1823	1824	1825
United States	Mild recession	Revival	Prosperity	Prosperity; panic; recession
England.....	Revival; prosperity	Prosperity	Prosperity	Prosperity; recession; panic
	1826	1827	1828	1829
United States	Depression; revival	Moderate prosperity	Prosperity; recession	Depression; revival
England.....	Depression	Revival	Prosperity	Recession; depression
	1830	1831	1832	1833
United States	Moderate prosperity	Prosperity	Moderate prosperity	Prosperity; panic; recession
England.....	Slow revival	Recession; depression	Depression	Revival
	1834	1835	1836	1837
United States	Mild depression	Revival; prosperity	Prosperity	Prosperity; panic; recession; depression
England.....	Prosperity	Prosperity; stock exchange panic	Prosperity; financial panic	Recession; panic; depression
	1838	1839	1840	1841
United States	Depression; slight revival	Revival; panic; recession	Depression	Depression
England.....	Depression	Depression	Depression	Depression
France.......	....	....	Revival	Prosperity
	1842	1843	1844	1845
United States	Depression	Depression; revival	Revival; prosperity	Prosperity; brief recession
England.....	Depression	Revival	Mild prosperity	Prosperity
France.......	Prosperity	Prosperity	Prosperity	Prosperity; bourse panic
	1846	1847	1848	1849
United States	Recession; mild depression	Revival; prosperity; panic; recession	Mild depression; revival	Prosperity
England.....	Prosperity	Prosperity; panic; recession	Depression	Depression; revival
France.......	Prosperity	Recession; panic	Depression; panic	Depression
	1850	1851	1852	1853
United States	Prosperity	Prosperity	Prosperity	Prosperity; recession
England.....	Prosperity	Prosperity	Prosperity	Prosperity
France.......	Depression	Depression	Revival	Prosperity
Germany....	....	....	....	Revival

TABLE 32—(*Continued*)

CONSPECTUS OF BUSINESS FLUCTUATIONS IN VARIOUS COUNTRIES

	1854	1855	1856	1857
United States	Recession; depression	Depression; revival	Prosperity	Prosperity; panic; recession; depression
England.....	Recession	Mild depression	Revival; prosperity	Prosperity; panic; recession
France.......	Prosperity; brief recession	Prosperity	Brief recession	Moderate prosperity; panic; recession
Germany....	Prosperity	Prosperity	Prosperity; bourse panic	Prosperity; panic; recession

	1858	1859	1860	1861
United States	Depression	Revival	Prosperity; recession	Mild depression; revival
England.....	Depression	Revival	Prosperity	Uneven prosperity
France.......	Depression	Revival	Prosperity; recession	Recession
Germany....	Recession; depression	Depression	Revival	Mild prosperity

	1862	1863	1864	1865
United States	War activity	War activity	War activity	Boom; recession
England.....	Uneven prosperity	Uneven prosperity	Uneven prosperity; financial strain	Prosperity
France......	Mild depression	Uneven depression	Depression; financial panic	Depression
Germany....	Uneven prosperity	Moderate prosperity	Moderate prosperity	Prosperity

	1866	1867	1868	1869
United States	Mild depression	Depression	Revival	Prosperity; monetary difficulties
England.....	Recession; panic; depression	Depression	Depression	Revival
France.......	Revival	Recession; mild depression; bourse panic	Depression; revival	Prosperity;
Germany....	Prosperity; recession; depression	Depression; revival	Revival	Prosperity bourse panic
Austria......	....	Revival	Moderate prosperity	Prosperity; panic; recession

TABLE 32—(*Continued*)

CONSPECTUS OF BUSINESS FLUCTUATIONS IN VARIOUS COUNTRIES

	1870	1871	1872	1873
United States	Recession; mild depression	Revival; prosperity	Prosperity	Prosperity; panic; recession
England	Prosperity; panic	Prosperity	Prosperity	Prosperity; recession
France	Prosperity; recession; depression	Depression; panic	Revival	Recession; depression
Germany	Prosperity; brief recession	Prosperity	Prosperity	Prosperity; panic; recession; depression
Austria	Slow recession	Mild depression	Revival; prosperity	Prosperity; panic; recession

	1874	1875	1876	1877
United States	Depression	Depression	Depression	Depression
England	Depression	Depression	Depression	Depression
France	Mild depression	Revival	Gradual recession	Mild depression
Germany	Depression	Depression	Depression	Slow revival
Austria	Deep depression	Depression	Depression	Depression

	1878	1879	1880	1881
United States	Depression; revival	Revival; prosperity	Prosperity	Prosperity
England	Deepening depression	Depression; revival	Slow revival	Mild prosperity
France	Depression	Revival; bourse panic	Prosperity	Moderate prosperity
Germany	Recession; depression	Depression; revival	Recession; mild depression	Renewed revival
Austria	Depression	Depression	Revival	Mild prosperity

	1882	1883	1884	1885
United States	Prosperity; slight recession	Recession	Depression	Depression; revival
England	Mild prosperity	Slow recession	Depression	Depression
France	Recession; panic	Depression	Depression	Depression
Germany	Prosperity; recession	Mild depression	Depression	Depression
Austria	Moderate prosperity; bourse panic	Prosperity	Recession	Mild depression

	1886	1887	1888	1889
United States	Revival	Prosperity	Brief recession	Prosperity
England	Depression; slight revival	Revival	Moderate prosperity	Prosperity
France	Depression	Revival	Moderate prosperity	Moderate prosperity; financial strain
Germany	Depression; revival	Revival	Moderate prosperity	Prosperity
Austria	Depression; revival	Revival	Prosperity	Prosperity

TABLE 32—(*Continued*)

CONSPECTUS OF BUSINESS FLUCTUATIONS IN VARIOUS COUNTRIES

	1890	1891	1892	1893
United States	Prosperity; recession	Depression; revival	Prosperity	Recession; panic; depression
England.....	Prosperity; panic; recession	Industrial recession; financial prostration	Depression	Deep depression
France.......	Recession; mild depression	Mild depression	Depression	Depression
Germany....	Recession	Depression	Depression	Depression
Austria......	Uneven prosperity	Prosperity	Recession	Revival
Russia.......	Mild prosperity	Recession, depression	Depression	Revival
Sweden......	Prosperity	Prosperity	Recession, mild depression	Depression
Netherlands..	Mild prosperity	Recession	Depression	Depression
Italy........	Depression	Depression; panic	Depression	Depression; panic
Argentina....	Recession; depression	Depression; panic	Revival, recession	Mild depression
Brazil.......	Depression	Depression	Uneven depression	Depression
Canada......	Mild depression	Depression; revival	Mild prosperity	Recession; depression
South Africa.	Prosperity; recession; depression	Depression	Rapid revival	Prosperity
Australia.....	Recession; depression	Depression	Depression	Depression; panic
India........	Mild depression	Depression	Uneven depression	Depression
Japan.......	Recession; depression	Depression	Depression	Mild depression
China.......	Mild depression	Mild depression	Depression deepens	Depression

TABLE 32—(*Continued*)

CONSPECTUS OF BUSINESS FLUCTUATIONS IN VARIOUS COUNTRIES

	1894	1895	1896	1897
United States	Deep depression	Depression; revival	Recession; depression	Depression; revival
England	Depression	Depression; revival last half-year	Revival; prosperity	Prosperity
France	Depression	Depression; revival	Revival	Moderate prosperity
Germany	Depression; revival	Revival	Prosperity	Prosperity
Austria	Recession; mild depression	Mild depression	Mild depression	Mild depression
Russia	Prosperity	Prosperity	Prosperity	Prosperity
Sweden	Mild depression	Revival	Prosperity	Prosperity
Netherlands	Depression	Depression	Revival	Mild prosperity
Italy	Depression	Depression	Depression; slight revival	Revival
Argentina	Depression	Lessening depression	Revival	Revival retarded
Brazil	Revival	Mild prosperity	Recession; panic; depression	Depression; panic
Canada	Acute depression	Depression	Lessening depression	Revival
South Africa	Prosperity	Prosperity; recession	Depression	Depression
Australia	Depression	Depression; slight revival	Strong revival	Mild prosperity; agricultural depression
India	Uneven revival	Mild prosperity	Recession	Depression
Japan	Revival; recession	Revival	Prosperity	Prosperity; recession
China	Depression	Revival	Prosperity	Gradual recession

TABLE 32—(*Continued*)

CONSPECTUS OF BUSINESS FLUCTUATIONS IN VARIOUS COUNTRIES

	1898	1899	1900	1901
United States	Revival; prosperity	Prosperity	Prosperity, brief recession	Prosperity
England	Prosperity	Prosperity	Prosperity; recession, summer	Mild depression
France	Prosperity	Prosperity	Prosperity; recession	Depression
Germany	Prosperity	Prosperity	Prosperity; recession; depression	Depression
Austria	Mild depression; revival	Mild prosperity	Recession; depression	Depression
Russia	Prosperity	Prosperity; panic; recession	Recession; depression	Depression
Sweden	Prosperity	Prosperity	Prosperity	Recession; depression
Netherlands	Prosperity	Prosperity	Prosperity	Recession; mild depression
Italy	Uneven prosperity	Mild prosperity	Prosperity; brief recession	Prosperity
Argentina	Mild prosperity	Prosperity	Recession; depression	Depression
Brazil	Depression deepens	Depression; revival	Revival; panic; recession	Mild depression
Canada	Prosperity	Prosperity	Prosperity; slight recession	Revival; prosperity
South Africa	Depression	Revival; recession	Depression	Revival
Australia	Prosperity	Prosperity	Prosperity	Recession
India	Slow revival	Moderate prosperity	Recession	Depression
Japan	Depression	Depression	Deeper depression	Depression; financial panic, spring
China	Mild depression	Revival; prosperity	Prosperity; recession; depression	Depression; revival

TABLE 32—(*Continued*)

CONSPECTUS OF BUSINESS FLUCTUATIONS IN VARIOUS COUNTRIES

	1902	1903	1904	1905
United States	Prosperity	Prosperity; recession	Mild depression; revival	Prosperity
England	Lessened depression	Depression deepens	Revival	Revival; prosperity
France	Depression	Revival	Moderate prosperity	Prosperity
Germany	Depression	Revival	Mild prosperity; recession	Revival; prosperity
Austria	Depression	Depression; revival	Revival	Mild prosperity
Russia	Depression	Depression; revival	Recession; depression	Depression
Sweden	Depression	Revival	Mild prosperity	Prosperity
Netherlands	Depression	Depression	Revival; prosperity	Prosperity
Italy	Moderate prosperity	Prosperity	Prosperity	Prosperity
Argentina	Depression; revival	Prosperity	Prosperity	Prosperity
Brazil	Mild depression	Depression deepens	Depression	Depression
Canada	Prosperity; financial distress	Prosperity	Uneven prosperity	Full prosperity
South Africa	Prosperity	Recession	Depression	Depression
Australia	Mild depression	Deepening depression	Revival	Mild prosperity
India	Revival	Prosperity	Prosperity	Prosperity
Japan	Slow revival	Revival	Prosperity	Prosperity; recession; depression
China	Mild prosperity	Mild prosperity	Mild prosperity	Mild prosperity

TABLE 32—(*Continued*)

CONSPECTUS OF BUSINESS FLUCTUATIONS IN VARIOUS COUNTRIES

	1906	1907	1908	1909
United States	Prosperity	Prosperity; panic; recession; depression	Depression	Revival; mild prosperity
England	Prosperity	Prosperity; recession	Depression	Revival
France	Prosperity	Prosperity	Recession; mild depression	Revival
Germany	Prosperity	Prosperity; recession; depression	Depression	Depression; revival
Austria	Prosperity	Prosperity	Recession; depression	Depression
Russia	Depression; slight revival	Revival	Recession; depression	Depression; revival
Sweden	Prosperity	Prosperity; recession; panic	Depression	Depression
Netherlands	Prosperity	Prosperity	Depression; revival	Revival; prosperity
Italy	Prosperity	Prosperity; recession	Depression	Depression
Argentina	Prosperity	Prosperity	Mild recession	Revival; prosperity
Brazil	Slow revival	Revival; recession, autumn	Depression	Revival
Canada	Prosperity peak	Prosperity; panic; recession	Depression; revival	Revival
South Africa	Depression	Depression deepens	Depression lessens	Revival
Australia	Prosperity	Prosperity	Recession; mild depression	Rapid revival; prosperity
India	Prosperity	Prosperity; recession	Depression	Depression; slight revival
Japan	Revival; prosperity	Prosperity; panic; recession	Depression	Depression; revival
China	Recession	Depression	Depression	Revival

TABLE 32—(*Continued*)

CONSPECTUS OF BUSINESS FLUCTUATIONS IN VARIOUS COUNTRIES

	1910	1911	1912	1913
United States	Recession	Mild depression	Revival; prosperity	Prosperity; recession
England	Prosperity	Prosperity	Prosperity	Prosperity; recession, last quarter
France	Prosperity	Prosperity	Prosperity	Prosperity; recession
Germany	Revival; prosperity	Prosperity	Prosperity	Prosperity; recession
Austria	Depression	Revival	Prosperity; recession; depression	Depression; panic
Russia	Prosperity	Prosperity	Prosperity	Prosperity except on bourse
Sweden	Revival	Prosperity	Prosperity	Prosperity; slight recession
Netherlands	Prosperity	Prosperity	Prosperity	Recession
Italy	Mild depression	Revival halted, autumn	Uneven prosperity	Mild prosperity; recession
Argentina	Prosperity	Recession; mild depression	Depression; revival, autumn	Recession
Brazil	Prosperity	Prosperity	Prosperity	Uneven prosperity
Canada	Prosperity	Prosperity	Prosperity	Prosperity; recession
South Africa	Prosperity	Prosperity	Prosperity	Uneven recession
Australia	Prosperity	Prosperity	Prosperity	Mild recession
India	Revival	Prosperity	Prosperity	Uneven prosperity
Japan	Revival; prosperity	Prosperity	Prosperity	Prosperity
China	Recession	Depression	Depression	Depression

TABLE 32—(*Continued*)

CONSPECTUS OF BUSINESS FLUCTUATIONS IN VARIOUS COUNTRIES

	1914	1915	1916	1917
United States	Depression	Revival; prosperity	Prosperity	Prosperity; war activity
England.....	Mild depression, deepens with war	War activity	War activity	War activity
France.......	Depression	War activity	War activity	War activity
Germany....	Mild depression; revival	War activity	War activity	War activity
Austria......	Depression	War activity	War activity	War activity
Russia.......	Recession; panic; depression	Uneven depression	War activity	Recession; depression
Sweden......	Recession; depression	Revival, prosperity	Prosperity	Recession
Netherlands..	Recession; panic; depression	Revival; uneven prosperity	Moderate prosperity	Recession
Italy........	Recession; panic; depression	Uneven depression	War activity	War activity
Argentina....	Depression; panic	Uneven depression	Depression; slow revival	Revival
Brazil........	Depression deepens	Depression; revival	Revival; prosperity	Prosperity
Canada......	Depression deepening with war	Depression; revival	War activity	War activity
South Africa.	Recession; depression	Slow revival	Rapid revival	Prosperity
Australia.....	Revival; recession	Mild depression; revival	War activity	War activity
India........	Prosperity: recession	Depression	Revival	Prosperity
Japan.......	Recession; depression	Revival; prosperity	Prosperity	Uneven prosperity
China.......	Depression deepens	Depression	Revival; prosperity	Uneven prosperity

TABLE 32—(*Continued*)

CONSPECTUS OF BUSINESS FLUCTUATIONS IN VARIOUS COUNTRIES

	1918	1919	1920	1921
United States	War activity; recession	Revival; prosperity	Prosperity; recession; depression	Depression
England.....	War activity; recession	Revival; prosperity	Prosperity; recession; depression	Deep depression
France.......	War activity; stagnation	Depression; revival; boom	Prosperity; recession; depression	Depression; revival
Germany....	War activity; disorganization, November	Depression	Depression	Revival, spring
Austria......	War activity; chaos	Depression	Slow revival	Revival
Russia.......	Depression	Depression	Depression	Depression
Sweden......	Depression	Depression; revival	Boom; recession; depression	Depression
Netherlands..	Depression	Revival; prosperity	Prosperity; recession; depression	Depression
Italy........	War activity; slight recession	Mild depression; revival	Recession; depression	Depression; panic
Argentina....	Moderate prosperity	Prosperity	Prosperity; recession	Depression
Brazil.......	Prosperity; brief recession	Prosperity	Prosperity; recession; depression	Severe depression
Canada......	War activity; recession	Revival; prosperity	Prosperity; recession	Depression
South Africa.	Prosperity; recession	Revival; prosperity	Prosperity; recession; depression	Deep depression
Australia.....	War activity	Prosperity	Prosperity; recession	Depression
India........	Prosperity; recession	Revival; prosperity	Prosperity; recession; depression	Depression
Japan.......	Uneven prosperity; recession	Depression; revival; prosperity	Prosperity; recession; depression	Depression
China.......	Uneven prosperity	Prosperity	Prosperity; recession; depression	Depression

TABLE 32—(*Continued*)

CONSPECTUS OF BUSINESS FLUCTUATIONS IN VARIOUS COUNTRIES

	1922	1923	1924	1925
United States	Revival; prosperity	Prosperity; recession	Mild depression; revival	Prosperity
England.....	Depression	Depression	Lessening depression	Depression
France.......	Revival	Prosperity	Prosperity	Prosperity
Germany....	Revival checked, summer; disorganization	Depression	Revival; temporary check, summer	Halting revival; recession
Austria......	Uneven recession	Depression	Depression; financial strain	Depression
Russia.......	Depression; slight revival	Revival; recession, October	Mild depression; revival	Uneven prosperity; recession
Sweden......	Depression; revival	Revival	Mild prosperity	Mild prosperity
Netherlands..	Depression	Depression	Revival	Mild prosperity
Italy........	Depression	Depression; revival	Moderate prosperity	Prosperity
Argentina....	Depression	Lessening depression	Revival	Prosperity
Brazil.......	Lessening depression	Revival	Mild prosperity; recession	Depression
Canada......	Depression; revival	Moderate prosperity	Recession; mild depression	Revival; prosperity
South Africa.	Depression	Revival	Mild prosperity	Prosperity
Australia.....	Slow revival	Revival; mild prosperity	Mild recession	Revival; prosperity
India........	Depression	Slow revival	Revival; mild prosperity	Mild prosperity
Japan.......	Depression	Depression	Depression	Depression; revival
China.......	Depression	Depression	Depression	Depression

2. How Closely the Cycles in Different Countries Agree.

Concerning the fact of fundamental interest in this inquiry, the conspectus of business conditions gives an exaggerated impression of century-long and world-wide similarity. Periods of prosperity, recession, depression and revival are here pictured as recurring in much the same way in every country and during every decade. The fuller form of the annals makes it clear, not only that this recurrence is nowhere the whole story of economic fluctuations, but also that it is farther from being the whole story in some countries than in others. The importance of business cycles as a factor in national life was less during the closing decades of the 18th century than during the opening decades of the 20th century in England and the United States. There is a similar difference between these two countries and China, Russia or Brazil at present. The more highly organized a country's business, the larger the proportion of its people who live by making and spending money incomes, the more important become the recurrent cycles of activity. Let us, however, take cyclical oscillations for granted, disregard their relative amplitudes, and inquire what influence the cycles in one country exercise upon cycles in other countries.

It has long been recognized that the great financial crises have an international sweep. Thus the conspectus shows that England and the United States shared in the crises of 1815, 1825 and 1837; that England, the United States and France (which now is represented in the annals) shared in the crisis of 1847; that these three countries, and Germany also, shared in the panic of 1857; that England, the United States, France, Germany and Austria shared in varying degrees the crisis of 1873. To these familiar facts our annals add that all five countries had mild recessions in 1882-84. Of the 17 countries included in the annals after 1890, 10 had recessions in 1890-91, 15 had recessions in 1900-01, 15 in 1907-08, 12 in 1912-13, 11 in 1918, and 14 in 1920. Further, the countries which escaped a share in these world reactions usually owed their exemption to an earlier turn for the worse. Thus South Africa and Japan had no recession in 1900-01 because they were already suffering from depres-

sion. The three countries of our 17 which escaped in 1920 were Germany, Austria and Russia.

Of course the experiences of the several countries were not identical in the years of crises and recessions. In the whole record there is no crisis which was equally severe everywhere. In 1873, for example, the United States, Germany and Austria suffered far more severely than England and France. In 1890, on the contrary, the financial strain was more severe in London than in New York or Berlin, while Vienna deferred its recession until 1892. The center of disturbance in 1900 seems to have been Germany; countries like the United States and Italy felt but repercussions of a foreign shock. In 1907 the gravest difficulties appeared in the United States. Probably the nearest approach to a severe world-wide crisis was made in 1920, and that case was obviously dominated by post-war readjustments. It is clear, however, that a financial crisis breaking out in any country of commercial importance produces financial strains in other countries, and that even mild recessions like those of 1882-83 and 1913 spread widely.

It has been less noticed that other phases of business cycles also propagate themselves. The long depressions of the 1870's, the checkered fortunes of the 1880's, the revival of the middle 1890's, the boom of 1906-7, the calmer prosperity of 1912, the hectic activity of the war years, and the severe depression after 1920 had much the same international character as the crises to which attention is often restricted.

Yet business cycles do not run a strictly parallel course in any two countries. Perhaps the best way to bring out the degree of likeness and difference in contemporary fortunes is to note the proportion of years in which conditions in different countries are described by the same terms in the conspectus, and the proportion of years in which conditions are described in unlike terms. An effort to carry out this plan shows that many years do not fall into either category. Business may be reviving in one country and already prosperous in another, depressed in one and entering depression in another; or conditions may be similar during the early part of a year and divergent in the closing months, or different at the start and convergent at the close. In such cases one cannot call the conditions quite similar or decidedly unlike. Thus it is necessary to recognize at least three types of relations between the synchronous phases of business cycles in different countries—agreement, partial agreement

and opposition. Arbitrary definitions may be adopted, and a statistical tabulation made of these relationships.[1]

Such a comparison of business conditions in the five countries for which we have annals running back of 1890 is provided by Table 33. Most of the comparisons here made show a preponderance of years in which the business cycles of the countries paired were passing through the same phases over years in which they were passing through opposite phases. The intimacy of relations is probably understated by the table; for it takes no account of the shifting relations of lead and lag in the influence exercised by business conditions in one country upon business conditions in the other country with which it is compared. As one would expect from England's position in international trade and finance, English cycles are more highly correlated with the cycles of other countries, than the cycles of other countries are correlated with each other. The closest agreements are found between English and French or English and German cycles; the loosest agreements are between Austrian and American cycles.

From the third section of the table, it appears that the international similarity of phase in business cycles increased on the whole with the passage of time. The breaking of economic bonds by the war, and the tardiness of their restoration after the Armistice, interfered with this process of synchronizing cycles. But the non-economic factors, which played so large a rôle after 1914, had much the same character and influenced business among all the belligerents in much the same way, so long as hostilities lasted. Since 1918, economic

[1] The rules followed by Dr. Thorp in preparing the data for the following table are as follows:

Agreement includes

1. Years in which two countries pass through the same phase or phases of a cycle.
2. Years in which two countries pass through at least two corresponding phases, though one may enter a third phase. Example: "Prosperity; recession" in one country, and "Prosperity; recession; depression" in another.

Partial agreement includes

Years in which two countries pass through phases of the cycle which succeed one another. Example: "Revival" in one country, and "Prosperity" in another; or "Recession" in one country, and "Recession; depression" in another.

Opposition of phases includes

Years in which opposite phases of cycles occur, whatever intermediate phases are noted. Example: "Prosperity; recession; depression" in one country, and "Depression; revival" in a second.

War activity is interpreted in this tabulation as corresponding to prosperity.
The relative severity of recessions in different countries is not taken into account.

TABLE 33.

AGREEMENT AND DIFFERENCE OF PHASE IN ENGLISH, FRENCH, GERMAN, AUSTRIAN AND AMERICAN BUSINESS CYCLES

Various Periods

	Period Covered		Number of Years of			Percentage of Years of		
	Dates	Number of Years	Agreement in Phase	Partial agreement	Opposition in Phase	Agreement in Phase	Partial agreement	Opposition in Phase
I								
English and French cycles.	1867–1925	59	32	20	7	54	34	12
English and German cycles	" "	59	33	22	4	56	37	7
English and Austrian cycles	" "	59	27	21	11	46	36	19
English and American cycles	" "	59	28	18	13	47	31	22
French and German cycles.	" "	59	27	25	7	46	42	12
French and Austrian cycles	" "	59	19	21	19	32	36	32
French and American cycles	" "	59	23	23	13	39	39	22
German and Austrian cycles	" "	59	23	24	12	39	41	20
German and American cycles	" "	59	21	20	18	36	34	31
Austrian and American cycles	" "	59	18	23	18	31	39	31
II								
England and four other countries	1867–1925	236	120	81	35	51	34	15
Germany and four other countries	" "	236	104	91	41	44	39	17
France and four other countries	" "	236	101	89	46	43	38	19
United States and four other countries	" "	236	90	84	62	38	36	26
Austria and four other countries	" "	236	87	89	60	37	38	25
III								
English and American cycles	1790–1857	68	21	28	19	31	41	28
	1857–1925	68	33	21	14	49	31	21
English and French cycles..	1840–1882	43	12	17	14	28	40	33
	1883–1925	43	28	11	4	65	26	9
English and German cycles.	1853–1888	36	19	15	2	53	42	6
	1889–1925	37	21	13	3	57	35	8
English and Austrian cycles.	1867–1895	29	14	12	3	48	41	10
	1896–1925	30	13	9	8	43	30	27

fortunes have diverged widely. Presumably the business forces tending toward convergence are gradually resuming their wonted sway.

In treating the period when the annals include 17 countries, a more significant method of presenting the relations among their business cycles is feasible. For the cycles since 1890 have an international pattern simple enough to be carried in mind, and applied to the experience of one country after another. This pattern may be sketched as follows:

1st cycle, 1890-91 to 1900-01
Recession in 1890-91; depression in 1891-95; revival in 1895-96; prosperity in 1896-00; recession in 1900-01.

2nd cycle, 1900-01 to 1907-08
Recession in 1900-01; depression in 1901-03; revival in 1903-04; prosperity in 1905-07; recession in 1907-08.

3rd cycle, 1907-08 to 1913-14
Recession in 1907-08; depression in 1908-09; revival in 1909-10; prosperity in 1910-13; recession in 1913-14.

4th cycle, 1913-14 to 1918
Recession in 1913-14; depression in 1914-15; revival in 1915; prosperity in 1915-18; recession in 1918.

5th cycle, 1918 to 1920
Recession in 1918; very brief and mild depression early in 1919; quick revival in 1919; prosperity in 1919-20; recession in 1920.

6th cycle, 1920 to —— (unfinished)
Recession in 1920; severe depression in 1921-22; revival in 1922-23; mild prosperity in 1924-25.

During this period, of our 17 countries

Six have had 5 cycles and are now in a 6th: England, France, the Netherlands, Sweden, Italy and China.

Five have had 6 cycles and are now in a 7th: Austria, South Africa, Australia, Argentina and India.

Five have had 7 cycles and are now in an 8th: Germany, Russia, Canada, Brazil, and Japan.

One has had 10 cycles and is now in an 11th: the United States.

Thus no country in our list has had fewer business cycles since 1890 than the international pattern calls for; but the majority of

countries have had one or two more than that number. These additional cycles seldom result from failure to participate in the international movements of activity and depression, but rather from the intercalation of what we may call domestic recessions between the dates of international recessions. To take the most striking case: the United States had its share in all the recessions of the international pattern; but it also had domestic recessions in 1893, 1896, 1903, 1910, and 1923. When a country skips an international recession, it is usually because that country has recently suffered a domestic recession. Thus business was already depressed in Japan and South Africa when the international recession of 1900 began; South Africa and China escaped the international recession of 1907 for similar reasons; so too the European neutrals had recessions in 1917 and not in 1918.

The countries whose business cycles diverge most from the international pattern are Italy before say 1907, Russia, South Africa, Brazil and China—all countries rather backward in economic organization and predominantly agricultural. The countries whose cycles have followed the international pattern most closely, on the other hand, are countries of highly developed industry, trade, and finance—England, France, Germany (until 1919), Sweden, and the Netherlands. Australia and Canada lag but a little behind these European powers in conformity. Austrian cycles were being assimilated closely to those of her western and northern neighbors in the decade before the war. Even British India and Japan have followed the European pattern of cycles without very striking divergencies.

Another way of summing up the international relationships of business cycles since 1890 is to run down the columns of entries in Table 32 for each year. There is no year of the 36 covered in which the same phase of the cycle prevailed in all of the 17 countries. Uniformity is approached, however, in 1893, 1899, 1906, 1908, 1912, 1916, 1920, and 1921; and in most years there is a marked preponderance of entries of similar tenor.

A graphic presentation of these facts is given by Chart 27. The irregular bands of white and of black which run vertically across the chart are not quite continuous in any year from 1890 to 1925. But the existence of a general trend toward uniformity of business fortunes is plain.

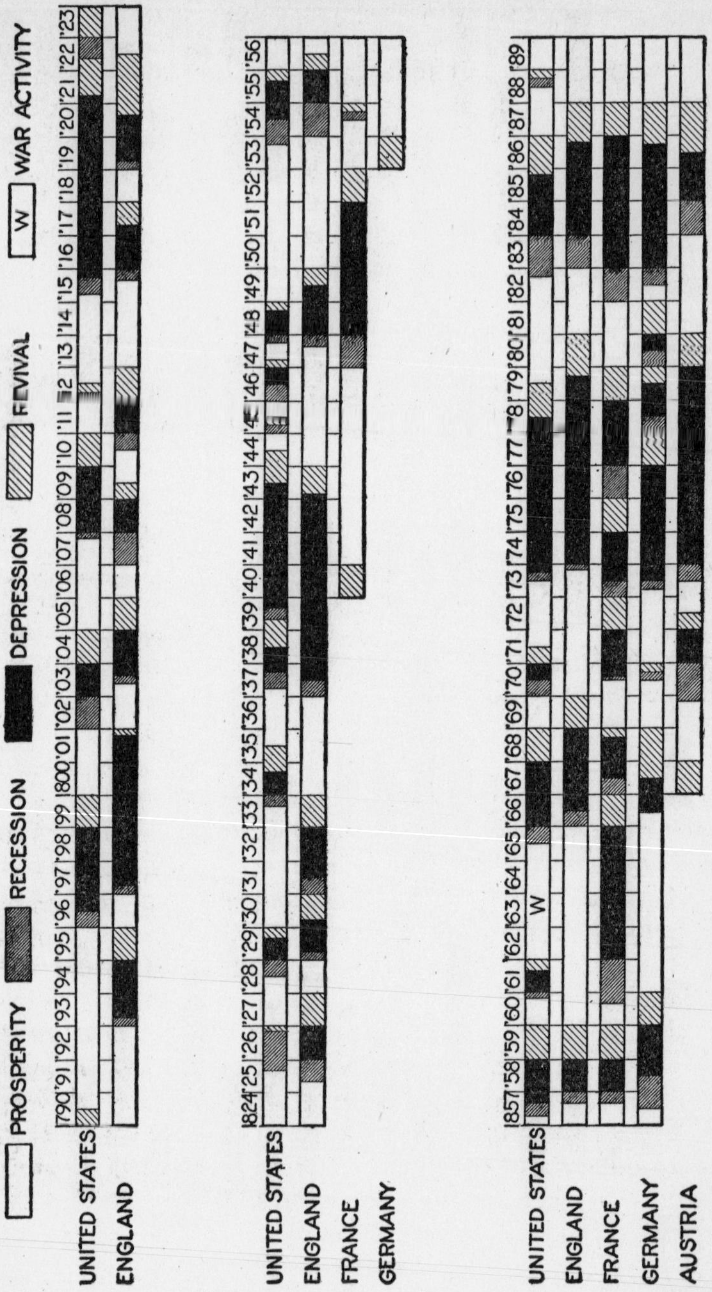

PROSPERITY
RECESSION
DEPRESSION
REVIVAL
W WAR ACTIVITY
UNITED STATES
ENGLAND
UNITED STATES
ENGLAND
FRANCE
GERMANY
UNITED STATES
ENGLAND
FRANCE
GERMANY
AUSTRIA

Chart 27. Conspectus of Business Cycles in Various Countries, 1790-1925—(*Continued*)

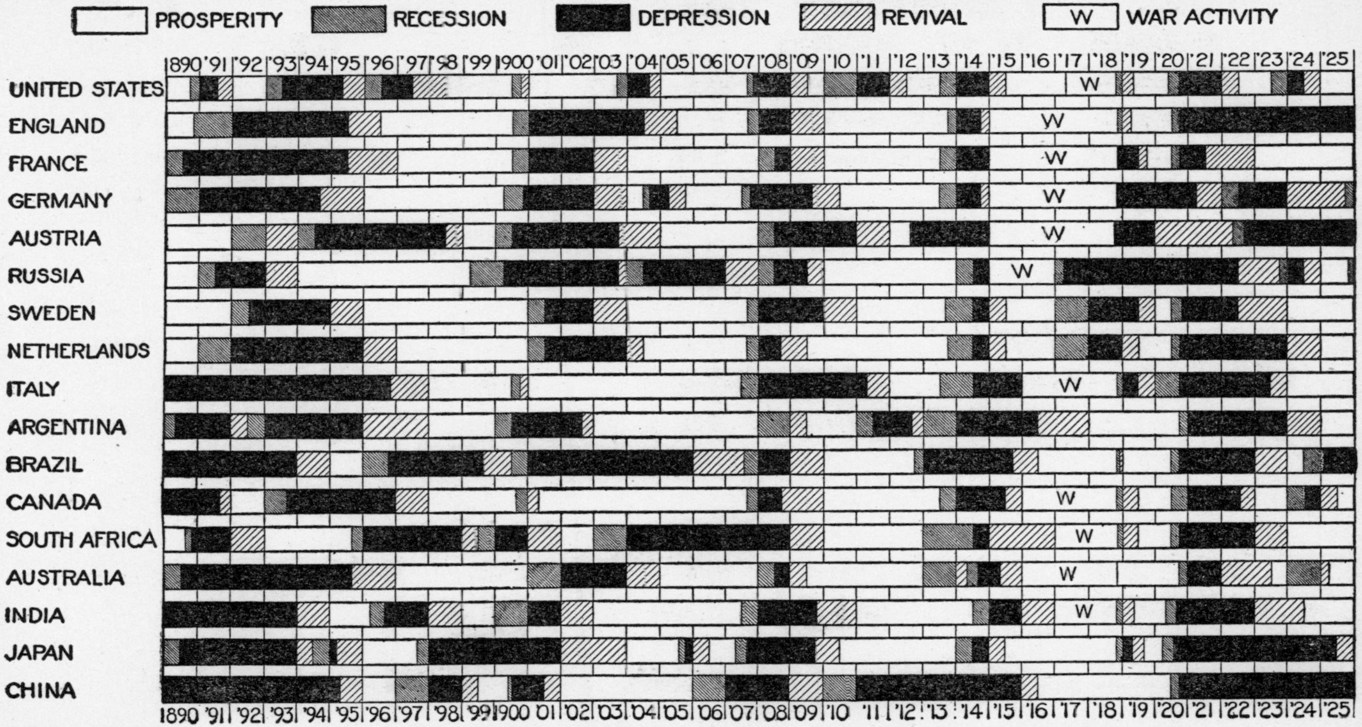

3. Domestic and Foreign Factors in Business Cycles.

Possibly this tendency to synchronize their phases, found in the business cycles of different countries, arises from some cosmic cause which affects all quarters of the globe in much the same way each year. Upon that daring hypothesis, our annals throw no light. But the annals do suggest certain tamer explanations, which account not only for the general resemblance among cycles in different countries, but also for their differences. These tamer explanations are not inconsistent with the cosmic hypothesis, but they do not depend upon it.

Whatever the causes of the recurrent fluctuations in economic activity may be, the annals suggest that these causes become active in all communities where there has developed an economic organization approximating that of western Europe. There appears to be a rough parallelism between the stage attained in the evolution of this organization by different countries, and the prominence of business cycles as a factor in their fortunes.

One characteristic of the type of organization in question is the wide area over which it integrates and coördinates economic activities. Bare as they are and short their span, the annals reveal a secular trend toward territorial expansion of business relations and a concomitant trend toward economic unity. For example, the American annals show how often the fortunes of the North, the South and the West diverged from one another in the earlier decades after the adoption of the Constitution, and how these divergencies have diminished in later decades. Not that business is ever equally prosperous or equally depressed in all states of the Union even now: always there are perceptible differences, and at times the differences are wide, particularly among the great farming "belts." Yet the annals picture the vastly greater population of to-day, spread over a vastly greater territory, as having more unity of fortune than had the people of the thirteen original states and the frontier settlements in 1790-1820.

Broadly speaking, the annals support a similar conclusion concerning the world at large. The network of business relations has been growing closer and firmer at the same time that it has been stretching over wider areas. The annals allow us to catch some glimpses of this double trend within the borders of a few countries besides the United States, and they show it clearly in the relations among different countries. As American business is coming to have one story, diversi-

fied by agricultural episodes, so, before the war shattered international bonds for a time, world business seemed to be approaching the time when it too would have one story, diversified by political and social as well as agricultural episodes in different countries.

The basis of this trend toward unity of economic fortunes among communities organized on the European model is that each phase in a business cycle, as it develops in any area, tends to produce the same phase in all the areas with which the first has dealings.

Prosperity in one country stimulates demand for the products of other countries, and so quickens activities in the latter regions. Prosperity also lessens the energy with which merchants, financiers, and contractors seek competitive business in neutral markets, and so gives a better chance to the corresponding classes in countries where the domestic demand is less active. Further, prosperity, with its sanguine temper and its liberal profits, encourages investments abroad as well as at home, and the export of capital to other countries gives an impetus to their trade. A recession checks all these stimuli. A severe crisis in any important center produces quicker and graver results. Demands for financial assistance raise interest rates and reduce domestic lending power in other centers; apprehensions regarding the solvency of international houses may start demands for liquidation in many places; the losses which bankruptcies bring are likely to be felt by business enterprises the world over. So, too, with depressions and revival; wherever they prevail, they exert influences upon business elsewhere which tend to produce depressions or revivals in all regions with which the center of disturbance trades.

Nor are these relations one-sided. The condition of business in every country not only influences, but is influenced by conditions in other countries. The trend toward international similarity of business cycles is enforced by an endless series of actions and reactions among the influences exerted and experienced by all the nations which deal with each other.

Of course, the degree of influence exerted by business conditions in a given area upon business elsewhere depends upon the importance of that area in international commerce and finance. Similarly, the sensitiveness of business in a given area to the influence of business conditions elsewhere is least in communities like interior China, whose economic activities are mainly self-contained, and greatest in communities which depend largely upon foreign markets, foreign invest-

ments, and foreign sources of supply, like England. It is also clear that a country of the latter type will reflect world conditions more faithfully, the more widely its foreign interests are distributed.

While this line of analysis explains the tendency of business cycles in different countries to synchronize their phases, it does not hide the obstructions which this tendency meets.

In so far as the people in any country buy and sell, lend and borrow only among themselves, they are likely to have economic vicissitudes all their own. Agricultural communities which live largely on what they produce suffer more from acts of nature than farming populations which trade extensively; but they have little share in the world dislocations of business. Even in countries where farmers are more business-like, we have noted that agriculture has a story of its own, dictated by the weather at home and abroad—a story which often differs from the story of mining, manufactures, transportation, wholesale trade, and finance.[1] Of course the agricultural story modifies the general tale. Fluctuations in the cost of raw materials and of foods, as well as fluctuations in the buying power of farm families, react upon the prosperity of other industries in proportion to the relative weight of agriculture in the country's total business. Hence, the larger the agricultural element in a given nation, the less likely are that nation's business cycles to fit neatly into the international pattern over a long series of years. For two nations with large farming interests are not likely to have closely similar harvest fluctuations year after year. The one development touching agriculture which most clearly tends toward unifying business fortunes is the decline in the proportion of families which depend on farming, and the concomitant increase in the proportion following industrial pursuits. Dr. Thorp's prefaces to the chapters of *Business Annals* show that this decline is world-wide.

While the rise of large-scale industry within a nation of cultivators, craftsmen and petty traders links its economic life to that of other nations, there may be a stage in this development when international influences seem to recede and domestic influences to grow more important. The first modern mines, factories, railways, and banks in such a country are likely to be foreign enterprises,

[1] In one way, the development of a "world market" for the great agricultural staples even increases the hazards of farming. A scanty yield of wheat in Canada, for example, does not always cause a compensatory rise of prices.

dependent upon foreign investors for their capital and perhaps upon foreign customers for their markets. During that stage, such business as the outside world recognizes in the new-old country will be peculiarly sensitive to foreign fluctuations in finance and commerce. Meanwhile, if the new ventures prosper, natives of the country will learn to practice modern methods and to consume modern products. Alongside the foreign-owned enterprises, domestic enterprises will multiply, drawing their capital from home sources and selling largely in the home market. After a time perhaps most of the early enterprises will be sold by their foreign owners to native business men. During this stage the country's business will seem to be emancipating itself from the domination of outside influences, and its business cycles will diverge more widely from the international pattern. But if the process of modernizing economic life continues until a considerable fraction of the population is affected, then a gradual reapproach toward world conditions will begin. Some such series of changes probably explains in part, but in part only, a curious feature of our Russian annals. In the earlier years covered by this record, Russian cycles followed the international pattern more closely than in the later years of the Tsarist régime.[2] Perhaps Chinese business will pass through similar stages in the not-distant future.

Besides differences in economic organization, in the proportion of people engaged in farming, and in harvest conditions, there is a host of more obvious causes of divergencies among business cycles, whether we consider successive cycles in the same country or synchronous cycles in different countries. Wars and civil disturbances play a prominent rôle in business annals, and that rôle is most erratic. Many of the differences of business fortune which the annals show seem ascribable to such factors; but we have had occasion to note that during its earlier stages, at least, the World War had a unifying effect upon conditions among both belligerents and neutrals. The after-effects of this war, however, were far from uniform in different nations. In the cycles of every country we can trace also the influence of changes in monetary conditions, banking organization and tariff acts domestic or foreign, if not the influence of changes in taxation, internal improvement plans and public regulation of business enterprises. Besides these governmental matters, it seems probable that

[2] For a fuller discussion of the relations between business cycles in Russia and in Western Europe, see S. A. Pervushin, *The Business Conjuncture*, Moscow, 1925, pp. 209-213. I am indebted to Dr. Simon S. Kuznets for a synopsis of Professor Pervushin's analysis.

differences of national habit in respect to enterprise and thrift affect the frequency and violence of business oscillations. Still other matters which may count are changes in the methods of managing investments, the integration of industry, the organization of labor, the development of social insurance. But there is little point in extending a list of factors whose relative importance we cannot weigh.

This much seems clear: business activity is influenced by countless developments in the realms of nature, politics and science, as well as by developments within the realm of business itself; few of these developments occur at the same time, in the same form and on the same scale in all countries. Thus there is no difficulty in understanding why business cycles vary in many ways from nation to nation, though it is quite impossible as yet to assign its relative importance to each (perhaps to any) cause of divergence. One's final reflection may be that the quiet business forces working toward uniformity of fortunes must be powerful indeed to impress a common pattern upon the course of business cycles in many countries. And the increasing conformity to an international pattern which the annals reveal in recent years shows that the international influences are gaining in relative importance.

CHAPTER V.

RESULTS AND PLANS.

I. The Concept of Business Cycles.

1. Evolution of the Concept.

To the early workers in our field the pressing problem was to account for the dramatic events which they called "commercial crises." Not only did they confine themselves mainly to this single phase of business fluctuations; also they confined themselves mainly to excogitating explanations. The occurrence of crises was known to everyone. What need was there of elaborate factual investigations? And why need one explain prosperity?

This approach led to a discussion which centered in the validity of rival doctrines, rather than in the characteristics of business fluctuations. The participants debated with each other on the basis of common knowledge, reënforced by occasional citations of evidence. Even in using evidence, their aims were oftener dialectical than positive. A second consequence was that the discussion tended to drift away from the main body of economic theory and to become a "specialty." For when crises are taken out of their setting in a continuous process of change, they appear to be "abnormal" phenomena. As such they lie on the edge, rather than in the center, of the theoretician's domain. In discussions of what were taken to be the leading problems of economics, changes in business activity were among the matters hidden from sight under the blanket assumption, "other things remaining the same." While chapters on the cause of crises appeared in some of the standard treatises which applied economic principles to practical issues, the topic had no place in "pure theory." Most of the contributions were monographs, and many of the writers had but slender knowledge of economics. As late as 1898, Böhm-Bawerk thought it necessary to argue that a theory of crises "should always form the last, or next-to-the-last, chapter in a system of eco-

nomic theory, written or unwritten."[1] The converse view, that ideas developed in the study of business fluctuations may lead to reformulations of economic theory, still strikes most economists as strange.[2]

A broader conception of the problem was implied by John Wade's casual observation, made in 1833, that "the commercial cycle," with its "alternate periods of prosperity and depression," had been running its course in England "during the last seventy years."[3] Probably the notion that trade fluctuations are cyclical occurred independently to other men; certainly it spread rapidly. Clement Juglar made this conception his own, and in 1860 sought to show the relations between the "three periods of prosperity, crisis, and liquidation," which "always follow one another in the same order." More than that, Juglar threw himself energetically into factual investigations, basing his conclusions largely upon analyses of changes in commodity prices, interest rates, and bank balances, supplemented by a history of crises since 1696.[4] His work marks a critical turning point in the study. But, though Juglar grasped the need of dealing with business cycles, he called his book *Des Crises Commerciales*. If to this day many writers (especially Europeans) follow his precedent in choosing titles for their books, they also follow his other precedent by making their theories of crises include a discussion of prosperity and depressions, if not also of revivals.[5]

Most of the changes made since Juglar's time in the conception of the problem have resulted from doing the kind of work he did on a larger scale and more intensively. Ideas implicit in his notions have become clear; matters which he passed over lightly have been emphasized; better methods of analyzing time series have been invented; terms have come into use which Juglar would not have under-

[1] See Böhm-Bawerk's review of Eugen von Bergmann's *Geschichte der Nationalökonomischen Krisentheorien*, in *Zeitschrift für Volkswirtschaft, Sozialpolitik und Verwaltung*, vol. vii, p. 112.

[2] Compare Dr. Adolf Löwe's elaborate argument that the problem of cyclical fluctuations cannot be treated by the "variation methods" of pure economics, and that it, among other problems, calls for the development of a dynamic theory, in which the concept of equilibrium will be replaced by the concept of cyclical oscillations. "Wie ist Konjunkturtheorie überhaupt möglich?" *Weltwirtschaftliches Archiv*, October, 1926, vol. xxiv, pp. 165-197.

[3] See Chapter I, section iii.

[4] To appreciate the scope of Juglar's long-continued labors, one must examine the second edition of his book, *Des Crises Commerciales*, Paris, 1889. The phrases quoted in the text are from p. 21.

[5] For example, see Mentor Bouniatian's remarks concerning the ground which should be covered by a theory of crises: *Les Crises Économiques*, Paris, 1922, p. 28.

stood. Both in seeming and in truth, the whole discussion is on a different plane; yet one can read many of the ideas which seem to us fresh between the lines of Juglar's book, if not in the text itself.

Juglar did not realize clearly that the intervals between crises frequently contain two, and sometimes contain three, alternations of prosperity and depression. Nor is this important fact firmly grasped by contemporary writers upon crises. It stands out sharply only when one analyzes appropriate time series, or reads business reviews with care. Of course, the reason why these brief cycles are overlooked by writers upon crises is that the cycles in question include no crises, in the traditional meaning of the term. A man who composes a treatise upon "Commercial Crises" may entertain the idea of "commercial cycles," plan to treat them, and yet not recognize a goodly part of the cycles revealed by his own materials. To minimize the danger of being thus misled, statistical investigators, who plume themselves upon following faithfully the indications of their data, have discarded what seemed to be the most firmly established term in the whole discussion. They call the transition from prosperity to depression a recession. It follows that the cycles which they recognize are briefer on the average than the cycles of the books on crises. Instead of thinking about periods seven or eight years long, they think of three- or four-year cycles as typical. But they are also concerned to find how the longer and shorter cycles are distributed about this mode, and how the average duration of cycles varies from period to period and from one country to another.

In word, at least, Juglar held that crises are "periodic": his full title runs *Des Crises Commerciales et de leur Retour Périodique en France, en Angleterre et aux États-Unis*. But his own history of crises in these three countries shows that in no one of them have the intervals between crises been regular. Theoretical writers frequently follow this inexact precedent, calling crises periodic in their titles and showing in their texts that the period varies widely.[6] Statistical

[6] Compare the titles of the following books with the passages cited in each: A. Aftalion, *Les Crises Périodiques de Surproduction,* Paris, 1913, vol. i, pp. 8-14; M. Bouniatian, *Les Crises Économiques—Essai de Morphologie et théorie des crises économiques périodiques,* Paris, 1922, pp. 42-45; J. Lescure, *Des Crises Générales et Périodiques de Surproduction,* 3d ed., Paris, 1913, pp. 1-288 (note the intervals between the dates of the crises described); Ludwig Pohle, *Bevölkerungsbewegung, Kapitalbildung, und periodische Wirtschaftskrisen,* Göttingen, 1902, statistics in the appendix, especially pp. 89-90.

This may be one more case in which we should explain what seems to be a verbal contradiction by observing that what a theorist takes to be "normally" true he does not expect to find historically true.

workers have avoided this loose use of a term which in other sciences implies strict regularity of timing. What they find to be regular is the recurrence of prosperity, recession, depression and revival, in that sequence. One of their leading aims, as said above, is to find out just how business cycles, and their constituent phases, vary in duration. Yet to this day an occasional critic treats the word "cyclical" as synonymous with "periodic," and imputes belief in the periodicity of fluctuations to writers upon business cycles.

John Wade spoke confidently of "the" commercial cycle; on occasion Juglar used the corresponding French phrase; [7] there are recent books upon "the" business cycle and "the" trade cycle.[8] Possibly the misleading implications which can be read into these phrases would have been accepted by their early users. John Wade may have conceived the commercial cycle as a single movement, or as a succession of grand, unitary swings from prosperity to depression and back again. Maybe a ghost of this dim notion still haunts the minds of some who trace business cycles to a single cause. But most of those who now speak of "the" business cycle, mean by it, not one phenomenon, but a congeries of interrelated phenomena. Increasing emphasis upon the diversities in respect to amplitude and timing found among the cyclical fluctuations of different processes is highly characteristic of recent work. Statistics provide no direct evidence of the existence of "the" business cycle; what they provide is evidence of cyclical fluctuations in hundreds of time series. Indeed, it is difficult to construct from the data, or even to conceive of constructing, any single index of "the general trend" in business activity.[9] But the more thoroughly investigators anatomize the business cycle, the more they need a general term to designate the whole.

Yet the words we use set traps for us. Starting with a vague conception of a group of seemingly related phenomena which we wish to study, we name it. That step is necessary, but dangerous. The definiteness of the name may conceal from us the indefiniteness of our knowledge. If the name is a compound of words familiar in other uses, we may take their implications for facts. Assuming tacitly that

[7] For example, "Le cycle est parcouru dans le monde entier sur toutes les places de commerce;" *Des Crises Commerciales*, 2d ed., p. 17.

[8] For example, Miss Dorothy S. Thomas calls her valuable study *Social Aspects of the Business Cycle*, and Mr. F. Lavington uses *The Trade Cycle* as a title.

[9] Compare Chapter III, section vi, 2 "A Critique of the Indexes of Business Conditions."

we know what we have named, we may begin contriving explanations, when we should be trying to find out what our words mean.[10]

All this was said at the beginning of the book. It explains why no definition of business cycles was given there. It explains why even the review of theories was made to emphasize a fundamental feature of business cycles, to indicate what detailed facts should be looked for, and how those facts should be studied. It explains the long chapters on economic organization, statistical methods, and business annals. It explains the present section on the evolution of the concept of business cycles. Even now, we can do no more than frame a working definition to use in trying to learn more—a definition which presumably will require modification as knowledge grows.

2. A Working Concept of Business Cycles.

To find out what business cycles are, we have looked at them through the eyes of economic theorists, through the eyes of economic statisticians, and through the eyes of business reporters. Each group of workers helps us to appreciate features of the common object which the other groups take for granted, or fail to see. It is by combining the three sets of observations that we can form the mental picture of business cycles most useful in the constructive work which lies before us.

(1) Elements derived from Business Reports.

Treated in one way, business reports give a most confusing view of business fluctuations; but treated in another way, they give the simplest view. When we wade through the commercial histories printed in financial papers or consular documents, we may get no general impression except that of infinite detail. But by careful planning and hard work, we can put these records in such form that they afford a view over wide areas and through decades. Then the details fade, and the broad features of commercial history become clear. Among these broad features, one of the most prominent is a pattern in the changes taking place in time—a pattern common to all countries which can be said to have a business history. Again and

[10] It seems to me that as a name for our subject "the business cycle" exposes us to these dangers rather more than does "business cycles." On that ground, I prefer the latter term in most contexts. Surely it is safer usage to speak of "commercial crises" than to speak of "the commercial crisis."

again in many lands, a period of active trade ends in a relapse; then dull times prevail; afterwards comes a quickening, and presently trade is active once more. This frequently recurring sequence, of which there are so many examples in the record slowly built up by the coöperation of numberless business reporters, is what men have in mind when they speak of the business cycle.

But business annals give us much more than this bare skeleton of a concept.

(1) Current commercial histories usually take nations as their units, but they make it clear that a given wave of prosperity or depression does not always sweep over all parts of a country, and that such a wave sometimes sweeps over the commercial world. So unequal are the areas affected by different waves that we cannot associate business cycles with any given geographical or political unit. For convenient discussion it seems wise to abide by the convention of our sources, and think of (say) Japanese cycles, Swedish cycles and Brazilian cycles. There is the more reason for this practice in that the record of business cycles in every country has its own peculiarities. But we must conceive of the phenomena as international, not only in the sense that they occur in many countries, but also in the sense that the state of trade prevailing in any country at any time actively promotes the development of a similar condition in all other countries with which the first has important business relations. On the other hand, we must recognize that in a large country whose economic organization is not highly integrated different sections sometimes have cyclical fluctuations more divergent than those of neighboring nations.

(2) The conception of prosperity or depression within a given country has the character of an average. Seldom does a detailed survey show that all branches of business are active, or all dull, at the same time. As a rule, the reporters are clear and unanimous concerning the "prevailing tone"; but sometimes they picture conditions as so mixed that it is hard to discover the trend. And sometimes when reporters agree concerning the prevailing tone, they agree also that certain industries present striking exceptions. In other words, a reader of commercial histories conceives of business cycles as a sequence of phases each of which is a highly complex aggregate of conditions in different industries—conditions which are never strictly uniform, and which are at times markedly divergent.

(3) Another characteristic of business cycles as pictured by com-

mercial histories is that they vary in intensity. The writers tell of wild panics and of quiet recessions, of sensational booms and of mild prosperity, of complete prostration and of mere dullness, of dramatic revivals and of long-drawn-out recuperations. These descriptive terms and their hundred variants cannot be interpreted with precision. We cannot even rank successive or contemporary cycles in the order of their intensities,—to say nothing of measuring degrees of intensity. But neither can we doubt the fact that cycles run the gamut from violent fluctuations to moderate swings. And if we follow these sources faithfully, we must drop crises from our conception of business cycles, for in the moderate swings no phase occurs which is fitly designated by that word.

(4) Concerning the wave-length of business cycles, commercial histories give us more definite impressions. We can measure approximately the intervals between successive recessions. There are doubtful cases, because the industrial complexity just referred to sometimes makes it hard to say whether a given set of difficulties was general enough to be called a recession; but these cases are not sufficiently numerous to cut much figure in the results.

Some cycles are found in the record which appear to have been nearer one year than two years in length. At the other extreme, we find a few cycles lasting 11 or 12 years. But the bulk of the cases fall within the three- to six-year range. And when a goodly number of observations are put together the measurements distribute themselves about their central tendency in a fairly regular, though not symmetrical, fashion.

Further, it appears that the phases of revival and recession, as reported in the sources from which business annals are compiled, are brief in comparison with the phases of prosperity and depression; that on the average prosperity lasts a little longer than depression; that this relation of prosperity to depression is accentuated when wholesale prices have a rising secular trend, and reversed when that trend declines; that the very long cycles are due more to the prolongation of depression than to the prolongation of prosperity.

(5) On reading the business records of any country year after year, one is impressed by the continuity of cyclical changes. In the sequence of prosperity, recession, depression and revival, any stage can be treated as the end of one cycle and the beginning of another. Yet it seems wiser to say that there is no beginning and no end; or better still, that there is a continuous movement which passes through

certain phases in an established order, but at a pace which varies from time to time and country to country.

(6) Current business commentators say many hasty things about the causes of changes in conditions which we cannot incorporate into a working conception of business cycles. But for one generalization along this line we have use: business cycles are highly sensitive phenomena, influenced by a host of factors not of business origin. Among such factors, wars, civil disturbances, inequalities in harvests, and epidemics play prominent rôles.

(7) Finally, a survey of business annals of countries at different stages of development, and of the business annals of the same country through successive stages, suggests that business cycles are associated with a certain form of economic organization. This suggestion is confirmed by a longer-range study of economic history.[1] While commercial and financial crises can be traced back a long time in England, the Netherlands, France, Southern Germany, and northern Italy, these early modern and late medieval crises appear to have been due far more largely to non-business factors than are modern recessions, and to have been less general in their incidence. Business cycles which affect the fortunes of the mass of people in a country, which succeed each other continuously, and which attain a semblance of regularity, do not become prominent in the economic history of a country until a large proportion of its people are living mainly by making and spending money incomes. Also, there is evidence that business cycles keep changing character as economic organization develops. The most violent manifestations are brought under control. Panics subside into crises, and crises into recessions. It seems probable that the average length of cycles grows shorter at one stage of institutional development, and at a later stage grows longer again. In fine, we must think of the recurrence of prosperity, recession, depression and revival as characteristic of economic activity only when economic activity is organized on the basis of what is here called "business economy."

Thus the conception of business cycles obtained from a survey of contemporary reports starts with the fundamental fact of rhythmical fluctuations in activity, and adds that these fluctuations are peculiar to countries organized on a business basis, that they appear in all

[1] See Chapter II, section i, "The Historical Connection between Business Cycles and the Use of Money."

such countries, that they tend to develop the same phase at nearly the same time in different countries, that they follow each other without intermissions, that they are affected by all sorts of non-business factors, that they represent predominant rather than universal changes in trend, and that, while they vary in intensity and duration, the variations are not so wide as to prevent our identifying different cases as belonging to a single class of phenomena.

(2) Elements Derived from Theories of Business Cycles.

What alterations in this concept are suggested by studying the theories of business cycles?

Read one after another in full detail, these theories are scarcely less confusing than are commercial reviews. It is feasible, however, to deal with the theories in much the same way as we have dealt with the business reports. Chapter I presents a collection of theoretical accounts, which can be set against the historical accounts summarized in Chapter IV. Treating one collection as we did the other, we can ask, What do the theories as a whole tell us about the phenomena?

First, the theories put fresh emphasis upon the exceeding complexity of cyclical fluctuations. But the complexity revealed by the theories is complexity of an order different from that revealed by commercial reports. While the latter deal with business conditions in different areas and different industries, the theories deal with different processes—processes which are supposed to run their course in, or to affect, all industries and all communities organized upon a business basis.

Among the processes so intimately involved in cyclical fluctuations that they have been made to yield explanations of business cycles, we noted the following:

Banking operations—particularly the processes of expanding or contracting bank loans, with their effects in enlarging or reducing the volume of credit currency; fluctuations in discount rates, and the fluctuations of bank reserves which result from changes in the public's use of coin and paper money, and from the banks' efforts to maintain solvency.

Saving and investing in their relation to the amount of construction work undertaken, the supply of consumers' goods sent to market, and the volume of retail buying.

The process of adjusting the current supply of goods of all sorts

to the demand for them, as that process affects business commitments, or is affected by (1) the uncertainties incident to all business planning, (2) changes in the marginal utilities of consumers' goods and the marginal utility of money, on the one hand, and, on the other hand, by changes in the demand for and in the operation of industrial equipment.

Disbursing money incomes to consumers and spending money by consumers, in relation to the processes of making and selling goods—relations which may be treated with reference to the influence of price fluctuations upon the incomes and purchasing power of different classes, with reference to the effect of saving by corporations and individuals upon the demand for consumers' goods, or with reference to the difficulty of providing liquid capital for business enterprises without reducing the demand for goods in general below the volume sent to market.

Making profits out of industrial operations—a process which is held to breed illusions concerning the volume of demand, to magnify the moderate fluctuations of retail buying into violent oscillations in production, or to cause the alternate marking up and writing down of the capital values at which business enterprises are rated and upon which loan credits are based.

Promoting new business ventures, or making revolutionary changes in business methods.

"Progress" at large, a characteristic of the age which makes it impossible to keep the rates at which different factors grow properly adjusted to each other.

In addition to these economic processes our attention has been called to:

Waves of optimism and pessimism, which are held by one writer to "give birth to one another in an endless chain," and by another writer to result from fluctuations in birth-, death-, and morbidity-rates.

Cyclical changes in weather, which affect business on one line of analysis because they affect crop yields, on a second line of analysis because they affect health and mental attitudes, and on a third line because they give the industries using organic materials a rhythm different from that of the industries using inorganic materials.

Of course not all of these theories of business cycles can be valid in the sense of their authors. Indeed, if any one theory really shows

the chief cause of cyclical fluctuations, none of the rival theories shows the chief cause. But we can take all of the theories into our working conception of business cycles in the sense that we can conceive of the recurrent sequences of prosperity, recession, depression and revival as involving cyclical fluctuations in each of the economic processes listed, and as affected by emotional and climatic conditions. Nor can we limit our view to the processes and conditions on which theories of business cycles have been erected. In working, we must be prepared to study any feature of modern life which appears to be intimately related to business fluctuations. But with every factor in the complex, whether suggested by others or discovered in our inquiry, we must deal critically. Among other things, this means that our conception of a multiplicity of processes involved in business cycles does not commit us in advance to any conclusion about the number of causes at work. If the evidence we find points in that direction, we can conclude that some single cause produces, directly and indirectly, the cyclical fluctuations in an uncounted list of processes.

While adding a significant feature to our conception of business cycles, the survey of theories sheds little light upon the suggestions derived from the survey of business annals. For the cycles explained by economic theorists are not the cycles recorded by business historians. Interested in establishing generalizations, a theorist passes lightly over the differences among successive cycles in the same country and synchronous cycles in different countries. He contemplates an ideal, or a typical, case, supposedly modeled on real cases and summing up all their really essential features. Nor is that procedure open to criticism, provided the theorist takes care to test his ideal construction for conformity to fact. Some modern theorists do so explicitly and at length; doubtless others believe that they have made adequate tests privately, though they spare their readers the heavy task of assessing their evidence. In any case, concentration upon an ideal case by a theorist does not mean that he denies the variability of the phenomena, but that he sets the variations aside in order to get a clearer view of what seem to him fundamentals.

On two points, however, most of the theories of business cycles are at variance with the concept derived from commercial reviews. These points were discussed in Chapter IV, and noted in the preceding section; but they must be mentioned in the present connection. (1) Most theorists take crises to be one of the phases of all business

cycles, though a few writers define "crisis" in a way which makes it equivalent to "recession." (2) By taking cycles as the intervals between crises, and not counting mild recessions as crises, most theorists make the duration typical of business cycles roughly twice the length we deduce as typical. On both these points, the conception suggested by business annals, confirmed as it is by statistical analysis, is more useful in constructive work than its rival.

Nor can the idea presented in many theories that business cycles represent an alternate rupture and restoration of economic equilibrium be included in our working conception. Men who take as their point of departure the theorem that economic forces tend to establish a stable equilibrium may conceive the main problem to be, how this fundamental tendency is overcome at times and how it presently reasserts itself. I have not chosen that point of departure. Hence it is no part of my task to determine how the fact of cyclical oscillations in economic activity can be reconciled with the general theory of equilibrium, or how that theory can be reconciled with facts.

Yet this does not dispose of the matter. Whatever his methodological assumptions, anyone who deals with crises is likely to think of a balance of forces, particularly if his explanation centers in some single process. "Over-saving," "over-production," "under-consumption," "a rate of interest higher than that economically justified," "optimistic error," "excess capacity,"—all such phrases imply the idea of an equilibrium which has been disturbed. They may or may not be conscious applications of a general economic theorem. But when we enlarge our problem to include numerous processes and all phases of the cycle, the idea of equilibrium becomes less helpful in conceiving the whole movement than in dealing with details. Provided we interpret equilibrium, not in the mechanical, but in the bookkeeping sense, as suggested in the closing section of Chapter II, we may compare one set of factors or forces with an opposing set, note which set exceeds the other for the time being, and inquire what consequences that excess produces. But in what useful way can we conceive of the equilibrium of the whole system we must contemplate, when that system includes factors which cannot be combined into two opposing totals—quantities of goods in physical terms, prices, pecuniary aggregates? If we could reduce every factor to its money value, the feat might be accomplished; but in the process we should bury qualitative distinctions of great moment. While we can relate all the qualitatively unlike factors in the problem to each other

through their bearing upon prospective profits, we cannot add them all together and get results which are illuminating.

(3) Elements Derived from Statistical Analysis.

Our collection of statistics is like our collection of business annals, and unlike our collection of theories, in that it deals with the cycles of history—fluctuations which have occurred in certain countries between certain dates. Hence the statistics can be used to test elements in our concept which are derived from commercial reviews. The tests confirm, with a welcome increase of definiteness, the view that business cycles run a continuous round; that they vary, but vary after the fashion characteristic of most social phenomena, in intensity, in duration and in the intensity and duration of their constituent phases; that the synchronous fluctuations in countries having business relations with one another tend to have a common pattern, and that the course of business changes is frequently altered by factors not of business origin.

On the other hand, our collection of statistics resembles our collection of theories, and differs from our collection of business annals, in that it deals with economic processes rather than with the fortunes of different industries. Hence, the impression derived from the theories, that a business cycle is a highly complex congeries of fluctuations in different processes, can be made clearer by appeal to statistics. And though statistics deal with historical cycles, to a limited extent we can combine the different cases they present in such a way as to test theoretical conceptions of what features of the historical cycles are typical, and what are exceptional.

Besides confirming certain elements in the concept derived from our other sources, the collection of statistics brings forcibly to our attention two elements which are traceable, rather than prominent, in business annals and in certain theories.

Time series show that the cyclical fluctuations characteristic of various economic processes differ in amplitude and timing; they show approximately how much these fluctuations differ in amplitude, and what order they follow in time.

Time series also show that the cyclical fluctuations of most (not all) economic processes occur in combination with fluctuations of several other sorts:—secular trends, primary and secondary, seasonal variations, and irregular fluctuations.

By developing special methods for segregating secular trends and seasonal variations, statisticians have enabled us to get a clearer view of cyclical fluctuations, though they have accomplished little toward isolating the irregular changes in their series. Thus we are forced to deal with materials, which, at best, show cyclical-irregular fluctuations in combination. Even so, we can sort the series into groups, based upon the regularity and the measure of agreement among their movements. There are some time series whose fluctuations, mild or violent, show slight traces of any rhythm. But there are enough series which show tolerably regular cyclical fluctuations, agreeing with one another and with our business annals in tenor, to give us confidence in the basic element of our conception—the recurrence of the prosperity-recession-depression-revival sequence.

3. Two Criticisms Considered.

One element in our working concept has been rejected by Dean Arthur B. Adams, who holds:

> It is a mistake to think that cyclical movements are continuous. . . . Each business cycle is, in a large measure, separate and distinct from the one preceding it and the other succeeding it. Considerable time may elapse between the ending of one cycle and the beginning of another.

Adams illustrates this contention by reference to American experience:

> No period of prosperity developed from 1893 until the industrial expansion of 1905-07. Again, following the Panic of 1907 no period of prosperity developed until the World War expansion of 1915-20.

Our annals, on the contrary, and the business indexes with which we have compared them, show between 1893 and 1907 a "submerged cycle" terminated by a recession early in 1896, a second period of somewhat greater activity terminated by a very mild reaction in 1900, and a third movement of expansion ending in the "rich man's panic" of 1903. Between 1907 and 1920, also, our annals and indexes show three cycles, marked off by recessions in 1910, 1913 and 1918.

Yet the difference between Dean Adams' view and the one taken here is more a difference in the use of terms than a difference con-

cerning facts. For Adams recognizes that between 1893 and 1905, and again between 1907 and 1915, there was "some oscillation of prices, credit and profits." He thinks, however, that

> these slight movements occurring within a few months were far too inconsequential to be designated as cyclical fluctuations.

What are here called business cycles of small amplitude, Dean Adams calls "periods of time covered by oscillating business equilibria." [1] In his terminology, no fluctuation is a business cycle unless the prosperous phase develops into a "boom."

Perhaps it does not matter greatly which of these contrasting usages is adopted, so long as the facts are kept in mind. On either view, one must face the problem why some revivals grow into intense and prolonged prosperity, and why in other cases prosperity is mild and brief. But one who takes the trouble to measure the amplitudes of successive fluctuations in many time series throughout considerable periods, finds his observations so distributed about their central tendency that he has no basis for contrasting business cycles and what Dean Adams calls "oscillating business equilibria." [2] Our inquiry will be more orderly if we treat all cyclical oscillations as belonging to one species of phenomena, and inquire into the variations characteristic of the species in respect to amplitudes, duration, and other measurable features.

Professor Irving Fisher doubts the validity of the whole conception with which we are concerned, and asks whether "the" business cycle is not a myth. His chief argument runs as follows:

> if by the business cycle is meant merely the statistical fact that business does *fluctuate* above and below its average trend, there is no denying the existence of a cycle—and not only in business but in any statistical series whatsoever! If we draw any smooth curve to represent the general trend of population, the actual population figures must necessarily rise sometimes above and sometimes below this mean trend line. . . . In the same way weather conditions necessarily fluctuate about their own means; so does the luck at Monte Carlo. Must we then speak of "the population cycle," "the weather cycle" and "the Monte Carlo cycle"?

[1] Arthur B. Adams, *Economics of Business Cycles,* New York, 1925, pp. 195-197, and 213.

[2] See "The Amplitude of Business Cycles" in Chapter III, sections vi, 3 (7).

> I see no more reason to believe in "the" business cycle. It is simply the fluctuation about its own mean. And yet the cycle idea is supposed to have more content than mere variability. It implies a regular succession of *similar* fluctuations, constituting some sort of *recurrence*, so that, as in the case of the phases of the moon, the tides of the sea, wave motion, or pendulum swing, we can forecast the future on the basis of a pattern worked out from past experience, and which we have reason to think will be copied in the future. We certainly cannot do that in predicting the weather, or Monte Carlo luck. Can we do so as to business? Not so long as business is dominated by changes in the price level! [3]

Professor Fisher has rendered a wholesome service to students of business cycles by challenging their basic concept in this vigorous fashion. To discuss the issue in full would involve repeating once again many of the facts set forth in the preceding chapters and summarized in the preceding sections. That is not feasible; but it is well to recall what groups of facts the challenge must face.

Even when economic time series are reduced to percentage deviations from their secular trends adjusted for seasonal variations, the fluctuations in some cases still seem as irregular as the fluctuations of the weather, or of "Monte Carlo luck." But there are many series of which this cannot be said. When charted, the fluctuations of pig-iron production, unemployment percentages, bank clearings, and building permits, to cite but a few examples, prove to be decidedly less irregular than the fluctuations of a weather chart, a chart of net gold shipments, or of potato crops. In no case are the fluctuations highly regular; but in many cases they are far from haphazard, despite the inability of statisticians to free what they call "cyclical" changes from what they call "irregular" perturbations. Further, the cyclical-irregular fluctuations of the series which individually show semblance of regularity are found to have tolerably regular relations with one another in respect to time, duration, and amplitude of movement—relations many of which have been suggested by economic theory. Finally, in timing and direction these inter-correlated fluctuations agree closely with the evidence given by business annals concerning a long-continued and wide-spread recurrence of prosperity, recession, depression and revival.

[3] Irving Fisher, "Our Unstable Dollar and the So-called Business Cycle," *Journal of the American Statistical Association,* June, 1925, vol. xx, pp. 191, 192.

To ascertain how regularly this sequence recurs, to learn all they can about its characteristics, causes, and consequences, is the problem upon which students of business cycles are working. They speak of cyclical fluctuations, instead of periodic fluctuations, just because the first term does not imply strict regularity of recurrence. To them "the cycle idea" does "have more content than mere variability"; but it does not have the content of periodicity. Anyone who makes business forecasts on the basis of a fixed time schedule is not applying their concept, but violating it. What they know about the recurrence does not yet enable them to make consistently successful business forecasts. But in that fact they see reason, not for giving up their work, but for pressing it further.

No competent judge questions the desirability of studying economic fluctuations in an objective fashion. Professor Fisher himself is one of the distinguished workers in the field. But he thinks that the subdivision of this broad problem which is called "business cycles" in America and "trade cycles" in England would flourish better under some other name. Perhaps a new name can be found which is equally apt and less subject to misconstruction. If so, it should be adopted. But no such blanket term as "economic undulations," "industrial fluctuations," "business oscillations," or "theory of conjunctures" will meet the needs of current research. For we have seen that various investigators believe they have discovered several different types of fluctuations in time series—secular trends, "long waves," secondary trends, generating cycles, commercial cycles (the commonest name for inter-crisis changes), business cycles, seasonal variations, irregular perturbations. Probably each of these types which withstands critical examination will become the object of intensive study by economic statisticians and by economic theorists, or better by men who unite these too-often separated interests. As knowledge grows, there will be increasing need of specific names to characterize each type of fluctuations and to differentiate each from the other types. To drop the name now widely used for one of the best established of these types, before a better substitute has been supplied, might cause more confusion than is now caused by misunderstanding of the word "cycles." Meanwhile, the general adoption of this word in other sciences to designate recurrent, but non-periodic, phenomena is familiarizing the intelligent public with its meaning.[4] Perhaps the

[4] See above, Chapter IV, section iii, 2; "Use of the Term 'Cycles.'"

course which will make the least trouble is for critics to observe what those who treat of business cycles mean by that term.

4. A Definition of Business Cycles.

In a systematic investigation of business cycles, all of the characteristics developed in the preceding pages by analyzing business annals, theoretical hypotheses and statistical data should be considered. But it is useful to have a brief definition summarizing those characteristics which show the generic type of the phenomena in question, and those characteristics which mark off business cycles from the other phenomena just mentioned with which they may be confused.

Business cycles are a species of fluctuations in the economic activities of organized communities. The adjective "business" restricts the concept to fluctuations in activities which are systematically conducted on a commercial basis. The noun "cycles" bars out fluctuations which do not recur with a measure of regularity.

The phenomena with which business cycles may be confused are (1) changes in business conditions which occur between the dates of "crises," (2) fluctuations which affect a minor portion of the economic activities of a business community, (3) fluctuations which recur every year, and (4) the less definitely established secondary trends and "long waves." From the first of these related species, business cycles are distinguished by the fact that each cycle includes one wave of rising and falling, or falling and rising activity, whereas the intervals between "crises" often include two and some times include three such waves. From the second species, business cycles are distinguished by their wider inclusiveness. From the third species they are distinguished by not recurring annually. From the fourth species they are distinguished by their briefer time-span.

Following the lines of this analysis, we indicate both the generic features and the distinguishing characteristics of business cycles by saying that they are recurrences of rise and decline in activity, affecting most of the economic processes of communities with well-developed business organization, not divisible into waves of amplitudes nearly equal to their own, and averaging in communities at different stages of economic development from about three to about six or seven years in duration.

Seldom can the interrelated species of social (or natural) phe-

nomena be marked off from one another with such precision as to leave no doubtful cases. Certainly our business annals and statistical indexes show some fluctuations which are difficult to classify on any scheme. If the definition suggested makes clear what is typical of the phenomena in question, it will serve its purpose.

II. Tentative Working Plans.

To give an intelligible account of business cycles, as we have come to conceive them, is the task of the second volume. The cycles with which the discussion will deal are neither the cycles of history, nor the cycles of some speculative construction, but cycles of an intermediate order. We shall seek to find what features have been characteristic of all or of most cycles, and to concentrate attention upon them, paying less attention to features which have been peculiar to one or a few cases. In this respect, our aim will be like that of economic theorists, and different from that of economic historians, commercial journalists, and business forecasters, who are concerned with particular cycles. But our way of finding what is typical and what is exceptional will be the way of the statistician and the historian who ventures to generalize. Of course, concentrating upon what is typical involves considering the way in which the various phenomena treated are distributed around their central tendencies. What this procedure shows to be typical may at times be equivalent to what an economic theorist would call "normal" features of business cycles; but there is no assurance that such correspondence will be common.

Materials for the discussion are supplied by the three collections from which our working conception of business cycles has been derived—the collection of business annals, the collection of statistical series, and the collection of theories. These are formal, objective sources which any student can exploit. In addition, like every other student of economic behavior, I shall draw upon my own store of experiences and observations—a queer mixture of generic and individual elements, the latter determined largely by chance and by personal equation.

The methods employed must be methods which make it possible to weave these diverse materials into a single fabric. We must be ready to consider concrete events such as historians treat; but we must array them in groups after the fashion of statisticians, and interpret them in the light of what we know about economic behavior, after

the fashion of economic theorists. Similarly, we must be ready to apply the mathematical technique of statisticians; but we must guide our statistical investigations by rational hypotheses, and eke out our statistical observations by recourse to historical records. So, too, while we must be ready on occasion to analyze imaginary cases with the theorists, these cases should be arranged whenever possible with an eye upon the historical and statistical data by which speculative conclusions may be tested. Of course, it is an error to think that free use of factual materials reduces the need for careful reasoning. In our effort to give an intelligible account of business cycles, reasoning must be our chief concern; but it should be reasoning which deals, and squares, with observations, and the observations should have as wide a sweep as we can get from history, as much precision as we can get from statistics, and as much subtlety as we can get from personal experience.

The concept of business cycles developed in this volume suggests that the leading question of the second volume be put in the form "How do business cycles run their course?" rather than in the form "What causes business cycles?" What we are seeking to understand is a complex of recurrent fluctuations in numerous interrelated processes. To learn what we can about the workings of these processes in their relations to one another and as a whole is the next step. When we have taken that step, it will be time to see what the question about the cause of business cycles means, and in what sense it can be answered.

Meanwhile, we need not hesitate to speak about causal relationships among the numerous factors in the processes whose fluctuations we are tracing, whenever such language seems appropriate. Men phrase their statements concerning economic relations in various ways. One may say that under certain circumstances an increase of orders for goods is followed by a rise of prices, or that it permits sellers to raise prices, or that it tends to produce a rise of prices, or that it occasions a rise, or that it causes prices to rise. Each of these phrases has implications somewhat different from the others—implications of which we seldom stop to think in the midst of our constructive work. The only statement in the list which we can test adequately is the colorless statement that one event is followed by another. We should be on the safest ground if we confined ourselves strictly to tested allegations concerning past sequences. Yet in our searches for sequences

to test, and in our thinking about probable future developments, it would be foolish to contend against the settled habit of thinking in terms of cause and effect. Many of our keenest guesses at new truth come to mind in this dubious form, just as many stimulating insights are suggested by analogies. We avail ourselves of analogies both in making investigations and in stating their results, though we all know that analogy is not proof. So we think and write in causal terms, though we admit the impossibility of establishing a necessary connection between antecedent and consequent.

Whatever causal connections we may work into our account of business cycles, that account will remain an analytic description of interrelated processes. Of necessity, the causal relationships will appear most complicated. A phenomenon which crops up first as an effect turns presently into a cause, and since we shall be following a continuous process we must treat it first as the one and then as the other. Even that is a simplified version of the facts: in truth every factor in the situation at every moment is being influenced by, and is influencing, other factors—it is not first cause and then effect, but both cause and effect all the time. Further, we cannot follow single chains of causal influence. The interactions among economic processes are so important that we cannot set them aside. Almost every effect with which we deal will appear to be the joint product of numerous causes, and to be one among several causes of numerous effects. In view of these complications, it will prove more helpful to treat our problem at large in terms of the relations among a number of complex variables, rather than in terms of cause and effect.

A cardinal illustration of our difficulties, and of the way out, is provided by Chapter II. To avoid getting lost in the maze of processes which Chapter I showed we must follow, we sought to find some general scheme for viewing these processes in systematic relation to one another. The scheme suggested was to relate every factor to the current and prospective profits of business enterprises. Profits are net mathematical resultants of many plus and minus items in a computation. We do not analyze profit and loss statements in terms of cause and effect, though we often give causal explanations of changes in certain items. So, when we put the scheme of Chapter II to use in the second volume, we shall concentrate attention upon the net resultants of interrelated changes in many variables and relegate causal analysis to incidental uses.

The best framework for a discussion of how business cycles run their course is that provided by the phases of these cycles—prosperity, recession, depression, and revival. Our collections of business annals and of theories lend themselves readily to this plan; for the annals mark changes in the tides of activity, and most current theories explain crises by what happens in prosperity and revivals by what happens in depression. But statistical time series are continuous. How shall we break them into parts for use in a discussion which treats first all periods of prosperity as a unit, then all periods of recession, and so on?

Most of the statistics which the National Bureau is collecting come from the United States, England, France and Germany—countries included in our volume of *Business Annals*. For each of these countries Dr. Thorp has drawn up a table which marks off, not only successive cycles, but also the successive phases of each cycle. As they stand, or with such modifications as prove advisable when we enter into full detail, his divisions will be used as a basis for breaking up the time covered by each series used, first into cycles, second into periods of prosperity, recession, depression and revival. That is, we plan to analyze all the time series for a given country on the basis of a standard pattern derived from the business annals of that country, not on the basis of the various patterns which might be derived from study of the several series themselves. In most cases we anticipate that the cycles and phases of the individual series will correspond fairly well with the standard patterns of the countries from which they come. But there will be cases of notable divergence in timing—cases which our plan will throw into high relief, and from which we shall learn much of interest.

The cycles with which we are working run from trough to trough; that is, they show a business cycle as a wave which rises, breaks and subsides. We might equally well have taken the cycles from peak to peak, representing each as a decline, followed by a rise. Our chief reason for preferring the former plan is that it may enable us to include a few more recent cases than would its rival.

When a series has been divided into cycles on this basis, we plan to ascertain its mean value in each cycle, and to turn the original figures for every month or quarter of each cycle into relatives on the basis of this mean value as 100. This step will put all the series into comparable form, and give us numerical results which can be used in many ways. Then each cycle in each series will be repre-

sented by four charts, one showing its relative fluctuations during the prosperous phase, one during the phase of recession, a third during depression, and a fourth during revival. These charts will be drawn with overlaps at either end; for example, the charts for revivals of activity will include the latter part of the preceding depression and the earlier part of the succeeding prosperity.

Charts drawn in this manner, with logarithmic vertical scales, can be used in many combinations. We can compare the fluctuations of a given series in a given country in successive periods of given phase, and contrast its fluctuations in opposite phases. We can study the movements of similar series from different countries in the same phases of the same cycles. We can take different series from the same country in the same phase of the same cycle. And so on.

By using the average value of each series during each cycle as the base for computing relatives, we eliminate most of the secular trend. Otherwise, the plan involves a minimum of "adjustments" in presenting data. But though simple, it can be elaborated at will. At need, the seasonal variations of series can be ascertained by any of the standard methods, and eliminated. Or a series can be turned into percentage deviations from its secular trend before it is broken up into cycles. Our percentage fluctuations about the mean values of a series in a given cycle can be reduced to multiples of their own standard deviations. Indeed, we can utilize almost any technical device which the work of other investigators, or our own experience, shows to be helpful.

A special advantage of the plan is that it helps us to deal with the most baffling problem encountered in analyzing time series—the problem of segregating cyclical from irregular fluctuations. In no single case will our procedure effect such a segregation; but when we assemble charts showing the movements of some variable during (say) the prosperous phase of numerous cycles in several countries, we should be able to make out with some confidence what changes are characteristic and what are exceptional. In some cases we may be able to go further, and connect deviations from the common course with disturbing factors of which we read in non-statistical sources.

Of course, our fundamental problem in using statistics will be to find out what relations subsist between the cyclical fluctuations characteristic of different economic processes. As pointed out in Chapter III, the possible relationships are of many types. We are accustomed to asking whether it is the total magnitude of one variable which

affects a second, a change in the direction of its movement, or the amount of change from one date to the next, or the percentage rate of change. We are learning to ask whether it is the changes accumulated over a period of time that should be looked into, or the amount of the variable in excess of a critical range, or its ratio to some other variable. These are but a few of the possibilities which statisticians may soon be considering. Moreover, the effects upon the second variable may be changes in total amount, in direction of movement, in amount of movement, in percentage rise or fall, or in any of the other indefinitely numerous possibilities. Again, a given variable may affect a second variable in one way while it affects a third and fourth in other ways. So, too, a given variable may be affected in unlike ways by two or more processes which bear upon it. All these problems are further complicated by the need of finding how promptly an effect is exercised, how that effect is distributed through time, and whether the effect is constant in character through all phases of business cycles, or whether it changes from phase to phase.

There are important problems relating to business cycles which cannot be treated within the framework which has been sketched. Hence the analysis of what happens in periods of prosperity, recession, depression and revival must be supplemented by discussions in which certain hypotheses are tested with reference to long periods of time, in which business annals are considered in their wider sweep, and in which statistical series are taken as wholes instead of in segments. But these problems will stand out far more clearly after the successive phases of business cycles have been analyzed in detail than they do at present.

No group of workers in the present generation can hope to cover the field marked out by these suggestions. The task of finding, case by case, the best form of stating the relations among different economic processes is a task on which an increasing number of increasingly skillful investigators will be working for a long time to come—how long no one can guess. But what our successors can accomplish will depend upon the stage at which we pass on the problem. Our task is to use as best we can the means at our disposal—the insights given by economic theory as it now stands, the statistical and historical data now available, and all the suggestions we can get.

ADDENDA

Work upon business cycles is progressing so rapidly in so many quarters that a manuscript falls somewhat behind date while it is passing through the press. As partial remedy, I add notes on a few developments of which I have learned too late for mention in the proper place. Before the volume reaches its first readers, doubtless I shall be wishing that I might supplement these addenda. Not all the omissions are items of recent date. Probably the most serious are matters of which I should have known long ago, but of which I am still ignorant.

A Russian paper by Albert Wainstein on *Harvests, Meteorological and Economic Cycles, and the Problem of Economic Forecasting*, Moscow, 1926, reviews the recent literature upon weather theories of business cycles. Among the contributions noticed is a series of articles, otherwise unknown to me, published by Axel F. Enström in the *Teknisk Tidskrift* (Veckoupplagen), 1916. From the French synopsis of Wainstein's paper, supplemented by notes which Dr. Kuznets has made, I judge Enström's investigations to merit more attention than they have received. By repeated smoothing and differentiation of numerous time series, most of which run back to 1830, Enström finds non-synchronous cycles of 8 to 9 years in wholesale prices, crops, production, temperature and sunspots. Between sunspot and temperature cycles he gets a correlation coefficient of —.94. He attributes the lagging cycles in economic activities to the cycles in temperature, and believes that the sequences are sufficiently regular to afford a basis for forecasting economic cycles from solar observations.

In the new volume of *Der moderne Kapitalismus*, "Das Wirtschaftsleben im Zeitalter des Hochkapitalismus" (Munich and Leipzig, 1927), Professor Werner Sombart gives a fresh exposition of his theory of business cycles, showing the relation between the factor which he stresses (the different conditions under which organic and inorganic goods are produced) and other processes.

This discussion, Chapter xxv, also throws light upon the historical connection between business cycles and the form of economic organization. In treating that theme, I ought to have referred to Chapters xvi and xvii in the second volume of *Der moderne Kapitalismus,* 3rd ed., Munich and Leipzig, 1919. Sombart there points out the characteristics which differentiate the economic perturbations of the 16th, 17th and 18th centuries from the business cycles of the 19th and 20th centuries.

Professor A. C. Pigou's treatise on *Industrial Fluctuations,* mentioned in Chapter I as forthcoming, has been published in London. A hasty examination of the copy I have just received suffices to show that the book fulfills the high expectations with which it has been awaited.

Mr. R. G. Hawtrey's article in the May, 1927, issue of the *Quarterly Journal of Economics* on "The Monetary Theory of the Trade Cycle and Its Statistical Test" contains not only a concise statement of his own views, but also a criticism of Pigou's "psychological theory," which Hawtrey seems to regard as the only serious "rival" of the "monetary theory."

An interesting variant of the "profits theory" has been suggested by Professor F. Schmidt of the University of Frankfurt in *Die Industriekonjunktur—ein Rechenfehler.* (Zeitschrift für Betriebswirtschaft, 2. Sonderheft, Berlin and Vienna, 1927.)

The gist of Schmidt's contention is that illusions concerning current profits arise from a technical defect in bookkeeping. When the price level rises, profits are overstated, because no allowance is made for the increasing unit costs of replacing the raw materials, current supplies, and other goods which enterprises are continually using up. The whole difference between aggregate buying prices and aggregate selling prices is set down as profits, although the replacement of the necessary working supplies will absorb a larger part of the receipts than in the preceding turnover period. When the price level is falling, profits are minimized, or losses magnified, because no account is taken of the diminished unit costs of replacing the goods used up. This illusory element in profits leads to over-borrowing, over-confidence, and over-extension of industrial equipment in the one case, and to their opposites in the other case.

Dr. Matsuyo Takizawa's *Penetration of Money Economy in Japan and its Effects upon Social and Political Institutions* has now been published by the Columbia University Press.

The American estimate, cited in Chapter II, that savings have averaged about one-seventh of national income, may be compared with the new British estimate by Professor Bowley and Sir Josiah Stamp. "Total savings expressed as a proportion of total social income was . . . 16 per cent in 1911, and 12 or 13 per cent in 1924. If the unemployed are absorbed in industry, and we reach a year of good trade, the pre-war proportion of saving may well be again attained." *The National Income, 1924,* by Arthur L. Bowley and Sir Josiah Stamp, Oxford, 1927, p. 57.

A study of secondary trends, by Dr. Charles A. R. Wardwell of the University of Pennsylvania, will soon be published in Philadelphia under the title, *An Investigation of Economic Data for Major Cycles.* I have seen only the first draft of the manuscript. Dr. Wardwell uses methods different from those of de Wolff, Kondratieff, or Kuznets, and gets from his American data, which run by quarters from 1866 or later to the present, "major cycles" averaging about 15 years in duration. Smaller samples of English and German series also give "major cycles," but somewhat briefer ones.

My remark in Chapter I, that "no one has yet devised a satisfactory method of measuring . . . cyclical fluctuations directly," has been made questionable by Dr. Martin Allen Brumbaugh. His doctoral dissertation, published at the University of Pennsylvania and in New York in 1926, is entitled *Direct Method of Determining Cyclical Fluctuations of Economic Data.*

"The method developed arrives at the relatives of cyclical differences in two major operations, first, the division of each item of data by the item of the same season of the preceding year, and secondly, the correction for trend residue. The first step removes the seasonal variations, reduces the data to relative form and, since it is a chain index, removes the normal growth. The second step removes the small residual trend element which represents the increase of one year. . . .

"In the final result we have not measured cycles but cyclical differences. . . . We have demonstrated that the relative cyclical

differences lead to a wave curve whose periodic changes conform to those of a curve of relative cycles. Further, that the amplitudes of the curve of cyclical differences express rapidity of change whereas the amplitudes of the curve of relative cycles express amounts which are the results of such change." (Pp. 71, 72.)

Dr. Brumbaugh recognizes that the final test of his method "must come from an appeal to business conditions." In his judgment, the method "has satisfactorily fulfilled every reasonable requirement for the cases to which it has been applied." (P. 73.)

Mr. A. W. Flux publishes a valuable paper upon "Indices of Industrial Productive Activity" in the latest issue of the *Journal of the Royal Statistical Society,* vol. xc, part ii, pp. 225-271.

Mr. Carl Snyder has brought together in one volume his numerous studies of cyclical fluctuations (of which such free use is made in Chapters III and IV), and added valuable new results to the papers already published. *Business Cycles and Business Measurements: Studies in Quantitative Economics,* by Carl Snyder, New York, 1927.

In "The Summation of Random Causes as the Source of Cyclic Processes" (*Problems of Economic Conditions,* vol. iii, part i, published by the Conjuncture Institute in Russian with an English summary, Moscow, 1927), E. E. Slutsky presents two theses:

> (a) that cyclic . . . processes may originate owing to a summation of mutually independent chance causes, and (b) that these chance waves may show a certain regularity, being an imitation in lesser or greater degree, of strictly periodical fluctuations.

The first thesis, which is supported by a most interesting analysis of a random series from numbers drawn in a lottery, has a bearing upon my inference from the distribution of cycle durations (see above pp. 419, 420). But Mr. Slutsky thinks that I am not justified in treating the variability of cycle durations

> as a reason for denying the regular periodicity of cycles . . . for a similar result could be obtained also for many curves composed from regular sine curves.

The preliminary annals for 1926, prepared by Dr. Willard L. Thorp and published in the National Bureau's *News-Bulletin* for May 20, 1927, indicate that recessions occurred last year in France, Italy, and Argentina. These reports add three new observations upon the duration of business cycles to the collection analyzed in Chapter IV. All three of the cycles just terminated lasted about 6 years.

INDEX

[illegible]
70

F.U.A.N.E.M? Germany
S.V.A.M! winter
F U A N E X? Germany
S V A X! winter
O K M + Xs germany